ORGANIZATIONAL BEHAVIOR AND THE PRACTICE OF MANAGEMENT

REVISED

The Scott, Foresman Series in Management and Organizations

Charles E. Summer, Advisory Editor
University of Washington

ORGANIZATIONAL BEHAVIOR AND THE PRACTICE OF MANAGEMENT

REVISED

David R. Hampton
California State University, San Diego

Charles E. Summer
University of Washington

Ross A. Webber
University of Pennsylvania

Scott, Foresman and Company
Glenview, Illinois   Brighton, England

To Dorothy, Carol, and Mary Lou

Library of Congress Catalog Card Number: 72-97197
ISBN: 0-673-07823-X

Copyright © 1973, 1968 Scott, Foresman and Company
Glenview, Illinois.
Philippines Copyright 1973 Scott, Foresman and Company.
All Rights Reserved
Printed in the United States of America.

Regional offices of Scott, Foresman and Company are located
in Dallas, Texas; Glenview, Illinois; Oakland, New Jersey;
Palo Alto, California; Tucker, Georgia; and Brighton, England.

Preface

Modern societies do things—produce and distribute goods and services, educate people, provide health care, and so on—by using special-purpose organizations. Through this social invention, people cooperate effectively to get work accomplished. Indeed, organizations are the hallmark of a modern society. Since managers are the key operators of organizations, they are important people in organizational societies. How well they perform their work affects how well organizations perform theirs, and, consequently, how well societies accomplish their objectives.

Most people who read this book are headed for or have already begun work careers in organizations. Our purpose in this second edition of *Organizational Behavior and The Practice of Management* is to assist them in that endeavor in two ways. First, we want to help them understand the territory of organizations—individual behavior, interpersonal behavior, group behavior, and the interplay of human and nonhuman factors. Second, we want to help them see how this knowledge can help them manage effectively. Accordingly, our emphasis in this book is not to "cover" the behavioral sciences, but to *uncover* the deeper structure of behavior in organizations, and to apply that knowledge to designing, managing, and leading organizations.

We have revised the book to take advantage of new developments in research and theory. New features of the second edition include:

New Concepts in Motivation. The chapter on individual behavior has been expanded to include such topics as expectancy theory and cognitive dissonance.

Communication and Influence. Two new chapters analyze the vital processes of communication and influence. Located between chapters on individual and group behavior, these chapters focus on interpersonal relations.

Group Decision Making. A new chapter reflects recent research on decision making in groups.

Technology and Structural Design. Two new chapters explore alternative organizational designs based on a consideration of tasks, human behavior, and environment.

Administrative Systems Design. Two new chapters explore methods of planning, controlling, leading, and rewarding, based upon behavioral-science knowledge of motivation and cognition.

Conflict Management. In addition to a chapter on the nature of conflict, a new chapter explores techniques for using and containing conflict in organizations.

Organization Development. A new chapter explores techniques for planned intervention in organizations, to improve interpersonal competence and organizational effectiveness.

Cases. Two short discussion cases have been added to each chapter, a total of twenty-four in all.

Though the book has been modified, as these new features indicate, it continues its distinctive use of concepts and research findings in organizational behavior as a foundation for the practice of management.

We should like to express our gratitude to all those who have helped us to prepare the book. Many authors and publishers have kindly permitted us to reprint selections of their work in this volume. It would be fitting if our use of their works will draw deserved attention to the whole books or articles from which we have borrowed parts.

Many users of the first edition and other reviewers have generously shared their thoughts with us. James Walker, Robert Pethia, George Strauss, Jonathan Monat, Frank Paine, and John Hornaday are among those who have helped. We thank them. We also express our thanks to Robert Runck of Scott, Foresman and Company for his outstanding editorial assistance.

David R. Hampton
Charles E. Summer
Ross A. Webber

Contents

PART THREE
MANAGEMENT OF CONFLICT AND CHANGE

Introduction

As Francis Bacon once observed: "Nature, if it is to be commanded, must be obeyed." The engineer cannot expect water to run uphill; the physician cannot expect a chronic ailment to go away; and a manager cannot expect people to cooperate and produce—all merely for the asking. Yet each can achieve his goal if, and only if, he harnesses the lawful course of the processes involved.

The engineer, if he is to cause water to run uphill, must understand the factors—water, gravity, etc.—with which he works. The physician, if he is to cure a patient, must understand the anatomy and physiology of the system in which he would intervene. The manager, if he is to design and operate an organization, must understand the parts and processes of the organizational system. The power of these professionals to command results is increased proportionally as their actions are better fitted to the nature of the systems—machines, people, organizations—with which they cope.

The manager's system is called the organization. Its anatomy includes individuals, pairs of individuals, groups, technology, organization structure, and such administrative components as plans, controls, rewards, and leadership. The organization's processes include all of the physiology—the interaction of the parts to achieve goals within a larger environment. The objective of this book is to help people learn to fit managerial actions to the nature of organizational behavior. To paraphrase Bacon, the objective is to help people learn how to obey the nature of organizations so that they can command or manage them.

Professional education which neglects the nature of the subject system—the person, the machine, the organization—enfeebles the practitioner by depriving him of necessary knowledge. This was the gist of the famous and influential Flexner (1910) report on the state of medical education in America early in this century. This report revealed that the existing system of having senior practicing physicians teach medical students had a serious weakness. The veteran practitioners could indeed help pass along existing knowledge and skills, but they inevitably passed along information and ideas that were out of date. They were out of date because the growing discoveries in the underlying disciplines—physiology, chemistry, biology, and the like—made them obsolete. Practicing doctors whose education was completed in advance of vital discoveries simply could not communicate the results of such discoveries to their younger colleagues. Similar problems have at various times weakened the training of engineers and managers.

The remedy is not to throw out all senior professionals, but to channel developing knowledge into the training of students. Textbooks provide one such channel. Faculty members who know the underlying sciences as well as the applied discipline provide another. Curriculums which require science courses provide still another.

Nevertheless, balanced preparation for work in any of the applied disciplines—engineering, medicine, management—is an elusive goal. The effective manager, for example, like the skillful physician, needs a feeling for the key properties of particular situations, as well as more general knowledge. Perhaps this skill is formed more by experience than by academic study. Yet books like this one do try to nurture this ability through the use of cases and other devices.

But what is distinctive about this book is its selection and arrangement of knowledge about organizational behavior, and its application of that knowledge to the processes or functions of management—organizing, planning and controlling, leading, rewarding, and coping with conflict, innovation, and development. Unfortunately, the word "knowledge" suggests a quality of final truth which is misleading. In many cases, only a few laboratory or field studies provide the newer knowledge. Consequently, making even tentative statements of how to manage based on this knowledge means skating on thinner ice than one might hope for. Still, if education is, as Alfred North Whitehead * suggested, "the acquisition of the art of the utilization of knowledge," then our effort to use what knowledge is available may help you learn to use it in creating your own style.

Part I of the book concentrates on illuminating and explaining individual, interpersonal, and group behavior in organizations. Motivation theory and research guides our examination of individual behavior. Communication and influence theory and research guides our study of interpersonal processes. Interaction theory guides our study of groups. Many other concepts, as you will see, play a part in making the behavior of people at work understandable.

Parts II and III concentrate on management. Part II begins with a chapter which explores the interrelations of tasks, technology, and structure. It is followed by a series of three chapters which consider the management processes of organizing, planning, controlling, leading, and rewarding. Here is where we begin to put to work knowledge about organizational behavior in the practice of management. As you will see, what motivation theory, for example, reveals about human nature provides a base for logically designing structures, goals, controls, leadership, and rewards calculated to influence behavior.

Part III begins with a chapter which explores the roots of conflict in organizations. It is followed by a chapter on the management of conflict. This chapter puts to work some findings about individual, interpersonal, and group behavior and about methods of organization and administration.

Finally, since organizations are living systems with changing internal and external conditions, they must adapt, cope, and create. They develop or die. The last chapter considers this problem and techniques for organizational development.

A word of caution: Many of the techniques we discuss may *seem* quite easy to institute. For example, management by objectives has enjoyed widespread popularity in recent years—even to the point of becoming a fad. Likewise, American business managers went through a period when decentralization seemed to be the obvious answer to the elusive "best" way to manage. We now

---

* *The Aims of Education* (The Free Press, 1967), p. 4.

know that decentralization is more complicated to carry out than originally thought, and is furthermore applicable only to certain situations in certain companies at certain times. This same oversimplification has been characteristic of the era of delegation, the era of planning and control, the age of authority, and the period of overemphasis on participative management.

One of the newest managerial technologies is organization development, which shows every sign of becoming the latest fad. Some disciples of this school treat it as if it were the long-awaited panacea to all the manager's problems. The wise manager recognizes that it has its proper place in the panorama of management processes, along with others. He also sees that it is more important to try to understand its true function, and its applicability under certain conditions, than it is merely to learn buzzwords such as "sensitivity," "feedback," or "climate."

Another caution: You should be wary of "getting religion" on any one managerial technology and forgetting the rest. If you find yourself doing this, it will be because you are paying more attention to your own experiences (or problems) than you are to the study of various alternatives for a particular organization with which you must deal in the future. There is not now, nor probably ever will be, any one technique of management which is best over periods of time and for diverse organizations. Any author who implies that there is such a technique is trying to make all organizations fit his own set of values and attitudes.

The applied techniques of management represent a *synthesis* of ideas, and give prescriptions for action. They are technologies, which draw on many behavioral forces at once. For example, drawing on concepts of motivation, communication, influence, group behavior, and conflict, the chapters on organization design and administration show alternative systems which involve all of these concepts. This presents problems of exposition, because there is no really systematic way to show how each managerial strategy affects each behavioral phenomenon. However, so long as you are prepared to see that each technique of management might simultaneously solve many of the problems uncovered through analysis, you will see that the techniques are indeed methods of synthesis.

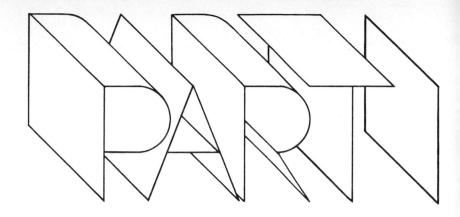

INDIVIDUAL AND GROUP BEHAVIOR

Chapter 1

Individual Motivation

In 1822 the English philosopher Jeremy Bentham wrote, "Nature has placed mankind under the governance of two sovereign masters, *pain* and *pleasure*" (Burtt, 1939, p. 791). The same thought had been expressed long before and has echoed long after Bentham. It can be found in Plato's *Protagoras,* and in modern terms, as a central assumption of motivation theory.

Man, like other animals, seeks to approach those states which are pleasurable and to avoid those which are painful. Historically, most of the research which has explored these ideas has concentrated on animals. Many of us remember from our psychology courses that animals do indeed try to obtain food when hungry, and to avoid electrical shocks and other unpleasant stimuli. Fortunately, however, knowledge of motivation is not restricted to knowledge of rodent motivation. There has been increased concentration on human motivation, and, of particular interest to us, human motivation and behavior in organizations. After all, ever since the United States rejected Thomas Jefferson's attractive but simplistic vision of a nation of independent yeomen and chose Alexander Hamilton's dream of a wealthy, complex, and interdependent society, most of us have had to work in an organization. So the pleasures and pains of organizational life are of personal concern to us.

A few basic facts will guide our exploration of individual behavior in organizations. First, behavior on the job is a function of what the person brings to the situation and what the situation brings to the person. When people come to work in organizations they do not come "empty handed," as it were. They bring a supply of energy or potential to perform. They bring various needs or motives which predispose them to release their energy or behave in particular ways—ways which seem to them likely to satisfy their needs.

What the person brings to the situation is but one blade of the scissors. The other blade is what the situation brings to the person. It is only as the blades come together that the pattern of behavior is cut. The characteristics of the organizational or work situation provide cues which can arouse particular tendencies to behave. Circumstances can signal to the individual that particular job-oriented behaviors may lead to satisfaction of his needs. The commission system can notify the salesman that selling more means more income. Not surprisingly in our society, the prospect of more income may mean to the salesman increased status, esteem, and other pleasures.

In this chapter we take a close look at the needs people bring with them into organizations. We discuss how motives develop. We also discuss how motives dispose people to behave in particular ways, and how managers can profit by matching task requirements and behavioral predispositions. Since motives do

3

not express themselves in behavior without the related processes of perception and thought, we also consider the cognitive side of human nature. Specifically, we consider expectancy and dissonance theories. Our central interest is how individual predispositions and situational characteristics come together to produce particular ways of behaving on the job. Finally, we preview the subject of how managers can behave skillfully to increase the probability that subordinates will perform effectively—a subject we return to later in the book.

Needs Theory: The Hierarchy of Needs

The early needs theorists, such as Murray (1938), suggested lists of needs that may be of academic interest, but that hold out little promise of providing any readily usable tool for understanding the everyday task performances of people at work. But such a tool was forthcoming. It was the hierarchy of needs concept developed by Abraham Maslow (1943) and popularized by numerous management writers, the foremost being Douglas McGregor (1960).

Maslow's hierarchy of needs is simplicity itself. The central idea is that man's needs—physiological, safety, love, esteem, and self-actualization—are arranged in a hierarchy of prepotency. Physiological needs are at the bottom of the hierarchy, and self-actualization needs at the top. Though man is in a state of want all of the time, according to the theory, what he wants is a function of his pattern of need satisfactions in the hierarchy. He can start out with lofty aspirations relative to love, esteem, and self-actualization, but be driven to more basic needs if those more basic needs become unsatisfied.

A tragic episode in American history provides an illustration. In the early 1800s, a band of pioneers led by a man named Donner crossed the western plains with ox-drawn covered wagons, and climbed into the Sierra Nevada. For most of the party, the trip ended there. Marooned by enormous snow drifts and slowly freezing on the wind-swept slopes, they were unable to move forward or back. As they exhausted their supply of food, the party gradually deteriorated.

Some years ago, a diary kept by a member of the party was published (Croy, 1955), in which the writer described his compatriots at the beginning of the journey as "salt of the earth"—God-fearing and individualistic, but cooperative and concerned for each other's welfare. During the protracted ordeal in the mountains, they withdrew upon themselves: concern shifted from the larger group to the immediate family; then to the individual; finally, as in McKinlay Kantor's (1955) description of a Civil War prison camp, the strong began to prey on the weak for personal survival, and the ultimate horror emerged—cannibalism.

To the party, food eventually came to be all important and all motivating. If one is without food long enough, he becomes a sort of human piranha—thinking, dreaming, and hunting food without any other concern.[1] Such a food-seeking monster is not interested in building monuments, wearing fine clothes, or worshipping God. The satisfaction of the physiological drives is essential to the maintenance of life; thus Maslow described them as prepotent for the motivation of behavior.

Happily, the hierarchical model suggests that, as physical needs are met

---

[1]For a classic example of this kind of behavior, see Hamsun (1967).

(at least at a minimum level), new needs emerge to motivate behavior. We have seen that man is a "wanting creature," striving to satisfy many different needs in an order of potency as follows: (1) physiological, (2) safety, (3) love, (4) esteem, and (5) self-actualization. Therefore, just as unmet basic needs drove the Donner party down the hierarchy, satisfied basic needs open up higher level wants.

This dynamic quality of the needs hierarchy has important consequences for the motivation of people at work. As lower-level needs are relatively satisfied, they become less directly motivating for behavior. One is motivated mainly by the next level of unsatisfied need. Thus gratified needs, in a sense, disappear. They are not motivating. Since any manager attempts to influence human behavior, he must consider what needs are relatively unsatisfied, and hence can serve as levers for motivation. If workers are no longer starving or profoundly insecure, offering them work whose only rewards are seen to be food and safety will not arouse the motive power of unmet needs.

The question arises, then, of the relationship between work and such higher needs as love, esteem, and self-actualization. Historically, the primary source of satisfaction for love, or social needs, has been the family. But American families in the twentieth century have changed. We have fewer children than our grandparents did. More fundamentally, the consanguine family unit has become a conjugal family unit. Infrequently do grandparents, children, uncles, aunts, cousins, and grandchildren live together, as they used to. Often the separate generations do not even live in the same neighborhood, city, or state. This means that the family unit is smaller.

Inside this smaller unit, encouraged by the availability of bicycles, motor scooters, motorcycles, and "personal" cars, family members tend to turn to outside associates for recreation and for satisfaction of the needs for membership, affection, affiliation, and so on. Moreover, in our modern society, maintaining a family to supply love and social satisfaction requires a job and at least a modicum of economic stability. Thus the job has come to serve as the primary source of social satisfaction.

Employers of the nineteenth and early twentieth century saw no need for social satisfaction on the job. In office and shop their posted policies frequently included dictums forbidding "socializing," "idle gossip," or "conspiratorial meetings." When Frederick Taylor and scientific management came along, managers were advised to treat people strictly as individuals and to offer individual piece-rate incentive pay which would encourage each employee to produce to his maximum ability. Managers in the 1920s were aware, and in the famous Hawthorne plant studies at Western Electric academic researchers corroborated, that many workers (if not most) limited their personal effort in order to maintain their membership in an informal social structure (Homans, 1950; Roethlisberger and Dickson, 1939). At some point, for virtually everyone except the individualistic "rate-busters," the desire for communication, support, and friendship with associates on the job and during work hours became more important than the little bit of extra money that might be earned.

In addition to the two ways that the job aids in the satisfaction of the affiliation need (that is, maintenance of a family and of social relations with fellow workers), Freud (1962) suggested a third socializing contribution of the job. A job forces a person to set aside his own concerns and confront the world. A job imposes discipline. It requires interpersonal communication that assists the individual to learn about the norms of society around him—and to maintain a sense of reality, identity, and stability by continually testing his own views against societal norms. Not that these norms are always right, but the job and the contact with the world that the job requires enables a man to live more easily in that world and to find desired social satisfactions.

Research on the mental health and attitudes of long-term unemployed males (Ginzberg, 1943) support Freud's suggestions. These studies indicate very directly the relevance of the job to a man's sense of membership in society. Even though welfare and a variety of governmental programs remove their fears and anxieties about the satisfaction of physiological and security needs, unemployed men feel out of place. They are not members of society; they are not fulfilling the requirements of the head of a household. In many cases they become withdrawn and depressed, unable even to take satisfaction in their families. They are simply not confronting the world in ways that the culture values.

When social needs are relatively satisfied, however, the desire for esteem tends to move into consciousness. And one's job plays a prominent part in determining one's self-esteem and the esteem received from others. Kenneth Clark (1965) has described the loss of self-esteem which is part of the under-employment experience of many black Americans (as well as others). Having a job is no guarantee of deriving feelings of pride and dignity from it. Elliot Liebow relates a memorable discussion with Tally of *Tally's Corner* which illustrates the point:

"You know that boy came in last night? That Black Moozlem? That's what I ought to be doing. I ought to be in his place."

"What do you mean?"

"Dressed nice, going to [night] school, got a good job."

"He's no better off than you, Tally. You make more than he does."

"It's not the money. [Pause] It's position, I guess. He's got position. When he finish school he gonna be a supervisor. People respect him. . . . Thinking about people with position and education gives me a feeling right here [pressing his fingers into the pit of his stomach]."

"You're educated, too. You have a skill, a trade. You're a cement finisher. You can make a building, pour a sidewalk."

"That's different. Look, can anybody do what you're doing? Can anybody just come up and do your job? Well, in one week I can teach you cement finishing. You won't be as good as me 'cause you won't have the experience but you'll be a cement finisher. That's what I mean. Anybody can do what I'm doing and that's what gives me this feeling. [Long pause] Suppose I like this girl. I go over to her house and I meet her father. He starts talking about what he done today. He talks about operating on somebody and sewing them up and about surgery. I know he's a doctor 'cause of the way he talks. Then she starts talking about what she did. Maybe she's a boss or a supervisor. Maybe she's a lawyer and her father says to me, 'And what do you do, Mr. Jackson?' [Pause] You remember at the courthouse, Lonny's trial? You and the lawyer was talking in the hall? You remember? I just stood there listening. I didn't say a word. You know why? 'Cause I didn't even know what you was talking about. That's happened to me a lot."

"Hell, you're nothing special. That happens to everybody. Nobody knows everything. One man is a doctor, so he talks about surgery. Another man is a teacher, so he talks about books. But doctors and teachers don't know anything about concrete. You're a cement finisher and that's your specialty."

"Maybe so, but when was the last time you saw anybody standing around talking about concrete?"[2]

The organization with which one is affiliated is also a possible source of self esteem. In reply to the question "What do you do?" Americans often respond with "I'm associated with IBM," or "I'm with General Electric." Fifty years ago the replies would have been "I'm a machinist," or "I'm an accountant." The earlier responses were a legacy of the traditional societies of Europe, where a man's craft has always been a major determinant of his self-esteem, status, or prestige. However, craft in these societies is generally determined by birth or family, which are the true determinants of status or prestige. The United States has always been a much less rigid society in terms of social class; for example, attitudes toward status distinctions vary with geography and socio-economic background—the criteria for social esteem in the Northeast among the middle class is quite different from those in the Southwest among the working class. But a man's association with a particular company of wide repute is a reliable source of status. Thus, in the United States, the corporation as a source of feelings of esteem and prestige has begun to obliterate the older tradition of status differentiation on the basis of vocation or craft.

Within the corporation, elaborated hierarchies of positions and their attendant status symbols and perquisites also reflect the desire for status differentiation. Management ignores at its peril the necessity to correlate pay, title, authority, and symbols of status. A large regional insurance office is a case in point. The two or three huge rooms stretch out like an airplane hangar, aisle after aisle. With clerks, secretaries, representatives, claims men, supervisors, and department heads all seated at seemingly identical desks row after row, the scene resembles a Franz Kafka novel in its mechanistic oppressiveness. Not surprisingly, the management has difficulty with superior-subordinate relations, and particularly with supervisory morale. Giving out important-sounding job titles—or even more money—would be inadequate to satisfy the desire for status on the job. One of the principal causes of dissatisfaction is the lack of physical manifestation of status differences, including individual offices to give quiet and privacy.

Finally, as Maslow (1943) puts it: "Even if all these needs are satisfied, we may still often (if not always) expect that a new discontent and restlessness will soon develop, unless the individual is doing what he is fitted for. A musician must make music, an artist must paint, a poet must write if he is to be ultimately happy. What a man *can* be, he *must* be. This need we may call self-actualization" (p. 382).

While Maslow's hierarchy-of-needs theory has proved very stimulating and useful to students of management (chiefly, it has made them carefully consider the relationship of the job to motivation), it has met with criticism. Some critics (Cofer and Appleby, 1964) have raised questions about the adequacy of Maslow's research. Maslow had selected examples and data "from among personal acquaintances and friends and from among public and historical

---

figures" (1954, p. 200). In addition, McClelland (1955) has expressed doubts about both the universality of the needs hierarchy and the adequacy of the concept of self-actualization. He suggests that many of the needs are not biological and universal, but are socially acquired and vary from culture to culture. What would be regarded as fulfilling or actualizing one's potential varies from society to society, and from beholder to beholder within one society.

Socially Acquired Motives

McClelland, Atkinson (1964), and others have contributed a quarter of a century of careful research on socially acquired motives. As a way of introducing the study of certain such motives, we would like to ask you to perform an easy and brief exercise.

Take a quick (10 to 15 seconds) look at the picture on the next page. Now, allowing yourself no more than five minutes, make up and write an imaginative story about what the picture suggests. Don't merely describe the picture, but relax and let your imagination fly. No one but you will see the story anyway.

To make sure you have a story plot, the following questions can serve as guides for your creative writing:

1. What is happening? Who are the people?
2. What has led up to this situation? That is, what has happened in the past?
3. What is being thought? What is wanted? By whom?
4. What will happen? What will be done?

Remember, only 10 to 15 seconds for looking at the picture, and no more than five minutes for writing your story.

This picture is one of a group of six pictures which make up the *Test of Imagination* (1968), a Thematic Apperception Test. Each of the pictures is ambiguous. People who look at them and then compose imaginative stories project their own needs into the story content. The story you wrote thus can tell something about your own motives (though we have no reason to think we have adequately sampled your own fantasies to describe your motives definitively). Under normal and adequate test conditions, each person would be asked to write six stories, each in response to a different picture. A total score would then be obtained.

Psychologists have developed reasonably reliable and valid means for analyzing and scoring the content of stories for this test and similar ones. The stories can be scored for three particularly important motives: the need for achievement, the need for affiliation, and the need for power. They are important, as we shall see, because they dispose people to behave in ways which critically affect the performance of many jobs and tasks.

The Achievement Motive

David McClelland, one of the psychologists who has contributed most to the study of the achievement motive, has discussed responses written by business executives to the particular picture you saw. Here is one of the stories and McClelland's (1962) analysis:

> The man is an engineer at a drafting board. The picture is of his family. He has a problem and is concentrating on it. It is merely an everyday occurrence—a problem which requires thought. How can he get that bridge to take the stress of possible high winds? He wants to arrive at a good solution of the problem by himself. He will discuss the problem with a few other engineers and make a decision which will be a correct one—he has the earmarks of competence (p. 101).

This author's thoughts are almost entirely on a specific task problem and how to solve it. He describes a problem, wants to solve it, thinks about how to solve it, thinks about obstacles, and thinks about people who might help. According to established protocols for scoring stories (Atkinson, 1958), each idea about a particular motive theme yields one point. This story would receive most of its points for n (need for) Achievement.

McClelland (1962, pp. 104–105) goes on to sketch the characteristics of the person with high n Achievement:

1. He likes situations in which he takes personal responsibility for finding solutions to problems.
2. He tends to set moderate achievement goals and to take "calculated risks."
3. He wants concrete feedback on how well he is doing.

The Affiliation Motive

"People who need people," as Barbra Streisand sings it, "are the luckiest people." Lucky or not, people certainly do vary in their needs for socializing. A person with high n Affiliation tends to think often about the quality of his personal relationships. He might savor the good times he has had with some people and be concerned about shortcomings in his relations with others. It is to these topics, rather than to defining and solving task problems, that his mind runs when he is daydreaming or not required to concentrate on anything in particular.

To illustrate, here is another story from McClelland (1962):

> The engineer is at work on Saturday when it is quiet and he has taken time to do a little daydreaming. He is the father of the two children in the picture—the husband of the woman shown. He has a happy home life and is dreaming about some pleasant outing they have had. He is also looking forward to a repeat of the incident which is now giving him pleasure to think about. He plans on the following day, Sunday, to use the afternoon to take his family for a short trip (p. 101).

McClelland explains that such a story emphasizes affiliative themes, since the author's thoughts are about relations with other people. This is the theme most people emphasize when they write stories about this picture.

Schachter (1959), a psychologist, has completed many ingenious experiments and field studies which have contributed much to understanding the affiliation motive. He has demonstrated the tendency of people to seek out others to gain confirmation for their own beliefs or to relieve the stress of uncertainties. In one experiment, he led the subjects to believe that they would experience some pain as part of the experiment. He told the subjects they would have to wait for that stage of the experiment. Then he asked each if he would prefer to wait alone or with other subjects. Most people in such a miserable predicament wanted company.

In another study, Festinger et al. (1956) observed a group ("cult" might be a better term) who believed the world would end but that they would be spared the disaster and removed to another planet by beings from that planet. When the zero hour arrived and passed and nothing happened, what did the group do? Disband? No, the members discussed their views and interpretations more vigorously than ever and intensified their efforts to interest outsiders in joining their group. The disappointment seemed to stimulate compensatory behavior to build a strengthened basis for the group's beliefs.

Though there is not nearly as much research on affiliative motivation as on achievement motivation, there is enough to suggest that there is a common goal in such behavior—social interaction with others. But such behavior has multiple origins. In some instances affiliative behavior is linked with anxiety reduction, as in the experiment which caused the subjects to anticipate pain. In others, affiliative behavior contributes more to securing social approval of one's views, as in the end-of-the-world cult.

Whatever the origins of the need for affiliation, the patterns of behavior it tends to produce are similar. Persons with a high need for affiliation seek the company of others and take steps to be liked by them. They try to project a favorable image in interpersonal relations. They smooth out disagreeable tensions in meetings. They help and support others and want to be liked in return.

The Power Motive

The kind of story about the man at the work table with the family picture which would seem rich in the preoccupation with power might go something like this:

> The man is an engineer. He is thinking of how he will present his plan at the design committee meeting. He wants to sell the idea and he knows he must persuade them to his view. He believes he will carry the day and refute any criticisms. He wants badly to get the new project manager job which will be opening up. He thinks if he can win this coming battle he will be in a strong position to move up the ladder. Then he will be able to get people moving in the right direction at long last.

As you can see, there is no notice of satisfaction in solving the technical problem (achievement), and no notice of the family (affiliation); there is only power—control and influence. Individuals high in n Power spend more time thinking about how to obtain and exercise power and authority than do those low in n Power. The former need to win arguments, to persuade others, to prevail. They feel uncomfortable without some sense of power.

One of the problems with the subject of power is its negative emotional connotations. We are accustomed to think of it as being at least a bit nasty. To manipulate, to be "Machiavellian," suggests something distasteful to most people. But possession of a strong power drive is not necessarily undesirable, the equivalent of a character defect. As McClelland (1970) has taken pains to point out, power really has two faces. The first is the one which arouses negative reaction. This face of power is the one concerned with dominance-submission, with having one's way, with having a strong impact in controlling others.

The other face of power is positive. It reflects the process by which persuasive and inspirational behavior on the part of a leader can evoke feelings of power and ability in subordinates. The active leader who helps his group form goals and who helps them in attaining their goals plays a part, not in subordinating and dominating people, but in aiding their expression of their strength and competence in reaching their goals. A selection by McClelland following this chapter develops the concepts of power more fully.

Given that individuals do differ in the relative potency of their needs for achievement, affiliation, and power, and that it is possible through tests or just sampling a person's conversation to get some idea of his motive pattern, one question remains: How do such needs develop? How do individuals come to exhibit differing configurations of n Achievement, n Affiliation, and n Power?

Development of Social Motives

Social motives are learned. They are not learned or acquired consciously in the way one learns the alphabet or addition. Rather, the acquisition of motives is accidental, a byproduct of behaving, of trying actively to cope with one's environment. It may be that while one is learning the alphabet or addition one tastes something of the pleasure of achievement.

That taste can be rewarding, and as behavioral psychologists have long known, rewards following an act reinforce the act, or in other words, increase the probability of its recurrence. Where the active, problem-solving behavior of the child operates on the environment to elicit satisfying results, more than the answer to the problem gets learned; the mode of behavior associated with success is reinforced as well. McClelland (1962) describes an experiment which illustrates some of the conditions which nurture behaviors associated with the need for achievement:

"A group of boys were blindfolded and asked to stack irregularly shaped blocks on top of each other with their left hands, at home in front of their parents. Separately, the mothers and fathers were asked how high they thought their sons could stack the blocks. Both parents of a boy with high n Achievement estimated that their boy should do better; they expected more of him than did the parents of a boy with low n Achievement. They also encouraged him more and gave him more affection and reward while he was actually doing the task. Finally, the fathers of boys with high n Achievement directed the behavior of their sons much less when they were actually stacking the blocks; that is, they told them less often to move their hands this way or that, to try harder, to stop jiggling the table, and so forth, than did the fathers of boys with low n Achievement" (p. 110).

Apparently, under conditions which encourage independence and moderate risk-taking, people can acquire the taste for challenges of manageable propor-tions—challenges which are likely to yield neither failure nor too easy success, but maximal feelings of achievement.

Similarly, a strong need for affiliation or power probably would be the product of a history of rewards being associated with sociable or dominant behavior. It takes a particular history to produce the view that "one learns from experience that being close and friendly with people is more important than career success" (Moment and Zaleznik, 1963). What has been learned by one who holds such a view is that, as one copes in the world, the most valuable rewards come through good social or interpersonal relations. It is easy to see how the affectionate and supportive fathers in the blockstacking experiment might have nurtured the affiliation motive. We can speculate, though, that the psychic rewards available to the boys high in *n* Achievement may have been contingent upon successful performance of ambitious goals.

To stick with the same example and with a mood of speculative interpretation, we can imagine that the more dominant and directive fathers behave the same way outside the experiment. Conceivably, their children, having a different model to emulate, may try more often to exercise power and direction over their playmates and, depending upon how successfully such modes operate on the environment, acquire or not acquire a need to relate to others in a dominating way. In any event, our purpose is only to suggest, not develop fully, some picture of how socially acquired needs are molded. In essence, they are one outcome of the whole of an individual's problem-solving or developmental history.

As White (1959) suggests, one of the mainsprings of human motivation is an interest in getting to know what the world is like and in learning to get what one wants from it. He calls this a competence motive, which probably underlies the development of the other motives already discussed. The teacher hopes that this drive (for competence) exists in his students as a desire to master an academic discipline, and in general expand themselves intellectually. Obviously, the competence motive may also take other directions. The reward of self-esteem may be derived from competence in a wide variety of vocational and avocational activities. A selection by White following this chapter expands on the competence motive.

This competence motive can be seen as active even in very young infants, in the fun of random fingering of objects, poking around, and touching whatever is in reach. Later, it is exploring, tinkering, taking things apart, putting them together, and the like. Whether an adult's sense of competence is strong or weak depends on the balance of successes and failures he has experienced in his various encounters with the world. Whether his needs for achievement, affiliation, and power are strong or weak depend upon their past associations with problem-solving performances and rewards. Lawrence and Lorsch (1969) summarize the process succinctly:

"As the individual system strives to master problems, certain behaviors turn out to be consistently rewarding; that is, they provide solutions to the problems the individual faces. Consequently, the next time the individual needs to solve a problem he tries the same pattern of behavior again. Over time, as some of these patterns are consistently rewarding, the individual learns to rely on them. Thus, we say that a person is highly motivated to compete against a standard of excellence (need for achievement), or has a higher need for warm friendly relations (need for affiliation), etc. As a result of this learning process, different individuals develop the different patterns of these motives already described" (pp. 68–69).

But there is at least one significant additional force at work in the learning process: anxiety. Learning not only takes place when acts are followed by positive states or rewards, but also when acts are followed by a reduction of negative states of unpleasant tension. There are states which are gratifying to avoid as well as states which are gratifying to approach. As Sullivan (1950) observes:

"The first of all learning is called out to avoid recurrence of the extremely unpleasant tension of anxiety, which is, and always continues to be, the very antithesis of everything good and desirable. . . . The child soon learns to discriminate *increasing* from *decreasing* anxiety and to alter activity in the direction of the latter. The child learns to chart a course by the anxiety gradient" (p. 95).

In part, then, the reduction of anxiety associated with successful problem-solving behavior contributes to the strengthening of such behavior. If competing against a standard of excellence pays off by relieving anxiety, the need for achievement is strengthened. If warm, friendly relations with others are associated with success, the need for affiliation is strengthened. If persuasiveness and dominance are associated with success, the need for power is strengthened.

Motives and Behavior

Different motives tend to express themselves in different behavior. When a need or motive is strong in a person, its effect is to predispose the person to behavior which has become associated with the satisfaction of that need. For example, having a high *n* Achievement predisposes the individual to engage in setting goals for himself, trying to improve performance to reach the goals, and realistically seeking and using feedback on performance; *n* Achievement has no emphasis on people.

The needs for affiliation and power are rather different. They both orient the individual towards interpersonal behavior. For *n* Affiliation, interpersonal relations, when they are good, are their own reward. For *n* Power, interpersonal relations provide the path to exercising influence over others.

These bits of information may be interesting, but we might ask why a practical hard-headed manager should want to know them. How can he behave more skillfully if he understands that socially acquired motives such as *n* Achievement, *n* Affiliation, and *n* Power mean readiness or predisposition to behave in particular ways? There are a great many things he can do. We explore a few here and expand our study of practical administrative implications in Chapters 8 and 9.

Suppose, for example, we could learn what sorts of behavior patterns are instrumental in the effective performance of particular tasks. With this knowledge we could then consider what motives predispose people to such behavior. We could seek out such people and hire them for the task. To illustrate, consider the behavioral manifestations of *n* Achievement in relation to two jobs: salesman and manager.

Where are the opportunities in a society for taking personal responsibility for problem solving, for taking calculated risks, and for obtaining concrete feedback on performance? Generally, business offers such opportunities on a large scale. One might expect, then, that people high in *n* Achievement might gravitate towards business. This is exactly what McClelland (1962) found: ". . . in three countries representing different levels and types of economic development, managers or executives scored considerably higher on the average in achievement thinking than did professionals or specialists of comparable education and background" (p. 102). And within business itself, there tends to be a concentration of men high in *n* Achievement where these opportunities are most clearly present: sales jobs. Successful salesmen, in particular, tend to be high in *n* Achievement.

On the other hand, there is the old saw that the best salesman may not make the best sales manager. Why? Because management involves planning, organizing, and leading people. And, as McClelland (1970) points out, "it is fairly clear that a high need to Achieve does not equip a man to deal effectively with managing human relationships" (p. 30).

Perhaps other motives better predispose individuals to effective managerial behavior: *n* Affiliation and *n* Power differ from *n* Achievement in that they are interpersonally oriented needs. The power motive impels a man to strive for a position where he can exercise influence; it may also aid him in being effective in that position. As J. Sterling Livingston (1971) puts it:

"Power seekers can be counted on to strive hard to reach positions where they can exercise authority over large numbers of people. Individual performers who lack this drive are not likely to act in ways that will enable them to advance far up the managerial ladder. They usually scorn company politics and devote their energies to other types of activities that are more satisfying to them. But, to prevail in the competitive struggle to attain and hold high-level positions in management, a person's desire for prestige and high income must be reinforced by the satisfaction he gets or expects to get from exercising the power and authority of a high office.

"The competitive battle to advance within an organization, as Levinson (1969) points out, is much like playing 'King of the Hill.' Unless a person enjoys playing that game, he is likely to tire of it and give up the struggle for control of the top of the hill. The power game is a part of management, and it is played best by those who enjoy it most" (p. 87).

Thus far, we have written about each motive as a pure case. This has facilitated exposition, but it may be misleading. To illustrate, here is a third story from McClelland (1962) about the picture we showed you earlier:

> A successful industrial designer is at his "work bench" toying with a new idea. He is "talking it out" with his family in the picture. Someone in the family dropped a comment about a shortcoming in a household gadget, and the designer has just "seen" a commercial use of the idea. He has picked up ideas from his family before—he is "telling" his family what a good idea it is, and "confidentially" he is going to take them on a big vacation because "their" idea was so good. The idea will be successful, and family pride and mutual admiration will be strengthened (p. 101).

In this case the author expresses a strong interest in interpersonal relations. However, he adds the innovation of a product. The introduction of this idea evidences some concern for achievement. He does not think only about people, but also about task accomplishment.

Thus, that a given individual might be high in one motive does not mean that he would necessarily score low in any other motive. For example, to score high in *n* Power is not necessarily to lack concern for people or achievement. It all depends on the mix and the situation. As Litwin and Stringer (1968) suggest: "A man with a strong *n* Power, little concern for warm, affiliative relationships, and strong authoritarian values would certainly tend toward autocratic and dictatorial action. On the other hand, a man with a strong *n* Power, considerable sensitivity to others' feelings, and a desire to give service to others would probably make an excellent Peace Corps worker or missionary" (pp. 19–20).

As Livingston has argued and as Litwin and Stringer's example suggests, some degree of *n* Power might be a critical attribute of managers or Peace Corps workers if their effectiveness required sustained effort to influence others. Similarly, some degree of *n* Affiliation would seem indispensable where task performance depended upon maintaining cordial interpersonal relations. It is difficult to conceive of any managerial position not requiring some degree of power and affiliation behavior. But what mixture is optimal can only be determined by analysis of the specific tasks to be performed.

The potential payoff is, of course, what was suggested: selecting and placing people whose motive patterns predispose them to behave in ways which contribute to task performance—managerial tasks or other tasks. Some recent research by Lawrence and Lorsch (1969) provides a straightforward illustration of how sensitivity to motive patterns may contribute to organizational effectiveness. In two cases, the researchers looked at not only the motive patterns of people in the organization but at the tasks they performed as well. Earlier research had led Lawrence and Lorsch to expect that a motivational analysis of both tasks and individuals could lead to improved placement. They said:

"We have found it useful to identify the behaviors which are required to perform a particular set of tasks effectively and then to determine what individual characteristics are most often associated with this behavior. For example, in attempting to achieve more effective performance on the part of "integrators" in an organization, it was learned, from an analysis of the task and an examination of personality characteristics of more and less effective performers in this job, that a relatively high need for affiliation, along with moderately high achievement, was associated with effectiveness. These jobs provided a high expectation of meeting these needs, and people with this need pattern found these jobs interesting and performed more effectively" (pp. 70–71).

With this much background, you can examine the following two selling tasks described by Lawrence and Lorsch (pp. 71–77) and see if you are able to identify the motive patterns associated with successful performance.

Case One: Selling Hospital Equipment

The medical division of a large, diversified manufacturing company produced and sold expensive ($5000 to $200,000) electromechanical devices and systems to hospitals. The equipment was used in hospital operating rooms. To carry out the sales task, the division was organized into three regions. Each region comprised ten or so district offices. Each district office was staffed with six to eight salesmen and sixteen to twenty servicemen. The latter group both installed and serviced equipment.

When the researchers studied what the selling task involved, they observed three distinguishable phases. The first of these, which could vary from one to fifteen years, was a period in which the salesman needed to develop good relations with hospital administrators and doctors. He needed to foster their trust and confidence in him. The second phase was a shorter period, six months to three years, of more concentrated selling. The salesman needed to create an opportunity to demonstrate and sell equipment. The third phase began with the installation of the equipment and continued with its servicing for many years, as many as twenty-five.

In terms of the existing measures of sales performance, there were some clear-cut differences between district offices. The researchers were able to make a comparison between four outstandingly successful district offices and four offices with average sales performance. What was compared were the motivation patterns of the salesmen. They were given Thematic Apperception Tests (TAT), and the tests were scored for *n* Achievement, *n* Affiliation, and *n* Power, the purpose being to see if there were any differences between the motives of the salesmen in the outstanding offices and salesmen in the average offices. What do you think the results were?

If you are like the researchers, you would have looked for a difference in achievement motivation to be the answer. After all, as we said earlier, successful salesmen tend to be high in *n* Achievement. In fact, while salesmen in both average and outstanding offices scored high in *n* Achievement, salesmen in average offices had the higher scores. The salesmen in the outstanding offices, however, scored higher in *n* Affiliation. Remember there seemed to be little opportunity for immediate, frequent, and tangible feedback on how well the salesman was doing in this particular sales task. The man high in *n* Achievement would not very readily get what he requires. On the other hand, those who enjoy and need good companionable relationships, those who find such relationships intrinsically satisfying and who require less performance feedback and fewer signposts of achievement, would seem better matched to performing the job successfully. They would seem better attuned to the behavior the task required. And that, indeed, proved to be the case.

Case Two: Selling Clothing to Retailers

In this case, the company was a medium-sized manufacturer of women's sportswear. Of its thirty salesmen, all paid on a commission basis, management observed performance differences; some salesmen were turning in unsatisfactory results. Top management retained consultants to investigate the sources of below-average performance.

The consultants studied the nature of the sales task. Though the orthodox view in the company seemed to be that the salesman's job was to write orders, the consultants found the task to be more complex. The salesmen had to help the retail store personnel in the selection and merchandising of goods. They had to help build the retail store's sales volume by showing store personnel how to display and move their merchandise. The task was more helping to operate the retail stores successfully through selling the manufacturer's products than it was simply taking orders.

Because the consultants suspected that testing procedures would be unwelcome and disruptive in this organization, they sought to assess the motive patterns of both outstanding and below-average salesmen by interviewing them. They queried the salesmen to see how they conceived of the sales task. The salesman's picture of his task, the consultants reasoned, would provide them with a basis for inferring motive patterns. What differences in motive patterns did they find?

The outstanding salesmen did conceive of their task as one of helping build the retailers' volume. This effort yielded satisfaction for them. By taking some risks in guiding store personnel in merchandise selection, they were able to obtain feedback in terms of sales-volume increases as a means of gauging their own performance and, of course, increasing their own commissions. The consultants interpreted this as evidence that the outstanding salesmen were high in n Achievement. Their less effective colleagues derived their main satisfaction from the commission check. They did not express satisfaction in the business-building process itself. The pattern of their remarks about their work persuaded the consultants that the less successful salesmen were lower in n Achievement. And although the consultants did not mention n Power, we might speculate that the need to influence the customer may play a part in successful performance of this task.

It would appear that n Achievement contributes primarily to entrepreneurial behavior rather than simply to any sort of selling behavior. So to the extent that any job (managerial or otherwise) contains entrepreneurial components, n Achievement, as a quality of people performing the job, may lead to greater effectiveness. Wainer and Rubin (1969) conducted a study based upon this line of thought. They measured the motive patterns of the heads of fifty-one small, technically based companies in the Boston area. They assumed that all of these jobs were entrepreneurial in nature and that high n Achievement would directly influence the entrepreneur's skill and his enterprise's performance. They did find that n Achievement levels were high among the leaders of the best-performing companies.

However, when all of the data were considered, the results were too complicated to assume any simple linear relationship between the leader's n Achievement and company performance; n Affiliation and n Power were combined in various ways with n Achievement in the leaders of the best-performing companies.

"In summary, the *highest performing companies* in this sample were led by entrepreneurs who exhibited a high n Achievement and a moderate n Power. Those entrepreneurs who had a high n Achievement coupled with a high n Power performed less well than their high n Achievement counterparts who exhibited only a moderate level of n Power. Within the moderate n Achievement group, higher performing companies were led by entrepreneurs who had high n Affiliation" (*ibid.*, pp. 182–183).

Wainer and Rubin speculate that a high n Power could produce autocratic or authoritarian leadership behavior. Such a pattern would interfere with making effective use of talented manpower in research and development activities. Therefore, high n Power could cancel out high n Achievement and make for less effective companies.

On the other hand, high n Affiliation could serve, indirectly, to compensate for moderate n Achievement. As Wainer and Rubin suggest: "It may be that for those individuals who have only a moderate level of n Achievement, a high level of n Affiliation enables them to form close interpersonal relationships with their colleagues. In this way, the moderate n Achievement individual may be

able to acquire the assistance he needs from his colleagues, some of whom may
well have a higher level of *n* Achievement than he himself has" (p. 184).

Expectancy Theory

Were we to characterize human behavior in organizations solely as a function
of the needs and corollary propensities to behave which people bring to their
organizational roles, we would be guilty of neglecting another extremely important side of man: cognition. At the beginning of this chapter we suggested
metaphorically that patterns of behavior in organizations are cut by two blades
of a pair of scissors, one blade being the needs and energies the person brings
to the job situation, and the other blade being the characteristics of the situation
itself. But how does the situation affect the person and become, in his mind,
grounds for action?

What psychologists call expectancy theories of motivation provide a particularly useful answer. Though expectancy theory is conceived of in a number
of different ways by different theorists at the present time, we can distill its
essence. Its central idea is that people behave as they do because they perceive
that the behavior will lead to a desired reward. They have an expectation or
expectancy: in this particular situation, right now, if I perform this way I will
obtain a reward I value.

Of course, this is simplified. Actually, behaving in any particular way will
lead to several consequences. For example, setting ambitious yet realistic goals,
taking risks, and striving hard may be a likely path to gaining feelings of
achievement, but it might also mean worry, overwork, and neglect of family.
An impressionistic calculus of pleasure and pains is involved.

There may be doubts about one's ability to perform. There may be doubts
that, in a particular situation, reward is really likely to follow performance.
Perhaps the reward will not be big enough to warrant all the bother.

Expectancy theory holds that merely having a particular motive or needing
a particular reward is not sufficient to turn a readiness to behave into behavior
and performance. It is also necessary that the individual perceive that his
situation will yield what he desires and that it will permit him to do what is
necessary to fulfill his desires and leave him with a net profit. Expectancy theory
stresses that the individual must believe or expect two things. First, efforts toward
performance can result in performance. (If he tries he can do it. The situation
is one in which it is possible to do it. And he has the ability to do it.) Second,
performance will result in reward. (If he does it, he will obtain the reward he
desires.) What motivation theory tells us is what people desire. What expectancy
theory tells us is how desire can become action.

We have already indicated that it makes sense for a manager to analyze
task requirements to see what behavior contributes to effective performance.
If a sales job calls for achievement-oriented behavior, then persons predisposed
to such behavior can be identified and placed on the job. Beyond that, the
objective characteristics of the situation can be examined to see if they are likely
to encourage the salesman to perceive and to believe that setting challenging
goals, taking moderate risks, and taking personal responsibility for results will
be rewarded. In Chapters 8 and 9 we discuss more fully the design of administrative practices to arouse motivation and encourage performance. Here, we need

only note that the objective characteristics of the situation—the structure, the performance standards, the rewards and punishments—are important inputs to the individual's cognitive world. Hence, they are important potential shapers of his expectancies, behavior, and task performance. A selection following this chapter explains expectancy theory more fully.

Dissonance Theory

Each individual lives in a world of his own perceptions, beliefs, and ideas—a cognitive world. Despite Ralph Waldo Emerson's belief that consistency is but a "hobgoblin of small minds," an important characteristic of an individual's cognitive world is its tendency towards unity or consistency. People do tend to maintain internally consistent relations among their beliefs, ideas, and actions. There are not many Minutemen who are simultaneously Weathermen, Black Panthers who hold memberships in the NAACP, or hippies who belong to Rotary.

Emerson notwithstanding, consistency seems to be something which people strive for. Apparently, consistency is something of an acquired need which most cultures strongly inculcate in people. As Zimbardo (1969) puts it: "In most cultures, consistency, if it is not prized in and for itself, is certainly reinforced as a general behavior underlying a multitude of specific responses. In our society, the 'golden rule' stresses interpersonal consistency, the hypocrite is derided because his actions are inconsistent with his words, our child-rearing practices build consistency into almost every aspect of human functioning, and our educational systems emphasize logical consistency and historical continuity. The imposition of the human concept of time on the flow of events makes causal consistency a reality and traps present behavior between past commitments and future obligations and expectations" (p. 280).

One consequence of valuing consistency is that its lack produces an uncomfortable tension. When internal conflicts or inconsistencies appear, particularly in important aspects of a person's cognitive world, an unpleasant reaction called *cognitive dissonance* occurs. Suppose, for example, a professor believes himself to be a highly skilled teacher and he reads a survey of student evaluations of his teaching which shows that he is regarded as a disorganized, inept instructor. The information gives rise to discrepant or dissonant ideas. It is difficult, to say the least, to believe that one is both competent and incompetent.

When a person experiences cognitive dissonance, he experiences a pain which he is motivated to reduce. But how? There are two major possibilities. He might change his beliefs or he might change his behavior. There are almost innumerable manifestations of each type of change. The professor, for example, might work hard to improve his teaching. He might endure videotaping and playback of his own lectures. He might diligently change his ways.

On the other hand, he might defend his original assessment and find fault with the student evaluation. He can restore a sense of balance among his ideas if he can discredit the new information. He can accomplish the same result by lowering his estimate of his own competence. Whichever course he pursues, dissonance theory predicts that he will choose one designed to reduce the inconsistency and restore some balance. A selection by Festinger following this chapter extends this discussion of dissonance theory.

The significance of cognitive dissonance for management is that, since it motivates behavior, it amounts to another determinant of how people function in organizational roles. There is a growing body of research which suggests practical implications for management. Specifically, there are indications that dissonance can be created by controls and rewards and that the resultant efforts to reduce dissonance can be either beneficial or detrimental to realizing organizational goals. The achievement arousal value of feedback has been mentioned. But it is also true that performance feedback emanating from management can also depress and discourage the recipient. Rather than nurture expectancies that efforts will result in performance and performance in rewards, feedback which brings only the news that performance is always below anticipated standards can result in not trying. It is probably easier for most of us to accept the idea that we failed but didn't really try hard than to accept the idea that we tried extremely hard and failed. It will be better to not try so hard next time.

Motivation and Management

The manager is employed to contribute to realizing organizational effectiveness. An important part of his challenge is to enlist the efforts of his subordinates to this same end. Argyris (1957) suggests that conventional management wisdom, in emphasizing such practices as task specialization and chain of command, does not provide the best guidance in coping with this task. Argyris describes the growth or development of human personality, and advances the idea that organizational arrangements are often incongruent with the fulfillment of human needs. The ways in which workers respond actively to this incongruence often lead managers to employ further directive leadership and more controls, which turn out to be counterproductive. More recently, Argyris has suggested that one way workers adjust to organizational pressures, seemingly successfully, is through apathy. This would hardly seem to lead to optimum organizational effectiveness, however.

The theories we have been considering lead to a more knowledgeable approach to motivation. Generally, if the manager can make task performance a path to need satisfaction, he raises the probability that employee effort will be committed to organizational purpose (assuming, of course, that the tasks are themselves well fitted to organizational objectives). Consider a few of the possibilities which come into view when the manager becomes sensitive to the particular patterns of needs possessed by subordinates. The more pronounced an individual's need to be liked and approved by others, the more susceptible he is to efforts to control his behavior by making approval contingent on producing the desired behavior. Just as one might better motivate someone high in n Achievement by offering the opportunity for setting goals, taking calculated risks, and obtaining feedback in his job, one might better motivate someone high in n Affiliation by offering the potential reward of social approval or increased friendly interpersonal contact. For the individual high in n Power, increased opportunity to influence others, obtained by winning promotions, for example, might be particularly attractive and rewarding. Similarly, for the individual with prepotent needs for esteem or security, influence can be increased by designing jobs and personnel policies which provide satisfaction of those needs in return for satisfactory performance.

Tailoring influence to subordinates' needs presupposes some basis for recognizing the pattern of those needs. The manager cannot go about administering and interpreting tests, so how is he to know what motives are stronger than others in specific individuals? The question is perhaps not so difficult to answer as one might think. Although motives are invisible, their presence can be inferred from behavior. What people do the manager can see. What they want he can infer from what they say and do. In essence, the manager can see in characteristic, established ways of behaving the expression of underlying motives. For example, if he reasons back from the visible signs of setting challenging goals, taking personal responsibility for results, taking moderate risk, and so on, the manager has a basis for believing *n* Achievement is probably at work.

Once the manager recognizes that he depends upon the volition of subordinates, and that his problem is to attune his leadership behavior and organizational goals, controls, rewards, and structures to human nature, he sharpens his awareness of his opportunities and constraints, and he can learn to provide stimuli more likely to become transformed, upon perception by subordinates, into personal motivation, behavior, and valued organizational consequences. More specifically, he can manage motivation by carefully forming the climate that characterizes the work situation.

Summary

Everyone has a history of behaving and of experiencing pleasures and pains. This history makes each person more likely to behave in some ways and less likely to behave in others. Being likely to behave in one way is what is meant when we say that someone has a need or a strong need of a particular type. A need amounts to a propensity to act in a certain way.

We have discussed several of these needs. Maslow's hierarchy of needs, for example, includes physiological needs, and needs for safety, love, esteem, and self-actualization. He suggested that these are arranged in an order of "prepotency," in which successive needs come into operation only as more basic ones are satisfied. Since satisfied needs do not motivate behavior, one implication for management is that jobs must appeal to unmet needs if they are to motivate employees.

Beyond this theory of motivation are other theories. Socially acquired needs for achievement, power, and affiliation, as well as the general need for competence, also identify patterns of behavior important to management. The behavior associated with each need can be instrumental in successful job performance. We saw, for example, that the need for achievement is associated with success at one type of sales task and that the need for affiliation is associated with success at another.

Two other needs are also important: the need to reduce anxiety and the need to reduce dissonance. The avoidance of these painful or unpleasant states also affects the behavior of people at work.

But motivation and successful performance depend upon more than needs. They depend upon the situation and how it interacts with the individual. There must be cues in the situation which encourage the belief or expectancy that effort will result in performance and performance will be rewarded. The more clearly managers understand what kind of behavior will lead to improved performance, the more carefully they can consider who is likely to behave that way and what administrative and organizational conditions will help stimulate that behavior.

References

Arendt, H. *The Human Condition.* University of Chicago Press, 1958.

Argyris, C. *Personality and Organization.* Harper & Row, 1957.

Atkinson, J. W. *An Introduction to Motivation.* Van Nostrand, 1964.

———, ed. *Motives in Fantasy, Action, and Society.* Van Nostrand, 1958.

Bentham, Jeremy. "An Introduction to the Principles of Morals and Legislation." In *The English Philosophers from Bacon to Mill,* ed. E. A. Burtt. Random House, 1939.

Campbell, J. P., M. D. Dunnette, E. E. Lawler. *Managerial Behavior, Performance, and Effectiveness.* McGraw-Hill, 1970.

Carlyle, Thomas. *Past and Present.* Macmillan, 1927.

Clark, K. B. *Dark Ghetto: Dilemmas of Social Power.* Harper & Row, 1965.

Cofer, C. N. and M. H. Appleby. *Motivation: Theory and Research.* Wiley, 1964.

Croy, H. *Wheels West.* Hastings House, 1955.

Festinger, L. *A Theory of Cognitive Dissonance.* Stanford University Press, 1957.

———, H. Riecken, and S. Schachter. *When Prophecy Fails.* University of Minnesota Press, 1956.

Freud, Sigmund. *Civilization and Its Discontents,* tr. J. Strachey. Norton, 1962.

Ginzberg, E., et al. *The Unemployed.* Harper & Row, 1943.

Hamsun, K. *Hunger* (1899). Farrar, Strauss & Giroux, 1967.

Homans, G. *The Human Group.* Harcourt Brace Jovanovich, 1950.

Kantor, M. *Andersonville.* World, 1955.

Lawrence, P. R., and J. W. Lorsch. *Developing Organizations: Diagnosis and Action.* Addison-Wesley, 1969.

Levinson, H. "On Becoming a Middle-Aged Manager." *Harvard Business Review,* Vol. 47, No. 4 (July-Aug. 1969), 51–60.

Liebow, E. *Tally's Corner.* Little, Brown, 1967.

Litwin, G. H., and R. A. Stringer, Jr. *Motivation and Organizational Climate.* Graduate School of Business Administration, Harvard University, 1968.

Livingston, J. S. "Myth of the Well-Educated Manager." *Harvard Business Review,* Vol. 49, No. 1 (Jan.-Feb. 1971), 79–89.

Maslow, A. H. "A Theory of Human Motivation." *Psychological Review,* Vol. 50, No. 4, July 1943, 370–396.

———. *Motivation and Personality.* Harper & Row, 1954.

McClelland, D. C. "Comments on Professor Maslow's Paper." In *Nebraska Symposium on Motivation III,* ed. M. R. Jones. University of Nebraska Press, 1955.

———. "Business Drive and National Achievement." *Harvard Business Review,* Vol. 40, No. 4 (July-Aug. 1962), 99–112.

———. "The Two Faces of Power." *Journal of International Affairs,* Vol. 24, No. 1 (1970), 29–47.

McGregor, D. *The Human Side of Enterprise.* McGraw-Hill, 1960.

Moment, D., and A. Zaleznik. *Role of Development and Interpersonal Competence.* Division of Research, Graduate School of Business Administration, Harvard University, 1963.

Murray, H. A. *Explorations in Personality.* Oxford University Press, 1938.

Roethlisberger, F. J., and W. J. Dickson. *Management and the Worker.* Harvard University Press, 1939.

Schachter, S. *The Psychology of Affiliation.* Stanford University Press, 1959.

Sears, R. R., E. L. Maccoby, and H. Levin. *Patterns of Child Rearing.* Harper & Row, 1957.

Sullivan, H. S. "Tensions, Interpersonal and International," in H. Cantril (ed.), *Tensions That Cause Wars.* University of Illinois Press, 1950.

Test of Imagination. Behavioral Science Center of the Sterling Institute, Boston, Massachusetts, 1968.

Wainer, H. A., and I. M. Rubin. "Motivation of Research and Development Entrepreneurs: Determinants of Company Success," Part I. *Journal of Applied Psychology,* Vol. 53, No. 3, June 1969, 178–184.

White, R. W. "Motivation Reconsidered: The Concept of Competence." *Psychological Review,* Vol. 66, September 1959, 297–334.

Zimbardo, P. G. *The Cognitive Control of Motivation.* Scott, Foresman, 1968.

Readings

The Two Faces of Power

DAVID C. McCLELLAND

For over twenty years I have been studying a particular human motive—the need to Achieve, the need to do something better than it has been done before. As my investigation advanced, it became clear that the need to Achieve, technically n Achievement, was one of the keys to economic growth, because men who are concerned with doing things better have become active entrepreneurs and have created the growing business firms which are the foundation stones of a developing economy.[1] Some of these heroic entrepreneurs might be regarded as leaders in the restricted sense that their activities established the economic base for the rise of a new type of civilization, but they were seldom leaders of men. The reason for this is simple: n Achievement is a one man game which need never involve other people. Boys who are high in n Achievement like to build things or to make things with their hands, presumably because they can tell easily and directly whether they have done a good job. A boy who is trying to build as tall a tower as possible out of blocks can measure very precisely how well he has done. He is in no way dependent on someone else to tell him how good his performance is. So in the pure case, the man with high n Achievement is not dependent on the judgment of others; he is concerned with improving his own performance. As an ideal type, he is most easily conceived of as a salesman or an owner-manager of a small business, in a position to watch carefully whether or not his performance is improving.

While studying such men and their role in economic development, I ran head on into problems of leadership, power, and social influence which n Achievement clearly did not prepare a man to cope with. As a one-man firm grows larger, it obviously requires some division of function and some organizational structure. Organizational structure involves relationships among people, and sooner or later someone in the organization, if it is to survive, must pay attention to getting people to work together, or to dividing up the tasks to be performed, or to supervising the work of others. Yet it is fairly clear that a high need to Achieve does not equip a man to deal effectively with managing human relationships. For instance, a salesman with high n Achievement does not necessarily make a good sales manager. As a manager, his task is not to sell, but to inspire others to sell, which involves a different set of personal goals and different strategies for reaching them. I shall not forget the moment when I learned that the president of one of the most successful *achievement*-oriented firms we had been studying scored exactly zero in n Achievement! Up to that point I had fallen into the easy assumption that a man with a high need to Achieve does better work, gets promoted faster, and ultimately ends up as president of a company. How then was it possible for a man to be head of

"The Two Faces of Power" by David C. McClelland, from *Journal of International Affairs,* Vol. 24, No. 1 (1970), 29–47. Reprinted by permission.

an obviously achieving company and yet score so low in *n* Achievement? At the time I was tempted to dismiss the finding as a statistical error, but there is now little doubt that it was a dramatic way of calling attention to the fact that stimulating achievement motivation in others requires a different motive and a different set of skills than wanting achievement satisfaction for oneself. For some time now, research on achievement motivation has shifted in focus from the individual with high *n* Achievement to the climate which encourages him and rewards him for doing well.[2] For no matter how high a person's need to Achieve may be, he cannot succeed if he has no opportunities, if the organization keeps him from taking initiative, or does not reward him if he does. As a simple illustration of this point, we found in our research in India that it did no good to raise achievement motivation through training if the trained individual was not in charge of his business.[3] That is to say, even though he might be "all fired up" and prepared to be more active and entrepreneurial, he could not in fact do much if he was working for someone else, someone who had the final say as to whether any of the things he wanted to do would in fact be attempted. In short, the man with high *n* Achievement seldom can act alone, even though he might like to. He is caught up in an organizational context in which he is managed, controlled, or directed by others. And thus to understand better what happens to him, we must shift our attention to those who are managing him, to those who are concerned about organizational relationships—to the leaders of men.

Since managers are primarily concerned with influencing others, it seems obvious that they should be characterized by a high need for Power, and that by studying the power motive we can learn something about the way effective managerial leaders work. If A gets B to do something, A is at one and the same time a leader (i.e., he is leading B), and a power-wielder (i.e., he is exercising some kind of influence or power over B). Thus, leadership and power appear as two closely related concepts, and if we want to understand better effective leadership, we may begin by studying the power motive in thought and action. What arouses thoughts of being powerful? What kinds of strategies does the man employ who thinks constantly about gaining power? Are some of these strategies more effective than others in influencing people? In pursuing such a line of inquiry in this area, we are adopting an approach which worked well in another. Studying the achievement motive led to a better understanding of business entrepreneurship. Analogously, studying the power motive may help us understand managerial, societal, or even political leadership better.

There is one striking difference between the two motivation systems which is apparent from the outset. In general, in American society at least, individuals are proud of having a high need to Achieve, but dislike being told they have a high need for Power. It is a fine thing to be concerned about doing things well (*n* Achievement) or making friends (*n* Affiliation), but it is reprehensible to be concerned about having influence over others (*n* Power). The vocabulary behavioral scientists use to describe power relations is strongly negative in tone. If one opens *The Authoritarian Personality,*[4] one of the major works dealing with people who are concerned with power, one finds these people depicted as harsh, sadistic, fascist, Machiavellian, prejudiced, and neurotic. Ultimately, many claim, the concern for power leads to Nazi-type dictatorships, to the slaughter of innocent Jews, to political terror, police states, brainwashing, and the exploitation of helpless masses who have lost their freedom. Even less political terms for power than these have a distinctively negative flavor—dominance-submission, competition, zero sum game (if I win, you lose). It is small wonder that people do not particularly like being told they have a high need for Power.

The negative reactions to the exercise of power became vividly apparent to me in the course of our recent research efforts to develop achievement motivation.[5] Out of our extensive research on the achievement motive, we conceived of possible ways to increase it through short intensive courses. At first people were interested and curious. It seemed like an excellent idea to develop a fine motive like n Achievement, particularly among under-achievers in school or relatively inactive businessmen in underdeveloped countries. But most people were also skeptical. Could it be done? It turned out that many remained interested only as long as they were really skeptical about our ability to change motivation. As soon as it became apparent that we could indeed change people in a relatively short period of time, many observers began to worry. Was it ethical to change people's personalities? Were we not brainwashing them? What magical power were we employing to change an underlying personality disposition presumably established in childhood and laboriously stabilized over the years? Once these questions were raised, we became aware of the fundamental dilemma confronting anyone who becomes involved in any branch of the "influence game." He may think that he is exercising leadership—i.e., influencing people for their own good—but if he succeeds, he is likely to be accused of manipulating people. We thought that our influence attempts were benign. In fact, we were a little proud of ourselves. After all, we were giving people a chance to be more "successful" in business and at school. Yet we soon found ourselves attacked as potentially dangerous "brainwashers."

To some extent, ordinary psychotherapy avoids these accusations because the power of the therapist seems to be relatively weak. Therapy does not work very well or very quickly, and when it does, the therapist can say that the patient did most of the work himself.

But consider the following anecdote. Johnny was a bright but lazy sixth-grade student in math. His parents were concerned because he was not motivated to work harder, preferring to spend his evenings watching television, and they were delighted when psychologists explained that they had some new techniques for developing motivation to which they would like to expose Johnny. Soon after the motivation training regime began, they noticed a dramatic change in Johnny's behavior. He never watched television, but spent all of his time studying, and was soon way ahead of his class in advanced mathematics. At this point, his parents began to worry. What had the psychologists done to produce such a dramatic change in their son's behavior? They had wanted him changed, but not *that* much. They reacted very negatively to the power that the psychologists seemed to have exercised over him.

This experience was enough to make us yearn for the position of the detached-scientist or consulting-expert so vividly described by John Gardner in *The Anti-Leadership Vaccine*[6] as the preferred role for more and more young people today. For the "scientist" ordinarily does not directly intervene—does not exercise power—in human or social affairs. He observes the interventions of others, reports, analyzes and advises, but never takes responsibility himself. Our research had led us to intervene actively in Johnny's life, and even that small, relatively benign exercise of influence had led to some pretty negative responses from the "public." My own view is that young people avoid socio-political leadership roles not so much because their professors brainwash them into believing that it is better to be a professional, but because in our society in our time, and perhaps in all societies at all times, the exercise of power is viewed very negatively. People are suspicious of a man who wants power, even if he does so for sincere and altruistic reasons. He is often socially conditioned to be suspicious of himself. He does not want to be in a position where he might be thought to be seeking power and influence in order to exploit others, and as a result he shuns public responsibility.

Yet surely this negative face of power is only part of the story. Power must have a positive face too. After all, people cannot help influencing one another. Organizations cannot function without some kind of authority relationships. Surely it is necessary and desirable for some people to concern themselves with management, with working out influence relationships that make it possible to achieve the goals of the group. A man who is consciously concerned with the development of proper channels of influence is surely better able to contribute to group goals than a man who neglects or represses power problems and lets the working relationships of men grow up unsupervised by men. Our problem, then, is to try to discern and understand two faces of power. When is power bad and when is it good? Why is it often perceived as dangerous? Which aspects of power are viewed favorably, and which unfavorably? When is it proper, and when improper, to exercise influence? And finally, are there different kinds of power motivation?

It will not be possible to answer all of these questions definitively, but the findings of recent research on the power motive as it functions in human beings will help us understand the two faces of power somewhat better. Let us begin with the curious fact that turned up in the course of what are technically "arousal" studies. When an experimenter becomes interested in a new motive, he ordinarily begins to study it by trying to arouse it in a variety of ways in order to see how it influences what a person thinks about. Then these alterations in thought content are worked into a code or a scoring system which captures the extent to which the thinking of the subject is concerned about achievement or power or whatever motive state has been aroused. For instance, Veroff,[7] when he began his study of the power motive, asked student candidates for office to write imaginative stories while they were waiting for the election returns to be counted. He contrasted these stories with those written by other students who were not candidates for office. That is, he assumed that the students waiting to hear if they had been elected were in a state of aroused power motivation and that their stories would reflect this fact in contrast to the stories of students not in such a state. From the differences in story content he derived a coding system for *n* Power (need for Power) based on the greater concern for having influence over others revealed in the stories of student candidates for election. Later arousal studies by Uleman[8] and Winter[9] further defined the essence of *n* Power as a concern for having a *strong impact on others*. That is, when power motivation was aroused in a variety of ways, students thought more often about people having strong impact on others. This was true not only for student candidates for office awaiting election returns, but also for student experimenters who were about to demonstrate their power over subjects by employing a winning strategy in a competitive game that they had been taught beforehand.[10]

What surprised us greatly was the discovery that drinking alcohol also stimulated similar power thoughts in men. This discovery was one of those happy accidents which sometimes occurs in scientific laboratories when two studies thought to be unrelated are proceeding side by side. When we began studying the effects of social drinking on fantasy, we had no idea that alcohol would increase power fantasies. Yet we immediately found that it increased sex and aggression fantasies, and one day it occurred to us that certain types of exploitative sex and certainly aggression were instances of "having impact" on others and therefore could be considered part of an *n* Power scoring definition. We later found that drinking alcohol in small amounts increased the frequency of *socialized* power thoughts while in larger amounts it promoted thinking in terms of *personalized* power. We began to notice that these two types of power concern had different consequences in action. For instance, Winter found that some college students with high *n* Power scores tended to drink more heavily while others held more offices in student organizations. These were not, however, the same people. That is, a student with high *n* Power either drank more heavily or he was a club officer, though he was usually not both, possibly because heavy drinking would prevent him from being elected to a responsible office. In other words, Winter identified alternative manifestations of the power drive—either heavy drinking or holding office. Later we found that the orientation of the power thoughts of these two types of people was quite different. Men whose power thoughts centered on having impact for the sake of others tended to hold office, whereas those whose thoughts centered on personal dominance tended to drink heavily, or to "act out" in college by attempting more sexual conquests or driving powerful cars fast, for example.

Other studies have further illuminated this picture, and while it is still not altogether clear, its main outlines can be readily sketched.[11] There are two faces of power. One is turned toward seeking to win out over active adversaries. Life tends to be seen as a "zero-sum game" in which "if I win, you lose" or "I lose, if you win." The imagery is that of the "law of the jungle" in which the strongest survive by destroying their adversaries. The thoughts of this face of power are aroused by drinking alcohol or, more socially, by putting a person in a personal dominance situation in which he is threatened. At the level of action, a personal power concern is associated with heavy drinking, gambling, having more aggressive impulses, and collecting "prestige supplies" like a convertible or a Playboy Club Key. People with this personalized power concern are more apt to speed, have accidents, and get into physical fights. If these primitive and personalized power-seeking characteristics were possessed by political office-holders, especially in the sphere of international relations, the consequences would be ominous.

The other face of the power motive is more socialized. It is aroused by the possibility of winning an election. At the fantasy level it expresses itself in thoughts of exercising power for the benefit of others and by feelings of greater ambivalence about holding power—doubts of personal strength, the realization that most victories must be carefully planned in advance, and that every victory means a loss for someone. In terms of activities, people concerned with the more socialized aspect of power join more organizations and are more apt to become officers in them. They also are more apt to join in organized informal sports, even as adults.

We have made some progress in distinguishing two aspects of the power motive, but what exactly is the difference between the way the two are exercised? Again a clue came from a very unexpected source. It is traditional in the literature of social psychology and political science to describe a leader as someone who is able to evoke feelings of obedience or loyal submission in his followers. A leader is sometimes said to have charisma if, when he makes a speech, for example, the members of his audience are swept off their feet and feel that they must submit to his overwhelming authority and power. In the extreme case they are like iron filings that have been polarized by a powerful magnet. The leader is recognized as supernatural or superhuman; his followers feel submissive, loyal, devoted, and obedient to his will. Certainly this is the most common description of what happened at mass meetings addressed by Hitler or Lenin. As great demagogues they established their power over the masses which followed loyally and obediently.

Winter wished to find out exactly, by experiment, what kinds of thoughts the members of an audience had when exposed to a charismatic leader.[12] He wanted to find out if the common analysis of what was going on in the minds of the audience was in fact accurate. So he exposed groups of business school students to a film of John F. Kennedy's Inaugural Address as President of the United States sometime after he had been assassinated. There was no doubt that this film was a highly moving and effective presentation of a charismatic leader for such an audience at that time. After the film was over he asked them to write imaginative stories as usual, and contrasted the themes of their stories with those written by a comparable group of students after they had seen a film explaining some aspects of modern architecture. Contrary to expectation, he did not find that the students exposed to the Kennedy film thought more afterwards about submission, following, obedience, or loyalty. Instead the frequency of power themes in their stories increased. They were apparently strengthened and uplifted by the experience. They felt more powerful, rather than less powerful and submissive. This suggests that the traditional way of explaining the influence which a leader has on his followers has not been entirely correct. He does not force them to submit and follow him by the sheer overwhelming magic of his personality and persuasive powers. This is in fact to interpret effective leadership in terms of the kind of personalized power syndrome described above, and leadership has been discredited in this country precisely because social scientists have often used this personal power image to explain how the leader gets his effects. In fact, he is influential by strengthening and inspiriting his audience. Max Weber, the source of much of the sociological treatment of charisma, recognized that charismatic leaders obtained their effects through *begeisterung,* a word which means "inspiritation" rather than its usual translation as "enthusiasm."[13] The leader arouses confidence in his followers. The followers feel better able to accomplish whatever goals he and they share. There has been much discussion of whether the leader's ideas about what will inspire his followers come from God, from himself, or from some intuitive sense of what the people need and want. But whatever the source of the leader's ideas, he cannot inspire his people unless he expresses vivid goals and aims which in some sense they want. Of course, the more he is meeting their needs, the less "persuasive" he has to be, but in no case does it make much sense to speak as if his role is to force submission. Rather it is to strengthen and uplift, to make people feel like origins, not pawns of the socio-political system.[14] His message is not so much: "Do as I say because I am strong and know best. You are children with no wills of your own and must follow me because I know better," but rather "Here are the goals which are true and right and which we share. Here is how we can reach them. You are strong and capable. You can accomplish these goals." His role is to clarify which goals the group should achieve and then to create confidence in its members that they can achieve them. John Gardner described these two aspects of the socialized leadership role very well when he said that leaders "can conceive and articulate goals that lift people out of their petty preoccupations, carry them above the conflicts that tear a society apart, and unite them in the pursuit of objectives worthy of their best efforts."[15]

Clearly the more socialized type of power motivation cannot and does not express itself through leadership which is characterized by the primitive methods of trying to win out over adversaries or exert personal dominance. In their thinking about the power motive, social scientists have been too impressed by the dominance hierarchies established by brute force among lower animals. Lasswell and other political scientists have described all concern with power as a defense, an attempt to compensate for a feeling of weakness. At best this describes the personalized face of the power motive, not its socialized face—and even at that, we can only say that the personalized power drive *perceives* the world in defensive terms, not that it originates as a defense. Personal dominance may be effective in very small groups, but if a human leader wants to be effective in influencing large groups, he must rely on much more subtle and socialized forms of influence. He necessarily gets more interested in formulating the goals toward which groups of people can move. And if he is to move the group toward achieving them, he must help define the goals clearly and persuasively, and then be able to strengthen the will of the individual members of the group to work for those goals.[16]

Some further light on the two faces of power was shed by our experience in trying to exert social leadership by offering achievement motivation development courses for business leaders in small cities in India. As noted above, when we began to succeed in these efforts, some observers began to wonder whether we were coarsely interfering in people's lives, perhaps spreading some new brand of American imperialism by foisting achievement values on a people that had gotten along very well without them. Their reaction was not unlike the one just described in which an outsider seeing a leader sway an audience concludes that he must have some mysterious magical power over the audience. Did we have a similar kind of *power over* the Indian businessmen who came for motivation training? Were we psychological Machiavellians?

Certainly we never thought we were. Nor, we are certain, did the businessmen perceive us as very powerful agents. How then did we manage to influence them? The course of events was very much like the process of social leadership described by John Gardner. First, we set before the participants certain goals which we felt would be desired by them—namely, to be better businessmen, to improve economic welfare in their community, to make a contribution in this way to the development of their country as a whole, to provide a pilot project that the rest of the underdeveloped world might copy, and to advance the cause of science. These goals ranged all the way from the specific and personal—improving one's business—to improving the community, the nation, and the world. While a selfish appeal to personal power generally has not been as effective as an appeal which demonstrates that increased personal power leads to important social goals, the goals which we presented certainly were objectives that interested the businessmen we contacted. Second, we provided them with the means of achieving these goals, namely, the courses in achievement motiva-tion development which we explained were designed to make them personally better able to move quickly and efficiently towards these objectives. We offered new types of training in goal setting, planning, and risk taking which research had shown would help men become more effective entrepreneurs. No one was pressured to undergo this training or pursue these goals. If there was any pressure exerted, it was clearly in the eyes of the outside observer noting the effects of our "intervention"; it was not in the minds of the participants at the time. Third, the major goal of all of our educational exercises was to make the participants feel strong, like origins rather than pawns. Thus we insisted that the initial decision to take part in the training sessions must be their own, and that they not come out of a sense of obligation or a desire to conform. In fact, we depicted the training as a difficult process, so that a high degree of personal involvement would be necessary to complete it. During the training, we never set goals for the participants, but let them set their own. We made no psychological analyses of their test behavior which we either kept for our private diagnosis or presented to them as evidence of our superior psychological knowledge. Rather we taught them to analyze their own test records and to make their own decisions as to what a test score meant. After the course they set up their own association to work together for common community goals. We did not provide them with technical information about various types of new businesses they might enter, but let them search for it themselves. We had no fixed order of presenting course materials, but constantly asked the participants to criticize the material as it was presented and to direct the staff as to what new types of presentations were desired. Thus, in our ceaseless efforts to make the participants feel strong, competent, and effective, we behaved throughout the entire experiment like effective socialized leaders. We expressed in many ways our faith in their ability to act as origins and solve their own problems. In the end many of them justified our faith. They became more active, as we expected them to, and once again validated the ubiquitous psychological findings that what you expect other people to do they will in fact tend to do.[17] Furthermore, we have good evidence that we succeeded only with those businessmen whose sense of personal efficacy was increased. This demonstrated the ultimate paradox of social leadership and social power: to be an effective leader, one must turn all of his so-called followers into leaders. There is little wonder that the situation is a little confusing not only to the would-be leader, but also to the social scientist observing the leader-ship phenomenon.

Now let us put together these bits and pieces of evidence about the nature of power, and see what kind of a picture they make. The negative or personal face of power is characterized by the dominance-submission mode: if I win, you lose. It is *primitive* in the sense that the strategies employed are adopted early in life, before the child is sufficiently socialized to learn more subtle techniques of influence. In fantasy it expresses itself in thoughts of conquering opponents. In real life it leads to fairly simple direct means of feeling powerful—drinking heavily, acquiring "prestige supplies," and being aggressive. It does not lead to effective social leadership for the simple reason that a person whose power drive is fixated at this level tends to treat other people as pawns rather than as origins. And people who feel that they are pawns tend to be passive and useless to the leader who is getting his childish satisfaction from dominating them. Slaves are the poorest, most inefficient form of labor ever devised by man. If a leader wants to have far-reaching influence, he must make his followers feel powerful and able to accomplish things on their own.

The positive or socialized face of power is characterized by a concern for group goals, for finding those goals that will move men, for helping the group to formulate them, for taking some initiative in providing members of the group with the means of achieving such goals, and for giving group members the feeling of strength and competence they need to work hard for such goals. In fantasy it leads to a concern with exercising influence *for* others, with planning, and with the ambivalent bitter-sweet meaning of many so-called "victories." In real life, it leads to an interest in informal sports, politics, and holding office. It functions in a way that makes members of a group feel like origins rather than pawns. Even the most dictatorial leader has not succeeded if he has not instilled in at least some of his followers a sense of power and the strength to pursue the goals he has set. This is often hard for outside observers to believe, because they do not experience the situation as it is experienced by the group members. One of the characteristics of the outsider, who notices only the success or failure of an influence attempt, is that he tends to convert what is a positive face of power into its negative version. He believes that the leader must have "dominated" because he was so effective, whereas in fact direct domination could never have produced so large an effect.[18]

There is, however, a certain realistic basis for the frequent misperception of the nature of leadership. In real life the actual leader balances on a knife edge between expressing personal dominance and exercising the more socialized type of leadership. He may show first one face of power, then the other. The reason for this lies in the simple fact that even if he is a socialized leader, he must take initiative in helping the group he leads to form its goals. How much initiative he should take, how persuasive he should attempt to be, and at what point his clear enthusiasm for certain goals becomes personal authoritarian insistence that those goals are the right ones whatever the members of the group may think, are all questions calculated to frustrate the well-intentioned leader. If he takes no initiative, he is no leader. If he takes too much, he becomes a dictator, particularly if he tries to curtail the process by which members of the group participate in shaping group goals. There is a particular danger for the man who has demonstrated his competence in shaping group goals and in inspiring group members to pursue them. In time both he and they may assume that he knows best, and he may almost imperceptibly change from a democratic to an authoritarian leader. There are, of course, safeguards against slipping from the more socialized to the less socialized expressions of power. One is psychological: the leader must thoroughly learn the lesson that his role is not to dominate and treat people like pawns, but to give strength to others and to make them feel like origins of ideas and of the courses of their lives. If they are to be truly strong, he must continually consult them and be aware of their wishes and desires. *A firm faith in people as origins prevents the development of the kind of cynicism that so often characterizes authoritarian leaders.* A second safeguard is social:

democracy provides a system whereby the group can expel the leader from office if it feels that he is no longer properly representing its interests.

Despite these safeguards, Americans remain unusually suspicious of the leadership role for fear that it will become a vehicle of the personal use and abuse of power. Students do not aspire to leadership roles because they are sensitive to the negative face of power and suspicious of their own motives. Furthermore, they know that if they are in a position of leadership, they will be under constant surveillance by all sorts of groups which are ready to accuse them of the personal abuse of power. Americans probably have less respect for authority than any other people in the world. The reasons are not hard to find. Many Americans originally came here to avoid tyranny in other countries. We have come to hate and fear authority in many of its forms because of its excesses elsewhere. As a nation, we are strongly committed to an ideology of personal freedom and non-interference by government. We cherish our free press as the guardian of our freedom because it can ferret out tendencies toward the misuse or abuse of personal power before they become dangerous to the public. In government, as in other organizations, we have developed elaborate systems of checks and balances of divisions of power which make it difficult for any one person or group to abuse power. In government, power is divided three ways—among the executive, the legislative, and the judicial branches. In business it is divided among management, labor, and owners. And in the university, among trustees, administration, and students. Many of these organizations also have a system for rotating leadership to make sure that no one acquires enough power over time to be able to misuse it. A Martian observer might conclude that as a nation we are excessively, almost obsessively worried about the abuse of power.

It is incredible that any leadership at all can be exercised under such conditions. Consider the situation from the point of view of a would-be leader. He knows that if he takes too much initiative, or perhaps even if he does not, he is very likely to be severely attacked by some sub-group as a malicious, power hungry status-seeker. If he is in any way a public figure, he may be viciously attacked for any mis-step or chancy episode in his past life. Even though the majority of the people are satisfied with his leadership, a small vociferous minority can make his life unpleasant and at times unbearable. Furthermore, he knows that he will not be the only leader trying to formulate group goals. If he is a Congressman, he has to work not only with his fellow Congressmen, but also with representatives of independent sources of power in the executive branch and the governmental bureaucracy. If he is a college president, he has to cope with the relatively independent power of his trustees, the faculty and the student body. If he is a business manager, he must share power with labor leaders. In addition, he knows that his tenure of office is likely to be short. Since it is doubtful that he will ever be able to exert true leadership, there seems little purpose in preparing for it. Logically, then, he should spend his time preparing for what he will do before and after his short tenure in office.

Under these conditions why would any promising young man aspire to be a leader? He begins by doubting his motives and ends by concluding that even if he believes his motives to be altruistic, the game is scarcely worth the candle. In other words, the anti-leadership vaccine, which John Gardner speaks of, is partly supplied by the negative face that power wears in our society and the extraordinary lengths to which we have gone to protect ourselves against misused power. It is much safer to pursue a career as a professional adviser, assured some continuity of service and some freedom from public attack—because, after all, one is not responsible for decisions—and some certainty that one's motives are *good,* and that power conflicts have to be settled by someone else.

How can immunity against the anti-leadership vaccine be strengthened? Some immunity surely needs to be built up if our society is not to flounder because of a lack of socialized leadership. Personally, I would not concoct a remedy which is one part changes in the system, one part rehabilitation of the positive face of power, and one part adult education. Let me explain each ingredient in turn. I feel least confident in speaking about the first one, because I am neither a political scientist, a management expert, nor a revolutionary. Yet as a psychologist, I do feel that America's concern about the possible misuse of power verges at times on a neurotic obsession. To control the abuses of power, is it really necessary to divide authority so extensively and to give such free license to anyone to attack a leader in any way he likes? Doesn't this make the leadership role so difficult and unrewarding that it ends up appealing only to cynics? Who in his right mind would want the job of college president under most operating conditions today? A president has great responsibility—for raising money, for setting goals of the institution that faculty, students, and trustees can share, for student discipline, and for appointment of a distinguished faculty. Yet often he has only a very shaky authority with which to execute these responsibilities. The authority which he has he must share with the faculty (many of whom he cannot remove no matter how violently they disagree with the goals set for the university), with the trustees, and with students who speak with one voice one year and quite a different one two years later. I am not now trying to defend an ineffective college president. I am simply trying to point out that our social system makes his role an extraordinarily difficult one. Other democratic nations, Britain, for example, have not found it necessary to go to such extremes to protect their liberty against possible encroachment by power-hungry leaders. Some structural reform of the American system definitely seems called for. It is beyond the scope of this paper to say what it might be. The possibilities range all the way from a less structured system in which all organizations are conceived as temporary,[19] to a system in which leaders are given more authority or offered greater protection from irresponsible attack. Surely the problem deserves serious attention. If we want better leaders, we will have to find ways of making the conditions under which they work less frustrating.

The second ingredient in my remedy for the anti-leadership vaccine is rehabilitation of the positive face of power. This paper has been an effort in that direction. Its major thesis is that many people, including both social scientists and potential leaders, have consistently misunderstood or misperceived the way in which effective social leadership takes place. They have confused it regularly, we have pointed out, with the more primitive exercise of personal power. The error is perpetuated by people who speak of leaders as "making decisions." Such a statement only serves to obscure the true process by which decisions should be taken. It suggests that the leader is making a decision arbitrarily without consulting anyone, exercising his power or authority for his own ends. It is really more proper to think of an effective leader as an educator.

The relationship between leading and educating is much more obvious in Latin than it is in English. In fact the word *educate* comes from the Latin *educare* meaning *to lead out*. An effective leader is an educator. One leads people by helping to set their goals, by communicating them widely throughout the group, by taking initiative in formulating means of achieving the goals, and finally, by inspiring the members of the group to feel strong enough to work hard for those goals. Such an image of the exercise of power and influence in a leadership role should not frighten anybody and should convince more people that power exercised in this way is not only not dangerous but of the greatest possible use to society.

My experience in training businessmen in India has led me to propose the third ingredient in my formula for producing better leaders—namely, psychological education for adults. What impressed me greatly was the apparent ease with which adults can be changed by the methods we used. The dominant view in American psychology today is still that basic personality structure is laid down very early in life and is very hard to change later on. Whether the psychologist is a Freudian or a learning theorist, he believes that early experiences are critical and shape everything a person can learn, feel, and want throughout his entire life span. As a consequence, many educators have come to be rather pessimistic about what can be done for the poor, the black, or the dispossessed who have undergone damaging experiences early in life. Such traumatized individuals, they argue, have developed non-adaptive personality structures that are difficult, if not impossible, to change later in life. Yet our experience with the effectiveness of short term training courses in achievement motivation for adult businessmen in India and elsewhere does not support this view. I have seen men change, many of them quite dramatically, after only a five-day exposure to our specialized techniques of psychological instruction. They changed the way they thought, the way they talked, and the way they spent their time. The message is clear: adults can be changed, often with a relatively short exposure to specialized techniques of psychological education. The implication for the present discussion is obvious. If it is true, as John Gardner argues, that many young men have learned from their professors that the professional role is preferable to the leadership role, then psychological education offers society a method of changing their views and self-conceptions when they are faced with leadership opportunities. The type of psychological education needed will of course differ somewhat from the more simple emphasis on achievement motivation. More emphasis will have to be given to the means of managing motivation in others. More explanations will have to be given of the positive face of leadership as an educational enterprise, and will have to provide participants with a better idea of how to be effective leaders. These alterations are quite feasible; in fact they have been tried.

Repeatedly we have discovered that leaders are not so much born as made. We have worked in places where most people feel there is not much leadership potential—specifically, among the poor and dispossessed. Yet we have found over and over again that even among people who have never thought of themselves as leaders or attempted to have influence in any way, real leadership performance can be elicited by specialized techniques of psychological education. We need not be as pessimistic as is usual about possibilities for change in adults. *Real leaders* have been developed in such disadvantaged locations as the Delmarva peninsula of the United States, the black business community of Washington, D.C., and the relatively stagnant small cities of India. Thus I can end on an optimistic note. Even if the leadership role today is becoming more and more difficult, and even if people are tending to avoid it for a variety of reasons, advances in scientific psychological techniques have come at least partly to the rescue by providing society with new techniques for developing the socialized and effective leaders that will be needed for the prosperity and peace of the world of tomorrow.

Notes and References

1. David C. McClelland. *The Achieving Society* (Van Nostrand, 1961).
2. George H. Litwin and Robert A. Stringer. *Motivation and Organizational Climate* (Harvard University, Graduate School of Business Administration, Division of Research, 1968).
3. David C. McClelland and D. G. Winter. *Motivating Economic Achievement* (The Free Press, 1969).
4. Theodor W. Adorno, E. Frenkel-Brunswick, D. J. Levinson, and R. N. Sanford. *The Authoritarian Personality* (Harper & Row, 1950).
5. McClelland and Winter, *op. cit.*
6. John W. Gardner. *The Anti-Leadership Vaccine* (1965 Annual Report, The Carnegie Corporation of New York).
7. Joseph Veroff. "Development and Validation of a Projective Measure of Power Motivation." *Journal of Abnormal and Social Psychology,* No. 54, 1957, 1–8.
8. J. Uleman. *A New TAT Measure of the Need for Power* (Unpublished Doctoral Dissertation, Harvard University, 1965).
9. D. G. Winter. *Power Motivation in Thought and Action* (Unpublished Doctoral Dissertation, Harvard University, 1967).
10. Uleman, *op. cit.*
11. David C. McClelland et al. *Alcohol, Power and Inhibition* (Van Nostrand, 1969).
12. Winter, *op. cit.*
13. For a fuller discussion of what Weber and other social scientists have meant by charisma, see Samuel N. Eisenstadt, *Charisma, Institution Building, and Social Transformation: Max Weber and Modern Sociology* (The University of Chicago Press, 1968); also Robert C. Tucker, "The Theory of Charismatic Leadership." *Daedalus,* No. 97, 1968, 731–56.
14. Richard deCharms. *Personal Causation* (Academic Press, 1968).
15. Gardner, *op. cit.*
16. To be sure, if he is a gang leader, he may display actions like physical aggression which are characteristic of the personalized power drive. But to the extent that he is the leader of a large group, he is effective because he is presenting, by personal example, objectives for the gang which they find attractive, rather than because he can keep many people in line by threatening them.
17. Robert Rosenthal and Lenore Jacobson. *Pygmalion in the Classroom* (Holt, Rinehart and Winston, 1968).
18. Why is a successful influence attempt so often perceived as an instance of personal domination by the leader? One answer lies in the simplifying nature of social perception. The observer notices that a big change in the behavior of a group of people has occurred. He also can single out one or two people as leaders in some way involved in the change. He does not know how the leaders operated to bring about the change since he was not that intimately involved in the process. As a result, he tends to perceive the process as an instance of the application of personal

power, as founded on a simple dominance-submission relationship. The more effective the leader is, the more personal power tends to be attributed to him, regardless of how he has actually achieved his effects.

19. Warren G. Bennis and Philip E. Slater. *The Temporary Society* (Harper & Row, 1968).

Motivation Reconsidered: The Concept of Competence

ROBERT W. WHITE

When parallel trends can be observed in realms as far apart as animal behavior and psychoanalytic ego psychology, there is reason to suppose that we are witnessing a significant evolution of ideas. In these two realms, as in psychology as a whole, there is evidence of deepening discontent with theories of motivation based upon drives. Despite great differences in the language and concepts used to express this discontent, the theme is everywhere the same: Something important is left out when we make drives the operating forces in animal and human behavior.

The chief theories against which the discontent is directed are those of Hull and of Freud. In their respective realms, drive-reduction theory and psychoanalytic instinct theory, which are basically very much alike, have acquired a considerable air of orthodoxy. Both views have an appealing simplicity, and both have been argued long enough so that their main outlines are generally known. In decided contrast is the position of those who are not satisfied with drives and instincts. They are numerous, and they have developed many pointed criticisms, but what they have to say has not thus far lent itself to a clear and inclusive conceptualization. Apparently there is an enduring difficulty in making these contributions fall into shape.

In this paper I shall attempt a conceptualization which gathers up some of the important things left out by drive theory. To give the concept a name I have chosen the word *competence,* which is intended in a broad biological sense rather than in its narrow everyday meaning. As used here, competence will refer to an organism's capacity to interact effectively with its environment. In organisms capable of but little learning, this capacity might be considered an innate attribute, but in the mammals and especially man, with their highly plastic nervous systems, fitness to interact with the environment is slowly attained through prolonged feats of learning. In view of the directedness and persistence of the behavior that leads to these feats of learning, I consider it necessary to treat competence as having a motivational aspect, and my central argument

Robert W. White, from "Motivation Reconsidered: The Concept of Competence." *Psychological Review,* Vol. 66, No. 5, 1959, 297–334. Copyright © 1959 by the American Psychological Association, and reproduced by permission.

will be that the motivation needed to attain competence cannot be wholly derived from sources of energy currently conceptualized as drives or instincts. We need a different kind of motivational idea to account fully for the fact that man and the higher mammals develop a competence in dealing with the environment which they certainly do not have at birth and certainly do not arrive at simply through maturation. Such an idea, I believe, is essential for any biologically sound view of human nature.[1]

Effectance

The new freedom produced by two decades of research on animal drives is of great help in this undertaking. We are no longer obliged to look for a source of energy external to the nervous system, for a consummatory climax, or for a fixed connection between reinforcement and tension-reduction. Effectance motivation cannot, of course, be conceived as having a source in tissues external to the nervous system. It is in no sense a deficit motive. We must assume it to be neurogenic, its "energies" being simply those of the living cells that make up the nervous system. External stimuli play an important part, but in terms of "energy" this part is secondary, as one can see most clearly when environmental stimulation is actively sought. Putting it picturesquely, we might say that the effectance urge represents what the neuromuscular system wants to do when it is otherwise unoccupied or is gently stimulated by the environment. Obviously there are no consummatory acts; satisfaction would appear to lie in the arousal and maintaining of activity rather than in its slow decline toward bored passivity. The motive need not be conceived as intense and powerful in the sense that hunger, pain, or fear can be powerful when aroused to high pitch. There are plenty of instances in which children refuse to leave their absorbed play in order to eat or to visit the toilet. Strongly aroused drives, pain, and anxiety, however, can be conceived as overriding the effectance urge and capturing the energies of the neuromuscular system. But effectance motivation is persistent in the sense that it regularly occupies the spare waking time between episodes of homeostatic crisis.

In speculating upon this subject we must bear in mind the continuous nature of behavior. This is easier said than done; habitually we break things down in order to understand them, and such units as the reflex arc, the stimulus-response sequence, and the single transaction with the environment seem like inevitable steps toward clarity. Yet when we apply such an analysis to playful exploration we lose the most essential aspect of the behavior. It is constantly circling from stimulus to perception to action to effect to stimulus to perception, and so on around; or, more properly, these processes are all in continuous action and continuous change. Dealing with the environment means carrying on a continuing transaction which gradually changes one's relation to the environment. Because there is no consummatory climax, satisfaction has to be seen as lying in a considerable series of transactions, in a trend of behavior rather than a goal that is achieved. It is difficult to make the word "satisfaction" have this connotation, and we shall do well to replace it by

[1]For an elaboration of these points, omitted here, the reader is referred to pp. 297–321 of the original.

"feeling of efficacy" when attempting to indicate the subjective and affective side of effectance.

It is useful to recall the findings about novelty: the singular effectiveness of novelty in engaging interest and for a time supporting persistent behavior. We also need to consider the selective continuance of transactions in which the animal or child has a more or less pronounced effect upon the environment—in which something happens as a consequence of his activity. Interest is not aroused and sustained when the stimulus field is so familiar that it gives rise at most to reflex acts or automatized habits. It is not sustained when actions produce no effects or changes in the stimulus field. Our conception must therefore be that effectance motivation is aroused by stimulus conditions which offer, as Hebb (1949) puts it, difference-in-sameness. This leads to variability and novelty of response, and interest is best sustained when the resulting action affects the stimulus so as to produce further difference-in-sameness. Interest wanes when action begins to have less effect; effectance motivation subsides when a situation has been explored to the point that it no longer presents new possibilities.

We have to conceive further that the arousal of playful and exploratory interest means the appearance of organization involving both the cognitive and active aspects of behavior. Change in the stimulus field is not an end in itself, so to speak; it happens when one is passively moved about, and it may happen as a consequence of random movements without becoming focalized and instigating exploration. Similarly, action which has effects is not an end in itself, for if one unintentionally kicks away a branch while walking, or knocks something off a table, these effects by no means necessarily become involved in playful investigation. Schachtel's (1954) emphasis on focal attention becomes helpful at this point. The playful and exploratory behavior shown by Laurent is not random or casual. It involves focal *attention* to some object—the fixing of some aspect of the stimulus field so that it stays relatively constant—and it also involves the focalizing of *action* upon this object. As Diamond (1939) has expressed it, response under these conditions is "relevant to the stimulus," and it is change in the *focalized* stimulus that so strongly affects the level of interest. Dealing with the environment means directing focal attention to some part of it and organizing actions to have some effect on this part.

In our present state of relative ignorance about the workings of the nervous system it is impossible to form a satisfactory idea of the neural basis of effectance motivation, but it should at least be clear that the concept does not refer to any and every kind of neural action. It refers to a particular kind of activity, as inferred from particular kinds of behavior. We can say that it does not include reflexes and other kinds of automatic response. It does not include well-learned, automatized patterns, even those that are complex and highly organized. It does not include behavior in the service of effectively aroused drives. It does not even include activity that is highly random and discontinuous, though such behavior may be its most direct forerunner. The urge toward competence is inferred specifically from behavior that shows a lasting focalization and that has the characteristics of exploration and experimentation, a kind of variation within the focus. When this particular sort of activity is aroused in the nervous system, effectance motivation is being aroused, for it is characteristic of this particular sort of activity that it is selective, directed, and persistent, and that instrumental acts will be learned for the sole reward of engaging in it.

Some objection may be felt to my introducing the word *competence* in connection with behavior that is so often playful. Certainly the playing child is doing things for fun, not because of a desire to improve his competence in dealing with the stern hard world. In order to forestall misunderstanding, it should be pointed out that the usage here is parallel to what we do when we connect sex with its biological goal of reproduction. The sex drive aims for pleasure and gratification, and reproduction is a consequence that is presumably unforeseen by animals and by man at primitive levels of understanding. Effectance motivation similarly aims for the feeling of efficacy, not for the vitally important learnings that come as its consequence. If we consider the part played by competence motivation in adult human life we can observe the same parallel. Sex may now be completely and purposefully divorced from reproduction but nevertheless pursued for the pleasure it can yield. Similarly, effectance motivation may lead to continuing exploratory interests or active adventures when in fact there is no longer any gain in actual competence or any need for it in terms of survival. In both cases the motive is capable of yielding surplus satisfaction well beyond what is necessary to get the biological work done.

In infants and young children it seems to me sensible to conceive of effectance motivation as undifferentiated. Later in life it becomes profitable to distinguish various motives such as cognizance, construction, mastery, and achievement. It is my view that all such motives have a root in effectance motivation. They are differentiated from it through life experiences which emphasize one or another aspect of the cycle of transaction with environment. Of course, the motives of later childhood and of adult life are no longer simple and can almost never be referred to a single root. They can acquire loadings of anxiety, defense, and compensation, they can become fused with unconscious fantasies of a sexual, aggressive, or omnipotent character, and they can gain force because of their service in producing realistic results in the way of income and career. It is not my intention to cast effectance in the star part in adult motivation. The acquisition of motives is a complicated affair in which simple and sovereign theories grow daily more obsolete. Yet it may be that the satisfaction of effectance contributes significantly to those feelings of interest which often sustain us so well in day-to-day actions, particularly when the things we are doing have continuing elements of novelty.

The Biological Significance of Competence

The conviction was expressed at the beginning of this paper that some such concept as competence, interpreted motivationally, was essential for any biologically sound view of human nature. This necessity emerges when we consider the nature of living systems, particularly when we take a longitudinal view. What an organism does at a given moment does not always give the right clue as to what it does over a period of time. Discussing this problem, Angyal (1941) has proposed that we should look for the general pattern followed by the total organismic process over the course of time. Obviously this makes it necessary to take account of growth. Angyal defines life as "a process of self-expansion"; the living system "expands at the expense of its surroundings," assimilating parts of the environment and transforming them into functioning parts of itself. Organisms differ from other things in nature in that they are "self-governing entities" which are to some extent "autonomous." Internal processes govern them as well as external "heteronomous" forces. In the course of life there is a relative increase in the preponderance of internal over external forces. The living system expands, assimilates more of the environment, transforms its surroundings so as to bring them under greater control. "We may say," Angyal writes, "that the general dynamic trend of the organism is toward an increase of autonomy. . . . The human being has a characteristic tendency toward self-determination, that is, a tendency to resist external influences and to subordinate the heteronomous forces of the physical and social environment to its own sphere of influence." The trend toward increased autonomy is characteristic so long as growth of any kind is going on, though in the end the living system is bound to succumb to the pressure of heteronomous forces.

Of all living creatures, it is man who takes the longest strides toward autonomy. This is not because of any unusual tendency toward bodily expansion at the expense of the environment. It is rather that man, with his mobile hands and abundantly developed brain, attains an extremely high level of competence in his transactions with his surroundings. The building of houses, roads and bridges, the making of tools and instruments, the domestication of plants and animals, all qualify as planful changes made in the environment so that it comes more or less under control and serves our purposes rather than intruding upon them. We meet the fluctuations of outdoor temperature, for example, not only with our bodily homeostatic mechanisms, which alone would be painfully unequal to the task, but also with clothing, buildings, controlled fires, and such complicated devices as self-regulating central heating and air conditioning. Man as a species has developed a tremendous power of bringing the environment into his service, and each individual member of the species must attain what is really quite an impressive level of competence if he is to take part in the life around him.

We are so accustomed to these human accomplishments that it is hard to realize how long an apprenticeship they require. At the outset the human infant is a slow learner in comparison with other animal forms. Hebb (1949) speaks of "the astonishing inefficiency of man's first learning, as far as immediate results are concerned," an inefficiency which he attributes to the large size of the association areas in the brain and the long time needed to bring them under sensory control. The human lack of precocity in learning shows itself even in comparison with one of the next of kin: as Hebb points out, "the human baby takes six months, the chimpanzee four months, before making a clear distinction between friend and enemy." Later in life the slow start will pay dividends. Once the fundamental perceptual elements, simple associations, and conceptual sequences have been established, later learning can proceed with ever increasing swiftness and complexity. In Hebb's words, "learning at maturity concerns patterns and events whose parts at least are familiar and which already have a number of other associations."

This general principle of cumulative learning, starting from slowly acquired rudiments and proceeding thence with increasing efficiency, can be illustrated by such processes as manipulation and locomotion, which may culminate in the acrobat devising new stunts or the dancer working out a new ballet. It is especially vivid in the case of language, where the early mastery of words and pronunciation seems such a far cry from spontaneous adult speech. A strong argument has been made by Hebb (1949) that the learning of visual forms proceeds over a similar course from slowly learned elements to rapidly combined patterns. Circles and squares, for example, cannot be discriminated at a glance without a slow apprenticeship involving eye movements, successive fixations, and recognition of angles. Hebb proposes that the recognition of visual patterns without eye movement "is possible only as the result of an intensive and prolonged visual training that goes on from the moment of birth, during every moment that the eyes are open, with an increase in skill evident over a period of 12 to 16 years at least."

On the motor side there is likewise a lot to be cumulatively learned. The playing, investigating child slowly finds out the relationships between what he does and what he experiences. He finds out, for instance, how hard he must push what in order to produce what effect. Here the S-R formula is particularly misleading. It would come nearer the truth to say that the child is busy learning R-S connections—the effects that are likely to follow upon his own behavior. But even in this reversed form the notion of bonds or connections would still misrepresent the situation, for it is only a rare specimen of behavior that can properly be conceived as determined by fixed neural channels and a fixed motor response. As Hebb has pointed out, discussing the phenomenon of "motor equivalence" named by Lashley (1942), a rat which has been trained to press a lever will press it with the left forepaw, the right forepaw, by climbing upon it, or by biting it; a monkey will open the lid of a food box with either hand, with a foot, or even with a stick; and we might add that a good baseball player can catch a fly ball while running in almost any direction and while in almost any posture, including leaping in the air and plunging forward to the ground. All of these feats are possible because of a history of learnings in which the main lesson has been the effects of actions upon the stimulus fields that represent the environment. What has been learned is not a fixed connection but a flexible relationship between stimulus fields and the effects that can be produced in them by various kinds of action.

One additional example, drawn this time from Piaget (1952), is particularly worth mentioning because of its importance in theories of development. Piaget points out that a great deal of mental development depends upon the idea that the world is made up of objects having substance and permanence. Without such an "object concept" it would be impossible to build up the ideas of space and causality and to arrive at the fundamental distinction between self and external world. Observation shows that the object concept, "far from being innate or readymade in experience, is constructed little by little." Up to 7 and 8 months the Piaget children searched for vanished objects only in the sense of trying to continue the actions, such as sucking or grasping, in which the objects had played a part. When an object was really out of sight or touch, even if only because it was covered by a cloth, the infants undertook no further exploration. Only gradually, after some study of the displacement of objects by moving, swinging, and dropping them, does the child begin to make an active search for a vanished object, and only still more gradually does he learn, at 12 months or more, to make allowance for the object's sequential displacements and thus to seek it where it has gone rather than where it was last in sight. Thus it is only through cumulative learning that the child arrives at the idea of permanent substantial objects.

The infant's play is indeed serious business. If he did not while away his time pulling strings, shaking rattles, examining wooden parrots, dropping pieces of bread and celluloid swans, when would he learn to discriminate visual patterns, to catch and throw, and to build up his concept of the object? When would he acquire the many other foundation stones necessary for cumulative learning? The more closely we analyze the behavior of the human infant, the more clearly do we realize that infancy is not simply a time when the nervous system matures and the muscles grow stronger. It is a time of active and continuous learning, during which the basis is laid for all those processes, cognitive and motor, whereby the child becomes able to establish effective transactions with his environment and move toward a greater degree of autonomy. Helpless as he may seem until he begins to toddle, he has by that time already made substantial gains in the achievement of competence.

Under primitive conditions survival must depend quite heavily upon achieved competence. We should expect to find things so arranged as to favor and maximize this achievement. Particularly in the case of man, where so little is provided innately and so much has to be learned through experience, we should expect to find highly advantageous arrangements for securing a steady cumulative learning about the properties of the environment and the extent of possible transactions. Under these circumstances we might expect to find a very powerful drive operating to insure progress toward competence, just as the vital goals of nutrition and reproduction are secured by powerful drives, and it might therefore seem paradoxical that the interests of competence should be so much entrusted to times of play and leisurely exploration. There is good reason to suppose, however, that a strong drive would be precisely the wrong arrangement to secure a flexible, knowledgeable power of transaction with the environment. Strong drives cause us to learn certain lessons well, but they do not create maximum familiarity with our surroundings.

This point was demonstrated half a century ago in some experiments by Yerkes and Dodson (1908). They showed that maximum motivation did not lead to the most rapid solving of problems, especially if the problems were complex. For each problem there was an optimum level of motivation, neither the highest nor the lowest, and the optimum was lower for more complex tasks. The same problem has been discussed more recently by Tolman (1948) in his paper on cognitive maps. A cognitive map can be narrow or broad, depending upon the range of cues picked up in the course of learning. Tolman suggests that one of the conditions which tend to narrow the range of cues is a high level of motivation. In everyday terms, a man hurrying to an important business conference is likely to perceive only the cues that help him to get there faster, whereas a man taking a stroll after lunch is likely to pick up a substantial amount of casual information about his environment. The latent learning experiments with animals, and experiments such as those of Johnson (1953) in which drive level has been systematically varied in a situation permitting incidental learning, give strong support to this general idea. In a recent contribution, Bruner, Matter, and Papanek (1955) make a strong case for the concept of breadth of learning and provide additional evidence that it is favored by moderate and hampered by strong motivation. The latter "has the effect of speeding up learning at the cost of narrowing it." Attention is concentrated upon the task at hand and little that is extraneous to this task is learned for future use.

These facts enable us to see the biological appropriateness of an arrangement which uses periods of less intense motivation for the development of competence. This is not to say that the narrower but efficient learnings that go with the reduction of strong drives make no contribution to general effectiveness. They are certainly an important element in capacity to deal with the environment, but a much greater effectiveness results from having this capacity fed also from learnings that take place in quieter times. It is then that the infant can attend to matters of lesser urgency, exploring the properties of things he does not fear and does not need to eat, learning to gauge the force of his string-pulling when the only penalty for failure is silence on the part of the attached rattles, and generally accumulating for himself a broad knowledge and a broad skill in dealing with his surroundings.

References

Angyal, A. *Foundations for a Science of Personality.* Commonwealth Fund, 1941.

Bruner, J. S., J. Matter, and M. L. Papanek. "Breadth of Learning as a Function of Drive Level and Mechanization." *Psychological Review,* Vol. 62 (1955), 1–10.

Diamond, S. "A Neglected Aspect of Motivation." *Sociometry,* Vol. 2 (1939), 77–85.

Hebb, D. O. *The Organization of Behavior.* Wiley, 1949.

Johnson, E. E. "The Role of Motivational Strength in Latent Learning." *Journal of Comparative Physiology and Psychology,* Vol. 45 (1953), 526–530.

Lashley, K. S. "The Problem of Cerebral Organization in Vision." In *Visual Mechanisms,* ed. H. Kluver, pp. 301–322. Jacques Cattell, 1942.

Piaget, J. *The Origins of Intelligence in Children,* tr. M. Cook. International University Press, 1952.

Schachtel, E. G. "The Development of Focal Attention and the Emergence of Reality." *Psychiatry,* Vol. 17 (1954), 309–324.

Tolman, E. C. "Cognitive Maps of Rats and Men." *Psychological Review,* Vol. 55 (1948), 189–208.

Yerkes, R. M., and J. D. Dodson. "The Relation of Strength of Stimulus to Rapidity of Habit-Formation." *Journal of Comparative Neurology,* Vol. 18 (1908), 459–482.

Expectancy Theory

JOHN P. CAMPBELL, MARVIN D. DUNNETTE,
EDWARD E. LAWLER III, KARL E. WEICK, JR.

Early Cognitive Theories

Concomitant with the development of drive x habit theory, Lewin (1938) and Tolman (1932) developed and investigated cognitive, or expectancy, theories of motivation. Even though Lewin was concerned with human subjects and Tolman worked largely with animals, much of their respective theorizing contained common elements. Basic to the cognitive view of motivation is the notion that individuals have cognitive *expectancies* concerning the outcomes that are likely to occur as the result of what they do, and that individuals have preferences among outcomes. That is, an individual has an "idea" about possible consequences of his acts, and he makes conscious choices among consequences according to their probability of occurrence and their value to him.

Thus, for the cognitive theorist, it is the anticipation of reward that energizes behavior and the perceived value of various outcomes that gives behavior its direction. Tolman spoke of a *belief-value* matrix that specifies for each individual the value he places on particular outcomes and his belief that they can be attained.

Atkinson (1964) has compared drive theory and expectancy theory. Although he points out some differences, he emphasizes that both theories are actually quite similar and contain many of the same concepts. Both include the notion of a reward or favorable outcome that is desired, and both postulate a learned connection contained within the organism. For expectancy theory this learned connection is a behavior-outcome expectancy, and for drive theory it is an *S-R* habit strength.

However, the theories differ in two ways which are important for research on motivation in an organizational setting. For example, they differ in what they state is activated by the anticipation of reward. Expectancy theory sees the anticipation of a reward as functioning selectively on actions expected to lead to it. Drive theory views the magnitude of the anticipated goals as a source of general excitement—a nonselective influence on performance.

Expectancy theory is also much looser in specifying how expectancy-outcome connections are built up. Drive theory postulates that *S-R* habit strengths are built up through repeated associations of stimulus and response; that is, the reward or outcome must actually have followed the response to a particular stimulus in order for the *S-R* connection to operate in future choice behavior. Such a process is sufficient but not necessary for forming expectancy-outcome relationships. An individual may form expectancies vicariously (someone may tell him that complimenting the boss's wife leads to a promotion, for example) or by other symbolic means. This last point is crucial since the symbolic (cognitive) manipulation of various *S-R* situations seems quite descriptive of a great deal of human behavior.

These two differences make the cognitive or expectancy point of view much more useful for studying human motivation in an organizational setting. In fact, it is the one which has been given the most attention by theorists concerned with behavior in organizations.

Instrumentality-Valence Theory

Building on expectancy theory and its later amplifications by Atkinson (1958), W. Edwards (1954), Peak (1955), and Rotter (1955), Vroom (1964) has presented a process theory of work motivation that he calls *instrumentality theory*. His basic classes of variables are expectancies, valences, choices, outcomes, and instrumentalities.

Expectancy is defined as a belief concerning the likelihood that a particular act will be followed by a particular outcome. Presumably, the degree of belief can vary between 0 (complete lack of belief that it will follow) and 1 (complete certainty that it will). Note that it is the perception of the individual that is important, not the objective reality. This same concept has been referred to as *subjective probability* by others (e.g., W. Edwards, 1954).

Valence refers to the strength of an individual's preference for a particular outcome. An individual may have either a positive or a negative preference for an outcome; presumably, outcomes gain their valence as a function of the degree to which they are seen to be related to the needs of the individual. However, this last point is not dealt with concretely in Vroom's formulation. As an example of these two concepts, one might consider an increase in pay to be a possible outcome of a particular act. The theory would then deal with the valence of a wage increase for an individual and his expectancy that particular behaviors will be followed by a wage increase outcome. Again, valence refers to the perceived or expected value of an outcome, not its real or eventual value.

According to Vroom, outcomes take on a valence value because of their *instrumentality* for achieving other outcomes. Thus he is really postulating two classes of outcomes. In the organizational setting, the first class of outcomes might include such things as money, promotion, recognition, etc. Supposedly, these outcomes are directly linked to behavior. However, as Vroom implicitly suggests, wage increases or promotion may have no value by themselves. They are valuable in terms of their instrumental role in securing second level outcomes such as food, clothing, shelter, entertainment, and status, which are not obtained as the direct result of a particular action.

According to Vroom, instrumentality, like correlation, varies between $+1.0$ and -1.0. Thus a first level outcome may be seen as always leading to some desired second level outcome $(+1.0)$ or as never leading to the second level outcome (-1.0). In Vroom's theory the formal definition of valence for a first level outcome is the sum of the products between its instrumentalities for all possible second level outcomes and their respective valences.

To sum up, Vroom's formulation postulates that the motivational force, or effort, an individual exerts is a function of (1) his expectancy that certain outcomes will result from his behavior (e.g., a raise in pay for increased effort) and (2) the valence, for him, of those outcomes. The valence of an outcome is in turn a function of its instrumentality for obtaining other outcomes and the valence of these other outcomes.

A Hybrid Expectancy Model

Since his formulation first appeared, a number of investigators have attempted to extend Vroom's model to make it more explicit and more inclusive in terms of relevant variables (Graen, 1967; L. W. Porter & Lawler, 1968). Although we shall not discuss the contributions of these writers in detail, we would like to incorporate a number of their ideas in our own composite picture of an expanded expectancy model. However, any imperfections in what follows should be ascribed to us and not to them.

One major addition to Vroom's model is the necessity for a more concrete specification of the task or performance goals toward which work behavior is directed. Graen (1967) refers to this class of variables as *work roles*, but we prefer to retain the notion of *task goals*. Task goals may be specified externally by the organization or the work group, or internally by the individual's own value system. Examples of task goals include such things as production quotas, time limits for projects, quality standards, showing a certain amount of loyalty to the organization, exhibiting the right set of attitudes, etc.

We would also like to make more explicit a distinction between first and second level outcomes. First level outcomes are outcomes contingent on achieving the task goal or set of task goals. A potential first level outcome is synonymous with the term "incentive," and an outcome which is actually realized is synonymous with the term "reward." The distinction is temporal. Like task goals, first level outcomes may be external or internal. Some examples of external first level outcomes granted by the organization are job security, pay, promotions, recognition, and increased autonomy. An individual may also set up his own internal incentives or reward himself with internally mediated outcomes such as ego satisfaction.

As pointed out in the discussion of Vroom's model, first level outcomes may or may not be associated with a plethora of second level outcomes; that is, the externally or internally mediated rewards are instrumental in varying degrees for obtaining second level outcomes such as food, housing, material goods, community status, and freedom from anxiety.

The concepts of valence for first and second level outcomes and the instrumentality of first for second level outcomes are defined as before, but the notion of expectancy decomposes into two different variables. First, individuals may have expectancies concerning whether or not they will actually accomplish the task goal if they expend effort (expectancy I); that is, an individual makes a subjective probability estimate concerning his chances for reaching a particular goal, given a particular situation. For example, a manufacturing manager may think the odds of his getting a new product into production by the first of the year are about 3 to 1 (i.e., expectancy I $= 0.75$). Perhaps the primary determiner of expectancy I is how the individual perceives his own job skills in the context of what is specified as his task goals and the various difficulties and external constraints standing in the way of accomplishing them. Certainly, then, an employee's perceptions of his own talents determine to a large degree the direction and intensity of his job behavior. This first kind of expectancy should be more salient for more complex and higher level tasks such as those involved in managing.

Second, individuals possess expectancies concerning whether or not achievement of specified task goals will actually be followed by the first level outcome (expectancy II). In other words, they form subjective probability estimates of the degree to which rewards are *contingent* on achieving task goals. The individual must ask himself what the probability is that his achievement of the goal will be rewarded by the organization. For example, the manufacturing manager may be virtually certain (expectancy II $= 1.0$) that if he does get the new product into production by the first of the year, he will receive a promotion and a substantial salary increase. Or, and this may be the more usual case, he may see no relationship at all between meeting the objective and getting a promotion and salary increase.

None of the authors cited so far have explicitly labeled these two kinds of expectancies. Indeed, in a laboratory or other experimental setting the distinction may not be necessary since the task may be so easy that accomplishing the goal is always a certainty (i.e., expectancy I is 1.0 for everybody) or the contingency of reward on behavior may be certain and easily verified by the subject (i.e., expectancy II is 1.0 for everybody). Vroom (1964) defines expectancy as an action-outcome relationship which is represented by an individual's subjective probability estimate that a particular set of behaviors will be followed by a particular outcome. Since Vroom presents no concrete definitions for the terms "action" and "outcome," his notion of expectancy could include both expectancy I and expectancy II as defined above. Thus effort expenditure could be regarded as an action, and goal performance as an outcome; or performance could be considered behavior, and money an outcome. Vroom uses both kinds of examples to illustrate the expectancy variable and makes no conceptual distinction between them. However, in the organizational setting, the distinction seems quite necessary. Rewards may or may not be contingent on goal accomplishment, and the individual may or may not believe he has the wherewithal to reach the goal. A schematic representation of this hybrid model is shown in Figure 1.

We have purposely been rather vague concerning the exact form of the relationships between these different classes of variables. This schematic model is in no way meant to be a formal theory. To propose explicit multiplicative

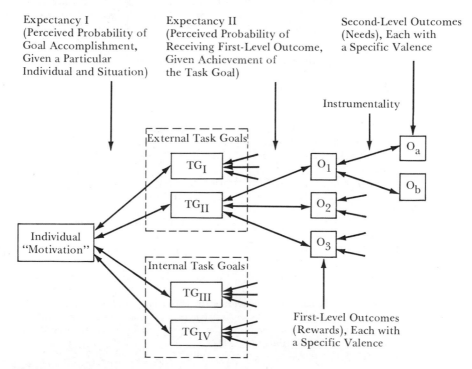

Figure 1   A Schematic Representation of a Hybrid Expectancy Model of Work Motivation Outlining the Determinants of the Direction, Amplitude, and Persistence of Individual Effort

combinations or other configural or higher order functions is going a bit too far beyond our present measurement capability. Rather, we shall sum up the relationships contained in our expanded model as follows:

1. The valence of a first level outcome (incentive or reward) is a function of the instrumentality of that outcome for obtaining second level outcomes (need satisfactions) and the valences of the relevant second level outcomes.

2. The decision by an individual to work on a particular task and expend a certain amount of effort in that direction is a function of (*a*) his personal probability estimate that he can accomplish the task (expectancy I), (*b*) his personal probability estimate that his accomplishment of the task goal will be followed by certain first level outcomes or rewards (expectancy II), and (*c*) the valence of the first level outcomes.

3. The distinction between external and internal goals and rewards leads to a number of potential conflict situations for the individual. For example, an individual might estimate his chances for accomplishing a particular task as virtually certain (i.e., expectancy I = 1.0). However, the internal rewards which are virtually certain to follow (i.e., expectancy II = 1.0) may have a very low or even negative valence (e.g., feelings of extreme boredom or distaste). If external rewards, such as a lot of money, have a very high valence, a serious stress situation could result from outcomes which have conflicting valences. It would be to an organization's advantage to ensure positive valences for both internal and external rewards. Other conflict situations could be produced by high positive valences for outcomes and low estimates of type I expectancies (i.e., the individual does not think he can actually do the job).

References

Atkinson, J. S., Ed. *Motives in Fantasy, Action and Society.* Van Nostrand, 1958.
————. *An Introduction to Motivation.* Van Nostrand, 1964.
Edwards, W. "The Theory of Decision Making." *Psychological Bulletin,* Vol. 51 (1954), 380–417.
Graen, G. B. *Work Motivation: The Behavioral Effects of Job Content and Job Context Factors in an Employment Situation.* Unpub. Ph.D. dissertation, University of Minnesota, 1967.
Lewin, K. *The Conceptual Representation and the Measurement of Psychological Forces.* Duke University Press, 1938.
Peak, H. "Attitude and Motivation." In *Nebraska Symposium on Motivation,* ed. M. R. Jones, pp. 149–188. University of Nebraska Press, 1955.
Porter, L. W., and E. E. Lawler III. *Managerial Attitudes and Performance.* Dorsey-Irwin, 1968.
Rotter, J. B. "The Role of the Psychological Situation in Determining the Direction of Human Behavior." In *Nebraska Symposium on Motivation, op. cit.,* 1955.
Tolman, E. C. *Purposive Behavior in Animals and Men.* Century (by permission of the University of California Press, 1932).
Vroom, V. H. *Work and Motivation.* Wiley, 1964.

Theory of Dissonance

LEON FESTINGER

It has frequently been implied, and sometimes even pointed out, that the individual strives toward consistency within himself. His opinions and attitudes, for example, tend to exist in clusters that are internally consistent. Certainly one may find exceptions. A person may think Negroes are just as good as whites but would not want any living in his neighborhood; or someone may think little children should be quiet and unobtrusive and yet may be quite proud when his child aggressively captures the attention of his adult guests. When such inconsistencies are found to exist, they may be quite dramatic, but they capture our interest primarily because they stand out in sharp contrast against a background of consistency. It is still overwhelmingly true that related opinions or attitudes are consistent with one another. Study after study reports such consistency among one person's political attitudes, social attitudes, and many others.

There is the same kind of consistency between what a person knows or believes and what he does. A person who believes a college education is a good thing will very likely encourage his children to go to college; a child who knows he will be severely punished for some misdemeanor will not commit it or at least will try not to be caught doing it. This is not surprising, of course; it is so much the rule that we take it for granted. Again what captures our attention are the exceptions to otherwise consistent behavior. A person may know that smoking is bad for him and yet continue to smoke; many persons commit crimes even though they know the high probability of being caught and the punishment that awaits them.

Granting that consistency is the usual thing, perhaps overwhelmingly so, what about these exceptions which come to mind so readily? Only rarely, if ever, are they accepted psychologically *as inconsistencies* by the person involved. Usually more or less successful attempts are made to rationalize them. Thus, the person who continues to smoke, knowing that it is bad for his health, may also feel (a) he enjoys smoking so much it is worth it; (b) the chances of his health suffering are not as serious as some would make out; (c) he can't always avoid every possible dangerous contingency and still live; and (d) perhaps even if he stopped smoking he would put on weight which is equally bad for his health. So, continuing to smoke is, after all, consistent with his ideas about smoking.

But persons are not always successful in explaining away or in rationalizing inconsistencies to themselves. For one reason or another, attempts to achieve consistency may fail. The inconsistency then simply continues to exist. Under such circumstances—that is, in the presence of an inconsistency—there is psychological discomfort.

First, I will replace the word "inconsistency" with a term which has less of a logical connotation, namely, *dissonance*. I will likewise replace the word "consistency" with a more neutral term, namely, *consonance*. A more formal definition of these terms will be given shortly; for the moment, let us try to get along with the implicit meaning they have acquired as a result of the preceding discussion.

The basic hypotheses I wish to state are as follows:

1. The existence of dissonance, being psychologically uncomfortable, will motivate the person to try to reduce the dissonance and achieve consonance.
2. When dissonance is present, in addition to trying to reduce it, the person will actively avoid situations and information which would likely increase the dissonance.

Before proceeding to develop this theory of dissonance and the pressures to reduce it, it would be well to clarify the nature of dissonance, what kind of concept it is, and where the theory concerning it will lead. The two hypotheses stated above provide a good starting point for this clarification. While they refer here specifically to dissonance, they are in fact very general hypotheses. In place of "dissonance" one can substitute other notions similar in nature, such as "hunger," "frustration," or "disequilibrium," and the hypotheses would still make perfectly good sense.

In short, I am proposing that dissonance, that is, the existence of nonfitting relations among cognitions, is a motivating factor in its own right. By the term *cognition*, I mean any knowledge, opinion, or belief about the environment, about oneself, or about one's behavior. Cognitive dissonance can be seen as an antecedent condition which leads to activity oriented toward dissonance reduction just as hunger leads to activity oriented toward hunger reduction. It is a very different motivation from what psychologists are used to dealing with but, as we shall see, nonetheless powerful. . . .

The Occurrence and Persistence of Dissonance

Why and how does dissonance ever arise? How does it happen that persons sometimes find themselves doing things that do not fit with what they know, or having opinions that do not fit with other opinions they hold? An answer to this question may be found in discussing two of the more common situations in which dissonance may occur.

1. New events may happen or new information may become known to a person, creating at least a momentary dissonance with existing knowledge, opinion, or cognition concerning behavior. Since a person does not have complete and perfect control over the information that reaches him and over events that can happen in his environment, such dissonances may easily arise. Thus, for example, a person may plan to go on a picnic with complete confidence that the weather will be warm and sunny. Nevertheless, just before he is due to start, it may begin to rain. The knowledge that it is now raining is dissonant with his confidence in a sunny day and with his planning to go to a picnic. Or, as another example, a person who is quite certain in his knowlege that automatic transmissions on automobiles are inefficient may accidentally come across an article praising automatic transmissions. Again, at least a momentary dissonance is created.

2. Even in the absence of new, unforeseen events or information, the existence of dissonance is undoubtedly an everyday condition. Very few things are all black or all white; very few situations are clear-cut enough so that opinions or behaviors are not to some extent a mixture of contradictions. Thus, a midwestern farmer who is a Republican may be opposed to his party's position on farm price supports; a person buying a new car may prefer the economy of one model but the design of another; a person deciding on how to invest his money may know that the outcome of his investment depends upon economic conditions beyond his control. Where an opinion must be formed or a decision taken, some dissonance is almost unavoidably created between the cognition of the action taken and those opinions or knowledges which tend to point to a different action.

There is, then, a fairly wide variety of situations in which dissonance is nearly unavoidable. But it remains for us to examine the circumstances under which dissonance, once arisen, persists. That is, under what conditions is dissonance not simply a momentary affair? If the hypotheses stated above are correct, then as soon as dissonance occurs there will be pressures to reduce it. To answer this question it is necessary first to have a brief look at the possible ways in which dissonance may be reduced.

Since there will be a more formal discussion of this point later on in this chapter, let us now examine how dissonance may be reduced, using as an illustration the example of the habitual cigarette smoker who has learned that smoking is bad for his health. He may have acquired this information from a newspaper or magazine, from friends, or even from some physician. This knowledge is certainly dissonant with cognition that he continues to smoke. If the hypothesis that there will be pressures to reduce this dissonance is correct, what would the person involved be expected to do?

1. He might simply change his cognition about his behavior by changing his actions; that is, he might stop smoking. If he no longer smokes, then his cognition of what he does will be consonant with the knowledge that smoking is bad for his health.

2. He might change his "knowledge" about the effects of smoking. This sounds like a peculiar way to put it, but it expresses well what must happen. He might simply end up believing that smoking does not have any deleterious effects, or he might acquire so much "knowledge" pointing to the good effects it has that the harmful aspects become negligible. If he can manage to change his knowledge in either of these ways, he will have reduced, or even eliminated, the dissonance between what he does and what he knows.

But in the above illustration it seems clear that the person may encounter difficulties in trying to change either his behavior or his knowledge. And this, of course, is precisely the reason that dissonance, once created, may persist. There is no guarantee that the person will be able to reduce or remove the dissonance. The hypothetical smoker may find that the process of giving up smoking is too painful for him to endure. He might try to find facts and opinions of others to support the view that smoking is not harmful, but these attempts might fail. He might then remain in the situation where he continues to smoke and continues to know that smoking is harmful. If this turns out to be the case, however, his efforts to reduce the dissonance will not cease. . . .

The terms "dissonance" and "consonance" refer to relations which exist between pairs of "elements." It is consequently necessary, before proceeding to define these relations, to define the elements themselves as well as we can.

These elements refer to what has been called cognition, that is, the things a person knows about himself, about his behavior, and about his surroundings. These elements, then, are "knowledges," if I may coin the plural form of the word. Some of these elements represent knowledge about oneself: what one does, what one feels, what one wants or desires, what one is, and the like. Other elements of knowledge concern the world in which one lives: what is where, what leads to what, what things are satisfying or painful or inconsequential or important, etc.

It is clear that the term "knowledge" has been used to include things to which the word does not ordinarily refer—for example, opinions. A person does not hold an opinion unless he thinks it is correct, and so, psychologically, it is not different from a "knowledge." The same is true of beliefs, values, or attitudes, which function as "knowledges" for our purposes. This is not to imply that there are no important distinctions to be made among these various terms. Indeed, some such distinctions will be made later on. But for the definitions here, these are all "elements of cognition," and relations of consonance and dissonance can hold between pairs of these elements.

There are further questions of definition one would like to be able to answer. For example, when is an "element of cognition" *one* element, or a group of elements? Is the knowledge, "the winter in Minneapolis is very cold" an element, or should this be considered a cluster of elements made up of more specific knowledge? This is, at present, an unanswerable question. Indeed, it may be a question which does not need answering.

Another important question concerning these elements is, how are they formed and what determines their content? At this point we want to emphasize the single most important determinant of the content of these elements, namely, *reality*. These elements of cognition are responsive to reality. By and large they mirror, or map, reality. This reality may be physical or social or psychological, but in any case the cognition more or less maps it. This is, of course, not surprising. It would be unlikely that an organism could live and survive if the elements of cognition were not to a large extent a veridical map of reality. Indeed, when someone is "out of touch with reality," it becomes very noticeable.

In other words, elements of cognition correspond for the most part with what the person actually does or feels or with what actually exists in the environment. In the case of opinions, beliefs, and values, the reality may be what others think or do; in other instances the reality may be what is encountered experientially or what others have told him.

But let us here object and say that persons frequently have cognitive elements which deviate markedly from reality, at least as we see it. Consequently, the major point to be made is that *the reality which impinges on a person will exert pressures in the direction of bringing the appropriate cognitive elements into correspondence with that reality*. This does not mean that the existing cognitive elements will *always* correspond. Indeed, one of the important consequences of the theory of dissonance is that it will help us understand some circumstances where the cognitive elements do not correspond with reality. But it does mean that if the cognitive elements do not correspond with a certain reality which impinges, certain pressures must exist. We should therefore be able to observe some manifestations of these pressures. This hypothesized relation between the cognitive elements and reality is important in enabling measurement of dissonance, and we will refer to it again in considering data.

It is now possible to proceed to a discussion of the relations which may exist between pairs of elements. There are three such relations, namely, irrelevance, dissonance, and consonance. They will be discussed in that order.

Two elements may simply have nothing to do with one another. That is, under such circumstances where one cognitive element implies nothing at all concerning some other element, these two elements are irrelevant to one another. . . .

Let us consider two elements which exist in a person's cognition and which are relevant to one another. The definition of dissonance will disregard the existence of all the other cognitive elements that are relevant to either or both of the two under consideration and simply deal with these two alone. *These two elements are in a dissonant relation if, considering these two alone, the obverse of one element would follow from the other.* To state it a bit more formally, x and y are dissonant if not-x follows from y. Thus, for example, if a person knew there were only friends in his vicinity and also felt afraid, there would be a dissonant relation between these two cognitive elements. Or, for another example, if a person were already in debt and also purchased a new car, the corresponding cognitive elements would be dissonant with one another. The dissonance might exist because of what the person has learned or come to expect, because of what is considered appropriate or usual, or for any of a number of other reasons. . . .

It may be helpful to give a series of examples where dissonance between two cognitive elements stems from different sources, that is, where the two elements are dissonant because of different meanings of the phrase "follow from" in the definition of dissonance given above.

1. Dissonance could arise from logical inconsistency. If a person believed that man will reach the moon in the near future and also believed that man will not be able to build a device that can leave the atmosphere of the earth, these two cognitions are dissonant with one another. The obverse of one follows from the other on logical grounds in the person's own thinking processes.

2. Dissonance could arise because of cultural mores. If a person at a formal dinner uses his hands to pick up a recalcitrant chicken bone, the knowledge of what he is doing is dissonant with the knowledge of formal dinner etiquette. The dissonance exists simply because the culture defines what is consonant and what is not. In some other culture these two cognitions might not be dissonant at all.

3. Dissonance may arise because one specific opinion is sometimes included, by definition, in a more general opinion. Thus, if a person is a Democrat but in a given election prefers the Republican candidate, the cognitive elements corresponding to these two sets of opinions are dissonant with each other because "being a Democrat" includes, as part of the concept, favoring Democratic candidates.

4. Dissonance may arise because of past experience. If a person were standing in the rain and yet could see no evidence that he was getting wet, these two cognitions would be dissonant with one another because he knows from experience that getting wet follows from being out in the rain. If one can

imagine a person who had never had any experience with rain, these two cognitions would probably not be dissonant. . . .

All dissonant relations, of course, are not of equal magnitude. It is necessary to distinguish degrees of dissonance and to specify what determines how strong a given dissonant relation is. . . .

One obvious determinant of the magnitude of dissonance lies in the characteristics of the elements between which the relation of dissonance holds. *If two elements are dissonant with one another, the magnitude of the dissonance will be a function of the importance of the elements.* The more these elements are important to, or valued by, the person, the greater will be the magnitude of a dissonant relation between them. Thus, for example, if a person gives ten cents to a beggar, knowing full well that the beggar is not really in need, the dissonance which exists between these two elements is rather weak. Neither of the two cognitive elements involved is very important or very consequential to the person. A much greater dissonance is involved, for example, if a student does not study for a very important examination, knowing that his present fund of information is probably inadequate for the examination. In this case the elements that are dissonant with each other are more important to the person, and the magnitude of dissonance will be correspondingly greater. . . .

Let us consider now the total context of dissonances and consonances in relation to one particular element. Assuming momentarily, for the sake of definition, that all the elements relevant to the one in question are equally important, *the total amount of dissonance between this element and the remainder of the person's cognition will depend on the proportion of relevant elements that are dissonant with the one in question.* Thus, if the overwhelming majority of relevant elements are consonant with, say, a behavioral element, then the dissonance with this behavioral element is slight. If in relation to the number of elements consonant with the behavioral element the number of dissonant elements is large, the total dissonance will be of appreciable magnitude. Of course, the magnitude of the total dissonance will also depend on the importance or value of those relevant elements which exist in consonant or dissonant relations with the one being considered. . . .

The Reduction of Dissonance

The presence of dissonance gives rise to pressures to reduce or eliminate the dissonance. The strength of the pressures to reduce the dissonance is a function of the magnitude of the dissonance. In other words, dissonance acts in the same way as a state of drive or need or tension. The presence of dissonance leads to action to reduce it just as, for example, the presence of hunger leads to action to reduce the hunger. Also, similar to the action of a drive, the greater the dissonance, the greater will be the avoidance of situations that would increase the dissonance.

In order to be specific about how the pressure to reduce dissonance would manifest itself, it is necessary to examine the possible ways in which existing dissonance can be reduced or eliminated. In general, if dissonance exists between two elements, this dissonance can be eliminated by changing one of those elements. The important thing is how these changes may be brought about. There are various possible ways in which this can be accomplished, depending upon the type of cognitive elements involved and upon the total cognitive context.

Changing a Behavioral Cognitive Element

When the dissonance under consideration is between an element corresponding to some knowledge concerning environment (environmental element) and a behavioral element, the dissonance can, of course, be eliminated by changing the behavioral cognitive element in such a way that it is consonant with the environmental element. The simplest and easiest way in which this may be accomplished is to change the action or feeling which the behavioral element represents. Given that a cognition is responsive to "reality" (as we have seen), if the behavior of the organism changes, the cognitive element or elements corresponding to this behavior will likewise change. This method of reducing or eliminating dissonance is a very frequent occurrence. Our behavior and feelings are frequently modified in accordance with new information. If a person starts out on a picnic and notices that it has begun to rain, he may very well turn around and go home. There are many persons who do stop smoking if and when they discover it is bad for their health. . . .

Changing an Environmental Cognitive Element

Just as it is possible to change a behavioral cognitive element by changing the behavior which this element mirrors, it is sometimes possible to change an *environmental* cognitive element by changing the situation to which that element corresponds. This, of course, is much more difficult than changing one's behavior, for one must have a sufficient degree of control over one's environment—a relatively rare occurrence. . . .

Whenever there is sufficient control over the environment, this method of reducing dissonance may be employed. For example, a person who is habitually hostile toward other people may surround himself with persons who provoke hostility. His cognitions about the persons with whom he associates are then consonant with the cognitions corresponding to his hostile behavior. The possibilities of manipulating the environment are limited, however, and most endeavors to change a cognitive element will follow other lines. . . .

Adding New Cognitive Elements

It is clear that in order to eliminate a dissonance completely, some cognitive element must be changed. It is also clear that this is not always possible. But even if it is impossible to eliminate a dissonance, it is possible to reduce the total magnitude of dissonance by adding new cognitive elements. Thus, for example, if dissonance existed between some cognitive elements concerning the effects of smoking and cognition concerning the behavior of continuing to smoke, the total dissonance could be reduced by adding new cognitive elements that are consonant with the fact of smoking. In the presence of such dissonance, then, a person might be expected to actively seek new information that would reduce the total dissonance and, at the same time, to avoid new information that might increase the existing dissonance. Thus, to pursue the example, the person might seek out and avidly read any material critical of the research which purported to show that smoking was bad for one's health. At the same time he would avoid reading material that praised this research. (If he unavoidably came in contact with the latter type of material, his reading would be critical indeed.) . . .

Before moving on, it is worth while to emphasize again that the presence of pressures to reduce dissonance, or even activity directed toward such reduction, does not guarantee that the dissonance will be reduced. A person may not be able to find the social support needed to change a cognitive element, or he may not be able to find new elements which reduce the total dissonance. In fact, it is quite conceivable that in the process of trying to reduce dissonance, it might even be increased. This will depend upon what the person encounters while attempting to reduce the dissonance. The important point to be made so far is that in the presence of a dissonance, one will be able to observe the *attempts* to reduce it. If attempts to reduce dissonance fail, one should be able to observe symptoms of psychological discomfort, provided the dissonance is appreciable enough so that the discomfort is clearly and overtly manifested.

Resistance to Reduction of Dissonance

If dissonance is to be reduced or eliminated by changing one or more cognitive elements, it is necessary to consider how resistant these cognitive elements are to change. Whether or not any of them change, and if so, which ones, will certainly be determined in part by the magnitude of resistance to change which they possess. It is, of course, clear that if the various cognitive elements involved had no resistance to change whatsoever, there would never be any lasting dissonances. Momentary dissonance might occur, but if the cognitive elements involved had no resistance to change, the dissonance would immediately be eliminated. Let us, then, look at the major sources of resistance to change of a cognitive element.

Resistance to Change of Behavioral Cognitive Elements

The first and foremost source of resistance to change for *any* cognitive element is the responsiveness of such elements to reality. If one sees that the grass is green, it is very difficult to think it is not so.

Certainly much behavior has little or no resistance to change. We continually modify many of our actions and feelings in accordance with changes in the situation. If a street which we ordinarily use when we drive to work is being repaired, there is usually little difficulty in altering our behavior and using a different route. What, then, are the circumstances that make it difficult for the person to change his actions?

1. The change may be painful or involve loss. A person may, for example, have spent a lot of money to purchase a house. If for any reason he now wants to change, that is, live in a different house or different neighborhood, he must endure the discomforts of moving and the possible financial loss involved in selling the house. . . .

2. The present behavior may be otherwise satisfying. A person might continue to have lunch at a certain restaurant even though they served poor food if, for example, his friends always ate there. . . .

3. Making the change may simply not be possible. It would be a mistake to imagine that a person could consummate any change in his behavior if he wanted to badly enough. It may not be possible to change for a variety of reasons. Some behavior, especially emotional reactions, may not be under the voluntary control of the person. For example, a person might have a strong reaction of fear which he can do nothing about. Also, it might not be possible to consummate a change simply because the new behavior may not be in the

behavior repertory of the person. A father might not be able to change the way he behaves toward his children simply because he doesn't know any other way to behave. A third circumstance which could make it impossible to change is the irrevocable nature of certain actions. . . .

Resistance to Change of Environmental Cognitive Elements

Here again, as with behavioral cognitive elements, the major source of resistance to change lies in the responsiveness of these elements to reality. The result of this, as far as behavioral elements go, is to tie the resistance to change of the cognitive element to the resistance to change of the reality, namely, the behavior itself. The situation is somewhat different with regard to environmental elements. When there is a clear and unequivocal reality corresponding to some cognitive element, the possibilities of change are almost nil. If one desired, for example, to change one's cognition about the location of some building which one saw every day, this would indeed be difficult to accomplish.

In many instances, however, the reality corresponding to the cognitive element is by no means so clear and unambiguous. When the reality is basically a social one, that is, when it is established by agreement with other people, the resistance to change would be determined by the difficulty of finding persons to support the new cognition.

There is another source of resistance to change of both behavioral and environmental cognitive elements. We have postponed discussion of it until now, however, because it is a more important source of resistance to change for environmental elements than for others. This source of resistance to change lies in the fact that an element is in relationship with a number of other elements. To the extent that the element is consonant with a large number of other elements and to the extent that changing it would replace these consonances by dissonances, the element will be resistant to change. . . .

Limits of the Magnitude of Dissonance

The maximum dissonance that can possibly exist between any two elements is equal to the total resistance to change of the less resistant element. The magnitude of dissonance cannot exceed this amount because, at this point of maximum possible dissonance, the less resistant element would change, thus eliminating the dissonance.

This does not mean that the magnitude of dissonance will frequently even approach this maximum possible value. When there exists a strong dissonance that is less than the resistance to change of any of the elements involved, this dissonance can perhaps still be reduced for the total cognitive system by adding new cognitive elements. In this way, even in the presence of very strong resistances to change, the total dissonance in the system could be kept at rather low levels.

Let us consider an example of a person who spends what for him is a very large sum of money for a new car of an expensive type. Let us also imagine that after purchasing it he finds that some things go wrong with it and that repairs are very expensive. It is also more expensive to operate than other cars, and what is more, he finds that his friends think the car is ugly. If the dissonance becomes great enough, that is, equal to the resistance to change of the less resistant element, which in the situation would probably be the behavioral element, he might sell the car and suffer whatever inconvenience and financial loss is involved. Thus the dissonance could not exceed the resistance the person has to changing his behavior, that is, selling the car.

Now let us consider the situation where the dissonance for the person who bought a new car was appreciable but less than the maximum possible dissonance, that is, less than the resistance to change of the less resistant cognitive element. None of the existing cognitive elements would then be changed, but he could keep the total dissonance low by adding more and more cognitions that are consonant with his ownership of the car. He begins to feel that power and riding qualities are more important than economy and looks. He begins to drive faster than he used to and becomes quite convinced that it is important for a car to be able to travel at high speed. With these cognitions and others, he might succeed in rendering the dissonance negligible. . . .

Avoidance of Dissonance

The discussion thus far has focused on the tendencies to reduce or eliminate dissonance and the problems involved in achieving such reduction. Under certain circumstances there are also strong and important tendencies to avoid increases of dissonance or to avoid the occurrence of dissonance altogether. Let us now turn our attention to a consideration of these circumstances and the manifestations of the avoidance tendencies which we might expect to observe.

The avoidance of an increase in dissonance comes about, of course, as a result of the existence of dissonance. This avoidance is especially important where, in the process of attempting to reduce dissonance, support is sought for a new cognitive element to replace an existing one or where new cognitive elements are to be added. In both these circumstances, the seeking of support and the seeking of new information must be done in a highly selective manner. A person would initiate discussion with someone he thought would agree with the new cognitive element but would avoid discussion with someone who might agree with the element that he was trying to change. A person would expose himself to sources of information which he expected would add new elements which would increase consonance but would certainly avoid sources which would increase dissonance.

If there is little or no dissonance existing, we would not expect the same kind of selectivity in exposure to sources of support or sources of information. In fact, where no dissonance exists there should be a relative absence of motivation to seek support or new information at all. This will be true in general, but there are important exceptions. Past experience may lead a person to fear, and hence to avoid, the initial occurrence of dissonance. Where this is true, one might expect circumspect behavior with regard to new information even when little or no dissonance is present to start with.

The operation of a fear of dissonance may also lead to a reluctance to commit oneself behaviorally. There is a large class of actions that, once taken, are difficult to change. Hence, it is possible for dissonances to arise and to mount in intensity. A fear of dissonance would lead to a reluctance to take action—a reluctance to commit oneself. Where decision and action cannot be indefinitely delayed, the taking of action may be accompanied by a cognitive negation of the action. Thus, for example, a person who buys a new car and is very afraid of dissonance may, immediately following the purchase, announce his conviction that he did the wrong thing. Such strong fear of dissonance is probably relatively rare, but it does occur. Personality differences with respect to fear of dissonance and the effectiveness with which one is able to reduce dissonance are undoubtedly important in determining whether or not such avoidance of dissonance is likely to happen. The operational problem would be to independently identify situations and persons where this kind of a priori self-protective behavior occurs.

Questions for Discussion

1. In much of West Africa, managers have had great difficulty in attracting and holding natives in factory work. They work a few weeks, collect their money, and go back to their villages. Why?

2. The graduated personal federal income tax (rising above 90 percent at upper levels) severely limits the executive's ability to increase his take-home pay by salary increases at the top organizational levels. Recently, the Internal Revenue Service has been attempting to tax stock dividends and bonuses at the same income tax rate. Do you think that such taxes adversely affect business management? In particular, do you think such taxes limit the business world's ability to attract and motivate ambitious and hard-working men?

3. In spite of repeated efforts to organize them, most engineers and professors have refused to join unions. Many might even agree that strong collective action would help them as a body, but they do not want to join. Why?

4. Harry Levinson reported the following observation in "Is There an Obsolescent Executive in Your Company—Or in Your Chair?" (*Think*, Jan.–Feb. 1968): "Some years ago I taught at a widely known university which offered two advanced graduate programs for executives. One group of men was between 30 and 38 years old, and the other between 45 and 55. The older group seemed less willing to learn and less able to look at alternative courses of action. They seemed to have more at stake in already fixed positions which they did not want to examine." Why might this be so?

5. In many organizations there is little or no consistent relationship between pay, promotion, and performance. Discuss the motivational implications of this condition. What theory of motivation helps explain these implications?

6. Discuss the needs or motives that would predispose an individual to perform effectively each of the following tasks: union business agent or union steward, college textbook salesman, high school student counselor, insurance salesman, mass production line foreman.

7. A not uncommon reaction of students receiving a low grade from a once favored, or at least approved, professor is to shift to a lower opinion of the professor. What theory of motivation might account for such opinion change and how would the theory explain the change?

8. Often, the basis for selecting a sales manager out of the sales staff is performance as a salesman. Why might picking a highly effective and highly achievement-oriented salesman for the job of sales manager be a mistake?

Short Cases for Discussion

The Community of Scholars

When I was working on my MBA degree I became involved with a group of fellow students in publishing a student evaluation of professors. This was done as a project of the Business Students Association. We informally solicited opinions from students on all faculty members. There was no standard questionnaire, no systematic sampling; we just asked people at coffee, in classes, and around the campus. We got together and pooled our inputs.

Next we decided to organize the information in three categories: quality of instruction, grading, and workload. We gave grades for quality of instruction: A for excellent, B for good, C for average, and D for poor. We gave numbers for grading and workload. For grading 1 meant stringent, 4 meant liberal, 2 and 3 meant degrees in between. For workload 1 meant heavy, 4 meant light, 2 and 3 meant degrees in between.

We dropped the bomb in the middle of the spring quarter. That is, we printed the evaluation and mailed a copy to each student, administrator, and faculty member. The reaction we got was unbelievable. Here are excerpts from a few letters, written in reaction by professors and administrators, all of which were critical of our action:

"Since you 'solicit and encourage input from the administration, faculty members . . .' let me provide you with some. As you know, I have encouraged your organization to work on some means of reporting to us on your classroom experiences.

"I feel, however, that your initial attempt will impede rather than assist your efforts in providing significant feedback. The evaluation seems to be more a product of haste than care."

"In reply to the gross distortions contained in the recent BSA release, entitled 'Faculty Evaluation,' first, let me assure you that I am very much in favor of faculty evaluations so long as they are conducted professionally, scientifically, and under officially recognized and qualified supervision. Furthermore, the University has provided that faculty evaluations be regularly made so there is no real need for an additional evaluation, unless someone has a personal reason for developing his own. The Evaluation stated it was evaluating courses but ended in evaluating faculty. Why?"

"I have had some discussions with the officers of the BSA concerning the Faculty Evaluation that was published by the Association and distributed to the faculty at the beginning of the week, and have come to the conclusion that this was not the result of a scientific evaluation of the faculty's teaching abilities. My view concerning this Evaluation as it now stands is that it has no validity whatsoever, and it is my hope that the faculty will totally disregard the ratings."

I had conversations with several professors (who did not know I was involved in the evaluation) and noted the following reactions:

"Students should never have been allowed to do this."

"I think this thing is just the last straw. The legislature is against us, the public, the governor, and the trustees are giving us a very bad time, and now the students have turned on us. It just touched a sore spot and while we can't react to all our other adversaries we can react to this one."

"One of our political animals, Professor Blank, was partly to blame for this. He spent a lot of time with the BSA students who prepared the Evaluation, before they did it. It would be altogether out of character, I think, for him to spend his time in this way out of an innocent desire to encourage student participation."

"I think the ratings were about 90 percent accurate. I can't think of a single instance where anybody was any more than one grade off."

"The Dean's comment about achieving scientific validity was crass hypocrisy. Does he mean scientific validity equal to that we achieve when we grade students? But I am not going to tell him—I haven't got tenure."

"I was surprised to see myself as being somewhat liberal in grading and really surprised, not happily, to see myself as giving a light workload. I'll have to do something about that."

Questions

1. What accounts for the intense reactions of faculty and administrators?
2. What concepts in the chapter might explain some of the reactions?

Adamson Advertising

Adamson Advertising Agency is a middle-size agency in a large southern city. I worked there as an artist for six years.

When I started at Adamson, the departments were organized along functional lines. All the creative types were in one major creative group. It was divided into such departments as art, copy, television and radio production, and newspaper and magazine production. The other major groups were marketing and account executives.

An account executive was assigned to manage each account. He was to direct a team drawn from creative and marketing personnel and provide service for the client. For several reasons this arrangement was not working well.

We kept adding and losing accounts rapidly. The creative and other employees were supposed to approach the client only after checking with the account executive, but they were making independent contacts. Sometimes the account executive was the last to hear about changes.

To cope with all of these problems, top management reorganized the agency. The old functional departments were broken up into new organizational units built around each client. This strengthened the position of the account executive, and he was able to control his team better.

Employees were physically regrouped according to the new organization. This meant that artists no longer sat with other artists exclusively. More likely the artist sat with a copywriter, a market research man, a television production man, and so on.

I noticed after several months that another change had occurred. Formerly a man had been evaluated mostly on his skill as a professional. Now, what seemed more important was his ability to satisfy the client. Meeting a deadline was valued more than the niceties of art work. I suppose that this was good for the business, but it had serious effects on those people whose job satisfaction came mostly from being good artists, writers, or whatever.

In fact, the creative personnel grumbled a great deal, and several of them quit within a year, saying that the job just was not what it used to be.

Question

How might motivational concepts discussed in this chapter explain the reaction of the creative employees who grumbled and quit?

Chapter 2

Interpersonal Communication

The department manager and his staff engineer were sitting in their glass-walled cubicle in the new continuous processing polyester plant. Outside the door a lone figure in white sat at a desk watching a myriad of dials and recoding graphs indicating temperatures, pressures, flow rates, densities, and so on. On the floor above, two men were repairing a vibrating casting belt, while below a single man was operating an automatic loading machine. That was it: the total complement of people in this modern chemical plant producing millions of pounds of product and millions of dollars of income. The department manager was worried, but not about his gleaming equipment. He was worried about relations with his men. Turning to his visitor, he exclaimed: "If only we could get rid of *all* the men, then I'd have no problems!"

This wishful thought of the technocratic manager reflected several conditions: a looming power confrontation with the union, the unpredictability of humans as compared with machines, and the difficulties that he was experiencing in his interpersonal relations. Like the autistic child, he wished for a world where *he* was the only person; the only person whose time was valuable, whose thoughts were correct, and whose plans should be fulfilled. Such an outlook is a threat to all achievement-oriented managers intent on making things happen. Some are tempted to look upon other people as obstacles to their achievement, and upon necessary interpersonal relations as a waste of time. This is a dangerous perspective, however, for effective interpersonal relations are central to political and organizational leadership. Even in highly automated plants where technology eliminates subordinates, the number of people with whom managers must maintain relations does not necessarily decrease. Those workers who are no longer required are replaced by systems engineers, computer programmers, executive assistants, and staff specialists. Relations with the latter may be more subtle and stressful than relatively clear-cut, boss-subordinate confrontations. Accordingly, interpersonal relations remain central to managerial careers and to organizational effectiveness.

Communicating and influencing behavior are the two aspects of interpersonal relations of most concern to managers. Communicating clearly consumes most of their time—some 50 to 90 percent (Horne and Lupton, 1965). (See Exhibit 2-1.)

Interpersonal relations do not constitute all organizational communications, of course. In addition, the complete communication system includes technology and structure. In later chapters we discuss structure and organizational communications, particularly in the context of planning, controlling, and changing.

Exhibit 2-1   Typical Distribution of Managerial Communication, Mean Hours per Week   (Webber, 1966)

Incoming (initiated by)	Outgoing (initiated to)
2.5 hr (superiors)	2.1 hr (superiors)
2.9 hr (people outside the organization)	3.6 hr (people outside the organization)
5.4 hr (diagonal and lateral associates)	6.3 hr (diagonal and lateral associates)
6.7 hr (subordinates)	7.1 hr (subordinates)

In this chapter, our concern is with a general communication model and the interpersonal dimension.

By interpersonal communication we mean all exchanges between people. Such communication can be official or unofficial, formal or informal. It can take place by word of mouth, memoranda, through meetings, or over the telephone. As we shall see, problems result mainly because people see things differently, say things differently, and interpret things differently. In this chapter, we assume that the essential purpose of communicating is *understanding*—ensuring that the other person understands what the sender is trying to communicate. In actuality, understanding may be less important to managers than influencing others' behavior, but we defer this until the next chapter. Understanding is our concern here.

A General Model of Communication

Consider the general model of communication shown in Exhibit 2-2 (Korzybski, 1962), and then examine all the blockages to understanding.

Exhibit 2-2   General Communication Model

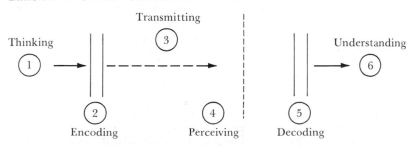

1. *Thinking:* the genesis and framing of the idea or message in the sender's mind.
2. *Encoding:* putting the thought into some form for possible communication. Ideation and encoding are closely related. On many matters we think in terms of language, but on others we experience feelings that we may encode in

facial expressions, body movements, art, or music, as well as in words. Thus, we can communicate in three ways: (a) by actual physical touch (a tap on the shoulder, a pat on the back, a slap on the cheek, a handshake); (b) by visible movements of some part of our bodies (a finger pointing, a wink of an eye, a nod of the head, a smile, grimace, or scowl, perhaps even posture, crossing legs and folding arms); (c) by symbols which stand for something we experience internally (audible symbols such as crying, speaking, and music, and visible symbols such as pictures, sculpture, and writing).

3. *Transmitting the signal:* the actual broadcasting of the message via some medium. If the sender encodes into language, he may transmit it orally (in person, over the phone, or by other electronic means) or write it (in longhand, have it typed, published, and so on).

4. *Perceiving:* the receiver must perceive—see, hear, or feel—the incoming communication with one or more of his senses.

5. *Decoding:* the receiver puts the incoming communication into some form that will make it understandable to him.

6. *Understanding.*

Thus, the following steps occur in a communication: the sender develops and encodes his message; that is, he takes the information, thought, or idea he wants to share and expresses it in a form that can be transmitted. The message is sent in the form of gestures, facial expressions, speech, written words, drawn diagrams, pictures, radio pulses, or other symbols. The message is (the sender hopes) perceived, decoded, and understood by the receiver.

Barriers to Understanding

The model is fairly simple, but the possibilities for blocking or distorting communication are many.

Sender's Assumptions

The sender's idea may be confused and contradictory, so clear encoding and transmission are impossible because he makes certain erroneous assumptions which contribute to all communication barriers. What is said, how it is said, what is left unsaid, often appear to depend on basic assumptions characterizing the sender: assumptions about himself, other people, and the communication process. Nilsen (1954) summarizes these assumptions and their effect on behavior as follows:

I *Sender's assumptions about his own motivation*
A) *Pattern of assumptions:* (1) sender's own psychological needs do not influence his words or actions; (2) his reasons for his behavior are "logical"; (3) he is motivated only by a desire to do what is best for the company and its personnel.

B) *Resulting pattern of behavior:* (1) sender's talking and acting fails to indicate an awareness of the meaning of events for others; (2) he lacks awareness of own bias; (3) he often lacks tact and courtesy, gives arbitrary orders, or withholds information (he does not recognize that his behavior may satisfy his needs).

II *Sender's assumptions about responses of his receivers*

A) *Pattern of assumptions:* (1) receiver "sees" the situation the same way sender does; (2) receiver understands what is said; (3) receiver feels, or should feel, as sender does; (4) receiver's responses are, or should be, "logical."

B) *Resulting pattern of behavior:* (1) sender does not check the reception and understanding of his statements; (2) he neglects receiver's perspective; (3) he deals with people as if they all see the same "facts" as facts; (4) he fails to provide opportunities for the expression of feelings by subordinates.

III *Sender's assumptions about the character of the environment*

A) *Pattern of assumptions:* (1) environment is unchanging, or ought to be; (2) events are fundamentally simple, not complex; (3) most events can be placed in one or other of two categories, e.g., "good" or "bad," "right" or "wrong"; (4) people respond the same way in different contexts or at different times.

B) *Resulting pattern of behavior:* (1) sender treats personnel problems as if once "solved" they will stay solved; (2) he deals with people as if their attitudes and beliefs did not change; (3) he deals with people the same way in different contexts and at different times; (4) he jumps to conclusions about problems; (5) he looks for *the* one cause of personnel problems; (6) he does not attempt to anticipate problems; (7) he does not recognize degrees of value in policies and people.

IV *Sender's assumptions about the process of communication*

A) *Pattern of assumptions:* (1) process of communication itself is not something that requires examination; (2) sender already knows enough about communicating; (3) communication process in a given situation has little or no relation to other events in the same situation; (4) communication processes are, or should be, independent of the attitudes of the people communicating; (5) words used mean the same to the receiver as to the sender.

B) *Resulting pattern of behavior:* (1) sender fails to examine or study the communication procedures of the organization; (2) he does not provide structured opportunities for personnel to express their points of view and to participate in planning; (3) he does not verify the reception and understanding of his communications; (4) he does not consider consistency between what is *said* and what is *done.*

These kinds of misleading assumptions and the associated sender behavior contribute to all of the other communication barriers.

Inconsistent or Improper Transmission

"I didn't mean it," "You always hurt the one you love," and so on all reflect the common notion that we often communicate what we do not intend to—and in fact may be contradictory to our intention. Often these are factors about ourselves that we are not entirely aware of. These communication ambiguities create what Bennis (1961) terms an "arc of distortion." For example, in Exhibit 2-3, we see that A is really communicating at least two things to B, the intended as well as the selectively unintended. This makes it difficult for B to determine how he should respond. Receivers usually attempt to discover at which level the sender would like to communicate, and then reciprocate.

Exhibit 2-3   The Arc of Distortion

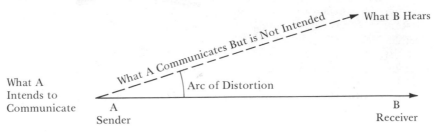

Inconsistency between message content and style of transmission is a common contributor to the arc of distortion. For example, a young research scientist enters the laboratory director's office with a letter from another organization offering a job. After some miscommunication between the two, the director heatedly exclaims: "I'm not disturbed. If you think it is best for you to go somewhere else, that is OK with me. We can get another plasma physicist any day, just as good as you. They are standing in line to get in here" (Zaleznik and Moment, 1964). Obviously, the words and manner of communication are at odds. The real message seems to be that the laboratory director is offended that one of his workers might leave him and afraid that others might lower their opinion of him because he can't hold on to his people.

"The medium is the message" is the popular McLuhan phrase. While exaggerated, the point has validity; the way a message is transmitted may carry more meaning than the sender's words. Research on face-to-face communication (Mehrabian, 1970) suggests that only a small portion of the information is contained in the words, perhaps seven percent. Most of the message apparently is transmitted by facial expression and physical posture (55 percent) and vocal intonation and inflection (38 percent). Consider the academician who tells his students of the glories of democracy and citizen participation, but delivers his message via a lecture from a platform above the students who are sitting in fixed seats all facing forward and from whom no questions are invited or even recognized. The method of transmission is so markedly at variance with the intended message that the sender may be dismissed as a hypocrite or fraud. Such inconsistency between message and medium characterizes much intergenerational and superior-subordinate communication.

The manner of transmission also has symbolic value that may aid or hinder the communication. In a memorable passage in the Bible, King David and his troops are described as setting up camp after a wearying day's march in the burning sun. His aid brings him a globlet and plate, but David refuses so he can make a tour of his army to see that they have refreshed themselves. Many great leaders such as Gandhi and Martin Luther King so mastered symbolic communication. Thus the aphorism that "actions speak louder than words" recognizes the symbolic component of behavior as communication.

For example, when a government researcher (Hall, 1966) was conducting interviews with managers about company views on equal opportunity employment, the men who kept him waiting and who never seemed to have as much time as planned were suggesting that they were not pleased about the program—

a point doubly made by the managers who remained sitting behind their desks during the entire visit.

Other examples: A recently installed president of a German manufacturing company had his executives change from their traditional Prince Albert coats to ordinary business suits in order to dramatize the shrinking gulf between levels; an American company president eliminated a relic of nineteenth-century capitalism, payment by the hour, in favor of a weekly salary for everyone. Such actions communicate more about the desired climate of the organization than speeches on the "one big happy family" theme.

The transmission of content and medium should be consistent and appropriate to the situation and people involved. President John F. Kennedy was reported to be a verbal person; he liked to call people directly. Yet, in spite of his position and power, he apparently found the Department of State unresponsive to his telephone calls. State's system was geared to written communication. Kennedy learned to send memos whenever he wanted a response (Schlesinger, 1965). The opposite characterized President Nixon. He reportedly disliked the "laying on of tongues" as White House locution had it, and much preferred to spend three minutes reading a memo to hearing someone out in person for a quarter hour (*N.Y. Times*, Dec. 12, 1969).

We know very little about what communication media are preferred by what people. One survey (Spector et al., 1971) suggests that in development projects in rural communities, women respond more favorably to radio broadcasts while men prefer audio-visual presentations. It would appear, however, that individuals and organizations have favored forms for receiving and transmitting information.

Psychological Interference

On a surface level, interference may reflect the receiver's thinking about other matters. At a professor's lecture on the first day of the fall semester when it is hot and uncomfortable, many students' thoughts may be on the recent past of cool waters, cool drinks, and cool companions. One academic experiment (Cameron, 1968) suggests that at any given instant in the college lecture hall, 20 percent of both men and women are thinking about sex, and only about 20 percent are concentrating on the professor.

As common as such inattention is, however, a more fundamental and disturbing psychological interference exists. The professor may be obviously conservative and establishmentarian. He could be tuned out because some students don't want to hear what he has to say. It is all "biased" or "irrelevant"—so they may think and so they may perceive the communication. For a sadder example, consider that the largest number of telephone calls that a major television network ever received occurred at a world series game when Jose Feliciano sang the national anthem. Thousands of viewers were apparently offended by his long hair, his guitar, and his distinctive personal styling of the song. They refused to see and hear the deep-felt emotion and love of country that the blind singer was attempting to communicate.

An even more unfortunate tale of similar miscommunication comes out of the United States' ill-fated involvement in the Cuban invasion of 1961 (Schlesinger, 1965). The planners were receiving communications about internal conditions in Cuba from three sources: (1) Cuban refugees disenchanted with

Castro; (2) CIA operatives and paid informers inside Cuba; and (3) neutrals with diplomatic stations in Havana. The first two indicated that Castro's popularity was declining, that the people were demoralized, and that a landing would spark spontaneous support from the island's inhabitants. The third source disputed these conclusions. Evaluating the sources, government officials believed the reports they wanted to believe. Because the doubtful messages came mainly from persons representing socialist governments whose sympathy with U.S. interests was suspect, their messages were dismissed.

We all tend to evaluate the sender and judge his communications accordingly. This is rational, except when the receiver is unaware of how his bias distorts his perception. Bass (1965) summarizes the impact of various perceptions of the sender: "If the communicator is labeled extremist before he presents his point of view, he is less likely to bring about change in the attitudes of the audience than the communicator who is seen as moderate [Weiss, 1958]. In the same way an impartial speaker who draws conclusions for his audience is likely to be most effective in changing audience attitudes. . . . These effects occur despite the fact that both the speaker labeled as impartial and the speaker who is perceived as biased present identical communications [Hovland and Mandell, 1952]. Again, a well-liked, esteemed, trustworthy communicator can accomplish more change by advocating a greater change. On the other hand, an audience is likely to disagree more with a disliked communicator who presents identical messages [Hovland and Weiss, 1951–52]. However, this is complicated by the 'sleeper effect.' Messages are remembered longer than the sources of the messages. Therefore, over time, messages originally rejected because the communicator was disliked tend to increase in acceptability because the communicator has been forgotten" (p. 291).

The receivers' skepticism about messages from senders thought to have biased attitudes results in the paradox that unintended communications carry greater weight than intended transmissions. Zajonc (1966) distinguishes between three kinds of communications: instrumental, consummatory, and incidental. Instrumental communication is goal directed; the sender seeks to achieve definite effects in the receiver. Such communication is *transmitted.* Consummatory communication arises as a consequence of an emotional or motivational state of the sender—his joy, anger, fear, and so forth; it is merely the spontaneous expression of this state. Such communication is *emitted.* Incidental communication imparts information to another without the sender having any intention of doing so, and often, without his knowledge that he does. The classic theatre provides numerous examples of misdelivered letters and overheard conversations that change the course of the drama. Such fortuitous occurrences may be poor writing, but they reflect an established fact that information overheard unintentionally (or when the receiver perceives the message as not intended for him) is more likely to be believed than similar instrumental communication.

Another experiment demonstrated that an audience rejects an open attack on its beliefs, but is more likely to believe something overheard incidentally. Festinger and Maccoby (1964) give an interesting explanation of this phenomenon: "Let us first try to understand the cognitive behavior of a person who, strongly committed to an opinion, listens to a vigorous, persuasive communication that attacks that opinion. Certainly, such a listener is not passive. He does not sit there listening and absorbing what is said without any counteraction on his part. Indeed, it is most likely that under such circumstances, while he is listening to the persuasive communication, he is actively, inside his own mind, counterarguing, derogating the points the communicator makes, and degrading the communicator himself. In other words, we can imagine that there is really an argument going on, one side being vocal and the other subvocal. Let us imagine that one could somehow prevent the listener from arguing back while listening to the persuasive communication. If one created such a passive listener, it seems reasonable to expect that the persuasive communication would then have more of an impact. The listener, not able to counterargue, would be influenced and would be less likely to reject the communication" (p. 360).

Berelson (1950) points out that there is certain psychological gratification from overhearing something not meant for you. Such a communication may affect the receiver inadvertently because he does not believe that the sender intended to influence him. The receiver's defenses are not alerted and aroused. Thus, overhearing persons talking about the dangers of smoking seems to have a greater impact on young people than formal lectures designed to warn, frighten, and dissuade (Allyn and Festinger, 1961). In spite of the subtle advantages of incidental communication, however, it is of minor importance to managers and organizations as a formal device. Our major concern is with instrumental communication directed by the sender to an intended receiver. As the above passage suggests, the sender may have substantial difficulty.

Clearly, then, we evaluate every incoming communication by evaluating the sender. Such authoritative or evaluative attitudes on the part of the receiver sometimes get back to the sender—particularly if the sender is an organizational subordinate. In this case, the superior may be so anxious about protecting and enhancing his position that he is unwilling to accept communication about the negative effects of his behavior. He will shift such conversation away from negative content toward the goodness or loyalty of the *bearer* of the message (he symbolically endeavors to slay the bearer of bad tidings—as sometimes actually occurred in antiquity). Such a boss is likely to get his way. He will hear nothing bad from his employees—until they resign or the creditors foreclose. This tendency to evaluate, to discourage negative information, and to categorize the communication and its sender prematurely is one of the major barriers to understanding.

Gibb (1966) described the problem of psychological interference as "defensive behavior." This is behavior which occurs when an individual perceives or anticipates threat. Its arousal prevents the listener from concentrating on the message. There are six categories of defensive and supportive climates which retard or facilitate communication shown in Exhibit 2-4.

Being able to listen without evaluation and premature criticism is particularly appropriate for organizational superiors. Shortly after the death of Winston Churchill, Lord Avon (the former Anthony Eden) discussed what he considered Churchill's outstanding leadership characteristic. He said that the indefatigable former Prime Minister always seemed to be available, he was ready to listen, he never cut off a suggestion with a curt dismissal but encouraged elaboration. To be sure, the great man was often formidable and abusive to subordinates who made mistakes in policy implementation; and he could be dictatorial in ordering the conduct of his own policy. But he was invariably receptive to new ideas. It was not a threatening experience to broach a new matter to Churchill.

Exhibit 2-4 Climate and Communication Effectiveness (Gibb, 1966)

Defensive Climate	Interference	Supportive Climate
Evaluation	Speech or other behavior which appears evaluative increases defensiveness	Description
Control	Speech which is used to control the listener evokes resistance	Problem orientation
Strategy	When the sender is perceived as engaged in a strategem involving ambiguous and multiple motivations, the receiver becomes defensive	Spontaneity
Neutrality	When neutrality in speech appears to the listener to indicate a lack of concern for his welfare, he becomes defensive	Empathy
Superiority	When a person communicates to another that he feels superior in position, power, wealth, intellectual ability, physical characteristics, or in other ways, he arouses defensiveness	Equality
Certainty	Those people who are dogmatic, seem to know the answers, or seem to require no data, tend to put others on guard	Provisionalism

The next day he might assert that the proposal was unacceptable, but the initial presentation was respected. Consequently, he was approached—and some of the unsolicited ideas were good.

Perhaps similar behavior characterizes effective business executives. In spite of the importance of initiating communication, executives may depend even more upon others to bring information to them. One study (Webber, 1966) suggests that higher rated executives spend more time talking with people *who come to them* than do lower rated executives. As a result, the latter spend more time initiating conversations.

This same research also suggests that effective executives conduct more of their numerous discussions in intimate, two-person talks than in group meetings or via correspondence. They seem to throw out invitations for individuals to come see them personally rather than waiting for the next scheduled meeting. Such a style may facilitate the frank expression of opinions and ideas. Exhibit 2-5 summarizes the distribution of time for these managers.

Exhibit 2-5   Some Executive Communications   (Webber, 1966)

	Executives Rated Less Effective (n = 6)	Executives Rated More Effective (n = 3)
Mean hours per week advising and discussing with others who have called or come to them	9.5	16.0
Mean hours per week consulting and discussing when they have initiated the conversation	11.3	6.5
Mean hours per week in two-person oral communication	12.6	21.2
Mean hours per week in group meetings	19.9	12.1

Differences between less effective and more effective executives is significant at 0.05 level. Categories of effectiveness were based on the subjective performance evaluations of superiors and an external consultant.

Perceptual Distortion

The "arc of distortion" may be further confounded by the receiver's selective inattention. It may be that he "hears" the sender saying something which is not intended and which in fact may not have been communicated. As an unfortunate extreme example, the paranoiac typically complains that others are rejecting him and persecuting him; he tends only to hear hostility and aggression whether it is present or not. What is involved in many of our examples of faulty communication is perceptual distortion resulting from the ways in which we "see" things. "I believe only in what I can see and touch" has always been the slogan of the man who considers himself pragmatic and realistic. But seeing, like all perceiving, is not necessarily reality. The major points of perceptual distortion result from expectations, needs, fears, and organizing schema.

Perception is affected by a person's needs, motivations, and experience. Thus the difference between the trained observer and the layman is largely a matter of differential selectivity: the pathologist examining the microscope slide concentrates on the familiar and expected microbe, while the novice sees an undifferentiated mass. In addition, there is heightened awareness of relevant stimuli and depressed awareness of irrelevant ones. A hungry man looks for food and seeks out signs of it—ignoring things of lesser importance. Relevant stimuli reach awareness more readily than neutral ones. So, words that have a sexual as well as nonsexual connotation (e.g., "screw") tend to be more quickly identified in unclear carbon copies when they have been recently experienced in the sexual rather than the neutral context (Wiener, 1955). The implications of this for the sender are significant because the potential receiver's interest in the message is more important for understanding than anything the communicator can do about his style, language, or delivery (Higham, 1957).

Research (Blum, 1954) suggests that pleasant or sympathetic messages are sought out, while threatening ones are actively avoided. Mildly threatening or unpleasant stimuli are not perceived until they are *very* dangerous, and then perception is heightened.

In addition to selectively perceiving, we tend to organize and complete fragmented and partial perceptions. Even the simplest perception is organized by the perceiver; the perceived characteristics of any part are a function of the whole to which it appears to belong. Apparently, one of the chief functions of the mind is filling up gaps. That is, we constantly try to connect new material into an old pattern in order to make it meaningful. We seem to prefer the simple and the regular to the complex and irregular; to organize what is received into tidy bundles. This is one reason why it is so difficult to communicate a new idea, because it has to be fitted into the existing structure of the mind. Barlett (1951) writes: "Our mental habits persist and may help or hinder us; they will only do the former if we can link what we have to say onto what our listeners already know; for in that way, the new can be assimilated to the old." (p. 158). In the blooming confusion that is life with its multiple stimuli, such organization and simplification is essential, though dangerous.

For example, we tend to perceive people as stereotypes, and this categorization is an important determinant of how their subsequent behavior will be interpreted. Jews, blacks, and other minorities have long been convenient scapegoats for those in fear of society's complexities. The world appears simpler if one assigns people to distinct categories and then ignores the individual. If you don't bother to learn how clean, industrious, and patriotic is a particular long-haired, bearded student, your hippie stereotype is not disturbed and you can maintain the illusion that you understand current university turmoil.

Research on the authoritarian personality indicates that some people are especially predisposed to categorize in this manner—those with a low tolerance for ambiguity (Adorno et al., 1950). One test of this characteristic consists of flashing a series of small dots on a screen. Initially, everyone agrees that the dots form a dog. Then the configuration is slowly modified so that the figure changes. People with low tolerance for ambiguity tend to lag in perceiving and recognizing a new shape; they hold on to the perception of the dog. In contrast, subjects with higher tolerance for ambiguity can relinquish the familiar shape, tolerate a period during which they do not know the shape, and recognize sooner the emerging form of a cat. In addition, when examining photographs of people, those low in ambiguity tolerance tend to categorize more of them as Jews, Negroes, and so on than do subjects with greater ambiguity tolerance (Scodel and Austrin, 1954).

This research on prejudice was originally considered in relation to American Jews. Recent classroom experiments where normally neatly dressed and clean-shaven students donned wigs, false beards, and hippie garb for a few days show that such distortion is still with us. They were refused credit more often than before their masquerade, as well as receiving more traffic tickets and general harassment, although their behavior had not changed.

A simple example of perceptual distortion in business is offered by evidence that busy managers distort their perceptions of their own behavior. They tend to see themselves as being busier than they really are, of doing more of certain things than they actually do, and especially of communicating more with subordinates than the latter perceive (Webber, 1970). For example, here is how sixty pairs of managers and subordinates perceived their communications with each other:

Superior perceives:	4.1 hours per week communicating with the subordinate
Subordinate perceives:	3.0 hours per week communicating with the superior
Actual (estimated from sample observations):	2.8 hours per week that superior and subordinate communicated with each other

Perhaps superiors are vaguely aware that their relations with subordinates are inadequate, so they defensively exaggerate their perceptions. Or, perhaps they feel so harried that they overestimate everything that they do. In any case, managers should be a little skeptical about how they think they communicate—and recognize that others probably do not see it as they do. Most important, they should recognize that communication breakdowns are not due to stupidity. Both parties may consider their perceptions valid.

A more involved example of large-scale perceptual distortion is the ill-fated Edsel automobile (Brooks, 1963). When the initial design of the new vehicle was unveiled to company executives in 1954, there was standing applause from the audience. The designer was praised for catching just the right combination of size, luxury, and gaudiness to compete with General Motors' midline cars. Yet, four years later when the project was in shambles and the Edsel near death, much of the blame fell on the designer for his "obvious" blunder. Just another example of corporate backstabbing? Perhaps, but more likely, executives *did like* the design in 1954. Subsequent events gradually changed their perception. (The more valid reason for the car's demise would seem to be an economic recession and the launching of Russia's Sputnik in October 1957—an event which shocked the United States and produced reexamination of national goals and strategies. For a time, at least, we tended toward more austere, conservative, and compact cars.)

The well-known Rorschach ink-blot test depends upon the tendency of people to perceive and organize according to their needs and personalities, which they project into their description of the ink blot. Thus, a cartoon illustrates a portly, bald-headed business executive looking at an ink-blot card and exclaiming, "I see creeping socialism, chiselers on relief, and the erosion of fiscal integrity in government!"

Erroneous Translation

An old adage says, "There are only three races: men, women, and children, and none of them speak the same language." Unfortunately there are many more languages than three, perhaps as many as there are individuals in the world. Thus, even if sender and receiver ostensibly know the same language, erroneous decoding may occur. The problem is twofold: first, each individual's "language" is a reflection of his experience, and second, words are ambiguous. Let us consider both briefly.

The originator of a message can encode it only within the framework of his own experience and knowledge. Similarly, the receiver can decode only within his own experience. Exhibit 2-6 illustrates this: If the circles do not meet, there are no common experiences or empathic psychological sets; communication is impossible.

In addition to the problem of experience gaps, words are troublesome.

Exhibit 2-6 Commonness of Experience Necessary for Communication (Vardaman and Halterman, 1968)

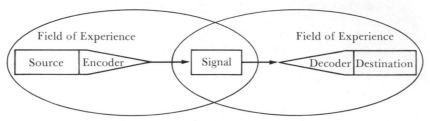

Words themselves do not have meanings. The words "police" or "pig" are not the things they name. Only people have meanings which they attach to words. A pioneer semanticist was once being interviewed by a magazine reporter. The scholar said, "Language is a very tricky thing; words don't mean what you think." The reporter asked, "What do you mean?" "Well, it's like this," went the reply, "when a young woman says you are 'going too far,' what she really means is that you are 'coming too close'" (Guthrie, 1958). Today young women are unlikely to use such an old-fashioned phrase, but certain words which they use can create common misunderstanding. Junior high school girls refer to certain classmates as "whores," which while frightening to the parents involved seems to mean that the teenagers in question flirt with other boys while going steady. The so-called generation gap may be wider in vocabulary than in actual beliefs or behavior.

Such words as "police," "pig," "law and order," "school busing," "boy," "lady," even "democracy," have different meanings and different impacts on certain whites, blacks, males, and females. The sender may believe that he has encoded in the proper language, but the receiver's understanding may be different from that intended. The newspaper columnist Russell Baker (Feb. 3, 1972) offers a humorous illustration of miscommunication between parents and children:

> The parent in Chicago looks across the table at the big new person who worries him. "What are you going to do?" he asks.
>
> "I may go to Boston to see about getting some guys to get up a camper trip to Winnipeg," comes the answer.
>
> To the parent the answer sounds insane. To "do" in his old vocabulary means to put down roots, to make something, to act—this for the purpose of building, maintaining and sitting fast by hearth-and-home, where the Depression can't touch him and war is far away.
>
> To the big new people, however, it often means "to be in motion." When a parent says, "What are you going to do?" he is asking, "How are you going to go about settling down?" What the big new people often hear is "Where are you off to next?" Not surprisingly, conversation collapses, sometimes in shrieks.

The problem of mismatching vocabularies is particularly common in organizations where staff specialists tend to utilize arcane terminology such as "stochastic variables" when the line manager wants to know the odds.

If you were to speak with different people who had heard Feliciano sing the Star Spangled Banner, observed the schoolgirl behavior, or been in on the Cuban invasion planning, you would probably hear very different words which would make it difficult for you, the outsider, to know what really happened. Because of selective perception and differing meanings attributed to words, individual experiences are never the same. Many problems in communication arise from forgetting this. When an admiring or irate observer talks about an event, he is talking about his inference, an event that occurred *inside* him, not about reality. Reality and communication can only be approximated, and only if many observers tend to agree on their inferences.

Distortions From the Past

There is another form of psychological interference that is also destructive of understanding. This is interference from the past in the form of rigidities of interpretation and response, which are principal obstacles to valid communications. The perception and interpretation of incoming communications are sometimes distorted to suit these rigidities, which stem from anxious early experiences carried over into new situations where they are inappropriate. We are "time-bound" in this respect, in that we tend to transfer and repeat such experiences. Transference is the reexperiencing of past relationships in the present with full affective force. We all perceive and decode communications through a mechanism laden with yesterdays. Frequently, influential events and people from our individual histories are transferred to the present as if they were still before us. Thus, the research scientist may be antagonistic toward his boss because the older man provides a way of getting even with his domineering father. And the laboratory director's anger may be an acting out of his hurt suffered from a son who disappointed him. The stress that many males feel while working under a female superior may run much deeper than the sexist attitudes that the women's liberation movement complains of; it may reflect the burden of mother and son experiences from which many men never escape. The repetition compulsion is expressed through repeating experiences which have been painful, apparently in an effort to master the original experience—frequently with no success.

Toward Perfect Understanding

Mutual understanding seems to be both cause and effect of perfect communication. Understanding of self and understanding of others are closely related.

Congruence and Communication

An individual can be considered to have three levels of reality: experience, awareness, and intention (see Exhibit 2-7). Experience is the deepest reality; it is the existential being, what he really feels or thinks—guilt, fear, love, and so on. Awareness is what he thinks he is; it is what he admits to his conscious level. The most superficial level is what he intends to communicate, the words that he broadcasts. Roger's (1961) general law of interpersonal relationships suggests that communication between two people will be most effective and understanding most complete when each is congruent. That is, what A intends to broadcast, what he is aware of, and what he truly experiences are all the

Exhibit 2-7   Levels of Communication

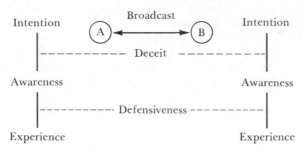

same. And if B is also congruent within himself, he will be able to understand and reciprocate.

For example, infants are fantastic communicators within a limited range of messages. If they feel hunger, fear, or joy, the feeling floods their consciousness and is automatically broadcast. The cry or the gurgle is understood by adults who find the young child's congruence very appealing. Unfortunately, or perhaps fortunately, most of us lose our congruence to some degree as we mature. The emotionally maladjusted person provides a sad example of personal incongruity. Because of gaps between his internal levels, communication within himself has broken down. As a result, communication with others is damaged. But to some extent we all share this problem, for we all have our gaps. The gap between what is admitted to awareness and what is really felt has been labeled *defensiveness*. It is what is repressed to the unconscious. The gap between awareness and what is intended for communication has been labeled *deceit*. This term suggests the sender's effort to communicate something different or less than he is aware of. Much psychotherapy rests upon the assumption that if the counselor is congruent, his congruence will gradually draw out the patient and move him toward congruence because of the climate of security, understanding, and liking. Gradually, the relationship grows mutually satisfying.

We can consider this matter in another way with the following simple matrix of interpersonal disclosure:

	Known to self	*Unknown to self*
Known to other	Announced (intended broadcast)	Denied (defensiveness)
Unknown to other	Concealed (deceit)	Unknown

Communication is most effective when the pertinent aspects of oneself are admitted to consciousness and are announced. However, concealment, deceit, denial, and defensiveness hinder true understanding. Look back at the harsh words of the laboratory director to his ambitious subordinate. The manager's lack of congruity and his effort to deny anger and hurt feelings undermines his communication with the young researcher.

Full disclosure can be threatening, however. Do I dare communicate my congruence? Do I dare announce my experience? Will I be rejected if my fear is known? Do I have the courage to enter into a relationship that may change me? If a person can answer these questions affirmatively, he is probably a self-actualizing person. The self-actualizing or fully functioning person *is* congruent; he is open to himself without excessive anxiety, hence open to others and to authentic communication.

Congruency and full disclosure suggest ways for improving interpersonal understanding especially relevant to parents, spouses, and counselors. In these situations, congruity aids disclosure and understanding. Indeed, the spontaneity and sincerity that are associated with this model have become extremely attractive to many groups, especially the young, and something of a fad through sensitivity training and encounter groups. "Letting it all hang out" has its attractions.

Short of extended therapy and T-groups, however, the most promising system for promoting such two-way understanding is old and simple, but still difficult: an evaluative tendency is avoided, and real communication facilitated, when each attempts to express ideas and attitudes from the other person's point of view. Obviously easier said than done, but perhaps approximated by restating the other person's position to him accurately and to his satisfaction. Perfect understanding can be approached only by sharing experiences, not by superficial verbalization. Anderson (1970) summarizes the criteria of giving feedback to an individual regarding his behavior and one's perception of it:

"I think the first, most general, and most significant criterion that 'helpful feedback' must meet is simply that it be intended to be helpful to the recipient. That is, the sender of the message should ask himself beforehand, 'Do I really feel that what I am about to say is likely to be helpful to the other person?' I need to examine my own motivation, that is, and be sure that I am not simply about to unload a burden of hostility from my own breast and for my own personal benefit, quite regardless of the expected effect on the receiver. Otherwise, I may convince myself that my only obligation is to be open and honest— that the name of the game is 'candor'—and that so long as I truly and completely 'level,' I have fulfilled the only necessary obligation. If my objective is to help the recipient of the feedback, then, three things are necessary:

1. The other person must understand what I am saying.
2. He must be willing and able to accept it.
3. He must be able to do something about it if he chooses to.

"To summarize: to be maximally useful to the recipient, feedback should meet the following criteria. It should be:

1. Intended to help the recipient.
2. Given directly and with real feeling, and based on a foundation of trust between the giver and receiver.
3. Descriptive rather than evaluative.
4. Specific rather than general, with good, clear, and preferably recent examples.
5. Given at a time when the receiver appears to be in a condition of readiness to accept it.

6. Checked with others in the group to be sure they support its validity.
7. Inclusive of only those things that the receiver might be expected to be able to do something about.
8. Not be more than he can handle at any particular time."

Manager's Problem

A manager, however, has a different problem than does the parent, husband, or therapist. Understanding through communicating is usually only a means for the manager; the end is influence. One communication adviser (Deunk, 1967) concludes, "If we can free ourselves from our need to influence and direct others to our way of thinking, we can then begin to listen to others with understanding." Probably true, but a manager/leader can never completely give up the need to influence others. It is at the center of his role and often of his personality. Thus, tension between communication and influence is at the heart of management.

Influencing people and events is more important for managers (and politicians) than is understanding through communication. If this sounds harsh, you should recognize that communication and influence are not necessarily in conflict or mutually contradictory. It is just that a certain degree of concealment or deceit may be essential. No man of responsibility can reveal everything that underlies a communication. To do so might hinder his effectiveness and unnecessarily frighten and hurt people.

Note that a need for modest deceit is not peculiar to men of power. It affects everyone. As children, we learn from our parents not to be quite so congruent; not to tell old Aunt Belle that she has bad breath and an ugly nose, and that we hate it when she tries to kiss us. We are told to bear it in silence so as not to hurt her feelings. Similarly, most parents control their impulse to tell their children to get lost because they cannot stand them, nor does the husband tell his wife of his attraction to his cute secretary. Parents and spouses know that their feelings will pass, to be replaced by a happier state, so useless hurt is avoided by deceit. Indeed, in the case of the child with his aunt, society labels it not deceit, but "courtesy," "manners," or "concern." As the old French diplomat Clemenceau put it, "Etiquette is nothing but hot air, but that is what our automobiles ride on and look how it smooths out the bumps!"

There is no perfect resolution to the tension between communication, influence, and concern. Congruence probably leads to better communication and understanding, but

- Personal defensiveness is difficult to overcome even with sensitivity training or psychological counseling.
- Some deceit may be essential to incorporate concern for others.
- Managers as managers tend to be more concerned with influencing behavior than with perfect understanding.

Yet the more a sender departs from congruence, the more difficult it probably will be to communicate understanding.

Lively controversy continues as to how much openness is desirable or possible in organizational relationships. By virtue of their achievement-oriented personalities and time-pressured positions, most managers tend to be quite task-oriented. This leads them to discourage nontask communication and the demonstration of emotion. Their attention is focused on the task, but such intellectual preoccupation tends to restrict their exercise of the faculty of observation. Consequently, they are frequently insensitive to others' behavior—especially nonverbal behavior. Lamb and Turner (1969) argue that it would indeed be desirable if managers could be more spontaneous and less intellectually disciplined about their behavior, but they recognize the essential difficulty:

"Those who argue cultishly for a more 'natural' life are wrong in thinking that Valhalla will be obtained only by rejecting the preoccupations of contemporary life and attaining some relaxed and mystical state. Clearly none of this concerns the manager. He has got to continue to apply intellectual disciplines and they will become increasingly more demanding with the increased complexity and specialization of work procedures. They cannot help but be increasingly applied, also, to dealings with people. The big question is, however, can some way be found to exercise enhanced observation without loss of intellectual control?" (p. 7).

To test empirically whether there is any relationship between open communication and company performance, Willets (1967) examined interpersonal relations among top executives in 20 small manufacturing concerns. He found it necessary to differentiate among three kinds of communication:

1. Open communication of *task-oriented* ideas between executives was correlated significantly with higher company performance.
2. Open communication *about* feelings in a rational, nonemotional way was correlated with higher company performance.
3. Spontaneous, emotional communication *of* feelings was *not* associated with higher performance (and there may be a negative association).

We consider this issue further in Chapter 12 when we examine organization development.

Critical Communication and Organizational Structure

Communication difficulties have their impact on the structure and management of organizations. Indeed, hierarchical structures and centralized decision making partially reflect communication problems.

Based upon his analysis of the German Socialist Party many years ago, Michels (1959) formulated his famous "Iron Law of Oligarchy." Part of his argument was that hierarchies become strong and organizations autocratic because of different personal abilities and ambitions among members. In addition, however, there was another theme in his argument. Simply put, this was that it is impossible to keep everyone informed no matter how much the members may desire democracy. Only a few can monitor the necessary information flows and know enough about what is going on to participate in organizational decisions. These few who occupy critical communication points emerge as leaders who make decisions that affect others.

Communication in Various Networks

Support for Michels' observation is reported by more recent behavioral research on communication networks. A number of researchers have investigated how the structure of organization affects speed and accuracy in solving problems. In the initial work on communication nets, Bavelas (1950) calculated an "index of relative centrality." The larger the index number (illustrated in Exhibit 2-8), the more central the position is in the communication flow and the more likely the incumbent is to exercise influence and control in the group. His research indicated that the network with the least centralized structure (circle) made the most errors on a relatively simple task; and that errors decreased as the structure became more centralized (Y and wheel). As the centralization increased, so too did agreement on who was the leader (the one highest on the centrality index). Finally, those persons most satisfied were the most central.

Exhibit 2-8 Communication Nets (Bavelas, 1950)

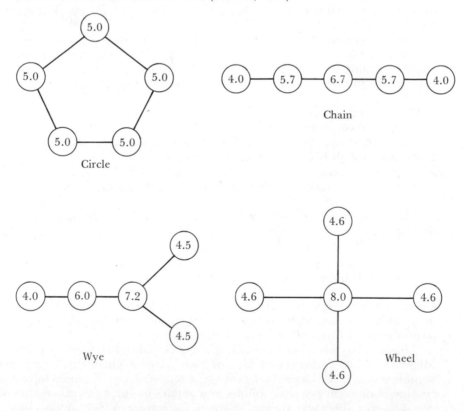

In a group structured as a wheel, the man at the hub can communicate with all of the men on the spokes. The latter, however, can communicate only with the hub. After repeated problems, the man at the hub, regardless of personality, emerges as the decision maker or leader. A "natural leader" at one of the spoke positions may attempt to lead, but among all groups tested, the spoke man came to recognize that the hub man must be the decision maker. Why? Because the man at the hub can get all the necessary information easier than anyone else. In a simple problem such as identifying a solid-color marble held by all five participants, the hub man collects the colors from all others, compares, decides, and simply informs the others of the answer. Since he occupies a critical communication link, he becomes manager.

Later network research (Guetzkow and Simon, 1955) added an "all-channel" group. Everyone can communicate with everyone else, as indicated in Exhibit 2-9. Yet, in a series of trials, most of the all-channel men find it impractical to operate on this basis, so they transform themselves into a wheel network. Voluntarily, they restrict their communication links. In most groups, some individual emerges as the occupant of the critical communication point at the hub. The others communicate only with him. The process is facilitated if one individual is clearly more articulate and analytical. Nonetheless, even when the members of the group are balanced in personality and prestige, the all-channel net tends to convert itself to the wheel. In short, management emerges because of the difficulty and inefficiency of transmitting all information to every member of the organization.

Exhibit 2-9 All-Channel Communication Network

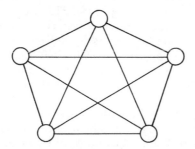

As found in the earlier Bavelas research, the more central a person is in the net, the more satisfied he is likely to be. His centrality means that he receives and sends more communications and is better able to solve problems. Centrality is satisfying because he knows more about what is going on. Such centrality rapidly develops in the wheel net; there is little room for spontaneity. A hierarchy emerges that conforms to the formal demands of the system in which the central person sends and receives information from all. Thus on simple, repetitive problems, centrality assists in the development of problem-solving procedures that complete the tasks faster, with fewer errors, and less communication (Glanzer and Glanzer, 1961).

The advantages of centralization depend upon the nature of the task, however. For example, if mottled-color agates are substituted for solid-color marbles, the groups have trouble. Finding the common marble is just about impossible for the wheel. The hub man in the wheel is overwhelmed because the perception and communication problems are just too great. He collects all the marble descriptions—but no two are alike! The all-channel nets also have difficulty, but *some* are able to find a solution because of their feedback advantages. By remaining all-channel and not restricting their communications as they did with simple problems, everyone can listen in so that freer exchange of perceptions is possible.

Task requirements tend to determine network communications, and groups adapt as necessary. Faucheux and MacKenzie (1966) conducted an experiment in which all-channel groups first worked a sequence of eight simple, routine problems and then a series of four very difficult problems involving inference. Most of the groups centralized (formed wheel networks) for the easier problems; speed increased, errors decreased, and the groups showed higher satisfaction. When the more difficult problem was given to the same group, however, the heavy pressure on the central position led to quick decentralization (return to the all-channel net) by every group.

Need for Hierarchy

Human limitation as well as technical problems force us to restrict communication. As March and Simon (1958) have pointed out, human beings have quite limited information-processing capability. We can consider only a relatively few factors at a time; others in the system are assumed to be constant. Much perceptual research indicates that we must focus our attention. Our communications are thus limited, because "a human being is more nearly a serial than a parallel information processing system" (p. 476). Although teenage girls would seem to be exceptions, we can carry on only one conversation at a time. A one-way announcement or lecture can be addressed to a mass audience, but most other forms of social interaction are sharply limited. Again, as Simon (1962) suggests, "most roles impose tasks and responsibilities that are time-consuming. One cannot, for example, enact the role of 'friend' with large numbers of other people" (p. 477).

Drawing on his laboratory research with groups, tasks, and communication nets, Mackenzie (1967) explains the development of hierarchical structure and its advantages in dealing with communications and conflict over limited resources: "The major structural characteristic of a hierarchy is that it is a concatenation of wheel structure subgroups. Interactions will usually occur on channels other than those to the chief executive, but those communications involving the resolution of conflict and the exercise of authority flow along the channels between the chief executive and his subordinates. The first-level subordinates in turn are centers of wheels with second-level subordinates, etc. Of course not all subordinates on one level have assistants on the next because some are staff and secretarial personnel. The answer why hierarchies form must be explained by why wheel structures occur.

"There are two main features of a wheel structure. First, a wheel has the minimum number of channels necessary to connect a group. . . . Second, the wheel is the most centralized primary group. Let us examine the implications of these two features.

"Let us assume that in order to minimize conflict and to have the benefits of a division of labor each participant in a group has nearly autonomous roles and each is necessary for survival. Assume further that resources are scarce and that each participant has the goal of maximizing his share. Then any intersection among the participants sets up conditions for conflict among the participants due to attempts to extend his control into the realm of another. In such a situation the network which has the minimum number of intersections (connections) would tend to reduce the potential for conflict. . . . If, as assumed, resources are scarce and each participant wishes to maximize his share, it is clear that some form of procedure for allocating the resources is necessary. . . . In a wheel structure, by virtue of one center with intersections with all the others, there is little possibility of the subordinate positions engaging in uncontrolled competition for resources. The center acts as the allocator of resources by resolving conflicts and balancing the costs and benefits of each post. He must give a sufficient amount to survive in pursuit of his own self interests. . . . The more centralized a group is, the greater the control of the center. Hence a wheel structure is preferable in the described situation over all others because it is the most centralized.

"Stability of structure tends to reduce interaction time and to allow increased span of control by the center. But if the group continues to grow, there comes a point when the capacity of the center is exceeded. The group is faced with an emergency because the center can no longer control the allocation of resources. Linkages begin to form among some of the subordinate positions in order to obtain the necessary resources or to get more than required. This endangers the others. Conflict again arises between and within the new coalition or subgroups. The process of wheel formation begins again. But who is to control the subwheel from disruptive competition? The solution is to form a hierarchy with two levels of wheels. The center of the original wheel (if he kept his position during the reorganization period) or his successor (if he did not) forms a wheel with the subgroup leaders as his subordinates. They in turn have their wheel subgroups made up of members of the coalition. Thus a hierarchy is born. As the group continues to grow more layers are added. The need for control of resources becomes even more necessary because of the increased dependence of the subgroups. Roles tend to become fixed" (pp. 24–26).

In short, because of communication difficulties, hierarchy may be essential and inevitable. The basic form is found in atoms and galaxies, in living organisms and inanimate computers. Simon (1962) writes, "Empirically, a large proportion of the complex systems we observe in nature exhibit hierarchical structure. On theoretical grounds we would expect complex systems to be hierarchies in a world in which complexity has to evolve from simplicity. . . . Hierarchy is one of the central structural schemes that the architect of complexity uses" (pp. 481–482).

Communication Problems of Hierarchies

Thus hierarchies develop partially because of communicational necessity; they foster task performance on many kinds of jobs. Nonetheless, once developed, hierarchies also hinder the flow of communications. These hindrances result from two aspects of a multilayered structure: distortions in relaying communications and status anxiety.

The receiver of a message who in turn sends it on (especially by word of mouth) to the next person tends to distort the message in systematic ways (Bass, 1965).

Condensation: What he repeats tends to be shorter, simpler, and less detailed than what he received. Often only the salient points are passed on and in a condensed coded form (Campbell, 1958). Hence contrast is enhanced within messages by emphasizing some items, ignoring others. In particular, the beginnings and ends of the messages tend to be expanded at the expense of the middle portion.

Closure: As we have seen, receivers tend to fill in gaps when a message is ambiguous. This is particularly dramatic when the receiver must articulate these gaps when he relays a message. If he hears that someone from the home office may come next week, he may pass on the message as a fact that the vice president is coming; and the next relayer may add that Vice President Jones is coming to chew them out for being over budget.

Expectation: Again as we have seen, we tend to hear what we expected to hear. This is perpetuated in relaying because the first receiver tends to report what he expected to hear from the sender in the first place. Thus bias becomes the message for the second receiver to interpret through his own bias. It is readily apparent how communications become fantastically corrupted as they move along a lengthy chain of command.

Association: Guilt by association is a widespread distortion. If ill news or past errors have come from a certain person or department, similar current communications tend to be associated with them, sometimes without reason.

In addition, communications tend to be manipulated in the interest of the communicator or relayer. That is, people do or do not communicate in order to achieve some goal, to satisfy some personal need, or to improve their immediate situation. Jackson (1959) formulates three principles about communication flow:

1. In the pursuit of their work goals, people tend to communicate with those who will help them achieve their aims, and not with those who will retard or not assist their accomplishment.

In a study of a government agency (Jackson, 1953), it was found that people communicated far more with members of their own subgroups than to any other persons. They also preferred to communicate with someone of higher status than themselves, and tried to avoid communication with those lower in status. Among peers, communications were mainly directed to highly valued persons who might be helpful. Those who could make little contribution were avoided.

2. People tend to direct their communication toward those who can make them feel more secure and gratify their needs, and away from those who threaten them, make them feel anxious, or generally provide unrewarding experiences.

Studies (Burns, 1954; Mishler and Tropp, 1956) consistently demonstrate that most of us prefer to speak with higher status people who have the capacity to gratify or deprive us. These effects may be tangible decisions and rewards or merely expressions of approval and confidence.

3. Persons in an organization communicate to improve their positions.

Subordinates have been observed as reluctant to ask supervisors for help when they need it, because this might be seen as a threatening admission of their inadequacy. And superiors tend to delete from their communications to subordinates any references to their own mistakes or errors of judgment (Jackson, 1959).

In a study (Zander et al., 1957) of the role relations of three types of professionals who work together in mental health (psychiatrists, psychologists, and psychiatric social workers) the direction, amount, and content of communication to one another could be predicted largely from two factors: their perception of the other professions' power relative to their own; and how satisfied they were with their own power position compared to that of the other groups.

These controls particularly characterize a subordinate's initiation of communication upward. Mellinger (1956) reports a tendency to minimize actual disagreement—a situation immortalized in the terms "organization man" and "yes man." In a more sophisticated survey in three large industrial organizations, Read (1962) found that information communicated up the hierarchy is screened or filtered, particularly when the information might reflect upon the competence, security, or progress of the subordinates. And those who are most ambitious are the most inaccurate communicators. Read found a negative correlation between a person's mobility aspirations and the accuracy with which he communicates upward in the hierarchy. Low trust seems to exaggerate this inclination. Under such conditions, the primary goal of upward communication becomes the reduction of the sender's anxiety, rather than the accurate transmission of ideas.

Summary

Barriers to understanding in communication include:

- Sender broadcasts before adequate thought or clarification and without examining his assumptions.
- Transmission is noisy, unreliable, improper, or inconsistent with the message, situation, or people involved.
- Receiver evaluates the sender and distorts his perception of the message because of the existing situation or past experiences. He may (a) hear what he expects, (b) hear what he wants to hear, (c) ignore conflicting information, (d) ignore nonverbal cues.
- Receiver decodes the message incorrectly because his vocabulary is different from the sender's; they do not agree on the meanings (especially symbolic) of words and actions.

Congruence of the communicator's experience, awareness, and intention would seem to promote better understanding. Yet, most managers face a dilemma because their primary intention is less understanding than it is influencing others' behavior. Communicating is a means rather than an end.

Research on communication networks indicates that centrality is personally rewarding, and helpful for solving relatively simple and routine problems. Complex tasks tend to require more unstructured and decentralized communications.

In organizations, communication difficulties lead to hierarchical structures and formally prescribed communication channels. These are essentially intended for managing information overload, but hierarchical structure in turn leads to other communication problems: distortions in relaying messages, and self-seeking manipulation to protect and promote status.

References

Adorno, T. W., E. Frenkel-Brunswik, D. J. Levinson, and R. N. Sanford. *The Authoritarian Personality: Studies in Prejudice.* Harper & Row, 1950.

Allyn, J., and L. Festinger. "The Effectiveness of Unanticipated Persuasive Communications." *Journal of Abnormal and Social Psychology,* Vol. 62 (1961), 35–40.

Anderson, J. "Giving and Receiving Feedback." In *Organizational Change and Development,* ed. G. W. Dalton, P. R. Lawrence, and L. E. Greiner. Irwin Dorsey Press, 1970.

Barlett, F. C. *The Mind at Work and Play.* Allen and Unwin, 1951.

Bass, B. M. *Organizational Psychology.* Allyn and Bacon, 1965.

Bavelas, A. "Communication Patterns in Task-Oriented Groups." *Journal of the Acoustical Society of America,* Vol. 22 (1950), 725–730.

Bennis, W. G. "Interpersonal Communication," In *The Planning of Change,* ed. W. G. Bennis et al. Holt, Rinehart and Winston, 1961.

Berelson, B. "Communication and Public Opinion." In *Reader in Public Opinion and Communication,* ed. B. Berelson and M. Janowitz. The Free Press, 1950.

———— and G. A. Steiner. *Human Behavior: An Inventory of Scientific Findings.* Harcourt Brace Jovanovich, 1964.

Blum, G. S. "An Experimental Reunion of Psychoanalytic Theory with Perceptual Vigilance and Defense." *Journal of Abnormal and Social Psychology,* Vol. 49 (1954), 94–98.

Boulding, K. E. *The Image: Knowledge in Life and Society.* University of Michigan Press, 1961.

Brooks, J. *The Fate of the Edsel and Other Business Adventures.* Harper & Row, 1963.

Burns, T. "The Directions of Activity and Communication in a Departmental Executive Group." *Human Relations,* Vol. 7 (1954), 73–79.

Cameron, P. Talk to the American Psychological Association, August 30, 1968.

Campbell, D. T. "Systematic Error on the Part of Human Links in Communication Systems." *Information and Control,* Vol. 1 (1958), 334–369.

Deunk, N. H. "Active Listening: A Forgotten Key to Effective Communication." *Hospital Administration,* Spring 1967, 34–45.

Fast, J. *Body Language.* M. Evans, 1970.

Faucheux, C., and K. MacKenzie. "Task Depending on Organizational Centrality; Its Behavioral Consequences." *Journal of Experimental Sociology and Psychology,* Vol. 2 (1966), 361–375.

Festinger, L., and N. Maccoby. "On Resistance to Persuasive Communications." *Journal of Abnormal and Social Psychology,* Vol. 68 (1964), 359–366.

Frenkel-Brunswik, E. "Intolerance of Ambiguity as an Educational and Perceptual Personality Variable." *Journal of Personality,* Vol. 18 (1949), 108–143.

Gibb, J. R. "Defensive Communication." *Journal of Communication* (March 1966), 141–148.

Glanzer, M., and R. Glanzer. " Techniques for the Study of Group Structure and Behavior: II. Empirical Studies of the Effects of Structure in Small Groups." *Psychological Bulletin,* Vol. 58 (1961), 1–27.

Guetzkow, H., and H. R. Simon. "The Impact of Certain Communication Nets Upon Organization and Performance in Task Oriented Groups." *Management Science,* Vol. 1, Nos. 3 and 4 (April–July 1955), 233–250.

Guthrie, W. "But . . . Is Anybody Listening?" Talk at the 13th Tecnifax Seminar-Workshop in Visual Communication, April 22, 1958.

Hall, E. T. *The Hidden Dimension.* Doubleday, 1966.

Hayakawa, S. I. *Language in Thought and Action.* Harcourt Brace Jovanovich, 1964.

Higham, T. M. "Basic Psychological Factors in Communication." *Occupational Psychology* (January 1957), 1–10.

Hilgard, E. R. *Introduction to Psychology,* 3rd ed. Harcourt Brace Jovanovich, 1962.

Horne, J. H., and T. Lupton. "The Work Activities of Middle Managers." *Journal of Management Studies,* Vol. 1 (1965), 14–33.

Hovland, C. I., and N. Mandell. "An Experimental Comparison of Conclusion-Drawing by the Communicator and by the Audience." *Journal of Abnormal and Social Psychology,* Vol. 47 (1952), 581–88.

—— and W. Weiss. "The Influence of Source Credibility on Communication Effectiveness." *Public Opinion Quarterly,* Vol. 15 (1951–1952), 635–650.

Jackson, J. M. "Analysis of Interpersonal Relations in a Formal Organization." Ph.D. thesis, University of Michigan, 1953.

—— "The Organization and Its Communications Problem." *Advanced Management* (February 1959), 17–20.

Korzybski, A. *Science and Sanity: An Introduction to Non-Aristotelian Systems and General Semantics,* 4th ed. Institute of General Semantics, 1962.

Lamb, W., and D. Turner. *Management Behavior.* International Universities Press, 1969.

Mackenzie, K. D. "Some Thoughts on the Span of Control Problems." Working Paper No. 66, Department of Industry, Wharton School, University of Pennsylvania, September 1967.

March, J., and H. Simon. *Organizations.* Wiley, 1958.

Maslow, A. *Motivation and Personality.* Harper & Row, 1954.

McClelland, D. C., and J. W. Atkinson. "The Projective Expression of Needs." *Journal of Psychology,* Vol. 25, 1948, 205–222.

Mehrabian, A. (of UCLA), cited in *The Denver Post,* August 25, 1970.

Mellinger, G. D. "Interpersonal Trust as a Factor in Communication." *Journal of Abnormal and Social Psychology,* Vol. 52 (1956), 120–129.

Michels, R. *Political Parties* (1915). Dover, 1959.

Mishler, E., and A. Tropp. "Status and Interaction in a Psychiatric Hospital." *Human Relations,* Vol. 9 (1956), 187–206.

Nilsen, T. R. "Some Assumptions That Impede Communication." *General Semantics Bulletin,* Nos. 14 and 15 (Winter–Spring 1954), 41–44.

Read, W. H. "Upward Communication in Industrial Hierarchies." *Human Relations,* Vol. 15 (1962), 3–15.

Rogers, C. R. *On Becoming a Person.* Houghton-Mifflin, 1961.

—— and F. J. Roethlisberger. "Barriers and Gateways to Communication." *Harvard Business Review,* Vol. 30, No. 4 (July–August 1952), 46–52.

Schlesinger, A. *A Thousand Days.* Houghton-Mifflin, 1965.

Scodel, A., and H. Austrin. "The Perception of Jewish Photographs by Non-Jews and Jews." *Journal of Abnormal and Social Psychology,* Vol. 19 (1954), 329–334.

Shannon, C. E., and W. Weaver. *The Mathematical Theory of Communication.* University of Illinois Press, 1949.

Simon, H. A. "The Architecture of Complexity." *Proceedings of American Philosophical Society,* Vol. 6 (1962), 467–482.

Spector, P., et al. "Communications Media in the Adoption of New Practices." *Human Organization,* Vol. 30, No. 1 (Spring 1971), 39–45.

Sullivan, H. S. *Conceptions of Modern Psychiatry.* William Alanson White Psychiatric Foundation, 1940; Tavistock Publications, 1955.

Vardaman, G. T. and Halterman, C. C. *Managerial Control Through Communication.* Wiley, 1968.

Walster, E., and L. Festinger. "The Effectiveness of 'Overheard' Persuasive Communications." *Journal of Abnormal and Social Psychology,* Vol. 65 (1962), 395–402.

Webber, R. A. "Managerial Behavior, Personality, and Organizational Structure." Ph.D. Dissertation, Columbia University, 1966.

————. "Perceptions of Interactions Between Superiors and Subordinates." *Human Relations,* Vol. 23, No. 3 (1970), 235–248.

Weiss, W. "The Relationship Between Judgements of a Communicator's Position and the Extent of Opinion Change." *Journal of Abnormal and Social Psychology,* Vol. 56 (1958), 380–384.

Wiener, M. "Word Frequency or Motivation in Perceptual Defense." *Journal of Abnormal and Social Psychology,* Vol. 31 (1955), 214–218.

Willits, R. D. "Company Performance and Interpersonal Relations." *Industrial Management Review,* Vol. 8, No. 2 (Spring 1967), 91–107.

Zaleznik, A., and D. Moment. *The Dynamics of Interpersonal Behavior.* Wiley, 1964.

Zajonc, R. B. *Social Psychology: An Experimental Approach.* Brooks/Cole, 1966.

Zander, A., A. R. Cohen, and E. Stotland. *Role Relations in the Mental Health Professions.* Institute for Social Research, University of Michigan, 1957.

Readings

Analyzing Interpersonal Communication: The Case of Mr. Hart and Bing

The case is presented in two versions, A and B. Version A presents Mr. Hart's point of view, and version B presents Bing's point of view.

The shop situation reported in this case occurred in a work group of four men and three women who were engaged in testing and inspecting panels for electronic equipment. The employees were paid on a piecework incentive basis. The personnel organization of the company included a counselor whose duty it was to become acquainted with the workers and talk over any problems they wished to discuss with him. The following statements of the views of two men consist of excerpts from five interviews that the counselor had with each of them within a period of about two weeks.

Version A (Mr. Hart)

Say, I think you should be in on this. My dear little friend Bing is heading himself into a showdown with me. Recently it was brought to my attention by the Quality Control checker that Bing has been taking double and triple set-up time for panels which he is actually inspecting at one time. In effect, that's cheatin', and I've called him down on it several times before. A few days ago it was brought to my attention again, and so this time I really let him have it in no uncertain terms. He's been getting away with this for too long and I'm gonna put an end to it once and for all. I know he didn't like my calling him on it because a few hours later he had the union representative breathin' down my back. But you know what talkin' to those people is like; they'll sometimes defend an employee, even though they think he's takin' advantage of the company. Well, anyway, I let them both know I'll not tolerate the practice any longer, and I let Bing know that if he continues to do this kind of thing, I'm gonna take official action with my boss to have the guy fired or penalized somehow. This kind of thing has to be curbed. Actually, I'm inclined to think the guy's mentally deficient, because talking to him has actually no meaning to him whatsoever. I've tried just about every approach to jar some sense into that guy's head, and I've just about given it up as a bad deal. I just can't seem to make any kind of an impression upon him. It's an unpleasant situation for everyone concerned, but I'm at a loss to know what more I can do about it.

I don't know what it is about the guy, but I think he's harboring some deep feelings against me. For what, I don't know, 'cause I've tried to handle that bird with kid gloves. But his whole attitude around here on the job is one of indifference, and he certainly isn't a good influence on the rest of my group. Frankly, I think he purposely tries to agitate them against me at times, too.

This case, Mr. Hart and Bing, was prepared by Harriet Ronkin under the direction of Professor George F. F. Lombard as the basis for classroom discussion and not to illustrate either effective or ineffective handling of an administrative situation. Copyright © 1949 by the President and Fellows of Harvard College. Used by specific permission.

It seems to me he may be suffering from illusions of grandeur, 'cause all he does all day long is sit over there and croon his fool head off. Thinks he's a Frank Sinatra! No kidding! I understand he takes singin' lessons and he's working with some of the local bands in the city. All of which is OK by me; but when his outside interests start interfering with his efficiency on the job, then I've gotta start paying closer attention to the situation. For this reason I've been keepin' my eye on that bird and if he steps out of line any more, he and I are gonna part ways.

I feel quite safe in saying that I've done all I can rightfully be expected to do by way of trying to show him what's expected of him. You know there's an old saying, "You can't make a purse out of a sow's ear." The guy is simply unscrupulous. He feels no obligation to do a real day's work. Yet I know the guy can do a good job, because for a long time he did. But in recent months, he's slipped for some reason and his whole attitude on the job has changed. Why, it's even getting to the point now where I think he's inducing other employees to "goof off" a few minutes before the lunch whistle and go down to the washrooms and clean up on company time. I've called him on it several times, but words just don't seem to make any lasting impression on him. Well, if he keeps it up much longer, he's gonna find himself on the way out. He's asked me for a transfer, so I know he wants to go. But I didn't give him an answer when he asked me, 'cause I was steamin' mad at the time, and I may have told him to go somewhere else.

I think it would be good for you to talk with him frequently. It'll give him a chance to think the matter through a little more carefully. There may be something that's troubling him in his personal life, although I've made every effort to find out if there was such a thing, and I've been unsuccessful. Maybe you'll have better luck.

Version B (Bing)

According to the system 'round here, as I understand it, I am allowed so much "set-up" time to get these panels from the racks, carry them over here to the bench and place them in this jig here, which holds them in position while I inspect them. For convenience's sake and also to save time, I sometimes manage to carry two or three over at the same time and inspect them all at the same time. This is a perfectly legal thing to do. We've always been doing it. Mr. Hart, the supervisor, has other ideas about it, though; he claims it's cheating the company. He came over to the bench a day or two ago and let me know just how he felt about the matter. Boy, did we go at it! It wasn't so much the fact that he called me down on it, but more the way in which he did it. He's a sarcastic bastard. I've never seen anyone like him. He's not content just to say in a manlike way what's on his mind, but he prefers to do it in a way that makes you want to crawl inside a crack in the floor. What a guy! I don't mind being called down by a supervisor, but I like to be treated like a man, and not humiliated like a school teacher does a naughty kid. He's been pullin' this stuff ever since he's been a supervisor. I knew him when he was just one of us, but since he's been promoted he's lost his friendly way and seems to be havin' some difficulty in knowin' how to manage us employees. In fact, I've noticed that he's been more this way with us fellows since he's gotten married. I dunno whether there's any connection there, but I do know he's a changed man over what he used to be like when he was a worker on the bench with us several years ago.

When he pulled this kind of stuff on me the other day, I got so damn mad I called in the union representative. I knew that the thing I was doing was permitted by the contract, but I was just intent on making some trouble for Mr. Hart, just because he persists in this sarcastic way of handling me. I'm about fed up with the whole damn situation. I'm tryin' every means I can to get myself transferred out of his group. If I don't succeed and I'm forced to stay on here, I'm going to screw him every way I can. He's not gonna pull this kind of kid stuff any longer on me. When the union representative questioned him on the case, he finally had to back down, 'cause according to the contract an employee can use any timesaving method or device in order to speed up the process as long as the quality standards of the job are met. During the discussion with me and the union representative, Mr. Hart charged that it was a dishonest practice and threatened to "take it up the line" unless the union would curb me on this practice. But this was just an idle threat, 'cause the most he can do is get me transferred out of here, which is actually what I want anyway.

You see, he knows that I do professional singing on the outside. He hears me singin' here on the job, and he hears the people talkin' about my career in music. I guess he figures I can be so cocky because I have another means of earning some money. Actually, the employees here enjoy havin' me sing while we work, but he thinks I'm disturbing them and causing them to "goof off" from their work. It's funny, but for some reason I think he's partial to the three female employees in our group. He's the same with all us guys as he is to me, but with the girls he acts more decent. I don't know what his object is. Occasionally, I leave the job a few minutes early and go down to the washroom to wash up before lunch. Sometimes several others in the group will accompany me, and so Mr. Hart automatically thinks I'm the leader and usually bawls me out for the whole thing.

So, you can see, I'm a marked man around here. He keeps watchin' me like a hawk. Naturally this makes me very uncomfortable. That's why I'm sure a transfer would be the best thing. I've asked him for it, but he didn't give me any satisfaction at the time. While I remain here I'm gonna keep my nose clean, but whenever I get the chance I'm gonna slip it to him, but good.

The Administrator's Skill: Communication

FRITZ J. ROETHLISBERGER

What is taking place when two people engaged in a common task interact? What do the actors involved perceive is taking place, what is a useful way for

"The Administrator's Skill: Communication," by F. J. Roethlisberger, Copyright © 1953 by the President and Fellows of Harvard College, reprinted, with omissions, by permission of the author and publisher from *Man-In-Organization: Essays of F. J. Roethlisberger,* Cambridge, The Belknap Press of Harvard University Press, 1968.

the executive to think about these interpersonal proceedings in which he is engaged, and what skills can he practice which will make him more effective as an administrator of people?

I want to discuss these questions in terms of a specific, down-to-earth case in an industrial plant—a case of misunderstanding between two people, a worker and a foreman. (It is not important that they happen to be foreman and worker; to all intents and purposes they might as well be superintendent and foreman or, for that matter, controller and accountant.)

A Case of Misunderstanding

In a department of a large industrial organization there were seven workers (four men and three women) engaged in testing and inspecting panels of electronic equipment. In this department one of the workers, Bing, was having trouble with his immediate supervisor, Hart, who had formerly been a worker in the department.

Had we been observers in this department we would have seen Bing carrying two or three panels at a time from the racks where they were stored to the bench where he inspected them together. For this activity we would have seen him charging double or triple setup time. We would have heard him occasionally singing at work. Also we would have seen him usually leaving his work position a few minutes early to go to lunch, and noticed that other employees sometimes accompanied him. And had we been present at one specific occasion, we would have heard Hart telling Bing that he disapproved of these activities and that he wanted Bing to stop doing them.

Views of Misunderstanding

Let me start with the simplest but the toughest question first: "What is going on here?" I think most of us would agree that what seems to be going on is some misunderstanding between Hart and Bing. But no sooner do we try to represent to ourselves the nature of this misunderstanding than a flood of different theories appear. Let me discuss briefly five very common ways of representing this misunderstanding: (1) as a difference of opinion resolvable by common sense, by simply referring to the facts; (2) as a clash of personalities; (3) as a conflict of social roles; (4) as a struggle for power; and (5) as a breakdown in communication. There are, of course, other theories too—for example, those of the interactionists, the field theory of Kurt Lewin, and even the widely held views of Adam Smith or Karl Marx. But for our purposes here the five I have mentioned will suffice.

Common Sense

For the advocates of common sense—the first theory, though most of them would not call it that—the situation resolves itself quickly:

Either Hart is right or Bing is right. Since both parties cannot be right, it follows that if Hart is right, then Bing is wrong; or if Bing is right, then Hart is wrong. Either Bing should or should not be singing on the job, carrying two or three panels at a time and charging double or triple setup time, and so on.

"Let us get these facts settled first," say the common-sense advocates. "Once ascertained, the problem is easily settled. Once we know who is doing what he should not be doing, then all we have to do is to get this person to do what he should be doing. It's as simple as that."

But is it? Let us look again at our case. Let us note that there are no differences of opinion between Hart and Bing about some matters. For example both would agree that Bing is taking double or triple setup time when he carries his panels two or three at a time to his bench for inspection. Both would agree that Bing sings on the job and occasionally leaves his work place a bit early for lunch.

Where they differ is in the way each *perceives* these activities. Hart perceives Bing's activities as "cheating," "suffering from illusions of grandeur," "thinking he is Frank Sinatra," "interfering with Bing's efficiency as well as the efficiency of other workers," "disturbing the other workers," "inducing them to goof off," and "influencing them against [Hart]." To Bing, on the other hand, these activities are "perfectly legal," "something we've always been doing," "something that is not disturbing the other workers," and so forth.

Among these many different conflicting claims and different perceptions, what are the facts? Many of these evaluations refer to personal and social standards of conduct for which the company has no explicit rules. Even in the case of taking double and triple setup time, there are probably no clear rules, because when the industrial engineer set the standards for the job, he did not envisage the possibility of a worker doing what Bing is now doing and which, according to Bing, is a time-saving device.

But we can waste effort on this question. For, even if it were clear that Hart is not exploring the situation, that he is not getting these important facts or rules which would settle who is right and who is wrong, it would still be true that, so far as Hart is concerned, he *knows* who is right and who is wrong. And because he *knows,* he has no reason to question the assumptions he is making about Bing's behavior.

Now this is very likely to happen in the case of advocates of the common-sense theory. Significantly, Hart himself is a good advocate of it. Does this have anything to do with the fact that he is not being very successful in getting Bing to do what he should be doing? Let us postpone this question for future consideration.

Clash of Personalities

For the second school of thought, what is going on between Hart and Bing can be viewed essentially as a clash of personalities—an interaction between two particular personality structures. According to this view, what is going on cannot be known in detail until much more information about these different personality structures is secured. Hence we can only speculate that what is going on may be something of this order:

Neither Hart nor Bing feels too sure of himself, and each seems to be suffering from feelings of inadequacy or inferiority. Being unable to recognize, admit, or accept these feelings, however, each one perceives the behavior of the other as a personal attack upon himself. When a person feels he is being attacked, he feels strongly the need to defend himself. This, then, is essentially what is taking place between Hart and Bing. Because of his feelings of inferiority, each one is defending himself against what he perceives to be an attack upon himself as a person. In psychology, the feelings of each man are conceived as being rooted somehow in his "personality."

That this theory is pointing to some very important phenomena can hardly be questioned. Certainly I will not argue its validity. I am only concerned with what it is telling us and what follows from it. As I understand it, this theory says that neither Hart nor Bing is aware of his own feelings of inadequacy and defense mechanisms. These are the important facts that each is ignoring. From this it follows that there is little hope of correcting the misunderstanding without helping Bing and Hart to become aware of these feelings and of their need to defend against them. Short of this, the solution lies in transferring Bing to a supervisor whose personality will be more compatible with Bing's, and in giving Hart a worker whose personality will be more compatible with Hart's.

Conflict of Social Roles

Let us look at the third explanation. Instead of viewing the misunderstanding as an interaction between two individual personality units, it can also be viewed as an interaction between two social roles:

With the promotion of Hart to the position of a supervisor of a group in which he had been formerly a worker, a system of reciprocal expectancies has been disturbed. Bing is expecting Hart to behave toward him in the same way Hart did when Hart was a worker; but by telling Bing to stop "crooning his fool head off," for example, Hart is not behaving in accordance with the role of a friend. Similarly, Hart, as the newly appointed supervisor, is expecting that Bing should do what he tells Bing to do, but by singing Bing is not behaving in accordance with the customary role of the worker.

According to this theory, as any recent textbook on sociology will explain, when two actors in a relationship reach differing definitions of the situation, misunderstanding is likely to arise. Presumably this is what is happening between Hart and Bing. The role-expectation pattern has been disturbed. Bing views his singing as variant but permissive; Hart views it as deviant. From these differing definitions of what each other's role should be misunderstanding results. According to this view, it will take time for their new relationship to work out. In time Bing will learn what to expect from Hart now that Hart is his supervisor. Also in time Hart will define better his role *vis-à-vis* Bing.

Struggle for Power

The fourth way of representing what is going on between Hart and Bing would be in terms of such abstractions as "authority" and "power":

When Bing refuses to stop singing on the job when Hart tells him to, Bing is being disobedient to the commands or orders of a holder of power. When this occurs, Hart, who according to this theory is a "power holder," has the right to exercise or apply sanctions, such as dismissal or transfer. But the threat to exercise these sanctions does not seem to be too effective in getting Bing to stop, because Bing is a member of the union, which also has power and the right to apply sanctions. By going to his union representative, Bing can bring this power structure into play.

In other words, what is going on in the case is not merely an interaction between two individual or social personalities; it is also a struggle between two kinds of institutionalized power. It is an issue between the management and the union which may even precipitate a strike. Management will charge that it cannot have workers in the plant who are disobedient to the orders of their foremen. The union will charge that Bing is merely introducing a labor-saving device which the foreman has not enough sense to recognize. To avoid things getting to this stage, the struggle-for-power theory would recommend that if Hart and Bing between them cannot settle their differences, they should refer them to the grievance machinery set up for this purpose by union and management.

According to this theory, Hart got into trouble not because he had authority but because when he tried to exercise it and was unsuccessful, he lost it. Authority ceases to exist when it cannot be exercised successfully.[1]

Breakdown in Communication

The fifth way of stating what is going on would be to say that Hart and Bing think they are talking about the same things when in fact they are not:

Hart assumes he understands what Bing is doing and saying; Bing assumes he understands what Hart is doing and saying. In fact, neither assumption holds. From this "uncritical assumption of understanding," misunderstanding arises.

Thus, when Hart tells Bing to stop "crooning his fool head off," Bing assumes that Hart is talking about Bing's singing when Hart may in fact be talking about his difficulties in maintaining his position as formal leader of the group. Hart assumes that Bing is singing deliberately to flaunt his authority, whereas in Bing's mind singing may be a way of relating himself to people and of maintaining his conceptions of himself.[2]

According to this theory, Hart and Bing are not on the same wave length, and as a result communication bypassing occurs. Each is behaving in accordance with the reality as he perceives it to be, but neither is aware of the assumptions that underlie his perceptions. Their misunderstandings arise as a result.

This theory strikes a new note that I should like to explore further.

Roots of Misunderstanding

So far our theories have explained well why there is misunderstanding and conflict; they have not shown so clearly how any new behavior patterns on the part of Hart or Bing or both can emerge or be encouraged to emerge from the present ones. In them we have found no responsible actor, no learner, and no practitioner of a skill.

Could it be that what is going on between Hart and Bing results also in part from the fact that nobody is taking any responsibility for what is going on? May we not assume that people can learn through experience how to determine their relationships with each other as well as be determined by them? Let us therefore look at these interpersonal proceedings from the point of view of a person who is responsibly involved in them and who may be capable of learning something from them.

From now on I shall be chiefly concerned with Hart, not because I think Hart is any more or less guilty than Bing of creating misunderstanding, but because I wish to develop a useful way of thinking for persons in a position of responsibility like Hart. This way of thinking, I hope, will not be in conflict with our other theories. It will merely spell out what a supervisor must learn if he is to take into account the significant processes which these other theories say have been going on.

So, instead of viewing Hart in his dealings with Bing as a supervisor expressing his personality, playing a social role, or exercising power, let us view him as a practitioner of a skill of communication. Let us see what skills, if any, he is using. And if we find, as I fear we may, that he has not been too skillful, let us see if he can learn to become a more skillful practitioner, and how this can be done.

Hart's Trouble

When we ask ourselves what Hart is doing to facilitate misunderstanding, we meet again a number of different theories. Although I am not sure that these theories are pointing to different things, each uses a slightly different terminology, so I shall state them separately:

1. *Hart is making value judgments*—According to one view, the biggest block to personal communication arises from the fact that Hart is making value judgments of Bing from Hart's point of view. Hart's tendency to evaluate is what gets him into trouble. Not only is he evaluating Bing, but he is trying to get Bing to accept his evaluation as the only and proper one. It is the orientation that angers Bing and makes him feel misunderstood.[3]

2. *Hart is not listening*—According to another and not too different view, Hart gets into trouble because he is not listening to Bing's feelings. Because he is not paying attention to Bing's feelings, he is not responding to them as such. Instead, we find him responding to the effect of Bing's feelings upon his own. Not only is he ignoring Bing's feelings, but also he is ignoring the effect of what he is saying upon them. This kind of behavior also leads to Bing's feelings of being misunderstood.[4]

3. *Hart is assuming things that may not be so*—Still another point of view says that Hart is getting into trouble because he is making assumptions about Bing's behavior that may not be so. Hart is confusing what he sees with what he assumes and feels.

When Hart sees Bing leaving early for lunch, for example, he assumes that Bing is doing this deliberately, intentionally, and personally to discredit him and to test his authority. Because of this assumption he feels angry and his feelings of anger reinforce his assumption. Now if Bing's going to lunch a few minutes early is such an attempt to discredit him, then Hart's anger and his attempt to retaliate make sense. But if he starts with this assumption and makes no attempt to check it, then his anger makes less sense. Hart may be assuming something that is not so.

Again, Hart shows he may be making assumptions that are not so by the way he talks in trying to get Bing to stop singing at work or to stop inspecting panels two or three at a time. When he uses phrases like "crooning your fool head off" and "cheating the company," is he not assuming that Bing should feel about these activities in the same way that he himself does? And if Bing does not feel this way, then obviously, in Hart's view, Bing must be a "fool," "defective," or a "sow's ear." To Hart, Bing *is* a sow's ear. And how does one feel toward a sow's ear? Toward such an entity one must feel (by definition) helpless and hopeless. Note that Hart's assumptions, perceptions, and feelings are of a piece; each reinforces the other to make one total evaluation.

In short, all of Hart's evaluations are suspect because he confuses what he sees with what he assumes and feels. As a result, there is no way for Hart to take another look at the situation. How can Hart check his evaluations when he is not aware that he is making them? By treating inferences as facts, there is no way for him to explore the assumptions, feelings, and perceptions that underlie his evaluations.[5] For Hart, Bing *is* the way he perceives Bing to be. There is no way for him to say that "because of the assumptions I make and because of the way I feel, I perceive Bing in this way."

4. *Hart is making his false assumptions come true*—A fourth theory emphasizes still another point. This theory says that the very kind of misevaluations which our last theory says Hart is guilty of must provoke *ipso facto* the very kind of behavior on the part of Bing of which Hart disapproves.[6] In other words, Hart is getting into trouble because, by his behavior, he is making his assumptive world come true.

Let us examine this theory first by looking at the effect of Hart's behavior on Bing. Very clearly Bing does not like it. Bing tells us that when Hart behaves in the way Hart does, he feels misunderstood, humiliated, and treated like a child. These feelings give grounds to his perception of Hart as "a sarcastic bastard," "a school teacher" pulling "kid stuff" on him. These perceptions in turn will tend to make Bing behave in the way that will coincide more and more with Hart's original untested assumptions about Bing's behavior. Feeling like a "marked man," Bing will behave more and more like a "sow's ear." Although he will try to "keep his nose clean," he will "slip it to [Hart], but good" whenever he gets the chance.

That this kind of misevaluation on the part of Hart will tend to produce this kind of behavior on the part of Bing is, according to this view, a fact of common experience. To explain it one does not have to assume any peculiar personality structure on the part of Bing—an undue sensitivity to criticism, defensiveness, or feeling of inferiority. All one has to assume is an individual personality with a need to maintain its individuality. Therefore, any attempts on the part of Hart which will be perceived by Bing as an attempt to deny his individual differences will be resisted. What Hart says about Bing is, from Bing's point of view, exactly what he is *not*. Bing *is* what he is from his own frame of reference and from the point of view of his own feelings, background, and situation. Bing *is* what he assumes, feels, and perceives himself to be. And this is just what Hart's behavior is denying.

In spite of the different terminology and emphasis of these theories, they all seem to point to certain uniformities in the interpersonal proceedings of Hart and Bing which should be taken into account regardless of the actors' particular personalities or social roles. For the misunderstandings that arise, Hart and Bing are not to blame; the trouble resides in the process of interpersonal communication itself.

Problem of Involvement

So far it would seem as if we had made Hart the villain in the piece. But let us remember that although Hart has been intellectually and emotionally involved in what has been going on, he has not been aware of this involvement. All of our theories have implied this. Hart's ego has been involved; his actual group memberships have been involved; his reference groups have been involved; his feelings, assumptions, and perceptions have been involved—but Hart is not aware of it. If any new behavior on the part of Hart is to emerge—and *all* our theories would agree to this—Hart must in some sense become aware of and recognize this involvement. Without such an awareness there can be no reevaluation or no change in perception. And without such a change no learning can take place.

How can this change be accomplished? Some theories would seem to imply that misunderstanding will be minimized only when Hart *logically understands* the nature of his involvement with Bing. Hart will learn to evaluate Bing more properly only when he understands better the personality structures of himself and Bing and the social system of which they are a part. Only by the logical understanding and critical probing of his and Bing's feelings of inadequacy and defense mechanisms can he make a proper evaluation and bring about any real change in his behavior.

But there is another view. It holds that logical understanding is not of the first importance. Rather, misunderstanding will be minimized when Hart learns to *recognize and accept* responsibility for his involvement. Better understanding will be achieved when Hart learns to recognize and accept his own and Bing's individual differences, when he learns to recognize and accept Bing's feelings as being different from his own, and when as a result he can allow Bing to express his feelings and differences and listen to them.[7]

Let me explore this second theory further, for it suggests that Hart might possibly learn to do a better job without having to become a professional social scientist or be psychoanalyzed. Moreover, it coincides with some facts of common experience.

How Can Hart Be Helped?

Some administrators have achieved the insights of the second theory through the school of "hard knocks" rather than through the help of books or by being psychoanalyzed. So should there not be simple skills which Hart can be taught, which he can learn and practice, and which would help him to recognize and accept his involvement and deal with it better?

Now it may be that Hart, because of certain personal deficiencies, is not able to recognize or accept his own feelings—let alone Bing's. That this holds for some supervisors goes without question. But does it apply to all? I do not think so, nor do I think it applies to Hart. Is it not possible that some supervisors may not be able to do these things because they have never learned how to do them?

The fact is, if our analysis up to this point is sound, that Hart does not get into trouble because he feels hopeless and helpless in the face of a worker who sings on the job, leaves early for lunch, and so on, and who refuses to stop doing these things when Hart tells him to. Any one of us who has had to deal with a worker behaving like Bing will recognize and remember feelings of inadequacy like Hart's only too well. We do not need to have very peculiar or special personality structures to have such feelings. Rather, Hart's trouble is that he assumes, and no doubt has been told too often, that he should *not* have feelings of inadequacy. It resides in the fact that he has not developed or been given a method or skill for dealing with them. As a result, these feelings are denied and appear in the form of an attribute of Bing—"a sow's ear."

In other words, I am suggesting that Hart gets into trouble partly because no one has assured him that it is normal and natural—in fact, inevitable—that he should have some feelings of inadequacy; that he cannot and *should* not try to escape from them. No one has helped him to develop a method of dealing with his own feelings and the feelings of Bing. No one has listened to him or helped him to learn to listen to others. No one has helped him to recognize the effect of his behavior on others. No one has helped him to become aware of his assumptions and feelings and how they affect the evaluations he makes.

Instead, too many training courses have told Hart what an ideal supervisor should be and how an ideal supervisor should behave. Both explicit and implicit in most of the instruction he receives is the assumption that an ideal supervisor should not become emotionally involved in his dealings with people. He should remain aloof, be objective, and deny or get rid of his feelings. But this goes against the facts of his immediate experience; it goes against everything upon which, according to our theories, his growth and development depend. Indeed, to "behave responsibly" and be "mature" in the way he is instructed to, without becoming emotionally committed, would be, to use the *New Yorker's* phrase, "the trick of the week!"

Is it any wonder, therefore, that Hart remains immature—socially, intellectually, and emotionally? He gets no understanding of how these frustrations and misunderstandings must inevitably arise from his dealings with others; he gets no help on how to deal with them when they do arise. He probably has had many training courses which told him how to recognize and deal with workers who are sow's ears. He probably has had no training course which helped him to see how his assumptions and feelings would tend to produce sow's ears by the bushel. He has not been helped to see how this surplus of sow's ears in modern industry might be diminished through the conscious practice of a skill. Thus he has not even been allowed to become intellectually involved and intrigued in the most important problem of his job. Yet there *are* training courses designed for just such a purpose, and they have worked successfully.[8]

Conclusion

Am I indulging in wishful thinking when I believe that there are some simple skills of communication that can be taught, learned, and practiced which might help to diminish misunderstanding? To me it is this possibility which the recent findings of general semantics and human relations are suggesting. They suggest that although man is determined by the complex relationships of which he is a part, nevertheless he is also in some small part a determiner of these relationships. Once he learns what he cannot do, he is ready to learn what little he can do. And what a tremendous difference to himself and to others the little that he can do—listening with understanding, for example—can make!

Once he can accept his limitations and the limitations of others, he can begin to learn to behave more skillfully with regard to the milieu in which he finds himself. He can begin to learn that misunderstanding can be diminished—not banished—by the slow, patient, laborious practice of a skill.

But we can expect too much from this possibility, so let me conclude by sounding two notes of caution:

1. Although these skills of communication of which I am speaking deal in part with words, they are not in themselves words, nor is the territory to

which they apply made up of words. It follows, then, that no verbal statement about these skills, however accurate, can act as a substitute for them. They are not truly articulate and never can be. Although transmissible to other persons, they are but slowly so and, even then, only with practice.

    2. Let us remember that these interpersonal proceedings between Hart and Bing, or *A* and *B* whoever they may be, are extremely complex. So far as I know, there exists no single body of concepts which as yet describes systematically and completely all the important processes that our separate theories have said are taking place and how they relate to each other. Let us therefore accept gracefully and not contentiously that these interpersonal proceedings, unlike the atom, have not been as yet "cracked" by social science. Only then can we as students of human behavior live up to our responsibility for making our knowledge fruitful in practice.

Notes and References

1. For an elaboration of this view see Robert Bierstedt, "An Analysis of Social Power," in *The American Sociological Review* (December 1950), 730.
2. For an analysis of this theory see Wendell Johnson, "The Fateful Process of Mr. A Talking to Mr. B," *Harvard Business Review* (January–February 1953), 49.
3. See Carl R. Rogers and F. J. Roethlisberger, "Barriers and Gateways to Communication," in *Harvard Business Review* (July–August 1952), 46–50.
4. Ibid., 50–52.
5. For a fuller explanation see Irving Lee, *How to Talk with People* (New York: Harper & Brothers, 1953).
6. For example, see Hadley Cantril, *The "Why" of Man's Experience* (New York: The Macmillan Company, 1950).
7. For a fuller explanation see Carl R. Rogers, *Client-Centered Therapy* (Boston: Houghton Mifflin, 1953).
8. See Kenneth R. Andrews, "Executive Training by the Case Method," and F. J. Roethlisberger, "Training Supervisors in Human Relations." *Harvard Business Review* (September 1951), 58 and 47.

Isomorphic Interrelationships Between Knower and Known

ABRAHAM H. MASLOW

My general thesis is that many of the communication difficulties between persons are the byproduct of communication barriers *within* the person; and that communication between the person and the world, to and fro, depends largely on their isomorphism (similarity of structure or form); that the world can communicate to a person only that of which he is worthy, that which he deserves or is "up to"; that to a large extent, he can receive from the world, and give to the world, only that which he himself is. As Kierkegaard said of a certain book, "Such works are like mirrors; if an ape peeps in, no apostle will look out." Goethe's contention was that we can fully understand only what we really love.

For this reason, the study of the "innards" of the personality is one necessary base for the understanding of what he can communicate to the world, and what the world is able to communicate to him. This truth is intuitively known to every therapist, every artist, every teacher, but it should be made more explicit.

Of course I take communication here in the very broadest sense. I include all the processes of perception and of learning, and all the forms of art and of creation. And I include primary process cognition (archaic, metaphorical, poetic, mythological cognition) as well as verbal, rational, secondary process communication. I want to speak of what we are blind and deaf to as well as what gets through to us; of what we express dumbly and unconsciously as well as what we can verbalize or structure clearly.

A main consequence of this general thesis—that difficulties with the outer parallel difficulties within the inner—is that we should expect communication with the outer world to improve along with improvement in the development of the personality, along with its integration and wholeness, and along with freedom from civil war among the various portions of the personality, i.e., perception of reality should improve. One then becomes more perceptive in the sense that Nietzsche says that one must have earned for oneself the distinction necessary to understand him.

Splits Within

First of all, what do I mean by failure of internal communication? Ultimately the simplest example is that of dissociation of the personality, of which the most dramatic and most usually known form is the multiple personality. The recent book and movie *Three Faces of Eve* is an excellent example. I have examined as many of these cases as I could find in the literature, and a few I had access to myself, along with the less dramatic fugues and amnesias. They seem to me to fall into a general pattern which I can express as a tentative general theory, which will be of use to us in our present task because it tells something about the splits in *all* of us.

In all the cases I know about, the "normal" or presenting personality has been a shy or quiet or reserved person, most often a female, rather conventional and controlled, rather submissive and even self-abnegating, unaggressive and "good," tending to be mousy, and easily exploited. In all cases, the "personality" that broke through into consciousness and into control of the person was the very opposite, impulsive rather than controlled, self-indulgent rather than self-abnegating, bold and brassy rather than shy, flouting the conventions, eager for a good time, aggressive and demanding, immature.

But this is a split that we can see in *all* of us in a less extreme form. This is the inward battle between impulse and control, between individual demands and the demands of society, between maturity and immaturity, between irresponsible pleasure and responsibility. Most of us manage to make better compromises or integrations between these opposites and so we don't split as dramatically as did Eve. To the extent that we succeed in being *simultaneously* the mischievous, childish rascal *and* the sober, responsible, impulse-controlling citizen, to that extent are we less split and more integrated. This, by the way, is the ideal therapeutic goal for multiple personalities, that is, to retain both or all three personalities, but in a graceful fusion or integration under conscious or preconscious control.

Each of these multiple personalities communicates with the world, to and fro, in a different way. Each talks differently, writes differently, indulges itself differently, makes love differently, selects different friends. "The willful child" personality in one case I had contact with had a big, sprawling child's handwriting and vocabulary and misspelling. The "self-abnegating, exploitable" personality had a mousy, conventional, good-schoolgirl handwriting. One "personality" read and studied books. The other couldn't, being too impatient and uninterested. How different would have been their art productions had we thought to get them.

In the rest of us too those portions of ourselves which are rejected and relegated to unconscious existence can and inevitably *do* break through into open effects upon our communication, both intake and output, affecting our perceptions as well as our actions. This is easily enough demonstrated by projective tests on one side and art expression on the other.

The projective test shows how the world looks to us, or better said, it shows how we organize the world, what we can take out of it, what we can let it tell us, what we choose to see and what we choose *not* to listen to or see.

Something similar is true on our expressive side. We express what we are (3). To the extent that we are split, our expressions and communications are split, partial, onesided. To the extent that we are integrated, whole, unified, spontaneous and fully functioning, to that extent are our expressions and communications complete, unique and idiosyncratic, alive and creative, rather than inhibited, conventionalized, and artificial, honest rather than phony. Clinical experience shows this for pictorial and verbal art expressions, and for expressive movements in general, and probably also for dance, athletic and other total bodily expressions. This is true not only for the communicative effects that we *mean* to have upon other people; it also seems to be true for the effects we don't mean to have.

Those portions of ourselves that we reject and repress (out of fear or shame) do not go out of existence. They do not die, but rather go underground. Whatever effects these underground portions of our human nature may thereafter have upon our communications tend either to be unnoticed by ourselves or else to be felt as if they were not part of us, e.g., "I don't know what made me say such a thing." "I don't know what came over me."

Other Splits Within the Personality

Pursuing this same theme, of the ways in which splits within the personality contaminate our communications to the world and from the world, I turn to several well-known pathological examples. I cite them also because they seem to be exceptions to the general rule that the healthy and integrated person tends to be a superior perceiver and expresser. There is both clinical and experimental evidence in large quantity for this generalization; for instance, the work of Eysenck and his colleagues. And yet, there are exceptions that force us to be cautious.

The schizophrenic is one in whom the controls and defenses are collapsing or have collapsed. The person then tends to slip into his private inner world, and his contact with other people and with the natural world tends to be destroyed. But this involves also some destruction of the communications to and from the world. Fear of the world cuts communication with it. So also can inner impulses and voices became so loud as to confuse reality testing. But it is also true that the schizophrenic patient sometimes shows a selective superiority. Because he is so involved with forbidden impulses and with primary process cognition (or archaic thinking), he is reported occasionally to be extraordinarily acute in interpreting the dreams of others or in ferreting out the buried impulses of others; for instance, concealed homosexual impulses.

It can work the other way about too. Some of the best therapists with schizophrenics were themselves "schizzy." And here and there we see a report that former patients can make exceptionally good and understanding ward attendants. This works on about the same principle as Alcoholics Anonymous. Some of my psychiatrist friends are now seeking this participant understanding by having an experience of being transiently psychotic with LSD or mescalin. One way of improving communication with a Y is to be a Y (4).

In this area we can learn much also from the psychopathic personalities, especially the "charming" type. They can be described briefly as having no conscience, no guilt, no shame, no love for other people, no inhibitions, and few controls, so that they pretty well do what they want to do. They tend to become forgers, swindlers, prostitutes, polygamists, and to make their living by their wits rather than by hard work. These people because of their own lacks are generally unable to understand in others the pangs of conscience, regret, unselfish love, compassion, pity, guilt, shame, embarrassment. What you are not, you cannot perceive or understand. It cannot communicate itself to you. And since what you are does sooner or later communicate itself, eventually the psychopath is seen as a cold, horrible, and frightening person, even though at first he seems so delightfully carefree, unneurotic, gay, and free.

But again we have an instance in which sickness, though it involves a *general* cutting of communications, also involves in specialized areas, a greater acuteness and skill. The psychopath is extraordinarily acute at discovering the psycho-pathic element in *us,* however carefully we conceal it. He can spot and play upon the swindler in us, the forger, the thief, the liar, the faker, the phony, and can ordinarily make a living out of this skill. They say, "You can't con an honest man," and seem very confident of their ability to detect any "larceny in the soul." (Of course, this implies that they can detect the *absence* of larceny, which means in turn that the character becomes visible in mien and demeanor, at least to the intensely interested observer, i.e., it communicates itself to those who can understand it and identify with it. Or as I have seen it said, "Time wounds all heels." The heels, thus visibly marked, are then able to know each other.)

Masculinity and Femininity

The close relationship between intra- and interpersonal communication is seen with especial clarity in the relations between masculinity and femininity. Notice that I do not say "between the sexes," because my point is that the relations *between* the sexes are very largely determined by the relation between masculinity and femininity *within* each person, male or female.

The most extreme example I can think of is the male paranoid who very frequently has passive homosexual yearnings, in a word, a wish to be raped and injured by the strong man. This impulse is totally horrifying and unacceptable to him, and he struggles to repress it. A main technique that he uses (projection) helps him to deny his yearning and to split it off from himself, and at the same time permits him to think about and talk about and be preoccupied with the fascinating subject. It is the *other* man who wants to rape him, not he who wishes to be raped. And so we get a suspiciousness in such a patient that can express itself in the most pathetically obvious ways, e.g., he won't let anyone get behind him, he'll keep his back to the wall, etc.

This is not so crazy as it sounds. Men throughout history have regarded women as temptresses, because they—the men—have been tempted by them. Men tend to become soft and tender, unselfish and gentle when they love women. If they happen to live in a culture in which these are nonmasculine traits, then they get angry at women for weakening them (castrating them), and they invent Samson and Delilah myths to show how horrible women are. They project malevolent intentions. They blame the mirror for what it reflects.

Women, especially "advanced" and educated women in the United States, are frequently fighting against their own very deep tendencies to dependency, passivity, and submissiveness (because this unconsciously and foolishly means to them a giving up of selfhood or personhood). It is then easy for such a woman to see men as would-be dominators and rapists and to treat them as such, frequently by dominating *them*.

For such reasons and others too, men and women in most cultures and in most eras have misunderstood each other, have not been truly friendly with each other. It can be said in our present context that their intercommunications have been and are still bad. Usually one sex has dominated the other. Sometimes they manage to get along by cutting off the women's world from the men's and making a complete division of labor, with concepts of masculine and feminine character that are very wide apart, with no overlapping. This makes for peace of a certain sort but certainly not for friendship and mutual understanding. What do the psychologists have to suggest about the improvement of understanding between the sexes? The psychological solution stated with especial clarity by the Jungians but also generally agreed upon is as follows: The antagonism between the sexes is largely a projection of the unconscious struggle *within* the person, between his or her masculine and feminine components. To make peace between the sexes, make peace within the person.

The man who is fighting within himself all the qualities he and his culture define as feminine will fight these same qualities in the external world, especially if his culture values maleness more than femaleness, as is so often the case. If it be emotionality, or illogic, or dependency, or love for colors, or tenderness with babies, he will be afraid of these in himself and fight them and try to be the opposite. And he will tend to fight them in the external world too by rejecting them, by relegating them to women entirely, etc. Homosexual men who solicit or accost are very frequently brutally beaten up by the men they approach, most likely because of the fears they arouse by being tempting. And it certainly fortifies this conclusion when we learn that the beating up often comes *after* the homosexual act.

What we see here is an extreme dichotomizing, either-or, Aristotelian thinking of the sort that Korzybski considered so dangerous. My psychologist's way of saying the same thing is "Dichotomizing means pathologizing; and pathology means dichotomizing." The man who thinks you can be *either* a man, *all* man, *or* a woman, and *nothing but* a woman, is doomed to struggle with himself, and to eternal estrangement from women. To the extent that he learns the facts of psychological "bisexuality," and becomes aware of the arbitrariness of either-or definitions and the pathogenic nature of the process of dichotomizing, to the degree that he discovers that differences can fuse and be structured with each other, and that they needn't be exclusive and mutually antagonistic, to that extent will he be a more integrated person, able to accept and enjoy the feminine within himself (the "Anima," Jung calls it). If he can make peace with his female inside, he can make peace with the females outside, understand them better, be less ambivalent toward them, and even admire them more as he realizes how superior their femaleness is to his own much weaker version. You can certainly communicate better with a friend who is appreciated and understood than you can with a feared, resented, and mysterious enemy. To make friends with some portion of the outside world, it is well to make friends with that part of it which is within yourself.

(I do not wish to imply that one process necessarily comes before the other. They are parallel and it can start the other way about, i.e., accepting x in the outside world can help achieve acceptance of that same x in the inside world.)

Primary- and Secondary-Process Cognition

My final example of intrapersonal split which parallels split with the world is the dichotomizing of conscious and unconscious cognitive processes or, to use Freud's later terminology, of primary process and secondary process. Unconscious thinking, perceiving, communication are archaic (in Jung's sense), mythological, poetic, metaphorical, proverbial, often concrete rather than conceptualized. It is characteristic of our night and day dreams, of our imagination, of revery, of an essential aspect of all art, of the first stages of creative production, of free association, etc.

It is generally stigmatized by most well-adjusted, sane, sober adults in the West as childish, crazy, senseless, wild. It is therefore threatening to their adult adjustment to the outer world, is regarded as incompatible with it and is therefore often repudiated. This means it can't be communicated with, and can't be used.

This repudiation of the inner psychic world in favor of the external world of common sense "reality" is stronger in those who *must* deal successfully with the outer world primarily. Also, the tougher the environment is, the stronger the repudiation of the inner world must be, and the more dangerous it is to a "successful" adjustment. Thus the fear of poetic feeling, of fantasy, of dreaminess, of emotional thinking, is stronger in men than in women, in adults than in children, in engineers than in artists.

Observe also that we have here another example of the profound Western tendency, or perhaps general human tendency to dichotomize, to think that between alternatives or differences one must choose *either* one or the other, and that this involves repudiation of the not-chosen, as if one couldn't have both (a sort of two-party system).

And again we have an instance of the generalization that what we are blind and deaf to within ourselves, we are also blind and deaf to in the outer world, whether it be playfulness, poetic feeling, aesthetic sensitivity, primary creativity, or the like.

This example is especially important for another reason, namely that it seems to me that reconciling this dichotomy may be *the* best place for educators to begin in the task of resolving *all* dichotomies. That is, it may be a good and practicable starting point for teaching humanity to stop thinking in a dichotomous way in favor of thinking in an integrative way.

This is one aspect of the great frontal attack upon an overconfident and isolated rationalism, verbalism, and scientism that is gathering force. The general semanticists, the existentialists, the phenomenologists, the Freudians, the Zen Buddhists, the mystics, the Gestalt therapists, the humanistic psychologists, the Jungians, the self-actualization psychologists, the Rogerians, the Bergsonians, the art educators, the "creative" educationists, and many others, are all helping to point out the limits of language, of abstract thought, and of orthodox science. These have been conceived as controllers of the dark, dirty, dangerous, and evil human depths. But now as we learn steadily that these depths are the wellsprings not only of neuroses but also of health, of joy, of creativeness, we begin to speak of the *healthy* unconscious, of healthy regression, of healthy instincts, of healthy nonrationality, of healthy intuition. And we begin to desire to salvage these capacities for ourselves.

The general theoretical answer seems to lie in the direction of integration and away from splitting and repressing. (I warn you that all these movements I've mentioned can too easily become themselves splitting forces. Antirationalism, anti-abstractionism, antiscience, anti-intellectualism are also splits. Properly defined and conceived, intellect is one of our greatest and most powerful integrating forces.)

B-Cognition, Full Functioning, Spontaneity

We begin to know something in a scientific way about the more integrated personality as it affects receiving and emitting communications. For instance, the many studies of Carl Rogers (7) and his collaborators indicate that, as the person improves in psychotherapy, he becomes more integrated in various ways, and that he becomes more "open to experience" (more efficient in perceiving) and more "fully functioning" (more honestly expressive). This is our main body of experimental research, but there are also many clinical and theoretical writers who parallel and support these general conclusions at every point.

My own pilot explorations (not exact enough to be called researches in the contemporary sense) come to the same conclusions from another angle, i.e., the direct exploration of the relatively healthy personality. First of all, they support the finding that integration is one defining aspect of psychological health. Secondly, they support the conclusion that healthy people are more spontaneous and more expressive, that they emit behavior more easily, more totally, more honestly.

Thirdly, they support the conclusion that healthy people perceive better (themselves, other people, all of reality), although, as I have indicated, this is not a *uniform* superiority. A current story has the psychotic saying, "2 plus 2 equal 5," while the neurotic says, "2 plus 2 equal 4, but I can't *stand* it!" I might add that the valueless person—suffering from a new kind of illness—says, "2 plus 2 equal 4. So what!" And the healthier person says in effect, "2 plus 2 equal 4. How perfect!"

Or to put it in another way, Joseph Bossom and I have recently published an experiment (2) in which we found that secure people tended to see photo-graphed faces as more warm than did insecure perceivers. The question remains for future research, however, as to whether this is a projection of kindness, of naivete, or of more efficient perception. What is called for is an experiment in which the faces perceived have *known* levels of warmth or coolness. Then, we may ask, are the secure perceivers who perceive or attribute more warmth right or wrong? Or are they right for warm faces and wrong for cool faces? Do they see what they want to see? Do they want to like what they see?

Being Worthy of the Experience

A last word about what I have called B-cognition (cognition of Being). This seems to me to be the purest and most efficient kind of perception of reality (although this remains to be tested experimentally). It is the truer and more veridical perception of the percept because most detached, more objective, least contaminated by the wishes, fears and needs of the perceiver. It is noninterfering, nondemanding, most accepting. In B-cognition, dichotomies tend to fuse, cate-gorizing tends to disappear, and the percept is seen as unique.

Self-actualizing people tend more to this kind of perceiving. But I have been able to get reports of this kind of perception in practically *all* the people I have questioned, in the highest, happiest, most perfect moments of their lives (peak experiences). Now, my point is this. Careful questioning shows that, as the percept grows more individual, more unified and integrated, more enjoyable, more rich, so also does the perceiving individual grow more alive, more inte-grated, more unified, more rich, more healthy for the moment. They happen simultaneously and can be set off on either side, i.e., the more whole the percept (the world) becomes, the more whole the person becomes. And also, the more whole the person becomes, the more whole becomes the world. It is a dynamic interrelation. The meaning of a message clearly depends not alone on its content but also on the extent to which the personality is able to respond to it. The "higher" meaning is perceptible only to the "higher" person.

As Emerson said, "What we are, that only can we see." Only we must now add that what we see tends in turn to make us what it is and what we are. The communication relationship between the person and the world is a dynamic one of mutual forming and lifting-lowering of each other, a process that we may call "reciprocal isomorphism." A higher order of persons can understand a higher order of knowledge; but also a higher order of environment tends to lift the level of the person, just as a lower order of environment tends to lower it.

Notes

1. Angyal, A. *Foundations for a Science of Personality.*
2. Bossom, J., and Maslow, A. H. "Security of judges as a factor in impressions of warmth in others," *J. Abnorm. and Social Psychol.*, 1957, *55*, 147–8.

3. Maslow, A. H. *Motivation and Personality.* Harper, 1954.
4. Maslow, A. H. *Toward a Psychology of Being.* Van Nostrand, 1962.
5. Maslow, A. H. *Religions, Values and Peak-Experiences.* Ohio State University Press, 1964.
6. Murphy, G. *Human Potentialities.* Basic Books, 1950.
7. Rogers, C. *On Becoming A Person.* Houghton Mifflin, 1961.

Communication, Feedback, and Empathy

DAVID K. BERLO

We have spent a good deal of time talking about the ways in which communication sources and receivers behave. At the beginning, we defined communication as a process, and pointed out that it is on-going, dynamic, without starting and stopping points. This is true. Yet, we necessarily have talked at times as if communication were static, nondynamic. This has not been intentional, but it is impossible to avoid when we *talk about* communication, when we take it apart to see how it works.

At this point, we might profit from another look at the process viewpoint of communication. The behaviors of the source do not occur independently of the behaviors of the receiver or vice versa. *In any communication situation, the source and the receiver are interdependent.*

The concept of interdependence is itself complex and can be illustrated by defining the possible relationships between any two concepts, such as *A* and *B*. A *and* B *are independent if and only if neither affects the other.* For example, the color of a person's hair (*A*) and his left- or right-handedness (*B*) are independent. They do not affect each other. Blondes are just as likely to be right-handed as they are left-handed. So are brunettes or red-heads. Right-handed people are just as likely to be blondes as they are to be brunettes or red-heads. The same is true for left-handed people. Neither affects the other.

There is a dependency relationship between A *and* B *if* A *affects* B *but* B *does not affect* A, *or vice-versa.* For example, the production of the ragweed flower (*A*) and the incidence of hay-fever (*B*) are dependently related. The presence of ragweed affects some people by producing hay-fever. Hay-fever is dependent on the existence of ragweed. Ragweed is not dependent on the existence of hay-fever. People who have hay-fever do not affect the existence of ragweed. *A* is not affected by *B*, but *B* is affected by *A;* therefore, *A* and *B* are dependently related.

Interdependence can be defined as *reciprocal* or *mutual* dependence. If *A* affects *B and B* affects *A,* then *A* and *B* are interdependent. For example, in this country the farmer and the grocer are interdependent. The food the farmer grows affects the product the grocer can sell. On the other hand, the sales of the grocer affect the kind and amount of crops the farmer will grow. Each is dependent on the other, each affects the other.

There are varying levels of interdependence among concepts or events. Maximum interdependence is found in concepts that we have referred to as dyadic. For example, the concepts of father and child are interdependent for their existence, neither can exist without the other. The same is true for husband-wife, leader-follower, supervisor-supervisee, etc. This can be called *definitional interdependence*. Dyadic concepts refer to relationships between events which cannot exist alone.

Communication between two or more people requires an interdependent relationship; however, the levels of communicative interdependence vary from situation to situation. How do these levels differ?

Levels of Communicative Interdependence

For purposes of discussion, we shall distinguish four levels of communicative interdependence. Again, it must be emphasized that we are distorting the process of communication when we do this. The four levels discussed are themselves not independent. Any communication situation probably includes some aspect of each; however, there are differences in emphasis from situation to situation.

If we remember that we are distinguishing among levels to point out differences in emphasis rather than differences in kind, we will not be misled. If we assume that communication at one level of interdependence is *not* related to the other levels, we will *not* be taking the process aspect of communication into account.

Definitional-Physical Interdependence

If we reflect for a moment, it becomes clear that the communication concepts of source and receiver are dyadic. They depend on each other for their very definition. You cannot define a source without defining a receiver. You cannot define a receiver without defining a source.

In addition to their definitional interdependence, the functions of the source and receiver are *physically* interdependent, although the functions may be performed at different points in time and space. When two people are communicating, they rely on the physical existence of the other for the production or reception of messages. Occasionally, this is the only kind of mutual interdependence involved to any appreciable extent. For example, let us look at the following hypothetical conversation between an industrial foreman (Harry) and a plant worker (John). John and Harry work in the same department. They meet when they get to work in the morning, and have the following "conversation":

> JOHN: Harry, let me tell you about what happened last night at home . . .
> HARRY: Fine, John. You know, things aren't going well on that experimental assembly job on the line . . .
> JOHN: I came in last night, and everything hit me. The wife said that the kids had ruined some of the plants in the yard . . .
> HARRY: If we don't get into full production pretty soon on that job, I don't see how . . .
> JOHN: the plumbing stopped up in the basement . . .
> HARRY: we can fulfill the contract we're working on.

JOHN: and the dog tried to bite the little boy down the street.
HARRY: Things are sure rough.
JOHN: They sure are.

This set of messages is exaggerated slightly to demonstrate a point, but most of us have heard conversations like this one, or even participated in a few. John and Harry were interdependent. Without the presence of the other, neither would have encoded the messages that he did; however, their major functions were to serve as receivers for the other's messages.

The kind of interdependence emphasized in this kind of situation is merely definitional-physical. The two communicators were not even reacting to each other's message. They were only waiting their turn to encode.

We probably would not want to label this "good" or "effective" communication. It *is* a frequent kind of communication.

When we communicate this way, we are not talking *to* each other, we are merely talking. We do not feel right in encoding certain messages unless we are in the presence of another. We cannot continue to do this when we are with another unless he puts up with it, or uses the situation for his own purposes. We are interdependent—but only because of the dyadic nature of the concepts of source and receiver.

Action-Reaction Interdependence

In explaining what is meant by action-reaction interdependence, we can use any of several servo-mechanisms as an illustration. For example, take the relationship between the modern furnace and the thermostat which we keep in our living rooms. We can look on thermostat-furnace behaviors as a communication relationship. Both the thermostat and the furnace serve as a source and a receiver. Each encodes messages, each receives messages from the other. Each affects the other. They are interdependent, and this relationship is more than mere physical interdependence. The responses that each make are determined by the responses of the other. We can describe the communication situation between the thermostat and the furnace as follows: The thermostat has an intention, a purpose: to maintain the temperature of the room at a specific level, such as 68°. As long as the temperature remains at that level, the thermostat is silent. It encodes no message. When the temperature drops below that level, the thermostat transmits a message to the furnace—"turn on." *The thermostat acts.*

When the furnace receives the message "turn on," it decodes it and *reacts* to the message. The furnace allows oil or gas to enter its chambers, it increases the force of the pilot, it produces heat. When the air at the top of the furnace reaches a certain level, such as 150°, another thermostat starts.

None of these messages are transmitted to the thermostat. They are internal (covert) responses of the furnace. When the blower starts, however, the furnace begins to transmit a message to the thermostat—heat. The thermostat receives this message (a reaction by the furnace), decodes it and decides that its original purpose has been accomplished. The room temperature is now at the desired level.

On making this decision, the thermostat reacts to the heat it received by encoding another message—"turn off." The furnace reacts to this message by reducing oil or gas flow, lowering the pilot, shutting off the blower, and stopping the transmission of heat. In time, the thermostat reacts to the absence of heat, decides the temperature has dropped below the desirable level, and encodes another message—"turn on." The cycle begins again. Continual communication occurs between the furnace and the thermostat. Each transmits messages, each receives messages. Each reacts to the messages it receives.

The thermostat-furnace relationship is illustrative of many communication situations. Take the . . . example of a dinner table discussion between Bill and John. Bill had a purpose, he wanted John to pass him the salt. He encoded a message. ("Pass me the salt, please.") He performed some *action*. John decoded the message and *reacted* to it. He responded by producing the salt. His action was taken as a result of decoding Bill's message.

When Bill perceived John's reaction, he reacted to it by reaching his hand out for the salt and saying "Thank you" to John. Each of these behaviors was dependent on the behavior preceding it. Bill acted, John reacted, Bill reacted, and so on. Bill and John were interdependent. Each was affected by the action of the other.

Feedback. Communication terminology includes a term related to action-reaction interdependence to which we have already referred: "feedback." It is correct to say that the furnace reacted to the thermostat; however, if we analyze the situation from the thermostat's point of view, we can say that the reaction of the furnace was *fed back* to the thermostat. The thermostat can utilize the reaction of the furnace in determining its next message.

Feedback from the furnace was useful because it affected the next message that the thermostat produced. Without feedback from the furnace, the thermostat would not be able to determine whether it should tell the furnace to keep providing heat or to turn itself off. The thermostat needed feedback to ascertain whether it was being successful in its communication, whether it was having the desired effect.

The term "feedback" names a special aspect of receiver reaction. It names the use which the source can make of this reaction in determining its own success. For example, when Bill asked John to pass the salt, he could watch John to see if he did it. John's response was useful to Bill as feedback. It told him whether he had been successful in accomplishing his objective. If John did not pass the salt, Bill could have asked him again. If the furnace did not turn on, the thermostat would have repeated its message.

The source can use the reaction of the receiver as a check of his own effectiveness and a guide to his own future actions. The reaction of the receiver is a *consequence* of the response of the source. As a response consequence, it serves as feedback to the source.

Feedback provides the source with information concerning his success in accomplishing his objective. In doing this, it exerts control over future messages which the source encodes.

In the thermostat-furnace example, the reaction of each to the behavior of the other serves as feedback; however, these reactions can be utilized only in a limited way. The thermostat can repeat its message of "turn on" or "turn off." The furnace can repeat its message of "heat" or "no heat." No other alternative is available to either. Neither can communicate a different message; neither can alter the code, content, or treatment of its message. All feedback can do in this illustration is affect the repetition of a message.

In human communication, we can utilize feedback to a much greater extent. John's response to Bill was usable by Bill as feedback. It told him whether he had been successful or not. If John did not pass the salt, Bill could have changed his message, changed the code, the content, or the treatment. Bill could have changed channels and pointed. He could have changed receivers and asked someone else. He even could have changed his purpose and eaten his food without salt.

John also could get feedback. When he passed Bill the salt, he could observe Bill's response. If Bill smiled, and said "Thanks," or began to use the salt, that would be one thing. If Bill frowned, looked confused, said "What's that for," that would be another thing. All these responses could be used by John as feedback. *One consequence of a communication response is that it serves as feedback—to both the source and the receiver.*

In summary, communication often involves an action-reaction interdependence. The action of the source affects the reaction of the receiver, the reaction of the receiver affects the subsequent reaction of the source, etc. The source or the receiver can make use of the reactions of the other.

Reactions serve as feedback. They allow the source or receiver to check up on himself, to determine how well he is doing in accomplishing his purpose. Feedback also affects subsequent behavior, if the source and receiver are sensitive to it.

When a source receives feedback that is rewarding, he continues to produce the same kind of message. When he gets nonrewarding feedback, he eventually will change his message. In responding to a message, the receiver exerts control over the source. The kind of feedback he provides determines in part the next set of behaviors of the source. Speakers and audiences, actors and theatre-goers, sources and receivers generally can be interdependent through the mutual effects of their reactions on the other.

For example, suppose you are giving a talk, making a speech. At one point in your talk, you tell a joke. The audience is supposed to laugh. If they laugh, this can serve as feedback to you. It tells you that you were successful. It tells you to keep going, your messages are having an effect. On the other hand, suppose the audience does not laugh. Suppose it just sits. This, too, serves as feedback. It tells you that you are not getting what you want, your messages are not meeting with success. You might change your jokes, or stop telling jokes. *The audience exerts control over your future messages by the responses it makes.* These are fed back to you. You are dependent on the audience for feedback.

At the same time, members of the audience are dependent on feedback. If one person does not laugh at your jokes and all the other members of the audience do, these responses are fed back to the nonlaughing receiver. He begins to question his sense of humor—and often begins to laugh at succeeding jokes, whether they strike him as funny or not. Eventually, they may even begin to strike him as funny.

Communication sources and receivers are mutually interdependent, for existence and for feedback. Each of them continually exerts influence over himself and others by the kinds of responses that he makes to the messages he produces and receives. A newspaper affects its readers by selecting the news they are allowed to read. On the other hand, the readers also affect the newspaper (although probably not as much as some publishers would have us believe).

If readers do not buy the paper (negative feedback), it may change its selection and presentation of news.

Advertisers control the reasons given to the public for buying this or that product. But the consumer affects the advertiser—through feedback. If the public buys more (positive feedback), the advertiser keeps his messages. If the public quits buying the product (negative feedback), the advertiser changes his messages—or the stockholders get a new advertising manager.

We can separate one communication situation from another by the ease with which feedback is obtained. Clearly, person-to-person communication permits maximum feedback. All available communication channels can operate. The source has an opportunity to change his message on the spot as a result of the feedback he gets. On the other hand, communication forms that we refer to as the public media (newspaper, television, magazines, etc.) have minimum opportunities for feedback. The source and the receiver are separated in time and space. They have little opportunity to get feedback from the responses of the other.

Even in our own person-to-person communication situations, we overlook the importance of feedback. As students, we fail to realize the extent to which we can affect the teacher. When we indicate that we do not understand, he repeats, if he is sensitive to feedback. When we let him know we think he is a good teacher, he may become a better teacher. Any performer would testify that he gives a better performance when his audience reacts favorably, when they make responses which he can use as positive feedback.

We underestimate the value of feedback when we communicate with our friends and families. We neglect to tell them when we think they have done a good job or when we like them. These kinds of responses are useful to them as feedback. They affect future actions toward us.

Action-reaction relationships are significant in analyzing communication. Feedback is an important instrument of effect. The reactions of the receiver are useful to the source in analyzing his effectiveness. They also affect his subsequent behaviors because they serve as consequences of his prior responses. If the feedback is rewarding, he perseveres. If it is not rewarding, he changes his message to increase the chances of being successful.

An awareness and utilization of feedback increase the communication effectiveness of the individual. The ability to observe carefully the reactions others make to our messages is one of the characteristics of the person we designate as being good at "human relations," or "sensitive as a communicator."

It is true to say that one can find communication situations that fit this action-reaction level of interdependence between the source and the receiver. Granted, too, that it is useful to retain the action-reaction concept and the corresponding concept of communication feedback. Yet there are at least two possible pitfalls into which this kind of analysis can lead.

First, the concept of feedback usually is used to reflect a *source orientation* to communication, rather than a receiver orientation or a process orientation. When we talk about the receiver's responses as feedback for the source, we are observing communication situations from the point of view of the source. We are perceiving through his eyes, not as an external observer.

As we shall show, there are levels of interdependence higher than action-reaction. We do not have to look at the source-receiver relationship as a one-way relationship; however, the feedback concept emphasizes one-wayness, at the expense of a two-way analysis. When people are taught about feedback, they are likely to take a source orientation to communication. We talk about "getting feedback" to the source, or "using the receiver's behavior" as feedback for the source.

The term "feedback" implies a point of view. We have said that one individual makes a response, performs an act. This response is perceived by a second individual and responded to. We say that the second individual reacts to the original message. When we call this reaction "feedback," we are structuring it as if we were the original source. We are talking about a use we can make of a reaction, not the reaction itself. There is nothing inherently wrong with this kind of terminology. In fact, it is useful to think this way. Nevertheless, if we are not careful, we begin to think about all of the process from the source's point of view, and ignore the basic interdependence that produced the term "feedback" in the first place.

The second pitfall in the use of the action-reaction concept is concerned with our continuing reference to communication as a process. The terms "action" and "reaction" deny the concept of process. They imply that there is a beginning to communication (the act), a second event in communication (reaction), subsequent events, etc., with a final end. They imply an interdependence of events within the sequence, but they do not imply the kind of dynamic interdependence that is involved in the communication process.

People are not thermostats or furnaces. They have the capacity to make trial responses within the organism, to use symbols to anticipate how others will respond to their messages, to develop expectations about their own behavior and the behavior of others. The concept of *expectations* is crucial to human communication. It requires analysis at a third level of communication interdependence.

Interdependence of Expectations: Empathy

All human communication involves predictions by the source and receiver about how other people will respond to a message. Even in the minimal-interdependence situation that we have called physical interdependence, Bill and John had some expectations about each other. They made predictions about the language facility of the other, the length of time the other would tolerate listening rather than speaking, the social relationships that existed between them, etc. We can analyze expectations as a distinctive level of interdependence; however, to some extent this kind of interdependence is involved in all communication.

Every communicator carries around with him an image of his receiver. He takes his receiver (as he pictures him to be) into account when he produces a message. He anticipates the possible responses of his receiver and tries to predict them ahead of time. These images affect his own message behaviors. For example, the Madison Avenue advertiser has an image (accurate or inaccurate) of the American public. The Hollywood producer has an image of the movie-goer. Newspapers have expectations about how their readers will react to messages. Magazines can be distinguished on the basis of the images they have of their subscribers. Personnel managers have an image of the typical factory worker. Teachers have expectations about students.

The development of expectations of the receiver by the source has its counterpart in the development of expectations of the source by the receiver. Receivers have expectations about sources. When we observe the President, we expect him to behave in certain ways and not in others—because he is the President. Magazine readers have an image of the magazines they read. The public image of the *Ladies' Home Journal* is not the same as the image of *Fortune, Playboy,* or *True Story.* We expect different messages from these magazines, different message treatments.

Communication receivers select and attend to messages in part because of their images of the sources and their expectations as to the kind of message these sources would produce. The public has an image of business corporations, labor union leaders, educators, doctors, etc. One of the major missions of the public relations expert is the development of expectations about his client. People in this profession are paid to manipulate the receiver's image of a company, a public figure, a product.

As sources and receivers, we have expectations about each other that affect our communication behaviors. Behavior is also affected by our images of *ourselves.* Our self-images influence the kinds of messages we create and the treatment we give our messages. Our expectations about our own behavior affect which messages we attend to. Subscribers to *Harper's* may have self-images different from those of subscribers to *The Reader's Digest.* Republicans have different expectations about their own behavior than do Democrats—at least in some behavioral areas.

As sources and receivers, we carry around images of ourselves and a set of expectations about other people. We use these expectations in encoding, decoding, and responding to messages. We take other people into account in framing messages. We frame messages to influence a receiver, but our expectations about the receiver influence us and our messages.

Some of the more interesting studies in communication analyze the images which individuals or communicative organizations have of their receivers, and how these expectations affect the source's behavior. For example, what image does Madison Avenue have of the typical Iowa farmer, of Madison Avenue itself? What image does the corporation executive have of himself, of the average factory worker, etc.? These are research questions, and important ones. Their answers can help us explain why people treat their messages as they do, because a source's expectations influence the way he communicates.

In approaching the concept of expectations, we can return to our basic model of the communication process. The communication source and receiver each possess certain communication skills, attitudes, and knowledges. Each exists within a social system and a cultural context. These affect how they will react to messages. Communication represents an attempt to couple these two individuals, these two psychological systems. Messages are used to accomplish this coupling of the organisms.

In one sense, messages are all that the organisms have available to them. By using messages, we come to "know" other men, to know ourselves. We believe that we can understand in part what is going on *within* another person. We develop expectations about what is going on within others and what will go on within ourselves. The basic question is, how do we develop these expectations?

To put it another way, we often make statements of the order, "I know John," or "He won't accept that argument—I know him inside and out." How do we come to "know" other people, inside and out? For that matter, how do we come to "know" ourselves? What is the process underlying our ability to develop expectations about others, to predict how they will behave before a situation arises?

Clearly, we frequently face decisions requiring this kind of knowledge. We decide whether we should promote Jones, whether we should marry Mary, whether we should recommend Bill for a responsible job. When we make these kinds of decisions, we operate on the assumption that we "know" Jones or Mary or Bill. We make decisions which imply that we understand people, that we can predict how they will behave.

When we say that we "know" somebody, we mean more than that we can recognize him physically when we see him. We mean that we can predict correctly that he will believe certain things and not others, he will behave in certain ways and not in others, he will react in certain ways and not in others.

When we say we "know" somebody, including ourselves, we are saying that we understand how he operates as a psychological entity—as a person with thoughts, feelings, emotions, etc. In making these predictions, we have physical behaviors as our basic data. Each of us perceives how others behave. We can observe these behaviors. They are overt, public. Expectations involve more than this. They involve the private behaviors of man, his covert responses, his internal states, his beliefs, his meanings. When we develop expectations, when we make predictions, we are assuming that we have skill in what the psychologists call *empathy—the ability to project ourselves into other people's personalities.* How do we develop empathic ability?

This is a basic question for students of communication. Unfortunately, there is no definitive answer to the question. In any complete sense, we are still without enough research evidence to substantiate one position or another. There are theories of empathy which are plausible—and at least consistent with research evidence. Tomorrow may provide an adequate answer—but we have to operate on what we know today. *We can define empathy as the process through which we arrive at expectations, anticipations of the internal psychological states of man.* How does this occur?

There are three major points of view on empathy. One school of thought argues that there is no such thing, that we cannot develop expectations. Supporters of this position for the most part are believers in a simple one-stage (S-R) theory of learning. This kind of learning theorist argues that all we have in communication is a set of messages. A message is produced by one person, and perceived by another. In other words, there are stimuli and responses. And that is that. We argued [previously] that a simple S-R theory of learning may account for nonhuman animal learning, but not for the more complex learning behaviors of man. By the same argument, a simple S-R theory of empathy does not seem to account for man's communication behavior.

We *do* develop expectations, we *do* have the ability to project ourselves into the internal states of others. We cannot accept the argument that empathy does not have meaning for us, that we cannot develop expectations and predictions. Some kind of *interpretive* process occurs.

The development of expectations requires a special kind of talent. We need to be able to think about objects that are not available. *Expectations require decisions about the not-here and the not-now.* In order to have expectations, to talk about the not-here and the not-now, we create arbitrary symbols to represent the objects that are not available. We need to be able to produce these symbols and manipulate them.

Man is distinguished from other animals in that he has developed both of these talents. He can receive and manipulate arbitrary symbols. He can produce these symbols to serve his purposes. Because of this, he can represent the nonavailable, the not-here and not-now. As Thorndike put it, the use of arbitrary symbols allows "humans to think *about* things, not merely to think things." Man clearly has these talents, although there are individual differences among people.

Some of our games involve this kind of skill, the development of empathic ability. Chess is an example. A successful chess-player cannot rely on action-reaction. He develops expectations about the consequences of his behavior, and operates under those expectations. He predicts how the other man will react—often several events in advance. He debates moving a pawn. He reasons, if I move this pawn, my opponent probably will take my knight with his bishop—but if he does that, then I will checkmate his king with my queen, etc.

The same thing occurs in contract bridge. The good bidder anticipates possible answering bids from his partner or opponents before he makes his own bid. He also predicts how others will play their hands. The inclusion of this kind of skill is what prevents bridge from becoming a mechanical game that can be described in books. We differ in empathic ability. Some of us are better predictors than others.

We can reject the argument that we have no meaning for the concept of empathy. All of us anticipate the future, we make predictions about the relationships between (a) certain behaviors on our parts, (b) subsequent behaviors of other people, and (c) subsequent behaviors of our own. We do more than act and react. We develop expectations about others which affect our actions—before we take them. This is what we mean by empathy.

Theories of Empathy

There are two popular theories about the basis for empathy. Both theories agree that the basic data of expectations are physical behaviors produced by man; i.e., messages. Both theories agree that man's predictions about the internal psychological states of man are based on observable physical behaviors. Both agree that man makes these predictions by using symbols to represent these physical behaviors and by manipulating these symbols. At this point, the two theories of empathy differ sharply. We can best discuss them separately.

Inference Theory of Empathy

An inference theory of empathy[1] is psychologically oriented. It argues that man can observe his own physical behavior directly, and can relate his behavior symbolically to his own internal psychological states—his feelings, thoughts, emotions, etc. Through this process, man comes to have meanings (interpretations) for his own physical behavior. He develops a concept of *self,* by himself, based on his observations and interpretations of his own behavior.

Given a self-concept, he communicates with other people. He observes their physical behaviors. On the basis of his prior interpretations of himself, he makes *inferences* about the internal states of others. In other words, he argues to himself that if behavior on his part represented such and such a feeling, a similar behavior produced by somebody else would represent a similar feeling.

This view of empathy assumes that man has first-hand knowledge of himself and second-hand knowledge of other people. It argues that man has the ability to understand himself, through analysis of his own behaviors. From this analysis, man can make inferences about other people based on the similarities between their behavior and his own.

Let us take a simple example of this argument. Suppose you observe yourself making certain gestures; e.g., you repeatedly pound your hand on a table. You analyze how you felt when you perfomed this behavior. You conclude that you were angry, that you were upset. You discover a relationship between your overt behavior (table-pounding) and an internal state or feeling of anger. Then you observe somebody else pounding his hand on the table. From this behavior, you infer that he too is angry. You make assumptions about his internal state from (a) observing his behavior, and (b) comparing his behavior with similar behavior on your part which reflected anger in you.

This is the position of an *inference* theory of empathy. What are its assumptions?

1. Man has first-hand evidence of his own internal states. He can only have second-hand evidence of other people's internal states.
2. Other people express a given internal state by performing the same behaviors that you perform to express the same state.
3. Man cannot understand internal states in other people which he has not experienced himself. Man cannot understand emotions which he has not felt, thoughts which he has not had, etc.

Let us take these assumptions one at a time. First, an inference theory of empathy says that man's first-hand knowledge is of himself. All other knowledge is second-hand. As we shall find, the other major view of empathy contradicts this assumption directly. From currently available research evidence, we cannot resolve this issue; the assumption can be neither accepted nor rejected.

There is considerable evidence that conflicts with the second assumption, that all people express the same purposes by the same behaviors, that all people mean the same things by the behaviors they perform. Many breakdowns in communication stem from this belief. We often assume that another person attaches the same meaning to a word that we do, that a smile by another person expresses the same internal state as does a smile by us, that other people see the world in the same way that we do—just because they perform many of the physical behaviors that we perform.

It is true that we often get our ideas about the internal states of other people by inferring them from our own internal states, as related to our own behavior. But in so doing, we often err. We often fail to "know" the internal workings of others when we assume they are the same as ours.

When we look at the success we have in predicting and anticipating the behavior of others, it seems likely that we need to add another approach to empathy to provide a complete explanation of our success. We need an approach which does not assume that man's first-hand knowledge is always of use. People are not the same.

There also is evidence that contradicts the third assumption of inference theory: that we cannot understand internal states which we have not experienced ourselves. Few theorists would dispute the point that man understands best those things which he has experienced himself. Yet we can find many examples of the understanding (at least in part) of emotions which have not been experienced. For instance, we can empathize with a mother who has just lost her baby. We can have expectations about how she will behave, what her internal states are, even though we have never lost a baby. We can empathize with people who are in a state of great happiness over their coming marriage, even though we have not been married ourselves. Experience increases our understanding, but it does not seem to be essential to understanding.

These are the essential arguments of an inference theory of empathy. There seems to be some merit in the arguments; however, inference theory does not seem to explain empathy in terms that are completely satisfying. We can turn our attention to the second point of view, popularized by Mead and usually considered to be a sociological point of view. Mead labeled his theory as *role-taking*.

Role-Taking Theory of Empathy[2]

Let us not assume that man's first-hand knowledge is of himself, or even that man *has* a concept of self before he communicates with other people. We can examine some of the behaviors of man, and try to interpret their implications for empathy.

Let us look at the very young child, the infant. How does he behave, how does he develop his ability to empathize? The basic data that are observable to the infant are physical behaviors, message behaviors. The infant, like everyone else, can observe and produce physical behavior. The question is, how does the child develop interpretations of self and others, given observable physical behaviors?

Role-taking theorists argue that the new-born infant cannot distinguish himself from other people, cannot tell one person from another. In order to develop the concept of self, the infant must first look on himself as an object— must act toward himself as he acts toward other objects, other people. *In other words, the concept of self does not precede communication. It is developed through communication.*

The young child exhibits a good deal of imitative behavior. He observes other people's behavior. He tries to repeat the behavior as well as he can. Some of the behavior he imitates is behavior directed toward him. His mother makes sounds (speaks) in his presence. He begins to imitate the sounds. The father moves his face (smiles) in his presence. He begins to imitate these facial movements.

In imitating behaviors directed toward him, the infant begins to act toward himself as others act toward him, but he has no interpretation for these actions, no meaning for the actions. This is the beginning of role-taking, the beginning of the development of a concept of self. *In the first stage of role-taking, the infant actually plays other people's roles without interpretation.* He imitates the behavior of others. He is rewarded for these role-playing responses; therefore he retains them.

As the child develops, he increases his role-playing behavior. He increasingly acts toward himself in the same way that other people act toward him. At the same time, he learns to produce and manipulate a set of symbols, significant symbols, symbols for which he and other people have meanings. Equipped with a set of significant symbols, the infant can begin to understand the roles that he takes. He can understand how other people behave toward him. He can begin really to put himself in other people's shoes, to look at himself as other people do.

Those of you who have watched small children know what is meant by this. The child at age two or three will play by having a make-believe tea party. At the tea party, he will reprimand himself—produce messages such as "Todd, you mustn't do that or I'll send you up to bed," or "No, no, Sandy, that's not the way to sit at the table." When the child behaves like this, he is looking at himself as an object of behavior—as an external object. He is playing the role of the parent, putting himself in the shoes of the parent. *This is the second stage of role-taking, in which the infant plays other people's roles—with understanding.*

As the child matures, he engages in more complex role-playing. He begins to play games with several other people. In playing games, the child must take a large number of roles at the same time. In hide-and-seek, the child must put himself in the shoes of the person who is "it," must, simultaneously, take the roles of all the other children who are hiding.

It now becomes impossible physically to *play* all these roles. The child cannot imitate all the related behaviors. Through the use of symbols, however, he hypothesizes what it would be like to behave as the other children do. He infers their roles, he takes their roles in his own mind, rather than playing the roles physically. *This is the third stage of role-taking, in which the child begins to put himself in other people's shoes symbolically, rather than physically.*

By putting himself in the places of all the other children, the child develops expectations about his own behavior—about what is expected of him in this situation. He then behaves according to his expectations, as determined by *taking* the roles of others. If he has done a good job of role-taking, his behavior conforms to the expectations the others have, and they reward him, they let him play, they like him. If he has not done a good job of role-taking, his behavior does not conform to the expectations of the other children and he is not rewarded. He is rejected, punished.

As the child continues to participate in group activity, he takes the roles of many other people. In so doing, he looks on himself as a receiver, as an object of behavior. Gradually, he begins to *generalize* the roles of others. He starts to get a general concept of how other people behave, how they interpret, and how they act toward him. We can call this the concept of the generalized other. *The generalized other is an abstract role that is taken, the synthesis of what an individual learns of what is general or common to the individual roles of all other people in his group.*

Each of us develops a concept of the generalized other, based on our experiences in a specific social environment and in the successive roles of other people that we take. The generalized other provides us with a set of expectations as to how we should behave. This is our meaning for the concept of self. *Our self-concept is the set of expectations that we have as to how we should behave in a given situation.* How do we develop a self-concept? Through communication, through taking the roles of others, through acting toward ourselves as an object of communication, through the development of a generalized other.

Inference theory *assumes* a concept of self, and suggests that we empathize by using the self-concept to make inferences about the internal states of other people. Inference theory suggests that the self-concept determines how we empathize. Role-taking theory argues the other way around. It suggests that the concept of self does not determine empathy. Rather, communication produces the concept of self and role-taking allows for empathy. Both theories place great importance on the nature of language, significant symbols, in the process of empathy and the development of a concept of self.

Which are we to believe? How does man empathize? Here, we will take the position that *man utilizes both these approaches to empathy.* We can argue that man's first approach is through role-taking. Each of us takes roles of other people. Each of us develops a concept of the generalized other. The way that we look on ourselves, our definition of ourselves, is determined by our concept of the generalized other, the social context in which we exist, the expectations which we perceive others to have about our own behaviors.

As we develop and mature, we construct a concept of self. Then we operate on it. We now begin to make inferences about other people, based on our concept of self. We lessen our use of role-taking, and increase our use of inferences. We make the assumption that other people are like us, and that their behaviors reflect the same internal states that our behavior reflects. We do this until we do not find it rewarding.

When we empathize by making inferences and are not rewarded, we are forced to do one of two things. Either (1) we distort the behaviors of others that we perceive, and make them correspond to our expectations, or (2) we take another look at our images of ourselves, we redefine self, we return to role-taking.

If we take the first solution, distorting the world that we perceive, we become mentally ill, we have "delusions," we end up in an institution. This is not desirable. Yet we can predict that much of the problem of mental health is related to man's inability or unwillingness to change his own image of himself when he finds that it is not rewarded in his social environment.

What about the second alternative, a redefinition of self? To do this, we have to return to role-taking, we again have to take the role of others, to develop a new concept of the generalized other, a new set of expectations for our own behavior. In so doing, we redefine ourselves, change our behaviors accordingly, and again begin to make inferences about other people.

We often engage in role-playing when we are revising our role-taking or self concepts. Again, the mentally ill can use role-playing as a technique to increase their ability to make useful hypotheses about how others would react, and how they should react in a given situation.

As we play the role of another, we combine the inference and role-taking points of view. When we role-play, we actually perform certain behaviors. From these, we can infer our own internal states, we can make inferences from our own behavior which are pertinent to the behavior of another. We then can use these inferences in taking the role of another.

This process of role-taking, inference, role-taking, inference goes on continually. It is what we mean when we say that man is adjustable, adaptable, able to alter his behavior to fit the situation, the social environment in which he finds himself. He develops expectations by taking the roles of others, or by making inferences about himself, or both.

When do we often find it necessary to redefine self? When we enter a new social situation, a new group, a different social environment. For example, when a teen-ager enters the university, he finds himself in a new social situation. His inferences about other people are no longer valid. He makes false predictions, has hazy expectations. Often, he begins to ask himself who he really is.

What does the teen-ager begin to do? He reverts to role-playing, often at a primitive stage. He begins to imitate the behavior of others—without meaning. Gradually, he takes the roles of others (students, teachers, etc.) and is able to put himself in other people's shoes, to look at himself through their eyes. In so doing, he develops a new concept of the generalized other, a new set of expectations about his own behavior. He redefines self and begins to behave in accord with his new definition.

This kind of process is required of us many times in our lives. When we enter a new community, join a new group, travel to a different culture, our predictive power is weakened. We find it difficult to make inferences from self-knowledge. If we are to operate effectively in a changing social situation, we need to be able to take other people's roles, to redefine ourselves. In part, this is the mark of the adjusted man.

Interaction: The Goal of Human Communication

One necessary condition for human communication is an interdependent relationship between the source and the receiver. Each affects the other. At one level of analysis, communication involves only a physical interdependence; i.e., source and receiver are dyadic concepts, each requires the other for its very definition, each requires the other for its existence.

At a second level of complexity, interdependence can be analyzed as an action-reaction sequence. An initial message affects the response that is made to it, the response affects the subsequent response, etc. Responses affect subsequent responses because they are utilized by communicators as feedback—as information that helps them determine whether they are achieving the desired effect.

At a third level of complexity, communication analysis is concerned with empathic skills, the interdependence produced by expectations about how others will respond to a message. Empathy names the process in which we project ourselves into the internal states or personalities of others in order to predict how they will behave. We infer the internal states of others by comparing them to our own attitudes and predispositions.

At the same time, we engage in role-taking. We try to put ourselves in the other person's shoes, to perceive the world as he sees it. In doing this, we develop the concept of self that we use to make inferences about others. In communicating, we shift from inferences to role-taking as a basis for our predictions. The expectations of the source and receiver are interdependent. Each affects the other, each is in part developed by the other.

A final level of interdependent complexity is interaction. The term *interaction* names the process of reciprocal role-taking, the mutual performance of empathic behaviors. *If two individuals make inferences about their own roles and take the role of the other at the same time, and if their communication behavior depends on the reciprocal taking of roles, then they are communicating by interacting with each other.*

Interaction differs from action-reaction in that the acts of each participant in communication are interrelated with each other, they affect each other through the development of hypotheses about what these acts will be, how they fit the purposes of the source and receiver, etc.

The concept of interaction is central to an understanding of the concept of process in communication. Communication represents an attempt to couple two organisms, to bridge the gap between two individuals through the production and reception of messages which have meanings for both. At best, this is an impossible task. Interactive communication approaches this ideal.

When two people interact, they put themselves into each other's shoes, try to perceive the world as the other person perceives it, try to predict how the other will respond. Interaction involves reciprocal role-taking, the mutual employment of empathic skills. The goal of interaction is the merger of self and other, a complete ability to anticipate, predict, and behave in accordance with the joint needs of self and other.

We can define interaction as the ideal of communication, the goal of human communication. All communication is not interactional, or at least does not emphasize this level of interdependence. . . . Much of our social behavior involves attempts to find substitutes for interaction, to find less energy-consuming bases for communication.

We can communicate without interacting to any appreciable extent; however, to the extent that we are in an interactional situation, our effectiveness, our ability to affect and be affected by others increases. As interaction develops, expectations become perfectly interdependent. The concepts of source and receiver as separate entities become meaningless, and the concept of process becomes clear.

References

1. The major source of this theory is Solomon Asch. *Social Psychology* (Englewood Cliffs, N.J.: Prentice-Hall, Inc., 1952), 139–169.
2. The major source of this theory is the work of George H. Mead. Much of the discussion is taken from George H. Mead, *Mind, Self and Society* (Chicago: University of Chicago Press, 1934).

Benefits of Poor Communication

CHARLOTTE OLMSTED KURSH

In this day and age one of the most popular forms of piety has to do with communication, somewhat narrowly defined. An ailment called "lack of communication" has taken the place of original sin as an explanation for the ills

Reprinted from *The Psychoanalytic Review,* Vol. 58, No. 2, 1971, through the courtesy of the author, the editors and the publisher, National Psychological Association for Psychoanalysis, New York, N.Y.

of the world, while "better communication" is trotted out on every occasion as a universal panacea. It is guaranteed to appear at least once, and usually several times, on any TV panel discussion. Usually it is offered with the mock modest air of one who is making a substantial contribution which is bound to be well received, while the correct response is solemn nods all around, strongly reminiscent of the amens in church. Indeed, ritualization of the whole sequence is far advanced.

Yet some of the basic assumptions underlying these popular views deserve more examination than they have had. One is the way in which poor communication resembles original sin: both tend to get tangled up with control of the situation. Although if one defines communication as mutual understanding, this does not imply control for either party and certainly not for both. The equation of good communication with control appears in the assumption that better communication will necessarily reduce strife and conflict. Each individual's definition of better communication, like his definition of virtuous conduct, becomes that of having the other party accept his views—which would reduce conflict at that party's expense. As long as both feel this way the struggle can continue indefinitely, but strictly speaking has very little to do with communication difficulties per se. A better understanding of the situation might serve only to underline the differences rather than to resolve them. Indeed many of the techniques thought of as poor communication were apparently developed with the aim of bypassing or avoiding confrontation, and some of them continue to be reasonably successful in this aim.

Another assumption that grows from this view is that when a conflict has gone on for a long time and shows every sign of continuing, lack of communication must be one of the basic problems. Usually if the situation is examined more carefully, plenty of communication will be found to be going on; the problem is again one of equating communication with agreement.

Still a third assumption, somewhat related but less squarely based on the equation of communication with control, is that *it is always in the interest of at least one of the parties to an interaction, and often of both, to attain maximum clarity as measured by some more or less objective standard.* Aside from the difficulty of setting up this standard—whose standard? and doesn't this give *him* control of the situation?—there are some sequences, and perhaps many of them, in which it is to the interests of both parties to leave the situation as fuzzy, amorphous and undefined as possible.

A final assumption is that poor communication is primarily a matter of *faulty techniques* of speaking, writing, listening or reading, that improvements in technique can be learned and in every case will vastly improve the quality of social life. While it is usually recognized that these "faulty techniques" were learned in a situation where they were probably more or less functional, the possibility is hardly considered that they might still be functional, or what that function might be.

Let us consider the relatively simple case of the conscious lie. Although there is grudging agreement that a lie can be of benefit to the liar at least temporarily, it is usually considered to be damaging, if not fatally so, both to the lied-to and to the communication system as a whole. Lies do have a number of effects on the system aside from their immediate benefits to the liar, but by no means are all of them as negative as is sometimes assumed.

When the butler says, or used to say: "Mrs. Jones is not at home," her physical presence on the property was not germane to the issue and both the butler and the visitor understood the statement to mean: "We don't want any visitors right now, or at any rate don't want you as a visitor. Go away quietly without making a fuss." It can hardly be classified as a lie any longer, regardless of its truth or falsity as a report on the physical presence of Mrs. Jones. No deception was either intended or achieved, but a face-saving formula had evolved for coding a request that worded differently might have been offensive in that particular society.

Although a society in which no one's statements can ever be taken uncritically at face value has a communication system which can be tiresomely intricate for the decoder, at least it helps to develop an altogether healthy skepticism. A society in which all reports were as honest as the reporter could make them might well engender a dangerous credulity and a tendency to equate the known good faith of the reporter with the correctness and the adequacy of his report. Authority can be, though honest, as misleading as a conscious liar—but one is far less likely to spot the mistakes if one has not learned to doubt the good intentions.

Aside from the value of lies in developing a listener's skills and in forcing him to look independently at the real world instead of blindly depending on the word of someone else, of course, they can also act as social lubricants. Indeed, such is the function of nearly all white lies. This is sometimes seen as intolerable hypocrisy, but this seems to be largely the complaint of a lazy and ill-informed listener, and an expression of the unconscious premise that the alternative to hypocrisy is a Utopia of true good will, rather than enmity differently expressed. There are many social situations where this kind of hypocrisy, suitably masked enmity, is just about as functional as true good will for the immediate moment—although, of course, much less global and not to be depended on outside that particular interaction. One major disadvantage of openly acknowledged enmity and eyeball-to-eyeball confrontations is that all the attention tends to get diverted to them. In casual or peripheral encounters or in purely instrumental encounters they can be great time wasters.

Another useful field for the lie is in the dominance-dependency struggle. Like the Colt revolver, the lie is a great equalizer. Because the situation is defined in such a way that they are not encouraged, or even allowed, to give direct orders to the dominant, the dependent usually rely upon manipulating the information they supply to the dominant, as a means of countercontrol. Most of their orders and requests, in other words, are recoded as statements. These statements may or may not be referentially truthful. In general the higher the proportion of truthful statements, the more effective they are likely to be as commands. But almost any dependent will make use of untruthful statements if sufficiently hard pressed, and even a dependent who is anxious to preserve his reputation for credibility for the sake of future orders and requests is unlikely to feel many qualms about selective reporting.

The dominant also often maintain their control by manipulating information. They may supply considerable amounts of false information in the course of this activity. One could make quite a good case for the statement that all deliberate distortion of information occurs in the course of some sort of dominance-dependency struggle, whether it takes the form of actual lies or of selective reporting of one sort and another. This is because the motivation for distortion is nearly always to influence the attitude and/or future behavior of the other—to control him, in a word. It consists of commands and requests recoded as statements without regard for their referential truth.

This shades over into another weapon often used, that of "meaningless" speech. The *meaningless* is in quotes because this type of speech, while notably lacking in solid referents and, often, coded commands or requests, cannot simply be nonsense syllables strung in random order. It is as bound by the rules of grammar as any other speech and the words it contains, however obscure their usage, are usually duly listed in the dictionary; these elements are typically artfully arranged so that they *seem to* convey more information than they actually do; they are not successful if the "meaninglessness" is casually apparent. Extreme examples are called, interestingly enough, "double talk"—interesting because the lack of referential meaning makes them, if anything, *less* double than ordinary speech. However, the more vague and ambiguous a statement is, the more different meanings can be read into it by the puzzled listener, so that this is the probable explanation of the term.

The fuzziness, the lack of clarity, the meaninglessness of the ordinary political speech, can be an important tool in getting a working majority—and a consensus, however arrived at, may be vital for the well-being or even existence of a nation.

But there is still another type of sequence in which *neither* effective speaking nor effective listening is rewarded, yet which is usually characterized by a real flood of noisy words. For this reason it will be called a *pseudocommunicational event*—not to suggest that no communication takes place, since communication cannot be avoided in any interaction, but to indicate that its primary function is as a public demonstration that no communication is or can be possible between the interacting parties; both are intent on demonstrating that the other party is *ineffective.*

Occasionally the only people involved are the principal parties, and that part of themselves that desires a stable self-image forms the only audience. Commonly, however, one or both are attached to some primary group with a strong stake in preserving its members' attitudes, opinions and future plans intact, regardless of anything that may take place in the interaction. The individual who allowed anything in this particular interaction to affect him in any way, even the most trivial, would be considered by that much to be disloyal, treacherous and unstable.

All the same, since one cannot avoid communicating with someone with whom one is interacting, the two principals are communicating with one another all the time under the surface, and are frequently cooperating as well. Their message is something like the following: "I am a member of *my* group and you are a member of *your* group and neither of us wants it otherwise; if we form a temporary new group it will be dangerous for us both. Let's put on a good show for the folks back home! I will show I can't and won't understand you, and you can do the same for me, since we both know that our own groups could never understand or forgive our reaching an understanding here."

Meaningless speech and the pseudocommunicational event are what most people seem to mean by poor communication. In neither case is the problem primarily one of *faulty techniques;* they both take considerable skill to deploy effectively.

Indeed, even if group-therapy-techniques and other measures aimed at "better communication" were entirely successful, one suspects that the conflict of interests between listener and speaker would soon resurrect all the old problems under a new guise. For what is the purpose of "good communication"? Listeners desire more explicit information from speakers in order to construct more effective speech themselves, and the effectiveness of speech is judged not by the information it imparts but by the extent to which the implicit commands and requests of the speaker are obeyed. The realistic and sensible victim who has had his own communications used against him once or twice understandably retreats into the comparatively safe, if sometimes obscure and thorny, thickets of "poor communication." There is a real basic problem in that the exercise of power is incompatible with good communication, but good communication unrelated to any action or exercise of power is useless.

Questions for Discussion

1. Add a "feedback loop" to the general communication model in the beginning of Chapter 2. Describe how such a loop should affect the communication process.

2. Attendees at professional meetings are often dismayed by their inability to understand the speakers or are bored by the presentations. What speakers' assumptions frequently interfere with communication?

3. Describe and analyze a faulty communication exchange in which you were involved. What went wrong? How might the exchange have been handled differently?

4. Undergraduates at many U.S. colleges have been lobbying for the elimination of all foreign-language course requirements in the curriculum. What benefits might be derived from such study that would improve communication in one's own tongue?

5. An old song title goes "Your lips tell me no, no, but your eyes say yes, yes." Observe and describe a communication situation demonstrating inconsistency between verbal and nonverbal communication, or between message content and style of transmission.

6. As the enormously sucessful show "Hair" demonstrated, hair communicates. But what? Discuss the possible reasons for the depth and breadth of older people's opposition to long hair on young people.

7. An older, traditional professor (but not one to be dismissed lightly) has observed that currently young people constitute the most inarticulate generation in decades. Much of their talk is punctuated with "you know," profanity, and unfinished sentences, all of which reflect an inability to communicate. What do you think about this phenomenon?

8. Describe an example (one for each) of instrumental, consummatory, and incidental communication.

9. Describe the behavior of a person you know (or a situation) demonstrating "defensive behavior" in communication.

10. Describe the behavior of a person you know (or a situation) demonstrating "supportive climate" in communication.

11. The world is busy and confusing, initiating multiple stimuli for everyone. People simplify incoming stimuli and communication in order to handle the confusion. Discuss how they do it.

12. In the operation of communication networks, what seem to be the general relationships of task nature, group leadership, communication, and decision making? What determines "centrality"?

13. Describe situations in which you have been involved that approximate the wheel and all-channel networks.

14. How do communication difficulties contribute to the development of hierarchy? That is, how does hierarchy solve communication problems?

15. In a popular book published some years ago, Vance Packard wrote about *The Status Seekers*. The motivation to seek status is apparently widespread in organizations. How is communication manipulated to protect or promote status?

Short Cases for Discussion

A Bungled Negotiation

As I walked to my 10:00 a.m. meeting in the conference room at company headquarters in New York, it seemed to me that this particular session would be more interesting than the many previous ones. The topic was still very much the same—that of negotiating a six-month joint research working arrangement with an outside firm. In the past, however, they had been all U.S. companies. This morning I was to set up such an agreement with Mr. Sato of Asahi Chemical Company in Japan.

I had been on the project since its inception nearly three years before, and for the past year we had been negotiating similar cooperative working agreements with other chemical firms. Our basic objective was to select those firms whose strength lay in areas other than ours, jointly to divide up the research effort which would be necessary, and to meet regularly to discuss results and make further plans. Although this was only my third year with the company, I already felt that such meetings were fairly routine. This particular meeting, our first with a foreign company, was to have been handled by my supervisor. However, because of unexpected illness, he had called only an hour before and requested that I handle the matter.

All I knew about Mr. Sato was what my boss's secretary had told me: that he was a distinguished-looking, greying executive with the title of "Director of Joint Ventures." Nonetheless, as I walked to the meeting I was confident that I could conduct the meeting effectively and reach an agreement expeditiously.

Mr. Sato was introduced to me by our Tokyo sales manager, who had accompanied him to the United States, and who was responsible for arranging all local meetings for him. Since such arrangements required constant rescheduling and briefings, our Tokyo representative left the meeting shortly after the introductions and promised to return for lunch with us.

Mr. Sato was an impeccably dressed, middle-aged executive—most impressive looking. His command of the English language was not exactly fluent, however, and I did not speak any Japanese, so the meeting progressed somewhat more slowly than usual. Anticipating a time problem, I attempted to get directly to the business at hand. Mr. Sato in contrast did not appear to be similarly worried about the time. The meeting became increasingly frustrating. It often seemed that he did not understand many of the points I was trying to make. Yet, each time he would nod in agreement. Five minutes later, however, he would ask about the same topic as if he had never heard of it. He also questioned me about my supervisor's opinion on nearly every question, and he constantly referred to his boss in Japan as his "superior."

There was one point on which I was unyielding. Many of our past joint programs had lacked direction and close correlation because we had been unable to extract a definite commitment from our co-partners. It seemed that whenever the working agreement was not strictly defined in our meetings, the results were disappointing. Feeling that such problems would be magnified in our relationship with foreign companies because of the cultural and physical distances involved, I pushed to get Sato to commit Asahi Chemical to a definite program. He, however, consistently stated that the company would notify us officially of their commitment only after his return, and he did not wish to be so specific at this meeting. I thought that such an attitude was an attempt to shift the major workload to our side, as many U.S. firms had tried to do, and pressed him further. After all, I thought, the man had a very impressive title on his business card. Certainly he had the little authority which was necessary to consummate the agreement. There seemed to be no good reason for his hesitancy. Yet, as the meeting wore on, he became more withdrawn and, finally, I dropped the matter. We continued our general discussion until 1:30 p.m. at which time our sales manager reappeared for lunch.

After the meeting, I took our Tokyo sales manager aside and expressed my belief that the meeting was a complete bust as far as any future results were concerned. Worse than that, I felt that I had personally affronted Mr. Sato, but could not really determine how. He recommended that I join him and Sato for cocktails that evening to discuss the matter further. At that point, a stiff drink seemed very appealing.

Question

Discuss the communication breakdown in the meeting.

Communications at the Southern Textile Company

Southern Textile Company is a relatively small, community owned, single-plant company located in the south. It manufactures fabric used mainly in men's clothing. A large volume line is a mixture of wool and Dacron for men's suits. Southern Textile does not manufacture the suits and it does no advertising. It sells the fabric to clothing manufacturers.

Scene 1: Executive Committee Meeting Room, Southern Textile Company

J. P. (President): Gentlemen, we have two subjects to discuss today. First, the shortage of Dacron for our textile manufacturing operation, and second, our future management problems. Bob, what's the story with Dacron?

Bob (V.P. Manufacturing): Well, as you know, we sell fabric containing Dacron and wool to various clothing manufacturers. Dacron is widely accepted and in great demand. It seems that everybody wants it, so Du Pont, who owns the trade name, doesn't seem to be able to keep up with production. We just can't get enough, so we checked with a Japanese manufacturing concern and they can supply the material and at a price about 30% lower than Du Pont charges.

J.P.: Well, what's the problem?

Mike (V.P. Marketing): We can't sell anything but Dacron and wool. If we use another name or tell people that the fiber is from Japan, we won't sell any. I think we'd better sell it as Dacron. We've got to maintain the company's reputation.

J. P.: Yes, but suppose its quality is not as good as Dacron?

Bob: But it is; we've run every test. It meets them all. It's really just as good as Dacron.

Mike: I think we should sell it as Dacron and wool. Bob, you can keep making tests to see that it is just as good as Dacron and I'll keep the purchasing agent trying to get Dacron from Du Pont. This could be only a temporary policy in order to meet our responsibilities to our stockholders and customers and to maintain the integrity of the organization. What do you think, J. P.?

J. P.: I'll think about it, and let you know. Okay, let's talk about the second issue. Gentlemen, as you all know, we're all getting along. I'm 65; both of you are approaching my age. We're really a bunch of old fogies.

Bob: Yes, and we have very few younger, capable managers coming along.

J. P.: Right, and that's my concern. We've got to develop our younger men; got to find promising young fellows in their thirties among our people and give extra attention to bringing them along. It's important that we find some loyal and interested younger managers. Jim Kuhn, the personnel director, has told me about the great MBA program up at Old Ivy University. They really give a man training in top-level management policy making. They spend a great deal of time studying and talking with professors, visiting executives, and talking among themselves. John Chappel over at Stevens Textile has sent two of his men up there in the last ten years, and he thought very highly of the results. One of his men is only 40 and is now Executive V.P. of the company. We could send one of our good young men up there at half pay. By working hard he should be able to finish in 18–20 months.

Mike: I think it sounds like a good idea, and I think the man to go is Bill Murphy. He's young, but knowledgeable and hard working. He's the best man I have.

J. P.: That's a good suggestion, Mike. I had also thought of Bill. Send him around next week and I'll talk to him.

Scene 2, Office of the President, one week later

J. P.: Bill, I've called you in to discuss your future and our future. As you know, the top management of this company is all growing old together. In a few years we'll all be gone. Since there have been a number of years in which relatively few managers were hired, we are very concerned about the training of our future replacements. We think you have the ability; we think you have the potential to move up in this organization. What do you think about Southern Textile Company?

Bill (Promising Young Manager): I like it very much here, sir. We have a good organization climate and an enjoyable group of people. Perhaps more important, we have a reputation in the market for quality and integrity.

It means a lot to me. Yes sir, I'm glad to cast my lot with Southern Textile Company, and I look forward to many years here.

J. P.: Fine, Bill. Because we think you can offer a lot, we want to move you into some jobs where you will get good, broad training. Also, we'd like to send you up to the Old Ivy Business School to get your MBA. We'll pay your tuition and half your salary while you're up there. You'd have an unrivaled opportunity to develop yourself and your abilities for management decision-making.

Bill: That seems like an excellent opportunity, sir.

J. P.: It is, Bill, and since the program will cost us about $30,000, making this offer to you reflects our confidence that, in the future, on the basis of your experiences in this program, you'll be able to move right up into the executive suite, here.

Bill: I look forward to it (leaves).

J. P. (to himself): Well, that's taken care of. Now, what do I do about that damned Dacron matter? Use the Japanese stuff or not? If I don't, we're going to lose some customers, that's for sure. And that means some men will be out of work around here.

Scene 3, Old Ivy Business School, 18 months later

Bill: Boy, Frank, this has been an exciting time! I'm sorry it's ending.

Frank (Classmate at Old Ivy): So am I, Bill, although I didn't take to the work as well as you did. I didn't know, and I bet you didn't either, that you were such a scholar. You've really impressed everyone here. You must rank very high in the class.

Bill: Well, the classes and reading were challenging.

Frank: I've told my boss about you, Bill. He says he'd like to hire you. I should keep my big mouth shut; you'll probably get my job.

Bill: Don't worry. I'm happy with Southern Textile. There's a great opportunity there, and it's a fine company. My wife especially likes the fact that it is a stable company located in a nice, small city. No traveling and some real opportunities for activity with the kids. The pay is not the best, but should get better for me.

Frank: I'm glad to hear that. But my boss will be up here next week, and he made me promise to line up a meeting with you. I'd be grateful if you'd talk to him.

Bill: Okay, but it's a waste of time.

Scene 4, Old Ivy Business School, a week later

P. R. (President of B.I.G. Electronics, and an energetic salesman type): Bill, Frank has told me so much about you, I feel I know you already. I've been asking around, and you've made quite an impression on the professors and other students up here.

Bill: It's nice of you to say that.

P. R.: Bill, I'll put it right on the table. I can offer you a terrific opportunity in a dynamic company in one of the fastest growing industries in America.

We need a driver, a go-getter, to keep up with our tremendous expanding market. We want you.

Bill: But I'm happy at Southern Textile.

P. R.: I know, Bill, but we offer growth, challenge, and innovation. Our profits and potential profits are such that we can offer some real financial advantages. I know that money isn't your primary interest, but our position is such that we can jump you from your present salary—it's about $13,000 a year, isn't it?—up to $22,000 right now. In addition, our top management salaries are two to three times what they are at Southern Textile. It'll mean moving and a good bit of traveling, but, most important, I can offer you a chance to join the most exciting management team in America. Think about it.

Bill: Well, okay, I'll consider it.

Scene 5, Office of the President, Southern Textile Company, a month later

Mike: J. P., things have gone just great since you decided to use the Japanese fiber. We've kept the production lines going and sales clicking. Almost wish Du Pont wasn't upping their production. I understand they'll be able to meet all our needs in a couple of months. Well, I've got to run. I hope to close a big deal on Dacron and wool with Botany 500. Let you know how it comes out (leaves).

J. P. (turning to Bill): Bill, how are things going since you've been back from Old Ivy? We're really proud of your record up there. You did a good job. I think your future's really bright here at Southern. In fact, I think you'll see a nice raise in your pay check next month.

Bill: Thanks very much, sir. That's very kind of you, and the job is going well enough. But I have something to tell you. I've decided to accept an offer with B.I.G. Electronics.

J. P. (interrupting in an agitated manner): But you can't do that, Bill! It's not right. It's not ethical. We sent you up to Old Ivy; we spent good money; we made plans.

Bill: I know, sir, but the opportunity looks too great. I owe it to my family to take the financial advantages this will present. The opportunities at B.I.G. Electronics look greater than Southern Textile would ever be able to offer. The president there makes three times what you do, sir.

J. P.: Bill, have you no sense of loyalty, have you no ethics? You can't just leave us in the lurch.

Bill: Loyalty and ethics have their price. As far as I am concerned, B.I.G. Electronics is paying the price.

Question

Analyze the communications of the President of Southern Textile and of Bill Murphy (and any others in this case that appear interesting).

Chapter 3

Organizational Influence

A central aspect of a manager's role is to "influence" others to do certain things. In this chapter we consider the process of influence in interpersonal relations from four perspectives:

Influence as the presence of others.
Influence as basic interpersonal attitudes.
Influence as appeal to human needs.
Influence as social exchange.

Management is concerned mainly with intentional influence. Nonetheless, there are some factors that influence behavior which are less susceptible to rational control. We first consider these types briefly, then move on to the more controllable processes.

The Presence of Others: Social Facilitation

With other creatures, man shares an apparently deep-seated attribute: we are all social. The mere presence of others seems to affect us. Consider the following (from Zajonc, 1966):

A single ant in the presence of earth commences to dig. While alone, he moves a substantial volume of earth (232 gm per six hours). Yet, when another ant is introduced into the same enclosure, the first ant works even harder (765 gm per six hours). When a third ant is included, the first ant continues at the same pace (778 gm per six hours). Finally, when the original ant's companions are removed, he falls back to his initial level (182 gm per six hours). Note that the ants do not appear to help one another. They merely work individually in the same area, but the presence of others seems to improve the single ant's performance of his appointed task.

A lone cockroach can learn the path through a maze and thus escape from unwanted light into protective darkness rather quickly (four minutes on the tenth trial). A pair learns more slowly (six minutes) and a group of three even more slowly (ten minutes). The presence of others seems to impede the cockroach's learning.

Goldfish are even cleverer than cockroaches. An isolated goldfish demonstrates a similar learning curve in mastering a maze (35 minutes on fourth trial). Yet, when he has learned the way, he can apparently impart his knowledge, because ignorant companions introduced into the tank with him learn more quickly than he did (seven minutes for group of four on fourth trial).

Research with humans produces similar results. The presence of others tends to improve performance of tasks that the subject knows well. This is the familiar heightening of a beneficial tension felt by a well-rehearsed actor or trained athlete before a large audience. In contrast, an audience seems to interfere with someone's learning a new task. If the learning group is composed of equally ignorant members, the presence of others seems to interfere with individual learning. However, if one member of the group is knowledgeable about the task, the ignorant members learn more quickly.

Explaining these human reactions in terms of human needs does seem plausible, because most people strive for esteem and fear ridicule. Yet something more fundamental is involved. The presence of others facilitates the dominant response: correct behavior on well-learned tasks; mistakes when trying to learn. Thus, the presence of others may aid or hinder performance, depending on the task and the characteristics of the others.

Influence from Basic Interpersonal Attitudes

As indicated in the preceding chapter, men are time bound. Attitudes derived while maturing are deep-seated, quite stable, and tend to affect present relations. Thus, attitudes regarding trust, autonomy, initiative, industry, identity, intimacy, and generativity developed during the stages of growth are part of each person's unique personality (Erikson, 1950). Although each man is unique, certain interpersonal attitudes and problems are nonetheless discernible and general.

Attitudes Toward Authority
Man faces two big problems when he comes into contact with others. The first is the problem of authority relationships—commonly referred to as the pecking order. Based on their authority orientations, there are apparently three kinds of human beings (Schutz, 1955):

1. Dependents, people who have a pronounced feeling of comfort in having others be leaders, or in having rules and procedures.
2. Counterdependents, people with pronounced feelings of discomfort toward other people in authority, or toward rules and regulations.
3. Independents, people with lesser feelings on both dimensions, who have the ability to watch real people without stereotyping them.

If a person falls in one of the first two groups—either accepting or rejecting *all* authority systems—he begins to develop certain other deeper views of man. For example, the man who on the surface trusts all bosses as being helpful may cling to this comforting view, but since the world is not really like this, he may also develop an underlying distrust of authority systems. He will vacillate between the extremes of submissiveness and rebelliousness. The same is true of the compulsive counterdependent. Believing that all authority figures and systems are bad in spite of the fact that there are some good leaders and organizations, he too may vacillate between wanting more direction (submissiveness) and hating all direction (rebelliousness).

Attitudes Toward Intimacy

An additional problem which all men face is that of intimacy. Again there are three classes, with differing views of man. The first (personal) cannot rest until he has stabilized a relatively high degree of intimacy with others. The second (counterpersonal) tends to avoid any intimacy with others and to be uncomfortable at any show of feelings, whether it be hostility or affection. The third (independent) has a realistic view of other men. As in relation to authority, those people who have strong tendencies to be either personal or counterpersonal are frequently destructively competitive, exploit relations with other people, and are deeply distrustful.

Implications for Behavior

When a person joins an organization, he may reveal himself to be crippled in his ability to work with others and solve problems because he has one of four stereotyped notions about authority and intimacy: dependent, counterdependent, personal, or counterpersonal. These are his fixed orientations about how he should treat others and how they will treat him. Some of these orientations are accurate, in that the belief represents what is "out there"; others are wrong, in that they are distortions. In the latter case, they are perpetuations of past maladaptive defense mechanisms, as if the person were learning the wrong lesson over and over again.

We can of course propose what this man *ought* to be like (and perhaps can be helped to be like through therapy and training). He ought to be more capable of looking at himself, other people, and relationships for what they *are*. He should not be so prone to engage in rebellion, submission, destructive competition, or exploitation of others. In addition to causing unhappy stress, such behavior may interfere with work and hinder the ability of an organization to move toward its goal.

Whether people's orientations are realistic or unrealistic, they affect behavior mainly below the level of intention—unintentionally, nonrationally (not "irrationally"), perhaps even as a reflex. For example, Leary (1957) has suggested a scheme for classifying interpersonal behavior along two axes: dominance-submission and affection-hostility. He developed 16 categories of behavior which fit into this scheme. Point 1 in Exhibit 3-1 illustrates a strong affection but dominance toward the other person—"smotherly love"; point 2 describes hateful submissiveness; and so on.

What has been suggested is that to each behavioral act of one person toward

Exhibit 3-1   Classification of Interpersonal Behavior

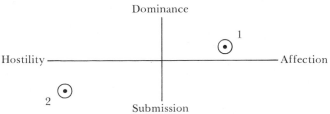

another, the latter responds with a complementary act and attitude. Along the vertical axis—dominance/submission—acts of one kind tend to evoke opposites: submissive behavior evokes domination; domination evokes obedience. Along the horizontal axis—affection/hostility—acts of one kind tend to evoke the same kind of act: seeking friendship evokes affection, acting hostile evokes hostility.

In short, one person's interpersonal mechanisms tend to "pull" a complementary reflex from the other. Of course, the process is not as simple or mechanical as we have described it, because the behavior of a particular person will not only be automatic but will also reflect the time, the place, and his needs. Thus, the individual's definition of the situation or his own personality will influence his response to a domineering act by another. That is, he may be more likely to give a passive or submissive response (be well out on the submission axis) if the domineering other is his father or his boss. In contrast, he will probably give a competitive response (probably just above zero on the dominance axis) to a domineering friend or peer.

Even this short description of the interpersonal reflex process gives some indication of the dynamic tension in social relationships. There are always forces operating to modify the terms of exchange of behavior and attitudes. This has important implications for the willingness of two persons to work together cooperatively. Such cooperation demands some harmony in their perceptions of the work situation, and such concurrence is influenced by the exchange of attitudes and behavior.

For example, Newcomb (1953) has pointed out that we tend to agree with those we like and like those with whom we agree. We also tend to disagree with those we dislike and dislike those with whom we disagree. Newcomb has formalized these ideas into a theoretical model that summarizes many of the concepts in this area. (See Exhibit 3-2.) Two persons (A and B) are engaged in interaction about one or more objects (X), which can be ideas, machines, or people. The arrows are A's Attitudes Toward B and X, and B's Attitudes Toward A and X.

Exhibit 3-2   Two-Person Interaction

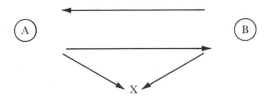

The set of attitudes which A and B have about each other and about X constitutes a system of interrelated parts. This set of attitudes is a system because the parts are interdependent: when one part changes, other parts are likely to show compensatory changes. In fact, there may be movement toward certain patterns of attitudes that are balanced or in equilibrium. These balanced states would be:

1. Mutual attraction between A and B, along with agreement about X.
2. Mutual rejection between A and B, along with disagreement about X.

All other states are unstable states and will tend toward one or another of the equilibrium patterns. For example, if A and B like each other and have good relations, disagreement about X will tend to be resolved into some compromise on which they can agree. They move toward the first balanced state above. In contrast, if A and B dislike each other but agree about X, there may be some pressure to move toward either of the equilibrium states—and it is difficult to predict which.

Influence as Appeal to Needs

In Chapter 1 we considered man's hierarchy of needs. If you are going to influence another, this is what you have to work with. You must influence through appeal to one or more of these needs. If you are holding a gun to my head, and if the gun is loaded, and if you communicate a willingness to fire, the chances are that I will do what you ask. The odds are stacked in your favor. But certainly history demonstrates many people in similar situations who have chosen *not* to obey. The implication is clear. The influence process depends upon the follower as much or more than it depends upon the leader. It is a decision by the follower whether to respond or not. Perhaps he does not have much choice, and perhaps it is not always consciously considered, but it is still his decision whether or not to go along. Therefore, what is the process of "followership," the reasons why a person would allow himself to be influenced?

Exhibit 3-3 illustrates a continuum of such reasons related to the need hierarchy. At the bottom of the influence continuum, the follower has no understanding of the *reasons* for directives; agreement is irrelevant and participation nonexistent. At the top end of the continuum, the follower understands and agrees because he participated in the formulation of the directive.

Exhibit 3-3 Influence Processes

Hierarchy of Needs	Influence Process		Influencer's Style
Self-actualization	Self-determination	↑	Abdicative
Competence, achievement	Joint determination		Democratic
Power, autonomy	Rational agreement	Understanding of reason for desired behavior	Collaborative
Esteem, prestige	Rational faith		Persuasive
Social, affiliation	Blind faith		Manipulative
Safety, security	Tradition		Authoritarian
Physiological	Fear		Autocratic

There are six fundamental reasons why people respond to influence: fear, tradition, blind faith, rational faith, rational agreement, and self-determination.

Influence by Fear

Across the span of human history and in most societies even today, fear is one of the most common influence systems. Fear of being hurt physically or psychologically has long characterized families, tribes, armies, and kingdoms. In business organizations, fear often takes the form of anxiety about losing a job. In the early nineteenth century during the fledgling industrial revolution, managers were told to pay only subsistence wages, to pay only enough to allow workers to obtain minimum food and shelter. Paying subsistence wages enabled managers to maximize their use of fear because employees were always on the knife edge of starvation. Because they had not been able to put any money aside, they would begin to starve immediately upon dismissal. Employers could appeal very immediately to insecurity and the needs for physiological necessities.

Under influence by fear, it makes no difference whether subordinates understand the reasons for directives or agree with them. Agreement or disagreement is simply irrelevant. All that the influencer cares about is whether subordinates understand what they are supposed to do. Coercion will lay less heavily on subordinates if they understand and agree with the directive, but understanding and agreement do not fundamentally alter the situation.

A prominent British government minister recently made a speech in which he bemoaned the apparent decline of fear as a motivator in British industry. He felt that somehow people just do not work hard enough because they do not fear loss of their jobs. Perhaps social legislation, full employment, and governmental guarantees against starvation have reduced the ability of the British employer to utilize fear. Fear as a motivator at work also declines during full employment when other jobs are available. Much the same thing is probably also true in the United States. Of course the elimination of job-loss fear has been a prime purpose of government and labor unions for many years. Nonetheless, managers from time to time may wistfully wish for the simplicity of using influence by fear.

In spite of its attractiveness, however, fear as a device has one great handicap: it is expensive. A leader must monitor his followers closely to see that they are doing what they are told, and that they are not departing from their instructions. If noncompliance is detected, the leader must punish in order to maintain the follower's fear. This process of policing and punishing can be exceedingly expensive. Hitler's Minister of Economics, Albert Speer, observes in his memoirs (1970) that he made a mistake in using slave labor in some Nazi manufacturing plants. Of course he did—he was imprisoned for twenty years on the charge—but his conclusion is on economic grounds.

A study of a slave-manned bomb manufacturing plant (Kogan, 1947) demonstrates what Speer meant, showing the sabotage that can be accomplished by resistant workers even under conditions most oriented around fear. They hindered production by withholding the simplest personal judgments and persistently asking for detailed instructions on what to do next. In addition, they were able to sabotage production by improperly fitting the bomb fuses. The sabotage was evident only when the weapon was dropped; duds were numerous. Their insubordination was impossible for the guards to detect unless they stood directly over the workers. Therefore, in order to influence the slaves to behave as desired, it became necessary to increase their probability of being caught—and this required more guards. The plant soon had almost as many guards as slaves. It would have been more sensible to eliminate the slaves and assign the guards to the work.

Most applications of fear suffer from the expense of monitoring performance and applying sanctions. It is essential that the influencer maintain the conviction that he will detect and punish transgressions. The crime syndicate loan shark must convey to his clients the mixed message of absolute honesty and commitment to the contract—in both directions. The potential deadbeat must know with certainty that retribution will follow. And in law enforcement it appears that a high probability of detection and a certainty of modest punishment is a greater deterrence to crime than low probability of detection and uncertain severe punishment. The problem is that detection is more expensive than punishment.

In addition, fear seems to be self limiting. Under prolonged stress of fear, people tend to lose their sensitivity to it. Inaction, indifference, or even acceptance of death may be the response to unlikely rewards and likely punishment over a period of time.

The use of fear as a managerial tool can be inverted in many modern organizations. A history of IBM (Rogers, 1969) says that Thomas Watson, Sr., made a conscious effort to eliminate the use of fear in management's relations with blue-collar and clerical workers, while encouraging fear of ridicule and dismissal as a primary motivator of managerial personnel. Because of their high pay and organizational prestige, middle managers may be particularly subject to fear. In addition, they have no union to represent their interests, and usually no due-process appeal procedures.

A study of the advertising business (Bensman, 1967) suggests that management's sensitivity to fear depends upon age and career stage. Little fear exists at low levels because pay is relatively poor and because interorganizational mobility is accepted practice. Being dismissed is not a serious blot on a young account executive's record. But managers and professionals aged 30 to 45, the period of greatest earnings and living expenses, become anxious and receptive to motivation through fear. They are locked in because it is unlikely that they can move to new positions with equal pay and because their life style depends on substantial income. In time, however, many manage to save enough so that the power of fear declines. If an executive lasts in advertising until age 45 or so, he has probably accumulated enough capital that he can work elsewhere for less money. In the past, some dismissed or disillusioned older advertising men went into teaching. The modest pay, along with their substantial savings, enabled them to maintain their homes in suburbia without too much sacrifice. Such financial and job mobility is of course affected by general economic conditions and job opportunities.

Perhaps the most dramatic reversal in the use of fear occurred in the United States Army. The "new" army attempted to improve life for enlisted men, preparatory to converting to an all-volunteer army. The use of threats and punishment by officers was discouraged. In Vietnam in the late 1960s and early 1970s, enlisted men in substantial numbers turned to fear as a control mechanism to keep their superiors in line. Threats of violence and actual "fraggings" (tossing a fragmentation grenade into an officer's quarters) all but completely reversed the balance of power and fear in the field. An army judge (Linden, 1972) argued that once an officer is intimidated by even the threat of fragging, he is useless to the military because he can no longer carry out orders. Through intimidation and scare stories, fragging became so influential that virtually all officers had to take into account the possibility of retaliation before giving an order to the men under them.

Influence by Tradition

Tradition has probably been the most common influence mechanism in human history. One obeys the king because he is the king, or because he is a representative of God, or as in ancient Egypt, because he *is* God. St. Paul expressed the basis for such influence in Romans 13:1, "Let everyone submit himself to the ruling authorities, for there exists no authority not ordained by God." Response is quasi-automatic, almost unconscious, the kind of habitual obedience that is the intent of close-order drill learned during the first weeks in military training (Timasheff, 1938). Perhaps tradition starts out as mainly fear, and perhaps there is even some implicit recognition of the power of authority, but the response becomes institutionalized and inculcated into the class structure and ideology of the society (Bendix, 1956). One responds out of respect for one's betters or because there is some natural social order that is customary. Adolf Eichmann obeyed because his culture had trained him to respond without question to an authoritarian directive.

Responding to traditional authority is not simply habit, of course. In the United States Marines, it draws on the follower's internalized sense of responsibility to all those who fought at Montezuma, Tripoli, Tarawa, or Vietnam; the young private is part of them, and he would feel guilty if he did not do his duty. Thus, the great advantage of a tradition-based influence system is that it offers positive motivation instead of the negative orientation of fear. It says, in effect, "respect authority, be obedient, and do what you're told—and if you do, you will be rewarded with acceptance into the community." Such acceptance means security and affiliation.

The submergence of self into the group for short periods of time during games, while singing in a choir, marching in a protest demonstration, even at times in military drill, is attractive to many people. A deeply traditional, ascriptive society may extend this to all existence. It can offer the greatest degree of certainty that is possible in human society, because it specifies who has authority, defines each person's obligations, and relieves most people of much onerous decision making. In effect, a tradition-based system can perpetuate childhood. As Fromm (1941) pointed out, and as Vroom (1964) later documented, many people find such a state most attractive. For such people, the influence mechanism is not even perceived as imposed; it is absorbed and integrated into their personality so thoroughly that they feel that they are exercising free choice. Influence and control is highest when it is least apparent.

Tradition as the basis for obedience was commonly assumed in nineteenth-century management practice, when a firm's management structure was closely allied with the class structure of the society (Fayol, 1949). It was assumed that lowers should respond to uppers. At first, those higher up were assigned certain obligations for the well-being of people lower down, but this ethic was gradually dropped in favor of Social Darwinism, in which success was rewarded with lesser responsibility. Yet the assumption remained: inferiors should respond to their betters. The manager should create esprit de corps, but fundamentally subordinates should respond because that is their obligation. Under this influence system, as with fear, it makes no difference whether the follower understands the reason for the directive or agrees, and he certainly has not participated in formulation of the directive.

Although we Americans like to think of ourselves as egalitarian, we do have many superior-subordinate relationships which attempt to program obedience: parent-child, teacher-student, employer-employee, and all have in common some traditional feeling that within certain limits the subordinate will respond to the superior's suggestions. The great Russian leader Nicolai Lenin observed at the beginning of Communist rule in Russia that the Russian economy was built upon fear, and that this had grave defects. What Russia needed in 1919, according to Lenin, was "Soviet Americanism"; and what Lenin meant by Soviet Americanism was his idea that American workers tended to do what they were told at work, and tended to work consistently without being policed because they expected to. In 1938 the president of a large American corporation observed that the average worker expected to do what he was told within certain limits (Barnard, 1938). Within his "zone of indifference" he was willing to do as he was directed. Those limits have probably narrowed in the last thirty years. We are less willing than we once were automatically to respond to authority and do what we are told. A decline in respect for authority in American society may be reflected in a decline in response to an authority figure just because he is an authority figure.[1]

Lenin thought that the United States was characterized by a high degree of respect for authority. Actually, this country has probably demonstrated less respect for authority than most nations. As far back as the early colonies, and as illustrated by Alexis de Tocqueville in the early nineteenth century, foreign observers have commented on the anti-authority climate in America. Children were disrespectful to parents, buildings were torn down not long after completion, and a secular religion of progress ruled the land. Common explanations for this situation include (1) our youth as a nation and the intention to forge a new history rather than just continuing the English past, (2) our distrust of central government, (3) the shortage of labor which provided opportunity, and (4) the availability of land. In the early United States, a son did not have to live indefinitely with a stern father, waiting to take over the farm. The boy could leave, and he did—for a job in the city or his own piece of land. The myth of the frontier and the man with the gun had enough reality to help shape attitudes toward authority in the developing nation.

Thus, prevailing attitudes toward authority and responsiveness to tradition are cultural phenomena. Two examples:

1. In 1959 a survey of German and American mothers (*Newsweek,* Sept. 23, 1968) asked them to rank ten favorable attributes in their children in order of desirability. The list included such characteristics as sociability, creativity, obedience, popularity, and so on. German mothers ranked obedience first. U.S. mothers ranked obedience last; desirable, but not as much as social compatibility, respect for others' rights, and self-confidence, among others. (Some observers have suggested that since 1959, we got what we asked for.) A current survey

[1] A Harris poll comparing public respect for the leadership of major American institutions in 1966 and 1971 demonstrated significant declines in just five years (*Philadelphia Inquirer,* Oct. 25, 1971).

might rank obedience higher (in reaction to perceived over-permissiveness), but its low ranking in 1959 seems consistent with America's past attitudes toward authority.

2. Uri Bronfenbrenner (1970) offers insights into the United States as compared with the Soviet Union. He probed teen-agers' willingness to engage in antisocial or anti-authority behavior (such as cheating on examinations, breaking street lights, stealing public property, etc.), under three conditions:

    a) when teachers or parents were to be told of the act.

    b) when only their friends were to be told.

    c) when no one but themselves was to know.

Soviet girls indicated virtually no willingness to engage in anti-authority behavior under any circumstances. In the United States, young girls were much less willing to engage in such behavior than were boys. Soviet boys were willing to perform these acts if no one was to know, much less if teachers/parents were to be told, and *least* if friends were to know. The Soviet culture, reinforced by fear or tradition, holds such behavior in low regard. Such is apparently not the case in the United States. American boys were *most willing* to engage in anti-authority behavior when their friends were to know—*even more than if no one were to know.* Apparently such public behavior brings admiration and prestige because of its bravado.

Note that in the traditional system the follower responds to the leader's position. In the army the officer is identified by his uniform and his insignia. One obeys the order, regardless of the characteristics of the person giving the order, because the position is respected. Whether the officer is tall or short, fat or thin, black or white is irrelevant; the follower responds to the position. This impersonality of influence and its associated stability and predictability constitute the great advantages of tradition as a means of influence.

Influence by Blind Faith

Influence through blind faith is a kind of Alexander or Napoleon syndrome. One responds to the great leader who has "charisma" (Weber, 1964). In the past, charisma was considered a gift of God, a gift of grace, or magical powers that were given to a few favored men. Only fools would not respond to the charismatic leader. But what is a charismatic leader today? Have we not moved away from the ignorance and superstition of earlier blind followers? Or have we just shifted the source of authority from magic to psychology? Consider the following: (a) Name a person who best symbolizes the concept of hero. That is, what contemporary person best represents the concept for you? He may be living or deceased, but contemporary with your lifetime. (b) Why? What two or three characteristics cause you to name this person? Exhibit 3-4 summarizes the responses of a number of groups of executives, managers, and students to these questions. Older executives tend to name Eisenhower or Truman, sometimes MacArthur or Churchill. Students most frequently cite John F. Kennedy. The transition is clearly seen in a group of young managers who respond equally with Eisenhower and Kennedy.

We might expect people of different ages to name different people. After all, Eisenhower is not really contemporary with college students. But it is interesting to see the differences in their reasons. All groups admire courage, and attribute this characteristic to their admired leader. The older executives also admire the ability to make a decision. Young managers admire integrity

Exhibit 3-4   Admired Heroes

Groups Responding	Mean Age	Persons Cited Most By Each Group	Attributes Cited Most By Each Group
(1) Business executives (n = 70)	42	Eisenhower, Truman	Courage, decisiveness
(2) Career army officers and managers (n = 42)	43	Eisenhower, MacArthur	Leadership, decisiveness
(3) Middle-level business managers (n = 51)	33	Eisenhower, Kennedy	Conviction, courage, integrity
(4) Graduate business students (n = 84)	23	Kennedy	Courage, conviction, perseverance
(5) Undergraduate college students (n = 203)	19	Kennedy	Courage, individuality, drive
(6) Suburban high school students (n = 33)	17	Many, including Kennedy, Jimi Hendrix, M. L. King, and others	Courage, independence
(7) Urban high school students (n = 37)	16	Many, including Kennedy, M. L. King, Malcolm X, and others	Compassion, concern, helpfulness

and conviction, belief in a cause. College students tend to cite individuality. Suburban high school students point to independence.

Each group attributes to their admired persons characteristics they themselves would like to have. High executives would like to be decisive; it is a critical part of their lives—the ability to make a decision and then to go on without being overly concerned about whether or not it was a mistake. One corporation vice-president in this survey suggested it was precisely this pressure for decisiveness that made him sometimes wonder why he had not remained a $15,000 per year accountant.

Younger middle-level managers encounter difficulty in reconciling their personal and organizational objectives, so they admire a person who believes in what he is doing, who demonstrates integrity of self and conviction in his cause. A young (32) manager stated that he was pleased with his income and status, but after five years he wondered just how important it was to get a box of "Admiral Zoom" cereal on every breakfast table.

College undergraduates are in a process of breaking out of the mass society characterizing education in America: They are also at the stage of self-identification in preparation for dealing with life. Young managers admire John Kennedy for his conviction, but undergraduates admire him for his individuality.

White, suburban high school students are obviously longing for independence, freedom from mother, dad, and a stifling society. They name a great many people, but most project a desired image of independence. In contrast, poor black and Puerto Rican students in an urban high school seem to admire the leader who offers concern, understanding, and compassion—attributes they find lacking in their environment.

Thus, people respond to the leader who has characteristics they admire, to the person who is a super model of what they would like to be. Perhaps most fundamentally, they respond out of strong emotional attachment, even love for the leader in whom they have blind faith. The relationship is personal rather than general, because charisma is not simply an attribute of the leader but the fit between his characteristics and the follower's needs. Lawrence of Arabia possessed charisma for the Arabs in World War I, but his dramatic, stylistic behavior offered no appeal to postwar Britons who did not support him in his bid for political office. In contrast, Winston Churchill's brand of charisma was not felt widely until Great Britain faced extinction in 1940; then his personal attributes matched people's concerns. These attributes became less relevant with the end of the European war in 1945, and Churchill was voted out of office.

Seventy years ago management literature asserted that one was born either a manager or a follower. Either one had natural leadership abilities or he did not. There is less belief in this argument now, because charismatic, natural leaders seem all too rare. They do exist in business, of course, but we cannot depend on their being in abundant supply. Business and government simply require more managers than there are charismatic people. It is now believed that people can develop into effective managers through education and experience. Indeed, in highly structured bureaucracies, personal charisma might even be a handicap in getting ahead. Nonetheless, business still seems to want attributes associated with "natural leadership" and "command presence": witness one finding that starting salaries for men over six feet tall were $1000 per year more than for men under that magic height!

Some great leaders combine different influence techniques. General Patton was not above using fear, if necessary. A believer in tradition, he wore the uniform and the emblems of a traditional position, but he was also a charismatic leader who generated faith among his men. Such charismatic leaders tend to be individualistic. They demonstrate unique styles and affectations (Patton's ivory-handled revolvers, John Kennedy's refusal to wear an overcoat or hat, Robert Kennedy's touseled hair) as a method of distinguishing themselves.

The basic difference between traditional and blind-faith influence systems is impersonality as opposed to personality. Classical management theory rests upon the traditional model—an hierarchical structure in which authority resides in positions, and interpersonal relations follow the chain of command. From this model flow the so-called principles of unity of command, chain of command, and not bypassing intermediate levels when communicating. The assumed organization shape is the pyramid. (See Exhibit 3-5.) In contrast, the implied shape in the charismatic organization is more ambiguous.

The charismatic leader influences people through his personality, not his position. Therefore, he endeavors to bring himself in direct interaction with many people throughout the organization. He bypasses the chain of command because he wants to tie people to himself, not to his lieutenants. Franklin Roosevelt was often criticized as being a poor manager because his assignment of duties was sloppy, and he evidenced little respect for the structure of government. He would personally contact people throughout the system and give them projects unknown to their peers or superiors. He cultivated individual, personalized relationships, not organizational, impersonal positions (Schlesinger, 1959). Gen. Robert Johnson of the Johnson & Johnson Company demonstrated

Exhibit 3-5   Authority Structure and Type of Influence

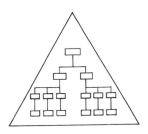

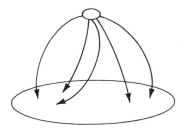

Tradition-Based Organization   Blind-Faith-Based Organization

quite similar behavior. He would descend on his plants unannounced, bypass the resident manager in charge, and move directly to individuals at various levels whom he cultivated personally. Such behavior can be upsetting to organizationally minded people, but it can create a sense of identification with the top and a willingness to sacrifice which can be very powerful. It may also be more effective in generating change than fear or tradition-based systems.

Nonetheless, influencing through fear, tradition, or blind faith are all essentially authoritarian situations. The leader tells the follower to do something; the follower responds either because he fears being punished or hurt, because he feels a responsibility to obey authority figures and do his part in society, or because he loves the authority figure and believes in his abilities. But in all three of these instances it is essentially one-way authoritarian communication. Thus followers respond to charismatic influence (at least for a while) without questioning whether specific directives are in their interests. They neither understand the reasons for the orders nor is their agreement relevant. Nevertheless, there is a difference between blind faith and fear or tradition because the power of the charismatic leader is not without limit. His authority depends in part on performance. If he has a series of failures, his charisma will fade away, and no longer will he have the power to generate acceptance by his subordinates. In this case he would have to use fear, or convert his influence process into something perhaps farther up the continuum of Exhibit 3-3.

The fear, tradition, and blind-faith influence processes all draw upon what Timasheff (1938) called the power phenomenon. He suggested that most people are characterized by a predisposition to submission. Whether this is instinctual or learned behavior is not clear—is it derived from the ancient experience of the species, going back to the primeval dominance of the tyrant ape (Morris, 1966), or does it reflect child-rearing patterns (Erikson, 1950)? The essential argument, however, is that most men have an automatic, unconscious, and hypnotic response to dominators just because they are dominant. Certain rituals, symbols, tones of voice, etc., reinforce the dominator and cue inhibiting forces which supposedly block out the parts of the rational mind that might interfere with automatic response. Whether because of this process, security from freedom, or avoidance of pain, authority-oriented influence systems based on fear, tradition, or charisma have been most common. Some political observers suggest that American society has so matured that our leaders must move beyond the old uses of fear, tradition, and blind faith to more rational explanations in attaining agreement from voters. This remains to be seen, but greater education does tend to undermine the use of these authoritarian influence styles.

Influence by Rational Faith

If we could count the number of influence incidents in modern organizations, especially among managers and professionals, we would probably find the most common influence process to be rational faith. Followers respond because, on the basis of evidence that he has knowledge and ability, they believe the leader knows what he is talking about. This is similar to your relationship with a doctor. You can make a fairly rational judgment that he is qualified, from the diplomas, license, and certificates on his office walls. It is even possible to learn about the quality of his medical school and residency hospital. You can ask friends about their experiences with him. In general, then, you can decide that he knows what he is talking about and that he has your interests at heart. Nonetheless, however rational your decision about the man, your response to his specific suggestions is based pretty much on faith. You probably cannot even read his handwriting on the prescription form, much less know precisely how the medicine will help you. In most cases you must simply accept it.

For a business example of this process, consider the following incident:

> A young staff specialist is hired to provide expertise to a number of production managers. Initially, the only influence process available to the specialist is persuasion—gaining the rational agreement of the managers. To be effective he prepares elaborate, clear presentations (even rehearsing with a colleague to anticipate any questions). By data, logic, and argument, he attempts to gain the agreement of his superiors. After a year of this kind of relationship, he goes one day to talk with one of the managers. An hour has been reserved for the presentation. He arrives and begins his pitch. After a couple of minutes, however, the busy manager interrupts: "I'm just too busy to go over this. We'll *do whatever you want to do.*"

The manager is presumably being rational, but he is also acting on faith. The rationality is based on his prior experience with the specialist; the staff man's track record is good. His past advice has helped the production department, so the manager decides that he is competent and concerned. Nonetheless, in accepting the latest proposal without detailed examination, the manager is acting on faith that it is as good as earlier ones.

This process of influence by acceptance of the person is widespread because it is time saving, and because it recognizes that authority based on knowledge must be reconciled with authority based on position. The man with certain knowledge impresses the man with position; the latter accepts the former's influence. The specialist derives great satisfaction from this situation, because it appeals to his needs for esteem, competence, power, and achievement—a potent combination. Of course, danger threatens the line manager in this relationship. He may unwittingly abdicate his effective authority and control to the specialist because he does not have time to question the specialist's ideas, or even because he loses his ability to do so.

Influence based on rational faith is perhaps an unstable state. Disappointing results undermine the faith, so the influencer is forced to resort to other processes.

Influence by Rational Agreement

Influence on the basis of rational agreement is implicit in the foregoing discussion, because it is closely related. One obeys because he understands the reason why the action is necessary, and agrees that it is the proper thing to do. The leader has been persuasive, able to explain rationally why an activity must be performed. Obviously this process consumes more time than any of the influence means discussed so far. The explanations imply substantial discussion, and even two-way conversations, in contrast to the one-way broadcasts characterizing authoritarian styles.

In trying to convince or persuade the follower, a leader is paying a compliment to the follower. In effect he is saying, "I think you have the ability and the knowledge to understand what I am asking, and I respect you enough to take the time to explain." Thus, the follower may feel that he is being treated in a somewhat more adult manner. The follower's needs for esteem and competence are at least appealed to. The only power he possesses, however, is the power of nonagreement, which would confront the influencer with a dilemma: a different argument or a different influence process.

The widespread existence of this influence style, even at high management levels, is well illustrated by the words of President Harry S Truman (Rossiter, 1956): "And people talk about the powers of a President, all the powers that a Chief Executive has, and what he can do. Let me tell you something—from experience!

"The President may have a great many powers given to him in the Constitution and may have certain powers under certain laws which are given to him by the Congress of the United States; but the principal power that the President has is to bring people in and try to persuade them to do what they ought to do without persuasion. That's what I spend most of my time doing. That's what the powers of the President amount to."

Influence by Joint and Self Determination

Near the end of the sad riot at Columbia University in 1968, the police bodily dragged students out of the administration building which they had been occupying. Amid the kicking, screaming, and swearing, one young female student in the grip of an officer exclaimed, "God, how exciting; that's the first time I've ever felt part of anything in my life!" Her words are testimony to the power and satisfaction that people find in collective action, where they perceive that they have participated in determining the group's actions.

Since the imaginative and influential research of Lewin (1948), most students of organizational behavior have come to accept that a person's participation in setting a goal increases the likelihood that he will act to insure that the goal is met. Presumably, when the follower has participated in determining what is to be done, he should understand and agree that a certain course of action is necessary and proper. In this participation, some quite high-level needs on the part of the follower are involved. He exercises some power and he has an opportunity to express himself and his abilities. Ideally, there is voluntary implementation through this participation and determination.

If practicing managers are less enthusiastic about participation (Haire et al., 1966), it is partly because of the difficulty of applying such an influence mechanism and of creating the sense of virtual ownership that motivates the employee to participate and contribute. In addition, even more than rational agreement, this influence style can be very time consuming. The leader also runs a grave risk of abdicating his authority by turning over control of the followers to the followers themselves.

Application of Influence

Note that we have not said that any one basis of followership is better than another. Fear, tradition, and faith have the great advantage of being quick. The follower should respond immediately to a curt directive. Nonetheless, they have drawbacks: fear is offensive to many, and it can be expensive to maintain the necessary police mechanism; tradition may be suffering because of declining respect for positional authority; faith suffers from the drawback that people who can generate this emotional response are rare.

Influence through rational agreement has some great attractions, but it is time consuming, and the leader is not always sure that he has the right reasons or that he can explain in a rational way. He may simply feel that something must be done, and this feeling can be difficult to convey. Participation is also very time consuming, and what is attractive to one follower is not always attractive to everyone. Not every person wants to take the time to participate in solving what he may really see as the leader's problems.

Each of the influence processes discussed is logical. Because they all appeal to certain human needs, they all can work; this is the central feature of influencing behavior. If the influencer works out a consistent plan, any of the techniques might work. Whether the plan chosen actually will work depends on the people and situation. For example, French and Raven (1959) defined the basis of power as the relationship between a person subject to power and a person exercising that power. They specify five power bases:

1. Reward power, based on a subordinate's perception that a superior has the ability to mediate rewards for him.
2. Coercive power, based on a subordinate's perception that a superior has the ability to mediate punishments for him.
3. Legitimate power, based on internalized values which dictate that there is a legitimate right to influence and an obligation to accept this influence.
4. Referent power, based on the desire of a subordinate to identify with a superior. The identification can be maintained if he behaves, believes, or perceives as the superior does.
5. Expert power, based on a subordinate's perception that a leader has special knowledge or expertise.

Student (1968) related the categories to eight production performance measures in a manufacturing firm.

Referent power was related to five of the measures.

Expert power was related to four of the measures.

Reward power was related to two of the measures.

Coercive power was related to two of the measures.

Legitimate power was not related to any measures.

Bachman et al. (1966) investigated salesmen's performance. The most effective groups were those in which the superior relied more on expert and referent power (as opposed to legitimate, reward, or coercive power).

Ivancevich (1970) studied agencies in a life insurance company. He found that the reasons for compliance with the agency manager's directives were, in order: legitimate power, expert power, referent power, reward power, coercive power. This study also suggested that satisfaction with status, autonomy, and growth was most associated with the manager's use of referent and expert power.

Gargir (1972) studied the power of three kinds of staff specialists in 14 production organizations. The specialists were industrial engineers, production planners, and quality controllers. The factors below are listed in order of degree of association with "the staff's influence as perceived by line supervisors." All factors listed, however, seem to be significantly correlated with the perception of influence.

Industrial engineering staff power over line supervisors (their ability to influence supervisors as perceived by the supervisors) was associated with the following:

1. Supervisor's feelings of trust toward the staff.
2. Man-controlled rather than automated production technology.
3. Plant manager's perception of need for specialization.
4. Staff's formal authority.
5. Supervisor's perception of staff's personal contacts with higher management.
6. College education of staff.

Production planning staff power over line supervisors was associated with the following:

1. Plant manager's perception of need for consistency.
2. Number of employees in the plant.
3. Staff's formal authority.
4. Smaller number of different lots produced per week.
5. Supervisor's feelings of trust toward staff.

Quality control staff power over line supervisors was associated with the following:

1. Plant manager's perception of need for consistency.
2. Plant manager's perception of need for specialization.
3. Staff's formal authority.

Influence as Social Exchange and Mutual Control

Our discussion of influence processes implies a unidirectional flow from the leader to the follower. This is not the case; the influence flow is mutual. Even in the classic influence of operant conditioning, influence flows both ways. If a scientist places a pigeon in a box with a feeding mechanism, the hungry bird will peck in various places in the box. When he accidentally pecks a red button, the scientist reinforces the behavior by giving the pigeon a piece of corn. When the pigeon pecks the red button again, he once more receives corn, and so on. Soon the pigeon will peck the button repeatedly. The scientist is controlling the pigeon, but the pigeon is also controlling the scientist. All the bird has to do is peck a button and the scientist gives him food. What is cause and effect?

Thus, influence is reciprocal. To control, one must be controlled to some extent. That is, the influencer must be influenced. The fear-dispensing dictator *must* punish insubordination or he will lose his credibility—others' belief that he will respond to (be controlled by) the offense. Similarly, a tradition-based system will collapse unless it provides its loyal, obedient supporters with warmth and security. The charismatic leader expecting blind faith must respond to certain follower demands. Basically, he must give of himself. He must allow his followers to see him, meet him, hear him, even talk to him. (Fidel Castro's leadership of Cuba is a classic example of this kind of behavior.) Every influence mechanism and every leader thus implies two-way influence, some mutual control. A former Assistant Secretary of State has written of his awareness of the two sides of control during his first days in office (Frankel, 1969):

"The taste of power, or whatever it was that I tasted the first day, went to my head too, but not quite as I had been warned it would. I had come into the office with projects and plans, and I was caught in an irresistible movement of paper, meetings, ceremonies, crises, trivialities. There were uncleared paragraphs and cleared ones, and people waiting for me to tell them what my plans were, and people doing things that had nothing to do with my plans. I had moved into the middle of a flow of business that I hadn't started and wouldn't be able to stop. There were people in place to handle this flow, and established machinery in operation to help me deal with it. The entire system was at my disposal. In a word, I had power. And power had me."

This mutuality has an important implication: influence is expandable. It is not a fixed pie that can only be divided; it is not a zero-sum game requiring one person to lose influence when another person gains. Both may gain influence as they mutually benefit from a relationship. Even more important, some research (Patchen, 1962) suggests that influence downward may be enhanced, rather than reduced, by influence upward. For example, see Exhibit 3-6. B's influence on C seems to be a function of C's perception of both C's influence on B *and* B's influence on A.

Exhibit 3-6   Reciprocal Influence Pattern

One study (Ries) indicates that *both* managers and workers in more effective organizations perceived themselves as having greater influence. In other words, the more total influence everyone has in the system, the greater the total system effectiveness.

All of this suggests that influence is a social exchange process. Homans (1958) summarizes this perspective: "Social behavior is an exchange of goods, material goods but also non-material ones, such as the symbols of approval or prestige. Persons that give much to others try to get much from them, and persons that get much from others are under pressure to give much to them. This process of influence tends to work out at equilibrium to a balance in the exchanges. For a person engaged in exchange, what he gives may be a cost to him, just as what he gets may be a reward, and his behavior changes less as profit, that is, reward less cost, tends to a maximum. Not only does he seek a maximum for himself, but he tries to see to it that no one in his group makes more profit than he does. The cost and the value of what he gives and of what he gets vary with the quantity of what he gives and gets. It is surprising how familiar these propositions are; it is surprising, too, how propositions about the dynamics of exchange can begin to generate the static thing we call 'group structure' and, in so doing, generate also some of the propositions about group structure that students of real-life groups have stated.

"In our unguarded moments we sociologists find words like 'reward' and 'cost' slipping into what we say. Human nature will break in upon even our most elaborate theories. But we seldom let it have its way with us and follow up systematically what these words imply. Of all our many 'approaches' to social behavior, the one that sees it as an economy is the most neglected, and yet it is the one we use every moment of our lives—except when we write sociology."

Not all aspects of the bargains one makes with people and organizations are stipulated and discharged in economic terms. Many matters are worked out in social terms: vaguely specified obligations grow which are not neatly dischargeable with money; inducements and rewards for special informal contributions evolve; and so on. For example, if you are on good working terms with the company's electronics laboratory, you might get your television set repaired free. Someone who is on good terms with the purchasing staff might get tires for his own car at a discount. The examples are endless, but every organization seems to have an unofficial rewards system, an amazing variety of exchange patterns involving material goods and services.

In non-material terms, an equally wide array of exchanges of behavior and sentiment are involved in daily life in organizations. Positively, one might give help and receive gratitude. Negatively, one might give punishment and receive resentment. One might give help and get help, give punishment and get punishment, and so on. Social exchanges are more or less costly, more or less rewarding, and on balance more or less profitable to the parties involved.

The terms of exchange between two persons would be as shown in Exhibit 3-7. For A:

$$\text{Profit}_A = \text{Receipts (A from B)} - \text{Contributions (A to B)}$$

If A's profit is satisfactory to him, he will tend to maintain the relationship unchanged. However, if his receipts or contributions change to undermine his profit, A will probably attempt to adjust the balance.

Exhibit 3-7　Social Exchange

This model is intuitively realistic, if a little simplistic and cynical about human nature. The cynical assumption that everyone attempts to manipulate others is less disturbing when one realizes the complexity of what is being exchanged. Apples and oranges are involved; simple addition or subtraction is impossible, yet somehow sentiments and goods are compared and weighed. Does every man have his price? The point is debatable, but people who have contributed behavior and sacrificed respect for money are not unknown; some even have devoted their lives for the love of others. And all of us frequently exchange goods and actions.

Social exchange is essentially what is involved in motivating by appeal to human needs. The autocratic manager exchanges income and temporary security for specified behavior; the traditional hierarchical organization exchanges membership and greater security for behavior and loyalty; the charismatic leader exchanges affection, membership, and vicarious esteem for commitment and obedience; the collaborative leader exchanges power and autonomy for contribution.

To illustrate, consider the relations between an engineering manager and his subordinate staff assistant. The superior assigns routine work and supervises it closely. In short, he gives the subordinate uninteresting activities and no autonomy or independence in performing them. The subordinate complains and performs poorly. That is, the subordinate gives the supervisor a worsening behavior pattern. In this case the costs for each party are high, the rewards are low, and the resultant profit for each is little.

With a little imagination, the case could be rewritten to illustrate a situation in which the exchange is a more profitable one. The subordinate could be doing challenging work with relatively greater autonomy. He could be turning in an impressive performance. The supervisor could be giving general assignments and receiving a highly valued contribution. Whatever the facts of the case, each party's behavior and sentiments are reciprocal parts of the exchange pattern.

According to the social exchange perspective, the manager is a kind of bargainer, and management is a kind of brokerage of activity and sentiment. The manager's problem is to make the best exchanges or bargains he can. If the work of a manager is conceived in these terms, the formula for human relations is "to give the other man behavior that is more valuable to him than it is costly to you and to get from him behavior that is more valuable to you than it is costly to him." The manager faces the challenge of learning how costly or how valuable different behavior patterns are to all concerned—to himself, to other individuals, and to groups of several persons as well. Different standards of value are involved, as are different degrees of bargaining power. So formulated, the manager's lot is not an easy one, but one in which he can build his skill by focusing on the analysis and management of his exchange patterns.

Uncertainty of Influence

All of the influence processes can work if logically and consistently applied. Nonetheless, it is not certain that *any* will work in a particular situation with particular people. We are dealing with probabilistic processes, not mechanical systems. Thus, whether an influence process will motivate a person to behave in the desired way depends on his perception and judgment of whether the effort will lead to the reward (or lack of punishment) *and* whether the reward will satisfy a fundamental need (Vroom, 1964). Thus, the more complete influence model is as shown in Exhibit 3-8. The follower's motivation/effort depends upon:

a) his estimate of the probability that effort will meet the influencer's objective.
b) his estimate of the probability that meeting the objective will result in the primary outcome (that the influencer will dispense his rewards—or withhold punishment).
c) his estimate of the probability that the primary outcome will result in the secondary outcome.
d) how much he values the secondary outcome (satisfaction of his needs).

The follower's motivation and effort will be great if need satisfaction is highly valued, *and* if he thinks the influencer's rewards will be instrumental to satisfying these needs, *and* if he thinks that his efforts will meet the influencer's objectives so that he is rewarded. For example, B is likely to work hard if he thinks he can meet A's desired productivity and if he is quite certain that the money or promotion which A offers will be granted and will satisfy his needs for security and esteem.

Breaking the system at any point undermines the leader's influence. Thus, if job security is viewed as unrelated to productivity (because it depends upon

Exhibit 3-8 Influence Model

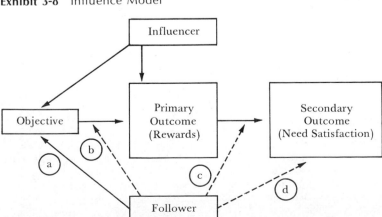

seniority and/or economic conditions), B is not likely to be motivated to work above the minimum level necessary. He may even believe that higher productivity will lessen his security. Or, if B's really important needs are for competence and achievement, he is unlikely to put forth much effort in a routine job if all A offers for high productivity is money. Finally, if B distrusts A's promise of rewards or doesn't believe his threats, A has no influence.

In short, the exchange of goods, activities, interactions, and sentiments between influencer and influenced is filtered through perceptions and subjective probability estimates of the relationships among effort, objective, primary outcome, and secondary outcomes.

Summary

Influence is the central dimension in a manager's interpersonal relations. He should be aware of the uncontrollable and controllable aspects of influence processes. People are subject to influence from the pressure of others and from basic interpersonal attitudes—especially toward authority and affiliation. These factors are less conscious and controllable than appeal to needs through a social exchange process. In many instances, a person allows himself to be influenced because certain needs are satisfied. Fear, tradition, and blind faith reflect basically authoritarian influence processes which have been effective and common in the past. Rational faith, rational agreement, and joint or self determination are influence processes of increasing relevance in modern organizations. All influence processes are logical, and if they are consistently applied, they may be effective—if people perceive their behavior as achieving goals that satisfy their fundamental needs. The effectiveness of influence processes depends on the meshing of style, people, task, and situation—these are topics to be examined in later chapters.

References

Bachman, J. G., C. G. Smith, and J. A. Slesinger. "Control, Performance and Satisfaction: An Analysis of Structural and Individual Effects." *Journal of Personality and Social Psychology,* Vol. 4 (1966), 127–136.

Barnard, C. I. *The Functions of the Executive.* Harvard University Press, 1938.

Bendix, R. *Work and Authority in Modern Industry.* Wiley, 1956.

Bensman, J. *Money and Sense.* Macmillan, 1967.

Bronfenbrenner, U. *Two Worlds of Childhood.* Russell Sage Foundation, 1970.

Erikson, E. H. *Childhood and Society.* W. W. Norton, 1950.

Fayol, H. *General and Industrial Management.* London: Pitman, 1949.

Frankel, C. *High on Foggy Bottom.* Harper & Row, 1969.

French, J. R. P., and B. H. Raven. "The Bases of Social Power." In *Studies in Social Power,* ed. D. Cartwright. University of Michigan Press, 1959.

Fromm, E. *Escape From Freedom.* Holt, Rinehart and Winston, 1941.

Gargir, J. "Staff Power: An Investigation of the Power Relationships Between Staff and Production Departments." Unpub. Ph.D. thesis, Wharton School, University of Pennsylvania, 1972.

Haire, M., E. Ghiselli, and L. Porter. *Managerial Thinking.* Wiley, 1966.

Homans, G. "Social Behavior as Exchange." *American Journal of Sociology,* Vol. 62 (May 1958), 597–606.

Ivancevich, J. M. "An Analysis of Control, Bases of Control, and Satisfaction in an Organizational Setting." *Academy of Management Journal* (December 1970), 427–436.

Kelman, H. C. "Processes of Opinion Change." *Public Opinion Quarterly,* Vol. 25 (1961), 57–78.

Kogan, E. *Der SS Staat.* Bermann-Fischer, 1947. Cited in Bendix, *op. cit.*

Leary, T. *Interpersonal Diagnosis of Personality.* Ronald, 1957.

Lewin, K. *Resolving Social Conflicts: Selected Papers on Group Dynamics.* Harper & Row, 1948.

Linden, E. "The Demoralization of an Army." *Saturday Review* (January 8, 1972), 12.

Morris, D. *The Naked Ape.* McGraw-Hill, 1966.

Newcomb, T. M. "An Approach to the Study of Communicative Acts." *Psychology Review,* Vol. 4 (1953), 183–214.

Patchen, M. "Supervisory Methods and Group Performance Norms." *Administrative Science Quarterly* (December 1962), 275–293.

Rogers, W. H. *Think: A History of IBM and the Watsons.* Stein & Day, 1969.

Rossiter, C. *The American Presidency.* Harcourt Brace Jovanovich, 1956.

Ries, V. "Influence Structure in Yugoslav Enterprise." *Industrial Relations,* Vol. 9 (1970), 148–166.

Schlesinger, A. M., Jr. *The Coming of the New Deal.* Houghton Mifflin, 1959.

Schutz, W. C. "What Makes Groups Productive?" *Human Relations,* Vol. 8, No. 4 (1955), 429.

Speer, A. *Inside the Third Reich.* Macmillan, 1970.

Student, K. R. "Supervisory Influence and Work-Group Performance." *Journal of Applied Psychology,* Vol. 52 (1968), 188–194.

Timasheff, N. S. "The Power Phenomenon." *American Sociological Review,* Vol. 3 (August 1938), 499–509.

Vroom, V. *Work and Motivation.* Wiley, 1964.

Weber, M. *The Theory of Social and Economic Organization.* The Free Press, 1964.

Zajonc, R. B. *Social Psychology: An Experimental Approach.* Brooks/Cole, 1966.

Readings

Influencing Attitudes and Changing Behavior

PHILIP ZIMBARDO, EBBE EBBESEN

A. The Persuader

1. There will be more opinion change in the desired direction if the communicator has high credibility than if he has low credibility. Credibility is:
   a. Expertise (ability to know correct stand on issue).
   b. Trustworthiness (motivation to communicate knowledge without bias).
2. The credibility of the persuader is less of a factor in opinion change later on than it is immediately after exposure.
3. A communicator's effectiveness is increased if he initially expresses some views that are also held by his audience.
4. What an audience thinks of a persuader may be directly influenced by what they think of his message.
5. The more extreme the opinion change that the communicator asks for, the more actual change he is likely to get.
   a. The greater the discrepancy (between communication and recipient's initial position), the greater the attitude change, up to extremely discrepant points.
   b. With extreme discrepancy, and with low-credibility sources, there is a falling off in attitude change.
6. Communicator characteristics irrelevant to the topic of his message can influence acceptance of its conclusion.

B. How to Present the Issues

1. Present one side of the argument when the audience is generally friendly, or when your position is the only one that will be presented, or when you want immediate, though temporary, opinion change.
2. Present both sides of the argument when the audience starts out disagreeing with you, or when it is probable that the audience will hear the other side from someone else.
3. When opposite views are presented one after another, the one presented last will probably be more effective. Primacy effect is more predominant when the second side immediately follows the first, while recency effect is more predominant when the opinion measure comes immediately after the second side.
4. There will probably be more opinion change in the direction you want if you explicitly state your conclusions than if you let the audience draw their own, except when they are rather intelligent. Then implicit conclusion drawing is better.

From Philip G. Zimbardo and Ebbe B. Ebbesen, *Influencing Attitudes and Changing Behavior,* 1969, Addison-Wesley, Reading, Mass. Reprinted by permission of Addison-Wesley Publishing Company, Inc.

5. Sometimes emotional appeals are more influential, sometimes factual ones. It all depends on the kind of audience.
6. Fear appeals: The findings generally show a positive relationship between intensity of fear arousal and amount of attitude change, if recommendations for action are explicit and possible, but a negative reaction otherwise.
7. The fewer the extrinsic justifications provided in the communication for engaging in counter-norm behavior, the greater the attitude change after actual compliance.
8. No final conclusion can be drawn about whether the opening or closing parts of the communication should contain the more important material.
9. Cues which forewarn the audience of the manipulative intent of the communication increase resistance to it, while the presence of distractors simultaneously presented with the message decreases resistance.

C. The Audience as Individuals

1. The people you may want most in your audience are often least likely to be there. There is evidence for selective seeking and exposure to information consonant with one's position, but not for selective avoidance of information dissonant with one's position.
2. The level of intelligence of an audience determines the effectiveness of some kinds of appeals.
3. Successful persuasion takes into account the reasons underlying attitudes as well as the attitudes themselves. That is, the techniques used must be tailored to the basis for developing the attitude.
4. The individual's personality traits affect his susceptibility to persuasion; he is more easily influenced when his self-esteem is low.
5. There are individuals who are highly persuasible and who will be easily changed by any influence attempt, but who are then equally influenceable when faced with countercommunications.
6. Ego-involvement with the content of the communication (its relation to ideological values of the audience) decreases the acceptance of its conclusion. Involvement with the consequences of one's response increases the probability of change and does so more when source-audience discrepancy is greater.
7. Actively role-playing a previously unacceptable position increases its acceptability.

D. The Influence of Groups

1. A person's opinions and attitudes are strongly influenced by groups to which he belongs and wants to belong.
2. A person is rewarded for conforming to the standards of the group and punished for deviating from them.
3. People who are most attached to the group are probably least influenced by communications which conflict with group norms.
4. Opinions which people make known to others are harder to change than opinions which people hold privately.
5. Audience participation (group discussion and decision-making) helps to overcome resistance.

6. Resistance to a counter-norm communication increases with salience of one's group identification.
7. The support of even one other person weakens the powerful effect of a majority opinion of an individual.
8. A minority of two people can influence the majority if they are consistent in their deviant responses.

E. The Persistence of Opinion Change

1. In time, the effects of a persuasive communication tend to wear off.
   a. A communication from a positive source leads to more rapid decay of attitude change over time than one from a negative source.
   b. A complex or subtle message produces slower decay of attitude change.
   c. Attitude change is more persistent over time if the receiver actively participates in, rather than passively receives, the communication.
2. Repeating a communication tends to prolong its influence.
3. More of the desired opinion change may be found some time after exposure to the communication than right after exposure (sleeper effect).

Leaders' Control and Members' Compliance
AMITAI ETZIONI

A Classification of Power

Power is an actor's ability to induce or influence another actor to carry out his directives or any other norms he supports.[1] Goldhamer and Shils state that "a person may be said to have power to the extent that he influences the behavior of others in accordance with his own intentions."[2] Of course, "his own intentions" might be to influence a person to follow others' "intentions" or those of a collectivity. In organizations, enforcing the collectivity norms is likely to be a condition determining the power-holder's access to the means of power.

Power positions are positions whose incumbents regularly have access to means of power. Statements about power positions imply a particular group (or groups) who are subject to this power. For instance, to state that prison guards have a power position implies the subordination of inmates. In the following analysis we focus on power relations in organizations between those higher and those lower in rank. We refer to those in power positions, who are higher in rank, as *elites* or as organizational *representatives*. We refer to those in subject positions, who are lower in rank, as *lower participants*.

Power differs according to the means employed to make the subjects comply. These means may be physical, material, or symbolic.[3]

Coercive power rests on the application, or the threat of application, of physical sanctions such as infliction of pain, deformity, or death; generation of frustration through restriction of movement; or controlling through force the satisfaction of needs such as those for food, sex, comfort, and the like.

Remunerative power is based on control over material resources and rewards through allocation of salaries and wages, commissions and contributions, "fringe benefits," services, and commodities.

Normative power rests on the allocation and manipulation of symbolic rewards and deprivations through employment of leaders, manipulation of mass media, allocation of esteem and prestige symbols, administration of ritual, and influence over the distribution of "acceptance" and "positive response." (A more eloquent name for this power would be persuasive, or manipulative, or suggestive power. But all these terms have negative value connotations which we wish to avoid.)

There are two kinds of normative power. One is based on the manipulation of esteem, prestige, and ritualistic symbols (such as a flag or a benediction); the other, on allocation and manipulation of acceptance and positive response.[4] Although both powers are found both in vertical and in horizontal relationships, the first is more frequent in vertical relations, between actors who have different ranks, whereas the second is more common in horizontal relations, among actors equal in rank—in particular, in the power of an "informal" or primary group over its members. Lacking better terms, we refer to the first kind as *pure normative power* and to the second as *social power*.[5] Social power could be treated as a distinct kind of power. But since powers are here classed according to the means of control employed, and since both social and pure normative power rest on the same set of means—manipulation of symbolic rewards—we treat these two powers as belonging to the same category.

From the viewpoint of the organization, pure normative power is more useful, since it can be exercised directly down the hierarchy. Social power becomes organizational power only when the organization can influence the group's powers, as when a teacher uses the class climate to control a deviant child or a union steward agitates the members to use their informal power to bring a deviant into line.

Organizations can be ordered according to their power structure, taking into account which power is predominant, how strongly it is stressed compared with other organizations in which the same power is predominant, and which power constitutes the secondary source of control.

Neutralization of Power

Most organizations employ all three kinds of power, but the degree to which they rely on each differs from organization to organization. Most organizations tend to emphasize only one means of power, relying less on the other two.[6] Evidence to this effect is presented below in the analysis of the compliance structures of various organizations. The major reason for power specialization seems to be that when two kinds of power are emphasized at the same time, over the same subject group, they tend to neutralize each other.

Applying force, for instance, usually creates such a high degree of alienation that it becomes impossible to apply normative power successfully. This is one of the reasons that rehabilitation is rarely achieved in traditional prisons, that custodial measures are considered as blocking therapy in mental hospitals, and that teachers in progressive schools tend to oppose corporal punishment.

Similarly, the application of remunerative powers makes appeal to "ideal-istic" (pure normative) motives less fruitful. In a study of the motives that lead to purchase of war bonds, Merton pointed out that in one particularly effective drive (the campaign of Kate Smith), all "secular" topics were omitted and the appeal was centered on patriotic, "sacred" themes. Merton asked a sample of 978 people: "Do you think that it is a good idea to give things to people who buy bonds?"

Fifty percent were definitely opposed in principle to premiums, bonuses, and other such inducements, and many of the remainder thought it a good idea only for "other people" who might not buy otherwise.[7]

By omitting this [secular] argument, the authors of her scripts were able to avoid the strain and incompatibility between the two main lines of motivation: unselfish, sacrificing love of country and economic motives of sound investment.[8]

It is possible to make an argument for the opposite position. It might be claimed that the larger the number of personal needs whose satisfaction the organization controls, the more power it has over the participants. For example, labor unions that cater to and have control over the social as well as the economic needs of their members have more power over those members than do unions that focus only on economic needs. There may be some tension between the two modes of control, some ambivalence and uneasy feeling among members about the combinations, but undoubtedly the total control is larger. Similarly, it is obvious that the church has more power over the priest than over the average parishioner. The parishioner is exposed to normative power, whereas the priest is controlled by both normative and remunerative powers.

The issue is complicated by the fact that the *amount* of each kind of power applied must be taken into account. If a labor union with social powers has economic power which is much greater than that of another union, this fact may explain why the first union has greater power in sum, despite some "waste" due to neutralization. A further complication follows from the fact that neutralization may also occur through application of the "wrong" power in terms of the cultural definition of what is appropriate to the particular organization and activity. For example, application of economic power in religious organizations may be less effective than in industries, not because two kinds of power are mixed, but because it is considered illegitimate to use economic pressures to attain religious goals. Finally, some organizations manage to apply two kinds of power abundantly and without much waste through neutralization, because they segregate the application of one power from that of the other. The examination below of combat armies and labor unions supplies an illustration of this point.

We have discussed some of the factors related to the tendency of organizations to specialize their power application. In conclusion, it seems that although there can be little doubt that such a tendency exists, its scope and a satisfactory explanation for it have yet to be established.

Three Kinds of Involvement: A Comparative Dimension

Involvement, Commitment, and Alienation

Organizations must continually recruit means if they are to realize their goals. One of the most important of these means is the positive orientation of the participants to the organizational power. *Involvement*[9] refers to the cathectic-evaluative orientation of an actor to an object, characterized in terms of intensity and direction.

The intensity of involvement ranges from high to low. The direction is either positive or negative. We refer to positive involvement as *commitment*[10] and to negative involvement as *alienation*.[11] (The advantage of having a third term, *involvement*, is that it enables us to refer to the continuum in a neutral way.[12]) Actors can accordingly be placed on an involvement continuum which ranges from a highly intense negative zone through mild negative and mild positive zones to a highly positive zone.[13]

Three Kinds of Involvement

We have found it helpful to name three zones of the involvement continuum, as follows: *alienative*, for the high alienation zone; *moral*, for the high commitment zone; and *calculative*, for the two mild zones. This classification of involvement can be applied to the orientations of actors in all social units and to all kinds of objects. Hence the definitions and illustrations presented below are not limited to organizations but are applicable to orientations in general.

Alienative Involvement   Alienative involvement designated an intense negative orientation; it is predominant in relations among hostile foreigners. Similar orientations exist among merchants in "adventure" capitalism, where trade is built on isolated acts of exchange, each side trying to maximize immediate profit.[14] Such an orientation seems to dominate the approach of prostitutes to transient clients.[15] Some slaves seem to have held similar attitudes to their masters and to their work. Inmates in prisons, prisoners of war, people in concentration camps, enlisted men in basic training, all tend to be alienated from their respective organizations.[16]

Calculative Involvement   Calculative involvement designates either a negative or a positive orientation of low intensity. Calculative orientations are predominant in relationships of merchants who have continuous business contacts. Attitudes of (and toward) permanent customers are often predominantly calculative, as are relationships among entrepreneurs in modern (rational) capitalism. Inmates in prisons who have established contact with prison authorities, such as "rats" and "peddlers," often have predominantly calculative attitudes toward those in power.[17]

Moral Involvement[18]   Moral involvement designates a positive orientation of high intensity. The involvement of the parishioner in his church, the devoted member in his party, and the loyal follower in his leader are all "moral."

There are two kinds of moral involvement, pure and social. They differ in the same way pure normative power differs from social power. Both are intensive modes of commitment, but they differ in their foci of orientation and in the structural conditions under which they develop. Pure moral commitments are based on internalization of norms and identification with authority (like Riesman's inner-directed "mode of conformity"); social commitment rests on sensitivity to pressures of primary groups and their members (Riesman's "other-directed"). Pure moral involvement tends to develop in vertical relationships, such as those between teachers and students, priests and parishioners, leaders and followers. Social involvement tends to develop in horizontal relationships like those in various types of primary groups. Both pure moral and social orientations might be found in the same relationships, but, as a rule, one orientation predominates.

Actors are means to each other in alienative and in calculative relations; but they are ends to each other in "social" relationships. In pure moral relationships the means-orientation tends to predominate; hence, for example, the willingness of devoted members of totalitarian parties or religious orders to use each other. But unlike the means-orientation of calculative relationships, the means-orientation here is expected to be geared to needs of the collectivity in serving its goals, and not to those of an individual.

Notes and References

1. T. Parsons. *The Social System* (New York: The Free Press of Glencoe, Inc., 1951), 121.
2. H. Goldhamer, & E. A. Shils. "Types of Power and Status" *American Journal of Sociology* (1939), 45:171.
3. We suggest that this typology is exhaustive, although the only way we can demonstrate this is by pointing out that every type of power we have encountered so far can be classified as belonging to one of the categories or to a combination of them.
4. T. Parsons. *The Social System* (New York: The Free Press of Glencoe, Inc., 1951), 108.
5. This distinction draws on the difference between social and normative integration, referred to by T. Parsons, R. F. Bales, & E. A. Shils, *Working Papers in the Theory of Action* (New York: The Free Press of Glencoe, Inc., 1953), 182, as the distinction between the "integrative" and the "latent pattern maintenance" phases. In volume in progress, Shils distinguishes between social and ideological primary groups (private communication). J. S. Coleman, "Multidimensional Scale Analysis," *American Journal of Sociology* (1957), 63:255, has pointed to the difference between group-oriented and idea-oriented attachments.
6. In more technical language, one can say that the three continua of power constitute a three-dimensional property space. If we collapse each dimension into high, medium, and low segments, there are 27 possible combinations or cells. Our hypothesis reads that most organizations fall into cells which are high on one dimension and low or medium on the others; this excludes 18 cells (not counting three types of dual structures discussed below).
7. R. K. Merton. *Mass Persuasion: The Social Psychology of a War Bond Drive* (New York: Harper & Row, Publishers, 1946), 47.
8. *Ibid.*, p. 45.
9. *Involvement* has been used in a similar manner by Nancy C. Morse, *Satisfactions in the White-Collar Job* (Survey Research Center, University of Michigan, 1953), 76–96. The term is used in a somewhat different way by students of voting, who refer by it to the psychological investment in the outcome of an election rather than in the

party, which would be parallel to Morse's usage and ours. See, for example, A. Campbell, G. Gurin, and W. E. Miller, *The Voter Decides* (New York: Harper & Row, Publishers, 1954), 33–40.

10. Mishler defined *commitment* in a similar though more psychological way: "An individual is committed to an organization to the extent that central tensions are integrated through organizationally relevant instrumental acts." Cited by C. Argyris, *Personality and Organization* (New York: Harper & Row, Publishers, 1957), 202.

11. We draw deliberately on the associations this term has acquired from its usage by Marx and others. For a good analysis of the idea of alienation in Marxism, and of its more recent development, see D. Bell, "The 'Rediscovery' of Alienation," *Journal of Philosophy,* 56 (1959), 933–52. And D. Bell, *The End of Ideology,* (New York: The Free Press of Glencoe, Inc., 1960), 335–68. See also D. G. Dean, "Aliena- tion and Political Apathy," *Social Forces,* 38 (1960), 185–89.

12. An example of empirical indicators which can be used to translate the involvement continuum into directly observable terms is offered by E. A. Shils, and M. Janowits, "Cohesion and Disintegration in the Wehrmacht in World War II," *Public Opinion Quarterly,* 12 (2), (1948), 282–83. They classify "modes of social disintegration" in the armed forces as follows: desertion; active surrender; passive surrender; routine resistance; "last-ditch" resistance. In the terms used here, these measures indicate varying degrees of involvement, from highest alienation (desertion) to highest commitment (last-ditch resistance).

    Nettler (1958) has developed a 17-item unidimensional scale which measures alienation from society. It seems that a similar scale could be constructed for measuring alienation from or commitment to organizational power without undue difficulties. A. Kornhauser, H. L. Sheppard, and A. J. Mayer, *When Labor Votes* (New York: University Books, 1956), 147–48, have developed a 6-item scale, meas- uring the orientation of union members to their organization, which supplies another illustration of the wide use and measurability of these concepts, which are central to our analysis.

13. Several sociologists have pointed out that the relationship between intensity and direction of involvement is a curvilinear one: the more positive or negative the orientation, the more intensely it is held. L. Guttman, "The Cornell Technique for Scale and Intensity Analysis," *Education and Psychology Measurement J* (1947), 247–79.

14. H. H. Gerth, and C. W. Mills. *From Max Weber: Essays in Sociology* (New York: Oxford University Press, 1946), 67.

15. K. Davis. "The Sociology of Prostitution," *American Sociological Review,* 2 (1937), 748–49.

16. For a description of this orientation in prisons see D. Clemmer, *The Prison Community* (New York: Holt, Rinehart & Winston, Inc., 1958), 152ff. Attitudes toward the police, particularly on the part of members of the lower class, are often strictly alienative. See for example, E. Banfield, *The Moral Basis of a Backward Society* (New York: The Free Press of Glencoe, Inc., 1958).

17. G. M. Sykes. *The Society of Captives* (Princeton: Princeton University Press, 1958), 87–95.

18. The term moral is used here and in the rest of the volume to refer to an orientation of the actor; it does not involve a value-position of the observer. See T. Parsons, and E. A. Shils, *et al. Toward a General Theory of Action* (Cambridge, Mass.: Harvard University Press, 1952), 170ff.

Authority: Its Nature and Motives

HERBERT A. SIMON, DONALD W. SMITHBURG, VICTOR A. THOMPSON

From a psychological standpoint the exercise of authority involves a relationship between two or more persons. On the one side we have a person who makes proposals for the action of others. On the other side we have a person who accepts the proposals—who "obeys" them. Now a person may accept another's proposals under three different sets of circumstances:

1. He may examine the merits of the proposal, and, on the basis of its merits become convinced that he should carry it out. We shall exclude such instances of acceptance from our notion of authority, although some writers on administration have called this the "authority of ideas."
2. He may carry out the proposals without being fully, or even partially, convinced of its merits. In fact he may not examine the merits of the proposal at all.
3. He may carry out the proposal even though he is convinced it is wrong—wrong either in terms of personal values or of organizational values or both.

We will treat both the second and third cases as instances of the acceptance of authority. Of course in any actual instance all three of the "pure types" of acceptance listed above may be combined in various proportions. In actual practice authority is almost always liberally admixed with persuasion.

Because the person who accepts proposals may do so for a variety of motives, there will be seen in any organization a number of different types of authority relationships, corresponding to these different motives for acceptance.

People accept the proposals of persons in whom they have great confidence. In any organization there are some individuals who, because of past performance, general reputation, or other factors, have great influence or authority. Their proposals will often be accepted without analysis as to their wisdom. Even when the suggestions of such a person are not accepted, they will be rejected reluctantly and only because a stronger authority contradicts them.

The authority of confidence may be limited to a special area of competence in which a person has acquired a reputation.

The willingness to accept authority on the basis of confidence, both within and outside organizations, goes even one step further. Not only is the layman generally unable to judge the quality of the advice he is getting from the specialist, but he often is in no position to judge the competence of the specialist, except on the basis of certain superficial and formal criteria that give the specialist his *status*.

There are at least two kinds of status, which may be called *functional status* and *hierarchical status*. It is with functional status that we are concerned at the moment. A person has functional status in a particular area of knowledge when

From *Public Administration*, by Herbert A. Simon, Donald W. Smithburg and Victor A. Thompson. Copyright © 1950 by Herbert A. Simon, Donald W. Smithburg and Victor A. Thompson. Reprinted by permission of Alfred A. Knopf, Inc.

his decisions and recommendations in that area are accepted as more or less authoritative.

In the established professions, status is generally conferred on the basis of standards developed by the profession itself. The M.D. degree is conferred on the young doctor by the medical profession (acting through an "accredited" medical school). Law and engineering degrees and the certificate of the public accountant are awarded in much the same way. In other cases, job experience in a particular field confers functional status in that field. A person with long experience in a professional position in the Interstate Commerce Commission may acquire status as a transportation economist.

Confidence can be a powerful support for hierarchical as well as for non-hierarchical authority. A subordinate will much more readily obey a command of a superior if he has confidence in the intelligence and judgment of that superior or if he believes that the superior has knowledge of the situation not available to himself.

In particular, where a problem requiring decision affects the work of several units in an organization, the superior who has hierarchical authority in the formal organization plan over all the units involved is often accepted as the person best located—because he has the "whole picture"—to make the decision. Hence, the coordinating functions that are commonly performed by those in hierarchical authority are based, in part at least, upon the authority of confidence—upon the belief of subordinates that the superior is the best informed about the situation as a whole.

The most generally recognized weapon of the superior is the sanction—the ability of the superior to attach pleasant or unpleasant consequences to the actions of the subordinate.

The relationship of the authority of sanctions with the organizational hierarchy can be viewed from a more general standpoint. When a person joins an organization he is accepting a system of relationships that restricts his individuality or his freedom of action. He is willing to do so because he feels that, in spite of the organizational restraints, being a member of the organization is preferable to other alternatives available to him. To continue as a member of the organization, he must continue, to some extent, to abide by the complex of procedures which constitutes the organization. Although, increasingly, the power to discharge an employee is not lodged in any specific superior (because of merit systems, central personnel offices, labor unions, etc.), nevertheless, this power resides somewhere in the organization, being, in fact, one of its working procedures. The sanctions discussed in this section are increasingly *organization* sanctions, brought into play through the working procedures of the organization, and not the special prerogatives or powers of *individual superiors*.

For the most part the authority of sanction rests on the behavior responses that are induced by the *possibility* that a sanction may be applied. An organization member is seldom presented with an ultimatum "to do so and so or suffer the consequences." Rather, he anticipates the consequences of continual insubordination or failure to please the person or persons who have the ability to apply sanctions to him, and this anticipation acts as a constant motivation without expressed threats from any person.

There is another reason why employees accept the proposals of other organization members—a reason less rationalistic but probably more important than the desire to avoid the organization sanctions discussed above. People accept "legitimate" authority because they feel that they *ought* to go along with the "rules of the game."

Throughout their development to maturity and after, people are educated in the beliefs, values, or mores of society. They learn what they ought to do and what they ought not to do. One of the values with which they are indoctrinated is that a person should play according to the rules of the game. This ethic is acquired very early. When a child enters a ball game in the sand lot he does not expect the game to be altered at various points to suit his convenience. Rather he expects to adjust his behavior to the rules of the game. Although there may be disputes as to what the rule is on some point, once this is established, the proposition that he should abide by the rule is unquestioned.

Likewise, when people enter organizations most of them feel that they ought to abide by the rules of the game—the working procedures of the organization. These working procedures define how the work will be done; how working problems will be solved when they arise; how conflicts will be settled. They prescribe that on such and such matters the individual will accept the suggestions of this or that person or organization; secure the advice of such and such unit; clear his work with so and so; work on matters that come to him in such and such a way; etc.

The working procedures of an organization prescribe that the individual member will accept the proposals of other members in matters assigned to them. This acceptance is one of the rules of the game which he feels he should abide by. Thus, individuals in organizations also accept the authority of other persons because they think they *ought* to accept it.

The working relationships in an organization designated by the term "hierarchy" constitute a particular organization procedure for handling the authority of legitimacy. Acceptance of the working procedures of an organization by a member includes acceptance of the obligation to go along with the proposals of an hierarchical superior, at least within a limit of toleration—the "area of acceptance." Thus, whether the other reasons for obedience are operating or not (confidence, identification, or sanctions), organization members will feel that they ought to obey their superiors. Legitimacy is one of the most important sources of the authority of the hierarchical superior.

The feeling that hierarchical authority is legitimate is immensely strengthened by previous social conditioning. Hierarchical behavior is an institutionalized behavior that all organization members bring to the organization with them. Like the players in the Oberammergau Passion Play who begin to learn their roles in early childhood, "inferiors" obey "superiors" because they have been taught to do so from infancy, beginning with the parent-child relationship and running through almost constant experience with social and organizational hierarchies until death brings graduation from this particular social schooling. Hierarchical behavior involves an inferior-superior role-taking of persons well versed in their roles. "Inferiors" feel that they ought to obey "superiors"; "superiors" feel that they ought to be obeyed.

Our society is extremely hierarchical. Success is generally interpreted in terms of hierarchical preferment. Social position and financial rewards are closely related to hierarchical preferment, as also are education and even perhaps romantic attainment. Advancement up a hierarchy is generally considered a

sign of moral worth, of good character, of good stewardship, of social responsibility, and of the possession of superior intellectual qualities.

Hierarchy receives a tremendous emphasis in nearly all organizations. This
is so because hierarchy is a procedure that requires no training, no indoctrination, no special inducements. It rests almost entirely on "pre-entry" training—a training so thorough that few other organization procedures can ever
compete with it. Furthermore, hierarchy is a great simplification.

Theory X and Theory Y

DOUGLAS McGREGOR

Theory X: The Traditional View of Direction and Control

Behind every managerial decision or action are assumptions about human
nature and human behavior. A few of these are remarkably pervasive. They
are implicit in most of the literature of organization and in much current
managerial policy and practice:

1. *The average human being has an inherent dislike of work and will avoid it if he can.*

    This assumption has deep roots. The punishment of Adam and Eve for
eating the fruit of the Tree of Knowledge was to be banished from Eden into
a world where they had to work for a living. The stress that management places
on productivity, on the concept of "a fair day's work," on the evils of feather-
bedding and restriction of output, on rewards for performance—while it has
a logic in terms of the objectives of enterprise—reflects an underlying belief that
management must counteract an inherent human tendency to avoid work. The
evidence for the correctness of this assumption would seem to most managers
to be incontrovertible.

2. *Because of this human characteristic of dislike of work, most people must be coerced,*
    controlled, directed, threatened with punishment to get them to put forth adequate effort
    toward the achievement of organizational objectives.

    The dislike of work is so strong that even the promise of rewards is not
generally enough to overcome it. People will accept the rewards and demand
continually higher ones, but these alone will not produce the necessary effort.
Only the threat of punishment will do the trick.

    The current wave of criticism of "human relations," the derogatory com-
ments about "permissiveness" and "democracy" in industry, the trends in some
companies toward recentralization after the postwar wave of decentralization—all these are assertions of the underlying assumption that people will only
work under external coercion and control. The recession of 1957–1958 ended

a decade of experimentation with the "soft" managerial approach, and this assumption (which never really was abandoned) is being openly espoused once more.

3. *The average human being prefers to be directed, wishes to avoid responsibility, has relatively little ambition, wants security above all.*

This assumption of the "mediocrity of the masses" is rarely expressed so bluntly. In fact, a good deal of lip service is given to the ideal of the worth of the average human being. Our political and social values demand such public expressions. Nevertheless, a great many managers will give private support to this assumption, and it is easy to see it reflected in policy and practice. Paternalism has become a nasty word, but it is by no means a defunct managerial philosophy.

I have suggested elsewhere the name Theory X for this set of assumptions.

Theory X provides an explanation of some human behavior in industry. These assumptions would not have persisted if there were not a considerable body of evidence to support them. Nevertheless, there are many readily observable phenomena in industry and elsewhere which are not consistent with this view of human nature.

Such a state of affairs is not uncommon. The history of science provides many examples of theoretical explanations which persist over long periods despite the fact that they are only partially adequate. Newton's laws of motion are a case in point. It was not until the development of the theory of relativity during the present century that important inconsistencies and inadequacies in Newtonian theory could be understood and corrected.

The growth of knowledge in the social sciences during the past quarter century has made it possible to reformulate some assumptions about human nature and human behavior in the organizational setting which resolve certain of the inconsistencies inherent in Theory X. While this reformulation is, of course, tentative, it provides an improved basis for prediction and control of human behavior in industry.

Some Assumptions about Motivation

At the core of any theory of the management of human resources are assumptions about human motivation. This has been a confusing subject because there have been so many conflicting points of view even among social scientists. In recent years, however, there has been a convergence of research findings and a growing acceptance of a few rather basic ideas about motivation. These ideas appear to have considerable power. They help to explain the inadequacies of Theory X as well as the limited sense in which it is correct. In addition, they provide the basis for an entirely different theory of management.

Man is a wanting animal—as soon as one of his needs is satisfied, another appears in its place. This process is unending. It continues from birth to death. Man continuously puts forth effort—works, if you please—to satisfy his needs.

Human needs are organized in a series of levels—a hierarchy of importance. At the lowest level, but preeminent in importance when they are thwarted, are the physiological needs. Man lives by bread alone, when there is no bread. Unless the circumstances are unusual, his needs for love, for status, for recognition are inoperative when his stomach has been empty for a while. But when he eats regularly and adequately, hunger ceases to be an important need. The sated man has hunger only in the sense that a full bottle has emptiness. The same is true of the other physiological needs of man—for rest, exercise, shelter, protection from the elements.

A satisfied need is not a motivator of behavior! This is a fact of profound significance. It is a fact which is unrecognized in Theory X and is, therefore, ignored in the conventional approach to the management of people. I shall return to it later. For the moment, an example will make the point. Consider your own need for air. Except as you are deprived of it, it has no appreciable motivating effect upon your behavior.

When the physiological needs are reasonably satisfied, needs at the next higher level begin to dominate man's behavior—to motivate him. These are the safety needs, for protection against danger, threat, deprivation. Some people mistakenly refer to these as needs for security. However, unless man is in a dependent relationship where he fears arbitrary deprivation, he does not demand security. The need is for the "fairest possible break." When he is confident of this, he is more than willing to take risks. But when he feels threatened or dependent, his greatest need is for protection, for security.

The fact needs little emphasis that since every industrial employee is in at least a partially dependent relationship, safety needs may assume considerable importance. Arbitrary management actions, behavior which arouses uncertainty with respect to continued employment or which reflects favoritism or discrimination, unpredictable administration of policy—these can be powerful motivators of the safety needs in the employment relationship at every level from worker to vice president. In addition, the safety needs of managers are often aroused by their dependence downward or laterally. This is a major reason for emphasis on management prerogatives and clear assignments of authority.

When man's physiological needs are satisfied and he is no longer fearful about his physical welfare, his social needs become important motivators of his behavior. These are such needs as those for belonging, for association, for acceptance by one's fellows, for giving and receiving friendship and love.

Management knows today of the existence of these needs, but it is often assumed quite wrongly that they represent a threat to the organization. Many studies have demonstrated that the tightly knit, cohesive work group may, under proper conditions, be far more effective than an equal number of separate individuals in achieving organizational goals. Yet management, fearing group hostility to its own objectives, often goes to considerable lengths to control and direct human efforts in ways that are inimical to the natural "groupiness" of human beings. When man's social needs—and perhaps his safety needs, too—are thus thwarted, he behaves in ways which tend to defeat organizational objectives. He becomes resistant, antagonistic, uncooperative. But this behavior is a consequence, not a cause.

Above the social needs—in the sense that they do not usually become motivators until lower needs are reasonably satisfied—are the needs of greatest significance to management and to man himself. They are the egoistic needs, and they are of two kinds:

1. Those that relate to one's self-esteem: needs for self-respect and self-confidence, for autonomy, for achievement, for competence, for knowledge.

2. Those that relate to one's reputation: needs for status, for recognition, for appreciation, for the deserved respect of one's fellows.

Unlike the lower needs, these are rarely satisfied; man seeks indefinitely for more satisfaction of these needs once they have become important to him. However, they do not usually appear in any significant way until physiological, safety, and social needs are reasonably satisfied. Exceptions to this generalization are to be observed, particularly under circumstances where, in addition to severe deprivation of physiological needs, human dignity is trampled upon. Political revolutions often grow out of thwarted social and ego, as well as physiological, needs.

The typical industrial organization offers only limited opportunities for the satisfaction of egoistic needs to people at lower levels in the hierarchy. The conventional methods of organizing work, particularly in mass production industries, give little heed to these aspects of human motivation. If the practices of "scientific management" were deliberately calculated to thwart these needs—which, of course, they are not—they could hardly accomplish this purpose better than they do.

Finally—a capstone, as it were, on the hierarchy—there are the needs for self-fulfillment. These are the needs for realizing one's own potentialities, for continued self-development, for being creative in the broadest sense of that term.

The conditions of modern industrial life give only limited opportunity for these relatively dormant human needs to find expression. The deprivation most people experience with respect to other lower-level needs diverts their energies into the struggle to satisfy *those* needs, and the needs for self-fulfillment remain below the level of consciousness.

Now, briefly, a few general comments about motivation:

We recognize readily enough that a man suffering from a severe dietary deficiency is sick. The deprivation of physiological needs has behavioral consequences. The same is true, although less well recognized, of the deprivation of higher-level needs. The man whose needs for safety, association, independence, or status are thwarted is sick, just as surely as is he who has rickets. And his sickness will have behavioral consequences. We will be mistaken if we attribute his resultant passivity, or his hostility, or his refusal to accept responsibility to his inherent "human nature." These forms of behavior are *symptoms* of illness—of deprivation of his social and egoistic needs.

The "carrot and stick" theory of motivation which goes along with Theory X works reasonably well under certain circumstances. The *means* for satisfying man's physiological and (within limits) safety needs can be provided or withheld by management. Employment itself is such a means, and so are wages, working conditions, and benefits. By these means the individual can be controlled so long as he is struggling for subsistence. Man tends to live for bread alone when there is little bread.

But the "carrot and stick" theory does not work at all once man has reached an adequate subsistence level and is motivated primarily by higher needs. Management cannot provide a man with self-respect, or with the respect of his fellows, or with the satisfaction of needs for self-fulfillment. We can create conditions such that he is encouraged and enabled to seek such satisfactions for himself, or we can thwart him by failing to create those conditions.

Theory Y: The Integration of Individual and Organizational Goals

To some, the preceding analysis will appear unduly harsh. Have we not made major modifications in the management of the human resources of industry during the past quarter century? Have we not recognized the importance of people and made vitally significant changes in managerial strategy as a consequence? Do the developments since the twenties in personnel administration and labor relations add up to nothing?

There is no question that important progress has been made in the past two or three decades. During this period the human side of enterprise has become a major preoccupation of management. A tremendous number of policies, programs, and practices which were virtually unknown thirty years ago have become commonplace. The lot of the industrial employee—be he worker, professional, or executive—has improved to a degree which could hardly have been imagined by his counterpart of the nineteen twenties. Management has adopted generally a far more humanitarian set of values; it has successfully striven to give more equitable and more generous treatment to its employees. It has significantly reduced economic hardships, eliminated the more extreme forms of industrial warfare, provided a generally safe and pleasant working environment, *but it has done all these things without changing its fundamental theory of management.* There are exceptions here and there, and they are important; nevertheless, the assumptions of Theory X remain predominant throughout our economy.

Management was subjected to severe pressures during the Great Depression of the thirties. The wave of public antagonism, the open warfare accompanying the unionization of the mass production industries, the general reaction against authoritarianism, the legislation of the New Deal produced a wide "pendulum swing." However, the changes in policy and practice which took place during that and the next decade were primarily adjustments to the increased power of organized labor and to the pressures of public opinion.

Some of the movement was away from "hard" and toward "soft" management, but it was short-lived, and for good reasons. It has become clear that many of the initial strategic interpretations accompanying the "human relations approach" were as naïve as those which characterized the early stages of progressive education. We have now discovered that there is no answer in the simple removal of control—that abdication is not a workable alternative to authoritarianism. We have learned that there is no direct correlation between employee satisfaction and productivity. We recognize today that "industrial democracy" cannot consist in permitting everyone to decide everything, that industrial health does not flow automatically from the elimination of dissatisfaction, disagreement, or even open conflict. Peace is not synonymous with organizational health; socially responsible management is not coextensive with permissive management.

Now that management has regained its earlier prestige and power, it has become obvious that the trend toward "soft" management was a temporary and relatively superficial reaction rather than a general modification of fundamental assumptions or basic strategy. Moreover, while the progress we have made in the past quarter century is substantial, it has reached the point of diminishing returns. The tactical possibilities within conventional managerial strategies have been pretty completely exploited, and significant new developments will be unlikely without major modifications in theory.

The Assumptions of Theory Y

There have been few dramatic break-throughs in social science theory like those
which have occurred in the physical sciences during the past half century.
Nevertheless, the accumulation of knowledge about human behavior in many
specialized fields has made possible the formulation of a number of generalizations which provide a modest beginning for new theory with respect to the
management of human resources. Some of these assumptions were outlined in
the discussion of motivation in [the section on Theory X]. Some others, which
will hereafter be referred to as Theory Y, are as follows:

1. *The expenditure of physical and mental effort in work is as natural as play or rest.* The
   average human being does not inherently dislike work. Depending upon
   controllable conditions, work may be a source of satisfaction (and will be
   voluntarily performed) or a source of punishment (and will be avoided if
   possible).
2. *External control and the threat of punishment are not the only means for bringing about
   effort toward organizational objectives. Man will exercise self-direction and self-control
   in the service of objectives to which he is committed.*
3. *Commitment to objectives is a function of the rewards associated with their achievement.*
   The most significant of such rewards, e.g., the satisfaction of ego and self-
   actualization needs, can be direct products of effort directed toward organizational objectives.
4. *The average human being learns, under proper conditions, not only to accept but to seek
   responsibility.* Avoidance of responsibility, lack of ambition, and emphasis on
   security are generally consequences of experience, not inherent human characteristics.
5. *The capacity to exercise a relatively high degree of imagination, ingenuity, and creativity
   in the solution of organizational problems is widely, not narrowly, distributed in the
   population.*
6. *Under the conditions of modern industrial life, the intellectual potentialities of the average
   human being are only partially utilized.*

These assumptions involve sharply different implications for managerial
strategy than do those of Theory X. They are dynamic rather than static: They
indicate the possibility of human growth and development; they stress the
necessity for selective adaptation rather than for a single absolute form of
control. They are not framed in terms of the least common denominator of
the factory hand, but in terms of a resource which has substantial potentialities.

Above all, the assumptions of Theory Y point up the fact that the limits
on human collaboration in the organizational setting are not limits of human
nature but of management's ingenuity in discovering how to realize the potential
represented by its human resources. Theory X offers management an easy
rationalization for ineffective organizational performance: It is due to the nature
of the human resources with which we must work. Theory Y, on the other hand,
places the problems squarely in the lap of management. If employees are lazy,
indifferent, unwilling to take responsibility, intransigent, uncreative, uncooperative, Theory Y implies that the causes lie in management's methods of organization and control.

Beyond the Teaching Machine: Operant Conditioning in Management

WALTER R. NORD

The work of B. F. Skinner and the operant conditioners has been neglected in management and organizational literature. The present paper is an attempt to eliminate this lacuna. When most students of management and personnel think of Skinner's work, they begin and end with programmed instruction. Skinner's ideas, however, have far greater implications for the design and operation of social systems and organizations than just the teaching machine. These additional ideas could be of great practical value.

While neglecting conditioning, writers in the administrative, management, and personnel literature have given extensive attention to the work of other behavioral scientists. McGregor and Maslow are perhaps the behavioral scientists best known to practitioners and students in the area of business and management. Since the major concern of managers of human resources is the prediction and control of the behavior of organizational participants, it is curious to find that people with such a need are extremely conversant with McGregor and Maslow and totally ignorant of Skinner. This condition is not surprising since leading scholars in the field of what might be termed the applied behavioral sciences have turned out book after book, article after article, and anthology after anthology with scarcely a mention of Skinner's contributions to the design of social systems. While many writers who deal with the social psychology of organizations are guilty of the omission, this paper will focus primarily on the popular positions of Douglas McGregor, Abraham Maslow, and Frederick Herzberg to aid in exposition.

Almost every book in the field devotes considerable attention to Maslow and McGregor. These men have certainly contributed ideas which are easily understood and "make sense" to practitioners. Also, many practitioners have implemented some of these ideas successfully. However, the belief in the Maslow–McGregor creed is not based on a great deal of evidence.

By contrast, the work of Skinner (1953) and his followers has been supported by millions of observations made on animals at all levels of the phylogenetic scale, including man. Over a wide variety of situations, behavior has been reliably predicted and controlled by operant and classical conditioning techniques.

Why then have the applied behavioral sciences followed the McGregor–Maslow approach and ignored Skinner? Several reasons can be suggested. First is the metaphysical issue. Modern Americans, especially of the managerial class, prefer to think of themselves and others as being self-actualizing creatures operating near the top of Maslow's need-hierarchy, rather than as animals being

"Beyond the Teaching Machine: The Neglected Area of Operant Conditioning in the Theory and Practice of Management" by Walter R. Nord from *Organizational Behavior and Human Performance,* Vol. 4, 1969. Reprinted by permission of the author and Academic Press, Inc.

controlled and even "manipulated" by their environment. McGregor (1960) developed his argument in terms of Maslow's hierarchy. Skinner's position is unattractive in the same way the Copernican theory was unattractive. Second, Skinner's work and stimulus-response psychology in general appear too limited to allow application to complex social situations. Certainly, this point has much merit. The application of S-R theory poses a terribly complex engineering problem, perhaps an insoluble one in some areas. Nevertheless, the designs of some experimental social systems, which will be discussed later in this paper, demonstrate the feasibility of the practical application of Skinnerian psychology to systems design. A third possible reason for the acceptance of the McGregor and Maslow school and rejection of Skinner may stem from the fact that the two approaches have considerable, although generally unrecognized, overlap. As will be shown below, McGregor gave primary importance to the environment as the determinant of individual behavior. Similarly, although not as directly, so does Maslow's hierarchy of needs. The major issue between Skinner and McGregor–Maslow has to do with their models of man. Skinner focuses on man being totally shaped by his environment. Maslow–McGregor see man as having an essence or intrinsic nature which is only congruent with certain environments. The evidence for any one set of metaphysical assumptions is no better than for almost any other set. Empirically, little has been found which helps in choosing between Skinner's and McGregor's assumptions. Further, since most managers are concerned mainly with behavior, the sets of assumptions are of limited importance. It should be noted, however, that if McGregor's writings were stripped of Maslow's model of man, his conclusions on the descriptive and proscriptive levels would remain unchanged. Such a revision would also make McGregor's ideas almost identical with Skinner's. With more attention to contingencies of reinforcement and a broader view of the possibilities of administering reinforcement, the two sets of ideas as they apply to prediction and control of action would be virtually indistinguishable.

Perhaps the more humanistic tone of McGregor's writing or his specific attention to managerial problems faced in business is responsible for his high esteem among students of management relative to that accorded Skinner. While metaphorically there is great difference, substantively there is little. It would seem, however, that metaphors have led practitioners and students of applied behavioral science to overlook some valuable data and some creative management possibilities.

By way of summary to this point, it appears that more humanistic social scientists have been preferred by managers to behaviorists such as Skinner in their efforts to improve the management of human resources. Perhaps the oversight has been due to the congruence between their values and the metaphysics of people such as McGregor and Maslow. The differences between McGregor and Skinner do not appear to involve open conflict.

To the extent the two approaches agree, the major criterion in employing them would seem to be the degree to which they aid in predicting and controlling behavior toward organizational goals. The work of Skinner and his followers has much to offer in terms of the above criterion. In particular, McGregor's followers might find Skinner's work an asset in implementing Theory Y. The remainder of this paper will develop some of the major points of the Skinnerian approach and seek to explore their potential for industrial use.

Conditioning: A Synthesis for Organizational Behavior

The behavioral psychology of Skinner assumes, like Theory Y, that rate of behavior is dependent on the external conditions in which the behavior takes place. Like Theory X, it stresses the importance of the administration of rewards and punishments. Unlike Theory X, Skinnerian psychology places emphasis on rewards. Like Theory Y it emphasizes the role of interdependence between people in a social relationship and thus views the administration of rewards and punishments as an exchange. For those who are unfamiliar with the work of Skinner and his followers, a brief summary follows. Like any summary of an extensive body of work, this review omits a lot of important material. A more detailed, yet simple, introduction to conditioning can be found in Bijou and Baer (1961) and Skinner (1953). Extensions of this work by social exchange theorists such as Homans (1961) suggest that the conditioning model can be extended to a systems approach, contrary to McGregor's (1966) belief.

Generally, conditioned responses can be divided into two classes. Each class is acquired in a different fashion. The first class, generally known as respondent or classically conditioned behavior, describes the responses which are controlled by prior stimulation. These responses, generally thought of as being involuntary or reflexive, are usually made by the "smooth muscles." Common ones are salivation and emotional responses. Initially, the presentation of an unconditioned stimulus will elicit a specific response. For example, food placed on one's tongue will generally cause salivation. If a bell is sounded and then food is placed on the tongue, and this process is repeated several times, the sound of the bell by itself will elicit salivation. By this process, stimuli which previously did not control behavior, such as the bell, can become a source of behavior control. Many of our likes and dislikes, our anxieties, our feelings of patriotism, and other emotions can be thought of as such involuntary responses. The implications of emotional responses are of major importance to the management of human resources and more will be said about them later. However, the second class of responses, the operants, are of even greater importance.

The rate of operant responses is influenced by events which follow them. These events are considered to be the consequences of behavior. The responses, generally thought to be voluntary, are usually made by striped muscles. All that is necessary for the development of an operant response is that the desired response has a probability of occurring which is greater than zero for the individual involved. Most rapid conditioning results when the desired response is "reinforced" immediately (preferably about one-half second after the response). In other words, the desired response is followed directly by some consequence. In simple terms, if the outcome is pleasing to the individual, the probability of his repeating the response is apt to be increased. If the consequence is displeasing to the individual, the probability of his repeating the response is apt to be decreased. The process of inducing such change (usually an increase) in the response rate is called operant conditioning. In general, the frequency of a behavior is said to be a function of its consequences.

The above description of operant conditioning is greatly simplified. The additional considerations which follow will only partially rectify this state. One crucial factor has to do with the frequency with which a given consequence follows a response. There are several possible patterns. Most obviously, the consequence can be continuous (for example, it follows the response every time the response is made). Alternatively a consequence might follow only some of the responses. There are two basic ways in which such partial reinforcement can be administered. First, the consequence can be made contingent on a certain number of responses. Two sub-patterns are possible. Every nth response may be reinforced or an average of $1/n$ of the responses may be reinforced in a random pattern. These two related patterns are called ratio schedules. The former is known as a fixed ratio and the latter is known as a variable ratio. Ratio schedules tend to generate a high rate of response, with the variable-ratio schedule leading to a more durable response than both the fixed-ratio and continuous patterns. A second technique of partial reinforcement can be designed where the consequence follows the response only after a certain amount of time has elapsed. The first response made after a specified interval is then reinforced, but all other responses produce neutral stimulus outcomes. This pattern can also be either fixed or variable. Generally, interval schedules develop responses which are quite long lasting when reinforcement is no longer given, but do not yield as rapid a response rate as ratio schedules do. Obviously, mixed patterns of ratio and interval schedules can also be designed.

A second consideration about operant conditioning which deserves brief mention is the concept of a response hierarchy. All the responses which an individual could make under a given set of conditions can be placed in order according to probability that they will be made. In this view, there are two basic strategies for getting an individual to make the desired response. First, one could attempt to reduce the probability of all the more probable responses. Second, one could attempt to increase the probability of the desired response. Of course, some combination of these two approaches may often be used.

Strategies for changing the probability of a response can be implemented by punishment, extinction, and positive reinforcement. Generally punishment and extinction are used to decrease the occurrence of a response whereas positive reinforcement is used to increase its probability. An understanding of these three operations in behavior control is important, not only for knowing how to use them, but chiefly because of their unanticipated consequences or their side-effects.

Punishment is the most widely used technique in our society for behavior control. Perhaps, as Reese (1966) said, the widespread use of punishment is due to the immediate effects it has in stopping or preventing the undesired response. In this sense, the punisher is reinforced for punishing. Also, many of us seem to be influenced by some notion of what Homans (1961) called distributive justice. In order to reestablish what we believe to be equity, we may often be led to punish another person. This ancient assumption of ". . . an eye for an eye . . ." has been widely practiced in man's quest for equity and behavior control.

Whatever the reason for punishing, it can be done in two ways, both of which have unfortunate side-effects. First, punishment can be administered in the form of some aversive stimulus such as physical pain or social disapproval. Secondly, it can be administered by withdrawing a desired stimulus. The immediate effect is often the rapid drop in frequency of the punished response. The full effects, unfortunately, are often not clearly recognized. Many of these consequences are crucial for managers of organizations.

Punishment may be an inefficient technique for controlling behavior for a number of reasons. First, the probability of the response may be reduced only when the threat of punishment is perceived to exist. Thus, when the punishing agent is away, the undesired response may occur at its initial rate. Secondly, punishment only serves to reduce the probability of the one response. This outcome does not necessarily produce the desired response, unless that response is the next most probable one in the response hierarchy. Really, what punishment does is to get the individual to do something other than what he has been punished for. A third effect is that the punishment may interfere with the responses being made under desired circumstances. For example, if an organizational member attempts an innovation which is met with punishment by his superiors because they did not feel he had the authority to take the step, it is quite possible that his creative behavior will be reduced even in those areas where his superiors expect him to innovate.

In addition to these effects there are some other important byproducts of punishment. Punishment may result in a person's making responses which are incompatible with the punished response. Psychological tension, often manifested in emotional behavior such as fear or anxiety, is often the result. Secondly, punishment may lead to avoidance and dislike of the punishing agent. This effect can be especially important to managers who are attempting to build open, helping relationships with subordinates. The roles of punishing agent and helper are often incompatible. Many line-staff conflicts in organizations undoubtedly can be explained in these terms. Finally, punishment may generate counter-aggression. Either through a modeling effect or a justice effect, the punished person may respond with aggressive responses towards the punishing agent or towards some other stimulus.

The second technique for behavior change, commonly called extinction, also focuses primarily on reducing the probability of a response. Extinction arises from repeated trials where the response is followed by a neutral stimulus. This technique generates fewer byproducts than punishment. However, like punishment, it does not lead to the desired responses being developed. Furthermore, to the extent that one has built up an expectation of a reward for a certain response, a neutral consequence may be perceived as punishing. Thus, extinction may have some advantages over punishment, but has many of the same limitations.

Positive reinforcement is the final technique for changing behavior. Under conditions of positive reinforcement, the response produces a consequence that results in an increase in the frequency of the response. It is commonly stated that such a consequence is rewarding, pleasing, or drive-reducing for the individual. The operant conditioners, however, avoid such inferences and define positive reinforcers as stimuli which increase the probability of a preceding response. Positive reinforcement is efficient for several reasons. First, it increases the probable occurrence of the desired response. The process involves rewarding approximations to the direct response itself immediately after it is made. The desired behavior is being directly developed as opposed to successive suppression of undesired acts. Secondly, the adverse emotional responses associated with punishment and extinction are apt to be reduced, and in fact favorable emotions may be developed. Since people tend to develop positive affect to others who reward them, the "trainer" is apt to become positively valenced in the eyes of the "learner."

By way of summary, Skinner's (1953) approach suggested that the control of behavior change involves a reduction in the probability of the most prepotent response and/or an increase in the probability of some desired response. Punishment and extinction may be used. These means can only reduce the probability of the unwanted responses being made. Also, they may have undesired side effects. The third technique, positive reinforcement, has the important advantage of developing the desired response rather than merely reducing the chances of an undesired one. Also, positive reinforcement is apt to produce favorable rather than unfavorable "side effects" on organizational relationships.

This approach seems to suggest that both or neither Theory X and Theory Y assumptions are useful. This section suggested that conditioning may be both Theory X and Theory Y. Perhaps since the operant view does not make either set of assumptions, it is neither Theory X nor Theory Y. Operant conditioning is consistent with Theory Y in suggesting that the limits on human beings are a function of the organizational setting, but like Theory X, implies something about human nature; namely that deprivation or threat of some sort of deprivation is a precondition for behavior to be controlled. From the managerial perspective, however, the nomonological question is of little significance. The important thing to managers is behavior and the major point of this approach is that behavior is a function of its consequences. Good management is that which leads to the desired behavior by organizational members. Management must see to it that the consequences of behavior are such as to increase the frequency of desired behavior and decrease the frequency of undesired behaviors. The question becomes, how can managers develop a social system which provides the appropriate consequences? In many ways the answer to this question is similar to what Theory Y advocates have suggested. However, there are some new possibilities.

Applications of Conditioning in Organizations

The potential uses of the Skinnerian framework for social systems are increasing rapidly. The approach has far more applicability to complex social systems than has often been recognized. McGregor's rejection of the stimulus-response or the reward-punishment approach as inadequate for management because it does not allow for a systems approach is quite inconsistent with this general trend and his own environmentally based approach. Recent work in the field of behavioral control has begun to refute McGregor's position. The Skinnerian view can be and has been used to redesign social systems.

The most complete redesign was envisioned by Skinner (1948) in his novel, *Walden Two*. In this book, Skinner developed a society based on the use of positive reinforcement and experimental ethics geared to the goal of competition of a coordinated social unit with its environment. In other words, the system is designed to reward behaviors which are functional for the whole society. Social change is introduced on the basis of empirical data. As a result of the success of this system, man is enabled to pursue those activities which are rewarding in themselves. Although the book is a novel, it can be a valuable stimulus for thought about the design of social organization.

In addition, Skinner (1954) has taken a fresh look at teaching and learning in conventional educational systems. He noted that the school system depends heavily on aversive control or punishment. The use of low marks and ridicule have merely been substituted for the "stick." The teacher, in Skinner's view, is an out of date reinforcing mechanism. He suggested the need to examine the reinforcers which are available in the system and to apply them in a manner which is consistent with what is known about learning. For example, control over the environment itself may be rewarding. Perhaps grades reinforce the wrong behavior and are administered on a rather poor schedule. It would seem that a search for new reinforcers and better reinforcement schedules is appropriate for all modern organizations.

These speculations suggest the potential for great advances. *Walden Two* is in many ways an ideal society but has been a source of horror to many readers. The thoughts about changes in teaching methods are also a subject of controversy. However, the environment can be designed to aid in the attainment of desired ends. People resist the idea that they can be controlled by their environment. This resistance does not change the fact that they are under such control. Recently, evidence has begun to accumulate that the Skinnerian approach can be employed to design social systems.

Much of this evidence was collected in settings far removed from modern work organizations. The reader's initial response is apt to be, "What relevance do these studies have to my organization?" Obviously, the relationship is not direct. However, if, as the operant approach maintains, the conditioning process describes the acquisition and maintenance of behavior, the same principles can be applied to any social organization. The problem of application becomes merely that of engineering. The gains may well be limited only by an administrator's ingenuity and resources.

Much of the evidence comes from studies of hospitalized mental patients and autistic children, although some has been based on normal lower class children. A few examples from these studies will serve to document the great potential of the conditioning methods for social systems. Allyon and Azrin (1965) observed mental patients' behavior to determine what activities they engaged in when they had a chance. They then made tokens contingent on certain responses such as work on hospital tasks. These tokens could be exchanged for the activities the patients preferred to engage in. The results of this approach were amazing. In one experiment five schizophrenics and three mental defectives served as *Ss*. They did jobs regularly and adequately when tokens were given for the job. Such performance was reported to be in sharp contrast to the erratic and inconsistent behavior characteristic of such patients. When the tokens were no longer contingent on the work, the performance dropped almost to zero. In a second experiment, a whole ward of 44 patients served as *Ss*. A similar procedure was followed and 11 classes of tasks observed. When tokens were contingent upon the desired responses, the group spent an average of 45 hours on the tasks daily. When tokens were not contingent on responses, almost no time was spent on the tasks. The implications seem rather clear. When desired behavior is rewarded, it will be emitted, when it is not rewarded, it will not be emitted.

A great deal of related work has been reported. Allyon (1966) and Wolf, Risley, and Mees (1966) have shown how a reinforcement procedure can be effective in controlling the behavior of a psychotic patient and of an autistic child respectively. These are but a few of the many studies in a growing body of evidence.

More important for present purposes are the applications of this approach in more complex social situations. The work of Hamblin *et al.* (1967) shows some of the interesting possibilities of the conditioning approach for school classes and aggressive children. A token system was used to shape desired behavior. Through the application of the conditioning approach to the school system, gains may be made in educating children from deprived backgrounds. Two examples will illustrate these possibilities.

The first example comes from a recent newspaper story. A record shop owner in a Negro area of Chicago reported seeing the report card of a Negro boy. The owner thought the boy was bright, but the report card showed mostly unsatisfactory performance. He told the boy he would give him $5 worth of free records if he got all "excellents" on the next report card. Ten weeks later the boy returned with such a card to collect his reward. The owner reported that similar offers to other children had a remarkable effect in getting them to study and do their homework. The anecdote demonstrates what everyone knows anyway: people will work for rewards. It also suggests the converse: people will not work if rewards do not exist. The problems of education in the ghetto, and motivation to work in general, may be overcome by appropriate reinforcement. Further support for this statement comes from the work of Montrose Wolf.

Wolf (1966) ran a school for children, most of whom were sixth graders, in a lower class Negro area of Kansas City. The children attended this school for several hours after school each day and on Saturday. Rewards were given in the form of tickets which could be saved and turned in for different kinds of things like toys, food, movies, shopping trips, and other activities. Tickets were made contingent on academic performance within the remedial school itself, and on performance in the regular school system. The results were remarkable. The average school grade of the students was raised to C from D. The results on standard achievement tests showed the remedial group progressed over twice as much in one year as they had done the previous year. They showed twice as much progress as a control group. Other gains were also noted. Wolf reported that a severe punishment was not to let the children attend school. They expressed strong discontent when school was not held because of a holiday. He further noted that when reading was no longer rewarded with tickets, the students still continued to read more than before the training. Arithmetic and English did not maintain these increments. Thus, to some extent, reading appeared to be intrinsically rewarding.

A final point concerns the transferability of skills learned in such a school to society at large. Will the tasks that are not rewarding in themselves be continued? The answer is probably not, unless other rewards are provided. The task then becomes to develop skills and behavior which society itself will reward. If this method is applied to develop behavior which is rewarded by society, the behavior is apt to be maintained. The same argument holds for organizational behavior. It will be fruitless to develop behavior which is not rewarded in the organization.

In summary, evidence has been presented to show the relevance of the Skinnerian approach to complex social systems. Certainly the evidence is only suggestive of future possibilities. The rest of this paper attempts to suggest some of these implications for organizational management.

Management Through Positive Reinforcement

The implications of the systematic use of positive reinforcement for management range over many traditional areas. Some of the more important areas include training and personnel development, compensation and alternative rewards, supervision and leadership, job design, organizational design, and organizational change.

Training and Personnel Development

The area of training has been the first to benefit from the application of conditioning principles with the use of programmed learning and the teaching machine. An example of future potential comes from the Northern Systems Company Training Method for assembly line work. In this system, the program objectives are broken down into subobjectives. The training employs a lattice which provides objective relationships between functions and objectives, indicates critical evaluation points, and presents a visual display of go-no-go functions. Progress through various steps is reinforced by rewards. To quote from a statement of the training method ". . . the trainee gains satisfaction only by demonstrated performance at the tool stations. Second, he quickly perceives that correct behaviors obtain for him the satisfaction of his needs, and that incorrect behaviors do not (p. 20)." Correct performance includes not only job skills, but also the performance of social interaction which is necessary in a factory setting. The skills taught are designed to allow for high mobility in the industrial world. The Northern Systems' method develops behavior which the economic and social system will normally reinforce, and has been successful in training people in a wide variety of skills. Its potential in training such groups as the "hardcore" unemployed seems to be limited only by the resources and creativity of program designers.

The Skinnerian approach seems to have potential for all areas of personnel development, not only for highly programmed tasks. Reinforcement theory may be useful in the development of such behaviors as creativity. The work of Maltzman, Simon, Raskin, and Licht (1960) demonstrated this possibility. After a series of experiments employing a standard experimental training procedure with free association materials, these investigators concluded that a highly reliable increase in uncommon responses could be produced through the use of reinforcement. The similarity of their results to those of operant experiments with respect to the persistence of the responses and the effect of repetitions led them to conclude that originality is a form of operant behavior. Positive reinforcement increased the rate at which original responses were emitted.

Support is also available for the efficacy of operant conditioning to more conventional personnel and leadership development. Three such contributions are discussed below. The first concerns the organizational environment as a shaper of behavior of which Fleishman's (1967) study is a case in point. He found that human relations training programs were only effective in producing on-the-job changes if the organizational climate was supportive of the content of the program. More generally it would appear that industrial behavior is a function of its consequences. Those responses which are rewarded will persist; those responses which are not rewarded or are punished will decrease in frequency. If the organizational environment does not reward responses developed in a training program, the program will be, at best, a total waste of time and money. As Sykes (1962) has shown, at worst such a program may be highly disruptive. A second implication of operant conditioning concerns the content of personnel development programs in the area of human relations. If, as Homans (1961) and others have suggested, social interaction is also influenced by the same operant principles, then people in interaction are constantly "shaping" or conditioning each other. The behavior of a subordinate is to some degree developed by his boss and vice-versa. What more sensible, practical point could be taught to organizational members than that they are teaching their fellow participants to behave in a certain manner? What more practical, sensible set of principles could be taught than that, due to latent dysfunctions generated, punishment and extinction procedures are less efficient ways to influence behavior than positive reinforcement? Clearly, the behavioral scientists who have contributed so greatly to organizational practice and personnel development have not put enough emphasis on these simple principles. The third implication for personnel development is added recognition that annual merit interviews and salary increments are very inefficient development techniques. The rewards or punishments are so delayed that they can be expected to have little feedback value for the employees involved. More frequent appraisals and distribution of rewards are apt to be far more effective, especially to the degree that they are related to specific tasks or units of work.

Job Design

Recently, behavioral scientists have emphasized the social psychological factors which need to be attended to in job design. McGregor and others have suggested job enlargement. Herzberg (1968) has argued that job enlargement just allows an individual to do a greater variety of boring jobs and suggests that "job enrichment" is needed. For present purposes, job enlargement and job enrichment will be lumped together. Both of these approaches are consistent with the conditioning view if two differences can be resolved. First, the definitions of motivation must be translated into common terms. Second, reinforcers operating in the newly designed jobs must be delineated and tested to see if the reinforcers postulated in the newly designed jobs are really responsible for behavioral changes or if there are other reinforcers operating.

With respect to the definitions of motivation, the two approaches are really similar in viewing the rate of behavior as the crucial factor. The major differences exist on the conceptual level. Both job enlargement and job enrichment are attempts to increase motivation. Conceptually, McGregor and Herzberg tend to view motivation as some internal state. The conditioning approach does not postulate internal states but rather deals with the manipulation of environmental factors which influence the rate of behavior. Actually, some combination of the two approaches may be most useful theoretically as Vinacke (1962) has suggested. However, if both approaches are viewed only at the operational level, it is quite probable that rates of behavior could be agreed on as an acceptable criterion. Certainly from the practitioner's viewpoint, behavior is the crucial variable. When a manager talks about a motivated worker, he often means one who frequently makes desired responses at a high rate without external prompting from the boss. The traditional view of motivation as an inner drive is of limited practical and theoretical value.

If both approaches could agree on the behavioral criterion, at least on an operational level, the operant approach could be employed to help resolve some practical and theoretical problems suggested by the work of McGregor and Herzberg. Since, generally speaking, the external conditions are most easily manipulated in an organization, attention can be focused on designing an environment which increases the frequency of the wanted responses. As a result, practitioners and students of organization could deal with motivation without searching for man's essence. We can avoid the metaphysical assumptions of Maslow and McGregor until they are better documented. The issue of a two-factor theory of motivation proposed by Herzberg, which recently has been severely challenged by Lindsay, Marks, and Gorlow (1967) and Hulin and Smith (1967), among others, can also be avoided. Attention can be confined to developing systems which produce high rates of desired behavior. Thus the conceptual differences about motivation do not cause unresolvable conflict at the present time.

The second area of difference between McGregor–Herzberg and the operant explanation of the effects of job enrichment stems from the failure of Herzberg and McGregor to recognize the great variety of possible rewards available in job design. The Skinnerian approach leads to the development of a more comprehensive discussion of the rewards from enriched or enlarged jobs. In terms of the operant approach, both job enrichment and job enlargement are apt to lead to what would generally be called greater motivation or what we will call higher rates of desired behavior. McGregor and Herzberg suggest feelings of achievement and responsibility explain these results. The reinforcement approach leads to a search for specific rewards in these newly designed jobs.

Job enlargement can be viewed simply as increasing the variety of tasks a person does. Recent research on self-stimulation and sensory deprivation has suggested that stimulation itself is reinforcing, especially when one has been deprived of it. The increased variety of tasks due to job enlargement may thus be intrinsically rewarding due to a host of reinforcers in the work itself rather than to any greater feeling of responsibility or achievement. These feelings may be a cause of greater productivity or merely correlates of the receipt of these intrinsic rewards from stimulation. The evidence is not clear, but the effects of job enlargement can at least be partially explained in operant terms.

Some additional support from this idea comes from Schultz's (1964) work on spontaneous alteration of behavior. Schultz suggested that spontaneous alteration of human behavior is facilitated (1) when responses are not reinforced and/or are not subjected to knowledge of correctness, (2) by the amount of prior exercise of one response alternative, and (3) by a short interval. Low feedback and reinforcement, short intervals between responses, and the frequent repetition of one response are all characteristic of many jobs which need enlargement. Merely making different responses may be rewarding to a worker, thereby explaining some of the benefits noted from job enlargement. It has also been noted that people create variation for themselves in performing monotonous tasks. For example, ritualized social interaction in the form of social "games" is a form of such alteration workers developed noted by Roy (1964).

By way of summary, much of the current work on job enlargement and enrichment has attributed the effects to feelings of achievement or responsibility, without taking into account numerous other possible reinforcers which may be more basic. Further research to determine the efficacy of these various possibilities is needed before definite conclusions can be drawn. Do the feelings of achievement or responsibility operate as reinforcers in an operant manner? Do these feelings come from other more basic rewards as task variety? Present data do not permit answers to these questions.

With respect to the benefits noted from job enrichment, an operant model may provide further insights. Herzberg (1968) maintained that some jobs can not be "enriched" or made more motivating in themselves. It is the contention of this paper that it is not the tasks which are the problem, but it is the reinforcement schedules. For example, what could be more boring, have less potential for achievement and realization of Herzberg's satisfiers than the game of bingo? Yet people will sit for hours at bingo, often under punishing conditions (since the house takes in more than it pays out) and place tokens on numbers. Similar behavior is exhibited at slot machines and other gambling devices. Most operational definitions of motivation would agree that these players are highly motivated. The reason is clear from the operant viewpoint. The reinforcement schedule employed in games of chance, the variable ratio schedule, is a very powerful device for maintaining a rapid rate of response. With respect to job design, the important requirement is that rewards follow performance on an effective schedule.

The type of rewards Herzberg (1968) called satisfiers may be important motivators because they are distributed on a variable ratio schedule. Herzberg's data does not rule out this explanation. Take achievement, for example. If a person is doing a job from which it is possible to get a feeling of achievement, there must be a reasonably large probability that a person will not succeed on the task. Oftentimes, this condition means that some noncontinuous schedule or reinforcement is operating. An individual will succeed only on some variable ratio schedule. In addition, successful completion of the task is often the most important reward. The reward is, of course, immediate. A similar statement could be made about tasks which are said to yield intrinsic satisfaction, such as crossword puzzles or enriched jobs. Thus the factors Herzberg called motivators may derive their potency from the manner in which the rewards are administered. The task is immediately and positively reinforced by the environment on a variable ratio schedule. Often the schedule is one which rewards a very small fraction of a large number of responses. Since behavior is a function of its consequences, if jobs can be designed to reinforce desired behavior in the appropriate manner, "motivated" workers are apt to result. Some of Herzberg's results may be explained without resort to a two-factor theory more parsimoniously in terms of schedules of reinforcement. Herzberg's (1966) finding that recognition is only a motivator if it is contingent on performance further documents the operant argument.

Another suggestion for job design from the operant tradition was suggested by Homans. He explored the relationship of the frequency of an activity and satisfaction to the amount of a reward. He concluded that satisfaction is generally positively related to the amount of reward whereas frequency of an activity is negatively related to the amount of reward the individual has received in the recent past. In order to have both high satisfaction and high activity, Homans (1961) suggested that tasks need to be designed in a manner such that repeated activities lead up to the accomplishment of some final result and get rewarded at a very low frequency until just before the final result is achieved.

Then the reinforcement comes often. For example, consider the job of producing bottled soda. An optimal design would have the reward immediately on the completion of putting the caps on the bottles, but the task would be designed such that all the operations prior to capping were completed before any capping was done. Near the end of a work day, all the capping could be done. High output and satisfaction might then exist simultaneously. In general then, the operant approach suggests some interesting possibilities for designing jobs in ways which would maximize the power of reinforcers in the job itself.

A similar argument can be applied to some problems faced in administration and management. For example, it is commonly recognized that programmed tasks tend to be attended to before unprogrammed ones. It is quite obvious that programmed functions produce a product which is often tangible. The product itself is a reinforcer. An unprogrammed task often requires behavior which has not been reinforced in the past and will not produce a reward in the near future. It may be beneficial to provide rewards relatively early for behavior on unprogrammed tasks. This suggestion will be difficult to put into practice because of the very nature of unprogrammed tasks. Perhaps the best that can be done is to reward the working on such tasks.

Compensation and Alternative Rewards

Although whether money is a true "generalized reinforcer," as Skinner suggests, has not been demonstrated conclusively, for years operant principles have been applied in the form of monetary incentive systems. Opsahl and Dunnette (1966) concluded that such programs generally do increase output. However, the restriction of output and other unanticipated consequences are associated with these programs. Many writers have attributed these consequences to social forces, such as the desire for approval from one's peers. Gewitz and Baer (1958), for example, have shown that social approval has the same effects as other reinforcers in an operant situation. Dalton's (1948) famous study on rate-busters may be interpreted to show that people who are more "group-oriented" may place a higher value on social approval and hence are more apt to abide by group production norms than are less "group-oriented" people. Thus, it is not that money in piece-rate systems is not a potential reinforcer, but rather other reinforcers are more effective, at least after a certain level of monetary reward.

The successful use of the Scanlon Plan demonstrates the value of combining both economic and social rewards. This plan rewards improved work with several types of reinforcers, and often more immediately and directly than many incentive systems. The Scanlon Plan combines economic rewards, often given monthly, with social rewards. The latter are given soon after an employee's idea has been submitted or used.

Related arguments can be made for other group incentive programs. Often jobs are interdependent. The appropriate reinforcement for such tasks should be contingent upon interdependent responses, not individual ones. Even if the jobs are independent, the workers are social-psychologically interdependent. Social rewards are often obtainable by restricting output. It is hardly surprising that individual incentive programs have produced the unanticipated consequences so often noted. Further, since rewards and punishments from the informal group are apt to be administered immediately and frequently they are apt to be very powerful in controlling behavior.

In general, then, money and other rewards must be made contingent on the desired responses. Further, the importance of rewards alternative to money must be recognized and incorporated into the design of the work environment. The widely known path-goal to productivity model expresses a similar point.

Another problem of compensation in organizations is also apparent in an operant context. Often, means of compensation, especially fringe benefits, have the unanticipated consequences of reinforcing the wrong responses. Current programs of sick pay, recreation programs, employee lounges, work breaks, and numerous other personnel programs all have one point in common. They all reward the employee for not working or for staying away from the job. These programs are not "bad," since often they may act to reduce problems such as turnover. However, an employer who relies on them should realize what behavior he is developing by establishing these costly programs. Alternative expenditures must be considered. If some of the money that was allocated for these programs were used to redesign jobs so as to be more reinforcing in themselves, more productive effort could be obtained. This idea is certainly not new. A host of behavioral scientists have suggested that resources devoted to making performance of the job itself more attractive will pay social and/or economic dividends.

Another interesting application of conditioning principles has to do with the schedule on which pay is distributed. The conventional pay schedule is a fixed interval one. Further, pay often is not really contingent on one's performance. The response needed to be rewarded is often attending work on pay day. Not only is pay often not contingent upon performance, but the fixed interval schedule is not given to generating a high response rate. In a creative article, Aldis (1966) suggested an interesting compensation program employing a variable ratio schedule. Instead of an annual Christmas bonus or other types of such expected salary supplements, he suggested a lottery system. If an employee produced above an agreed upon standard, his name would be placed in a hat. A drawing would be held. The name(s) drawn would receive an amount of money proportionate to the number of units produced during that period of time. This system would approximate the desired variable ratio schedule.

In addition to the prosperity of the owners of gambling establishments, there is some direct evidence that variable ratio schedules will be of use to those charged with predicting and controlling human behavior. A leading St. Louis hardware company, although apparently unaware of the work of the operant conditioners, has applied an approximate variable ratio schedule of reinforcement to reduce absenteeism and tardiness. Although the complete data are not available, the personnel department has reported surprising success. A brief description of the system will be presented below and a more detailed study will be written in the near future.

Under the lottery system, if a person is on time (that is, not so much as $\frac{1}{2}$ minute late) for work at the start of his day and after his breaks, he is eligible for a drawing at the end of the month. Prizes worth approximately $20 to $25 are awarded to the winners. One prize is available for each 25 eligible employees. At the end of six months, people who have had perfect attendance for the entire period are eligible for a drawing for a color television set. The names of all the winners and of those eligible are also printed in the company paper, such that social reinforcement may also be a factor. The plan was introduced because tardiness and absenteeism had become a very serious problem. In the words of the personnel manager, absenteeism and tardiness ". . . were lousy before." Since the program was begun 16 months ago, conditions have improved greatly. Sick leave costs have been reduced about 62 percent. After the first month, 151 of approximately 530 employees were eligible for the drawing. This number has grown larger, although not at a steady rate, to 219 for the most recent month. Although the comparable figures for the period before the program were unfortunately not available, management has noted great improvements. It would appear that desired behavior by organization participants in terms of tardiness and absenteeism can be readily and inexpensively developed by a variable ratio schedule of positive reinforcement. The possibilities for other areas are limited largely by the creativity of management.

The operant approach also has some additional implications for the use of money as a reward. First, many recent studies have shown money is not as important as other job factors in worker satisfaction. Herzberg (1968), among others, has said explicitly that money will not promote worker satisfaction. Undoubtedly, in many situations, Herzberg is correct. However, crucial factors of reward contingencies and schedules have not been controlled in these studies. Again, it appears that the important distinction that can be made between Herzberg's motivators and hygiene factors is that the former set of rewards are contingent on an individual's responses and the latter are not. If a work situation were designed so that money was directly contingent on performance, the results might be different. A second point has to do with the perception of money as a reward. Opsahl and Dunnette (1966) have recently questioned pay secrecy policies. They maintained that pay secrecy leads to misperception of the amount of money that a promotion might mean. The value of the reinforcers is underestimated by the participants' suggesting that they are less effective than they might otherwise be. Certainly, alternative rewards are likely to be "over chosen." By following policies of pay secrecy, organizations seem to be failing to utilize fully their available monetary rewards.

In addition to underutilization of money rewards, organizations seem to be almost totally unaware of alternative reinforcers, and in fact see punishment as the only viable method of control when existing reinforcers fail. What are some alternatives to a punishment-centered bureaucracy? Some, such as job design, improved scheduling of reinforcement, and a search for new reinforcers have already been suggested. There are other possible reinforcers, a few of which are discussed below.

The important thing about reinforcers is that they be made immediately contingent on desired performance to the greatest degree possible. The potential reinforcers discussed here also require such a contingent relationship, although developing such relationships may be a severe test of an administrator's creativity. One of the more promising reinforcers is leisure. It would seem possible in many jobs to establish an agreed-upon standard output for a day's work. This level could be higher than the current average. Once this amount is reached, the group or individual could be allowed the alternative of going home. The result of experiments in this direction would be interesting to all concerned. Quite possibly, this method might lead to a fuller utilization of our labor force. The individual may be able to hold two four-hour jobs, doubling his current contribution. Such a tremendous increase in output is quite possible, as Stagner and Rosen (1966) have noted, when the situation possesses appropriate contingencies. Certainly, the problems of industrial discipline, absenteeism, and grievances which result in lower productivity might be ameliorated. Another possible reinforcer is information. Guetzkow (1965) noted that people have a strong desire to receive communication. Rewarding desired performance with communication or feedback may be a relatively inexpensive reinforcer. Graphs, charts, or even tokens which show immediate and cumulative results may serve this function. Some of the widely accepted benefits from participative management may be due to the reinforcing effect of communication. Certainly the "Hawthorne effect" can be described in these terms. In addition, social approval and status may be powerful reinforcers. Blau's classic study described by Homans (1961) on the exchange of approval and status for help is but one example. People will work for approval and status. If these are made contingent on a desired set of responses, the response rate can be increased. At present, often social approval is given by one's peers, but is contingent on behavior which is in conflict with organizational goals.

In addition to these reinforcers, there are certain social exchange concepts such as justice, equity, reciprocity, and indebtedness which deserve attention. Recent research has demonstrated that an unbalanced social exchange, such as one which is inequitable or leaves one person indebted to someone else, may be tension-producing in such a way that individuals work to avoid them. In other words, unbalanced exchanges are a source of punishment. Relationships, such as those involving dependency, which result in such social imbalance can be expected to have the same latent consequences as punishment. Techniques which employ social imbalance to predict and control behavior can be expected to be less efficient in most respects than ones based on positive reinforcement.

The crucial variable in distributing any reward is contingency. Managers have been quick to point out that the problem with a "welfare state" is that rewards do not depend on desired behavior. This point is well taken. It is surprising that the same point has not been recognized in current management practices.

Organizational Climate and Design

Important aspects of human behavior can be attributed to the immediate environment in which people function. The potential then exists to structure and restructure formal organizations in a manner to promote the desired behavior. Once this point is recognized and accepted by managers, progress can begin. The reaction of managers to this approach is often, "You mean my organization should reward people for what they ought to do anyway?" The answer is that people's behavior is largely determined by its outcomes. It is an empirical fact rather than a moral question. If you want a certain response and it does not occur, you had better change the reinforcement contingencies to increase its probable occurrence.

The first step in the direction of designing organizations on this basis involves defining explicitly the desired behaviors and the available reinforcers. The next step is to then make these rewards dependent on the emission of the desired responses. What are some of the implications of such reasoning for organizational design?

Already the importance of organizational climate has been discussed in connection with human development. Some additional implications merit brief consideration. A major one concerns conformity. Often today the degree to which people conform to a wide variety of norms is lamentably acknowledged and the question is asked, "Why do people do it?" The reasons in the operant view are quite clear: conformity is rewarded, deviance is punished. People conform in organizations because conformity is profitable in terms of the outcomes the individual achieves. In fact, Nord (in press) and Walker and Heyns (1962) presented considerable evidence that conformity has the same properties as other operant responses. If managers are really worried about the costs of conformity in terms of creativity and innovation, they must look for ways to reward deviance, to avoid punishing nonconformity, and to avoid rewarding conformity. Furthermore, the way in which rewards are administered is important. Generally, if rewards are given by a person or group of people, a dependency relationship is created, with hostility, fear, anxiety, and other emotional outcomes being probable. Dependence itself may be a discomforting condition. It is therefore desirable to make the rewards come from the environment. Rewards which have previously been established for reaching certain agreed-upon goals are one such means. Meaningful jobs in which achievement in itself is rewarding are another way. In general, to the degree that competition is with the environment or forces outside the organization, and rewards come from achievement itself, the more effective the reinforcers are apt to be in achieving desired responses.

A final point concerns the actual operation of organizations. Increasingly it is recognized that a formal organization, which aims at the coordination of the efforts of its participants, is dependent on informal relationships for its operation. As Gross (1968) noted, "In administration, also, 'the play's the thing' and not the script. Many aspects of even the simplest operation can never be expressed in writing. They must be sensed and felt. . . . Daily action is the key channel of operational definition. In supplying cues and suggestions, in voicing praise and blame, in issuing verbal instructions, administrators define or clarify operational goals in real life" (p. 406).

More generally, what makes an organization "tick" is the exchange of reinforcers within it and between it and its environment. The nature of these exchanges involves both economic and social reinforcers. Many of these are given and received without explicit recognition or even awareness on the part of the participants. The operant approach focuses attention on these exchange processes. As a result, it may prove to be an invaluable asset to both administrators and students of administration and organization.

A final advantage of the operant approach for current organizational theory and analysis may be the attention it focuses on planned and rational administration. Gouldner (1966) noted "Modern organizational analysis by sociologists is overpreoccupied with the spontaneous and unplanned responses which organizations make to stress, and too little concerned with patterns of planned and rational administration (p. 397)." The Skinnerian approach leads to rational planning in order to control outcomes previously viewed as spontaneous consequences. This approach could expand the area of planning rational action in administration.

References

Aldis, O. "Of Pigeons and Men," in R. Ulrich, T. Stachnik and J. Mabry (eds.), *Control of Human Behavior*. Glenview, Ill.: Scott, Foresman, 1966, 218–221.

Ayllon, T. "Intensive Treatment of Psychotic Behavior by Stimulus Satiation and Food Reinforcement." In R. Ulrich, T. Stachnik and J. Mabry (eds.), *Control of Human Behavior*. Glenview, Ill.: Scott, Foresman, 1966, 170–176.

Ayllon, T., and Azrin, N. H. "The Measurement and Reinforcement of Behavior of Psychotics," *Journal of the Experimental Analysis of Behavior,* 1965, 8, 357–383.

Bijou, S. W., and Baer, D. M. *Child Development*. Vol. 1. New York: Appleton-Century-Crofts, 1961.

Dalton, M. "The Industrial 'Rate-Buster': A Characterization." *Applied Anthropology,* 1948, 7, 5–18.

Fleishman, E. A. "Leadership Climate, Human Relations Training, and Supervisory Behavior." In Fleishman, E. A. (ed.), *Studies in Personnel and Industrial Psychology*. Homewood, Ill.: Dorsey, 1967, 250–263.

"Free Records Given for E's, Pupils' Report Cards Improve." *St. Louis Dispatch,* December 3, 1967.

Gewirtz, J. L., and Baer, D. M. "Deprivation and Satiation of Social Reinforcers as Drive Conditions." *Journal of Abnormal and Social Psychology,* 1958, 57, 165–172.

Gouldner, A. W. "Organizational Analysis." In Bennis, W. G., Benne, K. D., and Chin, R. (eds.), *The Planning of Change*. New York: Holt, Rinehart, and Winston, 1966, 393–399.

Gross, B. M. *Organizations and Their Managing*. New York: Free Press, 1968.

Guetzkow, H. "Communications in Organizations." In March, J. G. (ed.), *Handbook of Organizations*. Chicago: Rand McNally, 1965, 534–573.

Hamblin, R. L., Bushell, O. B., Buckholdt, D., Ellis, D., Ferritor, D., Merritt, G., Pfeiffer, C., Shea, D., and Stoddard, D. "Learning, Problem Children and a Social Exchange System." Annual Report of the Social Exchange Laboratories, Washington University, and Student Behavior Laboratory, Webster College, St. Louis, Mo., August, 1967.

Herzberg, F. "One More Time: How Do You Motivate Employees?" *Harvard Business Review,* January–February, 1968, 53–62.

Herzberg, F. *Work and the Nature of Man*. Cleveland: World, 1966.

Homans, G. C. *Social Behavior: Its Elementary Forms*. New York: Harcourt, Brace and World, 1961.

Hulin, C. L., and Smith, P. A. "An Empirical Investigation of Two Implications of the Two-Factor Theory of Job Satisfaction." *Journal of Applied Psychology,* 1967, 51, 396–402.

Lindsay, C. A., Marks, E., and Gorlow, L. "The Herzberg Theory: A Critique and Reformulation." *Journal of Applied Psychology,* 1967, 51, 330–339.

Maltzman, I., Simon, S., Roskin, D., and Licht, L. "Experimental Studies in the Training of Originality." Psychological Monographs: General and Applied, 1960, 74 (6, Whole No. 493).

Maslow, A. *Eupsychian Management*. Homewood, Ill.: Dorsey, 1965.

McGregor, D. *The Human Side of Enterprise*. New York: McGraw-Hill, 1960.

McGregor, D. *Leadership and Motivation*. Cambridge, Mass.: M. I. T. Press, 1966.

Nord, W. R. "Social Exchange Theory: An Integrative Approach to Social Conformity." *Psychological Bulletin,* (in press).

Northern Systems Company. "A Proposal to the Department of Labor for Development of a Prototype Project for the New Industries Program." Part One.

Opsahl, R. L., and Dunnette, M. D. "The Role of Financial Compensation in Industrial Motivation." *Psychological Bulletin,* 1966, 66, 94–118.

Reese, E. P. *The Analysis of Human Operant Behavior.* Dubuque, Iowa: William C. Brown, 1966.

Roy, D. F. "Banana Time—Job Satisfaction and Informal Interaction." In Bennis, W. G., Schein, E. H., Berlew, D. E., and Steele, F. I. (eds.), *Interpersonal Dynamics.* Homewood, Ill.: Dorsey, 1964, 583–600.

Schultz, D. P. "Spontaneous Alteration Behavior in Humans, Implications for Psychological Research." *Psychological Bulletin,* 1964, 62, 394–400.

Skinner, B. F. *Science and Human Behavior.* New York: Macmillan, 1953.

Skinner, B. F. "The Science of Learning and the Art of Teaching." *Harvard Educational Review,* 1954, 24, 86–97.

Skinner, B. F. *Walden Two.* New York: Macmillan, 1948.

Stagner, R., and Rosen, H. *Psychology of Union-Management Relations.* Belmont, Cal.: Wadsworth, 1966.

Sykes, A. J. M. "The Effect of a Supervisory Training Course in Changing Supervisors' Perceptions and Expectations of the Role of Management." *Human Relations,* 1962, 15, 227–243.

Vinacke, E. W. "Motivation as a Complex Problem." *Nebraska Symposium on Motivation,* 1962, 10, 1–45.

Walker, E. L., and Heyns, R. W. *An Anatomy of Conformity.* Englewood Cliffs, N.J.: Prentice-Hall, 1962.

Wolf, M. M. Paper read at Sociology Colloquium, Washington University, December 5, 1966.

Wolf, M. M., Risley, T., and Mees, H. "Application of Operant Conditioning Procedures to the Behavior Problems of an Autistic Child." In R. Ulrich, T. Stachnik and J. Mabry (eds.), *Control of Human Behavior,* Glenview, Ill.: Scott, Foresman, 1966, 187–193.

Employee Performance and Employee Need Satisfaction: Which Comes First?

ROBERT A. SUTERMEISTER

Assuming Maslow's hierarchy of needs theory is correct,[1]

- What is the cause and effect relationship between employee performance and need satisfaction?
- Does high performance result in satisfaction of needs?
- Does satisfaction of needs result in improved performance?
- Or is there a circular relationship, each contributing to the other and each being affected by the other?

These are difficult questions. Brayfield and Crockett established in 1955 that "satisfaction with one's position in a network of relationships need not imply

"Employee Performance and Employee Need Satisfaction—Which Comes First?" by Robert A. Sutermeister. Copyright © 1971 by The Regents of the University of California. Reprinted from *California Management Review,* Vol. 13, No. 4, pp. 43–47, by permission of the author and of The Regents.

strong motivation to outstanding performance within that system."[2] Roberts et al. conclude there is no present technique for determining cause and effect of performance and satisfaction.[3] Porter and Lawler state that the greatest future research need is for data to provide evidence on the direction of causality in their model relating performance and satisfaction (see Figure 1).[4]

Figure 1   Porter-Lawler Theoretical Model (Reprinted with permission from L. W. Porter and E. E. Lawler, *Managerial Attitudes and Performance,* Homewood, Ill.: Richard D. Irwin, Inc., 1968 ©, p. 165.)

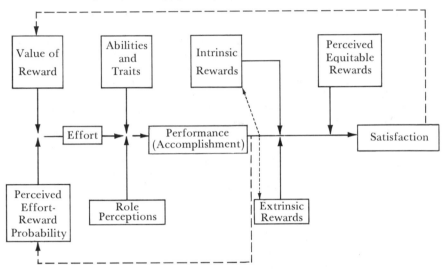

A number of authors state or imply that satisfaction contributes to improved performance and productivity. Herzberg et al. examined studies in which the effect of job attitudes on productivity was measured. They found "that in 54 percent of the reported surveys high morale was associated with high productivity" although the correlations in many of these studies were low; they concluded there was "frequent evidence for the often suggested opinion that positive job attitudes are favorable to increased productivity."[5] Sorcher and Meyer in a study of factory employees found that giving more meaning to routine jobs, making them more satisfying, and meeting some of the human needs of workers resulted in greater productive motivation and higher quality workmanship.[6] Pigors and Myers state a working hypothesis that job satisfaction of a certain kind and at a given level may have a positive relationship to individual productivity.[7] And Sutermeister proposes a generalization for individuals who have strong egoistic needs: that the chances of motivating good employee performance are greater if the egoistic needs are fairly well satisfied on a continuing basis or if the employees feel that their present activities will lead to such satisfaction in the future.[8] The suggestion is that satisfaction (now or anticipated) of needs (especially egoistic) leads to improved performance.

Other authors state or imply a different point of view: that outstanding performance leads to greater satisfaction of needs. Miles, Porter, and Craft state that work satisfaction may improve as a by-product of subordinates' making full use of their resources; that satisfaction is intrinsic in the work; that subordinates get a major portion of their rewards merely from their own feelings of accomplishment and doing the job well.[9]

The Porter and Lawler Model

Porter and Lawler devised perhaps the most complete model of a satisfaction-performance relationship in their study of managerial attitudes and performance. Their model *predicts* that satisfaction results from performance itself, the rewards for performance, and the perceived equitability of those rewards.[10] (Ideally rewards come as a result of performance, but actually people can and often do receive rewards unrelated to performance.) However, they are careful to point out that the direction of causality the model predicts remains to be validated in future research.

In the Porter and Lawler model, if an individual is attracted by the value of the reward he envisions for a higher level of performance, and if he perceives as highly probable that increased effort will lead to that reward, he will increase his effort. And, if he has the required abilities and accurate role perceptions, his performance or accomplishment will improve. If the intrinsic and extrinsic rewards he receives from improved performance are perceived as equitable, then satisfaction will result, satisfaction being the difference between perceived equitable and actual rewards. In short, the model predicts that performance leads to satisfaction rather than satisfaction to improved performance.

The Cycle Concept

It may be useful to think of the performance-satisfaction relationship in terms of a series of cycles. The Porter-Lawler study did not collect data to predict how "changes in level of need satisfaction affect the future values of certain rewards." This is a major area well worth further study and research.

Since psychologists seem agreed that a satisfied need is no motivator, one could hypothesize that if an individual's needs are met and satisfaction has been achieved, he would not be motivated to improve his performance. Such an hypothesis overlooks the possibility that higher level needs may become activated, and the individual may now be motivated to satisfy them. It may be helpful to view satisfaction in the Porter and Lawler model as the end of one cycle and as the beginning of another.

It is difficult, of course, to pinpoint the end of one cycle and the start of another. In general it might be said one cycle ends when the individual receives his rewards, whether intrinsic, extrinsic, or both. Some people whose satisfaction depends mostly on pay (as an extrinsic reward) receive their rewards annually at pay increase time. Other people whose satisfaction depends mostly on intrinsic rewards may receive their rewards in the form of recognition and accomplishment at annual performance review time (which may be different from pay increase time). For others, who view their most important rewards as meeting challenges and self-fulfillment through utilization of their highest capacities, the rewards may be self-bestowed and come at any time. Thus various individuals are likely to have different times for ending one performance-reward cycle and starting the next.

Life Cycle and Aspiration Level

In addition to considering a performance-satisfaction cycle, it is convenient to consider a "life cycle" through which each person passes.

The young man getting out of school and embarking on his career is likely to be eager and enthusiastic and his aspiration level high. The role which he plays during these early years in his career may be quite different from the roles he plays later on. Money may be an important incentive as he tries to carve out his niche among his peers. On the other hand, some individuals are more interested in the opportunities a job offers than in its immediate financial reward. If they feel the job is "leading to something," represents a path to a goal they have set for themselves, the money may be of secondary importance.

A man's turning point often comes in the middle of his career. Here he may find a definite fork in the road. If he has accumulated a string of successes in achieving his goals, he may follow one fork and set his cap for a higher goal; or if he has become thwarted in achieving his goals, he may follow the other fork and resign himself to something less than he had started out to achieve. This is a critical period in which the "climber" may change into the "conserver," when reality may replace idealism and one may compromise or settle for less than earlier goals.[11] The level of aspiration a person now adopts will depend on whether he has achieved his previously set levels of aspiration or whether he has failed to reach them and now therefore lowers his aspirations.

In his late career a man is even more likely to become a conserver and hold on to what he has. He may feel that insufficient years remain for him to achieve the high-level goals sought in his youth, so he may be tempted to ride out his career until retirement at 65.

This description of a life cycle represents, of course, a general pattern. Specific individuals vary widely from the described scheme. Many men are going strong at 65 and have distinguished careers into their 80's and 90's. Others become conservers and "retire" at 30. The important point is not that there is a single pattern the same for everyone, but rather that the position one occupies in his life cycle is likely to have a great bearing on his level of aspirations.

Level of Needs. At the end of a cycle, and referring only to needs activated on the job, have the individual's needs been fully met or are they unfulfilled? Has the fulfillment of certain egoistic needs been followed by activation of higher-level needs? For some individuals higher-level needs are never completely satisfied. Fulfillment of one need simply activates a higher-level need in a never-ending striving for complete self-fulfillment.

Alternatives for the Unsatisfied

Let's assume for the moment that at the end of a cycle the individual's needs are not satisfied (see Figure 2). Whether he begins a search for a way to satisfy them depends upon his level of aspiration, which in turn is affected by his position in his life cycle.

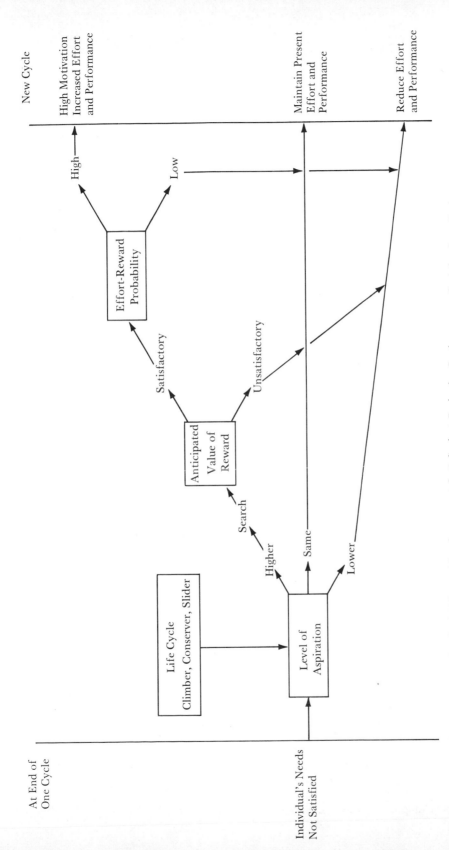

Figure 2 Alternatives for the Individual Whose Needs are not Satisfied at End of a Performance-Satisfaction Cycle

- A person late in his life cycle may have become a conserver or a backslider and have lowered his level of aspiration; or,
- Even if he is a climber in his life cycle, his failure to satisfy his needs in the previous cycle could lower his level of aspiration in the new cycle; or,
- He may have a high level of aspiration and intensify his need-satisfaction search.

He may do this by seeking a different job in the same firm or in a new firm. He may do this by exerting greater effort on his present job, provided, in accordance with the Porter-Lawler model, the value of the reward he anticipates in the next cycle is high enough, and the effort-reward probability strong enough.

If he becomes convinced that his chances of satisfying his needs are not good or are not worth the effort, he may give up his search. Thus his actual behavior will be strongly influenced by his level of aspiration, which in turn is affected by what happened in the previous performance-satisfaction cycle and by his place in his life cycle.

Alternatives for the Satisfied

Now let's assume that when the individual receives his reward he perceives it as equitable and is satisfied (see Figure 3). He now has to plan his behavior for the next cycle.

- Will his effort drop to a lower level?
- Will he maintain it at the present level?
- Will he try to improve it?

If a satisfied need is no motivator, his initial reaction may be to reduce his effort. His decision again will depend on a number of factors.

- What is the individual's level of aspiration as influenced by his position in his life cycle?
- Have higher-level needs been activated?
- If so, is the anticipated value of the reward in the next cycle satisfactory?
- And, is the effort-reward probability perceived as satisfactory?

For some individuals higher level needs may become activated. They may be in a climbing period in their life cycles, or for other reasons have high aspiration levels; and if the value of reward and perceived effort-reward probability are satisfactory, they may be motivated to greater effort and improved performance. (A unionized worker may find his higher level needs activated. But if his rewards come from higher pay, and pay is determined through union negotiations and not through personal effort, there is low probability of effort leading to reward. In the new cycle, then, his effort and performance are not likely to be high.)[12]

A second group of individuals may decide that they would like only to continue enjoying their present satisfaction. They may be in the middle of their life cycles, and have become conservers, wishing merely to retain their present level of power, prestige, and income. Their needs are satisfied, but this does

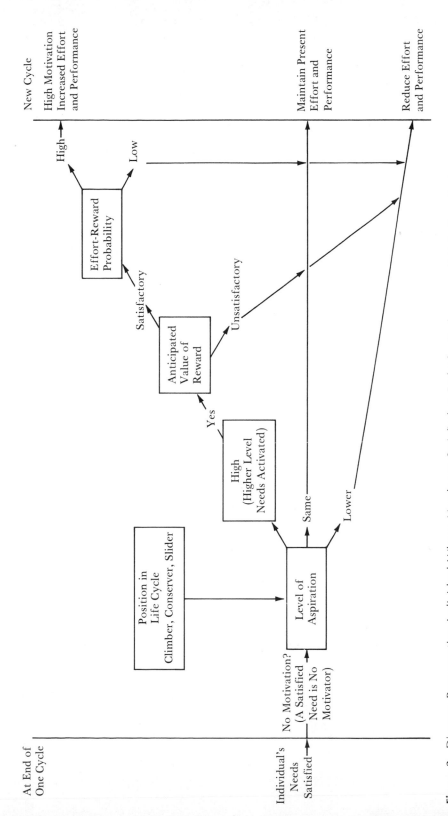

Figure 3 Diagram Representing Individual Whose Needs are Satisfied at End of a Performance-Satisfaction Cycle

not mean that they have no motivation. Rather they are motivated to continue their efforts at a level which will retain the rewards they now enjoy, provided, of course, the value of the reward and the perceived effort-reward probability remain the same.

A third group of individuals may decide to lower their levels of aspiration. Perhaps they are far along in their life cycles and desire to ease up on their efforts and be satisfied with a lower reward. In this case the value of the reward and the perceived effort-reward probability, even if high, are of little concern.

Conclusion

The degree of satisfaction at the end of one performance-satisfaction cycle and the individual's position in his life cycle will affect his level of aspiration in the new performance-satisfaction cycle. If his level of aspiration is raised, and if the value of the reward and the perceived effort-reward probability appear satisfactory to him, he will be motivated to improve his effort and performance in the new cycle. If his level of aspiration remains the same, and value of reward and perceived effort-reward probability remain the same, he will be motivated to continue his previous level of effort in the new cycle. And if his level of aspiration is lowered, he will reduce his effort in the new cycle regardless of the value of reward and perceived effort-reward probability.

We may theorize, then, that effort and performance affect satisfaction, and that satisfaction by its influence on level of aspiration affects subsequent effort and performance. Thus it would seem as if the satisfaction-productivity relationship is circular, as the final figure shows.

Figure 4 Satisfaction-Productivity Relationship

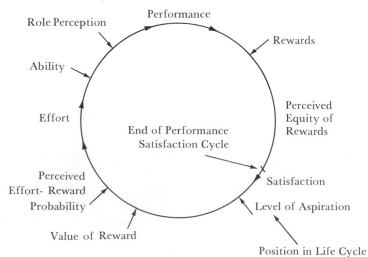

References

1. A. H. Maslow. "A Theory of Human Motivation." *Psychological Review,* 50 (1943), 370–396.
2. Arthur H. Brayfield and Walter H. Crockett. "Employee Attitudes and Employee Performance." *Psychological Bulletin,* 52:5 (1955), 415–422.
3. Karlene Roberts, Raymond E. Miles, and L. Vaughn Blankenship. "Organizational Leadership Satisfaction and Productivity: A Comparative Analysis." *Academy of Management Journal,* 11:4 (December 1968), 401–414.
4. Lyman Porter and Edward E. Lawler. *Managerial Attitudes and Performance* (Homewood, Ill.: Irwin, 1968), 167.
5. F. Herzberg *et al., Job Attitudes: Review of Research and Opinion* (Pittsburgh: Psychological Service of Pittsburgh, 1957), 103.
6. Melvin Sorcher and Herbert H. Meyer. "Motivating Factory Employees." *Personnel* (Jan.–Feb. 1968), 22–28.
7. Paul Pigors and Charles Myers. *Personnel Administration.* 6th ed., (New York: McGraw-Hill, 1969), 160–161.
8. Robert A. Sutermeister. *People and Productivity.* 2d ed. (New York: McGraw-Hill, 1969), 54–55.
9. Raymond E. Miles, Lyman Porter, and Joseph A. Craft. "Three Models of Leadership Attitudes." In Paul Pigors, Charles Myers, and F. T. Malm, *Management of Human Resources* (New York: McGraw-Hill, 1961), 48–49.
10. Porter and Lawler, p. 165.
11. The terms "climber" and "conserver" are from Anthony Downs, *Inside Bureaucracy* (Boston: Little Brown, 1967), 92 and 96.
12. See Porter and Lawler. "What Job Attitudes Tell About Motivation." *Harvard Business Review* (Jan.–Feb. 1968), 121.

Questions for Discussion

1. Describe a situation in which you observed or felt the action of social facilitation; that is, the effect of others on your learning or performing effectiveness.

2. Attitudes or feelings are only partially controllable. Describe three situations demonstrating the interdependence of personal attitudes, agreement/disagreement, and external "facts":
   a) where there is mutual attraction between A and B along with agreement about X.
   b) where there is mutual rejection between A and B along with disagreement about X.
   c) an unstable state.

3. Describe a situation in which you were involved (or that you observed) where fear was the primary influence mechanism. What needs were appealed to? Did it work?

4. Describe a situation in which you were involved (or that you observed) where tradition was the primary influence mechanism. What needs were appealed to? Did it work?

5. Describe a situation in which you were involved (or that you observed) where blind faith was the primary influence mechanism. What needs were appealed to? Did it work?

6. Describe a situation in which you were involved (or that you observed) where rational faith was the primary influence mechanism. What needs were appealed to? Did it work?

7. Describe a situation in which you were involved (or that you observed) where joint determination was the primary influence mechanism. What needs were appealed to? Did it work?

8. What is the central difference between fear and tradition as influence mechanisms?

9. Describe a person who has "charisma" *for you.* What attributes do you admire? How does he or she behave?

10. Describe the various bases of power between people. Give an example of each from your own experience or observation.

11. Discuss the theoretical relationship between influence through self-determination and the power and achievement needs discussed in Chapter 1.

12. Discuss how influence extends upward as well as downward in organizations—and how the two directions are interdependent.

13. Describe two examples of influence situations in which you were involved (or that you observed) which fit the probabilistic influence model.

Short Cases for Discussion

An Attempt to Consolidate Cooperatives in Ecuador

A credit cooperative is known to most persons in the United States as a credit union or a savings and loan cooperative. Members place their savings in the cooperative, as they would in a bank, but loans are available only to members at, they hope, a lower rate of interest. Yearly, all profits are returned to the members, divided on the basis of the amount of savings they have in the cooperative.

A cooperative is normally governed by a five-member board elected from the membership. These members include a president, vice president, treasurer, and the heads of the credit and supervisory committees. The credit committee approves all loans and the supervisory committee insures that the cooperative is being operated according to its bylaws. Professional managers can be hired by the cooperative, but this is feasible only when the cooperative is large.

Credit cooperatives have been formed in many underdeveloped areas because of the lack of credit at reasonable interest rates for the small merchant and farmer. Credit cooperatives provide it. At the same time, they mobilize capital in the community by teaching the members the importance of regular saving.

Credit cooperatives were started in Ecuador for these purposes. Ecuador is a small country, larger only than Uruguay in South America, with a population of about five million. It is an extremely poor country, relying on the export of bananas for most of its income. It has a geographic handicap for future economic development because the Andes mountains run completely through the center of the country. The ruggedness of these mountains makes trade and communication between areas very difficult, and may partially explain why the coastal region of Ecuador has had a better record of cooperative development than has had the mountain region.

As a young American member of the Peace Corps, I was assigned to work with the credit cooperatives in Cuenca, the third largest city in Ecuador, with a population of about 80,000. Cuenca is situated in the mountain region, eight hours from the coast and fifteen hours from the capital city, Quito. Thus, it is not surprising that the cooperatives in Cuenca have been doing so poorly that most people in the city had never even heard of them.

There were three formally organized cooperatives in Cuenca. After an initial period of growth, two of them were stagnating. The third cooperative had failed completely, although it had not been disbanded.

The best of the three cooperatives was called "La Merced," after the patron saint of the neighborhood in which the cooperative was formed. The president, Sr. Caldera, and the treasurer, Sr. Marchan, were knowledgeable in the mechanics of operating a cooperative, but were not aggressive in promoting the concept. As a result, the cooperative had only 100 members and $100 in capital. Most of its members were women, small businessmen, and merchants, which hampered the economic growth of the cooperative. If the cooperative was to give its intended service, the membership had to be expanded. Unfortunately, the cooperative had not attracted many new members in the past six months.

The other functioning cooperative in Cuenca was headed by Sr. Mendosa. Sr. Mendosa exhibited tremendous pride in being the founder and president of an organization of this kind. He ran the entire show and he took great pride in doing so. He was not only the president, but the treasurer; he approved all the loans (which, by the way, was illegal). He did not delegate any authority and he resented criticism of his operation by anyone. He restricted membership to only his friends and spoke of his role as one of looking out for their welfare, but of course their voice in the cooperative was insignificant.

The third cooperative was made up of local carpenters. It failed because the membership did not seem to understand what a credit cooperative was or how it was to operate. The cooperative was never officially disbanded, and only a complete transfusion could save it, but even this was doubtful, since it had a reputation of failure.

After having worked with these cooperatives for a few months, I felt that Cuenca should have more people involved in credit unions that just the 200 then participating. I thought the idea of a single large cooperative for the entire city was desirable and feasible. Instead of independently improving the three existing cooperatives, I thought it would be more sensible to merge them into one. This would result in a nucleus of trained personnel to manage the cooperative and a base of 200 members from which to convince others that the cooperative was a success.

Greatly excited because I thought I could make a substantial contribution to the economic life of the city, I set up appointments with the presidents of the three cooperatives.

I approached each of the cooperatives with my idea. Sr. Mendosa strongly rejected the plan and dismissed me, saying that the other cooperatives should be dissolved, with their members joining his organization. The other two cooperatives in turn rejected Mendosa's position, but they did agree to discuss consolidation of their two groups.

When the meeting was held, the purpose of the merger was explained and how it was to be accomplished was carefully detailed. Each cooperative would officially withdraw from the National Federation and a new one would immediately be established so that there would be no loss in services for the present members. With the larger amount of members and capital, the new cooperative would be able to make larger loans to its members with greater regularity. All old officers of the two cooperatives would resign and a new directorship would be elected by the new, combined membership.

At this point the idea began to run into difficulties. The president of "La Merced," Sr. Caldera, did not like the idea of disbanding his cooperative, because the name would be changed. He felt that the name had religious significance and should be retained. The president of the carpenters, Sr. Maldonado, on the other hand, did not want to retain the name of "La Merced" because it would seem as if they were being forced to capitulate to the other cooperative—and besides he did not like the religious association. The subsequent argument forced a polarization of those present, each backing the position of their own cooperative; each side became more adamant in their position as time went by.

When the discussion turned to the election of officials, fear was expressed that if one cooperative outnumbered the other, their directors might be completely re-elected, leaving the other cooperative without representation. This problem was partially bypassed when it was suggested that the president should be elected from one cooperative, a vice president from the other, etc. This, however, met with resistance on the point of which cooperative was to elect the president. Each cooperative wanted to retain its own president, and neither president wanted to accept the second position in favor of the other. The mistrust by members of one cooperative toward the members of the other gradually became obvious.

The meeting was finally adjourned with no progress toward consolidation but with heightened suspicion and animosity between the two cooperatives. Later, when I met with individuals in each cooperative, I could see that they did not want to discuss the matter further. Future plans were dropped and the idea died.

Question

Discuss why the North American failed to influence the Latin Americans.

Frank Perriman's Appointment

Indefatigable Mutual Insurance is a large national company with more than ten thousand employees in fifty states and Canada. Its basic organization has been as shown in Exhibit 1.

Each regional vice president had access to the president if he so desired, but most actual communication between the field and home office were with the functional vice presidents, who set policy and monitored performance in their respective functional areas. The two senior vice presidents have acted as staff to the president in their areas of expertise; one in actuarial and statistical matters, the other in investments and finance. In general, Indefatigable has been a highly centralized, regionally dispersed organization.

Frank Perriman has had exceptional and striking success at Indefatigable. After experience primarily in sales, Frank was appointed vice president of the middle western region at age 35—the youngest such appointment in the company's history. One annual report contained an individual picture of Frank (the only regional V.P. so honored) with a caption describing him as an example of what could happen to young men at Indefatigable. In general, however, most company executives were fairly old.

Exhibit 1   Organization Chart for Indefatigable Mutual Insurance Company

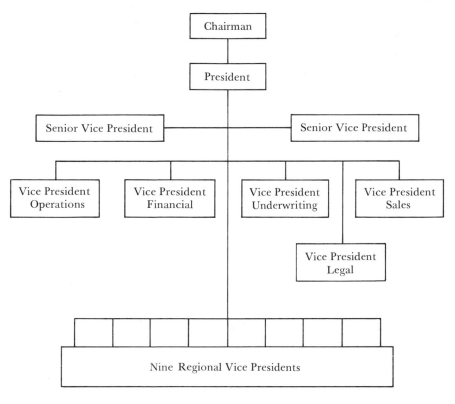

After eight years as regional vice president, Frank was promoted in June to senior vice president (thus making three senior V.P.'s) and transferred to the home office in charge of regional activities. The president sent out the following notifications:

GENERAL ORGANIZATION BULLETIN #349   June 29

Effective August 1, Mr. Frank Perriman, Vice President and Manager, Middle-western Region, will transfer to the President's staff at the home office.

Mr. Perriman will be responsible to the President for achieving Division performance in accordance with Company policies and objectives.

Mr. Perriman will assist Regional Managers in obtaining well-coordinated efforts by all departments and will establish and use measurements of results for each Division.

Regional Vice Presidents will report to and be responsible to Mr. Perriman.

Thomas Achison
President

GENERAL ORGANIZATION BULLETIN #351   July 14

Effective July 14, the Board of Directors made the following election:
Mr. Frank Perriman, Senior Vice President.

Thomas Achison
President

Question

Discuss any problems that Perriman might have in establishing his authority and influence in his new post.

Chapter 4

Group Dynamics

Man abhors vacuum, instability, and chaos. Void is replaced by activity, instability by equilibrium, and disorder by order. In our human relationships, we attempt to create structure and impose predictability. This phenomena appears at its most dramatic in the rich elaboration of complex patterns in small groups. "What is distinctly human," state Berelson and Steiner (1964), "comes from the primary fact that man lives his life in groups with other people." Behavioral scientists, therefore, have given a great deal attention to groups—from families to military squads to work groups.

We here consider the emergent or informal organization as it exists within the formal organization. Actually, the dichotomy is false; there is only one organization—the holistic, "real" organization. Nonetheless, since "reality" and "wholeness" are illusive concepts, we need to focus on partial aspects of the total organization. The aspects of concern in this and the following chapter are the unplanned, emergent, frequently unanticipated dynamics of face-to-face relationships and decision-making processes in human groups.

Informal Organization and the Individual

In a fascinating study, Schein (1956) suggests the essential purposes of informal organization and groups. During and after the Korean War in the early 1950s, widespread concern was voiced about the behavior of U.S. Army prisoners of war in North Korea. Since there were few escapes, many deaths from disease, and numerous instances of apparent collaboration, many Americans in this country were distressed. POW behavior was interpreted to indicate that America's youth were decadent, soft, ignorant of their mission, and unpatriotic (Kinkead, 1959). The implication: unless U.S. moral fiber stiffens, all will be lost to Communism.

It is probably true that the men fighting in Korea were not as clear about the issues involved as were the soldiers in World War II. Schein, nonetheless, suggests other reasons for the problems of death, escape, and collaboration in the Korean camps.

First-hand observers were impressed by the different attitudes characterizing newly liberated American prisoners in Korea as compared with American prisoners freed in Germany. Cheering, jubilation, and happiness characterized the latter; quiet, sullenness, and anxiety the former. Subsequent investigation indicated differences in the conditions, treatment, and organization of the prisoners in Nazi Germany and Communist Korea:

In the Nazi camps sharp disparities existed between the conditions of prisoners and guards. The prisoners received worse food, clothing, and shelter.

The Nazis dealt with the prisoners through a military structure by recognizing rank, requiring American officers to police and maintain the internal organization.

When interrogating, prisoners were brought in individually, questioned, and returned to the unit. If any torture had been applied, the theory was that the unfortunate sufferer would serve as an example to frighten the others and induce them to talk when they were brought in.

Under these conditions, there was a relatively low death rate from illness, almost no instances of collaboration, and many escapes.

Conditions in Korea were very different:

Many of the prisoners were taken after the Chinese attacked across the Yalu River and the Americans retreated in one of the few routs in U.S. Army history. Disorganized, separated from their units, wandering in a strange land, the soldiers were captured by the Chinese and marched to prison camps. On the march the Chinese continually reminded them that they were the Americans' friends and that the prisoners were lucky to have been captured by the Chinese. If they had been taken by the North Koreans, the Chinese maintained, the Americans would have been killed because as capitalist imperialists they had attacked the homeland of the North Koreans.

During the march there were few contrasts between conditions for the prisoners and for their guards. The Chinese captors shared their limited food and medicine and, by and large, had things about as bad as the prisoners.

At the prison camps, officers were separated from enlisted men. In some instances lower ranking men were intentionally placed in charge of noncommissioned officers.

Groups were systematically broken up and people transferred between barracks in order to forestall the development of a military or informal organization.

With some notorious exceptions, the Chinese used relatively little physical torture, and even their so-called brain washing techniques were relatively simple. After a man was interrogated, however, he was not sent back to his old unit. He would reappear elsewhere in the camp, perhaps with new clothes. This meant that the prisoners in the barracks did not know what kind of experience they were facing or what kind of questions they were going to be asked. It was difficult for them to prepare themselves psychologically for the experience. Finally, there was some suspicion over how their former buddy had behaved.

Under these conditions, there was low morale, much illness and a high death rate, few escapes, and compromising answers in the interviews.

The major problems in the Communist prisoner of war camps resulted from inadequate military or social structure; neither support nor discipline was given to the individual. In the German camps, on the other hand, there was a structure which enabled a prisoner to prepare himself and to gain some strength from his buddies prior to interrogation. He also had to come back to his friends, which would be difficult and dangerous if he compromised himself to the Nazis. In the Chinese camps the prisoner did not have adequate preparation for the interviews, and he did not have to go back to face his barracks mates. Consequently, when asked questions that sounded rather unimportant and innocuous, or when told that his friend had provided information, the soldier tended to respond more than he should.

Escapes were rare in Korea, according to Schein, because escape is a group activity; trust is essential. The men simply could not get organized. Because of frequent transfers, they did not have time to develop the cooperative efforts necessary for escape. In addition, of course, they were Occidentals in an Oriental country, and this made escape much more difficult than it had been for American prisoners in Germany. So, in the Communist prisoner of war camps, morale was low, the will to survive declined, and the death rate was greater than physical differences between the Chinese and Nazi camps would explain. Friends can help a man to fight even germs.

What the Group Offers the Individual

The foregoing narrative indicates that the group serves three functions for the individual: (1) the satisfaction of complex social needs, (2) emotional support in identifying oneself and dealing with the world, and (3) assistance in meeting goals. The Korean memoirs of General William Dean (1954) well describe some of these functions. General Dean won the Congressional Medal of Honor for his heroism in Korea. Nonetheless, he points out that he talked to his captors more than he should have. After prolonged solitary confinement and existence on poor rations slipped under a door, Dean had an overwhelming compulsion to talk when taken to the Chinese interrogator. He responded positively to his interrogator even though he knew the man was his enemy.

Satisfaction of Social Needs

Most fundamentally, men join groups because of a need for affiliation. The basis of affiliation ranges from simple enjoyment of other human beings to more complex desires for group affirmation of an individual's self-conception. Thus, affiliation can either be a means to an end or an end in itself. For General Dean, desires for companionship flowed automatically from the human relationship—even between the prisoner and his keeper. Similarly, veteran soldiers comment on the tendency of new recruits to stick together for friendship and support when under stress—even though they know it increases rather than decreases the danger.

Research indicates that employees who have no opportunity for social contact find their work unsatisfying. This lack of satisfaction may reflect itself in low production, high turnover, and absenteeism. In the earliest of his classic research efforts, Mayo (1946) observed that employees in a textile plant who worked in isolated jobs were highly dissatisfied and consistently failed to meet production standards. When the company permitted these workers to take rest periods as a group, production and satisfaction increased. Similarly, other observers have suggested that maids in hospitals feel uncomfortable when they work only in the company of doctors and nurses (Burling et al., 1956). Some hospitals have discovered that, when three or four maids are grouped together as a team, turnover is reduced and a more effective job is done. And Roy (1960) has vividly described the enjoyment and assistance derived from informal games, banter, and horseplay on the job.

Identification and Emotional Support

Our prisoner of war examples do not mean that compromise and collaboration are inevitable just because man craves affection; the process is more subtle. As

General Dean points out, he simply was not sure what was right and what was wrong. Isolated from human companionship and communication, he lost touch with the essential basis and support for ethical behavior—social corroboration of individual conscience. Even the development of that conscience is heavily influenced by social contact, because self-identification is greatly affected by others. This is clear in the teenager, for example. He tries to be everything his friends say he should be. His choices of styles in music, clothes, and hair all reflect the teenager's efforts to define himself in terms of his companions. Self-image derives from social image.

"Absolute abstinence from sexual activity" is the prime requisite for joining the Esoteric Fraternity of California (Hillinger, 1971). This hardly suggests that it would be successful, but this informal organization has existed continuously for almost a hundred years, during which it has published books and pamphlets still in demand. Of course it never included more than a dozen members, and now numbers only two brothers, both over ninety. Yet it succeeded because it provided acceptance, support, and certitude for those few who joined—in this case, certainty that the kingdom of God would be established on earth "when man gives up the sex act." The Communist Party has managed to enroll more members than the Esoteric Fraternity, but with a similar appeal to some. A member might derive strength and a sense of identity from his self-definition as part of the vanguard of the proletarian revolution and as an agent of historical destiny.

In a wartime prison camp, a strong group could assist the individual to define the basis of ethical behavior. So also in the shop and office, the group can guide the individual in knowing what is desirable and undesirable behavior. How much time should he take for a coffee break? Is it all right to talk to fellow employees while the boss is in the room? Must all copy be shown to the advertising manager? Even where there are established rules, a question remains: is everyone expected to live by the letter of the law? Most employees do not want to violate the generally accepted rules of the game; at the same time, they do not want to conform to restrictive rules that everyone else ignores. They want to know the right thing to do. The group fills an important function by providing its members with a kind of guide to correct behavior—not correctness in terms of written policies but in terms of what is actually acceptable.

Research in military units indicates that the group can give support, perhaps even courage, to the individual in a dangerous situation. Young Joe Marm, a second lieutentant on duty in South Vietnam in the autumn of 1965, grabbed up two side arms and a pile of grenades, ran up a hill alone, and attacked and destroyed a machine gun nest, killing eight Viet Cong. Upon being recommended for the Congressional Medal of Honor, Marm was asked why he made the attack. His reply was simple: "What would the fellows have thought of me if I had been afraid to do it?" (New York Times, Nov. 17, 1966). Similarly, in studies of soldiers in World War II, there is evidence that those men closely tied to cohesive groups were more responsible in carrying out their duties, more confident of being able to perform well as soldiers, less fearful in battle, and less likely to capitulate or surrender under stress (Shils, 1950). These studies also indicated that the soldier's willingness to show bravery and make sacrifices was correlated not with loyalty to country or understanding of the war issues but with loyalty to the immediate group. In other words, men who performed heroic acts were motivated largely by the desire not to let their buddies down.

The case of Lieutenant Marm would seem to indicate that things have not changed.

Of course, some people have stronger self-identification and conscience than others. They could stand against a group or initiate action on their own. Nonetheless, the group can assist most individuals, if not all, in being true to themselves. Support of the group in maintaining morale and identity was critical in the Korean prisoner of war situation; its absence helped to explain why there was so much distrust, sickness, and death among the prisoners. As the poet John Donne said, "No man is an island entire of itself."

Life in the business organization is not so dangerous. Nonetheless, group support can be just as necessary to the individual—especially to the low-skilled worker who, as one person, is relatively unimportant to management. Katz (1965) describes how informal work groups at low levels serve as a vehicle for expressing independence from management and help bind blue-collar workers to the formal organization: "This produces continuity between the workman's outside life and his participation in the work setting—a setting to which he [may have] very limited allegiance."

Assistance in Meeting Objectives

Groups do more than just satisfy social, psychological, and metaphysical needs. The group can assist in solving very specific problems and protect the individual from his mistakes. A new sales clerk may not be sure about how to handle a complicated problem of returning merchandise. A lab technician may be hesitant about asking his boss to repeat instructions yet be afraid he may ruin the experiment unless he receives additional information. In each case the employee turns to his fellow workers for assistance; most prefer this source of help. Blau (1955) has illustrated how federal agents consistently prefer getting assistance from fellow employees as opposed to going to their manager. Indeed, this ability to provide assistance is a source of substantial prestige for the giver.

So far, we have emphasized what the group can do for the individual; in addition, a group as a collectivity develops goals. The behavior of groups in pursuit of these goals is of primary concern to the manager. Before we consider this, however, let us investigate the development of informal organization on the job.

The Development of Informal Organization

Theoretically, management is only concerned with the formal aspects of organization: the duties, behavior, and communications of people. If there is any concern with feelings or sentiments, it is usually an unstated hope that everyone will be cooperative and emotionally neutral. A manager assigns certain duties to individuals as part of their jobs. In carrying out these activities, they customarily interact or communicate with others. Theoretically, this is all the manager need be concerned about—whether they perform the activities effectively and efficiently, communicating as necessary. Nonetheless, it does not stop here. Unplanned sentiments inevitably emerge. People dislike or like (and rarely are neutral about) the people with whom they work. In turn, these sentiments encourage them to elaborate their communications and activities with others in a variety of unplanned and informal patterns (Homans, 1950). The process can be illustrated as shown in Exhibit 4-1.

Exhibit 4-1 Interaction of Activities and Sentiments

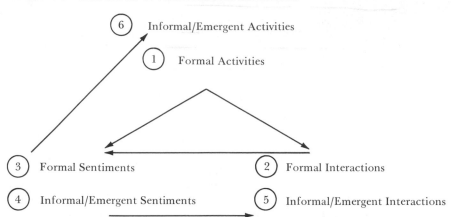

Thus, when management brings people together in the office or plant where it expects them to communicate and work together, inevitable elaboration occurs. It does not always follow the numerical order in the figure, but as interaction theory suggests, the individuals are related in a system of activities, interactions (communications), and sentiments. These elements form a social system which implies mutual dependency; that is, a change in any one affects the others. Sayles and Strauss (1966) describe this development:

"Employees form friendship groups based on their contact and common interest—and these groups arise out of the life of the organization. Once these groups have been established, however, they develop a life of their own that is almost completely separate from the work process from which it arose. This is a dynamic, self-generating process. Brought together by the formal organization, employees interact with one another. Increasing interaction builds favorable sentiments toward fellow group members. In turn, these sentiments become the foundation for an increased variety of activities, many not specified by the job description: special lunch arrangements, trading of job duties, fights with those outside the group, gambling on paycheck numbers. And these increased opportunities for interaction build stronger bonds of identification. Then the group becomes something more than a mere collection of people. It develops a customary way of doing things—a set of stable characteristics that are hard to change. It becomes an organization in itself" (p. 89).

Membership in a group is thus related to technology and work flow. There has to be some physical proximity and communication opportunity in order for people to form mutually interacting groups. People who communicate are more likely to develop mutual sentiments and hence become attached to each other in some informal structure.

Informal Status Systems

Most men have need for affiliation and membership. Yet once they have established mutual relationships, many individuals want to be better than their companions. Everyone wants to be equal, but as George Orwell put it in *Animal*

Farm, "some want to be more equal than others." With affiliation, a new need emerges—desire for social esteem, prestige, or status—that is, some differentiation of social position from associates and peers.

Prestige or status are frequently defined as a set of unwritten rules about the kind of conduct that people are expected to show in one's presence: what degree of respect or disrespect, familiarity or unfamiliarity, reserve or frankness. Notwithstanding the barbs of contemporary social critics, prestige seeking is not solely a twentieth century American phenomenon. Mankind has apparently always created social structure, differentiating the power and glory of his fellows. "Like it or not," Gellerman (1963) tells us, "people have evidently been sorting themselves out into chiefs and Indians, nobles and peasants, executives and hourly workers from time immemorial, and they show no signs of stopping (p. 151)." The classless society is yet to appear, and as the Yugoslav Milovan Diljias (1957) courageously showed us, the Communist states also develop class distinctions.

Even within the small informal group, subtle status differences begin to emerge. The type of membership and status within a work group that a person enjoys depend upon factors that he brings to the organization, and factors derived from his job.

External Factors   What a man brings to the workplace influences what his status will be on the job. This pertains to who and what a man is, not what he does. When one of the authors worked in a large chemical manufacturing company, a fellow engineer was the second largest stockholder in this large company. Stock ownership was widely dispersed and his inherited ownership was less than 1%, but it still constituted a large fortune. In the formal organization, however, he was only an engineer with no real indication that his stock ownership was going to help him directly in his hierarchical career. Nonetheless, he obviously had status in the plant regardless of what he did—especially since he prominently displayed on his desk Christmas cards received from the chairman of the board.

Among the off-the-job qualities that confer status are education, age, seniority, sex, and ethnic background. Typically, in business, women and blacks have been accorded low status. Other ethnic groups are also arranged according to a status hierarchy, with Anglo-Saxons usually at the top, and people of southern European background near the bottom. However, the relative positions on this status ladder may vary from one community to another. For example, to be a "regular" at one plant requires Irish extraction, regardless of other personal characteristics. At other plants, one might find it helpful to be Polish, and so on (Zaleznik et al., 1958).

Personality also plays a role, although research findings in this area are not clear. Among informal student groups there is evidence that higher status is associated with physical size, appearance and dress, self-confidence and self-assurance, sociability or friendliness, and intelligence—although the leaders must not exceed their followers by a very large margin in any of these characteristics (Stogdill, 1948). The importance of these factors in determining status changes from time to time and with cultures. We have asked many classes of American students for factors determining informal group status. Age is seldom mentioned, and if it is, only as the last item. In most of history and in most societies, age has been the major determinant of formal and informal status—as witness Japanese industry (Takezawa, 1966).

Internal Factors   The job also influences the status system. In fact, when management creates an organization, it consciously creates a status system based primarily on pay and authority. Titles, job descriptions, evaluation programs, pay systems, and work-measurement practices all influence the informal social structure.

- *Job title*—Obviously a superintendent is more important than a general foreman, and a general foreman outranks a foreman. Engineers outrank technicians; secretaries are above stenographers. In almost every organization, although organizations are certainly not consistent on this, job titles are subtly graded according to levels of status, and the status of each individual depends in part on the job he holds.
- *Pay*—This is one of the most important determinants of status. Higher pay means higher status, and even a difference of a few cents per hour may have a significant effect on a job's status. How one is paid also helps to determine status. Being a salaried man on a monthly payroll may be less convenient, but it carries much more prestige than getting a weekly or daily wage.
- *Work schedules*—The freedom to choose one's hours, or being excused from punching the time clock, is a mark of distinction. Working a day schedule is usually thought of as a higher-status job than a shift schedule.
- *Mobility*—Generally, a job which allows a man to move around freely, interacting and communicating with many different people, is thought of as having higher prestige than a position that allows no autonomy or discretion over one's movements. This mobility is also related to autonomy or freedom from close management supervision. Again, this is a status factor generally giving higher prestige in the informal social structure.
- *Symbols of office*—There is a vast range of physical factors which are desirable in themselves but which also serve as symbols for higher status. These include such things as in which company lunchroom you can eat. Can you leave the building for morning coffee? Do you have a reserved parking space? What kind of clothing do you wear in the office? Also the type of office—what kind of furnishings do you have? telephone? desk? carpeting? and so on.

What we are suggesting is that people on the job structure themselves in various relationships, integrating on-job and off-job status factors. An informal social structure will be created; employees will look up to certain people and consider certain jobs attractive; they may even plan their careers around movement through these positions. The highest status positions will tend to be occupied especially by people high in both external and internal status factors. This informal status system may approximate the formal structure of the company, but it will probably deviate in a number of ways, as we shall illustrate later in this chapter.

Group Cohesion

The success of informal groups in achieving their objectives depends to an important extent upon the internal strength or cohesion of the group. Part of the difficulty in the Korean prisoner of war camps was inadequate group cohesion. That is, stable values and standards of behavior never developed; group members could not work together in mutual dependency. Cohesion is both cause and consequence: it aids the pursuit of group objectives, and, at the same time, it can be strengthened by the sharing of concerted effort. But the sources of cohesion are many and varied, as the following summary suggests.

Homogeneity   One of the most cohesive work groups we ever observed was composed entirely of an ethnic or national group called the "West of Englanders." All of the six to seven people in the group had come from the southwest—Land's End—section of England many years before, and they maintained their sense of identification—perhaps because they were very much an ethnic minority among Italians and Poles. The ethnic tie was so strong that this group was one of few we observed that contained both male and female members. (This combination usually destroys cohesion.) These production workers (including a foreman) held a stable set of values and assistance expectations; they controlled production (at a fairly high level) and were remarkably successful in getting management to respond to them.

In contrast, groups whose members have different interests and backgrounds are often less effective in promoting their interests. When, for example, people with sharp differences in rates of pay and job duties work near each other, the resulting group is seldom cohesive. The group may often be characterized by conflicting cliques, which hinder common action.

Even when doing similar work, competition among members of a group will often hinder cohesion—unless the group can agree to regulate the competition. At a large automobile dealer's, the bottom three of twenty-five salesmen are fired every month, regardless of their sales. Under these circumstances, the salesmen would hardly constitute a cohesive group. On the other hand, where expulsion depends upon absolute rather than relative performance, a basically homogeneous group with good cohesion will assist the poor performer in improving his output.

Stable membership contributes to higher cohesion. With time, the members come to know each other, they learn the values and expectations of the group, and they learn how to behave. This was one of the problems in the prisoner-of-war camps referred to earlier. Where the barracks groups were systematically broken up, no cohesive groups could develop. "A tightly knit group," Lasswell and Kaplan (1950) maintain, "significantly means both a group difficult to enter and one whose members closely identify with one another. The less permeable the group, the more value attaches to membership and, in turn, the more intense the adherence to group perspective" (p. 35).

Communication   To be a group, people must be able to talk with one another. Only in this way can their similarities and common interests be developed, their values and standards established, and joint action initiated. Groups in which the members can communicate easily with one another are more likely to be cohesive. Internal group unity can be thwarted in such areas as noisy steel mills, long assembly lines, or even quiet offices, where "gossiping" is frowned upon, and there is no privacy for conversation.

Isolation   Physical isolation from other groups tends to build cohesiveness. Familiar to the student is the contrast between the school spirit of a college isolated in the country and the nonchalance characterizing students in large, urban universities in New York, Los Angeles, Chicago, Washington, D.C., or Philadelphia. Miners have demonstrated, in countless lengthy strikes, that isolated workers will stick together more stubbornly than workers who are socially integrated with the rest of the community.

Even simple physical boundaries on a group may be essential for cohesion. If a group can't identify its members and clearly differentiate itself, cohesion will be low. This is another of the problems in long assembly lines: it is difficult to distinguish logical groups. A large insurance company has a one-story office building which resembles nothing so much as an airplane hangar—or a setting from a Kafka novel. Several hundred clerical and supervisory personnel work together in one large area with no physical boundaries between people. It is difficult for cohesive groups to emerge.

Size   This insurance office also illustrates that too many people hinder development of cohesive groups. Larger groups hinder communication, lower homogeneity, and encourage breaking up into small cliques. Small departments, therefore, tend to be more closely knit than large ones. Loyalty, as in the military, is a product of frequent, face-to-face contacts. It is simply easier to have close relationships with all members of a small group than with all members of a large one.

Outside Pressure   We have already mentioned how members of groups tend to herd together under stress. Continuous outside pressure from management may produce high cohesion. Under organizational stress, lateral and peer communications tend to increase while vertical communications decrease. Personal differences are minimized when threatened by a common danger—or a tough supervisor. And this closeness may remain after the threat is relieved. Perhaps the most closely knit army veterans of World War II are those of the 11th Armored Division, which was so badly mauled by the Germans in the Battle of the Bulge. They still publish a newsletter, meet frequently, hold annual conventions, and maintain high camaraderie, in spite of great differences among the members in economic and social achievement since the war.

A tough management policy towards personnel may well encourage them to form strong informal groups as a protective and retaliatory device. On the other hand, the more sophisticated and manipulative manager who, like the Korean War captors, systematically promotes internal competition, transfers people, and prevents communication will hinder the development of group cohesion.

Status of the Group   Our earlier discussion of individual needs suggests that people often prefer to identify with high-status groups. This means that people are more likely to feel loyalty toward a high-status group than toward a low-status group. The factors conferring status upon a group as a whole are very much the same as those giving status to the individual within the informal organization. They include special skills, monopoly control over certain functions, responsibility and autonomy, opportunities for promotion out of the area, physical location and working conditions, influence of the supervisor in organization affairs, and so on.

Although it is true that high-status groups tend to have higher cohesion, it is not clear whether status *per se* is the cause of high cohesion—or whether the factors conferring status (such as seniority, ease in communication, autonomy, and freedom from close supervision) simply allow cohesion to develop.

Management and Informal Groups

Like it or not, every manager must deal with informal organizations and work groups. They will exist. Managers simply cannot treat everyone as individuals, as they might prefer, because they will unwittingly create problems. Managers should understand emergent sentiments, activities, and interactions, for two reasons: (1) so that they do not inadvertently transgress the informal system, causing reactive behavior that blocks the achievement of formal objectives; and (2) in order to draw on the informal system to contribute positively to formal objectives; that is, to integrate the formal and emergent systems. These objectives are hindered when distributive justice is offended and when formal and informal norms conflict.

Distributive Justice

Men usually infuse the social exchange process with moral/ethical content. What *is* or *has been* for some time becomes more than just a rational exchange; it becomes a matter of justice. With time, the exchange becomes judged on the basis of precedent more than on the basis of exchange balance. Thus the offended manner of the husband whose wife of fifteen years unilaterally modifies the terms of their relationship. If he would or could analyze his contribution and his wife's contribution after the change, he might discover that they are in balance. But he seldom does this, because his perception of the situation is based on past experience. Hence, any change in his wife's behavior is perceived as unbalancing.

The employee tends to view his relationship with his employer similarly. His perception of contribution and costs is based on the past, supplemented by continuously increasing experience or seniority which he feels should be reflected in continuously increasing rewards from his employer. Thus the exchange is seen as continuously expanding. In fact, and often unfortunately, the employee's contribution to the exchange may be decreasing for various reasons (personal obsolescense, decline of his specialty, infirmities of age). Yet, an employer's unilateral attempt to revise the terms of the exchange usually produces outrage and accusations of injustice.

Justice is thus a matter of past and future, of memories and expectations. When their expectations are not fulfilled, men tend to feel angry. As Homans points out (1967):

"Remember: in the end and always, the sense of injustice is invariably grounded on a defeat of expectation, and expectations in the long run are always grounded on what actually happens. Reexamining one of our examples: if, over a period of time, older persons do not generally get better jobs than younger ones, then an older man's sense of injustice, when he does not get a good job, will eventually disappear. Whatever is, is right—if only what is will stay put long enough, which it usually does not. It is change that makes the trouble.

Thus a person or group that has, for any reason, come to expect a steady increase in rewards, will, when the increase is checked or reversed, feel angry, even if they are better off absolutely than they were in the beginning. In psychologists' language, their level of aspiration has risen. This is a fertile source of revolt and one very hard to cope with, for how can anyone go on increasing rewards indefinitely?"

The problem of distributive justice is of great concern to managers because the danger of inadvertently or even intentionally transgressing it multiplies with the number of people involved. Each person compares himself with others. Each expects equality in the ratio of contributions/costs to rewards/receipts. A wants to feel that:

$$\frac{\text{A Rewards/Receipts}}{\text{A Contributions/Costs}} = \frac{\text{B Rewards/Receipts}}{\text{B Contributions/Costs}}$$
$$= \frac{\text{C Rewards/Receipts}}{\text{C Contributions/Costs}} = \frac{\text{D Rewards/Receipts}}{\text{D Contributions/Costs}}$$

A asks himself if he is getting enough rewards/receipts in view of his contributions/costs *in comparison* with others. Thus, all other things being equal, if A and B put in the same number of hours, they expect to receive the same pay—and more than C and D, who put in fewer hours. If A receives less than any of the others he is offended, and suffers from a sense of relative deprivation, regardless of what absolute amount he is paid.

Of course, "all other things" are seldom equal, so the exchanges and comparisons are much more complex. If we are "better" or contribute more, we expect more; if we think the other person is "better" or contributes more, we are not offended if *he* gets more. The main problem is the dimension of "better." Contributions or costs include the effort devoted to the organization, but also that which a person is or brings to the job: age, seniority, education, ability, alternatives, even apparently irrelevant factors like sex, ethnicity, and race. The higher the value on any of these factors, the greater the expected rewards/receipts.

Status Incongruency

A is also likely to be offended when there is inconsistency or incongruity between external and internal status factors—that is, between the attributes a man brings to the job (such as age, seniority, sex, ethnicity, education) and the rewards he expects to get from the job (pay, working conditions, privileges, formal status, and informal prestige).

For example, consider the problems of blacks in business. Their effort to climb to higher positions does create some perceived status incongruity by whites, however illegitimate the perception. Some whites still assign low external status to blacks. Historically, this has been consistent with the jobs blacks have filled—low skilled, low paying, dirty, and monotonous. There was consistency between off-job and on-job status factors. At present, however, one of the most demanded persons in American society is the black MBA graduate. How far he will climb in business is still undetermined, but the black college graduate's movement into positions of relative importance, high on internal status (in such factors as pay, skill, authority, office furnishings, etc.), brings status incongruity—in the opinion of some whites. Because a white man thinks he brings higher external status factors to the job, he may be upset when he has lower job status.

Some companies who want to hire and promote blacks and women attempt to maintain the white male perception of status congruity, either by rewarding the blacks and women with less or by requiring greater contributions on their part. Tobacco companies in the Carolinas apparently have had some success in putting black supervisors over white workers at relatively low levels. To be black implies low external status, but those appointed are brighter, harder working, and better educated than the whites working under them.

White males are less offended by a black (or female) receiving equal rewards if it is patently obvious that the latter is superior. Of course, blacks and females are increasingly offended by this inequity. Status congruity is preserved for white males, but it is intentionally violated for others. If they feel inferior and really believe they have less to offer, they may not care, or they may not have complained in the past because they needed the work (in general, blacks have been more willing to accept jobs below their capabilities).

Obviously, these days are ending. Blacks and females are awakening to the injustice of *their* status incongruence. The solution is the elimination of race and sex as sources of external status relevant to work, but we are dealing with informal factors here that come from outside the organization.

A manager's ability to hire, transfer, and promote people is hindered to the extent that people are upset by incongruent status comparisons. Of course, we are not implying that management should limit its activity because of fear of status incongruity and the resulting stresses. What we do say is that the manager should be aware of possible causes and consequences of such status comparisons when he takes actions that affect the informal status system within the organization.

Conflicting Formal and Informal Status Systems

Difficulty is created for management when formal organizational structure conflicts with an informal status system—that is, when management evaluation of jobs and positions does not correspond to group evaluation. For example, Exhibit 4-2 illustrates the formal and informal status of jobs in one chemical plant before and after a technological change.

The job of handler required a semi-skilled, manual operator to sort raw and finished materials. Working conditions were good, the area was clean and well lighted, but the job required relatively little training and skill. The pay rate was $2.00 per hour. The next higher position, tank room operator, was responsible for a batch chemical process, using eight large tanks in another room in the same building. He had to add chemicals, control flows, and make various tests. The job was a promotion from handler: it paid $2.50 an hour and required greater skill and experience, including some fairly sophisticated knowledge of chemical tests. In addition, the tank room operator had greater autonomy and responsibility. However, his working conditions were atrocious. Since various digestive processes using organic enzymes were percolating in open vats, the area was like the inside of a stomach. The smell, heat, and humidity all detracted from the desirability of the job.

Exhibit 4-2   Formal and Informal Job Status

Formal Status System *Before* Change	Informal Status System *Before* and *After* Change	Formal Status System *After* Change
Assistant foreman . . . . salary ↑	Assistant foreman . . . . salary ↑	Assistant foreman . . . . salary ↑
Head operator of continuous processing . . . $2.75/hr ↑	Head operator of continuous processing ↑	Tank room operator . . . . . $3.00/hr ↑
Tank room operator . . . . . $2.50/hr ↑	Tank room operator ↑	Head operator of continuous processing . . . $2.75/hr ↑
Handler $2.00/hr	Handler	Handler $2.00/hr

The most desirable job in the department was head operator of continuous processing equipment. A precursor of the "white coverall" worker of the future, the head operator received $2.75 an hour for manipulating a console and making some important decisions regarding chemical flows, times, temperatures, and so forth. He performed very little manual work. His work area was clean, well lighted, and much cooler than the tank room.

For years, the informal social structure and the formal organizational hierarchy were similar. Management and the men agreed on which jobs were more desirable. The wage rates reflected both management and group judgments of job status. Each worker saw his career as progressing up through these positions—from handler to tank room operator to head operator. In general, the more senior people were head operators, the next in seniority were tank room operators, and the newer people were handlers.

One day the harmony ended. Because of technological developments in another department, it was necessary to redesign some of the operations in the tank room, increasing the responsibilities of the tank room operator and the skill and technical sophistication necessary. Greater decision-making discretion and autonomy were given to the tank room operator. The wage and salary administrator revaluated the job, and pay was increased to $3.00 an hour—more than the head operator received. However, working conditions were not improved. The tank room was still dirty, smelly, and unpleasant. The formal status structure now went from handler to head operator to tank room operator. Unfortunately, the work group refused to modify their own status hierarchy. The pay increase for the tank room operator was not enough to give that job higher status than the head operator's position. The men could not see the high point of their careers as moving to the tank room. They still wanted to progress from handler to tank room operator to head operator—and were willing to take a cut in pay to move to the last job.

An additional problem was created. Because the wage and salary staff refused to increase the head operator's rate, the junior men in the tank room were now making more money than the senior operators—thus creating status incongruity. Eventually, the only way management was able to solve this problem was to make extensive physical modifications in the tank room to improve working conditions. These changes made the working conditions in the tank room roughly similar to the head operator's, which in turn raised the informal status of the tank room operator's job. In other words, management was able to solve the problem only by modifying the status factors to make informal and formal status systems congruent.

Summary

There is a rich fabric of emergent relationships in organizations and small groups. Groups offer individuals substantial benefits: satisfaction of social needs, identification and emotional support, and assistance in meeting objectives. Informal structure emerges from the formal structure as activities, interactions, and sentiments are elaborated into a status system. An individual's status in the informal system depends on the external or personal factors which he brings to the job, and internal factors such as pay, title, working conditions, etc.

Managers should understand informal organization for two reasons: first, so that they do not inadvertently transgress the informal system, producing reactive behavior that blocks formal objectives; second, in order to integrate the formal and emergent systems for better performance. Of particular concern to management are problems of offended equity, when people do not perceive equality and balance in their contributions/costs and rewards/receipts to and from the organization. Improper reward distribution, status incongruency, and conflicting formal and informal status systems sometimes result.

We are not saying that management must always accommodate informal groups and shift formal organization, policy, and procedures to satisfy them. Rather, managers may attempt to change the norms of the informal group. But to do this successfully requires understanding of informal group dynamics.

References

Berelson, B., and G. Steiner. *Human Behavior—An Inventory of Scientific Findings.* Harcourt Brace Jovanovich, 1964.

Blau, P. *The Dynamics of Bureaucracy.* University of Chicago Press, 1955.

Burling, T., E. Lentz, and R. Wilson. *The Give and Take in Hospitals.* Putnam, 1956.

Dean, W. F. *General Dean's Story* (as told to W. L. Worden). Viking Press, 1954.

Diljias, M. *The New Class.* Praeger, 1957.

Gellerman, S. *Motivation and Productivity.* American Management Association, 1963.

Hillinger, C. "The Last of the Esoteric Fraternity." *International Herald Tribune,* April 27, 1971.

Homans, G. C. *The Human Group.* Harcourt Brace Jovanovich, 1950.

———. "Fundamental Processes of Social Exchange," from Chapter 1 in *Sociology,* ed. N. Smelser. Wiley (1967), 27–78.

Katz, F. E. "Explaining Informal Groups in Complex Organizations," *Administrative Science Quarterly,* Vol. 10, No. 2 (September 1965), 204–221.

Kinkead, E. *In Every War But One.* Norton, 1959.

Lasswell, H. D., and A. Kaplan. *Power and Society: A Framework for Political Inquiry.* Yale University Press, 1950.

Mayo, E. *The Human Problems of an Industrial Civilization.* Graduate School of Business Administration, Harvard University, 1946.

Roy, D. "Banana Time—Job Satisfaction and Informal Interaction." *Human Organization,* Vol. 18 (1960), 158–168.

Sayles, L. R., and G. Strauss. *Human Behavior in Organizations.* Prentice-Hall, 1966.

Schein, E. "The Chinese Indoctrination Program for Prisoners of War." *Psychiatry,* Vol. 19 (1956), 149–172.

Shils, E. A. "Primary Groups in the American Army." In *Continuities in Social Research: Studies in the Scope and Method of the American Soldier,* ed. R. K. Merton and P. F. Lazarsfeld. Free Press (1950), 16–39.

Stogdill, R. "Personal Factors Associated with Leadership: A Survey of the Literature." *Journal of Psychology,* Vol. 25 (1948), 35–71.

Takezawa, S. "Socio-Cultural Aspects of Management in Japan." *International Labour Review,* Vol. 94, No. 2, August 1966.

Zaleznik, A., C. R. Christensen, and F. J. Roethlisberger. *The Motivation, Productivity and Satisfaction of Workers: A Prediction Study.* Graduate School of Business Administration, Harvard University, 1958.

Readings

Banana Time: Job Satisfaction and Informal Interaction

DONALD F. ROY

This paper undertakes description and exploratory analysis of the social interaction which took place within a small work group of factory machine operatives during a two-month period of participant observation. The factual and ideational materials which it presents lie at an intersection of two lines of research interest and should, in their dual bearing, contribute to both. Since the operatives were engaged in work which involved the repetition of very simple operations over an extra-long workday, six days a week, they were faced with the problem of dealing with a formidable "beast of monotony." Revelation of how the group utilized its resources to combat the "beast" should merit the attention of those who are seeking solution to the practical problem of job satisfaction, or employee morale. It should also provide insights for those who are trying to penetrate the mysteries of the small group.

Convergence of these two lines of interest is, of course, no new thing. Among the host of writers and researchers who have suggested connections between "group" and "joy in work" are Walker and Guest, observers of social interaction on the automobile assembly line.[1] They quote assembly-line workers as saying, "We have a lot of fun and talk all the time,"[2] and, "If it weren't for the talking and fooling, you'd go nuts."[3]

My account of how one group of machine operators kept from "going nuts" in a situation of monotonous work activity attempts to lay bare the tissues of interaction which made up the content of their adjustment. The talking, fun, and fooling which provided solution to the elemental problem of "psychological survival" will be described according to their embodiment in intra-group relations. In addition, an unusual opportunity for close observation of behavior involved in the maintenance of group equilibrium was afforded by the fortuitous introduction of a "natural experiment." My unwitting injection of explosive materials into the stream of interaction resulted in sudden, but temporary, loss of group interaction.

My fellow operatives and I spent our long days of simple repetitive work in relative isolation from other employees of the factory. Our line of machines was sealed off from other work areas of the plant by the four walls of the clicking room. The one door of this room was usually closed. Even when it was kept open, during periods of hot weather, the consequences were not social; it opened on an uninhabited storage room of the shipping department. Not even the sound of work activity going on elsewhere in the factory carried to this isolated work place. There were occasional contacts with "outside" employees, usually on matters connected with the work; but, with the exception of the daily calls of

From *Human Organization*, Vol. 18, No. 4 (1960), 158–168. Reprinted by permission of the author and The Society for Applied Anthropology.

one fellow who came to pick up finished materials for the next step in processing, such visits were sporadic and infrequent.

Moreover, face-to-face contact with members of the managerial hierarchy were few and far between. No one bearing the title of foreman ever came around. The only company official who showed himself more than once during the two month observation period was the plant superintendent. Evidently overloaded with supervisory duties and production problems which kept him busy elsewhere, he managed to pay his respects every week or two. His visits were in the nature of short, businesslike, but friendly exchanges. Otherwise he confined his observable communications with the group to occasional utilization of a public address system. During the two-month period, the company president and the chief chemist paid one friendly call apiece. One man, who may or may not have been of managerial status, was seen on various occasions lurking about in a manner which excited suspicion. Although no observable consequences accrued from the peculiar visitations of this silent fellow, it was assumed that he was some sort of efficiency expert, and he was referred to as "The Snooper."

As far as our work group was concerned, this was truly a situation of laissez-faire management. There was no interference from staff experts, no hounding by time-study engineers or personnel men hot on the scent of efficiency or good human relations. Nor were there any signs of industrial democracy in the form of safety, recreational, or production committees. There was an international union, and there was a highly publicized union-management cooperation program; but actual interactional processes of cooperation were carried on somewhere beyond my range of observation and without participation of members of my work group. Furthermore, these union-management get-togethers had no determinable connection with the problem of "toughing out" a twelve-hour day at monotonous work.

Our work group was thus not only abandoned to its own resources for creating job satisfaction, but left without that basic reservoir of ill-will toward management which can sometimes be counted on to stimulate the development of interesting activities to occupy hand and brain. Lacking was the challenge of intergroup conflict, that perennial source of creative experience to fill the otherwise empty hours of meaningless work routine.[4]

The clicking machines were housed in a room approximately thirty by twenty-four feet. They were four in number, set in a row, and so arranged along one wall that the busy operator could, merely by raising his head from his work, freshen his reveries with a glance through one of three large barred windows. To the rear of one of the end machines sat a long cutting table; here the operators cut up rolls of plastic materials into small sheets manageable for further processing at the clickers. Behind the machine at the opposite end of the line sat another table which was intermittently the work station of a female employee who performed sundry scissors operations of a more intricate nature on raincoat parts. Boxed in on all sides by shelves and stocks of materials, this latter locus of work appeared a cell within a cell.

The clickers were of the genus punching machines; of mechanical construction similar to that of the better-known punch presses, their leading features were hammer and block. The hammer, or punching head, was approximately eight inches by twelve inches at its flat striking surface. The descent upon the block was initially forced by the operator, who exerted pressure on a handle attached to the side of the hammer head. A few inches of travel downward established electrical connection for a sharp, power-driven blow. The hammer also traveled, by manual guidance, in a horizontal plane to and from, and in an arc around, the central column of the machine. Thus the operator, up to the point of establishing electrical connections for the sudden and irrevocable downward thrust, had flexibility in maneuvering his instrument over the larger surface of the block. The latter, approximately twenty-four inches wide, eighteen inches deep, and ten inches thick, was made, like a butcher's block, of inlaid hardwood; it was set in the machine at a convenient waist height. On it the operator placed his materials, one sheet at a time if leather, stacks of sheets if plastic, to be cut with steel dies of assorted sizes and shapes. The particular die in use would be moved, by hand, from spot to spot over the materials each time a cut was made; less frequently, materials would be shifted on the block as the operator saw need for such adjustment.

Introduction to the new job, with its relatively simple machine skills and work routines, was accomplished with what proved to be, in my experience, an all-time minimum of job training. The clicking machine assigned to me was situated at one end of the row. Here the superintendent and one of the operators gave a few brief demonstrations, accompanied by bits of advice which included a warning to keep hands clear of the descending hammer. After a short practice period, at the end of which the superintendent expressed satisfaction with progress and potentialities, I was left to develop my learning curve with no other supervision than that afforded by members of the work group. Further advice and assistance did come, from time to time, from my fellow operatives, sometimes upon request, sometimes unsolicited.

The Work Group

Absorbed at first in three related goals of improving my clicking skill, increasing my rate of output, and keeping my left hand unclicked, I paid little attention to my fellow operatives save to observe that they were friendly, middle-aged, foreign-born, full of advice, and very talkative. Their names, according to the way they addressed each other, were George, Ike, and Sammy.[5] George, a stocky fellow in his late fifties, operated the machine at the opposite end of the line; he, I later discovered, had emigrated in early youth from a country in Southeastern Europe. Ike, stationed at George's left, was tall, slender, in his early fifties, and Jewish; he had come from Eastern Europe in his youth. Sammy, number three man in the line, and my neighbor, was heavy set, in his late fifties, and Jewish; he had escaped from a country in Eastern Europe just before Hitler's legions had moved in. All three men had been downwardly mobile as to occupation in recent years. George and Sammy had been proprietors of small businesses; the former had been "wiped out" when his uninsured establishment burned down; the latter had been entrepreneuring on a small scale before he left all behind him to flee the Germans. According to his account, Ike had left a highly skilled trade which he had practiced for years in Chicago.

I discovered also that the clicker line represented a ranking system in descending order from George to myself. George not only had top seniority for the group, but functioned as a sort of lead man. His superior status was marked in the fact that he received five cents more per hour than the other clickermen, put in the longest workday, made daily contact, outside the workroom, with the superintendent on work matters which concerned the entire line, and communicated to the rest of us the directives which he received. The narrow margin of superordination was seen in the fact that directives were always relayed in the superintendent's name; they were on the order of, "You'd better let that go now, and get on the green. Joe says they're running low on the fifth floor," or, "Joe says he wants two boxes of the 3-die today." The narrow margin was also seen in the fact that the superintendent would communicate directly with his operatives over the public address system; and, on occasion, Ike or Sammy would leave the workroom to confer with him for decisions or advice in regard to work orders.

Ike was next to George in seniority, then Sammy. I was, of course, low man on the totem pole. Other indices to status differentiation lay in informal interaction, to be described later.

With one exception, job status tended to be matched by length of workday. George worked a thirteen-hour day, from 7 a.m. to 8:30 p.m. Ike worked eleven hours, from 7 a.m. to 6:30 p.m.; occasionally he worked until 7 or 7:30 for an eleven and a half- or a twelve-hour day. Sammy put in a nine-hour day, from 8 a.m. to 5:30 p.m. My twelve hours spanned from 8 a.m. to 8:30 p.m. We had a half hour for lunch, from 12 to 12:30.

The female who worked at the secluded table behind George's machine put in a regular plant-wide eight-hour shift from 8 to 4:30. Two women held this job during the period of my employment; Mable was succeeded by Baby. Both were Negroes, and in their late twenties.

A fifth clicker operator, an Arabian *emigré* called Boo, worked a night shift by himself. He usually arrived about 7 p.m. to take over Ike's machine.

The Work

It was evident to me, before my first workday drew to a weary close, that my clicking career was going to be a grim process of fighting the clock, the particular timepiece in this situation being an old-fashioned alarm clock which ticked away on a shelf near George's machine. I had struggled through many dreary rounds with the minutes and hours during the various phases of my industrial experience, but never had I been confronted with such a dismal combination of working conditions as the extra-long workday, the infinitesimal cerebral excitation, and the extreme limitation of physical movement. The contrast with a recent stint in the California oil fields was striking. This was no eight-hour day of racing hither and yon over desert and foothills with a rollicking crew of "roustabouts" on a variety of repair missions at oil wells, pipe lines, and storage tanks. Here there were no afternoon dallyings to search the sands for horned toads, tarantulas, and rattlesnakes, or to climb old wooden derricks for raven's nests, with an eye out, of course, for the tell-tale streak of dust in the distance which gave ample warning of the approach of the boss. This was standing all day in one spot beside three old codgers in a dingy room looking out through barred windows at the bare walls of a brick warehouse, leg movements largely restricted to the shifting of body weight from one foot to the other, hand and arm movements confined, for the most part, to a simple repetitive sequence of place the die, —— punch the clicker, —— place the die, —— punch the clicker, and intellectual activity reduced to computing the hours to quitting time. It is true that from time to time a fresh stack of sheets would have to be substituted for the clicked-out old one; but the stack would have been prepared by someone else, and the exchange would be only a minute or two in the making. Now and then a box of finished work would have to be moved back out of the way, and an empty box brought up; but the moving back and the bringing up involved only a step or two. And there was the half hour for lunch, and occasional trips to the lavatory or the drinking fountain to break up the day into digestible parts. But after each momentary respite, hammer and die were moving again: click, —— move die, —— click, —— move die.

Before the end of the first day, Monotony was joined by his twin brother, Fatigue. I got tired. My legs ached, and my feet hurt. Early in the afternoon I discovered a tall stool and moved it up to my machine to "take the load off my feet." But the superintendent dropped in to see how I was "doing" and promptly informed me that "we don't sit down on this job." My reverie toyed with the idea of quitting the job and looking for other work.

The next day was the same: the monotony of the work, the tired legs and sore feet and thoughts of quitting.

The Game of Work

In discussing the factory operative's struggle to "cling to the remnants of joy in work," Henri de Man makes the general observations that "it is psychologically impossible to deprive any kind of work of all its positive emotional elements," that the worker will find *some* meaning in any activity assigned to him, a "certain scope for initiative which can satisfy after a fashion the instinct for play and the creative impulse," that "even in the Taylor system there is found luxury of self-determination."[6] De Man cites the case of one worker who wrapped 13,000 incandescent bulbs a day; she found her outlet for creative impulse, her self-determination, her meaning in work by varying her wrapping movements a little from time to time.[7]

So did I search for *some* meaning in my continuous mincing of plastic sheets into small ovals, fingers, and trapezoids. The richness of possibility for creative expression previously discovered in my experience with the "Taylor system"[8] did not reveal itself here. There was no piecework, so no piecework game. There was no conflict with management, so no war game. But, like the light bulb wrapper, I did find a "certain scope for initiative," and out of this slight freedom to vary activity, I developed a game of work.

The game developed was quite simple, so elementary in fact, that its playing was reminiscent of rainy-day preoccupations in childhood, when attention could be centered by the hour on colored bits of things of assorted sizes and shapes. But this adult activity was not mere pottering and piddling; what it lacked in the earlier imaginative content, it made up for in clean-cut structure. Fundamentally involved were: a) variation in color of the materials cut, b) variation in shape of the dies used, and c) a process called "scraping the block." The basic procedure which ordered the particular combination of components employed could be stated in the form: "As soon as I do so many of these, I'll get to do those." If, for example, production scheduled for the day featured small, rectangular strips in three colors, the game might go: "As soon as I finish a thousand of the green ones, I'll click some brown ones." And, with success in attaining the objective of working with brown materials, a new goal of "I'll get to do the white ones" might be set. Or the new goal might involve switching dies.

Scraping the block made the game more interesting by adding to the number of possible variations in its playing; and, what was perhaps more important, provided the only substantial reward, save for going to the lavatory or getting a drink of water, on days when work with one die and one color of material was scheduled. As a physical operation, scraping the block was fairly simple; it involved application of a coarse file to the upper surface of the block to remove roughness and unevenness resulting from the wear and tear of die penetration. But, as part of the intellectual and emotional content of the game of work, it could be in itself a source of variation in activity. The upper left-hand corner of the block could be chewed up in the clicking of 1000 white trapezoid pieces, then scraped. Next, the upper right-hand corner, and so on until the entire block had been worked over. Then, on the next round of scraping by quadrants, there was the possibility of a change of color or die to green trapezoid or white oval pieces.

Thus the game of work might be described as a continuous sequence of short-range production goals with achievement rewards in the form of activity change. The superiority of this relatively complex and self-determined system over the technically simple and outside-controlled job satisfaction injections experienced by Milner at the beginner's table in a shop of the feather industry should be immediately apparent: "Twice a day our work was completely changed to break the monotony. First Jennie would give us feathers of a brilliant green, then bright orange or a light blue or black. The "ohs" and "ahs" that came from the girls at each change was proof enough that this was an effective way of breaking the monotony of the tedious work."[9]

But a hasty conclusion that I was having lots of fun playing my clicking game should be avoided. These games were not as interesting in the experiencing as they might seem to be from the telling. Emotional tone of the activity was low, and intellectual currents weak. Such rewards as scraping the block or "getting to do the blue ones" were not very exciting, and the stretches of repetitive movement involved in achieving them were long enough to permit lapses into obsessive reverie. Henri de Man speaks of "clinging to the remnants of joy in work," and this situation represented just that. How tenacious the clinging was, how long I could have "stuck it out" with my remnants, was never determined. Before the first week was out this adjustment to the work situation was complicated by other developments. The game of work continued, but in a different context. Its influence became decidedly subordinated to, if not completely overshadowed by, another source of job satisfaction.

Informal Social Activity of the Work Group: Times and Themes

The change came about when I began to take serious note of the social activity going on around me; my attentiveness to this activity came with growing involvement in it. What I heard at first, before I started to listen, was a stream of disconnected bits of communication which did not make much sense. Foreign accents were strong and referents were not joined to coherent contexts of meaning. It was just "jabbering." What I saw at first, before I began to observe, was occasional flurries of horseplay so simple and unvarying in pattern and so childish in quality that they made no strong bid for attention. For example, Ike would regularly switch off the power at Sammy's machine whenever Sammy made a trip to the lavatory or the drinking fountain. Correlatively, Sammy invariably fell victim to the plot by making an attempt to operate his clicking hammer after returning to the shop. And, as the simple pattern went, this blind stumbling into the trap was always followed by indignation and reproach from Sammy, smirking satisfaction from Ike, and mild paternal scolding from George. My interest in this procedure was at first confined to wondering when Ike would weary of his tedious joke or when Sammy would learn to check his power switch before trying the hammer.

But, as I began to pay closer attention, as I began to develop familiarity with the communication system, the disconnected became connected, the nonsense made sense, the obscure became clear, and the silly actually funny. And, as the content of the interaction took on more and more meaning, the interaction began to reveal structure. There were "times" and "themes," and roles to serve their enaction. The interaction had subtleties, and I began to savor and appreciate them. I started to record what hitherto had seemed unimportant.

Times

This emerging awareness of structure and meaning included recognition that the long day's grind was broken by interruptions of a kind other than the formally instituted or idiosyncratically developed disjunctions in work routine previously described. These additional interruptions appeared in daily repetition in an ordered series of informal interactions. They were, in part, but only in part and in very rough comparison; similar to those common fractures of the production process known as the coffee break, the coke break, and the cigarette break. Their distinction lay in frequency of occurrence and in brevity. As phases of the daily series, they occurred almost hourly, and so short were they in duration that they disrupted work activity only slightly. Their significance lay not so much in their function as rest pauses, although it cannot be denied that physical refreshment was involved. Nor did their chief importance lie in the accentuation of progress points in the passage of time, although they could perform that function far more strikingly than the hour hand on the dull face of George's alarm clock. If the daily series of interruptions be likened to a clock, then the comparison might best be made with a special kind of cuckoo clock, one with a cuckoo which can provide variation in its announcements and can create such an interest in them that the intervening minutes become filled with intellectual content. The major significance of the interactional interruptions lay in such a carryover of interest. The physical interplay which momentarily halted work activity would initiate verbal exchanges and thought processes to occupy group members until the next interruption. The group interactions thus not only marked off the time; they gave it content and hurried it along.

Most of the breaks in the daily series were designated as "times" in the parlance of the clicker operators, and they featured the consumption of food or drink of one sort or another. There was coffee time, peach time, banana time, fish time, coke time, and, of course, lunch time. Other interruptions, which formed part of the series but were not verbally recognized as times, were window time, pickup time, and the staggered quitting times of Sammy and Ike. These latter unnamed times did not involve the partaking of refreshments.

My attention was first drawn to this times business during my first week of employment when I was encouraged to join in the sharing of two peaches. It was Sammy who provided the peaches; he drew them from his lunch box after making the announcement, "Peach time!" On this first occasion I refused the proffered fruit, but thereafter regularly consumed my half peach. Sammy continued to provide the peaches and to make the "Peach time!" announcement, although there were days when Ike would remind him that it was peach time, urging him to hurry up with the mid-morning snack. Ike invariably complained about the quality of the fruit, and his complaints fed the fires of continued banter between peach donor and critical recipient. I did find the fruit a bit on the scrubby side but felt, before I achieved insight into the function of peach time, that Ike was showing poor manners by looking a gift horse in the mouth. I wondered why Sammy continued to share his peaches with such an ingrate.

Banana time followed peach time by approximately an hour. Sammy again provided the refreshments, namely, one banana. There was, however, no four-way sharing of Sammy's banana. Ike would gulp it down by himself after surreptitiously extracting it from Sammy's lunch box, kept on a shelf behind Sammy's work station. Each morning, after making the snatch, Ike would call out, "Banana time!" and proceed to down his prize while Sammy made futile protests and denunciations. George would join in with mild remonstrances, sometimes scolding Sammy for making so much fuss. The banana was one which Sammy brought for his own consumption at lunch time; he never did get to eat his banana, but kept bringing one for his lunch. At first this daily theft startled and amazed me. Then I grew to look forward to the daily seizure and the verbal interaction which followed.

Window time came next. It followed banana time as a regular consequence of Ike's castigation by the indignant Sammy. After "taking" repeated references to himself as a person badly lacking in morality and character, Ike would "finally" retaliate by opening the window which faced Sammy's machine, to let the "cold air" blow in on Sammy. The slandering which would, in its echolalic repetition, wear down Ike's patience and forbearance usually took the form of the invidious comparison: "George is a good daddy! Ike is a bad man! A very bad man!" Opening the window would take a little time to accomplish and would involve a great deal of verbal interplay between Ike and Sammy, both before and after the event. Ike would threaten, make feints toward the window, then finally open it. Sammy would protest, argue, and make claims that the air blowing in on him would give him a cold; he would eventually have to leave his machine to close the window. Sometimes the weather was slightly chilly, and the draft from the window unpleasant; but cool or hot, windy or still, window time arrived each day. (I assume that it was orginally a cold season development.) George's part in this interplay, in spite of the "good daddy" laudations, was to encourage Ike in his window work. He would stress the tonic values of fresh air and chide Sammy for his unappreciativeness.

Following window time came lunch time, a formally designated half-hour for the midday repast and rest break. At this time, informal interaction would feature exchanges between Ike and George. The former would start eating his lunch a few minutes before noon, and the latter, in his role as straw boss, would censure him for malobservance of the rules. Ike's off-beat luncheon usually involved a previous tampering with George's alarm clock. Ike would set the clock ahead a few minutes in order to maintain his eating schedule without detection, and George would discover these small daylight saving changes.

The first "time" interruption of the day I did not share. It occurred soon after I arrived on the job, at eight o'clock. George and Ike would share a small pot of coffee brewed on George's hot plate.

Pickup time, fish time, and coke time came in the afternoon. I name it pickup time to represent the official visit of the man who made daily calls to cart away boxes of clicked materials. The arrival of the pickup man, a Negro, was always a noisy one, like the arrival of a daily passenger train in an isolated small town. Interaction attained a quick peak of intensity to crowd into a few minutes all communications, necessary and otherwise. Exchanges invariably included loud depreciations by the pickup man of the amount of work accomplished in the clicking department during the preceding twenty-four hours. Such scoffing would be on the order of "Is that all you've got done? What do you boys do all day?" These devaluations would be countered with allusions to the "soft job" enjoyed by the pickup man. During the course of the exchanges news items would be dropped, some of serious import, such as reports of accomplished or impending layoffs in the various plants of the company, or of gains or losses in orders for company products. Most of the news items, however, involved bits of information on plant employees told in a light vein. Information relayed by the clicker operators was usually told about each other, mainly in the form of summaries of the most recent kidding sequences. Some of this material was repetitive, carried over from day to day. Sammy would be the butt of most of this newscasting, although he would make occasional counter-reports on Ike and George. An invariable part of the interactional content of pickup time was Ike's introduction of the pickup man to George. "Meet Mr. Papeatis!" Ike would say in mock solemnity and dignity. Each day the pickup man "met" Mr. Papeatis, to the obvious irritation of the latter. Another pickup time invariably would bring Baby (or Mable) into the interaction. George would always issue the loud warning to the pickup man: "Now I want you to stay away from Baby! She's Henry's girl!" Henry was a burly Negro with a booming bass voice who made infrequent trips to the clicking room with lift-truck loads of materials. He was reputedly quite a ladies' man among the colored population of the factory. George's warning to "Stay away from Baby!" was issued to every Negro who entered the shop. Baby's only part in this was to laugh at the horseplay.

About mid-afternoon came fish time. George and Ike would stop work for a few minutes to consume some sort of pickled fish which Ike provided. Neither Sammy nor I partook of this nourishment, nor were we invited. For this omission I was grateful; the fish, brought in a newspaper and with head and tail intact, produced a reverse effect on my appetite. George and Ike seemed to share a great liking for fish. Each Friday night, as a regular ritual, they would enjoy a fish dinner together at a nearby restaurant. On these nights Ike would work until 8:30 and leave the plant with George.

Coke time came late in the afternoon, and was an occasion for total participation. The four of us took turns in buying the drinks and in making the trip for them to a fourth floor vending machine. Through George's manipulation of the situation, it eventually became my daily chore to go after the cokes;

the straw boss had noted that I made a much faster trip to the fourth floor and back than Sammy or Ike.

Sammy left the plant at 5:30, and Ike ordinarily retired from the scene an hour and a half later. These quitting times were not marked by any distinctive interaction save the one regular exchange between Sammy and George over the former's "early washup." Sammy's tendency was to crowd his washing up toward five o'clock, and it was George's concern to keep it from further creeping advance. After Ike's departure came Boo's arrival. Boo's was a striking personality productive of a change in topics of conversation to fill in the last hour of the long workday.

Themes

To put flesh, so to speak, on this interactional frame of "times," my work group had developed various "themes" of verbal interplay which had become standardized in their repetition. These topics of conversation ranged in quality from an extreme of nonsensical chatter to another extreme of serious discourse. Unlike the times, these themes flowed one into the other in no particular sequence of predictability. Serious conversation could suddenly melt into horseplay, and vice versa. In the middle of a serious discussion on the high cost of living, Ike might drop a weight behind the easily startled Sammy, who hit him over the head with a dusty paper sack. Interaction would immediately drop to a low comedy exchange of slaps, threats, guffaws, and disapprobations which would invariably include a ten-minute echolalia of "Ike is a bad man, a very bad man! George is a good daddy, a very fine man!" Or, on the other hand, a stream of such invidious comparisons as followed a surreptitious switching-off of Sammy's machine by the playful Ike might merge suddenly into a discussion of the pros and cons of saving for one's funeral.

"Kidding themes" were usually started by George or Ike, and Sammy was usually the butt of the joke. Sometimes Ike would have to "take it," seldom George. One favorite kidding theme involved Sammy's alleged receipt of $100 a month from his son. The points stressed were that Sammy did not have to work long hours, or did not have to work at all, because he had a son to support him. George would always point out that he sent money to his daughter; she did not send money to him. Sammy received occasional calls from his wife, and his claim that these calls were requests to shop for groceries on the way home were greeted with feigned disbelief. Sammy was ribbed for being closely watched, bossed, and henpecked by his wife, and the expression "Are you man or mouse?" became an echolalic utterance, used both in and out of the original context.

Ike, who shared his machine and the work scheduled for it with Boo, the night operator, came in for constant invidious comparison on the subject of output. The socially isolated Boo, who chose work rather than sleep on his lonely night shift, kept up a high level of performance, and George never tired of pointing this out to Ike. It so happened that Boo, an Arabian Moslem from Palestine, had no use for Jews in general; and Ike, who was Jewish, had no use for Boo in particular. Whenever George would extol Boo's previous night's production, Ike would try to turn the conversation into a general discussion on the need for educating the Arabs. George, never permitting the development of serious discussion on this topic, would repeat a smirking warning, "You watch out for Boo! He's got a long knife!"

The "poom poom" theme was one that caused no sting. It would come up several times a day to be enjoyed as unbarbed fun by the three older clicker operators. Ike was usually the one to raise the question, "How many times you go poom poom last night?" The person questioned usually replied with claims of being "too old for poom poom." If this theme did develop a goat, it was I. When it was pointed out that I was a younger man, this provided further grist for the poom poom mill. I soon grew weary of this poom poom business, so dear to the hearts of the three old satyrs, and, knowing where the conversation would inevitably lead, winced whenever Ike brought up the subject. . . .

Serious themes included the relating of major misfortunes suffered in the past by group members. George referred again and again to the loss, by fire, of his business establishment. Ike's chief complaints centered around a chronically ill wife who had undergone various operations and periods of hospital care. Ike spoke with discouragement of the expenses attendant upon hiring a housekeeper for himself and his children; he referred with disappointment and disgust to a teen-age son, an inept lad who "couldn't even fix his own lunch. He couldn't even make himself a sandwich!" Sammy's reminiscences centered on the loss of a flourishing business when he had to flee Europe ahead of Nazi invasion.

But all serious topics were not tales of woe. One favorite serious theme which was optimistic in tone could be called either "Danelly's future" or "getting Danelly a better job." It was known that I had been attending "college," the magic door to opportunity, although my specific course of study remained somewhat obscure. Suggestions poured forth on good lines of work to get into, and these suggestions were backed with accounts of friends, and friends of friends, who had made good via the academic route. My answer to the expected question, "Why are you working here?" always stressed the "lots of overtime" feature, and this explanation seemed to suffice for short-range goals.

There was one theme of especially solemn import, the "professor theme." This theme might also be termed "George's daughter's marriage theme"; for the recent marriage of George's only child was inextricably bound up with George's connection with higher learning. The daughter had married the son of a professor who instructed in one of the local colleges. This professor theme was not in the strictest sense a conversation piece; when the subject came up, George did all the talking. The two Jewish operatives remained silent as they listened with deep respect, if not actual awe, to George's accounts of the Big Wedding which, including the wedding pictures, entailed an expense of $1000. It was monologue, but there was listening, there was communication, the sacred communication of a temple, when George told of going for Sunday afternoon walks on the Midway with the professor, or of joining the professor for a Sunday dinner. Whenever he spoke of the professor, his daughter, the wedding, or even of the new son-in-law, who remained for the most part in the background, a sort of incidental like the wedding cake, George was complete master of the interaction. His manner, in speaking to the rank-and-file of clicker operators, was indeed that of master deigning to notice his underlings. I came to the conclusion that it was the professor connection, not the straw-boss-ship or the extra nickel an hour, which provided the fount of George's superior status in the group.

If the professor theme may be regarded as the cream of verbal interaction, the "chatter themes" should be classed as the dregs. The chatter themes were hardly themes at all; perhaps they should be labelled "verbal states," or "oral autisms." Some were of doubtful status as communication; they were like the howl or cry of an animal responding to its own physiological state. They were exclamations, ejaculations, snatches of song or doggerel, talkings-to-oneself, mutterings. Their classification as themes would rest on their repetitive character. They were echolalic utterances, repeated over and over. An already mentioned example would be Sammy's repetition of "George is a good daddy, a very fine man! Ike is a bad man, a very bad man!" Also, Sammy's repetition of "Don't bother me! Can't you see I'm busy? I'm a very busy man!" for ten minutes after Ike had dropped a weight behind him would fit the classification. Ike would shout "Mamariba!" at intervals between repetition of bits of verse, such as:

Mama on the bed,
Papa on the floor,
Baby in the crib
Says giver some more!

Sometimes the three operators would pick up one of these simple chatterings in a sort of chorus. "Are you man or mouse? I ask you, are you man or mouse?" was a favorite of this type.

So initial discouragement with the meagerness of social interaction I now recognized as due to lack of observation. The interaction was there, in constant flow. It captured attention and held interest to make the long day pass. The twelve hours of "click, —— move die, —— click, —— move die" became as easy to endure as eight hours of varied activity in the oil fields or eight hours of playing the piece-work game in a machine shop. The "beast of boredom" was gentled to the harmlessness of a kitten.

Black Friday: Disintegration of the Group

But all this was before "Black Friday." Events of that dark day shattered the edifice of interaction, its framework of times and mosaic of themes, and reduced the work situation to a state of social atomization and machine-tending drudgery. The explosive element was introduced deliberately, but without prevision of its consequences.

On Black Friday, Sammy was not present; he was on vacation. There was no peach time that morning, of course, and no banana time. But George and Ike held their coffee time, as usual, and a steady flow of themes was filling the morning quite adequately. It seemed like a normal day in the making, at least one which was going to meet the somewhat reduced expectations created by Sammy's absence.

Suddenly I was possessed of an inspiration for modification of the professor theme. When the idea struck, I was working at Sammy's machine, clicking out leather parts for billfolds. It was not difficult to get the attention of close neighbor Ike to suggest *sotto voce*, "Why don't you tell him you saw the professor teaching in a barber college on Madison Street? . . . Make it near Halsted Street."

Ike thought this one over for a few minutes, and caught the vision of its possibilities. After an interval of steady application to his clicking, he informed the unsuspecting George of his near West Side discovery; he had seen the professor busy at his instructing in a barber college in the lower reaches of Hobohemia.

George reacted to this announcement with stony silence. The burden of questioning Ike for further details on his discovery fell upon me. Ike had not elaborated his story very much before we realized that the show was not going over. George kept getting redder in the face, and more tight-lipped; he slammed into his clicking with increased vigor. I made one last weak attempt to keep the play on the road by remarking that barber colleges paid pretty well. George turned to hiss at me, "You'll have to go to Kankakee with Ike!" I dropped the subject. Ike whispered to me, "George is sore!"

George was indeed sore. He didn't say another word the rest of the morning. There was no conversation at lunchtime, nor was there any after lunch. A pall of silence had fallen over the clicker room. Fish time fell a casualty. George did not touch the coke I brought for him. A very long, very dreary afternoon dragged on. Finally, after Ike left for home, George broke the silence to reveal his feelings to me: "Ike acts like a five-year-old, not a man! He doesn't even have the respect of the niggers. But he's got to act like a man around here! He's always fooling around! I'm going to stop that! I'm going to show him his place! . . . Jews will ruin you, if you let them. I don't care if he sings, but the first time he mentions my name, I'm going to shut him up! It's always 'Meet Mr. Papeatis! George is a good daddy!' And all that. He's paid to work! If he doesn't work, I'm going to tell Joe!"

Then came a succession of dismal workdays devoid of times and barren of themes. Ike did not sing, nor did he recite bawdy verse. The shop songbird was caught in the grip of icy winter. What meager communication there was took a sequence of patterns which proved interesting only in retrospect.

For three days, George would not speak to Ike. Ike made several weak attempts to break the wall of silence which George had put between them, but George did not respond; it was as if he did not hear. George would speak to me, on infrequent occasions, and so would Ike. They did not speak to each other.

On the third day George advised me of his new communication policy, designed for dealing with Ike, and for Sammy, too, when the latter returned to work. Interaction was now on a "strictly business" basis, with emphasis to be placed on raising the level of shop output. The effect of this new policy on production remained indeterminate. Before the fourth day had ended, George got carried away by his narrowed interests to the point of making sarcastic remarks about the poor work performances of the absent Sammy. Although addressed to me, these caustic depreciations were obviously for the benefit of Ike. Later in the day Ike spoke to me, for George's benefit, of Sammy's outstanding ability to turn out billfold parts. For the next four days, the prevailing silence of the shop was occasionally broken by either harsh criticism or fulsome praise of Sammy's outstanding workmanship. I did not risk replying to either impeachment or panegyric for fear of involvement in further situational deteriorations.

Twelve-hour days were creeping again at snail's pace. The strictly business communications were of no help, and the sporadic bursts of distaste or enthusiasm for Sammy's clicking ability helped very little. With the return of boredom, came a return of fatigue. My legs tired as the afternoons dragged on, and I became engaged in conscious efforts to rest one by shifting my weight to the other. I would pause in my work to stare through the barred windows at the grimy brick wall across the alley; and, turning my head, I would notice that Ike was staring at the wall too. George would do very little work after Ike left the shop at night. He would sit in a chair and complain of weariness and sore feet.

In desperation, I fell back on my game of work, my blues and greens and whites, my ovals and trapezoids, and my scraping the block. I came to surpass Boo, the energetic night worker, in volume of output. George referred to me as a "day Boo" (day-shift Boo) and suggested that I "keep" Sammy's machine. I managed to avoid this promotion, and consequent estrangement with Sammy, by pleading attachment to my own machine.

When Sammy returned to work, discovery of the cleavage between George and Ike left him stunned. "They were the best of friends!" he said to me in bewilderment.

George now offered Sammy direct, savage criticisms of his work. For several days the good-natured Sammy endured these verbal aggressions without losing his temper; but when George shouted at him "You work like a preacher!" Sammy became very angry, indeed. I had a few anxious moments when I thought that the two old friends were going to come to blows.

Then, thirteen days after Black Friday, came an abrupt change in the pattern of interaction. George and Ike spoke to each other again, in friendly conversation: I noticed Ike talking to George after lunch. The two had newspapers of fish at George's cabinet. Ike was excited; he said, "I'll pull up a chair!" The two ate for ten minutes. . . . It seems that they went up to the 22nd Street Exchange together during lunch period to cash pay checks.

That afternoon Ike and Sammy started to play again, and Ike burst once more into song. Old themes reappeared as suddenly as the desert flowers in spring. At first, George managed to maintain some show of the dignity of superordination. When Ike started to sing snatches of "You Are My Sunshine," George suggested that he get "more production." Then Ike backed up George in pressuring Sammy for more production. Sammy turned this exhortation into low comedy by calling Ike a "slave driver" and by shouting over and over again, "Don't bother me! I'm a busy man!" On one occasion, as if almost overcome with joy and excitement, Sammy cried out, "Don't bother me! I'll tell Rothman! [the company president] I'll tell the union! Don't mention my name! I hate you!"

I knew that George was definitely back into the spirit of the thing when he called to Sammy, "Are you man or mouse?" He kept up the "man or mouse" chatter for some time.

George was for a time reluctant to accept fruit when it was offered to him, and he did not make a final capitulation to coke time until five days after renewal of the fun and fooling. Strictly speaking, there never was a return to banana time, peach time, or window time. However, the sharing and snitching of fruit did go on once more, and the window in front of Sammy's machine played a more prominent part than ever in the renaissance of horseplay in the clicker room. In fact, the "rush to the window" became an integral part of increasingly complex themes and repeated sequences of interaction. This window rushing became especially bound up with new developments which featured what may be termed the "anal gesture."[10] Introduced by Ike, and given backing by an enthusiastic, very playful George, the anal gesture became a key component of fun and fooling during the remaining weeks of my stay in the shop: Ike broke wind, and put his head in his hand on the block as Sammy grabbed a rod and made a mock rush to open the window. He beat Ike on the head, and George threw some water on him, playfully. In came the Negro head of the Leather Department; he remarked jokingly that we should take out the machines and make a playroom out of the shop.

Of course, George's demand for greater production was metamorphized into horseplay. His shout of "Production please!" became a chatter theme to accompany the varied antics of Ike and Sammy.

The professor theme was dropped completely. George never again mentioned his Sunday walks on the Midway with the professor.

Conclusions

Speculative assessment of the possible significance of my observations on information interaction in the clicking room may be set forth in a series of general statements.

Practical Application

First, in regard to possible practical application to problems of industrial management, these observations seem to support the generally accepted notion that one key source of job satisfaction lies in the informal interaction shared by members of a work group. In the clicking-room situation the spontaneous development of a patterned combination of horseplay, serious conversation, and frequent sharing of food and drink reduced the monotony of simple, repetitive operations to the point where a regular schedule of long work days became livable. This kind of group interplay may be termed "consumatory" in the sense indicated by Dewey, when he makes a basic distinction between "instrumental" and "consumatory" communication.[11] The enjoyment of communication "for its own sake" as "mere sociabilities," as "free, aimless social intercourse," brings job satisfaction, at least job endurance, to work situations largely bereft of creative experience.

In regard to another managerial concern, employee productivity, any appraisal of the influence of group interaction upon clicking-room output could be no more than roughly impressionistic. I obtained no evidence to warrant a claim that banana time, or any of its accompaniments in consumatory interaction, boosted production. To the contrary, my diary recordings express an occasional perplexity in the form of "How does this company manage to stay in business?" However, I did not obtain sufficient evidence to indicate that, under the prevailing conditions of laissez-faire management, the output of our group would have been more impressive if the playful cavorting of three middle-aged gentlemen about the barred windows had never been. As far as achievement of managerial goals is concerned, the most that could be suggested is that leavening the deadly boredom of individualized work routines with a concurrent flow of group festivities had a negative effect on turnover. I left the group, with sad reluctance, under the pressure of strong urgings to accept a research fellowship which would involve no factory toil. My fellow clickers stayed with their machines to carry on their labors in the spirit of banana time.

Theoretical Considerations

Secondly, possible contribution to ongoing sociological inquiry into the behavior of small groups, in general, and factory work groups, in particular, may lie in one or more of the following ideational products of my clicking-room experience:

1. In their day-long confinement together in a small room spatially and socially isolated from other work areas of the factory the Clicking Department employees found themselves ecologically situated for development of a "natural" group. Such a development did take place; from worker intercommunications did emerge the full-blown sociocultural system of consumatory interactions which I came to share, observe, and record in the process of my socialization.

2. These interactions had a content which could be abstracted from the total existential flow of observable doings and sayings for labelling and objective consideration. That is, they represented a distinctive subculture, with its recurring patterns of reciprocal influencings which I have described as times and themes.

3. From these interactions may also be abstracted a social structure of statuses and roles. This structure may be discerned in the carrying out of the various informal activities which provide the content of the subculture of the group. The times and themes were performed with a system of roles which formed a sort of pecking hierarchy. Horseplay had its initiators and its victims, its amplifiers and its chorus; kidding had its attackers and attacked, its least attacked and its most attacked, its ready acceptors of attack and its strong resistors to attack. The fun went on with the participation of all, but within the controlling frame of status, a matter of who can say or do what to whom and get away with it.

4. In both the cultural content and the social structure of clicker group interaction could be seen the permeation of influences which flowed from the various multiple group memberships of the participants. Past and present "other-group" experiences or anticipated "outside" social connections provided significant materials for the building of themes and for the establishment and maintenance of status and role relationships. The impact of reference group affiliations on clicking-room interaction was notably revealed in the sacred, status-conferring expression of the professor theme. This impact was brought into very sharp focus in developments which followed my attempt to degrade the topic, and correlatively, to demote George.

5. Stability of the clicking-room social system was never threatened by immediate outside pressures. Ours was not an instrumental group, subject to disintegration in a losing struggle against environmental obstacles or oppositions. It was not striving for corporate goals; nor was it faced with the enmity of other groups. It was strictly a consumatory group, devoted to the maintenance of patterns of self-entertainment. Under existing conditions, disruption of unity could come only from within.

Potentials for breakdown were endemic in the interpersonal interactions involved in conducting the group's activities. Patterns of fun and fooling had developed within a matrix of frustration. Tensions born of long hours of relatively meaningless work were released in the mock aggressions of horseplay. In the recurrent attack, defense, and counterattack there continually lurked the possibility that words or gestures harmless in conscious intent might cross the subtle boundary of accepted, playful aggression to be perceived as real assault. While such an occurrence might incur displeasure no more lasting than necessary for the quick clarification or creation of kidding norms, it might also spark a charge of hostility sufficient to disorganize the group.

A contributory potential for breakdown from within lay in the dissimilar "other group" experiences of the operators. These other-group affiliations and identifications could provide differences in tastes and sensitivities, including appreciation of humor, differences which could make maintenance of consensus in regard to kidding norms a hazardous process of trial and error adjustments.

6. The risk involved in this trial and error determination of consensus on fun and fooling in a touchy situation of frustration—mock aggression—was made evident when I attempted to introduce alterations in the professor theme. The group disintegrated, *instanter.* That is, there was an abrupt cessation of the interactions which constituted our groupness. Although both George and I were solidly linked in other-group affiliations with the higher learning, there was not enough agreement in our attitudes toward university professors to prevent the interactional development which shattered our factory play group. George perceived my offered alterations as a real attack, and he responded with strong hostility directed against Ike, the perceived assailant, and Sammy, a fellow traveler.

My innovations, if accepted, would have lowered the tone of the sacred professor theme, if not to "Stay Away From Baby" ribaldry, then at least to the verbal slapstick level of "finding Danelly an apartment." Such a downgrading of George's reference group would, in turn, have downgraded George. His status in the shop group hinged largely upon his claimed relations with the professor.

7. Integration of our group was fully restored after a series of changes in the patterning and quality of clicking-room interaction. It might be said that reintegration took place *in* these changes, that the series was a progressive one of step-by-step improvement in relations, that re-equilibration was in process during the three weeks that passed between initial communication collapse and complete return to "normal" interaction.

The cycle of loss and recovery of equilibrium may be crudely charted according to the following sequence of phases: (a) the stony silence of "not speaking"; (b) the confining of communication to formal matters connected with work routines; (c) the return of informal give-and-take in the form of harshly sarcastic kidding, mainly on the subject of work performance, addressed to a neutral go-between for the "benefit" of the object of aggression; (d) highly emotional direct attack, and counter-attack, in the form of criticism and defense of work performance; (e) a sudden rapprochement expressed in serious, dignified, but friendly conversation; (f) return to informal interaction in the form of mutually enjoyed mock aggression; (g) return to informal interaction in the form of regular patterns of sharing food and drink.

The group had disintegrated when George withdrew from participation; and, since the rest of us were at all times ready for rapprochement, reintegration was dependent upon his "return." Therefore, each change of phase in interaction on the road to recovery could be said to represent an increment of return on George's part. Or, conversely, each phase could represent an increment of reacceptance of punished deviants. Perhaps more generally applicable to description of a variety of reunion situations would be conceptualization of the phase changes as increments of reassociation without an atomistic differentiation of the "movements" of individuals.

8. To point out that George played a key role in this particular case of re-equilibration is not to suggest that the homeostatic controls of a social system may be located in a type of role or in a patterning of role relationships. Such controls could be but partially described in terms of human interaction; they would be functional to the total configuration of conditions within the field of influence. The automatic controls of a mechanical system operate as such only under certain achieved and controlled conditions. The human body recovers from disease when conditions for such homeostasis are "right." The clicking-room group regained equilibrium under certain undetermined conditions. One of a number of other possible outcomes could have developed had conditions not been favorable for recovery.

For purposes of illustration, and from reflection on the case, I would consider the following as possibly necessary conditions for reintegration of our group: (a) Continued monotony of work operations; (b) Continued lack of a comparatively adequate substitute for the fun and fooling release from work tensions; (c) Inability of the operatives to escape from the work situation or from each other, within the work situation. George could not fire Ike or Sammy to remove them from his presence, and it would have been difficult for the three middle-aged men to find other jobs if they were to quit the shop. Shop space was small, and the machines close together. Like a submarine crew, they had to "live together"; (d) Lack of conflicting definitions of the situation after Ike's perception of George's reaction to the "barber college" attack. George's anger and his punishment of the offenders were perceived as justified; (e) Lack of introduction of new issues or causes which might have carried justification for new attacks and counter-attacks, thus leading interaction into a spiral of conflict and crystallization of conflict norms. For instance, had George reported his offenders to the superintendent for their poor work performance; had he, in his anger, committed some offense which would have led to reporting of a grievance to local union officials; had he made his anti-Semitic remarks in the presence of Ike or Sammy, or had I relayed these remarks to them; had I tried to "take over" Sammy's machine, as George had urged; then the interactional outcome might have been permanent disintegration of the group.

9. Whether or not the particular patterning of interactional change previously noted is somehow typical of a "re-equilibration process" is not a major question here. My purpose in discriminating the seven changes is primarily to suggest that re-equilibration, when it does occur, may be described in observable phases and that the emergence of each succeeding phase should be dependent upon the configuration of conditions of the preceding one. Alternative eventual outcomes may change in their probabilities, as the phases succeed each other, just as prognosis for recovery in sickness may change as the disease situation changes.

10. Finally, discrimination of phase changes in social process may have practical as well as scientific value. Trained and skillful administrators might follow the practice in medicine of introducing aids to re-equilibration when diagnosis shows that they are needed.

Notes and References

1. Charles R. Walker and Robert H. Guest. *The Man on the Assembly Line.* Harvard University Press, Cambridge, 1952.
2. *Ibid.,* 77.
3. *Ibid.,* 68.
4. Donald F. Roy. "Work Satisfaction and Social Reward in Quota Achievement: An Analysis of Piecework Incentive." *American Sociological Review,* XVIII (October 1953), 507–514.
5. All names used are fictitious.
6. Henri de Man. *The Psychology of Socialism.* Henry Holt and Company, New York, 1927, 80–81.
7. *Ibid.,* 81.
8. Roy, *op. cit.*
9. Lucille Milner. *Education of An American Liberal.* Horizon Press, New York, 1954, 97.
10. I have been puzzled to note widespread appreciation of this gesture in the "consumatory" communication of the working men of this nation. For the present I leave it to clinical psychologists to account for the nature and pervasiveness of this social bond.
11. John Dewey. *Experience and Nature.* Open Court Publishing Co., Chicago, 1925, 202–206.

Informal Work Groups and Autonomy in Structure

FRED E. KATZ

A generation after the Hawthorne studies, no one questions the existence of informal groups in complex organizations. Numerous studies have documented their existence, especially among employees in the lowest ranks. But the task remains of developing an adequate *conceptual* explanation of how persons in the lowest ranks, with their limited career prospects in their work and slight opportunity for advancement, are incorporated into work organizations on a relatively permanent basis. Stated differently, how can one account for the integration of organizations that include a large number of persons who are largely disenfranchised from the organization's reward system? How can one account for the apparent collaboration, if not loyalty, of persons who, since the time of Marx, have been described as being alienated from their work?[1] A brief, though oversimplified answer is that workers need work and factories need workers. One can hardly argue with this statement. Yet, the economic interdependence of workers and factories does not clarify the nature of the structural arrangement under which the interdependence is worked out.

Fred E. Katz, "Explaining Informal Groups in Complex Organizations: The Case for Autonomy in Structure," *Administrative Science Quarterly,* Vol. 10, No. 2 (September 1965), pp. 204–221. Reprinted by permission. "Autonomy in Structure" has been more fully developed in Katz, *Autonomy and Organization,* Random House, 1968.

The proposed answer to the question of how workers are incorporated into complex organizations has two aspects: (1) Workers have considerable autonomy within the confines of the organization. Even when their work is prescribed in exact detail, the work role tends to be defined narrowly. This leaves a considerable portion of the worker's life within the work organization *undefined.* (2) Workers tend to use this autonomy to bring their working-class culture into the organization, even though this is alien to the bureaucratic ethos of the higher echelons of the organization. This produces continuity between the workman's outside life and his participation in the work setting—a setting to which he has very limited allegiance.[2] This continuity in turn promotes workers' integration into work organizations. After a general presentation of this perspective, it is illustrated through a detailed review of one of Donald Roy's case studies of factory workers. No attempt will be made to assess the degree of fit of this perspective to particular types of industries.

The guiding perspective is that the culture of informal work groups is a manifestation of autonomy within the confines of the organization, and that autonomy is an aspect of organizational structure that needs systematic study. Autonomy is defined as independence from external control. Here, it means that the activities of workers within the organization are not fully controlled by the organization. This leaves room for development of informal patterns of various sorts—those that lessen boredom of workers, those that help get work done, as well as those that are alienative to the organization. I shall attempt to view autonomy as an aspect of the very structure of organizations, as spheres of independence which are delegated by the organization. Direct and indirect delegation of autonomy suggest themselves. The first refers to specific rules that delimit an area of autonomy. For example, a rule specifying that the foreman can decide who will work the night shift indicates a sphere in which the foreman has autonomy, one in which he exercises discretion. By contrast indirect delegation of autonomy results from the absence of rules; in a sphere where no clear rules exist, autonomy exists by default. Both direct and indirect delegation of autonomy promotes spheres of activity that are not closely controlled by the organization. The present thesis is that the resulting autonomous behavior needs to be considered as an aspect of organizational structure, not merely as deviance. This paper will mainly examine autonomy based on indirect delegation, since this seems to characterize informal patterns among workers.

Worker autonomy can be regarded as part of the barter arrangement between workers and the organization, where limited affiliation with the organization is exchanged for a degree of autonomy. The arrangement has important adaptive functions for both parties. For the organization it is a way of promoting the affiliation of some of its employees with the organization, while at the same time excluding them from certain vital spheres of organizational activity. For workers it permits continuation of the working-class style of life and provides ties of sociability in a context that in many ways is alien to the workman's culture. In short, the autonomy appears to have adaptive and pattern-maintenance functions for the workers, and adaptive and goal-attainment functions for the organization. It must be noted that worker autonomy, although enacted *in* the work organization is essentially *external* to his work role. This contrasts with the autonomy pattern for white collar workers, that is, all those who—from the lowliest clerk to the president—make up the administrative hierarchy. They have greater autonomy *within* their work role, but their role is more broadly defined than that of the worker.[3] In a sense the white-collar worker takes his work role *outside* the organization; the blue-collar worker brings his nonwork role *into* the organization.

The definition of formal organization focuses on a planned system, and the definition of informal organization on actual behavior. This is a weak distinction, theoretically. Actual behavior is undoubtedly relevant to planned systems; and system characteristics, even planned ones, are relevant to actual behavior. The distinction seems to need refocusing to enable orderly analysis of structure and ongoing behavior. I would suggest the following perspective: Organizational structure includes relatively controlled and relatively autonomous spheres. The controlled sphere is based on direct specification of behavior; the autonomous sphere is based on both direct and indirect specification of behavior. Direct specification of behavior approximates the formal organization concept; but it allows spheres of autonomy as well as spheres of controlled activity. The indirect specification of behavior approximates the traditional informal organization, but under comparable conceptual footing with the planned formal system.

The writings of Chester Barnard illustrate that autonomous and controlled behavior coexist within organizations and that the executive must fuse them together.[4] He notes that autonomy among personnel is not necessarily a disaster to executive control but may, in fact, be an asset to administrative processes. He suggests that the executive must rely on the "willingness to serve"[5] of those under his command; he must recognize that there is a "zone of indifference"[6] in which persons are prepared to accept orders, and beyond which they are prone to oppose orders. Informal patterns, in Barnard's view of the executive, are not divisive forces, but instead, are "expansion of the means of communication with reduction in the necessity for formal decisions, the minimizing of undesirable influences, and the promotion of desirable influences concordant with the scheme of formal responsibilities."[7] From Barnard's perspective both formal and informal patterns can be harnessed in the service of a "co-operating system." But it seems that the real point is not the blending of formally and informally organized behavior, but the blending of controlled and autonomous behaviors that exist within organizations. Barnard's model of the organization is suffused with autonomy patterns that can serve the whole organization; some of these patterns proceed from direct official specification of behavior and some come from indirect specification.

The Worker's Place in the Organization

Workers are here viewed as being permitted to develop relatively autonomous subcultures and subsystems of social interaction in their day-to-day routines. The autonomous patterns diverge from the officially prescribed patterns, but are very much in line with the workman's style of life and culture outside the organization. The culture of the working-class man is in many ways alien to the decorum and demeanor expected of the white-collar members of the organization. In the routinized work of the white-collar worker there is no room for the sudden display of anger of the working-class male; in the face-the-public white-collar worker there is little scope for the pervasive sexual allusions of the working-class male. Yet within the working clique inside the organization the workman can enact the culture patterns of his life outside the organization. He can, for example, indulge freely in what is perhaps the workman's major form of creative mental activity: verbal play, imaginative exploits, and the romanticism on the theme of sex.[8] Indeed, the workman has a large sphere of verbal freedom, since much of what he says "doesn't count," so far as his work is concerned. Unlike the white-collar worker, whose work consists of a world of words, written and spoken, the worker is basically measured by the contributions of his hands. Therefore, his verbal jostlings, such as the razzing of the lowest person on the prestige totem pole, are not considered part of his job. There is every indication (as is shown in the review of the study by Donald Roy), that the content of the verbal banter contains reference to the workman's niche in the social order and the conditions of his social existence.[9] These are also reflected in patterns of practical jokes and prankish physical contact, which are characteristic of the workman's culture, but taboo in the culture of the white-collar worker.[10]

By contrast, the white-collar workers, whether senior executive or junior administrators, have a broad affinity for the organizational style of behavior. They are likely to be members of the middle or upper class, where they have learned the demeanor and proprieties of manner they will be expected to exercise in their position in the organization.[11] There is little abrupt discontinuity, for instance, between the style of dress and speech of their social class and that associated with the bureaucratic style of behavior. Stated differently, they can carry over elements of their external life into the organization and apply them to their job without having to make fundamental adjustments in their general style of behavior; although this does not mean that they have nothing to learn in their work. The organization-man thesis makes the same point in converse terms: The work habits and interests of the white-collar worker spill over into his family and community life. For the white-collar worker, the organization is less clearly differentiated from the culture of his private world than it is from the private world of the worker; the organization is not the enemy camp. The blue-collar worker, on the other hand, is eager to leave his work behind him as he leaves the gates of the factory.[12]

How does autonomy in the role of white-collar worker differ from that of the blue-collar worker? Briefly stated, white-collar workers have greater autonomy *in their task-related activities* than does the blue-collar worker; the time clock; the regimentation involved in feeding a machine and gearing one's work to the pace of a machine, of doing one's work exclusively at the location of a particular machine—these apply to the blue-collar worker to a far larger extent than to the white-collar worker. For the latter, work is defined more broadly than it is for the blue-collar worker, requiring a more diffuse commitment. This means that for the white-collar worker a broad range of activities and personal attributes are defined as relevant to work, from personal grooming to getting along with others. Organizing a Little League baseball team, the fate of the local community chest drive, and participation in college alumni affairs—a good organization man's allegiance to the organization and his style of work include taking part in these activities after working hours and communicating these interests to his work peers. It is difficult to assess which activities are regarded as clearly *external* to his work role. On the other hand, the worker's tasks are defined more narrowly, leaving scope for activity that is defined as *external* to his work, but enacted while he is at his place of work.

The limited bases for the worker's *allegiance* to the work organization are given tacit recognition not only in the worker being excluded from administrative decision making, but also in his being allowed to bring into the work setting working-class culture patterns and to fashion them into relatively autonomous subcultures. In short, the worker's external affiliations, i.e., with the working-class style of life, are permitted to intrude into the organization that employs him. This can be viewed as part of the exchange (in addition to monetary pay) for limited forms of reward and participation that the worker is allowed by the employing organization. In view of the differentiation between worker subculture and bureaucratic culture, the worker's immersion in working-class patterns may serve to perpetuate his disenfranchisement from the administrative sphere, resulting in a vicious cycle.

The empirical study of workers in factories has been a favorite of sociologists and social psychologists. The focus of many of these studies is on what actually goes on in work settings. Among the most eloquently descriptive studies of the culture and interaction patterns of workers are those by Donald F. Roy. Roy's article ["Banana Time: Job Satisfaction and Informal Interaction"] is perhaps a culmination in a series of research findings that, since the days of the Hawthorne studies, have pointed to the demise of the economic man without, however, completing the task of making social organization the focus of analysis. The early studies, in their opposition to the economic-man thesis, pointed out that the individual was not guided only by his own monetary self-interest. Indeed, he could be guided against his own self-interest by his worker peer group; the individual worker might actually lose income by following the output control patterns of his peers. It was emphasized that there was a "group factor" in work situations; but an individualistic, social psychological focus was retained for this group factor. In the Hawthorne studies there was much concern with changes in attitude toward work; the meaning of work was considered a basic factor in individuals' performance; and work groups were considered in molding the meaning and attitudes for members of the group.[13] Roy's interpretation of his findings is similarly social psychological. It is that the informal patterns serve primarily to provide job satisfaction by relieving *boredom.* Along with many students of industrial relations in the last thirty years, he notes the existence of relatively distinct subgroups that have relatively distinct culture and interaction patterns, and that are separate from the formal structure in the factory. Yet, the basic interpretation is in individualistic, psychological terminology: it relieves boredom. Even if one accepts the psychological perspective, one must question whether routine, repetitive work is necessarily conducive to boredom. For example, Chinoy's study of automobile assembly-line workers suggests that workers' response to routine, repetitive work is perhaps better characterized by irritation over lack of control over one's work than by boredom.[14] To realize that routine, repetitive activity does not necessarily lead to boredom, one should allow for the influence of culture. The researcher may be exaggerating the activistic theme of Western societies. The Jicarilla Apache, for example, "have an infinite capacity for not being bored. They can sit for hours on end and apparently do nothing; they certainly don't intellectualize about doing nothing."[15]

The focus of the present paper suggests attention to what seems to be a basic feature in the social organization of the work situation, the autonomy enjoyed by the work group.[16] It does this on Roy's evidence that *considerable structuring of the work situation is done by the workers themselves*. What, then, is the content of the autonomous group culture? As Roy describes it, the work situation includes a great variety of behaviors that are not directly connected with *work*. Many of these fit Simmel's description of play forms of social reality.[17] Subjects that are of serious concern, such as economic security, sexual virility, health and death, submission to the authority of other men, family loyalty, and status aspirations, are examined in a context where they are stripped of their serious content. But the manner in which attention is paid to these subjects is particularly important. Flitting from one topic to another—from the deeply serious to the comic, from the immediately practical to the remotely romantic—indicates the decided irrelevance of the practical, concrete reality in which each of the subjects is embedded. Perhaps it is because members are simultaneously engaged in serious work that they feel free to treat other concerns so detachedly. Roy's group appears to be a veritable haven for the enactment of play forms. Elements of life that are largely beyond the control of the individual are exposed and, in a fashion, are dealt with. All this is most clearly evident in the verbal themes. In addition to play forms, it may well be that the various social interaction patterns—the "razzing" of Sammy, the paternalism of George—are reiterations of serious realities in the larger social context in which the men find themselves. It is noteworthy that it is Sammy, the newest immigrant (all three men are immigrants) who is the scapegoat; it is George, the only Gentile, who quietly occupies the superior status; it is the Negro handyman who is the object of stereotypical banter about uncontrolled sexuality.

These elements, whether they are fairly explicit reiterations or play forms of the workman's life outside the factory, are continuities between life outside the factory and life inside the factory and therefore are important for understanding the nature of the bond between the worker and the organization in which he is employed. Work peers participate in a common culture, which relies heavily on their common fate both within and *outside* the organization. In their commonality they retain a fundamental alienation from the white-collar ranks in the organization. This appears to be demonstrated in Chinoy's findings of workers' widespread lack of interest in becoming foremen or white-collar workers.[18] It is also supported by Walker and Guest's study of assembly-line workers. They found largely favorable reaction by workers to their immediate job, but intense dissatisfaction with the factory as a whole.[19] Although there is lack of affiliation with the white-collar ranks of the organization, the worker *does* form bonds within the organization—with his own work peers.[20] For the organization, this dual relationship provides an uneasy truce without lessening the fundamental internal antithesis, and manifests itself in problems of morale and communications. At the same time the structure of the situation—the existence of two cultures—assures the continuity of the basic antithesis.

Roy points out that the group had developed a "full-blown sociocultural system." The group was to a considerable extent a separate and distinct system, one in which the members had active, at times even creative, participation—in sharp contrast to their minimal participation in the larger organization. But it does not seem that *work* was at all a major focus of this sociocultural system! If one accepts this point, one gains a tool for reconciling the dilemma as to whether factory workers are strongly alienated from their work.[21] It appears that work is *one of a variety* of topics around which Roy's group had developed behavioral patterns, but work was by no means the central point of attention of this "full-blown sociocultural system."

The contention that work is not a central feature of Roy's work group differs considerably from traditional explanations of informal groups. Although no claim is made about the representativeness of the Roy group, it must be understood that the sort of data he presented has traditionally been interpreted largely in terms of its relevance to *work.* Statements to the effect that informal activities give meaning to dull, routine factory work[22] and that "work output is a function of the degree of work satisfaction, which in turn depends upon the informal social patterns of the work group"[23] are typical examples. These statements provide a social-psychological explanation of the group's mediating effect between the individual and his work, but they are hardly adequate in providing a structural explanation of the place of informal groups in a complex organization.

In addition to the social-psychological interpretations, there are well-documented studies—by Roy and others—which show production control and worker collusion against management by informal groups of workers.[24] Here there can be no doubt that informal patterns are relevant to work. But it is not certain, even here, that informal groups exist primarily for the worker's control over work or whether the explanation should not be reversed: that control over work exists because of the presence of informal groups which, in turn, exist because of the worker's relative autonomy.

In summary, it is suggested that Roy's work group exhibits a rich sociocultural system that is made possible by substantial worker autonomy. The autonomy exists by default; worker's roles are narrowly defined, leaving a considerable sphere of undefined action within the confines of the organization. The content of worker's sociocultural system is made up of a variety of elements from the culture and social context of workers outside the factory. These elements manifest themselves as direct reiterations as well as play forms of the reality. They provide continuity between the workman's life outside the factory and his participation within the factory.

In using the Roy study to illustrate autonomy patterns among informal groups, certain cautionary statements must be made. The group Roy studied may be atypical in the small amount of managerial supervision and in the degree of isolation from the rest of the factory, which might allow a disproportionately high degree of autonomy, as compared with other work groups. One can only answer that this requires investigation; it has not been demonstrated at this time. Also, worker autonomy structure is evident in other studies, as implied, for example, in Gouldner's conception of the managerial "indulgency pattern" toward workers,[25] and Bensman and Gerver's study of "deviancy in maintaining the social system" in a factory.[26] In addition, autonomy patterns among employees who are operating on higher echelons than laborers have been explored by Chester Barnard[27] and in the various writings of Peter Blau;[28] but these are outside the scope of the present paper.[29]

Note on the Theory of Integration of Complex Organizations

Complex organizations must have ways of procuring and integrating the services of a variety of participants. On a common-sense level one can see the process of procurement and integration accomplished most readily in organizations that have coercive means at their disposal. Prisons can force inmates to peel potatoes. But organizations that do not have coercion at their disposal provide a problem for the analyst. There can be little doubt that most complex organizations do, in fact, solve the problem. How is it accomplished?

The concern of this paper has been the integration of a particular segment of the membership of complex organizations, namely blue-collar workers in factories. The particular issue, here, is how these persons are recruited and integrated into the organization, which offers them few of the rewards that it can bestow. The answer is that a federalistic type of solution exists: Workers are permitted ample separation from the total organization and, to a considerable extent, their integration into the larger system is left to them. Informal work group cultures are the concrete structures that make up the solution.

The separation of workers from the employing organization provides workers with flexibility and options as to the degree of alienation from the whole organization. At the same time, the separation gives the organization freedom to adopt means and goals that are disparate, if not alien, to those of the workers. The federalistic balance of autonomy for the blue-collar workers as against the white-collar staff allows flexibility to both sides; but it is also a potential source of divergence and conflict, which finds nurture in the separate subcultures.

In contrast to the form of integration suggested here, other writings have shown much concern with models of organization that dwell on lessening internal differentiation. Workers and the white-collar staff are seen as diverging in interest and this divergence can *and needs to be* lessened if the organization is to operate effectively.[30] These writings differ from the present essay both in theoretical and practical focus. On the theoretical side, the present exposition is based strongly on the view that autonomy can be viewed as a structural principle of organizations, which can have positive or negative consequences for the operation of organizations. Structured autonomy manifests itself in internal divergencies, but these are not necessarily disruptive and maladaptive for the whole organization or any part of it. As to practical goals, many writers, notably Whyte and Argyris,[31] are concerned with the problem of improving human relations in industrial concerns. The practical focus here is not on improving social relationships in complex organizations; it is on the problem of improving the analytic theory of complex organizations. I do not claim that this is a more worthy or pressing problem than that of improving human relationships in complex organizations, merely that it *is* a problem.

Notes and References

1. For a survey and research application of the theme of worker alienation, see Robert Blauner, *Alienation and Freedom: The Factory Worker and His Industry* (Chicago: University of Chicago, 1964).

2. For a summary of the literature on the limited commitment of workers to the complex organizations in which they work, as well as to work itself, see Chris Argyris,

Integrating the Individual and the Organization (New York: John Wiley, 1964). In Pt. IV the author provides a summary of the debate as to whether the worker is alienated. Argyris' book is addressed to the same general issue as the present paper, but his approach differs in that it focuses on the issue—a very important one—of developing organizational patterns so that there is congruence between the psychological needs of members and the administrative requirements of the organization. The present paper, in contrast, attempts to remain entirely on the level of social structure. See, also, R. Dubin, "Industrial Workers' World: A Study of the 'Central Life Interests' of Industrial Workers," in Erwin O. Smige (ed.), *Work and Leisure* (New Haven: College and University Press, 1963), 53–72.

3. This viewpoint is more fully developed in Fred E. Katz. "The School As a Complex Organization." *Harvard Educational Review,* 34 (Summer 1964).

4. Chester I. Barnard. *The Functions of the Executive* (Cambridge: Harvard University, 1938).

5. *Ibid.,* 83ff.

6. *Ibid.,* 167ff.

7. *Ibid.,* 227.

8. I am not suggesting that middle and upper class males do not engage in this form of mental sport, but I do suggest that for the working-class male it is a *major* creative outlet, and much less so for the middle and upper classes.

9. S. M. Miller and Frank Riessman suggest that the "factory 'horseplay,' the ritualistic kidding" are partly an expression of the working-class theme of person centeredness; see their "The Working-Class Subculture." In A. B. Shostak and W. Gomberg (eds.), *Blue Collar World* (Englewood Cliffs, N.J.: Prentice-Hall, 1964), 24–35.

10. Participating in physical contact—be it fighting, prankish shoving, or contact sports—are chiefly characteristic of male preadult culture. Presumably it is only at the low socioeconomic levels that this pattern continues into adulthood. It is not clear whether similar continuities exist between *preadult* and adult female culture among working-class women.

11. It makes little difference whether they are members of the middle or upper class or use these classes as a reference group to guide their behavior.

12. Robert Blauner, "Occupational Differences in Work Satisfaction." In R. L. Simpson and I. H. Simpson (eds.), *Social Organization and Behavior* (New York: John Wiley, 1964), 287–292.

13. Fritz J. Roethlisberger and William J. Dickson, *op. cit.,* and Edward Gross, *Work and Society* (New York: Thomas Crowell, 1958), ch. xiv.

14. Ely Chinoy. *Automobile Workers and the American Dream* (Garden City, N.Y.: Doubleday, 1955).

15. Personal communication from H. Clyde Wilson.

16. Focus on autonomy structure does not altogether avoid the pitfall of potentially overemphasizing one set of structures and one set of functions, just as social-psychological studies have done. But it should serve to broaden the existing basis of analysis.

17. K. H. Wolff (ed. and transl.), *The Sociology of George Simmel* (New York: Free Press, 1950).

18. Ely Chinoy, *op. cit.;* see especially ch. v. See also E. W. Bakke, *The Unemployed Worker* (New Haven: Yale University, 1940); and poll conducted by *Fortune* (May, 1947), both cited by Chinoy. Chinoy's explanation of the lack of desire for promotion is that workers have become so discouraged in the course of their work careers that they have given up. He notes that workers are reacting to "the limited opportunities available, to the uncertainties stemming from the informal procedures by which foremen were chosen, and to the nature of the foreman's job itself . . ." (p. 49). This explanation is not irreconcilable with the one offered here. The young factory worker, who does have visions of advancement, is presumably not sufficiently

knowledgeable about the culture wall between himself and the administrative bureaucrat.

19. Charles R. Walker and Robert H. Guest. *The Man on the Assembly Line* (Cambridge, Mass.: Harvard University, 1952); see, for example, 139–140.

20. Dubin's studies suggest, however, that workers' friendship bonds with work peers are less important than bonds with peers outside the work setting; see Robert Dubin, *op. cit.*

21. Argyris, *op. cit.*, believes that workers are strongly alienated; Walker and Guest, *op. cit.*, note that workers they studied were relatively contented doing simple, repetitive work.

22. Edward Gross, *op. cit.*, 526.

23. Reinhard Bendix and Lloyd H. Fisher. "The Perspectives of Elton Mayo." In Amitai Etzioni, (ed.), *Complex Organizations: A Sociological Reader* (New York: Holt, Rinehart, and Winston, 1961), 119.

24. See Donald Roy, "Efficiency and 'The Fix': Informal Intergroup Relations in a Piecework Machine Shop." In S. M. Lipset and N. J. Smelser (ed.), *Sociology: The Progress of a Decade* (Englewood Cliffs, N.J.: Prentice-Hall, 1961), 378–390; also his "Quota Restriction and Goldbricking in a Machine Shop," *American Journal of Sociology,* 57 (March 1952), 427–442.

25. Alvin W. Gouldner. *Wildcat Strike* (Yellow Springs, Ohio: Antioch Press, 1954).

26. Joseph Bensman and Israel Gerver. "Crime and Punishment in the Factory: The Function of Deviancy in Maintaining the Social System." *American Sociological Review,* 28 (August 1963), 588–598.

27. Chester Barnard, *op. cit.*

28. Peter M. Blau, "Structural Effects," *op. cit.*, and *The Dynamics of Bureaucracy, op. cit.*

29. A broader formulation of autonomy structure has been attempted in Fred E. Katz, *op. cit.*

30. Argyris, *op. cit.*, and other writings by the same author. See also the writings of W. F. Whyte; for example, *Patterns of Industrial Peace* (New York: Harper and Row, 1951) and *Money and Motivation* (New York: Harper and Row, 1955).

31. *Ibid.*

On Norms

JOHN W. THIBAUT, HAROLD H. KELLEY

Conceptualization of Norms

Consider two people in a dyadic relationship and assume that the pattern of their outcomes is such that they cannot achieve their best outcomes at the same time. For example, this might be a husband and wife whose problem is that the wife likes to go dancing in the evening and the husband prefers that they go to the movies. The outcomes are illustrated in Figure 1. It is apparent that trading is necessary if both are to obtain good outcomes even occasionally.

Trading can be established through exercise of the power that each possesses,

Figure 1   Illustration of Relationship Requiring Trading

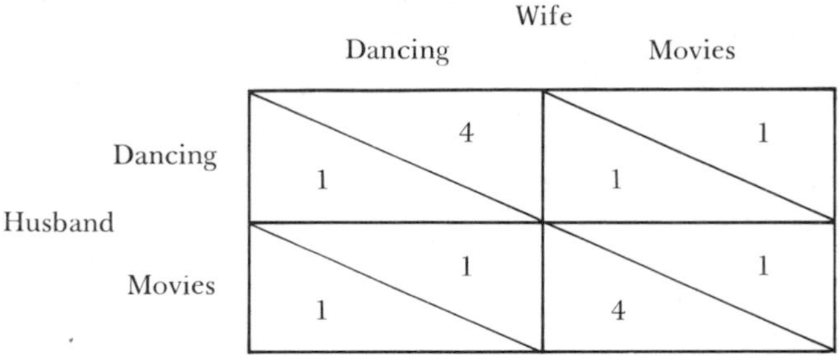

if this power is adequate. For example, the husband can use his control over the wife's outcomes by promising to go dancing if she will go with him to the movies. Or he can threaten to go to the movies anyway if she fails to cooperate, in which case she will have poor outcomes. Similar influence opportunities exist for the wife.

The moment-to-moment use of personal power can be obviated if the two can agree upon some rule for trading. For example, they might agree that they will alternate between dancing and attending the movies, making the shift upon some mutually acceptable signal; for example, a word from the momentarily favored person to the effect that he or she is satiated with the present activity. Once agreement is reached on a rule of this sort, shifts are likely to proceed smoothly and predictably and, in view of the limitations inherent to the relationship (noncorrespondence of high outcomes), each person is likely to feel that his own outcomes are satisfactory.

Agreements of this sort may be matters of mere convenience, repeated for their immediate value in reducing the costs involved in face-to-face influence and in smoothing out the course of the interaction. However, as Waller and Hill (1951) so aptly put it, "The *usual* quickly becomes the *right* . . ." (p. 49). The rule is likely to take on the characteristics of a moral obligation (or even to have them from the start). This means, in brief, that conformity to agreements becomes rewarding in and of itself.

Just how this transformation occurs is a complex matter. It probably has some basis in the fact that conformity to rules and agreements has proven rewarding in past relationships in which some external agent has delivered extrinsic rewards for conformity. For example, two brothers disagree about what to play because they prefer different games. Their mother steps in and says, "Play what Jimmy wants for awhile, and, after you've done that, give Johnny a chance," and rewards them if they follow her rule. Agreement to rules is also reinforced by the value they have for the relationship in cutting costs and enhancing rewards. We shall elaborate this shortly.

These reinforcing conditions make it likely that the two boys will learn to value "fair play." They will *accept* the rule in the sense that their equitable turn-taking behavior will no longer occur simply as a result of their compliance to external sanctions but also because they have *internalized* the rule [see Kelman, 1961].

Thus a predisposition to value and abide by a trading rule may exist at the outset of the husband and wife relationship. Norms need not be invented anew for each relationship but may often be transferred from other ones. These learning conditions also make it likely that a general value for agreements and rules of this sort will be acquired.

When an agreement about a matter such as trading exists between the members of a dyad and when it is accepted to some degree by both, we would say that a norm exists. This would manifest itself to an outside observer in several ways:

(1) There would be regularity in behavior (in our example, a routinized sequence of shifts in activities of the pair).

(2) In the event of disruption of this regularity, the "injured" person would attempt to restore it by appealing, at least initially, to the rule and he would exercise his personal power as an enforcer of the rule.

(3) The person disrupting the regularity would be likely to feel some obligation to adhere to the agreement and might even exhibit some conflict or guilt about deviating from it, as if he were punishing himself for his nonconformity.

Once a norm exists, it appears to the pair almost as if a third agent had entered the relationship, a feeling which undoubtedly is reinforced by the fact that in earlier relationships the enforcers of rules often actually were third persons (e.g., the mother in the case of the two brothers). The third agent exercises power over each member in the usual sense of making it desirable for him to act in certain ways at certain times and does so in an impartial way without regard to the special interests of either one. This normative power, when the rule has been accepted or internalized, seems to be exclusively behavior control, except in the case we discuss later in which the person is unable to make the necessary discriminations or perform the specified behavior. In one sense this power accrues to the norm because the two persons give up some of their individual power to it. This is evidenced by their exercising personal power in the name of the norm rather than to advance their personal interests. In another sense, the norm may have power over them independently of their enforcement of it: to the degree that the norm is accepted by individuals to whom it applies, conformity is more rewarding, other things being equal, than nonconformity.

From the preceding discussion the reader can deduce our definition of norm. A norm is a behavioral rule that is accepted, at least to some degree, by both members of the dyad. (A rule which one person advances and tries to enforce but which the other person does not accept cannot be called a norm, at least in a dyad. In large groups, on the other hand, acceptance by all members is not an essential part of the concept, although acceptance by a sizable number is.) Thus both members feel some obligation to adhere to it. Nonadherence is met with the use of power to attempt to produce conformity, but the influence appeal is to a supra-individual value ("Do it for the group" or "Do it because it's good") rather than to personal interests ("Do it for me" or "Do it and I'll do something for you").

The reader may wish to compare the present treatment of norm with similar conceptualizations advanced by other social scientists. Most similar is Homans' (1950) definition:

"A norm, then, is an idea in the minds of the members of a group, an idea that can be put in the form of a statement specifying what the members or other men should do, ought to do, are expected to do, under given circumstances. . . . A statement of the kind described is a norm only if any departure of real behavior from the norm is followed by some punishment" (p. 123).

In the Lewinian tradition, Festinger, Schachter and Back (1950) give a definition in terms of forces: ". . . a uniform set of directions which the group induces on the forces which act on the members of the group" (p. 166). Rommetveit (1954) distinguishes carefully between the individual acting as enforcer of a norm, on the one hand, and the individual subject to it, on the other: "A social norm is a pressure existing between a norm-sender and a norm-receiver's behaviour in a category of recurrent situations" (p. 45). The last phrase excludes accidental and temporary interpersonal pressures. Pressure is said to be manifested in the norm sender's expectations that the norm receiver will behave in a specific way, or in his wish for this behavior, and in overt sanctions applied by the norm sender in response to the norm receiver's actions (pp. 45 ff.).

The general contention advanced above can be argued from a slightly different point of view. Consider a dyad in which one member, A, performs a certain special behavior that is highly rewarding to B. As long as A continues to perform this sequence, there will be no problem; B will come to *expect* it in the sense of predicting that A is likely to repeat it in the future. However, if A is somewhat undependable or even merely exhibits covert tendencies not to perform his special function, B's dependency upon him is dramatized and becomes somewhat difficult to tolerate. This might be explained by assuming the existence of a need for autonomy (Murray, 1938) that motivates people to avoid interpersonal situations in which they are dependent upon others. Perhaps it is simpler merely to suggest that dependency upon an unreliable person is cost increasing. In interaction with such a person one often begins behavioral sequences without being able to consummate them, and one frequently does things for him without getting anything in return. On the other hand, dependency is no problem with a perfectly reliable deliverer of rewards, for example, a bountiful environment or the corner grocer with his stable prices.

So B's problem is to strengthen A's tendency to perform the desired sequence without making too apparent his dependency upon A, that is, without suffering power loss. This is done by an appeal to a supra-individual value connected with the welfare of some third agent, set of persons, or organization rather than with B's own welfare. Such appeals as "Do it because it's good," "People expect it of you," or "Do it for the group" are essentially power-maintenance strategies. They play down the value of the behavior to the person making the appeal or request but at the same time insure that the performance will continue. Allport (1954) summarizes an extremely cynical version of this point, advanced by Le Dantec. Moral standards such as those expressed in the Ten Commandments are described as being promulgated merely for the convenience of those who have some interest to protect, as, for example, property owners—"Thou shalt not steal"—and persons who have sexual partners—"Thou shalt not commit adultery." Thus B attempts to change the basis for A's performing the behavior from that of doing B a personal favor to that of satisfying social or moral obligations.

This process of transforming the value basis for compliance is probably supported and reinforced by conflict reduction on the part of A, the performer. If he has impulses not to help his partner, he has a recurring conflict between incompatible activities, those rewarding to B versus those which are not. This conflict is costly and can be reduced by mobilizing powerful instigations to only one kind of behavior. These are provided by the moralistic or social value appeals used by B which give A a justification for overvaluing the desirability of the behavior. Thus acceptance of supra-individual, depersonalized values as the basis for behavior has functional value both for the actor and the one dependent upon his actions.

Norms have similar functional values in many dyads in which power is evenly distributed. In highly cohesive groups the great power the two members have over each other not only gives them ability to carry out strong influence measures but also to resist each other's influence. This situation potentially leads to interpersonal conflicts and unresolved "stand-offs" in which neither one is able to get the other to engage in desired activities. This type of conflict can be avoided by procedural rules in which power is transferred, so to speak, from personal agents to the norms. Then, when A tries to induce B to do something, B is expected to perceive the locus of causality for the influence attempt not as internal to a whimsical or self-aggrandizing A but as existing in the de-personalized norm on behalf of which A is acting. We might expect that the counterpower (or resistance) that B might mobilize against A's suggestion would not exist for an impersonal set of rules. Alternatively stated, in a highly cohesive dyad B's counterpower derives from his ability to affect A's fate; this source of resistance is eliminated when power is depersonalized by transfer to a set of procedures or rules. (Note the implication that norms will develop more rapidly and more surely in highly cohesive groups, assuming that the majority of the members have about the same degree of dependence on the group, than in less cohesive groups.) Frank (1944) provides evidence that an appeal to an impersonal value encounters less resistance than does the direct exercise of personal power.

Even if equal power does not lead to interpersonal impasses, the interaction process is likely to be characterized by a good deal of argument and informal litigation. Unless argument and uncertainty happen to be rewarding in themselves, they merely represent unnecessary costs. These costs can be substantially reduced by agreements that enable the individuals to run off their most frequent interaction sequences according to automatic routines, without moment-by-moment decision making. Green (1956) comments on this point, "What an utter chaos human life would be—it could not long endure—if every day we had to settle by family debate or authoritarian decision how many meals we would eat *this* day, at what hour of the day or night" (p. 75). In a similar vein, MacIver and Page (1949) write of norms, "Without them the burden of decision would be intolerable and the vagaries of conduct utterly distracting" (p. 207). It may also be noted that for both members of a dyad the necessity of invoking power on the one hand and the necessity of complying with it on the other tend to bring to mind and dramatize the dependence of each upon the other. As we have stated above, the feeling of dependence is probably something most people would rather avoid. To the extent that there is depersonalization of influence, the source of power and control being external to both individuals, the basic fact of their interdependence goes unstated and probably unnoticed.

In short, we may view norms as social inventions that accomplish more effectively what otherwise would require informal social influence. We do not intend to imply that norms are deliberately developed for this purpose. The contention is merely that there exists a basis for unconscious collusion between weaker and stronger persons, between controllers and the controlled, between persons highly dependent upon each other—a collusion that has the effect of bringing regularity and control into the relationship without the informal exercise of personal power.

Some Implications

This point of view has several important implications. *First,* if the central assertion is correct, that norms are means of influence and control which minimize the problems created by informal influence, then from a close examination of informal influence and its problems we should be able to infer the general *properties of norms.* This requires little explanation beyond that contained in the preceding pages. Norms are, in the first place, *rules about behavior.* They tell each person what is expected of him in certain situations, and in so doing they indirectly indicate requests that others may not properly make of him. In this way, he is protected from subjugation to another's whimsically exercised power. Norms are also *stable* so that the individual knows not only what is expected of him today but what will be expected of him tomorrow. Furthermore, norms are based upon *agreement or consensus* which reduces the necessity for thorough surveillance and, in large groups, distributes the responsibility for surveillance rather widely. The enforcement of norms often involves *appeals to impersonal values or suprapersonal agents,* which reduce the extent to which compliance is viewed as a matter of giving in to a more powerful person and thereby reduces resistance. Also these values are often *widely held* among the group members, so that once they have been associated with compliance it becomes directly rewarding and the need for exercise of external control is greatly reduced. Simmel (1902) puts the last point this way:

"In the morality of the individual, society creates for itself an organ which is not only more fundamentally operative than law and custom, but which also spares society the different sorts of costs involved in these institutions. Hence the tendency of society to satisfy its demands as cheaply as possible results in appeals to 'good conscience,' through which the individual pays to himself the wages for his righteousness, which otherwise would probably have to be assured to him in some way through law or custom" (p. 19n).

The *second* implication is this: If norms are to control or replace interpersonal influence, then they should have some relevance to the things about which this influence is exercised. What norms are about, that which is commonly called the *content of norms,* should be inferable from a consideration of the things about which group members find it necessary to influence each other.

References

Allport, G. W. *The Nature of Prejudice.* Addison-Wesley, 1954.

Festinger, L., S. Schachter, and K. Back. *Social Pressures in Informal Groups: A Study of a Housing Project.* Harper & Row, 1950.

Frank, J. D. "Experimental Studies of Personal Pressure and Resistance: II. Methods of Overcoming Resistance." *Journal of General Psychology,* Vol. 30 (1944), 43–46.

Green, A. W. *Sociology: An Analysis of Life in a Modern Society.* McGraw-Hill, 1956.

Homans, G. C. *The Human Group.* Harcourt Brace Jovanovich, 1950.

Kelman, H. C. "Processes of Opinion Change." *Public Opinion Quarterly,* Vol. 25 (1961), 57–78.

MacIver, R. M., and C. H. Page. *Society: An Introductory Analysis.* Holt, Rinehart and Winston, 1949.

Murray, H. A. *Explorations in Personality.* Oxford University Press, 1938.

Rommetveit, R. *Social Norms and Roles.* University of Minnesota Press, 1954.

Simmel, G. "The Number of Members as Determining the Sociological Form of the Group." *American Journal of Sociology,* Vol. 8 (1902–1903), 19n.

Waller, W., and R. Hill. *The Family: A Dynamic Interpretation.* Holt, Rinehart and Winston, 1951.

Sources of Power of Lower Participants in Complex Organizations

DAVID MECHANIC

It is not unusual for lower participants[1] in complex organizations to assume and wield considerable power and influence not associated with their formally defined positions within these organizations. In sociological terms they have considerable personal power but no authority. Such personal power is often attained, for example, by executive secretaries and accountants in business firms, by attendants in mental hospitals, and even by inmates in prisons. The personal power achieved by these lower participants does not necessarily result from unique personal characteristics, although these may be relevant, but results rather from particular aspects of their location within their organizations.

Informal Versus Formal Power

Within organizations the distribution of authority (institutionalized power) is closely if not perfectly correlated with the prestige of positions. Those who have argued for the independence of these variables[2] have taken their examples from diverse organizations and do not deal with situations where power is clearly comparable.[3] Thus when Bierstedt argues that Einstein had prestige but no power, and the policeman power but no prestige, it is apparent that he is comparing categories that are not comparable. Generally persons occupying high-ranking positions within organizations have more authority than those holding low-ranking positions.

"Sources of Power of Lower Participants in Complex Organizations," by David Mechanic from *Administrative Science Quarterly,* Volume 7, No. 2 (December 1962), pp. 349–364. Reprinted by permission of the author and *Administrative Science Quarterly.*

One might ask what characterizes high-ranking positions within organizations. What is most evident, perhaps, is that lower participants recognize the right of higher-ranking participants to exercise power, and yield without difficulty to demands they regard as legitimate. Moreover, persons in high-ranking positions tend to have considerable access and control over information and persons both within and outside the organization, and to instrumentalities or resources. Although higher supervisory personnel may be isolated from the task activities of lower participants, they maintain access to them through formally established intermediary positions and exercise control through intermediary participants. There appears, therefore, to be a clear correlation between the prestige of positions within organizations and the extent to which they offer access to information, persons, and instrumentalities.

Since formal organizations tend to structure lines of access and communication, access should be a clue to institutional prestige. Yet access depends on variables other than those controlled by the formal structure of an organization, and this often makes the informal power structure that develops within organizations somewhat incongruent with the formally intended plan. It is these variables that allow work groups to limit production through norms that contravene the goals of the larger organization, that allow hospital attendants to thwart changes in the structure of a hospital, and that allow prison inmates to exercise some control over prison guards. Organizations, in a sense, are continuously at the mercy of their lower participants, and it is this fact that makes organizational power structure especially interesting to the sociologist and social psychologist.

Clarification of Definitions

The purpose of this paper is to present some hypotheses explaining why lower participants in organizations can often assume and wield considerable power which is not associated with their positions as formally defined within these organizations. For the purposes of this analysis the concepts "influence," "power," and "control" will be used synonymously. Moreover, we shall not be concerned with type of power, that is, whether the power is based on reward, punishment, identification, power to veto, or whatever.[4] Power will be defined as *any force that results in behavior that would not have occurred if the force had not been present*. We have defined power as a force rather than a relationship because it appears that much of what we mean by power is encompassed by the normative framework of an organization, and thus any analysis of power must take into consideration the power of norms as well as persons.

I shall also argue, following Thibaut and Kelley,[5] that power is closely related to dependence. To the extent that a person is dependent on another, he is potentially subject to the other person's power. Within organizations one makes others dependent upon him by controlling access to information, persons, and instrumentalities which I shall define as follows:

Information includes knowledge of the organization, knowledge about persons, knowledge of the norms, procedures, techniques, and so forth.

Persons include anyone within the organization or anyone outside the organization upon whom the organization is in some way dependent.

Instrumentalities include any aspect of the physical plant of the organization or its resources (equipment, machines, money, and so on).

Power is a function not only of the extent to which a person controls information, persons, and instrumentalities, but also of the importance of the various attributes he controls.[6]

Finally, following Dahl,[7] we shall agree that comparisons of power among persons should, as far as possible, utilize comparable units. Thus we shall strive for clarification by attempting to oversimplify organizational processes; the goal is to set up a number of hypothetical statements of the relationship between variables taken two at a time, "all other factors being assumed to remain constant."

To state the hypothesis suggested, somewhat more formally:

H1   Other factors remaining constant, organizational power is related to access to persons, information, and instrumentalities.

H2   Other factors remaining constant, as a participant's length of time in an organization increases, he has increased access to persons, information, and instrumentalities.

While these hypotheses are obvious, they do suggest that a careful scrutiny of the organizational literature, especially that dealing with the power or counter-power of lower participants, might lead to further formalized statements, some considerably less obvious than the ones stated.

Sources of Power of Lower Participants

The most effective way for lower participants to achieve power is to obtain, maintain, and control access to persons, information, and instrumentalities. To the extent that this can be accomplished, lower participants make higher-ranking participants dependent upon them. Thus dependence together with the manipulation of the dependency relationship is the key to the power of lower participants.

A number of examples can be cited which illustrate the preceding point. Scheff, for example, reports on the failure of a state mental hospital to bring about intended reform because of the opposition of hospital attendants.[8] He noted that the power of hospital attendants was largely a result of the dependence of ward physicians on attendants. This dependence resulted from the physician's short tenure, his lack of interest in administration, and the large amount of administrative responsibility he had to assume. An implicit trading agreement developed between physicians and attendants, whereby attendants would take on some of the responsibilities and obligations of the ward physician in return for increased power in decision-making processes concerning patients. Failure of the ward physician to honor his part of the agreement resulted in information being withheld, disobedience, lack of co-operation, and unwillingness of the attendants to serve as a barrier between the physician and a ward full of patients demanding attention and recognition. When the attendant withheld co-operation, the physician had difficulty in making a graceful entrance and departure from the ward, in handling necessary paper work (officially his responsibility), and in obtaining information needed to deal adequately with daily treatment and behavior problems. When attendants opposed change, they could wield influence by refusing to assume responsibilities officially assigned to the physician.

Similarly, Sykes describes the dependence of prison guards on inmates and the power obtained by inmates over guards.[9] He suggests that although guards could report inmates for disobedience, frequent reports would give prison officials the impression that the guard was unable to command obedience. The guard, therefore, had some stake in ensuring the good behavior of prisoners without use of formal sanctions against them. The result was a trading agreement whereby the guard allowed violations of certain rules in return for co-operative behavior. A similar situation is found in respect to officers in the Armed Services or foremen in industry. To the extent that they require formal sanctions to bring about co-operation, they are usually perceived by their superiors as less valuable to the organization. For a good leader is expected to command obedience, at least, if not commitment.

Factors Affecting Power

Expertise

Increasing specialization and organizational growth has made the expert or staff person important. The expert maintains power because high-ranking persons in the organization are dependent upon him for his special skills and access to certain kinds of information. One possible reason for lawyers obtaining many high governmental offices is that they are likely to have access to rather specialized but highly important means to organizational goals.[10]

We can state these ideas in hypotheses, as follows:

H3   Other factors remaining constant, to the extent that a low-ranking participant has important expert knowledge not available to high-ranking participants, he is likely to have power over them.

Power stemming from expertise, however, is likely to be limited unless it is difficult to replace the expert. This leads to two further hypotheses:

H4   Other factors remaining constant, a person difficult to replace will have greater power than a person easily replaceable.
H5   Other factors remaining constant, experts will be more difficult to replace than nonexperts.

While persons having expertise are likely to be fairly high-ranking participants in an organization, the same hypotheses that explain the power of lower participants are relevant in explaining the comparative power positions of intermediate- and high-ranking persons.

As a result of growing specialization, expertise is increasingly important in organizations. As the complexity of organizational tasks increases, and as organizations grow in size there is a limit to responsibility that can be efficiently exercised by one person. Delegation of responsibility occurs, experts and specialists are brought in to provide information and research, and the higher participants become dependent upon them. Experts have tremendous potentialities for power by withholding information, providing incorrect information, and so on, and to the extent that experts are dissatisfied, the probability of organizational sabotage increases.

Effort and Interest

The extent to which lower participants may exercise power depends in part on their willingness to exert effort in areas where higher-ranking participants are often reluctant to participate. Effort exerted is directly related to the degree of interest one has in an area.

> *H6*   Other factors remaining constant, there is a direct relationship between the amount of effort a person is willing to exert in an area and the power he can command.

For example, secretarial staffs in universities often have power to make decisions about the purchase and allocation of supplies, the allocation of their services, the scheduling of classes, and, at times, the disposition of student complaints. Such control may in some instances lead to sanctions against a professor by polite reluctance to furnish supplies, ignoring his preferences for the scheduling of classes, and giving others preference in the allocation of services. While the power to make such decisions may easily be removed from the jurisdiction of the lower participant, it can only be accomplished at a cost—the willingness to allocate time and effort to the decisions dealing with these matters. To the extent that responsibilities are delegated to lower participants, a certain degree of power is likely to accompany the responsibility. Also, should the lower participant see his perceived rights in jeopardy, he may sabotage the system in various ways.

Let us visualize a hypothetical situation where a department concludes that secretarial services are being allocated on a prejudicial basis as a result of complaints to the chairman of the department by several of the younger faculty. Let us also assume that, when the complaint is investigated, it is found to be substantially correct; that is, some of the younger faculty have difficulty obtaining secretarial services because of preferences among the secretarial staff. If in attempting to eliminate discretion by the secretarial staff, the chairman establishes a rule ordering the allocation of services on the basis of the order in which work appears, the rule can easily be made ineffective by complete conformity to it. Deadlines for papers, examinations, and the like will occur, and flexibility in the allocation of services is required if these deadlines are to be met. Thus the need for flexibility can be made to conflict with the rule by a staff usually not untalented in such operations.

When an organization gives discretion to lower participants, it is usually trading the power of discretion for needed flexibility. The cost of constant surveillance is too high, and the effort required too great; it is very often much easier for all concerned to allow the secretary discretion in return for co-operation and not too great an abuse of power.

> *H7*   Other factors remaining constant, the less effort and interest higher-ranking participants are willing to devote to a task, the more likely are lower participants to obtain power relevant to this task.

Attractiveness

Another personal attribute associated with the power of low-ranking persons in an organization is attractiveness or what some call "personality." People who are viewed as attractive are more likely to obtain access to persons, and, once such access is gained, they may be more likely to succeed in promoting a cause. But once again dependence is the key to the power of attractiveness, for whether a person is dependent upon another for a service he provides, or for approval or affection, what is most relevant is the relational bond which is highly valued.

H8   Other factors remaining constant, the more attractive a person, the more likely he is to obtain access to persons and control over these persons.

Location and Position

In any organization the person's location in physical space and position in social space are important factors influencing access to persons, information, and instrumentalities.[11] Propinquity affects the opportunities for interaction, as well as one's position within a communication network. Although these are somewhat separate factors, we shall refer to their combined effect as centrality[12] within the organization.

H9   Other factors remaining constant, the more central a person in an organization, the greater is his access to persons, information, and instrumentalities.

Some low participants may have great centrality within an organization. An executive's or university president's secretary not only has access, but often controls access in making appointments and scheduling events. Although she may have no great formal authority, she may have considerable power.

Coalitions

It should be clear that the variables we are considering are at different levels of analysis; some of them define attributes of persons, while others define attributes of communication and organization. Power processes within organizations are particularly interesting in that there are many channels of power and ways of achieving it.

In complex organizations different occupational groups attend to different functions, each group often maintaining its own power structure within the organization. Thus hospitals have administrators, medical personnel, nursing personnel, attendants, maintenance personnel, laboratory personnel, and so on. Universities, similarly, have teaching personnel, research personnel, administrative personnel, maintenance personnel, and so on. Each of these functional tasks within organizations often becomes the sphere of a particular group that controls activities relating to the task. While these tasks usually are co-ordinated at the highest levels of the organization, they often are not co-ordinated at intermediate and lower levels. It is not unusual, however, for coalitions to form among lower participants in these multiple structures. A secretary may know the man who manages the supply of stores, or the person assigning parking stickers. Such acquaintances may give her the ability to handle informally certain needs that would be more time-consuming and difficult to handle formally. Her ability to provide services informally makes higher-ranking participants in some degree dependent upon her, thereby giving her power, which increases her ability to bargain on issues important to her.

Rules

In organizations with complex power structures lower participants can use their knowledge of the norms of the organization to thwart attempted change. In discussing the various functions of bureaucratic rules, Gouldner maintains that such rules serve as excellent substitutes for surveillance, since surveillance in addition to being expensive in time and effort arouses considerable hostility and antagonism.[13] Moreover, he argues, rules are a functional equivalent for direct, personally given orders, since they specify the obligations of workers to do things in specific ways. Standardized rules, in addition, allow simple screening of violations, facilitate remote control, and to some extent legitimize punishment when the rule is violated. The worker who violates a bureaucratic rule has little recourse to the excuse that he did not know what was expected, as he might claim for a direct order. Finally, Gouldner argues that rules are "the 'chips' to which the company staked the supervisors and which they could use to play the game";[14] that is, rules established a punishment which could be withheld, and this facilitated the supervisors' bargaining power with lower participants.

While Gouldner emphasizes the functional characteristics of rules within an organization, it should be clear that full compliance to all the rules at all times will probably be dysfunctional for the organization. Complete and apathetic compliance may do everything but facilitate achievement of organizational goals. Lower participants who are familiar with an organization and its rules can often find rules to support their contention that they not do what they have been asked to do, and rules are also often a rationalization for inaction on their part. The following of rules becomes especially complex when associations and unions become involved, for there are then two sets of rules to which the participant can appeal.

What is suggested is that rules may be chips for everyone concerned in the game. Rules become the "chips" through which the bargaining process is maintained. Scheff, as noted earlier, observed that attendants in mental hospitals often took on responsibilities assigned legally to the ward physician, and when attendants refused to share these responsibilities the physician's position became extremely difficult.[15]

The ward physician is legally responsible for the care and treatment of each ward patient. This responsibility requires attention to a host of details. Medicine, seclusion, sedation and transfer orders, for example, require the doctor's signature. Tranquilizers are particularly troublesome in this regard since they require frequent adjustment of dosage in order to get the desired effects. The physician's order is required to each change in dosage. With 150 patients under his care on tranquilizers, and several changes of dosages a week desirable, the physician could spend a major portion of his ward time in dealing with this single detail.

Given the time-consuming formal chores of the physician, and his many other duties, he usually worked out an arrangement with the ward personnel, particularly the charge (supervisory attendant), to handle these duties. On several wards, the charge called specific problems to the doctor's attention, and the two of them, in effect, would have a consultation. The charge actually made most of the decisions concerning dosage change in the back wards. Since the doctor delegated portions of his formal responsibilities to the charge, he was dependent on her good will toward him. If she withheld her co-operation, the physician had absolutely no recourse but to do all the work himself.[16]

In a sense such delegation of responsibility involves a consideration of reward and cost, whereby the decision to be made involves a question of what is more valuable—to retain control over an area, or to delegate one's work to lower participants.

There are occasions, of course, when rules are regarded as illegitimate by lower participants, and they may disregard them. Gouldner observed that, in the mine, men felt they could resist authority in a situation involving danger to themselves.[17] They did not feel that they could legitimately be ordered to do anything that would endanger their lives. It is probably significant that in extremely dangerous situations organizations are more likely to rely on commitment to work than on authority. Even within nonvoluntary groups dangerous tasks are regarded usually as requiring task commitment, and it is likely that commitment is a much more powerful organizational force than coercive authority.

Summary

The preceding remarks are general ones, and they are assumed to be in part true of all types of organizations. But power relationships in organizations are likely to be molded by the type of organization being considered, the nature of organizational goals, the ideology of organizational decision making, the kind of commitment participants have to the organization, the formal structure of the organization, and so on. In short, we have attempted to discuss power processes within organizations in a manner somewhat divorced from other major organizational processes. We have emphasized variables affecting control of access to persons, information, and facilities within organizations. Normative definitions, perception of legitimacy, exchange, and coalitions have all been viewed in relation to power processes. Moreover, we have dealt with some attributes of persons related to power: commitment, effort, interest, willingness to use power, skills, attractiveness, and so on. And we have discussed some other variables: time, centrality, complexity of power structure, and replaceability of persons. It appears that these variables help to account in part for power exercised by lower participants in organizations.

Notes and References

1. The term "lower participants" comes from Amitai Etzioni, *A Comparative Analysis of Complex Organizations* (New York, 1961) and is used by him to designate persons in positions of lower rank: employees, rank-and-file, members, clients, customers, and inmates. We shall use the term in this paper in a relative sense denoting position vis-a-vis a higher ranking participant.
2. Robert Bierstedt. An Analysis of Social Power. *American Sociological Review,* 15 (1950), 730–738.
3. Robert A. Dahl. The Concept of Power. *Behavioral Science,* 2 (1957), 201–213.
4. One might observe, for example, that the power of lower participants is based primarily on the ability to "veto" or punish. For a discussion of bases of power, see John R. P. French, Jr., and Bertram Raven. "The Bases of Social Power," in D. Cartwright and A. Zander, eds., *Group Dynamics* (Evanston, Ill., 1960), 607–623.

5. John Thibaut and Harold H. Kelley. *The Social Psychology of Groups* (New York, 1959). For a similar emphasis on dependence, see Richard M. Emerson, Inter-Dependence Relationships. *American Sociological Review,* 27 (1962), 31–41.

6. Although this paper will not attempt to explain how access may be measured, the author feels confident that the hypotheses concerned with access are clearly testable.

7. *Op. cit.*

8. Thomas J. Scheff. Control over Policy by Attendants in a Mental Hospital. *Journal of Health and Human Behavior,* 2 (1961), 93–105.

9. Gresham M. Sykes. "The Corruption of Authority and Rehabilitation." In A. Etzioni, ed., *Complex Organizations* (New York, 1961), 191–197.

10. As an example, it appears that 6 members of the cabinet, 30 important subcabinet officials, 63 senators, and 230 congressmen are lawyers (*New Yorker,* April 14, 1962, p. 62). Although one can cite many reasons for lawyers holding political posts, an important one appears to be their legal expertise.

11. There is considerable data showing the powerful effect of propinquity on communication. For summary, see Thibaut and Kelley, *op. cit.,* 39–42.

12. The concept of centrality is generally used in a more technical sense in the work of Bavelas, Shaw, Gilchrist, and others. For example, Bavelas defines the central region of a structure as the class of all cells with the smallest distance between one cell and any other cell in the structure, with distance measured in link units. Thus the most central position in a pattern is the position closest to all others. Cf. Harold Leavitt. "Some Effects of Certain Communication Patterns on Group Performance." In E. Maccoby, T. N. Newcomb, and E. L. Hartley, eds., *Readings in Social Psychology* (New York, 1958), 559.

13. Alvin W. Gouldner. *Patterns of Industrial Bureaucracy* (Glencoe, Ill., 1954).

14. *Ibid,* 173.

15. Scheff, *op. cit.*

16. *Ibid.,* 97.

17. Gouldner, *op. cit.*

Questions for Discussion

1. Perhaps the most group-oriented phase of life is the early teen years. For example, the decision to smoke or not is more strongly influenced by peers than by parents (even if the parents do not smoke). Discuss what groups do for the young teenager.

2. For the past 200 years, European observers have commented on the group orientation of Americans. In comparison with people in more tradition-directed countries, Americans seem more "other-directed" (in David Reisman's phrase). For example, a study of parents faced with a decision about rules for their children indicated that German parents would directly apply family or church teachings. In contrast, American parents were much more likely to consult friends and neighbors with children of similar ages. Discuss why you think Americans apparently have been and are so group-oriented.

3. Why is the distinction between "formal" and "informal" organization now considered artificial?

4. Describe and analyze the status system in any group of which you are a member or which you have observed: family, fraternity, club, team, job, etc.

5. Describe and analyze the cohesiveness of the group you selected. What factors strengthen its cohesion; what factors hinder it?

6. Describe a situation with which you are familiar where someone's sense of distributive justice was offended.

7. We live in an era when the prevalent social force has been described as "a revolution of rising expectations." Discuss the relationship of rising expectations and distributive justice during a period of economic slowdown after years of expansion.

8. A large, regional over-the-road trucking firm hires only college graduates as drivers. After joining the Teamsters Union and completing a training program, they immediately earn more than $20,000 a year (compared with an average of approximately $9000 for new college graduates). Most of them claim that they will drive for only a few years. The management of the trucking firm likes them because they dress well, carry attache cases, and communicate well with customers. Discuss the status incongruency of these drivers. Do you think it will be a problem for them, or for their management?

9. Most organizations not directly supported by tax money attempt to keep the salaries they pay a secret within the organization, so that (theoretically)

managers and professionals do not know how much their co-workers are paid. Discuss this policy from the perspective of distributive justice and status congruence.

10. A study of a state employment office a few years ago found that interviewers preferred most to interview well-dressed black men. Apparently this was so because such men were most likely to accept job offers for which they were over-qualified. Discuss.

Short Cases for Discussion

The Dying Fraternity

Omega Alpha Sigma is a mess—at least physically if not socially. The living room of its ramshackle house has never really recovered from last fall's post homecoming game bash when a keg of beer leaked all over the floor (and nearly drowned two brothers sleeping there). The upstairs is just as bad, with leaking pipes, dirty bathrooms, and bedrooms looking like a Portnoy's mother's nightmare. In fact, a high point (or low point depending on one's perspective) was achieved when Whitney Framingham's parents arrived uninvited and unannounced one Saturday afternoon to find Whit in bed with a coed in a room strewn with dirty clothes. His mother screamed, his father cursed, and both abruptly departed with threats of discontinuing the monthly checks. Whit was not sure what upset them more, his bed companion or the messy room, but the money did stop. He is getting by for the rest of his senior year, however, through loans from his more fortunate brothers whose parents have not made uninvited visits.

We are all that way—helpful and respectful of each other's rights; no one butts in. I have never been to any brother's home, and I'm not sure where most even come from, but we are all close when at school. Tennis, squash, and soccer are the principal nonparty activities of the fraternity. The key players on all three varsity teams are in $\Omega A \Sigma$, and the school is nationally ranked in all three sports. Scholastic concerns are a poor third.

In addition, there is Crazy Max. Max is not his real name, but he is crazy. He was a student two years ago. Apparently, he has never really recovered from a bad acid trip, never attended class since, and never gone home. He lives in the house on free room and board and handouts while trying to hide from the green devils he sees everywhere.

The acceptance of Max has an ironic contrast in the only rule the fraternity seems to have: no hard drugs, or even pot, to be used in the building. The fine of $50 is never imposed, but the rule is more observed than not.

Omega Alpha Sigma is near extinction. Fraternity membership in general at this university has been shrinking—down from 75 to 25 percent of the male students in less than ten years. The university administration has been lukewarm toward them for some time. Several fraternity houses on which the school held mortgages have been torn down and the land used for dormitory apartments. $\Omega A \Sigma$ has enrolled no pledges this year. In spite of the president's begging, the brothers have neither appointed a pledge chairman nor organized any effort to obtain new members. The budget is in balance only because four brothers' girlfriends have moved in, contributing funds and cooking skills.

In an effort to bring the chapter back to the straight and narrow, the middleaged chairman of the national council visited the house one night earlier this year. He lighted the white candles; we all repeated the mystic oath and sang the secret song. He left feeling encouraged, but somehow we are not seeking new members nor fixing up the building as we solemnly promised that we would.

Question

Discuss the state of this organization—e.g., its purpose, structure, and cohesion.

Demilitarized Zone

Battalion Landing Team 1/3, U.S. Marines, had been formed in Da Nang in February. The 1st Battalion of the 3rd Marine Regiment had been pulled in from Khe Sanh to provide a nucleus to which were added a battery of 105 mm howitzers, a battery of 4.2 in. mortars, and a platoon each of tanks, antitanks, amphibian tractors, plus various other small service and support elements. All of these units were veterans of long months (years in some cases) of combat; all were under strength and sorely in need of equipment repair and replacement. It was at this juncture that I, a young first lieutenant, was ordered to the 105 battery after having served 10 months with the "grunts" (infantry) as an artillery forward observer and fire support coordinator. Somewhat "salty" as a result of my combat experience, I was looking forward to the brief rest the BLT refitting would bring.

We sailed out to Okinawa. Here, no mortar or rocket attacks, no firefights, mud, or cold chow. Here, instead, barracks, hot water, plenty of money which had been piling up "on the books" and a happy horde of bar girls to help you invest it. Work, certainly—rebuild and replace worn-out gear, join new troopers fresh from the U.S. and train them—but play hard too, play with the hedonistic fatalism of a Roman gladiator. Marine, you're going back to "Nam" soon, back to combat.

Even given these distractions, I think we developed an effective team. My three senior noncommissioned officers were Gunnery Sergeant Laplace, operations chief; Sergeant Von Polske, assistant operations chief; and Staff Sergeant Rivera, communications chief.

Laplace was a young man, at 28 just a few years older than I. He was brilliant, and during his eight-year career had amassed a greater knowledge of fire direction and gunnery than I have encountered before or since. A fantastic promotion record accompanied this knowledge. He had "broken me in" as a Fire Direction Officer and I had the professional admiration for him that you have for a good teacher. I relied heavily on his technical knowledge in the FDC and delegated much of this activity to him.

Von Polske, on the other hand, was old for his rank (mid 30's), having been "busted" several times. He was a brown little bear of a man with a black handlebar mustache; roguish humor masked a violent temper. Yet he was to display an impressive cool in battle and, at times, astounding bravery which exerted a very strong influence on the troopers.

Rivera, too, was in his mid 30's, very professional and a calm, likeable sort. A Puerto Rican, he was a "loner" and tended to stay with his men and their radio equipment, thus earning a reputation as an empire builder. But I appreciated his competence, so I left him alone. Later, I felt I owed him a debt for unhesitatingly following me forward under fire in the nightmare of our first battle.

In April we somehow crammed all that gear we never knew we rated aboard A Navy ship. A brief sniff of Taiwan, a cancelled exercise in the Philippines, and we left Subic Bay as Special Landing Force Alpha, the amphibious strike force for I Corps, the five northernmost provinces of the Republic.

Late that month, we were taken by helicopter into the now-infamous Que Son Valley on Operation Union. The battery, now half filled out with green troopers (many of our vets had rotated home from Okinawa), had been attacked and surrounded in a landing zone by a battalion of main-force Viet Cong. Casualties had been miraculously light, but a close call gets to you after it's over.

Now, only a day or two out of Operation Union, we are to take part in the first Allied invasion of the DMZ, assaulting the beach just south of the Ben Hai River. The rifle companies are helo-lifted inland, and sweep north to the river. The battery goes ashore in amphibian tractors and sets up among the sand dunes just in from the beach. North Vietnamese shore batteries throw a few rounds at the shipping, but our landing goes otherwise unopposed. It is strange, quiet, eerie. We dig in, but you can't really, not in beach sand—it's like digging in a bowl of salt.

Suddenly the "grunts" knock heads with heavy NVA forces, and we begin to receive requests for fire. In my Fire Direction Center (FDC) we acknowledge the requests, hurriedly compute the firing data, and send it down to the guns. The 105's bark. A lull comes, a short moment to relax.

Then we hear a faint boom, somewhere off to the north. For an eternal second we stare at each other in disbelief. Boom! Boom! Then realization: "Incoming! Incoming!" Kick your Marines in the ass to get them into their flak jackets and helmets and the unnecessary ones out of the FDC and into those pitiful sand trenches amid banshee screams of arriving shells. Eeeeyow, wham! Shrapnel whistles. Terror, stone cold terror. You've been under mortars before, but they don't howl at you on the way in—the screaming strikes you with paralytic fear. Incredibly, you move, act, function (thank God for ingrained training), compute data to return fire.

After 24 hours of intermittent dueling we are ordered south, out of the DMZ and we hope out of range. Our "grunts" have fought their way to the river and are now sweeping south.

Our new position is among the ruins of what was once apparently a small French plantation house. Ironically, it's a pretty spot. But something has died here recently—we can smell it. My FDC is established in a corner formed by two parts of standing wall; the troops sandbag the rest of it, then turn to digging foxholes for themselves. It is late afternoon and quiet. We speak in low voices. We are like a dog in a corner, licking its wounds. Weary, I roll up in my poncho to sleep.

I am startled awake in the darkness. Standing near me and apparently unaware of my presence, several men are arguing violently. I recognize the voices of Gunnery Sergeant Laplace, Sergeant Von Polske, and Staff Sergeant Rivera.

Laplace: "What the hell you use for brains, Rivera? You saw how many of your radios got knocked out back up the beach. I have *got* to have comm with Dong Ha, or else they don't know where we are!"

Rivera: "I'm the Comm Chief in this battery, and if anybody talks to Dong Ha it'll be me, not you!"

Laplace: "It's my FDC! I run it and all the comm gear in it! If I tell you to put another radio in my FDC, you damn well . . ."

Von Polske, breaking in: "Shut up, Frenchy. Listen, you motherless Puerto Rican idiot, I been watchin' you hoard your precious damn radios over there with your damn communicators. You act like an old damn lady, Rivera. I'm gonna break you (cocking his fist) . . ."

Me, by this time on my feet and in among the three men: "Shut up, all three of you. Von Polske, go get in your foxhole. Rivera, get back over to Comm where you belong and send back a radio set on Dong Ha's frequency. Laplace, get back in the FDC and put that radio up when it gets there."

A few days later, Von Polske asked for a transfer out of the battery. I was never able to regain Rivera's confidence or full cooperation. Laplace seemed to come around, but I was never totally sure of him after having overheard his part in the argument. What had previously seemed to me to be a smooth working relationship had broken down, never to be fully regained.

Question

Analyze the relation between the formal and informal status systems in this unit. What did the lieutenant do?

Chapter 5

Group Behavior and Decision Making

In describing group development, we emphasized what social organizations provide for the individual—affiliation, self-identification, and assistance. Once a social structure develops, however, it takes on a life of its own. A group pursues objectives which may contribute to individual goals—but which may also limit the individual.

Attitude and Behavior Expectations

At several universities, undergraduate students voted against adoption of academic honor systems which would have abolished faculty proctoring of examinations. Considering the widespread and well-publicized activities in support of greater student participation in university administration, these rejections seem contradictory. The explanation lies with the proposals voted upon. They placed individual responsibility on the student not to cheat but also required him to take some action if he observed someone else cheating. At one Ivy League university, the required action was a report either to a faculty committee or to a student group. The students rejected this proposal because it conflicted with an underlying student norm—one should not "fink" on classmates. Indeed, in the Air Force Academy cheating scandals, the parents of several cadets suspended for not reporting code infractions were vociferous in support of this norm as applying to American society as a whole: one should not be punished for not reporting a crime if one didn't commit it (*Newsweek*, Feb. 1, 1965; *Time*, March 3, 1967).

After the first defeat at the Ivy League university referred to above, the honor system was amended to make optional the report to the faculty and to require only that the student tell the cheater that he has been observed. He did not have to take any further action, although he did have the option. Again, the proposal was defeated. The undergraduates were apparently not willing to approve any system that required them to exercise any control over their peers. It contradicted their conception of proper behavior.

On a more positive note, among junior faculty members at many universities, there is an informal social expectation that one will read and comment on a colleague's rough draft articles. The colleague unwilling to conform to this expectation is not well regarded.

Informal groups, then, develop attitudinal norms and standards of behavior. That is, people in groups tend to think and act alike; continuous association leads to shared values and norms. The shared values include those associated with education, age, class, or ethnicity; beyond that, they reflect such matters as attitudes, tastes, beliefs, and behavioral norms. As Homans (1950) puts this general point: "Interaction between persons leads to sentiments of liking, which express themselves in new activities, and these in turn mean further interaction. . . . The more frequently persons interact with one another, the stronger their sentiments of friendship for one another are apt to be. . . . The more frequently persons interact with one another, the more alike in some respects both their activities and sentiments tend to become" (pp. 119, 120, 133).

Group expectations grow out of needs to maintain the group, remove sources of stress, and promote cooperation. They are functional for the group even if dysfunctional to certain individuals and to the larger organization. For example, Stanford University pioneered in coed dormitories where males and females could live in an intersexual setting. Surprisingly, many students maintained that there was less sexual intimacy than under the old system. What reportedly happened is that an "incest taboo" developed. Residents tended to form platonic friendships, as traditional sexual roles broke down under the close living. "It's like a brother-sister relationship with sexual overtones" is how one coed put it (*Daily Pennsylvanian*, Nov. 18, 1969). The "taboo" makes for easier living because it promotes naturalness and lessens intrasex competition. Without such rules, the dorm life would be too stressful.

To a greater or lesser extent, all informal groups are characterized by such attitudinal norms and behavioral expectations. Of special importance in work groups are attitudes toward assistance and effort. As mentioned, one of the reasons for the development of informal groups is mutual assistance. Accordingly, most work groups value and expect cooperation and helpfulness among regular members of the group—hints on how to machine parts, assistance on difficult jobs, warning against management inspection, assistance in camouflaging mistakes, and a whole host of informal practices. In order to maintain standing in a group and receive its benefits, this aid must be given.

If the basic attitude of the group towards the company is positive, informal expectations can greatly assist management. If the group is fundamentally interested in getting the job done, the workers will fill in the gaps and work out the ambiguities in management assignments. They will be willing to shift with the varying demands of the job in order to assist hard-pressed colleagues without specific management direction. Even under the best conditions, however, a strong informal group will oppose some of management's desires. And when basic attitudes towards management are adverse, the group's behavioral expectations may be directed against management's desires in a variety of amazing ways—ways that managers and workers develop to compensate for inadequacies in the formal system of rewards.

Output and Effort Standards

Limitation of output has long been a prominent anti-management behavior pattern. A wide variety of studies, starting with the Hawthorne research of the late 1920s, has demonstrated how informal groups limit their output (Roethlisberger and Dickson, 1939). Indeed, much earlier, Frederick W. Taylor (Dale, 1970) devoted much of his life to attempting to stamp out the widespread "soldiering," which he thought endangered the very existence of the United States.

The term "soldiering" connoted anti-management motivation, but this need not be the case. Any group of individuals tends to develop some conception of a "fair day's work." In the absence of piece rates, in particular, a group tends to develop agreement on how much should be done. To be sure, not everyone concurs, but among both students and crate handlers, there is a tendency to define what should be done so that there is relative equality of effort. The definition of output is not always harmful to management; the level of effort decided upon by the group may be higher than some individuals would demonstrate. In addition, the group's standard of performance may facilitate management's prediction of output, thus simplifying scheduling and costing.

Spectacular tests of will may result, however, when group output norms are below management expectations. Such disagreements can lead to protracted ill feeling. We well remember a ten-month controversy when a closely knit group of women film splicers disagreed with management about how many rolls of eight-millimeter film they should be able to process. The girls simply thought that management's output desires on a new product were unreasonable. No fear of unemployment and no union were involved. Employer-employee relations were outstanding—but both sides had to redefine proper output. This was not done, however, until many rolls of amateur eight-millimeter film were "accidentally" dropped, to roll around the floor and become entangled in serpentine knots.

Group Discipline

Like all societies, informal groups at work develop common values and behavioral expectations—management is dangerous, don't fink on your buddies, don't goof off, but don't work too hard. Whether the members of the group act or don't act upon these norms and standards depends upon whether the individual wants to be a member of the group and whether the group can enforce its desires. The more eager an individual is to be a member of a group, the more he will conform to its norms of behavior, and the easier it will be to enforce group rules. As Festinger (1950) put it: "If a person wants to stay in a group, he will be susceptible to influences coming from the group, and he will be willing to conform to the rules which the group sets up" (p. 91).

Withdrawal of the group's contribution to the individual is the primary method of enforcement. The group strongly influences the behavior of its members by providing them with support, reinforcement, security, encouragement, protection, rationale, rationalization, etc., for their "proper" behavior, and by punishing them for deviations through the use of ridicule, hostility, threat of expulsion, etc. When an individual is genuinely attached to a group and in close and continuous contact with it, his behavior and beliefs are extremely resistant to change by forces outside the group. In such circumstances the group can exercise firm control over him.

In addition, among some informal social groups there is indication that popularity is associated with respect for the group's norms. One study (Argyle, 1957) concludes, "Deviates are rejected while conformers become popular (p. 155)." The closer an individual conforms to the accepted norms of the group, the better liked he will be; the better liked he is, the closer he conforms; the less he conforms, the more disliked he will be. To the extent that these judgments (based upon observations of teenage groups) are general, people like to be liked, so they tend to engage in actions that will maintain or increase the esteem received from those around them. This means that there is always a tendency to go along with a group—a tendency that is realized unless there are strong countervailing influences.

If an independent soul refuses to abide by group values and standards, initial group reaction may simply be gentle ribbing or good-natured sarcasm. If these fail to alter the individual's behavior, more serious reasoning, discussion, and persuasion result, followed by more heated arguments. At the same time some of the social benefits derived from group membership, such as assistance and socializing, may be reduced. The member's status in the group is thereby reduced. If he still does not conform, overt coercion or complete ostracism may be used, depending upon the importance of the issue and the moral standards of the group. To quote Homans (1961) again:

"Men give social approval, as a generalized reinforcement, to others that have given them activity they value, and so make it more likely that the others will go on giving the activity. One of the kinds of activity some men find valuable is that their own behavior and that of others they are associated with in a group should be similar in conforming to a norm. . . .

"People that find conformity valuable reward conformers with social approval, but they withhold approval from those that will not conform, or even express positive dislike for nonconformists as having denied them a reward they had a right to expect.

"Some members of a group conform for the norm's sake, . . . and some for the approval's sake, but both will come to say that they do it for the norm. The more a member values an activity incompatible with conformity . . . and the more valuable are his sources of social approval other than the conformers in his group, the less likely he is to conform" (p. 129).

 If the errant individual does not derive satisfaction or benefits from the group, if he has alternative sources of satisfaction, or if he just does not give a damn, the group's ability to enforce its norms and standards is weakened.

Regulars, Isolates, and Conformity

Clearly, individuals have differing relationships with the informal organization and its norms and standards. Regulars are those who conform most closely to all informal expectations, perhaps because they need the group more and obtain more satisfactions from it. Research suggests that a majority (70–80 percent) of people may be regulars where there are fairly cohesive work groups. In Dalton's (1955) study of 84 production workers, 50 were classified as regulars on the basis of their behavior; they restricted production to the 100–150 percent level that was the informal norm. Most of the regulars were from the dominant ethnic background, were sons of working class, labor-union fathers, had grown up in the city, were Catholic, voted Democratic, lived in similar neighborhoods, and were socially active and friendly off the job. The informal leaders were also regulars and shared these attributes, although they tended to have more ability. Fulfilling the restricted quota in less time was a source of status (as was ostentatious goofing off while still making quota).

The term "isolate" would suggest that such uncommon people are entirely independent, free from the work group's attractions, and free to pursue their own personal interests. In fact, the "isolate" may not be free at all. Rather, he may be marching to a different drummer (in Thoreau's felicitous phrase).

The drummer is a specific or even indefinite group with which he identifies. From this reference group, he derives some values and behavioral norms which he may attempt to follow (Hyman and Singer, 1968). Somehow, following these perceived norms (however distorted the perception) and "living up to" the values of others perceived as one's betters is satisfying. Thus patterns of drinking, for example, tend to reflect the socioeconomic group that one identifies with or aspires to. Dalton (1955) showed that the 10 percent who were considered rate-busting isolates averaged over 150 percent of the group norm. They tended to consider themselves middle-class, to vote Republican, to live in different neighborhoods, and to be from rural backgrounds. Similarly, a study of retail salesmen indicated that the highest performers identified with wealthier groups, even to purchasing more expensive homes than they could afford (French, 1960).

The distant reference group unknowingly influences the would-be member much as the group regular conforms to the expectations of his immediate associates. Of course there is a difference. The regular gets frequent feedback from his group to the effect that they accept him and reward him for his conformity. The problem for the isolate who identifies with a distant reference group *is* distance. The reference group may not be physically close enough to reward him with friendship and support; in fact, the reference group may not even know of the isolate's existence. Continued identification thus requires enormous fortitude and persistence.

Society is ambivalent about an isolate who demonstrates such courage in stubbornly refusing to give in to his immediate associates. If we are among those associates, we tend to condemn him as untrustworthy, a scab, a fink, or worse. Yet when we read about such people, whose reference group is a group with whom *we* identify, we laud them as a hero or saint. In no other area are people more inconsistent. We admire the true Christian who rejects the tinseled irrelevancy of contemporary American society, but most of us don't really want him around, because he makes us uncomfortable.

Cohesion and Work Group Behavior

Leonard Sayles (1958) has described four kinds of groups, based on the nature of group relation to management authority—as he puts it: ". . . on the level of acceptance of and cooperation with management decisions, or, contrariwise, on the frequency and nature of the challenge issued by the group to management (p. 7)." The four kinds of groups are apathetic, erratic, strategic, and conservative.

Apathetic groups are least likely to exert concerted pressure on management. They manifest low cohesiveness and widely distributed leadership.

Erratic groups behave inconsistently towards management. There seems to be no relation between the seriousness of their grievances (from the point of view of the employees themselves) and the intensity of their protest. The kinds of activities they indulge in are apparently not contrived to solve their problems, but seem to be emotional reactions to frustration, which blinds them to their failure to deal effectively with reality. These groups tend to seek individual, autocratic leaders who are likely to be active in the organizing phase of union growth but shunted aside when more reasonable and stable union-management relations are required.

Strategic groups are shrewdly calculating pressure groups, who never tire of objecting to unfavorable management decisions, of seeking loopholes in existing policies and contract clauses that would redound to their benefit, and of comparing their benefits to those of other departments in the plant. They demand constant attention to their problems and can reinforce their demands by group action. Departments so classified seem to be highly cohesive. The leadership consists of a small core of highly active and influential group members, each of whom specializes in such functions as dealing with management, dealing with the union, maintaining internal unity, or taking the lead in voicing dissatisfaction.

Conservative groups are a secure, powerful elite, relatively independent of union activities. Their jobs usually involve critical skills. They are self-consciously assured, successful, and relatively stable in their external relations with management as well as in their internal affairs.

Sayles lists the following factors as most influential on the overall behavior of groups towards management:

1. Relative position of the group on the formal status hierarchy.
2. Relative size and importance of the group.
3. Similarity of jobs and the degree of independence or interdependence within the group.
4. The degree to which the group's work is indispensable in the functioning of the plant and department.
5. The precision with which management can measure work load and pace for the group.

This typology of group behavior need not be restricted to blue-collar workers; it may extend to office employees and even professionals. For example, New York City school teachers can be described by the model. Elementary school teachers are an apathetic group. They have engaged in little active union organizing or agitation. Why? They tend to be women with a lesser stake in the job, perhaps seeing it merely as supplementary income or as a vehicle for expressing their desires to contribute to society. In either case, concrete steps to improve social-economic conditions are not seen as desirable. Nor, in fact, do these teachers probably have the power and the cohesion to successfully undertake such action.

The junior high school teachers are an erratic group. This is the most difficult teaching level in the New York City system. Many of the delinquency problems such as truancy, lack of control, and violence occur among these pupils. By senior high school, many of the worst pupils have left or have been expelled. Some junior high school teachers have been the firebrands in the development of an independent labor union to improve the lot of teachers (and perhaps quality of education); many are just caretakers, rather apathetic about the situation.

The high school teachers are a strategic group—especially in the competitive-admission high schools. Their power has given them certain privileges in pay and working conditions, so they have not been very active in the union movement, preferring to favor the professional association.

The conservatives are the professors in the city university, whose importance and irreplacability have insured them a preferential position. Their contracts are tied to high school pay, guaranteeing a certain spread, and college pay increases if lower echelon teachers are successful in union agitation.

Individuals, Groups, and Decisions

As we pointed out earlier, the dichotomy between emergent (or informal) and formal organization is artificial. Informal group behavior and formal job duties intermesh. Nowhere is this more true than with group decision making. The decision may be a requirement of the formal organizational task, but the interpersonal processes in reaching the decision reflect the emergent phenomena we have been discussing. To explore the relationships between individual and group decision making, we will examine the nature of decisions, and then compare individuals and groups.

Rational Decision Making

The conditions for ideally rational decision making may be summarized as follows: (1) an individual is confronted with a number of different, specified alternative courses of action; (2) to each of these alternatives is attached a set of consequences; and (3) the individual possesses criteria that permit him to rank all sets of consequences according to preference so that he may select the alternative that has the preferred consequences (Miller and Starr, 1960).

Given these conditions, the process of decision making includes the following steps:

1. Diagnose—identify and clarify the problem's nature and causes. Give the requirements for a satisfactory solution and indicate limits within which the solution must function.
2. Find alternative solutions—alternatives range from doing nothing to finding a way around the difficulty, removing the difficulty, or even modifying the objective.
3. Analyze and compare alternatives—compare alternatives as to advantages and disadvantages. Ensure that the alternatives from which a choice is to be made are really the ones that should be under consideration.

The rational model of decision making assumes that the decision maker (1) is aware of the problem, (2) is aware that he must make a decision, (3) has a set of alternatives, and (4) possesses a criterion for making the decision. But these are significant assumptions. Problems seldom pop up with identifying flags. Frequently, managers just do not know that they have problems; the problems are not "felt." If managers are pressed for time and operating satisfactorily, they simply do not use present time to search for future problems (Moore and Anderson, 1954). Few managers systematically search for or consider alternatives unless their present course is creating stress. But creative problem solving must be preceded by continuous saturation, search, and scanning.

The ideal model of rational decision making also assumes that the decision maker is aware of all possible alternatives and that he decides after examining all of them. Obviously this is impossible because time is limited. Managers cannot determine all or even most possibilities; they must pursue a focusing strategy. So they draw up a partial list based on their own experience, that of associates, articles, and advertisements, and hopefully some creative thought. Frequently, managers fail to postpone evaluation until all alternatives are listed; they evaluate as they develop alternatives. The search for alternatives may cease as soon as a satisfactory one is found, even though all possibilities have not been exhausted and a better solution might remain unexamined. Of necessity, time limits search and leads managers to seek satisfactory rather than optimal answers (March and Simon, 1960). All of this makes sense, but it limits rationality.

In the broad sense, managers tend to place action ahead of diagnosis and to reward speed. Many managers frequently shortcut the decision-making process by combining causal determination with problem definition. For example, in a case we have discussed with numerous executive groups, a vice president has constructed a new assembly line to which he has assigned a rather passive and reluctant engineer as foreman. The new unit is not producing at the desired rate. When considering this situation, time and again managers start with the conclusion that the foreman's weakness is the problem. Such premature judgment dangerously distorts further thought about the matter. The foreman is not the *problem;* the problem is a growing backlog of orders and customer cancellations stemming from lagging production. The weak foreman may be the *cause* of inadequate production, but he is not the problem. This is an important distinction. Defining the foreman as the problem tends to focus subsequent thought on how to change or dismiss him. Seeing him as a cause will at least allow thinking to explore what other causative factors may be involved (such as faulty selection of operators, inadequate training, and equipment bugs).

A further illustration of this distortion can be drawn again from the Cuban invasion in 1961. In the deliberations about Cuba, government officials defined the problem as Castro. Therefore, solutions were oriented around how to get rid of him—since he seemed immune to exhortations to change his ways. But Fidel was not the problem. He was a cause, but only one of several having historical roots well before he appeared. The problem was the threat of Cuba's geography and personnel. How might the land be used against American interests (a point that became all too evident later in the missile crisis) and how could Cuban agents foment terror and revolution in Latin America (as Che Guevara attempted to do)? These were the problems, not Castro. If Cuba could have been isolated from the rest of the world, its land denied to others, its agents confined, Castro's presence would have been irrelevant to the United States. The proper solution is unknown, of course, but defining Fidel as the problem was misleading and dangerous. Time pressure encourages decision makers to confuse problems, causes, and solutions.

In contrast to the perfectly rational model of decision making, Alexis and Wilson (1967) summarize the actual process as follows:

1. Problem solving of necessity entails the use of *strategies* (plans or patterns) of search behavior when the slightest degree of complexity prevails. The greater the *cognitive strain* imposed by problem constraints such as time, information retention, and recall activities, the simpler are the search rules. The problem solver may minimize cognitive strain in part by choices of strategies.

2. Problem-solving behavior is *adaptive*. Individuals start with a tentative solution, search for information, modify the initial solution, and continue such processes until there is some balance between expected and realized behaviors.
3. In even the most restricted problem-solving situation, the problem solver's personality and his aversion or preference for risk enter into his choice of strategies, his use of information, and his ultimate solution.

Decision makers may move more slowly as they gain in experience, wisdom, and assurance. As discussed in Chapter 3, some executives were requested to name the contemporary figure that they most admired and why. The two men mentioned most frequently were Dwight Eisenhower and Harry Truman. The reasons given were similar for both: courage and decisiveness. Some people have criticized President Eisenhower as not being decisive, but few question President Truman in this regard. If anything, he made decisions too easily without sufficient diagnosis, but he never shrank from a decision and he rarely worried about past ones. He said that he always went to sleep shortly after his head touched his pillow (Truman, 1955). Obviously, these executives admired this ability. It was an attribute they wished they had in their own jobs. In his own memoirs, however, Truman's Secretary of State Dean Acheson (1969) observed that Truman gradually slowed down his decision making, overcame his tendency to jump immediately into action, and expanded the period of diagnosis. Yet he still retained the ability to reach a decision by a deadline. Acheson advanced some sarcastic observations on a tendency of later presidents not to decide, but to struggle "to keep their options open." For Acheson, this was merely indecision.

More systematic research with scientists indicates that more creative men work slowly and cautiously while they are analyzing the problem and gathering basic data. Once they obtain data and approach synthesis and decision, they work rapidly. Less creative men spend less time analyzing the problem but more time in attempting to synthesize their material (Bem et al., 1965).

Comparing Individual and Group Decision-Making Performance

"A camel is a racehorse designed by a committee." So goes one of many aphorisms on the inadequacies of groups as decision makers. In spite of the fun in such complaint, however, committees continue to make decisions, because they offer advantages in breadth of experience, varied knowledge, absorption of antagonism, and mutual support (Maier, 1967).

To compare some aspects of individual versus group performance, numerous exercises have been conducted with managers and students. In Webber's (1972) research, five-person research groups take longer than the average of individuals working alone (50 percent longer), but over three-fourths of the groups produce better performance (an average of 30 percent better). Most groups, however, are worse than the best individual in the group. (See Exhibit 5-1.)

These findings support Shaw's (1932) early contention that a group may be an advantage where being correct or avoiding mistakes is of greater importance than speed. The group does seem to improve on the performance of most people (Lorge et al., 1958). In short:

1. The best individuals are usually better than groups as to accuracy, speed, and efficiency.

Exhibit 5-1   Comparison of Individual and Group Performance   (Webber, 1972)

	Individual $n_1 = 240$	Group $n_2 = 48$
Mean time to complete vocabulary test	4.5 min	6.8 min
Mean score (number correct out of 25 questions)	13.2	17.5
Mean errors (number incorrect)	11.8	7.5
Mean efficiency—number right per minute	3.0	2.6

2. The average individual is faster and more efficient than most groups, but he makes more errors.
3. Groups are more accurate but slower than most individuals.

The superiority of groups over individuals, however, depends on prior experience and training. Hall's research (1971), utilizing a "lost on the moon" exercise, presents findings very similar to Webber's vocabulary test: the mean individual score for Hall was 47.5 (0 is perfect, 112 is totally wrong); the mean score for *ad hoc* groups was 34. In addition, Hall found that improved performance followed the reading of a one-page handout on developing group consensus—the mean score of such instructed groups was 26. Of the instructed groups, 75 percent produced group decisions that surpassed even the best individual decisions. Only 25 percent of the uninstructed groups did this.

Age and position level also seem to affect group performance on exercises. (See Exhibit 5-2.) Various groups participated in Webber's research: among others, they included high-level general executives averaging 47 years of age, 40-year-old middle managers, 32-year-old managers, and graduate and undergraduate business students about 25 and 20 years old respectively. The findings are distinctive. There were no significant differences in task performance among the different categories of people when they worked as individuals. *Yet, lower level young men were more effective in utilizing group decision making than older, higher level managers.* The difference between group performance and average individual performance decreased with increasing age and level of the group members. Younger groups improved more on individual performance. In fact, college students constituted the *only groups* that had higher group scores than their best individual. Among all the others, the best individual was better than the group.

So younger people seem to be more effective in utilizing groups for decision making than older and higher level managers. Time and age seem to weaken the ability to work jointly with others—or perhaps the younger students came through an educational system that placed greater emphasis on group activity. The reasons why might also include less sensitivity to status, more personal flexibility, greater willingness to express opinions, and more "team spirit." Nonetheless, all age groups offered advantages and disadvantages compared to most individuals—more correct answers, fewer errors, but slower progress.

Exhibit 5-2 How Age/Position Level Is Related To Individual and Group
Performance   (Webber, 1972)

Subjects	Mean Score (no. correct)	Mean Time (min)	Mean Group Effectiveness (group score minus mean of indivs. in group)	Mean Group Excellence (group score minus best indiv. score in group)
Executives mean age 47				
40 indiv.	13.4	4.0		
8 groups	15.8	9.0	+1.8	−1.4
Middle managers mean age 40				
55 indiv.	13.3	4.2		
11 groups	15.1	6.2	+1.7	−2.9
Young managers mean age 32				
90 indiv.	13.2	4.2		
18 groups	15.3	5.3	+2.3	−3.1
M.B.A. students mean age 25				
90 indiv.	14.3	4.7		
18 groups	16.3	6.0	+3.7	0
B.S. students mean age 20				
40 indiv.	11.5	5.5		
8 groups	17.5	6.0	+3.5	+1.5

Factors Affecting Group Performance

Undoubtedly, personality affects the task performance of groups, but research
here is quite rare because most group study is concerned with the relation
between individual personality and individual behavior rather than group
behavior (McGrath and Altman, 1966). The general findings on personality and
task performance are mixed.

Homogeneity of attitudes is thought to be desirable (Schutz, 1958). In
Schutz's research, it did not seem to matter whether any or all group members
subscribed to a particular attitude. Performance of group tasks was equally
effective as long as members of the same group shared the same attitude.
However, group task performance was likely to be less effective when the group
was composed of individuals who were mixed in their attitudes.

In contrast, other research (Hoffman, 1959; Hoffman and Maier, 1961)
suggests that groups with heterogeneous personality types are more successful
in solving problems than groups containing individuals similar in personality.

In three-person groups, Ghiselli and Lodahl (1958) found that the most
effective groups were composed of one highly dominant individual with two
others of average or low dominance scores. Similarly, another study (Haythorne,
1953) of two-man groups indicated the most effective combination of cooperative

task assignments was a highly dominant individual paired with a submissive individual.

Sociability or extroversion seems also to be related to performance. In one study (Gurnee, 1937), group errors were greater when the groups were composed of "nonsocial, solitary and independent individuals."

Most of the studies referred to above must be interpreted cautiously, because the tasks involved were mainly simple and repetitive, rather than the complex problems that characterize much managerial decision making. A recent combined laboratory and field experiment (Bither, 1971) utilized a management game to simulate more realistic problem complexity and its relationship to members' personalities. Bither concludes (pp. 59–61):

"The results of this research suggest that the greater the degree to which individuals in a task group involved in complex decision making possess skills that enable them to deal effectively with other group members, the greater will be the success of the group. This in no way implies that groups homogeneous in need patterns will be more successful than heterogeneous groups. Neither does it imply that individuals who like one another will be more successful in a group than any other mixture of individuals. Thus the common remark, 'I don't have to like him—I just have to work with him' may contain a good deal of truth in terms of successful group operations.

"A second implication of this research is that the degree to which individuals in the group possess needs for dominance will have a powerful effect upon the structure of the group. In addition, a limited amount of evidence is presented which suggests that the personality need-dispositions of the most dominant individual in the group may have great influence upon the success of the group. Although the evidence is limited, it appears that if the dominant individual has a high need for social recognition and a low need for autonomy, the group is more likely to be successful. Finally, the degree to which the dominant individual possesses skills in social intelligence is likely to influence the success of the group positively.

"These findings do not suggest that personality is a substitute for ability. They do indicate that, when ability is either unknown or relatively equal among possible candidates for complex group task assignments, a consideration of the mix of personalities to be assigned to the group is likely to pay off in terms of increased group effectiveness.

"The data of this study suggest that a low score on the personality characteristic of need for autonomy and high scores on two other characteristics—the need for social recognition and the trait of social intelligence—may be important characteristics for the dominant individual to possess if his membership group is to attain high achievement on complex decision tasks."

Blau and Scott (1963) maintain that groups are superior to individuals on certain types of problem solving because social interactions (1) provide an error-correcting mechanism, (2) furnish social support to group members, and (3) foster competition among peers for respect of their peers. And Argyle (1957) observes: "The collective judgment of a group is superior to the judgment of most of the individuals. Two distinct processes are involved—firstly, discussion leads to the improvement of individual judgments, and secondly, the combination of individual judgments is advantageous." However, Berelson and Steiner (1964) point out that this advantage exists only under certain conditions (p. 355):

- There is little expression of personal, self-oriented needs.
- Whatever self-needs are expressed tend to be satisfied during the course of the meeting.
- There is a generally pleasant atmosphere and the participants recognize the need for unified action.
- The group's problem-solving activity is understandable, orderly, and focused on one issue at a time.
- Facts are available and used.
- The participants feel warm and friendly toward each other in a personal way.
- The chairman, through much solution proposing, aids the group in penetrating its agenda problems.

In general, both the effectiveness of the group and the satisfaction of its members are increased when the members see their personal goals as being advanced by the group's success. When members push their own needs, both satisfaction and effectiveness decline. Of course, the successful dominator may be *more* satisfied, and herein lie many problems with group problem solving. Because of his personality, organizational position, or personal status, one individual may be excessively dominant (Smelser, 1961). For example, in hierarchically differentiated groups, the presence of the senior manager tends to inhibit problem diagnosis and discussion. Lower status members are sometimes reluctant to participate. This speeds the decision-making process, of course, because the leader can push right along to the selection state. Nonetheless, the advantage of group participation in problem analysis is lost. Awareness of this phenomenon may explain why Alfred Sloan (1964), when he headed General Motors, established committees with himself as chairman, but did not attend early group meetings. It appears that by his absence, he wanted to facilitate open and candid discussion during the analytical stage of the problem-solving process. Only when progress toward a solution was deemed desirable and possible did he participate.

A high-status person such as a certified expert may continue to dominate a group after its attention has shifted to a problem outside his area of expertise (Doyle, 1971). An experience in the classroom dramatically demonstrated this distortion. Five-person teams were participating in a vocabulary-type exercise. Since one team was short an individual, a psychology professor was drafted to complete the team. On the first set of words, the students deferred to the professor's judgment—even when some were skeptical. They deferred because he was of higher status and possessed impressive academic credentials. By chance, however, he also happened to have a rather poor vocabulary. The group did badly. When the students became aware of his inadequacies, they rejected him as leader (and even as a valuable team member).

Under the pressures of hierarchical or status differences, some group members may conform merely for social approval; conformity and agreement may set in so early that all opinions are not considered; and group members may become so dependent on other persons for knowledge and information that they cannot make contributions on their own. All these developments hinder group performance.

Concern over these negative aspects of status, hierarchy, and personality differences in face-to-face groups has led to the development of more impersonal group decision procedures (Van de Ven and Delbecq, 1971). The Delphi technique (Dalkey, 1969) represents one of the most promising efforts to eliminate factors other than knowledge from group problem solving. It (1) keeps group membership anonymous, and/or (2) lists members but keeps specific communications anonymous, and (3) allows only written communication. Each member takes a position. The central thrust of those positions (usually two thirds distribution) is communicated to all members. On the second round, each can modify his position or not—but he must give specific written reasons for departing from the central range of the other responses. This iterative process is continued for several rounds. Dalkey reports that such a process leads to better decisions than face-to-face groups.

Breinholt and Webber (1972) replicated the Hall research, using his "lost on the moon" exercise, but they included Delphi groups. Combined with Hall's results, their preliminary evidence is shown in Exhibit 5-3. The face-to-face groups instructed on how to derive a group consensus performed better than the uninstructed groups. The Delphi groups progressed to better performance than either of Hall's categories and better than Breinholt and Webber's uninstructed groups. Eliminating personality and status from group deliberations via a Delphi-like technique does seem promising. Nonetheless, it should be pointed out that the very best group performance in the research (score of 16) occurred with an uninstructed group where apparently a very knowledgeable member was able to dominate.

Exhibit 5-3   Comparing Different Groups on "Lost on the Moon" Problems

	Hall (3-7 person teams)	Breinholt and Webber (5-person teams)
Mean individual score	47.5 (n = 80)	
Mean score, uninstructed face-to-face groups	34 (n = 16)	29 (n = 8)
Mean score, instructed face-to-face groups	26 (n = 16)	23 (n = 7)
Mean score, Delphi groups (after fourth round)		25 (n = 8)

Groups and Risk Taking

Surprising, but still controversial, is the finding that groups may be more willing to take risks than individuals. Many people, especially business managers, argue that group decision making inhibits daring and risk taking, and promotes a conservative course when a choice must be made between more or less risky actions. A group's apparent ability to reduce errors suggests the conservative stance. Nonetheless, laboratory experiments indicate the opposite effect: group decisions following discussion tend to be riskier than individual decisions (Bem et al., 1965). Perhaps the individual can better hide his responsibility in the group (Wallach et al., 1964), or perhaps resonance from other group members overcomes uncertainty and builds courage (*ibid.*, 1962)—or facilitates self-delusion—but in the experimental setting with ad hoc groups created by the researcher, the risk orientation is quite consistent.

What actually occurs does not seem to be that groups invariably promote risky decisions. Rather, they reinforce the prevailing cultural or climatic attitude (Marquis, 1968). If the initial individual attitudes are on the conservative side of a neutral point, subsequent group discussion moves the decision toward more decisive conservatism. Similarly, if the average attitude is slightly risk taking, group discussion tends to produce a "risk shift." This shift is particularly pronounced because most people tend to think that they are personally less conservative and more risk oriented than "average" others. Consequently, they may be quite surprised to discover that those others are not as conservative as expected. This leads to a shift of personal positions in the direction of greater risk.

Obviously, one must be cautious about extrapolating from laboratory research to real life—especially on the subject of risk. Some researchers (Lewin and Weber, 1966) have argued that ad hoc groups of college students temporarily together in an afternoon class are very different from teams of executives who have a past and future of working together and established status relationships that influence their deliberation. Such "traditional" or real-life groups may handle risk very differently.

Combined Group and Individual Decision Making

The choice of group or individual decision making is not really an either-or proposition. It may depend on the stage within the decision process. Bales (1951) has developed a model of group problem solving which emphasizes three operational phases: orientation, evaluation, and control:

"*Orientation.* In this particular phase it is assumed that each member of the group has some relevant facts about the problem to be solved. In addition, however, each member has some degree of ignorance and uncertainty about the problem-solving situation. Thus the phase of orientation entails the distribution of information among the members. Interactions specifically involve asking for and giving information.

"*Evaluation.* In this phase, it is assumed that members will attempt to harmonize differences in opinions and interests with the purpose of reaching a solution. Interactions involve expressing feelings, giving opinions, and developing an analysis.

"*Control.* Directional interactions occur at this stage. Interactions designed to pressure members into line and toward a group decision are common. Ideas, suggestions, and possible alternatives are weighed and ranked in terms of the group's task."

In addition to identifying basic phases, Bales' interaction analysis codes the reaction of group participants as negative or positive. Negative reactions are defined as disagreements, tension, and antagonisms. Generally, in each phase, both negative and positive reactions may occur. However, as the problem-solving process moves toward the final phase (control), negative reactions tend to increase. Once preliminary success is experienced, the positive reactions tend to increase. From that point there is an even distribution between the number of negative and positive reactions.

A clue to how this works is offered by the following incident: A group of young women were working on an exercise problem which went well until they reached the solution stage. At this point, one of the girls (an extremely bright Phi Beta Kappa graduate) jumped up exclaiming, "I can't stand this anymore!" With that, she bolted from the room. To everyone's surprise, she returned quickly with a correct solution. She explained that she left when she had enough information; the group's questions and talk were a hindrance after this. The noise and confusion interfered with her thought—so she left.

What happens is that the group is helpful in diagnosis—analyzing the problem, the objective, and the limits on the solution. This is apparent in the pattern of questions: they are asked in batches, with one person's triggering off three or four from others; then a silence follows; then another cluster of questions; and so on. Everyone feels free to utilize the information developed by others. So the group aids in collecting information necessary to solve the problem, but tends to interfere with the detailed formulation of a solution. In short, a group may be helpful in the analytical stage of decision making (perhaps three fourths of the total time to make the decision), but a hindrance to final evaluation and selection.

Summary

Emergent groups develop expectations about proper attitudes and behavior which members generally respect and conform to. Of special importance to management are restrictions on effort and output which groups impose on members. Nonconformance results in group sanctions to force recalcitrants into line. Regulars tend to conform, isolates not to. Hence the latter are rejected and isolated. Some nonconformists are attempting to conform to the standards of other, more distant reference groups.

Work groups tend to fall into limited behavioral categories. Apathetic, erratic, strategic, and conservative groups have been described, along with factors conducive to group cohesiveness: homogeneity, easy communication, group isolation, limited size, outside pressure, and formal status.

There are important differences in decision making by individuals and by groups. Groups offer advantages on certain kinds of problems when conditions are favorable—mainly on specific problems with clear-cut answers when open communication is facilitated because status and hierarchical distinctions are absent or not important. Training, experience, age, and personality also affect group effectiveness, but groups tend to make fewer errors, to be willing to take higher risks, and to improve on the performance of average individuals—but not always on that of the best group members.

Whether the advantages of group decision making justify the additional time required depends on three critical factors: (1) whether speed is essential (as when a military unit is under attack or a prospective customer is threatening to terminate negotiations); (2) whether an incorrect decision can be tolerated (as it cannot when making important defense decisions in Washington or styling decisions in Detroit); and (3) whether the organization has an exceptional individual who would be hindered by a group (as the United States had with President Lincoln, or as a few corporations have had with entrepreneurial giants).

References

Acheson, D. *Present at the Creation: My Years in the State Department.* W. W. Norton, 1969.

Alexis, M., and C. Z. Wilson. *Organizational Decision-Making.* Prentice-Hall, 1967.

Argyle, M. *The Scientific Study of Social Behavior.* Methuen, 1957.

Bales, R. F., and F. L. Strodtbeck. "Phases in Group Problem-Solving." *The Journal of Abnormal and Social Psychology,* Vol. 46, 1951.

Bem, D. J., M. A. Wallach and N. Kogan. "Group Decision Making Under Risk of Aversive Consequences." *Journal of Personality and Social Psychology,* Vol. 1 (1965), 453–460.

Berelson, B., and G. Steiner. *Human Behavior.* Harcourt Brace Jovanovich, 1964.

Bither, S. W. "Personality as a Factor in Management Team Decision Making." Center for Research of the College of Business Administration, Pennsylvania State University, 1971.

Blau, P., and W. E. Scott. *Formal Organizations.* Chandler, 1963.

Breinholt, R., and R. A. Webber. "Comparing Delphi Groups, Uninstructed and Instructed Face-to-Face Groups." 1972.

Bruner, J. S., J. J. Goodnow and G. A. Austin. *A Study of Thinking.* Wiley, 1960.

Collins, B., and H. Guetzkow. *A Social Psychology of Group Processes for Decision-Making.* Wiley, 1964.

Dalkey, N. C. "The Delphi Method: An Experimental Study of Group Opinion." Rand Corporation Memorandum RM 5888-PR, June 1969.

Dalton, M., cited in W. F. Whyte, *Money and Motivation.* Harper & Row, 1955.

Doyle, W. "Effects of Achieved Status of Leader on Productivity of Groups." *Administrative Science Quarterly,* Vol. 16, No. 1 (March 1971), 40–50.

Festinger, L., S. Schachter and K. Back. *Social Pressure in Informal Groups.* Harper & Row, 1950.

French, C. J. "Correlates of Success in Retail Selling." *American Journal of Sociology,* Vol. 66, No. 2, 1960.

Ghiselli, E. E., and T. M. Lodahl. "Patterns of Managerial Traits and Group Effectiveness." *Journal of Abnormal and Social Psychology,* Vol. 57 (1958), 61–66.

Gurnee, H. "A Comparison of Collective and Individual Judgments of Facts." *Journal of Experimental Psychology,* Vol. 21, 1937.

Hall, J. "Decisions." *Psychology Today* (November 1971), 51ff.

Haythorne, W. "The Influence of Individual Members on the Characteristics of Small Groups." *Journal of Abnormal and Social Psychology,* Vol. 48 (1953), 276–284.

Hoffman, L. R. "Homogeneity of Member Personality and its Effect on Group Problem Solving." *Journal of Abnormal and Social Psychology,* Vol. 58 (1959), 27–32.

———— and N. R. Maier. "Quality and Acceptance of Problem Solutions by Members of Homogeneous and Heterogeneous Groups." *Journal of Abnormal and Social Psychology,* Vol. 62 (1961), 401–407.

Homans, G. C. *Social Behavior: Its Elementary Forms.* Harcourt Brace Jovanovich, 1961.

————. *The Human Group.* Harcourt Brace Jovanovich, 1950.

Hyman, H. H., and E. Singer, eds. *Readings in Reference Group Theory and Research.* The Free Press, 1968.

Lewin, A. Y., and W. L. Weber. "Risk Taking in Ad Hoc and Traditional Groups." Paper presented to Institute of Management Science, September 8, 1966.

Lorge, I., D. Fox, J. Davitz, and M. Brenner. "A Survey of Studies Contrasting the Quality of Group Performance and Individual Performance 1920–1957." *Psychological Bulletin,* Vol. 55, 1958.

Maier, N. R. F. "Assets and Liabilities in Group Problem-Solving: The Need for an Integrative Function." *Psychological Review,* Vol. 74 (1967), 239–248.

March, J. G., and H. A. Simon. *Organizations.* Wiley, 1960.

Marquis, D. G. "Individual and Group Decisions Involving Risk." *Industrial Management Review,* Vol. 9, No. 3 (Spring 1968), 69–75.

McGrath, J. E., and I. Altman. *Small Group Research.* Holt, Rinehart and Winston, 1966.

Miller, D. W., and M. K. Starr. *Executive Decision and Operations Research.* Prentice-Hall, 1960.

Moore, O. K., and S. B. Anderson. "Search Behavior in Individual and Group Problem Solving." *American Sociological Review,* Vol. 19, 1954.

Roethlisberger, F. J., and W. Dickson. *Management and the Worker.* Harvard University Press, 1939.

Sayles, L. R. *Behavior of Industrial Work Groups.* Wiley, 1958.

Schutz, W. C. *FIRO: A Three Dimensional Theory of Interpersonal Behavior.* Holt, Rinehart and Winston, 1958.

Shaw, M. E. "A Comparison of Individuals and Small Groups in the Rational Solution of Complex Problems." *American Journal of Psychology,* Vol. 44, 1932.

Sloan, A. P., Jr. *My Years with General Motors.* Doubleday, 1964.

Smelser, W. T. "Dominance as a Factor in Achievement and Perception in Cooperative Problem-Solving Interactions." *Journal of Abnormal and Social Psychology,* Vol. 62 (1961), 535–542.

Taylor, F. W. Lectures given at Harvard University 1909–1914, cited by E. Dale in *Readings in Management,* 2nd ed. McGraw-Hill, 1970.

Truman, H. S. *Memoirs, Years of Decision.* Vol. 1, Doubleday, 1955.

Van de Ven, A., and A. L. Delbecq. "Nominal Versus Interacting Group Processes for Committee Decision-Making Effectiveness." *Academy of Management Journal* (June 1971), 203–211.

Wallach, M. A., N. Kogan, and D. J. Bem. "Group Influence on Individual Risk Taking." *Journal of Abnormal and Social Psychology,* Vol. 65 (1962), 75–86.

———, ———, and ———. "Diffusion of Responsibility and Level of Risk Taking in Groups." *Journal of Abnormal Social Psychology,* Vol. 68 (1964), 263–274.

Webber, R. A. *Time and Management.* Van Nostrand Reinhold, 1972.

Readings

Conformity and Nonconformity

EDWIN P. HOLLANDER, RICHARD H. WILLIS

When Thoreau voiced the suspicion that the apparent nonconformer was merely marching to a more distant drummer, he provided an insight which has been rather surprisingly disregarded in much of the contemporary research on conformity. Cooley (1922), pursuing the same point, asserted that there is no definite line between conformity and nonconformity, and that both should be considered together as normal and complementary phases of human activity.

Despite these long-standing and astute observations, the dominant focus of most current research on social influence has been to ascertain what can be systematically shown to occasion conforming behavior. Nonconformity is typically ignored or at least not considered conscientiously. What makes this a curious emphasis is that conformity is usually the modal response. Hence, this work tells us less than it might about individual differences in reactions to social pressures. Introducing conditions favoring the possibility of nonconformity, by contrast, can reveal a good deal more about the idiosyncratic patterning of responses that we are accustomed to terming "personality," for quite often there are several ways in which one can not conform but only one way of conforming.

An Overview

The essential task of this paper is to redress this present imbalance in research on conformity and nonconformity, and to explicate several concepts and distinctions which clarify certain basic features of such research. In documenting the importance of these concepts and distinctions here, we cite a rather large number of studies. However, these citations are illustrative, rather than exhaustive, of what is a considerable literature.

In this connection, it should be noted that although the literature on conformity and closely related topics has reached Brobdingnagian proportions (cf., e.g., Allen, 1965; Berg & Bass, 1961; Graham, 1962; Willis, 1961), it remains disparate in many of its implications. Mann (1959), for example, reported a marked degree of inconsistency concerning the relationship between stable attributes of personality and conformity in the 27 studies he surveyed. Conformity was found to be a positive function of certain personality variables in some of these studies and uncorrelated or a negative function of these same variables in other studies. This strongly suggests the desirability of reexamining most carefully the differential meaning of "conformity" and "nonconformity" as they are currently conceptualized, and as they have been operationalized in psychological research.

Edwin P. Hollander and Richard H. Willis, "Some Current Issues in the Psychology of Conformity and Nonconformity," abridged from *Psychological Bulletin,* Vol. 68, 1967, pp. 62–76. Copyright © 1967 by the American Psychological Association, and reproduced by permission.

Throughout most of this paper we are concerned with conformity-nonconformity as social *response*—that is, we focus on the actor. Toward the latter part of the paper, in the discussion of the assumption of norm homogeneity, we move to a concern with conformity-nonconformity as social *stimulus*. That is, we consider how the actor is perceived by others.

Descriptive Criteria

Contemporary treatments of conformity usually fail to take account of the kind of distinction illustrated in Halla Beloff's (1958) contrasting of *conventionality* and *acquiescence* as modes of social response. The former is operationally defined as high *agreement* between an individual's response and the mean or modal response of his group or class, while the latter is operationally defined as the amount of *shift* from private to public opinion. Beloff comes as close as anyone known to us to making an explicit distinction between the two basic descriptive criteria of conformity-nonconformity that have been formally analyzed by Willis (1964) and labeled congruence and movement. At the purely descriptive level, the congruence criterion requires that conformity (or nonconformity) be measured in terms of the extent of agreement between a given response and the normative ideal. The movement criterion dictates the measurement of conformity (positive or negative) in terms of a change in response resulting in a greater or lesser degree of congruence.

When these two aspects of social response are not conscientiously differentiated, paradoxes can result. This may be readily shown in the recent work of Walker and Heyns (1962) in which conformity was quite explicitly defined in terms of, and only in terms of, movement: "Let us define conformity as movement toward some norm or standard and nonconformity as movement away from such a norm or standard (p. 5)."

The implication of this definition, standing alone as it does, is clearly that an individual complying fully with the norm or standard from the beginning *cannot* be considered to reveal conformity. Walker and Heyns evidently contemplated this dilemma, since later on the same page they stated, "To describe a person or a group as conformist on the basis of a single observation implies an earlier state in which the degree of agreement with the norm was not so great." This would mean that an individual who had moved only slightly from a position of extreme nonconformity would be considered more conforming than one who had from the outset matched the norm.

It becomes apparent, then, that congruence conformity and the potential for movement conformity are actually *perfectly and inversely* related! The mixing of these two aspects of conformity, or the failure to recognize one or the other, doubtless explains much of the confusion encountered in attempts to understand the workings of "conformity" at the global level. For purposes of understanding, it is accordingly essential to maintain a strict distinction between these inversely related aspects of conformity.

At a somewhat more psychological level, a roughly analogous distinction can be made between habituation to *past* social demands which have some continuity in the present, as exemplified by musical preferences and aversions (Beloff's "conventionality," the congruence criterion), or a reaction to an *immediate* influence, as exemplified by compliance with a request to leave the room (Beloff's "acquiescence," the movement criterion).

Unidimensional Approaches

Another inadequacy in the customary view of response to social influence is the tendency to cast it into a single dimension of response, with perfect conformity at one end and perfect something else, usually nonconformity or independence, at the other. Instructive in this connection is an observation made by DeSoto (1961) in reporting on his work on the predilection for single orderings: "In the theorizings of social scientists about society and culture [this predilection] shows up as a stubborn urge somehow to reduce discrepant orderings of people, or classes, or cultures, to single orderings (p. 22)."

These unidimensional approaches give rise to the classical bipolar conception of conformity-nonconformity, such as the J curve formulation of Floyd Allport (1934); or to the conformity-independence variant, seen in the work of Asch (1951, 1956), Marie Jahoda (1959), and many others. Throughout the literature on social influence, one sees a view of perfect conformity as an exact matching of one and only one group-approved position along the response continuum, which stands in contrast to an opposite response location, viewed either as nonconformity or independence. Although Walker and Heyns (1962) constitute an exception, there appears to be some tendency for those adopting the nonconformity contrast to think of conformity as *being* like others, while those employing the independence contrast typically view conformity as *becoming* more like others. Clearly, the first formulation is appropriately addressed to the congruence criterion, whereas the second applies to movement.

In what follows, we are concerned primarily with the movement criterion, the one customarily employed in experimental social psychology, particularly in studies of convergence. Nonetheless, we wish to stress our belief that, ultimately, both criteria must be rigorously analyzed, thoroughly investigated empirically, and fully interrelated with one another.

Bearing in mind specifically the movement criterion, consider the hypothetical case of an individual who consistently responds negatively to any and all social pressures. Where can he be located along the conformity-independence dimension? Obviously he is not a conformist, but, equally apparent, he cannot be considered independent. Nor can he be placed at any intermediate position. Actually, he is maximally dependent, since his behavior is highly predictable from a knowledge of the social pressures to which he is exposed, but at the same time he is minimally conforming. There is no place for this "anticonformist" and yet a place must be provided—not because such perfect anticonformists are known to exist, but because there is no logical reason that one could not exist, and also because such negativistic behavior tendencies have often been observed in more attenuated form. It can be shown that a two-dimensional model of social response is capable of resolving this dilemma.

A Two-Dimensional Approach

A two-dimensional model of social response, applying to the movement criterion and to binary judgments, has recently been suggested by Willis (1963) and adapted in research by Willis and Hollander (1964a) and Hollander and Willis (1964). This model stipulates two dimensions of response, the first of which is dependence-independence, or merely *independence*. The second is conformity-anticonformity, or *net conformity*. These are orthogonal of one another, not in the sense of being uncorrelated (the extent of the correlation being an empirical matter and varying from situation to situation), but rather in the same sense that one plots two such obviously correlated variables as height and weight against orthogonal coordinates. In the initial conception of the model, the response space, which defines the limits of possible patterns of responding over trials, is an isosceles triangle with vertices labeled Conformity and Anticonformity along the net conformity dimension, and Independence, at the vertex formed by the conjunction of the two equal sides. These vertices represent three basic modes of responding to social pressure, defined descriptively (operationally) as follows:

Pure conformity. Viewed relative to the movement criterion, this consists of maximal and completely consistent movement in the direction of greater congruence. This descriptive definition stands in contrast to the conceptual definition of conformity given earlier.

Pure independence. This behavior is describable within the triangular model as a total lack of movement from pre-exposure to post-exposure responses. In psychological terms, such behavior would occur when (but not only when) the individual perceives relevant normative expectancies, but does not rely upon them as guides to his behavior.

Pure anticonformity. This corresponds to movement that is maximal and completely consistent (like pure conformity), but in the direction of *lesser* congruence. Also like conformity, anticonformity implies dependence upon the normative expectancies, but of a negative kind.

Crutchfield has conceived of conformity and its alternatives in similar terms. Although he usually speaks of counterformity rather than anticonformity, essentially the same three modes of responding are considered to be interrelated as the vertices of a triangle (Krech, Crutchfield, & Ballachey, 1962, pp. 506–507). Crutchfield and his associates have not embarked upon experimentation on counterformity behavior, but he has discussed some of the personality characteristics of "the counterforming personality" (Crutchfield, 1962, 1963).

This concludes our descriptive analysis of conformity and nonconformity. In the following sections we turn to a consideration of both earlier and recent conformity research in light of the foregoing but at a more psychological (i.e., inferential or explanatory) level.

Studies of Movement Conformity

The classic study of Muzafer Sherif (1935) provided a model for much subsequent work on group conformity. Earlier, Arthur Jenness (1932a, 1932b) had conducted experiments in which subjects judged the number of beans in a bottle, then discussed this judgment with others to arrive at a single judgment, after which each made a second set of individual judgments. Results consistently indicated convergence (i.e., movement) towards a group standard. Sherif employed a comparable research paradigm but used the autokinetic phenomenon as the basis for his stimulus. In the absence of physical cues to distance and with the requirement for absolute judgments, he found a marked tendency for the perceptual judgments of subjects to converge in this highly ambiguous situation.

A number of studies followed which varied the Sherif procedure, employing a variety of stimuli and tasks, all within the framework of conformity in terms of perceptual convergence (e.g., Asch, 1951, 1956; Crutchfield, 1955; Schonbar, 1945). In a related vein, the studies of Mausner (1953, 1954a), Kelman (1950), and Luchins and Luchins (1961) manipulated the reinforcement of accuracy and the alleged characteristics of a partner in order to determine their effects on the degree of movement. In general, reinforcing the subject for accuracy of his own responses leads to a decrease in conformity as measured by the convergence procedure, and the net effect, therefore, seems to be to increase independence from the partner or group. Conversely, perceptions of the other(s) as more competent or of higher status than the subject usually result in greater conformity.

Such studies highlight the importance of the immediately preceding information supporting one's own accuracy in determining nonconformity. However, the source of this supporting information appears to be critical. Hollander, Julian, and Haaland (1965) have recently demonstrated that prior agreement from *other subjects*, rather than from the experimenter, leads to higher subsequent movement conformity. Furthermore, as predicted, the pattern of conformity varied over time. Thus, the condition with complete prior support produced more initial conformity than either of two conditions of less prior support, but the decrement in conformity over trials was also most marked for this condition.

Other studies have manipulated the credibility, prestige, or competence of the source of judgments and have found that subjects are affected by sources having these attributes more than by those who do not possess them (e.g., Croner & Willis, 1961; Gerard, 1954; Kidd & Campbell, 1955; Mausner, 1954b; Wolf, 1959). The results consistently indicate predictable situational sources of conformity and nonconformity in terms of the perception of the influence source—whether a co-worker, a group, or an experimenter.

By and large, even with its productive features, this line of investigation (i.e., the Sherif construction of conformity as perceptual convergence, and related approaches) has tended to further a view which is still in popular currency, namely, that there exists a general norm *equally applicable* to all group members. The limitations of this assumption of norm homogeneity, as we can term it, are considered in some detail in a later section. Briefly, it involves the conception of a standard of conduct as a place on a continuum where some consensus rests, and is associated historically with Floyd Allport's J curve description of conforming behavior on a collective level as an accumulation of approved responses at one end of the response continuum (Allport, 1934). A more adequate view allows the definition of conformity to vary as a function of the status of the actor (Hollander, 1958, 1959, 1960, 1961).

A second criticism that can be leveled against the traditional work on perceptual convergence is that it is heavily biased against the elicitation of nonconformity. It shares with almost all psychological experimentation the feature of very high experimenter status as measured relative to the subject. Typically, experimenters create influence assertions directed at producing movement conformity by the constructions of the situations they pose to subjects, especially through instructional sets and task materials. The demand characteristics (Orne, 1962) implicit in this subject-experimenter relationship tend to force one kind of modal response.

Milgram (1965) has recently reported an experiment closer to the substance of a real-life problem and involving a test of experimenter influence. It is illuminating in several ways. As the experimenter, he instructed subjects to administer what was falsely thought to be a painful shock to another (mock) subject. In one set of experimental conditions, two other mock subjects either agreed to administer the shock or refused to do so. He found significantly more subjects refusing to administer shock if the other "subjects" would not than he did when they were instructed to do so with no others present. What is particularly striking is that he found no significant differences in willingness to give shock between subjects run with two other compliant subjects and those run alone. The very presence of the experimenter so biased the situation in favor of compliance that results from the confederates-complying and the confederates-refusing conditions are not directly comparable.

Greater use of experimental procedures in which the experimenter is perceived by the subject as incompetent, obnoxious, vulgar, or *needlessly* cruel (a rationale was provided in the Milgram study) might reveal varieties of behavior that have been to date rarely observed in the psychological laboratory. The question of the ethics of deception, which has deservedly received much attention recently (e.g., Kelman, 1966), is bypassed here because of space limitations. We emphasize, rather, that customary experimental techniques conspire with well-channeled habits of unidimensional thinking to foster a pervasive fixation on the conformity end of the spectrum and a particular neglect of negativistic reactions.

On the more encouraging side, there appears to be increasing attention devoted to the study of *resistance* to influence, which is to say, the independence mode. In addition to the work of Asch and the Milgram experiment just noted, this tack is represented by Vaughan and Mangan (1963), Kiesler and Kiesler (1964), McGuire (1964), and McGuire and Millman (1965).

The Situation and Conformity

Among the situational variables that have been identified as affecting movement conformity are the ambiguity or difficulty of the stimuli; the greater status, power, or competence of the influence source; the observable unanimity of attractive others; and the general appropriateness of the act of conformity to achieving a desired goal (Asch, 1951, 1956; Blake, Helson, & Mouton, 1956; Goldberg, 1954; Jackson & Saltzstein, 1958; Mausner & Block, 1957; Thibaut & Strickland, 1956; Walker & Heyns, 1962). Further, the effects of these variables have usually been found to be enhanced by the requirement of a public response (e.g., Argyle, 1957; Gorden, 1952; Mouton, Blake, & Olmstead, 1956), although the seemingly simple distinction between public compliance and private acceptance is in fact a complex one (Asch, 1959; Jahoda, 1959; Kiesler, 1969).

The essential thrust of this work is towards the understanding of conditions in the situation which do lead to predictably greater conformity in the sense of convergence towards a group judgment. Psychologically, all of these effects appear to be explainable in terms of a heightened willingness to accept influence as a feature of dependence (cf. Berkowitz, 1957). In this regard, Blake and Mouton (1961) have said: "conformity behavior increases when it is necessary for an individual to rely more heavily on the responses of others in making his own adjustment. Attitudes are more easily shifted than are reactions to factual or logical items, probably because attitudes are more social in character. Increasing the difficulty of items, reducing external cues which provide objective information, and increasing the strength of command in the direction of the compliant behavior all serve to increase the effectiveness of conformity pressures in shifting a person's response" (p. 11).

While all of this may be demonstrably so, a question which requires additional study concerns the situational bases for *nonconformity*. Most theoretical treatments are very lopsided in this respect. French's (1956) otherwise instructive formal model of social power, for example, focuses almost exclusively on pressures towards increased consensus, with only the most oblique concern for factors affecting diversity. Zetterberg's (1957) axiomatic treatment of compliant actions also provides little consideration of motivational or situational factors which would prevent a state of perfect agreement in the long run.

There is another reason for this habitual neglect of nonconformity, over and above the constraints of the traditional experimental paradigm. It is the widespread and highly questionable assumption that the situational and motivational bases of nonconformity are identical to those of conformity, but working in reverse. Taken literally, this assumption leads to the notion that knowledge about conformity means knowledge about nonconformity. This assumption of symmetry, as it might be called, fails to take into account that there are usually multiple ways of not conforming opposed to any particular manner of conforming. Another source of asymmetry arises from the fact that in groups larger than two, perfect consensus (congruence conformity) is always possible in principle, but perfect dissensus is not.

Another entirely different kind of asymmetry that enters into social influence, and which has been very little investigated as yet, concerns the relationship between power *over* another and power to *resist* that other (Cartwright, 1959). It was found by Croner and Willis (1961) that perceptions of differential competence on a prior task within dyads resulted in significant differences in influence transmitted in each direction during a subsequent task, as would be expected, but it was also observed that task similarity was a critical factor. French (1963) has advanced the interesting idea that power to influence and power to resist will be positively correlated in the case of persuasive power but negatively correlated in the case of coercive power.

Personality and Conformity

Despite some voices raised to the contrary (e.g., Crutchfield, 1955; Hovland & Janis, 1959; Tuddenham, 1959), it is increasingly clear that the search for sovereign attributes of a conforming personality have not been especially fruitful. True, for any particular situation individual differences are invariably observed, and these are often substantial, but it is also true that conformity in one situation is not generally a very reliable predictor of conformity in other situations. Although Vaughan (1964), for example, found some consistency in conformity or nonconformity for 20% of the subjects he studied across four situations, the remainder were quite clearly affected differentially by the situations in terms of the amount of conformity manifested.

Additional examples are not lacking. Weiner and McGinnies (1961) conducted a study of the relative levels of conformity by authoritarians and non-authoritarians, finding no confirmation for their hypothesis that authoritarians conform more. Smith (1961) found no relationship between conformity and Barron's Ego-Strength Scale (Barron, 1953). Using several measures growing out of the work of Schroder and Hunt, an investigation by Wilson (1960) supported his predictions regarding personality determinants of conformity for some attitudinal stimuli, but not for a series of perceptual stimuli. These and similar studies often fall back on the necessity to look further at the charac-teristics of the situation, and how it is defined by the subjects, to account in principle for the apparent inconsistencies in the observed patterns of behavior. One can conform or not conform in the service of such a wide variety of personal needs and perceived instrumentalities as to permit only a very limited validity to the construct of the conforming personality.

The issue is reminiscent of the earlier one about leadership attributes. It will be recalled that a prolonged search for the general traits of leaders was sufficiently discouraging as to produce a thoroughgoing reorientation of thought on the topic, with the situational determinants of leadership receiving almost exclusive consideration for a time (see, e.g., Gouldner, 1950). Eventually the pendulum swung back to a more moderate position, and today the importance of the situation continues to be stressed while the role of personal attributes (temperamental, intellective, and physical) as group resources is also generally recognized (cf. Hollander & Julian, 1968).

Whether the issue is leadership or conformity, the recent penetrating treat-ment by Hunt (1965) is especially noteworthy, pointing out as it did that personality factors are more likely to be most important in their *interactions* with situational factors rather than in any sense of total primacy over them. For his data, which serve only an illustrative function, differences among situations accounted for somewhat more variance than differences among persons. More to the present point, however, is the fact that the interactions were more impor-tant than either, accounting for 4 to 11 times the variance due to persons! In Hunt's own words, "Thus, it is neither the individual differences among subjects, *per se,* nor the variations among situations, *per se,* that produce the variations in behavior. It is, rather, the interactions among these which are important (p. 83)."

Related to the idea of the conforming personality is that of the "conforming society." At least one experimental study (Milgram, 1961) has demonstrated consistent differences in amount of movement conformity between samples from two countries. Norwegian university students were observed to be more con-forming than French university students across all of five situations related to the Crutchfield procedure. Concerning these results, Milgram said, "No matter how the data are examined they point to greater independence among the French than among the Norwegians (p. 50)." He went on to relate this difference in "independence" to differences in the two national cultures.

Although it *may* be true that the French are the more independent, Mil-gram's data do not actually allow this conclusion. There exists another equally tenable interpretation. If it is recalled that anticonformity, like conformity, is a variety of *dependence* (cf. the triangular or diamond model of social response), it becomes apparent that one very real possibility is that the French group was exhibiting substantially stronger anticonformity tendencies than the Norwegian group. If so, it could well be that the French subjects were at the same time *less conforming but more dependent.* While the Norwegians felt less free to not conform, the French may have felt less free to conform. Or, if one may put it this way, the French may have been in some degree conforming to a norm of anti-conformity.

It should be borne in mind that this interpretation of the Milgram experiment remains speculative, because his data do not allow a direct test of it; and his data do not allow a test because they derive from experimentation based upon the conformity-independence paradigm. However, the main point is that conformity and dependence are not logically equivalent, and the distinction needs to be maintained both in the design of research and in conceptual analyses.

Whether or not Norway does in fact constitute a conforming society, a whole school of social criticism has developed around the theme that American culture can be so described (e.g., Riesman et al., 1950; Whyte, 1956). The most characteristic tack in such critiques is to describe conventional behavior in modern American society, label it conformity, invoke the "self-evident" premise that conformity is oppositional to individuality or independence, and therefore conclude that modern society and its component institutions hamper constructive initiative and are accordingly bad.

Apart from the value-laden feature of this literature, it neglects and indeed often hides the particular psychological utility of conformity behavior. Under many circumstances an objective analysis of possible courses of action leads to the conclusion that conformity will most effectively serve the individual's goals, whether these are social (e.g., need for approval) or nonsocial (e.g., need for food). From the assumption that all that qualifies as conformity, descriptively, is fully explainable in strictly social terms, an unfortunate confounding of description and explanation results which obscures the necessary and distinct place of each.

Although it is true that conformity and individuality are in opposition insofar as the perfect conformist cannot display individuality, they are in *very imperfect* opposition by virtue of the fact that even the most individualistic person often conforms. The hypothetical perfect individualist would not waste his energy and his status by not conforming in trivial ways—such as wearing red silk suits instead of gray flannel. Rather, he would feel free not to conform whenever something of importance to him was at stake, just as he would *feel free to conform* whenever this had instrumental value.

The distinction, already considered, between conventionality and acquiescence (or, more generally, between congruence and movement), is useful for liberating conventional behavior from the blanket stigma of acquiescent conformity. Thus, the convention of wearing clothes in public cannot be treated as slavish conformity in the same sense as accommodating to any and all fads, indiscriminately. The former represents a long-term habituation to a pattern which has obvious advantages as a necessary condition for normal social interaction of almost all kinds; the latter represents a series of short-term yieldings which, taken in the aggregate, do not have any general instrumentality. A mathematician is not considered lacking in initiative just because he adopts the conventional notation of mathematics, for this is obviously a necessary precondition for the demonstration of whatever professional skills he may have.

Clearly, then, much of the social criticism regarding conformity is misplaced in that what an individual's culture teaches him may severely limit alternatives that are socially and psychologically economical. His habits become conventionalized along the lines occasioned by cultural requirements that usually encourage the self-sufficiency of a particular mode of behaving. As Asch (1959) has put it:

"Each social order confronts its members with a selected portion of physical and social data. The most decisive feature of this selectivity is that it presents conditions lacking in perceptible alternatives. There is no alternative to the language of one's group, to the kinship relations it practices, to the diet that nourishes it, to the art it supports. The field of the individual is, especially in a relatively closed society, in large measure circumscribed by what is included in the given cultural setting" (p. 380).

Like the idea of a conforming personality, the conforming society concept appears to be of limited utility. A realistic assessment of the precise limits of the utility of these concepts will become possible only after the correction of such ambiguities and confusions as have been discussed here lead to a less superficial level of analysis.

Conformity-Nonconformity and Social Exchange

Another, very promising avenue to understanding conformity and nonconformity is to be found in recent conceptions of reciprocity and social exchange (Adams, 1965; Blau, 1964; Gouldner, 1960; Homans, 1958, 1961; Jones, 1964; Thibaut & Kelley, 1959), which has ties both to reinforcement theory and to game theory. The approach is applicable to a study of social behavior either as response or as stimulus, although in this section only the latter is considered.

The social-exchange view construes conformity as a social process in which positive effects are occasioned in interactions with others by manifestations of expected behavior. Seen in this light, conformity becomes either a *deserved reward to others* which smooths the path of interaction and provides for further prospects for rewarding exchange, or as a *payment in advance* for anticipated rewards. In this latter regard, Jones (1965) has called attention again to the various ways in which conformity may be used as a technique of ingratiation. The ingratiation concept indicates one instrumental basis for displaying conformity in interaction which forms a counterpart to the more basic "deserved reward" conception. Moreover, it emphasizes the potential *alteration* of expectancies which is an essential feature of social interaction in the full sense of the term.

Related to these schemes is the "idiosyncrasy credit" model (Hollander, 1958, 1964), which looks upon conformity as one input to the accumulation of status in the form of positive impressions or "credit" awarded by others. This credit then permits greater latitude for nonconformity under certain conditions. A basic feature of the idiosyncrasy credit model is the view that conformity and nonconformity are *not* invariably defined relative to a fixed norm to which everyone in the group is expected to comply equally, as in the Sherif paradigm. Rather, nonconforming behavior is seen to be variously defined by the group for any given actor depending upon how that actor is perceived. Conformity is thus considered to be to some degree person-specific and functionally related to status. That individuals of higher status or greater esteem have wider latitude for deviation has been widely observed and variously demonstrated in recent experiments by Berkowitz and Macaulay (1961), Hollander (1960, 1961), Julian and Steiner (1961), Sabath (1964), and Wiggins, Dill, and Schwartz (1965).

The consideration that when a person is perceived to have higher status his behavior is evaluated differently provides a useful bridge for understanding the relationship between conformity and the later potential for the kinds of deviancy associated with leadership. Thus, the apparent paradox that leaders are said to be greater conformers to group norms (Homans, 1950; Merei, 1949), while also being initiators of change reflected in seemingly nonconforming behavior, is handled within the idiosyncrasy credit model as a matter of sequence. Early conformity, in combination with such attributes as perceived competence, enhances acceptance of later nonconformity.

Nonconformity can also be viewed with regard to the distinction between common expectancies of a group regarding its members and those special expectancies associated with high status. While there is more tolerance of nonconformity for the high-status person in some directions, there are greater restrictions in others. These obligations are the particular role obligations associated with his position in the group. There are at least two reasons why the role obligations of high-status persons are more severely delimited (Hollander, 1964, p. 227). First, because high status is perceived to hold greater self-determination, those in high-status positions are assumed to be more responsible for their actions. Second, and no less critical, high status carries with it role demands which are more likely to affect important outcomes for the members of the group.

The visibility associated with higher status also means that the outcome of any given act of nonconformity will be judged not only in terms of intentions but also in terms of the rewards it produces for the group. Other things equal, the high-status group member's behavior is more likely to be perceived as providing good outcomes to the group, rather than bad. Norm violations are more often seen as instances of "productive nonconformity" in the terminology of Pepinsky (1961). Uppermost here, however, is the consideration that acts of an evidently nonconforming variety will be variously interpreted as a function of others' *perceptions of the actor* based on their past experience with him, and in particular their *imputation of motives* to him (cf. Heider, 1958). Thus it has been found that the high-status person who conforms is seen to do so for internally determined causes while the low-status person is seen to conform for externally determined causes (Thibaut & Riecken, 1955). Accordingly, the motives seen to underlie the action will vary as a function of the actor's perceived status and the related assumption that the high-status person is more in command of initiatives to do as he wishes.

It should follow, too, that when his actions are seen to hurt the group, the high-status person will be held more responsible than would a low-status member. This would hold in particular when some basic role requirement, specific to the position of the individual, is not met. It is true that the acts of the high-status person are less likely to be perceived negatively than those of a low-status person, but *given* that the evaluation of acts is equally unfavorable, the high-status person will pay the higher social price.

In sum, conformity and nonconformity are observed and evaluated as features of interaction which may influence the subsequent action of others toward the actor.

Conclusions and Implications

Let us now consider some salient conclusions.

1. *Current research on social influence is preoccupied with conformity to an extent sufficient to produce a relative neglect of nonconformity.* It should be evident from the numerous studies cited that conceptual and experimental work on nonconformity phenomena has received only a fraction of the attention devoted to the conformity side of the picture. The obvious implication is that a shift of emphasis is much needed.

2. *Current research is characterized by a failure to distinguish consistently between descriptive (phenotypic) and explanatory (genotypic) levels of analysis.* A mutual interdependence exists between the two levels of analysis, and refinements at either level can be expected to facilitate progress at the other. In the area of social influence, however, the distinction has not been maintained as conscientiously as it might. An unfortunate result is that it becomes very easy to overlook the fact that the same overt act, or the same kind of overt act, observed on different occasions, can correspond to a variety of underlying psychological states and processes. A second effect has been the almost total neglect of careful descriptive analysis; this in turn has led to the necessity of making the next point.

3. *Current research is characterized by a nearly universal failure to distinguish between two basically different descriptive criteria of conformity-nonconformity, here termed congruence and movement.* Of writers known to us, only Beloff (1958) has approached an explicit distinction of this kind. Her *conventionality* corresponds to congruence, while her *acquiescence* corresponds to movement—at least so it would seem from the kinds of measures she employed. She, like most others, considered only the conformity side of social influence.

From a strictly descriptive or operational point of view, congruence refers to the proximity between the position of the response along the response continuum and the point defining the normative ideal. Movement refers to changes in level of congruence from one occasion to another. The customary failure to distinguish between the two is roughly analogous to a failure to distinguish between hot and cold, since there is a perfect inverse relationship between the level of congruence and the potential for movement conformity.

4. *Current research is characterized by a persisting tendency to conceptualize conformity and its alternative(s) in an overly restrictive unidimensional manner.* Here two versions of a two-dimensional approach to movement conformity were described. The first, a triangular model, is similar to a less fully articulated conceptualization by Crutchfield and his associates. Conformity, independence, and anticonformity (or counterformity) are considered to be interrelated as the vertices of a triangle. A refinement of the triangular model, the diamond model, introduces a fourth mode of response, variability or self-anticonformity.

The unidimensionality of previous and current research was documented in a selective survey of the literature on movement conformity as a function of situational factors.

5. *Current thinking on conformity and nonconformity often indulges in unwarranted value judgments.* Here the reference was to the related "conforming personality" and "conforming society" points of view. The former fails to recognize that interactions between personality and situational factors are more important than personality variables per se. Both also fail to take into account the fact that

nonconformity, as well as conformity, can represent dependency. One must consider both the individual's freedom to not conform *and his freedom to conform*. At the societal level, a higher level of conformity does not necessarily imply a lower level of psychological freedom or individuality.

6. *Current thinking by social psychologists is frequently characterized by the simplistic and unwarranted assumption that conformity to the general group norms is defined alike for all members of the group.* This assumption of norm homogeneity fails to incorporate the effects of those group processes that produce variations in normative expectations as a function of the status of the actor. These processes were discussed in terms of the idiosyncrasy credit formulation, and related to the social-exchange view of interaction. From extensions of this kind, a more adequate understanding of the mechanisms producing such group phenomena as leadership, innovation, and deviance becomes possible.

References

Adams, J. S. "Inequity In Social Exchange." In *Advances In Experimental Social Psychology*, Vol. 2, ed. L. Berkowitz. Academic Press, 1965.

Allen, V. V. "Situational Factors in Conformity." *Ibid.,* 1965.

Allport, F. H. "The J-Curve Hypothesis of Conforming Behavior." *Journal of Social Psychology*, Vol. 5 (1934), 141–183.

Allport, G. W. *The Nature of Prejudice.* Addison-Wesley, 1954.

Argyle, M. "Social Pressure in Public and Private Situations." *Journal of Abnormal and Social Psychology*, Vol. 54 (1957), 172–175.

Asch, S. E. "Effects of Group Pressure Upon the Modification and Distortion of Judgments." In *Groups, Leadership, and Men*, ed. H. Guetzkow. Carnegie Press, 1951.

———. "Studies of Independence and Conformity: A Minority of One Against a Unanimous Majority." *Psychological Monographs*, Vol. 70 (9, whole no. 416), 1956.

———. "A Perspective on Social Psychology." In *Psychology: A Study of a Science*, Vol. 3, ed. S. Koch. McGraw-Hill, 1959.

Barron, F. "An Ego-Strength Scale Which Predicts Response to Psychotherapy." *Journal of Consulting Psychology*, Vol. 17 (1953), 327–333.

Beloff, H. "Two Forms of Social Conformity: Acquiescence and Conventionality." *Journal of Abnormal and Social Psychology*, Vol. 56 (1958), 99–104.

Berg, I. A., and B. M. Bass. *Conformity and Deviation.* Harper, 1961.

Berkowitz, L. "Liking for the Group and the Perceived Merit of the Group's Behavior." *Journal of Abnormal and Social Psychology*, Vol. 54 (1957), 353–357.

——— and J. R. Macaulay. "Some Effects of Differences in Status Level and Status Stability." *Human Relations*, Vol. 14 (1961), 135–148.

Blake, R. R., H. Helson, and J. S. Mouton. "The Generality of Conformity Behavior as a Function of Factual Anchorage, Difficulty of Task, and Amount of Social Pressure." *Journal of Personality*, Vol. 25 (1956), 294–305.

——— and J. S. Mouton. "Conformity, Resistance and Conversion." In *Conformity and Deviation*, ed. I. A. Berg and B. M. Bass. Harper, 1961.

Blau, P. M. *Exchange and Power in Social Life.* Wiley, 1964.

Cartwright, D. "Power: A Neglected Variable in Social Psychology." In *Studies in Social Power*, ed. D. Cartwright. Institute for Social Research, University of Michigan, 1959.

Cooley, C. H. *Human Nature and the Social Order.* Scribner's, 1902 (rev. ed., 1922); reprinted by The Free Press, 1956.

Croner, M. D., and R. H. Willis. "Perceived Differences in Task Competence and

Asymmetry of Dyadic Influence." *Journal of Abnormal and Social Psychology,* Vol. 62, (1963), 705–708.

Crutchfield, R. S. "Conformity and Character." *American Psychologist,* Vol. 10, (1955), 191–198.

———. "Conformity and Creative Thinking." In *Contemporary Approaches to Creative Thinking,* ed. H. E. Gruber, G. Terrell, and M. Wertheimer. Atherton, 1962.

———. "Independent Thought in a Conformist World." In *Conformity and Conflict: Control of the Mind,* ed. S. M. Farber and R. H. L. Wilson. McGraw-Hill, 1963.

DeSolto, C. B. "The Predilection for Single Orderings." *Journal of Abnormal and Social Psychology,* Vol. 62 (1961), 16–23.

French, J. R. P., Jr. "A Formal Theory of Social Power." *Psychology Review,* Vol. 63 (1956), 181–194.

Goldberg, S. C. "Three Situational Determinants of Conformity to Social Norms." *Journal of Abnormal and Social Psychology,* Vol. 49 (1954), 325–329.

Gorden, R. L. "Interaction Between Attitude and the Definition of the Situation in the Expression of Opinion." *American Sociology Review,* Vol. 17 (1965), 388–390.

Gouldner, A. W. "Situations and Groups: The Situationist Critique." In *Studies in Leadership,* ed. A. W. Gouldner. Harper, 1950.

———. "The Norm of Reciprocity: A Preliminary Statement." *American Sociology Review,* Vol. 25 (1960), 161–179.

Graham, D. "Experimental Studies of Social Influence in Simple Judgment Situations." *Journal of Social Psychology,* Vol. 56 (1962), 245–269.

Heider, F. *The Psychology of Interpersonal Relations.* Wiley, 1958.

Hollander, E. P. "Conformity, Status, and Idiosyncrasy Credit." *Psychology Review,* Vol. 65 (1958), 117–127.

———. "Some Points of Reinterpretation Regarding Social Conformity." *Psychology Review,* Vol. 65 (1959), 159–168.

———. "Competence and Conformity in the Acceptance of Influence." *Journal of Abnormal and Social Psychology,* Vol. 61 (1960), 361–365.

———. "Reconsidering the Issue of Conformity in Personality." In *Perspectives in Personality Research,* ed. H. P. David and J. C. Brengelmann. Springer, 1960.

———. "Some Effects of Perceived Status on Responses to Innovative Behavior." *Journal of Abnormal and Social Psychology,* Vol. 63 (1961), 247–250.

———. *Leaders, Groups, and Influence.* Oxford University Press, 1964.

——— and J. W. Julian. "Leadership." In *Handbook of Personality Theory and Research,* ed. E. F. Borgatta and W. W. Lambert. Rand McNally, 1968.

———, J. W. Julian, and G. A. Haaland. "Conformity Process and Prior Group Support." *Journal of Personality and Social Psychology,* Vol. 2 (1965), 852–858.

——— and R. H. Willis. "Conformity, Independence, and Anticonformity as Determiners of Perceived Influence and Attraction." In *Leaders, Groups, and Influence.* Oxford University Press, 1964.

Homans, G. C. *The Human Group.* Harcourt, 1950.

———. "Social Behavior as Exchange." *American Journal of Sociology,* Vol. 63 (1958), 597–606.

———. *The Nature of Social Science.* Harcourt, 1961.

Hovland, C. I., and I. L. Janis, eds., *Personality and Persuasibility.* Yale University Press, 1959.

Hunt, J. M. "Traditional Personality Theory in the Light of Recent Evidence." *American Scientist,* Vol. 53 (1965), 80–96.

Jackson, J. M., and H. D. Saltzstein. "The Effects of Person-Group Relationships on Conformity Processes." *Journal of Abnormal and Social Psychology,* Vol. 57 (1958), 17–24.

Jahoda, M. "Conformity and Independence: A Psychological Analysis." *Human Relations,* Vol. 12 (1959), 99–120.

Jenness, A. "Social Influences in the Change of Opinion." *Journal of Abnormal and Social Psychology,* Vol. 27 (1932), 279–297.

Jones, E. E. *Ingratiation.* Appleton-Century-Crofts, 1964.

———. "Conformity as a Tactic of Ingratiation." *Science,* Vol. 149 (1965), 144–150.

Julian, J. W., and I. D. Steiner. "Perceived Acceptance as a Determinant of Conformity Behavior." *Journal of Social Psychology,* Vol. 55 (1961), 191–198.

Kelman, H. C. "Effects of Success and Failure on 'Suggestibility' in the Autokinetic Situation." *Journal of Abnormal and Social Psychology,* Vol. 45 (1950), 267–285.

———. "Deception in Social Research." *Transaction,* Vol. 3 (1966), 20–24.

Kidd, J. S., and D. T. Campbell. "Conformity to Groups as a Function of Group Success." *Journal of Abnormal and Social Psychology,* Vol. 51 (1955), 390–393.

Kiesler, C. A. "Group Pressures and Conformity." In *Experimental Social Psychology,* ed. J. Mills. Macmillan, 1969.

——— and S. B. Kiesler. "Role of Forewarning in Persuasive Communications." *Journal of Abnormal and Social Psychology,* Vol. 68 (1964), 547–549.

Krech, D., R. S. Crutchfield, and E. Ballachey. *Individual in Society.* McGraw-Hill, 1962.

Luchins, A. S., and E. H. Luchins. "On Conformity with Judgments of a Majority or an Authority." *Journal of Social Psychology,* Vol. 53 (1961), 303–316.

McGuire, W. J. "Inducing Resistance to Persuasion." In *Advances in Experimental Social Psychology,* Vol. I, ed. L. Berkowitz. Academic Press, 1964.

——— and S. Millman. "Anticipatory Belief Lowering Following Forewarning of a Persuasive Attack." *Journal of Personality and Social Psychology,* Vol. 2 (1965), 471–479.

Mann, R. D. "A Review of the Relationship Between Personality and Performance in Small Groups." *Psychology Bulletin,* Vol. 56 (1959), 241–270.

Mausner, B. "Studies in Social Interaction: III Effect of Variation in One Partner's Prestige on the Interaction of Observer Pairs." *Journal of Applied Psychology,* Vol. 37 (1953), 391–393.

———. "The Effect of Prior Reinforcement on the Interaction of Observer Pairs." *Journal of Abnormal and Social Psychology,* Vol. 49 (1954), 557–560.

——— and B. L. Block. "A Study of the Additivity of Variables Affecting Social Interaction." *Journal of Abnormal and Social Psychology,* Vol. 54 (1957), 250–256.

Merei, F. "Group Leadership and Institutionalization." *Human Relations,* Vol. 2 (1949), 337–352.

Milgram, S. "Nationality and Conformity." *Scientific American,* Vol. 205, No. 6 (1961), 45–51.

———. "Liberating Effects of Group Pressure." *Journal of Personality and Social Psychology,* Vol. 1 (1965), 127–134.

Mouton, J. S., R. R. Blake, and J. A. Olmstead. "The Relationship between Frequency of Yielding and the Disclosure of Personal Identity." *Journal of Personality,* Vol. 24 (1956), 339–347.

Orne, M. T. "On the Social Psychology of the Psychological Experiment: With Particular Reference to Demand Characteristics and Their Implications." *American Psychologist,* Vol. 11 (1962), 776–783.

Pepinsky, P. N. "Social Exceptions That Prove the Rule." In *Conformity and Deviation,* ed. I. A. Berg and B. M. Bass. Harper, 1961.

Riesman, D., N. Glazer, and R. Denney. *The Lonely Crowd: A Study of the Changing American Character.* Yale University Press, 1950.

Sabath, G. "The Effect of Disruption and Individual Status on Person Perception and Group Attraction." *Journal of Social Psychology,* Vol. 64 (1964), 119–130.

Schonbar, R. A. "The Interaction of Observer-Pairs in Judging Visual Extent and Movement: The Formation of Social Norms in 'Structured' Situations." *Archives of Psychology,* Vol. 41, No. 299, 1945.

Sherif, M. "A Study of Some Social Factors in Perception," *Archives of Psychology,* Vol. 27, No. 187, 1935.

Smith, K. H. "Ego Strength and Perceived Competence as Conformity Variables."
   Journal of Abnormal and Social Psychology, Vol. 62 (1961), 169–171.
Thibaut, J. W., and H. H. Kelley. *The Social Psychology of Groups.* Wiley, 1959.
——— and H. W. Riecken. "Some Determinants and Consequences of the Perception
   of Social Causality." *Journal of Personality,* Vol. 24 (1955), 113–133.
——— and L. H. Strickland. "Psychological Set and Social Conformity." *Journal of
   Personality,* Vol. 25 (1956), 115–129.
Tuddenham, R. D. "Correlates of Yielding to a Distorted Group Norm." *Journal of
   Personality,* Vol. 27 (1959), 272–284.
Vaughan, G. M. "The Trans-Situational Aspect of Conformity Behavior." *Journal of
   Personality,* Vol. 32 (1964), 335–354.
——— and G. L. Mangan. "Conformity to Group Pressure in Relation to the Value
   of the Task Material." *Journal of Abnormal and Social Psychology,* Vol. 66 (1963),
   179–183.
Walker, E. L., and R. W. Heyns. *An Anatomy for Conformity.* Prentice-Hall, 1962.
Weiner, H., and E. McGinnies. "Authoritarianism, Conformity, and Confidence in a
   Perceptual Judgment Situation." *Journal of Social Psychology,* Vol. 55 (1961), 77–84.
Whyte, W. H. Jr. *The Organization Man.* Simon & Schuster, 1956.
Wiggins, J. A., F. Dill, and R. D. Schwartz. "On Status-Liability." *Sociometry,* Vol. 28
   (1965), 197–209.
Willis, R. H. "Social Influence and Conformity—Some Research Perspectives." *Acta
   Sociologica,* Vol. 25 (1961), 100–114.
———. "Two Dimensions of Conformity-Nonconformity." *Sociometry,* Vol. 26 (1963),
   499–513.
———. "Descriptive Models of Social Response." Technical Report, Washington
   University, Nonr 816(12), Office of Naval Research, November, 1964.
——— and E. P. Hollander. "An Experimental Study of Three Response Modes in
   Social Influence Situations." *Journal of Abnormal and Social Psychology,* Vol. 69 (1964),
   150–156.
Wilson, R. S. "Personality Patterns, Source Attractiveness, and Conformity." *Journal
   of Personality,* Vol. 28 (1960), 186–199.
Wolf, I. S. "Social Influence: Self-Confidence and Prestige Determinants." *Psychological
   Record,* Vol. 9 (1959), 71–79.
Zetterberg, H. L. "Compliant Actions." *Acta Sociologica,* Vol. 8 (1957), 179–190.

Individual and Group
Decisions Involving Risk

DONALD G. MARQUIS

An understanding of group risk taking—a phenomenon that heretofore has been
confused and controversial—now seems to be coming into focus. The results
of this and previous research indicate that individual familiarization with the

problem can lead to more cautious or more risky decisions, as can group discussion. The shift in decision is toward one or the other extreme and its direction is determined by the initial individual risk positions relative to the neutral midpoint.

Executives typically make decisions after consultation with colleagues and advisors, either individually or as a group. The effects of such consultation are ordinarily considered to be specific to the subject of the decision. But recent research indicates that there are some general and consistent effects on the riskiness of the decision. Contrary to common belief, committee decisions tend to be more risky than individual decisions.

In 1962 I published the first report of the surprising finding that groups reach joint decisions that are more risky than the average of the members' individual decisions prior to group discussion. The research was a replication and extension of the basic finding by Stoner. A review of the field by Kogan and Wallach lists 40 published research reports which stem from the original finding. On the basis of five studies carried out at the Sloan School as thesis projects, and with a valuable assist from Bateson, it is now possible to present a resolution of most of the questions raised by the unexpected finding.

The original research and most of the subsequent studies have made use of a set of 12 short case problems of which the following is a typical example:

> Mr. D, an electrical engineer, married, with one child, has been working for a large electronics corporation since graduating from college five years ago. Although he is assured of a life-time job with a modest but adequate salary and liberal pension, it is very unlikely that his salary will increase much. Mr. D is offered a job with a small, newly founded company with a highly uncertain future. The new job would pay more and would offer the possibility of a share in the ownership if the company survives competition from larger firms.
>
> Imagine that you are advising Mr. D. Listed below are several probabilities (from 0.1 to 1.0) that the new company will prove financially sound. Please check the lowest probability that you would consider acceptable to make it worthwhile for Mr. D to take the new job.

Since 1962, replications, extensions and modifications of the original study have demonstrated the generality of the shift in the direction of greater risk after group discussion. For example, in the problem above, the average individual selected a probability value of about 0.5, while the average group decided on a value of 0.3. The shift has been found with males and females, college students and senior executives, Americans, Englishmen and Israelis. It appears with case problems like the one above, which involve advice to a hypothetical person, and with problems where money is personally risked or where the stake involves an unpleasant experience. It has been demonstrated by investigations using group discussion without a group decision, or using written communication of individual decisions to the others, or merely exposing persons to a taped group discussion.

Several explanations for the risky shift have been proposed. An obvious hypothesis is that persons are free to take a more risky position when responsibility for the choice is diffused to the whole group. This hypothesis was first rejected on the basis of a study in which one individual was designated chairman and charged with the entire responsibility for the decision. After he had discussed the problem with his group, which did not try to reach consensus, his choice showed a risky shift equal to that observed in group decisions (Marquis).

Another hypothesis is that individuals who take a risky position initially will be most persuasive in influencing group opinion. No evidence in support of this explanation has been found (Wallach et al.).

On the basis of preliminary evidence, Brown hypothesized that group discussion would correct the impression held by most persons that they are more risky than others. Hinds had previously demonstrated that individuals do indeed consider that "200 others like you" would take a less risky position. In group discussion such individuals would learn that this notion is not true, and could shift in the risky direction to maintain their position relative to others.

The above hypotheses were formulated and tested on the assumption that groups are always more risky than individuals. But this has now been shown to be false. Nordhoy first demonstrated the existence of a shift in the opposite, or cautious, direction after group discussion for some questions. Following is an example of a case problem on which a consistently cautious shift occurs:

> A man is about to board a plane for an overseas trip to which he has been looking forward for some time. He awoke that morning with severe abdominal pains about which he is troubled but thinks may be due to nervousness since he has never flown before. He is not far from a hospital, but if he goes there he will miss his plane and this will seriously disrupt his vacation plans. The pain has gotten more severe in the last few minutes.

With respect to cautious shifts, Nordhøy hypothesized, "In the group, the impact of values which are commonly accepted in the culture to which the subjects belong will be reinforced (p. 19) . . . on questions where the cultural values support cautious talk or action, individual decisions made after group discussions will be more cautious than individual decisions made without any discussion" (p. 21).

Significant shifts in the cautious direction following group participation have been found in other situations. Zajonc et al. found in their experimental situation that groups showed consistent and significant shifts in the cautious direction.

Stoner (1968) modified the original case problem questionnaire to include six cautious questions and six of the original risky questions. He asked each subject to estimate what choice 200 other people like him would make for each situation. He also asked them to rank 18 social values "in the order in which they are important to you." The phrases were formulated to represent the values involved in the 12 case problems.

The results of this experiment support a relative value hypothesis, which had been proposed in various forms by Stoner (1961), Brown, and others. Those problems that elicited a risky shift were the ones for which people in general had ranked the social value of the outcome prize higher than that of the stake, and conversely for the six cautious questions. Those problems that elicited risky shifts were also the same ones for which people considered others to be less risky. Those problems for which people considered others to be more risky were the ones which elicited cautious shifts.

Theory took a different direction when Burns developed a hypothesis "that groups are more decisive (extreme) than individuals." This idea is in agreement with Teger and Pruitt's demonstration of a correlation between average initial risk level and amount of shift. Burns's model predicts shifts in riskiness, using only the distribution of the individuals' initial preferences as data. It is therefore applicable to a specific group considering a specific decision. The hypotheses state: (1) individuals with more extreme initial positions are more confident in their decisions and will influence the group in that direction, (2) the variance of initial positions will stimulate discussion in the group and result in a greater shift, and (3) the product of the initial extremity and variance determines the amount and direction of group shift. The model can be expressed mathematically as follows:

$$\hat{g} = k_1 EV + k_2$$

in which $\hat{g}$ is the group decision shift, k_1 the "responsiveness of the group to its shift potential," E the initial extremity (discrepancy between average initial position and a neutral mid-position n), V the initial variance, and k_2 a constant measuring a general risk bias. The model was tested on 361 group decisions and correctly predicted the exact shift in more than half the cases.

In 1966 Bateson showed that the risky shift could be produced without any group discussion. In his experimental procedure, the group discussion was replaced by a procedure for individual analytic study (familiarization). He wished to test the hypothesis that familiarization, without any group discussion, will lead to an increase in riskiness. The initial encounter with the problem might not leave the individual ready to commit himself since he did not have sufficient time to weigh all the pros and cons. He would therefore be inclined towards a cautious response at that time. After careful study of the problem, however, he might commit himself to a riskier decision instead of the "I don't know" that underlies the initial caution.

Bateson used five of the 12 case problems which yield risky group shifts. Individuals in the familiarization condition were asked first to record their decision and then to assume the role of a consultant and prepare a brief of the problem which listed the pros and cons, and lastly to make a final decision. Another set of subjects filled out the questionnaire alone initially and then met in groups, discussed the problem and filled out the questionnaire again.

The results of this study (subsequently confirmed by Flanders and Thistlethwaite) showed a risky shift not only in the group discussion condition, but also in the familiarization condition. Thus, analytic reflection on a problem seems to account for some of the risky shift.

The research to be reported in this paper compares the group discussion and the familiarization process, not only on problems yielding a risky shift but on others known to yield a cautious shift. Will the "familiarization" process work on cautious problems?

The Experiment

Forty-five students in the M.I.T. Alfred P. Sloan School of Management were treated in two groups, one for the group discussion condition and one for the familiarization condition. The design of the research is very small in scale, the time available being only two hours. Six questions were used, of which three were designed by Stoner to produce a cautious shift (representing cultural values associated with caution) and three were designed to produce risky shifts. All six of the questions have been previously shown to produce the expected shifts after group discussion (Stoner, 1968).

Procedure

Booklets with instructions were given to the 45 class members, and they were asked to record their individual decisions. The answers were collected after ten minutes. Five groups of five men each were then asked to report to five separate rooms with an experimenter. There they were given the same booklets and instructed to discuss the problems and come to a unanimous decision; that is, agreement by all and not just a majority vote. The groups had no leader or chairman. They were told to spend about five minutes on each question. The experimenter did not take part in the discussion. Each person indicated in the booklet the decision of the group, and then went back and recorded his own private or personal decision, which may or may not have agreed with that of the group.

The other 20 individuals remained in the classroom and were asked to analyze each problem, listing on a separate sheet of paper the pros and cons for taking the alternative action. They then indicated their personal decision choice for each problem.

Results

The average shift for the groups was calculated by taking the difference between the mean individual decision before and after the experimental procedure (Table 1). The average of the individual decisions made after the group discussion was used instead of the group decision in order to compare it to the familiarization condition in which there was no group decision.

Table 1 Average Individual Decision Under Four Experimental Conditions

	Group Discussion			Familiarization		
	Prior	After	Direction of Shift	Prior	After	Direction of Shift
3 risky problems	4.2	2.9	Risky	3.8	3.4	Risky
3 cautious problems	6.8	6.9[a]	Cautious	6.4	6.9	Cautious

[a] The shift is much smaller than has been obtained in other large-scale studies and must be attributed to the law of small numbers.

The only finding which is not a replication of previous research is the shift on cautious problems after the familiarization procedure. The number of individuals shifting cautiously on each problem (23 cautious shifts vs. eight risky shifts out of 64) is significant [p (one-tail) $< .01$].

Conclusion

An understanding of a phenomenon that heretofore has been confused and controversial now seems to be coming into focus after seven years. In the so-called "group risky shift," "group" is not an essential element, as demonstrated by the individual familiarization procedure; "risk" is also not an essential element as demonstrated by the cautious shift in some situations. The fact of a shift of some predictable direction and magnitude remains to be explained.

The findings reported in the paper, considered together with previous results, point to the following conclusions:

1. The direction of shift is determined by the average initial position relative to the mid-point, which in turn is determined by relative values of stake and prize.
2. The magnitude of the shift is determined by the size of the discrepancy between the average initial position and the neutral mid-point.
3. When the shift is the result of group discussion, its magnitude is also a function of the variance of the members' initial positions.

The process of executive decision making, which involves analytic reflection and group consultation, is thus not subject to any binding forces in either the risky or the cautious direction. The decision process moves from a less decisive position to a more decisive one on the same side of the neutral point.

References

Bateson, N. "Familiarization, Group Discussion and Risk Taking." *Journal of Experimental Social Psychology,* II (1966), 119–129.

Brown, R. *Social Psychology.* New York: The Free Press, 1965.

Burns, J. F. "An Extremity-Variance Analysis of Group Decisions Involving Risk." Unpublished doctoral thesis, Sloan School of Management, M.I.T., 1967.

Flanders, J. P., and D. L. Thistlethwaite. "Effects of Familiarization and Group Discussion Upon Risk Taking." *Journal of Personality and Social Psychology,* V (1967), 91–97.

Hinds, W. C., Jr. "Individual and Group Decisions in Gambling Situations." Unpublished master's thesis, Sloan School of Management, M.I.T., 1962.

Kogan, N., and M. A. Wallach. "Risk Taking as a Function of the Situation, the Person, and the Group." In *New Directions in Psychology, III.* Holt, Rinehart and Winston, 1967, pp. 113–278.

Marquis, D. G. "Individual Responsibility and Group Decisions Involving Risk." *Industrial Management Review,* III (Spring 1962), 8–23.

Nordhøy, F. "Group Interaction in Decision Making under Risk." Unpublished master's thesis, Sloan School of Management, M.I.T., 1962.

Stoner, J. A. F. "A Comparison of Individual and Group Decisions Involving Risk." Unpublished master's thesis, Sloan School of Management, M.I.T., 1961.

———. "Risky and Cautious Shifts in Group Decisions: The Influence of Widely Held Values." *Journal of Experimental Social Psychology,* 1968.

Teger, A. I., and D. G. Pruitt. "Components of Group Risk Taking." *Journal of Experimental Social Psychology,* III (1967), 189–205.

Wallach, M. A., N. Kogan, and R. B. Burt. "Are Risk Takers More Persuasive than Conservatives in Group Discussions?" *Journal of Experimental Social Psychology,* IV (1968), 76–88.

Zajonc, R. B., R. J. Wolosin, M. Wolosin, S. J. Sherman. "Individual and Group Risk-Taking in a Two-Choice Situation." *Journal of Experimental Social Psychology,* IV (1968), 89–106.

Group Problem Solving
NORMAN R. F. MAIER

A number of investigations have raised the question of whether group problem solving is superior, inferior, or equal to individual problem solving. Evidence can be cited in support of each position so that the answer to this question remains ambiguous. Rather than pursue this generalized approach to the question, it seems more fruitful to explore the forces that influence problem solving under the two conditions (9, 15). It is hoped that a better recognition of these forces will permit clarification of the varied dimensions of the problem-solving process, especially in groups.

The forces operating in such groups include some that are assets, some that are liabilities, and some that can be either assets or liabilities, depending upon the skills of the members, especially those of the discussion leader. Let us examine these three sets of forces.

Group Assets

Greater Sum Total of Knowledge and Information

There is more information in a group than in any of its members. Thus problems that require the utilization of knowledge should give groups an advantage over individuals. Even if one member of the group (e.g., the leader) knows much more than anyone else, the limited unique knowledge of lesser-informed individuals could serve to fill in some gaps in knowledge. For example, a skilled machinist might contribute to an engineer's problem solving and an ordinary workman might supply information on how a new machine might be received by workers.

Greater Number of Approaches to a Problem

It has been shown that individuals get into ruts in their thinking (6, 16, 44). Many obstacles stand in the way of achieving a goal, and a solution must circumvent these. The individual is handicapped in that he tends to persist in his approach and thus fails to find another approach that might solve the problem in a simpler manner. Individuals in a group have the same failing, but the approaches in which they are persisting may be different. For example, one researcher may try to prevent the spread of a disease by making man immune to the germ, another by finding and destroying the carrier of the germ, and still another by altering the environment so as to kill the germ before it reaches man. There is no way of determining which approach will best achieve the desired goal, but undue persistence in any one will stifle new discoveries. Since group members do not have identical approaches, each can contribute by knocking others out of ruts in thinking.

Norman R. F. Maier, "Assets and Liabilities in Group Problem Solving: The Need for an Integrative Function," *Psychological Review*, Vol. 74, No. 4, 1967, pp. 239–249. Copyright © 1967 by the American Psychological Association, and reproduced by permission.

Participation in Problem Solving Increases Acceptance

Many problems require solutions that depend upon the support of others to be effective. Insofar as group problem solving permits participation and influence, it follows that more individuals accept solutions when a group solves the problem than when one person solves it. When one individual solves a problem he still has the task of persuading others. It follows, therefore, that when groups solve such problems, a greater number of persons accept and feel responsible for making the solution work. A low-quality solution that has good acceptance can be more effective than a higher-quality solution that lacks acceptance.

Better Comprehension of the Decision

Decisions made by an individual, which are to be carried out by others, must be communicated from the decision maker to the decision executors. Thus individual problem solving often requires an additional stage—that of relaying the decision reached. Failures in this communication process detract from the merits of the decision and can even cause its failure or create a problem of greater magnitude than the initial problem that was solved. Many organizational problems can be traced to inadequate communication of decisions made by superiors and transmitted to subordinates, who have the task of implementing the decision.

The chances for communication failures are greatly reduced when the individuals who must work together in executing the decision have participated in making it. They not only understand the solution because they saw it develop, but they are also aware of the several other alternatives that were considered and the reasons why they were discarded. The common assumption that decisions supplied by superiors are arbitrarily reached therefore disappears. A full knowledge of goals, obstacles, alternatives, and factual information is essential to communication, and this communication is maximized when the total problem-solving process is shared.

Group Liabilities

Social Pressure

Social pressure is a major force making for conformity. The desire to be a good group member and to be accepted tends to silence disagreement and favors consensus. Majority opinions tend to be accepted regardless of whether or not their objective quality is logically and scientifically sound. Problems requiring solutions based upon facts, regardless of feelings and wishes, can suffer in group problem-solving situations.

It has been shown (32) that minority opinions in leaderless groups have little influence on the solution reached, even when these opinions are the correct ones. Reaching agreement in a group often is confused with finding the right answer, and it is for this reason that the dimensions of a decision's acceptance and its objective quality must be distinguished (22).

Valence of Solutions

When leaderless groups (made up of three or four persons) engage in problem solving, they propose a variety of solutions. Each solution may receive both critical and supportive comments, as well as descriptive and explorative comments from other participants. If the number of negative and positive comments for each solution are algebraically summed, each may be given a *valence index* (13). The first solution that receives a positive valence value of 15 tends to be adopted to the satisfaction of all participants about 85 percent of the time, regardless of its quality. Higher quality solutions introduced after the critical value for one of the solutions has been reached have little chance of achieving real consideration. Once some degree of consensus is reached, the jelling process seems to proceed rather rapidly.

The critical valence value of 15 appears not to be greatly altered by the nature of the problem or the exact size of the group. Rather, it seems to designate a turning point between the idea-getting process and the decision-making process (idea evaluation). A solution's valence index is not a measure of the number of persons supporting the solution, since a vocal minority can build up a solution's valence by actively pushing it. In this sense, valence becomes an influence in addition to social pressure in determining an outcome.

Since a solution's valence is independent of its objective quality, this group factor becomes an important liability in group problem solving, even when the value of a decision depends upon objective criteria (facts and logic). It becomes a means whereby skilled manipulators can have more influence over the group process than their proportion of membership deserves.

Individual Domination

In most leaderless groups a dominant individual emerges and captures more than his share of influence on the outcome. He can achieve this end through a greater degree of participation (valence), persuasive ability, or stubborn persistence (fatiguing the opposition). None of these factors is related to problem-solving ability, so that the best problem solver in the group may not have the influence to upgrade the quality of the group's solution (which he would have had if left to solve the problem by himself).

Hoffman and Maier (14) found that the mere fact of appointing a leader causes this person to dominate a discussion. Thus, regardless of his problem-solving ability a leader tends to exert a major influence on the outcome of a discussion.

Conflicting Secondary Goal: Winning the Argument

When groups are confronted with a problem, the initial goal is to obtain a solution. However, the appearance of several alternatives causes individuals to have preferences and once these emerge the desire to support a position is created. Converting those with neutral viewpoints and refuting those with opposed viewpoints now enters into the problem-solving process. More and more the goal becomes that of winning the decision rather than finding the best solution. This new goal is unrelated to the quality of the problem's solution and therefore can result in lowering the quality of the decision (12).

Factors That Serve as Assets or Liabilities, Depending Largely upon the Skill of the Discussion Leader

Disagreement

The fact that discussion may lead to disagreement can serve either to create hard feelings among members or lead to a resolution of conflict and hence to an innovative solution (8, 10, 12, 20, 22, 30). The first of these outcomes of disagreement is a liability, especially with regard to the acceptance of solutions; while the second is an asset, particularly where innovation is desired. A leader can treat disagreement as undesirable and thereby reduce the probability of both hard feelings and innovation, or he can maximize disagreement and risk hard feelings in his attempts to achieve innovation. The skill of a leader requires his ability to create a climate for disagreement which will permit innovation without risking hard feelings. The leader's perception of disagreement is one of the critical factors in this skill area (30). Others involve permissiveness (19), delaying the reaching of a solution (24, 33), techniques for processing information and opinions (22, 25, 31), and techniques for separating idea getting from idea evaluation (21, 22, 31).

Conflicting Interests Versus Mutual Interests

Disagreement in discussion may take many forms. Often participants disagree with one another with regard to solutions, but when issues are explored one finds that these conflicting solutions are designed to solve different problems. Before one can rightly expect agreement on a solution, there should be agreement on the nature of the problem. Even before this, there should be agreement on the goal, as well as on the various obstacles that prevent the goal from being reached. Once distinctions are made between goals, obstacles, and solutions (which represent ways of overcoming obstacles), one finds increased opportunities for cooperative problem solving and less conflict (11, 21, 22, 33, 40).

Often there is also disagreement regarding whether the objective of a solution is to achieve quality or acceptance (29), and frequently a stated problem reveals a complex of separate problems, each having separate solutions so that a search for a single solution is impossible (22). Communications often are inadequate because the discussion is not synchronized and each person is engaged in discussing a different aspect. Organizing discussion to synchronize the exploration of different aspects of the problem and to follow a systematic procedure increases solution quality (25, 31). The leadership function of influencing discussion procedure is quite distinct from the function of evaluating or contributing ideas (17, 19).

When the discussion leader aids in the separation of the several aspects of the problem-solving process and delays the solution-mindedness of the group (20, 22, 33), both solution quality and acceptance improve; when he hinders or fails to facilitate the isolation of these varied processes, he risks a deterioration in the group process (40). His skill thus determines whether a discussion drifts toward conflicting interests or whether mutual interests are located. Cooperative problem solving can only occur after the mutual interests have been established and it is surprising how often they can be found when the discussion leader makes this his task (18, 22, 23).

Risk Taking

Groups are more willing than individuals to reach decisions involving risks (42, 43). Taking risks is a factor in acceptance of change, but change may either represent a gain or a loss. The best guard against the latter outcome seems to be primarily a matter of a decision's quality. In a group situation this depends upon the leader's skill in utilizing the factors that represent group assets and avoiding those that make for liabilities.

Time Requirements

In general, more time is required for a group to reach a decision than for a single individual to reach one. Insofar as some problems require quick decisions, individual decisions are favored. In other situations acceptance and quality are requirements, but excessive time without sufficient returns also represents a loss. On the other hand, discussion can resolve conflicts, whereas reaching consensus has limited value (42). The practice of hastening a meeting can prevent full discussion, but failure to move a discussion forward can lead to boredom and fatigue-type solutions, in which members agree merely to get out of the meeting. The effective utilization of discussion time (a delicate balance between permissiveness and control on the part of the leader), therefore, is needed to make the time factor an asset rather than a liability. Unskilled leaders tend to be too concerned with reaching a solution and therefore terminate a discussion before the group potential is achieved (24).

Who Changes

In reaching consensus or agreement, some members of a group must change. Persuasive forces do not operate in individual problem solving in the same way they operate in a group situation; hence, the changing of someone's mind is not an issue. In group situations, however, who changes can be an asset or a liability. If persons with the most constructive views are induced to change the end-product suffers; whereas if persons with the least constructive points of view change the end-product is upgraded. The leader can upgrade the quality of a decision because his position permits him to protect the person with a minority view and increase his opportunity to influence the majority position. This protection is a constructive factor because a minority viewpoint influences only when facts favor it (17, 18, 32).

The leader also plays a constructive role insofar as he can facilitate communications and thereby reduce misunderstandings (18, 40). The leader has an adverse effect on the end-product when he suppresses minority views by holding a contrary position and when he uses his office to promote his own views (24, 27, 32). In many problem-solving discussions the untrained leader plays a dominant role in influencing the outcome, and when he is more resistant to changing his views than are the other participants, the quality of the outcome tends to be lowered. This negative leader-influence was demonstrated by experiments in which untrained leaders were asked to obtain a second solution to a problem after they had obtained their first one (25). It was found that the second solution tended to be superior to the first. Since the dominant individual had influenced the first solution, he had won his point and therefore ceased to dominate the subsequent discussion which led to the second solution. Acceptance of a solution also increases as the leader sees disagreement as idea producing rather than as a source of difficulty or trouble (30). Leaders who see some of their participants as troublemakers obtain fewer innovative solutions and gain less acceptance of decisions made than leaders who see disagreeing members as persons with ideas.

The Leader's Role for Integrated Groups

Two Differing Types of Group Process

In observing group problem solving under various conditions it is rather easy to distinguish between cooperative problem-solving activity and persuasion or selling approaches. Problem-solving activity includes searching, trying out ideas on one another, listening to understand rather than to refute, making relatively short speeches, and reacting to differences in opinion as stimulating. The general pattern is one of rather complete participation, involvement, and interest. Persuasion activity includes the selling of opinions already formed, defending a position held, either not listening at all or listening in order to be able to refute, talking dominated by a few members, unfavorable reactions to disagreement, and a lack of involvement of some members. During problem solving the behavior observed seems to be that of members interacting as segments of a group. The interaction pattern is not between certain individual members, but with the group as a whole. Sometimes it is difficult to determine who should be credited with an idea. "It just developed," is a response often used to describe the solution reached. In contrast, discussions involving selling or persuasive behavior seem to consist of a series of interpersonal interactions with each individual retaining his identity. Such groups do not function as integrated units but as separate individuals, each with an agenda. In one situation the solution is unknown and is sought; in the other, several solutions exist and conflict occurs because commitments have been made.

The Starfish Analogy

The analysis of these two group processes suggests an analogy with the behavior of the rays of a starfish under two conditions; one with the nerve ring intact, the other with the nerve ring sectioned (7, 35, 36, 39). In the intact condition, locomotion and righting behavior reveal that the behavior of each ray is not merely a function of local stimulation. Locomotion and righting behavior reveal a degree of coordination and interdependence that is centrally controlled. However, when the nerve ring is sectioned, the behavior of one ray still can influence others, but internal coordination is lacking. For example, if one ray is stimulated, it may step forward, thereby exerting pressure on the sides of the other four rays. In response to these external pressures (tactile stimulation), these rays show stepping responses on the stimulated side so that locomotion successfully occurs without the aid of neural coordination. Thus integrated behavior can occur on the basis of external control. If, however, stimulation is applied to opposite rays, the specimen may be "locked" for a time, and in some species the conflicting locomotions may divide the animal, thus destroying it (5, 36).

Each of the rays of the starfish can show stepping responses even when sectioned and removed from the animal. Thus each may be regarded as an individual. In a starfish with a sectioned nerve ring the five rays become members of a group. They can successfully work together for locomotion purposes by being controlled by the dominant ray. Thus if uniformity of action is desired, the group of five rays can sometimes be more effective than the individual ray in moving the group toward a source of stimulation. However, if "locking" or the division of the organism occurs, the group action becomes less effective than individual action. External control, through the influence of a dominant ray, therefore can lead to adaptive behavior for the starfish as a whole, but it can also result in a conflict that destroys the organism. Something more than external influence is needed.

In the animal with an intact nerve ring, the function of the rays is coordinated by the nerve ring. With this type of internal organization the group is always superior to that of the individual actions. When the rays function as a part of an organized unit, rather than as a group that is physically together, they become a higher type of organization—a single intact organism. This is accomplished by the nerve ring, which in itself does not do the behaving. Rather, it receives and processes the data which the rays relay to it. Through this central organization, the responses of the rays become part of a larger pattern so that together they constitute a single coordinated total response rather than a group of individual responses.

The Leader as the Group's Central Nervous System

If we now examine what goes on in a discussion group we find that members can problem-solve as individuals, they can influence others by external pushes and pulls, or they can function as a group with varying degrees of unity. In order for the latter function to be maximized, however, something must be introduced to serve the function of the nerve ring. In our conceptualization of group problem solving and group decision (22), we see this as the function of the leader. Thus the leader does not serve as a dominant ray and produce the solution. Rather, his function is to receive information, facilitate communications between the individuals, relay messages, and integrate the incoming responses so that a single unified response occurs.

Solutions that are the product of good group discussions often come as surprises to discussion leaders. One of these is unexpected generosity. If there is a weak member, this member is given less to do, in much the same way as an organism adapts to an injured limb and alters the function of other limbs to keep locomotion on course. Experimental evidence supports the point that group decisions award special consideration to needy members of groups (11). Group decisions in industrial groups often give smaller assignments to the less gifted (18). A leader could not effectually impose such differential treatment on group members without being charged with discriminatory practices.

Another unique aspect of group discussion is the way fairness is resolved. In a simulated problem situation involving the problem of how to introduce a new truck into a group of drivers, the typical group solution involves a trading of trucks so that several or all members stand to profit. If the leader makes the decision the number of persons who profit is often confined to one (27, 34). In industrial practice, supervisors assign a new truck to an individual member of a crew after careful evaluation of needs. This practice results in dissatisfaction, with the charge of *unfair* being leveled at him. Despite these repeated attempts to do justice, supervisors in the telephone industry never hit upon the notion of a general reallocation of trucks, a solution that crews invariably reach when the decision is theirs to make.

In experiments involving the introduction of change, the use of group discussion tends to lead to decisions that resolve differences (18, 19, 26, 28, 29). Such decisions tend to be different from decisions reached by individuals because of the very fact that disagreement is common in group problem solving and rare in individual problem solving. The process of resolving differences in a constructive setting causes the exploration of additional areas and leads to solutions that are integrative rather than compromises.

Finally, group solutions tend to be tailored to fit the interests and personalities of the participants; thus group solutions to problems involving fairness, fears, face-saving, etc., tend to vary from one group to another. An outsider cannot process these variables because they are not subject to logical treatment.

If we think of the leader as serving a function in the group different from that of its membership, we might be able to create a group that can function as an intact organism. For a leader, such functions as rejecting or promoting ideas according to his personal needs are out of bounds. He must be receptive to information contributed, accept contributions without evaluating them (posting contributions on a chalk board to keep them alive), summarize information to facilitate integration, stimulate exploratory behavior, create awareness of problems of one member by others, and detect when the group is ready to resolve differences and agree to a unified solution.

Since higher organisms have more than a nerve ring and can store information, a leader might appropriately supply information, but according to our model of a leader's role, he must clearly distinguish between supplying information and promoting a solution. If his knowledge indicates the desirability of a particular solution, sharing this knowledge might lead the group to find this solution, but the solution should be the group's discovery. A leader's contributions do not receive the same treatment as those of a member of the group. Whether he likes it or not, his position is different. According to our conception of the leader's contribution to discussion, his role not only differs in influence, but gives him an entirely different function. He is to serve much as the nerve ring in the starfish and to further refine this function so as to make it a higher type of nerve ring.

This model of a leader's role in group process has served as a guide for many of our studies in group problem solving. It is not our claim that this will lead to the best possible group function under all conditions. In sharing it we hope to indicate the nature of our guidelines in exploring group leadership as a function quite different and apart from group membership. Thus the model serves as a stimulant for research problems and as a guide for our analyses of leadership skills and principles.

Conclusions

On the basis of our analysis, it follows that the comparison of the merits of group versus individual problem solving depends on the nature of the problem, the goal to be achieved (high quality solution, highly accepted solution, effective communication and understanding of the solution, innovation, a quickly reached solution, or satisfaction), and the skill of the discussion leader. If liabilities inherent in groups are avoided, assets capitalized upon, and conditions that can serve either favorable or unfavorable outcomes are effectively used, it follows that groups have a potential which in many instances can exceed that of a superior individual functioning alone, even with respect to creativity.

This goal was nicely stated by Thibaut and Kelley (41) when they "wonder whether it may not be possible for a rather small, intimate group to establish a problem-solving process that capitalizes upon the total pool of information and provides for great interstimulation of ideas without any loss of innovative creativity due to social restraints" (p. 268).

In order to accomplish this high level of achievement, however, a leader is needed who plays a role quite different from that of the members. His role is analogous to that of the nerve ring in the starfish which permits the rays to execute a unified response. If the leader can contribute the integrative requirement, group problem solving may emerge as a unique type of group function. This type of approach to group processes places the leader in a particular role in which he must cease to contribute, avoid evaluation, and refrain from thinking about solutions or group *products*. Instead he must concentrate on the group *process*, listen in order to understand rather than to appraise or refute, assume responsibility for accurate communication between members, be sensitive to unexpressed feelings, protect minority points of view, keep the discussion moving, and develop skills in summarizing.

References

1. Argyris, C. "T-Groups for Organizational Effectiveness." *Harvard Business Review*, XLII (1964), 60.
2. ———. "Explorations in Interpersonal Competence II." *Applied Behavioral Science*, I, No. 3 (1965), 255.
3. ———. *Organization and Innovation*. Homewood, Ill.: Richard D. Irwin, Inc. 1965.
4. Blake, R. R., J. S. Mouton, L. B. Barnes, and L. E. Greiner. "Breakthrough in Organization Development." *Harvard Business Review*, XLII (1964), 135.
5. Crgzier, W. J. "Notes on Some Problems of Adaptation." *Biological Bulletin*, XXXIX (1920), 116–29.
6. Duncker, K. "On problem solving." *Psychological Monographs*, LVIII, No. 270 (1945).
7. Hamilton, W. F. "Coordination in the Starfish, III: The Righting Reaction as a Phase of Locomotion (Righting and Locomotion)." *Journal of Comparative Psychology*, II (1922), 81–94.
8. Hoffman, L. R. "Conditions for Creative Problem Solving." *Journal of Psychology*, LII (1961), 429–44.
9. ———. "Group Problem Solving," in *Advances in Experimental Social Psychology*. Vol. II, ed. L. Berkowitz. New York: Academic Press, Inc., 1965, pp. 99–132.
10. ———, E. Hamburg, and N. R. F. Maier, "Differences and Disagreement as Factors in Creative Group Problem Solving." *Journal of Abnormal and Social Psychology*, LXIV (1962), 206–14.
11. ———, and N. R. F. Maier, "The Use of Group Decision to Resolve a Problem of Fairness." *Personnel Psychology*, XII (1959), 545–59.
12. ———, and ———. "Quality and Acceptance of Problem Solutions by Members of Homogeneous and Heterogeneous Groups." *Journal of Abnormal and Social Psychology*, LXII (1961), 401–7.
13. ———, and ———. "Valence in the Adoption of Solutions by Problem-Solving Groups: Concept, Method, and Results." *Journal of Abnormal and Social Psychology*, LXIX (1964), 264–71.
14. ———, and ———. "Valence in the Adoption of Solutions by Problem-Solving Groups: II. Quality and Acceptance as Goals of Leaders and Members" (Unpublished manuscript, 1967 [mimeo]).
15. Kelley, H. H., and J. W. Thibaut. "Experimental Studies of Group Problem Solving and Process." In *Handbook of Social Psychology*, ed. G. Lindzey, Cambridge, Mass: Addison-Wesley Publishing Co., Inc., 1954, pp. 735–85.

16. Maier, N. R. F. "Reasoning in Humans. I: On Direction." *Journal of Comparative Psychology,* X (1930), 115–43.
17. ———. "The Quality of Group Decisions as Influenced by the Discussion Leader." *Human Relations,* III (1950), 155–74.
18. ———. *Principles of Human Relations.* New York: John Wiley & Sons, Inc., 1952.
19. ———. "An Experimental Test of the Effect of Training on Discussion Leadership." *Human Relations,* VI (1953), 161–73.
20. ———. *The Appraisal Interview.* New York: John Wiley & Sons, Inc., 1958.
21. ———. "Screening Solutions to Upgrade Quality: A New Approach to Problem Solving Under Conditions of Uncertainty." *Journal of Psychology,* IL (1960), 217–31.
22. ———. *Problem Solving Discussions and Conferences: Leadership Methods and Skills.* New York: McGraw-Hill Book Company, 1963.
23. ———, and J. J. Hayes. *Creative Management.* New York: John Wiley & Sons, Inc., 1962.
24. ———, and L. R. Hoffman. "Quality of First and Second Solutions in Group Problem Solving." *Journal of Applied Psychology,* XLIV (1960), 278–83.
25. ———, and ———. "Using Trained 'Developmental' Discussion Leaders to Improve Further the Quality of Group Decisions." *Journal of Applied Psychology,* XLIV (1960), 247–51.
26. ———, and ———. "Organization and Creative Problem Solving." *Journal of Applied Psychology,* XLV (1961), 277–80.
27. ———, and ———. "Group Decision in England and the United States." *Personnel Psychology,* XV (1962), 75–87.
28. ———, and ———. "Financial Incentives and Group Decision in Motivating Change." *Journal of Social Psychology,* LXIV (1964), 369–78.
29. ———, and ———. "Types of Problems Confronting Managers." *Personnel Psychology,* XVII (1964), 261–69.
30. ———, and ———. "Acceptance and Quality of Solutions as Related to Leaders' Attitudes Toward Disagreement in Group Problem Solving." *Journal of Applied Behavioral Science,* I (1965), 373–86.
31. ———, and R. A. Maier. "An Experimental Test of the Effects of 'Developmental' vs. 'Free' Discussions on the Quality of Group Decisions." *Journal of Applied Psychology,* XLI (1957), 320–23.
32. ———, and A. R. Solem. "The Contribution of a Discussion Leader to the Quality of Group Thinking: The Effective Use of Minority Opinions." *Human Relations,* V (1952), 277–88.
33. ———, and ———. "Improving Solutions by Turning Choice Situations into Problems." *Personnel Psychology,* XV (1962), 151–57.
34. ———, and L. F. Zerfoss. "MRP: A Technique for Training Large Groups of Supervisors and Its Potential Use in Social Research." *Human Relations,* V (1952), 177–86.
35. Moore, A. R. "The Nervous Mechanism of Coordination in the Crinoid Antedon Rosaceus." *Journal of Genetic Psychology,* VI (1924), 281–88.
36. ———, and M. Doudoroff. "Injury, Recovery, and Function in an Aganglionic Central Nervous System." *Journal of Comparative Psychology,* XXVIII (1939), 313–28.
37. Osborn, A. F. *Applied Imagination.* New York: Charles Scribner's Sons, 1953.
38. Schein, E., and W. Bennis. *Personal and Organizational Change Through Laboratory Methods.* New York: John Wiley & Sons, Inc., 1965.
39. Schneirla, T. C., and N. R. F. Maier. "Concerning the Status of the Starfish." *Journal of Comparative Psychology,* XXX (1940), 103–10.
40. Solem, A. R. "1965: Almost Anything I Can Do, We Can Do Better." *Personnel Administration,* XXVIII (1965), 6–16.
41. Thibaut, J. W., and H. H. Kelley. *The Social Psychology of Groups.* New York: John Wiley & Sons, Inc., 1961.

42. Wallach, M. A., and N. Kogan. "The Roles of Information, Discussion, and Consensus in Group Risk Taking." *Journal of Experimental and Social Psychology*, I (1965), 1–19.

43. ———, ———, and D. J. Bem. "Group Influence on Individual Risk Taking." *Journal of Abnormal and Social Psychology*, LXV (1962), 75–86.

44. Wertheimer, M., *Productive Thinking*. New York: Harper & Row, Publishers, 1959.

Committee Management

ALAN C. FILLEY

The committee is one of the most maligned, most frequently employed forms of organization structure. Despite the criticisms, committees are a fact of organization life. For example, a recent survey of 1200 respondents revealed that 94 percent of firms with more than 10,000 employees and 64 percent with less than 250 employees reported having formal committees.[1] And, a survey of organization practices in 620 Ohio manufacturing firms showed a similar positive relationship between committee use and plant size.[2] These studies clearly indicate that committees are one of management's important organizational tools.

My thesis is that committee effectiveness can be increased by applying social science findings to answer such questions as:

- What functions do committees serve?
- What size should committees be?
- What is the appropriate style of leadership for committee chairmen?
- What mix of member characteristics makes for effective committee performance?

Committee Purposes and Functions

Committees are set up to pursue economy and efficiency within the enterprise. They do not create direct salable value, nor do they supervise operative employees who create such value.

The functions of the committee have been described by business executives as the exchange of views and information, recommending action, generating ideas, and making major decisions,[3] of which the first may well be the most common. After observing seventy-five conferences (which were also referred to

"Committee Management: Guidelines from Social Science Research" by Alan C. Filley. Copyright © 1970 by The Regents of the University of California. Reprinted from *California Management Review*, Vol. 13, No. 1, pp. 13–21, by permission of the author and of The Regents. Adapted from Chapter 14 of *Managerial Process and Organizational Behavior* by A. C. Filley and R. J. House (Scott, Foresman, 1969).

as "committees"), Kriesberg concluded that most were concerned either with communicating information or with aiding an executive's decision process.[4] Executives said they called conferences to "sell" ideas rather than for group decision-making itself. As long as the executive does not manipulate the group covertly, but benefits by its ideas and screening processes, this activity is probably quite legitimate, for members are allowed influence and to participate, to some extent, in executive decision-making.

Some committees also make specific operating decisions which commit individuals and organization units to prescribed goals and policies. Such is often the province of the general management committee composed of major executive officers. According to one survey, 30.3 percent of the respondents reported that their firms had such a committee and that the committees averaged 8.6 members and met 27 times per year.[5]

Several of the characteristics of committee organization have been the subject of authoritative opinion, or surveys of current practice, and lend themselves to evaluation through inferences from small-group research. Current practice and authoritative opinion are reviewed here, followed by more rigorous studies in which criteria of effectiveness are present. The specific focus is on committee size, membership, and chairmen.

Committee Size

Current Practice and Opinion

The typical committee should be, and is, relatively small. Recommended sizes range from three to nine members, and surveys of actual practice seldom miss these prescriptions by much. Of the 1658 committees recorded in the Harvard Business Review survey, the average membership was eight. When asked for their preference, the 79 percent who answered suggested an ideal committee size that averaged 4.6 members. Similarly, Kriesberg reported that, for the 75 conferences analyzed, there were typically five or six conferees in the meetings studied.[6]

Committees in the federal government tend to be larger than those in business. In the House of Representatives, Appropriations is the largest standing committee, with fifty members, and the Committee on Un-American Activities is smallest, with nine. Senate committees average thirteen members; the largest, also Appropriations, has twenty-three.[7] The problem of large committee size is overcome by the use of subcommittees and closed executive committee meetings. The larger committees seem to be more collections of subgroups than truly integrated operating units. In such cases, it would be interesting to know the size of the subcommittees.

Inferences from Small-Group Research

The extent to which a number is "ideal" may be measured in part in terms of the effects that size has on socio-emotional relations among group members and thus the extent to which the group operates as an integrated whole, rather than as fragmented subunits. Another criterion is how size affects the quality of the group's decision and the time required to reach it. Several small experimental group studies have evaluated the effect of size on group process.

Variables related to changes in group size include the individual's capacity to "attend" to differing numbers of objects, the effect of group size on interpersonal relations and communication, its impact on problem-solving functions, and the "feelings" that group members have about proper group size and the nature of group performance. To be sure, the effects of these variables are interrelated.

Attention to the Group   Each member in a committee attends both to the group as a whole and to each individual as a member of the group. There seem to be limits on a person's ability to perform both of these processes—limits which vary with the size of the group and the time available. For example, summarizing a study by Taves,[8] Hare[9] reports that "Experiments on estimating the number of dots in a visual field with very short-time exposures indicate individual subjects can report the exact number up to and including seven with great confidence and practically no error, but above that number confidence and accuracy drop."

Perhaps for similar reasons, when two observers assessed leadership characteristics in problem-solving groups of college students, the raters reached maximum agreement in groups of six, rather than in two, four, eight, or twelve.[10]

The apparent limits on one's ability to attend both to the group and the individuals within it led Hare to conclude: "The coincidence of these findings suggests that the ability of the observing individual to perceive, keep track of, and judge each member separately in a social interaction situation may not extend much beyond the size of six or seven. If this is true, one would expect members of groups larger than that size to tend to think of other members in terms of subgroups, or 'classes' of some kind, and to deal with members of subgroups other than their own by more stereotyped methods of response.[11]

Interpersonal Relations and Communication   Given a meeting lasting a fixed length of time, the opportunity for each individual to communicate is reduced, and the type of communication becomes differential among group members. Bales et al.[12] have shown that in groups of from three to eight members the proportion of infrequent contributors increases at a greater rate than that theoretically predicted from decreased opportunity to communicate. Similarly, in groups of from four to twelve, as reported by Stephen and Mishler,[13] size was related positively to the difference between participation initiated by the most active and the next most active person.

Increasing the group size seems to limit the extent to which individuals want to communicate, as well. For example, Gibb[14] studied idea productivity in forty-eight groups in eight size categories from 1 to 96. His results indicated that as group size increases a steadily increasing proportion of group members report feelings of threat and less willingness to initiate contributions. Similarly, Slater's[15] study of 24 groups of from two to seven men each working on a human relations problem indicated that members of the larger groups felt them to be disorderly and time-consuming, and complained that other members became too pushy, aggressive, and competitive.

Functions and Conflict   An increase in group size seems to distort the pattern of communication and create stress in some group members, yet a decrease in group size also has dysfunctional effects. In the Slater study check-list responses by members rating smaller groups of 2, 3, or 4 were complimentary, rather than critical, as they had been for larger groups. Yet observer impressions were that small groups engaged in superficial discussion and avoided controversial subjects. Inferences from post hoc analysis suggested that small group members are too tense, passive, tactful, and constrained to work together in a satisfying manner. They are afraid of alienating others. Similar results have been reported in other studies regarding the inhibitions created by small group size, particularly in groups of two.[16]

Groups of three have the problem of an overpowerful majority, since two members can form a coalition against the unsupported third member. Four-member groups provide mutual support when two members oppose the other two, but such groups have higher rates of disagreement and antagonism than odd-numbered groups.[17]

The data reported above are not altogether consistent regarding the reasons for dysfunctional consequences of small groups. The "trying-too-hard-for-agreement" of the Slater study seems at odds with the conflict situations posed in the groups of three and four, yet both agree that for some reason tension is present.

Groups of Five   While it is always dangerous to generalize about "ideal" numbers (or types, for that matter), there does appear to be logical and empirical support for groups of five members as a suitable size, if the necessary skills are possessed by the five members. In the Slater study, for example, none of the subjects felt that a group of five was too small or too large to carry out the assigned task, though they objected to the other sizes (two, three, four, six, and seven). Slater concluded:

"Size five emerged clearly . . . as the size group which from the subjects' viewpoint was most effective in dealing with an intellectual task involving the collection and exchange of information about a situation, the coordination analysis, and evaluation of this information, and a group decision regarding the appropriate administrative action to be taken in the situation. . . .

"These findings suggest that maximal group satisfaction is achieved when the group is large enough so that the members feel able to express positive and negative feelings freely, and to make aggressive efforts toward problem solving even at the risk of antagonizing each other, yet small enough so that some regard will be shown for the feelings and needs of others; large enough so that the loss of a member could be tolerated, but small enough so that such a loss could not be altogether ignored."[18]

From this and other studies,[19] it appears that, excluding productivity measures, generally the optimum size of problem-solving groups is five. Considering group performance in terms of quality, speed, efficiency and productivity, the effect of size is less clear. Where problems are complex, relatively larger groups have been shown to produce better quality decisions. For example, in one study, groups of 12 or 13 produced higher quality decisions than groups of 6, 7, or 8.[20] Others have shown no differences among groups in the smaller size categories (2 to 7). Relatively smaller groups are often faster and more productive. For example, Hare found that groups of five take less time to make decisions than groups of 12.[21]

Several studies have also shown that larger groups are able to solve a greater variety of problems because of the variety of skills likely to increase with group size.[22] However, there is a point beyond which committee size should not increase because of diminishing returns. As group size increases coordination of the group tends to become difficult, and thus it becomes harder for members to reach consensus and to develop a spirit of teamwork and cohesiveness.

In general, it would appear that with respect to performance, a task which requires interaction, consensus and modification of opinion requires a relatively small group. On the other hand, where the task is one with clear criteria of correct performance, the addition of more members may increase group performance.

The Chairman

Current Practice and Opinion

Most people probably serve on some type of committee in the process of participating in church, school, political, or social organizations and while in that capacity have observed the effect of the chairman on group progress. Where the chairman starts the meeting, for example, by saying, "Well, we all know each other here, so we'll dispense with any formality," the group flounders, until someone else takes a forceful, directive role.

If the committee is to be successful, it must have a chairman who understands group process. He must know the objectives of the committee and understand the problem at hand. He should be able to vary decision strategies according to the nature of the task and the feelings of the group members. He needs the acceptance of the group members and their confidence in his personal integrity. And he needs the skill to resist needless debate and to defer discussion upon issues which are not pertinent or where the committee lacks the facts upon which to act.

Surveys of executive opinion support these impressions of the chairman's role. The Harvard Business Review survey stated that "The great majority [of the suggestions from survey respondents] lead to this conclusion: the problem is not so much committees in management as it is the management of committees." This comment by a partner in a large management consulting firm was cited as typical: "Properly used, committees can be most helpful to a company. Most of the criticism I have run into, while probably justified, deals with the way in which committees are run (or committee meetings are run) and not with the principle of working with committees."[23]

A chairman too loose in his control of committee processes is by no means the only difficulty encountered. Indeed, the chronic problem in the federal government has been the domination of committee processes by the chairman. This results from the way in which the chairman is typically selected: he is traditionally the member of the majority party having the longest uninterrupted service on the committee. The dangers in such domination have been described as follows:

"If there is a piece of legislation that he does not like, he kills it by declining to schedule a hearing on it. He usually appoints no standing subcommittees and he arranges the special subcommittees in such a way that his personal preferences are taken into account. Often there is no regular agenda at the meetings of his committee—when and if it meets . . . they proceed with an atmosphere of apathy, with junior members, especially, feeling frustrated and left out, like first graders at a seventh grade party."[24]

Inferences from Small Group Research

The exact nature of the chairman's role is further clarified when we turn to more rigorous studies on group leadership.

We shall confine our discussion here to leader roles and functions, using three approaches. First, we shall discuss the nature of task leadership in the group and the apparent reasons for this role. Then we shall view more specifically the different roles which the leader or leaders of the group may play. Finally, we shall consider the extent to which these more specific roles may be combined in a single individual.

Leader Control   Studies of leadership in task-oriented, decision-making groups show a functional need for and, indeed, a member preference for directive influence by the chairman. The nature of this direction is illustrated in a study by Schlesinger, Jackson, and Butman.[25] The problem was to examine the influence process among leaders and members of small problem-solving groups when the designated leaders varied on the rated degree of control exerted. One hundred six members of twenty-three management committees participated in the study. As part of an initial investigation, committee members described in a questionnaire the amount of control and regulation which each member exercised when in the role of chairman. Each committee was then given a simulated but realistic problem for 1.5 hours, under controlled conditions and in the presence of three observers.

The questionnaire data showed that individuals seen as high in control were rated as more skillful chairmen and as more valuable contributors to the committee's work.

The study also demonstrated that leadership derives from group acceptance rather than from the unique acts of the chairman. "When the participants do not perceive the designated leader as satisfactorily performing the controlling functions, the participants increase their own attempts to influence their fellow members."[26] The acceptance of the leader was based upon task (good ideas) and chairmanship skills and had little to do with his personal popularity as a group member.

The importance of chairman control in committee action has been similarly demonstrated in several other studies.[27] In his study of 72 management conferences, for example, Berkowitz[28] found that a high degree of "leadership sharing" was related inversely to participant satisfaction and to a measure of output. The norms of these groups sanctioned a "take-charge" chairman. When the chairman failed to meet these expectations, he was rejected and both group satisfaction and group output suffered. These studies do not necessarily suggest that committees less concerned with task goals also prefer a directive chairman. Where the committees are composed of more socially oriented members, the preference for leader control may be less strong.[29]

Leadership Roles   A second approach to understanding the leadership of committees is to investigate leadership roles in small groups. Pervading the research literature is a basic distinction between group activities directed to one or the other of two types of roles performed by leaders. They are defined by Benne and Sheats[30] as task roles, and as group-building and maintenance roles. Task roles are related to the direct accomplishment of group purpose, such as seeking information, initiating, evaluating, and seeking or giving opinion. The latter roles are concerned with group integration and solidarity through encouraging, harmonizing, compromising, and reducing conflict.

Several empirical investigations of leadership have demonstrated that both roles are usually performed within effective groups.[31] However, these roles are not always performed by the same person. Frequently one member is seen as the "task leader" and another as the "social leader" of the group.

Combined Task and Social Roles   Can or should these roles be combined in a single leader? The prototypes of the formal and the informal leader which we inherit from classical management lore tend to lead to the conclusion that such a combination is somehow impossible or perhaps undesirable. The research literature occasionally supports this point of view as well.

There is much to be said for a combination of roles. Several studies have shown that outstanding leaders are those who possess both task and social orientations.[32] The study by Borgotta, Couch, and Bales illustrates the point. These researchers assigned leaders high on both characteristics to problem-solving groups. The eleven leaders whom they called "great men" were selected from 126 in an experiment on the basis of high task ability, individual assertiveness, and social acceptability. These men also retained their ratings as "great men" throughout a series of different problem-solving sessions. When led by "great men" the groups achieved a higher rate of suggestion and agreement, a lower rate of "showing tension," and higher rates of showing solidarity and tension release than comparable groups without "great men."

When viewed collectively two conclusions emerge from the above studies. Consistent with existing opinion, the leader who is somewhat assertive and who takes charge and controls group proceedings is performing a valid and necessary role. However, such task leadership is a necessary but not a sufficient condition for effective committee performance. Someone in the group must perform the role of group-builder and maintainer of social relations among the members. Ideally both roles should probably be performed by the designated chairman. When he does not have the necessary skills to perform both roles, he should be the task leader and someone else should perform the social leadership role. Effective committee performance requires both roles to be performed, by a single person or by complementary performance of two or more members.

Committee Membership

The atmosphere of committee operations described in the classic literature is one where all members seem to be cooperating in the achievement of committee purpose. It is unclear, however, if cooperation is necessarily the best method of solving problems, or if competition among members or groups of members might not achieve more satisfactory results. Cooperation also seems to imply a sharing or homogeneity of values. To answer the question we must consider two related problems: the effects of cooperation or competition on committee effectiveness, and the effects of homogeneous or heterogeneous values on committee effectiveness.

Cooperation or Competition

A number of studies have contrasted the impact of competition and cooperation on group satisfaction and productivity. In some cases the group is given a cooperative or competitive "treatment" through direction or incentive when it is established. In others, competition and cooperation are inferred from measures of groups in which members are operating primarily for personal interest, in contrast with groups in which members are more concerned with group needs. These studies show rather consistently that "group members who have been motivated to cooperate show more positive responses to each other, are more favorable in their perceptions, are more involved in the task, and have greater satisfaction with the task."[33]

The best known study regarding the effects of cooperation and competition was conducted by Deutsch[34] in ten experimental groups of college students, each containing five persons. Each group met for one three-hour period a week for six weeks, working on puzzles and human relations problems. Subjects completed a weekly and post-experimental questionnaire. Observers also recorded interactions and completed over-all rating scales at the end of each problem.

In some groups, a cooperative atmosphere was established by instructing members that the group as a whole would be evaluated in comparison with four similar groups, and that each person's course grade would depend upon the performance of the group itself. In others, a competitive relationship was established by telling the members that each would receive a different grade, depending upon his relative contribution to the group's problem solutions.

The results, as summarized by Hare, show that: "Compared with the competitively organized groups, the cooperative groups had the following characteristics:

(1) Stronger individual motivation to complete the group task and stronger feelings of obligation toward other members.

(2) Greater division of labor both in content and frequency of interaction among members and greater coordination of effort.

(3) More effective inter-member communication. More ideas were verbalized, members were more attentive to one another, and more accepting of and affected by each other's ideas. Members also rated themselves as having fewer difficulties in communicating and understanding others.

(4) More friendliness was expressed in the discussion and members rated themselves higher on strength of desire to win the respect of one another. Members were also more satisfied with the group and its products.

(5) More group productivity. Puzzles were solved faster and the recommendations produced for the human-relations problems were longer and qualitatively better. However, there were no significant differences in the average individual productivity as a result of the two types of group experience nor were there any clear differences in the amounts of individual learning which occurred during the discussions."[35]

Similar evidence was found in the study of 72 decision-making conferences by Fouriezos, Hutt, and Guetzkow.[36] Based on observer ratings of self-oriented need behavior, correlational evidence showed that such self-centered behavior was positively related to participant ratings of high group conflict and negatively related to participant satisfaction, group solidarity, and task productivity.

In general, the findings of these and other studies suggest that groups in which members share in goal attainment, rather than compete privately or otherwise seek personal needs, will be more satisfied and productive.[37]

Homogeneity or Heterogeneity

The effects of member composition in the committee should also be considered from the standpoint of the homogeneity or heterogeneity of its membership. Homogeneous groups are those in which members are similar in personality, value orientation, attitudes to supervision, or predisposition to accept or reject fellow members. Heterogeneity is induced in the group by creating negative expectations regarding potential contributions by fellow members, by introducing differing personality types into the group, or by creating subgroups which differ in their basis of attraction to the group.

Here the evidence is much less clear. Some homogeneous groups become satisfied and quite unproductive, while others become satisfied and quite productive. Similarly, heterogeneity may be shown to lead to both productive and unproductive conditions. While the answer to this paradox may be related to the different definitions of homogeneity or heterogeneity in the studies, it appears to have greater relevance to the task and interpersonal requirements of the group task.

In some studies, homogeneity clearly leads to more effective group performance. The work of Schutz[38] is illustrative. In his earlier writing, Schutz distinguished between two types of interpersonal relationships: power orientation and personal orientation. The first emphasizes authority symbols. The power-oriented person follows rules and adjusts to external systems of authority. People with personal orientations emphasize interpersonal considerations. They assume that the way a person achieves his goal is by working within a framework of close personal relations, that is, by being a "good guy," by liking others, by getting people to like him. In his later work, Schutz[39] distinguished among three types of needs: *inclusion*, or the need to establish and maintain a satisfactory relation with people with respect to interaction and association; *control*, or the need to establish and maintain a satisfactory relation with people with respect to control and power; and *affection*, or the need to establish and maintain a satisfactory relation with others with respect to love and affection.

Using attitude scales, Schutz established four groups in which people were compatible with respect to high needs for personal relations with others, four whose members were compatible with respect to low personal orientation, and four which contained subgroups differing in these needs. Each of the twelve groups met twelve times over a period of six weeks and participated in a series of different tasks.

The results showed that groups which are compatible, either on a basis of personalness or counterpersonalness, were significantly more productive than groups which had incompatible subgroups. There was no significant difference between the productivity of the two types of compatible groups. As might be expected, the difference in productivity between compatible and incompatible groups was greatest for tasks which required the most interaction and agreement under conditions of high-time pressure.

A similar positive relationship between homogeneity and productivity is reported for groups in which compatibility is established on the basis of prejudice or degree of conservatism, managerial personality traits, congeniality induced by directions from the researcher, or status congruence.[40] In Adams' study, technical performance first increased, then decreased, as status congruence became greater. Group social performance increased continuously with greater homogeneity, however.

The relationship posited above does not always hold, however. In some studies, heterogeneous groups were more productive than homogeneous. For example, Hoffman[41] constructed heterogeneous and homogeneous groups, based on personality profiles, and had them work on two different types of problems. On the first, which required consideration of a wide range of alternatives of a rather specific nature, heterogeneous groups produced significantly superior solutions. On the second problem, which required primarily group consensus and had no objectively "good" solution, the difference between group types was not significant. Ziller[42] also found heterogeneity to be associated with the ability of Air Force crews to judge the number of dots on a card.

Collins and Guetzkow[43] explain these contradictory findings by suggesting that increasing heterogeneity has at least two effects on group interaction: it increases the difficulty of building interpersonal relations, and it increases the problem-solving potential of the group, since errors are eliminated, more alternatives are generated, and wider criticism is possible. Thus, heterogeneity would seem to be valuable where the needs for task facilitation are greater than the need for strong interpersonal relations.

Considering our original question, it appears that, from the standpoint of cooperation versus competition in committees, the cooperative committee is to be preferred. If we look at the effects of homogeneous or heterogeneous committee membership, the deciding factor seems to be the nature of the task and the degree of interpersonal conflict which the committee can tolerate.

Summary and Conclusions

Research findings regarding committee size, leadership, and membership have been reviewed. Evidence has been cited showing that the ideal size is five, when the five members possess the necessary skills to solve the problems facing the committee. Viewed from the standpoint of the committee members' ability to attend to both the group and its members, or from the standpoint of balanced interpersonal needs, it seems safe to suggest that this number has normative value in planning committee operations. For technical problems additional members may be added to ensure the provision of necessary skills.

A second area of investigation concerned the functional separation of the leadership role and the influence of the role on other members. The research reviewed supports the notion that the committee chairman should be directive in his leadership, but a more specific definition of leadership roles makes questionable whether the chairman can or should perform as both the task and the social leader of the group. The evidence regarding the latter indicates that combined task and social leadership is an ideal which is seldom attained, but should be sought.

The final question concerned whether committee membership would be most effective when cooperative or competitive. When evaluated from the standpoint of research on cooperative versus competitive groups, it is clear that cooperative membership is more desirable. Committee operation can probably be enhanced by selecting members whose self-centered needs are of a less intense variety and by directions to the group which strengthen motivations of a cooperative nature. When the proposition is evaluated from the standpoint of heterogeneity or homogeneity of group membership, the conclusion is less clear. Apparently, heterogeneity in a group can produce both ideas and a screening process for evaluating their quality, but the advantage of this process depends upon the negative effects of heterogeneous attitudes upon interpersonal cooperation.

References

1. Rollie Tillman, Jr. "Problems in Review: Committees on Trial." *Harvard Business Review*, 38 (May–June 1960), 6–12; 162–172. Firms with 1001 to 10,000 reported 93 percent use; 250 to 1000 reported 82 percent use.
2. J. H. Healey. *Executive Coordination and Control.* Monograph No. 78 (Columbus: Bureau of Business Research, The Ohio State University, 1956), p. 185.
3. "Committees." *Management Review*, 46 (October 1957), 4–10; 75–78.
4. M. Kriesberg. "Executives Evaluate Administrative Conferences." *Advanced Management*, 15 (March 1950), 15–17.
5. Tillman. *op. cit.*, 12.
6. Kriesberg, *op. cit.*, 15.
7. "The Committee System—Congress at Work." *Congressional Digest*, 34 (February 1955), 47–49; 64.
8. E. H. Taves. "Two Mechanisms for the Perception of Visual Numerousness." *Archives of Psychology*, 37 (1941), 265.
9. A. Paul Hare. *Handbook of Small Group Research.* (New York: The Free Press of Glencoe, 1962), p. 227.
10. B. M. Bass, and F. M. Norton. "Group Size and Leaderless Discussions." *Journal of Applied Psychology*, 35 (1951), 397–400.
11. Hare. *op. cit.*, 228.
12. R. F. Bales, F. L. Strodtbeck, T. M. Mills, and M. E. Roseborough. "Channels of Communication in Small Groups." *American Sociological Review*, 16, (1951), 461–468.
13. F. F. Stephen and E. G. Mishler. "The Distribution of Participation in Small Groups: An Exponential Approximation." *American Sociological Review*, 17 (1952), 598–608.
14. J. R. Gibb. "The Effects of Group Size and of Threat Reduction Upon Creativity in a Problem-Solving Situation." *American Psychologist*, 6 (1951), 324. (Abstract)
15. P. Slater. "Contrasting Correlates of Group Size." *Sociometry*, 21 (1958), 129–139.
16. R. F. Bales, and E. F. Borgotta. "Size of Group as a Factor in the Interaction Profile." In *Small Groups: Studies in Social Interaction*, A. P. Hare, E. F. Borgotta, and R. F. Bales, eds. (New York: Knopf, 1965, rev. ed.), pp. 495–512.
17. *Ibid.*, 512.
18. Slater, *op. cit.*, 137–138.
19. R. F. Bales. "In Conference." *Harvard Business Review*, 32 (March–April 1954), 44–50; Also A. P. Hare. "A Study of Interaction and Consensus in Different Sized Groups." *American Sociological Review*, 17 (1952), 261–267.
20. D. Fox, I. Lorge, P. Weltz, and K. Herrold. "Comparison of Decisions Written by Large and Small Groups." *American Psychologist*, 8 (1953), 351. (Abstract)
21. A. Paul Hare. "Interaction and Consensus in Different Sized Groups." *American Sociological Review*, 17 (1952), 261–267.

22. G. B. Watson. "Do Groups Think More Efficiently Than Individuals?" *Journal of Abnormal and Social Psychology,* 23 (1928), 328–336; Also D. J. Taylor and W. L. Faust. "Twenty Questions: Efficiency in Problem Solving as a Function of Size of Group." *Journal of Experimental Psychology,* 44 (1952), 360–368.

23. Tillman. *op. cit.,* 168.

24. S. L. Udall. "Defense of the Seniority System," *New York Times Magazine* (January 13, 1957), 17.

25. L. Schlesinger, J. M. Jackson, and J. Butman. "Leader-Member Interaction in Management Committees." *Journal of Abnormal and Social Psychology,* 61, No. 3 (1960) 360–364.

26. *Ibid.,* 363.

27. L. Berkowitz. "Sharing Leadership in Small Decision-Making Groups." *Journal of Abnormal and Social Psychology,* 48 (1953), 231–238; Also N. T. Fouriezos, M. L. Hutt, and H. Guetzkow. "Measurement of Self-Oriented Needs in Discussion Groups." *Journal of Abnormal and Social Psychology,* 45 (1950), 682–690; Also H. P. Shelley. "Status Consensus, Leadership, and Satisfaction with the Group." *Journal of Social Psychology,* 51 (1960), 157–164.

28. Berkowitz. *Ibid.,* 237.

29. R. C. Anderson. "Learning in Discussions: A Resume of the Authoritarian-Democratic Studies." *Harvard Education Review,* 29 (1959), 201–214.

30. K. D. Benne, and P. Sheats. "Functional Roles of Group Members." *Journal of Social Issues,* 4 (Spring 1948), 41–49.

31. R. F. Bales. *Interaction Process Analysis* (Cambridge: Addison-Wesley, 1951); Also R. M. Stogdill and A. E. Coons (eds.), *Leader Behavior: Its Description and Measurement,* Monograph No. 88 (Columbus: Bureau of Business Research, The Ohio State University, 1957); Also A. W. Halpin. "The Leadership Behavior and Combat Performance of Airplane Commanders." *Journal of Abnormal and Social Psychology,* 49 (1954), 19–22.

32. E. G. Borgotta, A. S. Couch, and R. F. Bales. "Some Findings Relevant to the Great Man Theory of Leadership." *American Sociological Review,* 19 (1954), 755–759; Also E. A. Fleishman, and E. G. Harris. "Patterns of Leadership Behavior Related to Employee Grievances and Turnover." *Personnel Psychology,* 15, No. 1 (1962), 43–56; Also Stogdill and Coons, *Ibid.;* Also H. Oaklander and E. A. Fleishman. "Patterns of Leadership Related to Organizational Stress in Hospital Settings." *Administrative Science Quarterly,* 8 (March 1964), 520–532.

33. Hare. *Handbook of Small Group Research, op. cit.,* 254.

34. M. Deutsch. "The Effects of Cooperation and Competition Upon Group Process." In *Group Dynamics, Research and Theory,* D. Cartwright and A. Zander, eds., (New York: Harper and Row, 1953).

35. Hare. *Handbook of Small Group Research, op. cit.,* 263.

36. Fouriezos, Hutt, and Guetzkow. *op. cit.*

37. C. Stendler, D. Damrin and A. Haines. "Studies in Cooperation and Competition: I. The Effects of Working for Group and Individual Rewards on the Social Climate of Children's Groups." *Journal of Genetic Psychology,* 79 (1951), 173–197; Also A. Mintz. "Nonadaptive Group Behavior." *Journal of Abnormal and Social Psychology,* 46 (1951), 150–159; Also M. M. Grossack. "Some Effects of Cooperation and Competition Upon Small Group Behavior." *Journal of Abnormal and Social Psychology,* 49 (1954), 341–348; Also E. Gottheil. "Changes in Social Perceptions Contingent Upon Competing or Cooperating." *Sociometry,* 18 (1955), 132–137; Also A. Zander and D. Wolfe. "Administrative Rewards and Coordination Among Committee Members." *Administrative Science Quarterly,* 9 (June 1964), 50–69.

38. W. C. Schutz. "What Makes Groups Productive?" *Human Relations,* 8 (1955), 429–465.

39. W. C. Schutz. *FIRO: A Three-Dimensional Theory of Interpersonal Behavior.* (New York: Holt, Rinehart and Winston, 1958).

40. I. Altman and E. McGinnies. "Interpersonal Perception and Communication in Discussion Groups of Varied Attitudinal Composition." *Journal of Abnormal and Social Psychology,* 60 (May 1960), 390–393; Also W. A. Haythorn, E. H. Couch, D. Haefner, P. Langham and L. Carter. "The Behavior of Authoritarian and Equalitarian Personalities in Groups." *Human Relations,* 9 (1956), 57–74; Also E. E. Ghiselli and T. M. Lodahl. "Patterns of Managerial Traits and Group Effectiveness." *Journal of Abnormal and Social Psychology,* 57 (1958), 61–66; Also R. V. Exline. "Group Climate as a Factor in the Relevance and Accuracy of Social Perception." *Journal of Abnormal and Social Psychology,* 55 (1957), 382–388; Also S. Adams. "Status Congruency as a Variable in Small Group Performance." *Social Forces,* 32 (1953), 16–22.

41. L. R. Hoffman. "Homogeneity of Member Personality and Its Effect on Group Problem-Solving. *Journal of Abnormal and Social Psychology,* 58 (1959), 27–32.

42. R. C. Ziller. "Scales of Judgment: A Determinant of Accuracy of Group Decisions." *Human Relations,* 8 (1955), 153–164.

43. B. E. Collins and H. Guetzkow. *A Social Psychology of Group Process for Decision-Making.* (New York: John Wiley and Sons, 1965), p. 101.

Questions for Discussion

1. Years ago, managers, industrial engineers, and personnel psychologists tended to criticize work groups for "irrationally" forgoing opportunities to make more money on incentive jobs by restricting production. How might such output restriction actually be "rational"?

2. What factors affect whether or not a person will conform to his group's expectations?

3. Describe a situation where you were (or someone you observed was) subjected to group pressures to conform. How did the group enforce discipline? Did it work? Why?

4. Describe groups with which you are familiar that could be characterized as apathetic, erratic, strategic, and conservative with respect to an authority structure?

5. How do we all depart from being "ideally rational" in our decision making?

6. Under what circumstances would you prefer individual decisions to group decisions?

7. Under what circumstances would you prefer group decisions to individual decisions?

8. In a comparative study of managerial attitudes, U.S. and German business managers were generally skeptical of group participation in decision making. In contrast, Japanese business managers and U.S. Foreign Service officers favored group decision making. How would you explain these contrasting views?

9. What factors seem to affect group performance in decision making?

10. What advantages *might* the Delphi decision-making technique have over face-to-face group communication and decision making?

11. Why might groups be willing to reach more risky decisions than individuals?

12. How and at what stage of decision making is the group sometimes helpful to the individual decision maker? When does the group tend to interfere?

Short Cases for Discussion

Flying High at Findley Wholesale Distributors Inc.

Oliver Findley considered himself a community-minded businessman. In spite of the deteriorating and crime-ridden area around his warehouse and office in North Philadelphia, Findley had rejected his personnel manager's suggestion that the company relocate to a modern facility in Bucks County. Most of his customers were in the city, although his suburban business was expanding more rapidly. More important, Findley wanted to provide jobs for local community residents. Yet, as his personnel manager pointed out, in spite of the substantial unemployment in the area (as much as 30% of all black youths 16–25), it was difficult to obtain permanent and reliable help. Since much of the goods handled were fragile, pilferable, or both, good employees were essential—especially on the evening shift when there was less supervision.

As a solution to his personnel problems and because he thought they deserved special consideration, Mr. Findley began to seek out local Vietnam veterans. He figured they would be more mature and stable—and perhaps more grateful for work. He soon had a total of 21 warehousemen: 14 blacks and 7 whites. About half were fairly recently discharged servicemen. He also hired two local college students who worked only on the evening shift.

Although the men did not turn out to be quite as reliable as he had hoped, Findley had no major complaints. Evening-shift work still lagged in productivity, however. Some of the foremen griped about a certain listlessness and horseplay, but nothing seemed dramatically wrong. Tom Smidt, one of his oldest foremen, commented that things were better now than in the old days, when there was much drinking before the men came to work and even during working hours. Tom said he had no problem with this anymore.

In late March, Mr. Findley's son, Oliver Jr., was having a coke in the student center at the University, where he was a junior. Charles Murray, one of the students who worked part-time for Mr. Findley, came up and joined him.

Ollie: Hey man, how's it going?

Chuck: I'm beat. Studying, working, and playing around has got me fagged out.

Ollie: Oh, my old man doesn't work you that hard.

Chuck: Maybe it's the fooling around that we do down there. Some of those 'Nam veterans are wild. I'll tell ya, we've flown high some nights down there when things go slow.

Ollie: I'd better tell my square pop that you guys are taking a few puffs and goofing off.

Chuck: Listen, don't say a thing. We only fool around when things are slow. We get the work out when we have to. Besides, I thought Acapulco Gold was great stuff, but some of that Saigon weed really beats it. Maybe I can fix you up!

On Thursday, May 21, at 11:30 p.m., Oliver Findley was sitting in the study of his comfortable Main Line home. He was a little concerned about Oliver Jr. being out in his new car after the argument they had had earlier that evening. It was the same old things: Ollie's hair, President Nixon, the war, and so on. As Findley rose from his desk to look out the window, the telephone rang. It was a very rare call from foreman Tom Smidt at the warehouse. Tom was obviously upset.

Tom: Boss, you'd better get down here right away. It's a mess!
Findley: What is, Tom? What's the problem?
Tom: Willy's been hurt bad. He's bleeding something awful. It was that lift truck. Those S.O.B.'s. I wish they'd . . . !
Findley: O.K. Tom, take it easy. Call the ambulance. I'll be there in 30 minutes.
Tom: They're on the way. Hurry up please.

As Findley drove into Philadelphia, he was annoyed and concerned. Upon arrival, Tom was talking to a police officer. They told Findley that the ambulance had just left with Willy Washington, who had been run over by a fork lift truck. It seemed that Roosevelt James and Chuck Murray had been racing their trucks when James' vehicle went out of control, running over the unfortunate Willy, who had been sleeping behind some cartons next to the weighing scale. Both of his legs received compound fractures.

While Findley, Smidt, and the officer were talking, another man came up. It was Sgt. O'Connell of the special narcotics squad. He reported that marijuana cigarettes had been found on Washington, and that a sobbing Chuck Murray had spilled out a tale of pot, being high, and just having some fun to pass away the long evening.

Findley drove home later with a heavy heart. Ringing in his ears was Sgt. O'Connell's matter-of-fact retelling of Murray's troubled confessions, along with Tom Smidt's apparently sincere protestations that he knew nothing about such things going on.

Question

Discuss the various social norms in this incident. Should Ollie have done anything?

Managerial Attitudes Toward Group
Influence and Decision Making

As part of a larger survey of managerial attitudes,* thousands of managers in many nations and organizations have responded to the following questions:

*M. Haire, E. Ghiselli, and L. Porter, *Managerial Thinking*, Wiley, 1966.

a) "In a work situation, if the subordinates cannot influence me, then I lose some influence on them" (check one).

| strongly agree | agree | undecided | disagree | strongly disagree |

b) "Group goal setting offers advantages that cannot be obtained by individual goal setting."

| strongly agree | agree | undecided | disagree | strongly disagree |

Haire, Ghiselli, and Porter suggest that agreement with these statements indicates a "democratic" belief in the desirability of subordinate participation in managerial decision making. Disagreement indicates an "autocratic" attitude.

We have given the same questionnaire to many additional managers, with results supplementing those of the original international study. On the axis shown in Exhibit 1, you will find a summary of some samples.

Our sample of managers in the Motorola Corporation agrees with Haire, Ghiselli, and Porter's larger sample of U.S. business managers; thus the questionnaire tends to be verified. The U.S. State Department sample includes several hundred Foreign Service officers in the lower and middle ranks. The Bata Shoe Company is a large multinational firm headquartered in Canada, but manufacturing and selling in many nations. The executives sampled were the company

Exhibit 1   Managerial Attitudes

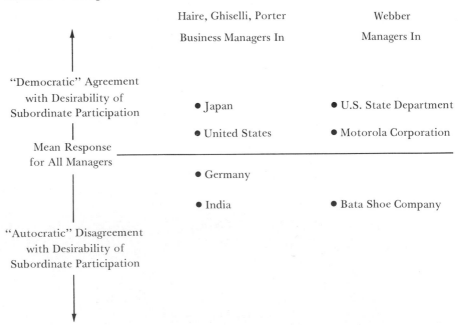

heads in various nations—the majority of which were relatively poor and still in the early stages of development.

The State Department agreement with the desirability of subordinate decision making is markedly different from all U.S. business managers questioned (including some not summarized on the diagram).

Question

Discuss why these managers might hold these attitudes toward group decision making and subordinate participation—particularly Bata and the State Department as compared with Motorola.

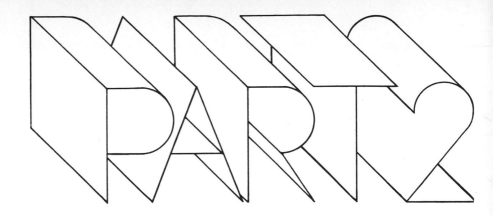

PART 2

TECHNOLOGY, STRUCTURE, AND ADMINISTRATION

Chapter 6

Tasks, Technology and Structure

Of the major factors that determine how people behave in organizations, this chapter takes up three powerful ones—the individual task to be done, the network of tasks tied to the organization's goal, and the authority and decision-making (coordinating) structure which exists in some form in all organizations. These factors are of equal importance with the factors already discussed if we are to gain a comprehensive understanding of the way people behave in complex organizations.

It hardly seems necessary to say that the work of a sales manager for Procter & Gamble is bound to influence his actions in certain ways. And these influences will be different from those which affect a factory employee for General Motors or a research chemist for the Food and Drug Administration. Likewise, a mechanical engineering student at Purdue is bound to have somewhat different motivations in his daily life than a law student at Michigan, a medical student at Indiana, or a forestry student at Oregon. Thus it is the purpose of this chapter to show how the individual task to be done, the network of tasks together, and the coordinating structure of the organization act as important influencers on organizational behavior.

Individual Jobs and Motivation

The accomplishment of any joint goal (except purely personal and social goals) requires some kind of rational relating of the work of one person to that of another. The most familiar way in which such specialized tasks are evident in business firms is the production line. Certainly the task of fitting the headlights to an automobile must be coordinated with prior tasks of assembling the chassis.

Originally, when organizations were very small, each individual performed a much more meaningful (to him) operation in the total organizational effort. If one could have watched Henry Ford and his work force building the first automobile, or Donald Douglas and his work force building the first DC-1 transport, there would have been considerable richness of problem solving, initiative, and skill exercised by the men on those projects, as compared with the thousands of specialists who produce today's Pintos or DC-10 jets. The dilemma faced in today's automobile and aircraft companies is illustrated forcefully if we imagine two people arguing the merits of Douglas of old versus Douglas today. "Today's aircraft production lines are reducing men to robots," says one man in this Platonic dialogue. "The work team back then, with Douglas and his men putting together an airplane in his garage shop, enabled the whole team, mechanics and engineer alike, to use their minds and become involved."

"But," answers the other man, "don't forget that Douglas in that garage couldn't produce a 747 jet transport. It has four and a half million parts."

A wealth of research and common sense supports the fact that large organizations in the industrial world of the 1970s do indeed involve people in specialized tasks and that, if the world wants advanced technology, one of the prices it pays is less satisfaction for people at work, especially at lower levels of the organization. The work of Douglas McGregor (1960) points to the futility of the "carrot and stick" form of compensation, under which salary and pay are used, in effect, to say "here is a specialized and meaningless job for which we will offer you money rewards. If you will spend eight hours a day doing something that does not offer intrinsic satisfaction, you may earn pensions for your old age and money to spend on holidays and weekends." The work of Argyris (1957) moved one step further, to argue that people in such jobs have a way of reacting to such frustrations. They may become aggressive toward the organization, or simply apathetic and disinterested. This sets in motion a chain reaction—an escalation of conflict between workers and managers. The managers look at such workers and think "people just don't seem to want to work. What is needed are more job studies, higher pay, and more rules." According to Argyris, this not only misses the cause of the problem, but actually compounds it. It offers more rules and technical planning handed down from above. Sooner or later, as workers and managers make successive counter moves, nobody really wins. The organization becomes a conflict arena in which labor battles management, or it becomes an apathetic place where people care little for satisfying work or for accomplishment of organization goals.

Organizations as Satisfiers of Needs

The other side of the dilemma in this case is that a person who lives in an industrial world needs an organization. He depends on an organization for his physical livelihood, for security of his loved ones, for a sense of accomplishment, or for many other needs. He also depends on an organization for the pleasure of social contact—working with other people on a project.

This need for organization can be seen even in primitive tribes, as many anthropological studies have shown. Fishermen in less developed island economies do in fact work, specialize, and socialize with their friends as they work together. It can also be shown by some of the more successful communes in present-day America. Those that survive involve more than love and friendship. They also involve working together on tasks and projects—both for a feeling of accomplishment and for the economic security of providing food and shelter.

The problem in modern, complex industrial organizations, then, is to find some way of providing tasks that men can use *themselves* as vehicles for getting what they want. Later we discuss some of the ways this might be done. One of the things we are most interested in in this chapter are the underlying motivational forces that accompany various types of job design—extreme specialization and meaningless jobs on the one hand, and enriched and meaningful tasks on the other.

Another way of stating our present objective is that the very first step in making work more satisfying is for the manager to be fully aware that there are two kinds of task structures available for designing a job (and writing the job description), and that each causes different motivational forces which act on the job holder.

In terms of both the attention it has attracted in the field of industrial psychology and the extent to which real-world business organizations have made use of it, the "motivation-hygiene" model developed by Herzberg (1968) must be included in any consideration of how jobs affect human beings. The theory can be criticized because factors other than the job itself (age, sex, level of education, level in the organization) might alter how well it works in any given situation. But there is enough fundamental truth in it that managers should take it seriously when designing jobs in organizations.

One thing Herzberg discovered that a person will work for, based on what it means in his life—i.e., which of his needs it satisfies—Herzberg calls "hygiene" factors. They meet the primary needs discussed in Chapter 1, and thus provide the necessary hygiene for the person to survive, exist, and be ready to go on to higher order accomplishment. A man who liked to ski (a higher order accomplishment) would have no hope unless he was healthy and possessed the necessary equipment. Therefore, he will be motivated to work, eat well, take exercise, and do a host of other things simply to *avoid* being in such an unhealthy physical and economic state that he has little hope of pursuing a positive accomplishment.

It is important to recognize that lower order needs are significant, and that hygiene factors are vital parts of total motivation in the organization. For example, take the necessity for a steady job. Organizations that provide some security and safety of employment are superior to those that hire a person today and fire him tomorrow. Or, take the example of pension plans. Organizations that pay pensions to workers when they are old and feeble are superior to those which use up the strength of a worker's best years and then dump him in the streets to beg or die when he is old.

Tasks as Satisfiers of Needs

In the U.S.A. today, however, we see many people who laugh at the idea of a steady job with a corporation, or at the idea of an employee pension plan which ties the employee to the organization. Why? Because the same things which are necessary to *avoid dissatisfaction* (avoid threat to primary needs) are not the same things people pursue for *positive* satisfaction. The skier does not brush his teeth and take exercise because all he wants from life are good teeth or muscles. (Can you imagine him sitting in a room day after day admiring his teeth and flexing his muscles?) And employees do not work from nine to five every day from age twenty to age fifty only to have a steady job and food when they are sixty-five.

The conditions under which a person may value his basic health and security are ones which enable him to attain higher order things out of life—to be involved and responsible, to feel inside that "I've done something worthwhile," to grow in ability and skill to cope with life. These factors Herzberg termed "motivating" factors. And they are realized in the jobs, tasks, and endeavors that are performed at work.

In the article accompanying this chapter, Herzberg shows that many jobs might be enriched by designing them in a way that builds into the job itself opportunities for feelings of responsibility, feelings of personal achievement, and learning important new skills for the future ("growing"). Two points need clarifying: his concept of vertical job loading (job enrichment); and the fact that job specialization can sometimes be highly rewarding.

Vertical job loading, or job enrichment, involves taking some task which might formerly have been done at higher levels in the organization and placing it within a standardized job that is creating very little feeling of accomplishment. For example, in the service department of a large automobile dealer, we might find a number of mechanics specializing in one kind of repair: brakes, cylinder blocks, tires, and so on. The head of the maintenance shop meets the customer as he drives in and discusses with him the nature of repair needed. He then does the job of deciding what repair to make, and passes on written orders— "replace carburetor" or "adjust carburetor"—to the man who specializes in fuel-system problems.

In order to enrich the latter job, the management of the dealership might well consider having the mechanic who does the work also perform part of the diagnosis of the problem. Procedures and job description might require that he be called to consult with the customer and decide what is causing the problem: to use his head (instead of the department manager's) in relating customer needs to mechanical activities. He might also acquire interpersonal skills for dealing with the public (instead of spending all of his time standing over a machine).

This is just one example of the meaning of job enrichment. Others, including the way job design might be applied to higher management positions via decentralization, are discussed later.

The other point for clarification is that not all job specialization lessens worker satisfaction. If the specialized task assigned to a person offers opportunity for future growth and success, it might result in improved motivation, not just increased efficiency. For example, a group of young women in a typing pool of a large pharmaceutical company had been typing miscellaneous letters and reports from scientists. Later, when management specialized the tasks of this department so that some women typed medical research materials and others typed letters to scientists in other institutions, both groups of women felt that their ability to find satisfying work in the future was increased because of the specialty. "There are much better jobs for medical secretaries and medical researchers than there are for run-of-the-mill typists," one said. "I hope to make a career of clerical and administrative work in a large medical school, and this job enables me to learn more of the knowledge and skill for that." Notice, however, that the common element which enriches jobs—whether it follows from moving from diverse duties to specialization, or from specialization to more diverse duties—is inclusion within the task of some subtask that is significant in the world outside the workplace. In the mechanic's case, he could use his head to relate customer needs to his knowledge of automobiles. In the medical typist's case, she could acquire skills now which would be useful in another job later.

Technology and Behavior

The job is one important influence on behavior, but there is another and more complex factor that must also be considered. It is *technology*, or the entire network of jobs taken together, along with the organization goal. This is a somewhat elusive concept, but in essence is quite simple. Let us take an example from sports in order to illustrate it.

Football is a game invented at some point but which has evolved over the years. It requires a ball of a certain shape. Nobody can play American football with a round object. It requires goal posts of certain measurements, placed geographically. Nobody can play football with a tennis net strung over the fifty-yard line. It is played by a team facing another team. Nobody could play football with two men using swords and face masks in a gymnasium. The goal is to run the ball over the goal line or to kick it between goal posts. Nobody could play football if he decided that the team should go fishing.

Up to this point, we should recognize that the technology of football requires a conscious objective (organization goal), that this objective in turn requires specifically and rationally designed capital equipment (ball, goals), and specifically trained manpower (the team). All three must exist as a total entity. Not only that, but they are related in a special way. The manpower and the equipment are means to an end. Teams and balls are means to scoring across the goal line. They are interdependent.

As the game has developed, there have come to be certain specialized tasks which make scoring easier. The team has a better chance of succeeding at what it sets out to do if one man is assigned to the position of guard, another to the position of center, and another to the position of quarterback. The job of each man must not only be performed in a certain way (the center passes the ball between his legs, he does not throw it over his shoulder), but many of the jobs must be performed in a certain time sequence (the guards must block on the scrimmage line before the passer can successfully throw the ball).

Two more elements of technology now emerge. First, there is a specialization of tasks. This particular *pattern of specialization* (guards, tackles, quarterbacks), rather than some other pattern, is related to final success as a means to a larger end. Second, there is a *pattern of interrelationships* that govern the quality of one job and the timing of it in relation to others. In other organizations, these are sometimes called rules or procedures.

The total taken together, along with the capital equipment and manpower, is the technology of football. It is a rationally integrated system of a final goal with a network of subparts and procedures to connect the parts. If any part is missing, or operates in a way not in accord with the logical design of the system, either there is no football game at all, or both the *team* and each *individual* player in his own job are less successful. This is to say that if technology is not present, the members of a team cannot "win." Furthermore, if both teams have sloppy technology, society (the public) cannot "win" either. Technology thus becomes a requirement of achievement for both people working in organizations and for people who depend on them.

Technology, Achievement, and Competence: A Simple Example

Imagine a college student who has the physical skill and mental desire for sports. Furthermore, his physical and mental characteristics tell him that football is the place that offers most satisfaction (tennis and basketball do not seem to fit as well). Suppose that he tries out and begins to play at a university with a good team, and that his position is quarterback. Everyone else is well trained. They are good at their own specializations, they work hard to know the interrelationships—the rules, the plays, the procedures. Our quarterback's achievement can come from three sources. One has to do with his own job or doing his own thing. Second, he is enabled to be a quarterback only because others are doing their own things. The third has to do with the organization's goal. He feels good when the team wins. The first of these sources of achievement is *personal accomplishment* and the other two are *organizational accomplishment.*

Now, imagine our man in another situation. He goes to a school offering only club football and is asked to play with a group of men with good physical characteristics but who have played little football. They are not "specialists" simply because no real technology exists. There is the usual snapping of the ball from the center, but the line is uncertain as to which way to run, how to block, or when to execute various plays. There may still be the social satisfaction of playing with friendly people, but there is very much less chance that our man can feel a sense of *personal* achievement in his own *individual* task. He may have been the greatest quarterback in the nation, but he cannot be as competent or achieve as much in his own eyes as in the previous situation. Nor can he ever feel the achievement that comes with winning games *as a team.* In short, the technology of football, though it may constrain his freedom to do as he pleases on the field, is an absolute requirement if he is to use his own abilities to feel competent and to feel high levels of achievement in this part of his life.

Notice that the technology of football is separate and distinct from the technology of basketball or tennis. They require different specializations for participants, different rules and procedures to govern the *interrelationships* of the players, and different capital equipment. But they cannot escape having technologies. And the performance of a basketball guard—his sense of personal competence and achievement—is bound to be affected by (1) the existence of a technology, and (2) every participant's reasonable compliance with it. The same can be said for the violinist in a symphony orchestra, the loader of an oceangoing ship at a dock, and the research chemist working in a large pharmaceutical company.

Technology and Other Values in Life

Before showing how the above analysis applies in complex organizations, there is an important question which should be answered. Do, in fact, many people place their jobs and careers foremost in their lives, relative to such other satisfactions as they gain from leisure, recreation, giving and receiving affection in the family, or engaging in social activities?

People do differ in this respect. Some are more career-oriented than others. The level and nature of jobs also differ in the extent to which they provide a sense of achievement (the studies reported later deal mostly with managers at all levels). Nevertheless, we can predict a considerable increase in the *probability* that all persons in an organization, from top to bottom, will feel competence and achievement in their work lives if organizations are technologically structured for success in each employee's own job, and success of the organization as a whole.

From Maslow's theory of needs, we might also predict that, since career achievement and competence are primarily a matter of self esteem and esteem of others, it is unlikely that people can take advantage of opportunities for achievement in well-designed technological organizations unless they have also been successful in satisfying their basic physical needs, safety needs, and social needs. A very hungry man, whether his hunger is for food, safety, or affection, is not likely to be able to think about, or be interested in, the work he is doing. Nor is he likely to feel a need for the technical coordination he must follow with others at work.

Finally, it should be pointed out that career interests are not an absolute matter for most persons. Few people are compulsive career slaves, on the one hand, or compulsive love and affection slaves, on the other. Life is a complex of trade-offs. Well-designed technologies simply offer a chance or avenue for achievement, competence, and self esteem. And when the individual strikes out to look for places to act out these needs, he often pays a price in giving his time in one direction rather than another.

Technology and Behavior in Industrial Organizations

In the past fifteen years, a considerable amount of research has been undertaken which identifies the different kinds of technology which are required to be successful in achieving different kinds of organizational goals. All of this research points to the facts that:

- The goal of one organization differs significantly from the goal of another organization. The crucial difference lies in whether the goal is relatively stable, known, and constant over time, or whether it is relatively unstable, chaotic, or changing.
- The subgoals and specializations in one organization (the means to the larger end) differ from those of another organization. The crucial difference lies in whether the *parts* of the organization are fairly close to one another in work and attitudes (relatively homogeneous), or relatively far apart (heterogeneous) in work and attitudes. From a total organization point of view, this factor is also a measure of simplicity versus complexity.

For example, take the goal of producing bread. It is a relatively stable goal. Though tastes change to a degree, and the organization must be somewhat flexible in producing raisin bread versus wholewheat bread, the external environment is fairly stable. Bread is bread. The organization does not have to worry about some competitor who will upset its entire technology (machines, job specializations, procedures) because people suddenly start eating plastic capsules. Furthermore, the three major functions which are subgoals of a baking company—product development, manufacturing, and sales—are, in the total spectrum of industry, relatively simple. The chemistry of bread baking is not too complex for a chemist, the production methods are not too complicated, and the selling is easier and more comprehensible than marketing jet airliners.

On the other end of the scale of stability-complexity, take the goal of producing electronic computers. It is relatively unstable, because competitors are very rapidly developing numerous important changes in the product. Not only this, but the diversity and complexity of the three basic functions are present in a much higher degree than in the case of bread. The people who do research and development have the whole field of electronics and mathematics to contend with, the people who produce the computers have a welter of technical processes and methods to contend with, and the people who do the selling have to know everything from the customer's product (e.g., banking) to his subfunctions (bookkeeping, check clearing, figuring of interest rates, etc.).

Stability of the final goal and diversity of the jobs necessary to attain it are important to the *human* side of enterprise. It determines (1) how specialized or different the people are in the various parts of the organization, (2) how difficult it is for them to coordinate the total technology, (3) what kinds of coordinating system they use, and (4) the attitudes of all those coordinated toward the coordinators and the system or coordinating process itself. This last point is especially important. For example, we shall see that when people pursue highly stable but simple goals (bread) there is a good chance that they feel satisfied when they have a line executive who possesses the knowledge of bread science, manufacture, and sales, and who conveys an "order" to them specifying what next week's or next year's production quotas will be. They would resent unnecessary "coordinators" being appointed to muddle up the system. On the other hand, when people pursue a highly unstable goal, or a goal requiring complex and diverse specialized jobs (computers), regarding which no one man could know all of the complex facts, they feel satisfied doing much of the coordinating themselves, or with the help of coordinators who serve as information centers. They would resent having a boss who could not possibly know all of the facts (even if he is president) pronouncing what the scientific characteristics of next year's product should be, whether a certain kind of machine could be used in the factory, and whether the customer will use it in preference to a competitor's product.

The following sections discuss how the organizational goal, differing as it does in stability and diversity, determines the character of the four other aspects mentioned above: the degree of diversity among various parts of the organization, the difficulty of coordinating the parts, the kinds of coordinating mechanisms used, and the attitudes of people toward the coordinating system.

Specialization and Diversity

Few organizational goals can be pursued without specialization of function. In the most noteworthy research on this subject to date, Lawrence and Lorsch (1967) found that container companies, producing packaging for other industries (a relatively stable and less complex goal), and plastics companies, producing a range of products (a relatively unstable and complex goal), both had to have three main specializing functions or parts—a product-development department staffed with scientists and engineers, a manufacturing department staffed with plant personnel, and a sales department staffed with marketing personnel.

Two crucial questions arise about these specialized parts. How do people with different specialties differ in their attitudes? Does the technology of producing containers cause people in a container company to be more different or less different from one another than the people in the plastics company with its different technology? In another sense, the second question asks how homogeneous or heterogeneous the people are in one organization compared to another.

The article by Lorsch and Lawrence accompanying this chapter describes how the different specialists in two of the plastics companies did indeed have different orientations, outlooks, and attitudes. Additional evidence from their original research is presented here (Lawrence and Lorsch, 1967).

The most obvious way people differed was in their orientations toward work goals and work objectives. Because their jobs dealt with sales, the people in marketing were naturally interested in and paid attention to customers, sales appeals, competitive practices, and the like. People in production were quite naturally preoccupied with such things as machinery, technical processes, and labor turnover in the plants.

Of more concern to us here is the attitude different specialists had toward interpersonal affairs at work. In the jargon of behavioral science research, were they *task-oriented* or *people-oriented?* In the production area, where engineers and plant managers dealt with rather certain and predictable actions in day-to-day operations, the people holding these jobs preferred interactions which were aimed at getting the job done, did not feel concerned about engaging in social relationships, and in case of difficulty with another person would simply feel "well, let's just get on with the job."

According to the researchers, the reason why a production person had this attitude was that production procedures and goals were there to coordinate his work with another person within the production department. And such a coordinating mechanism was effective because the production technology was relatively stable—the product was known, the amount and quality to be produced were known, and the various departments which had to process the materials were known.

This kind of motivation is similar to that which one feels when he stops at a traffic light and sees another car immediately behind. The traffic light is, of course, a predictable and orderly procedure which connects the actions of motorists. First, one does not necessarily feel any interest in social relationships with the other driver. The technology (traffic lights, sequence of cars stopping or moving on red or green) helps each driver do his own job (drive where he is going) as well as to coordinate drivers for the good of the organization (all cars stopped or moving are part of an organization to move traffic). Furthermore, if the driver behind shouts or blows his horn impatiently, it is easy to shrug one's shoulders, get on with the driving, and let him fume. Or, if he should come up to one's car and start engaging in friendly conversation when the light is red, one might wonder whether interpersonal communication is really necessary at that point.

Now let us look at an uncertain task and an uncertain goal. Driving over an interstate highway in Colorado in November, a person drives into an unexpected snowstorm. With no snow tires, he finds himself stuck at the foot of a mountain pass with other motorists. Not only is a great deal of technical interchange desired with those who have the goal of crossing the mountain range to Salt Lake City, but some exchange of friendly chatter would not seem out of place. Certainly any motorist who came from the other direction would be involved in considerable interchange.

This last illustration of a group of people with an unstable environment and goal, and no coordinating device, is not unlike what the researchers found in the sales specializations of the companies they studied. The sales and marketing people who were dealing with a relatively *uncertain* task and who were accustomed to being concerned about (note the attitude) maintaining social relationships with customers, also cared more about fostering positive social relationships with *coworkers inside the marketing department.*

Another attitude which differs between specializations is highlighted in this research: a person filling a position in one specialty tends to have a different orientation toward *time* than his fellow in another specialty. Sales personnel had the attitude that they had to solve problems and take action immediately (tomorrow's success or failure depended on it), and production specialists were similar. However, scientific personnel felt that their workday could be spent quite comfortably without solving an immediate problem. A crude synonym for this attitude might be "patience" versus "impatience" about actions or decisions.

Of the six plastics companies studied in depth, all specialists in the three functions exhibited the same types of attitudes. Regardless of which company or organization one belongs to, his special technology in one part of the organization, and its degree of certainty or stability, will tend to shape his attitudes toward goals, interpersonal relations, and time.

One of the important points highlighted in the research was that the most successful companies of the six studied had *pronounced* differences in departmental attitudes. Often, we read that "provincialism" or "bias" toward one's own work is bad for the organization. But here we see it as necessary to success. This is not too surprising. If a football team is to win, the tackle had better keep his mind on being a good tackle and not try to act like a quarterback.

Turning now to companies with different technologies, the plastics companies were compared with the container companies, in which no significant new products had been introduced for the past twenty years, and whose customers wanted proven containers that were produced regularly on high-speed automatic lines. As one executive said, "We and our competitors all use the same machines produced by the same company. The product has got to be virtually the same as your competitors, and there is not any price competition. All we have to know is how many cases does the customer want and when?" (*ibid.*, p. 92). The production technology was therefore certain, and the market goals were even more certain. Since the product development people had less turbulent goals than those in plastics, they were more like the drivers at the traffic light than the drivers on the mountain pass. In short, although the researchers found that the differences in attitude between specialists were the same in both plastics and container technologies, the differences were *less* in the stable container technology than in the more turbulent plastics technology. Salesmen still preferred interpersonal or social activities and production men were still more task-oriented. But salesmen and production men were more alike—homogeneous—in a container company than in a plastics company.

This diversity has far-reaching consequences for other human aspects of a company, as we shall see. It affects how people coordinate with each other in different companies—by themselves, in committees or task groups, relying on formal hierarchy to do the coordinating, or something in between (the use of special coordinating departments such as product managers, project managers, or the like). It also has an effect on how comfortable people feel with whatever mode of coordination is used.

Difficulties in Coordination

One of the great difficulties in the industrialized world, both from the standpoint of organizational success in reaching a goal and from the standpoint of human satisfaction (freedom from conflict) is that differences in specialization mean that people of widely different specialties cannot talk to each other and understand one another. Specialization is thus double-edged—we cannot do without it for organization success, and for each person achieving something in his own domain, but it potentially causes stress and conflict. Thorsten Veblen, a well known social critic of earlier in this century, said that people in one field often have a *trained incapacity* to deal with total problems in the real world. The very training for which they spend so much money and to which they devote so much effort, and which is so prized by other people (the organization), incapacitates them to solve a problem if it has factors in it from outside their field.

It is not surprising, therefore, that research scientists who develop products in the plastics industry, and who must develop products that the customer will buy, would have difficulty knowing and understanding customers, competitive prices, or sales appeals. Since they differ considerably in attitude from the people in the sales department, they are also not likely to find much common ground for engaging in direct and time-consuming interchange with marketing people. Nor is it surprising that, in the container companies, the coordination problem would be easier, since (1) each of the three functions—product development, sales, production—was more known and stable, and (2) the people in one or the other function were less different from their co-workers in another function. Let us see what effect this difference in degree of cooperation has on the way people coordinate their actions, and on how they feel toward the "system."

Structure and Behavior

Given the fact that people in different parts of an organization are cognitively different, and given the difficulties in technical and interpersonal relations that this creates, how have organizations evolved ways of coordinating potentially conflicting subtechnologies and people?

Formally Structured Coordination Systems

One way, particularly suitable for organizations with relatively stable goals and relatively homogeneous parts, is a formally structured organization. By structured we mean rationally worked out job descriptions for operating positions and people, policies and procedures for coordinating diverse jobs, and managerial positions and people specializing in effectuating the coordination itself.

The traffic system is an example. The requirements for a driver's license involve certain actions an *individual* driver is expected to carry out, including parking, entering a main thoroughfare, and the use of certain hand or light signals. This is the job description of the driver, and spells out his specialization. It is partly determined by how the automobile is constructed, and partly by requirements for *cooperation* among drivers operating automobiles. It sequentially spells out how one driver is related to others—it creates a coordinated organization.

The football team is another example. The guard has his specified actions as an *individual* specialist, but the *plays* connect each player's actions to the team. The quarterback is a coordinating specialist who relates the operating work of guards, ends, and other players. The man in this position decides (note the *decision-making* responsibility) which play to use.

In an industrial setting, the pilot who flies a commercial scheduled airliner from one airport to another has the technical operating responsibility of flying the airplane. His copilot and flight engineer have other technical operating duties to perform, as do the stewardesses in the cabin. Somewhere both the timing and the altitude of the flight in relation to other flights must be worked out in advance. This is done by someone (equivalent to a *staff* manager) in the Civil Aeronautics Board offices, who works out the traffic procedures between and around airports. To take care of detailed and unexpected events, someone must make ad hoc decisions and adjustments. This is the work of an air traffic controller in the airport tower, whose technical work is that of a *line* manager. Watching the various airplanes, he observes the standard traffic procedures, and calls signals to individual aircraft as he watches his radar and uses the radio to communicate with pilots.

Note that when some people are specialists in operating work and others are specialists in coordinating work, there is a separation of planning and decision making from operating. This does not mean that the pilot has no decisions to make, but that he is subject to coordinating decisions made by those who specialize in coordinating.

In the selection by Joan Woodward accompanying this chapter, the separation of coordinating from operating was found to be most pronounced in firms that operated in stable technologies—what she called continuous process technologies, such as in chemical or oil refining companies. We will look at some of her findings in the selection, from the full text of her initial studies (1965), and from her more recent studies (1970).

She studied one hundred manufacturing companies in a certain geographic area of England, to determine among other things whether all companies use formal organization structure as a means of managing. She found that some companies depend heavily on this kind of managerial coordination and others do not. This was an important finding at the time, since many management textbooks seemed to suggest that formal procedures and clear job descriptions with line managers and staff managers doing most of the decision making was the proper way to manage *all* enterprises.

She found that as companies move up the scale of diversity and complexity, and particularly when they deal with a stable and known product goal such as that of producing oil and chemical products for a mass market, there was indeed more and more separation of coordinating from operating. Furthermore, there was a separation within the coordinating function between those who *plan* production (coaches who develop the plays for a football game, or officials who work out traffic patterns for use around airports), and those who *supervise* production (quarterbacks who decide which play to use and call it to the players, or air traffic controllers who decide when an airplane is to enter the traffic pattern and call it to the pilot).

The size of the company made little difference in how many managerial positions there were. It was the stability of production and external environment that was the crucial determining factor. Some firms produced custom-made products, such as men's suits to order. They were most unstable of all, because the goal was always changing on the basis of customer needs, and entire production schedules and procedures had to be changed frequently. Others, which produced automobile parts in large batches or in mass production for a certain time period (such as a year's supply before a model change), were more stable in their goal and the system needed to achieve it. The most stable of all were the chemical and gasoline companies, which produced a steady flow of gasoline in standard units. A gallon this year is the same as a gallon next year. And quantities are produced for finished product inventories.

In the companies with custom-made products, the average number of levels in the managerial hierarchy was three, but it was four for large-batch product companies, and six for process industries such as chemicals. The ratio of managers to employees ranged among custom-product companies from $1:24$ to $1:49$; in large-batch industries from $1:14$ to $1:18$; and in process industries from $1:7$ to $1:8$. This increase in the number of managers may be in part a result of empire building or the proliferation of bureaucratic positions, as Parkinson's Law suggests. But it is also heavily influenced by the nature of the goal being pursued, and the complexity or change required in the entire interconnected network of operating specializations. Otherwise, there is no explanation of why bureaucrats in less stable companies did not build as many levels of management as those in more stable companies!

The same relationship between stability of goal and use of formal structures was found by Lawrence and Lorsch *within* a company. In six companies in the plastics industry, it was the manufacturing departments which had the most formalized structure. They had more levels in their managerial hierarchy, a higher ratio of supervisors to subordinates, and more frequent reviews of managerial performance.

At the other end of the formality spectrum, the research departments had fewer levels in the management hierarchy, more subordinates reporting to each supervisor, fewer managers for the same number of operators, and less reliance on formal job descriptions and procedures. The sales department, the goals of which were more stable than research but more changing and chaotic than production, fell between the two on these dimensions.

Effect of Structured Coordination on Behavior and Motivation

Structure—procedures, job descriptions, and coordinating direction—can have either positive or negative effects on people's feelings and emotions. We have already referred to the fact that people in *all* coordinating systems have a greater chance of achievement if the system fits the goal. If the goal calls for formal organization, those with high needs for achievement do not seem to mind. They may even welcome it. A football player cannot achieve much with his talents if he tried (or if someone tries to make him) to utilize the rules of golf, a game in which there is no synchronization between players in action.

In addition to achievement, we should recognize that, regardless of which human need one is using a job and career for, he can do so more easily if others do their part correctly. One might be using his job for money to buy housing and food, for security in an industrial world, or for status and prestige rather than for achievement in his task. If the goal of the organization, and therefore its technology, calls for formal organization, the person cannot be successful in achieving any of these human needs without the formal organization.

Though we shall see presently that people do resent hierarchies for various reasons, research evidence shows that many people go about behaving in formal or structured organizations with ease and apparent satisfaction. We have already seen, for example, that production men in organizations tend to prefer contacts with other men who are also task-oriented.

Woodward found that in companies which had very clear formal jobs and procedures "most of those interviewed seemed to resent authority less when exercised over them by the process than by a superior." This is not too surprising. We resent a traffic light much less than we would resent hundreds of cars with no rules of the road, or a policeman who had no rules to go by other than what he sees and decides himself. This is another way of saying that structural systems in one sense actually permit more delegation, and they do not require so much of one man's meddling into another man's work affairs. This same study showed that in three engineering companies moving from custom-type goals to more stable large-batch goals, the production managers spent more time coordinating procedures with their bosses (in one company, the manager increased this portion of his day from 34 percent to 47 percent), but *less* time talking to their subordinates (in one company this portion of the manager's time decreased from 33 percent to 16 percent). Because of this, people at successively lower levels simply felt less pressure from above, and were able to pursue their tasks without interference or changes directed from above.

Those familiar with Porter's famous "parable of the spindle" will recognize this phenomenon. He did research in a restaurant about conflict between the waitress who was giving "orders" to the cook, and the cook who had to give her the right item of food at the right time if she were to do her job correctly. In the particular restaurant, as no doubt in many others, there was frustration on the part of both people. With no rules and procedures, each was dependent on the whims of the other. In short, there was not much *stability* of expectation for the waitress or the cook. However, the friction was reduced considerably when a simple spindle was installed, with a procedure whereby the waitress clipped orders to the wheel in a certain order and the cook filled the orders in the same sequence. Each person was thereby freed *by the structure of technology* (a formally related network of jobs) to pursue his work.

The studies by Lawrence and Lorsch (1967) throw additional and important light on this kind of situation. They studied two container companies, both of which, you will recall, were pursuing a goal that was relatively stable. This in turn caused the *parts* of the company to be less diverse. One company was a high performer, with decision making concentrated at higher levels, and more clarity in procedures, rules, and job descriptions. The researchers found that, because its structure fit the requirements of the goal, the company was successful, and the morale and feelings of managers inside the company were better (they *felt* successful). "While a few managers indicated that they were unhappy because of their own lack of involvement, the vast majority saw the situation as necessary and conducive to their effectively performing their jobs. When conflicts arose, they knew that they would get them resolved by the top managers, who had both the knowledge of the environment and the influence required."

Here is a verbatim comment from a salesman in the more structured container company: "On new customers the sales vice president tells me whether we can do the business. However, the real person is the chief executive, because he wants to be updated immediately on everything, and does get himself involved in everything. He runs this place completely. And he gets fancy if something happens that he wasn't aware of and wasn't involved in. . . .

"I thought at first when I came here this was meddling. However, now, as I think about it, at least you have a guy who is going to give you decisions. If I want answers quickly, I'll go directly to him, keeping the other people tied in as I go . . ." (p. 118).

Dynamic Coordination Systems

A second way of coordinating is dynamic, carried out more by ad hoc, give-and-take communication than by operating according to stable and known procedures, or referring coordinating problems to higher line managers. Because of the information needed to deal with changing customer requirements, new scientific discoveries, new production methods, and the like, the coordination procedures used by Lawrence and Lorsch's plastics executives were much more temporary in nature than the more stable coordination procedures of, say, the container companies. Whereas the latter produces items which remain the same month in and month out, plastics managers may have to react to changes relatively frequently.

Consequently, the plastics companies tended to coordinate with a wide variety of task forces, committees, and informal groups. The people who coordinated the three parts (production, research, and sales) were those who had knowledge of the detailed and up-to-date information necessary to make decisions. Those who made up the task forces and committees were not always the top people in their departments' authority hierarchies. It happened that because production was the most stable of the three, the top men in production tended to have the necessary knowledge and thus represented their department in decision-making groups. But the opposite tended to be true in research. The individual scientists toward the bottom of the hierarchy were the only ones with the knowledge necessary to join a task force. In sales, it was a variety of middle-level sales managers who were most familiar with customers, advertising, or other marketing functions.

One of the characteristics of dynamic systems is that a wide variety of people engage in problem solving that is less structured along departmental lines, and less structured along vertical hierarchical lines. People seem to be less conscious of clear-cut job descriptions, and all those involved in coordination become somewhat involved in the functions of others. That is not to say that there is no formal organization. Individuals still maintain the orientations of their primary specialty, and line managers still have their say in affairs. However, it is they who have created the task forces and committees, who rely on them for coordination, and who appoint a different kind of coordinator—product manager, project manager, and similar positions. The people in these positions—serving as information centers for the specialist representatives, setting goals and targets, and occasionally "translating" one specialized department's needs for others—may write summary reports for top management, and try to get consensus among the operating departments.

Effect of Dynamic Coordination on Behavior and Motivation

If people in a dynamic system can achieve a reasonable degree of frankness and openness as they solve problems, and if they feel disposed to invest large amounts of emotional energy in problem solving and confrontation (two matters to be discussed later), such a system offers a number of positive motivations. One, the fact that an individual can perform his job regardless of what satisfactions he pursues, is similar to the motivation discussed in connection with well-designed structured systems. Relatively free interaction is the necessary way to proceed, in view of the fact that there are few stable goals and procedures on which to rely.

Another motivation—achievement and feelings of competence and involvement—is in some respects more likely in such a system than in more structured organizations. This can be explained by reference to Maslow's need hierarchy and McClelland's social motives, discussed in Chapter 1. There is opportunity for more influence on the total organization, and for involvement in a greater spectrum of the firm's decisions. Such involvement comes quite close to the motivating factors described by Herzberg earlier in this chapter.

It is also reasonable to assume that such systems offer greater opportunity for human interaction, and thus for satisfaction of social needs on the job.

That such an approach can work is evidenced by the following statement by a manager in one of the Lawrence and Lorsch's plastics companies (1967): "Our problems get thrashed out in our committees. We work them over until everybody agrees this is the best effort you can make. We may decide this isn't good enough. Then we decide to ask for more plant, more people, etc. We all have to be realistic and take a modification sometimes and say this is the best we can do.

"In recent meetings we have had a thrashing around about manpower needs. At first we didn't have much agreement, but we kept thrashing around and finally agreed on what was the best we could do" (p. 74).

Negative Motivations of Inappropriate Structures

The principal argument in this chapter is that the structure of an organization—the individual jobs themselves, and the total network of jobs tied together—has a higher probability of producing positive work motivation if it is designed so that it fits the *kind of goal* being pursued by the *particular organization.* The reason is simple: whatever the diverse personal motives of individuals in the company, they are more likely to pull in the right direction if the "right" structure is designed.

We can highlight this argument by looking at two kinds of situations which produce *negative* motivation. If we define "morale" as simply the positive or negative attitudes people have toward the organization they work in, negative morale can just as easily be caused by faults in the structure as positive morale can be caused by the structure which fits the goal. Many of the world's woes are caused by systems that are either overstructured or understructured.

Overstructured Systems

Suppose you drive to work each day on a four-lane superhighway carrying traffic between two small towns in western Nebraska. There is not an automobile in sight. There is hardly ever another automobile. Yet at each of five intersections between your home and your job there is a stoplight. After about a month, never having seen another car pull out into the highway, you lose some respect for the system, and run a red light. However, you find that there is a policeman stationed at each stoplight, and when you run the light he hauls you into court and the judge fines you fifty dollars. Regardless of how you feel about rules and authority in the beginning, if you are required to travel on that highway Monday through Friday in order to get to work, you might come to view the procedures and supervision with hostility.

This kind of situation has been depicted in much of the research done in industrial sociology and social psychology. The Argyris (1957) theory shows how managers may apply rules and regulations above and beyond what is required to get the job done. Employees, seeing this happen, may retaliate by forming negative attitudes toward the company and the coordinators. The selection by Thompson (1961) accompanying this chapter shows what can happen when an excessively formal organization of officials, lacking the knowledge necessary to coordinate a complex and changing situation, nevertheless insist on the rights of office instead of concentrating on the work to be done, the *necessary* technology, and the nature of the goal. These are "bureaucrats" in the bad sense of the word. Nobody wins. Those using their jobs only for security are frustrated anyway. Those seeking achievement find much less chance to do a good job.

One significant piece of research on this state of affairs is the study of firms in the English and Scottish electronics industries by Burns and Stalker (1961) and abstracted in a selection accompanying this chapter. Essentially, they found that people in organizations, especially managers, have four competing forces acting upon them which determine what decisions they make. They are workers with careers and jobs, they are members of groups that have sectional interests (which may lead to playing politics), they are individuals with rank and prestige (which may lead to defending prerogatives), and they are people with outside interests—home, sports, leisure, and so on.

In the stable electronics companies, which had been manufacturing simple electric switches or fuse boxes, the formal organization had been appropriate. People in various departments had their routines, they were not too far apart in attitudes and orientations, and they were willing to refer decisions up the line to a boss who knew most of the facts involved and who could make realistic decisions. However, when these companies tried to enter more complex markets, involving consumer products such as television and radio or parts for electronic computers, most of them failed because they would not give up the old structured approach and adopt a more dynamic approach.

Unstable and fast-changing goals and technologies are bound to cause anxiety, stress, and strain. This stress is likely to show up in excessive politics, defense of prerogatives, or simply devoting more energy to outside life than to career and work life. Unlike some earlier research (Argyris, 1957), Burns and Stalker did not find that all such frustrations lead to strife and organizational failure. Instead, some of the firms took the unstable conditions in stride. The anxiety and frustration which quite naturally accompany chaotic conditions outside a company were turned to productive work and goal accomplishment, rather than to bureaucratic politics and false authority.

To the extent that all organizations have some tendency toward rigidity when changing times upset established procedure, management must give serious attention to certain kinds of remedies. One is the provision for integrator positions to operate with task forces of different specialists; another is the designation of people who "know the facts," regardless of where they are in the hierarchy, to serve on task forces. A third is decentralization, wherein the whole company is split into task forces. These methods are more thoroughly discussed in Chapter 7. Organization development, or the breaking down of established formal structures and reformulating new and appropriate ones, is discussed in Chapter 12.

Understructured Systems

Suppose you drive to work each day on a four-lane highway connecting a suburb with a freeway. There are five intersections between your home and the freeway. Each is equipped only with four-way stop signs rather than traffic lights. There are hundreds of cars pulling out from these intersections each day during the rush hour. Since there is no stoplight, there are frequent traffic jams as each driver makes a stop or go decision from his own point of view. There even may be prolonged arguments, aimed at protection of status and prestige when one driver gets mad because another ignored him. After you have driven this route for a while, you begin to lose respect, not only for the system, but for many of your fellow "co-operators." If you must drive on that highway Monday through Friday week in and week out under these conditions, it would not be long before you might view a traffic light as a blessing, and a supervisor (policeman) as a desirable person to have around. Regardless of how much you like or dislike authority at the beginning, you would come to be more concerned about the task to be done and moved by the desire to get on with it.

Understructured organizations can be as devastating to human sensibilities (and to organization goals) as overstructured ones. This should be cause for concern by those who think that all organizations should use the greatest possible amount of human interaction and communication. Anyone who has heard derisive remarks about "too much committee management" will recognize the limitations of dynamic coordination systems.

Both Woodward, in her study of 100 diverse firms, and Burns and Stalker, in their study of electronic firms in England and Scotland, found that it takes large amounts of energy and commitment to engage in the dynamic, unstructured relationships necessary in the organic type of organization. Indeed, part of the reason (in addition to status and politics) why Burns' electronics managers did not enter into the amorphous relationships needed for swiftly moving events was that they were unwilling to commit the necessary time and energy to something totally unknown.

A very important series of incidents is reported by Lawrence and Lorsch (1967) to support this view. The researchers singled out two companies in the container industry with relatively stable goals and technologies, and two companies in the plastics industry with relatively diverse and changing technologies and goals. Each pair of companies contained one company that was very successful in its own industry and one company that was low in performance. In addition, the high-performance company in each industry seemed to have a system for coordinating which was appropriate to its technology. The high-performance plastics company had a dynamic system of coordinating and the high-performance container company had a more structured system of coordinating. Particularly, the latter coordinated by formal referral of coordination problems up to the line executives who had the requisite knowledge to solve them. This is roughly equivalent to centralized decision making, since a smaller group of executives toward the top made many of the coordinating decisions. On the other hand, the plastics company's more dynamic system involved a wider spread of people from various levels giving inputs to coordinating decisions through committees, task forces, and integrators. This is roughly equivalent to a decentralized or participative form of coordination.

At first, using only the data they obtained in plastics companies, the researchers hypothesized that the high-performance company had good coordination and good goal achievement because of two things: (1) improved motivation, energy, and goal commitment as a result of participative decision making; and (2) better technical and economic decisions because a wider range of knowledge was brought to bear on the technical problems of running the business.

But later they found that they could not use this hypothesis to explain why the high-performance container company was equally successful, because decision making was *not* spread downward in this manner. In fact, it was centralized at the top of the line hierarchy. They therefore concluded that it was the fact that decisions were made at a place on the decentralized-centralized continuum *appropriate to the tasks to be done* which caused the firms to prosper and be successful. It was the latter factor which made for effective system performance and good morale among those who worked in each company. The resolution of conflict was accomplished best with each company acting in its own appropriate way.

An interesting violation of this principle occurred in the low-performance container company: There had been a systematic attempt to get middle managers involved in making decisions about scheduling and other customer service issues. While this apparently gave them more feeling of having influence over these decisions than managers in the high performing (container) organization, it also left them with a feeling of frustration because they were not able to achieve any clear resolution. As one production manager said:

"Presently there are thousands of guys involved in the scheduling process around here. It just doesn't work with so many cooks in the stew. . . . What happens now is that when an order comes in it is my decision to take care of it and to schedule it into the first available production space and then give some other orders a later production date. This date usually goes back to the sales office, and they aren't happy, and they will start for the regional manager or the [integrating department] in headquarters to try to get this date improved. Consequently, the [integrating] guys are always dabbling with us about the schedule. This really gets frantic sometimes. On the other hand, there has to be a bit of this in the situation we are in. Hell, I don't know all the facts out here in an outlying plant. . . . It is just an order, and we don't know what's behind it or how important it is to the company. This, I think, also accounts for a lot of meddling in the scheduling."

What was happening in this company was that men down the line were being asked, either in the name of participative management or to satisfy the needs of overly dependent top executives, to make decisions that they did not and could not make because they did not have the necessary information.

This phenomenon also affected the sales department of the low-performance container company. One salesman complained that his regional sales manager had been turned into a production scheduler, and was so swamped with petty problems (i.e., problems away from his main job) that he could hardly keep his mind on the customers.

Finally, because the participative committees did not work for either the good of the company or the people, the decisions made at lower levels were frequently reversed at higher levels. The researchers conclude: "The managers at the middle levels were frustrated by their inability to handle these conflicts as they had been led to believe they should, and the problems intensified and festered as they were passed upward" (p. 117).

Whether higher level managers realized they were asking for participation but were not able to allow it is not clear. They probably believed that "good human relations means decentralized decision making." In any event, a person who is told that he can (and should) make more decisions, but is then not allowed to do so, might well conclude that he has been dishonestly manipulated by the system.

Summary and Conclusions

The vast majority of people in the world engage in some form of work or task. They may do so to satisfy any or all of the human needs discussed in Chapter 1. To the extent that people are able to work effectively together to achieve organizational goals, there is more chance for the individual in an industrial society to achieve his own goals, be they for security, status and prestige, personal achievement, or simply doing his own thing.

This is not to say that work is without strife. We see strife of various kinds in all organizations. Part of this strife can be caused by the psychological makeup a person brings to the organization. Recall that, in organizations that are an early part of life (including family, childhood groups, university classes, and so on), some people have learned to be comfortable with authority (dependent), some have learned to be discomfited by authority (counterdependent), and others have learned to accept a mix of authority and freedom (interdependent). Having acknowledged this, and the fact that people at either extreme (dependent-counterdependent) will have difficulty living in any organization, our purpose here is to show how the organization itself can make life better or worse for people. If there is a fit of the goal, the technology, and the coordinating system, chances are that the system will affect *all* participants' attitudes and satisfactions in a positive way. On the other hand, if there is *not* a fit of the goal, the technology, and the coordinating system, it affects all participants' attitudes and satisfactions in a negative way.

We have seen that there are different ways of structuring organizations. Sometimes they are structured so that there are detailed specifications for different tasks, and of the relationships of those tasks. Other times there is much less formal specification of tasks, and more reliance on people working things out informally, among themselves. Types of structures for organizations are taken up in some detail in Chapter 7.

At this point, one important condition for organization design should be explained. By the logic presented in this chapter, the manager does not start with the characteristics of people, and design a structure to fit them. Only in an organization with absolute congruence of individual objectives with the goals of the organization itself would this be possible. If the organization has output goals other than simply the friendly cooperation of internal participants, the structure must be designed to fit those goals.

References

Argyris, C. *Personality and Organization.* Harper & Row, 1957.
Burns, T., and G. M. Stalker. *The Management of Innovation.* London: Tavistock, 1961.

Herzberg, F. "One More Time: How Do You Motivate Employees?" *Harvard Business Review,* Vol. 46, No. 1, January–February 1968.

House, R. J., and L. A. Wigdor. "Herzberg's Dual-Factor Theory of Job Satisfaction and Motivation: A Review of the Evidence and a Criticism." *Personnel Psychology,* Vol. 20, No. 4, Winter 1967.

Lawrence, P. R., and J. W. Lorsch. *Organization and Environment.* Harvard University Graduate School of Business Administration, 1967.

Lorsch, J. W., and P. R. Lawrence. "Organizing for Product Innovation." *Harvard Business Review,* Vol. 43, No. 1, January–February 1965.

McGregor, D. *The Human Side of Enterprise.* McGraw-Hill, 1960.

Thompson, V. A. *Modern Organization.* Knopf, 1961.

Woodward, J. *Management and Technology.* London: Her Majesty's Stationery Office, 1958.

———. *Industrial Organization: Theory and Practice.* Oxford University Press, 1965.

———. *Industrial Organization: Behavior and Control.* Oxford University Press, 1970.

Readings

One More Time: How Do You Motivate Employees?

FREDERICK HERZBERG

How many articles, books, speeches, and workshops have pleaded plaintively, "How do I get an employee to do what I want him to do?"

The psychology of motivation is tremendously complex, and what has been unraveled with any degree of assurance is small indeed. But the dismal ratio of knowledge to speculation has not dampened the enthusiasm for new forms of snake oil that are constantly coming on the market, many of them with academic testimonials. Doubtless this article will have no depressing impact on the market for snake oil, but since the ideas expressed in it have been tested in many corporations and other organizations, it will help—I hope—to redress the imbalance in the aforementioned ratio.

'Motivating' with KITA

In lectures to industry on the problem, I have found that the audiences are anxious for quick and practical answers, so I will begin with a straightforward, practical formula for moving people.

What is the simplest, surest, and most direct way of getting someone to do something? Ask him? But if he responds that he does not want to do it, then that calls for a psychological consultation to determine the reason for his obstinacy. Tell him? His response shows that he does not understand you, and now an expert in communication methods has to be brought in to show you how to get through to him. Give him a monetary incentive? I do not need to remind the reader of the complexity and difficulty involved in setting up and administering an incentive system. Show him? This means a costly training program. We need a simple way.

Every audience contains the "direct action" manager who shouts, "Kick him!" And this type of manager is right. The surest and least circumlocuted way of getting someone to do something is to kick him in the pants—give him what might be called the KITA.

There are various forms of KITA, and here are some of them:

Negative Physical KITA

This is a literal application of the term and was frequently used in the past. It has, however, three major drawbacks: (1) it is inelegant; (2) it contradicts the precious image of benevolence that most organizations cherish; and (3) since it is a physical attack, it directly stimulates the autonomic nervous system, and this often results in negative feedback—the employee may just kick you in return. These factors give rise to certain taboos against negative physical KITA.

The psychologist has come to the rescue of those who are no longer permitted to use negative physical KITA. He has uncovered infinite sources of psychological vulnerabilities and the appropriate methods to play tunes on them. "He took my rug away"; "I wonder what he meant by that"; "The boss is always going around me"—these symptomatic expressions of ego sores that have been rubbed raw are the result of application of:

Negative Psychological KITA

This has several advantages over negative physical KITA. First, the cruelty is not visible; the bleeding is internal and comes much later. Second, since it affects the higher cortical centers of the brain with its inhibitory powers, it reduces the possibility of physical backlash. Third, since the number of psychological pains that a person can feel is almost infinite, the direction and site possibilities of the KITA are increased many times. Fourth, the person administering the kick can manage to be above it all and let the system accomplish the dirty work. Fifth, those who practice it receive some ego satisfaction (one-upmanship), whereas they would find drawing blood abhorrent. Finally, if the employee does complain, he can always be accused of being paranoid, since there is no tangible evidence of an actual attack.

Now, what does negative KITA accomplish? If I kick you in the rear (physically or psychologically), who is motivated? *I* am motivated; *you* move! Negative KITA does not lead to motivation, but to movement. So:

Positive KITA

Let us consider motivation. If I say to you, "Do this for me or the company, and in return I will give you a reward, an incentive, more status, a promotion, all the quid pro quos that exist in the industrial organization," am I motivating you? The overwhelming opinion I receive from management people is, "Yes, this is motivation."

I have a year-old Schnauzer. When it was a small puppy and I wanted it to move, I kicked it in the rear and it moved. Now that I have finished its obedience training, I hold up a dog biscuit when I want the Schnauzer to move. In this instance, who is motivated—I or the dog? The dog wants the biscuit, but it is I who want it to move. Again, I am the one who is motivated, and the dog is the one who moves. In this instance all I did was apply KITA frontally; I exerted a pull instead of a push. When industry wishes to use such positive KITAs, it has available an incredible number and variety of dog biscuits (jelly beans for humans) to wave in front of the employee to get him to jump.

Why is it that managerial audiences are quick to see that negative KITA is *not* motivation, while they are almost unanimous in their judgment that positive KITA *is* motivation? It is because negative KITA is rape, and positive KITA is seduction. But it is infinitely worse to be seduced than to be raped; the latter is an unfortunate occurrence, while the former signifies that you were a party to your own downfall. This is why positive KITA is so popular: it is a tradition; it is in the American way. The organization does not have to kick you; you kick yourself.

Myths about Motivation

Why is KITA not motivation? If I kick my dog (from the front or the back), he will move. And when I want him to move again, what must I do? I must kick him again. Similarly, I can charge a man's battery, and then recharge it, and recharge it again. But it is only when he has his own generator that we can talk about motivation. He then needs no outside stimulation. He *wants* to do it.

With this in mind, we can review some positive KITA personnel practices that were developed as attempts to instill "motivation":

1. *Reducing time spent at work*—This represents a marvelous way of motivating people to work—getting them off the job! We have reduced (formally and informally) the time spent on the job over the last 50 or 60 years until we are finally on the way to the "6½-day weekend." An interesting variant of this approach is the development of off-hour recreation programs. The philosophy here seems to be that those who play together, work together. The fact is that motivated people seek more hours of work, not fewer.

2. *Spiraling wages*—Have these motivated people? Yes, to seek the next wage increase. Some medievalists still can be heard to say that a good depression will get employees moving. They feel that if rising wages don't or won't do the job, perhaps reducing them will.

3. *Fringe benefits*—Industry has outdone the most welfare-minded of welfare states in dispensing cradle-to-the-grave succor. One company I know of had an informal "fringe benefit of the month club" going for a while. The cost of fringe benefits in this country has reached approximately 25% of the wage dollar, and we still cry for motivation.

People spend less time working for more money and more security than ever before, and the trend cannot be reversed. These benefits are no longer rewards; they are rights. A 6-day week is inhuman, a 10-hour day is exploitation, extended medical coverage is a basic decency, and stock options are the salvation of American initiative. Unless the ante is continuously raised, the psychological reaction of employees is that the company is turning back the clock.

When industry began to realize that both the economic nerve and the lazy nerve of their employees had insatiable appetites, it started to listen to the behavioral scientists who, more out of a humanist tradition than from scientific study, criticized management for not knowing how to deal with people. The next KITA easily followed.

4. *Human relations training*—Over 30 years of teaching and, in many instances, of practicing psychological approaches to handling people have resulted in costly human relations programs and, in the end, the same question: How do you motivate workers? Here, too, escalations have taken place. Thirty years ago it was necessary to request, "Please don't spit on the floor." Today the same admonition requires three "please"'s before the employee feels that his superior has demonstrated the psychologically proper attitudes toward him.

The failure of human relations training to produce motivation led to the conclusion that the supervisor or manager himself was not psychologically true to himself in his practice of interpersonal decency. So an advanced form of human relations KITA, sensitivity training, was unfolded.

5. *Sensitivity training*—Do you really, really understand yourself? Do you

really, really, really trust the other man? Do you really, really, really, really cooperate? The failure of sensitivity training is now being explained, by those who have become opportunistic exploiters of the technique, as a failure to really (five times) conduct proper sensitivity training courses.

With the realization that there are only temporary gains from comfort and economic and interpersonal KITA, personnel managers concluded that the fault lay not in what they were doing, but in the employee's failure to appreciate what they were doing. This opened up the field of communications, a whole new area of "scientifically" sanctioned KITA.

6. *Communications*—The professor of communications was invited to join the faculty of management training programs and help in making employees understand what management was doing for them. House organs, briefing sessions, supervisory instruction on the importance of communication, and all sorts of propaganda have proliferated until today there is even an International Council of Industrial Editors. But no motivation resulted, and the obvious thought occurred that perhaps management was not hearing what the employees were saying. That led to the next KITA.

7. *Two-way communication*—Management ordered morale surveys, suggestion plans, and group participation programs. Then both employees and management were communicating and listening to each other more than ever, but without much improvement in motivation.

The behavioral scientists began to take another look at their conceptions and their data, and they took human relations one step further. A glimmer of truth was beginning to show through in the writings of the so-called higher-order-need psychologists. People, so they said, want to actualize themselves. Unfortunately, the "actualizing" psychologists got mixed up with the human relations psychologists, and a new KITA emerged.

8. *Job participation*—Though it may not have been the theoretical intention, job participation often became a "give them the big picture" approach. For example, if a man is tightening 10,000 nuts a day on an assembly line with a torque wrench, tell him he is building a Chevrolet. Another approach had the goal of giving the employee a *feeling* that he is determining, in some measure, what he does on his job. The goal was to provide a *sense* of achievement rather than a substantive achievement in his task. Real achievement, of course, requires a task that makes it possible.

But still there was no motivation. This led to the inevitable conclusion that the employees must be sick, and therefore to the next KITA.

9. *Employee counseling*—The initial use of this form of KITA in a systematic fashion can be credited to the Hawthorne experiment of the Western Electric Company during the early 1930's. At that time, it was found that the employees harbored irrational feelings that were interfering with the rational operation of the factory. Counseling in this instance was a means of letting the employees unburden themselves by talking to someone about their problems. Although the counseling techniques were primitive, the program was large indeed.

The counseling approach suffered as a result of experiences during World War II, when the programs themselves were found to be interfering with the operation of the organizations; the counselors had forgotten their role of benevolent listeners and were attempting to do something about the problems that they heard about. Psychological counseling, however, has managed to survive the negative impact of World War II experiences and today is beginning to flourish with renewed sophistication. But, alas, many of these programs, like all the others, do not seem to have lessened the pressure of demands to find out how to motivate workers.

Since KITA results only in short-term movement, it is safe to predict that the cost of these programs will increase steadily and new varieties will be developed as old positive KITAs reach their satiation points.

Hygiene vs. Motivators

Let me rephrase the perennial question this way: How do you install a generator in an employee? A brief review of my motivation-hygiene theory of job attitudes is required before theoretical and practical suggestions can be offered. The theory was first drawn from an examination of events in the lives of engineers and accountants. At least 16 other investigations, using a wide variety of populations (including some in the Communist countries), have since been completed, making the original research one of the most replicated studies in the field of job attitudes.

The findings of these studies, along with corroboration from many other investigations using different procedures, suggest that the factors involved in producing job satisfaction (and motivation) are separate and distinct from the factors that lead to job dissatisfaction. Since separate factors need to be considered, depending on whether job satisfaction or job dissatisfaction is being examined, it follows that these two feelings are not opposites of each other. The opposite of job satisfaction is not job dissatisfaction but, rather, *no* job satisfaction; and, similarly, the opposite of job dissatisfaction is not job satisfaction, but *no* job dissatisfaction.

Stating the concept presents a problem in semantics, for we normally think of satisfaction and dissatisfaction as opposites—i.e., what is not satisfying must be dissatisfying, and vice versa. But when it comes to understanding the behavior of people in their jobs, more than a play on words is involved.

Two different needs of man are involved here. One set of needs can be thought of as stemming from his animal nature—the built-in drive to avoid pain from the environment, plus all the learned drives which become conditioned to the basic biological needs. For example, hunger, a basic biological drive, makes it necessary to earn money, and then money becomes a specific drive. The other set of needs relates to that unique human characteristic, the ability to achieve and, through achievement, to experience psychological growth. The stimuli for the growth needs are tasks that induce growth; in the industrial setting, they are the *job content*. Contrariwise, the stimuli inducing pain-avoidance behavior are found in the *job environment*.

The growth or *motivator* factors that are intrinsic to the job are: achievement, recognition for achievement, the work itself, responsibility, and growth or advancement. The dissatisfaction-avoidance or *hygiene* (KITA) factors that are extrinsic to the job include: company policy and administration, supervision, interpersonal relationships, working conditions, salary, status, and security.

A composite of the factors that are involved in causing job satisfaction and job dissatisfaction, drawn from samples of 1685 employees, is shown in Exhibit 1. The results indicate that motivators were the primary cause of satisfaction,

Exhibit 1 Factors Affecting Job Attitudes, As Reported in 12 Investigations

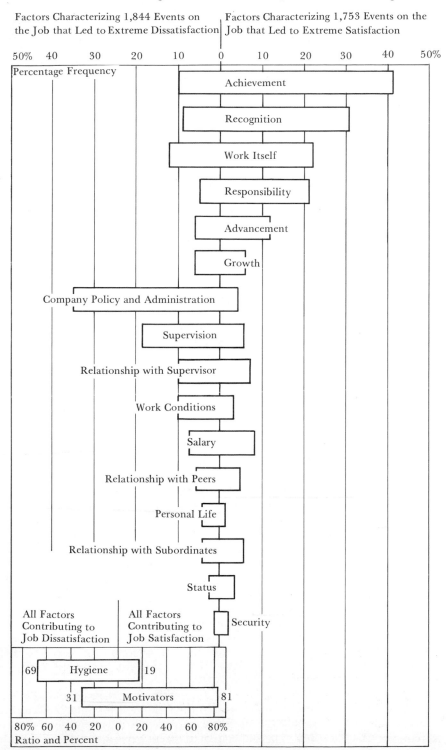

Factors Characterizing 1,844 Events on the Job that Led to Extreme Dissatisfaction

Factors Characterizing 1,753 Events on the Job that Led to Extreme Satisfaction

and hygiene factors the primary cause of unhappiness on the job. The employees, studied in 12 different investigations, included lower-level supervisors, professional women, agricultural administrators, men about to retire from management positions, hospital maintenance personnel, manufacturing supervisors, nurses, food handlers, military officers, engineers, scientists, housekeepers, teachers, technicians, female assemblers, accountants, Finnish foremen, and Hungarian engineers.

They were asked what job events had occurred in their work that had led to extreme satisfaction or extreme dissatisfaction on their part. Their responses are broken down in the exhibit into percentages of total "positive" job events and of total "negative" job events. (The figures total more than 100% on both the "hygiene" and "motivators" sides because often at least two factors can be attributed to a single event; advancement, for instance, often accompanies assumption of responsibility.)

To illustrate, a typical response involving achievement that had a negative effect for the employee was, "I was unhappy because I didn't do the job successfully." A typical response in the small number of positive job events in the Company Policy and Administration grouping was, "I was happy because the company reorganized the section so that I didn't report any longer to the guy I didn't get along with."

As the lower right-hand part of the exhibit shows, of all the factors contributing to job satisfaction, 81% were motivators. And of all the factors contributing to the employees' dissatisfaction over their work, 69% involved hygiene elements.

Eternal Triangle

There are three general philosophies of personnel management. The first is based on organizational theory, the second on industrial engineering, and the third on behavioral science.

The organizational theorist believes that human needs are either so irrational or so varied and adjustable to specific situations that the major function of personnel management is to be as pragmatic as the occasion demands. If jobs are organized in a proper manner, he reasons, the result will be the most efficient job structure, and the most favorable job attitudes will follow as a matter of course.

The industrial engineer holds that man is mechanistically oriented and economically motivated and his needs are best met by attuning the individual to the most efficient work process. The goal of personnel management therefore should be to concoct the most appropriate incentive system and to design the specific working conditions in a way that facilitates the most efficient use of the human machine. By structuring jobs in a manner that leads to the most efficient operation, the engineer believes that he can obtain the optimal organization of work and the proper work attitudes.

The behavioral scientist focuses on group sentiments, attitudes of individual employees, and the organization's social and psychological climate. According to his persuasion, he emphasizes one or more of the various hygiene and motivator needs. His approach to personnel management generally emphasizes some form of human relations education, in the hope of instilling healthy employee attitudes and an organizational climate which he considers to be felicitous to human values. He believes that proper attitudes will lead to efficient job and organizational structure.

There is always a lively debate as to the overall effectiveness of the approaches of the organizational theorist and the industrial engineer. Manifestly they have achieved much. But the nagging question for the behavioral scientist has been: What is the cost in human problems that eventually cause more expense to the organization—for instance, turnover, absenteeism, errors, violation of safety rules, strikes, restriction of output, higher wages, and greater fringe benefits? On the other hand, the behavioral scientist is hard put to document much manifest improvement in personnel management, using his approach.

The three philosophies can be depicted as a triangle, as is done in Exhibit 2, with each persuasion claiming the apex angle. The motivation-hygiene theory claims the same angle as industrial engineering, but for opposite goals. Rather than rationalizing the work to increase efficiency, the theory suggests that work be *enriched* to bring about effective utilization of personnel. Such a systematic attempt to motivate employees by manipulating the motivator factors is just beginning.

Exhibit 2   'Triangle' of Philosophies of Personnel Management

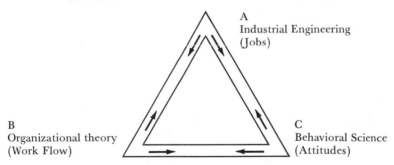

A
Industrial Engineering
(Jobs)

B
Organizational theory
(Work Flow)

C
Behavioral Science
(Attitudes)

The term *job enrichment* describes this embryonic movement. An older term, job enlargement, should be avoided because it is associated with past failures stemming from a misunderstanding of the problem. Job enrichment provides the opportunity for the employee's psychological growth, while job enlargement merely makes a job structurally bigger. Since scientific job enrichment is very new, this article only suggests the principles and practical steps that have recently emerged from several successful experiments in industry.

Job Loading

In attempting to enrich an employee's job, management often succeeds in reducing the man's personal contribution, rather than giving him an opportunity for growth in his accustomed job. Such an endeavor, which I shall call horizontal job loading (as opposed to vertical loading, or providing motivator factors), has been the problem of earlier job enlargement programs. This activity merely enlarges the meaninglessness of the job. Some examples of this approach, and their effect, are:

Challenging the employee by increasing the amount of production expected of him. If he tightens 10,000 bolts a day, see if he can tighten 20,000 bolts a day. The arithmetic involved shows that multiplying zero by zero still equals zero.

Adding another meaningless task to the existing one, usually some routine clerical activity. The arithmetic here is adding zero to zero.

Rotating the assignments of a number of jobs that need to be enriched. This means washing dishes for a while, then washing silverware. The arithmetic is substituting one zero for another zero.

Removing the most difficult parts of the assignment in order to free the worker to accomplish more of the less challenging assignments. This traditional industrial engineering approach amounts to subtraction in the hope of accomplishing addition.

These are common forms of horizontal loading that frequently come up in preliminary brainstorming sessions on job enrichment. The principles of vertical loading have not all been worked out as yet, and they remain rather general, but I have furnished seven useful starting points for consideration in Exhibit 3.

A Successful Application

An example from a highly successful job enrichment experiment can illustrate the distinction between horizontal and vertical loading of a job. The subjects of this study were the stockholder correspondents employed by a very large corporation. Seemingly, the task required of these carefully selected and highly trained correspondents was quite complex and challenging. But almost all indexes of performance and job attitudes were low, and exit interviewing confirmed that the challenge of the job existed merely as words.

A job enrichment project was initiated in the form of an experiment with one group, designated as an achieving unit, having its job enriched by the principles described in Exhibit 3. A control group continued to do its job in the traditional way. (There were also two "uncommitted" groups of correspondents formed to measure the so-called Hawthorne Effect—that is, to gauge whether productivity and attitudes toward the job changed artificially merely because employees sensed that the company was paying more attention to them in doing something different or novel. The results for these groups were substantially the same as for the control group, and for the sake of simplicity I do not deal with them in this summary.) No changes in hygiene were introduced for either group other than those that would have been made anyway, such as normal pay increases.

The changes for the achieving unit were introduced in the first two months, averaging one per week of the seven motivators listed in Exhibit 3. At the end of six months the members of the achieving unit were found to be outperforming their counterparts in the control group, and in addition indicated a marked increase in their liking for their jobs. Other results showed that the achieving group had lower absenteeism and, subsequently, a much higher rate of promotion.

Exhibit 3 Principles of Vertical Job Loading

Principle	Motivators Involved
A. Removing some controls while retaining accountability	Responsibility and personal achievement
B. Increasing the accountability of individuals for own work	Responsibility and recognition
C. Giving a person a complete natural unit of work (module, division, area, and so on)	Responsibility, achievement, and recognition
D. Granting additional authority to an employee in his activity; job freedom	Responsibility, achievement, and recognition
E. Making periodic reports directly available to the worker himself rather than to the supervisor	Internal recognition
F. Introducing new and more difficult tasks not previously handled	Growth and learning
G. Assigning individuals specific or specialized tasks, enabling them to become experts	Responsibility, growth, and advancement

Exhibit 4 illustrates the changes in performance, measured in February and March, before the study period began, and at the end of each month of the study period. The shareholder service index represents quality of letters, including accuracy of information, and speed of response to stockholders' letters of inquiry. The index of a current month was averaged into the average of the two prior months, which means that improvement was harder to obtain if the indexes of the previous months were low. The "achievers" were performing less well before the six-month period started, and their performance service index continued to decline after the introduction of the motivators, evidently because of uncertainty over their newly granted responsibilities. In the third month, however, performance improved, and soon the members of this group had reached a high level of accomplishment.

Exhibit 5 shows the two groups' attitudes toward their job, measured at the end of March, just before the first motivator was introduced, and again at the end of September. The correspondents were asked 16 questions, all involving motivation. A typical one was, "As you see it, how many opportunities do you feel that you have in your job for making worthwhile contributions?" The answers were scaled from 1 to 5, with 80 as the maximum possible score. The achievers became much more positive about their job, while the attitude of the control unit remained about the same (the drop is not statistically significant).

How was the job of these correspondents restructured? Exhibit 6 lists the suggestions made that were deemed to be horizontal loading, and the actual vertical loading changes that were incorporated in the job of the achieving unit. The capital letters under "Principle" after "Vertical loading" refer to the corresponding letters in Exhibit 3. The reader will note that the rejected forms of

Exhibit 4 Shareholder Service Index in Company Experiment (Three-month cumulative average)

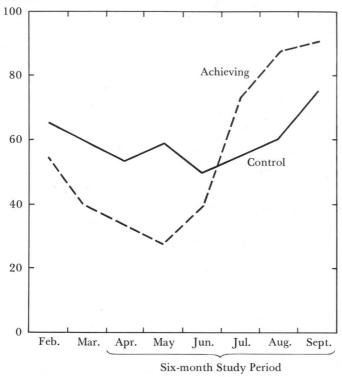

Performance Index

Six-month Study Period

Exhibit 5 Changes in Attitudes Toward Tasks In Company Experiment (Changes in mean scores over six-month period)

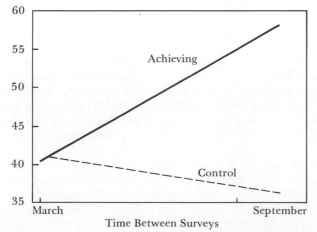

Job Reaction Mean Score

Time Between Surveys

Exhibit 6 Enlargement vs. Enrichment of Correspondents' Tasks in Company Experiment

Horizontal Loading Suggestions (rejected)	Vertical Loading Suggestions (adopted)	Principle
Firm quotas could be set for letters to be answered each day, using a rate which would be hard to reach.	Subject matter experts were appointed within each unit for other members of the unit to consult with before seeking supervisory help. (The supervisor had been answering all specialized and difficult questions.)	G
The women could type the letters themselves, as well as compose them, or take on any other clerical functions.	Correspondents signed their own names on letters. (The supervisor had been signing all letters.)	B
All difficult or complex inquiries could be channeled to a few women so that the remainder could achieve high rates of output. These jobs could be exchanged from time to time.	The work of the more experienced correspondents was proofread less frequently by supervisors and was done at the correspondents' desks, dropping verification from 100% to 10%. (Previously, all correspondents' letters had been checked by the supervisor.)	A
	Production was discussed, but only in terms such as "a full day's work is expected." As time went on, this was no longer mentioned. (Before, the group had been constantly reminded of the number of letters that needed to be answered.)	D
The women could be rotated through units handling different customers, and then sent back to their own units.	Outgoing mail went directly to the mailroom without going over supervisors' desks. (The letters had always been routed through the supervisors.)	A
	Correspondents were encouraged to answer letters in a more personalized way. (Reliance on the form-letter approach had been standard practice.)	C
	Each correspondent was held personally responsible for the quality and accuracy of letters. (This responsibility had been the province of the supervisor and the verifier.)	B,E

horizontal loading correspond closely to the list of common manifestations of the phenomenon listed earlier.

Steps to Job Enrichment

Now that the motivator idea has been described in practice, here are the steps that managers should take in instituting the principle with their employees:

1. Select those jobs in which (a) the investment in industrial engineering does not make changes too costly, (b) attitudes are poor, (c) hygiene is becoming very costly, and (d) motivation will make a difference in performance.

2. Approach these jobs with the conviction that they can be changed. Years of tradition have led managers to believe that the content of the jobs is sacrosanct and the only scope of action that they have is in ways of stimulating people.

3. Brainstorm a list of changes that may enrich the jobs, without concern for their practicality.

4. Screen the list to eliminate suggestions that involve hygiene, rather than actual motivation.

5. Screen the list for generalities, such as "give them more responsibility," that are rarely followed in practice. This might seem obvious, but the motivator words have never left industry; the substance has just been rationalized and organized out. Words like "responsibility," "growth," "achievement," and "challenge," for example, have been elevated to the lyrics of the patriotic anthem for all organizations. It is the old problem typified by the pledge of allegiance to the flag being more important than contributions to the country—of following the form, rather than the substance.

6. Screen the list to eliminate any *horizontal* loading suggestions.

7. Avoid direct participation by the employees whose jobs are to be enriched. Ideas they have expressed previously certainly constitute a valuable source for recommended changes, but their direct involvement contaminates the process with human relations *hygiene* and, more specifically, gives them only a *sense* of making a contribution. The job is to be changed, and it is the content that will produce the motivation, not attitudes about being involved or the challenge inherent in setting up a job. That process will be over shortly, and it is what the employees will be doing from then on that will determine their motivation. A sense of participation will result only in short-term movement.

8. In the initial attempts at job enrichment, set up a controlled experiment. At least two equivalent groups should be chosen, one an experimental unit in which the motivators are systematically introduced over a period of time, and the other one a control group in which no changes are made. For both groups, hygiene should be allowed to follow its natural course for the duration of the experiment. Pre- and post-installation tests of performance and job attitudes are necessary to evaluate the effectiveness of the job enrichment program. The attitude test must be limited to motivator items in order to divorce the employee's view of the job he is given from all the surrounding hygiene feelings that he might have.

9. Be prepared for a drop in performance in the experimental group the first few weeks. The changeover to a new job may lead to a temporary reduction in efficiency.

10. Expect your first-line supervisors to experience some anxiety and hostility over the changes you are making. The anxiety comes from their fear that the changes will result in poorer performance for their unit. Hostility will arise when the employees start assuming what the supervisors regard as their own responsibility for performance. The supervisor without checking duties to perform may then be left with little to do.

After a successful experiment, however, the supervisor usually discovers the supervisory and managerial functions he has neglected, or which were never his because all his time was given over to checking the work of his subordinates.

For example, in the R&D division of one large chemical company I know of, the supervisors of the laboratory assistants were theoretically responsible for their training and evaluation. These functions, however, had come to be performed in a routine, unsubstantial fashion. After the job enrichment program, during which the supervisors were not merely passive observers of the assistants' performance, the supervisors actually were devoting their time to reviewing performance and administering thorough training.

What has been called an employee-centered style of supervision will come about not through education of supervisors, but by changing the jobs that they do.

Concluding Note

Job enrichment will not be a one-time proposition, but a continuous management function. The initial changes, however, should last for a very long period of time. There are a number of reasons for this:

The changes should bring the job up to the level of challenge commensurate with the skill that was hired.

Those who have still more ability eventually will be able to demonstrate it better and win promotion to higher-level jobs.

The very nature of motivators, as opposed to hygiene factors, is that they have a much longer-term effect on employees' attitudes. Perhaps the job will have to be enriched again, but this will not occur as frequently as the need for hygiene.

Not all jobs can be enriched, nor do all jobs need to be enriched. If only a small percentage of the time and money that is now devoted to hygiene, however, were given to job enrichment efforts, the return in human satisfaction and economic gain would be one of the largest dividends that industry and society have ever reaped through their efforts at better personnel management.

The argument for job enrichment can be summed up quite simply: If you have someone on a job, use him. If you can't use him on the job, get rid of him, either via automation or by selecting someone with lesser ability. If you can't use him and you can't get rid of him, you will have a motivation problem.

Organizing for Product Innovation

JAY W. LORSCH, PAUL R. LAWRENCE

In this article we shall report the results of a pilot study on the problem of obtaining collaboration and coordination between research, sales, and production specialists involved in product innovation in two organizations producing basic plastic products. In presenting the findings we shall emphasize these points:

(1) The research, sales, and production specialists working on different tasks connected with product innovation develop different viewpoints and methods of operation and tend to work best in different kinds of organizational structures. This specialization and the differences associated with it are important for the effective operation of the separate sales, research, and production units, but they also contribute to the disagreements and differences of opinion between these departments which inevitably occur around the product-innovation process.

(2) Successful product innovation depends not only on this specialization but also on the development of methods of coordination which enable executives with diverse points of view to resolve their disagreements and achieve a unity of effort.

(3) One method of obtaining effective coordination is to establish a separate organizational unit which has as its primary task coordinating the activities of sales, production, and research. Such a unit is most effective when its members have a balanced point of view which enables them to work effectively with each of the specialist groups. By this we mean that the coordinators do not consistently favor the viewpoints of salesmen *or* researchers *or* production men but understand the interest of *all three* groups and can work back and forth effectively among them.

(4) A second method of improving collaboration is to use teams or committees in which the members have learned to fight constructively with each other, confronting their differences and resolving them rather than avoiding them. The members must have authority to make decisions—and they must not be too high up in the organization. Effective coordination seems to result when they are at a sufficiently low level in the company structure to have detailed technical and/or market knowledge bearing on the conflicts they try to resolve.

- How can we get our research people to be more responsive to the needs of the market?
- What can we do to get our salesmen more involved in selling new products and seeking new applications?
- Why are our production people so conservative when it comes to introducing new products?
- How can we get sales, research, and production people to pull in the same direction on product development?

Questions such as these have become of increasing concern to executives in companies operating in the many industries characterized by rapid technological and market change, in which new and improved products are the key to corporate success. Several years ago we were all concerned with obtaining effective research organizations. It was generally believed that if a climate could be developed in which talented scientists and engineers could work creatively, we would be assured of a constant flow of product improvements and new products. As companies have become successful in developing more effective research organizations, however, it has become increasingly apparent that creative, innovative researchers are not enough by themselves. What is needed, as the questions above indicate, is an organization which provides collaboration between scientific innovators and sales and production specialists, so that:

- The skills of the innovators can be directed at market needs and technological problems.
- Sales and production specialists can be actively involved in the commercialization of ideas developed in the laboratory.
- And, as a result, ideas can be transferred smoothly from laboratory prototype to commercial reality.

How Companies Innovate

We can begin our discussion of the problems of organizing for innovation by briefly examining the essential functions of any organization. Basically, an organization, whether it be the product division of a diversified chemical company or a corner drug store, provides a means by which more than one person can work together to perform a task that one individual could not perform alone. This means each individual or unit of the larger organization will be performing some specialized portion of the organization's task.

The first function of an organization, then, is to divide the total task into specialized pieces. The organization's second function is to provide a means by which units working on different parts of the total task may coordinate their activities to come out with a unified effort. While these processes of specialization and coordination are essential in any organization, they are particularly crucial for companies competing in developing new products.

Perhaps the best way to understand the specialization and coordination required in the innovation process is to describe the steps involved in developing products in the two plastics companies we studied. These were prominent companies in their industry, chosen to show similarities and contrasts in their organizational approach to product innovation. To protect their identity, we shall refer to them as the "Rhody" and "Crown" companies. It should be stressed that the two companies sold their products for industrial applications and there was, therefore, a constant demand not only for major new products but also for a flow of modifications in properties and processes that could improve the performance of old products and yield new applications for them. In our description of the innovation process we will be referring to the steps required for both types of innovation.

Required Collaboration

As we have already indicated, there are three major groups of specialists in each organization. Sales, production, and research specialists are each coping with a different sector of the organization's environment, and each should have a different portion of the total skills and knowledge required to discover a product idea and convert it into a tangible product:

- The sales department in dealing with the market environment should be in a position to extract information about market trends and customer needs.

- The research department in dealing with the scientific environment should be able to provide data about the technical and scientific feasibility of any new product development.
- The production department should have a store of knowledge about the limits of plant processes from the production environment.

Information from the sales department about customer needs and from production about processing limits has to be passed on to the research unit so that this information can be assimilated with the scientific feasibility of developing or modifying a product. Within the limits set by the needs of the customer and the capacities of the production process, the research units are then required to come up with a new development. If they succeed, it is then necessary to transfer information back to the sales department about product characteristics and to the production department about process specifications. With this information sales should be in a position to make and implement market plans, and production should have the data for planning and executing its task of manufacturing the product.

In short, product innovation requires close coordination between research and sales, on the one hand, and between research and production, on the other. This coordination is necessary not only to provide the two-way flow of technical information described earlier, but also to develop mutual trust and confidence between the members of the units which are required to collaborate in product development. Sales personnel must have confidence in research's knowledge of science, while research scientists must have confidence in sales' appraisal of the market. Similarly, there must be mutual confidence between research and production about production's ability to operate the process efficiently according to specifications and about research's capacity to develop a process that can be operated efficiently.

Product innovation, then, requires close collaboration between the sales and research units and the production and research units if the specialists involved are effectively to bring their separate skills to bear on a successful product development. However, the complexity and uncertainty of the factors which must be dealt with (at least in companies developing a multiplicity of new products) make it necessary for this coordination to take place at the *lower* levels of the organization. Executives in both Rhody and Crown indicate that it is difficult for managers at the upper levels of the organization to keep in touch with the multitude of rapidly changing factors which must be considered in the day-to-day process of developing many new products. Only the specialists on the firing line have the detailed knowledge of markets and technologies to make the frequent day-to-day decisions which the innovation process requires.

So far we have presented only a description of what *should* happen in both organizations if innovation is to be successfully accomplished. But our interests are in investigating not only what should happen but also, and more importantly, what *actually* happens in each organization as a result of the processes of specialization and coordination required for product innovation. We want to find out in what ways the groups of specialists working on diverse tasks in the two companies are different in their ways of thinking, in the ground rules they work by, and in terms of the organizational structures in which they work.

Dimensions of Specialization

When we undertook our study, we decided to find out first how groups of specialists actually were differentiated. We expected the differences to be related to the problems of obtaining coordination between units. Our findings about departmental differences are classified in terms of four main dimensions: (a) degree of departmental structure, (b) members' orientation toward time, (c) members' orientation toward others, and (d) members' orientation toward the environment.

Each of the differences between departments is seen to be a function of the characteristics of the environmental sector (market, science, or plant) with which a unit is coping in performing its task. Groups, such as production units, which have a very certain environment (as measured by the certainty of information at a given time, the rate of change in the environment, and the time range of the task) are highly structured. Because they are working with a highly stable environment, they tend to develop explicit routines and highly programmed ways of operating, adopt a directive interpersonal style, and also find a short-range time orientation useful for the performance of their task.

On the other hand, units, such as research, which are coping with less certain environments tend to be less structured, are characterized by a more permissive interpersonal orientation, and have a longer time orientation. These characteristics are consistent with an uncertain, nonroutine task, since effective performance of such a task requires opportunity for open consultation among colleagues in seeking solutions to problems and freedom to consider and attempt different courses of action.

Principal Patterns

How do the differences in orientation and structure characterize the departments in Rhody and Crown? Exhibit 1 summarizes our findings on this question. The data presented here are representative of the *general* pattern which exists in both organizations; some minor variations between the two organizations are not depicted. We see that:

Members of each department tend primarily to be oriented toward the sector of the environment with which their task involves them. Research people tend to be more oriented toward discovering new scientific knowledge, while sales people are more concerned with customer problems and market conditions, and production personnel indicate a primary concern with production costs and processing problems.

In time orientation, the research scientists tend to be more concerned with long-range matters which will not have an impact on company profits for several

Exhibit 1 Patterns of Specialization

	Departmental Structure	Orientation Toward Time	Orientation Toward Others	Orientation Toward Environment
Research	Low	Long	Permissive	Science
Sales	Medium	Short	Permissive	Market
Production	High	Short	Directive	Plant

years in the future. Sales and production specialists are primarily concerned with the more immediate problems which affect the company's performance within the current year.

The interpersonal orientations of the members of the units in both companies are also different. Research and sales personnel tend to prefer more permissive interpersonal relationships, while production specialists indicate a preference for a more directive manner of working with their colleagues.

As for the degree of departmental structure, the research units have the lowest amount and the production units have the highest. The sales units, which seem to be performing a task of medium certainty, have a structure which falls between the extremes represented by research and production.

What we find in both companies, then, are units which are quite different from each other both in terms of members' orientations and the structure in which the members work. These differences in ways of thinking about the job and in ground rules and operating procedures mean that each of these groups tends to view the task of innovation somewhat differently.

Impact on Ability

While we next want to examine the influence of these differences on the process of obtaining coordination, we should first emphasize a point which too often has been overlooked: The differences have a *positive* effect on the ability of each individual unit to perform its particular task. The common orientations and ground rules within a unit and a departmental structure which facilitate task performance direct the efforts of people in the unit to their segment of the organizational task and enhance their ability to carry out their mission. Because the units are performing different tasks, we have to expect that they will develop different departmental structures and that their members will be oriented differently. If attempts were made to standardize the structures of all units and to have all members of the organization oriented in the same direction, we would lose the benefits of specialization.

The two companies in our study recognize this fact to differing degrees. At Rhody the differences along the four dimensions tend to be greater than at Crown. Each department at Rhody not only has a structure conducive to the performance of its task, but also tends to be more highly concerned with a single task dimension or with a particular period of time than does the same unit at Crown. While in both organizations the specialization of units enables them to address their separate tasks, the units at Rhody, by virtue of their higher degree of specialization, often seem to be better able to perform their individual tasks.

Organizational Paradox

While specialized orientations and structures facilitate a unit's task performance, we would expect the patterns to be closely related to the problems of coordination in both firms. Because members of a given department hold common attitudes about what is important in their work and about dealing with each other, they are able to work effectively with each other. But to the extent that the ground rules and orientations held by members of one department are different from those held by members of another, we would expect the departments to have increased difficulty achieving the high degree of coordination required for effective innovation.

The data we collected through a questionnaire about the effectiveness of coordination between departments at Rhody and Crown confirm this expectation. When two units are similar in departmental structure and in the orientations of their members, we find that they have few problems in obtaining effective collaboration *with each other.* But when units tend to be on opposite poles along the four dimensions, we find that there are more problems in integrating their efforts. Within each organization there is clear evidence that the greater the differences in orientation and structure between any pair of units, the greater the problems of obtaining effective coordination.

Although this relationship holds within each company, we find an interesting paradox when the two organizations are compared. As already indicated, there is a higher degree of specialization and differentiation at Rhody than at Crown. Pairs of units which are required to collaborate at Rhody tend to be less similar than the comparable pairs of units at Crown. Since units at Crown are more similar, this *should* mean that Crown encounters fewer problems of coordination. However, this does not turn out to be the case. Rhody appears to be achieving better integration than Crown, even though it also has a higher degree of differentiation. In short, within each organization there is a relationship between the effectiveness of coordination and the degree of differentiation, but the organization which has the highest degree of specialization also has the most effective collaboration.

The significance of this paradox grows if we recall that specialization is a two-sided coin. Specialization is useful because it is necessary for the performance of individual departments; on the other hand, it can have negative consequences in that it is at the root of the problems of achieving the coordination required for innovation. At Rhody we have a situation in which one organization is able to have its cake (in the form of specialization) and to eat it too (in the form of coordination).

Contrasting Methods

Does the explanation reside in the methods used by the two organizations to facilitate coordination between units? We believe it does.

Attempts at devising methods to improve coordination between the specialized departments involved in product innovation are certainly not novel. New-product departments, or coordinating departments with other appellations, have been established in many organizations with the primary function of coordinating the activities of research, sales, and production specialists in the development of new products. Similarly, many firms have appointed liaison individuals who are responsible for linking two or more groups of functional specialists. Another frequent device has been to develop short-term project teams with representatives from the several functional departments to work on a new product. Finally, many companies have relied on permanent cross-functional coordinating teams to deal with the continuing problems of innovation around a given group of products.

Both Rhody and Crown have developed the same types of devices:
(1) In each company there is a coordinating department which has the

primary task of coordinating or integrating the innovation activities of the research, production, and sales units.

(2) Each company is making use of permanent cross-functional coordinating committees which have representatives from each of the basic departments and the coordinating department. The primary function of these committees is to serve as a setting in which coordination can take place.

Since both organizations are utilizing the same devices to achieve coordination, it is pertinent to ask whether there are differences in the functioning and effectiveness of these devices. The answer provided by our investigation is an emphatic *yes*.

We now turn to an examination of these differences, looking first at the coordinating departments, then at the committees.

Coordinating Departments

In addition to seeking teamwork among research, production, and sales, the coordinating departments at Rhody and Crown perform certain other tasks. At Crown the department is also involved in market planning and the coordination of sales efforts. At Rhody the coordinating department is also involved in technical service and market-development activities. As might be expected, both departments have developed orientations and structural characteristics somewhat different from those of the other units in the companies.

Key to Coordination

While various similarities exist between the two coordinating groups, there is also, as our measurements reveal, a major distinction:

At Rhody the coordinating department falls in a middle position on each of the four dimensions we have considered. That is, if we compare the department's degree of structure and its members' orientations with those of the sales, production, and research departments, it always has an intermediate value, never an extreme one. For instance, members of the coordinating department have a balanced orientation along the time dimension. They are equally concerned with the short-range problems of sales and production and the long-range matters with which research wrestles. Similarly, coordinating personnel have a balanced concern with production, scientific, and market environments. The degree of departmental structure and the interpersonal orientation of coordinating members also fall between the extremes of the other departments.

At Crown the coordinating department is in the middle along the structure and interpersonal dimensions but tends to be highly oriented toward short-range time concerns and toward the market environment. Personnel indicate a high concern with immediate sales problems, and less concern with longer-range matters or with research or production environments. On both the time and the environment dimensions, therefore, the coordinating department is not intermediate between the departments it is supposed to be linking.

The foregoing difference appears to be related to differences in the effectiveness of the two units. Our questionnaires and interviews indicate that the coordinating department at Rhody is generally perceived by members of that organization to be doing an effective job of linking the basic departments. On the other hand, the coordinating department at Crown is not perceived to be as effective as most members of the Crown organization think it should be.

Observations by Executives

The reactions of executives in the two companies pretty well explain for us why the intermediate position of the Rhody coordinating department is associated with effective coordination, while the imbalance in certain orientations of the Crown unit inhibits its performance. The following are a few typical comments from Rhody managers:

"The most important thing is that we have the coordinating department with its contacts with the customers and its technically trained people who are in contact with research. They are the kingpins. They have a good feel for research's ability, and they know the needs of the market. They will work back and forth with research and the other units."

"Generally speaking, the feeling of close cooperation between the coordinating unit and sales is echoed in the field. The top salesmen all get along well with the coordinating guys. You take a good coordinating fellow and a good salesman and that makes a powerful team. In our business the boys upstairs in the coordinating unit are top notch. They know what the lab can do, and they know the salesman's problems."

But at Crown the comments of executives have a different tone:

"My biggest criticism of our situation is that the coordinating department isn't a good enough mechanism to link the research activities to the customer. We need a better marketing strategy on certain products and some long-term plans. The lack of planning in the coordinating department is deplorable. One of our troubles is that the coordinating people are so tied up in day-to-day detail that they can't look to the future. They are still concerned with 1964 materials when they should be concerned with 1965 markets."

"Our problem is we can't clearly define the technical problems the customer is having. Theoretically the coordinating men should be able to handle this for research because they know the customer best. But they are so involved in present business that it takes all their time. They have a budget they have to live up to, and the best way to make money is to sell existing products. They know that selling existing products is more profitable than selling new products, so they keep on selling existing products to live up to the expectations of the budget."

In other words, we have a marked difference in reaction. What managers at Rhody are stressing is that the coordinating unit in their organization is effective because it has a familiarity with the problems, orientations, and ways of operating of the basic units it connects. At Crown the primary complaints about that organization's less-effective coordinating unit are that its members tend to be too oriented toward immediate sales matters.

The situation in these two organizations seems to indicate that for a coordinating department to be effective in linking the several specialized departments, it must be intermediate between any two along each of the several dimensions of orientation and structure. When a coordinating department is in this position, its members have more in common with members of the other units. Coordinating personnel tend to think and act in ways which are more understandable and agreeable to members of the other departments—and this facilitates collaboration. If members of the coordinating department have orientations and ground rules which are more suited to one specialized unit, as is the situation at Crown, their ways of thinking will necessarily be different from the other departments—and this situation will impair their effectiveness as coordinators.

Cross-Functional Groups

Even in an organization like Rhody, where the coordinating unit is doing an effective job of facilitating cooperation between the specialized units, certain disagreements between the various specialist units seem to be inevitable. Management's problem is to provide a setting in which attempts at resolving these disagreements can be made effectively. Both organizations in this study have turned to permanent cross-functional coordinating committees as devices for providing a setting in which to work at achieving coordination between units.

In investigating the functioning of these committees in the two organizations, we again want to obtain an assessment of their effectiveness as well as some understanding of the factors which might be related to their performance. If we listen to some of the comments made by members of both organizations, the differences between the devices in the two companies become apparent.

At the Rhody company, managers make comments such as these about the cross-functional teams:

"Our problems get thrashed out in committee. We work them over until everybody agrees this is the best effort you can make. We may decide this isn't good enough; then we may decide to ask for more people, more plant, and so forth. We all sometimes have to take a modification and be realistic and say this is the best we can do."

"I may want us to do some work on a particular new product. The coordinating guy may say, 'Let's get the customer to change his process instead.' A research guy may say we need both. It is the way we do it that becomes argumentative and rightfully so. These things take several meetings to work out, but we are never really stalemated. We have decided in our committee that we won't stalemate. There is more than one way to our ends. If I don't agree with the others, then I abdicate my position—sometimes gracefully and sometimes not.

"We had a disagreement about releasing confidential information to a customer and had quite a discussion about it. This was only the second time we had gotten so formal as to have a vote. I was outvoted three to one, but that afternoon I was the one who had to call the customer and give him the information as we had decided."

"Since we have had these committees, we are working more closely with other groups. It is really working out. In the past, production was reluctant to give us information, and they wanted to keep the prerogative of making process changes. Since this committee has been operating, there has been a greater exchange of information. . . ."

At Crown the executives speak differently about their experiences with cross-functional committees:

"Unfortunately, the committees are not decision-making groups as much as I would like. Generally there is a reporting session. We don't have time going over all these things to make some of the decisions which need to be made. I would like to see more hashing out of the problems and making of decisions. Of course we do make decisions every day between us."

"If I want something very badly and I am confronted by a roadblock, I go to top management to get the decision made. If the research managers are willing to go ahead, there is no problem. If there is a conflict, then I would go to their boss."

"I think these meetings only intensify the arguments. I haven't learned much that I didn't know already before I got to the meeting. It used to be that we had some knock-'em down, drag-out fights, but then we would get things settled. But this doesn't take place anymore, so there isn't any place for us to resolve our difficulties."

These and similar comments indicate that members of the Rhody organization find the cross-functional committees an important aid in achieving collaboration, while members of the Crown organization do not. They also indicate, as do our observations of meetings of these committees in both organizations, that there are at least two important differences between the functioning of these committees in the two organizations. Before going into these contrasts, however, we must first point to an important distinction in the organizational structures of the two companies.

The Crown organization tends to have a higher degree of structure (tighter spans of control, more specific rules and procedures, and so forth) in *all* its parts than does the Rhody organization. One important aspect of this difference is that the level at which decisions about product innovation are supposed to be made is much lower in the organizational hierarchy at Rhody than at Crown.

Decision Authority

The significance of this distinction becomes apparent if we turn to look at the teams at Rhody. In this organization team members are in most cases first-line supervisors who (being right down at the working level) have the detailed market and technical knowledge required to make decisions. They are the only persons who attend the meetings, and they usually have the formal authority to make decisions.

Our observation of meetings at Rhody, along with comments made by company executives, indicate that there are ground rules or norms operating in cross-functional committees which sanction the open confrontation of disagreement between members. Members of the committees tend to recognize their differences and seek ways of resolving them within the constraints of the situation with which they are dealing. This working through of disagreements often takes a great deal of emotional and intellectual effort, but members of the committees at Rhody tend to persevere until some resolution is reached. After decisions are made, the members of the committees are highly committed to them. As we learned from one executive, even though a member is not in initial agreement with the decision taken, he is expected to—and he does—carry out the actions worked out in the meetings.

In contrast with the situation at Rhody, we find at Crown (as we would expect from the greater degree of structure throughout this company) that members of the committees are at a higher level than their counterparts at

Rhody, but even these managers often do not have the authority to make decisions. Furthermore, because they are at a higher level, they usually do not have either the technical or market knowledge required to make the detailed decisions necessary to develop products.

As a consequence of this situation, members of the Crown committees often bring both their superiors and their subordinates to the meetings with them—the superiors in order to provide someone who has the authority to make decisions, the subordinates so that someone is present who has the detailed technical and market knowledge to draw on for decisions. Bringing in all these participants results in meetings two or three times as large as those at Rhody.

Resolving Conflict

Our observations of meetings at Crown and the comments of executives indicate that there are other shortcomings in the Crown committees. The norms of behavior in these groups sanction withdrawal from disagreement and conflict. Whenever there is a disagreement, the members tend to avoid discussing the matter, hoping it will magically go away. If this doesn't place the problem out of sight, they find another avenue of avoidance by passing it on to their superiors. As a consequence, many decisions which should be made at Crown seem to get dropped. They are not picked up again until they have festered for so long that somebody *has* to deal with them—and it is often too late by that time.

There will always be disagreements between members of departments which have highly different orientations and concerns. The problem facing members of coordinating committees is to learn to fight together constructively so that they can resolve these differences. At Rhody members of the cross-functional teams have developed this ability. They work at resolving conflict at their own level. They do not withdraw from disputes, nor do they try to smooth over their differences or arrive at some easy compromise. Rather, they seem willing to argue the issues involved until some understanding is reached about the optimal solution in a given situation.

In essence, the committees at Rhody have developed the ability to confront their differences openly and search persistently for solutions which will provide effective collaboration. At Crown, on the other hand, the committees avoid fights and forfeit the opportunity to achieve the coordination required for innovation.

Conclusion

The foregoing comparisons seem to provide an answer to the paradox of the Rhody organization achieving both greater specialization and more effective coordination than the Crown company does. The effective coordinating unit and cross-functional coordinating committees allow members at Rhody to concentrate on their specialties and still achieve a unity of effort. Sales, research, and production specialists are each able to address their separate departmental tasks and work in a climate which is conducive to good performance. At the same time, the men in the coordinating department, who have a balanced orientation toward the concerns of the three departments of specialists, help the three units to achieve a unity of effort. The cross-functional committees also provide a means by which the specialist groups and the coordinators can work through their differences and arrive at the best common approach.

At Crown, in spite of the fact that the specialist departments are more similar in orientation and structure than are the units at Rhody, there is more difficulty in obtaining unity of effort between them. Since the coordinators are overly concerned with short-term matters and sales problems, they do not effectively perform their function of linking the three groups of specialists. The cross-functional committees do not contribute much to coordination between these departments, either. They do not provide a setting in which problems can be solved, since authority to make decisions often resides in the higher levels of the organization and since norms have developed within the committees which encourage members to avoid conflict and pass it on to their superiors.

But what about the results the two companies have achieved in the market place? We have been asserting that both a high degree of specialization and effective coordination are important in achieving product innovation in this situation, but we have not presented any evidence that Rhody, with its greater specialization and more effective coordination, is in fact doing a better job of product innovation than is Crown. The following figures do show that the Rhody organization *is* achieving a higher level of innovation than Crown: At Rhody, new products developed in the last five years have accounted for 59% of sales. At Crown, the figure is only 20%, or just about one-third of Rhody's.

Part of this difference may have been due to some variation in market and technical factors confronting the two organizations. However, since these two organizations have been operating in the same industry and have been confronted by similar market conditions and technical problems, and because of the different levels of coordination and specialization achieved in each company, it seems safe to conclude that there is indeed a relationship between innovation performance and the internal organizational factors we have been discussing.

Management Challenge

While this discussion has been based on an examination of two organizations in the plastics industry, there is no question that the requirements for specialization and coordination are just as urgent in other industries confronted with the need for product innovation. It seems safe to generalize that, whatever the field or function, managers interested in improving their record with new products must recognize two essential organizational ingredients of success:

1. Specialists who are clearly oriented toward their individual tasks and who work in organizational structures which are conducive to task performance.

2. Effective means of coordination which permit specialists with diverse knowledge and orientations to work together. (There will be disagreements and conflicts among these specialists, but the organization must provide a means to resolve the conflicts in such a way that the full energy of research, sales, and production people can be brought to bear on innovation.)

Our discussion has focused on two devices to achieve this coordination—*coordinating departments* whose members have a balanced point of view enabling them to work effectively among the several specialist groups, and *cross-functional coordinating committees* in which members have learned to confront their differences and fight over them constructively so they can reach an optimal resolution. But other means of coordination are also available. The challenge confronting managers responsible for organizing for innovations is to work at developing means of coordination which permit effective specialization *and* effective coordination. This is the combination that is needed to produce the constant flow of innovations necessary for corporate growth in changing markets.

Management and Technology

JOAN WOODWARD

[The Human Relations Research staff of the South East Essex Technical College studied one hundred manufacturing firms in a certain area of England from 1955 to 1957. The objective of the research was to find out how these firms were organized and what caused them to organize in certain ways. The following extracts from the report of the researchers show what they found.]

The 100 firms in the survey were organized and run in widely different ways. In only about half did the principles and concepts of management theory appear to have had much influence on organizational development.

In 35 firms there was an essentially 'line' or 'military' type of organization; two firms were organized functionally, almost exactly as recommended by Frederick Taylor fifty years ago [*Shop Management,* 1910]. The rest followed in varying degrees a line-staff pattern of organization; that is, they employed a number of functional specialists as 'staff' to advise those in the direct line of authority.

The number of distinct levels of management between board and operators varied from two to twelve; while the span of control of the chief executive[1] ranged from two to nineteen, and that of the first line supervisor—i.e., the first level of authority that spent more than 50% of the time on supervisory duties— from seven to ninety. (An individual's span of control is the number of people directly responsible to him.)

Did any common thread underlie these differences? One possible explanation was that they reflected the different personalities of the senior managers, another that they arose from the historical background of the firms. While such factors undoubtedly influenced the situation, they did not adequately explain it; they were not always associated with differences in organizational patterns or in the quality of human relations.

A new approach lay in recognizing that firms differed not only in size, kind of industry and organizational structure, but also in objectives. While the firms were all manufacturing goods for sale, their detailed objectives depended on the nature of the product and the type of customer. Thus some firms were in more competitive industries than others, some were making perishable goods

From *Management and Technology,* by Joan Woodward. London, England: Her Majesty's Stationery Office, 1958. Excerpts from pp. 8–30.

1. The chief executive was in some cases the Chairman, in others the Managing Director, and in others the General or Works Manager. In every case he represented the highest level of authority operating fulltime on the spot.

that could not be stored, some produced for stock, and others to orders; in fact, marketing conditions were different in every firm. The underlying purpose varied too. For example, one firm had originally undertaken manufacture to demonstrate that the products of its mines could be effective substitutes for other more commonly used materials.

These differences in objectives controlled and limited the techniques of production that could be employed. A firm whose objective was to build prototypes of electronic equipment, for example, could not employ the technical methods of mass-production engineering. The criterion of the appropriateness of an organizational structure must be the extent to which it furthers the objectives of the firm, not, as management teaching sometimes suggests, the degree to which it conforms to a prescribed pattern. There can be no one best way of organizing a business.

This is perhaps not sufficiently recognized; management theorists have tried to develop a 'science' of administration relevant to all types of production. One result is that new techniques such as operational research and the various tools of automation have been regarded as aids to management and to industrial efficiency rather than as developments which may change the very nature of management.

The firms were grouped according to their technical methods. Ten different categories emerged. (See Exhibit 1.)

Exhibit 1 Production Systems in South Essex Industry

	I Production of simple units to customers' orders (5 firms)
Group I Small Batch and Unit Production (Types I through V)	II Production of technically complex units (10 firms)
	III Fabrication of large equipment in stages (2 firms)
	IV Production of small batches (7 firms)
	V Production of components in large batches subsequently assembled diversely (3 firms)
Group II Large Batch and Mass Production (Types V through VIII)	VI Production of large batches, assembly line type (25 firms)
	VII Mass production (6 firms)
	VIII Process production combined with the preparation of a product for sale by large-batch or mass-production methods (9 firms)
Group III Process Production (Types VIII through X)	IX Process production of chemicals in batches (13 firms)
	X Continuous flow production of liquids, gases, and solid shapes (12 firms)
	(8 firms unclassified because too mixed or changing)

Firms in the same industry did not necessarily fall into the same group. For example, two tailoring firms of approximately equal size had very different production systems; one made bespoke suits, the other mass-produced men's clothing.

Measurement of Technical Complexity

The ten production groups listed in Exhibit 1 form a scale of technical complexity. (This term is used here to mean the extent to which the production process is controllable and its results predictable.) For example, targets can be set more easily in a chemical plant than in even the most up-to-date mass-production engineering shops, and the factors limiting production are known more definitely so that continual productivity drives are not needed.

The analysis of the research revealed that firms using similar technical methods had similar organizational structures. It appeared that different technologies imposed different kinds of demands on individuals and organizations, and that these demands had to be met through an appropriate form of organization. There were still a number of differences between firms—related to such factors as history, background, and personalities—but these were not as significant as the differences between one production group and another and their influence seemed to be limited by technical considerations. For example, there were differences between managers in their readiness to delegate authority; but in general they delegated more in process than in mass-production firms.

Organization and Technical Complexity

Organization also appeared to change as technology advanced. Some figures showed a direct and progressive relationship with advancing technology (used in this report to mean 'system of techniques'). Others reached their peak in mass production and then decreased, so that in these respects unit and process production resembled each other more than the intermediate stage. Exhibits 2 and 3 show these two trends. (Details are given for the three main groups of production systems. See Exhibit 1.)

The number of levels of authority in the management hierarchy increased with technical complexity. (See Exhibit 2.)

The span of control of the first-line supervisor on the other hand reached its peak in mass production and then decreased. (See Exhibit 3.)

The ratio of managers and supervisory staff to total personnel in the different production systems is shown in some detail in Exhibit 4 as an indication of likely changes in the demand for managers as process production becomes more widespread. There were over three times as many managers for the same number of personnel in process firms as in unit-production firms. Mass-production firms lay between the two groups, with half as many managers as in process production for the same number of personnel.

The following characteristics followed the pattern shown in Exhibit 2—a direct and progressive relationship with technical complexity.

1. *Labour costs* decreased as technology advanced. Wages accounted for an average of 36 percent of total costs in unit production, 34 percent in mass production and 14 percent in process production.

Exhibit 2 The Number of Levels of Authority in Management Hierarchy

| Number of Levels of Authority | System of Production | | |
	Unit Production	Mass Production	Process Production
		Number of Firms	
8 or more		1	5
7		2	5
6		3	7 (median)
5		7	6
4	3	16 (median)	2
3	18 (median)	2	
2	3		

The median is the number of levels in the middle firm in the range—for instance, the sixteenth of the 31 mass-production firms.

2. *The ratios of indirect to direct labour* and of administrative and clerical staff to hourly paid workers increased with technical advance.

3. *The proportion of graduates* among the supervisory staff engaged on production increased too. Unit-production firms employed more professionally qualified staff altogether than other firms, but mainly on research or develop-

Exhibit 3 Span of Control of First Line Supervision

| Number of Persons Controlled | System of Production | | |
	Unit Production	Mass Production	Process Production
		Number of Firms	
Unclassified	1	1	
81–90		3	
71–80		1	
61–70		5	
51–60	1	4	
41–50	3	9 (median)	
31–40	4	5	2
21–30	8 (median)	2	5
11–20	6	1	12 (median)
10 or less	1		6

Exhibit 4   The Ratio of Managers and Supervisory Staff to Other Personnel

	Size of Firm		
System of Production	400–500 Employees	850–1000 Employees	3000–4600 Employees
Unit	1:22	1:37	1:25
Mass	1:14	1:15	1:18
Process	1:8	1:7	1:7

ment activities. In unit-production and mass-production firms it was the complexity of the product that determined the proportion of professionally qualified staff, while in process industry it was the complexity of the process.

4. *The span of control of the chief executive* widened considerably with technical advance.

The following organizational characteristics formed the pattern shown in Exhibit 3. The production groups at the extremes of the technical scale resembled each other, but both differed considerably from the groups in the middle.

1. *Organization was more flexible* at both ends of the scale, duties and responsibilities being less clearly defined.

2. The amount of *written, as opposed to verbal, communication* increased up to the stage of assembly-line production. In process-production firms, however, most of the communications were again verbal.

3. *Specialization between the functions of management* was found more frequently in large-batch and mass production than in unit or process production. In most unit-production firms there were few specialists; managers responsible for production were expected to have technical skills, although these were more often based on length of experience and on 'know-how' than on scientific knowledge. When unit production was based on mass-produced components more specialists were employed however. Large-batch and mass-production firms generally conformed to the traditional line-and-staff pattern, the managerial and supervisory group breaking down into two sub-groups with separate, and sometimes conflicting, ideas and objectives. In process-production firms the line-and-staff pattern broke down in practice, though it sometimes existed on paper. Firms tended either to move towards functional organization of the kind advocated by Taylor, or to do without specialists and incorporate scientific and technical knowledge in the direct executive hierarchy. As a result, technical competence in line supervision was again important, although now the demand was for scientific knowledge rather than technical 'know-how.'

4. Although production control became increasingly important as technology advanced, *the administration of production*—what Taylor called 'the brainwork of production'—was most widely separated from the actual supervision of production operations in large-batch and mass-production firms, where the newer techniques of production planning and control, methods engineering and work study were most developed. The two functions became increasingly reintegrated beyond this point.

The Effect of Technology upon Human Relations

The attitudes and behaviour of management and supervisory staff and the tone of industrial relations in the firms also seemed to be closely related to their technology. In firms at the extremes of the scale, relationships were on the whole better than in the middle ranges. Pressure on people at all levels of the industrial hierarchy seemed to build up as technology advanced, became heaviest in assembly-line production and then relaxed, so reducing personal conflicts. Some factors—the relaxation of pressure, the smaller working groups, the increasing ratio of supervisors to operators, and the reduced need for labour economy—were conducive to industrial peace in process production. Thus, although some managements handled their labour problems more skilfully than others, these problems were much more difficult for firms in the middle ranges than those in unit or process production. The production system seemed more important in determining the quality of human relations than did the numbers employed.

Size and Technology

No significant relationship was revealed between the size of the firm and the system of production. (See Exhibit 5.) There were small, medium, and large firms in each of the main production groups.

Exhibit 5   Production Systems Analysed by Number Employed

Production System	Number Employed: 101–250	251–1000	Over 1000	Total Number of Firms
Unit	7	13	4	24
Mass	14	12	5	31
Process	12	9	4	25
Totals	33	34	13	80

There were firms which employed relatively few people and yet had all the other characteristics of a large company, including a well-defined and developed management structure, considerable financial resources, and a highly paid staff with considerable status in the local industrial community. This was particularly true of the smaller process-production firms. Some of these employed less than 500 people but had more of the characteristics of large-scale industry than unit- or mass-production firms with two or three times as many employees. As indicated already the ratio of management staff to the total number employed was found to increase as technology advanced. It appeared also that the size of the management group was a more reliable measure of the 'bigness' of a firm than its total personnel.

Moreover, although no relationship was found between organization and size in the general classification of firms, some evidence of such a relationship emerged when each of the production groups was considered separately. For example, in the large-batch and mass-production group the number of levels of authority and the span of control of both the chief executive and the first line supervisor both tended to increase with size.

Structure and Success

Again, no relationship between conformity with the 'rules' of management and business success appeared in the preliminary analysis of the research data. The twenty firms graded as outstandingly successful seemed to have little in common.

When, however, firms were grouped on a basis of their production systems, the outstandingly successful ones had at least one feature in common. Many of their organizational characteristics approximated to the median of their production group. For example, in successful unit-production firms the span of control of the first line supervisor ranged from 22 to 28, the median for the group as a whole being 23; in successful mass-production firms it ranged from 45 to 50, the median for the group being 49; and in successful process-production firms it ranged from 11 to 15, the median for the group being 13. (See Exhibit 3.) Conversely the firms graded as below average in most cases diverged widely from the median.

The research workers also found that when the 31 large-batch and mass-production firms were examined separately there was a relationship between conformity with the 'rules' of management and business success. The medians approximated to the pattern of organization advocated by writers on management subjects. Within this limited range of production systems, therefore, observance of these 'rules' does appear to increase administrative efficiency. This is quite understandable because management theory is mainly based on the experience of practitioners in the field, much of which has been in large-batch and mass-production firms. Outside these systems, however, it appears that new 'rules' are needed and it should be recognized that an alternative kind of organizational structure might be more appropriate.

The Organizational Demands of Production Systems

What are the demands made by different technical methods? Is it possible to trace a relationship between a system of production and its associated organization pattern? To find answers to such questions as these, twenty of the firms included in the survey were picked out at intervals along the scale of technical complexity and studied in more detail. They included six unit or small-batch production firms, six large-batch or mass-production firms, five process-production firms, and three in which process production was combined with preparation of the product for sale by large-batch or mass-production techniques.

In each firm the research workers studied:

(1) The manufacturing process itself, analysing the subsidiary tasks necessary to the achievement of primary objectives.

(2) The number and nature of the decisions that had to be taken at each level of the management hierarchy.

(3) The kind of co-operation required between the various members of the management team.

(4) The kind of control which had to be exercised by senior executives.

The research workers then made an analysis of what they term the 'situational demands' in each firm. This means the demands on the organization of the technical situation, the system of techniques imposed by the firm's objectives. They also considered what organizational and operational expedients were likely to be effective in meeting the demands and how far the firms' existing organizational structures did in fact meet them.

The conclusions which follow derive both from these follow-up studies and from the case studies.

Co-ordination

Unit production appeared to demand co-ordination between functions on a day-to-day operational basis. In several firms product development was indistinguishable from production itself. In bespoke tailoring, for example, the cutter developed and produced at the same time, adjusting designs during manufacture to suit individual requirements.

Mass-production firms had elaborate and extensive research and development programmes, but staff responsible for research were not involved in day-to-day production problems or marketing activities. Any policy decisions taken as a result of their work were long-term and far-reaching and often involved considerable expenditure; thus they were taken only at the highest level of management. In some cases the functions were physically separated, research and development being undertaken on a separate site. In others, firms did no research or development at all; they relied for new ideas on outside research bodies or on more informal sources. But although day-to-day integration of functions did not appear to be necessary, and could be dangerously disruptive, co-operation in exchanging information was essential. Product-development staff relied upon information from marketing about the way customers were thinking and from production about manufacturing facilities for the new products. (All this refers only to research relating to the product and not to the development of production methods. Methods research is an integral part of the production function and obviously must be closely integrated with other production activities.)

In *process production* too, functions were in many cases independent of each other, though not as clearly as in mass production, because of the close relationship between product development and process development. More fundamental research on new products was almost entirely self-contained. It was not controlled by existing production facilities or by customers' requirements; indeed, in many cases a market had yet to be found. When development reached the pilot-plant stage, however, closer integration was required between research and production; in some cases this was needed on the job itself; in others co-operation in exchanging information was sufficient.

But while more co-ordination of the three basic tasks was normally required in unit production than in mass or process production, it was occasionally required in the two latter. For instance, in process production, development staff were required to work closely with marketing personnel when creating a market for a new product. In both process and mass production, development staff had to co-operate with production personnel when bringing a new product into large-scale manufacture.

Situational Demands

This discussion clarifies the action of "situational demands." For example, each technical situation requires a different kind of co-operation between the members of a management team. Consequently the system of communication through which cooperation is brought about must also differ from one situation to another. Communications systems cannot be good or bad in themselves; they are good only if they link people together in such a way as to further the objectives of the firm. Thus unit production requires a communication system which brings people together on a day-to-day operational basis; but in mass and process production such a system might well reduce efficiency.

Management Decisions

The number and nature of the decisions that had to be made also depended on the technical demands of the manufacturing process.

In *unit production*

(a) More decisions had to be made here than in other kinds of production, all of them relatively short-term and almost equal in importance. In many a firm a policy decision had to be made each time an order was accepted, but it committed the firm only for the period in which that article was produced. For large equipment such as television transmitters, the period could be as long as several years; even so it was shorter than that of many decisions in mass and process production.

(b) There was little distinction between policy decisions and problem-solving decisions, a problem-solving decision almost inevitably developing into a policy decision.

(c) A large proportion of the decisions made affected all the basic functions of manufacture. For example, when a raw material supply failed, the decision to use a substitute involved not only those concerned with production activities but also the development and marketing personnel; sometimes it was even necessary to reopen negotiations with the customer, too.

In *mass production,* decisions were more varied both in character and importance:

(a) Policy decisions about objectives, and the activities essential to achieving these objectives, were fewer but usually of greater importance than in unit production because they committed the firm further into the future and had to be based on a wider variety of background facts.

(b) Problem-solving decisions did not develop into policy decisions as often as they did in unit-production firms.

(c) As the basic functions of manufacture were more independent of each other, policy decisions sometimes affected one function only and could often be taken by the senior executive responsible for that function. The planning of a territorial sales organization, for example, normally involved decisions by the marketing personnel only. (One exception to this was found, however, in a firm where the area sales managers were linked with production units located in various parts of the country. Thus, any change made in the organization of the sales force affected the schedules of the production units and was therefore based on a joint decision of the two senior executives responsible for marketing and production respectively.)

(d) Decisions were also more predictable—not their exact content, of course, but at least the kind of decisions likely to occur.

In *process production*

(a) Policy decisions were fewer than in mass or unit production but committed the firms concerned further into the future. One firm was planning to erect a new plant which, it was estimated, would take three years to build and twenty years to give an adequate return on the investment. Production facilities, once determined, would be extremely inflexible, as in most other chemical plants. Success would depend, therefore, on an assured market for the product during the next twenty years. Even in process industry not all policy decisions were as long-term as this; nevertheless, many were too important to be the responsibility of one individual. The organizational framework had to allow for joint decisions by senior management and more of the decisions were made at board level than in other systems.

(b) Problem-solving decisions, on the other hand, had to be made as near as possible to the point at which the crisis occurred; they were normally associated with operational difficulties and were of great urgency. Policy decisions were even more distinct from problem-solving decisions than in mass production.

(c) Making decisions became an increasingly rational process. The imponderables became progressively fewer and the consequences of a particular course of action could be foreseen more exactly; management hunches were required less and less. This is probably the most important single factor linking technology with organization, and it has far-reaching implications.

The Effect on Human Relations

Technical complexity has been defined as the extent to which control can be exercised over the physical limitations of production. At the beginning of the technical scale, it seemed, physical limitations were so difficult to control that little attempt was made to do so; consequently people were subjected to relatively little pressure. No one, for example, tried to hustle the engineers engaged on the development of a complicated piece of equipment; on the contrary, it was traditional that they were unlikely to work well 'with a gun at their backs'.

In large-batch and mass production, continuous efforts to push back the limitations of production put considerable pressure on employees. Targets were set progressively higher, incentives of many different kinds were offered, and production tended to proceed by drives. But in the last resort the pace was still set by the amount of effort the operators were prepared to put into the job.

At the top of the scale the exercise of control was so mechanical and exact that pressure on people was again at a minimum. Productivity was related only indirectly to human effort; on the whole, people were hard-pressed only when things went wrong. Moreover, the plant itself constituted a framework of discipline and control. Any demands on the operators were in fact made by the process rather than by supervision. Most of those interviewed seemed to resent authority less when exercised over them by the process than by a superior.

As technology advances the entire concept of authority in industry may have to change. In process firms the relationship between superior and subordinate was much more like that between a travel agent and his clients than that between a foreman and operators in mass production. The process foreman's job was to arrange things within limits, set by the plant, which both he and the operators understood and accepted. This common understanding and appreciation of the demands of the job is much the same as that found in unit production.

There is, for example, a different attitude to time-keeping. In the mass-production firms visited, the foremen had to work hard to prevent their operators from slipping off to wash their hands or to gather at the clock before finishing time; but in the process firms operators would arrive early for the night-shift of their own free will in order to allow the men they were relieving to get away for a quick drink at the local before closing time. The process workers were aware that the plant could not be left unattended and they themselves made the necessary arrangements.

There appear to be considerable differences between production systems in the extent to which the 'situational demands' create conditions conducive to human happiness. Managers and supervisors get more satisfaction from their jobs at the advanced levels of technology; from the operator's point of view, too, it would appear that the relaxation of pressure and the higher quality of relationships between supervisor and subordinates will more than compensate for any increased monotony and boredom arising from monitoring occupations.

Bureaucracy and Bureaupathology

VICTOR A. THOMPSON

Some Characteristics of Modern Organizations

Modern organization has evolved from earlier forms by incorporating advancing specialization. In an earlier period organizations could depend much more on the "line of command." The superior could tell others what to do because he could master the knowledge and techniques necessary to do so intelligently. As science and technology developed, the superior lost to experts the *ability* to command in one field after another, but he retained the *right* as part of his role.

A great structure of specialized competencies has grown up around the chain of command. Organizations have grown in size because they must be able fully to employ the new specialists and the specialized equipment associated with them if the organizations are to meet their competition. As more specialists appear and the organization continues to grow in size, it becomes necessary to group employees into units, and the units into larger units. Some of the larger of these units in government have been called "bureaus," and so the kind of organization resulting from this process has been called "bureaucracy." (These units were called "bureaus" from the French word for writing table or desk.)

Bureaupathic Behavior

Dependence upon specialization imparts to modern organizations certain qualities. Among these are routinization, strong attachment to subgoals, impersonality, categorization, resistance to change, etc. The individual must adjust to these qualities because they cannot be eliminated from bureaucratic organization. In our society there are many people who have been unable to make this adjustment and who therefore find modern organization a constant source of frustration. They suffer from the social disease of "bureausis." In the last part of this article we shall try to diagnose this disease.

Personal behavior patterns are frequently encountered which exaggerate the characteristic qualities of bureaucratic organization. Within bureaucracy we often find excessive aloofness, ritualistic attachment to routines and procedures, and resistance to change; and associated with these behavior patterns is a petty insistence upon rights of authority and status. From the standpoint of organizational goal accomplishment, these personal behavior patterns are pathological because they do not advance organizational goals. They reflect the personal needs of individuals. To the extent that criticism of modern bureaucracy is not "bureaucratic," it is directed at these self-serving personal behavior patterns. Responsible criticism of bureaucratic pathology does not constitute a nostalgic longing to go back to a simpler era, but is an attempt to find the causes of pathological behavior with the hope of eliminating it. When people use the term "bureaucratic" in a critical sense, they are frequently referring to these personally oriented behavior patterns. Because the term is also used in a descriptive, noncritical sense, as Weber used it and as it has been used throughout this book, we shall avoid this critical use of the term and use in its stead a word which clearly denotes the pathological. We shall call these behaviors "bureaupathic."

The appropriation of major aspects of bureaucratic organization as means for the satisfaction of personal needs is pathological. It is a form of behavior which is functional for less than the system as a whole, including in this connection the clientele as part of the system. It involves a shifting in the costs[1] of the system by those with more authority to those with less, be they subordinates or clientele. It is a kind of behavior possible to those in the organization who have the best opportunity to use the organization to satisfy personal needs, namely, those in authority positions. It can only be exercised "downward." It cannot be exercised by clientele over authoritative officials, and it cannot be exercised by subordinates over superiors. It is, in short, a phenomenon of the system of authority, both hierarchical and nonhierarchical.[2]

Insecurity and the Need to Control

This pathological behavior starts with a need on the part of the person in an authority position to control those subordinate to himself. To "control" means to have subordinate behavior correspond as closely as possible with one set of preconceived standards. While the need to control arises in large part from personal insecurity in the superior, it has conceptual sources as well, which we shall briefly state.

In the United States, we have still the ghost of the absolute king in the guise of the theory of sovereignty. Sovereignty theory supports the monistic conception of bureaucratic organization, with its associated institution of hierarchy. The superior has the right, by delegation ultimately from the absolute sovereign, to obtain a unique outcome; and he has the duty, or the responsibility to his superior, to obtain it. In profit organizations, it is held that there is only one outcome which will satisfy profit maximization under the specific conditions of the market. It is also held that the duty to seek this outcome is an overriding one because only in this way can the welfare of all be best promoted, even though in individual instances it may not seem so. In the monocratic society of Russia, only one outcome can be tolerated because only one is consistent with the laws of history; only one is possible. (Why it is necessary to seek bureaucratic control in the face of this historical determinism has never been satisfactorily explained so far as we know.)

Although these conceptual sources for the need to control exist, they are hardly compelling. Much more important in explaining the authoritative need to control is personal insecurity.[3] Here we may well recap these sources of personal insecurity and anxiety in modern bureaucratic organization.

Hierarchical structure with its monopoly of "success" is a potent source of anxiety. The person in a superordinate position has a near final control over the satisfaction of subordinates' needs, their personal goals.[4] While at the bottom of the hierarchy the standards which must be met are frequently made explicit and objectively measurable, managerial personnel have generally resisted a like invasion of their own superordinate rights.[5] As we have said before, the objectivity of performance standards decreases as one mounts the hierarchy until at some point they become largely subjective. At the same time, we would expect an increasing concentration of success-hungry people in the upper reaches of the hierarchy. Strong status needs and strong doubts as to what will please the person who can satisfy those needs can only result in anxiety and, for many, in "automaton conformity"[6] to the wishes of the boss. Hierarchical anxiety is much like Calvinism in that it generates painful doubt as to who is chosen. Like Calvinism, these doubts can be reduced, not only by automaton conformity but by excessive activity and the appearance of extreme busyness.[7]

Anxiety is also associated with insecurity of function. To occupy a position not fully accepted by significant others in the organization tends to make one isolated, a minority in a hostile world. This kind of insecurity may result from a new specialty not yet fully accredited and accepted; or it may result from the authoritative assignment of jurisdiction (the delegation of nonhierarchical authority) in defiance of the needs of specialization.

Finally, the source of insecurity which is becoming the most significant in modern organizations is the growing gap between the rights of authority (to review, to veto, to affirm) and the specialized ability or skill required to solve most organizational problems. The intellectual, problem-solving, content of executive positions is being increasingly diverted to specialists, leaving hierarchical rights (and duties) as the principal components of executive posts.[8] Persons in hierarchical positions are therefore increasingly dependent upon subordinate and nonsubordinate specialists for the achievement of organizational (or unit) goals. The superior tends to be caught between the two horns of a dilemma. He must satisfy the nonexplicit and nonoperational demands of a superior through the agency of specialized subordinates and nonsubordinates whose skills he only dimly understands.[9] And yet, to be counted a success he must accept this dilemma and live with its increasing viciousness throughout his life. He must live with increasing insecurity and anxiety.[10] Although a particular person may have great maturity and general psychological security, an insecure superior at any point in the hierarchy above him can, and probably will, generate pressures which must inevitably be passed down the line, creating insecurity and tensions all the way to the botton.[11] Given a person's hierarchical relationship with his superior, he is always subject to blame for outcomes which he could control only remotely, if at all.

The Bureaupathic Reaction

Insecurity gives rise to personal (nonorganizational) needs which may be generalized in the need for control. This need often results in behavior which appears irrational from the standpoint of the organization's goals because it does not advance them; it advances only personal goals and satisfies only personal needs. In so doing, it creates conditions which do not eliminate the need for control but rather enhance it.[12]

Alvin W. Gouldner studied the succession to the position of plant manager by a man from outside the plant.[13] This man was obligated to upper management and felt dutybound to realize its efficiency and production values. He started out, therefore, with heavy pressure from above. Coming from outside, he did not understand the informal system prevailing in the plant and was unable to use it. As his insecurity and anxiety mounted, he turned more and more to the formal system of rules, defined competencies, impersonality, and close supervision. He met resistance and felt his position between the horns of the dilemma, between those above and those below, increasingly insecure. He reacted with increased aloofness and formality. He exaggerated the characteristics of bureaucratic organization. He became bureaupathic.

The example illustrates the circularity in the bureaupathic reaction. Since the manager's behavior was so strongly influenced by his personal needs to reduce his own anxiety, the employees' responses deviated more and more from organizational needs, thereby increasing the manager's anxiety and completing the circle. The mechanisms underlying this process are not difficult to understand. Control standards encourage minimal participation.[14] They encourage employees to meet the standards and no more. Furthermore, meeting the control devices tends to become the aim of the subordinates because that is how they manage their own insecurities and avoid sanctions. For example, if agents are rated on the number of violations they uncover, cases of compliance are not likely to give them great joy.[15] Strict control from above encourages employees to "go by the book," to avoid innovations and chances of errors which put black marks on the record. It encourages the accumulation of records to prove compliance, resulting in *paperasserie,* as the French call it.[16] It encourages decision by precedent, and unwillingness to exercise initiative or take a chance. It encourages employees to wait for orders and do only what they are told. It is not hard to understand, therefore, why the superior may come to feel that he must apply more control. If he is also subject to strict bureaupathic control from above, this situation is likely to contribute to ulcers, if not, indeed, to complete breakdown.

The Drift to Quantitative Compliance

An exaggerated dependence upon regulations and quantitative standards is likely to stem from a supervisor's personal insecurity in the parentlike role of the boss. It has been observed that women supervisors are more likely to insist upon strict compliance with all organizational rules and regulations than are men. The bureaupathic tendency of women has been attributed to their greater insecurity in the superordinate role because the general role of women in our society is somewhat subordinate.[17] A battery of regulations makes it unnecessary for the superior to give the detailed face-to-face order very often. Everybody, including the supervisor, is simply carrying out instructions imposed from above. If they are unpleasant instructions, it is not the supervisor's fault. For much the same reason, an insecure superior will probably appreciate a large number of quantitative control standards because his ratings of his subordinates then appear to be inevitable results of the performances of the subordinates, not merely the personal judgments of the superior. The anger and aggressions of the subordinates can then be displaced to the impersonal "system," and the superior can continue to get their indispensable co-operation upon which his own "success" depends.[18] Furthermore, disparities of power are hidden by the rules, and if punishment is meted out, it comes from the rules, not from the superior. In all of these ways, the rules and regulations make the parentlike role less uncomfortable for insecure people.[19]

Only the observable and measurable aspects of behavior can be controlled. These aspects are often the most trivial and unimportant from the standpoint of the long-range success of the organization. Where the need to control exists, therefore, it often manifests itself in procedures, reports, and clearances governing trivia, while at the same time very important matters are left to discretion because controlling them is not feasible. The need to control is sufficiently widespread to have given sometimes a petty and ludicrous quality to modern organization. We venture to predict that if one looks hard enough in any modern organization, he will find instructions just as ridiculous as those of the military on how to wash a dog, pick a flower, or use a fork.[20] Since the controls can successfully be applied only to the observable and measurable aspects of a job, and since the employee must concentrate on satisfying the control standards in order to reduce his own personal insecurities, his emphasis shifts from the more important, qualitative aspects of the job to the less important, quantitative aspects. In an employment office, for example, the goal shifted from good placement, in the beginning, to the highest possible number of people put to work. Interviewers felt constrained to use whatever sanctions they have to induce a client to take a job, whether he wanted it and was suited to it or not.[21]

Exaggerated Aloofness

Organizational relationships are by nature less warm and personal than the relations of friendship. It is only when this impersonality is exaggerated to cold aloofness and apparent disinterest that we can with any fairness call it pathological. As with other kinds of bureaupathic behavior, exaggerated aloofness can usually be attributed to personal insecurity.

A cold aloofness protects an insecure superior from commitments to his subordinates which he fears will be inconsistent with demands upon him from above. It makes it easier for him to mete out punishment or to perform other aspects of his hierarchical role, such as rating his subordinates. It protects him from the aggressions of his subordinates by maintaining a psychic distance between him and them. In extreme cases it can come close to a complete breakdown of communication between the superior and his subordinates.

The same considerations apply to relations between officials and clients. A certain impersonality is necessary both to protect the goals of the organization and to secure objective and therefore effective service to the client. This impersonality may be exaggerated into a cold disinterest by an insecure official. When officials are caught between demands or "rights" of clients and tight administrative controls from above, dissociation from the clients and disinterest in their problems may seem to be the only way out of the dilemma. Client hostility, generated by what appears to be official emphasis on the wrong goals, creates tension. Inconsiderate treatment of the clients may become a device for reducing tensions and maintaining the cohesion of the officials. Blau has shown how such a situation leads to backstage demeaning of clients which, by putting psychic distance between the officials and the clients, protects the officials. Officials then tend to seek satisfactions from the abstract values of the enterprise rather than from the concrete values of personal service to a client.[22]

Within the organization, technically unnecessary interdependence creates insecurity of function. As we have seen in previous chapters, authority is sometimes delegated for political rather than technical reasons, to meet personal rather than organizational needs. Because the resulting relationship is not accepted and is constantly under attack, the person with the delegated authority lives in insecurity. Here, also, patterns of cold and imperious aloofness are often observed, and abstract values rather than personal service become goals. Officials exercising such disputed, delegated authority frequently demean their clients as narrow-minded, if not stupid. Procedures to govern the relationship are elaborated and, because they stabilize the relationship, such procedures acquire an exaggerated value for these officials.

Resistance to Change

Bureaucratic organizations have to administer change carefully. Perhaps most people resist change just for the sake of change. The burden of proof is on the side of those advocating change. However, resistance to change may also be exaggerated by insecure officials; it may become bureaupathic. In an organizational context dominated by the need to control, innovation is dangerous because, by definition, it is not controlled behavior. It creates risks of errors and therefore of sanctions. To encourage innovation, an insecure superior would have to extend the initiative to subordinates and thereby lose control. Furthermore, in an insecure, competitive group situation, innovation threatens the security of all members of the group and for this reason tends to be suppressed by informal group action, as well as by the insecure superior. Innovation is facilitated by a secure, noncompetitive group administrative effort dominated by a professional outlook. Since this kind of situation is thought to be rare in modern bureaucracy, some people might regard excessive resistance to change as an inherent feature of bureaucratic organization, rather than as a form of bureaupathology. We feel, however, that excessive bureaucratic inertia is much less widespread than is supposed.[23] In an era of ever more rapid change, it seems unlikely that man has evolved a kind of organization which is particularly resistive to innovation. The traditionalistic organization was the kind most resistive, and in many places it had to be blasted off the scene by revolutionary action. The bureaucratic form replaced it, partly because it was able to accommodate to a changing world.

There is another source of resistance to change which is not bureaupathic and which is therefore subject to rational corrective procedures. The communication pattern determines who gets feed-back information. A particular official may never get intimate knowledge of the results of his own actions. Consequently, he may feel no need for a change which others who do have this knowledge think should be made. Bringing the "offending" official into direct communication with respondents might cure in a hurry this particular case of resistance to change.

Insistence on the Rights of Office

The bureaupathic official usually exaggerates the official, non-technical aspects of relationships and suppresses the technical and the informal. He stresses rights, not abilities. Since his behavior stems from insecurity, he may be expected to insist on petty rights and prerogatives, on protocol, on procedure—in short, on those things least likely to affect directly the goal accomplishment of the organization. For example, a rather functionless reviewing officer will often insist violently on his right of review and scream like an injured animal if he is by-passed. He will often insist on petty changes, such as minor changes in the wording of a document. If he has a counterpart at a higher organizational level, he will probably insist on exclusive contact with that higher clearance point. By controlling this particular communication channel he protects his authority and influence, even perhaps enhancing them somewhat by being the sole interpreter of the higher-clearance-point's requirements.[24] In like fashion and for the same reasons, an insecure superior can be expected to exert his right to the monopoly of outgoing and incoming communication. Everything must go through "formal channels." In this way he can hide his weakness and suppress information which might reveal his insecurity. He also hopes to maintain his influence and authority by suppressing the influence of external specialists, the "staff." One of the great difficulties of modern organization arises from the inescapable fact that specialist communication must break through such blockades.

Insistence upon the full rights of the superordinate role is what is meant by "close supervision." It seems to be related to doubts about the loyalty or ability of subordinates, combined with pressure from above.[25] Close supervision can be regarded as bureaupathic under conditions where the right to act and the ability to do so have become separated because of the advance of specialization. However, where the position has a great deal of technical content so that subordinates are technically dependent upon their supervisor, as in a railroad maintenance section, close supervision may be tolerated and even demanded by subordinates. It may be a necessary means to the organization's goal. The right to supervise closely gets further legitimation from the technical ability to do so.[26]

Bureaupathology and Organization Structure

Institutions are staffed by persons, and so personality is always an element in institutional behavior. It will account for differences of degree and minor variations in form. For the major outlines of institutional behavior, however, we must seek the causes in the institutions themselves. Bureaupathic behavior is caused by the structures and conditions within our bureaucratic organizations. To say this is not to deny the reinforcing impact of personality. Some people are undoubtedly more inclined than others to be aloof, to get enmeshed in details, to be officious, to be excessively cautious, to be insensitive to others, to be insecure. What we do deny is that there is a bureaupathic personality type, or that observed cases of bureaupathic behavior will always, or even usually, be associated with one type of person.[27] Any person, regardless of personality type, may behave in some or all of the ways we have just described under the appropriate conditions, and these conditions occur very frequently in the modern bureaucratic organization.

It has been argued that a kind of rigidity grows out of prolonged role enactment, and that bureaucrats, over a period of time, become insensitive to the needs of clients.[28] We have shown that a certain impersonal treatment is inherent in bureaucratic structure. The charge of insensitivity may therefore be a bureautic reaction. One must not forget that clients are notoriously insensitive to the needs of bureaucrats. The question is, when does bureaucratic insensitivity become pathological? In many bureaucratic organizations, relations with clients are warm and cordial, as for example, between the postman and the householder.

Although prolonged role enactment undoubtedly has a profound effect on a person,[29] what is the "bureaucratic role"? People move around quite freely in bureaucracies. They perform various roles. We do not think it makes sense to speak of the "bureaucratic role." We have emphasized specialist roles and hierarchical roles. In the hierarchy, people go from position to position as they advance. Specialists often move from organization to organization. The truly prolonged role is the entrepreneurial professional role, such as the physician. It seems doubtful that physicians, as a group, are "insensitive to the needs of clients."

Although there is no "bureaucratic role," there is bureaucratic structure. It is obvious that some people are able to achieve personal goals within this structure more easily and comfortably than others. These people have been called bureaucratic types; but they are not necessarily bureaupathic. In fact, it may be that the person who moves most easily within the bureaucratic structure is the one who can hide his insecurity, his "inner rumblings," as Whyte puts it. His insecurity may express itself internally as ulcers but not externally as bureaupathic behavior.

Bureaupathic behavior is one result of the growing insecurity of authority in modern organizations. This insecurity exists because nonhierarchical authority is so frequently delegated without regard to the ability to exercise it, such is the practice of politics.[30] More important, however, is the fact that the culturally defined institution of hierarchy, with its rather extreme claim of rights, is increasingly uncomfortable with advancing specialization. Hierarchical rights change slowly; specialization, the result of technology, changes with increasing speed. The situation is unstable. The legitimacy of organizational authority is in danger. Bureaupathic behavior is one result of this situation.

Bureaupathology and Routinization

The bureaupathic response to insecurity is facilitated by the routinization of organizational problem solving. When the development of appropriate routines is the dominant imperative, when technical problems must be solved, the emphasis must be on abilities rather than rights.[31] Charismatic patterns predominate. These facts are illustrated by wartime experience.

When World War II broke out, a large regulatory structure had to be quickly created. People with many types of skill, from many walks of life, and with many different statuses were quickly assembled in Washington. A whole host of brand new problems was given to them. In those early days, emphasis was on technical problem solving. Anyone who could come up with an idea on how to proceed "got ahead." Bureaupathic patterns were almost nonexistent. The emphasis was on what one could do, not on rights and prerogatives. People became quite scrambled up, with permanently low-status people temporarily elevated to high-status positions. Very young people found themselves in high positions.

Gradually technical problems were mastered and reduced to procedures and programs. Bureaupathic patterns became more pronounced. There were constant reorganizations, a growing volume of reports, increasing insistence upon clearance protocol, authority impressed for its own sake, not as a problem-solving device. Hierarchical dominance was pressed through a great variety of rituals— "control" boards, frequent staff meetings, calls to the "front office," progress reports, increasing insistence upon formal channels, etc.[32] These manifestations of authority were ritualistic because they were not related to winning the war, but to the "need for control." The organization product was not affected by them, because it was secured through an elaborate routine, of which no one comprehended more than a small part. Bureaupathic behavior occupied much more of the time of officials. They became kings' messengers after the kings were gone.[33]

Notes and References

1. The obligation to accept another's decision may have a number of negative aspects, or *costs*. First is the dislike of subordination itself. Furthermore, the decision may not accord with one's moral beliefs, or it may conflict with one's self-interest. It may not appeal to one's reason and is likely in any case to require some change in habits. Therefore, the possible costs involved in being a subordinate or a regulated client are subordination costs, moral costs, self-interest costs, rationality costs, and inertial costs. See Herbert A. Simon, Donald W. Smithburg, and Victor A. Thompson: *Public Administration* (New York: Alfred A. Knopf; 1959), ch. xxi.
2. Writers on bureaucracy like Merton, Selznick, Gouldner and others use essentially the same concept of "bureaucratic," although, except by Gouldner, the distinction between the descriptive and critical sense of the term is never made clear. In general,

they start with a need of some authority figure for control, followed by behavior which creates conditions exaggerating the need for control, etc., in a vicious circle. On this point see James G. March and Herbert A. Simon: *Organizations* (New York: John Wiley & Sons, Inc.; 1958) 36–46; and Chris Argyris: "The Individual and Organization: Some Problems of Mutual Adjustment." *Admin. Sci. Q.,* Vol. II (1957), 1–22, and "Understanding Human Behavior in Organizations: One Viewpoint," in Mason Haire, ed.: *Modern Organization Theory* (New York: John Wiley & Sons, Inc.; 1959).

3. Although the conceptual basis for the need to control is more thoroughly worked out in Russia, it has been observed that the attempt by Russian top management to concentrate power and control in its own hands results from insecurity generated by pressure from above. See Reinhard Bendix: *Work and Authority in Industry* (New York: John Wiley & Sons, Inc.; 1956), ch. vi.

4. For a theory of individual accommodation to the organization based on hierarchically generated anxiety, see Robert V. Presthus: "Toward a Theory of Organizational Behavior," *Admin. Sci. Q.,* Vol. III, No. I (June 1958), 48ff. See also Peter Blau: *The Dynamics of Bureaucracy* (Chicago: University of Chicago Press; 1955), 173.

5. This resistance was apparently the basis of the managerial opposition to Taylorism and Scientific Management generally. See Bendix: op. cit. 274–81.

6. See Erich Fromm: *Escape From Freedom* (New York: Holt, Rinehart and Winston, Inc.; 1941), 185. See also Clara Thompson: *Psychoanalysis: Evolution and Development* (New York: Thomas Nelson & Sons; 1950), 208. See also Fromm: *Man for Himself: An Inquiry into the Psychology of Ethics* (New York: Holt, Rinehart and Winston, Inc.; 1947), 72. Of 75 middle-management people questioned by Harold Leavitt, most thought that conformance to the wishes of the boss was the principal criterion for evaluating subordinates. Harold J. Leavitt: *Managerial Psychology* (Chicago: University of Chicago Press; 1958), 288.

7. See Rollo May: *The Meaning of Anxiety* (New York: The Ronald Press Company; 1950), p. 172.

8. For a discussion of this process in industrial management, see Bendix: op. cit., pp. 226ff. His discussion is based on a work by Ernest Dale: *Planning and Developing the Company Organization Structure* (New York: American Management Association, Inc.; 1952), Research Report No. 20. Advancing specialization in the problem-solving aspect of organizations is further reflected in these figures from Bendix: op. cit., 211ff. Between 1899 and 1947 the proportion of administrative to production workers in American industry increased from 7.7 percent to 21.6 percent. From 1910 to 1940 the work force in America increased by 49 percent. Entrepreneurs increased by 17 percent; manual workers, by 49 percent; and salaried employees, by 127 percent. Bendix sees bureaucratization in industry as the continuing subdivision of the functions of the early owner-manager.

9. Of course, the extent of the dilemma varies with position in the hierarchy and with the extent to which complex specialties are required by the particular organization. The ongoing process of specialization will move the dilemma down the hierarchy and to more and more organizations.

10. Middle-management executives interviewed by William H. Whyte referred to their lives as "treadmills" or "rat races," thereby expressing the tensions generated by this dilemma. *The Organization Man* (Garden City, New York: Doubleday & Company, Inc., 1953), 176.

11. William Caudill has shown that tensions starting at the very top of a mental hospital were easily communicated all the way down to the patients, creating symptoms in them that were generated entirely within the hospital. *The Psychiatric Hospital as a Small Society* (Cambridge: Harvard University Press; 1958).

12. March and Simon (op. cit.) criticize some of the sociological treatments of bureaupathic behavior because they feel that these theories do not explain why functional

learning on the part of authority figures does not take place. It will be recalled that these theories posit a need for control, followed by behaviors which create conditions which exaggerate the need for control. If this behavior is conceived as organization problem solving, there is indeed a problem of functional learning involved. However, bureaupathic behavior is functional in personal rather than organizational terms. It must be admitted that most of these sociological treatments do not clearly distinguish between personal and organizational goals—between bureaupathic and bureaucratic behavior. The "dysfunctional learning" involved is failure to learn that employees cannot very effectively be treated according to the machine model. However, this learning can be considered dysfunctional only by applying the machine model to management. If management operated like a rational machine, it would learn that employees are not machines. The basic methodological flaw of the "management" approach is that it assumes that persons described by the term "management" behave according to sociopsychological laws different from those governing the behavior of others—that the manager is an independent variable in the organization.

13. The following discussion of succession is taken from his *Patterns of Industrial Bureaucracy* (Glencoe, Illinois: The Free Press; 1954), Part Two.

14. Ibid., 174–6.

15. See Blau: op. cit., p. 192.

16. Walter Rice Sharp: *The French Civil Service: Bureaucracy in Transition* (New York: The Macmillan Co.; 1931), 446–50.

17. See Arnold W. Green and Eleanor Melnick: "What Has Happened to the Feminist Movement." Alvin W. Gouldner, ed.: *Studies in Leadership: Leadership and Democratic Action* (New York: Harper & Brothers; 1950), 277–302.

18. See Blau: op. cit., 175–6.

19. Gouldner: *Patterns of Industrial Bureaucracy,* ch. ix. On the relationship between ritualistic compliance with regulations and personal insecurity, see Rose Laub Coser: "Authority and Decision Making in a Hospital: A Comparative Analysis." *Am. Sociol. Rev.* (February 1958). See also Reinhard Bendix: *Higher Civil Servants in American Society* (Boulder, Colorado: University of Colorado Press; 1949), 14–19, 112–22.

20. There is another source of extreme, detailed controls in modern organizations, one which can be dealt with rationally. Units are frequently established whose goals are defined *entirely* in terms of writing instructions. Since they have nothing assigned to them except to write instructions, in time they can be expected to "cover" everything—even as a monkey, if given enough time on the typewriter, would eventually type out the complete works of Shakespeare. Involved in this situation is goal factoring, not bureaupathic behavior.

21. Blau: op. cit., 96.

22. Ibid., 91–5. See also Erving Goffman: *The Presentation of Self in Everyday Life* (Garden City, New York: Doubleday & Company, Inc.; 1959), 177.

23. In a state employment office and a federal enforcement agency, Blau found little evidence of resistance to change. The cases he did find were based upon the fear of a superior and fear of the loss of security in relations with subordinates or clients. (Op. cit., 184–9.) He found that new employees and less competent employees were more resistive to change than others. (Ibid., 197.) He found also that ritualistic compliance with rules and regulations stemmed from personal insecurity in important relationships at work. (Ibid., 188.) Secure officials welcomed change because it made their work interesting by providing new challenges.

24. See Victor A. Thompson: *The Regulatory Process in OPA Rationing* (New York: King's Crown Press; 1950), 298–303.

25. In addition to other references cited throughout this chapter, see Walter L. Dorn: "The Prussian Bureaucracy in the 18th Century." *Polit. Sci. Rev.*, Vol. XLVI (September 1931). See also Alexander Barmine: *One Who Survived* (New York: G. P.

Putnam's Sons; 1945); and "The Stewardship of Sewell Avery." *Fortune,* Vol. XXXIII (May 1946).

26. See D. Katy, N. Maccoby, G. Gurin, and L. G. Floor: *Productivity, Supervision and Morale among Railroad Workers* (Ann Arbor: Survey Research Center, University of Michigan; 1951). See also A. W. Halpin: "The Leadership Behavior and Combat Performance of Airplane Commanders." *J. Abnorm. and Soc. Psychol.,* Vol. XLIX (1954), 19–22.

27. For example, attempts have been made to show that "compulsive neurotics" predominate in bureaucracy. See Otto Sperling: "Psychoanalytic Aspects of Bureaucracy." *Psychoan. Q.,* Vol. XIX (1950), 88–100.

28. Theodore R. Sarbin: "Role Theory," in Gardner Lindzey, ed.: *Handbook of Social Psychology* (Reading, Massachusetts: Addison-Wesley Publishing Company, Inc.; 1954), Vol. I, 223–58. Sarbin points out that this proposition is only an hypothesis, and one would have to find these qualities of rigidity and impersonality in non-occupational behavior as well in order to demonstrate it. We might point out that one would also have to show that these qualities were not present at the beginning of the period of "prolonged role enactment." Sarbin relies somewhat on Robert K. Merton's well-known essay, "Bureaucratic Structure and Personality," in *Social Theory and Social Structure,* rev. ed. (Glencoe, Illinois: The Free Press; 1957). However, Merton does not seem to be talking about the interaction of self and role. Generally, he is explaining "bureaucratic" behavior by reference to bureaucratic structure (graded careers, seniority, *esprit de corps,* the appropriateness of secondary, i.e., impersonal, relations, etc.). He also suggests that the ideal patterns of bureaucratic behavior become exaggerated by being affectively backed, as we have argued. However, he does not explain the origin of this affect ("sentiments") to our satisfaction. We have argued that it comes from personal insecurity in an authority position. Merton does not distinguish between the descriptive and critical uses of the term "bureaucratic."

29. See Willard Waller: *The Sociology of Teaching* (New York: John Wiley & Sons, Inc.; 1932).

30. In organizational terms, politics means those activities concerned with the delegation of authority on bases other than a generally recognized ability to exercise it. It involves some kind of exchange between the person desiring the authority and the authority figure who has it to give. It is made possible by the fact that authority may be delegated. Since the specialist content of executive positions is increasingly attenuated as one mounts the hierarchy, so that ability criteria become less and less relevant, placement in these positions becomes more and more a political phenomenon, a matter of "office politics"; the incumbents are "political types." See Harold Lasswell: *Politics: Who Gets What, When, How* (New York: McGraw-Hill Book Co.; 1936).

31. Studies of decision-making groups in business and government show that the groups prefer strict and formal performances by the conference leader when the subject matter is trivial but not when the subject is important. L. Berkowitz: "Sharing Leadership in Small, Decision-Making Groups." *J. Abnorm. and Soc. Psychol.,* Vol. XLVIII (1953), 231–8.

32. See Victor A. Thompson: op. cit., Part Two.

33. The technical problem military organizations must solve is winning a war. In peacetime, with no technical problem to solve, bureaupathic patterns are more pronounced. Arthur K. Davis says they live and survive in peacetime on ritual. "Bureaucratic Patterns in the Navy Officer Corps." *Social Forces,* Vol. XXVII (1948), 143–53. He hypothesizes that "the effectiveness of military leaders tends to vary inversely with their exposure to a conventionally routinized military career." This study is reproduced in Merton, *et al.,* eds.: *Reader in Bureaucracy* (Glencoe, Illinois: The Free Press; 1952), pp. 380ff.

Management of Innovation

TOM BURNS, G. M. STALKER

The Preliminary Study

At this time, the rayon mill [described later] was growing and commercially prosperous. But two sets of circumstances which the study revealed did not seem easy to square with first-hand knowledge of other firms and with the conceptions of management available in the literature. Partly because of the lead given from the head office in London, the functions of each manager and worker were clearly specified; they were expected to follow, and did follow, the instructions which issued in a steady flow from the general manager and down through the hierarchy. Yet the system, lubricated by a certain paternalism, worked smoothly and economically, and there was no evidence that any individual felt aggrieved or belittled.

The other feature of interest lay in the comparative impotence of the Research and Development Laboratory. It was formally responsible for solving problems and curing faults in the process other than those which could be tended by people on the spot, for improving the existing process and products, and for introducing new products or methods. But its activities were regarded with much suspicion and some hostility by many production managers and supervisors; its studies were repetitive and often inconclusive; it was very largely occupied with finding answers to enquiries from the London office which arrived almost daily, and large arrears of which, at that time, had accumulated.

Very soon an opportunity presented itself of carrying out a similar study of the organization of an engineering concern with very large development interests. The wholly different conditions in which management acted, and the different codes of conduct and beliefs which individual managers brought to their jobs, were abundantly clear at the very beginning. As in the first concern, the study began with a series of interviews with managers and foremen, the principal purpose of which was to obtain descriptions of the jobs performed by individuals and the way in which they fitted in with others. After the first few such interviews a pattern appeared in them which was entirely unanticipated. The usual procedure was that after listening to the researchers, explaining his presence in the factory and his present purpose the informant would say, 'Well, to make all this clear, I'd better start from the beginning.' He would then proceed to give an account of his career in the firm, and of the activities and duties characteristic of the positions he had filled. This account was commonly lucid, well-organized, and informative, but would stop short at a point some months earlier. The question about his present functions, and whom they affected would then be framed again, rather more pointedly. There would be a pause. He would then explain, equally lucidly, what he would be doing when the present emergency had passed or the current reorganization or new development had matured, and his part of the concern could settle down to work as it was now planned.

Later, it became evident that ranks in the hierarchy of management as well

From *The Management of Innovation*, by Tom Burns and G. M. Stalker, 1961. Reprinted by permission of Tavistock Publications Ltd.

as functions were ill-defined, and that this was so because of the deliberate policy of the head of the concern. At this time, the most obvious consequence of this state of affairs was a pervasive sense of insecurity which was openly discussed by some managers and was also evident in individual conduct and in the formation of cliques and cabals.[1] Yet there was also the striking fact of the concern's commercial and technical success. Was there a causal connexion between the insecurity and stress displayed by individuals and the concern's effectiveness? An American study,[2] published about this time, suggested that there might be. Yet many of the actions arising from anxiety about career prospects and status were so clearly dissociated from the concern's tasks, even running counter to their accomplishment, and so much energy was consumed in internal politics, that it still seemed more plausible to regard insecurity, and the conduct to which it gave rise, as defects of the management system rather than its mainspring. Possibly, though, these defects were an inevitable concomitant of industrial change in the present state of our knowledge of organization.

This, at all events, was the view of the head of the concern. An organization chart was inapplicable, he believed, to the structure of management in the concern—it was 'probably a dangerous way of thinking about the way any industrial concern worked'. The first requirement of the management system was that it should make the fullest use of the capacities of its members; any man's job, therefore, should be as little defined as possible, so as to allow it to expand or contract in accordance with his special abilities. Any anxieties and frictions that might be generated were an inevitable circumstance of life as it is, and one could not 'manage them out of the organization'—not, at least, without neglecting or damaging some more vital interest.

Further study suggested, however, that 'initiative' no less than 'insecurity' and 'stress' might be dependent on the way in which management organized itself to carry out its task. The adaptation of *relationships* between individuals, rather than of individuals themselves, towards the requirements of the technical and commercial tasks of the firm became the focal point of the broader study which was then initiated, with the financial backing of the Department of Scientific and Industrial Research and in partnership with G. M. Stalker.

The Scottish Study

The Scottish Council (Development and Industry) is a voluntary body supported financially by industrial firms, local government bodies, and trade unions, and works in close touch with the Scottish Home Department and the Board of Trade. It has actively encouraged the growth in Scotland of industries using newer techniques. The declared purpose of the electronics scheme is to enable firms to acquire new technical resources and exploit them in commercial fields reasonably familiar to them. It is to this end that the firms are helped to build up laboratory teams on the basis of suitable contracts provided by defence ministries.

For our part, we hoped to be able to observe how management systems changed in accordance with changes in the technical and commercial tasks of the firm, especially the substantial changes in the rate of technical advance which new interests in electronics development and application would mean.

The major consideration for most firms entering the scheme was fear of shrinking markets or of keener competition in a static market; only one or two seemed prompted by an expansionist urge and the attraction of enterprise in new fields. A second distinction revealed itself between firms which negotiated a development contract before engaging a laboratory team, and those which began by investing in people who might be expected to produce ideas for development. Following roughly the same lines of division, a third distinction was visible between firms which confined the activities of their laboratory teams to work on defence contracts or on improving products developed elsewhere (to the extent of refusing to invest their own capital in development), and those prepared to exploit the team as a technical resource.

No firm attempted to match its technical growth with a comparable expansion of sales activities; in particular, no attempts were made at organized and thorough exploration of user needs for products which firms thought it possible to develop, or even for those which they had developed.

Most of the Scottish firms failed to realize their expectations. In half the cases, laboratory groups were disbanded or disrupted by the resignation of their leaders. Others were converted into test departments, 'trouble-shooting' teams, or production departments. Common to all predicaments was, first, the determined effort from the outset to keep the laboratory group as separate as possible from the rest of the organization; second, the appearance of conflicts for power, and over the privileged status of laboratory engineers; and third, the conversion of management problems into terms of personalities—to treat difficulties as really caused by the ignorance, stupidity or obstructiveness of the other side. These failures were interpreted by us as an inability to adapt the management system to the form appropriate to conditions of more rapid technical and commercial change.

There seemed to be two divergent systems of management practice. Neither was fully and consistently applied in any firm, although there was a clear division between those managements which adhered generally to the one, and those which followed the other. Neither system was openly and consciously employed as an instrument of policy, although many beliefs and empirical methods associated with one or the other were expressed. One system, to which we gave the name 'mechanistic', appeared to be appropriate to an enterprise operating under relatively stable conditions. The other, 'organic', appeared to be required for conditions of change. In terms of 'ideal types' their principal characteristics are briefly these:

In mechanistic systems the problems and tasks facing the concern as a whole are broken down into specialisms. Each individual pursues his task as something distinct from the real tasks of the concern as a whole, as if it were the subject of a sub-contract. 'Somebody at the top' is responsible for seeing to its relevance. The technical methods, duties, and powers attached to each functional role are precisely defined. Interaction within management tends to be vertical, i.e., between superior and subordinate. Operations and working behaviour are governed by instructions and decisions issued by superiors. This command hierarchy is maintained by the implicit assumption that all knowledge about the situation of the firm and its tasks is, or should be, available only to the head of the firm. Management, often visualized as the complex hierarchy familiar in organization charts, operates a simple control system, with information flowing up through a succession of filters, and decisions and instructions flowing downwards through a succession of amplifiers.

Organic systems are adapted to unstable conditions, when problems and requirements for action arise which cannot be broken down and distributed among specialist roles within a clearly defined hierarchy. Individuals have to perform their special tasks in the light of their knowledge of the tasks of the firm as a whole. Jobs lose much of their formal definition in terms of methods, duties, and powers, which have to be redefined continually by interaction with others participating in a task. Interaction runs laterally as much as vertically. Communication between people of different ranks tends to resemble lateral consultation rather than vertical command. Omniscience can no longer be imputed to the head of the concern.

The central problem of the Scottish study appeared to be why the working organization of a concern did not change its system from 'mechanistic' to 'organic' as its circumstances changed with entry into new commercial and technical fields. The answer which suggested itself was that every single person in a firm not only is (a) a member of a working organization, but also (b) a member of a group with sectional interests in conflict with those of other groups, and (c) one individual among many to whom the rank they occupy and the prestige attaching to them are matters of deep concern. Looked at in another way, any firm contains not only a working organization but a political system and a status structure. In the case of the firms we studied, the existing political system and status structure were threatened by the advent of a new laboratory group. Especially, the technical information available to the newcomers, which was a valuable business resource, was used or regarded as an instrument for political control; and laboratory engineers claimed, or were regarded as claiming, élite status within the organization.

Neither political or status preoccupations operated overtly, or even consciously; they gave rise to intricate manoeuvres and counter-moves, all of them expressed through decisions, or discussions about decisions, concerning the internal structure and the policies of the firm. Since political and status conflicts only came into the open in terms of the working organization, that organization became adjusted to serving the ends of the political and status system of the concern rather than its own.

The individual manager became absorbed in conflicts over power and status because they presented him with interests and problems more immediately important to him and more easily comprehended than those raised by the new organizational milieu and its unlimited liabilities. For increases in the rate of technical and commercial change meant more problems, more unfamiliar information, a wider range of work relationships, and heavier mental and emotional commitments. Many found it impossible to accept such conditions for their occupational lives. To keep their commitments limited meant either gaining more control over their personal situation or claiming exemption because of special conditions attached to their status. These purposes involved manoeuvres which persistently ran counter to the development of an organic system, and raised issues which could only be resolved by a reversion to a mechanistic system.

The Scottish study developed eventually into two complementary accounts of the ways in which the adaptation of management systems to conditions of change was impeded or thwarted. In one set of terms, the failure to adapt was attributed to the strength of former political and status structures. In other terms, the failure was seen as the consequence of an implicit resistance among individual members of concerns to the growth of commitments in their occupational existence at the expense of the rest of their lives.

The English Study

During the winter of 1955–6, the authors read papers dealing with some of the general findings of the Scottish study at a number of meetings. One of these was attended by senior officials of the Ministry of Supply. In later conversations with Burns, they suggested that major firms in the electronics industry in England might like to have an opportunity of hearing about the Scottish study and of discussing its implications for their own concerns. This suggestion led to a meeting in November 1957 at the Ministry of Supply, which was attended by managing directors and other senior members of eleven English firms, and by government officials.

While this discussion made it clear that the problems discussed in the summary report of the Scottish study were not unfamiliar, the ways in which the problems revealed themselves in different firms, and the responses and actions which they had evoked, were varied and idiosyncratic. Burns was therefore invited to make a brief study of each firm. Each of these studies concentrated on two topics: the management difficulties which seemed peculiar to firms engaged in rapid technical progress, and the particular problem of getting laboratory groups on the one hand (research—development—design) to work effectively with production and sales groups on the other.

The survey of English firms was completed in the first half of 1958 and the findings reported to the eight firms which had participated, out of eleven invited to do so. A general report was also distributed, and discussed at a one-day conference of the heads of firms and of government officials held at the Department of Scientific and Industrial Research in July 1958.

The eight English firms which eventually took part in the survey were not only much larger but much more committed to electronics development and manufacture than were the firms of the Scottish study, which were in the earliest stages of their careers in electronics. The situations available for study were more complicated; they were also more intimately related to the commercial and industrial destinies of the firms and to the lives of the people in them.

There was, for example, much more variety in the kind of group within the firm affected by an acceleration in the rate of technical change, and in the responses to change made by different firms. In firms which operated consciously on organic lines, changes from any direction were regarded as what they manifestly were—circumstances which affected every part of the firm and everybody's job, in some way. Organizational changes, additional tasks, and growth in any particular direction tended to be seen as the concerted response of the firm to a new situation; although debate and conflict were present, they were manifestly present and could be treated as part of the new situation to be reckoned with. In firms which operated according to mechanistic principles, the response to change was usually to create a new group, or to reconstitute the existing structure, or to expand an existing group which would be largely responsible for meeting the new situation, and so 'not disrupt the existing organization'.

This latter response, which in the Scottish firms characteristically led to the segregation of the new development team from the rest of management, was now visible in the way some firms dealt with big changes in market conditions. A Head Office sales department, or a new sales forecasting and market study group, might be created. Management might be reconstructed on product division lines, so as to extend the control of sales over the activities of the firm. Engineers might be recruited from development laboratories, or directorships offered to men of outstanding reputation from other firms. More significantly still, a new technical departure might be made the province of a newly created laboratory group independent of the laboratory concerned with the obsolescent techniques. In such cases, the confinement to a prescribed section of its organization of the total response of the firm to change meant that for the rest of the firm the challenge of the new situation became instead a threat offered by the 'new men' to the power, standing and career prospects they had hitherto enjoyed. This was especially the case with development engineers. Previously the element in every firm which had been identified with expansion and innovating change, they now saw their leading role passing—in part—to sales. The development-production conflicts typical of the Scottish study were overshadowed in the English firms by sales-development conflicts, by the resistance of the professional innovators to an innovating change.

Political conflict appeared to be clearly related to the particularism which was fostered by the separating out of the tasks of the firm according to specialist functions. Given a mechanistic system, changes of all kinds, including expansion, continually threw up new institutions within the firm which were intended to carry the whole of a new defined task and which themselves engendered political problems.

The conceptions of mechanistic and organic management have also proved useful in analysing the arrangements made inside firms for passing work through from the earliest stages of development to final manufacture. The tendency to regard the whole process as an articulated series of separate specialist functions made for the creation of 'hand over' frontiers between departments and for language barriers; it also went with a predilection for tethering functionaries to their posts. The need for communications beyond the formal transmission of instructions and drawings led to the appointment of liaison specialists— interpreters whose job was to move across the linguistic and functional frontiers and to act as intermediaries between the people 'getting on with the job.' Organic systems recognized the supreme importance of common languages and of each functionary's being able to seek out and interpret for himself the information he needed. The fewer distinguishable stages, the fewer interpreters and intermediaries, the more effectively were designs passed through the system.

Many of the insights generated by the English study were suggested in the first place by the distinctive response made by different concerns to a major change in market conditions as against techniques, as was the case with the firms in the Scottish study. The decline in government work and the increased emphasis on selling in the so-called 'commercial market' affected all concerns in the same way, although to a different extent. The first observable distinction was between the firms which saw that a sales function had been discharged by the laboratory engineer working on government development contracts, and that a similar role was equally necessary with commercial users, and those which overlooked this sales function in connexion with defence ministries and regarded market exploration and development as the province of salesmen. There were a number of aspects of this difference. Some concerns had always been wary of committing themselves too heavily to government work; others had allowed themselves to become educated into commercial unfitness by too complete a dependence on defence contracts. In general, it could be said that the first kind of firm tended to regard the market as a source of design ideas which the firm then attempted to realize, the second kind as a sink into which should be poured applications of techniques developed within the firm. Successful manufacturers of domestic radio and television receivers offered the most striking demonstration of the first principle. So much so, that in these firms not only the management system but the way in which individuals' jobs were defined, and the code of conduct prevailing in the concern, seemed to be generated by constant preoccupation with the market on the part of every member of management.

The differences between the two kinds of management system seemed to resolve themselves into differences in the kind of relationships which prevail between members of the organization, whether of the same or of different rank, and thus into the kinds of behaviour which members of an organization treat as appropriate in their dealings with each other. It was possible to distinguish various modes of behaviour used by individuals according to a single dimension of conduct: the bounds set to what—in the way either of requests, instructions, or of considerations and information—the individual would regard as feasible, acceptable, worth taking into account, and so forth. The observable way in which people in a concern dealt with each other—the code of conduct—could therefore be regarded as the most important element in a concern's organization, given the structure of the management hierarchy and the skills and other resources at its disposal. It expresses the framework of beliefs which decision-making invokes. In a realistic, operational sense, it *is* the organization.

In so far as differences in the obligations and rights attaching to different status within the concern are disputed, and in so far as the allocation of control over resources becomes a matter of political conflict, the style of conduct employed by the contending parties shows differences. That is to say, each side has differing beliefs about what considerations should enter into decisions, and about what are the feasible limits of the demands for action which may be made of themselves and which they may make on others. Conflicts thus wear the aspect of ideological disputes, whether these are conducted in overt terms or are implicit. The head of the concern enters at this point as a key figure who, in manifest or latent ways, denotes the code of conduct which should obtain.

Technical Progress and the Occupational Self

Organic systems are those which are best adapted to conditions of change. By common consent, such conditions are at present affecting a widening sector of industrial and occupational life. The code of conduct characteristic of organic systems—those better fitted to survive and grow in changing conditions—comprehends more eventualities than that necessary in concerns under stable conditions. More information and considerations enter into decisions, the limits of feasible action are set more widely.

The extension of the boundaries of feasible action and pertinent consideration makes for a fuller implication of the individual in his occupational role. As the pace of change, especially technical change, accelerates, and as the organic systems better equipped to survive under these conditions also expand, the occupational activities of the individual assume greater and greater importance within his life. This is in keeping with the commonly observed tendency for occupational status to assume an increasingly dominant influence over the location of individuals in British society. But it also denotes a greater subjection of the intellectual, emotional, and moral content of the individual's life to the ends presented by the working organizations of the society in which he exists.

Developing a system of organized industrial activity capable of surviving under the competitive pressures of technical progress, therefore, is paid for by the increased constraint on the individual's existence. In Freudian terms, men's conduct becomes increasingly 'alienated,' 'work for a system they do not control, which operates as an independent power to which individuals must submit.'[3] Such submission is all the more absolute when it is made voluntarily, even enthusiastically.

In the next chapter of this book it is suggested that a social technology, as exhibited in the institutional forms of modern society, has been developed *pari passu* with modern technology in the material sense. Modern organizational forms, governmental and industrial, represent the application of rational thought to social institutions in the same way that technology is the product of the rational manipulation of nature. In the same way, too, it congeals the processes of human affairs—'fixing' them so that they become susceptible to control by large-scale organizations. The reverse aspect of this tendency is the increasing subjection of the individual to the psychological and material domination of the social order, a domination increasingly objective and universal as civilization advances technically.

References

1. Burns, Tom. "The Reference of Conduct in Small Groups; Cliques and Cabals in Occupational Milieux." *Human Relations,* 8 (1955), 467–86.
2. Argyris, C. *Executive Leadership.* New York: Harper, 1953.
3. Marcuse, H. *Eros and Civilization.* London: Routledge, 1956.

Questions for Discussion

1. In studying English literature, one finds that some scholars refer to the eighteenth century as "The Age of Reason" (man was governed by reason and rationality) and to the nineteenth century as "The Age of Romanticism" (man was governed by emotions). Assume that the world really is as Chapter 6 posited: that man in organizations will be satisfied if the network of jobs fits the goal. Would you say this "man" is reasonable, emotional, or both?

2. How does the following argument (posed in Chapter 1) relate to the argument in Chapter 6 (which holds that people will be satisfied if working in an organization where technology, authority, and leadership fit the organization's goal)?

   "Behavior on the job is a function of what the person brings to the situation and what the situation brings to the person. When people come to work in organizations they do not come 'empty handed,' as it were. They bring a supply of energy or potential to perform. They bring various needs or motives which predispose them to release their energy or behave in particular ways—ways which seem to them likely to satisfy their needs."

   (Hint: you may also want to read the paragraph in the beginning of Chapter 1 which follows the one quoted above.)

3. According to Herzberg's motivation-hygiene theory, and drawing on your knowledge of human needs (and growth) from Chapter 1, why might the same routine lower-level job be positively motivating in an underdeveloped country such as Ethiopia, yet nonmotivating in a developed country such as Sweden or the U.S.A.?

4. Is it possible that a man may have a *task* (one individual at his workplace) which is negatively motivating, and at the same time be involved in a *technology* (many individuals in an interrelated network of tasks) which is positively motivating? Relate this answer to a term used in the military—*esprit de corps*. Is it possible for a nurse in a hospital or the manager of a branch bank to have this *esprit de corps?*

5. In fundamental terms, why does "the establishment" or "the system" exist? Do people want it to exist? (Hint: first clearly state what you mean by "establishment" or "system.")

6. According to the argument in Chapter 6, people join an organization and work in it for a variety of reasons. From the reasoning in Chapter 6, what is the *principal* reason why a person might find the system or the establishment unacceptable?

7. Why might a person resent the rules, job descriptions, and procedures in an organization structure, in terms of

a) what he brings to the situation (see also Chapter 1)?
b) what the situation brings to him in the way of "bad" technology (see Chapter 6, your answer to Question 6, and the Herzberg reading)?
c) what the boss brings to the situation that might create bad technology (see the Thompson reading)?

8. The following statement by a control-tower operator at a metropolitan airport indicates that job enrichment of the vertical type is of limited value in some instances. Why is this true? What do you think is positively motivating the airline pilot as he descends on the final approach?

"Particularly in weather with stratus clouds 8000 feet thick (from 200 feet above the runway up to 8200 feet), the pilot simply must do what he is told. He has his own radar set, and we have ours. We tell him exactly when to enter the traffic pattern behind other planes, when to descend more rapidly or cut his rate of descent, and when to stop his descent, increase power, and go around again (rather than continue landing). If I see that he is too close behind another plane landing, I give the order to pull up and go around. It would be unthinkable to ask him over the radio 'Would you like to make this decision?'"

Short Cases for Discussion

Autotronic Corporation of America

I am president of Autotronic Corporation of America, which produces a range of equipment for sports-car owners. Our largest selling item is a tachometer which measures the revolutions per minute (rpm) of the engine. We have found that the best way to get these to the consumer is by having salesmen call on two types of customers: large, chain discount stores; and repair garages run by independent owners (not repair departments of automobile agencies). Most of the latter use tachometers made by Datsun, Mazda, Porche, or other makes if the agency sells these cars.

We're having continuous trouble getting the plant personnel and the sales personnel to work together. Here is a typical instance which I call "provincialism." The sales manager and his salesmen go out and meet these garage owners. They know them personally, and go to a great deal of effort to give them what they want. They spend great amounts of time discussing sports cars, races, gadgets, and the like with managers and purchasing agents of discount chains. Because the salesman is a sports-car enthusiast and the customers are usually the same, they get along well.

Not long ago one of the discount-chain purchasing managers phoned the sales manager. He said they had, through error, computed their inventories of our TX-4 instrument and were out of stock with the summer season coming on. He wanted 650 instruments within a week. He told our sales manager it was really important to him.

Our sales manager went out to the factory personally. He got the production manager and said, "Mike, I've come this time with a must. We've got to have 650 TX-4's in 3 days."

The production manager told him he'd like to comply but that he only had 200 in stock. "Furthermore," he said, "we're working on a large run of model TX-13 for Sears. I could probably squeeze in a run of 400 TX-4's, but that would mean shutting down the production line, and taking a day to reset all of the tooling and machinery. We have scheduled production of the TX-4 about four weeks from now, when our machines will be set for another model close to that specification. The cost of setup time won't be great then. It will be now with that extra day. As you know, the financial V. P. holds us accountable for costs. If the plant cost for each instrument goes up, it reflects on us."

In a long conversation, each man simply tried to convince the other. They kept repeating their own arguments. In the end, the production manager just said he wouldn't do it.

The sales manager later told me he wouldn't go to see the financial V.P. because every time he'd been there in the past the man stressed cost cutting. He said he'd rather try to appease the customer than try to convince the financial V.P.

I've told them they're acting like prima donnas and that they've got to learn how to solve these kinds of questions for themselves.

Questions

1. What is going on in this situation and why is it going on?
2. Is the situation good or bad for the company, or for the individuals involved?

Roosevelt Hospital

Roosevelt Hospital is a large, privately endowed hospital in Louisville, Kentucky. The hospital cares for patients who pay for services as well as patients who do not have funds. The latter were referred to as "charity" patients; now, hospital personnel usually refer to them as "limited resource" patients. Money for such patients is provided by the city of Louisville, by the state and federal governments, and by endowment funds. Recently, the city of Louisville requested all hospitals receiving such funds to provide statistics on cost per patient per day for such items as room and board, pharmaceuticals, and doctors' fees. Because the hospital director knows that the city will channel funds to hospitals that do not show excessive costs, he has instituted certain control reports, such as a report on the total cost of drugs for one patient that exceeds $1000.

Two months ago, Dr. Gillam, a staff physician, decided to try experimentally a drug for one of his limited resource patients who had chronic arthritis. The drug, Milozene, was reported in medical journals as "a tentative help for severe arthritic conditions. It has passed all federal tests for safety, but we have not established that it actually results in patient improvement. That will not be known until clinical experiments have occurred over two to three more years."

The cost of Milozene is $150 per ounce. Gillam's estimate when he requisitioned the drug was 30 ounces for extended treatment. When the $4500 requisition reached Dr. Jackson, the hospital pharmacologist who acts as purchasing agent, the latter called Dr. Gillam to inquire why it was being purchased. Dr. Gillam explained his reasons and the pharmacologist ordered and paid for the requisitioned amount.

Dr. Prichard, the hospital director, asked Dr. Gillam, Mr. Travis, the financial director, and Dr. Jackson to come to his office for a general discussion of hospital costs, and said he had noticed a large number of high-cost requisitions made by Dr. Gillam.

Dr. Prichard: "John, of course I'm not questioning your judgment on treating patients. I just thought we'd understand better our cost situation if we took the Milozene requisition as a case in point. As you know, we're under public pressure to lower costs, and under city pressure in terms of further support."

Dr. Gillam: "Well, I did have the patient's interest in mind. I've used most of what is known in the way of medications. The patient responded somewhat. I know Milozene is an 'iffy' proposition, and that it may or may not help. In addition, I knew for sure I could include this in medical research. It is valuable research either way—if Milozene is found not to be an effective drug, that's as important to know as that it is effective. What I'm saying is that there's a payoff for our $4500, regardless of what the results are for the patient. We won't know for another year."

Dr. Prichard: "But don't you remember the decision of our board two years ago about the place of research in the hospital? It was agreed that we are primarily a health-care hospital, and not a research hospital. We leave that to the universities and the university hospitals. I'm surprised that you didn't consider that, and that Dr. Jackson didn't raise it at the time he saw the requisition."

Dr. Gillam: "In view of the possible benefit to the patient, I view it as health care."

Dr. Jackson: "Well, John gave me those reasons at the time we talked. I ordered the Milozene not on my own judgment, but his. It really isn't my job to treat patients. I'm here to check the specifications of items wanted by the staff and to make sure we get those exact specifications from manufacturers."

Mr. Travis: "As members of the Board of Trustees, Dr. Prichard and I have been troubled deeply about such costs. Both city and federal agencies have strongly intimated that charity and poverty funds may be channeled to Louisville General Hospital rather than to us, unless we can show we produce maximum care for the community for dollars invested. As of now, our costs exceed General by $13 per day per patient. We're $4 higher in doctor fees, $2 higher in rooms and meals, and $7 higher in drugs. I frankly believe Dr. Gillam made this decision on the basis of research, and that it was the wrong decision."

Dr. Gillam: "I said I had the patient's health in mind. If Dr. Prichard will give us some policy to follow, I'm more than glad to go along with it. I simply don't want to worry about decisions like this."

Dr. Prichard: "Of course we don't want to intrude on the prerogatives of the individual doctor."

Mr. Travis: "But don't you think we might work out some guidelines, or some procedures whereby the doctor gets a ruling on such matters from someone higher up? Or maybe we could simply have someone check with the doctor to help him clarify his own course of action."

Dr. Prichard: "I don't see how we could ever operate other than on the individual doctor's judgment. Maybe everyone should just bear in mind that we want good patient care and wise use of our precious dollars."

Dr. Jackson: "Well, I'd be glad to follow any procedure you may work out."

Dr. Prichard: "I thank you men for coming in. And I'm sure it was worth our time. Let's just think about what's been said, and from time to time talk among ourselves when these things come up."

The meeting broke up with usual good-natured comments about one another's golf game, the current political situation, and like matters. Each man returned to his own job. Later, Dr. Gillam commented: "Prichard is a gentleman and we all like him. Actually, he does conduct the most ineffective meetings in his office. If I'd thought about it carefully, I wouldn't have ordered the Milozene. But I simply cannot be a good doctor and researcher and be an economist-financier, too. I'm not interested in those things, know nothing about them, and cannot in the future worry during the day about such decisions. I'm bothered about the state of affairs in Louisville. I blame Roosevelt's rather bad reputation in part on Prichard. Some of us are also troubled because all of the best young doctors seem to be going to Louisville General. One of them told me he looks at Roosevelt as a good hospital, but one that is a little tired and messy to work in."

Questions

1. How is the environment of Roosevelt Hospital affecting its goals?
2. How are the various technical specialties influenced by these goals?
3. How are the motivations of people affected by the technology (goals plus tasks)?
4. What are the causes of the problems the men have in coordinating with one another?
5. Does the hospital seem overstructured or understructured?

Chapter 7

Structural Design
of Organizations

In Chapter 6, we introduced the problem of fitting the coordinating structures of an organization to the nature of its goals and the needs of its people. It is the purpose of this chapter to show how a manager might go about designing an organization structure that is viable in terms of (1) success for the organization in achieving its goals, and (2) success in providing individuals inside the organization with the opportunity for fulfilling whatever needs they are pursuing by working in the organization. The first is necessary if society is to support the organization and allow it to exist. The second is necessary if people are to contribute their efforts to the organization.

Philosophies of Organization Design

There are two "pure" types of organizations: the formal (sometimes called rational or mechanistic) and the informal (sometimes called democratic or organic). The first is characterized by clear-cut job descriptions (roles) for the people in specialized operating parts of the organization (e.g., research, manufacturing, sales); by a separation of the coordinating work from the operating work (thus creating coordinators such as line managers and staff managers); and by reliance of all concerned on policies and procedures (for example, production schedules) to achieve coordination of the operating technology. As explained in Chapter 6, typical coordinators figure out the way the technology is related to the organization goal and pass this on to operators. This method was invented by the military and is in wide use in the industrial world; it is Max Weber's "rational bureaucracy." (It forms the basis for "traditional" management theory, which grew up in the period from about 1920 to 1950.) This structural philosophy has been criticized on the grounds that it is too authoritarian and that it stifles individual initiative.

In spite of these criticisms (which in many cases have some truth in them), formal organization in fact exists in every work organization in the world. There are times when people want clear-cut decisions and a clear definition of their jobs. The student who asks for information on how grades are computed in a course ("Will there be a final examination? Will there be a term paper? About how long should the term paper be? How many absences are we allowed?") not only deserves answers but would be upset without such information.

The second structural philosophy is characterized by temporary or *ad hoc* roles for the operators and by integration of the coordinating work with the operating work (e.g., the sales, production, and research people do their own coordinating together, very much as a team of scientists work together inventing a television tube). There are still some coordinators, such as line executives and specialist advisors. And there are still some formal procedures. But the structure of positions and procedures is much broader and less detailed. People depend on talk among themselves to decide how procedures should be developed and operated to attain the organization goal.

This philosophy has steadily gained widespread support during the last twenty years in response to a number of dysfunctional effects which have occurred when formal organization is either misused or when it has been assumed to be *the only* viable form of organization. First, in some organizations with operating technologies that do not *require* formal structures, the managers holding power take over decision making unnecessarily, which is a case of misfit between the structure and the operating technology. This results in constriction of freedom, in conflict between the leaders and those led, and in conflict between knowledgeable operating people and generalist line executives with the "right" to command but without the knowledge. Second, some people entering organizations today bring problems of either overdependence or counterdependence (Chapter 3) from their previous lives. They categorize *all* formal structures as bad. Finally, behavioral scientists whose lives are spent studying psychology or small group sociology, who know little of technology, or have observed formal organization being used inappropriately, have concluded that human dynamics is the only (or the primary) method for coordinating.

How is the manager to reconcile all of this? The first step is to recognize that, while such an absolute dichotomy helps philosophize about organization design, and sets the stage for more intensive study, it is very misleading for anything but a start.

In order to overcome the limitations of such oversimplification, we look at some alternative structures which fit different conditions, different organizations, the same organization at different times, or even different parts of the same organization at any one time. Each of these organization design technologies is functional for a different kind of operating technology. Each is named according to the positions which do most of the coordinating work. In most of these structures, *many different* people do the coordinating work. But for convenience of analysis, the name specifies those *most responsible* for coordination. For each of the structures, we examine

- what kind of goal and technological conditions call for this type of structure.
- what kinds of formally described positions perform the coordinating work of the organization.
- what kinds of formally described positions perform the operating tasks of the organization.
- what kinds of behavior patterns are used by those doing the coordinating work and those doing the operating work.

We depend on previous chapters for an understanding of technological conditions (Chapter 6) and of human behavior (Chapters 1 through 5). Reference is made to these conditions when we consider each alternative, but we will not repeat in detail evidence presented earlier.

The order in which the five types of structures are discussed does not imply that any one type is "better" than the others. It seems easier to understand them if they are presented this way.

Centralized Organization Structures

The first three structures we consider may be called centralized structures, because for any one technology there is a clear division between those positions which specialize in primary operating activities and those which specialize in coordinating activities.

Line Managers as Integrators

Exhibit 7-1 shows a small printing company that produces booklets. Three *primary operating positions* are required: a typist, a mimeograph operator, and a proofreader. Primary operating positions deal directly with the main goals of the organization. Their function is to provide society with a useful product or· service. One *auxiliary service position* is required: a purchasing clerk. It is an auxiliary service position because the purchasing clerk specializes in buying all of the firm's supplies, including stencils used by the typist and paper used in the mimeograph operation. The function of an auxiliary service position is to facilitate primary operating work by producing a product or service for the operators. There is one coordinating position: the line manager. He coordinates the job technology of the firm.

This particular firm has a batch technology. If you study the figures carefully, you will see that customers order booklets in small quantities. One

Exhibit 7-1 Line Integrator of A. Dashed arrows (stencils or pages) represent sub-objectives in the input-output system.

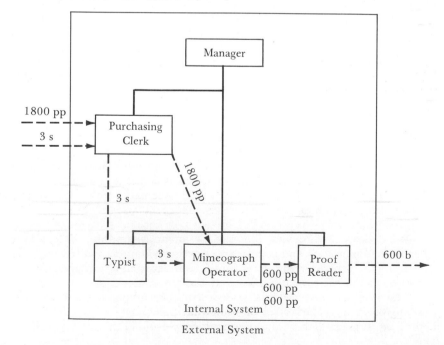

customer orders 600 booklets to be printed on blue paper to be delivered to the customer by 4 p.m. the following day. These are *organizational* goals. One can see that these goals are relatively unstable, since the next customer may want another kind of booklet in 800 copies on white paper by 10 o'clock in the morning.

The other numbers on Exhibit 7-1 indicate the subgoals or *departmental* goals. The typist, for example, has the goal of producing three stencils by 10 o'clock in the morning. The mimeograph operator has the goal of running the three stencils, page 1 on 600 sheets of paper, page 2 on another 600, etc. By 2 p.m. he delivers these to the proofreader who collates them, checks for quality, and ships them.

You can see how the technology for one booklet is an integrated whole. Each part is related to the goal of the company. If anyone does not do his job with the right timing and quality, the booklet does not get produced. The first job of the coordinator, therefore, is to coordinate current (day-to-day) operations. The task can also be called current planning or operating planning.

The second function of the manager is designing the parts themselves. This can also be called long-range planning, allocating fixed resources, capital budgeting, or strategic planning. We are talking about designing a fixed structure of resources, including manpower with specific talents and specializations, to synchronize with the quality and magnitude of the firm's expected future goal. If this firm is to be viable over the years, the fixed resources must match the future goals, in terms of the quality of products produced (booklets of various types), and in terms of quantity or magnitude of the goal.

For the company shown in Exhibit 7-1, whether by intuition, science, or simulation, the manager has gone through the following steps to match his internal resources with the external demands of society (customer requirements):

1. Estimate the output goal for the total organization (quantities, qualities) for a fixed time period—a month, a year, or even five years.
2. Break the total work to be done into parts.
3. Estimate the capacity of one person or department.
4. Divide the future output by the capacity of the person or department, thus computing how many units of resources (e.g., typists) are needed for that output.

There is a difference in the durability of the procedures and policies which result from the two types of management coordination, at least in a batch (changing) technology. Operating planning is *ad hoc* and somewhat informal. The plans for each booklet are temporary, since each new order is a different goal, calling for a slightly different technology. Thus, the operating planning for each new order may involve considerable give and take between the coordinator and the operators. He may have to act as expeditor if something goes wrong, seeking information, help, and advice from operators. He may, in turn, have to give one operator information about when the other people are scheduled to do their work, what is to be the next customer order, and so on. Notice that because some of the formal procedures are temporary, the behavior of manager and operators must be somewhat informal.

The frequent give and take among all personnel in *operating planning* gives this line manager the characteristics of an *integrator*. His behavior is more informal and dynamic, as he deals with operating people. Much of the research cited in Chapter 6 points out that there is a great deal of anxiety and energy involved in give and take. This is true in *any* social relationship except those that are highly structured (rituals, etc.). But the source of poor morale is more likely to be (1) too much coordination or too many coordinators, or (2) not enough coordination. An example of the former would be the line manager getting into too much detail, or perhaps appointing a new staff coordinator when he is not really needed. An example of the latter would be that when the mimeograph operator is ready to run his booklets, someone has forgotten to order the stencils.

The second kind of coordination—strategic planning—is a different matter. It is more formal. Let us first take an example of *informal* or *ad hoc* strategic planning. From it we can then draw conclusions as to why the more formal approach can be superior in many instances. It can be superior from the point of view of company success, from the point of view of the segment of society which depends on the company for products, and from the point of view of the people who work in the company.

The president (line manager) in our small printing company comes in one morning and says to the typist, who is quite competent in her work, "I've been thinking about going into the business of proofreading for a publisher down the street. Would you do a market survey, check with the banks to see if we can get the money, find out from a lawyer whether we would be legally liable for errors, decide how many proofreaders we'd have to hire, based on the number of titles they put out each year, check on the cost of renting office space, or whether it would be better to invest ourselves in a small building? By the way, try to get a list of all publishers in the eastern half of the U.S. And I guess you'll have to check with the purchasing agent to see how much those desks, chairs, special desk lamps, etc., would cost if we did go into this line of business."

There are two different problems presented by this manager in trying to involve the typist in an *ad hoc* strategic planning project which is not part of her formal job of typing. In terms of the technological success of the firm in the marketplace, such an excessive use of participation in strategic planning, if pursued too far, may well end up with no company at all. Since nobody is specializing in booklet production (operations), and nobody in current and strategic planning (coordination), customers may cease to reward the firm with orders.

In terms of human satisfaction, if strategic planning is attempted through such *ad hoc,* give-and-take, informal means, there is bound to be a negative effect on the morale of certain types of individuals. For one thing, people take jobs with a certain *expectation* of what they will be doing. The competent typist, who expects to pursue her specialty without the interruption of many new and foreign problems to solve, may feel that she is involved in a fairly chaotic existence. In addition, new and strange intrusions on one's accustomed routine, to say nothing of the energy and emotional strain of constantly dealing with other people who want one's attention or cooperation, are bound to exact a price in terms of anxiety—regardless of how interesting or "involving" the new project might be. If she is a good typist, enjoys her job, and her leisure time off the job, she just might say, "You're the one around here who's paid to do all that; I'll do my job and you do yours."

Staff Generalists as Integrators

In order to extend our knowledge of the small printer to the world of large corporations, it is only necessary to visualize a system such as the one depicted in Exhibit 7-2 for a firm that prints a wide variety of products—insurance-company policies, sales brochures for electric appliances, statistical forms for the government, and telephone books for the Bell system. Each of these is a different goal. And each requires a different technology—that is, different *specialized positions* and different *coordinating procedures* to get out the various products. Rationalizing the various stages in the work flow needed to produce one goal (brochures advertising washing machines) is different from designing the procedures necessary for a second goal (statistical forms for the government).

A chief line manager, who was our integrator in the small booklet shop,

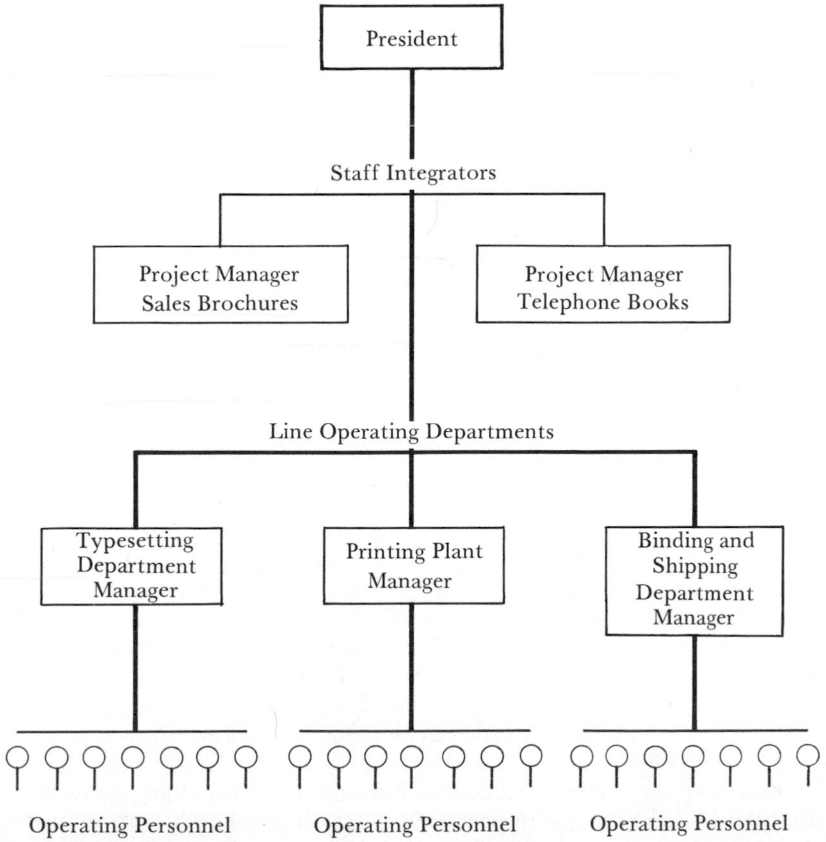

Exhibit 7-2   Staff Integrators in a Multitechnology Company

cannot possibly do all of this. At this point, the president creates integrators in the form of project or product managers, whose job it is to specialize in the detail work of strategic planning and operating planning *for one goal.* Such a system is described by Stewart (1965) in a selection following this chapter. This article describes product managers who are assigned to the sales organization. The product manager position is also applicable in technical organizations, in which the project managers report to the president instead of to the head of the sales division. A good example of the latter would be in the Boeing company, where the primary operating divisions (research and design of aircraft, manufacture of aircraft, sales, and government relations) are supplemented by project managers for both strategic and operating planning. One man would coordinate the 707 four-engine jet product, one the 747 jumbo-jet product, another the Bomarc guided missile, and so on.

The project manager is almost never regarded as having final authority over primary operating departments. This is a deliberate attempt by organization designers to provide for a great deal of give-and-take among all concerned, with operating specialists entering into a team effort with the project manager. This attempt, of course, is made because of the temporary and changing nature of the project goal (requiring a batch production technology) and because the operating specialists often have as much information about what ought to be done as the chief line officer or the project manager himself.

For multigoal or batch technologies, this design of structure has some obvious advantages from a human standpoint over an alternative in which the chief *line* executive, who could not possibly have expertise in all projects, nevertheless exercises control. For one thing, operating personnel have considerably more voice in the formulation of their own job technology. The structure allows those who are competent in each operating specialty to participate with a coordinating staff specialist who has time to devote to a specific project goal and technology. It also helps to prevent conflict between those operators with the *knowledge* to command and the chief line executive with the *right* to command (Chapter 6). The chance for operators to attain a sense of personal achievement and competence is greater. To the extent that a wider range of knowledge and experience is brought to bear on both current operating technology and strategic planning, such a company is more likely to be successful with the customer, to survive and to grow. This in turn means that the company is a better place to find secure jobs, safety in an industrial world, and even an *esprit de corps* from belonging to a successful organization. There is no doubt that in IBM, for instance, the joy of belonging to "the best" is a factor in the positive attitudes of those who are employed there.

The usefulness of the "integration" behavior pattern for different specialists when they are trying to solve problems jointly has been well known for many years. Those who wish to know more of this behavior pattern may consult the work of Follett (1942), and also study carefully the kinds of relationships described in Chapter 8. Those who wish a fuller understanding of how a very large corporation attempted to make integrators out of all of its line executives can consult the massive organization scheme devised by the General Electric Company (1953–55).

But there are disadvantages, too. There is a certain amount of role conflict generated because there is no clear-cut expectation of "who has the final say."

And the constant problem solving of *coordinating technology* creates anxiety when one is trying to solve problems in his *own specialty.* This effect of integrative staff structures has received considerable notice in the literature (e.g., Reeser, 1969).

Staff Specialists Who Provide Part of a Complete Technology

Organizations can become complex in yet another way. Not only can they have multiple technologies, but each technology *itself* can have its own specialized parts. In the project manager form of organization, we were talking about a company with a variety of goals. But it is one thing for a total organization to have multiple goals (goal complexity), and quite another for the organization to have one goal, yet an internal technology which itself becomes very complex in its pattern of specialization.

Such a company is pictured in Exhibit 7-3. Let us assume that this company is General Motors, producing only one automobile: Chevrolet. Assume further that it has the *primary operating* parts (functions, specialties, departments) shown at the bottom of the diagram.

Exhibit 7-3 Functional System of Technology with Staff Specialists

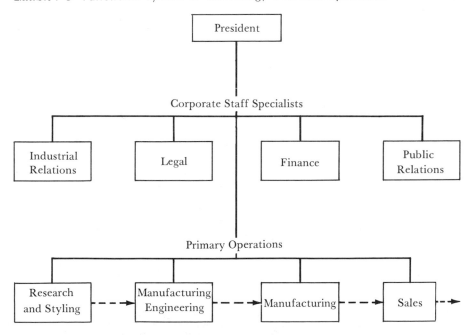

The research and styling department designs the automobile. Its goal is the production of blueprints which are delivered to the manufacturing engineering department. The latter's goal is the design and construction of plants and production lines for the manufacturing department. This department's goal is to manufacture cars and deliver them to the sales and distribution department.

But there are other parts of the technology—other activities. Staff specialist departments (middle row of Exhibit 7-3) are necessary to coordinate these other activities. Industrial relations experts are necessary to figure out everything from safety and medical programs to financial aspects of pension plans. Financial planners are necessary to see if the styling department is designing an automobile that the company can pay for with its cash flow, to collect money from customers and pay the foremen in the manufacturing department, to borrow money from banks to pay the salesmen, and to figure out a price that will pay all costs but not be so high that it will turn off prospective customers. Lawyers are needed to see that the salesmen, the research designers, the manufacturing executives, and everyone connected with the operating technology conforms to established laws of society.

Notice that these specialists are different from the generalist integrators discussed before. The latter coordinated a whole technology. These auxiliary staff experts are supposed to help operating managers in current operating planning. And they help top managers by advising on strategic planning. At this point, we see that a complete technology has three kinds of specialists: the top line coordinator, staff specialist coordinators, and operating managers.

There are two staff behavior patterns, formal and informal, each of which is appropriate for different types of organization goals. Appropriate in this case means that, when used properly under the right goal conditions, the behavior pattern will increase the probability that the goal is achieved successfully, and that the people in the system recognize the need for the intervention of staff experts. Formal staff behavior is discussed in the next section. Here we discuss informal staff behavior.

The article by Kolb following this chapter describes the staff man as a consultant, as opposed to the staff man as an influential representative of headquarters possessing either formal or implicit power.

When the designer of organizations uses a device such as informal staff coordinators, he does so for several reasons. First, it would be too costly in overhead if the designer duplicated a specialist of this type within each operating department. Second, such a structure is mandatory in an industrial world. If an automobile company decided to do away with its financial planners, leaving everything connected with the technology to people on the production line, there might be no cash next month to buy art supplies for the men designing the cars, or to pay salesmen for selling them. If the operators quit their jobs and tried to do finance work, there would be no product to finance.

The design of an organization using specialist staff coordinators also has powerful implications for some very important human needs—physical security, achievement, and job involvement.

Let us look at physical security first. It is somewhat difficult for those who live in an affluent society to see the effect on this need of good staff performance. This is not surprising, if we recall the need hierarchy described in Chapter 1. So we must imagine an automobile company in the U.S., France, or Germany that decides it will do away with staff specialists. It hardly seems necessary to point out that, with no financial planners, our hypothetical company would soon be a place that is very risky for a person to work. Given a complex industrial society, financial planners are a necessity if the organization is survive and have the money to pay wages, salaries, or old-age pensions to employees. In short, if General Motors' technological structure is well enough designed to insure that its employees will have enough to buy food, shelter, and other necessities of life, there is fortunately no need for most people employed there to worry about security of their physical needs.

When we turn to achievement, or feelings of competence and job involvement, it is likewise easier for people in advanced cultures to see the *dysfunctional* effects of big organizations on people than it is to see the need-satisfying effects. Conscious appreciation of staff specialist support can be seen in developing countries. Research done in newly forming companies in Iran, for example, show that individuals at all levels appreciate the existence of staff specialists (Summer, 1968). Interviews with operating personnel and staff engineers in a new tractor factory there show that they have a very great desire, not only to have a tractor factory, but to have line officers who know their technology and staff experts to tell them how to perform their jobs. Both Russian and American engineers went there to help design the procedural parts of the technology. In the short run, the Iranians showed appreciation for a place to work that would raise their standard of living. If you have had only primitive agriculture, hand work, no tools (capital "know how"), and a subsistence level of living, a job on a production line with an engineer to show you how to run it is something of value. Furthermore, both operators and staff specialists of local origin showed a great desire for technological training of *their own* engineers. They looked forward to the day when the Russians and Americans would leave—in many cases, not so much for nationalism, as for a feeling of competence and achievement. "We want to learn to do this ourselves. We don't want a *part of 'our' company missing*." Notice here the feeling of involvement with company goals, and the sense of achievement expressed because other specialists are doing their jobs.

Of course, the feeling of achievement and competence, as well as of growth (climbing Maslow's need hierarchy described in Chapter 1) is greatly increased if the specialists act as teachers, consultants, and informal advisors, rather than experts who figure out technological procedures which cannot be understood by the operators, and which are passed on as "givens." This is possible and appropriate when the goal of the organization is one that is not too complex technologically, or when even complex technologies require frequent checking with operating personnel to see that changing conditions (customers, processes, financing methods, etc.) are accommodated by the technology. The latter behavior results in a dynamic version of vertical job enrichment.

However, we will see later that if the technology is very complex but relatively stable, so that specialists have to "give orders" rather than consult and teach, it is *even then* possible to have operating people feel a sense of achievement.

Formal Line and Staff Coordinators

We turn now to a structure in which line and staff positions, using formal task-oriented behavior patterns, assume the largest share of the coordinating work in the organization.

This type of centralized structure looks similar to the one pictured in Exhibit 7-4. It is simplified to leave out the staff specialists (discussed above) who coordinate auxiliary parts of technologies, such as employee safety programs, accounting, labor relations, and pricing.[1]

---

[1] These parts are important, too, and also tend to operate more formally.

Exhibit 7-4 Line-Staff Formal Process Coordinators

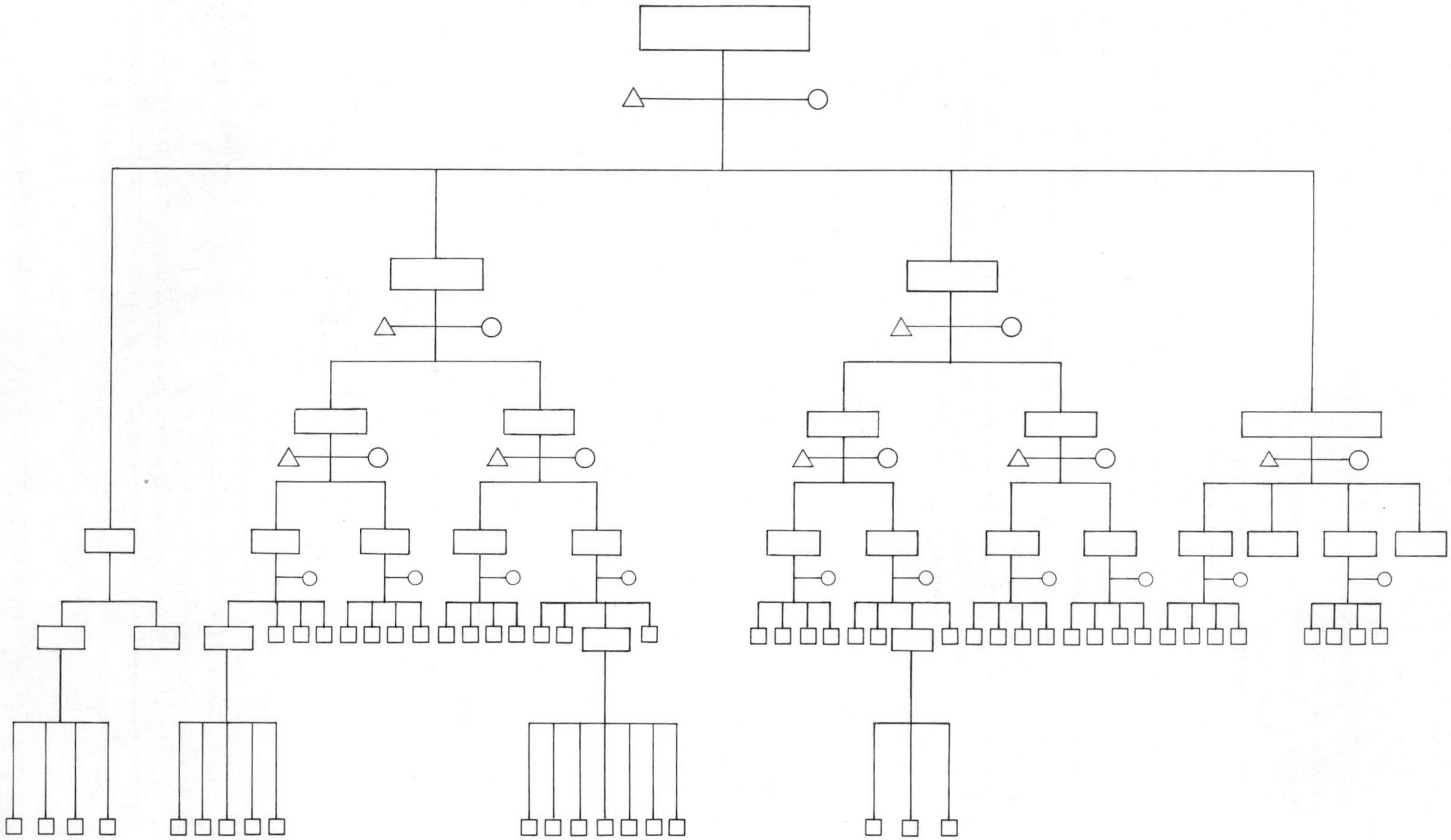

This kind of organization has a goal that requires a highly complex primary operating technology. The quality and quantity of work performed by each operating person and operating department is highly interdependent. Each person in an oil refinery, for example, must adjust his unit to receive an intermediate (half-finished) oil of exacting specifications from a previous person in the sequence. He then proceeds to change its chemical nature to a set of different chemical specifications and pipe it on to the next person, who does the same. This quantity and quality coordination is enormously complex; a modern refinery takes three or four streams of crude oil coming in from wells hundreds of miles away (that also have exacting goals), routes it through hundreds of different streams or channels within the plant, and spews out at the other end 400 products, ranging from gasoline and jet fuel to paraffin wax, 64 grades of grease, 90 lubricating oils, propane bottled gas, and ethylene for antifreeze.

The quality and quantity goals of each part, and their related procedures, are complex enough. But the *timing* and *sequencing* of the complete technology are not even comprehensible to middle-level coordinators, much less to lower level coordinators and operators. Twelve million gallons of liquids may flow through each day. There are 400 organizational goals, with 400 intricately related technologies which branch out in a web of interrelationships so complex that if one man turns the wrong valve, or turns the right valve at the wrong time, he may shut down part of the refinery. Depending on whether he is toward the beginning of the branching process or toward the end, he may shut down a small part of it or the whole thing.

Before we examine the behavioral characteristics of this structure, we need to know what kind of coordinating work is done by the managerial positions shown in Exhibit 7-4. They are all primary operating executives, because they deal directly with production, rather than with auxiliary specialist staff functions. The line executives are shown as square boxes. The staff coordinators of current production are shown as circles at the various levels. They rationalize the day-to-day (or perhaps minute-to-minute) production for their parts. In practice they are called production control engineers, process engineers, or plant balance engineers.

The triangles represent those who rationalize the fixed assets—they figure out how many machines are necessary, when the ethylene technology (one of the 400) will be switched over to newly developed machines and flows, and how many operators are required to monitor the control room of a catalytic cracker (this machine, incidentally, is seven stories high). These men are involved in strategic rather than current planning. Notice that the triangles disappear at about the middle of the chart. This means that *line* process coordinators probably know very little of equipment purchasing, construction costs, what new equipment is on the market, and so on.

Woodward found these characteristics in her studies of 100 manufacturing firms in England. She discovered the average number of levels in the formal command hierarchy in process industries was 6 and that some firms had 17 levels, compared to an average of 4 in batch-production firms. Further, she found that because of the technological expertise and effort required to coordinate such a system, the average span of control of managers was one manager coordinating 15 subordinates, rather than 48 subordinates, as was the case with batch-type firms. This same phenomenon is reflected in the fact that the ratio of all managers to all direct operators was one manager for every 7 or 8 operators, while batch firms average one manager for every 14 to 18 employees.

What kind of behavior patterns do the coordinators and the operators in this structure use? In order to understand their habit of getting along well with one another while preferring task-oriented (as opposed to social) behavior, we must see clearly the influence of technology on this kind of performance.

The goals of the company and their related technologies are relatively well known. A gallon of gasoline is a gallon of gasoline. A gallon of textile machinery lubricating oil is a gallon of textile oil. In addition, there is much research and development going on in the central research laboratories, which will mean structural or strategic change; and current production schedules must change, depending on the balance between the 400 different end products demanded by customers, or changes in availability of different crude oils flowing into refineries from far-away fields. Sometimes the internal plant technology is adjusted to run more kerosene and less gasoline, or more asphalt and less fuel oil. Or it is adjusted to run crude oil with a lower sulphur content than a previous supply. In short, here are relatively known technologies, but they are highly complex and changing, in timing, sequencing, and quantities.

Everyone in the system recognizes that successively higher levels of coordinators are specialists in knowing how one part of the system affects another, and that successively lower levels of coordinators and operators are specialists in knowing how to coordinate or operate one part of the technology. In short, they recognize their interdependence. Higher level managers and strategic planning staffs are the only ones who can "know" the information necessary to coordinate major strategic changes such as the introduction of new fuels with their complex machines, chemical processes, technologies, and manpower requirements. Higher and middle managers are the only ones who can know how each part of the process affects every other part, and how to balance current production schedules. Notice in Exhibit 7-4 that, as we move down the coordinating hierarchy, the strategic staff coordinators (the triangles) disappear at one point. Further down, even the staff process coordinators (the circles) disappear, and line managers perform the coordinating roles.

Also, because there is not nearly as much integrating to do each day in a process technology, there is not as much need for integrators or staff specialists down the line. That is another reason why the process coordinators begin to disappear as we move down the organization in Exhibit 7-4. The line managers can handle the whole job. Woodward found in her studies that there were fewer staff process coordinators in the process type of company than in batch-type companies, that line executives tended to know their part of the technology well, that there seemed to be a higher degree of delegation in process firms than in batch firms, and that there was less "organization consciousness." People were not so concerned about power, authority, and prerogatives of status or prestige.

The important point for behavior is that whenever the job to be done requires vast *suboperating* parts, whenever the system balance for one part can only be known by the top people in that part or department, the people in the system tend to be more task-oriented. They prefer their contacts to be aimed primarily at getting the job done. The line executives do more of the coordinating than in other types of firms: once the technology has been planned, there is not nearly as much on-the-spot *ad hoc* adjustment to be made in the technology by means of informal contacts. The typist in our small printing company would have many informal interactions with the line manager as the different custom-made technologies were invoked for different customers each day. But if she typed a previously run type of booklet when she reported for work, there would be less need for informal interaction.

Why do individuals prefer less social and more task-oriented behavior in a process organization than in a batch-type firm? If there were no changed condition from "normal," they would proceed along, simply observing their usual technology, and observing the supra-technology set by the company. They do not wish to stop and have a gabfest with other workers about how to do the job. On the other hand, if one goes to work each day in a different situation, he wants to talk with various coordinators to see what is going on and to get information on the proper action to take.

This is the same phenomenon found by Porter in his "parable of the spindle." The waitress and the cook in the restaurant were always having hostile confrontations about the sequencing and quality of meals ordered by customers. When a simple spindle (a technological sequencer) was installed by the owner (line coordinator), both individuals seemed to accept the job to be done without further incident. If there was a great deal of cooking going on in the kitchen, the cook no doubt tired of constant social conversations with the waitress each time she brought a slip to the order window.

This does not necessarily mean that people in such structures are completely lacking in social contacts during the work day. In fact, we have observed workers in a refinery with rather large amounts of leisure time using this time in talking on the phone with friends, cooking gourmet meals on steam equipment, even growing vegetable gardens outside the control room. These workers had an eye on the monitoring devices of their unit, in case something went wrong. At the same time, successively higher managers were observed to be discussing, frequently and vigorously, the coordination of the refinery with peers on their level, and with coordinators up the line. The observation that these men seemed to enjoy such "work-social" contacts (notice this is not the same as social work contacts!) supports Woodward's conclusion that there was considerable free and easy talk about the job to be done, a very permissive (rather than authoritarian) atmosphere to the relationship between men at different hierarchical levels, and less "organization consciousness."

There is strong evidence that human relations—attitudes of people toward their jobs, toward their peer workers, and toward managers—can be quite positive in such organization structures, if the structures are used when they are appropriate.[2] What are some of these feelings and attitudes?

In the interviews conducted in the previously mentioned tractor factory in Iran, it was found that line employees actually felt a sense of increased competence and achievement simply by doing their own job, *if they know that competent coordinators are also doing their own jobs*. The workers felt, when the Russian and American coordinators left and the jobs went to other Iranians, that they

---

[2] For those readers who are familiar with Taylor (1947), consider the analogy to his encounter with Schmidt, the uneducated Dutchman in the steel mill. Schmidt felt this same way. He faced an engineer who could show him how to do his job more successfully with the same effort. Perhaps he felt that he would develop better capabilities to cope with the industrial world, and would find his friendships or social satisfactions off the job rather than with his boss.

had achieved something, even though they were not themselves in coordinating positions. This suggests that people operating under formal line-staff coordination, receiving formal orders from above, do not necessarily need to be involved in coordinating themselves, or need to be treated informally in order to get a sense of competence and achievement from their work.

The following comment made by a line executive[3] of Mobil Oil Corporation is similar to comments made by people in IBM about Thomas J. Watson: "He (the president) is an absolute wizard. He started out as a financial planner, but has learned the oil business from stem to stern. When you add that kind of knowledge to a very sharp analytical mind, everybody in the company respects his decisions. You walk in his office with a complicated problem and he can cut through the confusion like nobody I've seen. We are lucky to have him."

The reverse is also true. "Democratic" or "committee" management can backfire, if used under inappropriate conditions, producing negative rather than positive effects on the feelings of people in the organization. In Chapter 6 it was noted that the management of one of the container companies instituted a lower management participation system. But because the technology was so complex, only specialists with the knowledge to plan could do the work effectively. Management could not understand why conflict resulted between the democratic planners at lower levels and the upper level coordinators, who frequently reversed the decisions made below.

The point that formal leadership can produce favorable human relationships *if the technology requires it* is substantiated in much of the research on leadership performed by Fiedler (1965). He found that there are many kinds of tasks in which groups want a strong leader, primarily those which can be performed with clear operating instructions. "We neither expect nor want the trusted airline pilot to turn to his crew and ask, 'What do you think we ought to check before takeoff?'" On the other hand, groups do not want such a leader if the task must be left nebulous or undefined. "It is easier to be the well-esteemed leader of a construction crew working from a blueprint than it is to be the disliked chairman of a volunteer committee preparing a new policy."

A revealing statement by an executive of a large electronics company in Yugoslavia serves to illustrate the kinds of attitudes we are talking about. In Yugoslavia, the officers of a firm are elected by the employees. This particular officer had just lectured to Western European executives attending a management course in Switzerland. He had explained how the employees elect him every two years. Somewhat astonished, a French executive said, "Such a system would be unthinkable in France. I'd not consider for a moment that my employees could elect me. Aren't you bothered by this election? Aren't you a bit afraid?"

The Yugoslavian's answer was, "Me, afraid? Why should I be? They know that the plant cannot exist without an executive vice president. They depend on me heavily while they do their work. I, in turn, depend on them heavily to get the work done. Of course it's a bother for me to put up with the time and energy of an election. But I do know that I have been elected several times, and that they therefore feel they need me."

This same type of question was later put to the waiter in a fashionable

---

[3]Interview with Mr. P. J. Boglioli, New York, March 1972.

resort hotel on the Adriatic. "I hear you elect the head of the hotel. Does this cause much excitement and interest when it happens? Do people have their favorite men, and do you, for example, ever want to be elected?" The answer was, "Why should I want to be elected? I am a waiter. I have been to one of the better hotel schools in the world to learn to be a waiter, and perhaps one day a *maitre d'hotel*. Mr. Dujmovik is paid to work very hard at a lot of things I don't want to worry about. He does a good job. Besides, a hotel has got to have a general manager."

These examples support Barnard's (1938) theory, discussed in a selection following this chapter, that authority is granted from below. Barnard was president of the New Jersey Bell Telephone Company, which has a highly complex and interdependent technology. He reasons that authority comes from below, but that the arrangement of formal communication is a necessary requisite to compliance by people down the line.

The selection by Koontz and O'Donnell accompanying this chapter discusses cases when formal authority might be given to staff men. We have already seen that such officers have a kind of natural authority from below, and that there is not too much "organization consciousness" in a process organization anyway. Furthermore, it is probable that a number of the so-called traditional management theory books have given entirely too much stress to the power, authority, and prestige of office in this type of organization (or in an integrator type of organization, for that matter). Nevertheless, the reading serves to illustrate in a practical way that many different kinds of formal staff coordinators might be used in designing an organization structure.

Does all of this mean that in such structures there is no human problem? Emphatically not. Many things can go wrong, such as conflict between line and staff (Dalton, 1950), conflict between line officers who have the right but not the knowledge to command (Thompson, 1961), a certain degree of boredom, or a rigid structure in which people cannot seem to talk openly when there is need to change the technology. To cope with these matters, there are devices other than structure available to the manager, such as training executives and workers, creating temporary informal systems within the formal structure, construction of proper reward systems, or other administrative practices. These are the subjects of Chapters 8 and 9.

Decentralized Organization Structures

We come now to another class of organization which involves the *sharing* of coordination between operating departments and coordinating departments. This involves essentially two types of structures: (1) formal decentralized structures which separate the operating planning from the strategic planning and spread the former among operating units; and (2) matrix structures which share both types of coordination between the coordinators and operators by emphasizing dynamic team problem solving. Each of these organization designs are examined separately.

Structural Decentralization and Job Enlargement

At lower levels, structural decentralization has been called "horizontal job enlargement" or "operating job enrichment." A look at Exhibit 7-5 shows how

Exhibit 7-5 Structurally Decentralized Organization. Dashed arrows represent sub-objectives of each part of the organization. All dashed arrows together represent current operating procedures, or rationalization of the current operating system.

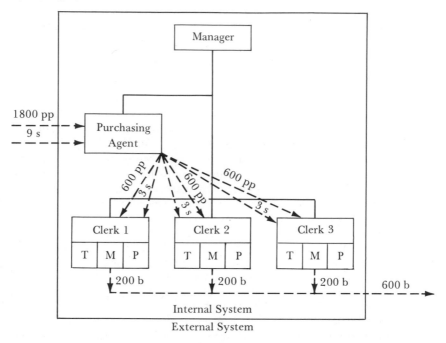

our small printing company would look if it were organized by structural decentralization. It is exactly the same company which appears in Exhibit 7-1. It would be well worth while to stop and study the two charts to see how they compare. First, there are decentralized *operating* parts which produce whole booklets. Instead of having the operating parts specialize in one part of the operating technology (typing, mimeo operating, and proofreading, as in Exhibit 7-1), we put one third of the organization's operating technology in each position (clerk 1, clerk 2, clerk 3). We decentralize the original complete operating technology into three complete operating subtechnologies.

Each part of the organization now has a subgoal which is stated in the same way as the total organization goal. For example, when the order for 600 booklets by 4 p.m. tomorrow came in from the customer, it was a total organization goal. In the former centralized structure, the goals of the typist were stated in terms of "three stencils by 10 o'clock tomorrow," and of the mimeograph operator in terms of "600 sheets run in three batches of 200 pages each, by 1 p.m. tomorrow." Now, each clerk has a goal of "200 booklets each by 4 p.m. tomorrow."

This fractionalization of organization goals into smaller final goals (rather than into functional goals stated as means to final goals) is one important hallmark of the structurally decentralized company. Another hallmark is the separation of the decision making to rationalize day-to-day operations (how to go about meeting the subgoal) from the strategic decision making necessary to rationalize longer run fixed parts of the technology (what the scale of operation will be, how many workers are necessary).

Since each clerk in the decentralized shop can now make his own decisions about timing of the three specialized operations (typing, mimeographing, proof reading), and only one overall objective is handed down by the management (200 booklets by 4 p.m.), we see how important the structure is for *management by objectives* (see the selection by McGregor following Chapter 8).

Structural Decentralization of Larger Organizations

A look at Exhibit 7-6 shows a structurally decentralized General Motors, with 500,000 employees. In the centralized structure of Exhibit 7-3, the primary operating components were a giant research and styling department, a giant manufacturing department, and a giant sales department. We now see that the primary operating components are Chevrolet, Buick, and Pontiac. Instead of having a welter of operating plans handed down from the president and his staff, together with budget and cost specifications, corporate headquarters can now "manage by objectives," simply by delegating the responsibility to produce Chevrolets profitably as measured by total return on investment. This is what is known as "profit center" decentralization.

How would General Motors ever get to this kind of organization design? It could grow large producing one model of automobile, as did Ford producing the Model T. In that case it would have somewhat the same characteristics as the oil refinery. Possessing only one goal with one technology, it would probably be organized similarly to the formal line-staff structure. As it adds more diverse goals, producing Buicks, Pontiacs, and Cadillacs, as well as Chevrolets, top management no longer has the knowledge to coordinate such diverse technologies (either current operations or strategic changes in technology). At this point, management has two alternatives. It might leave the *operating* structure the way it is, organized by giant functional departments—research and styling, engineering, manufacturing, and sales—but appoint product managers (vice president for Chevrolet, for example) on the president's staff. These managers, acting similarly to the staff integrators discussed previously, would then be responsible for acting as planners, informal communicators, and facilitators of coordination between the operating (functional) department heads (e.g., vice president, sales; vice president, manufacturing).

But as companies become very large and complex, the top management cannot even coordinate the coordinators! The Chevrolet team, composed of operating vice presidents plus the product-coordinating vice president for Chevrolet, may well develop a plan that is too costly for General Motors to execute without hurting *other* operating teams—the Cadillac or Buick teams, for example.

This is the point at which structural decentralization becomes a necessity. The pyramiding of coordinators who coordinate other coordinators becomes too complex for the top management or even for one product team to coordinate with five other product teams. The corporate staff grows to the point where everyone is stumbling over everybody else, and where nobody can take action or make a decision without checking first with a labyrinth of other people who are affected.

Exhibit 7-6 Structurally Decentralized Organization: Company Level

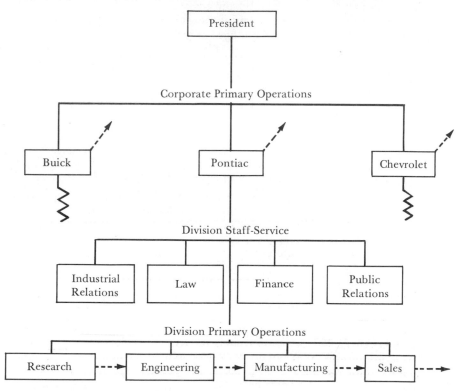

Structural decentralization, then, splits up the enterprise into separate complete technologies—separate autonomous divisions, each with a complete technology. Notice on Figure 7-6 that much of the corporate staff in the president's office has been disbanded. Its staff specialists (finance, law, public relations, etc.) who coordinate parts of technologies have been divided among the new decentralized divisions.

What remains at the top is strategic planning. The lower operating units have all of the talents and competencies to design, produce, and sell a given automobile. They even do a certain amount of strategic planning, such as changing their own product goals, for example. But the strategic matter of "when do we bring out a totally new car such as the Pinto or the Vega" is one dealt with by the corporate president and his staff.

Some important factors of human motivation and behavior appear with this kind of decentralization. For one thing, the lower line executive (vice president for Chevrolet) is much less *dependent* on the president and corporate staff vice presidents. He can feel more autonomy, strive for more achievement through his own efforts, and realize the joy of testing his skill in the marketplace.

Since the system of communications now involves only Chevrolet people (rather than the whole company, and dealing with other teams operating the Cadillac and Pontiac technologies), there is much less energy and anxiety connected with making any one decision. Finally, the chain of command is not so long. If an individual at any level within Chevrolet wishes to be heard on some matter, he need not have to go all the way to the top of the corporation, encountering more managerial levels who either do not want their existing operations upset or who feel defensive when new ideas are presented. True, he still has to go through many contacts within Chevrolet, but this is a much less formidable obstacle than taking on the entire General Motors system.

Viewed in another way, decentralization aids in overcoming two of the principal factors of bureaucratic rigidity. It relieves people down the line from the feeling of futility associated with giant organizations ("what's the use, I'll have to go all the way to the top and I'll never succeed"). It relieves some of the reluctance of top managers to change the whole system ("you can't do that in Chevrolet because you'll affect the people in Pontiac and Buick") simply by destroying some of the interdependencies between various technologies within the company. And the staff at headquarters is partially dispersed to the operating divisions.

Matrix Organization: Structure and Dynamics

Another form of decentralization stands halfway between informal coordination and formal structure as a coordinating mechanism. We have already seen that *all* methods of coordination have each of these two components in them. One of the main differences between different organization designs is how much one depends on formal versus informal behavior. *Matrix organization* comes somewhere near the middle. It is intended to depend slightly more on informal behavior rather than formal, but in practice the existence of formal departments and their clearly specific goals probably means that such a design depends equally on each. The essence of this design is that the integrators of *complete* technologies and the specialist staff coordinators of *part* of a technology are co-equal members of a team to produce a final organization goal. Neither has clear-cut prestige, authority, or precedence over the other. There are no distinctions between "operators" and "coordinators." In fact, in its purest form they are all advisors to each other. Exhibit 7-7 shows a matrix chart of General Motors organized in this fashion. It should be compared to Exhibits 7-3 (centralized GM) and 7-6 (decentralized GM) in order to see that each design represents a different philosophy of how people should behave within the structure. You may wonder what is in the squares. Actually, there is no position or person in the square. It represents a joint activity or joint decision to be performed by the two people on the vertical and horizontal axes.

It might be argued that simply drawing a chart differently, without rearranging the primary operating parts, will not cause anybody to behave differently inside the organization. This is to some extent true. But those who have worked for extended periods in organizations know that such a chart can be a powerful cognitive device to let the participants know what is desired by top management. To the extent that people want to reduce cognitive dissonance (Chapter 1), charts have their influence on behavior too.

Incidentally, General Motors is used for illustrative purposes only to compare with previous discussions. It is more likely that the structural decentraliza-

Exhibit 7-7 Matrix Organization

	Law	Research and Styling	Manufacturing	Sales	Industrial Relations
Buick					
Pontiac					
Oldsmobile					
Chevrolet					
Cadillac					

tion design fits this company's technology better than the matrix design. But in companies with fast-changing goals or technologies, such as aerospace companies, this form would be more applicable. Instead of the automobile operating divisions down the left side of the chart, there would appear the 747 Jet Transport program, the 707 Jet Transport program, the earth satellite program, and so on.

Summary

The manager facing a problem in organization design has available to him two broad philosophies. The first, formal organization (sometimes called rational or mechanistic) is characterized by clear-cut job descriptions, separation of coordinating work (decision making, planning) from the operating work, and spelled-out procedures and policies which connect one job to another. The second, informal organization (sometimes called democratic or organic), is characterized by temporary or *ad hoc* roles for operating jobs, by integration of planning, coordinating, and decision-making work with operating work, and by day-to-day *ad hoc* behavior as the team of organization members do the planning together.

Separation of organization design into these broad philosophies has value, but it also has dangers and limitations. Most organizations are a mixture of formal and informal behavior. It is therefore necessary to be more specific about the alternative designs a manager might use. This chapter poses six technologies of organization design. Each differs in terms of the *balance* between formal planning behavior and organic planning behavior.

In organizations depending primarily on general line managers to act as integrators, formal rules are rather broad, and managers act as facilitators or team builders. Such organizations are particularly applicable when there is an unknown or changing technology which must be developed by the operating specialists who have the appropriate knowledge. Companies with small batch or custom-made product technologies fall in this category.

A second type of structure uses headquarters staff generalists as integrators. They act with relatively informal leadership styles, to help the operating managers of diverse company functions make decisions as a team. Such a structure is particularly applicable when a given company has multiple technologies and goals (rather than a single product with its associated technology).

In organizations which depend heavily on specialist staff positions to contribute part of a technology, acting as teachers and consultants to operating personnel, emphasis is likewise on broad guidance and joint problem solving. This type of organization is appropriate when auxiliary specialization is needed (in finance, labor relations, and the like) and when the lower line manager has the diverse knowledge necessary to make general coordinating decisions.

The formal line and staff design, appropriate when only higher managers have the breadth of knowledge necessary to make coordinating decisions, envisions line officers and staff officers as decision makers who issue instructions. The job descriptions and the procedures necessary to connect diverse jobs together in a network tend to be more detailed, concrete, and inclusive. Behavior tends to be more task-oriented and formal. This design comes closest to the formal, or mechanistic philosophy.

Decentralized structures attempt to solve the coordinating problem by reserving strategic planning of the parts to top management, who set broad goals and act more formally. But decision making to coordinate current operating work is divided among self-contained operating divisions. This affects behavior in two ways. It eliminates a great deal of communication which would, under centralized structures, take place as the higher management attempts to coordinate current operations. Second, it makes possible smaller units of operation which then have more opportunity to engage in team planning of an organic nature. Such structures seem appropriate when the organization pursues relatively stable but diverse goals—so diverse that higher management cannot have the knowledge to coordinate current operations—and when the organization is large enough that it can afford the overhead costs of a separate management team for each division and technology.

Finally, matrix organization represents a half-way point between formal organization and informal organization. The coordinators and the operators are expected to work jointly, somewhat as colleagues pursuing a common goal. Such organizations are particularly appropriate when there are frequent changes in the product being produced, when flexibility of work procedures is mandatory, and when operating personnel are the only ones who have the knowledge to make coordinating decisions.

These, then, are the principal organization structures available for use in designing organizations. We shall see later (Chapter 12) that there is an additional organization system which has received considerable attention in theory and practice. It is organization development, sometimes called team management or group management. On the formal-informal continuum, it is the most informal and organic of all. In essence, it envisions a continuously changing technology and job structure, with the planning being done by any person in the organization with knowledge relevant to operations. The formal technology and job structure is supposed literally to "arise" out of informal communication.

References

Barnard, C. I. *The Functions of the Executive.* Harvard University Press, 1938.

Cordiner, R. J. *New Frontiers for Professional Managers.* McGraw Hill, 1956.

Dalton, M. "Conflicts Between Staff and Line Management Officers." *American Sociological Review,* June 1950.

Fiedler, F. E. "Engineer the Job to Fit the Manager." *Harvard Business Review,* Vol. 43, No. 5, September–October 1965.

Follett, M. P. "Constructive Conflict," in *Dynamic Administration,* edited by H. C. Metcalf and L. Urwick. Harper, 1942.

General Electric. *Professional Management in General Electric:* Book I, *General Electric's Growth,* 1953; Book II, *General Electric's Organization,* 1955; Book III, *The Work of a Professional Manager,* 1954.

Kolb, H. D. *Organizational Theory in Industrial Practice.* Wiley, 1962.

Koontz, H., and C. O'Donnell. *Principles of Management,* 4th ed., McGraw-Hill, 1972.

Lawrence, P. E. *The Changing of Organizational Behavior Patterns: A Case Study of Decentralization.* Division of Research, Harvard Business School, 1958.

Lawrence, P. R., and J. W. Lorsch. *Organization and Environment,* Harvard University Graduate School of Business Administration, 1967.

Reeser, C. "Some Potential Human Problems in the Project Form of Organization." *Academy of Management Journal,* December 1969.

Stewart, J. M. "Making Project Management Work," *Business Horizons,* Vol. 8, No. 3, Fall 1965.

Summer, C. E. *Industrial Development and Renovation Organization of Iran,* Institut pour l'Etude des Methodes de Direction de l'Entreprise, 1968.

Taylor, F. *Scientific Management.* Harper, 1947.

Thompson, V. A. *Modern Organization.* Knopf, 1961.

Woodward, J. *Industrial Organization Theory and Practice.* Oxford University Press, 1965.

Readings

Making Project Management Work

JOHN M. STEWART

With a good deal of local fanfare, a leading food producer opened a new plant in a small midwestern town. For the community it was a festive day. For top management, however, the celebration was somewhat dampened by the fact that the plant had missed its original target date by six months and had overrun estimated costs by a cool $5 million.

A material-handling equipment maker's latest automatic lift truck was an immediate market success. But a few more successes of the same kind would spell disaster for the company. An actual introduction cost of $2.6 million, compared to planned expenses of $1.2 million, cut the company's profits by fully 10 percent.

A new high-speed, four-color press installed by a leading eastern printing concern has enabled a major consumer magazine to sharply increase its color pages and offer advertisers unprecedented schedule convenience. The printer will not be making money on the press for years, however. Developing and installing it took twice as long and cost nearly three times as much as management had expected.

Fiascos such as these are as old as business itself—as old, indeed, as organized human effort. The unfortunate Egyptian overseer who was obliged, 5,000 years ago, to report to King Cheops that construction work on the Great Pyramid at Giza had fallen a year behind schedule had much in common with the vice-president who recoils in dismay as he and the chief executive discover that their new plant will be months late in delivering the production on which a major customer's contract depends. The common thread: poor management of a large, complex, one-time "project" undertaking.

But unlike the Egyptian overseer, today's businessman has available to him a set of new and powerful management tools with the demonstrated capacity to avert time and cost overruns on massive, complex projects. These tools, developed only recently, are not yet in common use outside the construction and aerospace industries, where such projects are a way of life. But there is already solid evidence that they can be successfully applied to a host of important, nonroutine business undertakings where conventional planning and control techniques fail—undertakings ranging from a new-product introduction or the launching of a national advertising campaign to the installation of an EDP system or a merger of two major corporations (Figures 1 and 2).

Project Management Organization

Commercial project management is <u>usually a compromise</u> between two basic forms of organization—pure project management and the more standard func-

Figure 1   Manpower Commitment to a New-Product Introduction Project

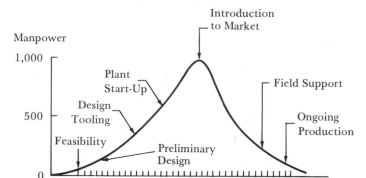

Figure 2   Manpower Commitment to a Merger Project

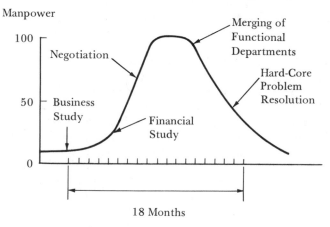

tional alignment. In the aerospace and construction companies (Figure 3), complete responsibility for the task, as well as all the resources needed for its accomplishment, is usually assigned to one project manager. In very large projects, the organization he heads, which will be dissolved at the conclusion of the project, resembles a regular division, relatively independent of any other division or staff group. Outside the aerospace and construction industries, however, the project manager is usually not assigned complete responsibility for resources (Figure 4). Instead, he shares them with the rest of the organization. He may have a project organization consisting of a handful of men on temporary assignment from the regular functional organization. The functional managers,

Figure 3 Typical Project Organization in the Aerospace and Construction Industries

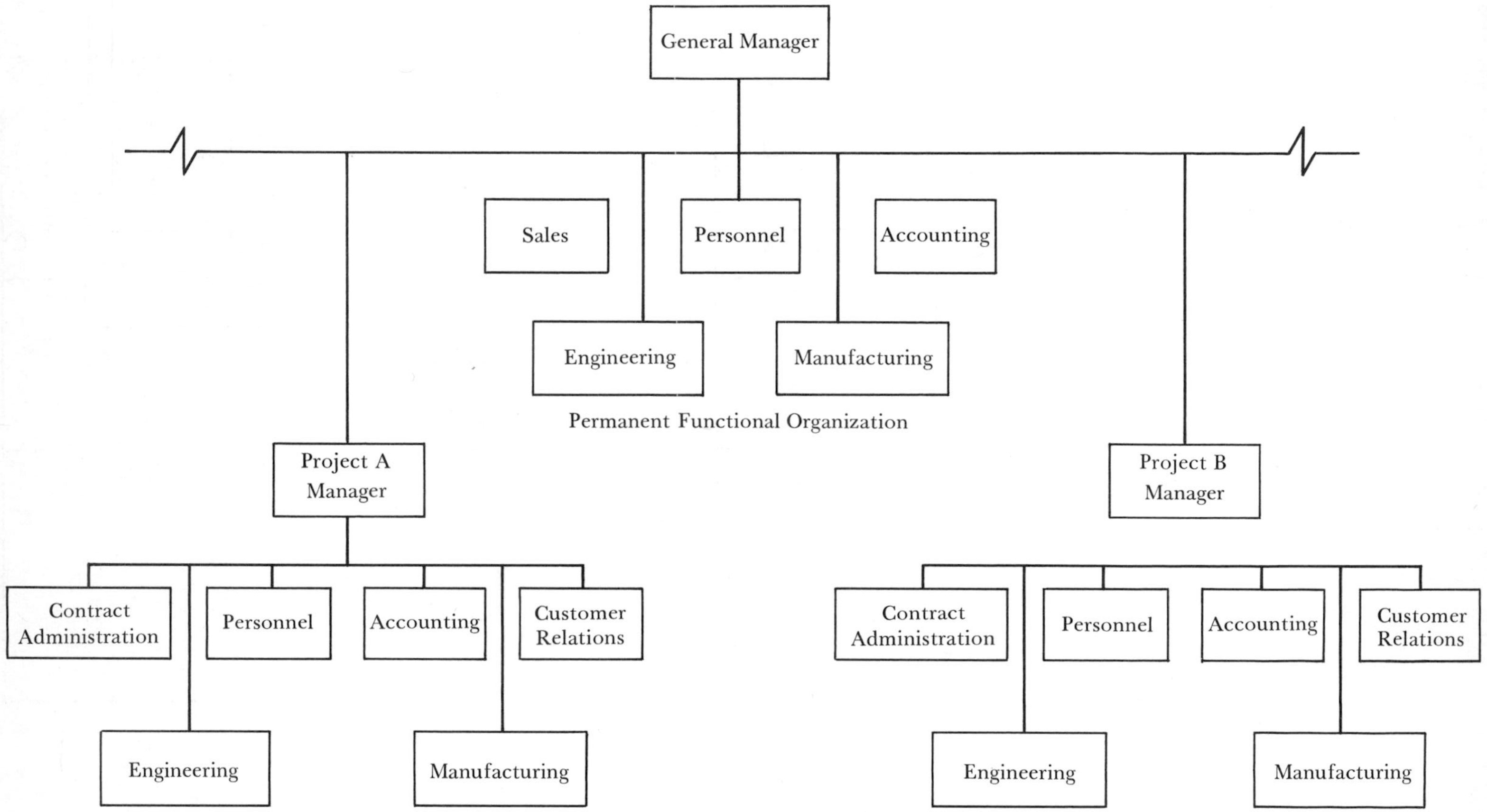

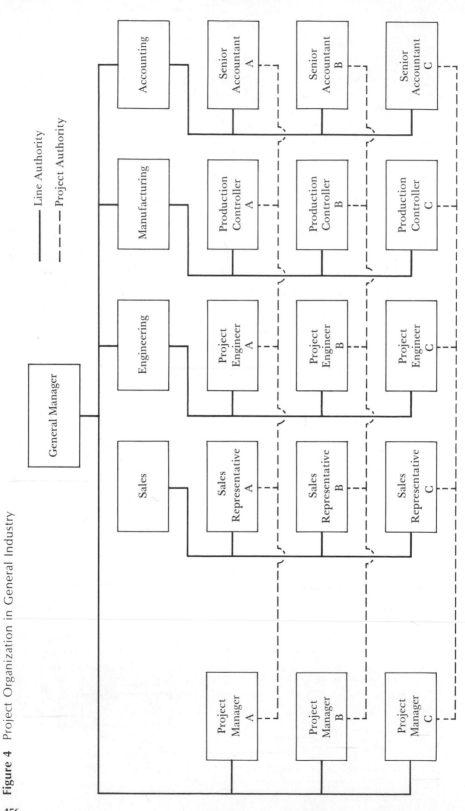

Figure 4 Project Organization in General Industry

however, retain their direct line authority, monitor their staffs' contributions to the project, and continue to make all major personnel decisions.

Reluctance to adopt new tools is typical in any industry; thus, one should not expect the tools of project management to gain instant acceptance. Outside the aerospace industry, few business executives appreciate their value and versatility. Fewer still are able to recognize the need for project management in specific situations, nor do they know how to use the powerful control techniques it offers. Meanwhile, the few companies that have grasped the significance of the new management concepts and learned to apply them enjoy an extraordinary, if temporary, advantage. They are bringing new products to market faster than their competitors, completing major expansions on schedule, and meeting crucial commitments more reliably than ever before.

Project management, however, is far from being a cure-all for the embarrassments, expenses, and delays that plague even the best-managed companies. First, project management requires temporary shifts of responsibilities and reporting relationships that may disturb the smooth functioning of the regular organization. Second, it requires unusually disciplined executive effort.

Basic to successful project management is the ability to recognize where it is needed and where it is not. When, in short, is a project a project? Where, in the broad spectrum of undertakings between a minor procedural modification and a major organizational upheaval, should the line be drawn? At what point do a multitude of minor departures from routine add up to the "critical mass" that makes project management operationally and economically desirable? Senior executives must have methods to identify those undertakings, corporate or divisional, that cannot be successfully managed by the regular functional organization working with routine planning and control methods. Although there are no simple rules of thumb, management can determine whether a given undertaking possesses this critical mass by applying four yardsticks: scope, unfamiliarity, complexity, and stake.

Scope

Project management can be profitably applied, as a rule, to a one-time undertaking that is (1) definable in terms of a single, specific end result, and (2) bigger than the organization has previously undertaken successfully. A project must, by definition, end at an objective point in time: the date the new plant achieves full production, the date the parent company takes over operating management of the new acquisition, or the date the new product goes on sale in supermarkets across the nation, to name a few.

The question of size is less easily pinned down. But where substantially more people, more dollars, more organizational units, and more time will be involved than on any other infrequent undertaking in the organization's experience, the test result is clearly positive. Such an undertaking, even though its component parts may be familiar, can easily overwhelm a divisional or corporate management. Project management forces a logical approach to the project, speeds decision making, and cuts management's job to a reasonable level. For example, a large service company, with years of experience in renovating district offices, established a project organization to renovate its 400 district offices over a two year period. Even though each task was relatively simple, the total undertaking would have swamped the administrative organization had it been managed routinely.

In terms of the number of people and the organizational effort it involves, a project could typically be charted over time as a wave-like curve, rising gradually to a crest and dropping off abruptly with the accomplishment of the end result. Consider, for example, the introduction of a new consumer product. The project begins with a few people studying the desirability of adding a product to the line. After some early decisions to proceed, perhaps a few dozen engineers are employed to design the product. Their work passes to scores of process planners, tool makers, and other manufacturing engineers, and finally involves entire manufacturing plants or divisions as the first month's production gains momentum. This momentum carries into the field as salesmen increase their effort to introduce the product successfully. Finally, the project effort ebbs as the new product is integrated into routine production and marketing operation.

Again, a merger typically shows a similar "growth and decay" project pattern. Initially, a few senior executives from each company may be involved in discussing the merger possibility. As interest grows, financial and legal advisors are engaged by both sides. Key inside executives are added to the task force to assist in planning. Then, as the deal moves toward completion, widening circles of executives, technical people, and analysts become involved in identifying the changes required after merger. Once the merger has been approved by the directors and stockholders of the two companies, the process of meshing the philosophies, structures, policies, and procedures of the two organizations must begin, possibly requiring the active participation of hundreds or even thousands of people. Eventually, as most of the changes are accomplished, employees return to their normal duties, and the corporation resumes its orderly march toward the end of the fiscal year. The merger project is at an end.

Unfamiliarity

An undertaking is not a project, in our sense of the term, unless it is a unique, or infrequent, effort by the existing management group. Lack of familiarity or lack of precedent usually leads to disagreement or uncertainty as to how the undertaking should be managed. In such a situation, people at the lower management levels need to be told more precisely what they are to do, while senior executives are justifiably troubled by a greater than usual sense of uncertainty about the realism of initial cost estimates, time commitments, or both.

Thus, though a single engineering change to one part of a product would not qualify for project management by this criterion, the complete redesign of a product line that had been basically unchanged for a decade would in most cases call for project management treatment. Individual managers could accomplish the first change easily, drawing on their own past experience, but each would have to feel his way by trial and error through the second.

Complexity

Frequently the decisive criterion of a project is the degree of interdependence among tasks. If a given task depends on the completion of other assignments in other functional areas, and if it will, in turn, affect the cost or timing of subsequent tasks, project management is probably called for. Consider the introduction of a hypothetical new product. Sales promotion plans cannot be completed until introduction dates are known; introduction dates depend upon product availability; and availability depends on tooling, which depends in turn on the outcome of a disagreement between engineering and product planning over performance specifications. There are many comparable interdependencies among marketing, engineering, manufacturing, and finance. If, as seems likely in this situation, no one person can produce a properly detailed plan on which all those concerned can agree; if estimates repeatedly fail to withstand scrutiny; or if plans submitted by different departments prove difficult to reconcile or coordinate, the critical mass of a project has probably been reached.

Stake

A final criterion that may tip the scales in favor of project management is the company's stake in the outcome of the undertaking. Would failure to complete the job on schedule or within the budget entail serious penalties for the company? If so, the case for project management is strong.

The corporate stake in the outcome of a project is commonly financial; that is, the failure of a $50,000 engineering project might jeopardize $12 million in annual sales. But it may also involve costs of a different kind. As more than one World's Fair exhibitor can attest, failure to meet a well-publicized project schedule can sometimes do real harm to a company's reputation. Again, failure to meet time and cost objectives may seriously disrupt corporate plans, as in the case of an equipment manufacturer who was obliged to abandon a promising new product line when a poorly-managed merger soaked up earnings that had been earmarked for R&D on the new line. In all such cases, the powerful controls of project management offer a much firmer prospect of meeting the time, cost, and quality objectives of the major one-time undertaking.

The specific advantages of project management for ventures that meet the criteria just discussed are easily summarized. Project management provides the concentrated management attention that a complex and unfamiliar undertaking is likely to demand. It greatly improves, at very small cost, the chances of on-time, on-budget completion. And it permits the rest of the organization to proceed normally with routine business while the project is underway. But these benefits are available only if top management clearly understands the unique features of project management, the problems it entails, and the steps required to make it work.

The Nature of Project Management

With respect to organization, project management calls for the appointment of one man, the project manager, who has responsibility for the detailed planning, coordination, and ultimate outcome of the project. Usually appointed from the middle management ranks, the project manager is supplied with a team, often numbering no more than half a dozen men for a $10 million project.

Team members, drawn from the various functional departments involved in the project, report directly to the project manager. For the duration of the project, he has the authority to insist on thorough planning, the freedom to challenge functional departments' assumptions and targets, and the responsibility to monitor every effort bearing on the successful completion of the project.

Within the limits of the project, the project manager's responsibility and authority are interfunctional, like that of top management for the company as a whole. Despite this similarity, however, his function cannot safely be superimposed on a top executive's normal workload. Every company I know that has tried giving operating responsibility for the management of a complex project to a division manager has found that he is soon swamped in a tidal wave of detail. Most projects call for more and faster decisions than does routine work, and clear precedents are usually lacking. Thus, a general manager who tries to run one of his own projects seldom has any guidelines for making reliable cost and time estimates, establishing cost control at commitment points, or setting adequately detailed targets for each department. Lacking precedents, he is obliged to invent them. This procedure may drain off far more of his time than the division can afford, without really providing the project with the concentrated attention it needs. He may well find that he is spending better than half his working time trying to manage a project representing less than a tenth of his division's annual budget, while divisional performance as a whole is slipping alarmingly. For these reasons, few projects are ever successfully managed on a part-time basis.

The essence of project management is that it cuts across, and in a sense conflicts with, the normal organization structure. Throughout the project, personnel at various levels in many functions of the business contribute to it. Because a project usually requires decisions and actions from a number of functional areas at once, the main interdependencies and the main flow of information in a project are not vertical but lateral. Up-and-down information flow is relatively light in a well-run project; indeed, any attempt to consistently send needed information from one functional area up to a common authority and down to another area through conventional channels is apt to cripple the project and wreck the time schedule.

Projects are also characterized by exceptionally strong lateral working relationships, requiring closely related activity and decisions by many individuals in different functional departments. During a major product development, for example, a design engineer will work more closely with the process engineering manager and the product manager from marketing than with the senior members of his own department. He will need common sense and tolerance to succeed in the scramble for available resources, such as test-cell time or the help of metallurgical specialists, without hurting relationships of considerable importance to his future career.

Necessarily though, a project possesses a vertical as well as a horizontal dimension, since those who are involved in it at various stages, particularly those who make the technical decisions that determine costs, must often go to their superiors for guidance. Moreover, frequent project changes underline the necessity of keeping senior executives informed of the project's current status.

Special Sources of Trouble

Understandably, project managers face some unusual problems in trying to direct and harmonize the diverse forces at work in the project situation. Their main difficulties, observation suggests, arise from three sources: organizational uncertainties, unusual decision pressures, and vulnerability to top-management mistakes.

Organizational Uncertainties

Many newly appointed project managers find that their working relationships with functional department heads have not been clearly defined by management. Who assigns work to the financial analyst? Who decides when to order critical material before the product design is firm? Who decides to delay design release to reduce unit cost? Who determines the quantity and priority of spares? All these decisions vitally concern the project manager, and he must often forgo his own guidelines for dealing with them. Unless he does so skillfully, the questions are apt to be resolved in the interest of individual departments, at the expense of the project as a whole.

Because of the number of decisions or approvals that may arise in the course of a large project, and the number of departments that have an interest in each, innumerable possibilities always exist for interdepartmental conflicts. Besides coping with these conflicts, the project manager must juggle the internal schedules of each department with the project schedule, avoid political problems that could create bottlenecks, expedite one department to compensate for another's failure to meet its schedule, and hold the project within a predetermined cost. Moreover, he must do all this singlehanded, with little or none of the experienced top-management guidance that the line manager enjoys.

Unusual Decision Pressures

The severe penalties of delay often compel the project manager to base his decisions on relatively few data, analyzed in haste. On a large project where a day's delay may cost $10,000 in salaries alone, he can hardly hold everything up for a week to perform an analysis that could save the company $5,000. He must move fast, even if it means an intuitive decision that might expose him to charges of rashness and irresponsibility from functional executives. Decisions to sacrifice time for cost, cost for quality, or quality for time, are common in most projects, and the project manager must be able to make them without panicking. Clearly, therefore, he has a special need for intelligent support from higher management.

Vulnerability to Top-Management Mistakes

Though senior executives can seldom give the project manager as much guidance and support as his line counterpart enjoys, they can easily jeopardize the project's success by lack of awareness, ill-advised intervention, or personal whim. The damage that a senior executive's ignorance of a project situation can create is well illustrated by the following example. A project manager, battling to meet a schedule that had been rendered nearly impossible by the general manager's initial delay in approving the proposal, found functional cooperation more and more difficult to obtain. The functional heads, he discovered, had become convinced—rightly, as it turned out—that he lacked the general manager's full confidence. Unknown to the project manager, two department heads whom he had pressured to expedite their departments had complained to the general manager, who had readily sympathized. The project manager, meanwhile, had been too busy getting the job done to protect himself with top management. As a result, project performance was seriously hampered.

Executive Action Required

Because of the great diversity of projects and the lack of common terminology for the relatively new techniques of project management, useful specific rules for project management are virtually impossible to formulate. From the experience of the aerospace and construction industries and of a handful of companies in other industries, however, it is possible to distill some general guidelines.

Guideline 1: Define the Objective

Performing unfamiliar activities at a rapid pace, those involved in the project can easily get off the right track or fall short of meeting their commitments, with the result that many steps of the project may have to be retraced. To minimize this risk, management must clarify the objective of the project well in advance by (1) defining management's intent in undertaking the project, (2) outlining the scope of the project, that is, identifying the departments, companies, functions, and staffs involved, and the approximate degree of their involvement, and (3) describing the end results of the project and its permanent effects, if any, on the company or division.

Defining Management's Intent What are the business reasons for the project? What is top management's motive in undertaking it?

A clear common understanding of the answers to these questions is desirable for three reasons. *First,* it enables the project manager to capitalize on opportunities to improve the outcome of the project. By knowing top management's rationale for building the new plant, for example, he will be able to weigh the one-time cost of plant start-up against the continuing advantage of lower production costs, or the competitive edge that might be gained by an earlier product introduction. *Second,* a clear definition of intent helps avert damaging oversights that would otherwise appear unimportant to lower-level managers and might not be obvious to the senior executive. One company failed to get any repeat orders for a unique product because the project team, unaware of the president's intent, saw their job only in terms of meeting their schedule and cost commitments and neglected to cultivate the market. *Third,* a definition of the intent of the project helps to avoid imbalance of effort at the middle-management level, such as pushing desperately to meet a schedule but missing cost-reduction opportunities on the way.

Outlining the Scope of the Project Which organizational units of the company will be involved in the project, and to what degree? Which sensitive customer relationships, private or governmental, should the project manager cautiously skirt? By crystallizing the answers and communicating them to the organization, the responsible senior executive will make it far easier for the project manager to work with the functional departments and to get the information he needs.

Describing the End Results Top managers who have spent hours discussing a proposed project can easily overlook the fact that middle managers charged with its execution lack their perspective on the project. An explicit description of how a new plant will operate when it is in full production, how a sales reorganization will actually change customer relationships, or how major staff activities will be coordinated after a merger, gives middle managers a much clearer view of what the project will involve and what is expected of them.

Guideline 2: Establish a Project Organization

For a functionally organized company, successful project management means establishing, for the duration of the project, a workable compromise between two quite different organizational concepts. The basic ingredients of such a compromise are (1) appointment of one experienced manager to run the project full-time, (2) organization of the project management function in terms of responsibilities, (3) assignment of a limited number of men to the project team, and (4) maintenance of a balance of power between the functional heads and the project manager. In taking these steps, some generally accepted management rules may have to be broken, and some organizational friction will almost inevitably occur. But the results in terms of successful project completion should far outweigh these drawbacks and difficulties.

Assigning an Experienced Manager   Though the project manager's previous experience is apt to have been confined to a single functional area of the business, he must be able to function on the project as a kind of general manager in miniature. He must not only keep track of what is happening but also play the crucial role of advocate for the project. Even for a seasoned manager, this task is not likely to be easy. Hence, it is important to assign an individual whose administrative abilities and skill in personal relations have been convincingly demonstrated under fire.

Organizing the Project Manager's Responsibilities   While some organizational change is essential, management should try to preserve, wherever possible, the established relationships that facilitate rapid progress under pressure. Experience indicates that it is desirable for senior management to delegate to the project manager some of its responsibilities for planning the project, for resolving arguments among functional departments, for providing problem-solving assistance to functional heads, and for monitoring progress. A full-time project manager can better handle these responsibilities; moreover, the fact that they are normally part of the executive job helps to establish his stature. A general manager, however, should not delegate certain responsibilities, such as monitoring milestone accomplishments, resolving project-related disputes between senior managers, or evaluating the project performance of functional department managers. The last responsibility mentioned strikes too close to the careers of the individuals concerned to be delegated to one of their peers.

For the duration of the project, the project manager should also hold some responsibilities normally borne by functional department heads. These include responsibility for reviewing progress against schedule; organizing for, formulating, and approving a project plan; monitoring project cost performance; and, in place of the department heads normally involved, trading off time and cost. Also, the senior executive must encourage the project manager to direct the day-to-day activities of all functional personnel who are involved fulltime in the project. Functional department heads, however, should retain responsibility for the quality of their subordinates' technical performance, as well as for matters affecting their careers.

Limiting the Project Team   Functional department heads may view the project manager as a potential competitor. By limiting the number of men on the project team, this problem is alleviated and the project manager's involvement in intrafunctional matters is reduced. Moreover, men transferred out of their own functional departments are apt to lose their inside sources of information and find it increasingly difficult to get things done rapidly and informally.

Maintaining the Balance of Power   Because the project manager is concerned with change, while the department head must efficiently manage routine procedures, the two are often in active conflict. Though they should be encouraged to resolve these disputes without constant appeals to higher authority, their common superior must occasionally act as mediator. Otherwise, resentments and frustrations will impair the project's progress and leave a long-lasting legacy of bitterness. Short-term conflicts can often be resolved in favor of the project manager and long-term conflicts in favor of the functional managers. This compromise helps to reduce friction, to get the job accomplished, and to prepare for the eventual phasing out of the project.

Guideline 3: Install Project Controls

Though they use the same raw data as routine reports, special project controls over time, cost, and quality are very different in their accuracy, timing, and use. They are normally superimposed upon the existing report structure for the duration of the project and then discontinued. The crucial relationship between project time control and cost control is shown graphically in Figure 5.

The project in question had to be completed in twenty months instead of the twenty and a half months scheduled by a preliminary network calculation. The project manager, who was under strict initial manpower limitations, calculated the cost of the two weeks' acceleration at various stages of the project. Confronted by the evidence of the costs it could save, top management approved the project manager's request for early acceleration. The project was completed two working days before its twenty-month deadline, at a cost only $6,000 over the original estimate. Without controls that clearly relate time to cost, companies too often crash the project in its final stages, at enormous and entirely unnecessary cost.

Time Control   Almost invariably, some form of network scheduling provides the best time control of a project. A means of graphically planning a complex undertaking so that it can be scheduled for analysis and control, network scheduling begins with the construction of a diagram that reflects the interdependencies and time requirements of the individual tasks that go to make up a project. It calls for work plans prepared in advance of the project in painstaking detail, scheduling each element of the plan, and using controls to ensure that commitments are met.

At the outset, each department manager involved in the project should draw up a list of all the tasks required of his department to accomplish the

Figure 5 Cost of Two Weeks' Acceleration at Various Project Stages

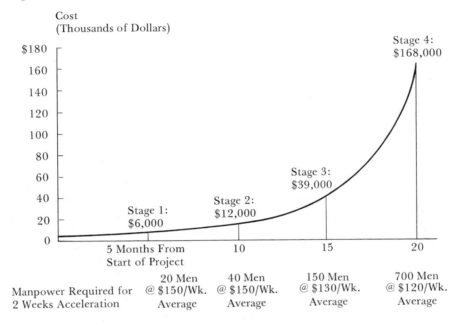

Cost
(Thousands of Dollars)

Stage 4:
$168,000

Stage 3:
$39,000

Stage 2:
$12,000

Stage 1:
$6,000

$180
160
140
120
100
80
60
40
20
0

5 Months From
Start of Project

10   15   20

Manpower Required for 2 Weeks Acceleration	20 Men @ $150/Wk. Average	40 Men @ $150/Wk. Average	150 Men @ $130/Wk. Average	700 Men @ $120/Wk. Average

project. Then the project manager should discuss each of these lists in detail with the respective departmental supervisors in order to establish the sequence in the project in relation to other departments. Next, each manager and supervisor should list the information he will need from other departments, indicating which data, if any, are habitually late. This listing gives the project manager not only a clue to the thoroughness of planning in the other departments but also a means of uncovering and forestalling most of the inconsistencies, missed activities, or inadequate planning that would otherwise occur.

Next, having planned its own role in the project, each department should be asked to commit itself to an estimate of the time required for each of its project activities, assuming the required information is supplied on time. After this, the complete network is constructed, adjusted where necessary with the agreement of the department heads concerned, and reviewed for logic.

Once the over-all schedule is established, weekly or fortnightly review meetings should be held to check progress against schedule. Control must be rigorous, especially at the start, when the tone of the entire project is invariably set. Thus, the very first few missed commitments call for immediate corrective action.

In critical path scheduling, one of the major network techniques, the diagram is similar in principle to that of Figure 6 for a very simple hypothetical project.

In the diagram, each arrow represents a defined task, with a clear beginning, end, and time requirement, that can be delegated to a single manager or supervisor. Each circle, or node (except the "start" node), represents the completion of a task. Task A, for example, might be "Define the technical objective

Figure 6   A Simple Critical Path Network

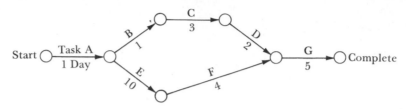

of the project." The numeral 1 indicates that the allotted time for its completion is one day.

The arrangement of the arrows is significant. As drawn here, B depends upon A; that is, it may not start until A is complete. Similarly, C may not start until B is complete. Also, while B and E may start at different times, neither may start until A is complete. Further along, G may not start until both D and F are complete. This diagram, then, is one of *sequence* and *dependency*.

The time required for the project corresponds to the longest path through the network from Start to Complete in terms of the time requirement associated with each task. In the diagram above, A-E-F-G is the critical path. To meet the over-all schedule, each of these tasks must begin as soon as its predecessor is completed and must end within its allotted time. To shorten the schedule, one or more of the tasks on the critical path must be accelerated.

There are other more complex varieties of network scheduling. Critical path method calculates both normal and crash schedules (and costs) for a project. Program evaluation and review technique (PERT) allows the use of multiple time estimates for each activity. PERT/Cost adds cost estimates, as the name implies. RAMPS (resource allocation and multiproject scheduling) adds the further refinement of a tool for allocating limited resources to competing activities in one or more projects. All, however, rest on the basic network concept outlined above.

Cost Control   Project cost control techniques, though not yet formalized to the same degree as time controls, are no harder to install if these steps are followed: (1) break the comprehensive cost summary into work packages, (2) devise commitment reports for "technical" decision makers, (3) act on early, approximate report data, and (4) concentrate talent on major problems and opportunities.

Managing a fast-moving $15 million project can be difficult for even the most experienced top manager. For a first-line supervisor the job of running a $500,000 project can be equally difficult. Neither manager can make sound decisions unless cost dimensions of the job are broken down into pieces of comprehensible size. Figure 7, which gives an example of such a breakdown, shows how major costs can be logically reduced to understandable and controllable work packages (usually worth $15,000 to $25,000 apiece on a major project), each of which can reasonably be assigned to a first-line manager.

Cost commitments on a project are made when engineering, manufacturing, marketing, or other functional personnel make technical decisions to take some

Figure 7 Breakdown of Project Cost Responsibility by Management Level

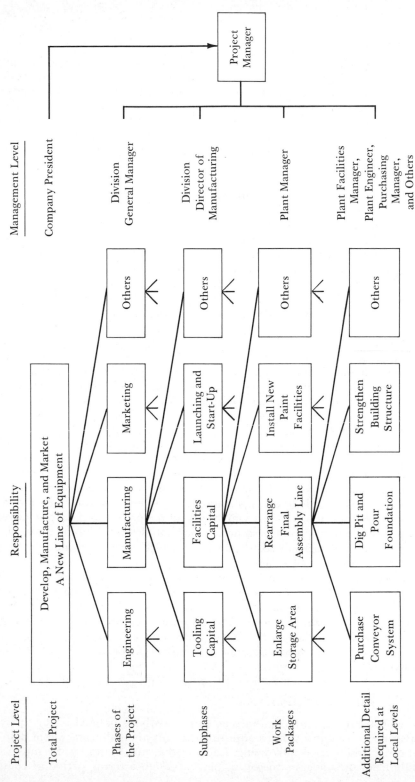

kind of action. In new-product development, for example, costs are committed or created in many ways—when marketing decides to add a product feature to its product; when engineering decides to insert a new part; when a process engineer adds an extra operation to a routing; when physical distribution managers choose to increase inventory, and so on. Conventional accounting reports, however, do not show the cost effects of these decisions until it is too late to reconsider. To enable the project manager to judge when costs are getting out of control and to decisively take the needed corrective action, he must be able to assess the approximate cost effect of each technical decision. In other words, he must have cost commitment reports at each decision stage.

Almost without exception, experience shows, 20 percent of the project effort accounts for at least 80 percent of the cost to which the company is committed. With the aid of a detailed cost breakdown and current information on cost commitment, the project manager is able, even after the project is underway, to take people off less important activities in order to concentrate more effort where it will do the most good in reducing costs. One company cut its product introduction costs by over $1 million in this way between the dates when the first print was released and the first machine assembled.

 Quality Control   Experience with a wide variety of projects—new-product introductions, mergers, plant constructions, introduction of organizational changes, to name a few—indicates that effective quality control of results is a crucial dimension of project success. Quality control comprises three elements: defining performance criteria, expressing the project objective in terms of quality standards, and monitoring progress toward these standards.

The need to define performance criteria, though universally acknowledged, is generally ignored in practice. Such quality criteria can, however, be defined rather easily, that is, simply in terms of senior executives' expectations with respect to average sales per salesman, market penetration of a product line, ratio of accountants to production workers, processing time for customer inquiries, and the like. If possible, these expectations should be expressed quantitatively. For example, the senior executive might expect the project to reduce emergency transportation costs from 15 percent to 5 percent of total shipping costs. Or he might expect a 30 percent reduction in inventory costs following installation of a mechanized control system.

Since achievement of these quality goals is a gradual process, the project manager should review progress toward them with the general manager monthly or quarterly, depending upon the length of the project. Sometimes there will be little noticeable change; in other cases major departures from expectation will be apparent. Here, as in the case of time and cost controls, the importance of prompt action to assure that the objectives will be met cannot be overemphasized.

Managing the Human Equation

The typical manager in a commercial business who is handed his first project management assignment finds adjustment to his anomalous new role painful, confusing, and even demoralizing. Lacking real line authority, he must constantly lead, persuade, or coerce his peers through a trying period of change.

Too often, in these difficult early weeks, he receives little support from senior management. Instead, he is criticized for not moving faster and producing more visible results. He may be blamed for flaws in a plan that, through the fault of top management, had to be rushed to completion mere days before the project began. Senior managers need to recognize that naming and needling the project manager is not enough. By giving him needed support at the start, by bringing a broad business perspective to bear on the over-all project plan, and by giving the project manager freedom in the details of the doing, the senior executive can greatly enhance his prospects of success.

Another critical point comes at the conclusion of the project, when its results are turned over to the regular organization and the project manager and his team must be returned to their permanent assignments. By virtue of the interfunctional experience gained under pressure, the project manager often matures in the course of a project, becoming a more valuable manager. But he may have trouble slowing down to a normal organizational pace. His routine job is likely to seem less attractive in terms of scope, authority, and opportunity to contribute to the business. Even the best project manager, moreover, can hardly accomplish his project objectives without antagonizing some members of management, quite possibly the very executives who will decide his future. In one instance, a project manager who had brought a major project from the brink of chaos to unqualified success was let go at the end of the project because, in accomplishing the feat, he had been unable to avoid antagonizing one division manager. Such difficulties and dissatisfactions often lead a retired project manager to look for a better job at this time, in or out of the company.

To retain and profit by the superior management material developed on the fertile training ground of the project, senior executives need to be aware of these human problems. By recognizing the growth of the project manager, helping him readjust to the slower pace of the normal organization, and finding ways to put his added experience and his matured judgment to good use, the company can reap a significant side benefit from every successfully managed project.

The Headquarters Staff Man in the Role of a Consultant

HARRY D. KOLB

Theories of organization underlying the American business corporation are not static. Fortunately, continuing process of change is at work. Thus, we find new concepts evolving while old, established ones are challenged and sometimes must give way.

Harry D. Kolb, "The Headquarters Staff Man in the Role of a Consultant," from *Organization Theory in Industrial Practice,* edited by M. Haire. Copyright © 1962 by John Wiley & Sons, Inc. Reprinted by permission.

Such is the nature of the subject of this paper. It deals with a changing idea as to what type of relationship should prevail between the staff man in a corporate headquarters and the various key managers he serves. It includes a change in role with respect to the corporate headquarters managers, but even more specifically a change in role with respect to the field organizations. It is in this arena that the internal (or "captive") consultant represents an emerging concept.

An example may illustrate the need. Consider a group of managers from a variety of field units meeting under the auspices of a headquarters staff department. If given an assignment to discuss what types of help they want from the headquarters staff group, the resulting discussion tends to be cautious and unenthusiastic. It is not difficult to imagine why. The headquarters staff man is normally seen as being in a controlling role rather than a consulting one. He sits in judgment. He has an inherent power of recommendation and communication to the headquarters line management. He has often failed to measure up to the expectations of those in the field who may have looked to him for help.

Even if the headquarters staff man should seek to operate in a new role, he still must deal with the experiences of the past. There have been a variety of roles taken by staff men. These include:

1. The auditor or inspector, who is concerned with enforcement, procedural compliance, faultfinding, and data collection for communication back to the headquarters.
2. The advisor or "helper" who offers unnecessary help and is less than fully responsible for the consequences of his advice.
3. The promoter or experimenter, whose interests are self-centered rather than designed for real problems in the field unit.
4. The technician who, though competent, is too rigid to be adaptable.

And now, the concept of "consultant" is being added as a new type of staff man from headquarters. In the past, field-unit managers have learned to recognize these various types of staff men and have built up their own procedures for dealing with them. The intent here is not to belittle the fundamental usefulness of all these activities; rather, it is to point out that when a new role is created, some light needs to be shed on what is intended and how this new type of staff man should be dealt with.

Field organizations have held certain stereotypes regarding the headquarters staff man. These are inherited and must be examined if a different type of relationship is intended. One of these stereotypes is that headquarters line managers rely on their staff men to provide information to them in order that the line managers can exercise their function of control. This type of staff behavior has to be changed under the consulting relationship that is intended. But, in order to accept this change, headquarters managers must first reexamine their own philosophy which says they need information from their staff people in order to exercise control. Fortunately, the newer consultant concept is an outgrowth of central managers relinquishing control to their field units. Thus, an implementation of true decentralization of control has both permitted and promoted the growth of the concept of the headquarters consultant. It is believed that the use of consultants will grow in proportion to the amount of progress a multi-plant corporation makes in this type of decentralization.

By decentralization is meant the transfer of latitude to the local field unit, particularly in terms of the methods, procedures, and emphasis it uses in how it tackles its job. This also includes the processes used to motivate and communicate and strengthen its own internal organization. It includes the way in which the organization develops its people, the philosophies that underlie its training efforts for its organization and, in general, its latitude in deciding how to utilize resources in order to accomplish its assigned mission.

When headquarters grants real latitude in these directions, it then faces a dilemma as to the amount and kind of staff help and direction which it should furnish, in order to avoid overcontrolling the activities of field managers. Some staff help is still intended, since the philosophy of decentralization does not mean abandonment. In addition, headquarters should provide staff help, first because of its responsibility for the business and, second, because of the inherent potential here for profit improvement.

Let us separate here certain types of staff service essential for financial procedures, for quality control, and for research and technical support. These are not usually areas in which there is as much doubt regarding appropriate staff behavior. More frequently, the question of the staff consulting role comes up in connection with headquarters departments in the fields of employee relations, public relations, organization planning, management development, and various advisory services. The following comments refer to staff work of these latter types of groups in which the focus is on human behavior.

The tradition of using a consulting role for such a staff man is not yet well developed. As a result, the staff man frequently falls into the pitfall of using inappropriate means in order to enhance his status and influence. This may constitute telling the local managers what they may or should not do. It involves utilizing the influence of headquarters management in order to constitute pressure on field units to get them to do what the staff man feels they should do.

The many types of inappropriate behavior are fairly clearly known. Although they may be regarded as inappropriate, even by those who indulge in them, what is not too clear is what alternative behavior is necessary first to be effective and, second, to be acceptable, both in the field and at headquarters.

The headquarters manager has his own concerns about what he should expect of the staff man. On the one hand, he feels the need for furnishing only such central services as can be really justified. On the other hand, he wants to rely on his staff to keep him informed wherever problem areas exist in the field, so that he can then be in a position of protecting the company's interests. This presupposes, therefore, that the staff group renders frequent and critical reports to the headquarters management. Yet doing so prevents growth of the type of consultant who is welcome in the field on the basis of being able to provide professional help, while at the same time maintaining a confidential relationship with his client. It is on this paradox of help to the headquarters manager and a confidential client relationship in the field that the problem is centered.

Herbert Shepard has commented in this direction as follows:

"Staff groups often try to enhance their influence by identifying themselves with groups that have formal authority in the organization. Thus some staff groups may be regarded as spies serving higher levels, as agents of headquarters authority, or as mechanisms for the prevention of decentralization.

"Sometimes this reputation is gained through indiscreet use of privileged communication, sometimes by the explicit operating principles of the staff man, as when he identifies himself as being responsible to a higher level.

"The temptation may be strong to use privileged communication or observations made in the field to build the staff's influence and reputation in the home office. Related to this is the tendency of the staff man, if he is unable to influence lower levels in the direction he thinks best, to try to get someone at higher level to lend his authority. This procedure may be momentarily effective, but turns the staff man into a threat rather than a resource for the future."

Professor Shepard goes on to point out that any indiscretion on the part of the consultant can very quickly render him of little further use. Therefore he concludes that: "If the staff man thinks certain kinds of information should be shared between groups or levels, his job is to help the parties communicate, rather than to communicate for them."

Headquarters management has to make up its mind whether or not it can rely on its field managers as the source of upward communication regarding problems, needs, and developments. The use of the staff system as a substitute for reliance upon direct upward communication has in the past subverted this more logical and appropriate direct upward channel.

Therefore, one of the essential conditions for an effective consultant role is this confidential relationship between the headquarters staff man and the field unit. The information which he gains regarding the operation of the field unit is not to be communicated by him within the headquarters. When he is in the field unit, he is serving the local manager in the same manner that an outside consultant would; he has a status of independence and, yet, he is working for the local manager.

Until the local unit accepts the fact that the consultant is not going to relay punitive information back to the headquarters, the consultant will not really gain access to reliable sources of information. If, however, this type of trust can be developed, then the staff man can be immensely more valuable to the local manager because he will be in a position to facilitate communication within the organization he is serving. His independence and freedom from immersion in the local organization's channels makes him a powerful mechanism for aiding the organization to surmount blockages that have been built up in its communication network.

If a headquarters management can accept the idea that its specialized consulting staffs do not make reports in the home office, how can it determine that such centralized services are justified or properly being used? The consultant has to rely upon the field management to communicate upward its own evaluation of his worth. This is, of course, risky and perhaps uncomfortable for the staff man. He is frequently by nature one who feels the lack of power in his position and, therefore, tends to want to draw attention to the usefulness of his work in order to enhance his own reputation. To the extent to which he develops a true consultant role, however, he will find less appropriate opportunity for doing this. Yet this can benefit the organization. If line management has to rely on appraisal of the effectiveness of staff work as judged by the clients (rather than as reported by the consultant), there can well be a lifting of standards of performance. Certain kinds of staff support which have been covered up, despite inadequacies in their quality, might by this system be revealed for what they are.

Thus far, we have dealt with the three-party relationship between the staff man, the local manager, and the headquarters manager. Considerably more is to be learned regarding the two-party relationship of the consultant with the local manager. Here is a man free from the bonds of organization channels and, therefore, free to approach the local manager directly. Does this mean that he concentrates his efforts at this spot in the organization, rather than working with lower echelons and rather than working with some counterpart local staff? The answer is not simple or clear-cut since all three types of concentration may be appropriate at different times.

There is no doubt that many an outside consultant has come to the conclusion that his effectiveness depends upon being able to communicate directly with the top man. However, this may be merely a question of strategy in order to get some initial commitment to a study or an undertaking. If the internal consultant is going to be useful, he needs to be able to bridge the gap between local staff and the local manager and to be a communication catalyst and link. Also, if the kinds of activities he is to engage in are those which rightly involve the total organization, he would be ill-advised to confine his contracts to just the top manager. A potential competitiveness exists between the consultant and any counterpart local staff. The effective consultant can recognize this, not be channel-bound because of it, and yet be supportive rather than destructive in order to enhance the position of the local staff man.

Another difficulty can arise when the consultant finds a local situation which is alarming, and yet sees his recommendations for improvement being ignored. What can he do? We have already seen that it would be inappropriate for him to communicate this to headquarters, and yet he is hardly so disinterested as to be able to ignore the situation. Few men are in the position that a famous outside consultant was in once when he rendered a report to a prominent American corporation regarding their labor-relations problems. With his report went his invoice for a substantial fee. Subsequently the president of the corporation called him in and said: "Here's the check for your fee, but we don't plan to do a damn thing about any of the recommendations in your report." Whereupon the consultant said, "If that's the way you feel, we don't need your check." Whereupon he tore up the check in front of the man and left.

This independence is commendable—and rare. Subsequent events proved the consultant right, and the firm recalled him and started to rely on his advice. Perhaps this does suggest that the internal consultant can only rely upon patience, while at the same time trying to maintain his independence and the integrity of his ideas. One of the continual worries is that the internal consultant will tend to sacrifice his own values as a result of pressure to conform, or to fit the requirements of a local situation. If this were to happen, in time the consultant's values would become synonymous with those of his client— frequently with the result that they would have become less valid and less useful to the company.

Another area of considerable interest is the extent to which the consultant should assume the role of an expert. If we are talking about a technician who is brought in to solve a problem of design, methods, or materials, it is normal to expect this staff man to come up with an expert's answer. But the problem changes with problems or changes affecting relationships, motivation, or organization behavior.

What happens if the consultant assumes the role of an expert in these situations? He may prescribe well, and yet accomplish little. The reason for this is clear. The matters we are dealing with here require more than clarity and accuracy of analysis in order for them to be accomplished. Any change affecting these organizational relationships, systems, climate, and standards of behavior will come about only when certain conditions prevail. Not just one person but all the participants themselves need to accept both the need for change and the desirability of a certain type of remedial action. The effectiveness of the change intended is dependent upon involvement of the total group affected. Thus, the consultant's job is more to accomplish this recognition and involvement than to prescribe the solution to the problem. One description of how the consultant should perform has been offered by Chris Argyris in a privately published report on the consultant role. Professor Argyris offers the following thoughts:

"The aim of the consultant is to help the participants become more aware of the blocks and barriers that prevent them from achieving their objectives. He also attempts to help the participants develop new diagnostic skills and take concrete actions to resolve their problems.

"The consultant strives hard to facilitate effective problem-solving without becoming the center of attention or the control mechanism for change. He attempts to help people by encouraging them to verbalize and clarify their views, to express their feelings, to become more open about their attitudes and beliefs.

"The consultant resists making the diagnosis, making alternate recommendations or taking the lead to plan further action. His objective is not to solve a particular problem for the managers. He realizes that the more problems he solves, the more dependent the organization can become upon him. . . . The more the consultant analyzes, recommends and suggests, the more he behaves in ways which are not consonant with self-diagnosis, self-growth, self-responsibility for action."

It is a rather disturbing thought to extend this idea to its logical conclusion. It states that the field unit which invites the consultant of this type in in order to get his help, finds that he is spending his efforts on getting them to solve their own problem rather than offering them a professional opinion or expert solution. Immediately, this creates some confusion. The consultant is brought in because of his superior knowledge, and yet submerges his own opinion in order to concentrate on a developmental job within the group. Obviously, this suggests the real difference here is that the consultant is looked upon as a trainer (or should be) rather than as a man who has a ready prescription.

It is difficult to know how consistently one could follow Argyris' definition. Field managers are in need of help. They are busy. They seek expert advice. They might well become annoyed or disinterested if instead of advice they get suggestions for involvement of their people in self-analysis work. No doubt frequently some compromise will have to occur. The consultant may find that, to stimulate action, he must take some initiative and provide a direction. At the same time, so long as he is concerned with human-behavior problems, he cannot escape the fact that solution to these problems requires a constructive process rather than a prescription. To this extent, as Argyris points out, "A consultant who is interested in helping the organization must give attention to the processes by which plans are developed, introduced, and made a part of the organization." This differs from many consulting relationships, where the ends are considered more important than the means.

Argyris believes that the effective consultant will tend to invite a greater degree of participation on the part of the members of the organization he is working with. He states:

"At the core of his relationships are such factors as openness, authenticity, the capacity to create minimal defensiveness, listening with minimum distortion, etc. Thus we find that even a consultant who provides help on such "hardware" tasks as incentive systems, cost reduction, and production problems may have to concern himself with authenticity and other interpersonal and group issues. Obviously the consultant whose objective is to provide help in the human factors area has no choice but to focus on creating authentic client-consultant relationships. In order to succeed in their work such consultants must be interested in the processes or means, as well as the ends."

What can be set forth as the objective of the consultant on problems involving human relationships? He must be a capable expert in his field, yet his expertness in this sense should also be related to his being able to develop the organization in its capacity to solve its own problems. Thus, the consultant could be said to have achieved his ultimate objective only when the following conditions prevail:

1. The organization has found an appropriate way to handle the problems which were of initial concern.
2. The organization has developed good procedures for identifying future problems.
3. The organization has recognized the benefits from periodic evaluation of its own effectiveness.
4. The organization has learned procedures which will help it maintain a healthy state of adaptability.

The development of internal consultants who meet this description represents a worthwhile objective for management. There is a potential here for effective help and service from a headquarters organization, in contrast with many of the presently acknowledged shortcomings of today's systems for central staff support. More specifically, there is potential for real development of field organizations toward greater self-sufficiency. Therefore, this represents a new and useful form of management development.

Certain specific steps by top management will be essential to its growth. There needs to be, for example, a clear understanding of the latitude available to field managers to use or not to use consultants on their own initiative. Likewise, local managers need to have full latitude with regard to the routes they pick for study, diagnosis, and involvement of their organization in activities of a developmental nature. Likewise, local units clearly need to have the latitude to collect data and yet not be forced to use it in ways amounting to self-incrimination. In place of this, there should be a clear understanding that the organization is judged on the basis of performance criteria rather than symptomatic data collected in its own work in problem diagnosis.

Management should anticipate paying a high premium for real skill and competence in the consultant function—and yet not settle for less in staffing this type of service. In view of apparent shortage of competent men at the present time, attention should be given to the selection and training of candidates with the range of skills needed.

An additional point to bear in mind deals with the importance of keeping the consultant group intact as a centralized staff. One might ask why, in view of a policy of decentralization, a consultant staff should not also be scattered and spotted in the various field units where it might be of help. One reason, of course, is the fact that there is an intermittent need for such help in the field, and therefore economy dictates some centralization. In addition, the highly skilled type of person that is needed further suggests that he be placed so that he can be utilized fully in a variety of locations.

But there are additional important reasons for not having the consultant located full-time and on a continuing basis in the field unit he is serving. To do so is running the risk that he will be absorbed into the unit, bound by organization channels and unable to exercise the independence of comment and judgment essential to a high-quality job. In fact, even when located in the headquarters, it takes special attention to maintain an attitude of true independence. There are the countervening influences of concern about status, reward, promotion into other lines of work, and pressure toward conformity. Is it really possible to accomplish true independence with internal consultants in a modern industrial organization? It is still too early to know. Meanwhile, hope is bright because the bits of experience to date have been encouraging—and the potential benefits are great.

Functional Authority

HAROLD KOONTZ, CYRIL O'DONNELL

Functional authority is the right which an individual or department may have delegated to it over specified processes, practices, policies, or other matters relating to activities undertaken by personnel in departments other than its own. If the principle of unity of command were followed without exception, authority over these activities would be exercised by their line managers, but numerous

reasons—including lack of special knowledge, lack of ability to supervise processes, and danger of diverse interpretations of policies—explain why they occasionally are not allowed to exercise this authority. In such cases, the line manager
is deprived of this limited authority. It is delegated by their common superior
to a staff specialist or a manager in another department.

Functional authority is not restricted to managers of a particular type of
department. It may be exercised by line, service,[1] or staff department heads,
more often the latter two, because they are usually composed of specialists whose
knowledge becomes the basis for functional controls.

Development of Functional Authority

The successive steps by which a line manager is deprived of his authority over
particular activities make an interesting study. The pure staff specialist offers
advice or recommendations to his line superior, who may issue them as instructions to be filtered down the organization hierarchy. The first modification of
this relationship may occur when the superior delegates authority to the staff
man to transmit information, proposals, and advice directly to the former's
subordinates. For example, a personnel assistant might be permitted to transmit
directly to the operating department heads information and advice on the
handling of labor grievances. Obviously, this saves the president time and
trouble and expedites the spread of the information.

A second modification might be to allow the staff specialist to consult with
operating managers and show them how the information should be used or put
into effect. For instance, the personnel assistant might be asked to advise line
personnel on procedures to eliminate mishandling of grievances. It will clearly
be advantageous to all concerned if the staff man can instruct the persons
responsible for this activity. Here, there is no question of his ordering them;
the agreement of the line executive concerned is needed; should this not be
forthcoming, he can appeal to his superior to issue the requisite instructions.
Even with the variations outlined above, the specialist is still operating wholly
in a staff capacity.

The transition to functional authority is accomplished when the assistant
is delegated specific authority to *prescribe* processes, methods, or even policy to
be followed in all subdivisions of either staff or operating departments. The
personnel assistant, for example, who once could only advise, now may be given
limited authority to supervise a special function or process of the line organization. He no longer merely advises his superior or the line organization
concerning handling grievances. Now, he may issue instructions *prescribing*
procedures. Or, to use another example, a corporation controller may be given
authority to prescribe the kind of accounting records to be kept by the sales
and manufacturing departments.

By limiting this authority to function, the factory manager—handling his
labor grievances in accordance with procedures prescribed by the personnel
manager—and the sales manager—keeping his records according to instructions
of the controller—are still primarily subject to the orders, supervision, and
control of their line superiors. The extent of their control by the staff officer
is governed by the latter's functional authority.

Functional Authority Delegation

Functional authority can perhaps be better understood if it is regarded as a small slice of the authority of the line superior. A corporation president, for example, has complete authority to manage the corporation, subject only to limitations placed upon him by such superior authority as the board of directors, the corporate charter and bylaws, and government regulations. In the pure staff situation, his advisers on personnel, accounting, purchasing, or public relations have no part of this authority, their duty being merely to offer counsel. But when the president delegates some of his authority to these advisers to issue instructions directly to the line organization as shown in Figure 1, that part is called "functional authority."

Figure 1   Functional Authority Delegation

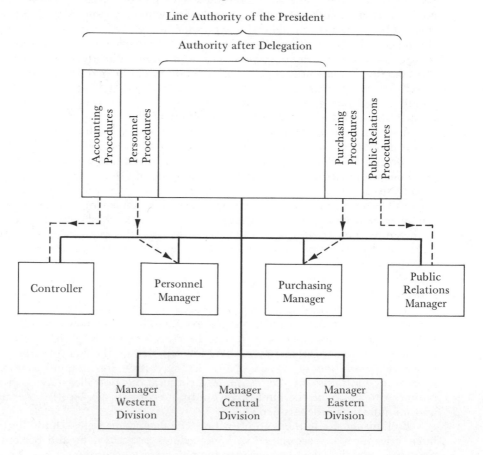

Line Authority of the President

Authority after Delegation

Accounting Procedures

Personnel Procedures

Purchasing Procedures

Public Relations Procedures

Controller

Personnel Manager

Purchasing Manager

Public Relations Manager

Manager Western Division

Manager Central Division

Manager Eastern Division

——————— Normal Line Relationships

- - - - - - - Delegation of Functional Authority from Line Authority of the President

As illustrated, the four staff executives have functional authority over the line organization with respect to procedures in the fields of accounting, personnel, purchasing, and public relations. What has happened is that the president, feeling it unnecessary that such specialized matters be cleared through him, has delegated his line authority to staff assistants to issue their own instructions to the operating departments. Likewise, of course, subordinate managers can use the same device, as when a factory superintendent sets up cost, production-control, and quality-control supervisors with functional authority to prescribe procedures for the foremen.

Functional Authority as Exercised by Operating Managers

Operating department heads sometimes have good reason to control some method or process of another line department. For example, the vice-president in charge of sales may be given functional authority over the manufacturing executives in scheduling customer orders, packaging, or making service parts available.

Where a company is organized along product lines, the exercise of functional authority over the product division managers by other executives is rather commonplace. All functions of sales, production, finance, or other so-called line functions (that is, "line" to the enterprise) may be placed under a division or product manager. In this case, certain top line officials in charge of a major function of the business might not have a direct line of authority over the product managers. But, to make sure that sales or financial policy is properly followed in the divisions, these officers may be given functional authority, as illustrated in Figure 2.

Area of Functional Authority

Functional authority should be carefully restricted. Such authority of the purchasing manager, for example, is generally limited to the procedures to be used in divisional or departmental purchasing. When he *conducts* certain purchasing activities of an over-all company nature, he is acting as head of a service department. The functional authority of the personnel manager over the general line organization is likewise ordinarily limited to the prescription of procedures for handling grievances, for sharing in the administration of wage and salary programs, and for handling vacation procedures and matters of a similar nature.

Functional authority is usually limited to the area of "how" and sometimes "when" and seldom applies to "where," "what," or "who." The reason for this limitation is not found in any logical demarcation between normal line authority and functional authority, since the latter *can* be made to apply to any aspect of operations. It is rather that the functionalization of management, if carried to extremes, would destroy the manager's job. Whenever a manager loses his authority to plan, organize, staff, direct, and control the activities within his department, he can no longer manage.

To some extent, this occurs when a staff or line executive has functional authority over some part of another manager's job. Even when the personnel manager requires the factory manager to follow seniority in layoffs or to grant employees definite pay and vacation allowances, he is interfering with some of

Figure 2 Functional Authority of Line Departments

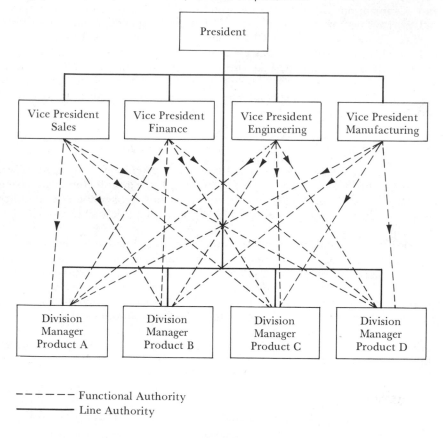

------ Functional Authority
————— Line Authority

the factory manager's prerogatives. When the accounting department requires district sales managers to file their expense accounts in a certain form, it is, to some extent, interfering with the authority of the general sales manager over his subordinates.

Therefore, well-managed concerns recognize that functional authority should be used sparingly and only where a real necessity exists. This necessity comes from both outside and inside influences. On the outside are such requirements as those of government agencies and labor union contracts that must be interpreted and administered by specialists. On the inside some matters are of such importance or complexity that the best possible grade of uniform action is required, necessitating in turn that the expert be given sufficient authority to carry out desired procedures. A rather thin line sometimes divides what should be controlled by the expert and what should be under the jurisdiction of the operating manager. Where there is doubt, good practice would seem to favor limiting the area of functional authority so that the operating manager's position is not weakened.

Unity of Command and the Flow of Functional Authority

Limiting the area of functional authority is, then, important in preserving the integrity of the managerial position. If a company had, as some do, executives with functional authority over procedures in the fields of personnel, purchasing, accounting, traffic, budgets, engineering, public relations, law, sales policy, and real estate, the complications of authority relationships could be great indeed. A factory manager or a sales manager might have, in addition to his immediate line superior, five, ten, or even fifteen functional bosses. Although much of the multiplication of command is unavoidable because of the demands for specialist prescription in complex areas, it is obvious that it can precipitate serious, and frequently intolerable, confusion and dispersal of responsibility.

Some semblance of unity of command can be maintained by requiring that the line of functional authority shall not extend beyond the first organization level below that of the manager's own superior. Thus, in Figure 3 the functional authority of the personnel or public relations director should not extend beyond the level of the vice-presidents in charge of finance, sales, and manufacturing. In other words, functional authority should be concentrated at the nearest possible point in the organization structure, to preserve, as much as possible, the unity of command of the line executives.

This principle is often widely violated. Top managers with functional authority sometimes issue instructions directly to personnel throughout the organization. Where the policy or procedure determination is so important that

Figure 3 Line and Functional Authority

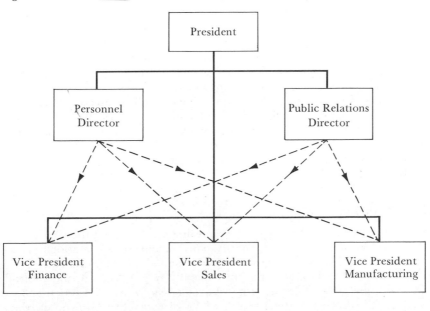

–––––– Functional Authority
——— Line Authority

there must be no deviation, both the prestige of the top manager and the necessity for accurate communication may make it necessary and wise to issue such instructions. Issuing them to the responsible line subordinate, as well as to the functional counterpart at the lower level, may not seem harmfully to increase the multiplicity of command. As will be noted later, there are forces of centralization of authority that may make this kind of exercise of functional authority unavoidable.

Lack of Clarification in Practice

It is surprising how many companies, even those otherwise well managed, fail to define the exact nature of the functional authority that a manager may have. Analysis by the authors of authority delegations in a large number of companies shows that adequate clarification in this area is rare. Most companies seem satisfied to say, for example, that the division managers are "administratively" responsible to the president, but "functionally responsible in accounting and similar matters" under the jurisdiction of the controller. This is an open invitation to confusion, compounded of ambiguity, lack of careful meaning and understanding, and the unsurprising tendency of specialists to see everything in a company through their own eyes. As a company controller once told one of the authors, "I realize that my authority in accounting matters throughout the company is limited; all I insist on approving is anything with a dollar sign attached."

The lack of clarification in the area of functional authority has been found in a number of studies. Studies of personnel managers, for example, have shown varying perceptions of the authority of this officer as between himself and his staff, his superior, and the various areas of the company subject to his influence.[2] Likewise, a recent study of company controllers with functional authority showed a high degree of confusion to exist between controller and noncontroller groups, and even within the controllers' departments, as to what the authority of the controller really was.[3] Other studies have shown the extensiveness of this lack of clarity and the conflict it engenders.[4]

Particularly in the light of the wide use and apparent inevitability of functional authority in all kinds of enterprises, lack of clarification is difficult to understand. It is true that many people can accommodate themselves to lack of clarity or work themselves through it by trial and error or persuasion. But if it is important to place functional authority in a position, it would appear to be a waste of time and resources not to make it clear.

Clarifying Functional Authority

Almost certainly the best means of avoiding some of the problems, confusions, and frictions of functional authority is to make sure it is clarified. Thus, it is not enough to say that a division or plant manager is "administratively responsible" to his line superior and "functionally responsible" to the controller. If the controller, like a few the authors have known, regards his functional authority over accounting matters to extend to all expenditures of funds, there is a built-in situation for undue conflict through multiplication of command. Or if a personnel manager interprets his delegation to cover anything concerned with people, the conflict potential is obvious. Likewise, if an operating manager regards the controller as being "staff" with no authority even to prescribe the form and nature of the company's accounting system, the controller cannot discharge his responsibility.

In order to obtain clarity, it is imperative that the exact functional authority delegated to a manager or to a department be clearly spelled out. This is necessary not only from the standpoint of the bearer's use and understanding of this specialized type of authority, but also for those operating managers who are on the receiving end. An example of one company's attempt to define the authority of the vice-president–controller is the following specific delegations to that officer, which delegations were thoroughly discussed with him and his subordinates and with key operating managers and their subordinates over whom he was expected to exercise such authority.

1. Authority to prescribe the corporate chart of accounts and the division's charts of accounts so far as they are supportive to and necessary for the corporation chart of accounts; authority to direct the development and maintenance of necessary procedures to insure the integrity of the company's accounts and statements; authority to see that the company's accounting policies and procedures are followed in the divisions.
2. Authority to prescribe policies and procedures in the handling of cash, including banking arrangements, methods of handling receipts and disbursements, and the requirements for bonding throughout the company.
3. Authority to prescribe policies, standards, and procedures with respect to inventory control matters which affect the integrity of accounting records.
4. Authority to prescribe the necessary form, procedures, and timing for the preparation and submission of profit plans.
5. Authority to require from the various divisions and departments of the company financial, accounting, and statistical reports and forecasts in a form and at times believed to be necessary for proper company planning and control.
6. Authority to approve the selection of the chief financial officer of any division or affiliate.
7. Authority to prescribe and undertake a program of internal auditing of financial, cash, credit, and accounting transactions, and an audit of corporate and divisional financial and accounting policies and procedures.

Line and Staff in Practice

The essential character of line and staff relationships becomes readily apparent in the study of well-managed enterprises. Although the semantics of management occasionally mislead the student (and, more often, those managing and being managed), a clear statement of authority relationships will identify the kind of authority—whether it be line, staff, or functional authority.

In one instance, one of the nation's leading management consulting firms spelled out the treasurer's authority in a fast-growing enterprise with territorial divisions for major line operations and a staff of top executives to control over-all policy as follows:

"The Treasurer has line authority over and is responsible for directing activities of such personnel as he requires to establish system policies and procedures for the functions under his jurisdiction and to administer system treasury and accounting functions which are reserved for his department. He has no direct line authority over the day-to-day activities of accounting personnel in the divisions and regions except as specifically delegated by the president. He is responsible for developing and interpreting budgeting, accounting, and financial policies to the divisions and regions for assisting these organizations in carrying out such policies, and for satisfying himself that such policies are correctly and ably administered in the field.

"At the request of division managements, or voluntarily when system welfare is materially concerned, the Treasurer shall make recommendations concerning the employment, promotion, dismissal, or change in compensation of supervisory personnel engaged in activities within his functional responsibility. Final action on such matters shall be taken by division managements when mutual agreement has been reached with department heads concerned."

This general description of authority is supplemented by a list of duties making clear that the treasurer's major assignments are establishing budgetary policy and procedures, instituting accounting policies and procedures for maintaining division records, and such other procedures as might be necessary for the discharge of his duties. The description and list make clear the line, staff, and functional authority relationships of the treasurer: He has line authority over his own department, staff relationship to top and divisional managers, and functional authority to require the major operating departments, the divisions, to follow good budgeting and accounting procedures.

Unavoidability of Functional Authority

In virtually every large enterprise, and in many smaller enterprises, some delegation of functional authority to staff departments seems unavoidable. Even though a manager may abhor and try to avoid this hybrid combination of line and staff authority, most major staff departments have some functional authority. This practice is largely due to the necessity for expert interpretation of policy and for formulation of procedures by specialists, which, in turn, results from the need for varying degrees of uniformity in accounting, labor, public relations, and other activities.

Of course, the line executive could maintain the separation of line and staff authority relationships in his organization structure if he were to insist on issuing all the instructions relating to matters required by specialized staff assistance. As a matter of fact, some corporation and division executives have done so. However, in most enterprises, this either taxes unduly the line manager's span of management, or, if he automatically accepts his staff's recommendations, it makes the apparent avoidance of functional authority a meaningless pretense. It is always good practice for the person actually making decisions to be plainly identified.

Notes and References

1. Some so-called staff departments are service departments. Since the latter reflect a special grouping of activities and since the discussion here is concerned with line and staff authority relationships, the analysis of service departments as a special organizational form is not discussed here.
2. See, for example, W. French and D. Henning, "The Authority-Influence Role of the Functional Specialist in Management," *Journal of the Academy of Management,* vol. 9, no. 3, pp. 187–203 (September, 1966); D. E. McFarland, *Cooperation and Conflict in Personnel Administration* (New York: American Foundation for Management Research, 1963); even J. A. Belasco and J. A. Arlutto, while professing to find that line-staff relationships in this area are less severe than usually believed, did find that "there may be a high conflict over 'how' the agreed upon role is performed." See "Line and Staff Conflicts: Some Empirical Insights," *Academy of Management Journal,* vol. 12, no. 1, pp. 469–477 (December, 1969).
3. See R. McIntire, "Functional Authority in the Controller's Position" (Ph.D. diss., University of California, Los Angeles, 1971).
4. See, for example, R. Golembiewski, *Organizing Men and Power* (Chicago: Rand McNally & Company, 1967).

A Theory of Authority

CHESTER I. BARNARD

The Source of Authority

If it is true that all complex organizations consist of aggregations of unit organizations and have grown only from unit organizations, we may reasonably postulate that, whatever the nature of authority, it is inherent in the simple organization unit; and that a correct theory of authority must be consistent with what is essentially true of these unit organizations. We shall, therefore, regard the observations which we can make of the actual conditions as at first a source for discovering what is essential in elementary and simple organizations.

Now a most significant fact of general observation relative to authority is the extent to which it is ineffective in specific instances. It is so ineffective that the violation of authority is accepted as a matter of course and its implications are not considered. It is true that we are sometimes appalled at the extent of major criminal activities; but we pass over very lightly the universal violations, particularly of sumptuary laws, which are as "valid" as any others. Even clauses of constitutions and statutes carrying them "into effect," such as the Eighteenth Amendment, are violated in wholesale degrees.

Violation of law is not, however, peculiar to our own country. I observed recently in a totalitarian state under a dictator, where personal liberty is supposed to be at a minimum and arbitrary authority at a maximum, many violations of positive law or edict, some of them open and on a wide scale; and I was reliably informed of others.

Nor is this condition peculiar to the authority of the state. It is likewise true of the authority of churches. The Ten Commandments and the prescriptions and prohibitions of religious authority are repeatedly violated by those who profess to acknowledge their formal authority.

These observations do not mean that all citizens are lawless and defy authority; nor that all Christians are godless or their conduct unaffected by the tenets of their faith. It is obvious that to a large extent citizens are governed; and that the conduct of Christians is substantially qualified by the prescriptions of their churches. What is implied is merely that which specific laws will be obeyed or disobeyed by the individual citizen are decided by him under the specific conditions pertinent. This is what we mean when we refer to individual responsibility. It implies that which prescriptions of the church will be disobeyed by the individual are determined by him at a given time and place. This is what we mean by moral responsibility. . . . .

We may leave the secondary stages of this analysis for later consideration. What we derive from it is an approximate definition of authority for our purpose: Authority is the character of a communication (order) in a formal organization by virtue of which it is accepted by a contributor to or "member" of the organization as governing the action he contributes; that is, as governing or determining what he does or is not to do so far as the organization is concerned. According to this definition, authority involves two aspects: first, the subjective, the personal, the *accepting* of a communication as authoritative, the aspects which I shall present in this section; and, second, the objective aspect—the character in the communication by virtue of which it is accepted—which I present in the second section, "The System of Coordination."

If a directive communication is accepted by one to whom it is addressed, its authority for him is confirmed or established. It is admitted as the basis of action. Disobedience of such a communication is a denial of its authority for him. Therefore, under this definition the decision as to whether an order has authority or not lies with the persons to whom it is addressed, and does not reside in "persons of authority" or those who issue these orders. . . .

Our definition of authority no doubt will appear to many, whose eyes are fixed only on enduring organizations, to be a platform of chaos. And so it is—exactly so in the preponderance of attempted organizations. They fail because they can maintain no authority, that is, they cannot secure sufficient contributions of personal efforts to be effective or cannot induce them on terms that are efficient. In the last analysis the authority fails because the individuals in sufficient numbers regard the burden involved in accepting necessary orders as changing the balance of advantage against their interest, and they withdraw or withhold the indispensable contributions.

We must not rest our definition, however, on general opinion. The necessity of the assent of the individual to establish authority *for him* is inescapable. A person can and will accept a communication as authoritative only when four conditions simultaneously obtain: (*a*) he can and does understand the communication; (*b*) *at the time of his decision* he believes that it is not inconsistent with the purpose of the organization; (*c*) *at the time of his decision,* he believes it to be compatible with his personal interest as a whole; and (*d*) he is able mentally and physically to comply with it.

(*a*) A communication that cannot be understood *can* have no authority. An order issued, for example, in a language not intelligible to the recipient is no order at all—no one would so regard it. Now, many orders are exceedingly difficult to understand. They are often necessarily stated in general terms, and the persons who issued them could not themselves apply them under many conditions. Until interpreted they have no meaning. The recipient either must disregard them or merely do anything in the hope that that is compliance.

Hence, a considerable part of administrative work consists in the interpretation and reinterpretation of orders in their application to concrete circumstances that were not or could not be taken into account initially.

(*b*) A communication believed by the recipient to be incompatible with the purpose of the organization, as he understands it, could not be accepted. Action would be frustrated by cross purposes. The most common practical example is that involved in conflicts of orders. They are not rare. An intelligent person will deny the authority of that one which contradicts the purpose of the effort as *he* understands it. In extreme cases many individuals would be virtually paralyzed by conflicting orders. They would be literally unable to comply—for example, an employee of a water system ordered to blow up an essential pump, or soldiers ordered to shoot their own comrades. I suppose all experienced executives know that when it is necessary to issue orders that will appear to the recipients to be contrary to the main purpose, especially as exemplified in prior habitual practice, it is usually necessary and always advisable, if practicable, to explain or demonstrate why the appearance of conflict is an illusion. Otherwise the orders are likely not to be executed, or to be executed inadequately.

(*c*) If a communication is believed to involve a burden that destroys the net advantage of connection with the organization, there no longer would remain a net inducement to the individual to contribute to it. The existence of a net inducement is the only reason for accepting *any* order as having authority. Hence, if such an order is received it must be disobeyed (evaded in the more usual cases) as utterly inconsistent with personal motives that are the basis of accepting any orders at all. Cases of voluntary resignation from all sorts of organizations are common for this sole reason. Malingering and intentional lack of dependability are the more usual methods.

(*d*) If a person is unable to comply with an order, obviously it must be disobeyed, or, better, disregarded. To order a man who cannot swim to swim a river is a sufficient case. Such extreme cases are not frequent; but they occur. The more usual case is to order a man to do things only a little beyond his capacity; but a little impossible is still impossible.

Naturally the reader will ask: How is it possible to secure such important and enduring cooperation as we observe if in principle and in fact the determination of authority lies with the subordinate individual? It is possible because the decisions of individuals occur under the following conditions: (*a*) orders that are deliberately issued in enduring organizations usually comply with the four conditions mentioned above; (*b*) there exists a "zone of indifference" in each individual within which orders are acceptable without conscious questioning of their authority; (*c*) the interests of the persons who contribute to an organization as a group result in the exercise of an influence on the subject, or on the attitude of the individual, that maintains a certain stability of this zone of indifference.

(*a*) There is no principle of executive conduct better established in good organizations than that orders will not be issued that cannot or will not be obeyed. Executives and most persons of experience who have thought about it know that to do so destroys authority, discipline, and morale. For reasons to be stated shortly, this principle cannot ordinarily be formally admitted, or at least cannot be professed. When it appears necessary to issue orders which are initially or apparently unacceptable, either careful preliminary education, or persuasive efforts, or the prior offering of effective inducements will be made, so that the issue will not be raised, the denial of authority will not occur, and orders will be obeyed. It is generally recognized that those who least understand this fact—newly appointed minor or "first line" executives—are often guilty of "disorganizing" their groups for this reason, as do experienced executives who lose self-control or become unbalanced by a delusion of power or for some other reason. Inexperienced persons take literally the current notions of authority and are then said "not to know how to use authority" or "to abuse authority." Their superiors often profess the same beliefs about authority in the abstract, but their successful practice is easily observed to be inconsistent with their professions.

(*b*) The phrase "zone of indifference" may be explained as follows: If all the orders for actions reasonably practicable be arranged in the order of their acceptability to the person affected, it may be conceived that there are a number which are clearly unacceptable, that is, which certainly will not be obeyed; there is another group somewhat more or less on the neutral line, that is, either barely acceptable or barely unacceptable; and a third group unquestionably acceptable. This last group lies within the "zone of indifference." The person affected will accept orders lying within this zone and is relatively indifferent as to what the order is so far as the question of authority is concerned. Such an order lies within the range that in a general way was anticipated at time of undertaking the connection with the organization. For example, if a soldier enlists, whether voluntarily or not, in an army in which the men are ordinarily moved about within a certain broad region, it is a matter of indifference whether the order be to go to A or B, C or D, and so on; and goings to A, B, C, D, etc., are in the zone of indifference.

The zone of indifference will be wider or narrower depending upon the degree to which the inducements exceed the burdens and sacrifices which determine the individual's adhesion to the organization. It follows that the range of orders that will be accepted will be very limited among those who are barely induced to contribute to the system.

(*c*) Since the efficiency of organization is affected by the degree to which individuals assent to orders, denying the authority of an organization communication is a threat to the interests of all individuals who derive a net advantage from their connection with the organization, unless the orders are unacceptable to them also. Accordingly, at any given time there is among most of the contributors an active personal interest in the maintenance of the authority of all orders which to them are within the zone of indifference. The maintenance of this interest is largely a function of informal organization. Its expression goes under the names of "public opinion," "organization opinion," "feeling in the ranks," "group attitude," etc. Thus the common sense of the community informally arrived at affects the attitude of individuals, and makes them, as individuals, loath to question authority that is within or near the zone of indifference. The formal statement of this common sense is the fiction[1] that authority comes down from above, from the general to the particular. This fiction merely establishes a presumption among individuals in favor of the acceptability of orders from superiors, enabling them to avoid making issues of such orders without incurring a sense of personal subserviency or a loss of personal or individual status with their fellows.

Thus the contributors are willing to maintain the authority of communications because, where care is taken to see that only acceptable communications in general are issued, most of them fall within the zone of personal indifference; and because communal sense influences the motives of most contributors most of the time. The practical instrument of this sense is the fiction of superior authority, which makes it possible normally to treat a personal question impersonally.

The fiction of superior authority is necessary for two main reasons: (1) It is the process by which the individual delegates upward, or to the organization, responsibility for what is an organization decision—an action which is depersonalized by the fact of its coördinate character. This means that if an instruction is disregarded, an executive's risk of being wrong must be accepted, a risk that the individual cannot and usually will not take unless in fact his position is at least as good as that of another with respect to correct appraisal of the relevant situation. Most persons are disposed to grant authority because they dislike the personal responsibility which they otherwise accept, especially when they are not in a good position to accept it. The practical difficulties in the operation of organization seldom lie in the excessive desire of individuals to assume responsibility for the organization action of themselves or others, but rather lie in the reluctance to take responsibility for their own actions in organization.

(2) The fiction gives impersonal notice that what is at stake is the good of the organization. If objective authority is flouted for arbitrary or merely temperamental reasons, if, in other words, there is deliberate attempt to twist an organization requirement to personal advantage, rather than properly to safeguard a substantial personal interest, then there is a deliberate attack on the organization itself. To remain outside an organization is not necessarily to be more than not friendly or not interested. To fail in an obligation intentionally is an act of hostility. This no organization can permit; and it must respond with punitive action if it can, even to the point of incarcerating or executing the culprit. This is rather generally the case where a person has agreed in advance in general what he will do. Leaving an organization in the lurch is not often tolerable.

The correctness of what has been said above will perhaps appear most probable from a consideration of the difference between executive action in emergency and that under "normal" conditions. In times of war the disciplinary atmosphere of an army is intensified—it is rather obvious to all that its success and the safety of its members are dependent upon it. In other organizations, abruptness of command is not only tolerated in times of emergency, but expected, and the lack of it often would actually be demoralizing. It is the sense of the justification which lies in the obvious situation which regulates the exercise of the veto by the final authority which lies at the bottom. This is a commonplace of executive experience, though it is not a commonplace of conversation about it.[2]

The System of Coordination

Up to this point we have devoted our attention to the subjective aspect of authority. The executive, however, is predominantly occupied not with this subjective aspect, which is fundamental, but with the objective character of a communication which induces acceptance.

Authority has been defined in part as a "character of a communication in a formal organization." A "superior" is not in our view an authority nor does he have authority strictly speaking; nor is a communication authoritative except when it is an effort or action of organization. This is what we mean when we say that individuals are able to exercise authority only when they are acting "officially," a principle well established in law, and generally in secular and religious practice. Hence the importance ascribed to time, place, dress, ceremony, and authentication of a communication to establish its official character. These practices confirm the statement that authority relates to a communication "in a formal organization." There often occur occasions of compulsive power of individuals and of hostile groups; but authority is always concerned with something *within* a definitely organized system. Current usage conforms to the definition in this respect. The word "authority" is seldom employed except where formal organization connection is stated or implied (unless, of course, the reference is obviously figurative).

These circumstances arise from the fact that the character of authority in organization communications lies in the *potentiality of assent* of those to whom they are sent. Hence, they are only sent to contributors or "members" of the organization. Since all authoritative communications are official and relate only to organization action, they have no meaning to those whose actions are not included within the coöperative system. This is clearly in accord with the common understanding. The laws of one country have no authority for citizens of another, except under special circumstances. Employers do not issue directions to employees of other organizations. Officials would appear incompetent who issued orders to those outside their jurisdiction.

A communication has the presumption of authority when it originates at sources of organization information—a communications center—better than individual sources. It loses this presumption, however, if not within the scope or field of this center. The presumption is also lost if the communication shows an absence of adjustment to the actual situation which confronts the recipient of it.

Thus men impute authority to communications from superior positions, provided they are reasonably consistent with advantages of scope and perspective that are credited to those positions. This authority is to a considerable extent independent of the personal ability of the incumbent of the position. It is often recognized that though the incumbent may be of limited personal ability his advice may be superior solely by reason of the advantage of position. This is the *authority of position.*

But it is obvious that some men have superior ability. Their knowledge and understanding regardless of position command respect. Men impute authority to what they say in an organization for this reason only. This is the *authority of leadership*. When the authority of leadership is combined with the authority of position, men who have an established connection with an organization generally will grant authority, accepting orders far outside the zone of indifference. The confidence engendered may even make compliance an inducement in itself.

Nevertheless, the determination of authority remains with the individual. Let these "positions" of authority in fact show ineptness, ignorance of conditions, failure to communicate what ought to be said, or let leadership fail (chiefly by its concrete action) to recognize implicitly its dependence upon the essential character of the relationship of the individual to the organization, and the authority if tested disappears.

This objective authority is only maintained if the positions or leaders continue to be adequately informed. In very rare cases persons possessing great knowledge, insight, or skill have this adequate information without occupying executive position. What they say ought to be done or ought not to be done will be accepted. But this is usually personal advice at the risk of the taker. Such persons have influence rather than authority. In most cases genuine leaders who give advice concerning organized efforts are required to accept positions of responsibility; for knowledge of the applicability of their special knowledge or judgment to concrete *organization* action, not to abstract problems, is essential to the worth of what they say as a basis of organization authority. In other words, they have an organization personality, as distinguished from their individual personality,[3] commensurate with the influence of their leadership. The common way to state this is that there cannot be authority without corresponding responsibility. A more exact expression would be that objective authority cannot be imputed to persons in organization positions unless subjectively they are dominated by the organization as respects their decisions.

It may be said, then, that the maintenance of objective authority adequate to support the fiction of superior authority and able to make the zone of indifference an actuality depends upon the operation of the system of communication in the organization. The function of this system is to supply adequate information to the positions of authority and adequate facilities for the issuance of orders. To do so it requires commensurate capacities in those able to be leaders. High positions that are not so supported have weak authority, as do strong men in minor positions.

Thus authority depends upon a cooperative personal attitude of individuals on the one hand; and the system of communication in the organization on the other. Without the latter, the former cannot be maintained. The most devoted adherents of an organization will quit it, if its system results in inadequate, contradictory, inept orders, so that they cannot know who is who, what is what, or have the sense of effective coördination.

This system of communication, or its maintenance, is a primary or essential continuing problem of a formal organization. Every other practical question of effectiveness or efficiency—that is, of the factors of survival—depends upon it. In technical language the system of communication of which we are now speaking is often known as the "lines of authority."

It has already been shown[4] that the requirements of communication determine the size of unit organizations, the grouping of units, the grouping of groups of unit organizations. We may now consider the controlling factors in the character of the communication system as a system of objective authority.

(*a*) The first is that *channels of communication should be definitely known.* The language in which this principle is ordinarily stated is, "The lines of authority must be definitely established." The method of doing so is by making official appointments known; by assigning each individual to his position; by general announcements; by organization charts; by educational effort, and most of all by habituation, that is, by securing as much permanence of system as is practicable. Emphasis is laid either upon the position, or upon the persons; but usually the fixing of authority is made both to positions and, less emphatically, to persons.

(*b*) Next, we may say that *objective authority requires a definite formal channel of communication to every member of an organization.* In ordinary language this means "everyone must report to someone" (communication in one direction) and "everyone must be subordinate to someone" (communication in the other direction). In other words, in formal organizations everyone must have definite formal relationship to the organization.[5]

(*c*) Another factor is that *the line of communication must be as direct or short as possible.* This may be explained as follows: Substantially all formal communication is verbal (written or oral). Language as a vehicle of communication is limited and susceptible of misunderstanding. Much communication is necessarily without preparation. Even communications that are carefully prepared require interpretation. Moreover, communications are likely to be in more general terms the more general—that is, the higher—the position. It follows that something may be lost or added by transmission at each stage of the process, especially when communication is oral, or when at each stage there is combination of several communications. Moreover, when communications go from high positions down they often must be made more specific as they proceed; and when in the reverse direction, usually more general. In addition, the speed of communication, other things equal, will be less the greater the number of centers through which it passes. Accordingly, the shorter the line the greater the speed and the less the error.

How important this factor is may be indicated by the remarkable fact that in great complex organizations the number of levels of communication is not much larger than in smaller organizations. In most organizations consisting of the services of one or two hundred men the levels of communication will be from three to five. In the Army the levels are: President, (Secretary of War), General, Major-General, Brigadier-General, Colonel, Major, Captain, Lieutenant, Sergeant, men—that is, nine or ten. In the Bell Telephone System, with over 300,000 working members, the number is eight to ten.[6] A similar shortness of the line of communication is noteworthy in the Catholic Church viewed from the administrative standpoint.

Many organization practices or inventions are used to accomplish this end, depending upon the purpose and technical conditions. Briefly, these methods are: The use of expanded executive organizations at each stage; the use of the staff department (technical, expert, advisory); the division of executive work into functional bureaus; and processes of delegating responsibility with automatic coördination through regular conference procedures, committees for special temporary functions, etc.

(*d*) Another factor is that, in principle, *the complete line of communication should usually be used.* By this is meant that a communication from the head of an organization to the bottom should pass through every stage of the line of authority. This is due to the necessity of avoiding conflicting communications (in either direction) which might (and would) occur if there were any "jumping of the line" of organization. It is also necessary because of the need of interpretation, and to maintain responsibility.[7]

(*e*) Again, the *competence of the persons serving as communication centers, that is, officers, supervisory heads, must be adequate.* The competence required is that of more and more *general* ability with reference to the work of the entire organization the more central the office of communication and the larger the organization. For the function of the center of communication in an organization is to translate incoming communications concerning external conditions, the progress of activity, successes, failures, difficulties, dangers, into outgoing communications in terms of new activities, preparatory steps, etc., all shaped according to the ultimate as well as the immediate purposes to be served. There is accordingly required more or less mastery of the technologies involved, of the capabilities of the personnel, of the informal organization situation, of the character and status of the subsidiary organizations, of the principles of action relative to purpose, of the interpretation of environmental factors, and a power of discrimination between communications that can possess authority because they are recognizably compatible with *all* the pertinent conditions and those which will not possess authority because they will not or cannot be accepted.

It is a fact, I think, that we hardly nowadays expect individual personal ability adequate to positional requirements of communication in modern large-scale organization. The limitations of individuals as respects time and energy alone preclude such personal ability, and the complexity of the technologies or other special knowledge involved make it impossible. For these reasons each major center of communication is itself organized, sometimes quite elaborately. The immediate staff of the executive (commanding officer), consisting of deputies, or chief clerks, or adjutants, or auxiliaries with their assistants, constitute an executive unit of organization only one member of which is perhaps an "executive," that is, occupies the *position* of authority; and the technical matters are assigned to staff departments or organizations of experts. Such staff departments often are partly "field" departments in the sense that they directly investigate or secure information on facts or conditions external to the organizations; but in major part in most cases they digest and translate information from the field, and prepare the plans, orders, etc., for transmission. In this capacity they are advisory or adjutant to the executives. In practice, however, these assistants have the function of semi-formal advice under regulated conditions to the organizations as a whole. In this way, both the formal channels and the informal organization are supplemented by intermediate processes.

In some cases the executive (either chief or some subordinate executive) may be not a person but a board, a legislature, a committee. I know of no important organizations, except some churches and some absolute governments in which the highest objective authority is not lodged in an *organized* executive group, that is, a "highest" unit of organization.

(*f*) Again, *the line of communication should not be interrupted during the time when the organization is to function.* Many organizations (factories, stores) function intermittently, being closed or substantially so during the night, Sundays, etc. Others, such as army, police, railroad systems, telephone systems, never cease to operate. During the times when organizations are at work, in principle the line of authority must never be broken; and practically this is almost, if not quite, literally true in many cases. This is one of the reasons which may be given for the great importance attached to hereditary succession in states, and for the elaborate provision that is made in most organizations (except possibly small "personal" organizations) for the temporary filling of offices automatically during incapacity or absence of incumbents. These provisions emphasize the non-personal and communication character of organization authority, as does the persistent emphasis upon the *office* rather than the *man* that is a matter of indoctrination of many organizations, especially those in which "discipline" is an important feature.

The necessity for this is not merely that specific communications cannot otherwise be attended to. It is at least equally that the *informal* organization disintegrates very quickly if the formal "line of authority" is broken. In organization parlance, "politics" runs riot. Thus, if an office were vacant, but the fact were not known, an organization might function for a considerable time without serious disturbance, except in emergency. But if known, it would quickly become disorganized.

(*g*) The final factor I shall mention is that *every communication should be authenticated.* This means that the person communicating must be known actually to occupy the "position of authority" concerned; that the position includes the type of communication concerned—that is, it is "within its authority"; and that it actually is an authorized communication from this office. The process of authentication in all three respects varies in different organizations under different conditions and for different positions. The practice is undergoing rapid changes in the modern technique, but the principles remain the same. Ceremonials of investiture, inaugurations, swearing-in, general orders of appointment, induction, and introduction, are all essentially appropriate methods of making known who actually fills a position and what the position includes as authority. In order that these *positions* may function it is often necessary that the filling of them should be dramatized, an essential process to the creation of authority *at the bottom,* where only it can be fundamentally—that is, it is essential to inculcate the "sense of organization." This is merely stating that it is essential to "organization loyalty and solidarity" as it may be otherwise expressed. Dignifying the superior position is an important method of dignifying *all* connection with organization, a fact which has been well learned in both religious and political organizations where great attention to the subjective aspects of the "membership" is the rule.

This statement of the principles of communication systems of organizations from the viewpoint of the maintenance of objective authority has necessarily been in terms of complex organizations, since in a simple unit organization the concrete applications of these principles are fused. The principles are with difficulty isolated under simple conditions. Thus, as a matter of course, in unit organizations the channels of communication are known, indeed usually obvious; they are definite; they are the shortest possible; the only lines of authority are complete lines; there is little question of authentication. The doubtful points in unit organization are the competence of the leader, never to be taken for granted even in simple organizations; and whether he is functioning when the

organization is in operation. Yet as a whole the adequately balanced maintenance of these aspects of simple leadership is the basis of objective authority
in the unit organization, as the maintenance of the more formal and observable
manifestations of the same aspects is the basis of authority in the complex
organization. . . .

Notes and References

1. The word "fiction" is used because from the standpoint of logical construction it merely explains overt acts. Either as a superior officer or as a subordinate, however, I know nothing that I actually regard as more "real" than "authority."
2. It will be of interest to quote a statement which has appeared since these lines were written, in a pamphlet entitled "Business—Well on the Firing Line" (No. 9 in the series "What Helps Business Helps You," in *Nation's Business*). It reads in part: "Laws don't create Teamplay. It is not called into play by law. For every written rule there are a thousand unwritten rules by which the course of business is guided, which govern the millions of daily transactions of which business consists. These rules are not applied from the top down, by arbitrary authority. They grow out of actual practice—from the bottom up. They are based upon mutual understanding and compromise, the desire to achieve common ends and further the common good. They are observed *voluntarily*, because they have the backing of experience and common sense.
3. See Chapter VII, p. 88 [*The Functions of the Executive*].
4. Chapter VIII, "The Structure of Complex Formal Organizations," beginning at p. 106 [*The Functions of the Executive*].
5. In some types of organizations it is not unusual, however, for one person to report to and to be subordinate to two or three "superiors," in which case the functions of the superiors are defined and are mutually exclusive in principle.
6. Disregarding the corporate aspects of the organization, and not including board of directors.
7. These by no means exhaust the considerations. The necessity of maintaining personal prestige of executives as an *inducement to them* to function is on the whole an important additional reason.

Decentralization: A Managerial Philosophy

RALPH J. CORDINER

Every company should be managed in accordance with some workable, ethically
responsible philosophy of management. That is, the managers of the company
should be in general agreement on a set of underlying principles that will guide
their work in providing leadership for the company.

For some companies, the set of principles that guide the managers may be tacitly understood, without ever being presented systematically. They may be part of the company's tradition or may even reflect the personal philosophy of the chief executive.

While General Electric's present philosophy of management has had a long evolution in Company tradition and reflects the personalities of its great leaders in years gone by, considerable effort has been devoted in the past ten years to "thinking through" and presenting this managerial philosophy in a systematic way.

I should like to discuss the results of these studies: the philosophy of decentralization, and how it has been applied by General Electric in building an organization structure to meet the challenges of an expanding economy.

Explosive Growth Raises Organizational Questions

Up until 1939, the Company was able to operate efficiently under a highly centralized form of management. During World War II, however, General Electric began a period of almost explosive growth which caused its managers to question whether it might not be necessary to evolve new techniques of organizing and managing the Company.

From 1920 to 1939, the Company's sales volume had risen slowly from $200 million to $342 million a year. By 1943, under the pressure of war production, it rose suddenly to $1,370,000,000 a year—over a four-fold increase in four years. Postwar experience and forecasts indicated that this was only the beginning of an opportunity for continuing, rapid growth in serving the nation's demands for electrical and related products. The Company produced over $3 billion worth of goods and services last year; and if we do the job we should do of satisfying customers, this figure may well rise—as the Company has publicly stated many times—to $6 billion early in the 1960's.

It is obvious that a company with such growth characteristics, and operating on such a scale, requires a different managerial approach than the company of the 1920's and '30's.

From the beginning of the study, it was apparent that the Company was going to require increasingly better planning, greater flexibility, and faster, more informed decisions than was possible under the highly centralized organization structure, which was suited for earlier and different conditions. Unless we could put the responsibility and authority for decision making closer in each case to the scene of the problem, where complete understanding and prompt action are possible, the Company would not be able to compete with the hundreds of nimble competitors who were, as they say, able to turn on a dime.

In addition, General Electric faced the need to develop capable leaders for the future; the need for more friendly and cooperative relationships between managers and other employees; the need to stay ahead of competition in serving the customers; and the very human need to make the work of a manager at all echelons of the organization more manageable. The work had to be made more manageable so that it could be understood and carried out by people of normally available energy and intelligence, thus leaving no requirement for the so-called indispensable man.

The Solution: Decentralization

In General Electric, decentralization is a way of preserving and enhancing these contributions of the large enterprise, and at the same time achieving the flexibility and the "human touch" that are popularly associated with—though not always attained by—small organizations.

Under this concept, we have undertaken decentralization not only according to products, geography, and functional types of work. The most important aspect of the Company's philosophy is thorough decentralization of the responsibility and authority for making business decisions.

Here is the underlying logic. The share owners, through their Board of Directors, delegate to the President responsibility for the conduct of the whole business. The responsibility carries with it all the authority required to get the work done, except such authorities as are specifically withheld by the Board and the share owners. The total responsibility also carries with it full accountability for results. General Electric may be unique in that the Board of Directors has issued a position guide for the President, stating in detail his responsibility, authority, and accountability.

Now, the President is of course unable to do all the work himself, and so he delegates the responsibility for portions of the total work through organization channels to individuals who have the talents and knowledge required to do it. This is done by planning and building the work of the Company into an organization structure which consists of all the necessary positions and components required to do all the work in the most effective and efficient manner.

Each employee thus takes on responsibility for some part of the over-all Company work. Along with this responsibility, each position naturally carries with it full accountability for measured results, and all the necessary authority required for the position except those authorities that are specifically stated as withheld. Therefore each employee of the Company has, in his position, full responsibility, authority, and accountability for a certain defined body of work and teamwork. Through teamwork he recognizes his relationships to the other employees who perform a share of the total work of the Company.

With this philosophy, General Electric achieves a community of purpose between leaders and their associates, and is able to attain that voluntary integration which is the hallmark of a free and decentralized enterprise.

In such compressed statement, this management philosophy may sound somewhat obscure, but its practical result is to put the responsibility for making business decisions not with a few top executives, but with the individual managerial and functional employees who have the most immediately applicable information required to make sound decisions and take prompt action. When such responsibility—along with commensurate authority and accountability—has been delegated according to a carefully planned organization of work, then each individual in the Company has a challenging and dignified position which will bring out his full resources and enthusiastic cooperation.

Ten Guiding Principles

Since philosophy is, by definition, a system of first principles, I should like to list for you ten principles which express General Electric's philosophy of decentralization.

1. Decentralization places authority to make decisions at points as near as possible to where actions take place.
2. Decentralization is likely to get best over-all results by getting greatest and most directly applicable knowledge and most timely understanding actually into play on the greatest number of decisions.
3. Decentralization will work if real authority is delegated; and not if details then have to be reported, or, worse yet, if they have to be "checked" first.
4. Decentralization requires confidence that associates in decentralized positions will have the capacity to make sound decisions in the majority of cases; and such confidence starts at the executive level. Unless the President and all the other Officers have a deep personal conviction and an active desire to decentralize full decision-making responsibility and authority, actual decentralization will never take place. The Officers must set an example in the art of full delegation.
5. Decentralization requires understanding that the main role of staff or services is the rendering of assistance and advice to line operators through a relatively few experienced people, so that those making decisions can themselves make them correctly.
6. Decentralization requires realization that the natural aggregate of many individually sound decisions will be better for the business and for the public than centrally planned and controlled decisions.
7. Decentralization rests on the need to have general business objectives, organization structure, relationships, policies, and measurements known, understood, and followed; but realizing that definition of policies does not necessarily mean uniformity of methods of executing such policies in decentralized operations.
8. Decentralization can be achieved only when higher executives realize that authority genuinely delegated to lower echelons cannot, in fact, also be retained by them. We have, today, Officers and Managers who still believe in decentralization down to themselves and no further. By paying lip-service to decentralization, but actually reviewing detailed work and decisions and continually "second-guessing" their associates, such Officers keep their organization in confusion and prevent the growth of self-reliant men.
9. Decentralization will work only if responsibility commensurate with decision-making authority is truly accepted and exercised at all levels.
10. Decentralization requires personnel policies based on measured performance, enforced standards, rewards for good performance, and removal for incapacity or poor performance.

Designing Organizational Structure

Now, given this philosophy, how can it be expressed in an organization structure suitable to the General Electric Company? In our experience, the following work must be done to attain a sound, flexible, and dynamic organization structure:

1. Determine the objectives, and the policies, programs, plans, and schedules that will best achieve those objectives; for the Company as a whole and in turn, for each component of the business.

2. Determine the work to be done to achieve these objectives, under such guiding policies.
3. Divide and classify or group related work into a simple, logical, understandable, and comprehensive organization structure.
4. Assign essential work clearly and definitely to the various components and positions in the organization structure.
5. Determine the requirements and qualifications of personnel to occupy such positions.
6. Staff the organization with persons who meet these qualifications.
7. Establish methods and procedures which will help to achieve the objectives of the organization.

General Electric's Organization Structure

In order to achieve these objectives on a continuing and profitable basis, an improved organization structure was devised in accordance with the principles of decentralization.

The organization of General Electric is essentially a three-part structure which carefully distinguishes between Operating work, Services work, and Executive work.

The Operating Components

First let us consider the Operating work. Today, General Electric's products are engineered, manufactured, and marketed by nearly a hundred decentralized Operating Departments, each of them bearing full operating responsibility and authority for the Company's success and profitability in a particular product or service field. The special skills and knowledge required for each operating business are thus brought to bear by a local business managerial team which can concentrate on the opportunities of a specific product or marketing area. Through these integrated managerial teams, each with a specific profit-and-loss responsibility for the operation of a defined business, we achieve the flexibility, drive, and the "human touch" that comes from direct participation in the daily problems of a business.

To demonstrate that the responsibility, authority, and accountability of these Operating Departments is real, not window dressing, consider their pricing authority. The price of a product can be raised or lowered by the managers of the Department producing it, with only voluntary responsibility on their part to give sensible consideration to the impact of such price changes on other Company products. In one area of General Electric products, the major appliances such as refrigerators, ranges, and home laundry equipment, there are two Divisions competing directly with each other. The Hotpoint Division in Chicago and the Major Appliance and Television Receiver Division in Louisville have different facilities, different product designs,.different distribution, and different prices. They compete at the market place very aggressively, and, incidentally, very profitably. Other Departments compete with each other by presenting different types of products that perform essentially the same function. For example, there is the competition between electronic tubes and transistors, or between room air conditioners and central air conditioning.

As further evidence of the freedom provided by decentralization to the Operating Departments, consider the fact that the operating budget of the General Electric Company is not a document prepared by the Executive Offices in New York. It is an addition of the budgets prepared by the Operating Department General Managers, with the concurrence of the Division General Managers and Group Executives. These budgets include planned sales volume, product development plans, expenditures for plant and equipment, market targets, turnover of investment, net earnings, projected organization structure, and other related items.

In the days when the Company had a centralized organization, it was the custom for Operating components to submit budgets which were promptly blue-penciled, modified, expanded or contracted, and "second-guessed" by the headquarters Executives. As a result, Operating people did not usually take their budgeting too seriously.

Now they are taking it seriously because they know they will be measured on their ability to achieve the budgeted results which they, themselves, have established as proper goals for their organizations.

We are frequently asked how these Operating Departments can do accurate forecasting and budgeting, and how the Executives can delegate this difficult function to persons less broadly experienced than themselves. The Operating Departments can do better forecasting and budgeting because they are intimately informed as to the conditions which prevail and will prevail in their line of business.

Since they are better informed, they are authorized to make whatever prudent commitments they should on materials, and we have recently increased the approval authority of the Operating Department General Managers over capital expenditures so that they can, by their own decision, make commitments up to $500,000.*

In such a diversified company as General Electric, it is impossible for the Executives in New York to have detailed knowledge of such a variety of businesses and markets. Executives can help by supplying some general aiming areas for the Company as a whole, and information as to the probable general trends of business. But this information is to be factored in, and not to dominate the budgeting of the Operating Departments, nor does it do so.

The fact is that the Operating Departments are now doing better budgeting than was done by headquarters in years gone by. Last year the Company as a whole was within 1% of its budgeted sales results, although some individual Departments were off by substantially greater percentages one way or another. . . .

It is important to emphasize the voluntary nature of a position in General Electric. For every position in the Company, including these Operating General Managers, a man has the personal right to accept or refuse the position—along with accountability for the results expected, and the risks involved in accepting such responsibilities. If for personal or other reasons he decides not to accept a particular position, there is no prejudice against him. He will receive other

---

*I believe that too much of a fetish has been made in the past of capital expenditures. A manager can lose a lot more money on inventory, foolish pricing policy, careless personnel staffing, or poor production scheduling. Let me illustrate. In General Electric, capital expenditures in 1955 amounted to $153 millions, but we bought $1,400 millions of materials and had a payroll of $1,200 millions.

offers for which he is qualified as such positions become available. Voluntary and wholehearted acceptance is of course a necessary condition if a man is to be held accountable for results in risk-taking ventures.

To assure that the Operating Departments and their customers will receive the full benefit of the Company's broad resources in knowledge and risk-taking capacity, two other types of work are provided for in the Company's over-all organization structure: Services work and Executive work.

The Services

The functional services are components at the corporate level, staffed with the Company's most experienced personnel in the major business functions: accounting, engineering, legal and corporate, management consultation, manufacturing, marketing, public and employee relations, treasury, and research. It is important to note that, in contrast with the powerful Operating authority wielded by headquarters functional Executives under the earlier centralized structure, these Services people have no authority whatsoever over the Operating Departments and Divisions, except the authority of knowledge. They have, instead, two Company-wide responsibilities: to do research, teaching, and long-range guidance in personnel development in their functional field; and to do such functional operating work for the Company as a whole as can best be done at the corporate level.

First, let us consider the research and teaching—what we call "Services functional work." In each business function, such as accounting or marketing, General Electric is trying to apply the same principles of fundamental research and creative study that have long kept it ahead in the area of science and technology. The Services have been deliberately freed of Operating responsibility so that they can think ahead, developing through research the most advanced knowledge, principles, and techniques in their functional field, as well as keeping abreast of current knowledge developed elsewhere.

Services also have the responsibility to convert this new knowledge into usable forms and patterns, and to make it available through advice and teaching, to the Operating Departments and Divisions. Services also help to formulate Company policies appropriate to their function, and maintain a "clearinghouse" of current practices and standards within the Company to help facilitate a free flow of functional knowledge across the entire organization.

Of course, communications should never bog down in channels. If a Section Manager in steam turbine engineering at Schenectady, for example, wants some information pertaining to the engineering of aircraft gas turbines in another section, in Evendale, he does not have to go all the way up through channels to a Group Executive and down the other channel. He is expected to get the information straight across the Company just by picking up the telephone and talking to the fellow in Evendale who has the information.

The duties of Services also include long-range personnel development planning, to assure a continuing supply of outstanding people with the required changing functional skills.

Thus the emphasis in Service functional work is on the future: anticipating future opportunities and future problems, so that when they arrive General Electric will have the personnel and knowledge ready to meet them unsurprised.

The other important duty of the Services is to perform such operating work as can best be done at the corporate level, for the Company as a whole.

This includes, for example, the work of Treasury Services in handling corporate financing and investment activities on an efficient basis. There would be great confusion if the 21 Operating Divisions or 100 Operating Departments were to deal with the banks entirely separately. It should be remembered, however, that the authority to deny the use of capital from the Company's treasury to Operating General Managers who wish prudently to invest is not part of the Treasurer's responsibilities.

Another example of Operating work in the Services is the conduct of public relations programs such as institutional advertising and television, preparation of the annual report, and similar informational activities that deal with the Company as a whole. It is important that Services perform such corporate operating work with great distinction, to serve as a high standard for functional work throughout the Company.

The Executives

Leadership and long-range planning for the Company as a whole constitute the Executive classification of work in the Company structure. To understand this Executive aspect of the General Electric organization, it is important to understand two unusual organizational devices: The President's Office and the Executive Office.

The President's Office is a group of Executives who share the work of the President. In addition to the President, it includes the Chairman of the Board, and five Executive Vice Presidents. The Chairman of the Board, in addition to the duties assigned him directly by the Board, represents the President in such areas as financial affairs, public and governmental liaison, and international matters, and each of the Executive Vice Presidents represents the President in relationships with a specific group of Operating Divisions. This unique organizational device was created in recognition of the fact that no one man would have the time and knowledge required to provide effective Executive leadership for the variety of businesses in a Company as large and as diversified as General Electric. Thus each Executive Vice President serves as the President in a defined Operating area, without in any sense relieving the President of the ultimate responsibility placed upon him by the Board of Directors for the success of the enterprise as a whole.

The Executive Vice Presidents, in General Electric, are true Executives. That is, they have been freed of Operating responsibility and administrative details so that they can devote their time to long-range planning, appraisal of current performance, bringing divisional objectives and plans into a working pattern with over-all Company needs, and making sure of the needed continuity of competent managerial and other personnel in the decentralized businesses.

These seven members of the President's Office, together with the nine Company Officers in charge of the Services, form what is known as the Executive Office. These Senior Officers deliberately set aside about 20% of their time to serve, not as Executives for their particular area of Operations or Services, but as a well-balanced group of general Executives who advise the President on matters that concern all functions and all operations—in other words, the

Company as a whole. In this way the Executive Office provides a melding of extensive business judgment and advanced functional knowledge to help the President plan the Company's management, growth, and course ten or more years ahead.

There you have the organizational structure of the General Electric Company: a three-part structure consisting of the Executives, who provide leadership and long-range planning for the Company as a whole; the Services, which provide leadership and advanced research in each functional field; and the Operating components, which have decentralized responsibility for the success, growth, and competitive profitability of the Company's diverse Operating businesses.

Changing Organizational Behavior Patterns

PAUL E. LAWRENCE

[Lawrence was engaged as a consultant to help the headquarters management of Food World, a large supermarket chain, effectively decentralize their chain of supermarkets. The management believed that decentralization would help Food World in competition with other grocery chains, and that it would make Food World a better place to work. Top managers had already decided upon the new organizational philosophy when Lawrence arrived.

Part of the problem lay in the increasing size of grocery stores. By about the time of this research, 11,000 small grocery stores had gone out of business. Their place was being taken by large stores—sixteen of the Food World stores did over $2 million sales a year (twenty years before, a trade magazine had estimated that if a store sold over $150,000 a year, operating efficiency and profits would fall off). There were over 100 stores in the Food World chain. Further, there were many changes taking place in ways of doing business. New product lines (frozen foods, drug items, more variety in staple lines) were emerging, and new merchandise methods (parking, customer service, etc.) had to be devised.

Food World had developed as a chain run essentially by one energetic man. He employed 60 superintendents, each supervising 10 of his 600 small stores. In his larger stores, three headquarters supervisors regularly visited to plan and supervise operations: a superintendent dealt with the store grocery manager, a headquarters produce manager dealt with the store produce manager, and a headquarters meat merchandiser dealt with the store meat manager. There was no overall general store manager in either the small or large stores. The

From Paul E. Lawrence, *The Changing of Organizational Behavior Patterns: A Case Study of Decentralization* (Boston: Division of Research, Harvard Business School, 1958), pp. 1–4, 62–68, 130–140. Reprinted by permission of the publisher.

small stores in effect shared the headquarters superintendent with other stores, as store manager. The large stores were supervised by the three functional headquarters managers.

As the company grew in volume (but decreased in number of stores to around 100), the headquarters reorganized with buyers (corporate staff) who specialized in groceries, meats, or produce. The operation of the stores (physical plant, merchandising, etc.) was headed by a vice-president for operations and a store operations manager. Top management at headquarters spent most of their time at the home office, planning what should happen in the stores and relaying orders to eight district managers.

The district managers were responsible for field supervision of the stores. They made regular supervisory visits to stores in their territory. First, they made an inspection tour. They then checked to see that adequate stocks were carried, checked on customer bad check losses, checked on sales of specific items, pointed out cleanliness measures that were needed, and in general spent most of their time relaying instructions from headquarters.

While the district manager was boss of all three store departments (grocery, meat, produce), he had staff assistants who specialized in meat and produce. Their behavior was somewhat like that of the district manager.

The five top men at headquarters had been worried because many employees in the stores were bright and experienced in the grocery business, but did not seem to produce. Many instances were found of district managers' instructions for improvement that were never carried out. Store personnel did not seem to be thinking about needed improvements themselves. Much hard work was being done, and morale seemed healthy, but somehow the attitude of the independent grocer, who could tailor his store to the needs of customers, was lost. Top management believed that the chains that would grow most would be those that could take advantage of the large-scale economies of a chain, yet preserve the interest, ability, and initiative of the local grocer.

This, essentially, was the reasoning behind the decentralization move. In the following, Lawrence describes how decentralization was visualized and what results it produced.]

Introduction

Upon undertaking the study, the researcher's first problem was to state and clarify the research questions that were to be answered and the research methods to be used in securing these answers. The researcher finally settled on two major sets of questions which in turn required the use of two quite different types of research methods. The early part of the research effort was concerned with the questions: What is the nature of the basic behavior patterns in this organization? What are the key factors involved in changing these patterns? These questions called for the use of the dual research methods of direct observation of behavior and interviews. The researcher spent many days talking to people at all levels in many parts of the organization and observing them going about their work. He kept voluminous field notes on what they said and did. His research interviews were open-ended—he was interested in what the individual thought was important to describe about his job and his work relationships. He observed what people did, with whom they dealt, and the way they handled themselves in these relationships.

The top management executives, in their roles as leaders of the Food World social system, wished to change some of the critical behavior patterns of the system. They were motivated to do this as a result of their observation of anticipated external pressures on the system and as a result of their perception of certain malfunctioning in the system itself that threatened its health and survival. They wanted their plans to have a significant effect on behavior throughout the entire organization. The researcher, however, could not hope to observe and measure all the effects of the reorganization. He chose, therefore, to concentrate his observations on two strategically critical positions; the store manager and the district manager. This choice was made on the assumption that the men in these positions would have to make the most changes in their behavior, and the desired results further down the line would be dependent upon their making these changes. We shall therefore be focusing our intensive study on the behavior of the people in these two strategic positions.

Members of top management stated their ideas about the desired behavior changes in terms of "decentralization" and "clear-cut administrative framework." They were not completely happy with these terms because they knew that they were subject to differing definitions, but regardless of the words they had a pretty clear idea of what they wanted. For our research purposes, however, we need to define these desired behavioral changes in more concrete and measurable terms. To do this we shall take the two key positions, the store manager and the district manager, and see in what specific ways management desired them to change their behavior. In other words, what were management's new requirements for the roles of these positions?

New Required Role: Store Manager

For convenience and clarity we shall subdivide the role requirements into the three elements of behavior—the kind of *activities* the store manager was to engage in, the kind of *interaction* he was to have with others, and the kind of *sentiments* he was to hold.

Activities Management expected the new store manager to spend considerable time in all departments of the store observing what was going on (in contrast to doing physical work). It expected him to analyze past performance and work out future plans and objectives.

Interactions Management expected the new store manager to interact down the line primarily with his three department heads (in contrast to working directly with clerks). These interactions were to be two-way, problem-solving conversations in which the subordinate participated in choosing departmental objectives and merchandising methods, and in making personnel decisions. It expected the store manager to initiate interactions with the staff merchandisers to seek their technical assistance in the perishable department but not to let themselves or their department managers be dominated by these merchandisers. As regards his superior, the district manager, he was expected not only to receive and interpret instructions from above but also to pass on ideas and problems.

Sentiments Management expected the store manager to conceive of himself as a businessman concerned with the over-all well-being of his store for the future as well as the present. He was to be loyal to the organization but feel more self-sufficient rather than dependent on his superiors. He was to have an enthu-siasm for the possibilities of the store that would be reflected in his subordinates' attitudes. He was to think of himself as a leader and developer of his subordinates rather than as a dominator of them.

In considering the required role described above, we need to remember that the organization plans called for recruiting most of the new store managers from positions as grocery managers or other departmental managers in stores. The new store manager role requirements are by no means the same thing as the existing pattern of activities, interactions, and sentiments practiced by depart-mental managers. In fact, it might be predicted that these changes are so great that they could not be successfully made without the intelligent and active support of his immediate supervisor, the district manager.

New Required Role: District Manager

The district managers had traditionally been a strong link between top man-agement and the store organization. They were traditionally giving their store personnel frequent and detailed supervision on the way top management wanted the work of the stores conducted. These were the men who were accustomed to making hundreds of detailed decisions about how the stores were to operate. They were giving instructions on how they wanted merchandise displayed, how they wanted work schedules handled, how they wanted the store plant main-tained, and the hundreds of other detailed items involved in good store opera-tion. The whole system worked so that the store people had been trained to be loyal and hard-working order takers, and, so far as they were concerned, these orders were emanating from the district manager who to them had always been their personal "big boss," who would have the dominant voice in deter-mining their own personal future with the organization. Under the new orga-nizational plan, these district managers were being asked to change drastically their traditional role. Top management's new role requirements for the district managers are spelled out below in terms of concrete behavior.

Activities The district manager was still expected to spend most of his time going from store to store in his territory observing and talking with his subordinates. He was, however, expected to spend more time looking over the perishable departments because of his loss of the assistant district managers. He was also expected to spend more time on planning functions and less on "fire fighting" current problems.

Interactions The district managers were expected to provide opportunities for their subordinate store managers to assume more decision-making functions. They would have to converse with their fledgling store managers so that these men would assume greater responsibilities and discharge them adequately. This meant that in their interactions with their subordinates they were expected to make a fundamental change toward adopting a more problem-solving, two-way type of communication. They would have to strike a relatively even balance between the amount of time they spent talking to their subordinates and the time their subordinates spent doing the talking to them. It was expected that the district managers would still be in frequent contact with the staff merchan-disers (their former assistant district managers), but instead of the traditional boss-subordinate pattern it was to be a relationship of a line-staff nature with the district manager calling on the merchandiser for advice and staff assistance and, in turn, teaching the store manager to use this staff assistance intelligently. The district manager was also to be expected to adopt different interaction practices with his superiors in the organization. This was most apparent in the way the plan called for conducting different types of headquarters meetings with the district manager group. These meetings were no longer to be primarily briefings where the district managers were told what top management orders they were to carry out, but rather they were now expected to do a more systematic job of keeping top management informed on the problems arising in the field and on the suggestions for improvement that were coming from the field. What is more, they were expected to participate more in making the plans and decisions that affected operations.

Sentiments   Like the store managers, the district managers were expected to conceive of themselves as more independent, self-sufficient businessmen who were concerned with the long-range well-being of their districts. They were even to think of their role as superiors, as being more that of teachers and developers of the capacities of their store managers.

These new role requirements were in considerable contrast to the customary ways of thinking and behaving that prevailed among these men. The district managers were, then, expected to change their role in the organization drastically—to change their behavior in every one of their key relationships, up, down, and sideways, that made up their daily work existence. These changes were strategically critical to the success of the entire reorganization plans since they were an essential prerequisite to changing the daily working practices of the people in the stores. It is for this reason that we shall be focusing in the succeeding chapters on the problems of change in the behavior of district managers in their relations with the new store managers, and certainly not because the individual district managers "ought" (in a moral sense) to change their behavior any more than anyone else.

Management Change Methods

The top management of Food World adopted a number of specific methods to clarify the new role requirements for store managers and district managers. The executives worked out new job definitions with the people concerned, gave speeches on what they expected of the new setup, wrote up various descriptions of what they wanted in the company's house organ, and redrew the company's official organization chart. They knew, however, that these customary steps to establish the new required roles had to be supplemented by other change methods—new work procedures and new incentives.

The new control procedures that required sales and expense goals to be agreed on at the store manager and district manager level were designed to foster the required interaction pattern. The same was true of the new procedure for having these supervisors participate in the systematic evaluation of their employees. Likewise the new type of management meetings were designed to give these supervisors a chance to practice filling the required roles.

Finally top executives gave their supervisors some explicit and implied incentives for behaving in terms of the new roles. They offered store departmental managers the incentive of a higher status title, "store manager," and increased pay for demonstrating that they could adequately meet the role requirements for store manager. With the district manager they implied that the larger, more desirable districts or even higher management jobs would go to those who could meet the new role requirements, while there was an implicit threat that failure to meet the requirements could result in demotion.

These, then, were the formal steps that management could and did make to translate the new required roles from the planning stage into the actual day-to-day behavior of the key supervisors. It remained to be seen if these formal steps were successful in making the plans a reality.

In early 1955 the observer heard a newly appointed store manager ask a kidding question of another store manager: "Have you heard the new definition of a store manager? It's a grocery manager with a raise in pay." This comment epitomized the question that was on the minds of many in the organization. Could management's plan get beyond the overt changes they could effect directly—the changes in title, in pay, and in job descriptions? Could it be transformed from a paper change into a basic change in the daily work habits of many people? Could it be a change of substance as well as of form?

Interaction Patterns: Three District Managers

The principal organizational changes that the top management group wished to make were in the overt behavior between superiors and subordinates at certain key spots in the organization. To succeed in effecting these changes, they had to get the members of their supervisory forces to actually change their interaction patterns—their customary conversational practices with their subordinates. Top management could not be content with gaining a mere intellectual under-standing of what they wanted, nor would it be enough to secure merely verbal agreement with their plans. And, since all the district managers spent most of their time talking to subordinates in the stores, the important question was not who the district managers talked to, but rather how they talked to their subor-dinates. The on-the-job, moment-to-moment, verbal behavior of people had to change or the new organizational model would not become a reality. Because this overt behavior was the true test of the success of the change, it also had to be the researcher's way of measuring the change. This fact ruled out the use of many research methods for checking the degree to which the change was actually implemented. It ruled out the use of questionnaires or various pencil and paper tests. It forced the researcher to search for ways to observe and record the overt interactions of the key individuals in the change.

In the last three chapters we have presented one way of reporting research on the behavior of people in an organization, the reporting of a sample of episodes of their behavior. This method has the advantage of helping us get a "feel" for these people and of seeing some of the dynamics of their behavior. However, this method used by itself leaves us with some doubts and short-comings. Was the sample biased? Can we be sure that a change has occurred between one point of time and another? To overcome these doubts and problems, the researcher decided to supplement his direct recording of behavior episodes with a way of quantifying the overt interaction pattern between a superior and a subordinate. This chapter will briefly describe this research method and then give the results of using it with our three key district managers.

The Research Method

On a somewhat trial-and-error basis and by borrowing ideas from Bales' interaction analysis methods (Robert Bales, *Interaction Process Analysis*, 1950), the
researcher evolved a research method that was simple enough to be practical
in making direct on-the-job observations and that provided a quantified measure
of the interaction pattern between a superior and a subordinate. In practice
the method worked as follows. The researcher entered a store with the supervising
district manager. Every time the district manager and the store manager engaged
in conversation with each other, the researcher noted: who talked; the length
of each separate speech; the category of speech involved (that is, was it (1) asking
a question, (2) supplying information, (3) giving an opinion, or (4) giving
directions or suggestions); the type of topic involved; and finally who initiated
new topics. The topic classifications that were used were, (1) discussion of people,
(2) merchandise, (3) record systems, (4) physical plant, and (5) small talk.

These observational categories follow closely the required changes in the
interaction aspects of the new supervisory role. It follows, then, that if we can
get reliable quantitative data on these items, we can measure the degree to which
the behavior of our three district managers is meeting the new role requirements
for interactions. The data will also serve as a check on the validity of the
descriptive analysis of the district managers' behavior presented in the preceding
three chapters.

The interaction patterns of our three key district managers were systematically observed over a period of five months in the summer and fall of 1955.
This was roughly the same time period in which the episodes occurred that are
reported in the three preceding chapters. At this time each of these men was
supervising the work of several newly appointed store managers. The theory
behind the store manager program had been fully explained to them. They
had had enough exposure to the new arrangements so that the first novelty
of the system had worn off. All the formal steps to implement the program had
been made, but it was still a very new thing. Our data should give us a measure,
then, of the degree to which the behavior of our three district managers coincides
with the new model at an early date, but after all the formal and direct
organizational steps had been taken to implement the new system.

The researcher was anxious to get a representative sample of the interactions
of each key district manager so that the resulting data would reflect accurately
the supervisory characteristics of the district manager and not other extraneous
factors. To do this, the district managers were observed working with several
different store managers to minimize the effect of the personality of a particular
store manager on the interaction pattern. The district managers were also
observed calling on stores on different days of the week, and for considerable
amounts of time. This was done to minimize the possibility of seeing a district
manager handling only a few types of problems in a store. Because of the need
to suit the job convenience of the district managers, it was not possible to
get a perfect distribution of observing time in all these factors, but, as is
indicated by Table 1, interactions were observed under a variety of circumstances to reduce the possibility that the differences between the three men
could be ascribed to factors other than the habitual interaction pattern of
the men themselves.

Table 1   Prevailing Conditions During Observation of DM Interaction Patterns

District Manager	Total Interaction Time Observed	Time Early in Week	Time Late in Week	No. of Separate Comments Recorded	No. of SMs Involved	No. of Separate Store Visits
DM1	227 min.	157 min.	70 min.	1,115	3	9
DM2	277 min.	134 min.	143 min.	1,173	3	5
DM3	466 min.	293 min.	173 min.	2,092	3	4

Results

The systematic observation of the interaction patterns of the three district managers turned up some striking differences between them. The most important differences are indicated by Figure 1. This figure presents a profile of each district manager's interaction pattern with three of his subordinate store managers and each district manager's average profile. The figure shows the percentage of total talking time that was used by each party to the conversation and the category of speech used. There are three observations that can be made from these data that are of special importance.

First, the total talking time used by each district manager relative to his subordinates indicates the degree of dominance of the district managers in these conversations. The relatively balanced talking time between DM1 and his store managers indicates that DM1's behavior most nearly coincides with the model requirement of two-way communication in this relationship. The figures indicate that DM3 deviates the most from the new organizational model. For DM3 the words going down the line are three times as much as those coming up the line.

Secondly, the breakdown of talking time into categories of speech gives us another check on the degree of balance in each district manager's interaction pattern. The breakdown indicates that DM1's interaction behavior was not only balanced over-all, but also relatively well balanced within each category of speech. This is especially evident in comparing DM1's record with the others in the categories of *questions, opinions,* and *suggestions or directions.* DM3's behavior is again the furthest from coinciding with the organizational model, going to an extreme of imbalance in the *suggestions or directions* category. For DM3 giving suggestions or directions was distinctly a one-way street.

Thirdly, the figure indicates the relative amount of time spent in each category of speech. This indicates the type of conversation that predominated in these exchanges and provides some clues to the problem-solving values of the conversations. When DM1 was talking with his store managers, most of the time was spent in exchanging *information,* with *opinions, suggestions or directions,* and *questions* following down in that sequence. This is the same sequence of time distribution followed by his average store manager and, in fact, by the averages of the store managers working for DM2 and DM3. This suggests that this particular sequence of time distribution among categories reflects a useful problem-solving type of discussion. This hypothesis, of course, could only be established by much more research. (The research studies of Robert Bales on problem-solving patterns in discussion groups tend to support this hypothesis.)

Figure 1 Percentage of DM and SM Talking Time by Categories

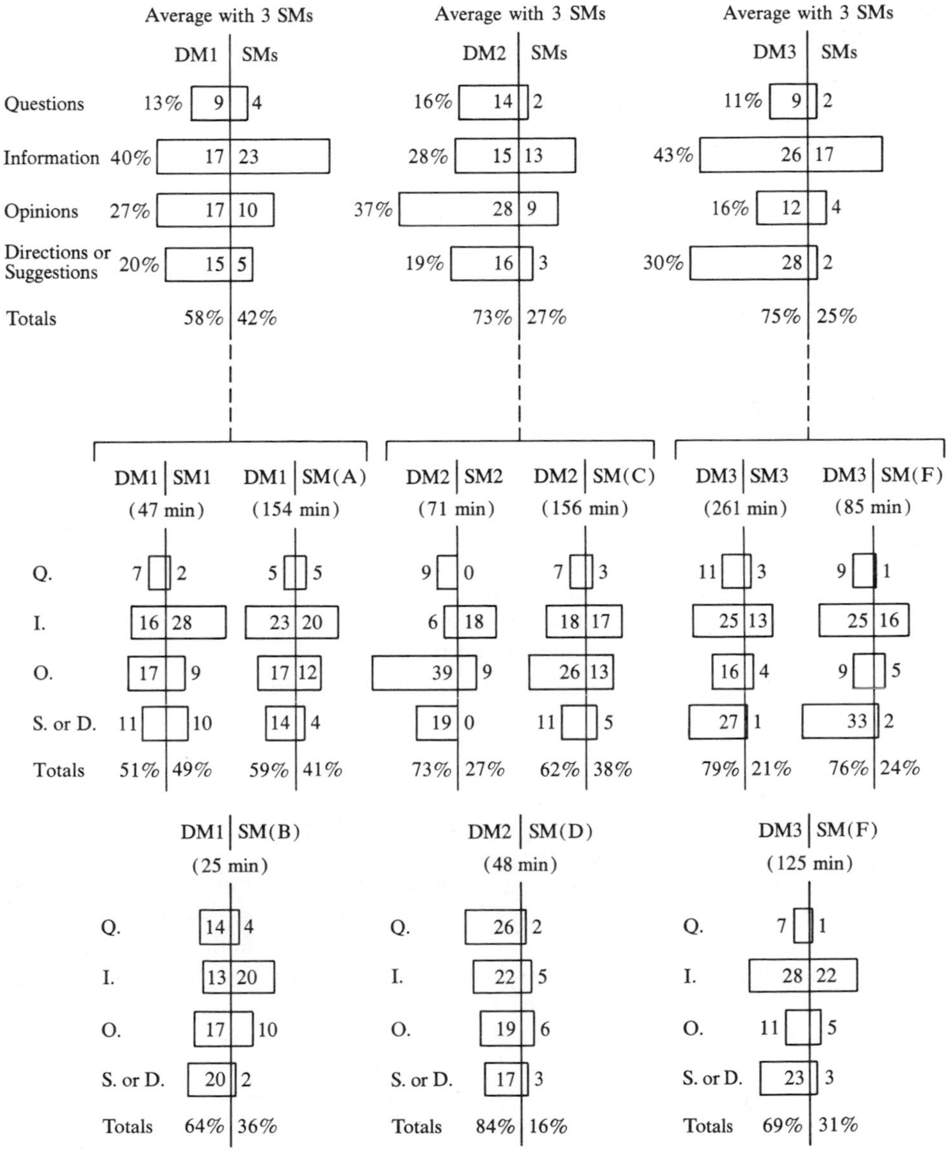

	Average with 3 SMs			Average with 3 SMs			Average with 3 SMs	
	DM1	SMs		DM2	SMs		DM3	SMs
Questions	13%	9	4	16%	14	2	11%	9	2
Information	40%	17	23	28%	15	13	43%	26	17
Opinions	27%	17	10	37%	28	9	16%	12	4
Directions or Suggestions	20%	15	5	19%	16	3	30%	28	2
Totals		58%	42%		73%	27%		75%	25%

	DM1 / SM1 (47 min)		DM1 / SM(A) (154 min)		DM2 / SM2 (71 min)		DM2 / SM(C) (156 min)		DM3 / SM3 (261 min)		DM3 / SM(F) (85 min)	
Q.	7	2	5	5	9	0	7	3	11	3	9	1
I.	16	28	23	20	6	18	18	17	25	13	25	16
O.	17	9	17	12	39	9	26	13	16	4	9	5
S. or D.	11	10	14	4	19	0	11	5	27	1	33	2
Totals	51%	49%	59%	41%	73%	27%	62%	38%	79%	21%	76%	24%

	DM1 / SM(B) (25 min)			DM2 / SM(D) (48 min)			DM3 / SM(F) (125 min)	
Q.	14	4	Q.	26	2	Q.	7	1
I.	13	20	I.	22	5	I.	28	22
O.	17	10	O.	19	6	O.	11	5
S. or D.	20	2	S. or D.	17	3	S. or D.	23	3
Totals	64%	36%	Totals	84%	16%	Totals	69%	31%

This sequence contrasts with DM2's which is very heavy on *opinions* and of DM3's which is heaviest on *suggestions or directions*. In summary, Figure 1 indicates that DM1's interaction pattern most nearly coincides with the organizational requirement of a two-way, problem-solving interaction pattern in this critical relationship. DM3's behavior coincides the least with this model.

Figure 2 presents the breakdown of the amount of DM-SM talking time

Figure 2   Percentage of DM and SM Talking Time by Topics

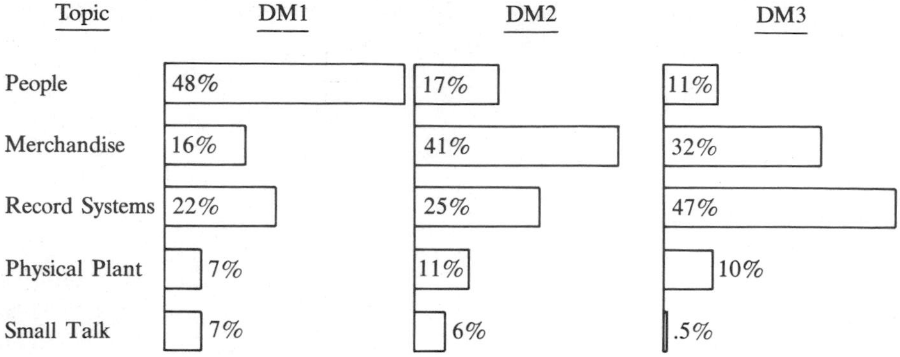

Topic	DM1	DM2	DM3
People	48%	17%	11%
Merchandise	16%	41%	32%
Record Systems	22%	25%	47%
Physical Plant	7%	11%	10%
Small Talk	7%	6%	.5%

that was devoted to the major topical headings. Again some clear differences emerge between the three district managers. These figures indicate the principal topical orientation that each district manager brought to his work. DM1 clearly put his emphasis on the handling and development of people. DM2 puts his chief stress on handling the merchandise, while DM3 was heavily oriented toward the record systems with a secondary emphasis on merchandise. All three gave about the same amount of time to the topic of the physical plant of the store. In the small talk category it is interesting how little time DM3 spent on this in relation to the other two men—DM3 stuck consistently to business in his conversations with subordinates.

It is not too easy to say which topical pattern most nearly coincides with the new organizational requirements since the model itself is hard to define in terms of topics. However, the emphasis of DM2 and DM3 on merchandise and record systems indicates their concern with the activities that had traditionally been the focus of management attention. While it is not quite so clear, DM1's emphasis on the topic of people would seem to indicate that he was giving conscious and explicit attention to discussing the interaction patterns (delegation, coaching, coordination procedures) and sentiments (morale, discipline, feelings about promotions, demotions, and transfers), all of which more directly involve the people in the business. In this sense DM1 seems to be most nearly following top management's model for changing organizational behavior.

Figure 3 shows the ratio between the number of new conversational topics initiated by the district managers and those initiated by their subordinate store managers. While each of the district managers initiated many more topics than their subordinates, DM1 was slightly more balanced on this score than his two colleagues. This provides another test for two-way communication.

Figure 4 gives the average length in minutes of a single speech (or comment) by the district managers and their store managers. The figure indicates what the earlier data would lead us to expect, namely that DM1 again shows the best balance in the average length of his single speech in relation to his subordinates and DM3 shows the least balance. DM1 gave the shortest single speeches of the three men and his subordinates gave the longest speeches. This would

Figure 3 Percentage of New Topics Initiated by DMs and SMs.

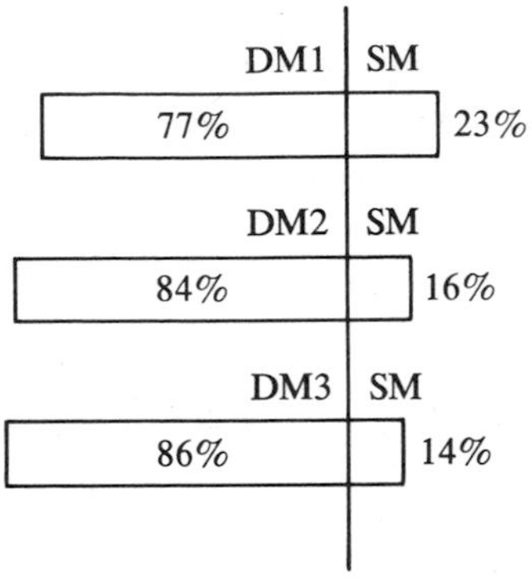

	DM1	SM	
	77%		23%

	DM2	SM	
	84%		16%

	DM3	SM	
	86%		14%

seem to indicate a relative lack of a sense of restraint on the part of DM1's subordinates in conversation with him and again indicates two-way communication.

The quantitative data given above consistently confirm [our] tentative conclusions. Without exception, every measure of the interaction pattern of all three district managers shows that DM1's behavior was most nearly coinciding with the desired model while DM3's was furthest from the new model.

The data in this article allow us to make some additional observations about the nature of the organizational behavior changes that were being attempted at Food World. First of all, the data help clarify an essential characteristic of the change that needs emphasis. The interaction pattern of our three district managers has been quantified by observing them making hundreds of discreet acts of speech at a rate of several per minute. It was this overt behavior pattern that top management wanted them to change. Changing this pattern is a far cry from the more customary changes, such as introducing new forms or work

Figure 4 Average Duration of a Single Comment in Minutes

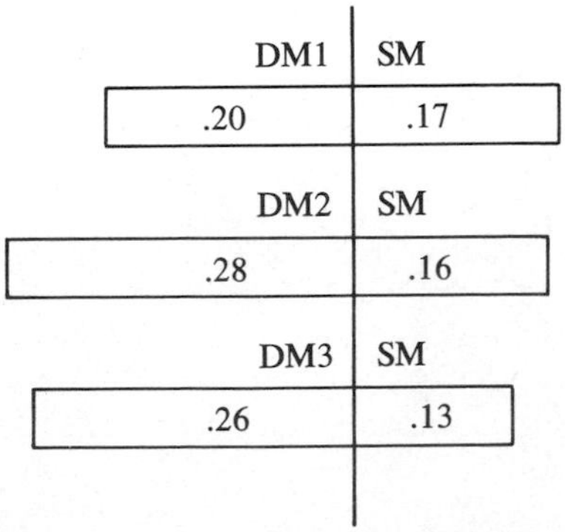

	DM1	SM	
	.20	.17	

	DM2	SM	
	.28	.16	

	DM3	SM	
	.26	.13	

procedures, changing the allocation of job time, transferring to a new district, and so on. Such changes, by comparison, would be easy to effect. The desired changes involve a man's intuitive, instantaneous responses to the entire range of supervisory issues. They involve some of a man's most intimate and persistent assumptions about himself and others. Of course, top management did not define in such concrete operational terms the changes they desired but, nevertheless, this is what their expectations meant in terms of actual behavior. The point is that the desired changes constituted severe demands on the key individuals involved.

One of the district managers used an analogy to explain to the researcher how difficult it was to make this transition: "This organizational switch-over that we are going through now is really tough. I can only make a rather earthy kind of comparison to give you an idea of how difficult it is. I think it is about like a woman who has lived with one man for thirty years suddenly becoming a widow and marrying a second husband. I think her adjustment in trying to live with that second husband and the difficulties that it must put her through is comparable to what we are going through."

Questions for Discussion

1. What three things constitute a rational organization? Give some examples that you have observed first hand, such as in an automobile dealership, a dentist's office, or a bank.

2. Suppose you were the director of Exxon Research Laboratories at Linden, New Jersey. You have about 500 Ph.D. chemists and engineers working in the laboratory. The president of the company requests that the laboratory develop a new gasoline that will not pollute the atmosphere as existing gasolines do. Which philosophy of organization design would you follow—the informal, the formal, or both? Give examples of how the organization would look to someone who came in to study it.

3. Suppose you were the superintendent of cable construction on a large bridge project to connect New York and New Jersey across the Hudson River, north of the George Washington Bridge. You have about 500 workers, including men with mechanical engineering degrees who are specialists in blueprint drawing and materials, experienced cable workmen, and experienced machine operators. Which philosophy of organization design would you follow—the informal, the formal, or both? Give examples of how the organization would look to someone who came in to observe it.

4. You have been made head librarian in a new college of business administration. The college will have 2400 students in five years. Make up a simplified example of your strategic plan, including the organization structure of the library.

5. Project management, as described in Chapter 7 and in the article by Stewart, involves both formal and informal organization. What formal arrangements does Stewart recommend, and why? What informal behavior patterns are recommended in the text chapter, and why?

6. Under what conditions would you design an organization structure which utilized formal staff specialists who "give orders" to lower line personnel, rather than act as teachers and consultants to them? Give an example of these conditions in real organizations.

7. Utilizing Barnard's theory of authority, explain why Swiss citizens traditionally obey most laws of their country to a greater extent than their counterparts just across the border in France (i.e., there are more frequent strikes against the French government, rebellions of French workers or farmers, etc.). Pay particular attention to the zone of indifference and the notions of inducements versus burdens-sacrifices.

8. It is often said that informal organization (day-to-day interaction of people with each other) is more powerful than formal organization. Is this true?

To examine this question factually, compare the formal plan of Food World supermarkets with the actual behavior of district manager 1 and district manager 3 (Lawrence reading). On a sheet of paper, arrange three columns. In the first, list the formal behavior plan under top management's decentralization concept. In the second column, describe how DM1 actually acted. In column three, repeat for DM3.

9. Ralph Cordiner states that the operating divisions of the company (e.g., the Hotpoint Division producing electric stoves, or the Television Division in Louisville) "can do better forecasting and budgeting" than the corporate headquarters. Using the two factors mentioned in the text chapter which cause people inside organizations to evolve decentralized structures, make up some illustrations from the electric stove business and the television business which prove *why* these G.E. divisions can perform the functions of forecasting and budgeting better.

10. Formal organization design includes a concept or philosophy about how an organization ought to operate, some rational steps to put the system into effect, some formal due-process procedures, and some kind of reward system to help insure that the design is followed in practice. Outline these steps as they occurred in the supermarket chain, Food World (Lawrence reading).

Short Cases for Discussion

Idlewild Hospital

Idlewild is a large hospital located in Detroit, Michigan. Over the years it has developed into an institution which specializes in three major areas of health care. Each is now a major department, headed by a full-time department head: (1) internal medicine (general medical practice), (2) heart surgery, and (3) bone surgery.

Two years ago, a committee of the board of trustees, working with the director, realized that long-range planning was needed to insure that expenditures for facilities, new equipment, and manpower were made so that the hospital could maintain excellence in all of its three chosen fields. The position of long-range planning coordinator was established, reporting to the director. It was stated in the job description that it was to be a staff position, the incumbent acting as an advisor and consultant to the three major department heads. They, in turn, were expected to perform a thorough analysis once each year which showed developments in society that might affect their departments, the strengths and weakness of their departments in light of these developments, and a strategic plan for any changes which should be made in their departments. Since conditions constantly change, it would be necessary to bring the plan up to date once a year, showing any changes in facilities, manpower, or equipment.

Two days before this year's presentation to the board, the head of Internal Medicine told the planning coordinator, "I must confess that the figures in this plan are not too meaningful. You and I have worked together enough that you know my situation. I have my hands full operating the department. We have thirty-eight doctors, and our workload is heavy. I must also keep my hand in with patients. Actually, the board wanted some figures and I pulled them together. They look good on paper, and that's what counts with the board. I doubt that we really will need the extra addition I propose to the hospital building, but I put it in because it is a possibility, and I have to have something to display in my presentation. Anyway, I just thought I'd let you know that the presentation to the board will be somewhat of a game or show we have to put on for them."

The coordinator was bothered by this conversation. He knew that the board had to decide where limited funds would be spent. He also knew that they would take the projections at face value. And he knew that funds badly needed by heart surgery would be cut so that internal medicine could have the building addition. He asked the head of internal medicine either to revise his figures, or frankly admit to the board that they were not ready yet. But the head insisted that "the show must go on."

The following day the coordinator met the director of the hospital in the cafeteria. The director said, "How are the departmental plans coming along? Will they all be in good shape by next week's meeting? Would you come over to my office this afternoon and tell me whether all departments are complying with our procedures?"

Questions

1. If you were the coordinator, what would you do in this situation if you wanted to make your position conform to the plan of organization originally visualized by the board and the director?
2. Think clearly about the characteristics of Idlewild Hospital's technology—its goals and the functions necessary to succeed in the Detroit society. Why might the coordinator want to serve as an informal staff integrator, rather than a formal staff planner himself? Why did the board and director envision this form of structure rather than a more formal one?
3. Be prepared to role play the coordinator. Role play 1: coordinator meets with the director. Role play 2: coordinator continues the conversation with the head of internal medicine.

Atlas Pharmaceutical Company

Atlas Pharmaceutical Company engages in the production and sale of proprietary drugs which may be sold over the counter without a prescription from a doctor. Employing 4000 people, the company produces 45 products, ranging from solutions for athlete's foot to anti-acid crystals for upset stomachs.

In recent years both the government and the public have demanded more strict attention to drug quality standards. The drug industry has experienced many instances when a particular drug was improperly manufactured (or improperly researched), sold, and subsequently caused illnesses or bad side-effects. The problem is complicated by the large volume of data which must be taken into account before a drug is released for sale. This falls into two categories: (1) technical research reports in pharmacology produced by medical schools; and (2) government regulations and reports on the legal and scientific standards which must be met.

One factory produces all Atlas products, and is organized by production processes. For example, powders and solids, liquids and emulsions, intravenous solutions, and the like. At present, both the sales department and the plant are required to keep abreast of the two kinds of information named above, and ensure that their operations are of a quality necessary to meet rigorous safety and health standards. The sales department has a four-man staff division which gathers information on products. It is the only department which can officially release a new product for sale. The plant staff section, which is responsible for quality, typically has been concerned with production specifications but has also looked into legal and consumer safety factors.

There occurred recently three instances which, in the words of the president, "were rather serious. We had to recall from all retailers a large quantity of Penthazone, a drug for the relief of an upset stomach. It caused slight increases in blood pressure. It could have been worse. Then another case simply involved legal registration—the government procedures for vitamin registration changed and nobody caught it. We didn't comply with red tape, and we were penalized by having to withdraw the drug from the market for six months until we did comply. That cost us $400,000 in profits.

"What I'm saying is that this business has become so complex that one department doesn't know what the other is doing, and each assumes that someone else is taking care of legal and technical safety. Furthermore, the cost to the company in prestige and reputation is a very serious matter.

"We have thought of pulling all personnel that are concerned with safety, now located in the sales and production divisions, into a central department of legal and quality control. We worry, though, about whether such a move is desirable, and if so, whether this staff department should have final authority over the operating divisions within sales and production."

Questions

1. What arguments might you advance to show the president of Atlas that a central department is needed?
2. Should the new quality control department operate primarily as an integrator unit, or as a formal decision-making and instruction-issuing unit? Explain and illustrate.

Chapter 8

Planning and Controlling

The structure of an organization, once selected or designed, is animated by the administrative practices of planning (goal setting), controlling, leading, and rewarding. In this chapter, we discuss planning and controlling. When the manager chooses goals and controls, he needs to choose those that support effective performance and lead to feelings of competence and achievement. Administrative practices might look satisfactory, even innocuous, from a technical, accounting, or information systems point of view. But organizations are not only technical, accounting, or information entities, they are *social* systems. So the manager needs to know how administrative practices affect motivation and behavior.

First, of course, the manager must identify the pattern of behavior which leads to effective performance. He may need salesmen more disposed to maintain contacts and friendly relations over the long term than to seek quick closing of many transactions. Having determined the behavior he wants and having tried to hire people whose motives lead them to act that way, the manager can consider the organizational climate in which his employees will work. Briefly, this refers to the subjective perceptions held by individuals of such objective organizational realities as structure, standards, leadership, and rules. What is important about climate is that it can arouse or suppress the motivational tendencies of individuals. Since administrative systems can foster good climate, they provide a key leverage point for management. The selection by Litwin and Stringer following this chapter is an extended discussion of organizational climate and its managerial implications.

In looking at alternative modes of planning and control, we are concerned with one central issue: How does each practice actually affect motivation, behavior, and organizational performance? Our aim is to select administrative inputs calculated to serve human and organizational requirements well.

Planning

Planning is the process of determining goals and how they are to be achieved. The differences in how managers conduct planning and related administrative processes are dramatic. Some approaches assume that goals are most effective when imposed from above and paired with threat, drawing on the influence process of fear, discussed in Chapter 3. Other approaches make directly opposing assumptions.

Directive Planning
The following is an example of the directive, threatening approach to goal setting. Richard Beeson, president of the beverage manufacturer, Canada Dry,

is describing what it is like to work for David Mahoney, chief executive at Norton Simon, Inc., which controls Canada Dry:

"'I had been on the job only a couple of weeks,' Beeson says, 'when we had a Canada Dry board meeting. I said to Mahoney, "Dave, we're a little bit below budget now, and I think we can hold that for the rest of the year. It won't get any worse."

'Dave looked at me, smiled, and said: "Be on budget by the six-month mark; be on by the year."

'"But Dave," I said, "there isn't enough time to get on by the *half*. I inherited this situation, after all."

'Still smiling, Dave looked at me and said: "Do I pay you a lot of money? Do I argue with you over what you want to spend? Do I bother you? Then don't tell me what the goals should be. Be on by the half; be on by the end of the year."

'"What if I can't, Dave?" I asked.

'"Then clean out your desk and go home."

"Beeson says he began running through the reasons why he couldn't meet the goals, but Mahoney said: 'Not interested. My board and my stockholders want me to make my numbers. The way I make my numbers is for you guys to make *your* numbers. Make your numbers!'" (*Forbes,* Feb. 25, 1972, p. 26).

The assumptions which support Mahoney's approach are interesting: goals are set by superiors, they are quantitative and inflexible (neither set nor modified by subordinates), and subordinates must meet them or face the organizational equivalent of capital punishment. Essentially the same assumptions and practices characterized the administration of the Soviet Union under Stalin during World War II. For example, during the siege of Leningrad, it was a common occurrence for quotas on everything from bread production to military advances to be set centrally and issued with the threat of death for any failure (Salisbury, 1969).

This sort of approach involves the callous willingness to arouse anxiety and harness to organizational purposes the need to reduce it. As Samuel Johnson once suggested, "Depend upon it, sir, when a man knows he is to be hanged in a fortnight, it concentrates his mind wonderfully." Formal education makes use of the same assumption, with its reliance upon periodic anxiety-fostering rituals called examinations. Whether they motivate you to study and learn in order to obtain the associated rewards (grades) or avoid hanging (bad grades) is best answered by reflection upon your own behavior in such circumstances. Most of us are responsive to the method.

Of course, planning and goal setting need not be performed only by superiors. Nor must goals or standards be paired with threat. Despite the facts that Beeson made the numbers and kept his job as president of Canada Dry, the Russians successfully defended Leningrad, and many of us do pass those stress-making examinations, there is no evidence that the directive, threatening method is the best for bottling soft drinks, for fighting wars, or for learning.

On the contrary, there is substantial evidence that, given clear-cut goals, too much motivation impairs performance. What happens is that people concentrate too narrowly upon the goal and ignore cues in the environment which might also help performance. There is even more evidence that stress-producing threats which create intense anxiety detract from performance (Vroom, 1964, pp. 204–209).

Supportive Planning

In sharp contrast to imposing goals from above and pairing them with threat is the supportive approach to planning described by McGregor (1960). He believed that "Genuine commitment is seldom achieved when objectives are externally imposed. Passive acceptance is the most that can be expected; indifference or resistance are the more likely consequences. Some degree of *mutual* involvement in the determination of objectives is a necessary aspect of managerial planning" (p. 868).

This approach to planning follows logically from the Theory Y view of human nature described by McGregor in a selection following Chapter 3. He stresses the importance of mutual discussion of goals between superior and subordinate. The superior is to interest himself in "helping the subordinate plan his own job in such a fashion that both personal and organizational goals will be achieved." Only then, McGregor reasons, will performance and satisfaction of higher level needs be served well.

Instead of fostering anxiety and using the human need to reduce it, a Theory Y approach creates a climate in which subordinates are provided with arousal cues for achievement, affiliation, power, and esteem. They are encouraged to set goals, to take calculated risks, to speak freely with superiors, to influence them, and to measure and adjust their own progress. Goals are not seen as inflexible, and the prospect of punishment is not salient.

The idea of quotas imposed and enforced from above is anathema to the democratic tendency to favor participation and self-control. Moreover, the faith is common and strong that motivation and hence performance can be better encouraged if the manager allows subordinates to share in the planning process. Jointly determined objectives, it is held, will lead to better results. But what is the evidence to support either approach—imposing quotas on subordinates or allowing them some say in goal setting?

Comparative Evidence

Studies by Locke and his associates (see references under Locke) show that in a series of laboratory experiments, subjects produced more when they set specific goals than when they were urged to "do your best." Also, the goals they set were always higher than the levels of performance they had achieved in prior practice efforts. The existence of clear-cut goals is thus associated with improved performance—a point which sales and production managers and other executives like Dave Mahoney of Norton Simon, Inc., intuitively recognize and use.

Goals are important. They specify intentions and standards. They direct the eye to targets. When subordinates set them, they tend to perform better. Still, the Locke studies do not show what would have happened to performance if superiors had set the goals.

Another study by Meyer et al. (1965) did compare a traditional superior-oriented performance appraisal system with a mutual goal-setting approach. In the latter condition, the emphasis was on mutual problem solving, not on rating performance or linking performance to pay. The study did *not* show that participative goal setting was superior to directive goal setting. Instead it showed that setting specific performance goals was the important factor. The existence of specific goals was associated with better performance; a particular means of setting goals was not.

Upon reviewing these studies and other related research, Campbell et al. (1970) conclude that prolonged discussions between superior and subordinates to set goals and explore means of arriving at them may not be more motivating, but *they may help the subordinate develop a much clearer idea of what he is supposed to do.* "Given two individuals with an equal desire to expend effort, the individual with the greater specific knowledge concerning the nature of the organization's goals and their priorities should perform at a higher level" (pp. 377–378). In other words, goal setting can have both cognitive and motivational effects, but a participative approach to planning may conceivably have more impact upon cognition than upon motivation. Nevertheless, the motive arousal potential of goals and goal setting is a strategic opportunity for powerful influence, one which the astute manager would not overlook.

Motivational Effects

Setting challenging goals in situations calling for personal responsibility for results can be especially stimulating to individuals high in *n* Achievement. As we explained in Chapter 1, persons high in *n* Achievement like to take personal responsibility for solving problems and accomplishing results, tend to set moderate (challenging, but not unrealistic) goals, and want feedback on performance.

Accordingly, it is possible to specify the characteristics of goals calculated to signal achievement opportunities. On the basis of research studies by Litwin and Stringer (1968), Stringer (1966) proposes the following:

1. *"Achievement motivation will tend to be aroused if the goals of the responsibility center are made explicit"* (p. 5). (If standards are explicit it should be easier for individuals to adopt them as their own internal standards of excellence.)
2. *"Achievement motivation will tend to be aroused if goals represent a moderate degree of risk for the individuals involved"* (p. 15).

The research findings of Hofstede (1968) on the motivational effects of budgeting (a means of goal setting) provide support for these ideas. Hofstede reports that where there is a realistically challenging budget and where it has been prepared with the financial staff taking a rather supportive role, the requirement of performance against budget standards often elicits the achievement motive and stimulates effective effort. Apparently, where budgeting can be accomplished to fit the needs of persons high in *n* Achievement for setting realistic goals and obtaining clear feedback on performance, the budget can be most helpful. Thus, from the point of view of the budgeted individual with certain personality characteristics, budgeting can be highly motivating if seen as a kind of achievement game. Hofstede, in a selection following this chapter, offers research-based, practical advice on how to maximize the achievement arousal effects of budgeting.

Setting realistic, challenging goals and obtaining performance feedback can do more than help release the propensity to achieve in persons strongly pre-disposed to achieve. The same techniques have the added virtue of enhancing the probability that those with milder needs to achieve will also be stimulated by what is plainly an achievement-oriented climate. Assuming that it makes sense to encourage the belief that achievement on the job leads to desirable ends, the whole process of planning and goal setting can be a rich source of signals to support that belief.

Achievement-oriented behavior seems important for those organizational tasks whose successful performance calls for taking personal responsibility for goals and using feedback realistically. So we have stressed the capacity of the planning process to arouse n Achievement. But, as you remember, in Chapter 1 we pointed out that the behavior which expresses n Achievement is task-oriented, not people-oriented. Since work in organizations involves interpersonal behavior, indeed depends absolutely upon it, the manager needs also to be concerned with the effects of administrative practices upon interpersonal behavior.

It is possible that too much administrative concern with individual goals and individual payoffs can provide an administrative context in which there is inadequate incentive to cooperate. University professors can be made so responsive to rewards for individual scholarship, e.g., winning grants and publishing, that they neither cooperate with one another to resolve problems of educational policy nor cooperate with students to facilitate learning. There are many reports of kindred phenomena in public and industrial organizations. For example, interviewers in a state employment office hid job openings from one another and hoarded them, so each alone would get credit for placement (Blau, 1963). The accounting office in a factory needed extra help for a special project beyond its capability, but people in other departments declined to help because there appeared to be nothing to gain by leaving their own work to help the accounting staff (Gross, 1953, p. 369). Everyone might be so busy "making his numbers" that needed cooperation is neglected.

The remedy for these problems lies in providing administrative reinforcements for necessary cooperation. Separate goals can divide groups; overriding goals pull them together, as we will see in Chapter 11. Cooperation can be fostered by nurturing the expectancy that it is a necessary part of the effort which leads to reward. In short, rewarding cooperation makes it known that rewards depend on cooperation.

Similarly, if the effective exercise of influence and persuasion is instrumental in successful task performance (as it must be in countless jobs where departmental interdependencies are complex and authority relationships ambiguous), then administrative practices must be geared to support these n-Power-based interpersonal behaviors. Goals must encourage efforts toward exerting influence over others in the organization where work progress can be aided by such influence. Bold negotiating efforts can be reinforced when they lead to desired organizational results.

Dangers of Oversimplification

Making goals especially salient in the organizational climate can lead to problems as well as to benefits. If the overall organizational goals are not well chosen, they can misdirect. Drucker (1954), for example, explained the dangers of a simplistic emphasis upon the goal of profit maximization in business enterprises:

"To emphasize only profit, for instance, misdirects managers to the point where they may endanger the survival of the business. To obtain profit today they tend to undermine the future. They may push the most easily saleable product lines and slight those that are the market of tomorow. They tend to short-change research, promotion, and the other postponable investments. Above all, they shy away from any capital expenditure that may increase the invested-capital base against which profits are measured; and the result is dangerous obsolescence of equipment. In other words, they are directed into the worst practices of management" (p. 62).

What is actually needed is a set of multiple objectives subject to revision as circumstances change. According to Drucker, the objectives need to be established for every area where performance critically affects the survival and prosperity of the organization. For a business firm, they include market standing, innovation, productivity, physical and financial resources, profitability, manager performance and development, worker performance and attitude, and public responsibility. Some of these goals deal with end results (market standing and profitability) and some of them deal with processes (innovation and manager performance and development) which contribute to those results. It is easy to see how these goals might conflict or have different priorities, some immediate and some deferrable. One of the contributions of a carefully wrought set of process and results objectives, and procedures for reviewing them, is to keep the questions of resource allocation and the conflicts of values salient and perennially, or at least periodically, up for reassessment.

Management by Objectives

One popular approach to goal setting and control, known as management by objectives (MBO), seeks to contain any tendency to overemphasize process at the expense of results. Instead of emphasizing compliance by devising controls which stress procedures and methods, MBO seeks to orient administration to results. Subordinates are encouraged to set their own goals and to assess their own performance, and stimulated to expect payoffs for results, not for process compliance. As you might expect, however, if the emphasis shifts too much and process compliance is neglected, impressive results may be obtained for a time until neglected processes bring the system to a halt. But MBO systems seek to avoid such neglect, and encourage goals and performance which provide balanced emphasis on both process and results (Odiorne, 1965; Hughes, 1965; Drucker, 1964b).

MBO can also help overcome another problem in organizations, particularly in those characterized by decentralized but highly goal-oriented operations. If goals set by individual units are not articulated, or integrated into more general goals, the accomplishments of individual units will not lead to organizational effectiveness. Where MBO is an overall company program, administered by top management, but participated in by lower level managers, the chances of interweaving subgoals and major goals into logically related objectives are increased. A selected reading at the end of the chapter by Levinson expands upon the practice of MBO. Levinson identifies some weaknesses and proposes means of making MBO more effective.

Program Management

Since plans and goals direct the eye to targets, MBO or any other approach to management which increases the salience of plans and goals can be a powerful leverage point for administrative influence. For example, suppose a manager must work with a firmly entrenched functional organization structure, yet he recognizes that effective overall performance of the organization's task would be better served by orienting managers (and others) less toward their department and more toward units of activity fitted into an overall program. Whether the organization is producing MBA's, food products, missiles, or patient services, it is possible to develop and superimpose program-oriented plans and goals over existing departmental structures.

The term "program management" has roots in the U.S. Department of Defense, and is usually associated with the innovations of its former secretary, Robert McNamara, and his colleagues, such as Charles Hitch, now president of the University of California. Program management is largely synonymous with project management, and is frequently associated with matrix organization structures. Its central characteristic is that it is an administrative system combining planning and control techniques to guide and coordinate all of the activities which contribute to one overall program or project. It has been used by the federal government to manage space exploration, weapons acquisition, and other programs involving many contributing organizations. It is also used by state and local governments and by individual firms to provide administrative integration of inputs from several sources, be they individuals, departments, or whole firms.

Some of the specific administrative techniques for program management include Program Evaluation Review Technique (PERT) and Program Planning and Budgeting (PPB). PERT begins with the compilation of a list of all the activities needed to accomplish an overall task. The next step consists of arranging these activities in a sequential network which depicts how much time it is estimated that each activity will take and which activities must be completed before others can begin. Actual progress can later be compared to the network. One of the possible psychological effects of PERT is to shift the cognitive and emotional orientation of managers away from differentiated departmental patterns to an integrated concept of the program into which their particular contributions must fit. These effects are not necessarily realized, however, unless the strength of the administrative forces pointing toward a program orientation are powerful enough to offset those which say, "Meet the department's standards even if they conflict with the program's, and you shall rise in this organization."

PPB begins with a similar identification of activities in a program across the whole set of departments involved. As a means of illustrating this idea, C. West Churchman (1968) drafted a matrix (Exhibit 8-1) which shows how various activities having to do with combating alcoholism are distributed among various departments in a state government.

Hours and/or dollars represented in each cell of the matrix where activity occurs can be estimated and summed in both directions. Thus, it is possible to find out how much, say, the Department of Motor Vehicles is spending on activities to combat alcoholism, and how much the activity of rehabilitation is costing all of the departments involved.

When it comes time to make up budgets, department heads can be brought together, perhaps by an integrator (e.g., the Alcoholism Program Manager) and the allocation of funds argued in terms of the mission and its accomplishment. Funding the mission or program can be made a special focus and not left to

Exhibit 8-1   PPB Matrix

Agency	Prevention	Educational	Legal	Economic	Remedial Activities	Detection	Screening & Evaluation	Treatment	Rehabilitation	Custody	Control	Medical	Economic	Legal	Social	Research	Support
Correction					X	X	X	X	X	X	X			X		X	X
Mental Hygiene					X	X	X	X	X								X
Social Welfare							X					X	X	X	X		X
Alcoholic Bev. Control	X	X	X	X							X	X	X				
Youth Authority	X	X			X	X	X	X	X	X	X			X			X
Public Health	X	X			X	X	X	X	X		X					X	X
Highway Patrol	X	X									X			X		X	X
TB Sanitaria Subvention						X	X		X	X	X	X					
Motor Vehicles											X			X			
Rehabilitation						X	X		X								X
Board of Equalization												X		X	X		
Alcoholic Bev. Cont. Appeals												X		X			
Education	X	X															X
Total	X	X	X	X	X	X	X	X	X	X	X	X	X	X	X	X	X

Source: C. West Churchman, *The Systems Approach,* Dell, 1968, p. 89.

somehow emerge from various, perhaps insufficiently integrated, departments. Requests for funds can be put to a cost-benefit analysis. Where funds are controlled by the program, the department managers will need to show contributions to the program to secure funds.

Program planning and budgeting is no panacea, but it can be employed to orient cognition and motivation to tasks and results. It and kindred activities like PERT can encourage setting goals, taking moderate risks, and utilizing feedback from a perspective which transcends a departmental one. It aligns administrative direction and payoffs to mission goals.

By the same token, planning, budgeting, and scheduling can be closely fitted to the structure of departments where differentiation rather than integration is to be emphasized. For example, in a department store where little or no interdependence exists between major departments, such as hardware and women's apparel, there would be little call for integrated transdepartmental program planning. Instead, administrative emphasis could be given to departmental orientations.

In either case, goals expressed in budgets, schedules, or standards can be a critical determinant of organizational behavior. But their capacity to motivate behavior also depends on their relationships to other administrative practices. Only when the associated controls support goal-achieving behavior is effective motivation likely to occur. Accordingly, we need to explore this related area of administration.

Standing Plans: Policies and Rules

Controls bear an intimate relationship to goals. Broadly conceived, controls include rules, regulations, policies, procedures, as well as schemes of measurement and evaluation to assure compliance and to reflect progress relative to goals or standards. Whether establishing and administering controls is more or less important than other managerial activities is a moot point, but to some observers of organizational behavior (Blau and Scott, 1962), "It appears that management's primary significance is no longer at the apex of the authority pyramid; rather its central function is to design, in collaboration with a staff of experts, appropriate impersonal mechanisms of control" (p. 185).

In its early days, a business may be quite successful by depending almost entirely on objectives, with few policies, procedures, or controls. Eventually, however, controls are necessary, and they do develop. The Xerox Company (*Newsweek*, 1965) is an example.

Xerox has been one of the most impressive organizations in American business. Between 1954 and 1964 the old family-dominated Haloid Company, manufacturing specialized photographic products, transformed itself into the modern Xerox Company—and jumped from 30 to over 300 million dollars a year in sales. In 1959 the company was chaotic. Offices were located all over Rochester, N.Y., over delicatessens and in abandoned schools. Job descriptions were few, policies broad, procedures ignored, and controls weak. Yet the company was successful. And it was successful because of top management's ability to point out direction. Chairman Sol Linowitz and President Joseph Wilson saw their roles as the laying down of objectives—long, intermediate, and short range. Wilson spent much of his time selling the Xerox Company to his own managers, describing the revolutionary and beneficial impact of its information technology on society—and also pointing out how each manager's own interest would be served if the company advanced. Given the fantastic expansion, he was aware that it would be impossible to control the entire company from the president's office. In order to take advantage of a divergent market and to exploit their technologically superior product, it was essential that managers at all levels be committed to manufacturing the product and getting it out to the market as quickly as possible. Premature policies, procedures, and controls would have interfered with the spontaneous cooperation and initiative demonstrated by Xerox management.

Nonetheless, standing plans and controls did emerge in the Xerox Company—and for good reason. First of all, why go on reinventing the wheel? Why must a company handle every problem as unique? Sam Jones wonders how Gil Smith has handled the problem of quality control on his gears. He asks about it. Gil's answer seems reasonable, and rather than search for new alternatives, Sam adopts Gil's procedure. Or Mike Stratton has had great success in handling rush orders within his production area. How does he do it? Some questioning will disclose his methods. Why not let everyone know about it? So an information memo is drafted and distributed. The basis for standing plans and procedures, then, rests upon an awareness of the usefulness of past experience. There is no reason why one should repeat the same mistakes over and over again without taking advantage of the accumulated knowledge of people in the organization. The famous words, in another context, of Oliver Wendell Holmes apply: "Three generations of idiots are enough!" The company decides to make some rules that trade upon experience and give guidance to people facing similar problems for the first time.

So in the beginning, procedures and policies are developed from the organization's own experience. After a while, however, management may feel that they should take advantage of experience outside the company as well. Experts can provide this knowledge, and so specialists, advisers, auditors, and controllers are hired. Once they are hired, there is a natural tendency for management to see that they are used, by giving them some authority to impose their experience on the rest of the organization.

At Xerox, the expansion of staff activities in the development of job descriptions, policies, and procedures was given impetus when management became concerned about internal efficiency. When their product is clearly superior and the market is fertile, management's main concern is getting the product made and out the door. Internal costs and efficiencies are of minor importance when production cost is a relatively small percentage of the selling or rental price. Xerox's main problem in the late fifties and early sixties was to get the jump on the competition and to put its machines into offices all over the world. Competition has developed, however, and although the price factor is apparently not critical yet, there has been increased concern within Xerox about manufacturing costs. Such concern inevitably means rationalization of production operations: rationalization means finding out what the best methods are, applying them throughout the organization, and seeing that people adhere to them—just as Taylor suggested many years ago.

A Xerox research and development engineer has indicated how such elaboration of procedures affected him. When he had an idea that required funds in 1959, he would walk into the office of the vice president with a scratch pad and pencil, sit down, and sketch out the idea. A decision would be made quickly, and the researcher would go to work. In 1967, however, the same researcher must complete, in multiple copies, a prescribed project form indicating potential equipment cost, material requirements, potential return, cash flow, etc. This is not simply red tape; multiple forms are not required just to complicate the lives of people in the organization. The decisions that have to be made about fund allocation are much more complex than they were in a simpler day. More and different projects are involved; they must be compared with one another on some consistent basis; and priority decisions have to be made about organizational objectives. Specific procedures for allocating capital funds facilitate comparison, prediction, and control—essential functions of management in any organization.

This development of job descriptions, policies, and procedures aids efficiency by promoting coordination and predictability. However fine the initiative of Xerox managers had been in the expansion stage, it was stressful and unstable. For a while, people will put up with instability, but order, regularity, and predictability become essential in the long run—especially if the rate of growth and promotional opportunities start to decline. Nor do managers necessarily dislike the development of standing plans and controls. Order is brought out of chaos and predictability out of instability, and simple relief from making the same mistakes over and over again is achieved. Indeed, many managers perceive the development of control procedures as progress.

Dysfunctional Consequences of Standing Plans and Controls

However inevitable and necessary the development of standing plans and controls, equally inevitable is the development of problems with those plans and controls. One of the so-called management principles of long repute has been the rule that delegated duties should be explicit and specific—with no gaps or overlaps. If this is true, and if standing plans are inclusive, theoretically each manager need only follow directions. No initiative is required.

Of course, we have described an impossible condition. Such perfect planning, delegating, and controlling is impossible. Therefore, spontaneity is essential. To a greater or lesser degree, every manager must fill in the gaps, work out the conflicts resulting from overlaps, and exercise discretion in following standing plans. If standing plans are followed blindly, the organization loses direction. There is an inversion of means and ends. To some people, following rules, plans, and controls becomes an end in itself, without a thought to whether or not they contribute to the organization's objectives. Indeed, in the eyes of many, such inversion of means and ends is almost synonymous with bureaucracy in an organization. Frequently, we assume such distortion to characterize governments and other public, nonprofit institutions. The comments of John Knowles, former Director of Massachusetts General Hospital, are illustrative: "In the teaching hospital, it has become set that the patient exists for the teaching programs, and not that the hospital exists for the patient" (De Hartog, 1966).

Such inversion of means and ends, however, also occurs in business. An advertisement in a prominent management journal once showed a hand holding a fancy notebook entitled "Policy Manual" over a wire-basket incinerator in which several similar notebooks were burning. Who was the advertiser? A management consulting firm. Its message? That one should not allow standing plans, policies, procedures, and controls to exist unchanged for too long, because they get out of date and hinder the organization instead of helping—better to burn them (and call in the consultant to write a new set).

Once established and accepted, standing plans and controls tend to limit flexibility and initiative. In the beginning, at least, standing plans are usually good, and an organization gains in coordination and predictability what it may lose in initiative. Nonetheless, it is difficult to keep policies, procedures, and controls up to date: policies no longer apply to new conditions; controls measure irrelevant factors; and those rational plans and controls which were developed to promote effectiveness begin to interfere with the accomplishment of objectives. If managers blindly follow these rules, spontaneity is lost.

Spontaneity may be maintained but direction still lost if control standards are misplaced or overly tight. In this case, managers develop elaborate devices for adapting to controls by meeting the standards on paper but not necessarily in ways that contribute to organizational effectiveness. Therefore, overly restrictive control systems are one of the gravest threats to organizational initiative. People will try to meet the numbers they are measured by. If they cannot meet these numbers by accepted and desirable behavioral patterns, undesirable patterns will be attempted.

In a pioneering study, Argyris (1957) examined the impact of budget controls on those being controlled. He gave repeated examples of short-run compliance with control standards that in either the short run or the long run had adverse cost consequences to the organization. He reported instances of people who worked under fixed quotas of output with some opportunity to select items to be worked on, choosing easy, rapidly completed jobs as fillers toward the end of a period in order to meet the quota. Blau (1963) reports similar behavior among law enforcement officials who maintain an established case load and who pick easy or fast cases toward the end of each month if they anticipate falling short of their quotas. Jasinski (1956) describes a similar adaptation in assembly-line production of foremen "bleeding the line" by stuffing all work in progress through the measuring point (using augmented crews) in order to meet a quota, but losing efficiency in the succeeding period until the line is refilled with work in progress.

Deliberate evasion is also a response. Jasinski describes "making out with the pencil" as a means of giving the appearance on paper of meeting expected standards without actually doing so. Dalton (1955) reports a comparable instance of evasion where local plant officials through blandishment of, and subsequent conspiracy with, the central office representative were able to evade cost-control checks imposed by the central office.

Such managerial adaptation to controls is not culture-bound. Granick (1960) points out that monetary rewards and glory attend the Soviet plant manager who sets a new production record. There is pressure to set a record at the expense of operating repairs and preventive maintenance. The result is lower output in the subsequent period while the delayed maintenance is attended to—or its effects are felt in breakdowns. Meanwhile, the manager has received his payoff for the over-quota output of the earlier period. In addition, Berliner (1956) and Richman (1965) note the practice in Soviet industry of "storming" production to meet output standards toward the end of a quota period, again at the expense of maintenance and balanced output.

Obviously there is a strong tendency to meet formal performance criteria, even if high but hidden costs are generated in so doing. It also seems highly probable that the severity of penalties for failure generates a proportional adaptive effort to show compliance, regardless of the other costs involved.

In all these examples, managers exercise spontaneous initiative to overcome control systems imposed on them. Perhaps even more dangerous for the organization is the disappearance of spontaneity. After a while, under restrictive control systems, some managers do not care if mistakes are avoided. If they feel that punishment awaits an unsuccessful departure from procedure, they may do what the book requires—and only that. No spontaneity will be demonstrated, and apathy will prevail.

Measuring and Evaluating Performance

As either a complement or an alternative to policies and rules, measurements can be another important means of influencing employees. The very act of measuring influences the behavior of the people being measured. When superiors measure subordinates' performance, they trigger a chain of cognitive and motivational effects. Subordinates tend to interpret the measurements as defining important aspects of the job. They respond by trying to make the measurements register at a level which will be rewarded.

Blau's (1963) classic study of a state employment agency, to which we have already referred, provides a useful example. Blau observed that the introduction of a set of statistical measurements of performance which counted referrals and placements as well as number of interviews (the latter was the only aspect of performance previously counted), resulted in increased referrals and placements. The purpose of introducing the new controls had not been to increase productivity, but that was the result, nonetheless. In effect, the new controls appeared to the interviewers to value productivity, i.e., placements. The measurements had another latent effect: they reduced discrimination against black clients better than any established rules prohibiting discrimination. As it happened, black applicants whose unemployment compensation had been exhausted were in abundant supply and were more eager to accept the low-paying jobs available than were white clients, a greater percentage of whom were still receiving unemployment benefits. Placing black clients, whatever the prejudices of the white employment office staff, apparently came to be regarded as a means of increasing productivity.

Cognitive Dissonance

One way of interpreting the behavior of the employment interviewers is to look at it in terms of the concept of cognitive dissonance (Chapter 1). From this perspective, an interviewer who believed that he ought to increase placements if he wanted to look good might be under the strain of dissonance. To reduce that strain he might logically try harder to place his clients.

What the interpretation suggests is that when controls provide performance feedback with respect to known goals, they can harness the motive power of cognitive dissonance. The employee who sees his performance as below standard, especially below a standard he himself has set, may feel a strong desire to improve his performance. If he believes it possible and wants the apparent reward, he is likely to try. Under less optimistic circumstances, of course, he might be discouraged and rationalize giving less effort.

Anxiety Reduction

Another possibility, one we have already suggested, is that measurement and evaluation of performance with respect to known standards can harness the power of the need to reduce anxiety. In Chapter 1 we discussed the motivational theory which holds that one learns to chart a course in life by the anxiety gradient, learning to do what reduces anxiety. In organizations, the policies, the goals, the rules, and the leader's preferences all specify expectations. Within limits, the more clearly the job performance expectations are specified (as in mechanistic or bureaucratic systems as opposed to organic systems) the easier it is to learn what to do to reduce anxiety. The controls will tell you if you are "making the numbers." If you are not, and especially if the boss has told you to "clean out your desk and go home" if you cannot make the numbers, it is not difficult to know what you must try to do if you wish to feel less anxious.

Need for Achievement

Of course, the atmosphere need not be so tense, nor is it necessary that controls only be linked to the avoidance of noxious states like dissonance and anxiety to be motivating. There are positive states such as achievement satisfaction to be cued by controls. As we explained earlier, one characteristic of the person high in *n* Achievement is that he wants concrete feedback on his performance, and uses it to adjust his behavior realistically. Based upon the Litwin and Stringer studies, Stringer (1966) proposes the following ideas to help signal achievement opportunities through controls and through their links with goal-setting:

1. *"A higher level of achievement motivation will tend to be aroused if provision is made in the management control process for adjusting specific goals when the chances of goal accomplishment change significantly (from the 50-50 level)"* (p. 14). (Remember, it is calculated, moderate risks that stimulate the achiever. If circumstances change to make the original goal unrealistic, the controls should adjust it so it is within range, yet still challenging.)

2. *"Achievement motivation will tend to be aroused if managers are evaluated in terms of their goal-setting behavior"* (p. 15). (The idea is to offer encouragement and support for setting ambitious but reasonable goals as distinct from unchallenging or unrealistic goals.)

3. *"Achievement motivation will tend to be aroused if individuals are given feedback of the progress they are making toward their goals"* (p. 15).

Unfortunately, there are risks as well as benefits involved in providing feedback on performance. Continually or periodically letting everyone know exactly where he stands may not be all that it is cracked up to be. Stedry (1960) and Caplan (1971), for example, have pointed out that budgeting practices which feed back and compare actual performance to budgeted performance produce mixed reactions. The news that actual performance compares unfavorably with budgeted performance—particularly over a prolonged period—may be very discouraging. The result can be that feedback depresses rather than arouses hopes of success.

The feedback which motivates one man positively can motivate another negatively. Therefore, the manager needs to develop some appraisal of the motivational characteristics of his subordinates and, insofar as is practicable, tailor the use of feedback to fit the individual. If he does not intervene and interpret impersonal feedback, he may fail to support those who need his help in withstanding discouragement. Similarly, he needs to intervene and interpret in some situations to prevent some individuals from resting on their laurels.

Redirecting Behavior

Measurements and evaluations can have other effects upon behavior and performance quite apart from their ability to raise or lower positive motivation. Controls can specify the direction in which effort is to be expended without changing the amount of effort expended. Experimental and field studies by Churchill and Cooper (1964) show that audits *per se* change the behavior of the persons audited. Generally, those whose work was audited tended to shift their behavior to conform to the auditor's criteria. They assumed that the auditor's criteria reflected certain organizational standards or goals. On the other hand, while some individuals led to anticipate an audit significantly decreased the errors they made, others made more errors.

The General Electric Company came up with an innovative system for avoiding the dysfunctional effects of audits. GE established a group of traveling auditors, who turned over the results of their annual audits to the heads of the profit-center divisions, rather than sending them in to headquarters. Thus, the audits were perceived as necessary operating information, rather than as possible ammunition for headquarters to use against the division head.

There is little doubt that controls affect behavior. The problem is to predict and shape those effects; otherwise controls make little contribution to control. As Drucker (1964a) reminds us, "In the grammar of social institutions the word 'controls' is not the plural of the word 'control'" (p. 186). More controls may yield a loss of control unless they contribute to the arousal of motivated, goal-directed behavior. If quantities measured are not to defeat qualities valued, managers must choose wisely what they will count and what feedback they will provide.

Management Systems and the Human Organization

One advocate of establishing new controls to replace those that misdirect employees and misinform managers is Likert (1967). He thinks of the organization as a system comprising three types of variables. *Causal* variables include the factors that managers shape and alter—such things as organization structure, controls, policies, and leadership behavior. *Intervening* variables include the attitudes, motivations, and perceptions of all of the workers. *End-result* variables include measures of organizational performance, such as productivity, costs, and earnings.

Most companies measure and evaluate end results. Company controls provide plenty of information on these variables. But most control systems pay little heed to the intervening variables. Consequently, managers manipulate the causal variables in response to information on end results only, not on the intervening factors which influence those end results.

Because of this information gap, Likert believes managers take actions which harm the human organization. They cut costs in response to a drop in earnings, for example. This shows a short-run improvement in earnings. But the long-run damage to attitudes and motivation is never measured. Nor is a measure taken of the long-term negative impact on earnings of the damage done to intervening variables by cost cutting.

Likert has devised new measurements which depict the systems state of an organization over time. The questionnaire which Likert has developed measures a core of items covering both causal and intervening variables. The questionnaire data graphically portray what Likert calls the "management system"—the cluster of factors including structure, controls, policies, and leadership behavior, plus the attitudes, motivations, and perceptions of organization members. End-result performance variables—productivity, costs, earnings—are also measured.

Out of the large number of studies already conducted along these lines by the Institute for Social Research under Likert's direction has come the identification of four types of management systems:

System 1, Exploitive-Authoritative
System 2, Benevolent-Authoritative
System 3, Consultative
System 4, Participative Group

The gist of Likert's thesis is that particular management systems are consistently associated with certain patterns of performance results over time. He expressed the idea cautiously in a technical article (1969): "The available and growing evidence justifies the view that further research very probably will demonstrate strong and consistent relationships among the causal, intervening, and end-result variables: that *certain leadership styles and management systems consistently will be found more highly motivating and yielding better organizational performance than others*" (p. 591; our italics). Specifically, System 4 appears to be consistently associated with more effective performance, and System 1 with less effective performance.

Studies of individual companies over several years show that as the management system shifts from a lower to a higher number, performance of the organization improves. Changes in the causal and intervening variables precede changes in the end-result variables. The time lag appears to vary according to organizational size, type of work, and organizational complexity. The larger or the more complex organization has a greater time lag.

Another important idea in the Likert scheme is that in tabulating the financial performance records of any firm, measures should be taken of such hitherto uncounted assets as the firm's human organization, its customer loyalty, its shareholder loyalty, its supplier loyalty, its reputation among the financial community, and its reputation in the community in which it has plants and offices. Some rough methods are in use for estimating the value of the firm's human organization (Brummett et al., 1969). They usually yield a value of three to five times payroll or fifteen to twenty times earnings. There is, in Likert's (1969) view, great need for a more comprehensive kind of accounting than we have now, because, "When all forms of human resources are ignored in a firm's accounting reports, as at present, the stated earnings can show a favorable picture for several years when the actual assets and true value are steadily *decreasing* by a substantial fraction" (p. 588). A selected reading at the end of the chapter discusses Likert's ideas further.

Summary

What may generally be termed the planning and controlling processes in organizations can be looked at in two ways. They might be considered impersonal, technical, information-gathering activities with no behavioral consequences. Or they might be viewed with an eye to their effects upon job-oriented behavior.

When examined for their behavioral implications, plans and controls tell a great deal about how the manager can make his influence effective. Planning or goal setting can be rich with cues which encourage taking personal responsibility for results, taking moderate risks, and other characteristic achievement-oriented behavior. Measurement and evaluation techniques can supplement these elements of organizational climate with feedback on performance—also likely to encourage task achievement. Where affiliation or power-oriented behavior is desired, plans and controls can be designed which cue collaborative behavior. Goals and evaluations can stress cooperative behavior. They can also stress exerting influence.

Devices such as management by objectives, program planning, and measurement of the management system and the human organization all have important behavioral consequences. They signal that certain behaviors are valued. They deemphasize others.

With skillful movement of the levers marked plans and controls, the manager can move the organization.

References

Argyris, C. *Personality and Organization.* Harper, 1957.

Berliner, J. S. "A Problem in Soviet Business Administration." *Administrative Science Quarterly,* Vol. 1 (June 1956), 87–101.

Blau, P. M. *The Dynamics of Bureaucracy.* University of Chicago Press, 1963.

——— and W. R. Scott. *Formal Organizations: A Comparative Approach.* Chandler, 1962.

Brummett, R. L., W. C. Pyle, and E. C. Flamholtz. "Human Resource Accounting in Industry." *Personnel Administration,* Vol. 32, No. 4 (July–August 1969), 34–46.

Campbell, J. P., M. D. Dunnette, E. E. Lawler III, and K. E. Weick, Jr. *Managerial Behavior, Performance, and Effectiveness.* McGraw-Hill, 1970.

Caplan, E. H. *Management Accounting and Behavioral Science.* Addison-Wesley, 1971.

Churchill, N. C., and W. W. Cooper. "Effects of Auditing Records: Individual Task Accomplishment and Organization Objectives." In *New Perspectives in Organization Research,* ed. W. W. Cooper, H. J. Leavitt, and M. W. Shelly II. Wiley, 1964.

Churchman, C. W. *The Systems Approach.* Dell, 1968.

Dalton, M. "Managing the Managers." *Human Organization,* Vol. 14 (Fall 1955), 4–10.

De Hartog, J. "What Money Cannot Buy." *Atlantic Monthly,* Vol. 218 (July 1966), 113.

Drucker, P. R. "Controls, Control, and Management." In *Management Controls: New Directions in Basic Research,* ed. Bonini, Jaedicke, and Wagner. McGraw-Hill, 1964a, pp. 286–296.

———. *Managing for Results.* Harper, 1964b.

———. *The Practice of Management.* Harper, 1954.

Granick, D. *The Red Executive.* Doubleday, 1960.

Gross, E. "Some Functional Consequences of Primary Controls in Formal Work Organizations." *American Sociological Review,* Vol. 18, No. 4 (August 1953), 368–373.

Hofstede, G. H. *The Game of Budget Control.* Tavistock, 1968.

Hughes, C. L. *Goal Setting: Key to Individual and Organizational Effectiveness.* American Management Association, 1965.

Jasinski, F. "Use and Misuse of Efficiency Controls." *Harvard Business Review,* Vol. 34, No. 4 (July–August 1956), 105–112.

Likert, R. *The Human Organization.* McGraw-Hill, 1967.

——— and D. G. Bowers. "Organizational Theory and Human Resource Accounting." *American Psychologist,* Vol. 24, No. 6 (June 1969), 585–592.

Litwin, G. H., and R. A. Stringer, Jr. *Motivation and Organizational Climate.* Harvard Graduate School of Business Administration, 1968.

Locke, E. A. "The Relationship of Intentions to Level of Performance." *Journal of Applied Psychology,* Vol. 50, No. 1 (February 1966), 60–66.

———. "The Motivational Effect of Knowledge of Results: Knowledge or Goal Setting?" *Journal of Applied Psychology,* Vol. 51, No. 4 (August 1967), 324–329.

———. "Toward a Theory of Task Motivation and Incentives." *Organizational Behavior and Human Performance,* Vol. 3, No. 2 (May 1968), 157–189.

———— and J. F. Bryan. "Cognitive Aspects of Psychomotor Performance: The Effect of Performance Goals on Level of Performance." *Journal of Applied Psychology,* Vol. 50, No. 4 (August 1966), 286–291.

———— and ————. "Knowledge of Score and Goal Level as Determinants of Work Rate." *Journal of Applied Psychology,* Vol. 53, No. 1 (February 1969), 59–65.

————, ————, and L. M. Kendall. "Goals and Intentions as Mediators of the Effects of Monetary Incentives on Behavior." *Journal of Applied Psychology,* Vol. 52, No. 2 (April 1968), 104–109.

McGregor, D. *The Human Side of Enterprise.* McGraw-Hill, 1960.

Meyer, H. H., E. Kay, and J. R. P. French, Jr. "Split Roles in Performance Appraisal." *Harvard Business Review,* Vol. 43, No. 1 (January–February 1965), 123–129.

Newsweek. "Copy Machine Boom—And Xerox Boom." Vol. 66 (November 8, 1965), 84–90.

Odiorne, G. *Management By Objectives—A System of Managerial Leadership.* Pitman, 1965.

Richman, B. M. *Soviet Management.* Prentice-Hall, 1965.

Salisbury, H. *The 900 Days: The Siege of Leningrad.* Harper, 1969.

Stedry, A. C. *Budget Control and Cost Behavior.* Prentice-Hall, 1960.

Stringer, R. A. "Achievement Motivation and Management Control." *Personnel Administration,* Vol. 29, No. 6 (November–December 1966), 3–5, 14–16.

Vroom, V. *Work and Motivation.* Wiley, 1964.

Readings

Motivation and Organizational Climate

GEORGE H. LITWIN, ROBERT A. STRINGER, JR.

Managers must control and direct the behavior of their subordinates, but such direction and control cannot be aimed only at *behavior*. Managers cannot afford to operate solely at the behavioral level. They must concern themselves with the determinants of behavior, that is, with *motivation*.

Managers can and do influence the thoughts, feelings, and desires of workers. It is these thoughts, feelings, and desires that arouse motivation and direct behavior. If managers are to become more effective, they must learn to understand and control some of the critical psychological factors in the work environment. In other words, *managers must manage motivation*.

There are managers who seem to be particularly sensitive to this aspect of the management function. These are "gifted" managers who know what influences make men work harder, who know what factors create high morale, and who know how to get the best out of each worker. It has been our experience that such managers are rare. For the vast majority, the job of managing motivation is a trial and error affair. Armed only with the logics of common sense and past experience, most managers must wait until late in their careers before they become experts in problems of motivating others. For most managers, a systematic framework for managing motivation is needed. We present such a framework, and—once understood—it may provide the needed perspective for more effective handling of problems of managing human motivation.

Key Elements of Managing Motivation

Our framework includes four of the critical variables that any manager must consider in managing motivation. These elements are not exclusive, nor are they independent. Each is—to a certain extent—beyond the control of the operating manager, but each represents a "leverage point" that the manager can use to influence the motivated performance of organization members. These four elements are:

1. The motives and needs the individuals bring to the situation;
2. The organizational tasks that must be performed;
3. The climate that characterizes the work situation; and
4. The personal strengths and limitations of the operating manager.

Personality differences account for much of the variation of individual behavior in organizations. We define these differences largely in terms of needs: for achievement, for power, and for affiliation. Individuals come to the work

From G. H. Litwin and R. A. Stringer, Jr., *Motivation and Organizational Climate*, Harvard Business School, Division of Research. © 1968 President and Fellows of Harvard College.

situation with different kinds of needs, and a manager cannot afford to overlook these differences.

The second element that a manager must consider in his efforts to manage motivation is the basic nature of the tasks to be performed. Different tasks involve or require different kinds of individual behavior and different patterns of motivation. For example, many sales tasks require risk taking, the assumption of individual responsibility, and so on, and achievement motivation seems especially relevant. Very routine tasks do not require this kind of motivation. Assembly lines are often most efficient when they are set up to afford the workers opportunities for mutual interaction, and affiliation motivation seems to be relevant.

We emphasize the importance of the third element in managing motivation, organizational climate. The climate that characterizes the work situation helps determine the kinds of worker motivation that are actually aroused. Climates tend to mediate between the task requirements and the needs of the individual. Sales tasks often require achievement-related behaviors, and thus salesmen should have high levels of achievement motivation. But, if the sales office climate fails to emphasize risk taking, responsibility, and flexible structure, then the salesmen's achievement concerns will not be stimulated. The capacity to influence the organizational climate is perhaps the most powerful leverage point in the entire management system. Because climates can affect the motivation of organization members, changes in certain climate properties could have immediate and profound effects on the motivated performance of all employees.

If the job of managing motivation revolves around managing organizational climate, then the manager's personal strengths and limitations must be considered. For the *manager's leadership style is a critical determinant of organizational climate.* Many managers, once they have diagnosed their motivational problems as climate-based, may find that they have to develop new skills in order to *change* the climate in the desired direction. A manager wishing to build stronger feelings of mutual support and encouragement (in order to arouse affiliation motivation, or in order to reinforce achievement motivation), may find that he is too aloof and impersonal in his dealings with his subordinates. This manager may decide to take a warmer and more personal interest in his men, and this may require skills and attitudes he does not presently possess.

Improving Our Diagnostic Abilities: Specific Examples

Below are several examples of motivation and motivated behavior that seem to contradict the "conventional wisdom." Using the conceptual framework we have developed, we are now prepared to analyze these examples systematically. At the same time, we will put ourselves into the position of the operating manager and decide which of the key elements are most important in each situation, and how he might develop an action plan to better manage the motivation of the workers in question.

1. The first example is of young girls working in an office where none of their dominant needs is being satisfied. They brought high n Achievement to the job, but this need was frustrated. The climate failed to emphasize flexible structure, individual responsibility, rewards, support, or group loyalty. The tasks that these workers performed were moderately challenging, but the elements

of challenge were not emphasized by management. This led to below-average performance and high levels of dissatisfaction and resentment. Two major alternative approaches to dealing with this problem include: (a) changing the needs of the workers; that is, hiring girls who would respond better to the highly structured office climate (girls high in *n* Power); and (b) changing the climate so that it tapped the achievement concerns of the employees.

2. The second example is more complicated. It illustrates the fact that many salesmen *are* made, rather than born. Salesmen were "turned into" top performers by the office climate in which they worked. In other offices, they had been mediocre performers. We must conclude that their success is due to the fact that their needs are now being satisfied and stimulated, whereas before they were being frustrated. The sales task is typically one that demands strong achievement motivation. Developing top-performing salesmen depends, then, on: (a) attracting men with high *n* Achievement; and (b) stimulating and satisfying this need once they are on board by creating an achieving climate in the sales office.

3. The final example involves the manager who had successfully innovated with "Theory Y" management principles. This success can be understood if we concentrate on the organizational climate that was created. The employees in this plant were not only performing well, but they were very enthusiastic about their work situation. There was a workable "match" between the task requirements, the needs of the workers, and the working climate. In addition, this particular manager seems to have evaluated and utilized his own strengths and weaknesses. He will probably find that future development of his organizational climate will depend on how well he is able to continue implementing his system without creating backlash in the larger corporation, with its more traditional philosophy.

These specific examples outline some of the potential applications of our motivation and climate framework. To facilitate diagnosis and action planning, a simpler means of measuring and evaluating the key elements is needed. In the next sections, we will present guidelines for managing motivation.

Human Motives: Their Measurement and Control

If a manager knew what the dominant needs of a man were, he would be in a much better position to satisfy these needs. When a man likes people, when he needs friendship, when he has a strong *need for affiliation*, it is certainly unwise to make him work alone. It is equally bad to make him work in a hostile atmosphere which discourages friendship and affiliation. When there is a job to be done that requires risk taking and responsibility, it is foolish to place a man with low *need for achievement* in that position.

Managers can control the motive patterns of organization members by careful recruitment and placement of personnel. To do so efficiently and effectively, a manager must learn to assess the strength of important human motives. The most straightforward method of measuring needs for achievement, affiliation, and power is through thematic apperception tests. Standardized test instruments, scored by content analysts trained in the McClelland-Atkinson procedures, provide measures of *n* Achievement, *n* Affiliation, and *n* Power.[1] These measures have been demonstrated to have reasonable reliability and considerable predictive validity (see Atkinson, 1958; McClelland, 1961).

Under some circumstances, the use of thematic apperception measures is not very practical. The alternative available to the operating manager involves his conducting a reaonably systematic assessment program. While this is time-consuming, it may also lead to real insights into the needs of organization members.

First, the manager may pay particular attention to the *thoughts and feelings* of individuals. How do they talk about their experiences? What seems to be on their minds when they are involved in a task? What do they seem to get the most satisfaction from? If the manager can train himself to "tune in" to these kinds of questions, he will soon find that he is able to judge the dominant motives of his men. He will be tuning in on the everyday imaginative material that people generate.

Let's take as an example a salesman who seems to be enthusiastic. He talks about his sales goals and seems to gain more satisfaction from reaching these goals than he does from receiving his commissions. He likes to call himself a planner, and he is proud of the detail that he goes into before he makes a sales call. Not only does he enjoy the competitive nature of his work, but he has commented to his boss several times that he appreciates the freedom and responsibility of his job. All these elements signify that this salesman is high in *need for achievement*. His co-worker talks mainly about the money he is earning (or not earning). He doesn't seem to enjoy the long hours he is forced to put in, and he talks about his job in terms of the people he has met and the friendliness of the other salesmen in the office. We might conclude from this small sample of thoughts and feelings that this man is motivated by a *need for affiliation,* rather than a *need for achievement.*

A second alternative involves paying close attention to the *behavior* of different workers under different circumstances. Since *behavior is a function of aroused motivation,* careful assessment of behavior should allow reasonable inferences about motivation patterns. The following list of key questions may help the manager identify different kinds of motivated behavior:

A. *High Achievement:*

When he starts a task, does he stick with it?

Does he try to find out how he is doing, and does he try to get as much feedback as possible?

Does he respond to difficult, challenging situations? Does he work better when there is a deadline or some other challenge involved?

Is he eager to accept responsibility? When he is given responsibility, does he set (and meet) measurable standards of high performance?

B. *High Power:*

Does he seem to enjoy a good argument?

Does he seek positions of authority where he can give orders, rather than take them? Does he try to take over?

Are status symbols especially important to him, and does he use them to gain influence over others?

Is he especially eager to be his own boss, even where he needs assistance, or where joint effort is required?

C. *High Affiliation:*

Does he seem to be uncomfortable when he is forced to work alone?

Does he interact with the other workers and go out of his way to make friends with new workers?

Is he always getting involved in group projects, and is he sensitive to other people (especially when they are "mad" at him)?

Is he an apple-polisher, and does he try hard to get personally involved with his superiors?

"Yes" answers to these questions mean that the motivation in question is strong.

Organizational Tasks: Their Measurement and Control

Even if a manager knew what the basic needs of his work force were, he would have to match these needs with the demands of each organizational task to get the most out of each person. It is a waste of human resources to hire a group of enthusiastic high school or college graduates to do relatively routine and repetitive tasks. It is poor management to promote a power-motivated individual into a position where *you know* he will have to take orders, rather than give them.

It is a fact of life that there are boring *and* exciting jobs to be done in business. For maximum long-run worker motivation and top performance, managers must *match* the needs of their subordinates with the various task demands. If it is impractical to shift personnel, then the attributes of the tasks might be altered somewhat. The problem is to measure the motivational demands of various jobs in the organization so that the manager knows *how* to change them and *where* to place different workers.

The following questions were designed to aid in the analysis of the motivational demands of tasks.[2]

Is It an Achievement Task?

1. How much latitude does a worker have in setting his work pace and work methods?
2. How much choice does a worker have when it comes to getting help or direction from someone else?
3. To what degree does errorless and efficient performance contribute to increased sales or company profits?
4. To what extent does the task challenge the abilities and skills of the worker?
5. Does the task provide clear, unambiguous feedback about the quality of performance?

Is It a Power Task?

6. How much opportunity does a worker have to personally direct his co-workers?

7. How much time is available for personal interactions while working?
8. To what degree does the task require the worker to deal directly with his superior?
9. How much control does the worker have over his work pace and work methods?
10. How many times can the worker leave his work area without reprimand?

Is It an Affiliation Task?

11. How many people *must* the worker interact with every two hours?
12. How many people *can* the worker interact with in his working area?
13. How dependent is successful task accomplishment on the cooperation of co-workers?
14. How much time is available for personal nontask interactions while working?
15. To what extent does the task allow for the maintenance of stable working relationships?

Rules for using these questions for task analysis are as follows:

1. Each task measured is to be ranked high, moderate, or low in response to each of the 15 questions.
2. A ranking of high   = 3 points
   A ranking of moderate = 2 points
   A ranking of low   = 1 point
3. For each question, standards will have to be set as to what constitutes a high, moderate, or low score. For example, high for question 11 would be 8 to 10 people, moderate would be 3 to 8, and low less than 3.
4. Total scores mean little. It is the relative scores in each of the three groups that measure the motivational demands of the task.

Exhibit 1 outlines a completed task analysis. The particular task being described is that of an assembly line worker in an electronic tube manufacturing plant. We can see from Exhibit 1 that this assembly line task taps affiliation motivation. This means that, *in and of itself,* the task is one that seems to satisfy a person's *need for affiliation.* If the workers on this assembly line have strong affiliative needs, then there is an appropriate *fit* between tasks and motives. If the workers were motivated by *n* Achievement or *n* Power, there is a poor *fit,* and the manager might consider altering certain aspects of the job. A task analysis can help him decide which aspects need to be changed.

Thus, the measurement scheme presented above can be used by the manager as part of an action-planning program to manage the motivation of his subordinates. By matching task demands with motives, the potential for high motivation and high performance is dramatically increased. But *this potential may never be realized.* High levels of worker motivation depend on the strength of the motive, the basic nature of the task, *and the arousal effects of the entire work situation. The expectancies and incentives that surround the work determine the level of aroused motivation.* And motivation level, in turn, determines how hard a subordinate will work, how long he will work, and what quality of work he will turn out. The final,

Exhibit 1   A Sample Task Analysis for an Assembly Line Worker

	High (3)	Moderate (2)	Low (1)
Is it an Achievement Task?			
1.			X
2.		X	
3.		X	
4.			X
5.			X
Total: 7			
Is it a Power Task?			
6.			X
7.		X	
8.		X	
9.			X
10.			X
Total: 7			
Is it an Affiliation Task?			
11.		X	
12.	X		
13.		X	
14.		X	
15.	X		
Total: 12			

and most powerful, leverage point available to the operating manager is his influence on expectancies and incentives.

Controlling Expectancies and Incentives in Specific Situations

Under certain circumstances the manager can have a strong influence on the worker's expectancies and incentives. In performance review meetings a manager can explain to his subordinates exactly what the rewards for top flight performance are. He can influence, to some extent, the worker's feelings and anticipations about his job, thus directly arousing motivation. In such one-to-one situations an effective manager can strongly arouse motivation, at least temporarily.

For example, if a manager knew that his subordinate was motivated by a strong *need for affiliation,* he could go out of his way to tap this need by creating a warm relationship. He could appeal to this "special relationship" in urging the worker to improve his performance. He could hold out specific affiliative rewards (more opportunities for interaction with his co-workers, a closer relationship with himself, etc.).

While such one-to-one interactions are an important leverage point in arousing motivation, they have several shortcomings:

1. They are time consuming.
2. They demand that the manager himself be present to manipulate the arousal cues.

3. Even if the manager succeeded in *arousing* the desired worker motivation, once the interaction was terminated other external factors might "erase" or destroy the arousal effects.

In other words, controlling expectancies and incentives in specific situations *may not be* the most efficient way of arousing and maintaining high levels of worker motivation. If the manager has successfully matched his organization's tasks with the needs of his workers, the most practical and powerful approach to the management of motivation involves controlling expectancies and incentives in nonspecific situations. The entire *organizational climate* must become the focus of management actions.

Climate: Measurement and Control

Controlling climate involves five action phases. *Phase one:* Deciding what kind of climate is most appropriate (given the nature of your workers and the jobs to be done). *Phase two:* Assessing the present climate. *Phase three:* Analyzing the "climate gap" and establishing a plan to reach the ideal climate. *Phase four:* Taking concrete steps to improve the climate. *Phase five:* Evaluating your effectiveness in terms of your action plan and (redirecting your climate control emphases).

Phase One

Deciding on the most appropriate or ideal climate involves an integration of the first two leverage points. If a work group is characterized by high *need for achievement,* and if there are achievement tasks to be performed, the ideal climate could be defined solely in terms of the achievement syndrome. Whenever there is a good task/motive fit, the ideal climate will emphasize those dimensions which arouse the motive in question.

However, when it is impossible to arrive at a good fit between a worker's dominant needs and the task demands, the ideal climate becomes more complicated. In such situations there are several alternative definitions of "ideal." Further research and experience are needed to determine the "optimum" and most useful solution to this problem, but two kinds of ideal climates may be described here.

The first kind of ideal climate would arouse the worker's dominant motive and *direct it toward task accomplishment*—even though the task normally requires some other pattern of motivation. The second kind of ideal climate would seek to arouse task-appropriate motivation even though it is not the worker's dominant need. To understand the strengths and weaknesses of these two alternative definitions of ideal climate, a brief example is outlined below.

A sales manager finds himself "stuck" with affiliation-oriented workers. He had attempted to hire achievement-oriented replacements but as yet has been unsuccessful. His sales tasks demand risk taking, use of performance feedback, and the like. They were achievement tasks and could not be altered. The manager might define his ideal climate as one that aroused affiliation motivation (high levels of warmth, friendliness, approval, support, and group identity). *He would then have to make sure that the workers received affiliative rewards for performing in achievement-related ways.* He would have to pay his salesmen "in friendship" for taking risks, using feedback, and setting high standards.

On the other hand, the manager might attempt to arouse the weaker achievement needs of his affiliation-oriented salesmen. In this case, he would define his ideal climate as an achieving climate, utilizing as many achievement arousal cues as possible. The induced achievement motivation would trigger task-related behavior without any special reinforcement or reward program, but the intensity or "energy investment" of the induced motivation would be only moderate (since the basic need was weak).

The first alternative (the affiliative climate) works with the strongest latent needs of the salesmen and should lead to highly motivated behavior. However, this alternative requires more supervision and direction, and it does not provide for the effective introduction of salesmen with stronger achievement needs. The second alternative (the achieving climate) should lead to less highly motivated behavior initially, but would allow for the recruiting and introduction of achievement-oriented salesmen. The choice among these alternatives should be based on an analysis of short-term and long-term organizational requirements, and on the manager's capacity to create one or the other kind of climate (or an effective combination).

Phase Two

Once the manager has decided on the general dimensions of his ideal climate, he must assess the "here and now" climate, and he should understand and believe in his measurement instrument.

The exact form of the questionnaire will depend on the specific needs of the manager. He may want to develop a special questionnaire, tailored to his measurement objectives and to the specific organization.

A sample of such a tailored climate questionnaire is presented below. The manager involved was a college professor interested in the secretarial climate in his department, and he restricted himself to the assessment of two aspects or dimensions of the climate, involving work standards and identification with the teaching group.

Work Standards

1. My boss sets explicit standards for me and my work in the office.
2. It's generally understood around here that secretaries are expected to be expert typists.
3. Around here there is considerable pressure to improve your secretarial skills.
4. None of the girls takes much pride in the way she does her work.
5. Most of the professors want an attractive and friendly secretary and don't care about the quality of the work.
6. If you want to be known as a good secretary, it's more important to be well-liked than it is to do good work.

Group Identification

7. As far as I can see, there is very little loyalty to this teaching group.
8. Most of the girls are proud of working for this teaching group.

9. I feel that my boss and I work together well.
10. All the secretaries around here are out for themselves.

Phase Three

By comparing the ideal climate with the here and now situation, the nature and size of the *climate gap* can be determined. There will usually be discrepancies between the ideal and the actual climate, and a manager will be able to see where his motivation arousal problems lie. For example, the college professor referred to above found that the secretaries were quite loyal to the teaching group, but perceived very little emphasis on high performance. For this professor, climate development seemed to center around raising the performance standards, *and communicating these higher standards to the secretaries.* This specific climate gap became the focus for action planning, as described below.

Phase Four

The action alternatives available to managers to control their organizational climate may be divided into four broad categories:

1. Spatial arrangement changes.
2. Changes in job and goal specifications.
3. Changes in communication/reporting patterns.
4. Changes in leadership style.

Some of the major action alternatives within each of these categories are outlined in Exhibit 2, along with a brief statement of the behavioral and climate effects that might be anticipated as a result of each action.

Spatial arrangement changes include the allocation of space to activities (and people) and the placement of desks, workbenches, and workers. As suggested in Exhibit 2, members of the organization could be placed close together, increasing interaction and cohesion, and leading to an affiliation-oriented climate. Or work partners and those who have to interact could be placed together, increasing task-related interaction and leading to a more achieving climate.

Changes in job and goal specifications include the extent to which job duties are defined in detail, the emphasis placed on prescribed job activities vs. performance goals, and the way goal-setting is handled. As indicated in Exhibit 2, the action alternatives in this area allow the creation of highly structured climates (through detailed job definition) or climates high in responsibility (through delegation and mutual goal-setting). In Exhibit 2, a distinction is made between delegation of overall job responsibility and infrequent review, which leads to a climate very high in personal responsibility but not very supportive or team-oriented and periodic mutual goal-setting, which leads to a climate characterized by responsibility, support, and team spirit.

Changes in communication/reporting patterns involve the kind of management control and information systems that are utilized, particularly the channels of communication, required reports (if any), and the typical quantity and content of communication. The major differences we have observed among communication/reporting patterns center around the emphasis on formal reporting through channels vs. informal sharing of information. As Exhibit 2

Exhibit 2   Action Alternatives for Controlling Climate

Category	Action Alternatives	Anticipated Behavioral Effects	Anticipated Effects on Climate[a]
Spatial Arrangements	Put people close together	Interaction and cohesion	Increase in Warmth, Support, Identity
	Put work partners close together	Task related interaction	Increase in Support, Identity, Responsibility
	Determined by status	Interaction within status levels	Increase in Structure, Responsibility
Job and Goal Specifications	Define job duties in detail	Constrained (stereotyped) behavior	Increase in Structure Decrease in Warmth, Responsibility
	Delegate overall responsibility and allow individual job planning	Individuality of work activity	Increase in Responsibility, Risk Decrease in Structure
	Set and review goals periodically	Mutual goal-oriented activity (of managers and subordinates)	Increase in Responsibility, Standards, Reward, Support
Communication/ Reporting Patterns	Establish formal channels and procedures	Constrained (stereotyped) behavior and decreased interaction	Increase in Structure Decrease in Warmth, Support
	Maintain informal contact	Manager-subordinate interaction and information sharing	Increase in Support, Reward, Identity
Leadership Style	Recognize and reward excellent performance	Increase in quality of output	Increase in Reward, Standards
	Provide coaching	Manager-subordinate problem solving	Increase in Support, Standards, Reward

[a] Climate effects are described as changes in the salience of dimensions.

suggests, formal communication/reporting systems will often lead to a highly structured climate and to a decrease in interaction and information flow. More informal systems, where the manager often uses himself as a channel, will be more likely to lead to increased warmth, support, and sense of reward, since the increased interaction allows more frequent personal recognition for goal performance.

Changes in leadership style involve the manager's behavior, his assumptions about people, his style of relating, and so on. In Exhibit 2 two aspects of leadership style which we have found to be important are described. The first of these involves the manager's ability to recognize and reward excellent performance. Throughout our studies, the emphasis placed on reward vs. punishment has been shown to be a critical determinant of achievement and affiliation motivation. Yet many managers fail to take advantage of opportunities to recognize and reward goal performance, often arguing that "money is the only reward people want." The second aspect of leadership style described in Exhibit 2 involves what we call *coaching* behavior. By coaching, we mean the extent to which a manager works *with* his people on the job (or in the field) to solve problems and encourage more effective goal-directed behavior. Coaching tends to lead to a climate characterized by very high support and team spirit.

Phase Five

Periodic assessment of changes in the organizational climate is the final phase of our action planning framework. This assessment allows the manager to "track" the development of certain climate characteristics and evaluate the effectiveness of attempts he has made to influence and change the climate. In a rapidly changing situation, it may be necessary to make fairly frequent assessments. Generally, we believe that a climate assessment should be conducted every six months. To avoid problems involved in too frequent administration of the questionnaire, it is desirable to create two or more reasonably representative groups of organization members, with each group completing no more than one questionnaire within a year.

The importance of periodic assessment cannot be overemphasized. A manager may *think* he is having the desired effect, but it is the *workers' perceptions* that count. In conversations and interviews, a manager may get positive (or negative) feedback on his actions, but this may or may not be confirmed by a systematic climate assessment. Without data that allow tracking changes in climate, a manager is unable to evaluate the impact of his actions or to establish revised goals for improving the climate. In business it is critical that a manager be aware of inventory, projected sales, cash flow, and available financial resources. Why is it any less important to be aware of the condition of the organizational climate, and the availability of motivational resources which climate represents?

Notes and References

1. The only professional scoring service we know of is operated by the Motivation Research Group, a division of the Behavioral Science Center, Suite 3750, Prudential Tower, Boston, Mass. This group also provides standardized test instruments and assessment packages. The scoring manuals are published in Atkinson (1958).

2. Parts of the following stem from the "Requisite Task Attributes" scheme developed by Turner and Lawrence (1965).

Atkinson, J. W. (ed.). *Motives in Fantasy, Action, and Society.* Van Nostrand, 1958.
McClelland, D. C. *The Achieving Society.* Van Nostrand, 1961.
Turner, A. N., and P. R. Lawrence. *Industrial Jobs and the Worker.* Division of Research, Harvard Business School, 1965.

Management by Integration and Self-Control

DOUGLAS McGREGOR

Let us consider in some detail a specific illustration of the operation of a managerial strategy based on Theory Y. The concept of "management by objectives" has received considerable attention in recent years, in part due to the writings of Peter Drucker. However, management by objectives has often been interpreted in a way which leads to no more than a new set of tactics within a strategy of management by direction and control.

The strategy to be illustrated in the following pages is an application of Theory Y. Its purpose is to encourage integration, to create a situation in which a subordinate can achieve his own goals *best* by directing his efforts toward the objectives of the enterprise. It is a deliberate attempt to link improvement in managerial competence with the satisfaction of higher-level ego and self-actualization needs. It is thus a special and not at all a typical case of the conventional conception of management by objectives.

This strategy includes four steps or phases:

1. The clarification of the broad requirements of the job.
2. The establishment of specific "targets" for a limited time period.
3. The management process during the target period.
4. Appraisal of the results.

Harry Evans is Vice President, Staff Services, for a manufacturing company with twenty plants throughout the Middle West and the South. The company is aggressively managed and financially successful; it is growing fairly rapidly through acquisition of smaller companies and the development of new markets for its products.

Evans was brought into the company three years ago by the President, who felt that the staff functions of the organization needed strengthening. One of the President's concerns was the personnel department, which had been something of a stepchild since it was established in the early forties. He felt that the management needed a lot of help and guidance in order to fulfill its responsibilities in this field.

Tom Harrison has been Director of Personnel Administration for a little less than a year. Evans selected him from among a number of candidates. Although he is not as well trained professionally as some of his colleagues, he appeared to have good promise as an administrator. He is in his young forties, intelligent, ambitious, personable, a hard worker with ten years of practical experience in personnel administration.

After Harrison had been on the job a few months, Evans had formed the following impressions about him:

1. He is overly anxious to make a good impression on top management, and this interferes with his performance. He watches too carefully to see which way the wind is blowing and trims his sails accordingly. He accepts even the most trivial assignments from any of the top management group, which makes a good impression but does little to strengthen the personnel function. He has done nothing to change the rather naïve top management expectation that personnel administration can be delegated to a staff department ("You take care of the personnel problems and we'll run the business.").

2. Harrison is a poor manager, somewhat to Evans' surprise, since he appeared to function well with more limited supervisory responsibilities. He uses his subordinates as errand boys rather than as resources, and he is much too ready to impose upon them his own practical and common-sense views of what should be done, brushing aside their specialized professional knowledge. He is anxious to reorganize the department, giving key responsibilities to men like himself who have practical experience but limited professional training.

These things added up, in Evans's eyes, to an inadequate conception of the nature of the personnel job and the proper role of the Department within the company. He recognized the value of management's acceptance of Harrison's practical orientation, but he felt that the real needs of the company would not be met unless management acquired a quite different point of view with respect to the function. He was not at all inclined to replace Harrison, since he believed he had the capacity to perform effectively, but he recognized that Harrison was not going to grow into the job without help. His strategy involved the four steps listed below.

Step 1: Determining the Major Requirements of the Job

Evans suggested to Harrison that he would like him to give some intensive thought to the nature of his job in the light of his experience so far. He asked him to list what he felt to be his major responsibilities, using the formal position description in his possession if he wished, but not limiting himself to it. He said, "I'd like to discuss with you at some length *your* view of your job after being on it for the past eight months."

The list of requirements which Harrison subsequently brought in for discussion with Evans was as follows:

1. Organization of the Department
2. Services to top management
    a. Awareness of company problems and provision of programs and policies for solving them

3. Productivity of the Department
   a. Efficient administration of personnel programs and services
   b. Definite assignments of projects to staff with completion dates and follow-up
   c. Periodic appraisals of the performance of department members, with appropriate action
4. Field relations
   a. Providing the field units with advice, adequate programs, information
   b. Periodic visits to assure the adequacy of field personnel units

Harrison and Evans had several lengthy discussions of this list of responsibilities. Evans began by saying, "Tom, I asked you to bring to this meeting a written statement of the major requirements of your job as you see them. Perhaps you expected me to define your job for you, to tell you what I want you to do. If I were to do so, it would not be your job. Of course, I don't expect that I will necessarily see eye to eye with you on everything you have written down. I do take it for granted that we have a common purpose: We both want yours to be the best damned personnel department anywhere.

"The difficulty we are likely to have in discussing your ideas is that if I disagree with you, you'll feel you have to accept what I say because I'm your boss. I want to help you end up with a list that we are both completely satisfied with, but I can't help if you simply defer to my ideas or if I don't express them for fear of dominating you. So try to think of me as a colleague whose experience and knowledge are at your disposal—not as your boss. I'm certain we can resolve any differences that may come up."

In the course of the discussion Evans did bring up his concerns, but he put major emphasis on encouraging Harrison to examine his own ideas critically. Evans talked quite frankly about the realities of the company situation as he saw them, and he discussed his conception of the proper role for a personnel department. He tried to persuade Harrison that his conception of the personnel function was too limited, and that his own subordinates, because of their training and experience, could help him arrive at a more adequate conception. Harrison held a couple of meetings with his own department staff to discuss this whole question, and after each of them he had further conversations with Evans.

The critically significant factor in these discussions was not their content, but the redefinition of roles which took place. Evans succeeded, by his manner more than by his specific words, in conveying to Harrison the essential point that he did not want to occupy the conventional role of boss, but rather, to the fullest extent possible, the role of a consultant who was putting all of his knowledge and experience at Harrison's disposal in the conviction that they had a genuine common interest in Harrison's doing an outstanding job.

As he began to sense this, and to believe it, Harrison's whole perception of his own role changed. Instead of seeking to find out, as would be natural under conventional circumstances, how Evans wanted him to define his job, what Evans wanted him to do, what Evans would approve or disapprove, Harrison began to think for himself. Moreover, with this greater sense of freedom about his own role (and with Evans's open encouragement) he began to perceive his own subordinates not as "hands," but as resources, and to use them thus.

The result, unrealistic as it may seem at first glance, was a dramatic change in Harrison's perception of himself and of his job. The true nature of the change that took place during these discussions with Evans and with his subordinates was revealed in his final statement of his responsibilities as he now perceived them:

1. Organization of the Department
2. Continuous assessment of both short- and long-run company needs through:
   a. Exploration in the field
   b. General awareness of management's problems
   c. Exploration of the views of members of the Department
   d. Knowledge of external trends
3. Professional help to all levels of management
   a. Problem solving
   b. Strategy planning
   c. Research studies
   d. Effective personnel programs and policies
   e. Efficient administration of services
4. Development of staff members
5. Personal development

This first step in Evans's managerial strategy with Harrison is thus consistent with his commitment to Theory Y. He believes that Harrison must take the major responsibility for his own development, but he believes he can help. He conceives of integration as an active process which inevitably involves differences of opinion and argument. He recognizes the likelihood that Harrison may accede too readily to his views without real conviction, and he does not want this to happen. Consequently he attempts to establish a relationship in which Harrison can perceive him as a genuine source of help rather than as a boss in the conventional sense. He knows that the establishment of this relationship will take time, but it is the long-term results which he considers important. Since he does not expect that Harrison will grow into his job overnight, he is prepared to accept a definition of Harrison's job which is considerably short of perfection. He is confident that it will be improved six months hence when they discuss it again.

If Harrison is going to learn and grow in competence, and if he is going to find opportunities to satisfy his higher-level needs in the process, it is essential that he find a genuine challenge in his job. This is unlikely if the job is defined for him by a formal position description or by a superior who simply tells him what he wants done. Thus, the principle of integration is important right at the start. It is not necessary in applying it to ignore the work of the organization planning staff. The necessity for a logical division of responsibilities within any organization is obvious. However, a position description is likely to become a strait jacket unless it is recognized to be a broad set of guidelines within which the individual literally makes his own job. The conception of an organization plan as a series of predetermined "slots" into which individuals are selectively placed denies the whole idea of integration.

The process involved at this step is similar, although more limited in scope, to the one so aptly described by Drucker as discovering "what business we are in." In the case of top management looking at the organization as a whole, this frequently is a highly instructive experience. The same thing can be true even in a limited setting such as this, especially if the superior can, by doing something like Evans is doing, encourage the subordinate to think creatively about his job.

Step 2: Setting Targets

When Evans and Harrison finished their discussion of the major requirements of Harrison's job, Evans suggested that Harrison think about some specific objectives or targets which he might set for himself and his department during the following six months. Evans suggested that he think both about improving the over-all performance of his unit and about his own personal goals. He asked him further to consider in broad terms what steps he proposed to take to achieve these targets. Evans said, "I don't want to tell you how to do your job, but I would like you to do some careful thinking about how you are going to proceed. Perhaps I can be helpful when we discuss your ideas." Finally, Evans asked Harrison to consider what information he would require, and how he might obtain it, in order to know at the end of the period how well he had succeeded in reaching his targets. He suggested that they get together to talk further when Harrison had completed his thinking and planning along these lines.

This is the planning phase, but again the process is one in which the subordinate is encouraged to take responsibility for his own performance. The conventional process is one in which objectives are conceived by higher levels and imposed on lower levels of the organization. The rationale is that only the higher levels have available the broader knowledge necessary for planning. To some extent this is true, but there is an important difference between the kind of planning in which a central group determines in detail what each division or department will do, and that in which the central group communicates what are believed to be the desirable over-all objectives and *asks* each unit to determine what it can contribute.

Even when general objectives are predetermined, they can usually be limited to certain aspects of performance such as production goals, costs, and profit margin. There are other aspects which are subject to local determination, as is, of course, the planning with respect to personal objectives.

The important theoretical consideration, derived from Theory Y, is that the acceptance of responsibility (for self-direction and self-control) is correlated with commitment to objectives. Genuine commitment is seldom achieved when objectives are externally imposed. Passive acceptance is the most that can be expected; indifference or resistance are the more likely consequences. Some degree of *mutual* involvement in the determination of objectives is a necessary aspect of managerial planning based on Theory Y. This is embodied in Evans's suggestions to Harrison.

In the discussion of targets, the superior again attempts a helping role rather than an authoritative one. His primary interest is in helping the subordinate plan his own job in such a fashion that both personal and organizational goals will be achieved. While the superior has a veto power by virtue of his position, he will exercise it only if it becomes absolutely necessary.

To be sure, subordinates will sometimes set unrealistic goals, particularly the first time they approach a task like this. Experience has indicated that the usual problem is that the goals are set too high, not too low. While the superior can, through judicious advice, help the subordinate adjust unrealistic goals, there may often be greater long-run advantages in permitting the subordinate to learn by experience than in simply telling him where his planning is unrealistic or inadequate.

The list of targets which Harrison brought for discussion with Evans was this:

1. Determination of major company needs, long and short range, by:
   a. Field visits and discussions with local management
   b. Intensive discussions with top management
   c. Exploration of the views of the personnel department staff
   A plan, with assignments of responsibility, and a time schedule will be worked out for this. I expect we can complete the study within six months, but a report and subsequent plans will probably not be completed by September.
2. Joint determination with department staff of current projects
   This will involve planning such as you and I are doing.
3. Development of departmental staff members
   Items 1 and 2 can be a vehicle for this. I need help in learning how to work better with my subordinates, and particularly on how to eliminate the friction between the old-timers and the college-trained youngsters.
4. Self-development
   a. I'd like to do some reading to improve my own thinking about personnel administration—or maybe take a university course. I'd like your advice.
   b. I guess I haven't gained as much skill as a manager as I need. I hear rumblings that some of my staff are not happy with me as a boss. I'd like to do something about this, but I'm not sure what is the best way to proceed.
5. Development of a good plan of organization for the department
   In working through some of the above projects, I think I'll get some good ideas about how we ought to be set up as a department.

Since the working relationship between the two men had been quite well established during their earlier discussions, there was a comfortable give and take at this stage. Evans saw the first target as a crucial one which could become the basis for an entirely new conception of the department's role. He felt also that it could be extremely educational for Harrison provided he tackled it with sensitivity and an open mind. Accordingly he spent several hours helping Harrison to think through his strategy for determining the needs of the company with respect to personnel administration. Harrison began to see that this project was a means by which he could work toward all the other targets on his list.

Evans had little difficulty after Harrison's earlier experiences in persuading him to involve his subordinates in developing plans for the project. He suggested that Harrison continue to meet with him to discuss and evaluate this process for a couple of months. He felt—and said—that this might be the best method for Harrison to begin improving his own managerial skills.

They agreed that Harrison would explore possible university programs during the next few months to see if some one of these might meet his needs a little later. Meanwhile, they worked out a reading list and a plan for an occasional session when Harrison could discuss his reading.

In view of the nature of the personnel function, and the particular problems facing Harrison, the targets did not lend themselves to quantitative measurement such as might have been possible in a production operation. Nevertheless, Harrison, under Evans's tutelage, worked out a fairly detailed plan with specific steps to be accomplished by the end of six months. Evans's interest was that Harrison would have a basis for evaluating his own accomplishments at the end of the period.

Evans brought into the discussion the question of their relationship during the ensuing period. He said, "I don't want to be in a position of checking up on you from week to week. These are your plans, and I have full confidence that you will make every effort to reach your targets. On the other hand, I want you to feel free to seek help if you want it. There are ways in which I believe my experience can be useful to you. Suppose we leave it that we'll get together on your initiative as often as you wish—not for you to report how you are doing, but to discuss any problems which you would like my help on, or any major revisions in your plans." Thus Evans helped Harrison still further to perceive the role that he wanted to occupy as a superior, and thus also to clarify his own responsibilities as a subordinate.

Step 3: The Ensuing Period

Since this is a managerial strategy rather than a personnel technique, the period between the establishment of targets and the evaluation of accomplishment is just as important as the first two steps. What happens during this period will depend upon the unique circumstances. The aim is to further the growth of the subordinate: his increased competence, his full acceptance of responsibility (self-direction and self-control), his ability to achieve integration between organizational requirements and his own personal goals.

In this particular situation Evans's primary interests were two: (1) the emergence throughout the company of a more adequate conception of the personnel function, and (2) the development of a competent department which would provide leadership and professional help to all levels of management with respect to this function. He felt that, as a result of steps 1 and 2 of his strategy, Harrison too was committed to these objectives. Moreover, he was persuaded that Harrison's project for assessing company needs in the field of personnel administration—as now conceived—was a highly promising means to these ends. He warned himself that he must be careful on two counts. First he must not expect too much too fast. The company situation was in no sense critical and there was no need for a crash program. Harrison's project was certain to be a valuable learning experience for him and his staff.

Second, Evans recognized that if the best learning was to occur, he must curb his natural tendency to step in and guide the project. Harrison would make mistakes; at his present level of sophistication he would quite possibly fail to appreciate the full scope of the task. Nevertheless, Evans decided more would be gained if he limited his influence to those occasions when Harrison sought his help.

This is what he did. His confidence in Harrison proved to have been justified. He and his staff tackled the project with more ingenuity and sensitivity than Evans would have imagined possible and began rather quickly to understand the true dimensions of the problem. Harrison came in one day to tell him that they had decided to extend their explorations to include visits to several university centers in order to take advantage of the point of view of some top-flight academic people. Also, they planned to test some of their emerging ideas against the experience of several other companies.

After this discussion, and the evidence it provided concerning the expansion of Harrison's intellectual horizons and the use he was making of the resources represented by his subordinates, Evans stopped worrying. He would bail them out if they got into trouble, but he anticipated no such necessity.

Step 4: Self-Appraisal

At the end of August, Harrison reminded Evans (not vice versa!) that the six months was up. "When do you want a report?" was his question. Evans responded that a report was not what he wanted, but Harrison's own evaluation of what he had accomplished with respect to the targets he had set six months earlier. Said Evans, "This can give you a basis for planning for the next six months."

A week later Harrison brought the following notes to a discussion with Evans.

Appraisal, September 1

1. Determination of major company needs:
   a. The field work is completed.
   b. My staff and I are working on a proposal that will involve a new conception of personnel administration in this company. We will have a draft for discussion with you within thirty days, and we want you to take a full day to let us present our findings and proposals to you.
   c. The results of our work make it clear that we have an educational job to do with top management, and I want to include a plan along these lines in my next set of targets.
2. Joint determination with staff of current projects. I am now conducting a set of target-setting meetings with my department staff as a whole in which we are laying out plans for the next year. All major projects—individual or group—are being discussed out in detail there. These department meetings will be followed by individual planning sessions.
3. Development of department staff members:
   a. The major project we have been carrying out has changed my ideas about several of my subordinates. I'm learning how to work with them, and it's clear they are growing. Our presentation to you next month will show you what I mean.
   b. I've appreciated how much your target-setting approach has helped my development, and I'm attempting to use it with each of my subordinates. Also, I think the departmental planning mentioned under 2 above is a developmental tool. I've been talking with some people in the B——— Company who do this and I'm excited about its possibilities in our own company.

4. Self-development

All I can say is I've learned more in the past six months than in the previous five years.

5. Departmental organization

I haven't done a thing about it. It doesn't seem very important right now. We seem to be able to plan our work as a department pretty well without developing a new setup. Perhaps we'll need to come back to this during the next six months, but there are more important things to be done first.

6. General comment

I would rate myself considerably lower than I would have six months ago in terms of how well I'm filling the responsibilities of my job. It's going to take me a couple of years to measure up to what you have a right to expect of the man in this spot, but I think I can do it.

The discussion of this self-appraisal went into considerable detail. Evans felt that Harrison had acquired quite a little insight into his own strengths and weaknesses, and they were able to discuss objectively where he needed to give thought to improving his competence further. Harrison, for example, opened up the whole problem of his "yes-man" attitude in dealing with top management and pointed out that his exploratory interviews with some of these men had resulted in increased self-confidence. He said, "I think maybe I can learn to stand up for my ideas better in the future. You have helped me to realize that I can think for myself, and that I can defend myself in an argument."

They agreed to postpone Harrison's discussion of plans for the next six months until after the one-day session at which Evans would meet with the whole department. "Then," said Harrison, "I want to talk over with you a new statement of my responsibilities which I'm working on."

The Game of Budget Control
G. H. HOFSTEDE

In this article practical advice is given to those in business who have to work—and live—with budgets and budgetary standards. This advice is based upon the situation of the manufacturing company. There are separate recommendations for:

1. Company top management
2. The top and middle management of the plant
3. The plant foremen or first-line managers

"The Game of Budget Control: Practical Recommendations" from *The Game of Budget Control* (1968), by G. H. Hofstede. Reprinted by permission of Tavistock Publications Ltd.

4. The company and/or plant controller
5. The budget accountant
6. The work study engineer
7. The personnel manager

Recommendations to Company Top Management

These recommendations are aimed at top management of a manufacturing company, which for its manufacturing operations either uses budget control and wants to improve its functioning, or does not use budget control and wants to introduce it. The recommendations in this chapter go to some extent beyond the immediate conclusions of this study. This is unavoidable, as any researcher will realize when he steps into a consultant role. My recommendations to company top management are:

Realize that the budget control system is *your* tool to manage your company. Its functioning depends primarily on you, not on your controller.

When setting budgets, have the decisions which must be taken at your level, like the choice of product lines and production volume, taken first and then communicated to your subordinates. Then ask your subordinates to prepare the draft budgets at the lowest possible level of management and have them consolidated at each next higher level. If they cannot be accepted and have to be revised, take the time to discuss this with your subordinates and to explain the reasons. Make sure they do the same with their subordinates. Realize that budgets have a coordinating and a motivating function and that especially in the larger corporations the way the coordination is felt at the lower levels can easily destroy motivation. It is therefore necessary to explain much more than you think you should.

Realize that budgets only motivate when they are tight enough to be a challenge, and that they only offer a challenge if there is a risk that they will not be fully met. If some budgets are not met this is only a sign that the system is healthy and it does not mean that somebody is at fault. If you take the habit of interpreting it in this latter way, budgets will all soon be met, but they will not motivate.

Realize that the fact that motivating budgets are not always met means that the same budget cannot be used both for coordinating and motivating. It will be necessary to reserve a risk percentage for average underattainment of budgets to arrive at actually expected figures which can be used for coordination.

Decide beforehand which percentage variance from the various budgets you can leave to the discretion of your subordinates before you will intervene and let them know this. In other words, set their control limits.

Be sensitive to the reactions of your subordinates to the budgets set for them and keep open grievance channels for those who see their standards as impossibly tight. Be ready to change budgets if this is the case; if you do not do it, actual results will be worse than if you do.

Eliminate the taboo on communicating financial information about budget results to the lowest levels of management, including plant foremen.

Discuss the functioning of the budget system with your controller and make sure he sees his role neither as an auditor nor as a data processor but as a systems architect and educator.

Recommendations to the Top and Middle Management of the Plant

Realize that the budget control system is *your* tool to manage your plant. Its functioning within the plant depends primarily on you, not on the controller or his department.

If possible, see to it that budgets and standards are set separately for the responsibility area of each of your foremen, but at least for each second-line manager. Then have your foremen participate in the setting of their technical standards and make their own draft expense budget. Let them have the assistance from the budget accountant they need, but let them do the actual figuring themselves.

If draft budgets are changed afterwards or cut, discuss this with your subordinates and explain the reasons.

If you are running a shift operation so that more foremen are responsible for the same department, the budgeting effort should be done by the lowest level which covers all shifts, but only after consultation with the foremen in meetings. If results can be split by shifts, then again the individual foremen can be the budgetees.

Decide beforehand which percentage variance from the various budgets and technical standards you will leave to the discretion of your subordinates before you will intervene and let them know this. These percentages are their control limits.

Be sensitive to the reactions of your subordinates on the budgets and standards set for them and keep open grievance channels for those who see their standards as impossibly tight. Be ready to change the standard if this is the case.

Take account of the age and personality structure of each of your subordinates in setting targets and standards for them: what will mean a challenge for a young man can mean a discouragingly tight objective for an older man.

Show interest in your subordinates' budget results also when they do not transgress their control limits, but be sure this is seen as interest, not as intervention.

If you have to intervene, get the full story from your subordinate first. Center the conversation around what should be done to correct the situation, not on who is at fault.

Show your subordinates that you consider meeting standards as part of their performance but be careful not to appraise by budget or standards results alone. Realize that while from your point of view results may be the only important factor, in the eyes of your subordinate it is his efforts which determine his merit.

If you are under pressure from your superiors, consider whether it is wise to send this pressure down to your subordinates. Protect your subordinates against influences from above which will in their situation only discourage and demotivate them. Perform your umbrella function.

When budgeting is first started in your plant, do not expect results immediately. Give your subordinates the time to learn to use this tool and learn to use it yourself: this may take a few years. See to it that the budget accounting staff interprets its role not as auditing or policing but as supporting and educating the line in the use of accounting information.

Discuss with your subordinates and with the budget and standards staff which feedback information is desirable from a line management point of view and which is available from a data processing point of view. Try to unite the two. Resist attempts of the line to ask, or of the staff to supply, more information than a normal human being can digest. Review periodically the information received and stop whichever part of it you do not use. Realize, however, that there are key points in your production process about which you should be informed, even if they are never off-standard. They may be off-standard tomorrow.

Realize that the essence of good budget control is cooperation and that you must meet the budget challenge with your subordinates as a team. Realize that the performance of your plant depends on their motivation. Try to develop a game spirit among your team. Show your enthusiasm and respect the responsibilities of your subordinates. Mistrust and undue pressure will destroy the game spirit.

Be sensitive to any signs of passing the buck, scapegoating, fighting the system, or other wasteful activities among your subordinates. If these things happen it is a sign that *you* have failed in leading the game the right way. Try again.

Make sensible use of group meetings with your subordinates. Do not handle problems here which can better be handled on a man-to-man basis, such as budget performances of individual departments. Use them for informal contact and team-building. Use them to supply general information about cost. Let your subordinates use the meetings to help each other in giving meaning to the standards and using them as management tools towards their own subordinates. Meetings can be powerful tools to influence your subordinates' attitudes. However, if you feel your meetings are not useful, it is better not to have them; they will do more harm than good.

Discuss the reorganizations in your management structure with your controller before they are carried out, so that the responsibility and account structures can remain mutually adapted.

Recommendations to the Foremen or First-Line Managers

Technical performance standards and budgets are a management tool for you to use. They are your guides in the management process and important yardsticks for your managerial achievement.

More and more the first-line manager will need the kind of information which is supplied by standards and budget systems. In many cases he will be able to do a better job if he gets insight into the financial results of his department as well as the technical results.

Although participation in the setting of an expense budget and sometimes other financial standards takes time and effort, this effort pays off in better budgets and a better understanding of how the business is run.

The foreman who is better informed himself will be able to do a better job at communicating results to the workers. There are many possibilities of involving the workers in the results feedback. The use of periodic meetings is one of them. This study has not included the cost-consciousness and standards fulfilment motivation of workers. From other studies it is clear that one important question is whether or not piece-rates or similar systems are used. Apart from this, the foreman is the key person in determining the cost-consciousness of his workers.

Recommendations to the Company and/or Plant Controller

The success of a budget system does not primarily depend upon the controller, but upon the top line executive. The controller's role is hygienic: he has to satisfy certain minimal requirements but has more scope in making the system fail than succeed. If he considers not only the accounting part but also the human part of the system as his specialty however, he can become the systems architect, catalyst and educator.

The same budget cannot be used for coordinating and for motivating managers. Coordinating budgets should represent actually expected performance; but budgets can be shown to have a motivating effect only when they involve a risk of not being attained. Budgets that are really motivating should be increased with an average risk percentage to arrive at actual expected performance.

Consider the use of statistical techniques in cost control and budgeting. From a point of view of motivation it is desirable that, for each budget, control limits are set which guarantee a certain free scope for managers at various levels before their superiors intervene. From a technical point of view this can be solved by statistical techniques like those used in quality control. Controllers should familiarize themselves much more with the possibilities of these techniques.

Split the account structure if possible as far as the responsibility of the individual foremen. Let the foreman draft his own expense budget but have him supplied with all the support from the budget accountant he needs. Eliminate the taboo on financial information in the plant.

Both the system in which individual plant departments are full profit centers buying from and selling to other departments and the system in which they are only expense centers have their drawbacks. In the first case the system is difficult to understand and use for line management and a continuous effort at simplification and instruction is necessary. In the second case expense budgets should be kept flexible enough to adapt to changes in technical performance and line management should have more support in taking economic decisions.

Management information reports should be separated from accounting consolidation reports. In management information there should be a periodic weeding out of over-information, and periodic consultations with management of various levels down to the foreman level about the understandability of information and the desirability of other information.

Establish a close cooperation between work study engineers and budget accountants, although it is not essential that the work study engineers report to the controller.

Man budget accounting departments in such a way that about 25% of total time is available for personal discussions with and support to line management.

When appraising budget accountants and other staff people for salary increases and promotion, ask the line managers with whom they cooperate for their impressions. This has a beneficial effect upon staff behavior and line-staff cooperation.

The best service to the line is given by budget accountants and other staff people who are competent in their speciality and also tactful.

Develop a career planning for your people.

Recommendations to the Budget Accountant

When budgets have to be set, let the line managers make the drafts. Assist them with all the information they need. Develop special information sources for this purpose; but let the actual figuring be done by line managers themselves.

Design the management information system yourself after thorough discussion about what line managers at various levels, down to the foreman level, need to know and what you can supply. Do not use reports that serve for accounting consolidation simultaneously for management information. Give more detailed information to lower management levels and more general information to higher management levels.

Have periodic consultations with line managers of the different levels about the management information system: desires for new information, improvement of understandability, weeding out of unnecessary information. Beware of over-information. Managers do not want to know everything; if they miss some information which they need, they will come and ask for it.

Make the management information reports yourself or if they are made by purely clerical people at least check them thoroughly before they are distributed. Managers will use figures only if they feel confident they are right. Frequent mistakes will spoil any information system.

Focus the information on efficiency variances. Omit variances that are caused by pure accounting causes.

Be informed about changes in the responsibility structure of the organization in due time so that you can adapt the account structure accordingly. Budgets should always follow management responsibility.

Be critical of the raw data you receive. Realize that if people feel they are measured by these data they will tend to make them look right. Data connected with a piece-rate system or which in any way directly influence pay are basically unfit for efficiency information. Always try to anchor the data you receive to actual cash movements, for instance wages paid, which cannot be faked.

Reserve about 25% of your time for personal contacts with the people who receive your management information. Take time to explain figures. Test whether they have understood the information. If they do not it does not mean that they are silly: it means that you have failed in speaking or writing a language they can understand. Try again.

Realize that the success of a budget and management information system is not in your hands: it is in the hands of line management. They will not be able to make it successful without your support, however. The success of *your job* depends on the quality of this support: upon your competence and the tactfulness with which you build up your contacts with line management.

Maintain good professional contacts with those responsible for the system of technical standards, such as work study engineers. Keep them informed about the financial side of efficiency results and always base your financial standards on their technical ones.

Recommendations to the Work Study Engineer

Set your standards always in close contact with line management. If line managers see you know your job and you behave tactfully, they will accept you. When they ask your support, always be ready to give it. A staff man should be happy when he is pulled and unhappy when he is pushing.

Base standards on external reference information wherever possible, but be careful about how you select these external reference points. If line management does not see them as legitimate and valid for their situation, they will do more harm than good. Take the time to discuss external data with the line managers and let them participate in finding valid reference points.

Realize that the success of your job depends to a large extent on how line people see you.

Maintain good professional contacts with the budget accountants and exchange information with them.

Recommendations to the Personnel Manager

Keep line management informed about any signs of discouragement of managers through standards that are seen as impossible, as well as about signs of interdepartmental conflict which may be adverse effects of the way the standards and budget system is used for management.

A system of job rotation between functions in line management or between line and staff can have its implications not only for the development of the people but also for the development of the control system.

Pay special attention to the development and career planning of staff people like budget accountants and work study engineers. For good line-staff cooperation, it is not essential that staff people have line experience; it is more important that they are competent in their speciality and behave tactfully. Include staff people in management development courses and in training in interpersonal relations.

Design the performance appraisal system for staff people for salary increases in such a way that their line counterparts are asked for their impression about the support they get from them and that this impression contributes to the appraisal of the staff man.

Management by Whose Objectives?

HARRY LEVINSON

Despite the fact that the concept of management by objectives (MBO) has by this time become an integral part of the managerial process, the typical MBO effort perpetuates and intensifies hostility, resentment, and distrust between a manager and subordinates. As currently practiced, it is really just industrial engineering with a new name, applied to higher managerial levels, and with the same resistances.

Obviously, somewhere between the concept of MBO and its implementation, something has seriously gone wrong. Coupled with performance appraisal, the intent is to follow the Frederick Taylor tradition of a more rational management process. That is, which people are to do what, who is to have effective control over it, and how compensation is to be related directly to individual achievement. The MBO process, in its essence, is an effort to be fair and reasonable, to predict performance and judge it more carefully, and presumably to provide individuals with an opportunity to be self-motivating by setting their own objectives.

The intent of clarifying job obligations and measuring performance against a man's own goals seems reasonable enough. The concern for having both superior and subordinate consider the same matters in reviewing the performance of the latter is eminently sensible. The effort to come to common agreement on what constitutes the subordinate's job is highly desirable.

Yet, like most rationalizations in the Taylor tradition, MBO as a process is one of the greatest of managerial illusions because it fails to take adequately into account the deeper emotional components of motivation.

In this article, I shall indicate how I think management by objectives, as currently practiced in most organizations, is self-defeating, and serves simply to increase pressure on the individual. By doing so, I do not reject either MBO or performance appraisal out of hand.

Rather, by raising the basic question, "Whose objectives?" I propose to suggest how they might be made more constructive devices for effective management. The issues I shall raise have largely to do with psychological considerations, and particularly with the assumptions about motivation which underlie these techniques.

The 'Ideal' Process

Since management by objectives is closely related to performance appraisal and review, I shall consider these together as one practice which is intended:

- To measure and judge performance.
- To relate individual performance to organizational goals.

- To clarify both the job to be done and the expectations of accomplishment.
- To foster the increasing competence and growth of the subordinate.
- To enhance communications between superior and subordinate.
- To serve as a basis for judgments about salary and promotion.
- To stimulate the subordinate's motivation.
- To serve as a device for organizational control and integration.

Major Problems

According to contemporary thinking, the "ideal" process should proceed in five steps: (1) individual discussion with his superior of the subordinate's description of his own job, (2) establishment of short-term performance targets, (3) meetings with the superior to discuss progress toward targets, (4) establishment of checkpoints to measure progress, and (5) discussion between superior and subordinate at the end of a defined period to assess the results of the subordinate's efforts. In *ideal* practice, this process occurs against a background of more frequent, even day-to-day, contacts and is separate from salary review. But, in *actual* practice, there are many problems. Consider:

No matter how detailed the job description, it is essentially static—that is, a series of statements.

However, the more complex the task and the more flexible a man must be in it, the less any fixed statement of job elements will fit what he does. Thus the higher a man rises in an organization and the more varied and subtle his work, the more difficult it is to pin down objectives that represent more than a fraction of his effort.

With preestablished goals and descriptions, little weight can be given to the areas of discretion open to the individual, but not incorporated into his job description or objectives.

I am referring here to those spontaneously creative activities an innovative executive might choose to do, or those tasks a responsible executive sees which need to be done. As we move more toward a service society, in which tasks are less well defined but spontaneity of service and self-assumed responsibility are crucial, this becomes pressing.

Most job descriptions are limited to what a man himself does in his work.

They do not adequately take into account the increasing interdependence of managerial work in organizations. This limitation becomes more important as the impact of social and organizational factors on individual performance becomes better understood. The more a man's effectiveness depends on what other people do, the less he himself can be held responsible for the outcome of his efforts.

If a primary concern in performance review is counseling the subordinate, appraisal should consider and take into account the total situation in which the superior and subordinate are operating.

In addition, this should take into account the relationship of the subordinate's job to other jobs, rather than to his alone. In counseling, much of the focus is in helping the subordinate learn to negotiate the system. There is no provision in most reviews and no place on appraisal forms with which I am familiar to report and record such discussion.

The setting and evolution of objectives is done over too brief a period of time to provide for adequate interaction among different levels of an organization.

This militates against opportunity for peers, both in the same work unit and in complementary units, to develop objectives together for maximum integration. Thus both the setting of objectives and the appraisal of performance make little contribution toward the development of teamwork and more effective organizational self-control.

Coupled with these problems is the difficulty superiors experience when they undertake appraisals.

Douglas McGregor complained that the major reason appraisal failed was that superiors disliked playing God by making judgments about another man's worth.[1] He likened the superior's experience to inspection of assembly line products and contended that his revulsion was against being inhuman. To cope with this problem, McGregor recommended that an individual should set his own goals, checking them out with his superior, and should use the appraisal session as a counseling device. Thus the superior would become one who helped the subordinate achieve his own goals instead of a dehumanized inspector of products.

Parenthetically, I doubt very much that the failure of appraisal stems from playing God or feeling inhuman. My own observation leads me to believe that managers experience their appraisal of others as a hostile, aggressive act that unconsciously is felt to be hurting or destroying the other person. The appraisal situation, therefore, gives rise to powerful, paralyzing feelings of guilt that make it extremely difficult for most executives to be constructively critical of subordinates.

Objectivity Plea

Be that as it may, the more complex and difficult the appraisal process and the setting and evaluation of objectives, the more pressing the cry for objectivity. This is a vain plea. Every organization is a social system, a network of interpersonal relationships. A man may do an excellent job by objective standards of measurement, but may fail miserably as a partner, subordinate, superior, or colleague. It is a commonplace that more people fail to be promoted for personal reasons than for technical inadequacy.

Furthermore, since every subordinate is a component of his superior's efforts to achieve his own goals, he will inevitably be appraised on how well he works with his superior and helps the latter meet his needs. A heavy subjective element necessarily enters into every appraisal and goal-setting experience.

The plea for objectivity is vain for another reason. The greater the emphasis on measurement and quantification, the more likely the subtle, nonmeasurable elements of the task will be sacrificed. Quality of performance frequently, therefore, loses out to quantification.

A Case Example   A manufacturing plant which produces high quality, high prestige products, backed by a reputation for customer consideration and service, has instituted an MBO program. It is well worked out and has done much to clarify both individual goals and organizational performance. It is an important component of the professional management style of that company which has resulted in commendable growth.

But an interesting, and ultimately destructive, process has been set in motion. The managers are beginning to worry because when they now ask why something has not been done, they hear from each other, "That isn't in my goals." They complain that customer service is deteriorating. The vague goal, "improve customer service," is almost impossible to measure. There is therefore heavy concentration on those sub-goals which can be measured. Thus time per customer, number of customer calls, and similar measures are used as guides in judging performance. The *less* time per customer and the *fewer* the calls, the better the customer service manager meets his objectives. He is cutting costs, increasing profit—and killing the business. Worse still, he hates himself.

Most of the managers in that organization joined it because of its reputation for high quality and good service. They want to make good products and earn the continued admiration of their customers, as well as the envy of their industry. When they are not operating at that high level, they feel guilty. They become angry with themselves and the company. They feel that they might just as well be working for someone else who admittedly does a sloppy job of quality control and could hardly care less about service.

The same problem exists with respect to the development of personnel, which is another vague goal that is hard to measure in comparison with subgoals that are measurable. If asked, each manager can name a younger man as his potential successor, particularly if his promotion depends on doing so; but no one has the time, or indeed feels that he is being paid, to thoroughly train the younger man. Nor can one have the time or be paid, for there is no way in that organization to measure how well a manager does in developing another.

The Missed Point

All of the problems with objectives and appraisals outlined in the example discussed in the foregoing section indicate that MBO is not working well despite what some companies think about their programs. The underlying reason it is not working well is that it misses the whole human point.

To see how the point is being missed, let us follow the typical MBO process. Characteristically, top management sets its corporate goal for the coming year. This may be in terms of return on investment, sales, production, growth, or other measurable factors.

Within this frame of reference, reporting managers may then be asked how much their units intend to contribute toward meeting that goal, or they may be asked to set their own goals relatively independent of the corporate goal. If they are left free to set their own goals, these in any case are expected to be higher than those they had the previous year. Usually, each reporting manager's range of choices is limited to his option for a piece of the organizational action, or improvement of specific statistics. In some cases, it may also include obtaining specific training or skills.

Once a reporting manager decides on his unit's goals and has them approved by his superior, those become the manager's goals. Presumably, he has committed himself to what he wants to do. He has said it and he is responsible for it. He is thereafter subject to being hoisted on his own petard.

Now, let us reexamine this process closely: the whole method is based on a short-term, egocentrically oriented perspective and an underlying reward-punishment psychology. The typical MBO process puts the reporting manager in much the same position as a rat in a maze, who has choices between only two alternatives. The experimenter who puts the rat in the maze assumes that the rat wants the food reward; if he cannot presume that, he starves the rat to make sure he wants the food.

Management by objectives differs only in that it permits the man himself to determine his own bait from a limited range of choices. Having done so, the MBO process assumes that he will (a) work hard to get it, (b) be pushed internally by reason of his commitment, and (c) make himself responsible to his organization for doing so.

In fairness to most managers, they certainly try, but not without increasing resentment and complaint for feeling like rats in a maze, guilt for not paying attention to those parts of the job not in their objectives, and passive resistance to the mounting pressure for ever-higher goals.

Personal Goals

The MBO process leaves out the answers to such questions as: What are the manager's personal objectives? What does he need and want out of his work? How do his needs and wants change from year to year? What relevance do organizational objectives and his part in them have to such needs and wants?

Obviously, no objectives will have significant incentive power if they are forced choices unrelated to a man's underlying dreams, wishes, and personal aspirations. For example:

If a salesman relishes the pleasure of his relationships with his hard-earned but low-volume customers, this is a powerful need for him. Suppose his boss, who is concerned about increasing the volume of sales, urges him to concentrate on the larger quantity customers rather than the smaller ones, which will provide the necessary increase in volume, and then asks him how much of an increase he can achieve.

To work with the larger quantity customers means that he will be less likely to sell to the individuals with whom he has well-established relationships and be more likely to deal with purchasing agents, technical people, and staff specialists who will demand of him knowledge and information he may not have in sophisticated detail. Moreover, as a single salesman, his organization may fail to support him with technical help to meet these demands.

When this happens, not only may he lose his favorite way of operating, which has well served his own needs, but he may have demands put on him which cause him to feel inadequate. If he is being compelled to make a choice about the percent of sales volume increase he expects to attain, he may well do that, but now under great psychological pressure. No one has recognized the psychological realities he faces, let alone helped him to work with them. It is simply assumed that since his sales goal is a rational one, he will see its rationality and pursue it.

The problem may be further compounded if, as is not unusual, formal changes are made in the organizational structure. If sales territories are shifted, if modes of compensation are changed, if problems of delivery occur, or whatever, all of these are factors beyond the salesman's control. Nevertheless, even with certain allowances, he is still held responsible for meeting his sales goal.

Psychological Needs

Lest the reader think the example we have just seen is overdrawn or irrelevant, I know of a young sales manager who is about to resign his job, despite his success in it, because he chooses not to be expendable in an organization which he feels regards him only as an instrument for reaching a goal. Many young men are refusing to enter large organizations for just this reason.

Some may argue that my criticism is unfair, that many organizations start their planning and setting of objectives from below. Therefore, the company cannot be accused of putting the man in a maze. But it does so. In almost all cases, the only legitimate objectives to be set are those having to do with measurable increases in performance. This highlights, again, the question, "Whose objectives?" This question becomes more pressing in those circumstances where lower level people set their objectives, only to be questioned by higher level managers and told their targets are not high enough.

Here you may well ask, "What's the matter with that? Aren't we in business, and isn't the purpose of the man's work to serve the requirements of the business?" The answer to both questions is, "Obviously." But that is only part of the story.

If a man's most powerful driving force is comprised of his needs, wishes, and personal aspirations, combined with the compelling wish to look good in his own eyes for meeting those deeply held personal goals, then management by objectives should begin with *his* objectives. What does he want to do with his life? Where does he want to go? What will make him feel good about himself? What does he want to be able to look back on when he has expended his unrecoverable years?

At this point, some may say that those are his business. The company has other business, and it must assume that the man is interested in working in the company's business rather than his own. That kind of differentiation is impossible. Everyone is always working toward meeting his psychological needs. Anyone who thinks otherwise, and who believes such powerful internal forces can be successfully disregarded or bought off for long, is deluding himself.

The Mutual Task

The organizational task becomes one of first understanding the man's needs, and then, with him, assessing how well they can be met in this organization, doing what the organization needs to have done. Thus the highest point of self-motivation arises when there is a complementary conjunction of the man's needs and the organization's requirements. The requirements of both mesh, interrelate, and become synergistic. The energies of man and organization are pooled for mutual advantage.

If the two sets of needs do not mesh, then a man has to fight himself and his organization, in addition to the work which must be done and the targets which have been defined. In such a case, this requires of him and his boss that they evaluate together where he wants to go, where the organization is going, and how significant the discrepancy is. The man might well be better off somewhere else, and the organization would do better to have someone else in his place whose needs mesh better with organization requirements.

Long-Run Costs

The issue of meshed interests is particularly relevant for middle-aged, senior-level managers.[2] As men come into middle age, their values often begin to change, and they feel anew the pressure to accomplish many long-deferred dreams. When such wishes begin to stir, they begin to experience severe conflict.

Up to this point, they have committed themselves to the organization and have done sufficiently well in it to attain high rank. Usually, they are slated for even higher levels of responsibility. The organization has been good to them, and their superiors are depending on them to provide its leadership. They have been models for the younger men, whom they have urged to aspire to organizational heights. To think of leaving is to desert both their superiors and their subordinates.

Since there are few avenues within the organization to talk about such conflict, they try to suppress their wishes. The internal pressure continues to mount until they finally make an impulsive break, surprising and dismaying both themselves and their colleagues. I can think of three vice presidents who have done just that.

The issue is not so much that they decide to leave, but the cost of the way they depart. Early discussion with superiors of their personal goals would have enabled both to examine possible relocation alternatives within the organization. If there were none, then both the managers and their superiors might have come to an earlier, more comfortable decision about separation. The organization would have had more time to make satisfactory alternative plans, as well as to have taken steps to compensate for the manager's lagging enthusiasm. Lower level managers would then have seen the company as humane in its enlightened self-interest and would not have had to create fearful fantasies about what the top management conflicts were that had caused a good man to leave.

To place consideration of the managers' personal objectives first does not minimize the importance of the organization's goals. It does not mean there is anything wrong with the organization's need to increase its return on investment, its size, its productivity, or its other goals. However, I contend that it is ridiculous to make assumptions about the motivations of individuals, and then to set up means of increasing the pressures on people based on these often questionable assumptions. While there may be certain demonstrable short-run statistical gains, what are the long-run costs?

One cost is that people may leave; another, that they may fall back from competitive positions to plateaus. Why should an individual be expendable for someone else and sacrifice himself for something that is not part of his own cherished dreams? Still another cost may be the loss of the essence of the business, as happened in the case example we saw earlier of the manufacturing plant which had the problem of deteriorating customer service.

In that example, initially there was no dialogue. Nobody heard what the managers said, what they wanted, where they wanted to go, where they wanted the organization to go, and how they felt about the supposedly rational procedures that had been initiated. The underlying psychological assumption which management unconsciously made was that the managers *had to be made* more efficient; ergo, management by objectives.

Top management typically assumes that it alone has the prerogative to (a) set the objectives, (b) provide the rewards and targets, and (c) drive anyone who works for the organization. As long as this reward-punishment psychology exists in any organization, the MBO appraisal process is certain to fail.

Many organizations are making this issue worse by promising young people they will have challenges, since they assume these men will be challenged by management's objectives. Managements are having difficulty, even when they have high turnover rates, hearing these youngsters say they could hardly care less for management's unilaterally determined objectives. Managements then become angry, complain that the young people do not want to work, or that they want to become presidents overnight.

What the young people are asking is: What about me and my needs? Who will listen? How much will management help me meet my own requirements while also meeting its objectives?

The power of this force is reflected in the finding that the more the subordinate participates in the appraisal interview by presenting his own ideas and beliefs, the more likely he is to feel that (a) the superior is helpful and constructive, (b) some current job problems are being cleared up, and (c) reasonable future goals are being set.[3]

The Suggested Steps

Given the validity of all the MBO problems I have been discussing to this point, there are a number of possibilities for coping with them. Here, I suggest three beginning steps to consider.

1. Motivational Assessment

Every management by objectives program and its accompanying performance appraisal system should be examined as to the extent to which it (1) expresses the conviction that people are patsies to be driven, urged, and manipulated, and (2) fosters a genuine partnership between men and organization, in which each has some influence over the other, as contrasted with a rat-in-maze relationship.

It is not easy for the nonpsychologist to answer such questions for himself, but there are clues to the answers. One clue is how decisions about compensation, particularly bonuses, are made. For example:

A sales manager asked my judgment about an incentive plan for highly motivated salesmen who were in a seller's market. I asked why he needed one, and he responded, "To give them an incentive." When I pointed out that they were already highly motivated and apparently needed no incentive, he changed his rationale and said that the company wanted to share its success to keep the men identified with it, and to express its recognition of their contribution.

I asked, "Why not let them establish the reward related to performance?" The question startled him; obviously, if they were going to decide, who needed him? A fundamental aspect of his role, as he saw it, was to drive them ever onward, whether they needed it or not.

A middle-management bonus plan tied to performance proved to be highly unsatisfactory in a plastic-fabricating company. Frustrated that its well-intentioned efforts were not working and determined to follow precepts of participative management, ranking executives involved many people in formulating a new one: personnel, control, marketing executives, and others—in fact, everyone but the managers who were to receive the bonuses. Top management is now dismayed that the new plan is as unsatisfactory as the old and is bitter that participation failed to work.

Another clue is the focus of company meetings. Some are devoted to intensifying the competition between units. Others lean heavily to exhortation and inspiration. Contrast these orientations with meetings in which people are apprised of problems and plan to cope with them.

2. Group Action

Every objectives and appraisal program should include group goal setting, group definition of both individual and group tasks, group appraisal of its accomplishments, group appraisal of each individual member's contribution to the group effort (without basing compensation on that appraisal), and shared compensation based on the relative success with which group goals are achieved. Objectives should include long-term as well as short-term goals.

The rationale is simple. Every managerial job is an interdependent task. Managers have responsibilities to each other as well as to their superiors. The reason for having an organization is to achieve more together than each could alone. Why, then, emphasize and reward individual performance alone, based on static job descriptions? That can only orient people to both incorrect and self-centered goals.

Therefore, where people are in complementary relationships, whether they report to the same superior or not, both horizontal and vertical goal formulation should be formalized, with regular, frequent opportunity for review of problems and progress. They should help each other define and describe their respective jobs, enhancing control and integration at the point of action.

In my judgment, for example, a group of managers (sales, promotion, advertising) reporting to a vice president of marketing should formulate their collective goals, and define ways both of helping each other and of assessing each other's effectiveness in the common task. The group assessment of each manager's work should be a means of providing each with constructive feedback, not for determining pay. However, in addition to his salary, each should receive, as part of whatever additional compensation is offered, a return based on the group effort.

The group's discussion among itself and with its superior should include examination of organizational and environmental obstacles to goal achievement, and particularly of what organizational and leadership supports are required to attain objectives. One important reason for this is that often people think there are barriers where none would exist if they initiated action. ("You mean the president really wants us to get together and solve this problem?")

Another reason is that frequently when higher management sets goals, it is unaware of significant barriers to achievement, leaving managers cynical. For example, if there is no comprehensive orientation and support program to help new employees adapt, then pressure on lower level managers to employ disadvantaged minority group members and to reduce their turnover can only be experienced by those managers as hollow mockery.

3. Appraisal of Appraisers

Every management by objectives and appraisal program should include regular appraisals of the manager by his subordinates, and be reviewed by the manager's superior. Every manager should be specifically compensated for how well he develops people, based on such appraisals. The very phrase "reporting to" reflects the fact that although a manager has a responsibility, his superior also has a responsibility for what he does and how he does it.

In fact, both common sense and research indicate that the single most significant influence outside himself on how a manager does his job is his superior. If that is the case, then the key environmental factor in task accomplishment and managerial growth is the relationship between the manager and his superior.

Therefore, objectives should include not only the individual manager's personal and occupational goals, but also the corporate goals he and his superior share in common. They should together appraise their relationship vis-à-vis both the manager's individual goals and their joint objectives, review what they have done together, and discuss its implications for their next joint steps.

A manager rarely is in a position to judge his superior's overall performance, but he can appraise him on the basis of how well the superior has helped him to do his job, how well he is helping him to increase his proficiency and visibility, what problems the supervisor poses for him, and what kinds of support he himself can use. Such feedback serves several purposes.

Most important, it offers the superior some guidance on his own managerial performance. In addition, and particularly when the manager is protected by higher level review of his appraisal, it provides the supervisor with direct feedback on his own behavior. This is much more constructive than behind-his-back complaint and vituperative terminal interviews, in which cases he has no opportunity either to defend himself or correct his behavior. Every professional counselor has had recently fired executive clients who did not know why they had been discharged for being poor superiors when, according to their information, their subordinates thought so much of them. In his own self-interest, every manager should want appraisal by his subordinates.

The Basic Consideration

When the three organizational conditions we have just seen do in fact exist, then it is appropriate to think of starting management by objectives with a consideration of each man's personal objectives; if the underlying attitude in the organization toward him is that he is but an object, there is certainly no point in starting with the man. Nor is there any point in trying to establish his confidence in his superiors when he is not protected from their rivalry with him, or when they are playing him off against his peers. Anyone who expressed his fears and innermost wishes under these circumstances would be a damned fool.

For reasons I have already indicated, it should be entirely legitimate in every business for these concerns to be the basis for individual objectives-setting. This is because the fundamental managerial consideration necessarily must be focused on the question: "How do we meet both individual and organizational purposes?" If a major intention of management by objectives is to enlist the self-motivated commitment of the individual, then that commitment must derive from the individual's powerful wishes to support the organization's goals; otherwise, the commitment will be merely incidental to his personal wishes.

Having said that, the real difficulty begins. How can any superior know what a subordinate's personal goals and wishes are if the subordinate himself—as most of us are—is not clear about them? How ethical is it for a superior to pry into a man's personal life? How can he keep himself from forming a negative judgment about a man who, he knows, is losing interest in his work, or is not altogether identified with the company? How can he keep that knowledge from interfering with judgments he might otherwise make, and opportunities he might otherwise offer? How often are the personal goals, particularly in middle age, temporary fantasies that are better not discussed? Can a superior who is un-trained in psychology handle such information constructively? Will he perhaps do more harm than good?

These are critically important questions. They deserve careful thought. My answers should be taken as no more than beginning steps.

Ego Concepts

Living is a process of constant adaptation. A man's personal goals, wishes, and aspirations are continuously evolving, and being continuously modified by his experiences. That is one reason why it is so difficult for an individual to specify concrete personal objectives.

Nevertheless, each of us has a built-in road map, a picture of himself at his future best. Psychologists speak of this as an *ego ideal,* which is comprised of a man's values, the expectations parents and others have held out for him, his competences and skills, and his favorite ways of behaving. A man's ego ideal is essentially the way he thinks he ought to be. Much of a person's ego ideal is unconscious, which is another reason why it is not clear to him.

Subordinate's Self-Examination   Although a man cannot usually spell out his ego ideal, he can talk about those experiences that have been highly gratifying, even exhilarating, to him. He can specify those rare peak experiences that made him feel very good about himself. When he has an opportunity to talk about what he has found especially gratifying and also what he thinks would be gratifying to him, he is touching on central elements of his ego ideal.

Given the opportunity to talk about such experiences and wishes on succes-sive occasions, he can begin to spell out for himself the central thrust of his life. Reviewing all of the occupational choices he has made and the reasons for making them, he can begin to see the common threads in those choices and therefore the momentum of his personality. As these become clearer to him, he is in a better position to weigh alternatives against the mainstream of his personality.

For example, a man who has successively chosen occupational alternatives in which he was individually competitive, and whose most exhilarating experi-ences have come from defeating an opponent or single-handedly vanquishing a problem, would be unlikely to find a staff position exhilarating, no matter what it paid or what it was called. His ideal for himself is that of a vanquishing, competitive man.

The important concept here is that it is not necessary that a man spell out concrete goals at any one point; rather, it is helpful to him and his orga-nization if he is able to examine and review aloud on a continuing basis his thoughts and feelings about himself in relation to his work. Such a process makes it legitimate for him to bring his own feelings to consciousness and talk about them in the business context as the basis for his relationship to the organization.

By listening, and helping him to spell out how and what he feels, the superior does not *do* anything to the man, and therefore by that self-appraisal process cannot hurt him. The information serves both the man and his superior as a criterion for examining the relationship of the man's feelings and his, however dimly perceived, personal goals to organizational goals. Even if some of his wishes and aspirations are mere fantasy and impossible to gratify, if it is legitimate to talk about them without being laughed at, he can compare them with the realities of his life and make more reasonable choices.

Even in the safest organizational atmosphere, for reasons already mentioned, it will not be easy for managers to talk about their goals. The best-intentioned supervisor is likely to be something less than a highly skilled interviewer. These two facts suggest that any effort to ascertain a subordinate's personal goals is futile; but I think not.

The important point is not the specificity of the statement that any man can make, but the nature of a superior-subordinate relationship that makes it safe to explore such feelings and gives first consideration to the man. In such a context, both subordinate and superior may come closer to evolving a man-organization fit than they might otherwise.

Superior's Introspection   A man-organization relationship requires the superior to do some introspection, too. Suppose he has prided himself on bringing along a bright young man who, he now learns, is thinking of moving into a different field. How can he keep from being angry and disappointed? How can he cope with the conflict he now has when it is time to make recommendations for advancement or a raise?

The superior cannot keep from being angry and disappointed. Such feelings are natural in that circumstance. He can express his feelings of disappointment to his protégé without being critical of the latter. But, if he continues to feel angry, then he needs to ask himself why another man's assertion of independence irritates him so. The issues of advancement and raises should continue to be based on the same realistic premises as they would have been before.

Of course, it now becomes appropriate to consider with the man whether—in view of his feelings—he wants to take on the burden of added responsibility and can reasonably discharge it. If he thinks he does, and can, he is likely to pursue the new responsibility with added determination. With his occupational choice conflict no longer hidden, and with fewer feelings of guilt about it, his commitment to his chosen alternative is likely to be more intense.

And if he has earned a raise, he should get it. To withhold it is to punish him, which puts the relationship back on a reward-punishment basis.

The question of how ethical it is to conduct such discussions as part of a business situation hinges on both the climate of the organization and on the sense of personal responsibility of each executive. Where the organization ethos is one of building trust and keeping confidences, there is no reason why executives cannot be as ethical as lawyers or physicians.

If the individual executive cannot be trusted in his relationships with his subordinates, then he cannot have their respect or confidence in any case, and the ordinary MBO appraisal process simply serves as a management pressure device. If the organization ethos is one of rapacious internal competition, backbiting, and distrust, there is little point in talking about self-motivation, human needs, or commitment.

Conclusion

Management by objectives and performance appraisal processes, as typically practiced, are inherently self-defeating over the long run because they are based on a reward-punishment psychology that serves to intensify the pressure on the individual while really giving him a very limited choice of objectives. Such processes can be improved by examining the psychological assumptions under-lying them, by extending them to include group appraisal and appraisal of superiors by subordinates, and by considering the personal goals of the individ-ual first. These practices require a high level of ethical standards and personal responsibility in the organization.

Such appraisal processes would diminish the feeling on the part of the superior that appraisal is a hostile, destructive act. While he and his subordinates would still have to judge the latter's individual performance, this judgment would occur in a context of continuing consideration for personal needs and reappraisal of organizational and environmental realities.

Not having to be continuously on the defensive and aware of the orga-nization's genuine interest in having him meet his personal goals as well as the organization's goals, a manager would be freer to evaluate himself against what has to be done. Since he would have many additional frames of reference in both horizontal and vertical goal setting, he would need no longer to see himself under appraisal (attack, judgment) as an isolated individual against the system. Furthermore, he would have multiple modes for contributing his own ideas and a varied method for exerting influence upward and horizontally.

In these contexts, too, he could raise questions and concerns about qualita-tive aspects of performance. Then he, his colleagues, and his superiors could together act to cope with such issues without the barrier of having to consider only statistics. Thus a continuing process of interchange would counteract the problem of the static job description and provide multiple avenues for feedback on performance and joint action.

In such an organizational climate, work relationships would then become dynamic networks for both personal and organizational achievements. No incidental gain from such arrangements is that problems would more likely be solved spontaneously at the lowest possible levels, and free superiors simulta-neously from the burden of the passed buck and the onus of being the purveyors of hostility.

References

1. "An Uneasy Look at Performance Appraisal," HBR May–June 1957, p. 89.
2. See my article, "On Being a Middle-Aged Manager," HBR July–August 1969, p. 51.
3. Ronald J. Burke and Douglas S. Wilcox, "Characteristics of Effective Employee Performance Reviews and Developmental Interviews," *Personal Psychology,* Vol. 22, No. 3, 1969, p. 291.

Sources

In the part of the article which defines the ideal process and the major problems inherent in it, I draw heavily on the work of these authors, in sequence:

Alva F. Kindall and James Gatza, "Positive Program for Performance Appraisal," HBR November–December 1963, p. 153.

Herbert H. Meyer, Emanuel Kay, and John R. P. French, Jr., "Split Roles in Performance Appraisal," HBR January–February 1965, p. 123.

Ishwar Dayal, "Role Analysis Techniques in Job Description," *California Management Review,* Vol. XI, No. 4, 1969, p. 47.

Stanley Sloan and Alton C. Johnson, "Performance Appraisal . . . Where Are We Headed?" *The Personnel Administrator,* Vol. 14, No. 5, 1969, p. 12.

Philip R. Kelly, "Reappraisal of Appraisals," HBR May–June 1958, p. 59.

Robert A. Howell, "A Fresh Look at Management by Objectives," *Business Horizons,* Vol. 10, No. 3, 1967, p. 51.

Albert W. Schrader, "Let's Abolish the Annual Performance Review," *Management of Personnel Quarterly,* Fall 1969, p. 20.

George H. Labovitz, "In Defense of Subjective Executive Appraisal," *Academy of Management Journal,* Vol. 12, No. 3, 1969, p. 293.

Larry E. Greiner, D. Paul Leitch, and Louis B. Barnes, "Putting Judgment Back Into Decisions," HBR March–April 1970, p. 59.

George Strauss and Leonard R. Sayles, *Personnel: The Human Problems of Management* (Englewood Cliffs, New Jersey, Prentice-Hall, Inc., 1967), p. 564.

Making Cost Control Work

RENSIS LIKERT, STANLEY E. SEASHORE

Many companies today are in a serious profit squeeze. They are struggling to maintain satisfactory earnings in a situation where costs are rising but price increases are becoming more and more difficult to obtain. Foreign and domestic competition as well as governmental efforts to prevent further inflation put serious restraints on additional price increases.

To maintain earnings in the face of these conditions, many companies are taking strong steps to reduce costs, eliminate waste, and increase productivity. Automation and improvements in technologies are helping to reduce costs but are often insufficient. The top managements of many companies, as a consequence, are putting pressure on their organizations at every point. Jobs are being timed and standards set in manufacturing departments where timing and standards did not exist previously. These procedures are also being extended into office operations. Budgets are being made more detailed; they are tighter and are controlled more rigorously. Economies are being sought all through the organization.

These developments are typical of a current emphasis in American business. The purpose of this article is to examine the consequence of these steps—long range as well as short range—and to propose an alternate course of action with more promising long-range results.

Prevailing Pitfalls

The price of most current methods of cost reduction is high and hidden. The impressive and immediate reduction in costs, increase in productivity, and improvement in earnings induced by pressure are only half the story. The other half is the price tag which management does not see—at least at first. It is obscured by several interrelated factors:

1. Cost-reduction procedures, such as setting standards and pressing for higher performance, are usually applied most vigorously and extensively to operations where automation and similar technological changes occur most often.

2. A much longer time interval than is generally recognized is required before the adverse effects from the usual approach to cost reduction begin to have an impact. As a consequence, the improvements in productivity and costs caused by automation and technological changes tend to hide, at least for a period of time, any unfavorable trends brought about by the usual cost-reduction procedures.

3. Not only the overlap in time but the character of accounting procedures tend to obscure the trends occurring simultaneously in the organization. The customary measurement and accounting procedures yield figures which reflect only the composite picture of all of the developments affecting the productivity and earnings of the company. Some of these developments may be internal and some external to the company; some may be favorable and some unfavorable. So long as the impact on productivity and costs of each causal variable is not measured separately, it is impossible to know from the accounting data alone whether serious, unfavorable developments are being masked by favorable developments of greater magnitude.

4. When the unfavorable trends in productivity, waste, and costs, and in such other factors as labor relations, finally become evident, there are no measurements which point to the true causes of the adverse shifts. As a consequence, a wrong diagnosis is often made, the wrong causes are blamed, and the corrective steps are focused on the wrong variables.

In order to examine the long-range costs of the usual approach to cost reduction, let us consider the sequence of events which would be likely to occur in a company if there were no technological changes or product changes. These changes, of course, do occur, and it is their effects which obscure the long-range consequences of cost reduction. To point up the total impact of cost-reduction efforts, the following discussion describes the sequence of developments which would probably occur in a company were the usual cost-reduction procedures introduced and *no technological changes or major product changes made during the total interval being examined.* This sequence of developments is shown in Exhibit 1.

Exhibit 1 How Conventional Pressures to Reduce Costs Affect Operations in a Well-Organized and Well-Managed Company

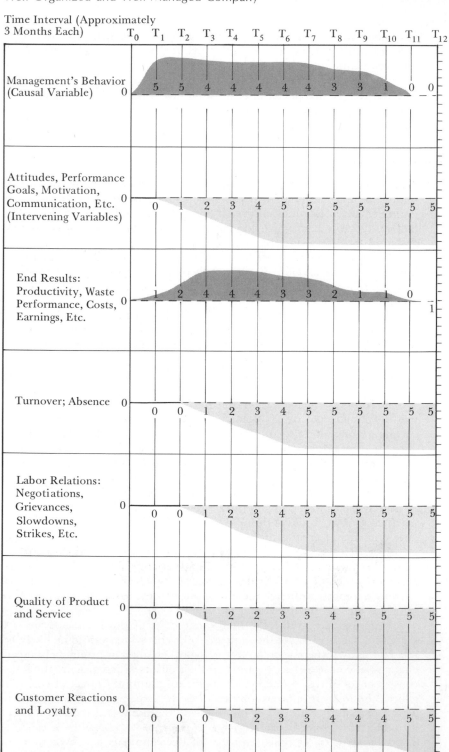

Time Interval (Approximately 3 Months Each)

	T_0	T_1	T_2	T_3	T_4	T_5	T_6	T_7	T_8	T_9	T_{10}	T_{11}	T_{12}
Management's Behavior (Causal Variable) 0		5	5	4	4	4	4	4	3	3	1	0	0
Attitudes, Performance Goals, Motivation, Communication, Etc. (Intervening Variables) 0		0	1	2	3	4	5	5	5	5	5	5	5
End Results: Productivity, Waste Performance, Costs, Earnings, Etc. 0		1	2	4	4	4	3	3	2	1	1	0	1
Turnover; Absence 0		0	0	1	2	3	4	5	5	5	5	5	5
Labor Relations: Negotiations, Grievances, Slowdowns, Strikes, Etc. 0		0	0	1	2	3	4	5	5	5	5	5	5
Quality of Product and Service 0		0	0	1	2	2	3	3	4	5	5	5	5
Customer Reactions and Loyalty 0		0	0	0	1	2	3	3	4	4	4	5	5

Cost-Reduction Sequence

The composite picture shown in Exhibit 1 is *hypothetical*. It shows trends with technological and product changes held constant—a condition which rarely exists. The exhibit is based on results from studies and field experiments conducted in many companies. Some of these studies have been conducted by the Institute for Social Research, and some by other research organizations and by individual companies. Some of them have been published (see Appendix); others are not yet in print. Many of those done by companies may never be published. Few of the studies deal with a time interval as long as that shown in Exhibit 1, but enough data are available to permit estimates of the trends. Only a few of all the studies drawn upon were focused specifically on the effect of cost-reduction programs on the organization; that effect was apparent in the data but not singled out as it is here.

Exhibit 1 is divided into vertical columns which represent time intervals of approximately three months' duration. The horizontal rows in the exhibit represent the different factors that must be weighed in evaluating a cost-reduction program. The dark gray areas represent improvement; the light gray areas represent an adverse trend.

In this article we shall refer to three broad classes of variables labeled, respectively, causal, intervening, and end-result:

The *causal* variables are the independent variables which determine the course of developments within an organization and the results achieved by the organization. These causal variables include the structure of the organization and management's policies, decisions, business and leadership strategies, and behavior.

The *intervening* variables reflect the internal state and health of the organization, e.g., the loyalties, attitudes, motivations, performance goals, perceptions, and skills of all members and their collective capacity for effective interaction, communication, and decision making.

The *end-result* variables are the dependent variables which reflect the achievements of the organization, such as its productivity, costs, scrap loss, and earnings.

First Steps and Early Gains

Cost reduction is generally initiated by decisions at the top of the organization. The efforts of management usually are not limited to a short time period, nor are they limited in scale. They customarily extend over a few years at least and deal with every part of the organization where it is believed that action can be taken. There is likely to be a reduction in personnel, especially in staff departments. In addition, these moves are likely to take place: standards are introduced or are extended to more jobs; increased pressure is applied to get performance up to standard; budgets are tightened and subject to closer control; maintenance and supply activities are often curtailed; and activities with uncertain or distant value such as research and development may be cut back. This abrupt change in behavior by top management with its resulting pressures on the organization is shown by the rapid rise in the dark gray area at T_1 in the first row of Exhibit 1. The duration of the cost-reduction effort is represented by the slow decline through time in the dark gray area, from 4 at T_7 to zero at T_{11}. (The units of gain or decline are, of course, arbitrary.)

The change in management's behavior usually results in an almost immediate improvement in productivity and reduction in costs in companies where reasonably good organization and management exist. This improvement in productivity and costs is shown in Exhibit 1 by the dark gray area at T_1 in the third row down, since it typically becomes apparent during that time period.

We have data from several situations which show that these cost-reduction efforts can result in continuing improvement in productivity and costs over some span of time, as shown in Exhibit 1.

But several months after the cost-reduction program starts, the lower levels of management and the nonsupervisory employees are apt to begin developing hostile reactions toward the cost-reduction program and toward higher levels of management. These reactions occur in response to the increase in direct, hierarchical pressure for greater productivity and decreased costs. (This negative shift in the intervening variables is shown by the increasing light gray area at times T_2 and T_3.) The changes in the intervening variables during the initial months of the cost-reduction effort are not as a rule of sufficient magnitude to produce measurable changes in such aspects of operations as employee turnover and absence, product quality, and service to customers.

After about one year, cost-reduction efforts will have been applied to many activities of the company, and the resulting benefits in such financial variables as productivity, costs, and earnings will be approaching their maximum as represented by the dark gray area for times T_3 to T_5 in Exhibit 1.

Second-Year Trouble Signs

During the last half of the first year and on through the second year of the cost-reduction effort, however, the continuing, extended, and increased pressure for improvement in productivity and costs causes a further deterioration in the intervening variables. Attitudes, performance goals, work motivation, and the adequacy and accuracy of communication continue to shift in an unfavorable direction. For example:

There is an increase in the proportion of both supervisory and nonsupervisory employees who resent the direct, hierarchical pressure for increased production and view it as "unreasonable pressure." They are apt also to react unfavorably to many of the other related actions taken by management. Anxieties also may arise from fears of unemployment or reduced employment. These anxieties and resentments produce serious changes in attitudes and behavior.

Confidence and trust in management decline further. Communication, both as sent and as received, becomes more filtered, biased, and distorted. The decision-making processes begin to deteriorate as the information available for company decision makers becomes less adequate and less accurate.

The unfavorable trends in the attitudinal, motivational, and other intervening variables begin, in turn, to be manifest in increased turnover and absence, poorer labor relations, more concerted effort to restrict production, and less satisfactory quality of product and of service. The entire organization's capacity to function effectively begins to decrease. The poorer quality of the product and the more hostile employee attitudes adversely affect customers, and an unfavorable shift in customer loyalty may begin to occur as early as the last quarter of the year. All these unfavorable developments are shown in Exhibit

1 as light gray areas at time T_3 and subsequently. The adverse trend falls steadily from 1 to 5 on the bottom half of the scale.

Trends in waste performance during these periods will depend on the attention given by management to waste control. If as much emphasis is placed on keeping waste to a minimum as is placed on achieving high productivity, then waste performance will be about as satisfactory as productivity. If not, then the adverse trend in the intervening variables is likely to cause waste performance to show a similar adverse trend.

Sometime during the second year a very important change begins to occur. Although pressure for cost reduction may remain high, the actual performance on costs and productivity starts to drop back from the favorable level achieved during the earlier phases of the cost push.

This drop in productivity and earnings stems from several unfavorable developments in the organization—absence and turnover increase (especially turnover among the more able employees); labor relations worsen; grievances increase, with slowdowns or wildcat strikes beginning to occur; and the quality of the product and services decreases, with customer satisfaction and loyalty suffering a further slump—with all that means for sales and profits.

About the end of the second year, a further important change begins. The increase in labor difficulties and in turnover among the better employees, and the greater scrap loss, poorer quality, and decreased customer satisfaction stimulate top management to start examining what is happening and why. This may lead to corrective action at that time, or such action may not occur for another several months.

Deterioration and Failure

Somewhat later, perhaps about the middle of the third year, top management is likely to be compelled to take corrective action and reduce substantially the pressure for higher productivity and lower costs. This is often precipitated by the serious labor difficulties or quality-control problems that have cropped up. (In one company, for example, distributors did not want products fabricated in a plant with a history of deteriorating employee relations.) If a particular plant or a decentralized division is the organizational unit involved, top management often responds by removing the manager of that operation. The new manager is often selected for his skills in dealing with people and handling "human relations" problems. Often such a manager is told that his job is to reduce scrap loss, improve product and service quality, and bring a major change in the labor climate. He is expected to reduce grievances, stop wildcat strikes, and correct similar manifestations of serious supervisory and labor dissatisfaction. Pressure for high productivity and cost control is discontinued at this time as priority is given to these other serious problems.

During the third and fourth years of such a cycle of events, even though the pressure for productivity and cost reduction is removed and attention is focused on improving human relations, there is likely to be little improvement in the intervening variables (attitudes, motivations, performance goals, capacity for effective interaction, communication, and decision making), and little improvement in such matters as turnover, absence, labor relations, restriction of output, quality, scrap loss, and customer loyalty. When hostile attitudes, uncooperative motivation, and distrust of management are widespread and deep-seated, it requires years for even an extremely competent manager to bring about any substantial improvement. Once middle management, supervisors, and nonsupervisory employees have lost faith in top management, the situation is hard to reverse. The same, of course, is also true of customer loyalty.

Negative Results

While no long-term study has as yet been conducted to verify the cycle just described and shown in Exhibit 1, nevertheless this cycle does conform, as earlier indicated, to the data obtained in a number of studies, and it conforms also to the experiences of executives who have survived such cycles. The cycle as described shows what is likely to occur if the usual approach to cost reduction is followed and *if there are no appreciable changes in the company's product or technology.*

Modifications in the pattern may occur for various reasons:

The duration of the cycle and of its different phases may vary depending on the history of the organization, the labor climate of the community, the degree of pressure exerted by management to reduce costs, the competitive situation in the industry, and comparable factors.

The full cycle described is apt to occur only when top management persists in its original strategy to reduce costs and increase productivity. In some situations, top management detects the unfavorable developments at an early stage and promptly modifies its approach. When this happens, the general sequence of events is modified accordingly.

If the company is poorly organized and under loose management, the initial response to cost reduction and tighter management is almost always favorable. Productivity will improve appreciably and so will the variables. Whether this initial improvement is followed by the cycle described in Exhibit 1 will depend on the extent to which management pursues the cost-reduction steps described above.

This cycle does not apply to all situations in which jobs are timed and standards set. It refers only to those situations in which top management is felt to be *changing* its behavior substantially. Such changes may involve introducing standards, extending standards, pressing for higher productivity, tightening budgets, or taking other similar steps toward aggressive cost reduction.

In those companies where measured work has been used for some time, with or without piece rates, and where there is a well-established process for setting and reviewing standards which all parties involved feel is equitable, the pattern shown in Exhibit 1 does not appear to be present. Employees working under standards may, and often do, have somewhat less favorable attitudes than employees not under standards, but marked changes seem to occur only in situations where management is changing its behavior by increasing pressure for higher productivity and lower costs.

Effects Obscured

If the long-range adverse consequences of the usual approach to cost reduction are as great as Exhibit 1 suggests, why do so many companies continue to use this approach rather than seek better alternatives? Why do they not recognize what is happening? As has been suggested, there appear to be several related reasons.

Impact of Automation   Most cost-reduction programs occur in the context of continuing technological innovation. New products are introduced, automation is extended, production facilities and processes are improved. These generally have immediate and marked effects on the overall cost performance of the company and tend to obscure the slowly developing organizational decay that may be occurring. Even where there is evidence of such developing counterforces to cost control as less favorable attitudes and increased grievances and other labor difficulties, these adverse developments are often neglected or are attributed to factors other than their true causes. Thus signs of growing organizational problems are often overlooked in the face of the certain evidence that cost improvements are in fact being achieved. It is common, for example, for technological changes and process improvements to result in a gain that is substantially less than that anticipated on purely technological grounds. Similarly, a program for innovation often takes considerably longer than planned. These developments, while sobering, are usually accepted as an inevitable accompaniment of major technological changes, and are not diagnosed as signs of serious deterioration in the quality of the human organization.

Information Gaps   To further obscure events, many firms are able to achieve continuing cost improvement over a span of several years and, understandably, come to rely increasingly on staff innovators to overcome the growing resistance to change and improvement rather than turning their attention equally to building a total organization oriented toward the optimum use of technological opportunities. Until accounting procedures are developed to the point where the cost gains from technological improvements are evaluated in the light of accurate estimates of the gains that should be obtained, the substantial expenses of organizational deterioration are not likely to be recognized or acted upon. These expenses are also obscured by the accounting practice of adding to the burden the costs incurred when plants are shut down because of wildcat strikes and similar events. These charges should be handled so that both their causes and their magnitude are immediately evident.

   If top management were to be confronted promptly with such information instead of having it buried in the burden, the likelihood of constructive action would be much greater, especially if the data made clear that management can choose to incur or not incur these costs.

   In addition, managers are handicapped by lack of systematic evidence revealing at an early stage adverse organizational trends. Sensitive managers may sense from scattered items of information the problems which are developing, but they lack data accepted as legitimate which would enable them to diagnose correctly the unfavorable developments occurring in their organizations and to obtain corrective action.

   A manager's cost reports, which come in monthly, or oftener, provide a sensitive barometer of the financial effects of actions taken under the urgency of a cost-reduction program. These immediate financial results have a compelling meaning. Information about the intervening variables concerning the motivation and behavior of his people is harder for a manager to get and harder to interpret. If top management is to be aware of the events pictured in Exhibit 1, there must be assessment of the causal and intervening variables in some manner that makes this kind of information available periodically and in a form that illuminates the trend of events. This is likely to require the measurement at regular intervals of all three kinds of variables, i.e., causal, intervening, and end-result, for the same operating units and the full analysis of the interrelationships and trends among these variables.[1]

Delayed Reaction A third reason for the frequent disregard of growing organizational problems arises out of the time delay pictured in Exhibit 1. Some of the adverse consequences of crash cost programs appear several months after the effort begins and are not easily associated with their earlier causes. The more dramatic consequences such as loss of key personnel or costly labor difficulties may not take place until long after the main cost push is past. To discern the connection between events so separated in time is not easy for busy managers who are under pressure for early results and are not often encouraged to take a longer perspective.

New System

If the current approaches to cost reduction and improved productivity tend to arouse negative forces which in the long run defeat the objectives sought, what other courses of action are there?

The usual approaches to cost reduction involve many highly effective and valuable procedures. The solution to achieving low costs and high productivity continuously is not to reject all aspects of current procedures but to develop a system of management which uses these procedures appropriately and in such a manner that cooperating rather than hostile motivations are created among both the supervisory and nonsupervisory members of the organization. A clue as to how this can be done and the nature of the resulting management system is provided by social science research coupled with the innovative insights and behavior of the most productive managers in American business.

A substantial number of objective, quantitative studies conducted by the Institute for Social Research and other investigators have demonstrated that there are important differences in behavior and management philosophy between those managers who achieve the highest productivity and best performance and those who attain mediocre results.

Characteristics of Approach

The highest producing managers, on the average, do not achieve their high-productivity, low-cost operations by putting direct, hierarchical pressure on their subordinates. They obtain high productivity levels by building cooperative organizations that have high motivation, high performance goals, efficient communication, and good teamwork, and that seek in every way to achieve the organization's objectives in the most economical and most efficient manner. Their methods of management are such that the noneconomic motives reinforce the economic motives rather than causing conflicting motivational forces. Such highly effective organizations, of course, are not built overnight. Their construction takes time.

There is increasing recognition that the highest producing managers use different principles of management from those used by less successful managers and place greater stress than other managers on building an organization with favorable attitudes and high loyalty and performance goals. There is much less awareness, however, that their principles and strategies can be used to achieve substantial and enduring cost reduction.

As might be expected, the highest producing managers in seeking low-cost performance typically do not introduce abrupt, high-pressure cost programs. These managers display a greater sensitivity and responsiveness to changes in the intervening variables and hold to a steady and long-range time perspective on all factors affecting costs and performance. They do not believe that successful and sustained cost reduction is achieved by instituting a high-pressure cost-cutting program or series of programs. Instead they seek to build an organization which has high productivity goals, is motivated to reduce waste and costs, and tries to discover and to use every possible avenue and resource to increase its performance in all respects. Cost concern is a continuous characteristic of the organization.

Four developments are taking place which should facilitate the general application of this more progressive approach to cost control:

1. The basic principles of management used by the highest producing managers are being understood increasingly well as a result of social science research.
2. Systematic integration of these principles into generalized statements is occurring.[2] These generalized formulations enable the basic principles to be more readily applied to a particular plant or operating situation.
3. There is a very small but growing body of data and experience to show that most managers who are earnestly motivated to do so and whose company situations permit it can learn to apply the principles used by the best managers and thereby improve the productivity and costs of their units.[3]
4. It is now possible to measure the causal and intervening variables. Having these data regularly available enables managers to work with confidence and with an adequate time perspective in achieving long-range cost control.

When a management seeks to achieve continuous cost control by applying an approach based on the principles followed by the highest producing managers, full use is made of all relevant existing technologies. Thus, effective use is made of work simplification, automation, setting of performance goals, and similar procedures. These resources are used, however, with a fundamentally different set of motivational assumptions and principles.

Limitations of Research

While we believe that an impressive case can be made for this alternate approach on the basis of the results it produces, we must stress that the research to date is far from complete. For one thing, experimental studies have been made in relatively few situations:

In some of these experimental studies, some departments of the organization employed an approach for increasing productivity and reducing costs based on the principles of management used by the highest producing managers, while other, matched departments employed more traditional approaches.

In other field tests, unfortunately, it was not possible to establish these highly desirable matched controls. In such instances, it was possible to measure only the changes over time in the intervening and end-result variables and to compare these changes with previous trends in the departments or plants involved and with general trends elsewhere in the corporation.

A few of the experimental field tests have involved an attempt to apply a relatively integrated and coordinated set of principles to most aspects of the operation. The majority of the experimental field tests, however, have dealt with modifying only limited, but important, parts of the system. For example, the supervisory and decision-making processes were changed but no change was made in the selection procedures.

The number of employees involved in the more carefully controlled studies has varied from approximately one hundred to several hundred. Some of the less rigorous applications have involved as many as several thousand employees. Most of the projects have involved several supervisory or managerial levels. Parts of these studies have been published, but much remains to be published.

An important conclusion has emerged from this research. All of the major organizational variables must be measured over a longer period of time than was thought to be necessary when the work was started. Unfortunately, this was not realized until after the first two of the more rigorous experimental studies were completed. As a consequence, none of the more carefully controlled field experiments which have been completed to date has continued to measure the causal, intervening, and end-result variables for as long a period of time as we now know is necessary to explore fully all the developments occurring as this proposed system of management is applied in an organization. All the variables need to be measured for at least three years and preferably five.

What is the sequence of developments which occurs when this approach to increasing productivity and reducing costs is applied in an organization? The trends shown in Exhibit 2 are based on data pieced together from many different sources. The time intervals and the particular sequence shown represent estimates of the overall pattern. The sequence of developments and the timing will, of course, vary from company to company and will depend on management's behavior as well as on the history and current situation of the company.

First Signs of Progress

The first steps in applying this new approach require that managers and supervisors learn the relevant principles, master their application, and develop the behavioral skills to use them on the job.[4] Several months, at least, are required for this to be done well enough for subordinates to notice any change in their superior's behavior. (Some managers, of course, will have already used many of the principles and practices of this new approach, and for them progress would be faster.) Actually, it will take about a year before supervisory and nonsupervisory employees experience a sufficient amount of change in a sufficient number of circumstances to be persuaded that management is *really* behaving more supportively, displaying greater confidence and trust, communicating more adequately, involving subordinates more fully in decisions about their work, and so forth. When this does happen, the situation as revealed by the intervening

Exhibit 2 How the Proposed System of Management Improves Performance and Reduces Costs

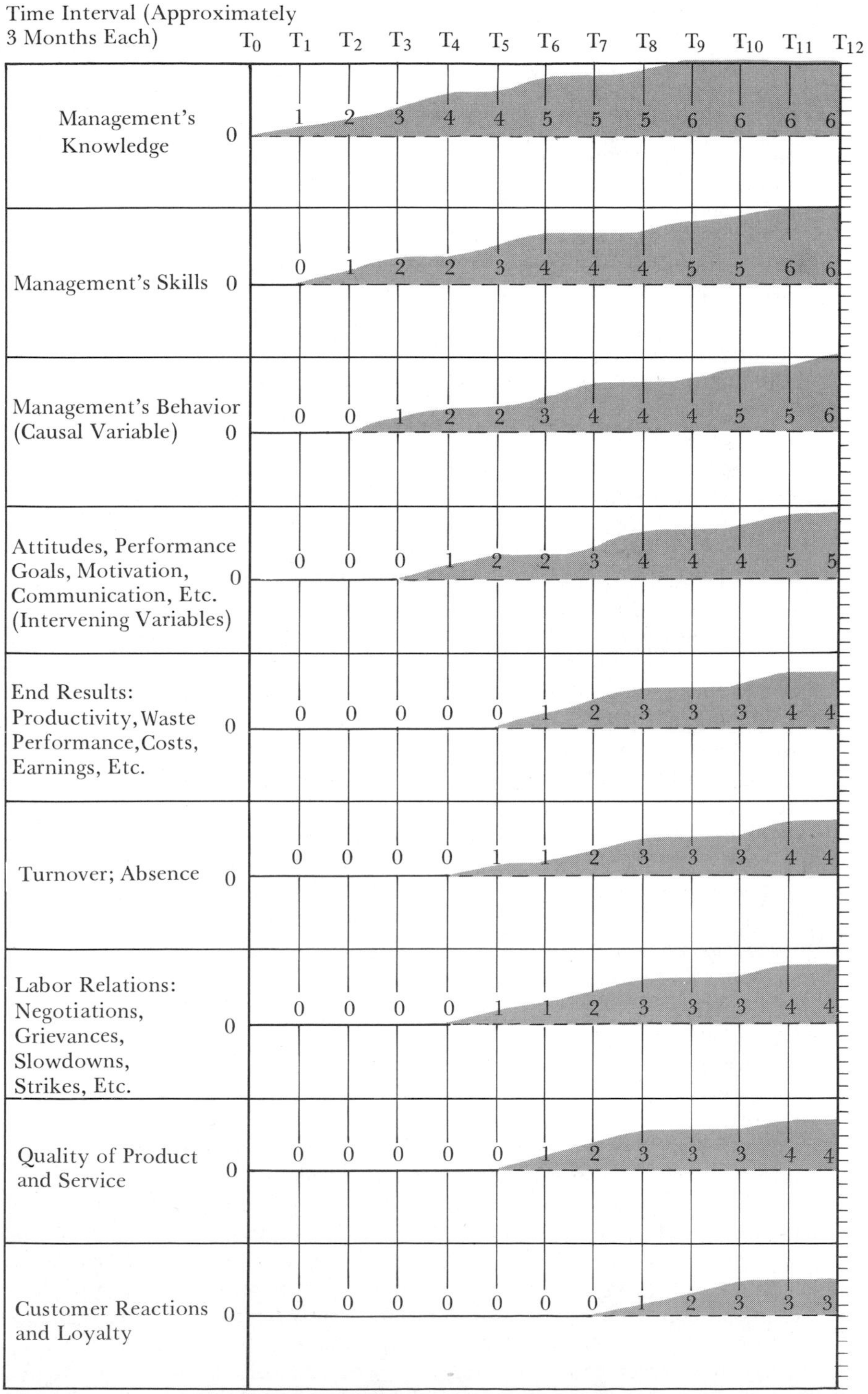

Time Interval (Approximately 3 Months Each)

	T_0	T_1	T_2	T_3	T_4	T_5	T_6	T_7	T_8	T_9	T_{10}	T_{11}	T_{12}
Management's Knowledge	0	1	2	3	4	4	5	5	5	6	6	6	6
Management's Skills	0	0	1	2	2	3	4	4	4	5	5	6	6
Management's Behavior (Causal Variable)	0	0	0	1	2	2	3	4	4	4	5	5	6
Attitudes, Performance Goals, Motivation, Communication, Etc. (Intervening Variables)	0	0	0	0	1	2	2	3	4	4	4	5	5
End Results: Productivity, Waste Performance, Costs, Earnings, Etc.	0	0	0	0	0	0	1	2	3	3	3	4	4
Turnover; Absence	0	0	0	0	0	1	1	2	3	3	3	4	4
Labor Relations: Negotiations, Grievances, Slowdowns, Strikes, Etc.	0	0	0	0	0	1	1	2	3	3	3	4	4
Quality of Product and Service	0	0	0	0	0	0	1	2	3	3	3	4	4
Customer Reactions and Loyalty	0	0	0	0	0	0	0	0	1	2	3	3	3

variables will show an improvement. (See the dark gray area starting about T_4 in the fourth row down in Exhibit 2.)

Improvement in the intervening variables, as reflected in their measurements, means that communication is improving, loyalty is greater, performance goals are higher, and the organization is more tightly knit. There is greater coordination of effort, decisions are based on more accurate information, and there is greater motivation to achieve the organization's objectives. This improvement in the organization—as shown by the measurements of the intervening variables—is not immediately reflected, however, in improved productivity, waste performance, and reduced costs.

Steady Gains

As managers and supervisors acquire more learning and skill in applying the proposed system of management and as information from the measurements of the intervening variables helps to guide their actions, their subordinates' experiences and perceptions become progressively more favorable. As a consequence, measurements of the intervening variables show steady improvement during the second year (note the wider dark gray area in Exhibit 2).

After substantial and continued improvement in attitudes, communication, confidence and trust, performance goals, and so on, increases in productivity and quality, and reduction in costs, scrap loss, and waste begin to occur. About this time, corresponding improvement in turnover, absence, and labor relations also becomes evident.

The general trend of steady but impressive improvement continues through the third and subsequent years. In other words, although improvement starts slowly with this approach to better management and reduced costs, it continues steadily until favorable levels are obtained. Customer reactions rise to 3 on the scale; the other end results rise to 4.

The contrast in developments with regard to supervisory and nonsupervisory attitudes and to labor relations under the old and new approaches is marked and substantial. The magnitude and importance of this difference are clarified and strengthened if one examines the history of managerial behavior in situations where prolonged strikes, frequent breakdowns in negotiations, and other manifestations of bitter, irreconcilable labor-management conflict exist. Although local labor climate and similar factors cannot be ignored as a source of problems, nevertheless, the plant management's past behavior is consistent with the cycle depicted in Exhibit 1. Further, the strikes, slowdowns, and prolonged negotiations now being experienced could have been predicted one or more years in advance from the trends in the intervening variables.

An important advantage of the proposed approach to cost control is that organizations which use it can make more timely, more rapid, and more successful use of automation, technological changes, and product changes.[5] This flexibility is due to the greater cooperative motivation and more effective communication and coordination present in such organizations. The motivation of the members of an organization can be crucial in determining whether labor-saving processes—computers or automated equipment—are made to work well or poorly. Supervisory and nonsupervisory employees, if they wish to do so, can make excellent equipment perform unsatisfactorily and with frequent failures. These employees can also, if they desire to do so, rapidly eliminate the "bugs" in new processes or equipment and have the operation running smoothly in a surprisingly short time.

The top management of many companies may share the point of view of one company officer who observed that to give a plant manager three to five years for building an effective organization is a long period of grace from full earning requirements. He felt this to be particularly unrealistic if the plant were manufacturing products or using a technology likely to become obsolete within that period of time. If we think in terms of any one product or technology, this point is valid. But if we think in terms of the viability of the organization, it is not. Any plant now manufacturing a product or using a process likely to become obsolete in the near future is necessarily going to have to introduce major product or process changes in order to survive. In such circumstances, it is especially important to have an organization capable of making these changes successfully. It would seem desirable for top management, consequently, to help the manager of such a plant to build an organization that is capable of introducing both product and technological changes smoothly, rapidly, and successfully.

Conditions of Success

The proposed system of management is more complex than other systems and requires greater learning and skill. To obtain the full benefit from this system, management must apply the general principles involved to all of the operating procedures and practices of the company or plant. Partial application is far less effective than total application because of the incompatibility of procedures, some of which are based on one set of motivational assumptions and theory of organization and others of which are based on a different set. Also, to emphasize a point made earlier, the unique conditions, traditions, and characteristics of the particular corporation or plant need to be taken into consideration when changes are made.

Introducing the proposed system of management in an organization is, however, not as difficult as it may sound. The management of most companies does not correspond in its entirety with either of the models portrayed. A wide range of management principles and practices is present in most organizations. The highest producing managers are behaving more like the Exhibit 2 pattern, the poorer managers more like the Exhibit 1 pattern. To change a company to the second approach in order to improve overall performance and cost control does not represent as drastic a shift in managerial style as the contrast between the two approaches to cost control suggests.

The top officers of very few companies are likely to persist in applying the proposed system of management in the face of competitive pressure and price-cost squeezes unless they have continuing evidence of encouraging progress. The only way to obtain this evidence is to measure the intervening variables regularly. These data are also needed for feedback to enable managers and supervisors to learn to manage in ways consistent with the newer approach. The measurement of the causal and intervening variables and the correct interpretation of these data are as complex, difficult, and subject to error as are the most complex problems in accounting. An organization seeking to use such measurements would be well-advised to obtain the assistance of a professionally qualified person.

Conclusion

Any company undertaking the proposed approach can expect to encounter tough problems and the lapse of a substantial period of time before experiencing an appreciable improvement in productivity, costs, and earnings. But once improvement starts, a competitor is unlikely to catch up by a crash program. Crash programs require the use of procedures which are opposite in character to the proposed system of management. They involve high levels of direct, hierarchical pressure for change and improvement and evoke hostility, resistance, and other counterforces. Crash programs, consequently, cause a company to move away from, rather than toward, the proposed system of management. Such approaches over the long range are therefore likely to be self-defeating.

Long-range success will go to those who use a long-range perspective. It will go to those who are guided by accurate information obtained by measuring regularly the different kinds of variables that affect and reflect performance.

Principles of Effective Management

Underlying the discussion of cost control in this article is a more general formulation of some principles and practices associated with effective management. This formulation is based on an extensive series of studies comparing exceptionally successful organizational units and their managers with similar organizational units that are getting only poor or mediocre results. The key concepts, which I [R. Likert] have spelled out in some detail in *New Patterns of Management* (McGraw-Hill, 1961), concern the problem of how to organize human activity so as to achieve the highest levels of coordinated, cooperative effort directed toward accomplishing an organization's goals. Here are some of the main points.

1. *The highest levels of productive and cooperative motivation are obtained when the noneconomic motives are made compatible with the economic motives.* To be effective, an organization must provide conditions which stimulate each member to make full use of his abilities and to grow to his full potential, and which give him both a sense of achievement and economic rewards in the form of an equitable and secure income. These conditions are required at all levels of the organization, not only among the top people.

2. *High levels of cooperative motivation can be attained by applying the principle of supportive relationships.* The leadership and other processes of the organization must be such as to ensure that in his interactions with other employees each member will, in the light of his background, values, and expectations, view the relationships as supportive ones—as tending to build and maintain his sense of personal worth and importance.

3. *High levels of cooperative motivation and the linking of such motivation to the goals of the common enterprise are achieved mainly through informal processes in face-to-face work groups.* It is therefore important that the formal structure of the organization place each member in one or more such groups that are to some degree stable in membership and that function so as to elicit group loyalty. Such groups must encourage effective work relationships, and they must also have linkages with other groups. The linkages occur through multiple or overlapping group membership such that most members of the organization share in the work of more

than one group. A department head, for example, may act as a member of a work group with other department heads, as a member of a work group with his own immediate staff and subordinates, and also as a member of several coordinating committees—thus serving a "linking pin" function that enables better coordination throughout the enterprise.

Seen in this way, the work groups are the building blocks of organization. The presence of multiple linkages provides a more dependable basis for coordination and upward communication than is commonly achieved through single "line of authority" linkages.

4. *The setting of goals and priorities and the assessment of accomplishments must be a continuing activity of the various groups.* While the general objectives of the organization are defined and clarified primarily by the upper-level people, these objectives need to be interpreted and elaborated in terms of the resources and functions of each lower-level group. Specific individual and group goals may then be set in a high but realistic manner and may be strengthened by open commitment to fulfill the goals. Some degree of involvement of each member in the decisions that affect him is necessary as a means for (a) achieving cooperative motivation, (b) developing coordination within and between groups, and (c) maintaining high goals.

5. *In applying these ideas to a particular organization, management should take account of the unique problems, objectives, conditions, and traditions of the company.* The application of the principle of supportive relationships, for example, will lead different firms to somewhat different operating policies and procedures (e.g., for compensation, decision making, communication, grievance handling, and so on) according to their unique traditions and the expectations that exist at the time.

The successful application of these concepts rests on helping the members, particularly supervisors and managers, develop a high level of skill and understanding in interaction with others. This includes, specifically, developing competence in leadership *and* in membership roles in groups. Successful application is usually accompanied by a widespread awareness of the importance of the organization as a system for interaction and influence. To that end, procedures for periodic self-assessment and corrective action are valuable. Periodic measurements of the health of the organization together with feedback of this information to the member are also effective in maintaining and improving the system.

References

1. Rensis Likert, "Measuring Organizational Performance," HBR March–April 1958, p. 41.
2. See Rensis Likert, *New Patterns of Management* (New York, McGraw-Hill Book Company, Inc., 1961); Douglas McGregor, *The Human Side of Enterprise* (New York, McGraw-Hill Book Company, Inc., 1960); and William F. Whyte, *Men at Work* (Homewood, Illinois, Irwin-Dorsey, 1961).
3. See, for example, D. G. Bowers, editor, *Applying Modern Management Principles to Sales Organizations* (Ann Arbor, Michigan, Foundation for Research on Human Behavior, 1963); L. Coch and J. R. P. French, Jr., "Overcoming Resistance to Change," in *Group Dynamics: Research and Theory*, edited by D. Cartwright and A. Zander (Evanston, Illinois, Row, Peterson & Company, 1960), pp. 319–341; Stanley E. Seashore and D. G. Bowers, *Changing the Structure and Functioning of an Organization* (Ann Arbor,

University of Michigan, Institute for Social Research, 1963); Nancy Morse and Everett Reimer, "The Experimental Change of a Major Organizational Variable," *Journal of Abnormal and Social Psychology,* January 1956, pp. 120–129; and Floyd C. Mann, "Studying and Creating Change: A Means to Understanding Social Organization," in *Research in Industrial Human Relations* (Madison, Wisconsin, Industrial Relations Research Association, 1957), pp. 146–167.

4. See, for example, Chris Argyris, *Interpersonal Competence and Organizational Effectiveness* (Homewood, Illinois, Irwin-Dorsey, 1962); W. G. Bennis, K. D. Benne, and R. Chin, *The Planning of Change* (New York, Holt, Rinehart & Winston, 1961); L. P. Bradford, J. R. Gibb, and K. D. Benne editors, *T-Group Theory and Laboratory Method* (New York, John Wiley & Sons, Inc., in press); R. Lippitt, Jeanne Watson and B. Westley, *The Dynamics of Planned Change: A Comparative Study of Principles and Techniques* (New York, Harcourt, Brace and World, 1958); and N. R. F. Maier and J. J. Hayes, *Creative Management* (New York, John Wiley & Sons, Inc., 1962).

5. See Coch and French, op. cit., pp. 319–341; and J. R. P. French, Jr., I. C. Ross, S. Kirby, J. R. Nelson, and P. Smyth, "Employee Participation in a Program of Industrial Change, *Personnel,* Nov.–Dec. 1958, p. 16.

Appendix

When management applies the usual cost-reduction procedures, the adverse results pictured in Exhibit 1 are likely (assuming no important changes in technology or products). This conclusion is based on a series of studies by various organizations. Many of these studies are discussed in some detail in the following publications:

Chris Argyris, *Personality and Organization* (New York, Harper & Brothers, 1957).

Peter Blau and W. Richard Scott, *Formal Organizations* (San Francisco, Chandler Publishing Company, 1962).

Saul W. Gellerman, *Motivation and Productivity* (New York, American Management Association, 1963).

Robert L. Kahn, "Human Relations on the Shop Floor," in *Human Relations and Modern Management,* edited by E. M. Hugh-Jones (Amsterdam, North-Holland Publishing Co., 1958), pp. 43–74.

Daniel Katz and Robert L. Kahn, "Some Recent Findings in Human Relations Research," in *Readings in Social Psychology,* edited by Guy E. Swanson, Theodore M. Newcomb, and Eugene L. Hartley (New York, Holt, Rinehart & Winston, 1952), pp. 650–665.

Rensis Likert, *New Patterns of Management* (New York, McGraw-Hill Book Company, Inc., 1961).

John G. March and Herbert A. Simon, *Organizations* (New York, John Wiley & Sons, Inc., 1958).

William F. Whyte, *Men at Work* (Homewood, Illinois, Irwin-Dorsey, 1961).

As for individual studies that have been published, some of the more relevant ones are:

David G. Bowers, editor, *Applying Modern Management Principles to Sales Organizations* (Ann Arbor, Foundation for Research on Human Behavior, University of Michigan, 1963).

Robert H. Guest, *Organizational Change* (Homewood, Illinois, Irwin-Dorsey, 1962).

Robert C. Hood, "Concern for Cost: A Participative Approach," *Manufacturing Series, No. 221* (New York, American Management Association, 1956), pp. 33–40.

Floyd C. Mann, *The Productivity of Work Groups* (Ann Arbor, Institute for Social Research, University of Michigan, 1963).

Floyd C. Mann, and Howard J. Baumgartel, *The Supervisor's Concern With Costs in an Electric Power Company* (Ann Arbor, Institute for Social Research, University of Michigan, 1953).

Louis C. McAnly, "Maytag's Program of Expense Reduction," *Manufacturing Series, No. 221* (New York, American Management Association, 1956), pp. 24–32.

Nancy Morse and Everett Reimer, "The Experimental Change of a Major Organizational Variable," *Journal of Abnormal and Social Psychology,* January 1956, pp. 120–129.

Stanley E. Seashore and David G. Bowers, *Changing the Structure and Functioning of an Organization* (Ann Arbor, Institute for Social Research, University of Michigan, 1963).

Questions for Discussion

1. What motivational and performance problems could result if the time span of administratively imposed goals and controls differs (is shorter, or longer) from the time typically required to perform the task? Why?

2. Compare and contrast the organizational climates of any two organizations (or any two college classes). How did your own motivation and behavior differ in the two situations, if it differed at all?

3. John Holt has said in *How Children Fail*, "It begins to look as if the test-examination-marks business is a gigantic racket, the purpose of which is to enable students, teachers, and schools to take part in a joint pretense that the students know everything they are supposed to know, when in fact they know only a small part of it—if any at all. Why do we always announce exams in advance, if not to give students a chance to cram for them? Why do teachers, even in graduate schools, always say quite specifically what the exam will be about, even telling the type of questions that will be given? Because otherwise too many students would flunk—What would happen at Harvard or Yale if a prof gave a surprise test in March on work covered in October? Everyone knows what would happen; that's why they don't do it." Discuss.

4. "It would be a good thing if every manager carried out his job on the assumption that he would continue to occupy that job for ten years." Discuss the advantages and disadvantages of this proposal.

5. In a large eastern state, high school teachers were once evaluated and rewarded by school administrators on the basis of their students' scores on statewide Regents' examinations. Discuss the advantages and disadvantages of such a measure.

6. What are the strengths and weaknesses of an administrative system like that exemplified in the anecdote about Dave Mahoney of Norton Simon, Inc. in Chapter 8? Under what circumstances might it be (a) better, and (b) worse, than a contrasting approach?

7. A sales manager desires to improve the quality of after-the-sale customer relations and service provided by his sales force. He can exhort his salesmen to pay more attention to this part of their job. He can even hire some new salesmen. But what planning and control changes can he initiate to improve after-the-sale customer relations and service?

8. What undesirable effects might result from a management by objectives program?

Short Cases for Discussion

Hell Week

The Navy has a jet pilot training station at Kingsville, Texas. About one half of the Navy's fighter and attack pilots must complete their training there before receiving their Navy wings. These symbols of completion of flight training are earned after approximately 350 hours of training in the air and countless hours of ground school and military training.

The other half of the Navy's fighter and attack pilots complete their formal training at nearby Beeville, Texas. Other types of training, such as anti-submarine warfare training, take place at Naval Air Stations in Corpus Christi and New Iberia, Louisiana. The headquarters for advanced training is located on the Naval Air Station at Corpus Christi.

One Tuesday morning each month, the commanding officers from the eleven advanced training squadrons are invited (command performance) to attend the admiral's conference. This conference covers general subjects of interest to the groups and progress reports on the status of each squadron in the production of naval aviators, with heavy emphasis placed on the previous week's statistical figures, shown in graphic and chart format. Various formulas are used—some complicated and confusing—to depict the amount of training performed in relation to several factors, such as the type of flying weather, aircraft availability, student and instructor availability, the number of students who completed flight training during the period, the use of flight simulators, and other things. Running totals are depicted, as are comparisons with the same periods of previous years.

Searching and detailed questions are asked the commanding officers of the squadrons whose charts show discrepancies and shortcomings which are not self-explanatory. Questions on any phase of the squadron's operation are asked. Those which cannot be answered by the commanding officer cause him great embarrassment and discomfort in front of the admiral, who must sign his personal evaluation report. Very few questions are asked concerning squadron training of those squadrons which have high production figures for the week preceding the meeting. Therefore, it becomes important to have high figures for at least this one week of the month, and so avoid questions.

Since the formula by which the graphs and charts are made is known to the squadrons, steps can be taken to beat the system. The graphs having the most variables are the easiest to manipulate. Even the figures for the weather can be controlled, since this is a variable used to reflect the differences in squadron training—i.e., 100% good flying weather for an instrument training phase might only be 20% good flying weather for a fighter tactics flight. The weather percentage is turned in by each squadron training officer, based on his own best judgment.

The number of flying days per week, when weather is not a factor, can be adjusted by subtracting time taken to perform military drills or inspections. Since the official work week is a five-day period, weekend flying does not add flying days to the figures, although it does add flight hours. Thus, problems during the week can be remedied by working six or seven-day weeks. For example, a squadron having flown only 300 hours during the official five-day week might add 200 hours to the total by flying Saturday and Sunday, thus getting credit for 500 hours for the five days.

The number of aircraft available for flight is an easy one to adjust. Aircraft which are out of commission awaiting parts at the beginning of the period and not counted as available can be put into commission by exchanging parts from other grounded aircraft. Extra aircraft above the normal squadron allowance are also assigned as a pool of replacements, and these have to be flown periodically. Instructors can combine instruction flights with minor test flights. All of these methods make aircraft available which are not chargeable against the squadron's use figures, but which improve the reported figures.

Other measures used in determining the squadron's standing on the graphs and charts can also be manipulated, and are not illegal, unsafe, or unrecognized by the admiral's staff. In fact, some of the maneuvers are condoned and recommended. The loophole provided by the Saturday and Sunday flying, for example, was intentional. It provides an incentive to work overtime to get the job done.

The week preceding the monthly conference attended by the commanding officers is appropriately called "hell week" by some instructors. No matter how bad the weather is or what the aircraft and personnel situation might be, this week is usually a six or seven-day work week. The flight day starts before sunrise and ends late at night, and all sorts of finagling takes place to improve the statistical figures. Since none of the personnel wants to work Saturdays and Sundays when it can be avoided, all of them contribute their part in boosting the figures which have to be reported. The mechanics work harder with fewer breaks for personal business; aircraft availability seems automatically to be higher. The line personnel refuel the aircraft and make minor adjustments and repairs more quickly, and more flights are flown. Fewer flights are cancelled for any reason. Instructor and student availability are improved with less illness, and more of the "can do" spirit prevails. More students are graduated during this particular week. The weather is always less than 100%.

The statistics used to produce the charts and graphs assume great importance. Squadron personnel tend to concentrate on those items which are reported and pay less attention to unreported ones. It becomes more important in some minds to have aircraft reported up and flyable than to be certain that aircraft meet rigid quality control inspections. Since the quality control people work for the men responsible for high aircraft availability, a relaxation of quality standards sometimes results. Some of the best qualified inspectors are transferred to head production units, with less qualified inspectors assigned to quality control units.

Students are often held over from the previous week so that student completions during "hell week" will be higher. Scheduling is arranged so that students who could have been completed the previous Friday are actually completed early in the following week. This sometimes fouls up their travel arrangements and lengthens their time in the squadron. Other students will be rushed to completion at an unnecessarily fatiguing pace.

Questions

1. Why does finagling with the numbers occur?
2. What are the advantages and disadvantages of the system of measurement and evaluation described in this case?

Performance and Cost Evaluation (PACE)

In early 1961 I was working for a large aerospace firm in California. Business and employment were at their peak, but costs were equally high. Because of the high costs, upper management decided to install a PACE program.

PACE was developed to assess performance and infer the management capability of an organization. It was started in 1958 by the manufacturing methods engineering department of the Norair Division of Northrop Corporation. Rather than measure the output of an organization as a basis for inferring management effectiveness, PACE was designed to measure certain selected inputs.

These inputs were actually losses in three factors related to the effective use of employees: (1) idleness, (2) out of area, and (3) group effort. Measures of these factors were combined into the PACE index. Then the index was used as a source of information to judge existing management control practices. PACE required a staff of people trained to observe the three inputs, using a random sampling technique.

Before PACE men observe in a firm, they are exposed to a period of indoctrination, during which they learn the group objectives, number of employees, assignments (who does what), and predicted activity. Before engaging in observation, the PACE man knows what the group is supposed to be doing. Each observer carries a 5 × 7 black book as he goes about his work. During his observations he records activities. After his walk and observation, he returns to his office and charts his calculations. For each period of observation, he usually spends half as much time in his office recording and charting.

The PACE observers and their management were brought into our firm for a period of indoctrination on the organization level. Then they were assigned to various areas and underwent further indoctrination at the group level. Measurements were to be taken at the working group level and combined to provide a program evaluation at the organizational level.

Of course, all of the measurements required some judgments. In measuring idleness, for example, the observer had to decide if an engineer sitting physically inactively at his desk was thinking about work or being idle. It was necessary for the observer to decide if people out of their own work areas were contributing to the task or were gone without contributing to the task.

Group effort was even more elusive to measure. For example, the PACE man was supposed to determine if a secretary talking on the phone was chatting excessively or presenting facts in a business-like manner, or if an engineer was strolling through the factory at leisure or walking at a business-like pace. (During his job training period, the PACE man was reportedly exposed to a mechanical walking machine which taught him to accurately measure walking speeds.) The total effort ratings of individuals provided a group effort rating.

At the end of each week, the PACE people met with group supervisors and called their attention to the charts and ratings. Each supervisor in turn called his group together in an effort to tighten their activities. This went on for several weeks in all areas in order to increase effectiveness.

My impression was that people reacted to PACE in some unanticipated and undesired ways. The PACE man was an intruder and a villain in the eyes of almost every employee. Supervisors returned from PACE meetings to say that there was idleness and a lack of group effort. In reaction to that, people did things like vigorously shuffle through papers and jot down numbers—any numbers—whenever the PACE man appeared. Machine operators performed unnecessary work to look busy. Such goings-on occurred frequently during the several months PACE was in operation.

The people felt as though they were under police observation. Tensions began to appear. Management made an attempt to convince the employees that the study was for the good of *their* company, but most of the people who were being observed found it difficult to associate the methods of evaluation with individual well-being. For instance, the workers didn't feel that the number of steps they took from one area to another was a significant measure of their ability to do a job. Since they felt that the measures were all wrong, employees just did not see how it was possible to get a fair rating of their performance.

One day the corporation president came to our plant and, after numerous meetings about PACE, dismissed the PACE people on the spot. Employees danced in the hallways and played darts in the chart room. From the workers' point of view, management had finally gathered their senses about them, after months of madness, and now everyone could quit playing games and get to work.

Question

How did PACE affect perceptions, expectancies, and motivation?

Chapter 9

Leading, Rewarding
and Consistency

In this chapter we consider the administrative practices of leading and reward-ing. We also discuss the relationships among all of the administrative inputs—plans, controls, leadership, and rewards—and an approach to overall, integrated administrative systems design.

In discussing leadership and rewards, our aim is not to provide exhaustive description and analysis. Instead, we look at each with an eye to leverage on the problem of managing motivation and behavior in organizations. We explore these questions: How can a leader behave toward his subordinates to encourage the likelihood that they will perform well and derive satisfaction from their work? How should pay and promotions be administered to reach the same objectives?

There is a mountain of research and opinion meant to answer each question. A discussion of most of it would be impossible and unproductive. Hence, we are highly selective and concentrate only on the most promising, practical guidelines which we can derive from research and other sources. First, let us look at leadership.

Leadership

The sum total of the behavior of an executive in his direct relations with subordinates could be termed "leadership." The "inhuman" side of adminis-tration, with its impersonal mechanisms of control, is far from the whole of administration. The rules, the policies, the evaluations come to life in the hands of the leader. How he behaves is central to the administrative system.

For all the importance of plans and controls, the impact of the leader can be decisive. Abraham Zaleznik (1966) suggests, "Leaders with brilliant ideas and the capacity to inspire thought and action in others are the main generators of energy. The effects of their personality induce a contagion to perform that is considerably stronger in directing organizations than depersonalized sys-tems . . ." (p. 4).

The same fascination with the mystique of charisma has led such students of society as Thomas Carlyle (1907) to adopt a "great man" approach to explaining historical events. It is undeniable that individual leaders have played a part in holding nations together under the most adverse conditions. Adolf Hitler, for example, was a key factor in prolonging the German Army's resistance in World War II. According to opinion polls taken long after Germany lost France and began even to lose Germany, captured German prisoners of war expressed great trust and confidence in Hitler's ability to set things right (Shils and Janowitz, 1948).

The Trait Approach

The apparent existence of charisma and its powerful effects led to a much used but singularly barren approach to the study of leadership: leadership traits. Essentially, this method involves trying to identify a set of personal characteristics (e.g., initiative, maturity, loyalty, decisiveness, and so on) shared by leaders somehow defined as effective. But effective leaders vary considerably in such traits. As a result, leadership trait studies have provided little of practical predictive value in selecting leaders.

The trait approach proved unproductive because it attempted to isolate one factor whose real significance was only in the way it was interwoven in a web of relationships with other factors. The leader's traits were only important, for example, insofar as they manifested themselves in ways of dealing with subordinates. Accordingly, researchers began to examine the ways leaders behaved toward subordinates, hoping that study would reveal consistent patterns of leader behavior linked to effective group performance of tasks.

Participative Leadership

There is a consensus in the behaviorally oriented management literature that participative leadership is generally desirable. Douglas McGregor (1960) advocates it in his Theory Y; Likert (1967) advocates it in his System 4; and Blake and Mouton (1964) imply it in the 9.9 sector of their managerial grid. This convergence of opinion seems to rest on the reasonable though often implicit assumption that most managers in a democratic society face what Fiedler (1965) calls "situations of intermediate difficulty." They lack absolute position power; they are not usually faced with completely hostile subordinates; and they must arrange for performance of a mixture of tasks, some of which are relatively unstructured.

However, the more or less explicit rationale for participative leadership rests upon the idea that leaders can permit subordinates to satisfy their higher level needs through the job. The participative leader encourages a subordinate to think about the problems of his job and his leader's job, and to take personal responsibility for problem solving and achieving results. As the subordinate functions in this way, he gains in competence, knowledge, and feelings of achievement.

Satisfaction of the higher order needs, achieved continually over time, fosters important feelings of self-confidence and self-esteem. At the same time, the subordinate who is in fact helping to solve organizational and managerial problems is a more mature person, growing in ability. Thus, prestige, status, and the respect of others are achieved, along with self-respect.

Even if no case could be made for participative leadership on motivational grounds, there are compelling reasons to consider participation an indispensable part of management. Organizational intelligence suffers if leaders do not hear the information possessed by those close to the scene and with knowledge of events. Decisions are made in lofty ignorance. For example, Harrison Salisbury (1969) reveals that numerous, authentic, and precisely correct reports were furnished Stalin and other Soviet leaders that the Germans planned to attack Russia long before they did so in World War II. Even the hour and location of the attack and the size of the attacking force were known. But Soviet leaders turned to their own agents an ear deaf from authoritarianism.

Those at the top need not abandon for all time a favored pattern of direction and control to capitalize upon intelligence from subordinates. Herbert Shepard (1967) reports on the skillful use of periodic shifts in leader behavior to suit the nature of the task at hand. A World War II military raiding unit in the Pacific alternated from open interaction among all participants, regardless of rank, to strict hierarchical command. The former system was used to generate ideas and plans for a raid and to rehash completed raids. But during the raid strict command ruled. The relaxed atmosphere was conducive to developing the best ideas—whether they came from the corporal or the colonel. The controlled atmosphere suited execution of the synchronized activities previously decided upon. Had the colonel declined to hear his juniors while planning, he would have limited his information arbitrarily. Thus, for the same leader, the situations in which he must fit people and tasks may be fluid. He needs to shift his own behavior accordingly.

Leadership Styles

One approach to leadership suggested by Fleishman et al. (1955) was concerned with two leadership styles: (1) the tendency to initiate structure and to direct group activities, and (2) the tendency to show consideration of subordinates' feelings and to take these into account in making decisions. Studies using this approach have yielded disappointing results, however. Korman's (1966) review of this research reveals that there is no conclusive evidence that either of these styles is consistently associated with more effective group performance.

Another approach tried to determine if such patterns of leader behavior as providing general supervision or providing close supervision, and being employee-centered or production-oriented, were consistently associated with effective group performance. There seemed to be some evidence, reported by Kahn (1956), that general supervision and employee-centered supervision more often accompanied better group performance. But other social scientists, such as Robert Dubin (1965), looked at the same data and concluded that the results are equivocal, because it is not evident that leader attentiveness to employee feelings or increased employee autonomy are conditions instrumental to effective performance of all jobs.

This problem is akin to the one the surveyor faces when he cannot measure the distance between two points directly. He needs a third point so that he can triangulate. Similarly, if we are to understand leadership, we need to see not only the traits of the leader or the characteristics of his position, or even this plus the relations between the leader and the subordinate. We also need to know the nature of the task. We need to know the three-way relations depicted in Exhibit 9-1.

Suppose, for example, that your job is to sell insurance policies. Would close and detailed supervision help or hinder you? A "classic" study by Likert (1961) suggests that it would hinder you. Those supervisors whose agents were allowed to function in an independent, entrepreneurial way fared better than did those who were more closely directed.

Alternatively, suppose you are an assembly-line worker in a plant manufacturing electric motors. The products have to be made to close tolerances and they flow sequentially in an integrated technology. Would general supervision and the autonomy it provides help or hinder productivity? A study by Argyle

Exhibit 9-1 Measuring Leadership Effectiveness

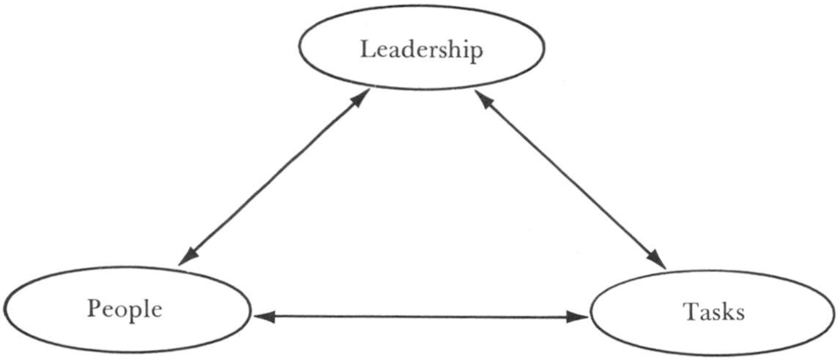

et al. (1957) of 90 foremen facing this situation in British factories showed no significant relationship between general supervision and productivity. General supervision did not help performance of this task.

Other studies have added measurements of the personalities of the people on the job. Vroom (1960), for example, studied supervisors and workers in a parcel delivery service firm. Different personality types preferred different amounts and types of interaction with their supervisors. Generally, people with a high need for independence and a low tendency toward authoritarianism responded to participative leadership with better motivation, attitudes, and performance than did people with the opposite qualities. Unless he discriminates among the people he supervises, the leader who applies one or another style of relating to his subordinates may aid some and merely interfere with or antagonize others.

Leadership and n Achievement

There is at least one laboratory study, by Misumi and Seki (1971), dealing with performance of an information-classifying task, which implies that effectiveness can be increased if leadership style varies with one characteristic of subordinates: their levels of *n* Achievement. Groups comprised of members low in *n* Achievement performed better under leaders who concentrated on task performance. Groups comprised of members high in *n* Achievement performed better under leaders who concentrated on both the quality of relations among members of the group *and* task performance. The explanation offered for high performance of the former groups was that the leader's stressing goal achievement helped overcome the low motivation. As the researchers point out, however, the leader stressing performance exclusively generated increasing hostility in his subordinates, which in a real organization might in time cancel out the short-run benefits realized during the experiment. The leader who stressed both performance and group maintenance presumably developed a climate which provided sufficient achievement arousal even for those high in *n* Achievement and, at the same time, avoided the buildup of hostile reactions.

Leadership style which exhibits warmth and support coupled with setting high standards has been associated with *n* Achievement in children (Rosen and D'Andrade, 1959). The leader's behavior can send out signals that taking risks and striving are desirable. And, as Litwin and Stringer (1968) observe, "Environmental cues which signify that an individual's activities are being supported, encouraged, and generally appreciated would tend to . . . increase the salience of achievement motivation and achievement-oriented activity" (p. 52). In contrast, the leader who somehow creates the feeling that he is watching over the subordinate's shoulder, ready to pounce at the first error, would inhibit venturesomeness. He would, instead, foster anxious compliance and avoidance of risks.

Still, if it is important for the leader to be mindful of the characteristics of his subordinates, it is equally important that his leadership be congruent with his own nature.

Congruence

The degree to which one's behavior is congruent or consistent with self and circumstance, according to such psychotherapists as Carl Rogers (1961, pp. 338–346), is one indicator of mental health. According to one critic of management education (Livingston, 1971), the universal promulgation of participative leadership, based on the works of behavioral scientists such as McGregor and Likert, encourages engaging in a prescribed leadership pattern rather than developing one's own style consistent with one's own leanings. Leadership vogues which ignore personal characteristics may thus foster incongruent behavior. The leader whose style is an artifice foreign to his nature will fool neither himself nor his subordinates.

What stands out above all else in emerging thought on the subject of leadership is the idea that effective leadership is contingent upon the degree to which it fits the situation. What is needed for effective performance and subordinate satisfaction is a fitting together of the three points: leadership, people, and tasks. An approach to leadership which seeks to optimize this fit may be called the situational or contingency approach to leadership.

The Contingency Approach

Fred Fiedler (1967), who has carried out a substantial amount of leadership research, has focused on three key factors upon which leadership effectiveness is dependent, or contingent: the leader-member relationship, the nature of the task, and the power of the leader's position. He has devised ways of measuring or judging all three. Questionnaires are used to assess members' feelings toward the leader. Task structure, or the degree to which the task is defined, is measured by rating the task on four aspects, namely, "decision verifiability—the degree to which the correctness of the solution can be demonstrated; goal clarity—the degree to which the desired outcome is clearly stated; goal path multiplicity—the number of possible methods for performing the task; and solution specificity— the degree to which there is more than one correct solution" (1965, p. 14). Position power is quantified by assessing the ability of the leader to promote or demote, and his special rank or title.

The better a leader's relations with his group, the more highly structured the task, and the greater the leader's position power, the more favorable the situation should be for the leader. The less the situation exhibits these conditions, the more unfavorable should be the situation for the leader. The question is: Which kind of leader, directive or permissive, will perform more effectively (achieve more effective performance of the group's primary task) under favorable, unfavorable, or intermediate conditions?

Though Fiedler's (1965) conclusions can only be regarded as tentative, they are interesting. In brief, his results suggest that "managing, controlling, directive leaders tend to be most effective in situations which are either very favorable for them or which are relatively unfavorable. Nondirective, permissive, considerate leaders tend to perform best in situations of intermediate difficulty" (p. 15).

For example, think of the elected chairman of a committee of senior professors convened to decide which junior professors shall be promoted. He cannot direct his colleagues, since his position power is negligible. He may be on reasonably good personal terms with the members of the committee; at least we might infer that, since they elected him chairman. At any rate, given these contingencies, he will likely fare best if he approaches this complex judgmental task in a participative style. On the other hand, the football team called into a huddle by the quarterback has come to receive direction. Players will be disturbed by the leader who does not provide it. Where time, performance, and expectations all call for direction, the leader who provides it will likely fare best.

An alternative view of the contingency approach is to concentrate on (1) the behavior required by the task for effective performance, and (2) the motive arousal effects of the leader's behavior. The leader's job is to help provide conditions which enable people to perform their work well. If the task calls for collaborative behavior, leadership which arouses affiliation is instrumental to success. If the task calls for entrepreneurial behavior, leadership which arouses achievement is instrumental to success. If the task calls for influential behavior, leadership which arouses power is instrumental to success.

In other words, by looking at the requirements of a task, we should be able to infer the behavior appropriate for successful performance, as we have done before. Now we can also look at the leader's behavior to see if it seems to encourage task-effective behavior. Consider, for example, the case of a state employment office studied by Peter Blau (1963) and see if you can select the leadership behavior (mingled with other task and people variables, as it inevitably is) associated with more effective performance.

Blau's Employment Agency Case

The state employment office studied by Blau was divided into three sections. Interviewers in Sections A and B performed the same standard duties. There were other interviewers in Section C, but they were concerned with the special task of helping handicapped persons find jobs.

Employers telephoned requests for workers to the agency. Whichever interviewer happened to answer the call recorded the job opening on an order form. The order forms were placed in alphabetical order in one of five boxes in Section A or, if the call was received in Section B, in one of two boxes there. The five boxes in Section A stayed on the desks of the five interviewers. The two boxes in Section B were moved from desk to desk by interviewers as needed. Cards indicating clients waiting for interviews were arranged in order of client arrival. The interviewer would assess the client's qualifications and attempt to locate a suitable job order on file in one of the boxes.

The only aspect of the performance of interviewers that was measured was the number of interviews held. This count alone seemed sufficient when jobs were abundantly available. But when jobs became scarce and more time and skill were necessary to match people and jobs, the bare count on interviews didn't reveal enough about interviewer performance. Even more serious were some unwanted effects on interviewer behavior.

In some instances, interviewers rushed applicants through the interview, thus securing a "point" quickly without careful assessment of qualifications and openings and without attentiveness to the unmeasured tasks of referral and placement. Unless the supervisor directly observed these shortcomings, he faced the task of evaluating interviewer performance ignorant of these problems. Instead, he had only quantitative evidence of good performance. It would be like a dean evaluating a professor by the number of articles published, without reading those articles or seeing the more subtle effects of teaching neglect possibly brought on by taking time to write the articles.

When a new department head took over Sections A and B of the agency, she introduced a new set of statistical records of performance. What was counted now included

1. the number of interviews held.
2. the number of clients referred to a job.
3. the number of placements (referred client was hired).
4. the proportion of interviews resulting in referrals.
5. the proportion of referrals resulting in placements.

Most interviewers in Section A were on probationary status at the time the new measures were introduced. Most interviewers in Section B were veterans and could not be terminated except for cause. Some of the veterans in Section B had begun work together at the end of World War II and received their initial training from a supervisor who placed special emphasis on carefully interviewing and professionally counseling the large number of returning veterans, as opposed to maximizing the quantity of interviews or placements with less concern for occupational guidance.

This same supervisor of Section B paid little heed to the new statistical measurements in evaluating interviewer performance. In contrast, the supervisor of Section A relied chiefly on the statistical records in evaluating interviewer performance.

In Section A, where the supervisor evaluated performance by seeing who had the best quantitative record, making more placements was a way of reducing anxiety about status evaluation. In contrast, those interviewers in Section B who made the most placements were not rated highest by their supervisor. Section B interviewers looked upon preoccupation with placements as a neglect of professional counseling duties and values. The definition of doing a better job in Section A was securing the most placements; the definition of doing a better job in Section B meant fewer placements.

Interviewers in Section A were less cohesive as a group than those in Section B, spending rest periods together less often than Section B interviewers, for example. The Section A interviewers who moved around and made more work-related contacts with others in Section A were the more productive. The number of contacts within Section B was not correlated so closely with productivity. Section A interviewers had to scurry around more to find openings.

The results: Interviewers in Section A behaved more competitively and less cooperatively than those in Section B. Their competitiveness was manifested in efforts to fill job openings before another interviewer could. In Section A, interviewers tended to monopolize the job openings employers had telephoned to them. In fact, Section A interviewers competed illegitimately in several ways to assure that they would fill the jobs and thereby receive credit. Sometimes, rather than put the job order in the box, they hid it under the blotter. They indicated experience requirements for low-paying jobs where no such require-ments existed—to discourage other interviewers who would believe experience was demanded of the applicant. If there were several openings on one order, an interviewer might file the order under "filled" after only one placement, thus monopolizing the remaining openings.

Which section, A or B, had the higher productivity as defined by the statistical measures of performance? Why?

In this case, though not necessarily in others, the better leader, i.e., the one whose group performed better, was the one who ignored "making the numbers." Section B achieved higher productivity by eight percent. This means, paradoxi-cally, that the group with what amounted to a norm against the narrow quanti-tative definition of productivity achieved greater productivity. The individ-ualistic, competitive practices of Section A interviewers yielded lower productivity for the section as a whole, though Section A had the most produc-tive single interviewer.

The greater cooperativeness of Section B seems to have aided efficient operations. Much greater interaction about work problems was necessary on the part of Section A interviewers to overcome individualistic concern for monopolizing job openings. The greater status anxiety of interviewers in Section A seems to have hampered efficiency by impairing cooperation. In contrast, the leadership style which supported and encouraged collaboration to make good placements was associated with making more placements, for the section as a whole.

Of course, our example does not include all of the complexities a leader might face. The leader must suit his own nature as well as that of his subordi-nates and the task they face, and most situations call for neither pure collabo-ration, entrepreneurship, or influence, but some mixture of all. Not all subordi-nates will respond similarly, and no leadership style can function without a reciprocal followership style. Nevertheless, an approximate leadership-people-task fit is obtainable in a wide range of situations. A selection by Tannenbaum and Schmidt following this chapter discusses the choice of leadership styles to achieve this fit.

Conclusion

We have seen that leadership can be a key to the arousal of motivation and behavior. It is the leader who interprets and applies plans and controls, and so can give them meaning to employees and relevance to the tasks they face. As we suggested earlier, the leader's impact can be decisive.

But a final qualification is necessary. It is possible that in a given situation, leadership accounts for only, say, five percent of the variance in productivity. If other factors account for ninety-five percent of output, then little can be gained by a very large improvement in leadership (Dubin, 1965). Other, perhaps technological, factors would be much more important levers to use in increasing productivity.

Since, however, the range of job situations in which leadership can help performance significantly would seem to be very great indeed, learning to improve the leadership-people-task fit would seem to be a top-priority goal for the skillful manager. It is for this reason that behavioral scientists such as McGregor (1960) and Herzberg (1966) have pointed the way to the motive-arousal opportunities inherent in leadership style, and its effect upon control systems and job enrichment. But concentration upon motivation through the job itself and through leadership, goals, and controls has had an interesting side effect. The capacity of other rewards, such as promotional opportunities and money, to motivate performance seems to have been neglected.

Formal Rewards

People do what they do because they find it rewarding. When behavior is followed by a reward from the environment, the behavior is reinforced; that is, the likelihood is increased that the behavior will occur again. On the basis of experience, people come to anticipate or expect a reward (even if it is only avoidance of punishment) and, under certain conditions, act to obtain it.

What is rewarding, moreover, is defined by the recipient, and therein lies the ultimate constraint upon administrative practices. Organizations are made up of people with their own ambitions, needs, and values. "No matter how 'totalitarian' the institution," Peter Drucker (1964) observes, "it has to satisfy the ambitions and needs of its members, and do so in their capacity as individuals but through institutional rewards and punishments, incentives and deterrents" (p. 294).

Drucker goes on to say, ". . . here is the real 'control' of the institution, that is the ground of behavior and the cause of action. People act as they are being rewarded or punished. For this, to them, rightly, is the true expression of the values of the institution and of its true, as against its professed, purpose and role. Employment selection and promotion decisions are the real 'controls.' In the employment selection an institution decides what kind of people it wants altogether. In the promotion decisions it makes operational its true and actual values and its real performance standards. A company that tells its foremen that the job is human relations but which then promotes the foreman who best does his paper work, makes it very clear to even the dumbest man in the shop that it wants paper work rather than human relations. And it will get paper work" (p. 295). It will get paper work to the extent that foremen aspire to be promoted. Those foremen who do not aspire to upward mobility would be less responsive to the message implicit in the promotion of foremen who excel in paperwork.

Money: A Negative View

What is perhaps a still more generalized reinforcer of behavior than selection and promotion is money: wages and salaries. But the relationship of money and motivation has been of surprisingly little interest to behavioral scientists. McGregor (1960) and Herzberg (1966), for example, seem to believe that money could contribute to the satisfaction of the lower level needs in Maslow's hierarchy: physiological and safety needs, or what Herzberg has referred to as hygiene or replenishment needs. But they do not see money as very important in contributing to higher level needs. As Opsahl and Dunnette (1966) put it, "Quite obviously, money serves to satisfy needs for food, clothing, and shelter, but it is much less obvious how money may be related to such other areas as *n* Achievement or *n* Power" (p. 114).

This lack of a clear-cut relationship between money and higher needs, combined with the managerial experience that no matter how good are the wages and fringe benefits that workers *receive,* the workers are still "unmotivated," seems to suggest that money simply is not the key to motivation. Money appears to secure only membership or participation in the organization. It does not assure meaningful performance or productivity within it.

As a result, most behavioral scientists have turned away from the topic of money and motivation. For Herzberg (1966), money, at best, can only stave off dissatisfaction temporarily. If workers are given an increase in pay it will cure their dissatisfaction momentarily. In time they will get hungry for an increase again. Then they will be as dissatisfied as they were before. All the while, however, the increases will not motivate them to perform better. What appears to be the practical implication? "Forget about money as a motivator. Let someone else take care of it because it must be done." But the manager should ". . . dig in exclusively on improving the nature of the job" (Ford, 1969, p. 33).

McClelland (1965) also seems to share the view that money has only a limited contribution to make to motivation. At least he points out that pay is not particularly effective in evoking effort and performance in people high in *n* Achievement. "The person with high *n* Achievement works hard anyway, provided there is an opportunity of achieving something. He is interested in money rewards or profits primarily because of the feedback they give him as to how well he is doing. Money is not the incentive to effort but rather the measure of its success for the real entrepreneur" (p. 7). It would appear that people would work in organizations with no pay at all, and they would *really* work if they had interesting jobs and carried them out in the context of well-designed goals and controls, and well-conducted leadership.

Not only is money unnecessary, but its use actually diminishes motivation, according to three experiments conducted by Edward Deci (see Vroom, 1971). He explored the effects that extrinsic rewards, specifically pay, have upon those rewards intrinsic to the performance of work. Common to each experiment was the following sequence:

First, subjects were put in a situation where their activity could be observed and taken as evidence of their intrinsic level of motivation. For example, a college sophomore who had agreed to be a subject in an experiment in human problem solving showed up for the first session, was told about the experiment, and given a puzzle to be worked out as his part in the study. The experimenter said he had to leave to attend to some other matters. He said he would be back in eight minutes and told the subject that he had 13 minutes to complete his puzzle assignment.

After the experimenter left to watch the subject through a one-way mirror, the subject observed that in addition to the puzzle, other items of interest were handy. There were the latest issues of *Playboy, Time, The New Yorker,* and other magazines. How long the subject worked on the puzzle rather than read magazines was measured and defined as his level of intrinsic motivation.

Next, the experimenter returned and started the second session. This time the subject was given a wage incentive, a dollar for each portion or configuration of the puzzle problem solved. The experimenter again said he had to leave. He went to the one-way mirror, took out his stop watch, and again measured how much time the subject worked on the puzzle. The third period was the same as the first. No money.

Control groups also underwent the experiment. For them all three periods were without money.

The question was: what effects will the extrinsic reward in period two have upon intrinsic motivation in period three? Will it drop, rise, or remain about the same when compared to the first period and to the control group? The answer: always, performance improved when pay was offered, but decreased when it was withdrawn.

Vroom (1971) comments upon Deci's research as follows: "The explanation of these findings is still problematical but let me give you mine. The introduction of pay for the performance of a task changes the meaning of a task for a person. Cognitively, it becomes something which he does for money, not because of its intrinsic enjoyment. This explanation is consistent with, if not derivable from, recent theories of cognitive dissonance" (p. 6). The point is that it becomes inconsistent in the third period to work hard for nothing. "It may mean, for example, that incentive compensation systems can increase performance but do so at the expense of intrinsic motivation that the person has for the performance of his job. Similarly, grading systems may be effective as motivators of students but may do so at the expense of student interest in learning for its own sake. The effects of these external control systems may be to change the person's perception of the locus of control over his behavior from himself to his environment" (p. 7).

Money: A Positive View

Perhaps all this emphasis on the vices of monetary rewards and the virtues of intrinsic rewards has been necessary to correct an earlier naive view that money is the only factor that can motivate people at work. We have overcorrected, however, and neglected the capacity of pay to function as a reward. Fortunately, a minority of behavioral scientists among the many who study organizations and management have concentrated on the relationships among money, motivation, and performance. Vroom (1964), Porter and Lawler (1968), and Lawler (1971), for example, have conducted research and developed practical recommendations, mainly within the framework of expectancy theory.

As we indicated in Chapter 1, the central idea of expectancy theory is that the likelihood that a person will act in a particular way is a function of how strong his expectancy is that the act will be followed by a reward and what value that reward holds for him. Like grades or marks in school, pay in organizations can be a desired or valued reward. It can also come to be seen as only available or contingent upon performing particular acts. Therein lies its power to motivate.

According to Lawler (1971, pp. 91–92), assuming that necessary abilities and other enabling conditions are present, pay can motivate good performance if employees

1. value pay highly.
2. believe that good performance results in high pay.
3. believe that by exerting effort they can improve their performance.

4. reckon that the advantages of working hard, performing well, and obtaining high pay exceed the disadvantages and psychic opportunity costs.
5. see good performance as the most attractive of all possible behaviors in the situation.

Porter and Lawler (1968) recommend a series of steps that managers can take to see if these conditions exist (pp. 173–182). First, managers should question people in the organization to find out just what they believe about pay, effort, and performance in the organization. What rewards do they want? Is additional pay strongly desired? Do employees believe that good performance really brings high pay in this organization? Do they believe that if they put forth greater effort it will affect their performance? What disadvantages are there to good performance?

Next, managers can try to cement the connection between pay and performance. By making it come true, they can support the subjective perception that pay varies positively with performance. To make the connection really effective requires flexible compensation practices so that the rewards offered can be varied to some extent to provide what individuals want. For example, some employees may prefer a greater share of their total pay package in retirement benefits and insurance. Others may want more in straight salary. Why not meet these individual preferences where the cost to the firm is equal? On top of this willingness to tailor compensation to individual preferences, it remains important to give superior performers both more extrinsic rewards (pay and/or benefits) and more intrinsic rewards (interesting assignments and/or promotions).

Finally, managers can continue to survey perceptions and preferences concerning pay and promotion practices. They can also measure other job attitudes. The results, when related to performance measures, can tell if the most satisfied employees are the best performers. If they are not, then the pay system may be out of control, rewarding organizational membership and not performance.

To provide a better alignment of pay and performance, Lawler (1971) has recommended a specific pay plan which he believes to be appropriate for a wide variety of organizations. The essence of his plan is to divide each employee's pay into three components. The first of these would be for the job to which the person is assigned. It would be equal for everyone assigned to that type of job. The second would comprise cost-of-living and seniority pay, to be paid everyone and adjusted annually. The third would be individually determined, based upon measurements of each person's performance during the preceding period. Lawler explains the third part this way:

"The poor performer in the organization should find that this part of his or her pay package is minimal, while the good performer should find that this part of his or her pay is at least as great as the other two parts combined. This would not be a raise, however, since it could vary from year to year, depending on the individual's performance during the last performance period. Salary increases or raises would come only with changes in responsibility, cost of living, or seniority. The merit portion of the pay package would be highly variable, so that if a person's performance fell off, his or her pay would also be decreased by a cut in the size of the merit pay. The purpose of this kind of system is, of course, to make a large proportion of an individual's pay depend upon performance during the current period. Thus performance is chronologically closely tied to large changes in pay" (p. 167).

There are, to be sure, problems to be resolved before such a plan could be implemented. Performance must be measurable; performance must in some way respond to effort; and management must support such a system. A critical aspect of administering pay for performance is the necessity that the system discriminate between success and failure. It must make performance success a contingency of reinforcement, in the best tradition of behavior modification theory (Skinner, 1969). If rewards follow failure as well, they cannot reinforce success.

Actually, the manager needs to consider even more about the situation before he can reasonably design payment plans. He needs to identify the behaviors best suited to the task. He needs to assess the motives of the people who are to perform the task. In fact, he needs to perform the same kind of triangulation for rewards that he needs to perform for leadership. This time the problem is one of fitting together the variables depicted in Exhibit 9-2.

Exhibit 9-2 Measuring Reward Effectiveness

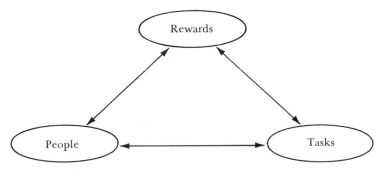

Suppose, for example, achievement-oriented behavior is instrumental to effective task performance, as it was in the case of the women's sportswear salesmen discussed in Chapter 1. For such a situation, sales commissions could be an effective achievement arousal cue, since they make pay clearly dependent upon entrepreneurial performance—the key to success on the job.

On the other hand, in the case of the hospital equipment sales job, in which success called for affiliative behavior, a better rewards-people-task fit might be obtained by a straight salary compensation system or a long-term bonus system. Short-term commissions could lead to premature attempts to close deals and hence loss of sales. Reinforcement for a longer time perspective would seem logical.

Appropriate rewards, like appropriate leadership styles, are those which encourage and enable people to do what is instrumental to successful task performance. Rewards in the short run for doing what is detrimental to success in the long run are not uncommon in organizations, but they are undesirable. Reward for individualistic achievement where collaborative effort is needed, or for departmental achievement where interdepartmental cooperation is necessary, is also common but undesirable. A selection by David McClelland following this chapter extends our discussion of rewards and recommends specific practices for specific situations.

Administrative Consistency

Our discussion of rewards, like our earlier discussions of plans, controls, and leadership, has emphasized the effects of each upon behavior. At times, we have not stressed the effects these separate administrative inputs have upon one another. We did indicate that leaders give the living reality to the other facets of administration, but there is more to the interactive effects of the parts of administration than that. The separate practices all fit together, or fail to fit together, in some way in real situations. Accordingly, we now need to consider the overall administrative system, its internal consistency or lack of it, and its role in effective management.

Administrative practices often show an internal logic and consistency. For example, a leadership style founded on mistrust of people will, other things being equal, likely favor a close and detailed network of controls. A reward system which reinforces rule-compliance may be expected to evoke supervisory efforts to enforce rules. In fact, the success of some administrative practices may depend critically on conditions provided by other administrative practices.

For example, the kind of pay plan recommended by Lawler (1971), with its incentive component, could not function without supporting leadership behavior, goal-setting practices, and controls. Goal-setting and appraisal would have to occur in a context where subordinate and superior trust one another and where they can influence one another. They would need jointly to determine reasonable and acceptable goals and means of measurement.

Similarly, the long term approach to measurement and control recommended by Rensis Likert (1967) would depend upon supportive leadership. Managers could not continue to gear their actions to enhancing the long-term value of the human organization by strengthening intervening variables—attitudes, motivations, and perceptions—if they were pressured to achieve incompatible short-run cost reductions. There can be no acquiescence to felt pressures to cut costs in reaction to a drop in earnings, if such cost cutting conflicts with the buildup of the state of intervening variables.

In short, administrative practices, if they are to reinforce consistent patterns of behavior, must come from consistent motivational assumptions and a coherent view of overall organizational climate. Just as gross parental inconsistency is thought to be associated with schizophrenia in children, administrative inconsistency seems to produce a bewildering and contradictory flow of signals to employees. The subordinate, be he manager or employee, faced with pressures to cut costs and to support moderately risky ventures, is moved to plead, "I can't do both. Which do you want?"

However desirable, administrative consistency is hardly automatic. Managers set goals and devise controls, rules, and patterns of reward aimed at stimulating and reinforcing goal-directed behavior. What happens, though, is that controls, rules, and patterns of reward sometimes displace goals. For example, Lawler (1971) points out that pay systems may be either results or process-oriented, or preferably some mixture of both (p. 172). If rewards are associated only with rule compliance, then rule compliance is the behavior that will be emphasized, at the expense of results. On the other hand, where rewards seem to depend only upon results—achieved even by means destructive to necessary processes—results will be emphasized at the expense of needed compliance to processes. Either way, some goals may be met at the expense of others, depending upon the weight of administrative influence.

A related problem is that goals can point in one direction and controls designed either to implement them or to perform mere information-collection can pull behavior in quite another direction. The practices of hoarding job openings and falsifying experience requirements in Blau's employment office were responses by anxious employees to statistical measurements of performance. These behaviors were in direct conflict with the goals of the organization— matching people and job openings in a given area.

In addition to devising administrative practices which work against one another, organizations sometimes introduce short-term emphases or crash programs which direct employees away from long-term goals. What often happens is that the mentality of management by drive or special emphasis triggers the organization to attack a particular problem. The object varies, but often includes either increasing sales, reducing costs, or improving quality.

To explore how management by drive affects organizations, Hampton (1970a; 1970b) investigated eight contests as a particular manifestation of the management by drive mentality in eight firms. In essence, he found that rather than increase total employee effort, contests simply drew it away from other goals. The contests were often successful in increasing whatever they sought to increase, but at some cost. They all engendered side effects. Specifically, they stimulated employees to neglect routine duties, conflict and compete with one another, and simply to cheat.

Time schedules with their tyranny of deadlines can be another source of unwanted consequences. However necessary they may be, time goals, *particularly when they are out of phase with the task cycle,* can introduce a serious inconsistency into the climate of an organization. The message perceived by the employee is that meeting the deadline is imperative (as well it may be), even at the expense of craftsmanship and procedural compliance. One study, conducted by Martin Patchen (1970) at the Tennessee Valley Authority, suggests that time limits interfere with achievement-oriented behavior. As a result, he advises, "Where it is necessary to establish time limits, their function as a standard against which achievement can be measured and rewards distributed, rather than merely as a noxious pressure, should probably be emphasized" (p. 235).

To summarize, there seems little point in permitting one administrative practice to undermine another. It may be necessary to stress a multiplicity of valued yet more or less conflicting objectives through administration, but a conscious concern for balance and overall direction should guide the design of administrative practices. Skillful administration does *not* consist of pushing a hodgepodge of short-run crash programs or proliferating policies, controls, and so on, ignorant of and incurious about their systemic ramifications. Instead, it involves the thoughtful provision of conditions, through goals, controls, leadership, and rewards, which influence desired behavior and performance. It also involves monitoring existing practices to identify and weigh their intended and unintended consequences, continuously attempting to foster the former and contain the latter.

A Contingency Approach to Administration

It is certainly to the good to try to avoid the catalog of dangers which attend administrative systems design. But it is even better to shape administration to affirmative action skillfully. And thanks to a number of studies, e.g., those of Burns and Stalker (1961), Lawrence and Lorsch (1967, 1969), and others, it is possible to spell out some guidelines to describe which pattern of administration best suits which situation.

"The beginning of administrative wisdom," wrote Burns and Stalker, "is the awareness that there is no one optimum type of management system" (p. 125). There is nothing intrinsically superior about a mechanistic system; nor is there anything intrinsically superior about an organic system. The real test of either is a pragmatic one. Which works best in a given situation?

Mechanistic administrative systems, as you recall, have such characteristics as specific goals, close measurement of performance, abundant rules, clear-cut procedures, and close supervisory enforcement of rules. In short, the pattern is the classic model of bureaucracy. It seems to fit better, that is, to be associated with effective task performance and high levels of individual satisfaction, when it is employed to regulate tasks which are routine, repetitive, and predictable, and whose accomplishment requires close interdependence where deviation must be kept within narrow tolerances.

Organic administrative systems show such characteristics as less specification of goals, less measurement, feedback and evaluation stressing compliance to process goals (rules and procedures), and general supervision. The opposite of bureaucracy, an organic system seems to fit better when applied to changing, uncertain, and unpredictable tasks whose accomplishment requires a greater measure of independent problem solving, innovation, and creativity.

Some of the differences between the administration of Sections A and B in Blau's employment agency are relevant. The nature of the interviewers' task could be described as requiring some measure of problem solving and creativity. The pattern of administration in Section B, which gave freer rein to interviewers to counsel, select, and place employees, was associated with greater productivity. In contrast, Section A's close preoccupation with individually "making the numbers" was associated with less productivity.

A study by John Morse (1970) adds more evidence to support a contingency approach to administration. Morse worked with two large companies, one having a set of comparable container manufacturing plants and one having a set of comparable research laboratories. He asked executives in each case to identify a high and a low-performing unit.

Morse found, upon examination of each plant, that the high performers had achieved a better fit of the administrative system to the task. The more effective container plant showed a highly mechanistic system applied to a routine, precisely specified production task. The less effective container plant had a more organic administrative system. The reverse was true in the research laboratories. Morse's findings are discussed in greater detail in a selection following this chapter.

The key to why mechanistic systems work where they do and why organic systems work where they do appears to be in their contribution to carrying out the job as it needs to be carried out. The lack of rules, controls, and specific direction was no help in a tightly interdependent production task requiring close tolerances. On the other hand, detailed controls and short-run goals hindered long-run R&D problem-solving efforts requiring flexibility and the absence of schedule pressures.

Where the administrative system arouses behavior instrumental to effective performance, employees show greater feelings of competence. Morse found that, while container plants and research laboratories had employees with rather different abilities, values, and predispositions, successful units had one thing in common. They achieved a good fit between task and administration. The better the fit, the higher the sense of competence and, it would appear, the better the chance for an effective organization and satisfied people within it.

The generalization these findings suggest is that the manager's problem is not to find one best way for all situations. Instead, he needs to achieve the best fit he can between the requirements of the task and the total administrative system. As a guide, he can seek to learn how people in the organization see its goals, controls, leadership, and rewards. Do these practices interfere with or facilitate performance? Do the people feel competent in this situation or do they not? Insofar as possible, he should seek to design the administrative system to aid people to carry out the task and to feel competent as they do so.

Suppose, for example, that analysis of task requirements had led to a decision to design a matrix organization structure to attain optimal integration and differentiation. Suppose, further, that the integrator, the program manager, was to play a critical part in the organization. At this point several questions can guide the design of the administrative system.

What are the appropriate objectives for the program manager? What standards should be used to measure his performance? How can it be measured? What rewards will reinforce cooperation which transcends departmental boundaries? Who will direct and evaluate the day-to-day work of individuals who are assigned to the program, but who belong to separate functional departments? What kind of budgeting, program or departmental, will best align resources and tasks?

There is no universal correct answer. There are, however, more or less effective answers in particular cases. The better answers lead to practices which more effectively arouse and support those patterns of behavior leading to task achievement. Departmental goals, controls, and rewards foster departmental patterns of thought and behavior. Project, product, or program goals, controls, and rewards foster project, product, or program patterns of thought and behavior. The desirable administrative pattern will not only be technically appropriate but will provide better perceptual, motivational, and behavioral consequences. Thus, the design of administrative systems can be sophisticated. That is, it can be rationally accomplished to create an organizational climate conducive to increased human satisfaction and organizational effectiveness.

Summary

When administrative practices are examined for their effects upon cognition, motivation, and behavior, strategic opportunities for the exercise of managerial influence come into view. It is possible to analyze tasks for their behavioral requirements. It is possible to analyze people for their behavioral propensities. And it is possible to select personnel to match the requirements and propensities. But it is also possible to design and utilize goals, controls, leadership, and rewards to strengthen further the likelihood that employees will behave in ways suited to task performance.

Planning and goal setting in a climate supportive of risks can help clarify approaches to tasks. These practices can also help arouse n Achievement. Similarly, leadership style and rewards can support venturesome behavior and reinforce effort and performance. Individualistic competition or group cooperation can be emphasized, depending upon the pattern of administrative practices. But that pattern can be identified and changed to modify behavior as desired.

The internal consistency of the administrative system can also be investigated. The explanation of baffling and "irrational" behavior is often found in understanding administrative inputs as employees understand them. When they learn what employees value, managers can design better rewards. When they learn how employees see goals and controls, managers can design them better. When they learn whether rewards, goals, controls, and leadership are consistent or inconsistent, managers can act to align them with their intentions. Finally, a situational or contingency approach to administrative systems design rather than a universal approach leads to better results. The key is to design administrative conditions which enable people to work competently, given the nature of their work.

References

Argyle, M., G. Gardner, and F. Ciofi. "The Measurement of Supervisory Methods." *Human Relations,* Vol. 10 (1957), 295–313.

Blake, R., and J. Mouton. *The Managerial Grid.* Gulf, 1964.

Blau, P. M. *The Dynamics of Bureaucracy.* University of Chicago Press, 1963.

Burns, T., and G. M. Stalker. *The Management of Innovation.* Tavistock, 1961.

Carlyle, T. *On Heroes, Hero-Worship, and the Heroic in History.* Houghton Mifflin, 1907.

Drucker, P. R. "Controls, Control, and Management." In *Management Controls: New Directions in Basic Research,* ed. Bonini, Jaedicke, and Wagner. McGraw-Hill, 1964, pp. 286–296.

Dubin, R. "Supervision and Productivity: Empirical Findings and Theoretical Considerations." In *Leadership and Productivity,* ed. R. Dubin, G. Homans, F. C. Mann, and D. C. Miller. Chandler, 1965.

Fiedler, F. C. "Leadership—A New Model." *Discovery,* Vol. 26, No. 4 (April 1965), 12–17.

———. *A Theory of Leadership Effectiveness.* McGraw-Hill, 1967.

Fleishman, E. F., E. F. Harris, and R. D. Burtt. *Leadership and Supervision in Industry.* The Ohio State University Press, 1955.

Ford, R. N. "The Obstinate Employee." *Psychology Today,* Vol. 3, No. 6 (November 1969), 32–35.

Hampton, D. R. "Contests as Misdirected Motivators." *Compensation Review,* Vol. 2, No. 2 (Second Quarter 1970a), 32–38.

———. "Contests Have Side Effects Too." *California Management Review,* Vol. 12, No. 4 (Summer 1970b), 86–94.

Herzberg, F. "The Motivation-Hygiene Concept and Problems of Manpower." *Personnel Administration,* Vol. 27, No. 1 (January–February 1964), 3–7.

———. *Work and the Nature of Man.* World, 1966.

Kahn, R. L. "The Prediction of Productivity." *Journal of Social Issues,* Vol. 12 (1956), 41–49.

Korman, A. K. "Consideration, 'Initiating Structure,' and Organizational Criteria—A Review." *Personnel Psychology,* Vol. 19, No. 4 (Winter 1966), 349–361.

Lawler, E. E., III. *Pay and Organizational Effectiveness: A Psychological View.* McGraw-Hill, 1971.

Lawrence, P. R., and J. W. Lorsch. *Developing Organizations: Diagnosis and Action.* Addison-Wesley, 1969.

———. *Organization and Environment: Managing Differentiation and Integration.* Harvard Graduate School of Business Administration, 1967.

Likert, R. *The Human Organization.* McGraw-Hill, 1967.

———. *New Patterns of Management.* McGraw-Hill, 1961.

——— and D. G. Bowers. "Organizational Theory and Human Resource Accounting." *American Psychologist,* Vol. 24, No. 6 (June 1969), 585–592.

Litwin, G. H., and R. A. Stringer, Jr. *Motivation and Organizational Climate.* Harvard Graduate School of Business Administration, 1968.

Livingston, J. S. "Myth of the Well-Educated Manager." *Harvard Business Review,* Vol. 49, No. 1 (January–February 1971), 79–89.

Maslow, A. H. *Motivation and Personality.* Harper & Row, 1954.

McClelland, D. C. "Achievement Motivation Can Be Developed." *Harvard Business Review,* Vol. 43, No. 6 (November–December 1965), 6–24, 178.

McGregor, D. *The Human Side of Enterprise.* McGraw-Hill, 1960.

Misumi, J., and F. Seki. "Effects of Achievement Motivation on the Effectiveness of Leadership Patterns." *Administrative Science Quarterly,* Vol. 16, No. 1 (March 1971), 51–59.

Morse, J., and J. W. Lorsch. "Beyond Theory Y." *Harvard Business Review,* Vol. 48, No. 3 (May–June 1970), 61–68.

Opsahl, R. L., and M. D. Dunnette. "The Role of Financial Compensation in Industrial Motivation." *Psychological Bulletin,* Vol. 66, No. 2 (August 1966), 94–118.

Patchen, M. *Participation, Achievement, and Involvement on the Job.* Prentice-Hall, 1970.

Porter, L. W., and E. E. Lawler III. *Managerial Attitudes and Performance.* Irwin, 1968.

Rogers, C. *On Becoming a Person.* Houghton Mifflin, 1961.

Rosen, B., and R. C. D'Andrade. "The Psychosocial Origins of Achievement Motivation." *Sociometry,* Vol. 22, No. 3 (September 1959), 185–218.

Salisbury, H. *The 900 Days: The Siege of Leningrad.* Harper & Row, 1969.

Shepard, H. A. "Innovation-Resisting and Innovation-Producing Organizations." *Journal of Business,* Vol. 60, No. 4 (October 1967), 470–477.

Shils, E. A., and M. Janowitz. "Cohesion and Disintegration in the Wehrmacht in World War II." *Public Opinion Quarterly,* Vol. 12, No. 2 (Summer 1948), 280–315.

Skinner, B. F. *Contingencies of Reinforcement: A Theoretical Analysis.* Appleton Century Crofts, 1969.

Vroom, V. "The Effects of Extrinsic Rewards on Intrinsic Motivation." Paper given at the Western Psychological Association, San Francisco, April 24, 1971.

———. *Some Personality Determinants of the Effects of Participation.* Prentice-Hall, 1960.

———. *Work and Motivation.* Wiley, 1964.

Zaleznik, A. *Human Dilemmas of Leadership.* Harper & Row, 1966.

Readings

Choosing a Leadership Pattern

ROBERT TANNENBAUM, WARREN H. SCHMIDT

The problem of how the modern manager can be "democratic" in his relations with subordinates and at the same time maintain the necessary authority and control in the organization for which he is responsible has come into focus increasingly in recent years.

Earlier in the century this problem was not so acutely felt. The successful executive was generally pictured as possessing intelligence, imagination, initiative, the capacity to make rapid (and generally wise) decisions, and the ability to inspire subordinates. People tended to think of the world as being divided into "leaders" and "followers."

Gradually, however, from the social sciences emerged the concept of "group dynamics" with its focus on *members* of the group rather than solely on the leader. Research efforts of social scientists underscored the importance of employee involvement and participation in decision making. Evidence began to challenge the efficiency of highly directive leadership, and increasing attention was paid to problems of motivation and human relations.

Through training laboratories in group development that sprang up across the country, many of the newer notions of leadership began to exert an impact. These training laboratories were carefully designed to give people a first-hand experience in full participation and decision making. The designated "leaders" deliberately attempted to reduce their own power and to make group members as responsible as possible for setting their own goals and methods within the laboratory experience.

It was perhaps inevitable that some of the people who attended the training laboratories regarded this kind of leadership as being truly "democratic" and went home with the determination to build fully participative decision making into their own organizations. Whenever their bosses made a decision without convening a staff meeting, they tended to perceive this as authoritarian behavior. The true symbol of democratic leadership to some was the meeting—and the less directed from the top, the more democratic it was.

Some of the more enthusiastic alumni of these training laboratories began to get the habit of categorizing leader behavior as "democratic" *or* "authoritarian." The boss who made too many decisions himself was thought of as an authoritarian, and his directive behavior was often attributed solely to his personality.

The net result of the research findings and of the human relations training based upon them has been to call into question the stereotype of an effective leader. Consequently, the modern manager often finds himself in an uncomfortable state of mind.

Often he is not quite sure how to behave; there are times when he is torn between exerting "strong" leadership and "permissive" leadership. Sometimes new knowledge pushes him in one direction ("I should really get the group to help make this decision"), but at the same time his experience pushes him in another direction ("I really understand the problem better than the group and therefore I should make the decision"). He is not sure when a group decision is really appropriate or when holding a staff meeting serves merely as a device for avoiding his own decision-making responsibility.

The purpose of our article is to suggest a framework which managers may find useful in grappling with this dilemma. First we shall look at the different patterns of leadership behavior that the manager can choose from in relating himself to his subordinates. Then we shall turn to some of the questions suggested by this range of patterns. For instance, how important is it for a manager's subordinates to know what type of leadership he is using in a situation? What factors should he consider in deciding on a leadership pattern? What difference do his long-run objectives make as compared to his immediate objectives?

Possible Leadership Behavior

Exhibit 1 presents the continuum or range of possible leadership behavior available to a manager. Each type of action is related to the degree of authority used by the boss and to the amount of freedom available to his subordinates in reaching decisions. The actions seen on the extreme left characterize the manager who maintains a high degree of control; those seen on the extreme right characterize the manager who releases a high degree of control. Neither extreme is absolute; authority and freedom are never without their limitations.

Now let us look more closely at each of the behavior points occurring along this continuum:

The manager makes the decision and announces it. In this case the boss identifies a problem, considers alternative solutions, chooses one of them, and then reports this decision to his subordinates for implementation. He may or may not give consideration to what he believes his subordinates will think or feel about his decision; in any case, he provides no opportunity for them to participate directly in the decision-making process. Coercion may or may not be used or implied.

The manager "sells" his decision. Here the manager, as before, takes responsibility for identifying the problem and arriving at a decision. However, rather than simply announcing it, he takes the additional step of persuading his subordinates to accept it. In doing so, he recognizes the possibility of some resistance among those who will be faced with the decision, and seeks to reduce this resistance by indicating, for example, what the employees have to gain from his decision.

The manager presents his ideas, invites questions. Here the boss who has arrived at a decision and who seeks acceptance of his ideas provides an opportunity for his subordinates to get a fuller explanation of his thinking and his intentions. After presenting the ideas, he invites questions so that his associates can better

Exhibit 1   Continuum of Leadership Behavior

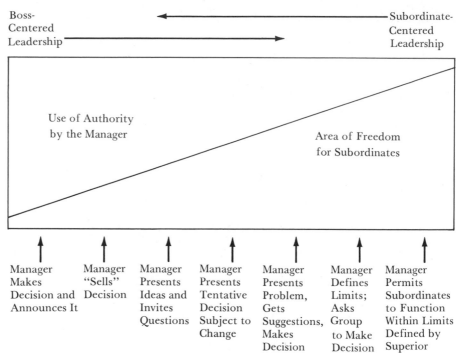

Boss-
Centered
Leadership

Subordinate-
Centered
Leadership

Use of Authority
by the Manager

Area of Freedom
for Subordinates

Manager Makes Decision and Announces It	Manager "Sells" Decision	Manager Presents Ideas and Invites Questions	Manager Presents Tentative Decision Subject to Change	Manager Presents Problem, Gets Suggestions, Makes Decision	Manager Defines Limits; Asks Group to Make Decision	Manager Permits Subordinates to Function Within Limits Defined by Superior

understand what he is trying to accomplish. This "give and take" also enables the manager and the subordinates to explore more fully the implications of the decision.

The manager presents a tentative decision subject to change. This kind of behavior permits the subordinates to exert some influence on the decision. The initiative for identifying and diagnosing the problem remains with the boss. Before meeting with his staff, he has thought the problem through and arrived at a decision—but only a tentative one. Before finalizing it, he presents his proposed solution for the reaction of those who will be affected by it. He says in effect, "I'd like to hear what you have to say about this plan that I have developed. I'll appreciate your frank reactions, but will reserve for myself the final decision."

The manager presents the problem, gets suggestions, and then makes his decision. Up to this point the boss has come before the group with a solution of his own. Not so in this case. The subordinates now get the first chance to suggest solutions. The manager's initial role involves identifying the problem. He might, for example, say something of this sort: "We are faced with a number of complaints from newspapers and the general public on our service policy. What is wrong here? What ideas do you have for coming to grips with this problem?"

The function of the group becomes one of increasing the manager's repertory of possible solutions to the problem. The purpose is to capitalize on the knowledge and experience of those who are on the "firing line." From the expanded list of alternatives developed by the manager and his subordinates, the manager then selects the solution that he regards as most promising.[1]

The manager defines the limits and requests the group to make a decision. At this point the manager passes to the group (possibly including himself as a member) the right to make decisions. Before doing so, however, he defines the problem to be solved and the boundaries within which the decision must be made.

An example might be the handling of a parking problem at a plant. The boss decides that this is something that should be worked on by the people involved, so he calls them together and points up the existence of the problem. Then he tells them: "There is the open field just north of the main plant which has been designated for additional employee parking. We can build underground or surface multilevel facilities as long as the cost does not exceed $100,000. Within these limits we are free to work out whatever solution makes sense to us. After we decide on a specific plan, the company will spend the available money in whatever way we indicate."

The manager permits the group to make decisions within prescribed limits. This represents an extreme degree of group freedom only occasionally encountered in formal organizations, as, for instance, in many research groups. Here the team of managers or engineers undertakes the identification and diagnosis of the problem, develops alternative procedures for solving it, and decides on one or more of these alternative solutions. The only limits directly imposed on the group by the organization are those specified by the superior of the team's boss. If the boss participates in the decision-making process, he attempts to do so with no more authority than any other member of the group. He commits himself in advance to assist in implementing whatever decision the group makes.

As the continuum in Exhibit 1 demonstrates, there are a number of alternative ways in which a manager can relate himself to the group or individuals he is supervising. At the extreme left of the range, the emphasis is on the manager—on what *he* is interested in, how *he* sees things, how *he* feels about them. As we move toward the subordinate-centered end of the continuum, however, the focus is increasingly on the subordinates—on what *they* are interested in, how *they* look at things, how *they* feel about them.

When business leadership is regarded in this way, a number of questions arise. Let us take four of especial importance:

Can a boss ever relinquish his responsibility by delegating it to someone else? Our view is that the manager must expect to be held responsible by his superior for the quality of the decisions made, even though operationally these decisions may have been made on a group basis. He should, therefore, be ready to accept whatever risk is involved whenever he delegates decision-making power to his subordinates. Delegation is not a way of "passing the buck." Also, it should be emphasized that the amount of freedom the boss gives to his subordinates cannot be greater than the freedom which he himself has been given by his own superior.

Should the manager participate with his subordinates once he has delegated responsibility to them? The manager should carefully think over this question and decide on his role prior to involving the subordinate group. He should ask if his presence will inhibit or facilitate the problem-solving process. There may be some instances when he should leave the group to let it solve the problem for itself.

Typically, however, the boss has useful ideas to contribute, and should function as an additional member of the group. In the latter instance, it is important that he indicate clearly to the group that he sees himself in a *member* role rather than in an authority role.

How important is it for the group to recognize what kind of leadership behavior the boss is using? It makes a great deal of difference. Many relationship problems between boss and subordinate occur because the boss fails to make clear how he plans to use his authority. If, for example, he actually intends to make a certain decision himself, but the subordinate group gets the impression that he has delegated this authority, considerable confusion and resentment are likely to follow. Problems may also occur when the boss uses a "democratic" facade to conceal the fact that he has already made a decision which he hopes the group will accept as its own. The attempt to "make them think it was their idea in the first place" is a risky one. We believe that it is highly important for the manager to be honest and clear in describing what authority he is keeping and what role he is asking his subordinates to assume in solving a particular problem.

Can you tell how "democratic" a manager is by the number of decisions his subordinates make? The sheer *number* of decisions is not an accurate index of the amount of freedom that a subordinate group enjoys. More important is the *significance* of the decisions which the boss entrusts to his subordinates. Obviously a decision on how to arrange desks is of an entirely different order from a decision involving the introduction of new electronic data-processing equipment. Even though the widest possible limits are given in dealing with the first issue, the group will sense no particular degree of responsibility. For a boss to permit the group to decide equipment policy, even within rather narrow limits, would reflect a greater degree of confidence in them on his part.

Practical Leadership Behavior

Now let us turn from the types of leadership that are possible in a company situation to the question of what types are *practical* and *desirable*. What factors or forces should a manager consider in deciding how to manage? Three are of particular importance: forces in the manager; forces in the subordinates; forces in the situation.

We should like briefly to describe these elements and indicate how they might influence a manager's action in a decision-making situation.[2] The strength of each of them will, of course, vary from instance to instance, but the manager who is sensitive to them can better assess the problems which face him and determine which mode of leadership behavior is most appropriate for him.

Forces in the Manager

The manager's behavior in any given instance will be influenced greatly by the many forces operating within his own personality. He will, of course, perceive his leadership problems in a unique way on the basis of his background, knowledge, and experience. Among the important internal forces affecting him will be the following:

1. *His value system.* How strongly does he feel that individuals should have a share in making the decisions which affect them? Or, how convinced is he

that the official who is paid to assume responsibility should personally carry the burden of decision making? The strength of his convictions on questions like these will tend to move the manager to one end or the other of the continuum shown in Exhibit 1. His behavior will also be influenced by the relative importance that he attaches to organizational efficiency, personal growth of subordinates, and company profits.[3]

2. *His confidence in his subordinates.* Managers differ greatly in the amount of trust they have in other people generally, and this carries over to the particular employees they supervise at a given time. In viewing his particular group of subordinates, the manager is likely to consider their knowledge and competence with respect to the problem. A central question he might ask himself is: "Who is best qualified to deal with this problem?" Often he may, justifiably or not, have more confidence in his own capabilities than in those of his subordinates.

3. *His own leadership inclinations.* There are some managers who seem to function more comfortably and naturally as highly directive leaders. Resolving problems and issuing orders come easily to them. Other managers seem to operate more comfortably in a team role, where they are continually sharing many of their functions with their subordinates.

4. *His feelings of security in an uncertain situation.* The manager who releases control over the decision-making process thereby reduces the predictability of the outcome. Some managers have a greater need than others for predictability and stability in their environment. This "tolerance for ambiguity" is being viewed increasingly by psychologists as a key variable in a person's manner of dealing with problems.

The manager brings these and other highly personal variables to each situation he faces. If he can see them as forces which, consciously or unconsciously, influence his behavior, he can better understand what makes him prefer to act in a given way. And understanding this, he can often make himself more effective.

Forces in the Subordinate

Before deciding how to lead a certain group, the manager will also want to consider a number of forces affecting his subordinates' behavior. He will want to remember that each employee, like himself, is influenced by many personality variables. In addition, each subordinate has a set of expectations about how the boss should act in relation to him (the phrase "expected behavior" is one we hear more and more often these days at discussions of leadership and teaching). The better the manager understands these factors, the more accurately he can determine what kind of behavior on his part will enable his subordinates to act most effectively.

Generally speaking, the manager can permit his subordinates greater freedom if the following essential conditions exist:

1. If the subordinates have relatively high needs for independence. (As we all know, people differ greatly in the amount of direction that they desire.)
2. If the subordinates have a readiness to assume responsibility for decision making. (Some see additional responsibility as a tribute to their ability; others see it as "passing the buck.")
3. If they have a relatively high tolerance for ambiguity. (Some employees prefer

to have clear-cut directives given to them; others prefer a wider area of freedom.)
4. If they are interested in the problem and feel that it is important.
5. If they understand and identify with the goals of the organization.
6. If they have the necessary knowledge and experience to deal with the problem.
7. If they have learned to expect to share in decision making. (Persons who have come to expect strong leadership and are then suddenly confronted with the request to share more fully in decision making are often upset by this new experience. On the other hand, persons who have enjoyed a considerable amount of freedom resent the boss who begins to make all the decisions himself.)

The manager will probably tend to make fuller use of his own authority if the above conditions do *not* exist; at times there may be no realistic alternative to running a "one-man show."

The restrictive effect of many of the forces will, of course, be greatly modified by the general feeling of confidence which subordinates have in the boss. Where they have learned to respect and trust him, he is free to vary his behavior. He will feel certain that he will not be perceived as an authoritarian boss on those occasions when he makes decisions by himself. Similarly, he will not be seen as using staff meetings to avoid his decision-making responsibility. In a climate of mutual confidence and respect, people tend to feel less threatened by deviations from normal practice, which in turn makes possible a higher degree of flexibility in the whole relationship.

Forces in the Situation

In addition to the forces which exist in the manager himself and in his subordinates, certain characteristics of the general situation will also affect the manager's behavior. Among the more critical environmental pressures that surround him are those which stem from the organization, the work group, the nature of the problem, and the pressures of time. Let us look briefly at each of these:

Type of Organization   Like individuals, organizations have values and traditions which inevitably influence the behavior of the people who work in them. The manager who is a newcomer to a company quickly discovers that certain kinds of behavior are approved while others are not. He also discovers that to deviate radically from what is generally accepted is likely to create problems for him.

These values and traditions are communicated in many ways—through job descriptions, policy pronouncements, and public statements by top executives. Some organizations, for example, hold to the notion that the desirable executive is one who is dynamic, imaginative, decisive, and persuasive. Other organizations put more emphasis upon the importance of the executive's ability to work effectively with people—his human relations skills. The fact that his superiors have a defined concept of what the good executive should be will very likely push the manager toward one end or the other of the behavioral range.

In addition to the above, the amount of employee participation is influenced by such variables as the size of the working units, their geographical distribution, and the degree of inter- and intra-organizational security required to attain company goals. For example, the wide geographical dispersion of an organization may preclude a practical system of participative decision making, even though this would otherwise be desirable. Similarly, the size of the working units or the need for keeping plans confidential may make it necessary for the boss to exercise more control than would otherwise be the case. Factors like these may limit considerably the manager's ability to function flexibly on the continuum.

Group Effectiveness   Before turning decision-making responsibility over to a subordinate group, the boss should consider how effectively its members work together as a unit.

One of the revelant factors here is the experience the group has had in working together. It can generally be expected that a group which has functioned for some time will have developed habits of cooperation and thus be able to tackle a problem more effectively than a new group. It can also be expected that a group of people with similar backgrounds and interests will work more quickly and easily than people with dissimilar backgrounds, because the communication problems are likely to be less complex.

The degree of confidence that the members have in their ability to solve problems as a group is also a key consideration. Finally, such group variables as cohesiveness, permissiveness, mutual acceptance, and commonality of purpose will exert subtle but powerful influence on the group's functioning.

The Problem Itself   The nature of the problem may determine what degree of authority should be delegated by the manager to his subordinates. Obviously he will ask himself whether they have the kind of knowledge which is needed. It is possible to do them a real disservice by assigning a problem that their experience does not equip them to handle.

Since the problems faced in large or growing industries increasingly require knowledge of specialists from many different fields, it might be inferred that the more complex a problem, the more anxious a manager will be to get some assistance in solving it. However, this is not always the case. There will be times when the very complexity of the problem calls for one person to work it out. For example, if the manager has most of the background and factual data relevant to a given issue, it may be easier for him to think it through himself than to take the time to fill in his staff on all the pertinent background information.

The key question to ask, of course, is: "Have I heard the ideas of everyone who has the necessary knowledge to make a significant contribution to the solution of this problem?"

The Pressure of Time   This is perhaps the most clearly felt pressure on the manager (in spite of the fact that it may sometimes be imagined). The more that he feels the need for an immediate decision, the more difficult it is to involve other people. In organizations which are in a constant state of "crisis" and "crash programing" one is likely to find managers personally using a high degree of authority with relatively little delegation to subordinates. When the time pressure is less intense, however, it becomes much more possible to bring subordinates in on the decision-making process.

These, then, are the principal forces that impinge on the manager in any given instance and that tend to determine his tactical behavior in relation to his subordinates. In each case his behavior ideally will be that which makes possible the most effective attainment of his immediate goal within the limits facing him.

Long-Run Strategy

As the manager works with his organization on the problems that come up day by day, his choice of a leadership pattern is usually limited. He must take account of the forces just described and, within the restrictions they impose on him, do the best that he can. But as he looks ahead months or even years, he can shift his thinking from tactics to large-scale strategy. No longer need he be fettered by all of the forces mentioned, for he can view many of them as variables over which he has some control. He can, for example, gain new insights or skills for himself, supply training for individual subordinates, and provide participative experiences for his employee group.

In trying to bring about a change in these variables, however, he is faced with a challenging question: At which point along the continuum *should* he act?

The answer depends largely on what he wants to accomplish. Let us suppose that he is interested in the same objectives that most modern managers seek to attain when they can shift their attention from the pressure of immediate assignments:

1. To raise the level of employee motivation.
2. To increase the readiness of subordinates to accept change.
3. To improve the quality of all managerial decisions.
4. To develop teamwork and morale.
5. To further the individual development of employees.

In recent years the manager has been deluged with a flow of advice on how best to achieve these longer-run objectives. It is little wonder that he is often both bewildered and annoyed. However, there are some guidelines which he can usefully follow in making a decision.

Most research and much of the experience of recent years give a strong factual basis to the theory that a fairly high degree of subordinate-centered behavior is associated with the accomplishment of the five purposes mentioned.[4] This does not mean that a manager should always leave all decisions to his assistants. To provide the individual or the group with greater freedom than they are ready for at any given time may very well tend to generate anxieties and therefore inhibit rather than facilitate the attainment of desired objectives. But this should not keep the manager from making a continuing effort to confront his subordinates with the challenge of freedom.

Conclusions

In summary, there are two implications in the basic thesis that we have been developing. The first is that the successful leader is one who is keenly aware of those forces which are most relevant to his behavior at any given time. He accurately understands himself, the individuals and group he is dealing with, and the company and broader social environment in which he operates. And certainly he is able to assess the present readiness for growth of his subordinates.

But this sensitivity or understanding is not enough, which brings us to the second implication. The successful leader is one who is able to behave appropriately in the light of these perceptions. If direction is in order, he is able to direct; if considerable participative freedom is called for, he is able to provide such freedom.

Thus, the successful manager of men can be primarily characterized neither as a strong leader nor as a permissive one. Rather, he is one who maintains a high batting average in accurately assessing the forces that determine what his most appropriate behavior at any given time should be and in actually being able to behave accordingly. Being both insightful and flexible, he is less likely to see the problems of leadership as a dilemma.

Notes and References

1. For a fuller explanation of this approach, see Leo Moore, "Too Much Management, Too Little Change," *HBR*, January–February 1956, p. 41.
2. See also Robert Tannenbaum and Fred Massarik, "Participation by Subordinates in the Managerial Decision-Making Process," *Canadian Journal of Economics and Political Science*, August 1950, pp. 413–418.
3. See Chris Argyris, "Top Management Dilemma: Company Needs vs. Individual Development," *Personnel*, September 1955, pp. 123–134.
4. For example, see Warren H. Schmidt and Paul C. Buchanan, *Techniques that Produce Teamwork* (New London, Arthur C. Croft Publications, 1954); and Morris S. Viteles, *Motivation and Morale in Industry* (New York, W. W. Norton & Company, Inc., 1953).

Pay in Organizations
EDWARD E. LAWLER III

In the last fifty years, scholars have advanced a number of rather completely developed yet different approaches to organization management (see, e.g., Miles, 1965; Scott, 1961). All of these approaches deal to some extent with pay administration. Not surprisingly, they tend to assign pay relatively different roles. The scientific management approach, for example, assigns it the primary role in motivating employees to follow the orders of their superiors, while modern management theory tends to ignore pay almost entirely or to see it as only one of a large number of possible influences on motivation (see, e.g., Likert, 1961).

Probably the one issue which should be considered by all organization theories is the relationship between pay and performance. Time and time again the issue has come up as a crucial issue in our discussion of pay and organizational effectiveness. No theory of organization can be said to be complete unless it deals with this issue. If the decision is made to try to relate pay to performance, then the issue of how this can be accomplished must also be dealt with. It is a difficult problem and one that is not adequately dealt with by most theorists.

Given our discussion of pay, it is difficult to argue with the view that relating pay to performance can contribute to organizational effectiveness. But it is also clear that under some conditions (e.g., subjective criteria, low trust) it cannot be done effectively. When pay is tied to performance, it can motivate performance. In addition, satisfaction will be related to performance, and as a result, turnover and absenteeism will be lower among high performers. Further, tying pay to performance leads to high pay satisfaction. Finally, it can increase the importance of pay. Figure 1 shows that tying pay to performance influences major psychological issues. It also shows that an organization can realize a number of tangible benefits from relating the two closely.

Figure 1   Effects of Relating and Not Relating Pay to Performance

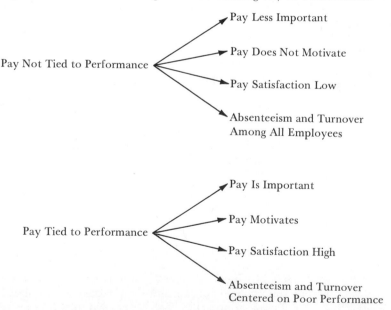

Theories of Organization and Pay

Not all theories of organization argue that pay should be tied to performance. Those that do differ widely on how they say this should be done and on how important they feel it is that it be done. Figure 2 shows one way of classifying the different approaches to administering pay in an organization. It presents a four-cell table that divides approaches according to whether they tie pay to

Figure 2 Management Style and the Relationship Between Pay and
Performance

Approach to Administering Rewards

	Authoritarian	Democratic
Pay Not Related to Performance	Paternalism	Human Relations Socialism
Pay Related to Performance	Scientific Management	

performance and according to whether pay is administered on a democratic
or an authoritarian basis.

In Figure 2 the names of different approaches to management and organizations are placed in three of the four cells. Paternalistic management is placed
in the cell where authoritarian control is practiced and pay is not related to
performance. This approach is called paternalistic because of the dependency
relationship this type of pay administration creates between employer and
employee and because, like the parent, the employer gives rewards for things
other than performance. Scientific management falls under the approach of
autocratically tying pay to performance: Taylor's work emphasizes the primary
role of management in setting piece rates and tying pay to performance. There
clearly is no room in Taylor's system for employee participation in discussions
about how pay should be administered. Using democratic or participative
management but not tying pay to performance is called the "human relations"
or "socialist management" approach. In one sense, neither of these labels perfectly fits this approach to adminstering pay. There is a strong current of this
kind of thinking in the writing of most writers who are identified with the human
relations movement (e.g., Mayo, Roethlisberger), and certainly there is an
element of this kind of thinking in the socialist management approach. The
socialist approach stresses involving the workers in administrative decisions and
relating their pay more to their needs than to their performance.

The name of no management style appears in the cell in which pay is
democratically tied to performance. The reason for this is simple: none of the
currently identifiable approaches to management have articulated this point
of view adequately. The spirit of this approach is partially contained in the

writings of many of the modern organization theorists. They are, however, far from unanimous in expressing this orientation toward pay administration. Many of them are more interested in the motivating power of higher-order needs, the importance of self-control, and the inappropriateness of the pyramidal structure.

Writers like Argyris (1964), Haire (1956), and McGregor (1960, 1967) are the exceptions here. They emphasize the importance of tying pay to perform-ance, and they also express a preference for participative management. But even these writers put forward only tentative views of how pay and performance are to be related. Typically, they single out the Scanlon Plan for praise and cite it as an example of what can be done. The Scanlon Plan is an interesting effort in this direction. Clearly, however, there are problems associated with it, and it is not universally applicable.

Most modern organization theorists concentrate their fire on building an organization in which people will be motivated by intrinsic rewards such as a desire for growth and competence. Indeed, as Schein (1965) has stated, they are concerned with motivating "self-actualizing man." There is, of course, some validity to this view, just as there is validity to the view of scientific management. Schein has said that organization theorists should think in terms of what he calls "complex" man. Such a view of man is necessary, particularly if we wish to see the role of pay in its proper perspective—somewhere between the high place given it by scientific management and the low place given it by many of the human relations movement writers. The research evidence shows that pay is important and that, if related to performance, it can contribute to organizational effectiveness. Still, some organizations probably should not try to relate pay to performance, and among those that should, widely different approaches are needed. As we shall see, such things as the climate, technology and structure of an organization strongly influence whether and how pay should be related to performance.

Organization Climate and Pay

The pay system in an organization must, above all, fit the human relations climate of that organization. Although it makes some sense to talk about general principles of pay administration, specific procedures must fit the conditions that exist in a particular organization. Consider for a moment the suggestion that salaries be made public. In the kind of organization that generally adopts a democratic or participative approach to management, this practice should develop naturally. As employees begin to participate more in evaluating them-selves and others, they will gradually come to know other people's salaries, as well as the general pay structure of the organization. On the other hand, in an autocratically run organization the policy of openness just will not fit. Salary openness demands trust, open discussion of performance, and justification of salaries. None of these are likely to occur in an authoritarian organization. They are, however, an integral part of a democratic approach to management. Participative performance appraisal is another practice that is necessary if salary is to be clearly tied to performance. It too is likely to fit well in a participative, but not in an authoritarian, style of management. Similarly, widespread em-ployee participation in a job evaluation program should present no problem in an organization that practices participative management day in and day out; but in one that does not, it may be quite impossible.

Piece rate plans with rates set by industrial engineers and other "semiautomated" payment plans were developed within the context of scientific management. Traditionally, such plans have been established as a management control device. Only with the advent of unions were workers given some say in how they were set up and administered. The fact that piece rate plans have typically been run in an authoritarian manner does not, of course, mean that they have to be. They could fit into a democratic approach to management if they were participatively developed and if greater self-control were built into the system. These plans are so strongly identified with more traditional styles of management, however, that it is difficult to convince people that they can be democratically administered. In fact, the traditional association of incentive pay and authoritarian management may account for the slight attention that many modern organization theorists have given to incentive plans.

What kind of pay incentive plan will work in an organization run on traditional lines? The evidence reviewed in this book suggests that the more "objectively" based the plan, the more likely it is to be successful. Plans that tie pay to "hard" criteria, such as quantity of output, profits, or sales, and thus require a minimum level of trust, stand a much better chance of succeeding in the traditional organization than approaches which depend on joint goal setting and soft criteria. Piece rate plans that are administered in a consistent and fair manner and have rates that are set fairly do work sometimes. So do sales bonuses for salesmen and profit-sharing plans in small organizations. But where trust is low, these plans seldom reach their full potential.

The problem for traditional organizations occurs in jobs where there are no hard criteria for measuring performance and where trust and participation are needed if pay is to act as an incentive. Here, the traditionally managed organization has difficulty in getting pay to work as a motivator because the conditions are not right for participative performance appraisal and joint goal setting. In this kind of job situation, a Theory Y organization is in a better position to use pay to motivate performance than is the traditional scientific management approach. In such job situations, this approach, which is built upon the idea of using pay as an incentive, cannot be used because it does not believe in employee participation or the other power-equalization approaches to management. On the other hand, many of the newer approaches to organization theory—approaches which were not designed to rely on pay to motivate—can use it. Many modern organization theorists do not capitalize on this advantage of their approach by actually saying how pay can be used to motivate performance within their system.

In summary, it has been argued that one of the factors which influences the type of pay plan an organization can use is the human relations climate or management style that exists in the organization. For illustrative purposes, organizations characterized by an authoritarian style of management were contrasted with those characterized by a more participative approach. It was stressed that the potential for using pay to motivate performance is greater in the latter than in the former, despite the fact that the authoritarian approach has given greater emphasis to the use of pay to motivate performance.

Technology and Pay

The human relations climate that exists in an organization is only one of the factors that determine how appropriate different pay plans will be. Certainly, the kind of product that is being produced must be considered, since it influences how an organization is technically organized, and this in turn influences the appropriateness of different pay plans.

Woodward (1965) distinguishes among industrial organizations that engage in mass production, unit production, and process production. Piece rate incentives probably can be used in unit and mass production plants, but they hardly make sense in a process production firm. Plantwide bonuses would seem to be well suited to many process production plants but not to most unit and mass production plants. This difference arises because of the difficulty of identifying individual contributions in process production. If we expand our discussion to include nonindustrial professionally staffed service organizations, such as hospitals and schools, this point becomes even more obvious. Neither of these types of organizations could use piece rate plans or organizationwide bonuses. They could, perhaps, use a system based upon participative performance appraisals and joint goal setting if the climate were right.

In short, the type of product an organization produces influences the technology and production method of the organization. Production methods in turn differ in the degree to which individual performance is identifiable and measurable, as well as in the degree to which cooperation among the members of the organization is necessary. Because of this, organizations that differ in the kinds of products they produce need different pay systems, even though they may be similar in other ways. For example, group plans lead to cooperation. In process production plants where cooperation is important and individual performance is difficult to measure, a group plan makes sense. In a consulting firm, however, where cooperation probably is not so important and individual performance is measurable, a more individualized plan makes sense, but not a piece rate plan, since individual performance in this situation probably does not lend itself to piece measurement.

Organization Structure and Pay

In addition to the human relations climate and technological factors, other characteristics affect the kind of pay system that will be appropriate for an organization. Size is a crucial variable. Another is the degree of centralization. Small organizations can do things that large organizations cannot. They can, for example, use incentive and bonus pay plans that are based upon organizationwide performance. In a small organization, most employees will feel that their behavior affects the performance of the total organization. In a large organization this is not likely to be so (except at the very top), and as a result an organizationwide plan is not likely to motivate performance. Pressures toward uniform policy statements and systematic pay and appraisal practices are also more prevalent in large organizations. Thus, it is more difficult to tailor an individual's pay package to his own situation. This is unfortunate, because much can be gained by individualizing fringe benefit packages and setting up individual pay incentive plans. People differ in how frequently they should be evaluated, in how they should be evaluated, and in the kind of pay system (i.e., bonus increase, stock options) that is most likely to motivate them. Using individualized pay programs to capitalize on these differences is difficult in large organizations because they entail tremendous increases in administrative overhead. They can be installed, however, in small organizations. In short, small organizations have a potential advantage over large organizations because they have more options open to them.

The degree of centralization-decentralization is relevant to pay administration because it affects the kind of performance criteria data that are available. In a centralized organization, for example, the performance of a subpart, or a particular plant, is often difficult to measure unless a decentralized responsibility-based accounting system is used. Even if it is possible to measure an individual plant's performance, this is often not a good criterion upon which to base pay, because the plant employees often are not in control of the plant. As a result they do not feel responsible for the plant's performance. If substantial decision-making power is vested in the central office, local plant management can hardly be evaluated on the basis of how the plant performs. In fact, the management may resent being evaluated on this basis. This is not true when decision making is decentralized and accounting data are gathered on subparts of the organization. This point is particularly important in a large organization. It means that pay plans that use large group, plantwide, or divisionwide performance as a criterion are practical only if the organization is to some extent decentralized. It is only within the context of a decentralized organization that this type of criterion can be meaningful.

Compared with firms with centralized authority, decentralized organizations have more pay administration options. As has already been mentioned, they can more easily use plantwide and subunitwide plans. In addition, they can more easily tolerate different pay practices in different parts of the organization. In fact, decentralization would seem to encourage different parts of an organization to establish different pay practices, while centralization would seem to discourage such tailoring. To the extent that it makes sense to tailor pay plans to fit the organization—which is the thesis on which this chapter is based—decentralization should have the advantage over centralization.

Table 1 attempts to summarize the points made so far on the relevance of organization factors to pay plans. The human relations climate of an organization, the type of production it engages in, its size, and its degree of centralization—all affect the kind of pay system that is appropriate for an organization. Each of these factors limits the possible types of merit pay plan that can be successfully used. Only certain kinds of plans are appropriate for large organizations, for example, and only certain kinds are appropriate for mass production organizations. In order to state what kind of plan can be used in a specific organization, one must classify the organization according to each of the four variables listed in Table 1. An organization might, for example, practice authoritarian management, engage in mass production, and be large and centralized. The pay plan that is appropriate for this organization is determined by all these factors. In other words, the plan that is chosen for this firm must be one that cannot be ruled out on the basis of any of these four characteristics.

Since each of the factors (being of a certain size, having a highly centralized administration, etc.) serves to rule out some kinds of pay plans, it is possible

Table 1 Relevance of Four Organizational Factors to Pay Plans

Human relations climate	Authoritarian	Need objective hard criteria; pay clearly tied to performance
	Democratic	Can use participative goal setting and softer criteria
Production type	Mass and unit	Can usually develop hard criteria; rewards on individual or small group basis
	Process	Need to encourage cooperation; individual performance not highly visible or measurable
	Professional organizations (i.e., hospital, school, consulting firms)	Individually based plans; soft criteria; high individual involvement in own evaluation
Size	Large	Organizationwide bonuses poor for all but a few top-level managers
	Small	Organizationwide bonuses possible in some situations
Degree of centralization	Centralized	Hard to base performance on subunit (i.e., plant) performance
	Decentralized	Pay can be based on profit center or subunit performance for members of management

that for some organizations there is no pay plan that can be labeled appropriate. Table 2 shows this by listing all the types of organizations that can be identified, using the crude classification system developed here. As indicated, in some (e.g., authoritarian, centralized, large, and professionally staffed service organizations), there is simply no type of merit or performance-based pay system that is appropriate. In these organizations, it is advisable not to try to base pay on performance, and to pay on the basis of attendance and membership. In fact, in many types of organizations there is no really satisfactory merit pay system, but it is possible to design merit pay systems that will be adequate (e.g., most authoritarian organizations).

The most important point that Table 2 illustrates is that pay systems exist in the context of organizations and that the characteristics of the organizations must be taken into account when pay systems are developed. No one pay system will fit all organizations; there are too many situational factors that must be considered. Our discussion has emphasized only a few of the most salient. There are others which, if considered, would further complicate the thinking shown in Table 2 (e.g., age of company, hiring policies, characteristics of workers). One of the problems with the research on pay is that little of it has tried to identify the relevant situational factors and to elaborate on their treatment. There is a good deal of research showing what basic conditions must exist if pay is to motivate (e.g., it must be important, and it must be related to performance) and what must happen if people are to be satisfied with their pay (e.g., inputs must match outcomes). Missing, however, is "developmental" research (Haire,

Table 2   Appropriate Merit Pay Plans for Various Types of Organizations

Authoritarian	Mass and unit	Large	Cent.	Individual basis; objective criteria
			Decent.	For workers—individual; for managers—group plan possible on profit center basis; for all objective criteria
		Small	Cent.	Individual basis; objective criteria
			Decent.	For workers—individual; for managers—group plan possible on profit center basis; for all objective criteria
	Process	Large	Cent.	None very appropriate; companywide bonus possible for managers
			Decent.	Group plan based upon objective subunit performance criteria
		Small	Cent.	Organizationwide bonus plan
			Decent.	Group plan based upon objective subunit performance measures
	Professional service	Large	Cent.	None appropriate
			Decent.	None appropriate
		Small	Cent.	None appropriate
			Decent.	None appropriate
Democratic	Mass and unit	Large	Cent.	Individual plans based on objective criteria as well as soft criteria, such as participatively set goals
			Decent.	Same as centralized, but for managers use data from their subpart of organization
		Small	Cent.	Some consideration to performance of total organization; individual plans based on objective criteria as well as soft criteria, such as participatively set goals
			Decent.	Same as centralized except subpart performance can be used as criteria in both individual and group plans
	Process	Large	Cent.	Organization wide plan based on objective and subjective criteria; individual appraisal based on soft criteria
			Decent.	Group plan based on plant performance; objective and subjective criteria
		Small	Cent.	Organizationwide plan based on company performance
			Decent.	Group plans based on subunit performance
	Professional	Large	Cent.	Design individual plans; high input from employees; joint goal setting and evaluation
			Decent.	Same as centralized but some consideration to performance of subparts
		Small	Cent.	Some consideration to performance of total organization; design individual plans; high input from employees; joint goal setting and evaluation
			Decent.	Same as centralized, except that data for subpart of organization may be relevant

1964)—that is, research concerned with (1) how these broad principles can be applied to the situations existing in particular organizations and (2) what the specific situational factors are that determine how the principles can be converted into practice. Investigators are showing a growing tendency to do research on the psychology of pay. It is hoped that the trend will continue and that this kind of research problem will be attacked.

Pay as a Change Agent

The discussion so far has emphasized the important relationship between organization climate and pay administration. We have said that the kind of climate that exists very much limits the kind of pay practices that an organization can use. Further, we have assumed that pay practices must be adjusted to fit the climate. This assumption is open to question. Is it not possible that the pay system can change the climate? There is some evidence that this has happened in companies that have tried the Scanlon Plan and the Lincoln Electric Plan. The installation of these plans seemed to help the organizations move toward a more democratic style of management. In effect, the pay plans seemed to be agents of change.

It is not difficult to see how pay administration policies can affect organization climate. Pay is important to people, and decisions about pay are carefully watched by everyone in an organization. Pay is a common language shared by all, and because of this it is a medium through which an organization can communicate with all its employees. Thus, pay practices can influence the whole climate of the organization. Pay administration is one place where management philosophy can be clearly and immediately converted into action. It is a concrete manifestation of leadership and management style. Because of this, changes in pay policy can be a direct indication to employees of a change in management thinking or management style. Actually delivering on promised pay raises or merit increases, for example, can be concrete evidence that management means what it says. Such acts can increase the credibility of management and potentially lead to greater trust between management and workers. Actually involving workers in pay decisions is a clear way to indicate that management is moving toward a more democratic climate. Similarly, giving employees a share of company profits is a clear way to indicate that the organization wants to establish a climate in which employee-employer relations are characterized by trust, cooperation, and, indeed, respect.

Little research has been done on the use of pay as a change agent in organizations. With the exception of the Scanlon Plan and a few others, pay plans simply have not been thought of as a way of changing organizations. This is unfortunate because potentially pay administration represents a powerful tool for effecting change. Interest in organization change at this time emphasizes interpersonal issues rather than structural changes. The typical change program seems to begin with management training, using T-groups, grid sessions, role playing, etc. This may be the best approach in many organizations, but in others, changes in organization policy or procedures may be better. At present, we know very little about which approach is more effective. In particular, we know little about when to choose a specific approach.

Even when an organization decides that the pay system is not a good place to start a change effort, it is important that the pay system not be forgotten or overlooked. In the long run, an anachronistic or inappropriate pay system can be a powerful retarding force. For example, where an attempt is being made to change toward a more participative style of management, keeping the traditional pay plan can slow progress considerably. Unfortunately, many attempts at organizational change have concentrated only on revising leadership styles or increasing interpersonal competence. For maximum effectiveness these changes should be accompanied by changes in the pay system; changes in the pay system can reinforce the other changes and make it clear that they are not just another management gimmick. Money speaks, and administered in a traditional way, it can say that an avowed move toward participative management is not sincere; administered in new ways, it can say that a real change is taking place. It is hoped that, as more is learned about the psychological aspects of pay administration, more people interested in organizational change will see pay system changes as an important element in any change effort.

Summary

The major theme of this chapter has been that a pay plan must fit the characteristics of an organization if it is to be effective; it must be individualized in terms of organization size, management style, etc. There are two ways organizations and pay systems can be matched. First, the task can be viewed as a problem of choosing the correct pay plan for an organization, taking into account the characteristics of the organization as it is presently administered. But as the last part of the chapter emphasized, there is a second way. Instead of fitting the plan to the organization, management can change the organization to fit the plan. The pay plan can be viewed as a stimulant or lever to effect change in the organization. A pay plan can be used to initiate movement toward a more participative management style. This can be done but we are just beginning to understand the process. The key would seem to be in choosing a pay plan that will start the organization moving and reinforce any movement that is made.

References

Argyris, C. *Integrating the Individual and the Organization.* Wiley, 1964.
Haire, M. *Psychology in Management.* McGraw-Hill, 1956.
———. "The Social Sciences and Management Practices." *California Management Review,* Vol. 6, No. 4 (1964), 3–10.
Likert, R. *New Patterns of Management.* McGraw-Hill, 1961.
McGregor, D. *The Human Side of Enterprise.* McGraw-Hill, 1960.
———. *The Professional Manager.* McGraw-Hill, 1967.
Miles, R. "Human Relations or Human Resources." *Harvard Business Review,* Vol. 43, No. 4 (July–August 1965), 148–163.
Schein, E. *Organizational Psychology.* Prentice-Hall, 1965.
Scott, W. R. "Organization Theory: An Overview and an Appraisal." *Journal of the Academy of Management,* Vol. 4, No. 1 (1961), 7–26.
Woodward, J. *Industrial Organization: Theory and Practice.* London: Oxford University Press, 1965.

Money as a Motivator: Some Research Insights

DAVID C. McCLELLAND

For nearly half a century, industrial psychologists have been demonstrating that money isn't nearly so potent a motivating force as theory and common sense suggest it ought to be. Elton Mayo's 1922 study of work output in a Philadelphia textile mill set the tone of what was to follow. Management had found that incentive payment schemes had not succeeded in increasing work or decreasing turnover in a department where the jobs were particularly monotonous and fatiguing. Mayo found, on the other hand, that allowing the men to schedule the work for themselves brought dramatic increases in productivity. Where money incentives hadn't proven effective, psychic rewards worked.[1]

Over and over again, later students[2] of industrial psychology emphasized the same point: Money isn't everything. Its meaning is in the eye of the beholder. It functions only as a symbol representing more important psychological factors in the work situation.

Why, then, in spite of all the evidence, do people still take money so seriously as a motivator? In the first place, money obviously is very important. Work, unless it is volunteer or "play," involves a contract between two parties "guaranteed" by the payment of money. The pay may symbolize the psychological realities of the contract imperfectly—which may be all the psychologists are saying. The employee may think he is working for it, and the manager may think he is using it to get the employee to work, but both are only partly right. To understand the situation better, particularly if we wish to manage motivation or behavior, we must penetrate beyond the money itself and consider what it really represents to employer and employee.

Money Misconceptions

But it is not just man's tendency to confuse symbols with realities that leads him to talk as if money were an end in itself. There are at least three other reasons why he does so. In the first place, no idea is more deeply entrenched in contemporary American psychology than the notion that in the end all learning is based on a few simple material rewards. I suspect practically all top managers today learned in Psychology I that there are so-called primary material rewards, such as food and water, and that all other rewards are "secondary," getting their "motivating value" from learned associations with the primaries. Money obviously falls into the secondary category.

This notion involves some major misconceptions, and there is no good reason why it should continue to shape the thinking of men who are interested in managing motivation. But it has persisted because of its appealing simplicity, and because the alternatives to it are hard to formulate so neatly.

Let me, however, illustrate one of these alternative approaches by a quick analogy. Think of what goes on in a man's mind as if it were a computer printout of a lot of miscellaneous material. In commonsense terms, a lot of thoughts buzz through a man's head during any given time. As anyone who has tried to do content analysis of computer printouts knows, the periods or other punctuation marks are of key importance. That is, if you are to search and simplify what is otherwise a bewildering mass of material, it is first necessary to break it up into units within which co-occurrences can be noted.

In real life, rewards or incentives are like punctuation marks. They break up sequences or call attention to them. In psychological terms, they are attention-getting, affect-producing mechanisms, rather than substitutes for something else. As such they are of tremendous importance in producing organization or order in thought and action. Note, however, that they are only one possible type of attention-getting mechanism. Bright lights and colors, changes in rest periods, reorganizations of work flow—all sorts of things—can also get attention.

In short, rather than being some kind of a substitute for simpler material rewards, money is more sensibly regarded as *one of a class* of attention-getters. And, like other members of its class, it can lose its attention-getting power with repetition.[3]

A second reason why managers go on thinking that money is a prime motivator is that most of them are highly achievement-oriented; in the psychologist's terms, they are "high in n Ach." We know that such men attach special significance to money rewards. They are strong believers in steeply increasing financial rewards for greater accomplishment. Because they themselves are particularly interested in some concrete measure that will sensitively reflect how well they have done, it is easy and natural for them to mistake this idea for a related one—namely, that the more money you offer someone the harder he will work.

Obviously, believing in more pay for more work is simply not the same as saying that more pay will lead *to* more work. But the fallacy in this reasoning is not only logical but psychological, for other experimental evidence shows that even men who score high in n Ach are not themselves spurred to greater efforts by money incentives. While they attribute greater importance to money as a motivator, it doesn't motivate *them* to work harder.

The apparent explanation: They seek financial reward, not for its own sake, but because it tells them how well they are doing. As Saul Gellerman has pointed out, the incentive value of top executive salaries must lie primarily in their "merit badge" quality, since high taxes result in rather minor differences in take-home pay at this level of compensation. So managers believe money is important in motivating others because they mistakenly think it motivates themselves. Actually, while it *is* more important to them as a measure of accomplishment, it doesn't really motivate them. And it doesn't motivate others either, except indirectly—as workers and others are ready to point out whenever they are asked.

Finally, the third reason why managers keep coming back to money as a way of motivating people is because at the practical level it is the one thing they can manipulate rather easily. After all, it is part of their job to motivate the people working for them, to get more work out of people, or at the very least to make sure that people aren't loafing. The higher their achievement motivation, the more they will want to show an improvement in the quality or quantity of the work done by their people. They may listen patiently to the psychologists and sociologists who seek to convince them that money isn't important for its own sake, but then what can they do to change those other psychological factors which are supposedly more important? Payment plans are real and manipulable. Plans for dealing with psychological factors often seem nebulous.

What, then, does all this add up to? Are we left with the conclusion that the nature of incentive plans makes no difference at all? Hardly. It is one thing to say that psychological factors will modify how incentive plans work; it is quite another to conclude that variations in incentive plans do not make any difference.

What we need is a change in orientation. The problem is managing motivation—not managing work, but managing the *desire* of men to work. This means seeing incentive plans as a particular means of achieving specific objectives within the larger framework of the work situation.

The Work Variables

It has recently been shown[4] that a work situation involves four sets of variables which must be accurately diagnosed before a "prescription" can be written for improvement:

1. The motives and needs of the persons working at the task.
2. The motivational requirements of the task they have to perform.
3. The motives (or strengths and limitations) of the manager.
4. The organizational climate.

Once a manager knows where he stands on these variables in a particular work situation, he is in a position to do various things. For example, if he finds that most of his workers are strongly achievement-oriented, while the tasks to be performed are assembly-line work that doesn't satisfy this motivation, he has an obvious mismatch. To bring the interests of the people into line with the motivational requirements of the job, he can get a different type of worker or change the nature of the task.

Our focus here, however, is narrower: Given different settings on these four types of variables, how can management use payment plans to help motivate men? Obviously, there can be no simple sovereign payment system that will work best for all people under all conditions. But we can give illustrations.

Variations in the Motives of Workers

Whether workers or managers are high or low in achievement motivation makes a real difference in the effectiveness of financial incentives. Several studies have shown that offering additional financial rewards for doing a task does not make strongly achievement-oriented people work harder or better.[5] A group of aggressive, achievement-minded salesmen would certainly be angry if their extra efforts were not recognized with a much greater financial reward; yet offering them bonuses is not what produces the extra effort. This may seem like a psychological distinction without a difference, but the interpretation of the meaning of the bonus plan genuinely affects performance, as a later example will show.

People with relatively low achievement motivation, on the other hand, *will* work harder for increased financial rewards. It is not the task itself that interests them, however, nor does the money they get by doing it interest them primarily as a measure of accomplishment. Rather, it has other values for them.

Two consequences flow from this simple fact. First, if there is any way to get the reward without doing the work, they will naturally tend to look for it. This means that managers who rely primarily on money to activate people who are low in achievement motivation will have a much harder job of policing the work situation than they would if the work satisfied certain other motivational needs. This conclusion will hardly come as news to managers who have been struggling with employee incentive plans over the past generation.

The second implication is that such employees will have to want something that the money can buy. Obviously, there are lots of important things that money *can't* buy: tolerable working conditions, friendship, and job security, to name a few. As a number of studies have shown, even the material possessions that most middle-class managers assume everyone wants, such as a home of one's own, are in fact not wanted by many of the people he is trying to motivate. It follows that if a manager must deal largely in financial incentives for these people, he will have to give some thought to creating psychological wants that money will satisfy—such as more education for children, a happier retirement, a more exciting (and expensive) vacation, etc.

But money can also have other values for people who are most strongly motivated by needs for social approval and solidarity with others in the work group. One study found, somewhat to the experimenters' surprise, that girls who scored high in n Affiliation actually worked harder for money prizes than girls who scored low on this factor, whereas there had been no difference between the two types of girls when the extra incentives were not offered.[6] Evidently the money helped to create a general expectancy on the girls' part that they should work hard to please the experimenters. The moral again is simple: For a working force that scores high on this factor, incentive plans and payments should be framed in terms of working together for the common good, not—as achievement-oriented managers nearly always assume—of working for one's own gain.

Finally, another study showed that college students who scored high in n Power spend more money on prestige supplies—expensive liquor, college insignia, powerful motorcycles or cars, etc.—in other words, on things which will make them feel or seem big, strong, powerful and respected.[7] If a manager finds his staff scores high in n Power, then he ought to administer his financial incentives in different ways, perhaps even presenting some of them in the form of prestige supplies—such as a trip to Europe or a new Cadillac—for especially outstanding performance.

One simple lesson to be learned from all these studies is that the motivational characteristics of the staff make a lot of difference. Even with the cost of incentives held constant, their form and meaning have to be shaped to fit the needs of the people they are designed to influence.

Variations in the Motivational Requirements of Tasks

Researchers have suggested some simple measuring devices for the motivational requirements of different tasks.[8] For instance, the job of an assembly-line worker has more "affiliation" than "achievement" elements, because workers must interact with each other. Successful task accomplishment depends on the co-operation of co-workers, stable working relationships over time, etc. If this is so, how can incentive plans help? Actually they are more likely to hinder, because most incentive plans are based on the assumption that all tasks primarily involve achievement. And in fact such plans usually make less than 10 percent of the people into "ratebusters," while they make the rest of the work force angry because the extra incentives reinforce behavior which is in direct opposition to the affiliation requirements of the task.[9] Such "gung-ho" achievers often disrupt normal working patterns and lower average productivity over the long run.

Even at the sales level this can be true. While, generally speaking, successful salesmen are strongly achievement and power-oriented and low in affiliation needs, at least one sales situation has been identified in which the very best salesmen scored only moderately high in achievement orientation, quite a bit higher in affiliation orientation than most salesmen, and lower in power orientation.[10] These particular salesmen were involved in a task which, in the researchers' words, required "a much greater emphasis on coordinating the efforts of the sales and service function, and on building long-term close customer relationships involving a high degree of trust, than on entrepreneurial selling." Here an incentive plan based on sales volume alone could easily attract the wrong men (those too high in n Ach) into sales, or influence existing salesmen to neglect the long-term consumer relationships that experience shows to be necessary for success in this job. Money payments have to fit not only the characteristics of the people in a work force, but also the nature of the jobs they have to perform.

Variations in the Motives of Managers

As we have seen, unless the manager understands his own motives, he may project them onto others. It is all too easy for a manager, in making plans for other people, to assume that they are like himself. But if he knows what *he* wants, he may be able to avoid falling into the trap. He may, for example, even be able to see when his own motivations are leading him to propose new ideas that have little chance of success. I have sometimes wondered how many personnel managers think up new incentive plans in order to convince *their* superiors that they are high achievers, deserving of a special bonus. Actually, a personnel man ought to be specially rewarded for picking and keeping outstanding men, but such day-to-day performance may be less promptly noticeable and rewardable than the installation of a brand-new incentive plan. Here again, the pay system may tend to distort the personnel job by treating and rewarding it as a straightforward achievement proposition.

Beyond such considerations, a manager must understand himself well enough to know what he can or should do in a given organizational situation. Thus he may discover that, while his staff is heavily affiliation-oriented and therefore wants and needs many signs of approval and friendship, he himself is rather aloof, priding himself that he got where he is today by not wasting time with "the boys." This kind of self-understanding should help him create the kind of climate that will make the incentive system work under a given set of conditions.

Variations in Climate

Two researchers, G. H. Litwin and R. A. Stringer, have identified some nine different dimensions on which organizational climates can vary.[11] They hypothesize that each of these variables has different effects on the motivations of people working in the organization. For example, a high degree of *structure* (rules, regulations, going through channels), reflecting an emphasis on power and control, should reduce affiliation and achievement needs among its employees, but at the same time make them more power-oriented. Similarly, a high degree of risk or challenge in the tasks to be performed should arouse achievement motivation but have little or no effect on workers' affiliation or power needs.

Consider how these climatic factors may operate when the incentive system is held constant. In one study[12] four outstanding sales offices were contrasted with four average sales offices, not only in terms of climate differences as perceived by the salesmen, but also in terms of actual observations of how managers interacted with their men during the day.

The incentive system in all offices was the same and men in the outstanding and the average offices were equally satisfied with it. Yet other climate variables apparently made for very different performance averages. The outstanding offices, as perceived by their salesmen, had more structure, evoked more identity and loyalty, and were warmer and friendlier. The salesmen from these outstanding offices also felt that higher standards were being set and that they were more often rewarded by the manager for their efforts than criticized for nonperformance. Their views were substantiated by observation of managers in the two types of offices. Those in the outstanding offices gave almost twice as much praise and encouragement as the managers from the average offices. To quote from the study,

". . . the outstanding manager makes it a habit to compliment a man sincerely on a job well done; a personal thank-you is always given over the phone and in person. He might also drop the man a note of congratulation and thanks for a successful sale. He also typically thanks the customer in the same manner and makes a real effort to visit the new installation with the salesman and compliment the salesman's efforts before the customer. In contrast, the average manager's attitude is that "these men are on very large commissions and that's what makes them hustle. They know they can go out on any day of the week and get a raise just by selling another piece of equipment. Oh, I *might* buy them a drink, but it's money that motivates these guys."[13]

Once again we see that nonfinancial, situational factors are important, but with a difference. Furthermore, we have a nice illustration of how too exclusive a concern for money can distract a manager's attention from other psychological variables that he ought to be taking into account.

Incentive Plan Variables

But it is no use repeating that everything depends on the way financial plans are perceived. If variations in the incentive plan really matter, we should be able to discover just what difference they make by investigating them while holding situational variables constant. Until such specific studies have been made, we cannot generalize very confidently about the important variables in the incentive plan itself. But on the basis of some theory and laboratory research it may be permissible to speculate about three of these variables: the probability of success (winning the incentive award), as perceived by participants in the plan; the size of the incentive offered; and the nature of the response-reward relationship.

Probability of Success

Experimental evidence indicates that moderate probabilities of winning an incentive reward produce better performance than either very low or very high probabilities.[14] In general, one researcher has shown, a person who has one chance in two of getting a reward will work harder than if he has a lower or higher probability of getting it, regardless of the strength of his achievement motivation or the size of the money incentive.[15] A study of my own confirmed the fact that students will work harder when the odds are lower than three chances out of four.[16] The generalization seems likely to hold for financial incentive plans, though the optimum probability for winning a special reward obviously would need to be worked out for each particular situation. John W. Atkinson's estimate that it is somewhere around the one-chance-in-two level is not a bad place to start.[17]

We know two further facts about this phenomenon. First, strongly achievement-oriented individuals work best under odds as slim as one in three, or even longer.[18] Thus, an incentive plan for a strongly achievement-oriented sales force should obviously offer a different set of odds from a plan designed for a group of clerical workers who score low in *n* Ach.

Second, we know that the perceived probability of success changes with experience. This is probably why achievement-oriented people work better under somewhat longer odds than the average person. They know from past experience that they tend to be more successful than the average person in tasks they undertake. Therefore, what to the outside observer is a one-in-three chance of winning for an average worker is correctly perceived by the high achiever as a one-in-two chance for him.

Many of the difficulties that incentive plans get into flow from the fact that experience changes the perceived probability of success. Suppose a salesman or a worker exposed to a new incentive plan works extra hard and gets a special bonus. Then what does he do in the next time period? If he notices that a lot of other people have made it, and if he makes it again, he may fear that management will raise the normal standard. Management, on its side, may wonder how it can keep the perceived probability of success at the optimal level without raising standards as individuals get better at their jobs. Most managers are unhappy if incentive plans stop working after a while. Yet, theory suggests that, because experience changes perceived probability of success, plans would have to be changed regularly in order to keep expectancies of winning at an optimal level for producing performance.

Size of Incentive

Offered $2.50 for the best performance, a group of college students solved more arithmetic problems than when they were offered only $1.25—regardless, again, of their level of achievement, motivation, or the odds under which they were attempting to win the prize.[19] Obviously, then, size of reward makes a difference.

Just as obviously, "size" is a relative matter—relative, that is, to one's own starting point and to what other people are getting. Five hundred dollars is much more of an incentive to a $5,000 wage earner than to a $50,000 executive. Almost certainly, the increment in money necessary to create a "just noticeable incentive" is some kind of constant fraction of the base. But, again, this function has yet to be determined for real-life situations. It would probably be easier to work out in a personnel recruiting context, where the incentive effect of additional pay is more obvious than that of incentives offered for increased output in a given work setting.

Many authors have recently turned their attention to how large a man perceives an incentive to be, in comparison not with his own starting level but rather with what others like him are getting.[20] Here, oddly enough, the yardstick seems to be more absolute than relative. That is, for a man earning $50,000, $500 may not seem like much of an incentive relative to his own past earnings, but it could become an important incentive if it puts him clearly ahead of another man whom he sees as a competitor.

One other finding relates to the size of incentives. In a couple of studies, managers receiving middle-level compensation scored higher in n Ach than either lower- or higher-paid managers.[21] The data are hard to interpret with any certainty but they are suggestive. One can infer that the managers with relatively low compensation (here, less than $20,000 a year) are those in the 35 to 50 age range who just haven't "made it." They are less successful, less achievement-oriented, and less rewarded. But why should the higher-paid managers (here, $25,000 a year and up) also be lower in achievement motivation? Older men, who may also get higher salaries, tend to become less achievement-oriented, but in this study age was controlled. Do the findings mean, then, that high financial rewards may lower motivation to achieve? Or do they mean that while high achievement motivation is necessary to get to the top, other motives are necessary for performing really well once one has gotten there?

Interestingly enough, the same pattern has been found in society: The middle-class people "on the way up" score highest in n Ach, whereas those from lower- and upper-class backgrounds are less achievement-oriented.[22] This might mean that very large financial rewards tend to decrease achievement motivation, perhaps not because they satisfy so many needs in the traditional sense but because they lead people to get interested in other things. At any rate, the possibility that very large rewards decrease motivation is intriguing and would seem to deserve further investigation.

The Response-Reward Relationship

Even in seniority systems where a man gets more pay as he grows older, the tacit assumption is that, with greater experience on the job, he is presumably doing the job better, even though it would be impractical to try to measure exactly how. This suggests the first variable in the incentive situation: how specifically the desired response is defined. If a person doesn't know what he is supposed to do to earn the reward, he will obviously be less able to do it.

So, in general, the supposition is that the more clearly specified the behavior, the greater the incentive value of the reward.

In some jobs—selling, for example—desired performance is relatively easy to define, while in others, such as the job of a personnel manager, it is quite difficult. In any case, it seems probable that successful incentive plans involve goals worked out as specifically as possible in advance, between superior and subordinate, so that the subordinate will know whether he is achieving his goals.

Two types of errors are commonly made in specifying the response for which the reward is offered. First, the manager may assume that the task primarily involves work output and may specify the expected responses in those terms, whereas a careful job analysis would show that other factors are important to success. A case in point is the sales offices mentioned previously, where too much emphasis on selling interfered with service functions and actually lowered performance.

Second, the manager may believe he is rewarding better performance from his staff, when in fact he is primarily rewarding other kinds of behavior, such as being loyal to him or "not rocking the boat." A comparative study of two large business organizations in Mexico provides an interesting illustration.[23] In Company A, where rewards were clearly given for better performance, men with high achievement motivation got significantly more raises over a three-year period. However, in Company P, where men were highly regarded if they were loyal to the boss and stayed in line, men who scored high in n Power were more often promoted. Company A was growing much more rapidly than Company P. Yet the president of Company P declared that he was interested in better performance for his top executives and couldn't understand why his company was not growing faster. He did not realize, though his subordinates did, that he was actually dispensing financial rewards primarily for loyalty to himself.

Another important characteristic of the response is whether it is expected from a group or from individuals. Should incentives be prorated on the basis of group performance, as in profit-sharing plans, or given for individual performance alone? No easy generalization is yet possible, though everyone agrees that each work situation should be carefully analyzed to see which type of performance it is most appropriate to reward in a given case. For example, where the staff is strongly affiliation-oriented and the job requires lots of interpersonal cooperation, some kind of group incentive plan would obviously be more effective than one rewarding individual excellence.

Still another important variable is the delay between the response and the reward. How often should bonus reviews be held—monthly, semiannually, or annually? Most studies with lower animals in simple learning situations suggest that the shorter the delay, the greater the incentive value of the reward. Applying this principle to the design of an industrial incentive plan could lead to "atomizing" expected improved responses so that a person could accumulate "points" every time he showed a better response, the points to be totaled and cashed in for money at regular intervals. The difficulty of measuring performance in a given work situation will almost certainly decide how often and how immediately rewards can be given. Generally speaking, such variations in timing are probably less important than the other variables mentioned, since most adults, and certainly most managers, are able to work for rewards deferred at least a month, and often a year or even longer.

In summary, then, money is one tool among many for managing motivation. It is a treacherous tool because it is deceptively concrete, tempting many managers to neglect variables in the work situation and climate that really affect productivity. In the near future, there will be less and less excuse for neglecting these variables, as the behavioral sciences begin to define them and explain to management how they can be manipulated just as one might change a financial compensation plan.

Incentive plans will continue to play an important role in the overall management framework. But the effective manager will also need to diagnose the needs of his staff, the motivational requirements of their jobs, his own motives, and the climate of the present organizational setup. Then he can rationally plan how to improve productivity by improving the climate; by developing certain motives in key people; by making a better match between the needs of the people and the needs of the job; or, finally, by specifically gearing incentive plans to the organizational situation.

References

1. Cf. S. W. Gellerman, *Motivation and Productivity,* New York: American Management Association, 1963.
2. Cf. R. Likert, "A Motivational Approach to a Modified Theory of Organization and Management" in *Modern Organization Theory,* M. Haire, ed., New York: Wiley, 1959; F. Herzberg, B. Mausner, and B. Snyderman, *The Motivation to Work,* 2d ed., New York: Wiley, 1959; W. F. Whyte, *Money and Motivation,* New York: Harper, 1955; D. McGregor, *The Human Side of Enterprise,* New York: McGraw-Hill, 1960. For review of these studies see *Motivation and Productivity,* op. cit.
3. See J. Kagan, "On the Need for Relativism," *American Psychologist,* 1967, pp. 22, 131–142.
4. G. H. Litwin and R. A. Stringer, *Motivation and Organization Climate,* Cambridge: Harvard, 1967.
5. J. W. Atkinson and W. R. Reitman, "Performance as a Function of Motive Strength," *Journal of Abnormal and Social Psychology,* 1956, pp. 53, 361–366; J. W. Atkinson, ed., *Motives in Fantasy, Action and Society,* Princeton, N.J.: D. Van Nostrand, 1958; C. P. Smith, "The Influence of Testing Conditions on Need for Achievement Scores and Their Relationship to Performance Scores," in *A Theory of Achievement Motivation,* J. W. Atkinson and N. T. Feather, eds., New York: Wiley, 1966, pp. 277–297.
6. *Journal of Abnormal and Social Psychology,* op. cit.
7. D. G. Winter, "Power Motivation in Thought and Action," unpublished Ph.D. thesis, Harvard University, 1967.
8. *Motivation and Organization Climate,* op. cit.
9. *Money and Motivation,* op. cit.
10. G. H. Litwin and J. A. Timmons, *Motivation and Organization Climate: A Study of Outstanding and Average Sales Offices,* Boston: Behavioral Sciences Center, 1966.
11. *Motivation and Organization Climate,* op. cit.
12. *Motivation and Organization Climate: A Study of Outstanding and Average Sales Offices,* op. cit.
13. Ibid, p. 13.
14. *Motives in Fantasy, Action and Society,* op. cit.; *A Theory of Achievement Motivation,* op. cit.
15. *Motives in Fantasy, Action and Society,* p. 296.
16. D. C. McClelland, *The Achieving Society,* Princeton, N.J.: Van Nostrand, 1961.

17. *Motives in Fantasy, Action and Society,* op. cit.
18. Ibid.; see also *The Achieving Society,* op. cit.
19. *Motives in Fantasy, Action and Society,* p. 293.
20. See R. L. Opsahl and M. D. Dunnette, "The Role of Financial Compensation in Industrial Motivation," *Psychological Bulletin,* 1966, pp. 66, 94–118.
21. See *The Achieving Society,* op. cit., p. 269.
22. B. C. Rosen, "Race, Ethnicity, and the Achievement Syndrome," *American Sociological Review,* 1959, pp. 24, 47–60.
23. J. D. W. Andrews, "The Achievement Motive in Two Types of Organizations," *Journal of Personality and Social Psychology,* June 1967.

Beyond Theory Y

JOHN J. MORSE, JAY W. LORSCH

During the past 30 years, managers have been bombarded with two competing approaches to the problems of human administration and organization. The first, usually called the classical school of organization, emphasizes the need for well-established lines of authority, clearly defined jobs, and authority equal to responsibility. The second, often called the participative approach, focuses on the desirability of involving organization members in decision making so that they will be more highly motivated.

Douglas McGregor, through his well-known "Theory X and Theory Y," drew a distinction between the assumptions about human motivation which underlie these two approaches, to this effect:

Theory X assumes that people dislike work and must be coerced, controlled, and directed toward organizational goals. Furthermore, most people prefer to be treated this way, so they can avoid responsibility.

Theory Y—the integration of goals—emphasizes the average person's intrinsic interest in his work, his desire to be self-directing and to seek responsibility, and his capacity to be creative in solving business problems.

It is McGregor's conclusion, of course, that the latter approach to organization is the more desirable one for managers to follow.[1]

McGregor's position causes confusion for the managers who try to choose between these two conflicting approaches. The classical organizational approach that McGregor associated with Theory X does work well in some situations, although, as McGregor himself pointed out, there are also some situations where it does not work effectively. At the same time, the approach based on Theory Y, while it has produced good results in some situations, does not always do so. That is, each approach is effective in some cases but not in others. Why is this? How can managers resolve the confusion?

A New Approach

Recent work by a number of students of management and organization may help to answer such questions.[2] These studies indicate that there is not one best organizational approach; rather, the best approach depends on the nature of the work to be done. Enterprises with highly predictable tasks perform better with organizations characterized by the highly formalized procedures and management hierarchies of the classical approach. With highly uncertain tasks that require more extensive problem solving, on the other hand, organizations that are less formalized and emphasize self-control and member participation in decision making are more effective. In essence, according to these newer studies, managers must design and develop organizations so that the organizational characteristics *fit* the nature of the task to be done.

While the conclusions of this newer approach will make sense to most experienced managers and can alleviate much of the confusion about which approach to choose, there are still two important questions unanswered:

1. How does the more formalized and controlling organization affect the motivation of organization members? (McGregor's most telling criticism of the classical approach was that it did not unleash the potential in an enterprise's human resources.)

2. Equally important, does a less formalized organization always provide a high level of motivation for its members? (This is the implication many managers have drawn from McGregor's work.)

We have recently been involved in a study that provides surprising answers to these questions and, when taken together with other recent work, suggests a new set of basic assumptions which move beyond Theory Y into what we call "Contingency Theory: the fit between task, organization, and people." These theoretical assumptions emphasize that the appropriate pattern of organization is *contingent* on the nature of the work to be done and on the particular needs of the people involved. We should emphasize that we have labeled these assumptions as a step beyond Theory Y because of McGregor's own recognition that the Theory Y assumptions would probably be supplanted by new knowledge within a short time.[3]

The Study Design

Our study was conducted in four organizational units. Two of these performed the relatively certain task of manufacturing standardized containers on high-speed, automated production lines. The other two performed the relatively uncertain work of research and development in communications technology. Each pair of units performing the same kind of task were in the same large company, and each pair had previously been evaluated by that company's management as containing one highly effective unit and a less effective one. The study design is summarized in Exhibit 1.

The objective was to explore more fully how the fit between organization and task was related to successful performance. That is, does a good fit between organizational characteristics and task requirements increase the motivation of individuals and hence produce more effective individual and organizational performance?

An especially useful approach to answering this question is to recognize

Exhibit 1   Study Design in "Fit" of Organizational Characteristics

Characteristics	Company I (Predictable Manufacturing Task)	Company II (Unpredictable R & D Task)
Effective performer	Akron containers plant	Stockton research lab
Less effective performer	Hartford containers plant	Carmel research lab

that an individual has a strong need to master the world around him, including the task that he faces as a member of a work organization.[4] The accumulated feelings of satisfaction that come from successfully mastering one's environment can be called a "sense of competence." We saw this sense of competence in performing a particular task as helpful in understanding how a fit between task and organizational characteristics could motivate people toward successful performance.

Organizational Dimensions

Because the four study sites had already been evaluated by the respective corporate managers as high and low performers of tasks, we expected that such differences in performance would be a preliminary clue to differences in the "fit" of the organizational characteristics to the job to be done. But, first, we had to define what kinds of organizational characteristics would determine how appropriate the organization was to the particular task.

We grouped these organizational characteristics into two sets of factors:

1. Formal characteristics, which could be used to judge the fit between the kind of task being worked on and the formal practices of the organization.

2. Climate characteristics, or the subjective perceptions and orientations that had developed among the individuals about their organizational setting. (These too must fit the task to be performed if the organization is to be effective.)

We measured these attributes through questionnaires and interviews with about 40 managers in each unit to determine the appropriateness of the organization to the kind of task being performed. We also measured the feelings of competence of the people in the organizations so that we could link the appropriateness of the organizational attributes with a sense of competence.

Major Findings

The principal findings of the survey are best highlighted by contrasting the highly successful Akron plant and the high-performing Stockton laboratory. Because each performed very different tasks (the former a relatively certain manufacturing task and the latter a relatively uncertain research task), we expected, as brought out earlier, that there would have to be major differences between them in organizational characteristics if they were to perform effectively. And this is what we did find. But we also found that each of these effective units had a better fit with its particular task than did its less effective counterpart.

While our major purpose in this article is to explore how the fit between task and organizational characteristics is related to motivation, we first want to explore more fully the organizational characteristics of these units, so the reader will better understand what we mean by a fit between task and organization and how it can lead to more effective behavior. To do this, we shall place the major emphasis on the contrast between the high-performing units (the Akron plant and Stockton laboratory), but we shall also compare each of these with its less effective mate (the Hartford plant and Carmel laboratory respectively).

Formal Characteristics

Beginning with differences in formal characteristics, we found that both the Akron and Stockton organizations fit their respective tasks much better than did their less successful counterparts. In the predictable manufacturing task environment, Akron had a pattern of formal relationships and duties that was highly structured and precisely defined. Stockton, with its unpredictable research task, had a low degree of structure and much less precision of definition (see Exhibit 2).

Exhibit 2   Differences in Formal Characteristics in High-Performing Organizations

Characteristics	Akron	Stockton
1. Pattern of formal relationships and duties as signified by organization charts and job manuals	Highly structured, precisely defined	Low degree of structure, less well defined
2. Pattern of formal rules, procedures, control, and measurement systems	Pervasive, specific, uniform, comprehensive	Minimal, loose, flexible
3. Time dimensions incorporated in formal practices	Short-term	Long-term
4. Goal dimensions incorporated in formal practices	Manufacturing	Scientific

Akron's pattern of formal rules, procedures, and control systems was so specific and comprehensive that it prompted one manager to remark:

"We've got rules here for everything from how much powder to use in cleaning the toilet bowls to how to cart a dead body out of the plant."

In contrast, Stockton's formal rules were so minimal, loose, and flexible that one scientist, when asked whether he felt the rules ought to be tightened, said:

"If a man puts a nut on a screw all day long, you may need more rules and a job definition for him. But we're not novices here. We're professionals and not the kind who need close supervision. People around here *do* produce, and produce under relaxed conditions. Why tamper with success?"

These differences in formal organizational characteristics were well suited to the differences in tasks of the two organizations. Thus:

Akron's highly structured formal practices fit its predictable task because behavior had to be rigidly defined and controlled around the automated, high-speed production line. There was really only one way to accomplish the plant's very routine and programmable job; managers defined it precisely and insisted (through the plant's formal practices) that each man do what was expected of him.

On the other hand, Stockton's highly unstructured formal practices made just as much sense because the required activities in the laboratory simply could not be rigidly defined in advance. With such an unpredictable, fast-changing task as communications technology research, there were numerous approaches to getting the job done well. As a consequence, Stockton managers used a less structured pattern of formal practices that left the scientists in the lab free to respond to the changing task situation.

Akron's formal practices were very much geared to *short-term* and *manufacturing* concerns as its task demanded. For example, formal production reports and operating review sessions were daily occurrences, consistent with the fact that the through-put time for their products was typically only a few hours.

By contrast, Stockton's formal practices were geared to *long-term* and *scientific* concerns, as its task demanded. Formal reports and reviews were made only quarterly, reflecting the fact that research often does not come to fruition for three to five years.

At the two less effective sites (i.e., the Hartford plant and the Carmel laboratory), the formal organizational characteristics did not fit their respective tasks nearly as well. For example, Hartford's formal practices were much less structured and controlling than were Akron's, while Carmel's were more restraining and restricting than were Stockton's. A scientist in Carmel commented:

"There's something here that keeps you from being scientific. It's hard to put your finger on, but I guess I'd call it 'Mickey Mouse.' There are rules and things here that get in your way regarding doing your job as a researcher."

Climate Characteristics

As with formal practices, the climate in both high-performing Akron and Stockton suited the respective tasks much better than did the climates at the less successful Hartford and Carmel sites.

Perception of Structure   The people in the Akron plant perceived a great deal of structure, with their behavior tightly controlled and defined. One manager in the plant said:

"We can't let the lines run unattended. We lose money whenever they do. So we make sure each man knows his job, knows when he can take a break, knows how to handle a change in shifts, etc. It's all spelled out clearly for him the day he comes to work here."

In contrast, the scientists in the Stockton laboratory perceived very little structure, with their behavior only minimally controlled. Such perceptions encouraged the individualistic and creative behavior that the uncertain, rapidly changing research task needed. Scientists in the less successful Carmel laboratory perceived much more structure in their organization and voiced the feeling that this was "getting in their way" and making it difficult to do effective research.

Distribution of Influence   The Akron plant and the Stockton laboratory also differed substantially in how influence was distributed and on the character of superior-subordinate and colleague relations. Akron personnel felt that they had much less influence over decisions in their plant than Stockton's scientists did in their laboratory. The task at Akron had already been clearly defined and that definition had, in a sense, been incorporated into the automated production flow itself. Therefore, there was less need for individuals to have a say in decisions concerning the work process.

Moreover, in Akron, influence was perceived to be concentrated in the upper levels of the formal structure (a hierarchical or "top-heavy" distribution), while in Stockton influence was perceived to be more evenly spread out among more levels of the formal structure (an egalitarian distribution).

Akron's members perceived themselves to have a low degree of freedom vis-à-vis superiors both in choosing the jobs they work on and in handling these jobs on their own. They also described the type of supervision in the plant as being relatively directive. Stockton's scientists, on the other hand, felt that they had a great deal of freedom vis-à-vis their superiors both in choosing the tasks and projects, and in handling them in the way that they wanted to. They described supervision in the laboratory as being very participatory.

It is interesting to note that the less successful Carmel laboratory had more of its decisions made at the top. Because of this, there was a definite feeling by the scientists that their particular expertise was not being effectively used in choosing projects.

Relations with Others   The people at Akron perceived a great deal of similarity among themselves in background, prior work experiences, and approaches for tackling job-related problems. They also perceived the degree of coordination of effort among colleagues to be very high. Because Akron's task was so precisely defined and the behavior of its members so rigidly controlled around the automated lines, it is easy to see that this pattern also made sense.

By contrast, Stockton's scientists perceived not only a great many differences among themselves, especially in education and background, but also that the coordination of effort among colleagues was relatively low. This was appropriate for a laboratory in which a great variety of disciplines and skills were present and individual projects were important to solve technological problems.

Time Orientation   As we would expect, Akron's individuals were highly oriented toward a relatively short time span and manufacturing goals. They responded to quick feedback concerning the quality and service that the plant was providing. This was essential, given the nature of their task.

Stockton's researchers were highly oriented toward a longer time span and scientific goals. These orientations meant that they were willing to wait for long-term feedback from a research project that might take years to complete. A scientist in Stockton said:

"We're not the kind of people here who need a pat on the back every day. We can wait for months if necessary before we get feedback from colleagues and the profession. I've been working on one project now for three months and I'm still not sure where it's going to take me. I can live with that, though." This is precisely the kind of behavior and attitude that spells success on this kind of task.

Managerial Style Finally, the individuals in both Akron and Stockton perceived their chief executive to have a "managerial style" that expressed more of a concern for the task than for people or relationships, but this seemed to fit both tasks.

In Akron, the technology of the task was so dominant that top managerial behavior which was not focused primarily on the task might have reduced the effectiveness of performance. On the other hand, although Stockton's research task called for more individualistic problem-solving behavior, that sort of behavior could have become segmented and uncoordinated, unless the top executive in the lab focused the group's attention on the overall research task. Given the individualistic bent of the scientists, this was an important force in achieving unity of effort. All these differences in climate characteristics in the two high performers are summarized in Exhibit 3.

Exhibit 3 Differences in "Climate" Characteristics in High-Performing Organizations

Characteristics	Akron	Stockton
1. Structural orientation	Perceptions of tightly controlled behavior and a high degree of structure	Perceptions of a low degree of structure
2. Distribution of influence	Perceptions of low total influence, concentrated at upper levels in the organization	Perceptions of high total influence, more evenly spread out among all levels
3. Character of superior-subordinate relations	Low freedom vis-à-vis superiors to choose and handle jobs, directive type of supervision	High freedom vis-à-vis superiors to choose and handle projects, participatory type of supervision
4. Character of colleague relations	Perceptions of many similarities among colleagues, high degree of coordination of colleague effort	Perceptions of many differences among colleagues, relatively low degree of coordination of colleague effort
5. Time orientation	Short-term	Long-term
6. Goal orientation	Manufacturing	Scientific
7. Top executive's "managerial style"	More concerned with task than people	More concerned with task than people

As with formal attributes, the less effective Hartford and Carmel sites had organization climates that showed a perceptibly lower degree of fit with their respective tasks. For example, the Hartford plant had an egalitarian distribution of influence, perceptions of a low degree of structure, and a more participatory type of supervision. The Carmel laboratory had a somewhat top-heavy distribution of influence, perceptions of high structure, and a more directive type of supervision.

Competence Motivation

Because of the difference in organizational characteristics at Akron and Stockton, the two sites were strikingly different places in which to work. But these organizations had two very important things in common. First, each organization fit very well the requirements of its task. Second, although the behavior in the two organizations was different, the result in both cases was effective task performance.

Since, as we indicated earlier, our primary concern in this study was to link the fit between organization and task with individual motivation to perform effectively, we devised a two-part test to measure the sense of competence motivation of the individuals at both sites. Thus:

The *first* part asked a participant to write creative and imaginative stories in response to six ambiguous pictures.

The *second* asked him to write a creative and imaginative story about what he would be doing, thinking, and feeling "tomorrow" on his job. This is called a "projective" test because it is assumed that the respondent projects into his stories his own attitudes, thoughts, feelings, needs, and wants, all of which can be measured from the stories.[5]

The results indicated that the individuals in Akron and Stockton showed significantly more feelings of competence than did their counterparts in the lower-fit Hartford and Carmel organizations.[6] We found that the organization-task fit is simultaneously linked to and interdependent with both individual motivation and effective unit performance. (This interdependency is illustrated in Exhibit 4.)

Exhibit 4 Basic Contingent Relationships

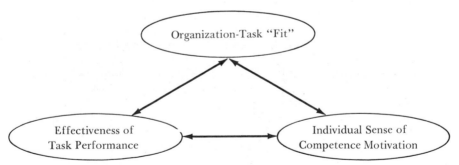

Putting the conclusions in this form raises the question of cause and effect. Does effective unit performance result from the task-organization fit or from higher motivation, or perhaps from both? Does higher sense of competence motivation result from effective unit performance or from fit?

Our answer to these questions is that we do not think there are any single cause-and-effect relationships, but that these factors are mutually interrelated. This has important implications for management theory and practice.

Contingency Theory

Returning to McGregor's Theory X and Theory Y assumptions, we can now question the validity of some of his conclusions. While Theory Y might help to explain the findings in the two laboratories, we clearly need something other than Theory X or Y assumptions to explain the findings in the plants.

For example, the managers at Akron worked in a formalized organization setting with relatively little participation in decision making, and yet they were highly motivated. According to Theory X, people would work hard in such a setting only because they were coerced to do so. According to Theory Y, they should have been involved in decision making and been self-directed to feel so motivated. Nothing in our data indicates that either set of assumptions was valid at Akron.

Conversely, the managers at Hartford, the low-performing plant, were in a less formalized organization with more participation in decision making, and yet they were not as highly motivated as the Akron managers. The Theory Y assumptions would suggest that they should have been more motivated.

A way out of such paradoxes is to state a new set of assumptions, the Contingency Theory, that seems to explain the findings at all four sites:

1. Human beings bring varying patterns of needs and motives into the work organization, but one central need is to achieve a sense of competence.

2. The sense of competence motive, while it exists in all human beings, may be fulfilled in different ways by different people depending on how this need interacts with the strengths of the individuals' other needs—such as those for power, independence, structure, achievement, and affiliation.

3. Competence motivation is most likely to be fulfilled when there is a fit between task and organization.

4. Sense of competence continues to motivate even when a competence goal is achieved; once one goal is reached, a new, higher one is set.

While the central thrust of these points is clear from the preceding discussion of the study, some elaboration can be made. First, the idea that different people have different needs is well understood by psychologists. However, all too often, managers assume that all people have similar needs. Lest we be accused of the same error, we are saying only that all people have a need to feel competent; in this *one* way they are similar. But in many other dimensions of personality, individuals differ, and these differences will determine how a particular person achieves a sense of competence.

Thus, for example, the people in the Akron plant seemed to be very different from those in the Stockton laboratory in their underlying attitudes toward uncertainty, authority, and relationships with their peers. And because they had different need patterns along these dimensions, both groups were highly motivated by achieving competence from quite different activities and settings.

While there is a need to further investigate how people who work in different settings differ in their psychological makeup, one important implication of the Contingency Theory is that we must not only seek a fit between organization and task, but also between task and people and between people and organization.

A further point which requires elaboration is that one's sense of competence never really comes to rest. Rather, the real satisfaction of this need is in the successful performance itself, with no diminishing of the motivation as one goal is reached. Since feelings of competence are thus reinforced by successful performance, they can be a more consistent and reliable motivator than salary and benefits.

Implications for Managers

The major managerial implication of the Contingency Theory seems to rest in the task-organization-people fit. Although this interrelationship is complex, the best possibility for managerial action probably is in tailoring the organization to fit the task and the people. If such a fit is achieved, both effective unit performance and a higher sense of competence motivation seem to result.

Managers can start this process by considering how certain the task is, how frequently feedback about task performance is available, and what goals are implicit in the task. The answers to these questions will guide their decisions about the design of the management hierarchy, the specificity of job assignments, and the utilization of rewards and control procedures. Selective use of training programs and a general emphasis on appropriate management styles will move them toward a task-organization fit.

The problem of achieving a fit among task, organization, and people is something we know less about. As we have already suggested, we need further investigation of what personality characteristics fit various tasks and organizations. Even with our limited knowledge, however, there are indications that people will gradually gravitate into organizations that fit their particular personalities. Managers can help this process by becoming more aware of what psychological needs seem to best fit the tasks available and the organizational setting, and by trying to shape personnel selection criteria to take account of these needs.

In arguing for an approach which emphasizes the fit among task, organization, and people, we are putting to rest the question of which organizational approach—the classical or the participative—is best. In its place we are raising a new question: What organizational approach is most appropriate given the task and the people involved?

For many enterprises, given the new needs of younger employees for more autonomy, and the rapid rates of social and technological change, it may well be that the more participative approach is the most appropriate. But there will still be many situations in which the more controlled and formalized organization is desirable. Such an organization need not be coercive or punitive. If it makes sense to the individuals involved, given their needs and their jobs, they will find it rewarding and motivating.

Concluding Note

The reader will recognize that the complexity we have described is not of our own making. The basic deficiency with earlier approaches is that they did not recognize the variability in tasks and people which produces this complexity. The strength of the contingency approach we have outlined is that it begins to provide a way of thinking about this complexity, rather than ignoring it. While our knowledge in this area is still growing, we are certain that any adequate theory of motivation and organization will have to take account of the contingent relationship between task, organization, and people.

Notes and References

1. Douglas McGregor, *The Human Side of Enterprise* (New York, McGraw-Hill Book Company, Inc., 1960), pp. 34–35 and pp. 47–48.
2. See for example Paul R. Lawrence and Jay W. Lorsch, *Organization and Environment* (Boston, Harvard Business School, Division of Research, 1967); Joan Woodward, *Industrial Organization: Theory & Practice* (New York, Oxford University Press, Inc., 1965); Tom Burns and G. M. Stalker, *The Management of Innovation* (London, Tavistock Publications, 1961); Harold J. Leavitt, "Unhuman Organizations," HBR July–August 1962, p. 90.
3. McGregor, op. cit., p. 245.
4. See Robert W. White, "Ego and Reality in Psychoanalytic Theory," *Psychological Issues,* Vol. III, No. 3 (New York, International Universities Press, 1963).
5. For a more detailed description of this survey, see John J. Morse, *Internal Organizational Patterning and Sense of Competence Motivation* (Boston, Harvard Business School, unpublished doctoral dissertation, 1969).
6. Differences between the two container plants are significant at .001 and between the research laboratories at .01 (one-tailed probability).

Questions for Discussion

1. Suppose you had the power to modify pay practices as you wished in the state employment agency discussed in Chapter 9. What changes would you propose to increase productivity, and how would they affect motivation and behavior?

2. Suppose you were the manager of three departments in an employment office such as the one discussed in Chapter 9, and you developed the strong impression that three of your subordinate supervisors had markedly different motive patterns. Each man supervised identical task groups, but Supervisor A is high in *n* Achievement, Supervisor B is high in *n* Affiliation, and Supervisor C is high in *n* Power. Assuming you had some flexibility, how might you style your own leadership and use of other administrative practices to motivate A, B, and C effectively?

3. Edward Lawler has argued that secrecy in compensation administration is undesirable, because it fosters guessing about pay rates and such guessing is often inaccurate. Thus, secrecy can lead to perceived inequity where none exists. Also, since subordinates often underestimate the pay of superiors, secrecy prevents a fact from being known which could motivate employees to work hard for promotion. Others say that where pay is not, in fact, related to performance (and it often is not), it might be a good idea to keep it a secret. Discuss the advantages and disadvantages of pay secrecy.

4. Commission schemes which link pay and sales volume have apparently been successfully used for years as motivators in such tasks as selling insurance and automobiles. But similar incentive schemes which link pay and output have often been extremely troublesome in manufacturing tasks (generating grievances, strikes, and restriction of output). What accounts for these varied reactions to similar pay schemes?

5. Advocates of participative management and related techniques are often frustrated by managers who say that economic and technological imperatives conflict with such "human relations" practices. In turn, the human-relations advocates say that managers who invoke these "necessities" are really fearful and reluctant to manage adults, and that excessive task specialization and routinization are really props for shaky executive psyches. Discuss.

6. One of the problems of leadership research is what might be called the chicken-or-egg issue. That is, which comes first, or which causes which, effective group performance or a leadership style? Researchers seem to assume that general supervision has caused good performance when they show only that it coexisted with good performance. Isn't it possible that causation runs the other way? Supervisors might not feel any need to direct subordinates closely as long as performance is acceptable, but poor performance might drive the supervisor to intervene more frequently. Discuss.

7. Suppose you were hired as a manager of a group of fourteen office equipment salesmen in one regional office. Your predecessor was a classic autocrat. Your own tendency is toward participative leadership. What advantages and disadvantages might there be in your proceeding directly to apply participative leadership?

8. The advocates of universal psychological approaches to management (Likert, McGregor, and Blake and Mouton, for example), seem at odds with those who advocate a contingency approach (Burns and Stalker, Woodward, and Lawrence and Lorsch, for example). The latter search for a best fit in a particular situation. Discuss the controversy between what might be called universalists and relativists.

Short Cases for Discussion

Wyatt Steel Fabricators

I was employed two consecutive summers by Wyatt Steel Fabricators. With the exception of one department, Wyatt was primarily concerned with the production of mobile-home trailer chassis, ranging from 14 feet to 60 feet long. The process from start to finish was spread throughout four departments. Department 1 was the parts fabrication department (9 men) whose purpose was to cut, bend, punch holes, or do whatever else was required to the flat sheet steel in order to prepare it as cross-members and outriggers (wings) for the trailer frames, and to make similar parts to be sold to independent trailer-frame manufacturers. Department 2 was the production department (17 men). Here the frames were built and tack-welded together by two men working on one of five jigs, and then hung on I beams to be completely welded by line welders. Department 3 was the assembly department (9 men), whose purpose was to put the undercarriages on the frames, paint them, and stack them for shipping. Department 4 was the shipping department. Since my case involves Departments 1 and 2, a brief diagram of their layout is shown in Exhibit 1 to better illustrate their relationship to one another.

Exhibit 1 Wyatt Steel Fabricators Department Layout

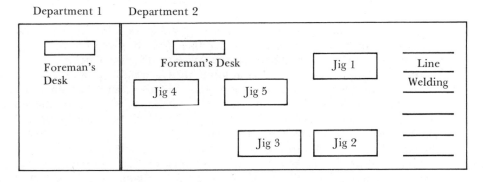

During the first summer I was a line welder on the day shift. All of the line welders and jig welders fell under the supervision of the Department 2 foreman, who was a very strict, unsociable, and production-oriented person. Higher management undoubtedly had a great influence on him. It was evident to most of the workers that the company's sole interest was production, with little or no concern for the workers.

The foreman's desk was located right within the department, so he kept a close eye on things. He was always walking through the shop to oversee everyone and make sure he was doing his job. We could always expect a dirty look or a few reprimanding words if we were caught conversing with our co-workers about anything except production. This meant there was very little conversation between the workers except during the coffee and lunch breaks.

The line welders had even less occasion than others to converse socially or informally with one another. Due to the routine nature of the job, there was no reason why we needed to converse with anyone the whole day. We knew we had to completely weld every frame that came off the jigs and that's all there was to it. Another reason why the line welders in particular were unable to have much social or informal contact with their co-workers was that the position was usually undermanned, which meant we were always behind and had no time to even think. This situation was created whenever someone quit or was absent on the jigs, which happened quite frequently, and men from the line were taken to fill the vacant places.

At the beginning of the following summer, an increased demand by independent trailer builders for parts manufactured in Department 1 promoted the creation of a swing shift for this department. At the same time, management wanted to reduce the amount of overtime (10 hours a day) being worked by the jig and line welders in Department 2. Management decided to have two experienced jig welders and one experienced line welder also work on the swing shift under the supervision of the Department 1 foreman, to alleviate the overload in Department 2.

I was asked to be the line welder on this shift and weld the frames tacked together in the jig by two welders I had worked with on the day shift in Department 2 the previous summer. In addition, I was given the responsibility of catching up on all uncompleted line welding left behind by the day crew, and of checking the blueprints of the frames to be built by the jig welders on the swing shift, so as to have all the necessary parts ready and available when they needed them.

The type and degree of supervision for the welders on the swing shift was almost completely opposite that of the day shift. Supervision of the three of us was very informal and unstructured. We weren't always being pressured for maximum production: in fact, the foreman was usually watching his men in Department 1 at the other end of the shop. He also showed an interest in our personal and social life, and on numerous occasions throughout the summer spent half an hour or so shooting the bull with us. Since the new foreman lacked knowledge of operations in Department 2, we were allowed more freedom in making decisions relevant to production. We were hardly supervised at all.

I felt that the fact that the shop superintendent or other higher managers were not around had a significant bearing on the relaxed working environment. But there were other reasons for the loose supervision, more directly attributable to the foreman himself. Before being moved up to the position of foreman, he was one of us; consequently, he was inclined to informality, since he still felt a part of the worker group, and had not yet associated himself and his leadership style with the higher management. Second, since his position was new to him, he was inexperienced, and so followed his own inclinations—he was a rather easygoing person in general.

The thing that has always puzzled me about these two summers is that my production was equally high on the swing shift as on the day shift. The same was true for the three other people with me on both shifts. The leadership was different, but we produced about the same amount. However, we were all happier on the second shift.

Question

How might similar results associated with different leadership be explained?

Universal Office Supply Company

The Universal Office Supply Company has its offices and major retail store in Los Angeles. Its commercial sales force consisted of eleven men, who called on business firms in western states. Six of the salesmen operated out of the Los Angeles headquarters and worked the Southern California territory.

The company had acquired a large supply of file folders purchased at an exceptionally low price from a bankrupt competitor. Universal's president and sales manager decided to develop a special month-long sales promotion to unload them. Along with the normal quota commission system, he added during the month of May a five-percent override on folders sold, and also staged a contest. First, second, and third prizes were $100.00, $75.00, and $50.00.

Normally, all of the eleven men worked on commission, amounting to 10 percent of the total dollar value of sales. Each salesman had his own monthly quota, based on a combination of his past sales record for that month in each of the past three years and a projected increase reflecting long-term trends. Normally, the salesmen met their quotas, each earning approximately $1000 per month.

After the contest ended, one salesman examined the daily sales and commission records for the month of May for the six salesmen working out of the Los Angeles office. He plotted the sales of folders per day for the three salesmen who finished highest, and the three who finished lowest in the file folder sales contest. Exhibit 1 shows what happened.

The salesman reported: "John, Harold, and I (George) get together every Friday afternoon for a drink after work. At the end of the first week I mentioned to the others that I thought my total sales were down. Harold said he was not pushing the special any more because it took too much time to sell and his other products would suffer. All three of us decided to stop pushing the folder special and return to our normal sales method and program, which put greater emphasis on more expensive items during customer contacts."

Indeed, as Exhibit 2 shows, those salesmen most responsive to the contest had lower sales, brought less revenue to the company, and less commission to themselves. As management, through its promotional contest, pushed the sale of file folders, time and sales effort were focused on a comparatively unprofitable line. Sales of the other merchandise (including many higher-priced items) were

Exhibit 1 File Folder Sales Per Day: Contest Winners and Losers

Folders Sold Per Day

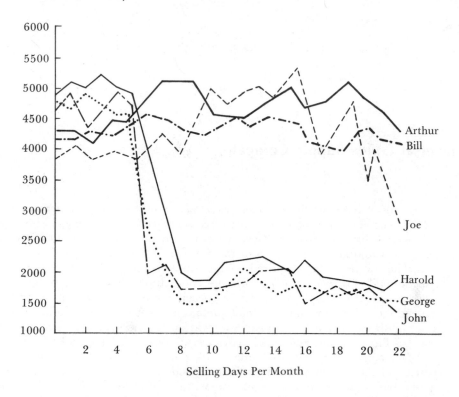

Selling Days Per Month

Exhibit 2 Percentage of Monthly Sales Quota: Contest Winners and Losers

Top Three in Special Sale		Bottom Three in Special Sale	
	Percent of Monthly Sales Quota		Percent of Monthly Sales Quota
Arthur	82	Harold	114
Bill	80	George	107
Joe	78	John	106

neglected, and this neglect brought down the total sales and commissions. In fact, the only real success came from ignoring the contest.

Questions

1. How does the concept of administrative consistency apply to this case?
2. How does the concept of goal displacement apply to this case?

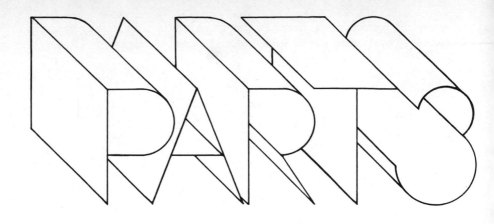

PART 8

MANAGEMENT OF CONFLICT
AND CHANGE

Chapter 10

Conflict in the Organization

"Life," as someone once observed, "is just one damned thing after another." For many people in organizations, a paraphrase is appropriate: Life is just one damned conflict after another! For conflict and stress are inevitable when such complex entities as individuals and small groups are brought together in formal organizations.

The common thread in our discussion of the need for hierarchy, the development of formal structure, and the elaboration of informal organization can be summed up in one word—interdependence. When there is interdependence, the parties involved must work out their relations across boundaries—between individuals and among groups in organizations. The process is, in the words of Walton and McKersie (1963), "The deliberate interaction of two or more complex social units which are attempting to define or redefine the terms of their interdependence" (p. 3). Such interaction is not infrequently accompanied by stress and conflict. Indeed, as Barnard (1950) suggested, the social patterns of stress, conflict, and bargaining are inevitable, because they seem "inherent in the conception of free will in a changing environment" (p. 36).

Evolving Attitudes Toward Conflict

A dramatic trend in the literature on organizations and management has been a reexamination of internal conflict. Conflict is increasingly perceived as inevitable, often legitimate, and perhaps even desirable. It does not necessarily indicate a breakdown of the organization or failure of management, as implied by classical management theory and human relations philosophy. Indeed, classical management says little about conflict among managers. One reason for this lack of comment might be the assumption that managers are basically rational, in contrast to workers. Such a view implies that, because of their rationality, managers can clearly see the objectives of their organization and can plan logically. Thus, it is assumed that management rationality is sufficient to bring about the required cooperation. The assumption is an illusion.

In an introduction to a study on conflict in research organizations, Evan (1965) advances three assumptions which characterize recent attitudes about conflict:

"An underlying assumption of this study is that conflicts are endemic in organizations because of a lack of consensus as to the expectations and prescriptions for various organizational positions or because of a lack of uniform commitment to organizational objectives.

"A second assumption is that some types of conflicts are detrimental and others are beneficial from the point of view of both organizational and individual goals.

"Thirdly, the principle of minimizing conflict subscribed to by some managers and social scientists may have some validity for crisis organizations, such as armies, or for so-called routine organizations, such as some manufacturing organizations. However, this principle may not be valid for knowledge- and technology-producing organizations, such as those engaged in research and development."

Bennis (1970) announces that formulating objectives for handling conflict and promoting collaboration is one of the eight major organizational objectives. And Kelly (1970) suggests that conflict and tension are beneficial (within certain limits) if they reflect commitment which promotes challenge, heightened attention, and effort. The emerging thesis is that too little manifestation of conflict is stagnancy, but uncontrolled conflict threatens chaos. Since individuals and organizations have differing abilities to withstand stress, an appropriate level is necessary. In short, it is not conflict itself that is alarming, but rather its mismanagement (Goser, 1956).

Nonetheless, many managers still emphasize organizational harmony and personal rationality. Zaleznik writes (1970): "There are few business activities more prone to a credibility gap than the way in which executives approach organizational life. A sense of disbelief occurs when managers purport to make decisions in rationalistic terms while most observers and participants know that personalities and politics play a significant if not overriding role" (p. 47).

Whether openness to conflict and rational response is more or less characteristic of real organizations today is impossible to determine, but it appears so. The "organization man" complaint seems much less common (among managers if not among youth) than it used to be (Porter, 1963). Matrix organizations have been designed which intentionally foster controlled conflict—but with resolution mechanisms. Lawrence and Lorsch (1962) have found empirical evidence that some managers pursue open confrontation, and that such a style is more effective than forcing conformity or denying differences. Indeed, many recent books and articles about various aspects of American life have proposed more open recognition and rational treatment of conflict. The goal of much marriage counseling (for example, in a volume entitled *The Intimate Enemy—How to Fight Fair in Marriage*), sensitivity training, psychoanalytic therapy, and so on, is not to eliminate conflict, but to manage it. In this chapter, we discuss forms, causes, and common settings for organizational stress and conflict. In Chapter 11, we consider various techniques for reconciling and managing conflict.

Forms of Conflict

The study of conflict and bargaining goes by many titles in the literature—conflict, social resolution, social negotiations, collective bargaining, and so on. Underlying all of these approaches, however, is an emerging commonality. The inaugural editorial in the *Journal of Conflict Resolution* (March 1957) stated:

"Many of the patterns and processes which characterize conflict in one area may also characterize it in others. Negotiations and mediation go on in labor disputes as well as international relations. Price wars and domestic quarrels have much the pattern of an arms race. Frustration breeds aggression both in the individual and the state. The jurisdictional problems of labor unions and the territorial disputes of states are not dissimilar. It is not too much to claim that out of the contributions of many fields a general theory of conflict is emerging" (p. 2).

Berelson and Steiner (1964) define social conflict as "the pursuit of incompatible, or at least seemingly incompatible, goals, such that gains to one side come about at the expense of the other" (p. 588), although perhaps it is not necessary that one side "lose," in the absolute sense. A general, if abstract, definition of conflict is two or more entities trying to occupy the same state/space, but only one can do so. This seems to include all kinds of conflict.

Intrapersonal Conflict

Conflicting Needs   The most common conflict is between and among various needs. You desire security, but also love. The latter, however, means exposing yourself to another who can then hurt you. Or you desire social prestige *and* self-esteem, but in some situations the former may require sacrifice of the latter. The dissonance of the person who seeks fame, finds it, and then bemoans his lack of privacy is well known.

Situational Frustration   This is the condition of the individual who knows what he wants, but is unable to obtain it because of external blocks, which may be human or nonhuman. Human interference may lead to interpersonal conflict or aggression; nonhuman interference is often manifest in role conflict and job dissatisfaction. Thus, the individual may have certain perceptions or desires about his role, but the situation prevents his behaving that way and achieving the desired rewards. Much frustration comes from a feeling of relative deprivation—the discrepancy between those desirable conditions of life to which people think they are justifiably entitled and those less favorable circumstances which they feel they will actually experience (Gurr, 1970).

When an external barrier stands between a motivated person and his goals, he normally tries to circumvent, remove, or otherwise master it. But when the barrier is not overcome or the motivation increases in intensity, the resulting frustration of goal-directed behavior may lead to aggression. The classical frustration-aggression hypothesis in psychology asserts that the occurrence of aggressive behavior presupposes the existence of frustration, and the existence of frustration leads to some form of aggression (Leavitt, 1972). The barrier itself may be attacked physically (common in boys, infrequent among politicians, almost unheard of among managers), symbolically (such as sticking pins in a voodoo doll or throwing darts at a picture of the boss), or organizationally (by "forgetting," spreading rumors, and—in extremis—sabotage).

Interpersonal Conflict

Individual versus Individual   The examples of individual conflict are legion: two individuals fighting over territory, two managers competing for the same promotion, two men vying for a beautiful woman, two executives arguing for a larger share of corporate capital, and so on. In every case, each is striving to possess the scarce resource by actually or symbolically eliminating the rival. The desired scarce resource may be a nonmaterial state: status, prestige, fame, power, etc.

The conflict may even be pleasurable in itself. It may be ritualistic and intrinsically rewarding. Adler's analysis of man's power motive implies certain love for conflict. On a more popular level, Eric Berne (1964) described several interpersonal games, including one entitled "Now I've Got You, You Son of a Bitch." In Berne's analysis, interpersonal conflict becomes satisfying in itself, not just a response to the inability to satisfy other needs.

Individual versus Group   Conflict sometimes occurs when an individual wishes to satisfy security, affiliative, or esteem needs through the group, but his associates demand excessive conformity or stressful behavior. Or such conflict may arise from an individual's efforts to promote his own interests, such as making more money by breaking the group's norms on permissible production. Such transgression of the emergent rules will often result in collective retaliation on the unfortunate offender.

Intergroup and Interorganizational Conflict

Down (1968) suggests a "law of interorganizational conflict—every organization is in partial conflict with every other social agent it deals with." Perhaps an exaggeration, but interdepartmental conflicts over authority, jurisdiction, and work flow are exceedingly common, as is labor-management strife, corporate competition, and national warfare. One reason for the frequency of intergroup conflict is the rarity of conditions necessary for intergroup cooperation. As summarized by Dalton (1963), these conditions are (1) internal social stability within each unit, (2) external value-sharing between parties; that is, they are aware of their interdependence and agree on the values and objectives of the larger unit of which they are a part, and (3) a legitimate authority hierarchy; both parties agree to relative status, authority, and interaction flow.

The situations leading to the breakdown or nondevelopment of these harmony-promoting conditions are discussed extensively in the remainder of the chapter and in the selected readings. Nonetheless, we can preview the problems by considering specific issues for each condition. For example, the difficulty of maintaining internal social stability may reflect the difficulty of reconciling needs for differentiation and integration. To deal with complexity, we resort to specialization and specialists—people with diverse cognitive and emotional orientations in the various functional areas. Such people frequently experience difficulty in communicating and cooperating. Yet, for the organization to act as a unity, we need integration or collaboration among the various departments. Thus, management frequently faces a problem: long-run performance requires substantial integration, but efforts to generate collaboration often produce short-run conflict. It is often easier simply to allow differentiation to dominate over integration.

Instances of inadequate sharing of values and of competing goals are numerous. Individual self-actualization versus collective will is one value conflict that has been and will be fought on many battlefields. At a business level, salesmen value company responsiveness to the customer, while production personnel value equilibrium and predictability; engineers value ingenuity and quality, while finance values the profit margin; marketing emphasizes gross income, while the credit department values minimum credit loss; and so on.

Also numerous are disagreements about relative status and authority, often manifest in conflict over the pattern of work and interactions between the parties—who initiates to whom, who responds. Production people sometimes feel that they are just as important, competent, and high in status as engineers. Therefore, they resent having to accept all the latter's initiations and changes.

Conflict Reinforcement

Once conflict and hostility exist, we tend to develop supporting stereotypes that maintain the conflict. Thus each side exaggerates the differences that exist—and once the perception is established, only small actual differences are necessary to maintain the stereotype. This is facilitated by a decrease in intergroup communication that accompanies conflict. If forced to interact, each side listens only to its own representatives. Indeed, in the absence of any shared goals, communication tends to reinforce stereotypes, and relations to deteriorate further. From their laboratory research on intergroup conflict, Blake and Mouton (1961) observed "two findings stemming from trends toward uniformities in membership behavior associated with protection of group interests which have unusual significance in determining barriers to the resolution of conflict between groups. They suggest that under competitive conditions members of one group perceive that they understand the other's proposal when in fact they do *not*. Inadequate understanding makes it all the more difficult for competing groups to view each other's proposals realistically. Areas they share in common are likely to go unrecognized and in fact be seen as characteristic of one's own group only. Under conditions of competition, areas of true agreement will go undiscovered" (p. 252).

Perceptual distortion thus exaggerates the differences between groups, so that actual overlap is underestimated. For example, even given their unreliability and questionable validity, intelligence tests in the past have suggested that the mean intelligence for whites slightly exceeded that for blacks (probably because of the latter's poorer schooling and less rich intellectual life in early childhood). Nonetheless, the differences were so narrow that perhaps one third of all blacks were superior to the average white on even the traditional IQ tests. It is doubtful that the "average white" would grant this. Similarly, differences in sexual mores and behavior between middle-aged adults and today's youth may exist, but they are probably less than perceived, with great variation on each side and substantial overlap. A sizable proportion of older people demonstrates more promiscuity than exists among average youth. Nonetheless, peering across the gap, many people exaggerate the differences.

Stereotyping also extends to the group. When in conflict with other groups, group solidarity and cooperation increases, and members tend to accept each other as honest, rational, and peace-loving. Most even think that their group is better than others. In Blake and Mouton's (1961) research, *all* groups rated themselves as better than average. A "superiority complex" seems to exist; regardless of what the group is really like, a member can say "poor though it may be, my group is at least above average!" We do not recognize the selective and self-protective distortion present. Consider the following statement of India's Prime Minister Indira Gandhi just days before the India–Pakistan war in 1971:

> "We have no animosity towards Pakistan even though they have campaigns—'crush India, conquer India'." She said that she did not know if pictures of these anti-India campaigns appeared in the United States, but

asserted that Pakistanis had bellicose stickers "on their cars." She said that her country "never had anything like this, and we never shall. We have not had anything against even China. China has attacked us, Pakistan has attacked us. On our side we have said we want friendship. But there has been no response forthcoming."

Thus competition heightens positive identification with the group. Its members close ranks, and become more single-minded. Now they have a clear goal—to win. Even after objective performance measurement, Blake and Mouton's groups tended toward more favorable subjective evaluation of their own performance and a downgrading of other groups.

In general, then, we tend to homogenize differences within the boundaries of our groups, and exaggerate the differences across boundaries. We also tend to reverse cause and effect. We say that the terrible characteristics of the other group justify our hostility and cause the conflict (e.g., Vietnamese "gooks" are dirty, lazy, and treacherous, hence we should either kill them or get out; welfare chiselers are shiftless and promiscuous, therefore they deserve no help). The social scientist sees the opposite causal direction: conflict leads to distorted perceptions in the interest of justifying hostility. Note that any differences may serve for stimulating hostility; the other side may be too dumb *or* too smart, too flexible (unprincipled) *or* too fixed (stubborn). It is difference that counts.

Most of the causes or settings for conflict are implicit in the foregoing discussion. However, three particularly important settings for organizational conflict are here considered in more detail: generalist-specialist relations; work flow; and role conflict.

Conflict of Specialists and Generalists

The expanded and still growing role of staff specialists is one of the salient aspects of modern organizations. In their comprehensive review of increasing organizational stress, Kahn et al. (1964) attributed much of the stress to the dominance of the physical sciences, which created a need for specialists; and the growth of large-scale organizations, which generated greater interdependence among members. Technological sophistication may demand specialists, but management also requires generalists. Fitting specialists into the organization and promoting their cooperation with generalists often involves stress and conflict.

Territorial Encroachment

The line manager may be fearful that the specialist is infringing on his job and taking away some of his power and status. The structural evolution of many organizations does suggest the expansion of specialist decisions, often at the expense of line authority and autonomy. Two of the most time-honored management "principles" are disappearing: "unity of command, or one should have only one boss" and "authority must equal responsibility." These long-time organizational postulates derive from common sense. A man cannot act on conflicting orders from more than one superior. What would he do first? How would he assign priorities? Even the Bible tells us that no man can serve two masters. Similarly, how can a manager be held responsible for performance if he does not have the tools or managerial powers to direct others? If a manager is going to be held responsible for achievement of certain objectives, he had better have enough authority to perform the necessary duties—or so the principle would suggest.

Nonetheless, the growth of specialization, sophistication, and complexity in modern organizations has made it virtually impossible to respect these old principles. The aeronautical engineering group leader responsible for developing an airframe depends on access to a wind tunnel controlled by a testing manager over whom he has no authority. It would be much too expensive for the group leader to have his own tunnel, nor does he have the necessary expertise to run it. Or a production manager is responsible for the productivity of his department, but he depends on planning specialists, industrial and mechanical engineers, and industrial relations men, over whom he has no authority. Although he presumably receives no orders from these staff men, he does receive "suggestions," "schedules," and "procedures." Under these conditions, conflict is not rare.

Interaction Patterns

The traditional theory of staff implies that the advisor will respond to inquiries from the generalist. Early in his career, however, a specialist learns that sufficient calls do not automatically come in—and not being busy is a mark of not being in demand and being of low status. Accordingly, the ambitious staff man begins to look around for places to "offer" his advice. He begins to initiate communications to line management. However, advice that has not been requested is often resented.

Conflicting Loyalties

When two interdependent parties must cooperate, divided loyalties always exist. This is not unique to generalist-specialist relations, but it is still a problem. Orientation toward a discipline versus loyalty to the organization sometimes characterizes professionals, specialists, and line managers. The researcher feels himself to be a chemist first and a member of the organization second; a production manager is first and foremost concerned with production. Not coincidentally, the "cosmopolitan" professional tends to be more critical of the organization than does the "local" manager.

Change versus Stability

Many managers simply fear change and see the staff specialist as embodying threats to present stability. The manager struggles to maintain equilibrium, while the specialist endeavors to demonstrate his ability and creativity. Usually, this requires a proposal of change. Most managers are not categorically opposed to change. The problem is that they feel no need for the specialist's proposed modification. There is no "felt need" on their part. In short, the specialist often "sees" problems needing correction when the managing generalist sees none, or sees different problems.

Incompatible Styles

Years ago, Dalton (1950) described the stress in line-staff relations which grew out of age and social differences. The younger, better educated staff man was frequently disliked and distrusted by older production managers who came up by what they perceived as a harder path. To make matters worse, the ambitious specialist sometimes betrayed condescension toward the generalist, whom he perceived as less able, less ambitious, and less promotable. Of course, many specialists were only putting on an act, attempting to appear more confident and influential than they really were. To support this image, they sometimes projected an aura of infallibility which severely hindered an open and free exchange of communications with their line clients. Insecurity about their real status and contribution led many specialists into elaborate charades. Indeed, Porter (1963) demonstrated that at all organizational levels, staff tended to feel greater anxiety and dissatisfaction than did line managers at comparable levels.

Dalton analyzed these conditions over twenty years ago. The adverse impact on organizational life has probably declined in the intervening years—but much still remains. The specialists' expertise may be more legitimate, but gaps still are common between them and generalist managers. For example, Doktor (1970) studied university students in engineering and liberal arts. Starting from quite similar patterns in the freshman year, they diverged. Engineering school seems to develop analytical ability and decrease creativity and integrative ability. In contrast, liberal arts does just the opposite. Subsequent work experience may continue the trend. Consequently, differing higher educational experiences may still lead to differing patterns of thought which hinder cooperation. The generalist may still think that the specialist is "too theoretical," "too impractical," or "too narrow."

Separation of Knowledge and Authority

For the line manager, the proliferation of staff advisors and specialists means that he no longer has complete control over his own operation. In particular, he may lack the specialized knowledge necessary to innovate. There seems to be a growing gap between knowledge and authority, paralleling the gap between ownership and control which took managerial authority from the owners as they multiplied and transferred it to professional management. It has been suggested that now the generalist manager is losing control to the specialist—and this generates stress, conflict, and anxiety. Thompson (1963) has described this development:

"Modern bureaucracy is an adaption of older organizational forms, altered to meet the needs of specialization. Modern specialization is grafted on to it, but old traces of the past remain. Along with technological specialization we find survivals of Genghis Khan and aboriginal war chiefs. We find the latest in science and technology associated with the autocratic, monistic, hierarchical organization of a simpler time. We find, in short, specialization and hierarchy together. . . .

"We have said that modern bureaucracy attempts to fit specialization into the older hierarchical framework. The fitting is more and more difficult. There is a growing gap between the right to decide, which is authority, and the power to do, which is specialized ability. This gap is growing because technological change, with resulting increase in specialization, occurs at a faster rate than the change in cultural definitions of hierarchical roles. This situation produces tensions and strains the willingness to cooperate. Much bureaucratic behavior can be understood as a reaction to these tensions. In short, *the most symptomatic characteristic of modern bureaucracy is the growing imbalance between ability and authority. . . .*

"More and more, organizational interdependence involves personal specialization and with it the dependence of higher status persons upon lower status persons. In these conditions, the high status persons must accord face-to-face accommodations to lower status persons. This accommodation violates status expectations. . . . Whereas the boss-man relationship is *formally* unilateral with rights running in one direction from the boss to the man, the advance of personal specialization is converting the relationship *informally* into a unilateral one with ability running from the man to the boss. Authority is centralized, but ability is inherently decentralized because it comes from practice rather than from definition. Whereas the boss retains his full right to make all decisions, he has less and less ability to do so because of the advance of science and technology. For these reasons the man-boss relationship has become curiously distorted and unstable; formally unilateral boss to man, informally unilateral man to boss" (pp. 5–6).

Work Flow Causing Stress and Conflict

Organizational structuring is the formal design of work flow, including the organization chart, authority allocation, policy and procedure manuals, job descriptions, and flow of materials. More fundamentally, structure determines the flow of interactions in the organization—who sees whom, who initiates and who responds, how often they do so, and so on. These structurally determined interaction patterns produce stress when they conflict with characteristic personality patterns.

Everyone has a fundamental pattern of interaction suitable to his personality. Such patterns of interaction at work are initially structured by our attempts to adapt or reconcile the work process to our own personalities, and then become stable through habit. Chapple and Sayles (1961) tell us that this basic activity pattern represents an equilibrium which may be disturbed when the individual encounters modifications in the work flow or the behavior of others, thus creating a stressful situation.

When stress does occur, we change our behavior to minimize the stress. For example, if a manager is transferred, his new job may require a different distribution of his time and contacts; if he continues to spend an accustomed amount of time consulting with and advising subordinates, his responsibilities for meeting with fellow department heads may be neglected. The first signs of trouble will be pressures coming from these other department heads. As the new pressures build up, our manager may modify his interactional patterns to reduce tension and dissatisfaction.

Not all stress should be eliminated from organization life, nor should the manager's role be to preside over an environment free of all threats and upsets. On the contrary, a crucial aspect of any manager's job is the intentional creation of stress as a dynamic, motivating force. But this stress should be calculated and controlled. If not, organizational life will deteriorate into a welter of long-run conflicts and short-run upsets. Three interaction patterns among organizational participants can be singled out as causing dysfunctional stress:

(1) unidirectional communication flow, (2) unpredictable or changing relationships, and (3) intermittent and infrequent interactions.

One-Way Patterns

Almost to a man, employees apparently resent always receiving communications, and responding to others (whether superiors, associates, or subordinates) with no opportunity to initiate. There is an adverse reaction to one-way initiation even if there is no other basis for bad feeling, but it is aggravated if the one-way flow is supplemented with criticism. A student who worked during the summer as a laborer suggests an example: "On Friday, the general foreman again criticized our foreman for his poor work. Mike then began to berate the laborers for their slowness and incompetence. . . . Under a constant barrage of criticism all day, the workers began to criticize each other's work. The frayed tempers of the laborers caused a further lowering of output."

In Guest's (1962) study of an automobile plant, unidirectional interaction characterized inefficient operations. Supervisors at middle and lower levels reported an overwhelming number of contacts initiated by superiors, mostly short directives, and communication taking place only in response to immediate technical and organizational emergencies.

Continual response to lower-status individuals or groups is especially disliked. A student's description of a summer spent working in a resort hotel restaurant demonstrates the adverse effects of unidirectional initiation, combined with ambiguous status differences:

"It was the policy of the management to employ college students wherever possible. . . . A great amount of antagonism was generated between the older kitchen staff and the waiters. . . . The reason for this friction probably was the upward initiation inherent in the work flow. The waiters, most of whom were new at the job, initiated activity for people who had been in the business for thirty years. The situation was trying for both groups, for both saw themselves superior to the other. The waiters, thinking themselves more intelligent, resented ridicule from such stupid cooks. The kitchen workers, thinking of themselves as masters of the trade, resented initiation from snotty kids. The cooks attempted to maintain their pride by humbling the waiters at every opportunity."

Work flow and environment were the sources of conflict in this case. Amid noise and confusion, the waiters initiated demands upon the chefs. To facilitate the cooks' understanding, orders had to be stated in a prescribed manner, but the waiters were never certain that they were heard. The lack of adequate response was disquieting. In addition, if the chef was slow or incorrect, it was the waiter who bore the customer's anger.

The pattern of initiation and response was also unpleasant for the chef. There is a general expectation that high-status people should initiate for lower (i.e., order them around). In this case, however, the veteran, highly paid chefs had to respond to youthful college students. This conflicts with the normal work expectations that older people, with seniority and higher pay, have higher status than temporary and inexperienced youngsters.

Unpredictable Patterns

Most people do not like adjusting to unexpected and uncontrollable changes in initiation and response patterns. An airline employee provides a rather terrifying illustration:

"Suppose that on a busy Sunday in July, I am working in reservations and, inadvertently, I oversell the 8:00 p.m. flight by five seats. The effects of such a blunder could easily reverberate throughout the entire system. At 7:30 the ticket counter agent will encounter 76 happy faces and five tigers, holding a total of 81 valid tickets for a plane which seats 76. His job is made that much more difficult, and the ensuing series of unpleasantries delays departure well past 8:00. This puts operations on the spot; a new clearance must now be obtained, necessitating further delay. Finally, the plane is airborne at 8:35.

"But this would only be the beginning of events that could be traced to my error. Because of greater traffic than would have been encountered with an on-time 55-minute flight, the trip requires 85 minutes in all, arriving in New York at 10:00 p.m. Over an hour late, fourteen passengers have missed connecting flights, and the ticket counter at Kennedy is inundated with angry fliers. Kennedy operations also has a problem; the same equipment was scheduled for the New York–Miami flight at 10:30, and the inbound delay will cause a similar delay outbound of one hour. This, in turn, will anger the 76 Miami-bound passengers and countless others waiting for them at Miami airport, and will wreak further havoc on those poor souls handling the ticket counter.

"To complicate matters, there was no way to pass off this feeling of pressure save for kicking the water cooler. We were instructed that a loss of temper in front of a passenger could result in dismissal. Many times I was forced to withstand such searing invective and abuse as would have bowled over a less hearty soul. Little wonder that one of the agents suffered a nervous breakdown while working the ticket counter."

In the foregoing example, unpredictable work flow results from dependence on people with whom there is little face-to-face contact, and on environmental conditions over which there is no control.

Unpredictability can also be caused by changes in personnel. We become familiar with the patterns of certain individuals; when new individuals move in, these expectations are upset. A period of learning and adaptation is necessary, during which initiation and response may be unpredictable. The turnover of brand managers in a marketing branch of a large household-products company illustrates how frequent personnel transfers generate unpredictability and stress:

"One of the most unsettling conditions was the frequent relocation of employees and the shifting of jobs. This was especially true of the brand men, although other jobs were also changed frequently. . . . As a consequence of this flux of personnel, the work flow was disturbed. The disruptions became most apparent in the relationships between agency account executives and brand men. Once a 'smooth working relationship' had been established, both men knew what projects were planned for the brand and what was the current status of copy, art work, research, and development. Both had become familiar with each other's working habits—how long it took on the average for each to come up with a solution to problems, how punctual they were, the type of suggestions each would automatically accept or reject, etc. The transfer of people upset these relationships, necessitating the building up of a new relationship between different men from scratch."

Changes in technology, organizational structure, and policy also modify interactional patterns. Especially when they are unexpected, changes can be stressful. Such was the case in a large electrical manufacturing company when a procedural change seriously damaged intergroup cooperation:

"The manager of an engineering department was concerned about the low productivity of an engineering section. . . . The engineers themselves complained about the time they had to spend with marketing personnel solving routine quotation problems. . . . Marketing relied on the engineers for sales engineering assistance. Individual marketing men consulted the engineers whenever they felt it necessary. These contacts included person-to-person discussion, written inquiries, and phone calls.

"The engineering manager issued a ruling that all marketing men should log in and out of the engineering section by signing a register. The stated purpose of the log was to measure the amount of time that marketing employees spent in the engineering section.

"When the first marketing man entered the engineering department after the order, he was advised by the engineering secretary to sign the log. The advice was ignored and the individual went to contact an engineer in the accustomed manner. The engineer refused to talk with the marketing man unless the register was signed. Higher-ups were brought in, an argument ensued, but the marketing man refused to sign and stomped away.

"In the next few days some of the marketing people signed the register but many refused. The engineering manager went to the marketing manager and demanded that all men sign the register, since the new policy would not work without complete cooperation. Each of the holdouts consented to sign when ordered to do so by their superior, but actually they ceased consulting the engineers.

"Relations between the two departments were further strained when individual engineers placed signs on their desks advising marketing men to sign the register. A previously healthy communication flow between the departments came to a screeching halt. Engineers sometimes contacted marketing men for specialized information, but the marketing department rebelled against the engineers by becoming very uncooperative. . . . Engineering, in reaction to hostile marketing actions, would not advise salesmen when special customers were delayed because of errors in ordering instructions. Several of the marketing men refused to request information from engineering. Naturally, company objectives suffered when salesmen advised their customers that they would not quote on products requiring engineering assistance. Refusal to quote enabled marketing men to avoid the engineering section but orders were lost in the process. . . .

"In talking to a sales manager who refused to sign the register, I discovered that he objected to the principle of the new arrangement. 'Why should I sign? Why can't the engineering secretary log marketing personnel in and out if it is so important? She doesn't do a day's work anyhow! If the manager of engineering had come to the marketing department and talked it over—O.K., I would have cooperated. Not now.'"

Apparently, stress is aggravated if (1) change implies a status relationship different from that previously accepted, (2) change is unilaterally imposed without consultation, or (3) the parties see no functional or technological reason for the change.

Inadequate Interaction

Closely related to unidirectional and unpredictable patterns is the situation in which individuals are expected to cooperate from time to time, even though the total interactional flow between them—both social and work-oriented—is fragmented and infrequent. This is especially relevant to relations between line and staff groups. An engineer in the atomic-power-equipment department of an electrical manufacturer comments:

"Essentially I was in a staff position, aiding the salesmen in their work and transmitting their needs to the production groups. . . . Through intimacy and frequency of contact, both social and job, and the use of technical skills, I could gain acceptance by many of the line personnel I worked with. . . . But even my friendliness and technical background didn't facilitate harmonious and efficient relations with the development engineers. I was never able to become friendly because I was always working with different groups of engineers. Maybe one, two, or three people in the group would be familiar, but new faces would be always appearing. In addition, we apparently had different aspirations. They looked upon me as an engineer bucking for a sales job. 'Why isn't he creative like one of us?' seemed to be an unspoken question. One or two of the new engineers in the group would be antagonistic to me, resulting in letters indicating distrust of my ability to meet the deadline, for one reason or another."

In addition, change in work flow is especially resented when it originates with people with whom there has been little habitual interaction:

"A project manager who I'd never worked with before dumped two huge brochures on my desk. After sending the work on through graphics, I learned he had changed a few pages. He wasn't the most organized fellow. I began stockpiling his text waiting for changes. After receiving two complaining memos, I told him in no uncertain terms he was disturbing me—my main allegiance was to the sales staff, not to him."

In our own experience, we have seen that it is possible to overcome adverse feelings originating in erratic and infrequent work interaction by developing vigorous social relationships. However, a great deal of time is required for such activity, and this may have an adverse effect on normal work flow. Moreover, stressful conditions can be aggravated by excessive social intercourse—often caused by crowded working conditions and the group's resultant expectation of friendliness. A laboratory research associate comments on the heightening of stress as a result of crowded physical conditions and the basic cohesiveness of the group: "Eight of us worked in an area more suitable for four. The result was that a disturbance for one became a disturbance for all. The interaction equilibrium level was high, requiring a large part of each individual's energy for gabbing and joking at the expense of work."

Although excessive social intercourse can be too demanding, there is widespread agreement that adequate social interaction is essential. Limitations on social interaction are experienced as stressful. In the reorganization of a food market chain to shift to customer self-service, the older employees were particularly upset; they all found out within a short time that it would be much more difficult to socialize with customers and even among themselves.

Not only is lack of social interaction stressful; scarcity of work communication is also disturbing. A worker comments adversely on the isolated aspects of his former job and tells how he went out of his way to initiate interaction; sometimes, this created extra work for other groups:

"I was a braider operator in a thread processing plant. I worked the 3 to 11 p.m. shift, so generally no one was around my end of the plant except the foreman, who came to see how I was doing two or three times a shift. He didn't talk to me but just waved from the end of the row of machines, because the noise was deafening. The 75 machines made braided string and my job was to keep them all going. A machine would automatically stop if one of the 16 threads broke or if a spool ran out. . . .

"The fact that I worked alone made the job uninteresting and dissatisfying. In order to get a chance to wander through the plant and talk with people, I tried to get all my machines working simultaneously—then I felt I could leave without being reproached. . . . This was difficult to do and occurred infrequently, because while I reloaded spools on stopped machines, others would stop at the other end of the row. Because I was isolated from other workers, I was reluctant to repair breakdowns that appeared to be serious. Since some machines were always broken, there were generally less than 75 of them running. The greater the number of machines shut down, the easier it was to keep the remaining ones running and the more I could wander through the plant. Actually, I could easily fix some breakdowns, but instead I would attach a red tag indicating that the mechanics should fix it the next day. I would have worked on them if there had been someone else around to talk to. I guess I was creating extra work for the mechanics."

We see that certain structurally and technologically determined interaction patterns are experienced as stressful. Now let us examine the behavioral manifestations or indications of such stressful conditions.

Symptoms of Stress

Under stress, people depart from their characteristic patterns of action. Their interactions become erratic, indicating the presence of stress by changes in volume, direction, and content.

Stress is often indicated by a stepping up of vertical and lateral communication. A disturbed manager will increase the frequency of interaction initiation with subordinates and associates, but they will be of shorter duration. "Whenever the operations officer became upset," comments a former naval officer, "he would soar to a high level of activity. Talking and moving about a great deal, he would go from one compartment to another, giving orders, shuffling papers, and griping." Stress may also be indicated by progressive withdrawal from interaction. Avoidance of contact with a specific individual is described by the same officer: "The executive officer's job was to check on my performance. I never liked having to respond to him. . . . I soon decided that to maintain my equilibrium I should avoid interaction with him if at all possible."

In a food market chain, under the stress of dissatisfaction among older employees, a new manager cut down on his direct relations with them. He required them to contact him "through the proper channels." Similarly, Richardson (1961) describes an electronics production supervisor who withdrew from all contact. Under technologically created stress, he tried to isolate himself in order to avoid interpersonal stress, and tried to find time to repair defective parts himself. This ineffective supervisor spent 50 percent less time communicating than did a successful manager.

Emphasis on vertical relations is an indication of stress and a common result of both increased interaction and withdrawal. As is implicit in the supermarket manager's order to stick to formal channels, this creates poor lateral and diagonal communication. Every job should include contacts outside the chain of command as a part of the normal work flow. In addition, a manager who confines his relations to vertical interaction is also likely to limit his attention to short-run, emergency problems. He will ignore more basic technological and structural issues. Richardson's poor supervisor had virtually no contacts with staff or other production groups. Similarly, Guest's ineffective supervisors in the automobile assembly plant constantly initiated interaction with subordinates, and resented any interaction with service groups because of the pressures of technological emergencies.

Stress is often accompanied by changed content in communication—what is said and how. Old-fashioned griping is indicative of stress in some cases (although it may also be a release mechanism that helps maintain relatively healthy relationships).

Change in the proportion of work and social content in interaction also characterizes stress situations. However, the direction of change is ambiguous. In a large chemical company, conflict between staff engineers and line supervision was characterized by reduced social contact. In contrast, in the same concern, conflict between staff engineers in different divisions was accompanied by increased social intercourse. Apparently, the engineers tried to avoid talking about technical matters but still wished to maintain contact. These observations imply that, under stress, vertical relations become more work related, while lateral relations become more superficial and unrelated to the job.

Under stress, verbal intercourse may grow more circumspect. In an engineering division, the inauguration of a budget charging system altered the content of interaction between engineering and production supervisors. Formerly, all engineering projects had been charged to general plant overhead. The new budget system was designed to allocate these hours to specific production departments. One effect was evasive relations between engineers and production supervisors. The engineers were uncertain whether they should publicize the value of their efforts, thereby raising fears about how much their service would cost, or whether they should minimize what they did and hope not to draw attention to their time charges. The results: selective bypassing in job requests, controlled distribution of final reports, avoidance of specific managers, and inadequate communication.

In his study of a food-store chain, Lawrence (1958) shows how stress is reflected in the changed proportions of interaction—more commands, and fewer questions and nondirective discussions. Similarly, when conditions were extremely chaotic and stressful in Guest's automobile plant, one-way or command interaction constituted virtually all communication. No one even had time to ask what was wrong.

Propagation of Stress

In any cooperative system each person tries to develop a stable pattern of work and interaction. When these stable patterns are disturbed, individuals experience stress—an uncomfortable feeling of pressure or dissatisfaction. This stress is characterized by (1) increased interactions downward, (2) increased interactions laterally among subordinates, (3) avoidance of specific people, and (4) changed content of interaction—fewer social contacts, more complaining, etc. These breakdowns in relations create further problems as individuals struggle to restore equilibrium. The expected responses from other individuals in the work sequence prove inadequate, and new problems of coordination arise. Not only do these disturbed interaction patterns indicate stress stemming from structural and technological problems; they also produce further stress.

When the press of technological and personnel problems becomes great, systematic interaction patterns tend to deteriorate: their volume becomes too great, their frequency too high, and the duration of each communication too short. In our earlier restaurant example, saturation of the channels between waiters, waitresses, and chefs compounded and aggravated the bad interactional flow. Under stress, the tempo of contacts becomes so rapid, the number of interactions so frequent, that the interacting individuals fail to communicate sufficiently to solve problems.

Regularities of actions and interactions disappear when stress occurs; erratic variation takes over. People react emotionally, and because more than one individual is involved, stress is reinforced. This wave-like motion of stress is graphically illustrated in the full account of our former naval officer:

"Whenever the operations officer became upset, he would soar to a high level of activity. Talking and moving about a great deal, he would go from one compartment to another, giving orders, shuffling papers and griping. Of course, this reaction to stress was detrimental to the efficiency and morale of the department as a whole. Aside from interrupting any work which may have been going on, many of the orders he gave while working off this reaction would be contradictory to those he had given previously.

"The results of this could be observed all the way down the line—to the lowest rated man in the department. Because of this pressure from above, a man would react by modifying his usual activity level. This upset person would react with someone else, and so on. As a result, the behavior of a great many men in the department was different than under normal conditions. Indeed, I could tell when the operations officer was upset simply by the behavior of my own men."

A vicious circle is established. Something happens in the work situation that causes the relationships of individuals to change or depart from the normal pattern. This creates stress, evincing either opposition or nonresponse, which is aggravated by the reactions of higher level supervisors and staff specialists.

Role Conflict

In Shakespeare's well-known words, "All the world's a stage and all the men and women merely players," attempting to fulfill the requirements of their various roles. The Bard's observation is perhaps too deterministic and pessimistic, but conceptualizing organizational behavior in terms of roles can be helpful. Each person in a formal organization is expected to behave in certain ways (role demands). These demands emanate from the various people with whom the actor comes in contact; these "role partners" collectively comprise his "role set." Nonetheless, he may not perceive the job in exactly similar terms as these others. His role perception may reflect wishful thinking, what he would like the role to be, which may of course be derived from his personality and basic values. The actual behavior or role performance grows out of the reconciliation of these factors. Role effectiveness is how well the behavior meets the role demands. Role satisfaction is how close behavior is to the role ideal. Exhibit

Exhibit 10-1 Elements of Role Behavior

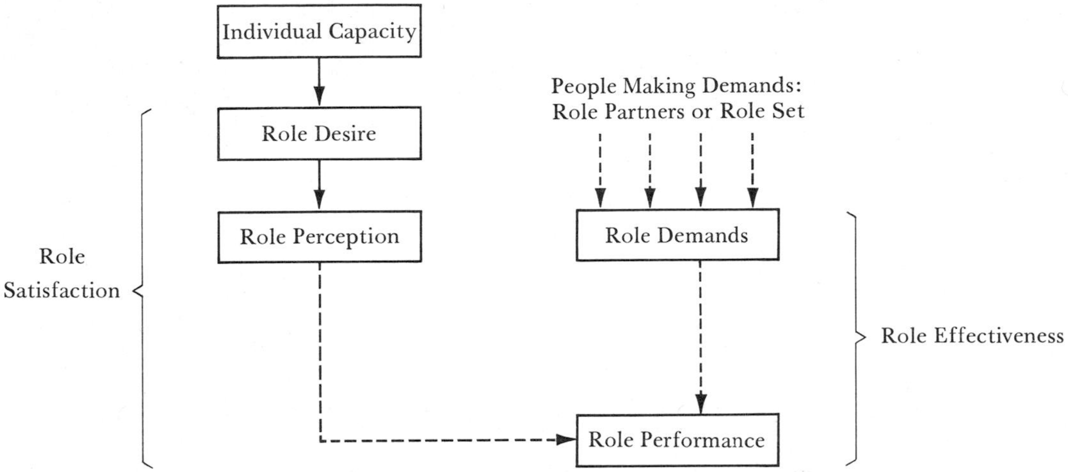

10-1 summarizes the elements. Simple as this model is, problems occur at various points.

Conflict of Individual Characteristics and Role Demands

If a person's characteristics and desires are largely unsuited to role demands, he is subject to stress, dissatisfaction, and probably poor performance. Even though many individuals may sublimate their own desires and behave as demanded, such conflict produces low job satisfaction and feelings of threat and anxiety. Hence, a quiet, passive, contemplative person may heartily dislike the pace and initiative required in a sales position. Or an achievement-oriented hard driver may have difficulty in teaching, where student progress is slow and so ambiguous that he receives little performance feedback. This is the familiar, if still difficult, problem of fit between man and job.

One way to visualize this problem is to compare personal capacity, role demands, and role performance as geometric shapes. In Exhibit 10-2, the circle is individual capacity, the square is role demand, and their overlap is role performance. For example, in 10-2(a), the position requirements are mostly outside the incumbent's capacity. His role performance is only a small part of role demand. This is the apocryphal military misassignment of personnel. The civilian truck driver is assigned to the mess hall as a cook; the former restaurant chef is ordered to become a radioman; the former television repairman is sent to the motor pool as a driver; and so on.

In 10-2(b), role demands are small compared with the incumbent's capacity. Performance draws on only part of his ability. This is the familiar stereotype of the narrowly defined blue-collar production job. However, research on the strikingly low morale among engineers indicates that this condition is widespread (Ritti, 1971). Many organizations have graduate engineers performing activities that consume time, but that do not draw on their abilities. Many of their role demands could better be met by lesser educated technicians. Indeed, Berg (1970)

Exhibit 10-2   Fit of Man and Job: Role Capacity, Demand, and Performance

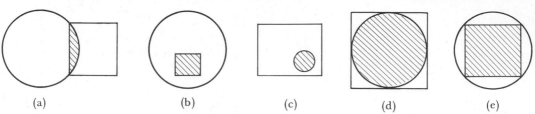

(a)   (b)   (c)   (d)   (e)

has demonstrated that overeducation for American jobs is exceedingly common, and that at each hierarchical level those people with less education have higher morale and equal performance to those at the same level with more education.

In 10-2(c), the position is much larger than the man. He is performing to his maximum capacity, but cannot meet all the role demands. The popular *Peter Principle* (Peter and Hull, 1969) maintains that everyone eventually faces this state. Supposedly, we all rise until we reach the job whose role demands are simply too great for us to meet—we have risen to our level of incompetence. The popularity of this concept suggests that it has some validity, but most of us probably use the "principle" to explain our superiors, not ourselves. The major weakness in Peter's idea is that it ignores the possibility of growth: expanding demands may challenge the incumbent and help him grow. Harry Truman rose initially to a level of incompetence, but then he seemed to develop into a competent (some say even outstanding) president (Rossiter, 1960). Somewhere, there is a job bigger than any one of us, but it is not necessarily in our hierarchy and we do not necessarily reach it.

In 10-2(d) and (e), there is an almost perfect match of individual capacity and role demands. But such compatibility is not necessarily static. In 10-2(d), where the role demands are slightly greater than the person's capacity, the challenge of self growth may be optimal. The incumbent has a feeling of moderate, invigorating stress which motivates developmental effort—rather than an overwhelming challenge that discourages him. In 10-2(e), where the incumbent's capacities are slightly greater than his role demands, this jobholder will probably attempt to expand his role. Creativity, innovation, and perhaps empire-building may be actively pursued.

These situations are fairly easy to conceptualize, and they are not rare in reality. Nonetheless, they are very difficult to predict and document. The problem is that we do not define role demands and individual characteristics in similar terms, so we find it difficult to measure either one very accurately. Intelligence, aptitude, and personality tests, in spite of their popularity, have not been very helpful in predicting the fit of person and job, especially for managers (Campbell et al., 1970).

Ambiguity or Incompatibility in Role Demands

The twin role of Dr. Jekyl and Mr. Hyde in Robert Lewis Stevenson's tale is an actor's dream. It is a challenge to portray the dual facets of one man's character, but he only has to play them sequentially, not simultaneously. Unfortunately, many people in organizations are under simultaneous conflicting demands.

All members of a person's role set depend in some way upon his perform-ance; they are rewarded by it, or they require it in order to perform their own tasks. Because they have a stake in his performance, they develop attitudes and expectations about what he should and should not do in his role. Unfortunately, these expectations do not always agree. Thus the members of the role set impose conflicting demands. The harried incumbent is expected to demonstrate contra-dictory or inconsistent behavior. In a way, we are all playing not to a single audience, but several.

For example, university dormitory advisors are graduate students expected to live with undergraduates, to be friend and advisor, while also serving as a communications link to the administration and enforcer of university regula-tions. However, it is difficult to be both friend and policeman. Being too conscientious in the latter destroys the former. Rigid enforcement of a school regulation against smoking marijuana, for instance, might end all candid communication.

The classic business example of role ambiguity has long been the production foreman described as a "man in the middle" and a "victim of doubletalk" (Gardner and Whyte, 1945; Roethlisberger, 1945). He is caught between his superiors who say that he is a member of management, the power residing in staff "advisors" who tell him what to do, and the pressures of his former work-ing companions who control much of his social satisfaction.

Some industrial engineers are expected to be advisors to line managers at the same time that they monitor production performance and set standards and budgets. But advising and monitoring are difficult to combine (Webber, 1967).

Line managers may expect routine cooperation and quick responsiveness from a staff specialist whose direct staff superior expects creative suggestions and elaborate reports.

Stockbrokers have especially knotty role conflicts. On various overlapping occasions, they are broker (agent), dealer (principal), investment advisor, un-derwriter, and even corporate director. The conflict between being a fiduciary agent and salesman is especially dangerous (Evan and Levin, 1966).

University professors often experience severe role conflict. They are expected to teach, and pressure is increasing from students and administrators to do a better job. They are expected to do research and to publish. In recent years, they have been expected to assist in the solution of social problems locally and nationally. Finally, they are frequently under pressure from themselves and their families to perform consulting, speaking, and writing for extra income.

In general, the problem of knowing who to play a role for and how to evaluate one's performance is widespread. Research (Dill et al., 1962) on the early careers of young managers suggests that the central problems are (1) ignorance and misunderstanding of the precise criteria by which their perform-ance is evaluated (i.e., ignorance of real role demands), and (2) insensitivity to the actual power system in the organization; a kind of naive acceptance of the organization chart, so that they do not know who are the important persons to satisfy (i.e., confusion about role demands and the role set).

In the complex theatre of modern life, most people play many roles—almost at the same time. This proximity of roles means it is difficult to keep them separate; they spill over into each other because they share common resources— the time, energy, and integrity of the incumbent. Thus, there can be conflict between two or more persons about two separate roles (a wife's expectation about her husband's devotion to the family and his employer's expectation about his commitment to the job), or conflict between the desires of one individual to perform in two different roles (the husband/employee may want to be both a good, attentive father and an ambitious, mobile manager). Yet, he has neither the energy nor the time to live up to his competing desires.

Response to Role Stress

Some great men may be all things to all people, but most of us cannot. Continuing ambiguous and conflicting role demands may have a marked impact on mental and physical health. Therefore, in the absence of changed role demands, individuals caught in the middle of role conflict attempt to alleviate their stress. They may formally resign from one or more roles.

They may develop "metaprescriptions." These are personal policies that are followed at all times, even though they are not exactly appropriate to a particular problem. For example, an executive might allot three nights per week to his family, regardless of job demands, but not depart from the pattern. Or he will always do what his superior says, without question. The advantage of such rules is that one does not have to analyze the specific situation before applying the prescription.

Gross et al. (1958) described three basic orientations for developing such rules: moral, expedient, and moral-expedient. The moral-oriented person emphasizes the legitimacy of the demands and responds to the authority figure perceived as most legitimate. The expedient-oriented person is most concerned with the rewards and punishments which could be exercised as a result of his conformity or nonconformity to expectations. Finally, the moral-expedient person takes both legitimacy and power into account and acts in accord with his perception of the net balance—some kind of compromise.

People may informally ignore one of the conflicting demands and avoid the person imposing it. For example, a dormitory advisor might avoid all communication with school administrators and informally stop enforcing regulations. Or a university professor may simplify his conflict by teaching as little as possible and literally hiding from students.

People may schedule conflicting demands in temporal sequence; that is, alternate concentrating on different aspects of the demands. A professor might devote Tuesdays and Thursdays entirely to his classes and students, not trying to do anything else on those days. Mondays and Wednesdays he might research and write, Fridays he might engage in community service or pursue extra income. Note that the intent of such arbitrary rules is to simplify the professor's life. By formulating the rules, he no longer must decide what to do with each demand; he simply fits it into a category. The approach works, but it still has a significant fault: the allocation of time is usually arbitrary and only loosely based on the real importance or priorities of the competing demands.

People may compromise on the conflicting demands by playing down the competitive elements. For example, a dormitory advisor might enforce only *major* rule violations and ignore the more numerous minor ones. Or a newly promoted foreman might exert pressure on his former workmates only when a crisis looms or only when higher management is physically present. Otherwise, he respects the group's informal code.

Not all individuals are equally sensitive to stress, nor does every individual respond to tensions in the same way. Kahn et al. (1964) view individuals as active agents, not passive victims, in stress situations. A person under stress confronts the following: (1) he must deal with the objective situation to reduce its stressful characteristics; (2) he must master the tension and negative emotions aroused by stress; (3) he often must cope with derivative problems of the situation. In this light, the authors examine the personality variables of neurotic anxiety, extroversion-introversion, and flexibility-rigidity, and also certain motivation orientations, in an effort to assess their impact on the individual's response to conflict situations. Their conclusions:

Neuroticism implies heightened sensitivity to stressful environmental conditions and a low degree of stress tolerance. A neurotic is characterized by excessive and conflicting motivation, emotional instability, inadequate coping procedures, and low self-esteem. At any given level of conflict, the reaction of neurotic individuals is more intense than those who are less anxiety-prone. Under stress, a neurotic experiences more job dissatisfaction, tension, and feelings of futility than others, and yet he is less likely to cut himself off from others because of his dependency needs. Neurotic and non-neurotic reactions to role conflict are substantially similar, and certain pressures produce neurotic symptoms in those who are not anxiety-prone.

On the extroversion-introversion dimension, the introvert is generally a sociable individual who characteristically prefers autonomy when experiencing stress or conflict. The introvert tends to be self-oriented, intellectual, artistic, idealistic, sentimental and passive in behavior. The extrovert is active, outgoing, pragmatic, and task-oriented. Both types of individuals seem to interact well socially. The extrovert is seldom troubled by tension or anxiety, even under stress, because he tends to perceive problems as existing within the environment, not in himself. The introvert is prone to anxiety, feels tension under stress, and typically withdraws. The introvert, when perceived as independent or unsociable by his role, faces strong role conflict and suffers high tension. Under severe stress, extroverts also withdraw. Such withdrawal may be successful in the short run, but may lead to further conflict in the long run.

On the dimension of flexibility-rigidity, the flexible person is characterized by other-directedness, open-mindedness, and emphasizes colleagueship in interpersonal relations. He tends to prefer variety and change in his job. The rigid person tends to be inner-directed, dogmatic, authoritarian, prefer routine in life, and therefore is well suited to systematic jobs. Because of the flexible's other-directedness, he tends to experience severe tension under stress. He encourages more conflict because of a desire to please, and thus often suffers from role overload by promising more than he can produce. The rigid person is more likely to feel stress when the situation is unstructured, ambiguous, or a breach in routine. Under such circumstances, he directs his tension outward by rejecting his role and withdrawing.

The three aspects of motivation considered were the desire for expertise in the job, the desire for status, and the desire for security. The first two types of individuals are similar, both being achievement-oriented, younger, more involved in their jobs, more confident, and more independent. The security-oriented individual is dependent, anxiety prone, and attributes high power to those whose favor he seeks. The organizational environment tends to be more hostile to the achievement-oriented person who, because of job involvement, becomes highly sensitive in the face of conflict and perceives it as ego-threatening. As a result he tends to cope by withdrawal, which creates more inner tension because he depends on his role for advancement. Security-oriented persons are least sensitive to role conflict, because they have less to lose.

Role ambiguity and conflict do not simply and consistently lead to organizational stress. It depends upon the organizational situation and climate. House et al. (1968) studied professionals in an organization that was perceived as having an unpleasant climate of inconsistent leadership, high role conflict, high role ambiguity, punitive management, ambiguous policies, low intrinsic job satisfaction, high stress, job pressure, fear, and high peer competitiveness.

The researchers related three independent variables (formalization, dysfunctions, and inflexibility) to measures of anxiety and departure. In general: (1) increased formalization (of plans, objectives, controls, methods, etc., in writing) is associated with *increased anxiety* but no greater departure; (2) dysfunctions (such as conflicting and inconsistent role demands) are associated with *less anxiety* and more job satisfaction; (3) inflexibility (higher management perceived as unresponsive to change) is associated with *less anxiety* and greater departures.

The researchers formulated two hypotheses to explain their findings. In the bureaucratic hypothesis, the effects of the independent variables (organizational formalization, dysfunctions) will be moderated by the amount of inflexibility experienced by the respondent. Specifically, the higher the inflexibility, the less favorable will be the individual reactions to formalization and the more favorable will be the individual reactions to dysfunctions. Their rationale: Under conditions of inflexibility, individuals will view formalization as a constraint on their freedom and will resist it where it exists by disregarding it or supporting dysfunctional behavior. Under conditions of flexibility, individuals will not resist formalization but will behave more consistently with formalized objectives, plans, and policies and not support dysfunctions.

In the stress hypothesis, the effects of the independent variables (organizational formalization, dysfunctions) will be moderated by the amount of stress experienced by the respondent. Specifically, the higher the stress, the less favorable will be the individual reactions to formalizations and the more favorable will be the individual reactions to dysfunctions. Their rationale: Individuals working under high stress conditions will prefer low formalization and high organizational dysfunctions because under nonformalized and disorderly conditions, they can evade formal control systems and cannot be held accountable, easily blamed, or punished. Under dysfunctional conditions, they can exercise more discretion in their work, pass the buck more easily, and spend time and energy according to their preferences rather than according to organizational requirements or boss's directions.

The researchers concluded that their data gave moderately strong support for the stress hypothesis and weak support for the bureaucratic hypothesis.

Summary and Conclusion

Organizations appear to be moving toward more open and rational handling of conflict. Conflict between two or more entities trying to occupy the same state/space comes in many forms: intrapersonal conflict, such as conflicting needs and frustration, and interpersonal, intergroup, and inter-organizational conflict. Role conflicts grow out of (1) conflict between individual capacity and role demands, (2) conflict between role desires and role demands, (3) ambiguity or incompatibility in role demands, and (4) conflict between the roles a person must play.

Work flow is also a source of stress and conflict. One-way and unpredictable patterns and inadequate interactions are reflected in various stress symptoms such as changes in normal communications. These symptoms tend to spread and themselves create new stress.

Conflict between specialists and generalists reflects (1) perceived or feared territorial encroachment, (2) stressful interaction patterns, (3) conflicting loyalties, (4) management's concern for stability versus staff's emphasis on change, (5) possible incompatible styles of thought, and (6) the growing separation of those with authority to act and those with the required knowledge.

We do not mean to add to the currently popular view of business and organization as arenas for political infighting and polite backstabbing. All organizational activity engenders some conflict—and business is no worse than any other area in this respect. Man is a political creature; this springs automatically from his social nature, his intelligence, and his ability to communicate. When competition and conflict appear, the manager must deal with them. Only by understanding the process can the manager use conflict constructively, to "make conflict *do* something for us," as Follett (1940) suggested many years ago.

References

Allport, G. W. *The Nature of Prejudice.* Addison-Wesley, 1954.

Barnard, C. *The Functions of the Executive.* Harvard University Press, 1950.

Bennis, W. G. *Organizational Development.* Addison-Wesley, 1970.

Berelson, B., and G. A. Steiner. *Human Behavior: An Inventory of Scientific Findings.* Harcourt Brace Jovanovich, 1964.

Berg, I. *Education and Jobs: The Great Training Robbery.* Praeger, 1970.

Berne, E. *Games People Play.* Grove Press, 1964.

Blake, R. R., and J. S. Mouton. "Reactions to Intergroup Competition Under Win-Lose Conditions." *Management Science,* Vol. 4, No. 4, July 1961.

Brim, O. G., and S. Wheeler. *Socialization After Childhood.* Wiley, 1966.

Campbell, J. P., M. D. Dunnette, E. E. Lawler, and K. E. Weick. *Managerial Behavior, Performance, and Effectiveness.* McGraw-Hill, 1970.

Campbell, D. T. "Stereotypes and the Perception of Group Differences." *American Psychologist,* Vol. 22, 1967, 818–829.

Chapple, E., and L. R. Sayles. *The Measure of Management.* Macmillan, 1961.

Dalton, G. W. "Diagnosing Interdepartmental Conflict." *Harvard Business Review,* September–October 1963.

Dalton, M. "Conflicts Between Staff and Line Managerial Officers." *American Sociological Review,* Vol. 15 (June 1950), 341–351.

Dill, W. R., T. L. Hilton, and W. R. Reitman. *The New Managers.* Prentice-Hall, 1962.

Doktor, R. H. "Some Cognitive Implications of Academic and Professional Training." *Experimental Publication System, American Psychological Assoc.,* Issue #7 (1970), 166–226.

Down, A. *Inside Bureaucracy.* Little, Brown, 1968.

Evan, W. M. "Conflict and Performance in R&D Organizations." *Industrial Management Review,* Vol. 7, No. 2 (Fall 1965), 37–46.

Evan, W. M., and E. G. Levin. "Status-Set and Role-Set Conflicts of the Stockbroker." *Social Forces,* Vol. 45, No. 1, September 1966.

Follett, M. P. *Dynamic Administration.* Harper & Row, 1940.

Gandhi, Indira, quoted in *Columbia Reports,* December 1971, on the occasion of her visit to Columbia University.

Gardner, B., and W. F. Whyte. "The Man in the Middle: Position and Problems of the Foreman." *Applied Anthropology,* Vol. 4, No. 2 (Summer 1945), 1–8.

Gellerman, S. W. *Motivation and Productivity.* American Management Association, 1963.

Gross, N., A. W. McEachern, and W. S. Mason. "Role Conflict and Its Resolutions," in E. E. Maccoby et al. (eds.), *Readings in Social Psychology.* Holt, Rinehart and Winston, 1958.

Guest, R. H. *Organizational Change: The Effect of Successful Leadership.* Irwin, 1962.

Gurr, T. R. *Why Men Rebel.* Princeton University Press, 1970.

Hilgert, R. L. "Interaction in an Industrial Plant: A Negative Hypothesis." *Human Organization,* Vol. 26, No. 4, Winter 1967.

House, R. J., J. R. Rizzo, and S. I. Lirtzman. "Organizational Stress and Inflexibility." Paper presented to Joint Meeting of the Institute of Management Sciences and Operations Research Society, College of Managerial Psychology, San Francisco, May 1968.

Ichheiser, G. "Misunderstandings in Human Relations." *American Journal of Sociology,* Vol. 55, No. 2, 1949.

Jennings, E. E. *The Mobile Manager.* Bureau of Industrial Relations, University of Michigan, 1967.

Kahn, R. L., D. M. Wolfe, R. P. Quinn, J. D. Snook, and R. A. Rosenthal. *Organizational Stress.* Wiley, 1964.

Kelly, J. "Make Conflict Work for You." *Harvard Business Review* (July/August 1970), 103–113.

Lawrence, P. *The Changing of Organizational Behavior Patterns: A Case Study of Decentralization.* Harvard Business School, 1958.

Lawrence, P. R., and J. W. Lorsch. *Organization and Environment.* Division of Research, Harvard Business School, 1962.

———. "New Management Job: The Integrator." *Harvard Business Review,* Vol. 45, No. 6 (November/December 1967), 142–151.

Leavitt, H. *Managerial Psychology,* 3rd ed. University of Chicago Press, 1972.

Lorenz, K. *On Aggression.* Harcourt Brace Jovanovich, 1966.

Melman, S. *Dynamic Factors in Industrial Productivity.* Blackwell, 1956.

Merton, R. K. *Social Theory and Social Structure,* rev. ed. The Free Press, 1957.

Peter, L. J., and R. Hull. *The Peter Principle.* Morrow, 1969.

Porter, L. "Where is the Organization Man?" *Harvard Business Review,* November/December 1963.

Richardson, F. L. W. *Talk, Work and Action.* Monograph No. 3, The Society for Applied Anthropology, 1961.

Ritti, R. *The Engineer in the Industrial Corporation.* Columbia University, 1971.

Roethlisberger, F. "The Foreman: Master and Victim of Doubletalk." *Harvard Business Review,* Vol. 23, No. 3 (May 1945), 283–298.

Rossiter, C. *The American Presidency,* rev. ed. Harcourt Brace Jovanovich, 1960.

Scodel, A., J. S. Minas, P. Ratoosh, and M. Lipetz. "Some Descriptive Aspects of Two-Person, Non-Zero Sum Games." *Journal of Conflict Resolution,* Vol. 3 (1959), 114–119.

Sherif, M. "Superordinate Goals in the Reduction of Intergroup Conflict." *American Journal of Sociology,* Vol. 63, No. 4, January 1958.

Stephenson, T. E. "The Causes of Management Conflict." *California Management Review,* Vol. 2, No. 2 (Winter 1960), 90–97.

Thompson, V. *Modern Organization.* Knopf, 1963.

Turner, R. "The Public Perception of Protest." *American Sociological Review,* Vol. 34 (1969), 815–831.

Walton, R. E., and R. B. McKersie. *A Behavioral Theory of Labor Negotiations—An Analysis of a Social Interaction System.* McGraw-Hill, 1963.

Webber, R. A. "Innovation and Conflict in Industrial Engineering." *Journal of Industrial Engineering* (May 1967), 13.

Zaleznik, A. "Power and Politics in Organizational Life." *Harvard Business Review* (May/June 1970), 47–60.

Readings

Taking Organizational Roles

DANIEL KATZ, ROBERT L. KAHN

Our description of role-sending and role-receiving is based on four concepts: *role expectations,* which are evaluative standards applied to the behavior of any person who occupies a given organizational office or position; *sent role,* which consists of communications stemming from role expectations and sent by members of the role set as attempts to influence the focal person; *received role,* which is the focal person's perception of the role-sendings addressed to him, including those he "sends" to himself; and *role behavior,* which is the response of the focal person to the complex of information and influence he has received.

Role Episode

These four concepts can be thought of as constituting a sequence or role episode. The first two, role expectations and sent role, have to do with the motivations, cognitions, and behavior of the members of the role set; the latter two, received role and role behavior, have to do with the cognitions, motivations, and behavior of the focal person. A model of the role episode is presented in Figure 1.

As the figure suggests, there is symmetry between the two complementary phases of the role episode—the cognitions and behavior of role senders on the one hand, and the cognitions and behavior of the focal person on the other. There is also a kind of orderliness to the model viewed in another way; boxes I and III represent processes of perception, cognition, and motivation—processes internal to the person, the role sender in box I, and the focal person in box III. Boxes II and IV represent behaviors—acts undertaken in expression of cognitive and motivational processes. These acts are viewed as role-sending when they are the behaviors of members of a role set under our observation, and as role behavior when they are the acts of a focal person (that is, any office occupant whom we have singled out for study).

The designation of an office or person as *focal* is, of course, a matter of convenience; it serves merely to identify our terms of reference for viewing some part of an ongoing organization. A complete study of an organization would require that each office in it be successively treated as focal, its role set identified, the role expectations and sent role measured, and the received role and role behavior similarly described. Every person in an organization receives role-sending from one or more others, and in most organizations each person is also a role sender for one or more others.

The ongoing life of a large organization involves many continuous cycles of sending, receiving, responding, evaluating, and sending again by persons in many overlapping role sets. In Figure 1, arrow 1 represents the process of

Figure 1 A Model of the Role Episode

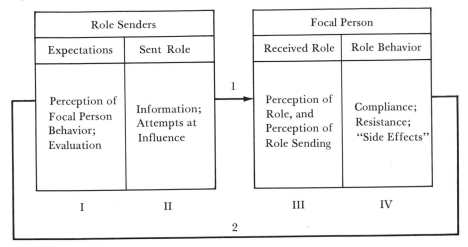

role-sending, and arrow 2 represents the process by which the role sender (a) estimates the degree of compliance which he has apparently induced on the part of the focal person and (b) prepares to initiate another cycle.

Arrow 2 is thus a feedback loop; the degree to which a person's behavior conforms to the expectations held for him at one point in time will affect the state of those expectations at the next moment. If his response is essentially a hostile counterattack, his role senders are apt to think of him and behave toward him in ways quite different than if he were submissively compliant. If he complies partially under pressure, they may increase the pressure; if he is obviously overcome with tension and anxiety, they may "lay off." In sum, the role episode is abstracted from a process which is cyclic and ongoing: the response of the focal person to role-sending feeds back to each sender in ways that alter or reinforce his expectations and subsequent role-sending. The current role-sendings of each member of the set depend on his evaluations of the response to his last sendings, and thus a new episode begins.

Even this brief description of the process of role-sending and role-receiving indicates that the model presented in Figure 1 is in many respects oversimplified. Three of these are of particular importance:

1. The notion of a role episode—neatly fulfilling the Aristotelian aesthetic requirements of beginning, middle, and end—is an abstraction. It is merely a convenient way of representing what we believe to be a complex ongoing process involving all the members of an organization. The convenience consists of assuming role expectations as a starting point, and presenting them as if the process of interaction were a sequence of discrete episodes.

2. A further simplification is the treatment of role expectations as if there were only a single role sender and he were completely consistent in his expectations, or as if there were consensus among role senders. In fact such consistency and consensus is not attained, and some degree of role conflict is characteristic of human organizations.

3. The third oversimplification inherent in the concept of the role episode is its abstraction from the larger context of organizational events. Every act of role-sending and role-receiving is in part determined by the context within which it occurs.

Of these three limitations, the first requires no further discussion; the second and third we will consider at greater length.

Role Conflict

To assert that some degree of role conflict is characteristic of human organizations does not imply violence as a way of organizational life. We define *role conflict* as the simultaneous occurrence of two (or more) role sendings such that compliance with one would make more difficult compliance with the other. In the extreme case, compliance with one expectation as sent would exclude completely the possibility of compliance with the other; the two expectations are mutually contradictory. For example, a person's superior may make it clear to him that he is expected to hold his subordinates strictly to company rules. At the same time, his subordinates may indicate in various ways that they would like loose, relaxed supervision, and that they will make things difficult if they are pushed too hard. Here the pressures from above and below are incompatible, since a style of supervision which satisfies one set of expectations violates the other set. Such cases are so common that a whole literature has been created on the problem of the first-line supervisor as "the man in the middle," the "master and victim of double-talk."

Several types of role conflict can be identified. One might be termed *intrasender:* the expectations from a single member of a role set may be incompatible, as for example when a supervisor orders a subordinate to acquire material which is unavailable through normal channels and at the same time warns him against violating those channels. A second type of role conflict we can call *intersender:* expectations sent from one sender are in conflict with those from one or more other senders. The foreman urged by his superior to supervise more closely and by his subordinates to allow them greater freedom fits the category of intersender conflict.

If we look beyond the organization, another type of role conflict becomes apparent—conflict between roles. Such *interrole* conflict occurs whenever the sent expectations for one role are in conflict with those for another role played by the same person. Demands from role senders on the job for overtime or take-home work may conflict with pressures from one's wife to give undivided attention to family affairs during evening hours. The conflict arises between the role of the focal person as worker and his role as husband and father.

All three of these types of conflict—intrasender, intersender, and interrole—are conflicts in the content of the role as sent; they exist as conflicts in the objective environment of the focal person. They give rise, of course, to psychological conflicts of some kind and degree within the focal person. Other types of conflict, however, are generated directly by a combination of externally sent role expectations and internal forces or role expectations which the focal person requires of himself. This fourth type of conflict, which we may call *person-role* conflict occurs when role requirements violate the needs, values, or capacities of the focal person. Pressures on an executive to conclude a profitable agreement in restraint of trade, for example, might be opposed by his personal code of ethics. In other cases of person-role conflict the person's needs and values may lead to behavior which is unacceptable to members of his role set; for example, an ambitious young man may be called up short by his associates for stepping on their toes in his haste to advance in the organization.

From these four basic types of conflict other complex forms of conflict sometimes develop. A very prevalent form of conflict in industrial organizations, for example, is role overload. Overload is typically encountered as a kind of intersender conflict in which the sent expectations of various members of the role set are legitimate and are not logically incompatible. The focal person, however, finds that he cannot complete all of the tasks urged on him by various people within the stipulated time limits and requirements of quality. He is likely to experience overload as a conflict of priorities or as a conflict between quality and quantity. He must decide which pressures to comply with and which to hold off. If it is impossible to deny any of the pressures, he may be taxed beyond the limit of his abilities. Thus overload involves a kind of person-role conflict, and is perhaps best regarded as a complex-emergent type combining aspects of conflict between role senders and conflict between senders and focal person.

The major issue with respect to role conflict, however, is not the typology which one chooses or constructs; it is the prevalence of role conflict as a fact. In a nationwide study of male wage and salary workers, Kahn and his colleagues (1964) found nearly half to be working under conditions of noticeable conflict. Forty-eight percent reported that from time to time they were caught between two sets of people who wanted different things from them, and 15 percent reported this to be a frequent and serious problem. Thirty-nine percent reported being bothered by their inability to satisfy the conflicting demands of their various role senders. The hierarchical and depersonalized nature of large-scale organization is also reflected in these data: 88 percent of all role conflicts reportedly involve pressures from above, and in 57 percent of these cases the spontaneous description of the source of these pressures was given in such impersonal terms as "the company" or "management."

Context of Role-Taking

The last of the oversimplifications to which we pointed in our model of the role episode was its abstraction from the context in which it occurs. That context can be thought of as consisting of all the enduring properties, the more or less stable characteristics, of the situation within which a role episode takes place. Some of these will be properties of the organization itself; some will be traits of the persons involved in the process of role-sending and role-receiving; some will be properties of the interpersonal relationships which already exist between the actors in the role episode.

These three additional classes of variables—organizational, personality, and interpersonal—can be conveniently represented in an enlargement and extension of Figure 1. That figure presented a causal sequence: role expectations (I) lead to role-sending (II), which leads to received role (III), which leads to behavior in response to the role as received (IV). That figure and the sequence it represents also forms the core of Figure 2.

The circles in Figure 2 represent not the momentary events of the role

Figure 2   A Theoretical Model of Factors Involved in the Taking of
Organizational Roles

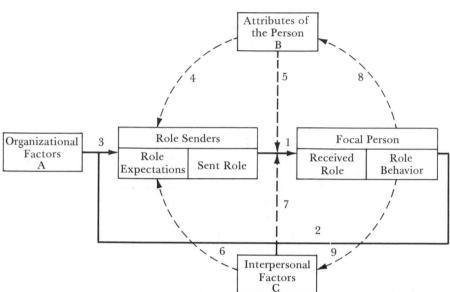

episode, but enduring states of the organization, the person, and the interpersonal relations between focal person and role senders. Such enduring properties are for the most part abstractions and generalizations based upon recurrent
events and behaviors. For example, characterizing a relationship as supportive
means simply that the parties to the relationship have behaved in a supportive
manner toward one another on a sufficient number of occasions so that we feel
justified in inferring supportiveness as a quality of the relationship. Such repetitions and patterns of events provide the basis and context within which each
new occurrence can best be understood.

To a considerable extent the role expectations held by the members of a
role set—the prescriptions and proscriptions associated with a particular office—
are determined by the broader organizational context. The technology of the
organization, the structure of its subsystems, its formal policies, and its rewards
and penalties dictate in large degree the content of a given office. What the
occupant of that office is supposed to do, with and for whom, is given by these
and other properties of the organization itself. Although human beings are doing
the "supposing" and rewarding, the structural properties of organization are
sufficiently stable so that they can be treated as independent of the particular
persons in the role set. For such properties as size, number of echelons, and rate
of growth, the justifiable abstraction of organizational properties from individual
behavior is even more obvious.

The organizational circle (*A*) in Figure 2 represents a set of variables. Some
of them characterize the organization as a whole; others describe some part of
it. Arrow 3 asserts a causal relationship between certain organizational variables
and the role expectations held about and sent to a particular position. For
example, there is an almost linear relationship between organizational size and

the amount of reported role conflict and tension in the organization (Kahn et al., 1964).

Enduring attributes of the person (circle B) refer to all those variables which describe the propensity of an individual to behave in certain ways—his motives and values, his defense preferences, his sensitivities and fears. Such factors affect the role episode in several ways. First, some traits of the person tend to evoke or facilitate certain evaluations and behaviors from his role senders (arrow 4). Second, the same sent role can be experienced differently by different people; that is, personality factors act as conditioning variables in the relationship between the role as sent and the role as received and responded to. Finally, we propose as a hypothesis that role behavior has effects on personality (arrow 8). This is simply the hypothesis that we become what we do, and in a sense we un-become what we do not do. The man who is required to play a subservient role, for example, cannot do so over an extended time without consequent changes in personality. Most abilities atrophy if unexercised.

As Figure 2 indicates, interpersonal relations (circle C) fulfill functions parallel to those already described for attributes of the person. The expectations held for and sent to a focal person depend to some degree on the quality of interpersonal relations between him and the members of his role set (arrow 6). He will also interpret differently the role-sendings he receives, depending on his interpersonal relations with the senders (arrow 7). Praise and blame have one set of meanings when they come from a trusted source, and another when they stem from untrusted sources. Finally, the behavior of the focal person feeds back to and has effects on his interpersonal relations with members of his role set (arrow 9). If he suddenly and persistently refuses to comply in any respect with their role-sendings, for example, we would predict not only an immediate change in their evaluation of his role behavior (arrow 2), but an enduring change in their liking for him (arrow 9).

The research evidence for this model of role-taking in organizations is substantial in quantity but irregular in quality and in relevance. That distinctive attitudes, values, and points of view are characteristically associated with different roles has been a part of human experience and folk wisdom for time beyond recollection, and within the past twenty years this fact has been well documented.

Stouffer and his colleagues (1949) reported sharp differences between officers and enlisted men in their attitudes toward the army, with officer opinions consistently more favorable. Jacobson (1951) showed similar differences among workers, foremen, and stewards in their attitudes toward the company and the union. Research on the differential perceptions of supervisors and subordinates shows consistently that role or position in the organization is related to perceptions no less than to attitudes and values. Mann's findings (Likert, 1961) that 76 percent of the foremen in a utility report that they "always or almost always get their subordinates' ideas in the solution of job problems" but that only 16 percent of the workers report being so consulted, is typical of such research.

Most such findings lend themselves to either of two interpretations or perhaps to a combination of both. One can argue that the role shapes the attitudes and perceptions of the individual, or that the individual is selected for his psychological goodness-of-fit to the role requirements. Lieberman (1956) has contributed the most definitive evidence for the former interpretation. He was able to measure the perceptions and attitudes of employees in two appliance plants three times during a period of three years: once when all were rank-and-file workers, a year later when 23 had become foremen and 35 had been elected stewards, and two years later still when about half of the new foremen and stewards had reverted to nonsupervisory jobs and half had continued in their new roles.

In their rank-and-file days, there were no significant differences between future foremen and future stewards, although both groups were more ambitious, more critical, and less unquestioningly loyal to the company than were the workers destined to become neither foremen nor stewards. On becoming foremen, Lieberman's subjects tended to report more favorably about the company as a place to work, to be more favorable in their perceptions of top management, and to endorse the principle of incentive pay. Those men who became union stewards became, according to their responses, more favorable toward unions in general, toward the top officers of their own union, and toward the principle of seniority rather than ability as a basis for wage payments. Those foremen and stewards who subsequently returned to the worker role tended also to revert to the perceptions and attitudes of workers; those who remained as foremen and stewards showed more sharply as time passed the kinds of differences described above. Mean differences between future foremen and future stewards on the numerous scales used were less than one percentage point at the time when all subjects were workers; 48 percent between the foremen and stewards after one year in role, and 62 percent after three years in role.

Even these data, however, leave unsupported many of the linkages stipulated in the model. Lieberman's data argue strongly for a causal relationship between the office an individual occupies in an organization (foreman, steward) and his expressed attitudes on job-relevant matters. Whether the characteristic changes in attitude are brought about because of the causal sequence of different role expectations, the sending of these expectations as attempts at influence, the receiving of such communications, and the subsequent response to them remains untested by Lieberman's research. The formulation of such a process with respect to the sending of norms was first proposed by Rommetveit (1954), but he was concerned with the religious attitudes and sex roles of Norwegian adolescents rather than the work situation and the organizational context. Other research, however, can be interpreted as supporting many of the hypotheses specified by the model. Let us consider some of this research, in the order suggested by the numbered arrows in Figure 2.

Relationship Between Role Expectations and Response (Arrow 1)

Sarbin and Williams (1953) conducted a laboratory experiment which demonstrated something of the expertise which people acquire in receiving and understanding communications from role senders. The subjects of the experiment listened to 38 sentences, each conveying some role expectation; their task was to determine the age, sex, and role of the sender, the intended receiver, and the action or role behavior which was being requested. Performance of the experimental subjects was so accurate that the resulting distributions showed the typical J-curve of conforming behavior.

Gross, Mason, and McEachern (1958), in their excellent study of school boards and school superintendents, demonstrated a number of significant relationships between the expectations and sending to members of a role set, on the one hand, and the perceptions and responses of the target or focal person on the other. Role-sending from the school board to the superintendent was associated with high job satisfaction on the part of the superintendent when the expectations of the board were consistent with his professional standards, and with low job satisfaction when they were not.

Kahn and his colleagues (1964), in their studies of role conflict and ambiguity, found that objective role conflict (measured by the statements of role senders that they wished for specific changes in the focal person's role behavior) was related to low job satisfaction, low confidence in the organization, and a high degree of job-related tension. The effects of role ambiguity (defined as lack of information regarding supervisory evaluation of one's work, about opportunities for advancement, scope of responsibility, and expectations of role senders) were in general comparable to those of role conflict. Persons subjected to conditions of ambiguity on the job tended to be low in job satisfaction, low in self-confidence, high in tension and in a sense of futility.

Gross and his colleagues (1958) also found that role conflict around such issues as hiring, promotion, teacher salaries, and budgetary matters was associated with low job satisfaction on the part of the superintendent. Getzels and Guba (1954) had previously demonstrated a relationship between role conflict and reduced teaching effectiveness in nine air force training schools.

Feedback Effect of Role Behavior on the Expectations of Role Senders (Arrow 2)

This effect, which is stipulated in the model, has yet to be appropriately tested. The required research would be longitudinal in design, in order to answer the question of whether the performance of the focal person in successive cycles of role-sending and response leads to modifications of the expectations of role senders. Some suggestive findings are available, however. Jacobson and his colleagues (1951) found that workers tended to express anti-union attitudes when their stewards failed to involve them in decision-making. Jacobson interpreted this to be the result of the workers' discovery that their initial expectations were unfulfilled, but the data permit other interpretations as well. Kahn and his colleagues (1964) found that role senders expressed fewer intentions to bring about change on the part of focal persons who were high in rigidity, presumably because the intractable performance of the focal person had led to a reduction of expectations on the part of his role senders.

Organizational Factors as Determinants of Role Expectations (Arrow 3)

This category of findings reminds us that role expectations and the process of role-sending do not arise as spontaneous and idiosyncratic expressions on the part of role senders nor as simple responses to some previous behavior of the focal person to whom the expectations were sent. Such factors serve only to mediate the major determinants of role-sending, which are to be found in the systemic properties of the organization as a whole, the subsystem in which the role senders are located, and the particular position occupied by each.

Gross, Mason, and McEachern (1958) found that organizational size was a determinant of the pattern of role expectations. Lack of consensus was more frequent in large school systems, and to some extent in communities which utilized complex organizational forms of decision-making rather than the open town meeting. Moreover, members of large school boards were less accepting of any deviation from established lines of authority.

Getzels and Guba (1954) had found earlier that, among the nine air force schools included in their study, strict adherence to military procedure as an organizational norm was associated with lesser role conflict. This finding they interpreted as a problem in normative congruence between system and super-system, asserting that those schools which maintained strict military procedure were consistent with the norms of the air force and the military establishment as a whole, while those schools which deviated from such procedure created problems of conflict for their staff, who were necessarily members of both the school and the larger military organization.

Kahn and his colleagues (1964) identified five dimensions of normative expectations which appeared to be characteristic of organizations as systems rather than of individual persons or roles. These included the extent to which one is expected to obey rules and follow orders, the extent to which supervisors are expected to show personal interest in and nurture their subordinates, the closeness or generality with which supervision is to be accomplished, the extent to which all relationships are conducted according to general (universalistic) standards, and the extent to which organization members are expected to strive strenuously for achievement and advancement.

Evidence is ample that expectations are shaped by position in organization, as well as by such organizationwide factors. According to the study of Jacobson and his colleagues (1951), almost 70 percent of the workers held the expectation that the steward should be active in representing the interests of his men rather than waiting until some grievance was presented to him. Only 30 percent of the foremen took this view of the steward's role, even though the foremen closely resembled the workers in demographic characteristics and had typically been workers in the same plant before their promotion to foreman.

In the studies of role conflict and ambiguity cited above (Kahn et al., 1964) the location of positions within the organization was found to be related to the degree of objective conflict to which the occupant of the position was subjected. In general, positions contained deep within the organizational structure were relatively conflict-free; positions located near the skin or boundary of the organization were likely to be conflict-ridden. Thus jobs involving labor negotiations, purchasing, selling, or otherwise representing the organization to the public were subjected to greater stress. Living near an intraorganization boundary—for example, serving as liaison between two or more departments—revealed many of the same effects but to a lesser degree.

The objective content of the role activities seems also to be related to the pattern of expectations and to the amount of conflict among them. Roles which demand innovative problem-solving are characterized by objective conflict and subjective tension. The occupants of such roles appear to become engaged in conflict primarily with the organizational old guard—men of greater age and power who want to maintain the status quo. Among the major role conflicts of such innovative jobs is the conflict of priority between the nonroutine activities

which are at the core of the creative job, and the routine activities of administration or paper work.

Finally, the same research discovered consistent relationships between
hierarchical position and the prevalence of conflicting role expectations. The
often heard assertion that the lowest levels of supervision are subjected to the
greatest conflict is not borne out; rather there is a curvilinear relationship in
which the maximum of conflict occurs at the upper middle levels of management. Supervisory responsibility, both direct and indirect, is associated with
conflict among role senders with respect to the appropriate style and requirements of the role.

The significant principle reflected by all these specific data is that characteristics of the organization as a whole, of its subsystems, and of the location
of particular positions act to determine the expectations which role senders will
hold and communicate to the occupant of a particular job. The holding and
sending of such expectations is personal and direct; their content is nevertheless shaped by systemic factors.

Personality Factors as Determinants of Role Expectations (Arrow 4)

The influence of personality on role-sending is one of those undeniable facts
of organizational life which nevertheless awaits measurement and documenta-
tion. Anyone who has worked under a number of different bosses has become
a student of such personality differences; anyone who has supervised a number
of subordinates has discovered how differently they respond to uniform tasks
and supervisory behavior. Gross and his colleagues (1958) measured the homogeneity of members of role sets on certain demographic and personality attributes and found some tendency for the degree of such homogeneity to be related
to their consensus on expectations for the school superintendent. The combined
correlation of political-economic conservatism, religious preference, and motivation to represent some constituent group was .54 with the measure of consensus
in role expectations.

Kahn and his coauthors (1964) report similar findings in the industrial
context. They found that people who were flexible rather than rigid were
subjected to greater pressures to change by their role senders. The behavior of
role senders toward extremely rigid focal persons seemed to reflect a judgment
of futility and acceptance and the abandonment of continuing attempts to
influence behavior in the direction of ideal performance. Role expectations and
role-sending were also related to the achievement-orientation of the focal person.
The greater the achievement-orientation, especially when such orientation took
on a cast of neurotic striving, the more likely were role senders to apply increased
pressures to change the style of the focal person.

Personality Factors as Mediators Between Role Expectations
and Response (Arrow 5)

During the past 15 years, the empirical evidence for the mediating influence
of enduring properties of the person (demographic, experiential, and personality)
has been steadily accumulating. Although such factors are still too often omitted
from organizational studies, thus increasing the unexplained variance in orga-

nizational behavior, their effects have been reported by dozens of research workers. Stouffer and Toby (1951), in an experiment based on Stouffer's earlier work (1949), found that the chosen behaviors indicated by their experimental subjects in hypothetical situations of role conflict tended to express the predisposition of subjects with respect to the norms of universalism or particularism. Jacobson and his colleagues in the same year (1951) found that the conflict experience of foremen was higher among those who had previously served as stewards, presumably because they had internalized the values of the earlier role.

Sarbin and various colleagues (Sarbin and Rosenberg, 1955; Sarbin and Hardyck, 1952; Albrecht and Sarbin, 1952; Sarbin and Stephenson, 1952) engaged in a series of laboratory experiments showing that the ability of individuals to respond appropriately to role expectations was a function of various personality attributes. The ability to perceive accurately demands of a role was related to a measure of neuroticism based on self-description. Role-taking ability was also related, apparently via the capacity to empathize, to such dimensions as equalitarianism-authoritarianism, and flexibility-rigidity. Extreme inability to take roles was manifested by schizophrenics and psychopaths, a finding consistent with Gough's (1948) earlier theory of psychopathy. He proposed that the characteristic problem of the psychopath is inability to empathize, that is to respond in the focal role *as if* he understood and felt the forces to which the role senders were subjected. Such an interpretation of psychopathy was given some support by Baker's (1954) small comparative study of psychopathic and nonpsychopathic prisoners. Questioning these subjects in terms which others used in appraising and describing them, Baker found that the psychopaths had significantly greater difficulty recognizing in themselves the ascribed traits.

Gross, Mason, and McEachern (1958) found that the effects of role conflict on job satisfaction and expressions of worry among school superintendents were consistently mediated by the characteristic anxiety level of the individual. They also utilized personality variables in attempting to predict the conflict-resolving behavior of the superintendents in four hypothetical situations, involving hiring and promotion, time allocation, salary recommendations for teachers, and budget recommendations. The personality predictor was based on a categorization of the superintendents as moralists, moral-expedients, or expedients —according to their predisposition to emphasize legitimacy or sanctions in response to a series of test items.

Kahn and his coauthors (1964) found that several personality dimensions mediate significantly the degree to which a given intensity of objective conflict is experienced as strain by the focal person. These personality dimensions include emotional sensitivity, introversion-extroversion, flexibility-rigidity, and the need for career achievement.

"For example, the effects of objective role conflict on interpersonal bonds and on tension are more pronounced for introverts. The introverts develop social relations which, while sometimes congenial and trusting, are easily undermined by conditions of stress. The preference of such people for autonomy becomes manifest primarily when social contacts are stressful, that is, when others are exerting strong pressures and thereby creating conflict for them. In similar fashion, emotional sensitivity mediates the relationship between objective conflict and tension, with emotionally sensitive persons showing substantially higher tension scores for any given degree of objective conflict. An individual who is strongly achievement-oriented exhibits a high degree of personal involvement with his job, and the adverse effects of role conflict are more pronounced for him than for those who are less involved" (p. 384).

Personality as Affected by Role Behavior (Arrow 8)

It is usual for psychologists to treat the characteristics of adult personality as relatively fixed, having been formed during earlier years of life and by earlier experiences. Our approach to personality is more dynamic than that; we believe the personality is essentially the product of social interaction, and that the process of personality formation continues throughout life. More specifically, the model of role-taking which we are proposing treats personality variables in three ways: as a determinant of the role expectations of others, as mediating factors between sent role and the ways in which it is experienced and responded to, and as factors which are affected by experience and behavior in organizational roles. It is the last of these three views of personality to which we now turn.

The empirical evidence for the effects of role experience and behavior on personality is thin, perhaps because it has not been often sought. The truth of the folk saying that "you become what you do" has yet to be put to systematic test. However, Cameron and Magaret (1951) reported that the absence of role-taking skills seemed to contribute to the development of paranoid symptoms. Gough and Peterson (1952) found that the number of roles played by an individual was related to his ability to be self-critical, and that deficiencies in role performance led to an increasing inability to see oneself in objective terms and to identify with the views of others. In an extended experiment involving the manipulation of the level of decision-making in a large clerical operation, Tannenbaum (1957) showed that both the autonomous and the hierarchical conditions produced significant changes in personality. The personality changes were in the direction of increasing congruence between role and person.

Earlier accounts of the effects of role on personality were unsupported by quantitative data, and were concentrated primarily on the dysfunctional effects of bureaucratic requirements. Veblen's discussion of "trained incapacity," Dewey's description of "occupational psychosis," and Warnotte's reference to "professional deformation" are perhaps the major examples of this line of argument. Merton (1957) builds on them in his own exposition of bureaucratic structure and personality, and concludes with a plea for "studies of religious, educational, military, economic, and political bureaucracies dealing with the interdependence of social organization and personality formation. . . ." The conclusion remains appropriate today.

The Significance of Interpersonal Relations in Role-Taking (Arrows 6, 7, and 9)

In theory, enduring properties of the interpersonal relationship between a focal person and members of his role set enter into the process of role-sending and response in ways analogous to enduring properties of the person. That is to say, we expect that the interpersonal relations between focal person and role senders will help to determine their role expectations, will intervene between sent role and received role, and will in turn be affected by the role behavior of the focal person. Some evidence for all three of these effects is available from the research on role conflict already cited (Kahn et al., 1964):

"The sources of pressure and conflict for a person can be expressed rather fully in terms of his interpersonal relations with these pressure sources (arrow 6). The greatest pressure is directed to a person from other people who are in the same department as he is, who are his superiors in the hierarchy, and who are sufficiently dependent on his performance to care about his adequacy without being so completely dependent as to be inhibited in making their demands known. The people who are least likely to apply such pressures are a person's peers and role senders outside his own department.

"The kinds of influence techniques which people are prepared to apply, as well as the degree of pressure they exert, vary with their formal relationship to the potential target of their pressures. To a considerable degree the actual power structure of organizations follows the lines of formal authority. Legitimate power, rewards, and coercive power over an organizational member are largely in the hands of his direct organizational superiors. Although a supervisor has coercive power available to him as a basis for influencing his subordinates, he is likely to refrain from using it where it might impede the performance of these subordinates and perhaps reflect upon the supervisor himself. On the other hand, the techniques used by subordinates to apply coercive power are precisely those which threaten the efficiency of the organization. They include the withholding of aid and information.

"The deleterious effects of role conflict are most severe where the network of an individual's organizational relations binds him closely to members of his role set (arrow 7). When a person must deal with others who are highly dependent on him, who have high power over him, and who exert high pressure on him, his response is typically one of apathy and withdrawal—psychological if not behavioral. Under such circumstances the experience of role conflict is intense and job satisfaction correspondingly low. Emotionally, the focal person experiences a sense of futility, and he attempts a hopeless withdrawal from his coworkers. Likewise, the costs of role conflict upon the focal person are most dear where there is a generally high level of communication between the focal person and his role senders.

"Since close ties to role senders with regard to functional dependence, power, and communication intensify the effects of an existing conflict, an obvious means of coping with conflict is to sever ties with one's role senders. Symptomatic of this pattern of withdrawal in the face of conflict is the tendency of an individual experiencing role conflict to reduce the amount of communication with his role senders, to derogate bonds with these senders (arrow 9). Although this pattern of coping with stress is common, its logic is questionable. Withdrawal may be successful in alleviating the effects of stress for a time; in the longer run it is likely to prove self-defeating. Withdrawal may not only leave the initial conflict unresolved, but may in addition set off a chain reaction of derivative conflicts" (pp. 382–383).

References

Albrecht, R., and T. R. Sarbin. "Contributions to Role-Taking Theory: Annoyability as a Function of the Self." Unpub. ms., 1952.

Baker, B. "Accuracy of Social Perceptions of Psychopathic and Non-psychopathic Prison Inmates." Unpub. ms., 1954.

Cameron, N., and A. Magaret. *Behavior Pathology.* Houghton Mifflin, 1951.

Getzels, J. W., and E. G. Guba. "Role, Role Conflict and Effectiveness: An Empirical Study." *American Sociological Review,* Vol. 19 (1954), 164–175.

Gough, H. G. "A Sociological Theory of Psychotherapy." *American Journal of Sociology,* Vol. 53 (1948), 359–366.

—— and D. R. Peterson. "The Identification and Measurement of Predispositional Factors in Crime and Delinquency." *Journal of Consulting Psychology,* Vol. 16 (1952), 207–212.

Gross, N., W. Mason, and A. W. McEachern. *Explorations in Role Analysis: Studies of the School Superintendency Role.* Wiley, 1958.

Jacobson, E., W. W. Charters, Jr., and S. Lieberman. "The Use of the Role Concept in the Study of Complex Organization." *Journal of Social Issues,* Vol. 7 (1951), 18–27.

Kahn, R. L., D. M. Wolfe, R. P. Quinn, J. D. Snoek, and R. A. Rosenthal. *Organizational Stress: Studies in Role Conflict and Ambiguity.* Wiley, 1964.

Lieberman, S. "The Effects of Changes in Roles on the Attitudes of Role Occupants." *Human Relations,* Vol. 9 (1956), 385–402.

Likert, R. *New Patterns of Management.* McGraw-Hill, 1961.

Merton, R. K. *Social Theory and Social Structure,* rev. ed. Free Press, 1957.

Rommetveit, R. *Social Norms and Roles.* University of Minnesota Press, 1955.

Sarbin, T. R., and C. Hardyck. "Contributions to Role-Taking Theory: Role Perception on the Basis of Postural Cues." Unpub. ms., 1953.

—— and B. G. Rosenberg. "Contributions to Role-Taking Theory: IV A Method for a Qualitative Analysis of the Self." *Journal of Social Psychology,* Vol. 42 (1955), 71–82.

—— and R. W. Stephenson. "Contributions to Role-Taking Theory: IV Authoritarian Attitudes and Role-Taking Skill." Unpub. ms., 1952.

—— and J. D. Williams. "Contributions to Role-Taking Theory: V Role Perception on the Basis of Limited Auditory Stimuli." Unpub. ms., 1953.

Stouffer, S. A., et al. *The American Soldier.* Princeton University Press, 1949.

—— and J. Toby. "Role Conflict and Personality." *American Journal of Sociology,* Vol. 56 (1951), 395–406.

Tannenbaum, A. S. "Personality Change as a Result of an Experimental Change of Environmental Conditions." *Journal of Abnormal and Social Psychology,* Vol. 55 (1957), 404–406.

Incompatibility and Instability in Organizational Evaluation and Authority

W. RICHARD SCOTT, SANFORD M. DORNBUSCH,
BRUCE C. BUSCHING, JAMES D. LAING

Incompatibility of Authority Systems

Given that participants attach some importance to the evaluations made of their performance by evaluators who influence the distribution of organizational

"Organizational Evaluation and Authority (Incompatibility and Instability)," by W. R. Scott, S. M. Dornbusch, Bruce C. Busching, and James D. Laing, from *Administrative Science Quarterly,* Vol. 12, No. 1 (June 1967), pp. 105–116. Reprinted by permission of the authors and the *Administrative Science Quarterly.*

sanctions, we make the important assumption that the participant will attempt to maintain, i.e., both achieve in the present and insure for the future, evaluations of his performance at a level which is satisfactory to him.[1] The minimal level of a performance evaluation for a given task which is satisfactory to a participant is the participant's *acceptance level* with regard to that evaluation. The acceptance level for an individual may change over time and may differ among participants; some may be satisfied with a rating of "fair," while others are satisfied only with "excellent." Moreover, the level of evaluation that is satisfactory to the participant being evaluated may not be the same level that satisfies the evaluator. Some participants may have higher expectations for themselves than their evaluators, whereas others may be satisfied with low evaluations even though their evaluators are dissatisfied.

An authority system is here called *incompatible* if it prevents the participant from maintaining his evaluations at or above his acceptance level and *compatible* if it does not prevent the participant from maintaining evaluations of his performance at his acceptance level. Thus, an authority system is incompatible if the set of exercised rights is either incomplete or contains elements that conflict in a way which causes the system to prevent the participant from maintaining his evaluations at a level satisfactory to him. Systems may also be ranked by degrees of incompatibility. In general, the more frequently incompatibilities occur for the participant, and the more important to him are the evaluations that cannot be maintained at a level acceptable to him, the greater is the incompatibility of the authority system.

If a given authority system is structural, then the structure may be compatible for some occupants of the position and incompatible for others because, as noted, individuals may have different acceptance levels. For instance, a structure that prevents maintenance of evaluations at the level of "excellent," but allows maintenance at the level of "good" is incompatible only for individuals with a very high acceptance level, thus perhaps being incompatible for only a few occupants of the structure. An authority structure is incompatible to the extent that occupants of its focal position are subjected to incompatibility.

Sources of Incompatibility

Four sources of incompatibility are identified: (*1*) contradictory evaluations, (*2*) uncontrollable evaluations, (*3*) unpredictable evaluations, and (*4*) unattainable evaluations. These four sources are expressed as four types of incompatibility.

Type I: Contradictory Evaluations

An authority system is incompatible if it places the participant in a situation in which the receipt of one performance evaluation at least equal to his acceptance level necessarily entails the receipt of another performance evaluation below his acceptance level.

This type of incompatibility is produced by a contradiction between the evaluations of two different evaluators, or the inconsistency of two different evaluations by a single evaluator. The participant finds that doing the kind of work required to receive one evaluation high enough to satisfy him necessarily involves incurring another evaluation so low as to make him dissatisfied. This problem may occur during the evaluation of a single task or of two or more tasks. An individual may be negatively evaluated for not working fast enough; yet if he were to increase his speed, he would be negatively evaluated for not working carefully enough. Or, evaluators may expect a participant to perform mutually exclusive tasks simultaneously.

This type of incompatibility may also occur when an individual receives evaluations both on his performance leading to an outcome and on the outcome itself. In this case, the contradiction may occur between the kind of performances allowed and the kinds of outcomes expected. Such a contradiction frequently occurs when a participant is allocated a task by directive but evaluated on the basis of a sample of outcomes. An appraiser may expect results that are impossible to achieve by following the particular course the allocator has directed. For this reason, a participant who receives allocations by directive is more likely to be subjected to incompatibility of this type if outcomes of his performance are sampled rather than the performance itself. The more routine the task, the more likely that criteria-setters will understand and agree on what can be expected of participants, and also the easier it is for the sampler to decide on samples that are representative; thus, the probability of this type of incompatibility is reduced with more routine tasks.

Complexity of the system also increases the probability of this type of incompatibility. The more differentiated the authority system, i.e., the greater the extent to which each of the rights are separately held, and the greater the number of participants exercising rights in the system, the greater the chance of failure in coordination.[2] For example, different allocators may allocate conflicting tasks to a participant. If this conflict is not considered by the evaluators, the participant may not be able to avoid receiving an evaluation below his acceptance level.

Type II: Uncontrollable Evaluations

An authority system is incompatible if it places the participant in a situation in which he receives evaluations below his acceptance level for performances or outcomes he does not control.

This type of incompatibility occurs when the outcomes that serve as a basis for the evaluation of a participant are not a regular function of that participant's performances from task to task. Therefore, to the extent that these uncontrollable outcomes are used as a basis for the evaluation of the participant's performance, he will be unable to control his evaluations through his performance. If this lack of control results in the participant receiving evaluations below his acceptance level, an incompatibility results.

The most obvious and simple instance of this failure occurs when an unsatisfactory performance or outcome is noted and the evaluation is wrongly assigned to a participant who neither performed the task nor had authority rights over the participant who did. (A nurse's aide may be negatively evaluated for mistakes committed by an orderly.)

Interdependence may be another source of this type of incompatibility. *Interdependence* is present when more than one participant contributes to a common outcome, which is used as the basis for evaluation. If evaluated outcomes are produced interdependently, they may not be related to a particular participant's performance; therefore, that participant may not be able to maintain his evaluation at his acceptance level because he cannot control the outcomes on which it is based. A competent decision maker may be prevented from maintaining evaluations satisfactory to him because of incompetent implementation of his decisions by others over whom he lacks authority rights. (An automobile designer is negatively evaluated for the poor appearance of the automobile, which is, actually, the result of inferior workmanship.) Conversely, a participant who implements another's faulty decision may be blamed incorrectly for an unsatisfactory outcome. (The workmanship is blamed for poor appearance, although the design is at fault.) Interdependence does not produce incompatibility if the participant has sufficient authority rights over the other contributors to control their common outcome; or if the performance of others is of such quality that the participant is not prevented from maintaining evaluations satisfactory to him. Given interdependence, the probability of this type of incompatibility increases to the extent that evaluations are based on outcomes rather than performance, particularly for those participants who have no rights over those with whom they are interdependent.

Attributes of the task may also produce this type of incompatibility. All tasks may be considered to involve the overcoming of some type of resistance. The resistance may be offered by nature, or by another person or a group. (A problem must be solved. A tunnel must be dug through rock. A company must produce a better product than its competitors.) If the resistance to a given task is known to be relatively constant from performance to performance, then the task is said to be *inert*. (A mile is to be run along the school track. Bills are posted in a ledger.) If the resistance is known to vary from performance to performance, then that task is considered to be *active*. (The general must capture a city. An election must be won.)

To evaluate the outcome of a task, the evaluator might employ standards that criteria-setters have determined by examining outcomes achieved by other performers on similar tasks. In the case of inert tasks, a valid inference to the quality of the performance can be made directly from comparisons of the outcome achieved relative to outcomes obtained by others on similar tasks. Active tasks, however, are difficult to evaluate, because the variability of the resistance complicates the problem of inferring the quality of performance from the nature of the outcome.[3] The outcome of a good performance need not be success and often is failure. (The patient may die, even though the operation was performed well.)

Active tasks fall into two categories, based upon the degree of knowledge about the resistance to be overcome. First, even though the resistance is variable, it is sometimes possible to have specific knowledge about it for a particular task performance. (The strength of the opposition meeting the general in a given battle is known. A tunnel is dug through strata of known composition.) The evaluation of each task performance can thus validly be based on the assessment of the outcome, if one also considers the resistance encountered in that particular task. Secondly, if the resistance encountered in a single performance is unknown, there may yet be some knowledge of the distribution of resistance over a succession of performances. This knowledge permits appraisers to take a probabilistic approach to the evaluations of these active tasks. The proportion of successful outcomes can be compared to the results of other performances under like circumstances. (The death rate for all premature babies provides a valid measure of the performance of a pediatrics unit, but only if the sample and comparison group do not differ in the assignment of difficult cases.)

Thus, given active tasks, the probability of this type of incompatibility increases to the extent that evaluations are based on outcomes rather than on performances, unless the resistance is considered, or probabilistic interpretations are made. Professionals employed by organizations are usually allocated more active tasks than are nonprofessionals. The professional, therefore, seeks direct measures of the quality of performance; or, if results are used, he demands probabilistic approaches to comparable outcomes.[4]

Type III: Unpredictable Evaluations

An authority system is incompatible if it places the participant in a situation in which he receives evaluations below his acceptance level because he is unable to predict the relationship between attributes of his performance and the quality of the evaluation.

This type of incompatibility occurs when the participant has insufficient or incorrect information about the properties, weights, and standards by which he is evaluated, and therefore is unable to adjust his performance to maintain evaluations at his acceptance level. Those being evaluated need not, of course, know all the details of the evaluation process, but only enough to be sufficiently able to predict evaluations from their performance so that they can make the adjustments in their behavior necessary to produce acceptable evaluations. Occupants of a position acting upon false information about the criteria used in their evaluation is an extreme instance of this type of incompatibility. (University faculty may be told and may act on the belief that community service, teaching, and research are all taken into account in the evaluations made of them, when, in practice, community service is not considered at all.) All those conditions which impede communication between the participant and his evaluators tend to increase the probability of this type of incompatibility.

Unpredictable evaluations may also be produced by an irregular relationship between the participant's performance and the evaluations he receives. To the extent that the sampler takes samples which are not representative of performance, the relationship between a performance and the evaluation of that performance will be irregular. Thus, those organizational conditions which increase the probability of unrepresentative samples also increase the probability of this type of incompatibility; therefore, the more frequently a participant's performance is sampled, the less the probability of this type of incompatibility.

Type IV: Unattainable Evaluations

An authority system is incompatible if it places the participant in a situation in which the standards used to evaluate him are so high that he cannot achieve evaluations at his acceptance level.

This type of incompatibility results when the participant lacks the facilities necessary to perform at a level that criteria-setters require if he is to achieve evaluations at his acceptance level; therefore, no matter how hard he tries, he cannot achieve evaluations acceptable to him. Facilities may consist of a certain level of skill or training (if a worker new to a job were expected to perform at the same level as more experienced workers, he would be subject to an incompatibility of this type) or physical equipment, such as tools. Facilities may also consist of authority rights themselves. If a participant is evaluated on his ability to control the performance of others, he must have sufficient rights and sufficient authorization to achieve the control; otherwise he may find it impossible to achieve the degree of control necessary to maintain evaluations at his acceptance level. (A university departmental chairman may be expected to ensure good teaching, but may lack important rights, such as the sampling right, over his faculty.) Thus, for a participant who is evaluated for his control over another, the greater the number of authority rights and the greater the degree of authorization of those rights, the less the chance of this type of incompatibility.

This type of incompatibility also may occur because the criteria setter has inadequate information about the task to select attainable standards. This is likely to occur if a task has been newly developed and if tasks similar to it have not been performed often enough to allow criteria setters to know what levels of performance can reasonably be expected. The variability of resistance encountered in performing an active task poses special problems to the criteria setter. If it is not possible to learn the nature of the resistance which occurred in a given performance of an active task, then it is necessary for the criteria setter to select standards on the basis of the frequency distribution of outcomes generated by past performances of the task in similar contexts. If such a comparison population is not available or is too small, then the criteria setter lacks information necessary for the selection of reasonable standards.

Incompatibility Produces Instability

Instability refers to the state of a system. A system is said to be *unstable* to the extent that it contains internal pressure for change. Highly unstable systems are, in short, in an "explosive" state and, as such, are highly susceptible to change. Stable systems do not contain internal pressures for change and, therefore, will change only as a result of external pressure.

We have assumed that participants will attempt to maintain their evaluations at or above their acceptance levels and have identified four ways in which an authority system can be incompatible with the focal participant's ability to succeed in this attempt. Participants so thwarted can be expected to be dissatisfied with the system and, therefore, are likely to engage in coping responses in an attempt to resolve the incompatibility. Some of these reactions to incompatibility represent internal pressures for change within the system. Thus the central proposition of the theory is that incompatible authority systems are unstable. The theory does not state that compatible systems are necessarily stable, for there are many other factors that may lead to system instability. For this reason, the theory cannot be advanced as a general explanation of the instability of authority systems; incompatibility is considered to be a sufficient but not necessary condition for instability.[5]

The instability of an authority system may become evident in various ways. The responses by the focal participant can be used to indicate pressures for change in the system; that is, as indices of instability. It is assumed that the set represents a sufficient variety of indices so that if a system is unstable, the instability will be indicated by the regular occurrence of at least one of them.

The indices are: dissatisfaction with some component of the system or with the system as a whole, expression of dissatisfaction with the system to others in the organization, suggestion to others in the organization that the system be changed, and noncompliance with the exercise of any authority right as a consequence of dissatisfaction with the system.

The interrelation of these indices is complex. If instability is indicated by one index, the probability of its being indicated by another may be changed. (The use of suggestions by the participant may reduce his use of noncompliance as a vehicle for effecting change in the system.) But aside from this interrelationship, it is expected that the greater the instability, the greater is the probability that each index is present and the greater its intensity. Thus, we make the empirical prediction that the greater the incompatibility of an authority system, the more likely participants are to be dissatisfied, and to express dissatisfaction, suggest changes, and fail to comply with the exercise of authority rights, and the more intense these responses will be.

There are a number of factors which influence the instability produced by incompatibility. One set of factors influences the form which instability will take in a particular system. For example, it is expected that occupants of positions with relatively high status in the organization will be more likely to respond to incompatibility by suggesting redefinition of the system components than will occupants of positions lower in status. Similarly, the absence of institutionalized mechanisms of appeal reduces the probability of suggestions for change. A second set of factors influences the amount of instability produced by incompatibility. For example, we expect there to be a "compositional effect"[6] in groups in which a large number of participants are subject to incompatibility. If a participant interacts with others who are subjected to incompatibility in systems similar to his own, he may begin to perceive a threat to his own ability to continue to maintain his evaluations above his acceptance level. Even though he is not thwarted by his system now, he comes to believe that he may be thwarted in the future, and is likely to begin reacting against his system. Also, in attempting to change his system, a participant subjected to incompatibility may succeed in enlisting the aid of others who are not themselves so subjected. Such compositional effects amplify the instability produced by a given amount of incompatibility.

Resolution of Incompatibility

The instability resulting from incompatibility can be expected to persist until the incompatibility is resolved. One resolution is for the participant to leave the system, either by moving to another system or by leaving the organization altogether, as would be indicated by high turnover rates. Another resolution is for him to reduce his acceptance level to that which can be maintained in the authority system as it is presently constituted. An incompatibility that produces an evaluation of "poor" may be resolved by the participant's reducing his acceptance level sufficiently that an evaluation of "poor" is satisfactory to him.

We are particularly interested in the resolution process which is activated by incompatibility when the participant neither leaves the organization nor lowers his acceptance level. In this case, resolution can be achieved only by reorganizing the system, either by changing the existing authorization or by changing the exercise of one or more of the existing rights. Thus, the theory would predict that newly emerging systems, and existing systems in which incompatibilities develop, continue to search through various distributions of regularly exercised rights until a compatible system is achieved.

This process is influenced by variables which affect the degree to which attempts to reorganize will be successful. For example, incompatible authority systems which are perceived as legitimate are expected to be less likely to provoke attack and to be more resistant to attacks that do occur than are systems perceived as illegitimate. It is also expected, however, that incompatible systems are more likely to become illegitimate than are compatible systems, therefore becoming more subject to attack and less resistant to change. The probability of success in attempts to change the authority system is also related to the degree to which the tactics utilized by participants succeed in causing others in the system to be subjected to incompatibility. If a participant resorts to noncompliance to resolve his own incompatibility, he places his superiors in an incompatible position to the extent that this noncompliance causes them to receive evaluations below their acceptance levels. These superiors can be expected to be more hospitable to negotiations aimed at reorganizing the authority system. In the final analysis, it may be possible to argue that, in an authority system which endangers one man's evaluations, no man is safe.

Notes and References

1. Alternative motivational assumptions could be considered in a similar theoretical framework. The participant's desire to have his evaluations be *appropriate*, i.e., accurately reflect the skill and effort he invests in his task performance, is an assumption which may be added in future formulations.
2. This reasoning provides a rationale for the unity of command principle of the traditional school of administrative management; type II and IV incompatibilities are relevant to the traditional responsibility and control principle.
3. Under type IV incompatibility, the effect of active tasks upon the setting of standards will be considered.
4. Everett C. Hughes has noted the probabilistic orientation of professionals in *Men and Their Work* (Glencoe, Ill.: The Free Press, 1958), p. 91.
5. It should also be clear that we are not studying effectiveness. Our empirical studies may uncover some degree of association between effectiveness, incompatibility, and instability, but effectiveness or productivity are not variables in the current theory. Indeed, a more effective structure may permit and encourage a higher level of certain behaviors indicative of instability, such as expression of dissatisfaction or suggestion of changes.
6. James A. Davis, Joe L. Spaeth, and Carolyn Huson, "A Technique for Analyzing the Effects of Group Composition," *American Sociological Review,* 26 (1961), 215–225. See also Peter M. Blau, "Structural Effects," *American Sociological Review,* 25 (1960), 178–193; P. M. Blau and W. Richard Scott, *Formal Organizations: A Comparative Approach* (San Francisco: Chandler, 1962), p. 101; and Paul F. Lazarsfeld and Herbert Menzel, "On the Relation between Individual and Collective Properties," in Amitai Etzioni (ed.), *Complex Organizations: A Sociological Reader* (New York: Holt, Rinehart, and Winston, 1961), chap. 16.

Power and Politics in Organizational Life

ABRAHAM ZALEZNIK

There are few business activities more prone to a credibility gap than the way in which executives approach organizational life. A sense of disbelief occurs when managers purport to make decisions in rationalistic terms while most observers and participants know that personalities and politics play a significant if not an overriding role. Where does the error lie? In the theory which insists that decisions should be rationalistic and nonpersonal? Or in the practice which treats business organizations as political structures?

Whatever else organizations may be (problem-solving instruments, socio-technical systems, reward systems, and so on), they are political structures. This means that organizations operate by distributing authority and setting a stage for the exercise of power. It is no wonder, therefore, that individuals who are highly motivated to secure and use power find a familiar and hospitable environment in business.

At the same time, executives are reluctant to acknowledge the place of power both in individual motivation and in organizational relationships. Somehow, power and politics are dirty words. And in linking these words to the play of personalities in organizations, some managers withdraw into the safety of organizational logics.

As I shall suggest in this article, frank recognition of the importance of personality factors and a sensitive use of the strengths and limitations of people in decisions on power distributions can improve the quality of organizational life.

Political Pyramid

Organizations provide a power base for individuals. From a purely economic standpoint, organizations exist to create a surplus of income over costs by meeting needs in the marketplace. But organizations also are political structures which provide opportunities for people to develop careers and therefore provide platforms for the expression of individual interests and motives. The development of careers, particularly at high managerial and professional levels, depends on accumulation of power as the vehicle for transforming individual interests into activities which influence other people.

Scarcity and Competition

A political pyramid exists when people compete for power in an economy of scarcity. In other words, people cannot get the power they want just for the asking. Instead, they have to enter into the decisions on how to distribute authority in a particular formal organization structure. Scarcity of power arises under two sets of conditions:

1. Where individuals gain power in absolute terms at someone else's expense.
2. Where there is a gain comparatively—not literally at someone else's expense—resulting in a relative shift in the distribution of power.

In either case, the psychology of scarcity and comparison takes over. The human being tends to make comparisons as a basis for his sense of self-esteem. He may compare himself with other people and decide that his absolute loss or the shift in proportional shares of authority reflects an attrition in his power base. He may also compare his position relative to others against a personal standard and feel a sense of loss. This tendency to compare is deeply ingrained in people, especially since they experience early in life the effects of comparisons in the family where—in an absolute sense—time and attention, if not love and affection, go to the most dependent member.

Corporate acquisitions and mergers illustrate the effects of both types of comparisons. In the case of one merger, the president of the acquired company resigned rather than accept the relative displacement in rank which occurred when he no longer could act as a chief executive officer. Two vice presidents vied for the position of executive vice president. Because of their conflicting ambitions, the expedient of making them equals drove the competition underground, but not for long. The vice president with the weaker power base soon resigned in the face of his inability to consolidate a workable definition of his responsibilities. His departure resulted in increased power for the remaining vice president and the gradual elimination of "rival camps" which had been covertly identified with the main contenders for power.

The fact that organizations are pyramids produces a scarcity of positions the higher one moves in the hierarchy. This scarcity, coupled with inequalities, certainly needs to be recognized. While it may be humane and socially desirable to say that people are different rather than unequal in their potential, nevertheless executive talent is in short supply. The end result should be to move the more able people into the top positions and to accord them the pay, responsibility, and authority to match their potential.

On the other side, the strong desires of equally able people for the few top positions available means that someone will either have to face the realization of unfulfilled ambition or have to shift his interest to another organization.[1]

Constituents and Clients

Besides the conditions of scarcity and competition, politics in organizations grows out of the existence of constituencies. A superior may be content himself with shifts in the allocation of resources and consequently power, but he represents subordinates who, for their own reasons, may be unhappy with the changes. These subordinates affirm and support their boss. They can also withdraw affirmation and support, and consequently isolate the superior with all the painful consequences this entails.

While appointments to positions come from above, affirmation of position comes from below. The only difference between party and organizational politics is in the subtlety of the voting procedure. Consider:

In a large consumer products corporation, one division received almost no capital funds for expansion while another division, which had developed a new marketing approach for products common to both, expanded dramatically. The head of the static division found his power diminished considerably, as reflected in how seriously his subordinates took his efforts at influence (e.g., in programs to increase the profit return from existing volume).

He initiated one program after another with little support from subordinates because he could not make a claim for capital funds. The flow of capital funds in this corporation provided a measure of power gains and losses in both an absolute and a relative sense.

Power and Action

Still another factor which heightens the competition for power that is characteristic of all political structures is the incessant need to use whatever power one possesses. Corporations have an implicit "banking" system in power transactions. The initial "capitalization" which makes up an individual's power base consists of three elements:

1. The quantity of formal authority vested in his position relative to other positions.

2. The authority vested in his expertise and reputation for competence (a factor weighted by how important the expertise is for the growth areas of the corporation as against the historically stable areas of its business).

3. The attractiveness of his personality to others (a combination of respect for him as well as liking, although these two sources of attraction are often in conflict).

This capitalization of power reflects the total esteem with which others regard the individual. By a process which is still not too clear, the individual internalizes all of the sources of power capital in a manner parallel to the way he develops a sense of self-esteem. The individual knows he has power, assesses it realistically, and is willing to risk his personal esteem to influence others.

A critical element here is the risk in the uses of power. The individual must perform *and* get results. If he fails to do either, an attrition occurs in his power base in direct proportion to the doubts other people entertained in their earlier appraisals of him.

What occurs here is an erosion of confidence which ultimately leads the individual to doubt himself and undermines the psychological work which led him in the first place to internalize authority as a prelude to action. (While, as I have suggested, the psychological work that an individual goes through to consolidate his esteem capital is a crucial aspect of power relations, I shall have to reserve careful examination of this problem until a later date. The objective now is to examine from a political framework the problems of organizational life.)

What distinguishes alterations in the authority structure from other types of organizational change is their direct confrontation with the political character of corporate life. Such confrontations are real manipulations of power as compared with the indirect approaches which play on ideologies and attitudes. In the first case, the potency and reality of shifts in authority have an instantaneous effect on what people do, how they interact, and how they think about themselves. In the second case, the shifts in attitude are often based on the willingness of people to respond the way authority figures want them to; ordinarily, however, these shifts in attitude are but temporary expressions of compliance.

One of the most common errors executives make is to confuse compliance with commitment. Compliance is an attitude of acceptance when a directive from an authority figure asks for a change in an individual's position, activities, or ideas. The individual complies or "goes along" usually because he is indifferent to the scope of the directive and the changes it proposes. If compliance occurs out of indifference, then one can predict little difficulty in translating the intent of directives into actual implementation.[2]

Commitment, on the other hand, represents a strong motivation on the part of an individual to adopt or resist the intent of a directive. If the individual commits himself to a change, then he will use his ingenuity to interpret and implement the change in such a way as to assure its success. If he decides to fight or block the change, the individual may act as if he complies but reserve other times and places to negate the effects of directives. For example:

In one large company, the top management met regularly for purposes of organizational planning. The executives responsible for implementing planning decisions could usually be counted on to carry them out when they had fought hard and openly in the course of reaching such decisions. When they seemed to accept a decision, giving all signs of compliance, the decision usually ended up as a notation in the minutes. Surface compliance occurred most frequently when problems involved loyalties to subordinates.

In one instance, a division head agreed to accept a highly regarded executive from another division to meet a serious manpower shortage in his organization. When the time came to effect the transfer, however, this division general manager refused, with some justification, on the grounds that bringing someone in from outside would demoralize his staff. He used compliance initially to respond to the problem of "family" loyalties to which he felt committed. Needless to say, the existence of these loyalties was the major problem to be faced in carrying out organizational planning.

Compliance as a tactic to avoid changes and commitment as an expression of strong motivation in dealing with organizational problems are in turn related to how individuals define their interests. In the power relations among executives, the so-called areas of common interest are usually reserved for the banalities of human relationships. The more significant areas of attention usually force conflicts of interest, especially competition for power, to the surface.

Interest Conflicts

Organizations demand, on the one hand, cooperative endeavor and commitment to common purposes. The realities of experience in organizations, on the other hand, show that conflicts of interest exist among people who ultimately share a common fate and are supposed to work together. What makes business more political and less ideological and rationalistic is the overriding importance of conflicts of interest.

If an individual (or group) is told that his job scope is reduced in either absolute or proportional terms for *the good of the corporation,* he faces a conflict. Should he acquiesce for the idea of common good or fight in the service of his self-interest? Any rational man will fight (how constructively depends on the absence of neurotic conflicts and on ego strength). His willingness to fight increases as he comes to realize the intangible nature of what people think is good for the organization. And, in point of fact, his willingness may serve the interests of corporate purpose by highlighting issues and stimulating careful thinking before the reaching of final decisions.

Secondary Effects

Conflicts of interest in the competition for resources are easily recognized, as for example, in capital budgeting or in allocating money for research and development. But these conflicts can be subjected to bargaining procedures which all parties to the competition validate by their participation.

The secondary effects of bargaining do involve organizational and power issues. However, the fact that these power issues *follow* debate on economic problems rather than *lead* it creates a manifest content which can be objectified much more readily than in areas where the primary considerations are the distributions of authority.

In such cases, which include developing a new formal organization structure, management succession, promotions, corporate mergers, and entry of new executives, the conflicts of interest are severe and direct simply because there are no objective measures of right or wrong courses of action. The critical question which has to be answered in specific actions is: Who gets power and position? This involves particular people with their strengths and weaknesses and a specific historical context in which actions are understood in symbolic as well as rational terms. To illustrate:

A large corporation, General Motors in fact, inadvertently confirmed what every seasoned executive knows: that coalitions of power to overcome feelings of rivalry and the play of personal ambitions are fragile solutions. The appointment of Edward Cole to the presidency followed by Semon Knudsen's resignation shattered the illusion that the rational processes in business stand apart or even dominate the human emotions and ties that bind men to one another. If any corporation prides itself on rationality, General Motors is it. To have to experience so publicly the inference that major corporate life, particularly at the executive levels, is not so rational after all, can be damaging to the sense of security people get from belief in an idea as it is embodied in a corporate image.

The fact that Knudsen subsequently was discharged from the presidency of Ford (an event I shall discuss later in this article) suggests that personalities and the politics of corporations are less aberrations and more conditions of life in large organizations.

But just as General Motors wants to maintain an image, many executives prefer to ignore what this illustration suggests: that organizations are political structures which feed on the psychology of comparison. To know something about the psychology of comparison takes us into the theory of self-esteem in both its conscious manifestations and its unconscious origins. Besides possibly enlightening us in general and giving a more realistic picture of people and organizations, there are some practical benefits in such knowledge. These benefits include:

Increased freedom to act more directly; instead of trying to "get around" a problem, one can meet it.

Greater objectivity about people's strengths and limitations, and, therefore, the ability to use them more honestly as well as effectively.

More effective planning in organizational design and in distribution of authority; instead of searching for the "one best solution" in organization structure, one accepts a range of alternatives and then gives priority to the personal or emotional concerns that inhibit action.

Power Relations

Organizational life within a political frame is a series of contradictions. It is an exercise in rationality, but its energy comes from the ideas in the minds of power figures the content of which, as well as their origins, are only dimly perceived. It deals with sources of authority and their distribution; yet it depends in the first place on the existence of a balance of power in the hands of an individual who initiates actions and gets results. It has many rituals associated with it, such as participation, democratization, and the sharing of power; yet the real outcome is the consolidation of power around a central figure to whom other individuals make emotional attachments.

Faulty Coalitions

The formal organization structure implements a coalition among key executives. The forms differ, and the psychological significance of various coalitions also differs. But no organization can function without a consolidation of power in the relationship of a central figure with his select group. The coalition need not exist between the chief executive and his immediate subordinates or staff. It may indeed bypass the second level as in the case of Presidents of the United States who do not build confident relationships within their cabinets, but instead rely on members of the executive staff or on selected individuals outside the formal apparatus.

The failure to establish a coalition within the executive structure of an organization can result in severe problems, such as paralysis in the form of inability to make decisions and to evaluate performance, and in-fighting and overt rivalry within the executive group.

When a coalition fails to develop, the first place to look for causes is the chief executive and his problems in creating confident relationships. The causes are many and complex, but they usually hinge around the nature of the chief executive's defenses and what he needs to avoid as a means of alleviating stress. For example:

The "palace revolt," which led to Semon Knudsen's departure from Ford Motor Company, is an illustration of the failure in the formation of a coalition. While it is true that Henry Ford II named Knudsen president of the company, Knudsen's ultimate power as a newcomer to an established power structure depended on forming an alliance. The particular individual with whom an alliance seemed crucial was Lee Iacocca. For some reason, Knudsen and Iacocca competed for power and influence instead of using cooperatively a power base to which both contributed as is the case with most workable coalitions. In the absence of a coalition, the alternate postures of rivalry and battle for control erupted. Ford ultimately responded by weighing his power with one side over the other.

As I have indicated, it is not at all clear why in Knudsen's case the coalition failed to develop. But in any failure the place to look is in the personalities of the main actors and in the nature of their defenses which make certain coalitions improbable no matter how strongly other realities indicate their necessity.

But defensiveness on the part of a chief executive can also result in building an unrealistic and unworkable coalition, with the self-enforced isolation which is its consequence. One of the most frequently encountered defensive maneuvers which leads to the formation of unrealistic coalitions or to the isolation of the chief executive is the fear of rivalry.

A realistic coalition matches formal authority and competence with the emotional commitments necessary to establish and maintain the coalition. The fear of rivals on the part of chief executives, or the jealousy on the part of subordinates of the chief executive's power, can at the extreme result in paranoid distortions. People become suspicious of one another, and through selective perceptions and projections of their own fantasies create a world of plots and counterplots.

The displacement of personal concerns onto substantive material in decision making is potentially the most dangerous form of defensiveness. The need for defenses arises because people become anxious about the significance of evaluations within existing power coalitions. But perhaps even more basic is the fear and the rivalry to which all coalitions are susceptible given the nature of investments people make in power relations. While it is easy to dismiss emotional reactions like these as neurotic distortions, their prevalence and impact deserve careful attention in all phases of organizational life.

Unconscious Collusions

All individuals and consequently groups experience areas of stress which mobilize defenses. The fact that coalitions embody defensive maneuvers on those occasions where stress goes beyond the usual level of tolerance is not surprising. An even more serious problem, however, occurs when the main force that binds men in a structure is the need to defend against or to act out the conflicts which individuals cannot tolerate alone.

Where coalitions represent the aggregation of power with conscious intention of using the abilities of members for constructive purposes, collusions represent predominance of unconscious conflict and defensive behavior. In organizational life, the presence of collusions and their causes often becomes the knot which has to be unraveled before any changes can be implemented.

The collusion of latent interests among executives can become the central theme and sustaining force of an organization structure of top management. For a collusion to take hold, the conflicts of the "power figure" have to be communicated and sensed by others as an overriding need which seeks active expression in the form of a theme. The themes vary just as do the structures which make a collusion. Thus one common theme is the need to control; another is the need to be admired and idealized; and still another is the need to find a scapegoat to attack in response to frustrations in solving problems.

If people could hold on to and keep within themselves areas of personal conflict, there would be far fewer collusions in organizational life. But it is part of the human condition for conflicts and needs to take over life situations. As a result, we find numerous instances of collusions controlling the behavior of executives. To illustrate:

A multidivisional corporation found itself with a revolution on its hands. The president was sensitive to the opinions of a few outside board members representing important stockholder interests. He was so concerned that he would be criticized by these board members, he demanded from vice presidents full information on their activities and complete loyalty to him. Over a period of years, he moved divisional chief executives to corporate headquarters so he could assure himself of their loyalty. Other executives joined in to gratify the president's need for control and loyalty.

The result of this collusion, however, was to create a schism between headquarters and field operations. Some of the staff members in the field managed to inform the board members of the lack of attention to and understanding of field problems. Discontent grew to such an extent that the board placed the president on early retirement.

Subsequently, the new president, with the support of the board, decentralized authority and appointed new division heads who were to make their offices in divisional headquarters with full authority to manage their respective organizations. One of the lingering problems of the new president was to dissolve the collusion at headquarters without wholesale firing of vice presidents.

Just as power distributions are central to the tasks of organizational planning, so the conservation of power is often the underlying function of collusions. Thus:

A manufacturing vice president of a medium-sized company witnessed over a period of 15 years a procession of changes in top management and ownership. He had managed to retain his job because he made himself indispensable in the management of the factory.

To each new top management, he stressed the importance of "home rule" as a means of assuring loyalty and performance in the plant. He also tacitly encouraged each supervisor to go along with whatever cliques happened to form and dominate the shop floor.

However, over time a gradual loss of competitive position, coupled with open conflict among cliques in the form of union disputes, led to the dismissal of the vice president. None of his successors could reassert control over the shop, and the company eventually moved or liquidated many of the operations in this plant.

'Life Dramas'

Faulty coalitions and unconscious collusions, as I have illustrated, can result from the defensive needs of a chief executive. These needs, which often appear as a demand on others to bolster the self-esteem of the chief executive, are tolerated to a remarkable degree and persist for a long time before harmful effects become apparent to outside stockholders, bankers, or boards of directors which ultimately control the distributions of power in organizations. Occasionally, corporations undergo critical conflicts in organizational politics which cannot be ignored in the conscious deliberations which affect how power gets distributed or used.

Intertwined with the various expressions of power conflicts in organizations are three underlying "life dramas" deserving careful attention:

The *first* portrays stripping the powers of a *parental figure.*

The *second* portrays the predominance of *paranoid thinking,* where distortions of reality result from the surfacing of conflicts which formerly had been contained in collusions.

The *third* portrays a *ritualistic ceremonial* in which real power issues are submerged or isolated in compulsive behavior but at the cost of real problem solving and work.

Parental Figure

The chief executive in a business, along with the heads of states, religious bodies, and social movements, becomes an object for other people. The term "object" should be understood, in a psychological sense, as a person who is the recipient of strong emotional attachments from others. It is obvious that a chief executive is the *object* because he controls so many of the levers which ultimately direct the flow of rewards and punishments. But there is something to say beyond this obvious calculation of rewards and punishments as the basis for the emotional attachments between leader and led as *object* and *subject.*

Where a leader displays unusual attributes in his intuitive gifts, cultivated abilities, or deeper personal qualities, his fate as the *object* is governed by powerful emotions. I hesitate to use the word "charismatic" to describe such a leader, partially because it suggests a mystique but also because, in its reference to the "great" man as charismatic leader, it expands to superhuman proportions what really belongs to the psychology of everyday life.

What makes for strong emotional attachments is as much in the need of the *subject* as in the qualities of the *object.* In other words, the personalities of leaders take on proportions which meet what subordinates need and even demand. If leaders in fact respond with the special charisma that is often invested in them at the outset, then they are parties to a self-fulfilling prophecy. Of course, the qualities demanded have to be present in some nascent form ready to emerge as soon as the emotional currents become real in authority relationships.

The emotional attachments I am referring to usually contain mixtures of positive and negative feelings. If the current were only of one kind, such as either admiration or hostility, then the authority relationship would be simpler to describe as well as to manage. All too often, the way positive feelings blend into the negative sets off secondary currents of emotion which intensify the relationships.

On the one side, subordinates cannot help but have fantasies of what they would do if they held the No. 1 position. Such fantasies, besides providing fleeting pleasures and helping one to regulate his ambitions, also provide channels for imaginative and constructive approaches to solving problems. It is only a short step from imagining what one would do as chief executive to explaining to the real chief executive the ideas which have been distilled from this flight into fantasy. If the chief executive senses envy in back of the thoughts, he may become frightened and choke off ideas which can be used quite constructively.

Critical Episode

But suppose a situation arises where not one but several subordinates enjoy the same fantasy of being No. 1? Suppose also that subordinates feel deprived in their relationship with the chief executive? Suppose finally that facing the organization there are substantive problems which are more or less out of control. With these three conditions, and depending on the severity of the real problems besetting the enterprise, the stage is set for a collusion which, when acted out, becomes a critical episode of displacing the parental figure. To demonstrate:

In November 1967, the directors of the Interpublic Group, a $700 million complex in advertising and public relations, moved for the resignation of the leader and chief executive officer, Marion Harper, Jr. Briefly, Harper had managed over a period of 18 years to build the world's largest conglomerate in market services, advertising, and information on the base of a personally successful agency career. In expanding from this base, Harper made acquisitions, started new companies, and widened his orbit into international branches and companies.

As often happens, the innovator and creative person is careless in controlling what he has built so that financial problems become evident. In Harper's case, he appeared either unwilling or unable to recognize the seriousness of his financial problems and, in particular, the significance of allowing cash balances to go below the minimum required in agreements with lending institutions.

Harper seemed careless in another, even more telling, way. Instead of developing a strong coalition among his executive group, he relied on individual ties to him in which he clearly dominated the relationship. If any of the executives "crossed" him, Harper would exile the offender to one of the "remote" branches or place him on partial retirement.

When the financial problems became critical, the aggrieved executives who had once been dependent on Harper and then cast out, formed their own coalition, and managed to garner the votes necessary to, in effect, fire the head man. Although little information is available on the aftermath of this palace revolution, the new coalition had its own problems—which, one would reasonably judge, included contentions for power.

A cynic viewing this illustration of the demise of a parental figure could conclude that if one seeks to maintain power by dominance, then one had best go all the way. This means that to take some but not all of the power away from rebellious sons sets the stage for a cabal among the deprived. With a score to settle, they await only the right circumstances to move in and depose the aggressor.

While this cynical view has its own appeal, it ignores the deeper issues of why otherwise brilliant men fail to recognize the realistic needs for coalitions in the relationships of superior and subordinates. To answer this question, we would need to understand how powerful people operate with massive blind spots which limit vision and the ability to maneuver in the face of realistic problems.

The one purpose that coalitions serve is to guard against the effects of blind spots, since it is seldom the case that two people have identical limitations in their vision and ability to respond. The need to control and dominate in a personalistic sense is perhaps the most serious of all possible blind spots which can affect a chief executive, because he makes it difficult for people to help him, while creating grievances which sooner or later lead to attacks on him.

The unseating of a chief executive by a coalition of subordinates seldom reduces the emotional charge built up in the uncertain attachments to the ousted leader. A new head man has to emerge and establish a confident coalition. Until the contentions for power subside and the guilt reactions attached to deposing the leader dissolve, individuals remain vulnerable to their own blind spots and unconscious reactions to striving for power.

The references to a parental figure in the preceding discussion may appear to exaggerate the meaning of power conflicts. In whatever ways it exaggerates, it also condenses a variety of truths about coalitions among executives. The chief executive is the central *object* in a coalition because he occupies a position analogous to parents in the family. He is at the nucleus of a political structure whose prototype is the family in which jealousy, envy, love, and hate find original impetus and expression.

It would be a gross error to assume that in making an analogy between the family and formal organizations the parental role is strictly paternal. There are also characteristics of the mother figure in certain types of chief executives and combinations of mother-father in the formation of executive coalitions.

Chief executives can also suffer from depersonalization in their roles and as a result become emotionally cold and detached. The causes of depersonalization are complex but, in brief, have some connections to the narrow definitions of rationality which exclude the importance of emotions in guiding communication as well as thought.

For the purpose of interpreting how defensive styles affect the behavior of leaders, there is some truth to the suggestion that the neutrality and lack of warmth characteristic of some leaders is a result of an ingrained fear of becoming the *object* for other people—for to become the *object* arouses fears that subordinates will become envious and compete for power.

Paranoid Thinking

This is a form of distortion in ideas and perception to which all human beings are susceptible from time to time. For those individuals who are concerned in their work with the consolidation and uses of power, the experience with suspiciousness, the attribution of bad motives to others, jealousy, and anxiety (characteristics of paranoid thinking), may be more than a passing state of mind.

In fact, such ideas and fantasies may indeed be communicated to others and may even be the main force which binds men into collusions. Organizational life is particularly vulnerable to the effects of paranoid thinking because it stimulates comparisons while it evokes anticipations of added power or fears of diminished power.

To complicate matters even more and to suggest just how ambiguous organizational decisions become, there may be some truth and substance in back of the suspicions, distrust, and jealousies which enflame thinking. Personality conflicts do affect decisions in allocating authority and responsibility, and an individual may not be distorting at all to sense that he had been excluded or denied an ambition based on some undercurrents in his relationships with others. To call these sensitivities paranoid thinking may itself be a gross distortion. But no matter how real the events, the paranoid potential is still high as a fallout of organizational life.

Paranoid thinking goes beyond suspiciousness, distrust, and jealousy. It may take the form of grandiose ideas and overestimation of one's power and control. This form of distortion leads to swings in mood from elation to despair, from a sense of omnipotence to helplessness. Again, when acted out, the search for complete control produces the tragedies which the initial distortions attempt to overcome. The tragedy of Jimmy Hoffa is a good case in point. Consider:

From all indications, Hoffa performed brilliantly as president of the teamsters' union. He was a superb organizer and bargainer, and in many ways a highly moral and even prudish man. There is little evidence to support allegations that he used his office to enrich himself.

Hoffa's troubles stemmed from his angry reactions when he could not get his way in managing the union's pension fund and from his relations with the government. In overestimating his power, Hoffa fell victim to the illusion that no controls outside himself could channel his actions. At this writing, Hoffa is serving a sentence in Lewisburg Penitentiary, having been found guilty of tampering with a jury.

It is interesting to note that Hoffa's successor delegated considerable authority to regional officers, a step that removed him from direct comparisons with Hoffa and served to cement a coalition of top officers in the teamsters.

Executives, too, can be victims of their successes just as much as of their failures. If past successes lead to the false sense of omnipotence which goes unchecked in, say, the executive's control of the board of directors, then he and his organization become the victims of changing times and competitive pressures along with the weakening in perception and reasoning which often accompanies aging.

One could speculate with some reason that paranoid distortions are the direct result of senility and the inability to accept the fact of death. While intellectually aware of the inevitability of death, gifted executives can sometimes not accept emotionally the ultimate in the limitations of power. The disintegration of personality in the conflict between the head and the heart is what we come to recognize as the paranoid potential in all forms of our collective relations.

Ritualistic Ceremonial

Any collective experience, such as organizational life with its capacity for charging the atmosphere in the imagery of power conflicts, can fall victim to rigidities. The rigidities I have in mind consist mainly of the formation and elaboration of structures, procedures, and other ceremonials which create the illusion of solving problems but in reality only give people something to act on to discharge valuable energies.

The best example of a ritualistic approach to real problems is the ever-ready solution of bringing people together in a committee on the naive grounds that the exchange of ideas is bound to produce a solution. There are even fads and fashions to ritualism as in the sudden appearance of favorite words like "brainstorming" or "synergism."

It is not that bringing people together to discuss problems is bad. Instead, it is the naive faith which accompanies such proposals, ultimately deflecting attention from where it properly belongs. Thus:

In one research organization, professionals faced severe problems arising from personal jealousies as well as differences of opinion on the correct goals and content for the research program. Someone would periodically suggest that the problems could not be solved unless people came together, preferably for a weekend away from the job, to share ideas and really get down to the "nitty-gritty" of the problem. (It is interesting to note that no one ever defines the "nitty-gritty.") The group would indeed follow such suggestions and typically end the weekend with a feeling of euphoria brought on by considerable drinking and a sumptuous meal.

The most concrete proposal for action was in the idea that the basic problem stemmed from the organization's increased size so that people no longer knew one another and their work. The solution which appeared, only shortly to disappear, was to publish a laboratory newsletter that would keep people abreast of their colleagues' newest ideas.

In a more general vein, ritualism can be invoked to deal with any real or fancied danger, with uncertainty, ambivalent attitudes, or a sense of personal helplessness. Rituals are used even in the attempt to manipulate people. That power relations in organizations should become a fertile field for ritualism should not surprise anyone.

As I have tried to indicate, the problems of organizational life involve the dangers associated with losses of power; the uncertainties are legion especially in the recognition that there is no one best way to organize and distribute power, and yet any individual must make a commitment to some form of organization.

Ambivalent attitudes, such as the simultaneous experience of love and hate, are also associated with authority relationships, particularly in how superior-subordinate become the subject and object for the expression of dependency reactions. In addition, the sense of helplessness is particularly sensitized in the events which project gains and losses in power and status.

Finally, superior and subordinate in any power structure are constantly tempted to manipulate each other as a way of gaining control over one's environment, and the more so when there is a lack of confidence and credibility in the organization's efforts to solve problems in realistic ways.

The negative effects of ritualism are precisely in the expenditure of energy to carry out the rituals and also in the childlike expectation that the magic formulas of organizational life substitute for diagnosing and solving real problems. When the heads of organizations are unsure of the bases for the exercise of power and become defensive, the easy solution is to play for time by invoking rituals which may temporarily relieve anxiety.

Similarly, when executives fail to understand the structure and potential of the power coalitions they establish (either consciously or unconsciously), they increasingly rely on rituals to deflect attention away from their responsibilities. And, when leaders are timid men incapable of initiating or responding, the spontaneous reaction is to use people to act out rituals. Usually, the content and symbolism in the rituals provide important clues about the underlying defensiveness of the executive.

Obsessional Leaders   The gravitational pull to ceremonials and magic is irresistible. In positions of power, obsessional leaders use in their public performances the mechanisms of defense which originate in their private conflicts. These defenses include hyper-rationality, the isolation of thought and feeling, reactive behavior in turning anger into moral righteousness, and passive control of other people as well as their own thought processes.

Very frequently, particularly in this day and age of psychologizing conflict, obsessive leaders "get religion" and try to convert others into some new state of mind. The use of sensitivity training with its attachment to "openness" and "leveling" in power relations seems to be the current favorite.

What these leaders do not readily understand is the fallacy of imposing a total solution for the problem of power relations where reality dictates at best the possibility of only partial and transient solutions. To force openness through the use of group pressure in T-groups and to expect to sustain this pressure in everyday life is to be supremely ritualistic. People intelligently resist saying everything they think to other people because they somehow have a deep recognition that this route leads to becoming overextended emotionally and, ultimately, to sadistic relationships.

Intelligent Uses of Power   The choice fortunately is not between ritualistic civility and naive openness in human relationships, particularly where power is concerned. In between is the choice of defining those partial problems which can be solved and through which bright people can learn something about the intelligent uses of power.

We should not lose sight of the basic lesson that people in positions of power differ from "ordinary" human beings mainly in their capacity to impose their personal defenses onto the stage of corporate life. Fortunately, the relationships are susceptible to intelligent management, and it is to the nature of this intelligence that I wish to address the conclusion of this article.

Coming Full Circle

The main job of organizational life, whether it concerns developing a new political pyramid, making new appointments to executive positions, or undergoing management succession at top levels, is to bring talented individuals into location for the legitimate uses of power. This is bound to be a highly charged event in corporate relationships because of the real changes in power distributions and the emotional reactions people experience along with the incremental gains and losses of power.

The demand, on the one hand, is for objectivity in assessing people and needs (as opposed to pseudorationality and rationalizing). This objectivity, on the other hand, has to be salvaged from the impact of psychological stresses which impel people to act out fantasies associated with power conflicts. The stresses of change in power relations tend to increase defensiveness to which counterreactions of rationalizing and of myth-making serve no enduring purpose except perhaps to drive underground the concerns which make people react defensively in the first place.

Stylistic Biases

Thought and action in the politics of organizational life are subject to the two kinds of errors commonly found in practical life: the errors of omission and those of commission. It is both what people do and what they neglect to do that result in the negative effects of action outweighing the positive. But besides the specific errors of omission and commission (the tactical aspects of action), there are also the more strategic aspects which have to be evaluated. The strategic aspects deal both with the corporate aims and objectives and with the style of the leaders who initiate change.

In general, leaders approach change with certain stylistic biases over which they may not have too much control. There is a preferred approach to power problems which derives from the personality of the leader and his defenses as well as from the realities of the situation. Of particular importance as stylistic biases are the preferences for partial, as contrasted with total, approaches and the preferences for substance over form.

Partial vs. Total   The partial approaches attempt to define and segregate problems which become amenable to solution by directive, negotiation, consensus, and compromise.

The total approaches usually escalate the issues in power relations so that implicitly people act as though it were necessary to undergo major conversions. The conversions can be directed toward personality structure, ideals, and beliefs, or toward values which are themselves connected to important aspects of personal experience.

When conversions become the end products of change, then one usually finds the sensitization of concerns over such matters as who dominates and who submits, who controls and who is being controlled, who is accepted and who is rejected. The aftermath of these concerns is the heightening of fantasy and defense at the expense of reality.

It may come as something of a disappointment to readers who are favorably disposed to psychology to consider the possibility that while organizations do have an impact on the attitudes of their constituent members, they cannot change personality structures or carry out therapeutic procedures. People may become more effective while working in certain kinds of organizations, but only when effectiveness is not dependent on the solution of neurotic conflict.

The advocates of total approaches seem to miss this point in their eagerness to convert people and organizations from one set of ideals to another. It becomes a good deal wiser, if these propositions are true, to scale down and make concrete the objectives that one is seeking to achieve.

A good illustration is in the attention given to decentralization of authority. Decentralization can be viewed in the image of conversion to certain ideals about who should have power and how this power should be used responsibly, or through an analytical approach to decide selectively where power is ill-placed and ill-used and to work on change at these locations. In other words, the theory of the partial approach to organizations asserts priorities and depends on good diagnostic observation and thought.

Substance vs. Form   Leaders can also present a stylistic bias in their preference for substance or form. Substance, in the language of organizations, is the detail of goals and performance—that is, who has to do what with whom to meet specific objectives. Form directs attention to the relationship of "who to whom" and attempts to achieve goals by specifying how the people should act in relation to each other.

There is no way in which matters of form can be divorced from substance.

But students of organization should at least be clear that attention to form *ahead of* substance threatens a person's sense of what is reasonable in undertaking actions. Attention to form may also present an implicit attack on one's conception of his independence and freedom from constraint.

Making form secondary to substance has another virtue: it can secure agreement on priorities without the need of predetermining who will have to give way in the ultimate give-and-take of the negotiations that must precede decisions on organization structure.

The two dimensions of bias, shown in the Exhibit 1 matrix, along with the four cells which result, clarify different executive approaches to power. The two dimensions define the executive's cognitive biases in: (1) selection of goals (partial vs. total), and (2) orientation toward action (form vs. substance).

Exhibit 1   Cognitive Management Styles in Organizational Life

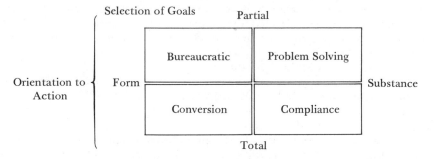

In the *bureaucratic* approach—that is, partial goals and attachment to form as a mode of acting—the emphasis is on procedure and the establishment of precedent and rule to control the uses of power.

The appeal of this approach is its promise of certainty in corporate relationships and in the depersonalization of power. The weaknesses of the bureaucratic approach are too familiar to need detailing here. Its major defect, however, is its inability to separate the vital from the trivial. It more easily commands energy over irrelevant issues because the latent function of the bureaucratic approach is to bypass conflict.

My contention here is that few important problems can be attended to without conflict of ideas and interests. Eventually organizations become stagnant because the bureaucratic approaches seldom bring together power and the vital issues which together make organizations dynamic.

The *conversion* approach (total-form) is notable through the human relations and sensitivity training movements as well as ideological programs, such as the Scanlon Plan and other forms of participative management. The popularity of "management by objectives" bears some scrutiny as a conversion movement directed toward power figures.

Another "total" approach which differs from conversion in its emphasis on substance is *compliance* with the directives of the powerful leader. This is the arena of the authoritarian personality (in both the leader, who has the power, and in the led, who seek submission), for whom personal power gets expressed in some higher goal that makes it possible for ends to justify means. The ideals may, for example, be race, as with dictator Adolf Hitler, or religion, as with Father Charles Coughlin, a dictator-type of the depression. In business, the illustrations are of a technological variety as with Frederick Winslow Taylor's "scientific management" and Henry Ford's automobile and assembly line.

Almost any technology can assume the proportions of the total approach if it is advanced by a charismatic leader and has deep emotional appeal. This explains the popularity of "management information systems," "value analysis," and "program planning and budgeting" which lead to a belief that the system itself is based on order, rationality, and control; therefore, the belief in turn helps to counteract the fears of chaos and lack of control which make people willing to demand total dependence and compliance in power relations. The effects of this fear on how people seek to arrange power relations in business, government, and the community cannot be overestimated.

Problem-Solving Approach

It should be perfectly obvious by now that my favored approach to organizational life combines the biases in Exhibit 1 of the partial substantive quadrant which I have designated "problem solving." From observation of competent business executives, we know it is precisely their ability to define problems worthy of thought and action and to use their organization to evolve solutions which characterize their style.

The contrary notion that executives are primarily caretakers, mediators, and seekers of consensus is more a myth than an accurate portrayal of how the competent ones attach themselves to power. To have power and not direct it to some substantive end that can be attained in the real world is to waste energy. The difficulties with the problem-solving approach are in risking power in favor of a substantive goal.

While there are no absolute right answers in problem solving, there are ways of evaluating the correctness of a program and plan. With a favorable average, the executive finds his power base enhanced and his ability to take risks increased.

The problem-solving approach to organization structure operates according to certain premises:

1. That organization structure is an instrument rather than an end. This means that a structure should be established or modified quickly instead of stringing out deliberations as though there actually exists a best and single solution for the problem of allocating power.

2. That organization structure can be changed but should not be tinkered with. This means that members of an executive organization can rely on a structure and can implement it without the uncertainty which comes from the constant modification of the organization chart.

3. That organization structure expresses the working coalition attached to the chief executive. In other words, the coalition has to be established de facto for the structure to mean anything. If the structure is out of line with the coalition, there will be an erosion of power and effectiveness. If no coalition exists in the minds of participants, putting it on paper in the form of an organization chart is nothing more than an academic exercise and a confusing one at that.

4. That organization structure represents a blend of people and job defini-

tions, but the priority is in describing the structure to accommodate competent people. The reason for this priority lies in the fact that competent executives are hard to find. Therefore, as an action principle, one should ensure the effective uses of the scarcest resources rather than conform to some ideal version of power relations.

5. That organization structure is a product of negotiation and compromise among executives who hold semiautonomous power bases. The more the power base of an executive is his demonstrated competence, the greater his autonomy of power and therefore capacity to determine the outcome in the allocations of power. The basic criticism of the problem-solving approach is in the danger of defining issues narrowly and ultimately undermining the moral-ethical basis of leadership. This criticism is valid, but as with so many problems in practical affairs, it can be overcome only by leaders who can see beyond the limits of immediate contingencies. In fact, I have tried to show throughout this article how the limitations of leaders, in both their cognitive and their emotional capacities, become the causes of power problems.

We have therefore come full circle in this analysis: because power problems are the effects of personality on structure, the solutions demand thinking which is free from the disabilities of emotional conflicts. This insight is often the margin between enduring with what exists or taking those modest steps which align competence with institutional authority in the service of human needs.

References

1. See my article, "The Management of Disappointment," HBR November–December 1967, p. 59.
2. See Chester Barnard, *The Functions of the Executive* (Cambridge, Harvard University Press, 1938), p. 167.

Innovation and Conflict in Industrial Engineering

ROSS A. WEBBER

As Horatio Alger might have said: "You can't keep a good idea down." Alger reflected the American feeling that the individual is the key to business success—especially in innovation. Either the top man is the source of creative ideas, or they originate with some engineer or manager in the lower regions of the organization. In the latter case, these ideas supposedly rise through the hierarchy to be recognized by those who make decisions. Even if ideas really did flow upward like this, the actual movement would be interesting. It is known, of course, that ideas are not helium-filled balloons forced up by their very difference

"Innovation and Conflict in Industrial Engineering" by Ross A. Webber from *The Journal of Industrial Engineering* (May 1967). Reprinted by permission of the American Institute of Industrial Engineers, Inc.

from surrounding environment. How many engineers have seen cherished ideas get nowhere? Most of them do not sit around in ivoried splendor just conjuring up new ideas. Their ideas grow out of their jobs; they are conceived within boundaries and constraints. They must proceed through staff and line hierarchies, and they must have some relation to what the business really needs. No matter how clever the thought, it means nothing if the company cannot use it.

What is being suggested here is that emphasis on the individual as the source of ideas may obscure other factors—organizational factors—of equal importance. An idea is not a goal but a means to more effective operations—and more profit. Acceptance of an idea is a function of time and company maturity. And it is related to social and economic forces operating on the firm through market preferences, technological advances, and political developments. Most important, the future of an idea depends upon organizational structure and the role that the innovator is able to play.

The subject is not just of academic interest. As Thompson [13] has pointed out, innovation, authority, and capacity to act have become increasingly fragmented in modern complex organizations. To an increasing extent, because of technological specialization, innovation must be a staff function more than an executive one [8]. This specialization, however, heightens the universal tension between information suppliers and decision-makers—between thinkers and doers. Since the Industrial Engineer is one of the key information suppliers and innovators in modern industry, he experiences such tension.

It was once fashionable to refer to the first-line foreman as "the man in the middle" [10]. With help, advice, and instruction coming from all sides, it is not surprising that a foreman can feel like the "monkey-in-the-middle" of the childhood game. But the foreman is not unique. Although one of the major sources of stress for the production foreman is the Industrial Engineer, the Industrial Engineer himself is buffeted by conflicting forces. He is caught between the demands of his staff supervisors and line clients—and also, caught between his ambitions as a professional engineer and his aspirations for production management. In this article, some of the stresses and strains in the Industrial Engineer's job will be examined and the impact they have on the engineer's contribution to organizational innovation will be indicated. As Schaffer [12, p. 1] points out:

"In all of this exhilarating expansion and forward movement [of Industrial Engineering techniques], relatively little attention has been paid to the strategy for maximizing the impact of those techniques on the real progress of the enterprise. As a whole, Industrial Engineering has concentrated on developing better weapons and providing its troops with the best equipment, but it has paid scant attention to how the war is to be won."

This war will be discussed in some detail. Specifically, three conflicts will be considered and the problems growing out of them:

1. Conflict between the objectives of Industrial Engineering and line departments.
2. Conflicts among the different functions that the Industrial Engineer must perform.
3. Conflicts in the career aspirations of the engineer.

It will be shown that all of these conflicts inhibit information flow and stifle creativity. This investigation may give some guidance concerning the proper location of innovators—centralized in insulated staff groups or decentralized in involved operational positions.

Conflicting Objectives

The author once set piece-rate standards on a group of middle-aged women— very middle-aged—and recalls this incident: "One day I brought a new standard rate card to the group's forelady. She glanced at it and told me that recently she had been purchasing meat at her butcher's when she looked into the refrigerator room. In chilling terms, she described how the great hanging carcasses were covered with ice and frozen blood. Because of the standards I had just set, she told me: 'Your heart must be just like that frozen meat!' I knew then that I was a successful Industrial Engineer."

As any other battered time and motion man will attest, conflict does exist between Industrial Engineers and various people in any business. No appeal to team spirit can eradicate the stress; what the Industrial Engineer tries to accomplish is often at odds with what other people want. Many of them attribute the conflict to personalities: "Bill just can't get along with anyone," or "Sam tries to block everything that we do." It is naive, however, to attribute this conflict solely to incompatible personalities. It is also an oversimplification to maintain that secret conspiracies are intentionally blocking Industrial Engineering from carrying out its job. No engineer can expect line personnel to be entirely happy with what he does; conflict is inherent in his relationships with operating people.

A new engineer has a rather naive belief in the traditional advisory concept of staff. He believes he will be called upon because of his superior training and knowledge. Most Industrial Engineering supervisors, however, envision the department not as a consultant or service group, but as a catalyst, a questioner of existing procedures, and a force in instituting new methods. Therefore, staff management tells the young engineer that he cannot sit around waiting for the phone to ring; it will not. He is encouraged to sell himself and his projects. Because the ambitious young man wants to impress his superiors and utilize his newly learned sophisticated techniques, he searches. He seeks a problem suited to his methods and then attempts to sell a project to production supervision.

This effort conflicts with the objectives of people with whom Industrial Engineers work. The typical foreman is interested in getting the work out—but without too much fuss. He wants to maintain stability among his personnel and equilibrium in his relationships. He is concerned only about problems that hinder him *now*. In contrast, the Industrial Engineer looks for problems that are not apparent to production people yet. To the foreman, the engineer seems to want to upset things—for no reason. It is easy to say that the foreman cannot see the forest for the trees, that he is shortsighted while the engineer looks ahead. But this is an oversimplified value judgment. Most foremen are rewarded for today's or this week's production, not next year's. His job is the here and now. He sees no real need for staff Industrial Engineering assistance in meeting his goal as rewarded by production management.

A production department head is also concerned with output, but this is supplemented by cost consciousness. His perspective is longer ranged than the foreman's, and he is interested in innovative change. Nonetheless, heaviest pressure is on relatively short-run costs. The average department head is not rewarded so much for long-term downtrends as for not exceeding weekly budgets. Industrial Engineering plays a major part in setting these budgets. Therefore, the department head's desire to have a loose budget clashes with the Industrial Engineer's desire to tighten the budget and show paper cost savings.

A higher level production supervisor usually has a greater interest in long-run costs and innovations, but frequently he is concerned with using mechanical, electrical, or chemical engineers whom he has on his own staff. He may maintain that this is cheaper, that he gets better work, and that he trains his future supervisory personnel at the same time.

Both Industrial Engineers and Industrial Engineering managers desire to broaden application of sophisticated techniques and to increase the power of the staff division to innovate. Selling Industrial Engineering services becomes essential. In many cases the engineer with his repertoire of techniques will simply try to find a problem to which he can apply his expertise. A Nobel physicist, Hans Bethe of Cornell, has commented that modern techniques have led to a tendency to think only about *how* to *solve* problems instead of *analyzing* the problems themselves. Among many Industrial Engineers, too much emphasis is placed on the techniques instead of the problems. Staff management aggravates this by overemphasizing Industrial Engineering as a professional discipline. Management may still proclaim loudly that Industrial Engineering is a "service" organization. Subtly, however, emphasis has shifted away from the often mundane problems of production departments. Rather, two objectives are pushed: first the development of a discipline; second, expansion in the power of Industrial Engineering to control and innovate.

If a man wants to sell something, naturally, he wraps up his product in the biggest and prettiest package. So it is with Industrial Engineering. In classic sales tradition, presentations are large and formal with aspirations of impressiveness. Emphasis is on completed staff work [9, p. 258], covering every alternative and requiring only management's signature for implementation. The results: assignments are overworked, overpolished, and diluted. Such effort is expended to impress line management with the caliber and completeness of Industrial Engineering work that embarrassing questions and radical viewpoints are minimized. Selling the solution rather than solving the problem is the objective. In addition, application of high-powered techniques to inappropriate and uneconomical situations leads to disappointing results—results which aggravate the difficulty of obtaining future jobs.

The primary fallacy of overemphasis on selling and image-making is that it bears little relevance to innovation or service. The staff tries to make decisions instead of determining and investigating alternatives. Of course, in any organization, selling is necessary to have legitimate alternatives considered. But, selling can be overdone. Salesmanship should not dominate the analysis and contemplation necessary for developing fresh ideas. In addition, it is not the function of a staff consulting department to formulate recommendations. Any staff group has a limited outlook; they are biased by their own skills and experience. Under ideal conditions, a decision-maker should receive studies of other staff groups. Each group should not recommend a solution. Rather, alternatives should be suggested that can be integrated into an overall plan of action. Industrial Engineering presentations frequently are designed to sell favored proposals to production supervision. In this way, the staff attempts to usurp decision-making responsibility at an inappropriate level and position.

Conflicting Functions

"Two-faced," "phonies," "actors," and "politicians," are epithets that production people have been heard to apply to Industrial Engineers. Their criticism is that Industrial Engineers sometimes are nice guys, other times are not. However appropriately these pejoratives may fit certain engineers, the real problem is not the personalities of engineers. It is the conflict built into the job.

Stress is produced because the Industrial Engineer's job is inconsistent; he must play different roles at different times. As advisory staff to a production department head, he answers questions about labor costs of various work methods. On another job, the same engineer serves as an auditor for a superior line superintendent by checking on the department head's reasons for using excess labor. On a third occasion, he exercises Industrial Engineering's authority over incentive plans by forcing through a maximum hour limit on a specific work crew. Finally, he is a salesman trying to convince manufacturing personnel to accept a new method of quality control. All of these relationships are made more difficult because the intervention of the engineer tends to be sporadic. As William F. Whyte has shown, production supervision reacts negatively to these unpredictable communications [14, p. 519].

In short, the Industrial Engineer often does not know where his job fits into the organization. Is he consultant to a production division superintendent, department head, or functionally responsible for installations of measured work plans? Is he adviser, auditor, controller, or innovator? In fact, he is all of these.

Most formal company procedures emphasize the Industrial Engineer's role as traditional advisory staff to a line authority. Staff management, however, points out that the engineer must sell himself and his projects. Selling requires frequent and vigorous initiation to production management. This is the reverse of the behavior required by an adviser—salesmen initiate, advisers respond. Moreover, in order to have something to sell, an engineer must have greater familiarity with departmental problems and possibilities than he would derive from passively waiting to be phoned. The growth of professionalism, the development of mathematical techniques, and the desires of new engineers all complement staff management's emphasis on salesmanship and innovation. This leads to search for problems, initiation from staff to line, and an innovative relationship not welcomed by production personnel.

In most companies Industrial Engineering once consisted mainly of work measurement. This legacy emphasizes the responsibility of IE for measured work plans everywhere in the company. There has developed a feeling that staff should control production departments to insure that line managers contribute to the company as a whole—and not work merely for their own departments. Staff management attempts to decide how production departments should contribute to corporate goals instead of what staff might do to help line supervisors best meet their own goals. As a result, many labor control plans require Industrial Engineering to act as inspector, controller, and auditor. In one company, for example, Industrial Engineering sets maximum hour limits for work crews. In order to pay his men, the production department head must request permission from an engineer. Because of varying production demands, it is not rare to exceed the allowed hours. The strain this puts on relations between the department head and Industrial Engineering is obvious: this interaction *must* be initiated by the department head to get Industrial Engineering action, and the authority relationship is just the reverse of that implied in the traditional advisory concept of staff.

Many Industrial Engineering supervisors also aggravate line-staff relations by their own behavior. They believe that production departments should be checked to see that they are contributing to company goals according to value criteria formulated by the Industrial Engineering division. Usually, there is no explicit justification for this attitude; it arises partly from the supervisor's experience and association with management people whose responsibilities do include such control, and partly as a result of insufficient job duties. Such a supervisor sits in his office checking budget figures and plant performance. Whenever he has a question, he notifies an engineer to call the production department and find out what happened. To answer his boss, the Industrial Engineer must call and question the production manager's activities. No manager likes to justify his performance to a staff man—much less to an inexperienced engineer who is younger and earns less money. The engineer may have worked hard to develop mutual trust and cooperation between himself and the production manager. Such checking can damage these relations.

The sensitive Industrial Engineer attempts to anticipate these questions from his supervisor so that he can answer without calling the production department. Because the staff supervisor influences advancement, the engineer wants to impress him with a ready answer. Also, he simply wants to avoid an unpleasant communication with the production department head. To have a ready answer requires a close relationship with the production department; otherwise, the engineer will not know what is going on.

It can be seen that the relationship between an Industrial Engineer and a production manager is characterized by confusion and inconsistency in communication patterns and organizational roles. Both the engineer and the production supervisor implicitly recognize that it is impossible to be a salesman, inspector, and consultant at the same time [14, p. 509]. The roles are incompatible. The engineer, therefore, is confused and anxious about his relations with the people he is supposed to serve.

So, armed with his arsenal of techniques, the engineer goes forth to find problems and "offer" his services to production supervision. He soon recognizes, however, that he cannot merely respond to staff management's call for selling. Selling stresses that the engineer is an outsider trying to get in. Geographic distance, social differences, and administrative centralization further emphasize the separation of Industrial Engineering from production. The engineer becomes aware that he must overcome this handicap of being a stranger to production people. To sell requires that the engineer have something of value. This should be an idea based upon observed conditions. Cultivation of these ideas is dependent upon search, and the search process requires an intimate knowledge of production activity. Besides, it is simply not possible to maintain a sufficient level of projects through search and selling only.

In short, the engineer realizes that he must cultivate requests from the production department for his services. He learns that he cannot be a remote Olympian oracle telling mere production mortals what to do. The engineer was taught to pursue change. To get things done, however, he needs to influence others to act. This requires a closer relationship than that of the expert.

To develop this closer relationship, the individual engineer attempts to camouflage his position as an outsider, minimize his selling, and increase his indispensability to production supervision. An example is the case of a junior Industrial Engineer who, without being requested, made a complete study of the future production trends, space requirements, and labor needs for a new product treatment area. A production department development engineer normally conducted such investigations but had not yet done so. The Industrial Engineer, at some risk, hid his hours in another assignment. When he presented the completed study to the production department head, the engineer became indispensable. He was consulted because he was a known information source. He also projected himself into consideration for a possible managerial post when and if the new product area expanded.

As Figure 1 illustrates, many Industrial Engineers desire a joint consultative-implementation relationship with production supervision: both would respond to the same department stimuli, 1, and either should be able to initiate consultation with the other, 2 and 3. Finally, engineers want to join in the implementation, 4.

It is apparent, then, that a staff group oriented toward solving problems and seeing the future as resting on demonstration of sophisticated knowledge will develop every avenue for obtaining access to production departments. Formal procedures will be given mock observance, but various methods of search

Figure 1 The Industrial Engineer's Desired Work Pattern

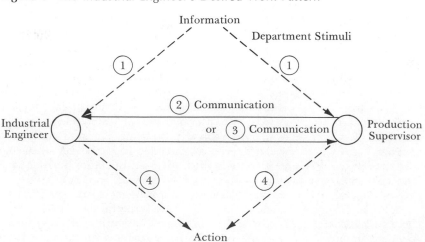

for problems and obtaining jobs will be explored. Inevitably, such activity creates stress and conflict.

Conflicting Career Aspirations

An additional source of stress for the Industrial Engineer is uncertainty about his career. Does he want management or engineering? Whom should he impress? Staff supervisors or production managers? This is a complex subject and extensive coverage is beyond the scope of this article. A few observations are pertinent, however. Unlike many professional employees (6), the Industrial Engineers who have been observed in large companies have been company and management rather than profession oriented. Many Industrial Engineering divisions historically have served as training areas for the whole company. Employment in Industrial Engineering has given promising people wide access to valuable contacts and experiences.

In one large chemical company, the normal period of service in the department was approximately three years after which the engineers generally moved into a production area—either as a manager or as a staff engineer directly assisting a production supervisor. The promotion path was definitely up the line hierarchy; few desired to stay in technical work. Such rapid turnover created problems for Industrial Engineering. In spite of high caliber young engineers, effective contribution was hindered by inexperience. In this company, as in many others, management decided to reduce promotions out of the department and emphasize careers in Industrial Engineering. By improving the performance of Industrial Engineering, they hoped that the engineers would be more effective in selling their ideas to production management. In addition, more engineers with advanced degrees in Industrial Engineering and Operations Research were recruited. In short, emphasis was placed on professional opportunity in Industrial Engineering.

Many companies have taken similar steps. Throughout Industrial Engineering there is a trend towards professionalism. Active research groups conduct courses in advanced mathematical techniques. Many engineers receive tuition refunds for graduate statistics, operations research, and industrial management programs. The natural desire of new graduates to use modern techniques is reinforced by the recognition given to those who demonstrate sophisticated applications. Invitations to give talks on their work to peers and supervisors, informal status, and formal staff promotions in recent years have tended to go to those who have had significant success in applying the more esoteric techniques.

Contemporary Industrial Engineers may be confused as to where their futures lie and whom they want to impress. The problem, however, may be resolved by the movement towards professionalism. The future Industrial Engineer may see his future in Industrial Engineering. He may not be frustrated by his inability to move out of the field. Accordingly, schizophrenia in the Industrial Engineer's aspirations may be eliminated. But such professionalism will aggravate the conflict between line and staff. The social and organizational gap will widen; the attempts of staff to control line will increase; and greater emphasis on professional development and sophisticated techniques will diminish the engineer's interest in assisting the production manager to solve the latter's mundane daily problems.

Inhibited Creativity

Creativity in problem-solving depends on memory, example, and analogy. Information plays a crucial role in all three aspects. The initial element of creativity is a search for problems and sources of information. When information is needed, most people start by asking someone else rather than searching through musty files and books. A man may turn around at his desk and ask the engineer sitting behind him in the cubicle. Or, he picks up the phone and calls some colleague. If pressed, he may rummage through his desk drawers to find some report or old copy of *Factory* magazine that has some information that he remembers vaguely. In order to locate information, however, he needs to know whom to ask and where to look. As March and Simon [6, p. 180] have observed:

"One important element of organizational structure is a set of understandings and expectations among the participants as to what bodies of information repose where in the structure. This set of expectations and understandings is a major determinant of the use of communication channels."

In addition, many observers comment that innovation requires emergence in the problem, long familiarity with all aspects, and extended thinking of possible alternatives, plus plain hard work [1]. Thomas Edison invented more by analogy and experimentation than imagination. He created by direct frontal assault—marshalling the widest array of facts and ideas and then carefully searching for previously unrecognized relationships between them. Similarly, Henry Eyring, drawing on his experience in various chemical laboratories, maintains that success is always related to and built upon the findings of others [3, p. 8]. Other observers define two more approaches to problem-solving:

1. Problem-solving is a cognitive process of learning and thinking.
2. Problem-solving is a manifestation of personality.

Essential for both approaches according to Ernest Hilgard [4, pp. 162–180] is a "mood" for the easy exchange of ideas.

These views emphasize the importance of free information flow among supervisors, subordinates, peers, and colleagues. Yet, Industrial Engineers experience extreme difficulty in obtaining information from production departments. The old "better communications" shibboleth is not being repeated here because it is not simply that two groups misunderstand each other. Engineers cannot search for and solve problems without free access to information. "But all you have to do is ask" is the reply of many production managers. In order to ask for information, however, the engineer has to know what he wants—and this is not possible in ambiguous situations, because what is valuable and pertinent is not known. To be innovative, an engineer must have access to all forms of departmental data: letters, production records, inspection reports, and engineering investigations. Engineers would prefer a running record of manufacturing department activities which they could peruse but it is difficult to obtain copies on a continuous basis. The department head "forgets" to tell his clerk to indicate Industrial Engineering as an information addressee, and the clerk "forgets" to send copies.

In addition, Industrial Engineers want to know what is going on in order to maintain and strengthen close relationships with the department. The desire to make oneself indispensable in order to increase requests initiated by production managers has already been described. The engineer can pursue this goal better if he is intimately familiar with production department activities.

Acquisition of this information frequently is hindered by the geographic and social isolation of the engineers. Industrial Engineers usually are located in one office separated from many of the production departments they serve. Distances are not great and do not seriously interfere with imperatives of the engineer's job, but they do influence the nature of communications with production supervisors. In many large companies, the distances discourage all but necessary business visits. Engineers do not often go out just to say hello or to have a cup of coffee. Thus, almost all visits and telephone calls initiated by Industrial Engineers are job-related. Indeed, Industrial Engineers are generally regarded as sticklers for work, both because of the "efficiency expert" connotation of their position and because of the job-oriented nature of their interactions.

Of course, some engineers have more energy than others, and these people do attempt to initiate informal relations. Social pressures, however, hinder them. Age, social, and educational differences between production supervisors and Industrial Engineers tend to minimize friendliness. On the one hand, young engineers tend to believe in respect for their elders—and most production supervisors are older. On the other hand, because Industrial Engineering requires college training, personnel and engineering managers seem to emphasize staff's higher status. There is even some pressure on engineers regarding dress; appearance is mentioned on some performance evaluation forms. In one company, production department supervisors wear ties and rough work jackets in the winter; in warm weather, they appear with no tie or jacket and sleeves rolled up. Engineers, in contrast, are expected to wear suits and keep jackets on at all times when in the plant. Completed with a felt hat, their appearance is less appropriate to a manufacturing department than it is to Madison Avenue.

These organizational, geographic, and social difficulties are not insurmountable obstacles to Industrial Engineers. They might be overcome by patience, sufficiently frequent trips to the production department, willingness to work in inadequate surroundings in making copies, and so forth. These factors, nonetheless, do reinforce the tendency to confine communications to specific job-related subjects. In addition, all these activities absorb energy and diminish the engineer's attention to problem-solving and innovation.

When the engineer has been given a specific problem that is of some concern to production management, he can overcome these information difficulties with energy and hard work. It is not so simple when the problems are not apparent and the staff group is searching for causes that will produce problems only in the future—if at all. Free movement of data and information is essential for such search [3, p. 12]. Some of this information flow should be without apparent relevance, without conscious request, and without specific purpose. It has been shown how various factors in Industrial Engineering relationships discourage such information flow and make it difficult to achieve the level of familiarity and commitment necessary for innovation. Valuable innovative effort depends on frequent discussion and information exchange between engineers and managers. By blocking information, the innovative process is hampered at its most critical stage—discovery of a problem.

Creativity, as with much human enterprise, prospers most in a friendly atmosphere of cooperation. This atmosphere frees individuals from pressure for uniformity and takes advantage of sympathetic "resonance" from contemporaries. A political scientist, Harold Laswell [5, p. 261], comments that the greatest boon to the innovator is an intellectual collaborator:

"In particular we are impressed by the peculiarly resonant relationships that successful innovators, at least, set up with individuals in their social environment. Similarly, although the means to which people resort in defeating themselves are devious and subtle, we suspect that potentially significant innovators are often stunted through lack of a friend to play the resonance role, and through dependence upon an environment only too willing to exert a dampening influence."

Resonance from production personnel available to Industrial Engineers in many organizations is very limited. In the initial stage of idea generation, the engineer's desire to maintain an air of knowledgeable superiority severely hampers discussion with production managers. Before they are talked about, the ideas of Industrial Engineers frequently freeze into proposals—proposals to be packaged and sold to dubious operating supervisors.

Alleviating the Conflicts

Three situations have been described that are of stress to the Industrial Engineer:

1. Conflict between his objectives and those of groups with whom he works.
2. Conflict among the functions he performs.
3. Conflict in his own career aspirations.

Finally, it has been shown how these conflicts inhibit communication flows and hamper creativity. With some oversimplification, two general methods of handling these problems are evident: first, centralization and increased authority for Industrial Engineering; second, decentralization and submission to stronger line control. The advantages and disadvantages of each in dealing with the problems raised will now be outlined.

The first problem—conflict between Industrial Engineering and other groups—is inevitable. In his innovating activities, the Industrial Engineer can always expect resistance from operating managers. Such conflict is inherent in organizations. "If I only had the power to . . ." often is the somewhat wistful refrain of the engineer. Perhaps vastly increased power to a centralized Industrial Engineering staff might enable them to persevere and force innovative changes. There are weaknesses in this approach, however. As many researchers have indicated [11], when power or authority is relied on exclusively to change behavior, the change is likely to be very superficial and half-hearted. No real effort will be exerted, ingenuity will be exercised *against* the change not *for* it, and compliance will be minimum. This tends to force the party with power to increase its observation, control, and power over the resistors. To concentrate such power in Industrial Engineering would probably be impossible, thankfully, because, if it were not, results would be disastrous. Complete breakdown in communication flow and cooperation would destroy the adviser-client relationship.

Unfortunately, the alternative of decentralization and submission to line authority also has its drawbacks. Frustration occurs daily in the engineer's life when his ideas are rejected arbitrarily without sufficient consideration—or so he thinks. A stagnant management may prevent innovative action long after a sensitive staff has recognized the need. So, the engineer must rely on persuasion to change behavior. If he is successful in convincing operating managers to make changes, the modifications are more likely to be made than if power were used. The use of persuasion, however, leads to the emphasis on salesmanship and other misdirected activities already described. No matter how aggravating IE's weakness may be, however, greater central power is not desirable.

When a person has multiple jobs or multiple roles to fill, one solution to conflicts between these roles is segregation or segmentation [2]. To eliminate the second problem of conflict among the Industrial Engineer's functions, the position might be broken up. For example, commercial bankers were once the largest stockbrokers and underwriters. In 1933, however, Congress and the Securities and Exchange Commission forced separation of the banking function from the underwriting activity. Similarly, there is current demand to separate the advisory functions of the present stockbrokers from their buying function. Such conflicts of interest lead to ethical problems. They were separated to resolve these conflicts.

Conflict of interests is not the problem for the Industrial Engineer as much as it is incompatibility between roles. As has been shown, the Industrial Engineer must be adviser, auditor, salesman, and innovator. Any of these roles are difficult to combine. Perhaps, a solution is to divide up the Industrial Engineer's functions among several positions.

Auditing or controlling interferes especially strongly with advising and innovating. As has been shown, the communication and authority relationships are directly contradictory; mutual trust and confidence are severely undermined. Therefore, control over incentive standards and payroll plans could be separated from the advisory and innovative roles. In a sense, this would be going back to the day when methods and measurement activities in Industrial Engineering were separate (a condition still existing in some companies). A problem here is that most engineers are not interested in careers in measurement because methods work is where the action is—where new analytical techniques are being applied and where big savings are possible. In addition, the distinction between the two types of Industrial Engineers interferes with communication and co-operation within Industrial Engineering. Proper methods are not installed before standards are set, methods men tend to get sloppy about labor costs, and so on. Neither the case for centralization nor decentralization is clearly stronger here.

Centralization, however, does offer some advantages for strengthening the Industrial Engineering profession and reducing career conflicts for the engineer. A centralized staff is usually associated with job variety, luxurious facilities, and organizational prominence. Of more importance, centralized Industrial Engineering encourages the development of a satisfying professional atmosphere. Formal training programs and informal bull sessions are facilitated; both promote technical performance. Such challenging and satisfying training experiences are extremely difficult when engineers are physically and administratively distributed among operating departments.

The last problem raised was the hindrance to creativity and innovation offered by communication barriers. The administrative, geographic, and social separation of Industrial Engineering from production supervision discourages the development of free communication flow essential for development of creative ideas. This is the most important question raised by consideration of the Industrial Engineer. Given the accelerated pace of innovation, the organizational location of innovative groups is of increasing importance. Just how closely should a staff group be involved in the operational problems of a production department?

The individual Industrial Engineer attempts to join in production department activities in order to make himself indispensable and to encourage line managers to initiate communication. Because of the technical and organizational familiarity and mastery essential for creativity, this closeness to production departments may facilitate innovation. Yet, there is a paradox. The more the innovative person becomes involved in handling operational problems, the greater the proclivity to accept the outlook of production people towards stability—just as long as no one is aware of any difficulty. Because an innovator must be dissatisfied when everyone else is satisfied, and because he must find problems before they are recognized as problems, such closeness to operations might stifle progress. In fact, it has been suggested that a requirement for innovation may be isolation of the innovator from operating pressures [3, p. 12].

Nonetheless, such isolation is not the answer. The innovator must be involved closely in the problems of the department or he will not become aware of possibilities. Innovation should not depend upon the efforts of centralized staff groups working in splendid isolation. These absent staff innovators cannot expect production personnel to respond amiably to their unpredictable appearances, cheerfully upsetting production because the engineer's proposals are rationally desirable. Rationality depends on whether one is getting or giving. At the same time, the harried production supervisor is not able to devote enough time to searching for problems that are not crucial and alternatives that are not apparent.

It is clear that neither centralization nor decentralization offers the perfect solution. There are advantages and disadvantages to both; neither extreme is justified; some balance is necessary. Detailed structural changes will not be proposed in this article, but one observation is pertinent. On the range from complete decentralization to complete centralization, it would appear that IE is too close to the centralized end. At least, the centralization of Industrial Engineering in a staff group should be reexamined. The biases, distortions, and overprofessionalism encouraged by such centralization may hinder organizational innovation. In short, consideration should be given to putting the Industrial Engineer closer—administratively, socially, and physically—to the people and technology he is trying to change.

References

1. Anderson, Harold (Editor), *Creativity and its Cultivation,* Harper & Row, New York, 1959.
2. Evan, William M., and Levin, Ezra G., "Status-set and Role-set Conflicts of the

Stockbroker: A Problem in the Sociology of Law," *Social Forces,* Volume 45, No. 1, September, 1966, pp. 73–83.

3. Eyring, Henry, "Scientific Creativity," *Creativity and its Cultivation,* Harper & Row, New York, 1959.

4. Hilgard, Ernest R., "Creativity and Problem Solving," *Creativity and its Cultivation,* Harper & Row, New York, 1959.

5. Laswell, Harold, "The Social Setting of Creativity," *Creativity and its Cultivation,* Harper & Row, New York, 1959.

6. March, James, and Simon, Harold, *Organizations,* John Wiley & Sons, New York, 1958.

7. Moore, David G., and Renck, Richard, "The Professional Employee in Industry," *Journal of Business,* January, 1955, p. 60.

8. Moore, Wilbert, "The Use and Misuse of Creative People and Ideas," *Individualism and Big Business,* McGraw-Hill Book Company, New York, 1963, pp. 119–125.

9. Newman, William, and Summer, Charles R., *The Process of Management,* Prentice-Hall, Englewood Cliffs, 1961.

10. Roethlisberger, Fritz J., "The Foreman: Master and Victim of Double Talk," *Harvard Business Review,* Volume 45, No. 5, September–October, 1965, p. 23ff.

11. Sayles, Leonard R., and Strauss, George, *Human Behavior in Organizations,* Prentice-Hall, Englewood Cliffs, 1966, pp. 184–209.

12. Schaffer, Robert H., *Maximizing the Impact of Industrial Engineering,* American Management Association, New York, Management Bulletin 82, 1966.

13. Thompson, Victor, *Modern Organizations,* Alfred A. Knopf, New York, 1963.

14. Whyte, William F., *Men at Work,* Irwin-Dorsey, Homewood, Illinois, 1961.

Questions for Discussion

1. Sit in a local restaurant and observe the flow of work. Plot the interactions. See if you can determine the points of stress and conflict. Discuss what causes it.

2. Have you ever been in a situation where you experienced stress from conflicting role demands? For example, in your role as son or daughter, friend, church member, etc. Discuss.

3. Describe and analyze a person you have observed who is experiencing role ambiguity or role conflict.

4. The eminent anthropologist Margaret Mead has commented that a central cause of the problems of teenagers and young adults in the United States is that our society postpones their adoption of successful life roles (e.g., they have to stay in school so long). What are the role ambiguities and conflicts of these years?

5. Thomas Jefferson once described the Presidency of the United States as "a splendid misery." To a lesser extent, this can be said of most high executive posts. Why?

6. In a recent study, it was reported that employee morale and job satisfaction tend to be lower in larger organizations than in smaller ones. As corporations grow larger, there is a significant decrease in satisfaction with the company, supervision, fellow employees, and the job. Other studies also report higher rates of absenteeism and turnover in large organizations. In contrast, another study indicated that management positions in larger organizations are seen as more rewarding and satisfying than those in smaller organizations. In addition, managers in larger organizations say that they have more freedom and autonomy (and less need for conformity) than in smaller companies. How would you explain these findings?

7. Why have hierarchical organizations in the past (and still to a large extent) tended to deny the presence of internal conflict?

8. What are the advantages of an organization "legitimizing" conflict; that is, dealing with it in an open and rational way? What are the potential disadvantages?

9. What factors and phenomena reinforce conflict between contending parties?

10. "If people would only communicate . . ." goes the old cliche. The assumption is that good communication would overcome most conflict, presumably because conflict is based on misunderstanding. Unfortunately, the wish is often a delusion. Improving communication is no guarantee of improved relations. Discuss why.

11. What are the mechanisms used by people to handle role conflict?

Short Cases for Discussion

Lakewood Community College

Lakewood Community College is a two-year, publicly supported urban institution of higher education. According to its statement of philosophy and purpose, its programs are designed to accommodate the diverse educational needs and aspirations of recent high school graduates and adults. The college believes that the key ingredient in a satisfactory experience for its students is excellence of classroom instruction. For this reason the college requires a commitment to college teaching as a fundamental qualification for its faculty. According to a recent statement of policy, each faculty member, in addition to holding professional credentials, must manifest a sincere interest in the instruction and counseling of students. The establishment of selection criteria and the actual hiring of staff is left to individual departments.

The college has no formal organization chart. Instead, the dean of instruction stated in a memo to department heads, "The college will arrive at its full divisional structuring via departmental paths and not by the filling in of a master organization chart." There are currently fifteen department heads, of which all report directly to the dean of instruction, who in turn reports to the president of the college. Also reporting to the president is a dean of students and a business manager.

The department of nursing provides a good illustration of the type of situation that characterizes many departments at Lakewood. The department consists of the following eight people:

Associate Professors:

| Gail Mauldin | 28 years old | 1st year faculty |
| Bill Gunner | 38 years old | chairman of the department (Teaches both 1st and 2nd years) |

Assistant Professors:

| Yvette Sturm | 40 years old | 1st year faculty |
| Jill Purdy | 27 years old | 2nd year faculty |

Instructors:

Pam Lowy	25 years old	2nd year faculty
Emerald Prince	33 years old	1st year faculty
Delores Rosenberg	30 years old	2nd year faculty
Frances MacDonald	32 years old	1st year faculty

The method of teaching used in the department has been described by the chairman (Bill Gunner) simply as group teaching. The faculty has been made to understand that no one is excused from any class unless the department chairman approves. In general, group teaching means that several faculty members are present in most classes.

The faculty members teaching first-year students and those teaching second-year students meet once each week to discuss issues common to both. Each group seems to regard the other with suspicion, or at best cool tolerance. At a recent joint meeting, the first-year faculty accused the second-year faculty of failing to establish "critical elements" (those elements considered critical to proper nursing performance). The second-year faculty retorted that the problem lay in the poor preparation the students received in their first year. Most of the exchange took place between Misses Mauldin and Purdy, who by virtue of their academic rank seem to have assumed the role of senior staff. Miss Mauldin admitted that the nursing students enter "a different world" during their second year. She stated, "It's probably because we don't get together to share exactly what we all teach."

During the past two months a crisis has developed in the first-year faculty. Apparently there had been dissension between Emerald Prince and the other first-year faculty almost from the time Mrs. Prince joined the faculty six months earlier (in September). Mrs. Prince is an R.N. and has a Master's degree in Nursing Administration, and confided that she had been unable to secure a position in that field because she is black. The faculty had been particularly anxious to hire a black instructor, as they felt it would be beneficial for their many black students. Mrs. Prince had been more closely associated with Gail Mauldin during the first semester than any of the other faculty, and Miss Mauldin had complained to Mr. Gunner on several occasions that Mrs. Prince was not competent.

The situation worsened at the beginning of the second semester when Yvette Sturm became the lead teacher for a unit on psychiatric nursing. (A faculty member is the "lead" teacher when her area of specialization is taught.) She and Mrs. Prince sharply disagreed on many issues, and were constantly waging verbal battles—at first in faculty meetings and later in student-faculty conferences. Mrs. MacDonald, otherwise a quiet person, frequently found herself acting as the mediator in these disputes. Although Mrs. MacDonald's efforts usually resulted in a temporary accord, disagreement would flare again. Miss Sturm found herself increasingly in the position of giving directives to Mrs. Prince. The disagreements between the two became sharper and more polar. Mrs. Prince always thought of nursing service (at a local hospital where the students gain clinical experience working), while Miss Sturm insisted that the students were in the agency for education, not service.

Students frequently complained that Mrs. Prince praised them and told them they were "doing fine," while Miss Sturm told them they *weren't* doing so fine. Miss Sturm insisted on correcting the tests and papers of Mrs. Prince's students after Mrs. Prince had already done so. Miss Sturm often marked the students' papers as much as twenty points lower. Mrs. Prince then would tell the students that she had no idea why they had been awarded such a grade. In sum, the students received "double messages" almost constantly.

In late February, the first-year students presented a letter to the faculty deploring the treatment of Mrs. Prince. Among other complaints the students listed inattention to her points of view, failure to solicit her ideas, and rude treatment of her by other faculty members in the classroom. The faculty members denied these charges and tried to reason with the students. Privately Mrs. Prince stated, "The students see how shabbily I am being treated." Meanwhile, other faculty members pointed out that Mrs. Prince's strong identification with nursing service (administration) often made her view completely incompatible with their own. Her comments in class appeared to embarrass and even stun them at times so that they did not always reply to her when she spoke.

Mr. Gunner talked with the dean of instruction and the president about the students' letter and about the worsening situation within the faculty. In describing his actions, Mr. Gunner said, "The dean isn't too strong a figure, so I usually end up going directly to the president. In fact, the president often issues directives right around the dean. Frequently I find myself writing a note to him explaining some action I'm taking or policy I'm implementing." In mid-March Mr. Gunner recommended that Mrs. Prince not be retained for the following school year. This proved to be somewhat of a problem, since notice of non-reappointment should have been given (according to policy) no later than March 1.

When the contracts went out on the first of April, Mrs. Prince did not receive one. The following day all but a handful of the first-year students failed to report for classes.

Question

Discuss the possible causes of conflict. (After reading Chapter 11, you may want to formulate recommendations for the president.)

The Young Venture Manager at J. R. Johnson, Inc.

J. R. Johnson is one of the largest manufacturers of wood products in the world. The company has five divisions, but the consumer products division is by far the largest, accounting for 70% of total sales. This division is headed by a company vice president, who has reporting to him, among others, a divisional vice president for marketing. Under marketing, there have been departments of marketing research, product management, and new products.

The new products department consisted of a director and four project managers, each charged with the development of specific products. As conceived, the position of project manager received assistance from marketing research as well as from the research and development division. The organization was as shown in Exhibit 1.

In the past decade, Johnson has seen substantial portions of important markets usurped by companies with improved products, and more recently by companies with highly successful new product divisions. Johnson has responded by making acquisitions in other businesses, and on occasion by marketing a

Exhibit 1   Organization Chart of J. R. Johnson, Inc.

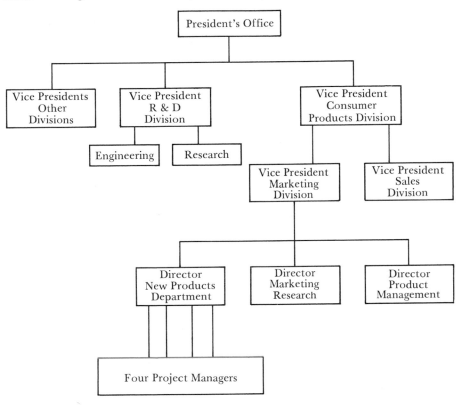

new product of its own making. Most new products were handled by the product management department, since they were not markedly different from current items. New products that were truly differentiated were given to the new products department. Several projects have produced marketable items, but overall the rate of commercial success has been distressingly low.

At 29, Bob Cole was the youngest of the four project managers in the new products department. As a project manager, Cole was given responsibility for the development of the product, but invariably relied on the assistance of R & D and marketing research. These areas were not organizationally responsible to the project manager, and had their own problems. The work they did for the project manager was done in spare time if at all. To expedite a project, it was necessary for the project manager to request the marketing division vice president to communicate the urgency of the project to marketing research and/or R & D. Bob Cole had often noted that such an organizational arrangement resulted in greatly extended development times and habitually poor work.

Johnson management recently became aware of the low productivity of its new products department and began studying a reorganization. It was management's expressed desire to replace the new products department with a concept more entreprenurial in nature. The decision was made to adopt an approach similar to that employed in venture capital undertakings. Bob Cole had been working on a project to which members of the R & D division and a marketing research consultant were assigned full time. This form of operation proved highly successful, with a product prepared for test marketing within one year (a significant improvement over past development periods). In view of this success, Bob was asked to write a job description for the venture managers who were to replace the new products department. When the description was finished, it included the following points:

1. The venture manager is to have full responsibility for the development of opportunities identified by the division of product planning and development.
2. The venture manager is to have authority for decisions on product form, advertising, pricing, and marketing strategy, subject to post-decision review by the divisional vice president of marketing.
3. Where personnel are needed from other areas of the company, the venture manager may request these people by name, and will have the final approval of selections. All personnel will be assigned to the project full time, and will be responsible to the venture manager for the duration of the project.
4. The venture manager will report to the vice president, product planning and development only for administrative matters, not for substantive reviews of his activities.

This description was sent to personnel and to top management of the division in September. In mid-February the company appointed a division vice president for product planning and development, and selected two additional men to join Bob Cole as venture managers. In the interim, Bob had continued to work on his project and had begun to make commitments for advertising and production. However, the increasing work load had caused Bob to conclude that an assistant was needed. In order to facilitate the writing of a job description for the new position, Bob asked the personnel department for a copy of his own job description. It was immediately apparent to Bob that significant changes had been made in the version he had originally submitted. These included a review of decisions on advertising, market planning, and production by the vice president, product planning and development; an assignment of specialized personnel on a basis in which they remained part of their functional area; and a limit on the amount of money the venture manager could commit without approval from the vice president, product planning and development.

    Bob could scarcely believe his eyes. The job description as it now read had reduced the position of venture manager to one not substantially different from the old project manager. Feeling obliged to discuss the situation with someone, Bob asked his new assistant to join him for lunch.

Bob: . . . so, Jim, I thought you should know what is taking place. The general reduction in authority seems totally inconsistent with the company's expressed intention to develop the type of entreprenurial spirit that characterizes the venture management concept. Even more important for the immediate future is the old problem of split responsibility created by retention of team members as part of their parent departments. Jim, I believe the success of the venture management idea is of crucial importance to the company.

Jim: I certainly agree with you, but quite frankly I am more concerned about the success of the project our team is already committed to. If we're not successful in cutting into Eaton's market share, we're going to be out in the cold on one of the fastest growing markets in the country.

Bob: That's true. And that reminds me that I hadn't even considered the commitments we've made to outside concerns. Suppose management doesn't agree with what we've done? We could be made to look pretty foolish.

Jim: And suppose other department heads discover that their people are not really ours after all? They wouldn't do anything immediately, but at the first sign that the project is in trouble, they would be calling Mr. Stone (divisional vice president for product planning and development) to get their people back.

Bob: Speaking of Stone: according to the revised description, he is to review all of our work before it goes to the division level. You know what that means—by the time he gets through with it nobody will be able to recognize the product package.

Jim: But Stone doesn't have the foggiest idea of what's involved in this project. Besides, we've nursed this thing for months, and to subject it to his O.K. will surely dilute the "fresh approach" that management has talked so much about.

Bob: Ted Stone never has been the type to work through others; he's always had to be the whole show. Why should he change his style now?

Jim: O.K. So what do we do?

Bob: As I see it, Jim, I have to weigh the risks of continuing to direct the project without formal authority against the difficulty of operating under the revised job description.

Jim: If I were you, I would also consider what effect that decision might have on my career with Johnson.

Question

Analyze Bob Cole's predicament.

Chapter 11

Managing Organizational Conflict

This chapter deals with three fundamental methods of managing the conflicts which inevitably arise in organizational life: dominance; the formation of hierarchies (and their use by participants to settle or avoid conflict); and bargaining. In addition, certain patterns of managerial leadership are described which contribute to the management of conflict.

Some of the most common methods for responding to conflict do not so much attempt to resolve it as to "handle" it in any way that will eliminate or obscure the problem. For example, avoidance or flight are probably the most common. Such actions are usually accompanied by psychological stress arising from conflict among the needs for safety, social esteem, and self-respect, so various rationalizations are developed to relieve it. We may simply reexamine our "real" desires and "rationally" conclude that overt conflict is not worth whatever we thought we wanted. Or we may convince ourselves that postponing conflict is desirable in order to allow time to prepare, frequently deluding ourselves that our objectives are so noble and important that we had better not run the risk of losing by premature conflict. Finally, we may feel that conflict avoidance is more mature and reasonable than "childish" argument. Knowing whether these judgments are valid or merely self-serving rationalizations is extremely difficult. Assuming that flight is not possible or desirable, what other general mechanisms for handling conflict exist? Three stand out: dominance, hierarchical appeal, and bargaining.

Dominance

Some definitions of conflict presuppose dominance as the method of handling it. Thus conflict is "a struggle over values or claims to status, power, and scarce resources, in which the claims of the conflicting parties are not only to gain the desired values, but also to neutralize, injure, or eliminate their rivals" (Coser, quoted in Turner, 1968). Eliminating the antagonist seems to take on an autonomous existence almost independent of the matters in conflict. Dominance may develop through individuals, coalitions, or majorities.

Individual Dominance

Many creatures settle conflict by individual dominance, based on fighting ability or physical strength. Conflict over territory or prospective mate results in the strongest or most aggressive individual obtaining his desires, while simultaneously promoting the survival of the species. Under such circumstances, "the strategy of conflict centers about injuring the other party without simultaneously injuring the self, while inhibiting and defending against retaliatory injury from the opponent" (Turner, 1969). As Lorenz (1966) has pointed out, the process is not as bloody as we might expect. Most animals, including man, replace actual injury or death with symbolic injury. Aggression is checked when both agree who is the loser. The loser follows the rules and withdraws from the conflict, usually going elsewhere to compete with less formidable foes. Among some group animals he may remain; however, he must never again strive for leadership, and he must demonstrate his obeisance to the rival who defeated him by symbolic acts of subservience.

In human organizations, many patterns of individual dominance are found. The dominating individual may be able to dominate because of his formal authority or power. Among groups of apparent peers, an individual may dominate by virtue of his personal attributes (height, appearance, education, etc.). Among college students, those who are uncertain about an issue frequently defer to the individual who expresses certainty; he is allowed to dominate.

In organizations, the loser is sometimes fired; more often, he resigns voluntarily or under pressure. One comparison of business and academia (Bensman, 1967) observes that conflict losers are more likely to leave the former, but remain in the latter. Because of tenure, the school is likely to have more "walking wounded." However, all organizations have individuals who have symbolically withdrawn from conflict. In the United States there tend to be people who have resolved their job-home conflict in favor of the latter, putting in minimal time and energy at work. Or they are apathetic older managers performing meaningless duties or working below their capacity. In short, we are not too effective in utilizing such losers. (How much easier it is in British politics! One of the Prime Minister's most comforting powers is the ability to cushion firing by enobling the victim. A good many peers in the House of Lords are politicians put out to pasture.) In Japan, such men are consciously and effectively utilized as "godfathers" to younger people in the organization to lend guidance and advice.

Coalition Dominance

The Bolsheviks' faith in ultimate success during the Russian Revolution rested less on Marxian inevitability than in belief that a minority coalition could prevail if it were willing to work harder, longer, and more intelligently than the majority. Coalitions of two or more persons are common because they can generate support out of proportion to their numbers. The presence of just one other supporter lends substantial strength to an individual's position.

Zaleznik (1970) suggests that no organization can function without a coalition that consolidates power around a central figure. "The failure to establish a coalition within the executive structure of an organization can result in severe problems such as paralysis in the form of inability to make decisions and to evaluate performance, and infighting and overt rivalry within the executive group" (p. 51). This is perhaps illustrated by the difficulty Semon Knudsen experienced at Ford Motor Company in the late 1960s. Knudsen had lost the contest for the presidency of General Motors. He could have remained at GM, but he left when Henry Ford III offered him the presidency at Ford. Knudsen lasted less than a year, however; apparently because he could not establish personal dominance and was unable to develop a strong coalition with Ford's vice presidents, who seemingly opposed him. Their coalition won.

Examination of business career paths (Jennings, 1967) suggests that sponsor-protege coalitions characterize the most upwardly mobile people. Mobile young managers are sensitive to superiors who have promotion potential, and effective in attaching themselves to them.

Majority Dominance

We sometimes refer to this process as democracy, but dominance is still the central element. The minority is expected to withdraw or go along. Usually, the majority hopes to obtain a consensus, which does not mean unanimity, but that the minority has so little power that it can safely be ignored.

Preference for Dominance

Research with student problem-solving groups under time pressure (Webber, 1972) suggests a preference for dominance techniques. A typical scenario runs as follows: First, there is an attempt to find consensus or unanimity through informal polling. The students seem to hope that there is no conflict. Even at this stage there is some majority dominance, in that some individuals do not express their disagreement when the majority seems against them.

Second: If there is no consensus, the group tends to respond to the dominant individual or the small coalition. The source of dominance may be perceived external status, but more frequently it is the degree of certainty demonstrated by an individual or pair. Where time is limited, certainty dominates uncertainty.

Third: Where status or certainty is absent, formal voting occurs. The majority dominates.

Fourth: If no majority results, the group tends to accept plurality coalition dominance without certainty, or gives up the conflict, does not solve the problem, and moves on to the next one.

The most rational steps toward problem solving are found during phase three. When no one is certain and before taking a vote, some discussion of individual thoughts and experiences in relation to the problem will occur. Substantive questions are raised: "What do the words mean?" "Has anyone ever been in this situation?" "Didn't some famous novelist talk about this?" and so on. Out of this discussion, a dominant position sometimes emerges.

Appeal to Hierarchy

One of mankind's great innovations was the transfer of conflict management from dominance to hierarchical appeal. For some scholars, it marks the beginning of civilization.

Appeal to God or Chance

Initially, the above shift was more philosophical than physical. The battle went on, but it was assumed that God's might was on the side of the right, that the human combat was just the vehicle for God's will. The efficiency of looking for the deity's wishes in less contentious ways was recognized some time ago, however. The stars, animal entrails, and tea leaves all served as communication media. Rationalists consider such appeals superstitious, but this is beside the point. Appeal to even a fictitious god made a major contribution to human advancement through its more efficient conflict management.

Appeal to chance also serves the same purpose, even if it is less philosophically and religiously satisfying. An external event not under the control of the contending parties is used to indicate which will dominate. The loser is expected to withdraw actually or symbolically.

Appeal to Positional Authority: Judicial and Bureaucratic Management

The difficulty with simple appeal to God or Lady Luck is that tremendous faith is necessary to believe that justice has been dispensed. Being of relatively little faith, civilized man began to look for justice in conflict management through more rational ways. Thus was born the idea of a judge or hierarchical superior who would resolve conflicts. A person in a recognized superior position is to listen to the parties in conflict, then decide who is correct.

If the principles of chain of command and unity of command are followed in society and its organizations, any two parties in conflict can find the common superior who links them and who can deal with the conflict. With all the attacks today on hierarchical authority systems, we do well to remember this central fact: this system was an enormous step forward in conflict management. This is perhaps the greatest contribution of hierarchy.

The judicial mechanism of courts, attorneys, judges, and juries are elaborations of the basic system to provide added protection to the defendant and to promote wisdom and justice, but the central feature is the same—the provision for difficult decisions through a judicial/bureaucratic, hierarchical structure. Persons are defined who have the authority and responsibility to make certain difficult and sometimes unpopular decisions.

Bargaining

Conflict may lead to some form of bargaining where the outcome depends upon the balance of power between the two parties. "Bargaining power," as Chamberlain (1955) tells us, "refers to another person's inducement to agree on your terms. Or, to put it in another way, your bargaining power is my cost of disagreeing on your terms relative to my cost of agreeing on your terms. This ratio measures the extent of my inducement to accept what you propose. Similarly, my bargaining power is your cost of disagreeing on my terms relative to your cost of agreeing on my terms" (p. 227). The power may have been bestowed by an external party—such as the power over working conditions given to the manager by his corporate directors, or the power to negotiate agreements delegated to elected union officers by the union membership. Or it may be power growing out of the relationship between the two parties—such as the power that management gives, perhaps inadvertently to any workers (especially to skilled workers) when it hires them and becomes dependent upon them.

Bargaining can be explicit or implicit. In the explicit situation, the two parties are aware that each is trying to influence the other, and that agreement is a function of the power they bring to the situation and their skill as bargainers. Where bargaining is implicit, at least one party does not consciously recognize the situation as one of bargaining. Leavitt (1972) describes this as a manipulative process: the manipulator attempts to develop a relationship of value to the other party, and then to trade on that relationship by threatening to terminate or change it. Such implicit bargaining is frequently associated with two individuals who have no formal power over one another, such as the production-line foreman and the maintenance manager. Nonetheless, an individual may attempt to bargain implicitly with a large number of people. A paternalistic manager who gives turkeys and bonuses at Christmas or builds an employee recreation park is often, consciously or unconsciously, attempting to manipulate subordinates into giving the firm greater loyalty.

The presence of a union is not essential for explicit bargaining, although employees do tend to create formal structures for dealing with management. As Zaleznik and Moment (1964) explain: "Where this problem (conflict) occurs *within* an interacting group, some communication channels exist or are possible for increasing the mutual understanding of real differences in task requisites, as well as the amount and kind of social differences required for group maintenance. When this problem occurs *between* socially isolated groups, such as managers and workers, the tendency is to resort to institutionalized means for resolving intergroup conflict in lieu of primary systems of communication" (p. 346). Nonetheless, conflict and bargaining do take place between management and employee groups, whether formal unions are involved or not.

Direct handling of conflicts by the conflicting parties is often difficult to distinguish from simple dominance. Employers once strove to eliminate unions physically by firing their leaders and exerting coercion (some still try this). The crucial difference between dominance and bargaining, however, is interdependence. In dominance, the dominator does not need the loser any longer. In bargaining, both sides recognize their mutual dependence; they must work together after the conflict. What we are dealing with is a continuum of attitudes: from open hostility to closer cooperation. Two perspectives along this continuum are distributive bargaining and integrative bargaining.

Distributive Bargaining

Distributive bargaining is somewhat like dominance, but with the recognition that the other party can hurt you and will remain after the round of conflict. In the short run, the relationship is viewed as a zero-sum game; what either side gains is at the expense of the other. Hence, it is bargaining over the pieces to be cut from the pie. The method of resolution is to find the size of slice for each that reflects each side's power and ability to harm the other, without totally disrupting the relationship.

Each side attempts to inflate its projected power and willingness to endure injury while endeavoring to discover the other's true minimum position. Confusion, obfuscation, and deception are inherent and necessary. When meaningful and substantive communication occurs, it is mainly on specifics of how much each side is willing to reduce its stated demands. Most labor-management bargaining falls in this category.

Integrative Bargaining

Integrative bargaining is a rare commodity. It is not a rejection of conflict because the parties still must look out for their own interests, but rather it is a transcendence of conflict, the conversion from bargaining to problem solving. The focus shifts from reducing demands toward expanding the pool of resources; away from how the small pie is to be sliced toward how to bake a larger pie so that both sides can increase their welfare. Ideally, the new satisfactions are bigger than the original demands.

This philosophy was communicated 70 years ago by Taylor (1911), who hoped to eliminate harmful "soldiering" and destructive conflict through scientific management. The new industrial engineering techniques were to be used to determine "the best way" to perform each task. Since the work measurement techniques were "scientific," labor and management would accept them, thus eliminating this argument. Bargaining could then be directed to expanding production and income so that both sides could gain.

Taylor's denial of inevitable class conflict and his philosophy of cooperation were typically American, stirring and idealistic. For the most part, however, the techniques caught on while the philosophy was rejected. Perhaps it is just too naive to expect rational agreement on distributing any limited resources, regardless of how large they are absolutely. Nonetheless, it may not be too much to expect collaborative efforts to improve the pool of resources upon which both sides must draw. Then the basis could shift to distributive bargaining. Thus integrative and distributive bargaining might alternate.

The problem, of course, is that keeping the two approaches separate is very difficult; the attitudes of distributive bargaining tend to poison the climate for integrative bargaining. In addition, entering a bargaining situation with an integrative perspective can be very dangerous if the other side views it from the distributive perspective. Integrative bargaining depends on candid disclosure which reduces the possibility of bluffing, therefore handicapping distributive bargaining but exposing one party to the other's exploitation.

Manager's Roles in Conflict Management

Drawing on his analysis of the settings and causes of organizational conflict as well as the various mechanisms for handling conflict, a manager can play a variety of roles. These include personal absorption of stress, judicial/bureaucratic resolution, restructuring of the system to prevent conflict, use of confrontation (matrix), introduction of transcendent objectives, shifting conflict to higher level, and facilitating bargaining.

Personal Absorption of Stress

A former Navy communications officer illustrates personal behavior as a means of alleviating and preventing the spread of stress: "I could tell when the operations officer was upset simply by the stressful behavior of my own men. I also discovered, however, that if I were the first one he came in contact with after he became upset, he could regain his equilibrium by just talking with me. I usually could make time to sit and listen to him while he cussed, complained, and told me his side of the story. After realizing I was an efficient buffer, I tried to make it a point to be the first one to encounter him after one of his go-rounds with the executive officer. In this way, I found I could aid in maintaining the equilibrium of the whole department." After a frustrating experience, the availability of a colleague to whom one can express pent-up feelings may facilitate a quick readjustment to stress.

Under the demands of stress situations, managers often reduce their contacts with others. This may be because they want to avoid the problem entirely or because they are concentrating on the problem area exclusively. In either case, stress is propagated. As much as possible, a manager should maintain his various communication links. Otherwise, reactivation will be difficult when the stress has passed.

Just as the manager must keep contacts in various directions, he should encourage communication laterally among his subordinates and upward to him. Richardson (1961) reports that poor managers are characterized by either very high or very low interaction levels relative to the usual level for that particular position and organization. In addition, poorer supervisors have far less diagonal and upward initiations than more effective supervisors. Research among 50 managers in all kinds of positions indicates only one significant difference in behavior between effective and ineffective managers—effective managers spend more time responding to their subordinates and associates. They are more readily available and receive more contact.

It is clear that the effective manager keeps lines of communication working in many directions. He tries to be consistent and stable in his behavior— especially under stress. Only in this way can the spread of trouble be blocked. Such a manager is described with admiration by a former garment factory employee: "I enjoyed working there, although I worked very hard. Arthur (the manager) was responsible for my pleasant work experience because he treated me fairly. Evidently, this policy has paid off for him because he has been able to maintain productivity at a high level.

"The man obviously had certain leadership qualities because his attitude and manner made you want to work harder. He encouraged everyone to make more money, treated everyone like a human being, and never browbeat an employee. I spoke to him long and often, and I came to the conclusion that he knew precisely what he was doing and why. But his secret always eluded me: how, as he was in the midst of fixing a garment and two girls screamed at him that their machines were jammed, while Ricco complained that he was not getting enough work, and Joe told him that his wife was on the phone in the office, while the machines were roaring, the weather 90 degrees in the shade, and the girls chattering away, *how* in all this, he could remain calm, patient, and composed, I was never able to understand. But whatever his secret, it was this that enabled him to make it a successful operation."

Judicial/Bureaucratic Resolution

By virtue of his formal authority, a manager can sometimes exercise dominance and dismiss one or more of the conflicting parties. This is a tempting step because it seems simple and complete. Richardson (1961) reports a managerial tendency to deal with production problems by replacing supervisors: "Of the twelve changes introduced by upper plant management during the ten-month period, eight were attempts to deal with situations diagnosed largely as problems of supervision. Of these eight, seven involved changes in supervisory personnel" (p. 10). To take another example: In a small steel mill the work and work process were modified. Interaction patterns were upset, stress resulted, and productivity suffered. The general manager was infuriated by the lag in output and by the fact that the welders had refused to work overtime for a few weeks, even though they would be handsomely paid. "Replace them all," he told the plant foreman. But to regard all problems as personnel problems is too limited—many problems are simply not solved by "getting a new man." Furthermore, personnel shifts may aggravate stress. Excessive transfers are both an indication of and a cause of stress. Personnel transfers cannot correct faulty work-flow design.

There is no question that judicious personnel selection and transfer are essential managerial functions. At times, the manager may successfully alleviate stressful conditions by shifting and replacing people. Primarily, however, he must redesign organizational work flow. Resilient mechanisms and routines must be developed by which the organization can absorb the compensatory interactional patterns of disturbed individuals.

If we have reservations about the widespread effectivenss of managerial dominance as a resolution device, this does not mean that managers must abdicate their judicial role. By virtue of their hierarchical positions, managers may still make traditional judgments. If the parties in conflict are his subordinates, the manager can listen to the arguments and render the difficult decision. As we saw in our discussion of charismatic leadership in Chapter 3, most experienced managers greatly admire the person who can demonstrate such courageous decisiveness. As admirable as it may be, however, such judicial decision making is not always sufficient nor desirable.

System Restructuring

Any organization involves the simultaneous coordination of people who must pass paper, materials, or ideas among themselves in some controlled sequence: giving orders, soliciting suggestions, responding to technological breakdowns, planning, etc. All of these activities and functions must be carried out through interactions with others. Thus, organizational structure is most fundamentally a design of human relationships and patterns of interaction.

Certain patterns are experienced as distressing—such as unidirectional, unpredictable, and intermittent or inadequate interactions. In responding to such unsettling conditions, participants demonstrate their stress by disturbed or erratic behavior, including changes in the volume, direction, and content of their interactions. In turn, these disturbed interactions upset other people and propagate the structure-based stress throughout the organization. Thus we see that the most basic functions of the manager include designing, maintaining, and stabilizing interrelated work loads so as to prevent organizational stress where possible and absorb it where necessary.

In order to minimize the adverse impact of stress on organizational effectiveness, managers must design and modify organizational structure to prevent upsetting work patterns. Several patterns are helpful.

Decoupling and Buffering   Since much conflict derives from interdependence, a manager can attempt to reduce this by "decoupling" the conflicting parties. He attempts to reduce their dependence on common resources or to provide iron-clad, impersonal rules for allocation. Giving each control of his own resources or introducing large buffer inventories can be expensive, but they do reduce interdependence. Thus state A in Exhibit 11-1 may be converted into state B.

Decoupling sometimes takes the form of duplicating the facilities of another department upon which one is dependent. For example, research may develop a small production unit under its control for pilot runs. Or a production department may recruit some engineers on its own to lessen its dependence on central engineering. State A in Exhibit 11-1 may be converted to state C.

It is tempting and common for managers to reduce interdependence by introducing excess resources or "organizational slack" at many stages. Extra men,

Exhibit 11-1 Reducing Conflict by System Restructuring

State A Interdependent

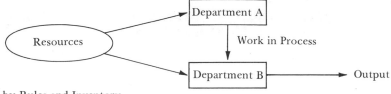

State B Decoupled by Rules and Inventory

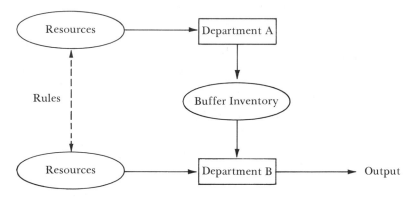

State C Decoupled by Duplication of Capability

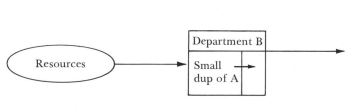

State D Buffered by an Intermediary Position

State E Unified Work Flow

money, and machines can make life easier. But such suboptimization may harm the whole organization.

Another form of buffering can be introduced in the form of an "expendable linker" (Dalton, 1963). This could be a fairly passive and low-status individual (or group) who serves as a communication link between conflicting parties. He is not personally threatening to any group, and they can vent their antagonisms on him without fear of retaliation. The go-between is sometimes an older man who clearly has little possibility of promotion and whose technical expertise is outdated. The linking role is usually informal with no official assignment of duties. Nonetheless, some formal linking groups do exist: field engineers standing between customers or sales representatives and design engineers; development engineers between research scientists and design engineers or production managers; order fillers between chefs and waiters; public relations or press representatives between political leaders and the press or public; directors of student activities between students and academic administrators.

Obviously, to play such a role can be extremely stressful. Many go-betweens are caught in the crossfire. The person must be able to absorb substantial stress or in fact not feel much stress because of a security guarantee or independent satisfaction.

Unifying Work Flow   Much stress and conflict stems from violation of the old organizational principle, "authority should equal responsibility." A manager feels upset because he does not control everything that he needs to perform his mission. Controlling *everything* is probably impossible, but the system might be restructured into more logical and complete work units which bring more control under one hierarchical position, thus decreasing ambiguity. This does increase unit size, and additional costs for internal coordination are necessary, but the benefits of defining a hierarchical judge may outweigh the costs. Thus state A in Exhibit 11-1 may be converted to state E.

The difference between states C and E is sometimes a matter of judgment and perception. Production might feel that developing its own small research or engineering capacity is logically unifying the task, while the other groups consider it inefficient, slack, and illegitimate empire building. The difference is subtle, but as a rule state C evolves informally, while state E is a formal organizational change. In fact, in most cases, state E may simply be legitimizing a previously existing state C.

Modifying Role Demands   To reduce or eliminate role conflict, a manager may simplify the demands imposed by eliminating conflicting elements. Or he may segregate the roles among different people. For example, a university may hire additional proctors to relieve a dormitory advisor of responsibility to enforce regulations; he can then concentrate on his advisory role. Management can separate monitoring from advising for a staff group by assigning the roles to different groups. Government or stock exchange action can segregate the roles of a stockbroker so that individuals and perhaps even institutions perform narrower roles—only sales, or advice, or underwriting. For university professors, the Carnegie Foundation has suggested that two doctoral degrees and two academic careers be created; one to concentrate on teaching, the other on research and writing.

Matrix Organization Perhaps the most persistent theme in recent literature on conflict management is confrontation. Limited research suggests that more effective managers facilitate conflict recognition and conciliation rather than "smoothing" conflict over by denying its reality or "forcing" solutions by superior power (Lawrence and Lorsch, 1967). Such managers recognize that conflict is inevitable if they create a climate where people express independent ideas rather than just conforming to the prevailing view. What is desired is that this conflict be expressed by following certain rules of confrontation.

Within organizations, a matrix structure offers one means for facilitating such confrontation. The most common matrix is shown in Exhibit 11-2. Such a structure is intended to promote the flexible use of specialized staff on interdisciplinary programs (e.g., a sophisticated product team drawing on various scientists and engineers in electronics, hydraulics, operations research, metallurgy, etc.). Just as important, however, is that the matrix defines a battlefield and its participants. It recognizes the competing interests of program and specialist departments, such as short-run program completion versus long-run career development. It provides separate managers to stand up for those interests. The overall executive's major role is to facilitate communication and bargaining, stepping in to be a judicial/bureaucratic decision maker only when absolutely necessary.

Exhibit 11-2 Matrix Organization

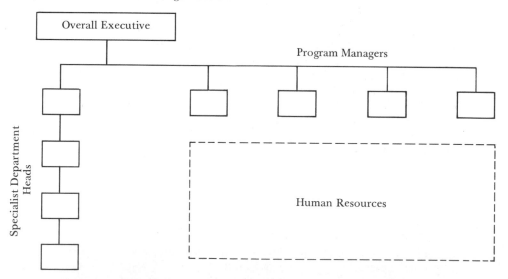

Based on survey data in research laboratories, Evan (1965) concluded that interpersonal conflict (i.e., personality conflict) is negatively associated with performance, while technical conflict (i.e., differences of opinion on design, technology, methods, etc.) is positively associated with performance. The matrix approach encourages technical conflict, while bringing interpersonal conflict out into the open where it can be seen.

There is some role ambiguity for the people involved, since they are in the middle of potential conflict. But overt conflict may be less debilitating than covert conflict. And research suggests that if they actively participate in reconciling the conflict, stress may still be high but job satisfaction will be increased. In this situation, stress from role ambiguity does not appear to affect performance adversely (Tosi, 1971).

Teamwork Through Conflict at TRW Systems   In recent years, TRW Systems (the high-technology aerospace operating group of TRW, Inc.) has drawn attention for its innovative management style. Team-building confrontation meetings, sensitivity training, and organization development meetings have been combined with their version of the matrix organization. An article in *Business Week* (March 20, 1970) examined their system:

"In July, 1960, the systems group, then called Space Technology Laboratories (with Ruben Mettler as its president), gave up its position as a captive think tank of the Air Force to become a hardware producer in a highly competitive market.

"That demanded a discipline of cost that was not much of a problem in the Air Force missile program. 'There,' James Dunlap, a vice president, explains, 'the name of the game was to get it done and not worry about costs.' But once Systems moved out to produce hardware on its own, the stakes and risks of losing were higher. Says Dunlap, 'We had to coordinate our activities and perform economically.'

"To get the work done, an unconventional management structure called Matrix was evolved, which was effective, though, only after OD was put in use. Matrix is a variation on the strict project organization of the aerospace industry. At Systems, each project office is not self-sufficient—it is only a minimum core group for overall planning, budgeting, coordination, and systems engineering. For the actual design and technical work, the project office calls on professionals from specialized departments.

"'Matrix is a way to get maximum utilization of highly technical and specialized resources on projects that do not always need these resources full-time,' says Richard D. DeLauer, TRW executive vice president. 'Our customers pay us for X number of people, but in reality they may be getting access to 20X people.'

"Matrix has its difficulties. One tradeoff for high utilization of resources is the loss of clear and permanent lines of authority. To get a job done, the project manager uses people over whom he has little authority. And each project office competes for resources and manpower. As one TRW employee puts it: 'The project office by nature has a hell-with-everyone-else attitude.' While the project office view is short-term, the departmental support groups' outlook is longer term. They must determine priorities and the necessary trading off to meet the requirements of several projects at once.

"'The project office and the departmental support group are fundamentally at cross purposes,' says D. R. McRell, an industrial relations staffer. 'The chief skill needed for Matrix is conflict management.'

"At TRW Systems, Matrix involves both permanent and temporary lines of authority [see Exhibit 11-3]. When these two kinds of authority meet, there are inherent conflicts. Ideally, organization development (OD)—a potpourri of

Exhibit 11-3 Management by Matrix

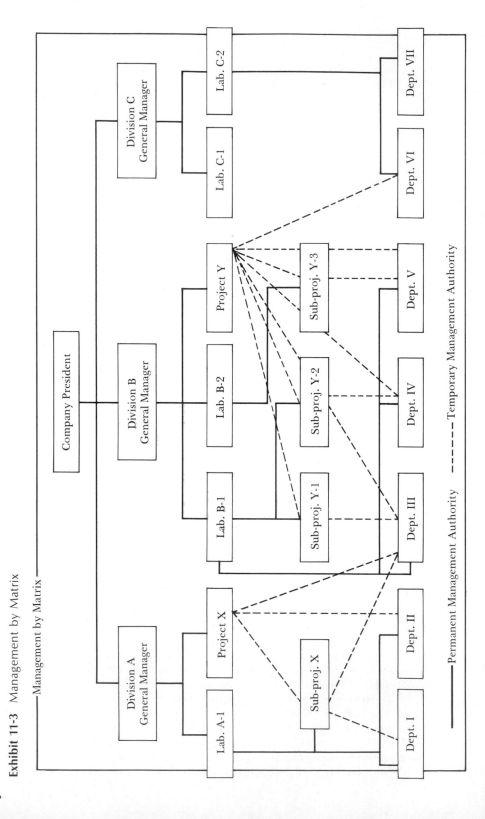

behavioral science techniques—keeps the communications channels open, minimizing the difficulties that result.

"The manager of Laboratory B-1 may agree, for example, at the start of Project Y that the project manager is the 'boss' of Depts. III, IV, and V as far as work on his Project Y is concerned. The laboratory manager also loans people from his lab to be subproject managers, who report to Project Y's manager and recruit expertise from any number of departments—including Depts. II or VI in other divisions.

"Under Matrix management, an engineer in Dept. III may work on several project teams at once and have any number of bosses. For instance, he may work for subproject manager Y-1 and project manager Y as well as for the head of Project X in another division."

Introducing Transcendent Objectives

Historically, introducing a transcendent objective has probably been the most common device of great leaders. Ideally, it renders existing conflict irrelevant by introducing a new superordinate objective that unites the conflicting parties. In William Golding's novel *Lord of the Flies,* the marooned boys were able to transcend their differences as long as they accepted the superordinate objective of keeping the signal fire lighted. When they gave up hope of rescue and the fire lost meaning as a common goal, the group decomposed into warring factions.

Sherif (1958) described superordinate goals as "compelling and highly appealing to members of two or more groups in conflict but which cannot be attained by the resources and energies of the groups separately." He concludes: "When individuals interact in a series of situations toward goals which appeal to all and which require that they coordinate their activities, group structures arise having hierarchical status arrangements and a set of norms regulating behavior in matters of consequence to the objectives of the group."

The creative conflict resolver looks for common, not divergent elements. For example, political leaders have long united squabbling followers by pointing out a common enemy who would destroy them all unless they fight together. (Think of George Washington and Europe, Castro and the United States, Mao and the Soviet Union.) Or the leader articulates the serious internal problems facing everyone, problems of such gravity that chaos will result unless petty dissension is dropped and cooperative behavior evidenced. (Think of Franklin Roosevelt and the Depression, Lyndon Johnson and civil rights, and numerous contemporary school administrators.) At a more mundane level, a manager can alter the reward system so that contending parties are rewarded for their cooperative performance rather than for their individual behavior. For example, rather than rewarding production department managers for performance on their departmental budgets, a plant-wide total cost index could be tied to a plant-wide bonus. The intent is to create an objective to which all parties are committed and which requires cooperative behavior to achieve.

Unfortunately, there is a limit to such expansion of objective. Where the transcendent objective becomes too large, encompassing a large number of individuals and groups, it tends to lose its motivating force. Each individual feels himself too small to really affect the whole; he thinks objective achievement does not significantly reflect his personal efforts. Hence he may give up. The individual worker or even a whole production department may simply not see a direct relation between his or their performance and the plant bonus. None-theless, the fact that the technique of offering transcendent, unifying objectives is used by demogogues and dictators as well as saints and democrats testifies to its potency as a mechanism for managing conflict.

Shifting Conflict to a Higher Level

To promote short-run cooperation and to buy time for more fundamental conflict resolution, a manager may attempt to assume the burden of conflict from his subordinates. He may tell competing subordinates that resolution does not rest at their level or at his level; that he will represent their interests upward in order to obtain more resources or a different distribution. Meanwhile, the subordinates should drop their fight and get on with the job. Such an approach looks dangerously like buck passing, but if the leader succeeds in resolving the conflict he assumes, it can reinforce his influence with his subordinates. It would appear that managers should be able to assume such stress from time to time.

Facilitating Bargaining

Not all conflict management depends exclusively on the manager's hierarchical position. He may allow and encourage conflicting subordinates to bargain directly. Chamberlain (1955) suggests that virtually all organizational decisions are made on the basis of the relative bargaining powers of those whose views and interests clash. Because of the complexity of these internal bargaining processes and their potential danger to organizational effectiveness, management must guide and control them: "Because of the number of individuals and groups involved, because of the number of issues concerned of which each has his preferences, because of the requirement that with respect to any issue only one resolution can be made, applying to all affected, and because of the further requirement that the decision on any issue must be consistent; and compatible with the decisions on all other issues—because of all these conditions it is necessary that there be a coordinator of the bargaining" (p. 228). This task—the coordination of the bargains of all those who compose the organization—is a unique function of management.

Mediation or conciliation is a way of fulfilling this function. The purpose of a mediator is not to decide who is right or what is just (an arbitrator or judge does that). Rather, a mediator attempts to stop the spiral of conflict by eliminating surrender as a demand and by encouraging each party to acknowledge that they have injured the other (in effect, to grant some justification for the other's hostility to them); he attempts to promote more authentic communication; and if requested, he suggests possible solutions.

Since "the key to all conflict resolution is the repair of previous injury and protection against future injury, conciliation is any act whose aim is to avert or discontinue conflict without either side asking or offering surrender" (Turner, 1969). By discovering and communicating the true positions of the parties, the mediator assists them in confronting their real differences and in discovering their common problems. As we have seen, the major tragedy in conflict is that efforts to injure the other party dominate the issues dividing the two. Hence, conflict shifts from item to item, philosophy to philosophy, and the original substantive matters may be forgotten. The mediating manager's great contribution can be to return the conflict to the real issues. He can articulate the potential damage to all parties if conflict continues.

Walton (1967) offers the following advice to managers for setting a proper example for handling conflict:

Confront, invite differences.
Listen with understanding rather than evaluation.
Clarify the nature of the issue.
Recognize and accept feelings.
Suggest a procedure for resolving differences.
Cope with threats to reasonable agreement.

He also points out that a mediator needs synchronization in confrontation. That is, he must make a judgment that the parties are both ready to confront each other and potentially willing to communicate. Premature confrontation may only promote escalation (a phenomenon long known to astute national leaders who delay "summit" conferences until agreement potential is high). Rejection of one party's overture to talk is viewed as particularly demeaning, which "justifies" strong attack from the rejected party (an event which has characterized many recent conflicts—Israel and Egypt, United States and North Vietnam, Pakistan and India).

The essence of successful mediation lies in making the warring parties realize they are dependent on each other, and in finding an area of common agreement (Henderson, 1971). Such an approach assumes that the issues to be resolved are objective and substantive, not merely reflections of irrational behavior by the contending parties. An objective definition of the problem, agreed upon by both sides, may be the single most important step in resolution (Blake and Mouton, 1961). Upon this common definition can sometimes be built a transcendent objective.

Substantial laboratory research under conditions where two parties apparently want to maximize their individual incomes indicates that many choices (almost 50 percent) are made *not* to maximize personal income, but to decrease the competitor's income. Relative standing seems more important then absolute benefits (Scodel et al., 1959). If the mediator can stretch the minds of quarreling individuals or groups so they can see how their parochial viewpoints fit into a much larger system, a higher understanding may be developed that integrates seemingly diverse goals. A sense of shared goals is critical.

Approaches to Reduction of Intergroup Tensions

Based upon Sherif's concepts of the importance of superordinate goals, Blake et al. (1961) outlined five approaches to reducing intergroup tensions:

1. *Negotiation by group members:* The critical limitation to seeking resolution through representative negotiation lies in the potential for conflict of interest. A representative who suffers defeat jeopardizes his own membership status; gaining victory enhances his membership position. Victory or defeat are, therefore, likely to be measured by reference to the position embraced by the group prior to negotiation. Where such conflict of interest occurs, loyalty overwhelms logic. Furthermore, since a chosen representative is likely to be an informal group leader, he is less free to negotiate than any other member of his group. Thus, the leader in his negotiations must behave in accord with the strictest interpretation of his group's norms.

2. *Exchange of persons:* The chances for increasing successful intergroup

collaboration through exchanges of *individuals* between groups is limited by two factors. People-to-people interaction across groups serves to make initially positive attitudes more positive, and initially negative attitudes more negative; therefore, only those individuals who are initially neutral are susceptible to influence. And social, political, and economic attitudes, rather than being based solely on individual personality, are significantly anchored in reference-group affiliations; the exchanged individual will resist influences which violate his group's norms. However, the exchange of *subgroups* may create a favorable background for future intergroup conflict resolution.

3. *Handing the conflict to judges:* While a judge is not usually subject to the "conflict of interest" problem, he is nearly as suspect by those whose position he defeats as is the representative who opposes his own group. Inherently, the judge's decision carries little force compared to the strength of the group's commitment to its position.

4. *Common goals with crisscross panels:* Several conditions are necessary to enhance the superordinate-goal approach. Both sides must *desire* a genuine solution, and there must be a single problem definition agreed upon by both sides prior to a statement of preferred solutions. However, the superordinate-goal approach is limited by the fact that it is difficult—if not in some cases impossible—for all members of competing groups to feel intimately involved in the drive toward attaining superordinate goals. Some system for choosing representatives is therefore necessary. The crisscross panel is one method of selection which minimizes status reductions that occur as a result of one representative's opposing his group's position.

Each side develops a list of nominees whom they consider qualified to represent them with respect to one particular source of friction. Next, from the total list of nominees, all group members elect an equal number of representatives from each side as a common decision-making panel. The panel then contains members who represent their own group and simultaneously represent the other group as well. By such a method of selection, representatives are able to confront the problem relatively free of the "hero-traitor" dynamic which is characteristic of the usual unilateral group orientation.

5. *Intergroup therapy:* Many problems, themselves subject to solution through the superordinate-goal approach, cannot even be faced until deeper animosities *between* groups have been resolved, or at least explored and neutralized. If emotion-laden negative attitudes and stereotypes are dealt with first, it becomes possible in a second phase to formulate and work toward the attainment of superordinate goals.

In private, each group discusses and seeks to agree on its perceptions of and attitudes toward the other group, and its perceptions of itself as well. Then *representatives* of both groups talk together in the presence of all members from both sides, who are obligated to remain silent. During this phase, representatives are responsible for accurate communication of the picture each group has constructed of the other and of itself. Representatives are used to maintain orderly communication and to increase the acceptance of responsibility for providing an accurate version of the situation. Members of both groups then discuss, *in private,* discrepancies in perception uncovered by their joint meeting. Finally, again working through representatives, each group helps the other to appreciate the bases of their differences, to correct invalid perceptions, and to consider alternative explanations of past behavior. The groups are now in an improved position to work toward superordinate goals.

Current Problems in Conflict Management

Man has always been tempted to resort to simple dominance to handle conflict. Violence and war are not necessarily more common today than in the past. Nonetheless, the complexity and interdependence of modern life mean that such solutions are less often restricted to the parties directly involved. Others are drawn in. In the sparsely populated and independent American frontier, two men "reconciling" their differences through gunplay was sad, but affected few people. Such behavior today threatens chaos. Accordingly, it is of ever increasing importance that we make alternative conflict management systems work. Unfortunately, they also present problems.

Judicial/Bureaucratic Resolution

We have already expressed our appreciation for the hierarchical decision maker as conflict resolver. He still has an important role, but it is shrinking. Optimal performance depends on a happy congruence of authority, knowledge, wisdom, and subordinate respect. When the decision maker cannot understand the issues, or the conflicting parties do not believe he does, nor respect his authority, his ability to resolve conflict is sharply curtailed. People will not accept the superior's judgment. They will attempt to fight it out without the judge; they will try to eliminate each other. Of course, a hierarchical superior can resort to his own dominance to force acceptance, but this sharply undermines the efficiency of the system.

The U.S. court system faces this crisis. Simple overload introduces delays until the conflict mechanism acts. And justice long delayed is not justice. In addition, substantial segments of society do not recognize the nation's laws as *their* laws and neither recognize nor respect the judge/jury's decisions. Most organization managers do not yet face problems of such great magnitude, but their ability to resolve conflict by hierarchical decisions is similarly eroding. Our discussion in Chapter 3 of the decline in traditional authority applies here.

An additional problem for hierarchical conflict management is that the neat departmental boxes are breaking down in and between organizations; boundaries are becoming indistinct. In short, most systems are expanding so that more and more people are in conflict who do not have a definite common superior to whom they can appeal. Who is the common superior of university alumni and administrators? Of government regulatory agencies and business executives? Of Ralph Nader's "raiders" and a company's management? Of a corporate president and dissenting vice presidents when the board of directors is mainly an inside board? A dramatic increase in unofficial advocacy groups has characterized U.S. society in recent years. Concern for the poor, for minorities, and for the environment has expressed itself in autonomous groups making demands on older, more formal organizations. Such confrontations are increasing, and they are not very susceptible to the traditional judicial/bureaucratic mode of conflict management.

Internal Organizational Bargaining

Managers increasingly must face the anxiety of presiding over conflicts below them as well as participating in bargaining themselves. Some will see bargaining as an improvement over dominance. Autonomous people can look out for their own interests and manage their own affairs. They are less dependent on a superior to resolve their difficulties. However, people new to bargaining attempt to dominate the other parties, so that coordination breaks down and the effects of conflict spread. The emphasis tends to be on distributive rather than integrative bargaining. This is the current state of affairs in many institutions where parties have begun to deal with each other directly: students and administrators, players and coaches, professionals and government bureaucrats, even enlisted men and officers. All of this is similar to the early days of labor-management negotiation before some unions and employers came to recognize the commonality of their problems.

In the words of the eminent labor economist and mediator George Taylor (1966), it is imperative that we come to see bargaining not as a game to be won or lost, but as a problem-solving process; that we need a new "philosophy of losing"—a philosophy that sees exchange in bargaining not as a defeat, but as a continuous process of conflict resolution.

However exasperating collective negotiations are, they represent one of the most important mechanisms of social conflict management. At its best, such bargaining signifies recognition and acceptance by the conflicting parties of each other's competing claims on resources within an orderly framework of law and custom. It appears that this mechanism will be expanded to many areas beyond labor and management relations. For inter-organizational conflicts, for example, there might be permanent panels of highly trained citizens to serve as "community mediation boards," appointed as quasi-public bodies and available at all times for any dispute that would otherwise fester, clutter court calendars, or be resolved by power plays (Henderson, 1971). The activities of most informal advocacy groups have been initially disruptive because they bring submerged issues to the surface, where they inevitably clash with established institutions and contrary public opinion. For this reason, they often trigger opposition and repression. But as they gain legitimacy and develop support, they will represent another means of resolving conflict between minority interests and the dominant culture.

Need for New Mechanisms

Finally, it appears that we need entirely new mechanisms for conflict management if we truly believe that such conflict is legitimate and potentially valuable. The ombudsman idea is not especially new and it is not a direct mechanism for conflict resolution, but it may be suggestive. The ombudsman stands outside the hierarchical structure so that he can facilitate communication and ensure that lower levels in the hierarchy can bring their problems up to the top. It may facilitate resolution of small conflicts before they expand.

Internal hearings and private courts are also not new, but are relatively rare within organizations. They may provide due process and more legitimate means to adjudicate what used to be strictly managerial decisions. A subordinate in conflict with a superior might have a body of peers to whom he could appeal.

A third old device is gaining new interest. This is the "expeditor" converted into "coordinator" or "integrator" (Lawrence and Lorsch, 1967). His role is to facilitate communication and coordination between interdependent and potentially conflicting departments. In most cases, he carries no substantial authority (other than right of access), but he has responsibility to promote, detect, and manage differences.

None of these devices are panaceas. We still need novel means of dealing with conflict. In few areas is the need for human ingenuity more critical.

Summary

We have considered the various social mechanisms man has developed for resolving conflict, including dominance (by individuals, coalitions, or majority), by appeal to a hierarchy (whether chance, God, or superior positions), and bargaining (both distributive and integrative).

The manager can play several roles in managing conflict. He might be a judicial/bureaucratic decision maker—although this aspect may be declining in importance. He might restructure the system by decoupling, buffering, or unifying contending departments. He might introduce superordinate objectives that transcend the conflict, or shift it to a higher level, thus unifying the contending parties. He might even facilitate bargaining by designing an appropriate matrix structure and acting as mediator.

We desperately need more effective conflict management. All of our mechanisms face difficulty because of changing patterns of authority and respect, because of emerging groups promoting change, and simply because of the large volume of conflicts to be managed. As Kahn et al. (1964) point out, our objective should be the "containment of conflict and ambiguity at levels and forms which are humane, tolerable, low in cost, and which at best, might be a positive contribution to the individual and the organization."

References

Bensman, J. *Dollars and Sense.* Macmillan, 1967.

Blake, R. R., and J. S. Mouton. "Reactions to Intergroup Competition Under Win-Lose Conditions." *Management Science,* Vol. 4, No. 4, July 1961.

Chamberlain, N. *A General Theory of Economic Process.* Harper & Row, 1955.

Dalton, G. W. "Diagnosing Interdepartmental Conflict." *Harvard Business Review,* September–October 1963.

Evan, W. M. "Conflict and Performance in R & D Organizations." *Industrial Management Review,* Vol. 7, No. 2 (Fall 1965), 37–46.

Henderson, H. "Toward Managing Social Conflict." *Harvard Business Review* (May–June 1971), 82–90.

Jennings, E. E. *The Mobile Manager.* Bureau of Industrial Relations, University of Michigan, 1967.

Kahn, R. L., D. M. Wolfe, R. P. Quinn, J. D. Snoek, and R. A. Rosenthal. *Organizational Stress.* Wiley, 1964.

Lawrence, P. R. "New Management Job: The Integrator." *Harvard Business Review,* Vol. 45, No. 6 (November–December 1967), 142–151.

———— and J. W. Lorsch. *Organization and Environment.* Division of Research, Harvard Business School, 1962.

———— and J. A. Seiler. *Organizational Behavior and Administration,* rev. ed. Irwin-Dorsey, 1965.

Leavitt, H. *Managerial Psychology,* 3rd ed. University of Chicago Press, 1972.

Lorenz, K. *On Aggression.* Harcourt Brace Jovanovich, 1966.

Piggott, S., ed. *The Dawn of Civilization.* McGraw-Hill, 1961.

Richardson, F. L. W. *Talk, Work and Action.* Monograph No. 3, The Society for Applied Anthropology, 1961.

Scodel, A., J. S. Minas, P. Ratoosh, and M. Lipetz. "Some Descriptive Aspects of Two-Person, Non-Zero Sum Games." *Journal of Conflict Resolution,* Vol. 3 (1959), 114–119.

Sherif, M. "Superordinate Goals in the Reduction of Intergroup Conflict." *American Journal of Sociology,* Vol. 63, No. 4, January 1958.

Skinner, B. F. *Beyond Freedom and Dignity.* Knopf, 1971.

Taylor, F. W. *The Principles of Scientific Management.* Harper & Row, 1911.

Taylor, G. W. "Ideas for Social Change." World Academy of Art and Science, Junk, The Hague, 1966.

Tosi, H. "Organization Stress as a Moderator of the Relationship Between Influence and Role Response." *Academy of Management Journal,* March 1971.

Turner, R. "The Public Perception of Protest." *American Sociological Review,* Vol. 34 (1969), 815–831.

Walton, R. E. "Third-Party Roles in Interdepartmental Conflict." *Industrial Relations,* Vol. 7, No. 1, October 1967.

——— and R. B. McKersie. *A Behavioral Theory of Labor Negotiations—An Analysis of a Social Interaction System.* McGraw-Hill, 1965.

Webber, R. A. *Time and Management.* Van Nostrand Reinhold, 1972.

Yoshino, M. *Japan's Managerial System.* The MIT Press, 1968.

Zaleznik, A. "Power and Politics in Organizational Life." *Harvard Business Review* (May–June 1970), 47–60.

——— and D. Moment. *The Dynamics of Interpersonal Behavior.* Wiley, 1964.

Readings

A Behavioral Theory of Negotiation
RICHARD E. WALTON, ROBERT B. McKERSIE

The Analytical Framework

Negotiation, as an instance of social negotiation, is comprised of four systems of activity, each with its own function for the interacting parties, its own internal logics, and its own identifiable set of instrumental acts or tactics.

We shall refer to each of the distinguishable systems of activities as a *subprocess.* The first subprocess is *distributive bargaining;* its function is to resolve pure conflicts of interest. The second, *integrative bargaining,* functions to find common or complementary interests and solve problems confronting both parties. The third subprocess is *attitudinal structuring,* and its functions are to influence the attitudes of the participants toward each other and to affect the basic bonds which relate the two parties they represent. A fourth subprocess, *intraorganizational bargaining,* has the function of achieving consensus within each of the interacting groups.

Distributive Bargaining

Distributive bargaining is a hypothetical construct referring to the complex system of activities instrumental to the attainment of one party's goals when they are in basic conflict with those of the other party. It is the type of activity most familiar to students of negotiations; in fact, it is "bargaining" in the strictest sense of the word. In social negotiations, the goal conflict can relate to several values; it can involve allocation of any resources, e.g., economic, power, or status symbols. What game theorists refer to as fixed-sum games are the situations we have in mind: one person's gain is a loss to the other. The specific points at which the negotiating objectives of the two parties come in contact define the issues. Formally, an *issue* will refer to an area of common concern in which the objectives of the two parties are assumed to be in conflict. As such, it is the subject of distributive bargaining.

Integrative Bargaining

Integrative bargaining refers to the system of activities which is instrumental to the attainment of objectives which are *not* in fundamental conflict with those of the other party and which therefore can be integrated to some degree. Such objectives are said to define an area of common concern, a *problem.* Integrative bargaining and distributive bargaining are both joint decision-making processes. However, these processes are quite dissimilar and yet are rational responses to different situations. Integrative potential exists when the nature of a problem permits solutions which benefit both parties, or at least when the gains of one party do not represent equal sacrifices by the other. This is closely related to what game theorists call the varying-sum game.

Attitudinal Structuring

Distributive and integrative bargaining pertain to economic issues and the rights and obligations of the parties, which are the generally recognized content of negotiations. However, we postulate that an additional major function of negotiations is influencing the relationships between parties, in particular such attitudes as friendliness-hostility, trust, respect, and the motivational orientation of competitiveness-cooperativeness. Although the existing relationship pattern is acknowledged to be influenced by many more enduring forces (such as the technical and economic context, the basic personality dispositions of key participants, and the social belief systems which pervade the two parties), the negotiators can and do take advantage of the interaction system of negotiations to produce attitudinal change.

Attitudinal structuring is our term for the system of activities instrumental to the attainment of desired relationship patterns between the parties. Desired relationship patterns usually give content to this process in a way comparable to that of issues and problems in distributive and integrative processes. The distinction among the processes is that whereas the first two are joint decision-making processes, attitudinal structuring is a socioemotional interpersonal process designed to change attitudes and relationships.

Intraorganizational Bargaining

The three processes discussed thus far relate to the reconciliation process that takes place between the union and the company. During the course of negotiations another system of activities, designed to achieve consensus within the union and within the company, takes place. Intraorganizational bargaining refers to the system of activities which brings the expectations of principals into alignment with those of the chief negotiator.

The chief negotiators often play important but limited roles in formulating bargaining objectives. On the union side, the local membership exerts considerable influence in determining the nature and strength of aspirations, and the international union may dictate the inclusion of certain goals in the bargaining agenda. On the company side, top management and various staff groups exert their influence on bargaining objectives. In a sense the chief negotiator is the recipient of two sets of demands—one from across the table and one from his own organization. His dilemma stems from conflict at two levels: differing aspirations about issues and differing expectations of behavior.

Distributive Bargaining

As we have stressed before, this process is basic to negotiations. However, the relative dominance of distributive bargaining activity in negotiations and the form it takes depends upon many contextual factors.

Basic Payoff Structure

Some basis for negotiations must exist before the parties can be motivated to bargain. This dependency can come about in several ways. First, the parties may enjoy a mutual advantage or *positive sum* because of such factors as market rigidities. The area of common interest is defined for them by their respective alternatives or by resistance points. In game terminology the joint gain is *fixed,* that is, it is determined by marketlike forces rather than by the efforts of the parties. A fixed-sum configuration usually produces distributive bargaining as the parties seek to divide the joint gain.

Whether the parties utilize power tactics and active coercion depends upon whether their respective aspirations for sharing the joint gain are compatible. When the terms of trade or norms for sharing the joint gain are relatively well established, there is little that the parties can or try to do except to define the situation and decide whether to enter into it or not.

In many instances the parties share a dependency because the relationship between two parties is an exclusive one—neither party has another relationship which can perform the same function for the party, or alternate relationships are available only at a substantial cost. However, in other situations one party may enjoy another alternative, and his dependency upon the relationship can be rather small. Therefore the basis for bargaining must come in a different manner.

When the environment does not establish dependency, it is often possible through bargaining to create mutual gain. Such a prospect produces integrative bargaining. The parties start with a zero-sum situation, but through their efforts they create a positive sum. The amount of gain created depends upon the inherent nature of the issues and the effectiveness of their problem solving. Thus over time the game may be positive and *varying sum* in character.

Of course, both parties seldom enter voluntarily into real-world bargaining situations unless good prospects exist for the zero-sum game to be transformed into a positive-sum game. If no relationship and no joint gain exist, it may be difficult to create a basis for bargaining merely on the chance that something beneficial might result. In many situations an initiating party would like to bargain, but the responding party refuses, realizing that he only stands to lose.

In such situations the first party has to create an incentive for the second party to enter negotiations. If no relationship exists, which is usually the case, and the absence of a relationship means the absence of trust, it is unlikely that the prospect of increasing mutual gain (through integrative bargaining) can be used as a meaningful basis for negotiations.

The basis for negotiations may have to come from coercion. In effect, the initiating party creates the prospect of harm for his opponent, the size of this expected loss being greater than the expected cost of the first party's demands. The opponent finds himself in the difficult configuration of avoidance-avoidance conflict. He agrees to participate in the *negative-sum* game because his only alternative produces a larger expected negative value. In effect, the substantive issue is *zero sum,* but when the threat of harm is added, the game payoffs for the responding party are all zero to negative in sum.

Labor Negotiations This context usually represents the positive-sum game, either fixed or varying in character, depending upon the issues and the orienta-tion of the parties. In labor-management negotiations, the parties are usually held together by a considerable area of joint dependency. Normally this depen-dency is balanced, and the union is as dependent upon management as vice versa.

However, there are certain situations in which the dependency in either direction can be rather thin. For example, the Teamsters are not dependent upon any small trucking company, and the area of mutual dependence is pretty much the dependence of the company upon the Teamsters. Contrastingly, in some industries in which the company is strong and the union is weak the area of dependency is very thin for the company. Some people feel that such is the case in the General Electric situation, in which the company has many alternatives (nonunion plants, etc.). Consequently, the union finds itself the dependent party.

The typical situation, however, is usually symmetrical both on positive gains (in the sense of both experiencing benefit from being in the relationship) and on the cost of a short-term breakdown (in the sense that both experience important sacrifices from a strike).

As we noted elsewhere, the incentive to negotiate may not come from market factors but from legislation. The requirements of the National Labor Relations Act (NLRA) may bring the parties together and induce them to negotiate an agreement.

The importance of this basis for bargaining can be inferred from the conduct of parties in situations not protected by the NLRA. For example, not-for-profit hospitals are exempted from the procedures of representation elections, designation of bargaining agents, and good-faith bargaining. Thus in 1959 and 1960 when a number of unions sought recognition for nonprofessional hospital workers, they were ignored in many instances. They possessed no means for creating a dependency on the part of the hospital management.

In New York City, the union created a basis for negotiations by striking against several hospitals and by disseminating to the public information about working conditions in hospitals. While most observers condemned these "strikes against the sick," the union's actions created such a severe crisis that the hospitals were forced to come to the bargaining table. The incentive to enter into negotiations did not come directly from the union but from the mayor and influential individuals who urged the hospitals to enter into discussions about employment conditions in order to end the crisis.

In Chicago at about the same time two hospitals were also struck. However, the campaigns were unsuccessful, since the striking workers allowed replacements and supplies to cross the picket line. Moreover, the mayor and influential citizens sharply criticized the union's action and thereby provided moral support for hospital management in its refusal to meet with the union.[1]

Thus a crucial factor in creating the basis for negotiations, as well as in affecting the outcome, is the role of third parties. We shall examine this structural factor shortly.

International Relations Although there are positive-sum possibilities, most manifest aspects of the payoff are zero sum with the presence of a negative-sum default alternative. An interesting point is that countries try to reduce areas of positive dependency and are particularly sensitive to asymmetrical structures. This is seen in the dispute between the United States and Panama over the arrangements for the Panama Canal. The United States has actively undertaken plans to build another canal in order to minimize its dependency upon the country of Panama for the Panama Canal. Shaping the area of dependency as the United States has done does not remove the basis for negotiations; it merely alters the resistance point for the United States and therefore the power equation.

The nuclear threat, however, creates mutual negative dependency insofar as both sides have a desire to avoid nuclear holocaust. In the Cuban crisis, as is typical in crisis encounters, the United States created the basis for negotiations between itself and Russia by convincing Russia that the cost of not entering negotiations (war) was greater than the cost of the concession involved.

Civil Rights   The substantive aspects of many civil rights encounters are also zero sum.[2] A change in public accommodations results in gains in freedom and dignity valued by one group and the loss of an arrangement needed and valued (although pathologically, perhaps) by another group. Voting rights and political power gained by Negroes take place at the expense of the political power and control of another group. Employment concessions which involve unneeded hires or preferential treatment may cost the employer flexibility and the loss of prerogatives that he values.

Because such items in civil rights are likely to be zero sum and since the target parties are expected to grant concessions, these groups are understandably reluctant to acknowledge the existence of a tacit bargaining situation, much less enter into explicit negotiations. Therefore, preliminary to establishing a bargaining relationship, the civil rights groups must first command the attention of the target party and also establish a basis for a *quid pro quo*. This usually involves threats of loss, inconvenience, or embarrassment.[3]

Although historically civil rights groups have had no negotiating base—no positive gains that they could offer nor any losses that they could threaten—this changed drastically during the 1960s. Most of the direct action that has taken place in the early 1960s must be seen as an attempt to create a situation in which the target eventually becomes dependent upon the civil rights movement, if only to have the demonstration or the boycott stopped.

An analysis of these direct-action techniques can be used to demonstrate both the variety of strategies for establishing a basis for negotiation and the range of contextual factors which influence the choice of strategy or weapon. A number of important weapons have been used: demonstrations, consumer boycotts, and sit-ins or lie-ins. In some respects these weapons possess similar characteristics, and in other respects they differ. They can be analyzed in terms of their leverage in creating immediate pressure on the target, their value in communicating degree of commitment, and their value in building internal strength within the protest group.

Of the three tactics the consumer boycott exerts the most leverage. Consumer acceptance is very important to most companies, and a boycott can hurt sales substantially. Moreover, the boycott involves an important dimension of power which enhances its effectiveness. The target company needs the influence of the civil rights movement to restore the company's good name in the Negro community. As a result an incentive exists to negotiate with the movement. In the case of demonstrations and sit-ins much of the damage may have already been done, and the employer stands to benefit very little by agreeing to explicit negotiations, if he has already made the critical concession to end the demonstration or sit-in, or if the police have ended it. In other words there is no further *quid pro quo*. However, the sit-in can be effective if it succeeds in blocking production, as it did in several cases in the North.

In terms of commitment, however, a different ordering of the tactics is involved. The sit-in represents the most costly form of protest to the participants since it involves personal hardship, and consequently it exhibits the highest degree of commitment. On the other hand, because it is easy to participate in a consumer boycott (there is not much entailed in shifting purchases to another product), this tactic does not express as much feeling or communicate as much resolution. A demonstration falls somewhere in between, since some costs are involved, namely, the time and money to get to the site and the personal discomfort to many people at appearing in public. But it does not usually entail the danger of arrest and the physical suffering present in a sit-in.

The weapons can be differentiated along a third dimension, the cultivation of group spirit. As we noted in collective bargaining, the taking of direct action (a strike) may be primarily designed to develop group solidarity and to prepare the rank and file for future action rather than as essentially a pressure tactic against the employer. Similarly, some of the direct-action tactics in the civil rights area are more functional for the developing of the "will to act" than they are for winning immediate concessions. The demonstration represents a very effective device for building *esprit de corps*. By its very nature a type of religious experience is involved. Many people participate, and a strong group spirit can develop. On this count the boycott is least effective in developing group solidarity, since the participation is on an individual basis and little group action takes place. The sit-in develops great solidarity among the participants, but since so few are involved, the effect on the total civil rights movement may be small.

The Number of Parties

In most situations the number of participants or the number of prime organizations in the bargaining process is not fixed. To the extent that additional organizations enter the deliberations, some important implications are raised for the whole process of negotiations. The alteration of the game from a two-party to a three or more-party configuration raises the possibility of coalition formation, which not only complicates the bargaining process for purposes of analysis but also opens up new avenues of influence. In a two-party confrontation, the only kind of instrumental power is that which works directly on the opponent, but in the three-party situation it may be possible to promise benefit or harm to the third party in order to enlist him in placing pressure on the opponent.

The third party can also take the initiative to change the sum of the game, by offering one or both parties some inducements in the way of bringing the negotiations to a conclusion. By offering positive inducements, he increases the sum of the game; negative inducements potentially subtract from the sum of the outcome.

Labor Negotiations The work-rules dispute in railroads, which reached a show-down during 1963–1964, provides a good illustration of an important change that can occur when three parties are involved in bargaining. The third party, of course, is the government and indirectly the public. As a result, each side (the brotherhoods and the carriers) directed its energies to winning support from mediation officials—Congress and the interested public. The forum for bargaining became the newspapers rather than the private meeting room.

The work-rules dispute was purely distributive as viewed by the unions and the companies. The unions felt that whatever changes took place in the work rules would be a direct loss to the membership in job security, income, etc. Similarly, the companies felt that whatever the unions blocked in the way of changes would be a direct impairment of their competitive position.

With the intervention of President Johnson in 1964 the nature of the game was affected quite fundamentally by the third party. The sum of the game changed—it increased. The President held out the possibilities to the companies that the Internal Revenue Service would reevaluate its tax policy on depreciation of tunnels and other "natural resources" owned by the railroads and that Congress would pass a bill giving the railroads greater flexibility in adjusting their rates in order to compete with other forms of transportation. Thus in terms of the direct transaction between unions and companies, the game remained fixed in sum, but in terms of possible side payments the game increased in value. The companies were induced to give up some of their key objectives (elimination of the 100-mile pay principle and freedom to operate interdivisional runs) in return for the promises by President Johnson.

International Relations The parallels in international relations to situations just described in collective bargaining are so numerous and familiar that we need not analyze them in detail. The Marshall Plan was a dramatic, massive, and relatively long-term effort by the United States to influence the negotiation outcome and process among European nations—we did this by contingent additions to the sums of their games. The United States and the United Nations have frequently used both techniques of military intervention and economic aid to influence the course of quarrels between small nations.

The United States and Russia are both conscious of world opinion, especially that of the neutral or uncommitted nations. To the extent that this third-party approval or disapproval is of value to the principal antagonists, the sum of the game is affected.

Civil Rights The public is almost always involved in encounters between the civil rights movement and the target group. How the public aligns itself is crucial to the outcome of a direct-action campaign. Thus, an important consideration in formulating strategy and tactics is to bring about a coalition between the movement, the public, and elected officials.

Some of the most effective campaigns have motivated public officials, perhaps against their will, to take action against employers. A demonstration at a construction site or a sit-in at a mayor's office, if properly publicized, can put an elected official under tremendous pressure to take action. Thus, the elected official may be induced to form a coalition with the civil rights movement. The role of the public is equally important; perhaps over the long run it is more important to the outcome of bargaining.

Being a minority force, the civil rights movement cannot achieve many of its objectives unless it wins the support of the larger community, which means the white public. The leadership of the movement knows that most white people endorse the objective of equal employment opportunity for Negroes. Thus, a key element in their strategy has been to play upon the conscience of the white community. The problem that they face, however, is that in dramatizing the lack of employment opportunities for Negroes, they cannot use means that violate the standards of the larger society. Thus, they are in a position of constantly testing the limits to which they can go in using extreme means to achieve noble ends.

What factors affect the response of the public? We can name several:

The first is the legitimacy of the objective—the more legitimate the objective, the more the public will tolerate questionable means. Civil disobedience has not been repressed as frequently in the North as in the South, since there is wider support for the idea of equal opportunity.

The same point can be made about the sit-down in the labor field: "They were tolerated in 1937, and even received substantial public support, mainly because large segments of American industry refused to accept collective bargaining. Trade unions were the underdogs and they were widely represented as merely attempting to secure in practice the rights that Congress had bestowed upon them as a matter of law."[4]

A second factor is the concreteness of the objective—when the objective is limited and stated concretely and is one that the target group can do something about, there is more tolerance for the tactics. This point explains the success of the Philadelphia ministers in securing employment opportunities through selective-buying campaigns and the lack of success of many of the New York City sit-ins. The latter gave the aura of general protest. By not stating their demands in concrete terms, they created an impression of anarchy.

A third matter is the duration of the disobedience—the more quickly the tactics can be accomplished, then the better the response by the public. One-shot demonstrations and short boycotts will be tolerated, while extended sit-ins will be disapproved. For example, when the sit-in demonstrators first appeared in Mayor Wagner's office, the public was not too opposed, but as the demonstrations continued, the public grew tired of the situation, and when Mayor Wagner had the demonstrators forcibly evicted, he was strongly supported by the public. In general one could say that the enthusiasm and interest of those who approve wanes, and the impatience and attention of those who disapprove mounts.

Fourth, the conduct of the participants is important. When the participants conduct themselves nobly and stand ready to accept punishment for their civil disobedience, there is less criticism of the movement. There is respect for participants when they express "the courage of their convictions," this courage being measured by the costs involved and the willingness of the participants to accept these costs. Thus there may be more public sympathy for "sit-iners" who stand (or sit) ready to be jailed than for the leaders of a consumer boycott who protect themselves through anonymity-creating devices.

A fifth factor is the representativeness of the organization conducting direct action. An organization like the NAACP speaks more authoritatively for the Negro community than narrowly based groups like CORE and SNCC do. As a result it may be less susceptible to public criticism when it initiates direct action.

A sixth factor is the prospect of greater turmoil—when the situation does not indicate still further disturbance, there will be a tendency to accept the tactics. The public often hopes that participation in the tactic will vent the displeasure of the minority and enable the society to return to normal. There may even be the hope that the means will be sufficiently successful to obviate the need for future action.

On the other hand the specter of future trouble can be a powerful motivator for a third party to try to influence the underlying conditions. This was an important consideration in the thinking of the Supreme Court when it declared the NLRA legal,[5] and it has been extremely important in inducing governmental authorities to seek to expand employment opportunities for Negroes.

Eliciting and Processing Clues

Compared with labor negotiations, the need to elicit and process clues regarding the others' intentions and capabilities is probably more important in international relations and less important in civil rights. This condition derives from differences along two dimensions of the total negotiating situation.

First, there are questions about the uncertainty of the other party's negotiating objectives, the means he will use to achieve them, and the timing of such moves. In international negotiations is the greatest uncertainty. The chief decision makers in the United States and Russia must be prepared to meet all contingencies—tactical moves of several different varieties (economic and political as well as other strategies) pursuant to a variety of several agenda items, including Berlin, NATO, shipping rights, nuclear tests, Cuba, Vietnam, Japan, etc.

In a civil rights confrontation there are only a few points of pressure, and there is little uncertainty about the general objectives of each side. The difficulty in civil rights arises because of the diversity of decision makers, particularly within the civil rights movement. There are many decision makers on each side, and there is therefore less agreement about short-term objectives and strategies. There is also less likelihood of getting advance information about the other side, and if obtained, it is less likely to be reliable.

Second, there are questions about the extent to which negotiating moves can be identified and interpreted. The more highly institutionalized the setting, the easier it is to discern and process clues. In international relations especially, the parties have highly developed techniques for gathering and processing such data. Several departments and agencies in the Federal government have this as their primary task. Moreover, in international relations there is relatively greater use of probing and testing through feelers and tentative moves.[6]

Concession Rules and Commitment Patterns

Several of the descriptive statements about concession rules in labor negotiations, which we presented in the chapter on distributive tactics, appear to apply to the postwar disarmament negotiations, including the tendency for concessions to be reciprocated during the same or following rounds. Indeed if they are not reciprocated in the same round, the first nation usually reduces its concessions in the next.[7] One distinctive feature of the disarmament negotiation not encountered in collective bargaining is the large number of retractions of concessions made previously. These reversals of position may reflect the extent to which the parties are using this setting for broader purposes than arriving at a decision on the stated agenda items.

The typical commitment pattern in the civil rights arena is an interesting one. In a given encounter the civil rights groups will often execute what we referred to earlier as an early-firm-commitment strategy. Here the strategy cannot be explained in terms of knowledge about the opponent's resistance point but must be explained primarily in terms of knowledge about one's own resistance point. In direct-action groups with militant members the leadership is well aware of the minimum expectations of the constituents.

The choice of early firm commitment in civil rights is also consistent with another hypothesis offered in Chapter III: commitment will approach the early-firm-commitment form when mechanisms are available for communicating this commitment. The availability of high-commitment weapons like sit-ins and going to jail makes it possible for civil rights groups to take a firm position.

We should not overlook another important dimension, that is, the belief of many direct-action people that human rights are not negotiable. In other words, they do not start from a position of demanding more than they expect to receive. When there is a principle at stake and a moral fervor behind the campaign, one should expect to find the early-firm-commitment approach to distributive bargaining. When issues are nonprinciple in character and there is discretion about how much more or less of something one receives, such as money, then the bargaining is more likely to take the form of gradually increasing commitment.

Integrative Bargaining

The main purpose of the discussion below is to explore the opportunities for this subprocess in different settings of social negotiations. Since we are already familiar with the problem agenda of collective bargaining, we turn directly to international relations and civil rights.

International Relations

There is tremendous integrative potential among the nations of the world. Superordinate goals for at least a large majority of these nations would include institutions for ensuring peaceful resolution of international disputes and progress in eliminating hunger, disease, poverty, and illiteracy. The UN is clear testimony in itself to these goals, and its agencies, conferences, committees, and programs are designed to facilitate problem solving and mixed bargaining toward these ends. UNESCO and its programs provide a well-known setting for integrative bargaining.

Shifting the focus to pairs of nations, integrative potential may arise because their interests have a consensual or symbiotic relationship for each other. An agricultural country and an industrialized country can readily increase their joint gain through mixed bargaining. Emigration-immigration offers integrative possibilities. For example, New Zealand, an underpopulated country, entered into an arrangement with the Netherlands, which is overpopulated, whereby they encouraged, subsidized, and supervised permanent migration to New Zealand. The decision processes which established the terms of this exchange must have been mixed bargaining. Both were interested in achieving migration but would have held different preferences for the characteristics of the migrants in terms of age, sex, skills, and family status as well as for the respective shares of the cost of transportation and other subsidies provided by the two governments.

In the examples above problem solving is likely to be the *main* process in the international interaction, distributive bargaining occurring as a complicating process. When the agenda contains mainly problems, the problem-solving process, not the distributive bargaining process, becomes the "cornerstone" for the theory. This emphasis is not inconsistent with the basic theory developed in this book, but it does require some reorientation to the theory.

It is significant that decision-making situations in international relations tend to have agendas which are either predominantly distributive or integrative. This appears to be a product of two tendencies. First, separate settings can be used to deal with issues and problems because they usually are not functionally interrelated. Second, they are separated out of an appreciation of the dilemmas created by dealing with a mixed agenda. Nevertheless, there are probably many matters which are mixed in nature and where progress can only be made by confronting the dilemmas.

Thus, we suspect that these areas of mixed agenda are not fully explored or exploited for additional reasons. The participants to international discussions may lack mixed bargaining skills (which are just now improving in labor negotiations). The limited trust which prevails between key nations like the United States and Russia is more constraining to mixed bargaining than to relatively pure problem solving. Finally, the complicated intraorganizational processes which the United States at least must contend with are major inhibitors in entering mixed bargaining.

Even though the mixed agenda is not typical, there are important examples. The series of meetings between the heads of the Allied countries before and after the end of World War II were classic examples of mixed bargaining. The postwar disarmament negotiations is another example of important and difficult mixed bargaining.

Still other important matters involving the basically antagonistic United States and Russia offer integrative possibilities. One which has been tentatively mentioned from time to time is the extremely costly exploration of space. The "space race" has been a competitive process, not only because of its military implications, but also because the parties chose to make it one. Space achievements could become a common venture, but only as a result of complex mixed bargaining.

Several matters of consensual interest are handled only tacitly thus far by the United States and Russia. There is a growing appreciation of the threat for both parties represented by Red China. A related matter is our joint interest in preventing the extension of nuclear weapons. These are part of the general desire held by the United States and Russia to preserve the *status quo,* growing out of the fact that both nations are prosperous and powerful. Although not discussed explicitly as agenda items, these matters are dealt with in tacit problem solving—even in the heat of such encounters as the Cuban crisis.

Civil Rights

By and large integrative bargaining has been absent from the civil rights situation. However, the government's regulations and its increasing enforcement of equal opportunities for Negroes have created for companies many problems on which the moderate groups can provide assistance.

Here and there a few innovative solutions have emerged as racial moderates have met with cooperative businessmen or public officials. Particularly in the areas of recruitment, training, and selection of Negroes some imaginative arrangements have been developed to accommodate (in a varying-sum manner) the need of the direct-action groups for immediate change and the need of the employer to effect orderly transition and protect the rights of the majority. These problems entered into the illustrative civil rights case above. We shall elaborate on them here.

The first problem area is that of recruiting Negroes. Many companies do not have Negroes working for them, simply because Negroes have not applied for employment. In one negotiation the company frankly asked the civil rights group how it could get the word out to the Negro community. The leaders advised the company in these terms:

"Simply saying that you are an equal-opportunity employer will not do any good; Negroes have learned over time that industry does not really want them, and hence they are not going to put themselves in the position of being embarrassed. You have to advertise in the Negro newspapers, you have to let us put the word out to the community, and you have to use other information posts in the ghetto such as churches, social service agencies, and fraternal organizations."

As a result of this advice, the company has been rather successful in generating a stream of Negro applicants.

After it has been made clear that a given company is interested in hiring Negro employees, the second problem becomes one of finding qualified applicants. At this point, an organization like the Urban League which has screening procedures can be helpful in referring qualified individuals to interested employers. But in many instances there are just not enough qualified Negroes to go around; the demand exceeds the supply. As a result, upgrading programs have been initiated to increase the supply of qualified Negroes. In Chicago, with the sponsorship of the Urban League, the Yellow Cab Company and the Shell Oil Company have run training programs for unemployed workers. These types of "prehire" programs have expanded rapidly around the country, and many of them have developed as a result of the search for solutions to the supply problem by civil rights leaders and employers.

A controversial issue is involved in the third problem, namely, selecting Negroes. The issue is one of preferential treatment for Negroes. All of the civil rights groups, including the Urban League, endorse some kind of preferential treatment for Negroes. As Whitney Young, of the Urban League, stated, ". . . white people have had special preference all along . . . it is time we instituted a special treatment for Negroes as compensation for generations of denial, at least for a while."[8]

Some interesting ideas have been advanced for fulfilling the spirit of preferential treatment but at the same time dealing with the inequities that may be involved. In one instance it was decided that preferential treatment could be achieved through extra effort and selective recruitment. In other words, whites would not be ignored, but extra attention would be given to developing a group of qualified applicants from the Negro community.

The "prehire" programs mentioned above represent another form of specialized attention to Negroes. The eligible group may be defined as the un-employed, but in most cities this means that the group will be heavily Negro.

Another solution which appears to be emerging, although it has not been put into practice, is the two-list system. This solution has relevance where there are whites on a waiting list. If Negroes are given exclusive preference, it means that they are advanced over the heads of whites who may have certain vested interests. One way of lessening this difficulty is to establish tandem lists from which applicants are taken in a stated proportion as openings develop.

Attitudinal Structuring

Before considering several structural variables which affect the importance and character of attitudinal structuring, a few general remarks about international relations and civil rights are in order.

There is no question that officials are conscious of the attitudinal components of the relationships between their nation and other nations. For the United States and Russia many international programs are designed specifically to improve mutual understanding and goodwill between the peoples of these countries. These programs include cultural and scientific exchange ventures as well as certain trade arrangements. However, the question is whether these international moves which effect substantive outcomes are also made with some thought about their influence on attitudes between the countries.

Certain treatments of the problem of tension management and attitude change in international relations are especially suggestive that attitudinal structuring is often a goal of officials engaged in international decision making.[9] The relationship between attitudinal and bargaining processes is pointed up by some of the balance tactics that have been suggested for changing United States–Russian relations: (1) renunciation by one party of an avowed objective having significance for the other party, (2) reduction in the absolute level of military forces and capabilities, (3) removal of provocative features of weapons or weapons systems, and (4) avoidance of certain subjects of discourse during negotiations.[10]

In the early 1960s attitudinal structuring was a part of social negotiations in the civil rights area but was not the dominant process by any means. In those geographic regions and with respect to those issues where there remained an assumption of basic conflict of interests, the civil rights groups were more concerned about building power and creating a negotiating base. In those instances in which the parties have actually entered into discussions or working arrangements, both sides have given more attention to the level of trust and friendliness. However, entering this phase does not signal the end of the need to create power and use it in bargaining over further objectives; therefore, in this phase there is an increase in the tension between the bargaining and the attitudinal structuring processes.

What we explore below are a few of the basic dimensions of the settings for social negotiations which affect the importance of attitudinal structuring within the overall process.

Nature of the Agenda

If the agenda contains a relatively larger proportion of problems to issues, relatively greater attention will be paid to the attitudinal structuring subprocess.

The parties will tend to resolve tactical dilemmas between distributive bargaining and attitudinal structuring in favor of the latter process. Similarly, they are more likely to follow the dictates of attitudinal structuring when they clash with intraorganizational bargaining.

Beyond the question of whether the agenda contains items which are inherently fixed sum or variable sum is the question about the emotional overtones involved in many issues. More may be at stake than economic resources allocation—human dignity, political freedom, rule of law, social class mobility, etc. Because of the critical nature of the stakes, the objectives of one party may go beyond usual self-interest; they may involve weakening or destroying the other. Thus, an important dimension of the agenda is the implication of the items for attitudinal structuring.

As we have stressed throughout this book, many collective bargaining issues have strong emotional overtones, they involve questions of personal dignity, personal security, managerial prerogatives and status, and democratic procedures. The labor movement is in large part a struggle for power and influence—a social revolution. Virtually the same general point applies to international relations and civil rights. Thus, the character of bargaining in all three settings is directly affected by the latent as well as explicit meanings in the agenda items.

Uncertainty of Performance under Agreement

In some bargains the transaction may be on the spot, immediate, or at least self-enforcing. This is the condition of many commercial transactions. In other cases it may involve understandings about rights and obligations and other conditions of future performance. Even if put into writing, the expectation may not be enforceable in any meaningful or complete way. What results then is uncertainty about fulfillment of the agreement terms.

Our assumption is that in those social negotiations in which performance under the agreement is relatively difficult to enforce and where it depends upon more or less voluntary compliance, the relatively greater attention will be paid to attitudinal structuring activities. Further, the tactical dilemmas between attitudinal structuring and other subprocesses will more frequently be resolved in favor of the attitudinal process.

In signing a labor contract, the union does not agree to deliver a depersonalized good or service. Rather, it agrees to a defined pattern of rights and obligations within which the employer can "expect" employee performance. The actual patterns and the performance delivered will be strongly conditioned by the attitudes of all concerned and the relationship which exists between the parties.

Similarly, in international relations some agreements contain great uncertainty about performance under any agreement. Nothing could illustrate that point better than the implementation of the four-power agreement on Berlin made at the end of the war. Moreover, in the Cuban situation we have had to continue overflights in order to be sure that the missiles were dismantled and removed from that island. An agreement without the presence of trust represents only a piece of paper. It is for this reason that the disarmament negotiations have proved to be so difficult. Since the feeling exists within the United States that "the Russians cannot be trusted," it has been the objective of the United States to negotiate a disarmament plan that would be fully enforceable through inspection, etc.

Sometimes the object of the transaction in civil rights agreements is specific and material: Negroes can take seats in the front of the bus; they can swim with police protection on certain beaches previously closed to them; a firm agrees to the immediate employment of five additional Negroes, etc. While in some cases these practices become self-enforcing, in many instances they raise issues of compliance, especially when more subtle objectives are involved, such as equal employment opportunity in white-collar jobs.

In passing, we should note that the presence of mechanisms for raising questions about compliance and intent under the agreement can eliminate much of the uncertainty about performance and thereby have an impact on the role of attitudinal structuring. In the labor area considerable emphasis has been placed on the right of the parties to submit grievances and in many cases to have these disputes about performance decided by a third party.[11]

Civil rights groups have expressed great concern that employers would not honor agreements, that they would grant concessions only to neutralize direct action, and that once the crisis passed, they would renege on their promises. Examples of this uncertainty about performance occurred frequently during the early days of the current civil rights revolution. For example, it was the practice of the Philadelphia ministers not to end a boycott until the requisite number of Negroes had been hired. A company's statement that it intended to hire a specified number of Negroes was not honored. In New York City when the referral committee of the construction industry made its first report about progress in introducing minority members, a civil rights spokesman commented: "self-serving rationalizations and half-truths."

In the international field, the UN and the World Court can serve to some extent the same function by handling complaints and misunderstandings between countries, although there is no way for the injured party to compel the other party to participate in the adjudication process. In the civil rights area, few formal mechanisms exist. Various human relations commissions attempt to mediate disputes, but they have little authority; they only operate at the pleasure of the parties. Where compliance mechanisms are largely absent or ineffective, attitudinal structuring performs a crucial function.

The acceptance of due process mechanisms by the parties reveals the extent of accommodation and the amount of attitudinal structuring that has already taken place. In other words, a measure of trust must be present before the parties will consent to live under a constitutional arrangement with established procedures for handling complaints about performance.

Pattern of Interaction

An important variable affecting the opportunities for attitudinal structuring is the interaction setting, especially whether the parties are face to face or removed, and whether the bargaining is continuous or one-shot.

Attitudinal structuring can take place much more readily when the negotiators meet in person than when they communicate through dispatches or intermediaries and also when the encounter is frequently repeated rather than when it represents an isolated transaction.

Labor negotiations, which are face to face and where there is a succession of contracts, present the most opportune setting for attitudinal structuring.

In international relations the chief negotiators seldom come face to face. While some of the encounters, such as the Cuban negotiations, are one-shot in character, diplomatic contact is maintained on a continuous basis, thereby providing some opportunity for attitudinal structuring.

The civil rights context has the most limited potential for attitudinal structuring. Very often the protagonists never come together—the encounter is an exercise in raw power without any face-to-face deliberations. However, once actual negotiations begin, there may be considerable attitudinal structuring, as the earlier case study illustrated. Moreover, a type of continuous interaction takes place between the civil rights movement and the general business community, the key leaders from both sides often developing a working relationship.

The pattern of interaction, its frequency and intensity, has another bearing on attitudinal structuring, particularly in its interrelationship with the other subprocesses. Continued interaction may produce positive attitudes, but it may also produce negative attitudes. It is unlikely that attitudes will remain neutral in the face of frequent encounters.

The tendency for extended interaction to move toward extreme states has been documented by various experimental studies. The important finding is that bargaining often follows a stochastic process, Party's actions being more a reaction to Opponent's than a predisposition to act in a certain way. As a result of the response-counterresponse dynamics, the tenor of bargaining evolves to either the stable state of cooperation or to defection.[12]

More importantly, frequent interaction also produces a pairing of distributive bargaining with hostile attitudes, and integrative bargaining with friendly attitudes. The point is that in a setting of frequent and intense interaction it is difficult for the configuration of distributive bargaining with positive attitudes to emerge. Either the self-oriented character of the distributive process produces hostile attitudes which are held stable by a type of reinforcement process between the parties, or the positive attitudes lead to a new approach to the substantive matters, i.e., integrative bargaining begins to emerge, and this also achieves stability through a type of reinforcement process.[13]

One would expect to find the hybrid arrangement, distributive bargaining with positive attitudes, only in situations in which the interaction could be carefully controlled, either because the parties communicated by dispatch, or because they negotiated agreements infrequently, or occupied highly specified roles which required emphasis on the self-interest objectives of the organization.

Intraorganizational Bargaining

Again, we turn directly to international relations and civil rights.

International Relations

The extent to which the international decision maker must attend to the problem of achieving internal consensus while he also acts appropriately in the international context is certainly an empirical question. Snyder and Robinson cite the divergent views on this matter when they report that "To talk to some policymakers is to come away with the impression that public opinion is a highly volatile force, omnipresent, unpredictable, a combination of shifting searchlights within which the policy-maker must function and which constitutes a basic limitation on what he can do. On the other hand, there are both poll data and frequent observations which suggest that the policy-maker is largely free to do what he wishes, and will do what he wishes, regardless of what those outside the government think or want."[14]

These two descriptions are applicable to the extreme cases, and the majority of international decision-making situations probably fall somewhere along a spectrum of public-opinion influence. Thus, we assert the generality of our assumptions made initially regarding the labor negotiator that "he occupies a position which has influence" but that "the activities and influence of the chief negotiator are constrained and shaped by internal organizational forces," and finally that "even with respect to the potential influence he does possess, he must choose and time his tactics wisely."

We can cite two ways in which the principals can affect the way the international negotiator conducts himself in integrative and distributive bargaining.

The negotiator, more than his principal, is cognizant of the need for the other to avoid losing face. In the Cuban crisis President Kennedy was more aware of this than the United States public was. Thus, he was less likely to insist upon an outcome which would be a victory for him and a defeat for the other. Contrastingly, the militants within the United States pressed for an all-out effort against Cuba. If Russia had not conceded, it would have been difficult for President Kennedy to have opposed the escalation of sanctions.

The negotiator, more than his principal, is aware of the possibility of an integrative solution in which neither side loses or in which one does not necessarily lose what the other gains. The American public and presumably other publics tend to keep almost daily score of the wins and losses in the diplomatic encounters between the United States and Russia, and the effect of this public preoccupation is to limit the negotiators' activity in mixed bargaining.

Civil Rights

The leader of a direct-action organization experiences many of the pressures and problems felt by a labor leader representing militant constituents. The Negro activist often finds himself in a role-conflict situation. As negotiations unfold, he becomes more cognizant of the problems of the employer, and he sometimes realizes that his extreme position is no longer tenable. Meanwhile, the constituents remain adamant and demand full measure for their position.

One technique for coping with this conflict involves "going through the motions," that is, acting aggressively and giving the constituents some release for their intense feelings. Such an approach works only when the employer understands that the outburst is for the benefit of constituents. "The furthering of race pride and racial solidarity is a means of diminishing internal strivings in the Negro community and of lining up the community into a working unity. Whites sometimes understand this, and there is, therefore, also a certain amount of 'tolerated impudence,' which a trusted and influential Negro can get away with even in the presence of whites."[15]

A second technique also similar to labor negotiations is to keep the constituents "in the dark" about developments in the bargaining room. In one situation in which the Negro leader was under pressure to obtain immediate concessions from the company, he spoke as a militant when confronted with the constituents but as a moderate when confronted by the employer. When challenged by his constituents, he scheduled additional meetings with the employer, but inside the meeting he acted in a moderate fashion. In many respects this approach resembles the first technique of going through the motions; the basic difference is in keeping the constituents in the dark about the approach being used on the employer.

A third technique is to avoid responsibility for a decision which may entail compromise by throwing the matter back to the constituency, in effect allowing them to experience the "essence of the situation." During discussions about the situation in the construction field in New York, James Farmer of CORE emerged from the bargaining room and predicted a settlement in the near future, but he added, "there will be no behind-the-door settlement, we will take it to the members for approval or rejection."

Intraorganizational bargaining operates at another level within the civil rights movement, namely, between groups within the movement. While it is the militant who experiences the brunt of intraorganizational pressures within a particular direct-action organization, it is the moderate who is sensitive to pressures within the movement.

The racial moderate faces a dilemma in maintaining his position in the larger Negro community. In many instances, the militants have seized the initiative and have forced the moderates into the background. The moderate becomes particularly troubled when the protest gets to the talking stage, especially when the militants have been successful in getting the attention of an employer with whom the moderates have been working for some time.

Confronted with this challenge, the moderate can ignore the activities of the direct-action group. The threat of direct action may even work to his advantage, since the company, convinced that it must do something, may rather make changes with the moderate on a calm, rational basis.

However, there comes a point at which the moderate must vie for control of the direct-action campaign. His personal position as well as the reputation of the institution he represents are at stake. How this was done in one situation was described earlier.

Size of Negotiating Group

The size of the organization is a crucial variable in affecting the complexity of the internal process and the extent to which intraorganizational bargaining is involved. Parties may be more than individuals; they may be complex social entities—groups, organizations, nations, coalitions, etc. The groups may be composed of more or less heterogeneous populations, in which subgroups hold differing biases and concerns about the issues of negotiations. The membership may have considerable influence over the objectives and strategies pursued in negotiations and varying degrees of opportunity for surveillance of the proceedings.

Generally speaking, larger organizations are more compartmentalized and are more likely to be characterized by divergence in outlook between the negotiators and the constituent groups. The larger the organization, then the more apt there is to be vertical and horizontal separation and the more prominent intraorganizational bargaining will be.

The size of the bargaining group in labor negotiations falls somewhere between international relations and civil rights. If the bargaining group is relatively large, e.g., multiunion councils or employer associations, then there are bound to be many internal differences, and the whole matter of achieving consensus within the organization becomes an important activity for the negotiator. On the other hand, if the effective decision-making unit includes only a few individuals, e.g., a small union or an authoritatively organized management group, there is likely to be little intraorganizational bargaining.

In the international relations field the size of the group is extremely large, often being the extent of the nation. It is for this reason that intraorganizational bargaining is such an important aspect of negotiations in this context.

The direct-action groups in the civil rights area are usually rather small, and the extent of intraorganizational bargaining is consequently limited. However, even within small cohesive groups, some people are not present at the deliberations, and the conduct of the negotiator may have to be shaped accordingly. At the level of the overall civil rights movement many differences exist in style between the moderates and the militants. Some interesting illustrations of divergence both within an individual direct-action organization and within the movement were presented earlier.

Notes and References

1. For an analysis of this campaign see: R. B. McKersie and Montague Brown, "Nonprofessional Hospital Workers and a Union Organizing Drive," *Quarterly Journal of Economics,* vol. 77 (August, 1963), pp. 372–404.
2. Much of the material contained in this section is based on the following study: McKersie, "The Civil Rights Movement and Employment," *op. cit.*
3. J. Q. Wilson, "The Strategy of Protest: Problems of Negro Civic Action," *Journal of Conflict Resolution,* vol. 5 (1961), pp. 291–303.
4. Walter Galenson, *The CIO Challenge to the AFL* (Cambridge, Mass.: Harvard University Press, 1960), pp. 146–147.
5. "Experience has abundantly demonstrated that the recognition of the right of employees of self-organization and to have representatives of their own choosing for the purpose of collective bargaining is often an essential condition of industrial peace. Refusal to confer and negotiate has been one of the most prolific causes of strife." *National Labor Relations v. Jones and Laughlin Steel Corporation* 301 U.S. 1 (1937).
6. See Daniel Schorr, "The Trojan Troika in Berlin," *Reporter* (Sept. 27, 1962), pp. 25–27.
7. Lloyd Jensen, "Soviet-American Bargaining Behavior in Post-war Disarmament Negotiations," *Journal of Arms Control,* vol. 1 (October, 1963), p. 622.
8. *The New York Times* (Monday, Aug. 12, 1963), p. 10. © 1963 by The New York Times Company. Reprinted by permission.
9. See C. E. Osgood, *Graduated Reciprocation in Tension-reduction: A Key to Initiative in Foreign Policy* (Urbana, Ill.: Institute of Communications Research. University of Illinois, December, 1960); and J. D. Singer, "Threat-perception and the Armament-tension Dilemma," *Journal of Conflict Resolution,* vol. 2 (1958), pp. 90–105.
10. R. C. Snyder and J. A. Robinson, *National and International Decision-making* (New York: The Institute for International Order, 1961), p. 136.
11. For a study of the bargaining process inherent in grievance administration see J. W. Kuhn, *Bargaining and Grievance Settlement* (New York: Columbia University Press, 1961).
12. See Marc Pilisuk and Anatol Rapoport, *A Non-zero-sum Game Model of Some Disarmament Problems* (Ann Arbor, Mich.: Mental Health Research Institute, University of Michigan, 1963).
13. R. E. Walton, "Theory of Conflict in Lateral Organizational Relationships," paper

presented to the International Conference on Operations Research and the Social Sciences, Cambridge, England, September 14, 1964.

14. Snyder and Robinson, *op. cit.,* p. 228.

15. Gunnar Myrdal, *An American Dilemma* (New York: Harper & Row, Publishers, Incorporated, 1944), p. 771.

Work Flow as the Basis of Organizational Design
ELIOT D. CHAPPLE, LEONARD R. SAYLES

In a business of any size, decisions that affect its organizational design are made almost daily. Constant changes in technology, markets, and financial conditions impel management to make decisions to keep the company on its course. The personalities of top management also shape the design; as its members come and go, changes are made to suit their private philosophies and their attitudes toward "proper" organization, although such changes are usually rationalized as fitting the demands of internal conflict or external forces.

For guides to decisions on organizational design, a manager has available the writings of experts in the "management movement" or he can call on a present-day consultant. Taken as generalizations from experience, the rules, doctrines, and principles of organization are thought-provoking. They represent the accumulated experience and wisdom of clinicians. Interpreted in the light of a specific problem, they often can help find the way to a solution. Yet, as in the comparable case of clinical medicine, they do not, in fact cannot, provide the precise criteria for diagnosis and therapy.

The medical axiom "Nature is the great healer" applies to organizations as well as to human beings. Far too many triumphs of clinicians stem from the persistence or inertia of the system. Thus, organizations often show extraordinary resistance to poorly considered attempts to change them. Surveys are made, often costing many hundreds of thousands of dollars; new charts and new manuals of procedure are prepared; and orders are issued to put the recommendations into action. Then, frequently within a few months, the enterprise sloughs off its new organizational skin, and only a few of the new titles remain. The expensive reports and manuals are put in an unused file, and the rest is abandoned.

Many organizations, both private and governmental, are reorganized almost yearly and usually by a different set of experts, each with their personal remedies for presumed organizational illness. The human damage is often great. People are fired, resign, or are moved from one end of the country to the other and back again. Yet, the organization holds together. The old habits are soon reestablished if they were ever put aside even temporarily. Employees with such ill-starred companies, which are often in a financially successful market position, soon develop the uneasy caution of the inhabitants of the Great Plains in the tornado season. At the barest tremor of the barometer or the first trace of blackness in the sky, they dive headfirst into the inactive safety of whatever organizational storm cellar they can find.

Toward a Science of Organization

Certainly there is no lack of clinical experience, but what is needed is a science of organization. To do the job, the criteria for decision on which the practitioner can call, as the physician relies on the laboratory to substantiate or overrule his clinical judgment, must be developed. Fortunately, most of the essentials are already at hand, the tools of measurement and accurate observation.

In the approach to be taken to organizational structure, two elements will appear. The technology or flow of work is the major criterion for designing the structure. This contrasts sharply with a well-established tradition of planning the organization from the top down. Secondly, any tendency to group people and activities together simply because they have or involve similar or purportedly similar functional responsibilities is avoided.

Traditionally, the scientific approach in studying any human group considers the environment and the technology developed to adapt to the environment. Each individual operation involves an implement or machine using some sort of power, a sequence of actions to accomplish the task, and possibly the interaction of several people in some kind of team activity. In this sense, the term "implement" can be applied to any object, a sheet of paper, a loom, an accounting machine, or a bulldozer. The products of business, or of any organization for that matter, result from interrelated techniques, some of which are essential and others secondary.

If an entire technique or series of techniques can be performed by a single individual, such as a silver craftsman who sells his wares himself, no organization results. But, if a division of labor occurs, some interaction between technicians must take place, and organization on the work level results. On the production level, a relatively large number of techniques may be linked together to make up the work flow through the plant, with a single owner-manager providing the entire management. If there is only a small number of employees and few demands on his time for other activities (for example, if he subcontracts for a larger corporation on a regular basis), the owner may have a foreman in the shop even though the operation does not require one. The ensuing growth of such enterprises usually comes about rather simply with the owner taking a partner who is often a relative. Then, the management begins to specialize, typically with one man selling and the other overseeing production.

Regardless of the type of business organization—a small retail shop, the trader or merchant acting as intermediary between buyers and sellers, or a bank—a similar elaboration of organization takes place. The division of labor on the work level may involve sales people, clerks recording transactions, or cashiers; as the division of labor proliferates, so does management. The development of specialized managers or of a management division of labor is clearly secondary in the evolution of business to the growth of specialization on the work-flow level. This sequence is of critical importance in designing the organization.

Yet, in many writings about modern business organizations, the prime and determining influence of technological process is lost sight of. In their writings, the designers of the organization, who are perhaps under the spell of a two-dimensional chart, start at the top. Beginning with the directors and the president, they work down, level by level, discussing the functions of the various divisions, considering the relationships of "staff" or "service" departments to the "line," weighing the importance of the "span of control," and defining their graphic representations by referring to the nature of executive authority and responsibility. They may casually mention the first-line supervisor, but what he supervises is usually incidental to their recommendations.

Clearly, a different approach to the problem of organizational design is needed. The structure built for members of management can be ignored for the moment to go back to the bottom where the work is done.

This requires looking at the way the technology separates out a series of jobs that must be accomplished if the product is to result. We may manufacture something, buy it for resale, or hire it, as in the case of money, but whatever the business—manufacturing, retailing, banking, or service—we follow certain techniques. There is a beginning, when the process starts, something is done, and the process ends. Put another way, something comes in the door, something is done to it, and it moves on its way out another door to the customer.

In the cases to follow, which are drawn from the authors' field studies, the problems created when the work-flow sequence is not used as a criterion of organizational design, as well as the techniques of analyzing the work process and identifying the work-flow sequences will be examined. By using a comparative point of view, we shall describe a method to isolate some general principles of organization.

The Sales-Credit Controversy

In this case, the general sales manager of a manufacturing company was engaged in a major battle with both the credit manager and the treasurer, who was the credit manager's boss. Such conflicts are not rare. Salesmen usually believe the credit department tries to prevent them from making sales, and credit personnel often think the salesmen will sell to anyone, no matter how bad the risk, to get their commissions. This case illustrates the nature of the problem and why management structure and work flow are too often incongruous.

Although interpreted by management as a clash of personalities, the argument between the sales manager and the credit manager stemmed from much more mundane sources. To understand it, it is necessary to look at the actual work flow through their departments and observe the way the work was organizationally split up. The key implement was the salesman's order, which he mailed in to the home office after filling out what the customer required and extending the dollar figures. Figure 1 illustrates what happened to the order and how the people who handled it were divided between the various functional divisions.

When the office opened in the morning, the mail was sorted in the mail room. Orders were separated and taken immediately by a mail boy to the sales office which occupied one section of the large, open general office of the com-

Figure 1

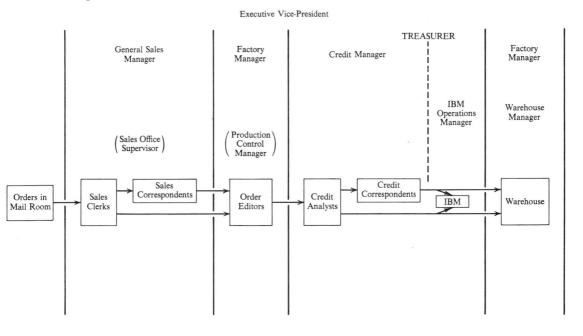

Executive Vice-President

pany, a one-floor layout. There, the clerks checked over the orders to see if there were any special problems of handling shipments or questions raised by the salesmen that might require correspondence. Any order presenting a problem was given to a sales correspondent who wrote to the customer or the salesman, if necessary.

When the sales department completed its work, the order was sent to what was called an order-editing department. This was under the jurisdiction of the factory manager because he superintended warehousing. The orders were checked to see that they were correct, the prices up-to-date, the arithmetic accurate, and the goods in stock at the warehouse nearest to the customer. A copy of the order was sent to another warehouse if the closest one did not have stock. If inventory records showed no stock available, the order editor made out a back-order form to be mailed to the customer.

Then one of the editors would take a batch of orders to the credit department, where credit analysts (clerks) checked the credit ratings to be sure each customer's credit was within the limits set by management. They ascertained whether it was permissible to sell on any other terms than C.O.D. and whether the volume of the order was within the limits of his credit rating. If there was a credit problem, i.e., a deviation, the order was given to a credit correspondent who wrote the customer, with a copy for the salesman, telling him his order could not be accepted and stating the terms, if any, on which he could still buy from the company. If the customer was a big-volume account whose credit rating had dropped, the credit manager would make a final decision before the correspondent wrote a letter. It should be mentioned that each salesman had a reference book of the credit ratings for all accounts in his territory and was not supposed to call on any account whose line of credit was below a specified level.

After this processing, the orders were assembled, one copy of each order was sent to the warehouses to be filled and another to be tabulated for accounting purposes. The IBM accounting processing was supervised by the treasurer, and the warehouses were, as mentioned above, under the manager of the factory. Work was organized so that, in theory at least, all of the orders were processed through this office work flow in one day. Thereafter, there was a definite break in timing because accounting did not receive the orders until a batch was completed at the end of each day. The same was true for the warehouses where goods were pulled for shipment and billed.

There was tension between the credit manager and the general sales manager because the credit department, following its procedure faithfully, occasionally canceled an order that a salesman had made, sometimes a large one. Because credit ratings fluctuate, this had happened recently to two large accounts, and the general sales manager was understandably furious. Both customers threatened not to buy from the company again. The situation was more embarrassing because the general sales manager had written each customer a personal letter to thank him for his confidence in their product after the sales correspondent handling the accounts called the orders to his attention.

Now let us look at a series of improvements in the organization. The first and most obvious change in the work flow of handling orders was to reverse the position of the sales and credit departments. If credit could not be extended, there was no point in checking the accuracy of an order or carrying out the "sales" functions involved. Moreover, this change would prevent recurrences of the kind of embarrassment the general sales manager had undergone. The rearrangement was also more efficient because it eliminated the processing of orders that ultimately would be thrown out. However, it did not deal with more basic issues.[1]

As the organization chart (Figure 1) indicates, three separate divisional heads, reporting to the executive vice-president, were involved in the movement of a piece of paper and its carbons from one clerical position to another in the general office. Not only were three separate divisions writing to the customer (sales, credit, and the order editor if he issued a back order) but also there was no assurance that there would be any coordination in what each said. Credit correspondents were accused by sales of being too brusque with customers and they, in turn, accused sales of promising too much.

Many other practical problems of management arose. The policy of the company was to clear the orders in a single day. Tight scheduling was sometimes necessary to get the work completed because volume fluctuates. Absenteeism, inadequate performance, or the assignment of other work to the people in a department would upset the even flow of work. If there was disagreement because one department was holding up another, the only recourse when the immediate supervisors could not agree was to settle the dispute on the level of the executive vice-president. Thus, in heated disagreements between the general sales manager and the credit manager, the executive vice-president had to listen not only to complaints about customer relations, but also to all the petty grievances each had about the performance or management of the other.

The difficulty was created when the work flow was divided into separate pieces on the basis of functional similarities. The solution was to put it back together as a single flow under a single supervisor. He would control the entire flow of an order from the time the paper arrived in the mail room until it left the general office to go to the tabulating department or the warehouse as well as credits, payments, and invoices after the billing was completed. He was responsible for individual performance and could move people around to fit the needs of fluctuating volume. He did not have to argue with other divisions on the management of the process. See Figure 2.

There was still the problem of functional responsibilities. Sales wanted and deserved some voice in the quality of letters sent to customers. Credit, too, had

Figure 2

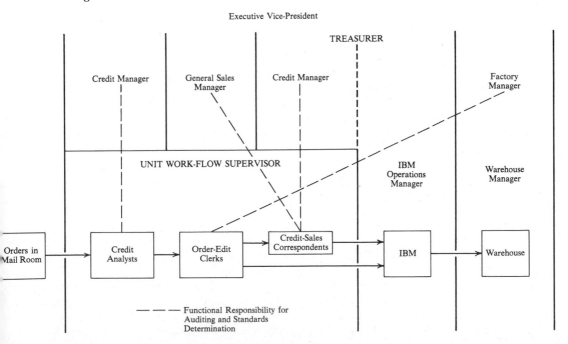

some legitimate concerns, primarily that company policies regarding credit be followed and any cases not under these policies be referred to higher authority. Both departments outlined standards and procedures that could be carried out by the new department. In this way, representatives of sales or credit would only come into the picture when an exceptional situation required higher-level attention. These procedures also included a periodic auditing program so the sales department could satisfy itself that the correspondents' letters to customers were not antagonistic. The credit department checked that this new work unit only made routine credit decisions and all exceptions needing the credit manager's decision actually got to him. As a result, only one correspondent, a credit-sales-order editing specialist, wrote to each customer although several did identical work. In turn, the correspondent was supervised, together with the clericals handling the proceduralized work flow of the order, by one individual. Credit, sales, and factory set the standards of action for which this single supervisor was responsible.

Handling the Training Function

The conflict between employment and training is a common problem in many personnel departments. At the simplest level, it is often a matter of scheduling because it is difficult to synchronize recruiting and hiring with the training necessary after the employee is hired. Training activities include both the initial training and indoctrination programs the individual receives before he is sent to a specific department and also on-the-job training that may include a wide range of activities from counseling to sales promotion or educational programs.

Here, the same pattern of functional specialization repeats itself. In this company all training was concentrated organizationally in a single department although the component parts were very different. The initial training program was actually a part of the employment process (Figure 3).

Large numbers of applicants applied in person at the employment department where they were given an application form by the receptionist. Those who passed a preliminary interview with a screening interviewer were sent to a systematic employment interview and a clerical stage where all the record forms were filled out. If several departments requisitioned personnel, the newly hired employees were sent to a training class that met the next day. Coordination was necessary if employees were to complete this stage and get on the payroll. When there were delays, some of the newly hired people did not come back because they became discouraged waiting for a class which would qualify them for the job. Furthermore, operating departments became impatient when requisitioned personnel had not been "processed" and were not ready when they were needed.

Within the training department, many pressures competed for the time available. Top management was constantly trying out new programs, some of them on a crash basis, although sometimes an existing program simply needed bolstering. Furthermore, there was never an even flow of ready-to-be-trained applicants. Sometimes there were too few for a class and at others a group too large for a single class was hired at once. Many times when classes were scheduled to tie in with requisitions for personnel, not enough qualified people applied.

Figure 3

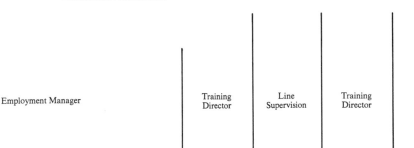

PERSONNEL DIRECTOR

At other times, people were hired simply because they made themselves available even though there were no pressing needs for new personnel. As a result, it was impossible to schedule classes on a regular basis. The training department complained they could not plan their work efficiently because they had no advance notice, and when they did plan, employment let them down. On the other hand, the employment people thought the training group was uncooperative and unwilling to be flexible in view of the difficulties inherent in the hiring operation. This pattern is typical of functional specialization that divides single work processes into organizational compartments.

The solution was to separate the initial induction training from the other training functions and combine it with the other employment operations described above. See Figure 4. As a result, a single supervisor now controlled the entire process by which an applicant at the "gate" was moved from the initial inquiry through all of the stages of the hiring procedure, largely eliminating the bickering between employment and training.

Identification of Unit Work Flow

Any organization that has more than one supervisor must decide which employees and, therefore, which processes should be under the jurisdiction or span of control of a given manager. This is the old question of who reports to whom.

Figure 4

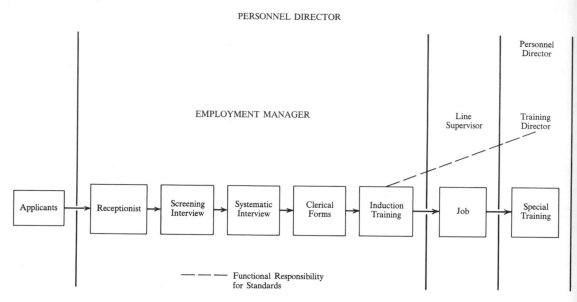

The preceding text was directed to finding some criterion upon which to base this crucial decision. The case studies were presented to illustrate the significance of technology as the critical determinant of this aspect of organizational structure.

But, this concept of technology needs a more careful explanation than the implications of the cases. It should be clear at the outset that the technology or work method of the organization does not refer primarily to the equipment or to the mechanical, electrical, or chemical processes utilized. Every organization has a method of performing work that involves some sequence of operations. These work flows, so crucial in the cases cited, can be identified wherever there is a sequence of techniques that must be performed in a regular or predetermined order by separate individuals. Thus the technology of the organization is the "who does what with whom, when, where, and how often."

These kinds of work flows are not the same as the work-flow analyses of the industrial engineer, which chart each operation in the production process chronologically. In constructing an organizational structure, the interest is in the person-to-person flow. Thus, one individual may perform what the engineer would identify as several separate operations before the work or paper goes to the next person in the production sequence.[2]

The next step is to separate the elements of the work flow that should be considered as a single supervisory unit, which will be called "unit work flows." The concern here is with the quantitative characteristics of the work flow regardless of whether that which "flows" is a person, paper, or material. These characteristics are necessary to set up criteria to identify the unitary work flows and to understand their implications behaviorally in organization design.

In broad terms, the flow of materials, in a manufacturing company for example, that begins at the receiving dock and finally appears at the shipping door as finished product ready for the customer could be considered a single work flow. However, the time coordinates of the complete process are generally too wide; sometimes a matter of weeks or months are needed to complete the manufacturing cycle. Besides the question of physical contiguity is relevant. Physical location or layout is an important factor in identifying the unit flows that make up an organizational design.

In the example of processing the salesman's order, a controlling factor in the separation of warehousing work flow from the office work flow was location. Although they are physically separate out of necessity, the warehouses could be contiguous. In this case they were located in various parts of the country. Consequently, there was a time lapse between the processing of the orders by the clerical groups and their receipt at the appropriate warehouses.

Yet, even if this time was reduced to a minimum and the location of the warehouse was, so to speak, at the end of the order-processing line, the order-filling work flow would still differ quantitatively from the order-processing work flow in its time characteristics. When the day's orders were received in the warehouse, they were sorted according to customer location and given to each order filler in groups having a common shipping route. He then assembled the order from bins or bulk locations and placed it with the order copy (with the amounts checked off) on a conveyer that moved the orders through a checking station, a manifest clerk, a packer, etc. The order-filling work flow did not begin until after the orders for an entire day were processed; the office work flow essentially was done one order at a time. Hence, this procedural difference caused a break in continuous flow similar to the one in geographical location.

If the existing procedural and locational discontinuities can be determined by time criteria, a total work flow can be divided into its unitary parts.[3] Obviously, by changing the technological system, the constituent techniques in a single unit flow can be varied and combined into more inclusive units, through the introduction of a conveyer, for example. Such changes are continually being made in business and require concurrent organizational changes to avoid creating management problems.

Sources of Stress in Organizations

A unit work flow becomes segmented and its parts placed under different chains of command largely, although not necessarily entirely, as a result of the emphasis on functional specialization in organizational design. Sales and credit managers were both responsible for the order-processing flow in one company, and chaos resulted. In the second case, the employment and training departments failed to coordinate the induction training procedure with the employment office functions. The true interrelationships among the processes, eventually merged under a single supervisor, had been disguised by artificial functional designations.

However, in one instance the problem was procedural not structural: the sequence within one group had not been thought through in terms of work flow. As a result, orders reached the credit checking clerks after they passed through earlier stages rather than at the beginning of the process which is more efficient.

Let us look more closely at the resulting organizational disturbances. In a situation requiring cooperative endeavors, whether it is a work group, employees and managers, or staff and line officials, each tries to develop a stable pattern of work, of interaction. When these stable patterns are disturbed, individuals experience stress or an uncomfortable feeling of pressure and dissatisfaction. A breakdown in the flow creates opposition as the individuals struggle to restore it. The expected responses from the individuals in the sequence prove inadequate, and new coordination problems arise.

The regularities of actions and interactions disappear when this stress occurs, and erratic variation takes over. The difference is obvious between a smoothly running operation and one with a problem. Under stress, people react emotionally, and, because more than one individual is involved, the reactions usually conflict with each other.

Thus, a vicious circle is established. Something happens in the work situation that causes the relationship of individuals to change or to depart from the normal pattern. This creates a stress, either of opposition or nonresponse, that is further complicated by higher levels of supervision and staff specialists whose unexpected interactions, i.e., outside the usual organization pattern, irritate the disturbed work-flow relations. People get upset; they become angry with each other and, depending on their individual characteristics, react temperamentally. These personality conflicts have direct ramifications in the work process because the emotional reactions change the pattern of contact and interaction. Joe is angry with Bill, so he does not check with him before starting a new experimental run. Consequently, a special test that should have been included in the run is left out, and the whole thing has to be done over. To complete the circle, these emotional disturbances damage the work-flow sequence, which causes additional personality stresses.

Robert Guest of the Yale Technology Project described this accurately when he said: "Foremen are always getting caught in this familiar vicious circle. Material inspection, say, has failed to spot some faulty pieces. Something goes wrong at a welding operation. The general foreman is on the foreman's neck to 'get it straightened out, or else!' The foreman drops everything to spend time on this one item. He cannot pay attention to the man he was breaking in on a new job. He cannot check on the stock bin which the stock man forgot to replenish. He meant to warn an operator about a safety condition. He knew another man was down in the dumps about a personal problem. By the time he has cleared up the original trouble and satisfied the boss, something else has blown up and the general foreman is roaring down the aisle again."[4]

What produced these stresses and where do these changes come from? They are not directly interactional on the worker level. With rare exceptions, the work flow does not require a direct interactional contact between two contiguous persons as team operations do. That is, the upsets and bickerings are not caused by people who occupy adjacent positions in the flow process and place pressures on one another. In fact, orders could be put on the next desk or on a conveyer without any real contact. Material or parts in an assembly operation usually move from one operator to the next on a conveyer. But, they may also be brought and taken away by service personnel, just as a mail boy may move orders from one group to the next in the office. In these examples, the flow of work does not cause any direct interpersonal problems,[5] except that the action of one person depends on the action of his predecessor, causing him not to act and thus breaking the sequence. As Guest indicates, however, the initiating sources of stress are primarily fluctuations in the rate at which work flows through the supervisory unit. The critical variable is time. Production schedules require tight coordination; holdups must be avoided. If they occur, production suffers and the relationships of the supervisor to his workers and of the workers among themselves change as a consequence.

The objective of any organizational structure is to minimize the incidence of deviations from the established interaction patterns of the work process. The realistic administrator knows complete stability is a never-to-be-achieved utopia. Equipment will always break down; employees will always be absent; and changes in procedures will be introduced continuously. Work will not always come through on time, or when it does, the quality may be so poor the normal process time must be increased significantly. Rush orders or a flood of work may press upon his unit. Whatever the type of fluctuation, his interaction patterns have to change. He may have to spend more time with individual workers, supervisors in other departments, engineers, mechanics, maintenance men, or various persons in control positions, such as production planners or factory cost controllers, who occupy a place in the paper-work flow of which the line supervisor also is a part. And, as a result, less time is available to maintain other vital contacts.

Even if his unit flow is not complicated by other supervisors who directly affect him, the supervisor will still have coordination and timing problems in his own unit and in his relations with those who give him work and to whom he transmits it. The possibility of stress is much greater if he does not have control over the key individuals who work directly with his segment of the flow and cannot get a response from them when he needs it, as in the case of the maintenance mechanics, or if he must constantly gear his segment to the next one, as in the examples of the material handling and inspection.

This is the major point of the discussion. Although the dynamic organization will always experience changes that cause variations in the work-flow system, most of these can be dealt with effectively by the supervisor affected. But, his job becomes almost impossibly difficult if there is no semblance of stability.[6] If the parts of a unit work flow are distributed among several supervisors, the individual manager cannot hope to maintain any stability in internal relationships because erratic changes are introduced by individuals whose behavior he cannot control. Because these other supervisors are meeting different organizational needs, they do not and cannot adjust to the requirements of any single manager. Significant irregularities in the rate of flow and significant changes in the interaction of the individuals concerned indicate the existence of a point of organization stress.

In companies where such problems are common, informal working arrangements usually develop over the course of time. Assuming the individual supervisors get along, i.e., the frequency or intensity of stress is not too great or their personalities are not obviously incompatible, they frequently get together to plan the work and discuss their mutual problems. The objective is for each supervisor to create the least upset to the next group in the line. Unfortunately, it is almost impossible because the segmentation of the work flow makes informal arrangements vulnerable to unexpected changes emanating from higher up.

Higher Level Management Problems

Because people, not lines on a chart, are the major concern, the elimination of points of stress within the work flow should be the first consideration of organization design. This means the traditional functional classification must be abandoned and each job analyzed as a part of one or perhaps, as in the case of an executive, many work flows. Merely recognizing that "informal" organization exists and hoping that management will grant it equal importance to the "formal" structure will not solve the problems.

Studies of the informal organization discuss how people actually relate themselves to each other in the process of getting the work done. Thus, the pattern of relationships that evolve in completing the job is what some observers consider the uncontrolled or spontaneous aspect of the organization. The authors believe this aspect must be the objective of the consciously contrived organizational structure. The organization must be designed for people—not in the hope that people will somehow fit into it.

Accordingly, the first step is to identify the unit work flows and set their boundaries, placing each one under a single supervisor. As stated previously, these work flows consist not only of the people through whom the material, paper, or person flows, but also all the individuals who help maintain the flow, the mechanics, service people, etc. All the factors required to get the work done should be concentrated under a single person with responsibility centered at the lowest managerial point, not at the highest, as in the examples where top management officials were constantly arbitrating interdepartmental disputes.

Span of Second-level Supervision

So far, a series of unit flows, each with its own supervisor, has been constructed. However, each still depends upon the other. Although the stress points within the unit work flows are eliminated by effective organizational design, areas of interdependence between these units necessarily remain. As noted above, the pace of the work generally shifts between unit work flows, there are different rhythms and sequences, and, as a result, the coordination problems are not as great, but there is still an obvious need to coordinate relationships. In the example, the application of quantitative criteria revealed that orders went to the warehouse or tabulating or material from a fabricating unit to assembly with a definable discontinuity. This indicates the need for at least one further level of supervision, a manager over the unit work-flow managers whose responsibility is to see that they are coordinated into a larger system.

Controls

Combining unit work flows into a work-flow system does not depend upon arbitrary assumptions as to the number of individuals such a manager can supervise. These factors are determined by analysis of the controls the manager has available to maintain the system, not by abstract formulas. Worthy pointed out that in the Sears organization a store manager may have thirty to forty department heads reporting to him.[7] This works not merely because the company does not want a manager spending too much time with any single department head but, more fundamentally, because the department store manager receives daily and weekly reports which are sufficient to tell him whether significant deviations are occurring in the ratio of stock (inventory) to sales, in markdowns, markups, etc. Consequently, he spends time with subordinates only in cases where managers are in trouble or where the reports suggest difficulties. As the theory of administrative controls is developed, similar control procedures can be adopted for any business operation.

Many companies find it difficult to organize for effective operation because their reporting systems do not adequately pinpoint responsibility. Most administrative controls are by-products of accounting controls. They were developed for financial record keeping, not management control. Consequently, they are issued by the controller as financial documents and, although completely accurate, they are usually so late as to be matters of ancient history and too general because costs are both prorated and arbitrarily assigned. As such, these reports have little use as operating tools.[8] Thus the number of unit work-flow supervisors reporting to the second management level is a function of the state of development of the organization's controls: the measures which assess how things are going in the production process. Primarily, controls signal troubles at the points where two unit work flows come into contact. These juncture points are the potential stress areas that the second level manager oversees. Improvements in management reporting technology, particularly by the computer, will substantially increase the span of control at this management level.

The use of controls is based on the same criterion utilized in defining each of the unit work flows, the time coordinates of the system. The controls should indicate when the individual unit flows are intermeshing with one another. If they show homogeneity, in the statistical sense, in the interrelationships of the component units, the system is operating as planned. If the sequential movement of goods, paper, or people between units is stabilized, as reported through appropriate controls, the manager can relax. He must go into action when his controls show stressful situations are developing that require attention and action to avoid complete breakdowns in the system.

Assuming some ingenuity is shown in the development of controls, the number of unit supervisors within the flow is of little significance, because each unit is self-sufficient.

Handling Staff-Line Relationships

What is to be done with specialists such as the chief mechanic, the chief inspector, the production planning manager, the training director, and the credit manager? As pointed out previously, the specialists are responsible for developing standards, the procedures to implement these standards, and auditing results. Although this was mentioned explicitly only in the case of the credit manager, each specialist also plays a part in one or more work flows. The significance of the specialists' development and auditing is that they have been removed from direct work-flow decision. The chief mechanic, for example, does not directly or through the foremen decide on what machine the mechanic is to work. He is responsible for the standards of mechanical repair, the program of preventive maintenance, and the evaluation of the mechanic's performance.

Thus, the unit work-flow supervisor and the chief mechanic have a dual responsibility for performance: the first, for the mechanic's contribution in maintaining the production flow, and the latter for the quality of his work. Both factors must be considered in evaluation and control. Otherwise, it is easy to overemphasize short-term gains in production at the cost of the long-run impact on the mechanical equipment.

Moreover, this shift in responsibility gives the specialist time to develop programs and to carry out his auditing responsibility. Otherwise, he is too busy with the day-to-day operating decisions to determine the source of the problems. Under the pressure of the immediate situation, his only interest would be to put the fire out; he would have little time to see what caused the problem in the first place.

However, the specialists need to be fitted into the organizational system. Because they are concerned with developing programs to expedite the work flow and eliminate stresses both within and between unit work flows that affect the total work-flow system, the specialists inevitably become the specialized assistants of the work-flow system manager. Their responsibility then is to act for him in their respective areas to improve the operation on the unit work-flow level. It is important to note the word "responsibility." In the usual sense of the word, specialists do not have staff responsibility with advisory or consultative relations to the line, nor do they have the responsibility of line supervisors, one step removed. They are actually *of* the staff of the manager and accountable to him for developing, installing, and auditing the results of programs in terms of the major objective of removing stress.

Conclusion: Work Flow and Organization Design

The type of organization design just described, based on the actual work flow within a technological and procedural framework, requires the complete use of time measurements as its basis. Not only is the delimitation of unit work flows dependent on the possession of quantitative criteria, but improvements of the technological process, in its broadest sense, require the examination of how each individual, whether worker, specialist, or supervisor, spends his time. The effective use of the method by any company depends also upon layout and location, the techniques by which paper, materials, or people are handled, and the controls used to signal real or impending deviations.

For example, if the record system is not or cannot be tied to individual responsibility, it is that much more difficult to locate points of stress and, in the absurd but common case, the supervisor may have to spend his time continually "on the floor" looking and listening because he does not routinely receive adequate information about his operation. The exception principle, one of the oldest in management, is useful in organizational planning only if the systems and procedures make its use possible.

The work-flow theory requires the specification of what each person does, when, where, with whom, how long, and how often. Therefore a type of job analysis or job description, to use a somewhat discredited term, is needed to outline the flows for each individual and to specify in quantitative measurements the duration of the action and interaction required to carry them out. These administrative patterns will be discussed in the next chapter, with the executive in mind, but similar, although much simpler, descriptions are necessary for the workers themselves. Any contact, whether it is a mechanic repairing a machine, a service boy bringing parts, or a set-up man making adjustments for a new run, involves some interaction, and the time involved is not simply a matter of the actual physical action.

The purpose here has been to suggest criteria upon which to base the design of an organization: the structure must be built from the bottom up and it must be superimposed upon a known technology. In fact, technology, as defined earlier, should be the basis for the distribution and assignment of supervision. Supervisory jobs are largely products of the time coordinates of the production process, regardless of the kind of work the organization does.

Notes and References

1. The reader may consider the illogical arrangement of having the credit checked after sales correspondents and order editors worked on an order as an obvious mistake that anyone should have recognized. However, because it was not recognized for many years in a relatively alert company, it reflects the strong attraction of organizing by functional specialty. All the sales activities were put together and handled first, with salesmen contacting their own departments. Then, and only then, was it time for the next function to begin, in this case, that of the credit department. Unfortunately, the logic of functional organization is rarely challenged in practice.

2. It is necessary, of course, to know the total time required by each person to complete his activities to determine the duration of that particular stage in the production sequence. This helps establish the rate at which the paper, material, or a person moves through the line. This rate is set by the time required to complete the slowest or longest step in the sequence.

3. With the use of statistical techniques, it is possible to determine the homogeneity of the measurements within any unitary flow and to develop accurate criteria to test for discontinuities.

4. Robert H. Guest, "Of Time and the Foreman," *Personnel,* May, 1956, pp. 478–486.

5. This contrasts with the usual conception of work-flow stress. Among the best-known studies in this area is William F. Whyte's work in the restaurant industry. Whyte found stress was caused by the direct pressure emanating from interworker contacts. "Lower-status" runners placed pressure and thus disturbed "higher-status" kitchen personnel, and demanding customers upset the waitress who could not tolerate a high frequency of demands. (William F. Whyte, *Human Relations in the Restaurant Industry,* McGraw-Hill Book Company, Inc., New York, 1948, pp. 49–59, 104–128.)

6. The degree to which the use of functional organization introduces stress and instability is cogently analyzed by James Worthy, Sears Roebuck and Co., in his paper, "Some Aspects of Organization Structure in Relation to Pressures on Company Decision-Making," in *Proceedings of Fifth Annual Meeting of the Industrial Relations Research Association* (ed. L. Reed Tripp), IRRA Publ. 10, 1953, pp. 69–79.

7. William F. Whyte, *Modern Methods in Social Research,* prepared for the Office of Naval Research under Contract Nonr-401 (2), pp. 25–28.

8. There is an increasing concern with what is called "management accounting."

However, present practice indicates it has by no means reached its declared goal of defining organizational responsibility within an accounting framework. Too many costs are still allocated and prorated. True managerial accounting cannot be achieved without loosening the bonds placed in the way of organizational change by poor accounting logic.

Third Party Roles in Interdepartmental Conflict

RICHARD E. WALTON

Almost inherent in specialization of skills and differentiation of functions performed by organizational units is the development of interunit differences. Reward systems, communication obstacles, status incongruity, and other factors often make it harder to achieve coordination and integration. Manifest or potential lateral conflict is a fact of organizational life. The growing literature on the subject has focused primarily on the determinants and dynamics of the conflict and has given relatively less attention to how this conflict is managed in the interest of organizational effectiveness.

The following article analyzes third party roles and interventions which are designed to assist in the resolution or control of interunit conflict; the paper reviews organizational studies which have implications for such an analysis.[1]

"Lateral conflict" refers to conflict between peer units, that is, where there are no superior-subordinate relations. The conflict may involve entire groups or merely unit representatives. It may have its foundation in stereotypes and emotional reactions or in organizational roles and forces. It may reflect differences over factors, methods, or goals.

"Third party" refers to any nonparticipant in the conflict who may facilitate the resolution or control of conflict between primary departments. In terms of organizational positions, potential third parties include: a higher organizational executive, a third peer department not directly involved in the interunit conflict, a separate unit formally assigned to coordinate the activities of two primary units, or an internal or outside organizational consultant. These various types of role relationships are depicted in Figure 1.

A focus on third party control and resolution of conflict assumes a diagnosis that the particular conflict involved has more dysfunctional than functional consequences. For example, the conflict may be more debilitating than energizing for the participants. Or it may tend to obscure rather than clarify alternatives available to the organization. The purpose in controlling conflict is to decrease or eliminate some of the more negative consequences.

"Third Party Roles in Interdepartmental Conflict," by Richard E. Walton from *Industrial Relations,* Vol. 7, No. 1 (October 1967). Reprinted by permission of the author and the Institute of Industrial Relations.

Figure 1 Role Relationships Between Third Parties and Principals

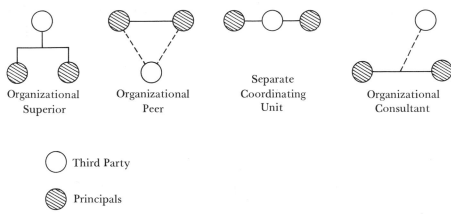

Organizational Superior	Organizational Peer	Separate Coordinating Unit	Organizational Consultant

○ Third Party

◎ Principals

    The discussion takes up four types of intervention: (1) to reduce or eliminate the conflict potential in a situation; (2) to resolve directly a substantive issue in dispute; (3) to facilitate the parties' efforts to manage a particular conflict, and (4) to help the parties change their conflict-prone relationship. A section follows which summarizes how and why each of these types of interventions is differentially available to superiors, peers, coordinative units, and consultants.

Reducing Conflict Potential

    A great many factors can contribute to interunit conflict. Frequently the conflict potential is inherent in the technology, organizational environment, or some essential administrative apparatus. In other cases, however, higher executives have latitude to modify the organizational structure or personnel assignment. For example:

    1. Organizational superiors may adjust the allocation of rewards, status symbols, and other resources in order to ameliorate some of the sharper sources of conflict;[2] and they may decrease the specificity of those individual unit performance measures which lead to a suboptimizing orientation.[3]

    2. They may reduce task load or increase capacity of units where an overload condition or task difficulty is creating bargaining or frustration among subordinate units.[4]

    3. Higher executives may take steps to stabilize organizational jurisdictions for a period of time in order to decrease the ambiguity surrounding departmental status which sometimes underlies competitive interunit maneuvering. Similarly, they may make explicit rules to assign final authority for decisions on interunit matters in order to depersonalize irritating lateral influence patterns, or they may develop rules to cover an increasing proportion of interunit transactions, confining interunit decision-making to exceptional situations.[5]

    4. Organizational designers may utilize mechanisms of segregation, including stricter role separation, between those organizational functions requiring affect and human relations and those requiring more impersonal social relations—because of the contradictory nature of these forms of relationship.[6]

5. Superiors may recruit, select, and assign personnel in ways that minimize the diversity of backgrounds which tends to create conflict among subordinate units[7] and that reduce the incompatibility of personalities or personal styles of unit representatives.

While the above list is not exhaustive, it includes the more important factors which both create conflict potential and are subject to the control of organizational architects or superiors.

Resolving Substantive Issues

Higher Executives

Brown emphasizes the frequency with which interunit conflict signals the need for superiors to become involved and to contribute to the substance of the decision. Often a disputed point between managers indicates that finely balanced judgments are involved. Only a manager with broader understanding and responsibility should make the judgments. Therefore, in Brown's experience, "rapid exposure of the disagreement at the cross-over point" is necessary. The cross-over point is the first executive to whom both departments report. As an extension of the superior's own power and judgment, he may bring in an outside technical expert to evaluate the merits of the positions of the contending parties.[8]

By taking an active role on substantive issues, executives offset the tendency for subordinates either to persist in or to compromise disagreements when the final decision should be made at a higher level. This pattern also satisfies a higher manager's need to be informed.[9]

According to Brown, higher managers are more likely to play this type of third party role in a timely and appropriate way if they avoid communicating that they regard subordinate conflict as personal failure, and, rather, communicate that they see the interunit conflict as reflecting inherent executive dilemmas or poor organizational policies, or both.[10]

Taking a somewhat different position, Blake, Shepard, and Mouton argue that third party judgments in win-lose struggles simply relieve the parties from the struggle itself, but not from the problems of defeat. They find that losers tend to feel an imposed decision was unfair, to suspect the third party, and to doubt his competence or understanding of the problem. These authors also mention third party use of fate mechanisms, such as the flip of a coin, to decide interunit conflicts regarded as inevitable. Even a superior's appeal to the disputants to accept his judgment in a "good sportsman-like way" is a subtle use of a fate mechanism.[11]

Separate Coordinating Units

Where basic departments which are interdependent in work-flow sequence are highly differentiated from each other, there is a tendency to use a permanent separate unit to help achieve coordination between them. In a study by Lawrence and Lorsch, such third party units used their own substantive analysis to influence decisions.[12] The authors differentiated three principal units— research, sales, and production—on four dimensions: (1) degree of structure, i.e., tightness of rules, narrowness of span of supervisory control, and frequency and specificity of performance review; (2) members' orientation toward time, i.e., length of time perspective; (3) members' orientation toward others, i.e., openness and permissiveness of interpersonal relationships; and (4) members' orientation toward different subgoals and segments of the organizational environment, i.e., new scientific knowledge versus customer problems and opportunities versus raw materials and processing costs. Thus, for example, a sales unit compared with the production unit may tend to be less structured, to have a longer time perspective, to be more permissive in interpersonal orientation, and to be more oriented toward the market environment.

Measurements of the degree of differentiation among the three departments were applied to firms in the plastics, food, and container industries. In plastics, the research, sales, and production departments were most differentiated; all six firms used a separate coordinating unit. In the food and container industries, only one of the two firms studied used a separate unit.

What factors influenced the effectiveness of these separate third party units? If a coordinating unit had an intermediate or balanced orientation to those factors which differentiated the basic departments, it was better able to facilitate interdepartmental decision-making. The managers of the basic departments apparently believed it was especially important for the third parties to have balanced time perspective and subgoal orientation.

Technical expertise is also important if third parties are to settle substantive disputes. The coordinating units in all six plastics firms studied by Lawrence and Lorsch had considerable power relative to their counterparts in the basic departments. However, in the two plastics firms where there was great respect for the technical competence of the third party personnel, there was also a higher level of integration. The experience of the food company's integrative unit was slightly different. At first its power was perceived by the basic departments as being based on its proximity to the president; however, as the basic departments gained respect for its expertise, the integrative unit made an increasingly positive contribution to conflict resolution.

What is the relative effectiveness of using a separate coordinating unit as opposed to relying on the crossover executive to resolve differences? Lawrence and Lorsch compared the way two container firms achieved interunit integration in the areas of scheduling and customer service, both frequently the subject of disagreement. One firm utilized a formal third party unit to facilitate coordination. The other firm relied on the crossover executive alone. The second arrangement was more effective in resolving conflict and more acceptable to the basic departments. Why? Although both arrangements provided a third party with a balanced orientation, the coordinating unit lacked the power and relevant information that the crossover executive had in the second firm (see Table 1).

Participation of a Peer Department

Still another potential source of third party influence on the substance of an interunit issue is a peer department which is not essentially involved.

Zald studied the pattern of interunit conflict among teachers, social service workers, and cottage parents in five delinquency institutions. The relative influence of the three types of units varied from institution to institution. The two lower influence departments tended to be more in conflict with the high influence department than with each other. Zald suggested that these conflict patterns reflected a tendency to balance off the high power of one department.[13]

Table 1   Relative Effectiveness of Coordinating Unit and
Crossover Executive in Dispute Resolution, Two Firms

	Attributes		
Third Parties	Balanced Orientation	Power	Relevant Information[a]
Coordinating unit	High	Low	Moderate
Crossover executive	High	High	High

Source: Based on Paul R. Lawrence and Jay W. Lorsch, *New Directions for Organizations* (Boston: Graduate School of Business Administration, Harvard University, 1967).
[a] About plant capacity and customer requirements.

Presumably the entry of a third party into an issue primarily between two units reduced unilateral decision-making and allowed the third party to exercise some substantive influence.

Dalton described the use of third party peer departments to force resolution of decisions which might otherwise represent an impass.[14] Whether or not this represents third party intervention in the sense of this paper depends on whether the third unit is interested primarily in helping to resolve the conflict or in entering into a coalition for the purpose of exchanging favors and influence.

Managing Manifest Conflict

The type of third party intervention described immediately above is concerned with the substance of the issues in dispute. In contrast, the interventions to help manage manifest conflict act on the *processes* of conflict and conflict management.

Influencing Gross Patterns of Contact

It is often possible to improve conflict management processes by affecting the gross pattern of interunit contact and coordination efforts. Some of these control techniques are available to the parties through their own initiative as well as at the initiative of a third party.

Sometimes control involves constraining interunit contact. In one production-sales relationship studied by Walton, Dutton, and Fitch, certain restrictions were designed to preserve a tenuously improving relationship. Interunit business transactions were channeled through the chief liaison personnel representing each department in order to reduce the likelihood of accidents or other provocative acts. For example, salesmen were not allowed to go onto the shipping dock or directly contact the shipping clerk.[15]

Direct contact between principals is sometimes reduced by using a low status, "expendable-linker" in interface activities.[16] This person elicits less hostility and absorbs the inevitable punishment more easily as he has less emotional energy invested in the relationship. In a similar vein, buffer inventories can be used to reduce the tightness of dependency and resulting need for frequent close coordination.[17]

In other instances, collaboration can be improved between departments by promoting interunit contacts. An obvious and basic way is to increase physical proximity. As an example, the ambassador of a large overseas mission reorganized office space and dispersed many sections of the AID mission in order to bring together physically the following and other combinations: assistant director of AID, economic counselor of the State Department, and the Treasury attaché; the AID capital development office and the Commerce attaché; etc. These changes facilitated functional coordination.[18]

Brown prescribes several roles for superiors who are aware of conflict between subordinates, including (1) ensuring that they confront their conflict, with a view toward resolving it; and (2) discussing with subordinates those lateral conflicts they fail to resolve on their own. Thus, the supervisor simply adds his own pressure for continued work on the conflict to that already inherent in the issues.[19] According to the "linking pin" concept of Likert, supervisors also can play an even more positive, social-emotional role in facilitating the resolution of conflict among subordinate units.[20]

In the overseas mission referred to above, the ambassador and his staff assistant had leadership patterns which combined to promote increased interunit contact and coordination. The ambassador let it be known that he had firm expectations that the separate agencies in the mission would find ways to coordinate their affairs and collaborate where appropriate. He asked for information about friction and was willing to exercise the force at his command to bring reluctant agencies into interagency contact. His staff assistant complemented the ambassador's harsh approach by encouraging, arranging, facilitating, and reinforcing interagency contacts and instances of coordination. He did use the influence of the ambassador, but subtly enough that his interpersonal and organizational skills at facilitation were the more apparent part of his approach. Thus, the moderately high power third party who punished instances of noncooperation was complemented by the low power, socially skillful third party who could facilitate the necessary interunit contacts. Both were more effective because their third party roles were combined and coordinated.

In other cases it is unclear whether the use of process intermediaries increases or decreases the gross rate of interunit interaction. Blake, Shepard, and Mouton cite a company in which a man was employed full time at the corporate level "for the sole purpose of trying to bring competing components of the organization into some reasonable alignment."[21] Burns and Stalker refer to "liaison specialists—whose job was to move across the linguistic and functional frontiers and to act as intermediaries between the people getting on with the job."[22] The use of such intermediaries was apparently a symptom of less effective organizations in the firms they studied.

Influencing the Approach to Issues in Dispute

A variety of distinctions have been made in how parties handle their differences. Schmidt and Tannenbaum cite avoidance, repression, sharpening into conflict, and transformation into problem-solving.[23] Blake, Shepard, and Mouton contrast a "win-lose" approach and problem-solving.[24] Walton elaborates two joint decision-making models, bargaining and problem-solving; these engagement approaches both contrast with a withdrawal posture.[25] Lawrence and Lorsch identify problem-solving, smoothing, and forcing.[26]

Common to all of these studies is problem-solving, where both parties strive toward: defining the problem in terms of underlying needs, exploring a wide range of alternatives, portraying accurately the strength of one's needs and preferences, and selecting alternatives that create the most joint gain. The outcomes of problem-solving are often integrative solutions rather than compromises. All authors appear to advocate strongly more frequent use of problem-solving, though they also acknowledge that under some conditions another approach makes sense. This general predeliction for confrontation and problem-solving appears to be justified in terms of the results of the Lawrence and Lorsch studies. The better performing firms tended to handle conflict by confronting it, rather than by smoothing it over or forcing outcomes.

Schmidt and Tannenbaum spelled out some of the third party interventions which facilitate problem-solving. The interventions are presumably available to superiors, consultants, and perhaps organizational peers.[27]

1. The third party can invite differences and stress their value in increasing the range of alternatives for the organization. To the extent that the parties perceive value to the confrontation process, each is less likely to define success in terms of attaining the particular outcome which he preferred initially.

2. The third party can listen with understanding rather than evaluation. The conflicting parties themselves usually don't listen to one another. Each is too busy trying to be understood. By listening and understanding, the third party can contribute to the parties' understanding of each other's position. Also, the third party's listening example is frequently followed by the participants themselves.

3. The third party can clarify the nature of the issue, e.g., whether it revolves around different perceptions of facts, methods, values, or goals. Disputants themselves often depart from the original issue by chasing a tangential point or by transposing the issue. The more detached third party can perform a welcome function by helping the disputants develop a common understanding of the issue and by repeatedly bringing them back to it.

4. The third party can recognize and accept the feelings of the individuals involved. Interunit disagreements are often compounded by the irrational feelings they generate, such as fear, jealousy, anger, or anxiety. When a third party communicates to a person that he can understand and accept these feelings he assists both participants to accept these feelings and to analyze their impact on the outstanding disagreement. The risk associated with identifying these "negative" feelings is that the person who is identified with them will feel criticized and become more defensive.

5. The third party can suggest procedures for resolving differences—the particular techniques depending on whether facts, methods, goals, or values are at issue. Walton and McKersie also suggest a variety of techniques to promote problem-solving when the mixed motive nature of the issue also requires some bargaining: differentiating the two types of interunit decision processes by fractionating the issue, by interunit representatives, by time, by ground rules, etc.[28]

6. Blake, Shepard, and Mouton, who approach interdepartmental and union-management conflict in similar ways, emphasize inter*group* dynamics. The third party can help the groups cope with what the authors call the "traitor threat," which involves loss of status and rejection of any representative who concedes points to the other group. The third party can influence the composition of the intergroup meeting or help regulate meeting caucuses and recesses in order to allow more continuous interchange between representatives and other members of their respective units.[29]

Facilitating Changing the Relationship

Now, rather than analyzing interventions which act either on the substance or process of conflict, we treat third party interventions which enable two units to perceive and move toward a new equilibrium—a relationship in which there is less emotional conflict and a generally improved capacity to solve differences.

In a Task Leadership Context: Interagency
Relations in Washington and Overseas

Many different departments and agencies of the U.S. government play a role in the conduct of foreign affairs: State, Defense, Agriculture, AID, Peace Corps, Commerce, CIA, to mention merely the more important ones. The agencies are coordinated in the field missions by the ambassador and his country team. Also, interdepartmental groups, comprised of several of these departments and chaired by an assistant secretary of state, have been created in Washington to coordinate foreign affairs on a regional basis. However, with very few exceptions, no such mechanism in Washington exists for coordinating these agencies' interest pertaining to an individual country. Generally the separate efforts are not well integrated, considerable mutual suspicion and low regard exists among agencies, and no well developed problem-solving mechanisms exist for resolving interagency differences.

Walton studied the innovative efforts of one country director (i.e., the ambassador's counterpart in the Washington, D.C., organization of the State Department) who has tried to increase interdepartmental integration and coordination at his level.[30] Beginning in May 1966, he scheduled meetings on a monthly basis, inviting representatives from about a dozen agencies—those persons directly concerned with the affairs of the same foreign country.

The country director, who did not have the power to compel membership or attendance, relied on his own skill in managing the sessions to make discussions productive and valuable to individual members. Many meetings featured informal presentations by persons with unique knowledge about the country, followed by round-table discussions of the issues raised. His method of handling meetings included relating himself to members directly and personally; urging continuity in the personnel representing an agency, differentiating one-time observers from regular members; encouraging, accepting, and helping develop views which differed from his own; and not keeping minutes on the meetings.

By the way he managed the sessions he gradually achieved certain states that in turn improved the problem-solving and conflict resolution capacity of this interagency network. Common exposure of the agency representatives to experts and to each other, and their own mutual education and information exchange activities, decreased the likelihood of future interagency conflict based on differences in perceived facts and tended to break down many negative intergroup stereotypes that exist about Peace Corps, Military, CIA, and State, etc. The development of personal relationships among agency representatives increased their tendency to check with each other for specific advice, information, and to coordinate activities generally. Encouragement of dissent and challenge in the absence of compelling policy or action decisions was effective in setting a group norm of sharpening, accepting, and exploring differences—a norm which could carry over into solving specific problems. A corollary group norm was one of identifying the additional information which the group would need if it were to choose between the alternative views. The agency representatives not only achieved a better understanding from State Department officials of overall goals for U.S. relations with the country in question but also became more committed to them by virtue of a sense of identification with the interagency group. This enhanced sense of membership in the group and commitment to superordinate goals increased a member's personal discomfort whenever his agency's actions ignored the interests of other agencies.

Interagency matters pertaining to a given country are somewhat better coordinated in the field than in Washington.[31] For example, the country team, comprised of the top officials of the important agencies and headed by the ambassador, is an established concept and usually provides some integration. Nevertheless, the amount of coordination is limited by many pervasive factors: (1) interagency stereotypes; resentments about incongruities among formal status, actual influence, and privileges (such as automobile allowances and invitations to diplomatic parties); (2) an agency's fears that its programs' identities will be blurred, its personnel misused, and its program activities oversupervised.

In the overseas mission studied, the ambassador and his staff had been relatively effective in encouraging interagency contacts. The third party roles they normally played are described above. An additional important experimental device for achieving a higher and more creative level of integration of the many strands of foreign affairs activities was referred to as the "Think Tank." It was an informal weekly meeting of a group drawn from many agencies to think imaginatively about problems of concern to the foreign affairs community as a whole. The ambassador's staff assistant had played a key role in initiating the idea. The group also included a second staff assistant to the ambassador, the deputy director of AID, an assistant director of AID, two military men, and a second level official from USIS. A ground rule for members was that they were to address the problems rather than represent their respective agencies' viewpoints.[32] Generally this group included bright young men below the country team level. Apparently group meetings not only weakened stereotypes but also increased members' confidence in their similar goals and the complementary competencies of their respective agencies. At the time of the study, they had identified some new potential areas of collaboration which they intended to recommend pursuing.

The examples of the country director in Washington and the staff assistant in the overseas mission both illustrate a third party whose relationship to the other person involved slightly greater organizational power, somewhat higher status, and higher access to information. Their interventions centered on task activities which did not require immediate action outside the group, but were nevertheless immediately gratifying to members. Their critical intervention strategy was to build a social system and their process tactics ensured that the system had norms and other attributes which facilitated the productive use of differences.

In a Behavioral Science Consulting
Context: An Intergroup Laboratory

Modifying the barriers to interunit collaboration is part of the more general problem of planned organizational change.[33] Blake, Shepard, and Mouton have utilized sensitivity training laboratory methods to improve intergroup relations in industry. Illustrative of their change strategy is the following account of their efforts which focused on the relations between headquarters and a field unit of a diversified and moderately decentralized industrial firm. This particular interunit relationship had attributes of both vertical and lateral relationships. The headquarters unit of Tennex Corporation performed staff as well as supervisory functions for the large Scofield unit.

The behavioral science consultants called in to help improve relationships first acquainted themselves with key management in both locations and the patterns of interactions, frustrations, and stereotypes in a generally deteriorating relationship.

"Headquarters personnel felt the division managers were 'secretive' and 'unresponsive.' The division was looked upon as unwilling to provide information that headquarters felt it needed. In turn, Scofield division management saw the headquarters management as 'prying' and 'arbitrary.' For example, headquarters was critical of the labor relations practices of the division. The division management resented the criticism, regarding it as prejudiced and ill-informed. Again, headquarters felt that Scofield managers had been 'dragging their feet' in implementing corporate marketing policies. Scofield felt that headquarters' demands in this area were unrealistic and that the corporate marketing group was behaving 'unilaterally,' and so on."[34]

The first of two basic types of intervention was training in group and intergroup dynamics. Separate three-day conferences with each group were designed to provide members with laboratory experiences which were in many respects analogous to those they face in their organizational roles. In this somewhat protected context, the consultants could identify the social dynamics while they were occurring, increase managers' awareness about how they were coping with them, and provide theory which generalized the experience and made credible its application to other situations.

". . . First, managers were able to see the headquarters-field problem in sufficient perspective to analyze the destructive consequences of the win-lose trap which had been dictating their actions. Second, an intergroup experiment and its analysis created a degree of openness within each group of managers that enabled them to review their own intragroup relationships and to develop greater mutual understanding and acceptance. This teamwork training is an important prelude to intergroup confrontation, because friction, 'politics,' or inability to level within each team clouds and confuses intergroup communication when the two groups are brought together."[35]

The second basic intervention was a three-day conference in which the two groups met together. This intervention involved the following phased activities:

Phase I: meeting together the groups listed and assigned priorities to those issues they felt required joint problem-solving.

Phase II: meeting separately each group prepared a description of itself as viewed by its members, constructed a verbal image of the other group, and finally built a description of their mutual relationships. These images supplemented the previously developed list of substantive issues, by providing an inventory of existing perceptions and feelings which needed to be examined, understood, and overcome.

Phase III: each group in turn exposed its own image of itself and in turn listened to the image as perceived by the other group. By their previous interventions, the consultants had created among participants a spirit of inquiry and a desire to listen for understanding rather than evaluation. As a result, the present activity of bringing these images into the open increased the general feelings of being understood and accepted. Then the participants again reviewed the substantive issues between the units.

Phase IV: several subgroups were formed of headquarters and field personnel with corresponding functional responsibilities. They first explored interpersonal issues and then tabled the functional problems they shared.

Phase V: a review was made of the progress in subgroups and between the units as a whole, and an analysis followed of the kinds of changes required in order to bring about actual improvements. One of the results of Phases IV and V was that headquarters personnel saw more clearly the alternative of conceiving themselves as "consultants" to the field rather than as persons who "control" field operations. They also better perceived the advantages of more mutual influence on policy-making and more continuous feedback about implementation. The groups agreed to reconvene for review and evaluation after a period of implementation.

By the end of phase V the groups had increased their mutual trust, respect, and understanding. In addition, they had made a number of commitments to new ways of either preventing or handling interunit differences.

Interpersonal Confrontation Between Key Personalities

Walton has described and analyzed the functions performed by a behavioral science consulting intervention which facilitated the confrontation of differences between the officials of two interdependent units in a government agency.[36]

The confrontation occurred between two program officers, whom we shall refer to as Bill and Lloyd. Bill's unit had overall project responsibility for designing an organizational system. Lloyd's unit provided many of the professional personnel engaged in the design work of the project. Lloyd himself had only recently assumed responsibility for supervising his unit's activities on the systems project. Friction had developed immediately between them. Bill decided to arrange a meeting with Lloyd specifically to review the working relationship between them and their respective units. He invited the consultant to participate as a third party. Lloyd agreed to the arrangement.

When the three of them met, Lloyd's initial statement of their difficulty stressed several intergroup issues. He asserted that his unit's personnel were being used below their capabilities and should be used more strategically. He felt that his unit had too little decision influence. He also believed that his own leadership position within his group was undermined by Bill's operating style. For his part, Bill was annoyed and harassed by what he regarded as dominating patterns of behavior by Lloyd in a combined group meeting. He objected to a similar pattern in their current interaction.

With the help of the third party they identified and discussed the issues which separated them, testing whether the differences were real or only apparent. Interestingly, as Lloyd realized that he was being listened to and understood and that the initially stated intergroup issues were being taken seriously, he began to identify more personal concerns about his own role and identity. For example, he did not feel sufficiently "connected" with the total project; moreover, he believed his own relevant experience and competence were not being recognized by Bill. It became apparent that these interpersonal concerns were an underlying part of the intergroup issues stated initially.

The confrontation was regarded by both participants and the consultant as successful. Some differences were resolved, and although other differences persisted, both principals believed they had established a basis for continuing to work on the issues. Further reports confirmed that the confrontation had been a significant factor in the improvement which occurred in their relationship and indicated that the consultant had played an important role in the confrontation.

Analysis of the confrontation suggests the functions performed by the third party. First, the consultant's presence facilitated openness in the confrontation, which enabled the parties to get the issues out and to redefine intergroup issues as interpersonal problems where appropriate. Both previously had participated in separate one-week sensitivity training workshops where high openness is normative. The consultant who was identified with sensitivity training emphasized the relevance of that prior sensitivity experience and made other attempts to invoke the norm of openness.

Second, the consultant was a synchronizing element. Arranging for the consultant's presence for a specific meeting served to create and confirm mutual expectations that they would confront their outstanding differences. Different expectations and different degrees of readiness often result in one person feeling "caught off guard" by another's attempt to raise the issues. The person who isn't prepared or doesn't recognize the other's attempt at confrontation certainly won't respond satisfactorily. Then the person whose attempt to confront is not reciprocated subsequently may well feel he overexposed himself and react by himself avoiding discussion of their issues in the future. Once Bill and Lloyd were into an exploration of their differences, the limited time availability of the consultant added further pressure to somewhat offset a natural tendency for the participants to smooth over their differences.

Third, the participants perceived the consultant as possessing behavioral skills and techniques which they could call upon if necessary. They believed that they ran less risk that the confrontation would bog down, get repetitive, and result in more frustration and bitterness. As a result, they entered into the meeting with more readiness.

Finally, the consultant both helped diagnose the underlying issues and provided an ingredient of emotional support for the participants. The third party listened to each discuss his views and feelings and sharpened what he understood to be an issue; the participants then responded in ways which tended to confirm or disconfirm that this was the underlying issue. An effort was made to state the issues in ways which made each person's position understandable, legitimate, and acceptable. One apparent effect of this was to encourage Lloyd to go on to identify the more personal concerns he had about not being involved and not being recognized as a competent person with experience relevant to the project.

Role Attributes and Interventions: A Summary

A third party may be related to the principals as an organizational superior, consultant, separate coordinating unit, or peer. These four role relationships differ in many respects, including the magnitude and types of power available to the third party, the degree of impartiality likely to be attributed to the third party, and the degree of relevant knowledge possessed by the third party. We can summarize how these and other aspects of the role relationships of a third party govern which of the four types of interventions are available to him.

Superiors

Superiors are the only third parties likely to have the organizational power to reduce conflict potential by restructuring the organization or reassigning personnel. Also, assuming that a superior's responsibility embraces both units, his view would be balanced enough to play this third party role. The main difficulty is that superiors often do not have an adequate information base or diagnostic framework by which to assess the dysfunctional consequences of conflict and the basic underlying causes. Moreover, elimination of the factors which induced the dysfunctional conflict in the first instance may not significantly reduce the conflict because of the number of self-reinforcing and regenerating processes involved in the relationship pattern.[37] Hence, structural interventions to reduce conflict potential need to be accompanied by process or clinical interventions to facilitate the change in lateral relationships.

Organization superiors can be too little or too much involved in the substance of a dispute. If deciding the issue requires unique judgment, he should be involved. He is more likely to be brought into the conflict if he tends to view interunit differences as based on task realities rather than arising from the emotional interreactions of line subordinates. However, substantive intervention by superiors runs the risk of creating "win-lose" reactions on the part of subordinates, especially if his action on the issue is intended merely to avoid further effects of the conflict process rather than to contribute unique knowledge.

Superiors sometimes facilitate the process of confronting and solving differences. To do this, a superior needs certain behavioral skills rather than unique knowledge about the issue in dispute. High organizational power is a mixed blessing to him in promoting problem-solving. On the one hand, he can require subordinates to change their gross pattern of interunit contact. On the other hand, his high power may inhibit the participants and discourage them from taking the personal risks associated with sharpening the issues in dispute. Similarly, high organizational power complicates a third party's attempts to create a nonevaluative social-emotional climate conducive to identifying and working through negative interunit attitudes.

Organizational Consultants

The organizational consultant lacks the superior's power to modify directly the conflict potential factors or to decide the substantive issues in dispute. However, he is usually in a relatively better position to influence the interaction processes. This is true to the extent that the consultant is perceived to have little or no preference regarding the outcome of a dispute, to have both objectivity and expertise which make him a fruitful source of diagnostic insight, to be nonevaluative, to be a source of emotional support, and to have high skills in facilitating interaction processes. The consultant can be used first to help the subordinate departments identify the organizational factors contributing to the conflict. Then, in association with organizational changes designed to reduce conflict potential, the consultant third party can facilitate the change in actual relationships.

Although we have not treated the problem here in any detail, it should be noted that the interpersonal styles and institutional props which create the appropriate role identity for consultant third parties are often as important as his active interventions.

Coordinating Units

Given the need for interdepartmental coordination, the more differentiated are the basic department's orientations, the more likely it is that a continuous, specialized third party can contribute to the resolution of inter-unit conflicts. If organizational differentiation is not great the interventions of a third party can reduce rather than enhance coordination.

The separate coordinative units studied were all intended to manage interdepartmental differences via substantive contributions to decision-making. The requisite role attributes for this type of intervention are balanced (or intermediate) orientation, high substantive knowledge, and moderately high organizational power (relative to the basic departments).

Peer Units

There is very little evidence of peer organizational units performing neutral third party roles. Perhaps there is little reward and high risk associated with informally taking on third party functions. A peer organizational unit may have certain inherent disadvantages. First, it would not have the high power of a superior. Second, it would not have the substantive expertise of a coordinative unit. Third, typically, it would have an even more difficult time than a superior or a separate coordinative group in convincing the disputants that it had a balanced orientation. Fourth, it probably would not possess the process skills of the organizational consultant.

Ambiguous Organizational Role Relationships

The State Department's relationship to the other foreign affairs agencies is an ambiguous mixture of the various types treated here. It is primarily a peer unit, but with legitimacy for certain supervisory and coordinative functions. State lacks authority to modify the basic structure within which the agencies deal with each other. Nevertheless, State personnel have an opportunity to design certain joint task activities and provide task leadership.

The studies reported on here focused on officials who had relatively high behavioral skill which they used to improve interagency relationships. In particular, they took advantage of slightly higher organizational power and status and higher task information in order to design and lead collaborative task activities, which in turn created group membership and norms more favorable to the constructive management of interagency differences.

Conclusion

The present treatment is tentative and less than comprehensive in treating the range of issues involved in third party analysis. Under what conditions is it useful to intervene? What are the optimum third party role attributes for resolving types of conflicts? How are these role attributes established? By individual? Or by organization? When should an intervention be specific to a dispute? When should it treat the relationship? When should it focus on the conflict potential in the organizational context? These questions are important enough to warrant much additional research.

Notes and References

1. This research was supported by AF 49(638)–1751, ARPA contract for "The Role of Third Parties in Conflict Resolution and Control."
2. James D. Thompson, "Organizational Management of Conflict," *Administrative Science Quarterly,* IV (1960), 389–409.
3. Richard E. Walton, "Theory of Conflict in Lateral Organizational Relationships," in J. R. Lawrence, editor, *Operational Research and the Social Sciences* (London: Tavistock, 1966), pp. 409–428.
4. *Ibid.*
5. Wilfred Brown, *Explorations in Management* (London: Tavistock, 1960); Henry A. Landsberger, "The Horizontal Dimension in a Bureaucracy," *Administrative Science Quarterly,* VI (1961), 298–333.
6. Eugene Litwak, "Models of Bureaucracy Which Permit Conflict," *American Journal of Sociology,* LXVII (1961), 177–184.
7. Thompson, *op. cit.*
8. Brown, *op cit.,* p. 69.
9. George Strauss, "Work-Flow Frictions, Interfunctional Rivalry, and Professionalism: A Case Study of Purchasing Agents," *Human Organization,* XXIII (1964), 137–149.
10. Brown, *op. cit.*
11. Robert R. Blake, Herbert A. Shepard, and Jane S. Mouton, *Intergroup Conflict in Organizations* (Ann Arbor, Mich.: Foundation for Research on Human Behavior, 1964).
12. Paul R. Lawrence and Jay W. Lorsch, *New Directions for Organizations* (Boston: Graduate School of Business Administration, Harvard University, 1967).
13. Myer N. Zald, "Power Balance and Staff Conflict in Correctional Institutions," *Administrative Science Quarterly,* VII (1962), 22–49.
14. Melville Dalton, *Men Who Manage* (New York: Wiley, 1959).
15. Richard E. Walton, John M. Dutton, and H. G. Fitch, "A Study of Conflict in the Process, Structure, and Attitudes of Lateral Relationships," in Albert Rubenstein and Chadwick Haberstroh, editors, *Some Theories of Organization* (Rev. ed.; Homewood, Ill.: Irwin, 1966), pp. 444–465.
16. John A. Seiler, "Diagnosing Interdepartmental Conflict," *Harvard Business Review,* XLI (September–October, 1963), 121–132.
17. Louis R. Pondy, *Organizational Conflict: Concepts and Models* (mimeographed, Graduate School of Business, University of Pittsburgh, 1965).
18. Richard E. Walton, *Interagency Coordination in the Overseas Mission* (mimeographed, 1966).
19. Brown, *op. cit.*
20. Rensis Likert, *New Patterns of Management* (New York: McGraw-Hill, 1961).
21. Blake, Shepard, and Mouton, *op. cit.,* p. 109.
22. Tom Burns and G. M. Stalker, *The Management of Innovation* (London: Tavistock, 1961).
23. Warren Schmidt and Robert Tannenbaum, "The Management of Differences," *Harvard Business Review,* XXXVIII (November–December, 1960), 107–115.
24. Blake, Shepard, and Mouton, *op. cit.*
25. "Theory of Conflict . . ."

26. Lawrence and Lorsch, *op. cit.*

27. Schmidt and Tannenbaum, *op. cit.*

28. Richard E. Walton and Robert B. McKersie, "Behavioral Dilemmas in Mixed Motive Decision Making," *Behavioral Science*, XI (1966), 370–384.

29. Blake, Shepard, and Mouton, *op. cit.*

30. Richard E. Walton, *A Centripetal Force in Foreign Affairs* (mimeographed, 1967).

31. Walton, *Interagency Coordination.* . . .

32. The "Think Tank" is very similar to an informal problem-solving and strategic-thinking group at Case Institute of Technology, which referred to itself as the "Hats Group" because each person was expected to leave his departmental hat at the door.

33. Chris Argyris, *Interpersonal Competence and Organizational Effectiveness* (Homewood, Ill.: Dorsey, 1962); Edgar H. Schein and Warren G. Bennis, *Personal and Organizational Change Through Group Methods: The Laboratory Approach* (New York: Wiley, 1965).

34. Blake, Shepard, and Mouton, *op. cit.*, p. 116.

35. *Ibid.*, p. 117.

36. Richard E. Walton, "Interpersonal Confrontation and Basic Third Party Roles: A Case Study," *Journal of Applied Behavioral Science* (1967).

37. John M. Dutton and Richard E. Walton, "Interdepartmental Conflict and Cooperation: Two Contrasting Studies," *Human Organization*, XXV (1966), 207–220.

Appeal Systems in Organizations

WILLIAM G. SCOTT

An Issue in Managerial Justice

Classical organization theorists defend the principles of hierarchy as vigorously as some modernists condemn them. What both overlook is that the scalar principle, the unity of command principle, and the rights of command authority are regularly and systematically overridden by many business and non-business undertakings.

The grapevine and other informal channels of communication in formal organizations are familiar. Almost equally well-known are the "overlays" of power, influence, and decision making which are the unanticipated modifications of bureaucratic structures by the people in them. These phenomena are discussed widely by human relationists and behavioral scientists.

What is unexplored is the formal and official violation of classical principles by policy makers through the establishment of appeal systems for organizational members. This research study concerns the nature of such appeal systems in business and non-business organizations. A major purpose of this study is the development of an *explanation* for the existence of formal appeal systems in organizations.

Formal circumvention of supervisors occurs frequently and is allowed as

Reprinted with permission from William G. Scott, *The Management of Conflict* (Homewood, Ill.: Richard D. Irwin, Inc., 1965 ©), pp. 1–14 and pp. 114–126.

a matter of policy in organizations where the chain of command is thought inviolate. The policies which permit "bypassing the boss" are found in a segment of personnel practice dealing with the administration of complaints and grievances. To provide alternative channels of upward communication for conflict resolution, policy makers often legitimatize the bypassing of immediate superiors. Appeal systems are, however, more than anomalous personnel practices which run counter to sacred management principles. They touch upon an area of law which heretofore has been largely unnoticed.

The law has two major segments. One part is public, both civil and criminal, and is supported by the sanctions of the state. The other is sociological in conception. It is concerned with the norms which are privately and locally evolved to regulate the affairs of organizations with each other and the relations between the person and the organization of which he is a member.

Our interest is in intraorganizational law. Laws in this category are found in one of two subdivisions. The first relates to the organization's expectations and the rights of its membership as stated in official documents like union constitutions, employee handbooks, or government personnel manuals. The other relates to specific guarantees to an organization's membership that redress is available if those in authority usurp or violate the rights of such membership. Organizational due process is a way to insure that redress against arbitrary authority will be available. As Wendell French clearly puts it, ". . . organizational due process consists of established procedures for handling complaints and grievances, protection against punitive action for using such established procedures, and careful, systematic, and thorough review of the substance of the complaints and grievances."[1] The focus of this study is upon the systems of due process as French defines them.

Thus appeal systems must be thought of within the context of intraorganizational law. They are part of the judicial function which insures equity in the administration of "legislated" policies, constitutions, or agreements. Some of these judicial systems may originate in the benevolence of the executives of an organization; or they might be traced to a "grass roots" movement for redress among organizational participants; others may stem from sources which could be labeled interorganizational, such as a business firm's installing an appeal system to forestall a threat of unionization. Still other plans may come from public law itself like certain categories of appeal in the federal civil service system.

To sum it up then, we deal with a subject which can be narrowly thought of as a personnel practice or more widely conceived in the sociology of law. A great deal of work has been done in analyzing, discussing, and describing the legislative (policy-making) and executive (action-evoking) activities of managers. But there is little empirical, analytical, and descriptive information on the *managerial judicial function.* This book is a systematic analysis of this neglected subject.

The Aims and Hypotheses of This Study

Our concern is with those appeal systems which have been granted to members of organizations as a *unilateral* act of administration. Bilaterally negotiated grievance procedures between unions and management *are excluded.* Unilateral appeal systems are far from unknown to administrators regardless of the type of organization in which they practice their art. As a personnel manager friend told me, "They are as common as fleas on a dirty dog." While not exactly an accurate simile it is descriptive of the prevalence of the type of program considered on the remaining pages.

Appeal systems have stayed largely within the province of management practitioners. Though not ignored by students of organization and administration, there are significant gaps in our understanding of the concept of appeal and its implementation in private organizations. We may legitimately ask such questions as the following: How prevalent are these kinds of programs in business? What are the procedural patterns followed by business and non-business appeal systems? What are the similarities and differences between business and non-business programs in terms of origin, policy, and form of implementation? What explanations can be offered for the existence of these programs? What relationship is there between organization size, the opportunities for individual mobility, and the existence of formal appeal procedures?

To this end, we are concerned with the following propositions which refer to size, mobility, and ubiquity:

1. Formal appeal systems are associated with large organizations in the sense that the larger the organization the more likely it is to have an appeal system.

2. Formal appeal systems arise out of the structural and environmental determinants of reduced mobility and increased dependency of organizational participants.

3. Formal appeal systems are indifferent to organizational objectives. They are found in private business, union, religious, military and government organizations.

Appeal systems are not new subjects in the professional literature of management and the behavioral sciences. They have been discussed by specialists in both areas for some time.[2] The treatment of the *issues* underlying appeal systems has been submerged, however, in the ideology of industrial humanism. To appraise the present status of the notion of appeal, it is necessary to deal with it at first on the terms of industrial humanism. We do not necessarily accept the validity of these terms. It is simply that the industrial humanists are the only ones who have had much to say about the philosophy of appeals.

The Appeal Issue

This book demonstrates that numerous organizations recognize the *right* of the individual to seek redress of complaints and grievances and provide for the exercise of this right through formal policies and procedures aimed at conflict resolution. Now, of course, due process is well established in civil society and more than adequately explained in traditional jurisprudence. It does not, however, have the same status in theories of administrative organizations. The most comprehensive attempt to explain the right of appeal in such organizations has been undertaken by a group I call the industrial humanists. While I find their position unacceptable, it is essential that their explanatory system receives a fair exposition.

To the industrial humanist the imperative in administrative effort is the design of the work environment so that a maximization of human satisfaction is realizable. Evidence of this goal is found in the writings of Roethlisberger,

Likert, McGregor, Argyris, and many others who reject the appropriateness of the mechanistic-competitive model of human motivation in business. The criticisms and recommendations of these scholars are well-known. Theory Y, job enlargement, communication, participation, and democratic leadership are familiar remedies for offsetting some of the restrictions on human satisfaction imposed by industrial employment. Lesser known is the stand of this group on the general subject of managerial justice and the specific matter of organizational appeal systems.

Justice and Appeal as Seen by the Industrial Humanist   The industrial humanist's conception of justice must not be equated with organizational appeal systems. Managerial justice to him is much more than this. The industrial humanist sees the just executive as one who promotes subordinates' psychological maturity, self-awareness, and security through a climate of democratic leadership, participation, sensitivity, and good communication. Within this broad conception of justice, organizational appeal systems play their role. Douglas McGregor's statement of twenty years ago is still appropriate.

"There are occasions when subordinates differ radically, but sincerely with their superiors on important questions. Unless the superior follows an 'appeasement' policy there exists in such a disagreement the possibility of an exaggerated feeling of dependence and helplessness in the minds of the subordinates. They disagree for reasons which seem *to them* sound; yet they must defer to the judgment of one person whom they know to be fallible.

"If these occasions are too frequent, the subordinates will be blocked in their search of independence, and they may readily revert to a reactive struggle. The way out of the dilemma is to provide the subordinate with a mechanism for appealing his superior's decisions to a higher level of the organization. The subordinate can then have at hand a check upon the correctness and fairness of his superior's actions. His feeling of independence is thereby increased.

"This is one of the justifications for an adequate grievance procedure for workers. All too often, however, there is no similar mechanism provided for management. To safeguard the individual against retaliative measures by his immediate superior is impossible, but it is possible to guarantee a reasonable degree of protection.

"If the relationship between subordinate and superior is a successful one, the right of appeal may rarely be exercised. Nevertheless, the awareness that it is there to be used when needed provides the subordinate with a feeling of independence which is not otherwise possible."[3]

McGregor bases the need for organizational appeal systems on three potential dangers:

1. dependency of the subordinate on the superior, resulting in,
2. the frustration of the subordinate's freedom of self-expression, leading to,
3. the blocking of the individual in his search for satisfaction through work.

Thus an organizational member would be happier and more productive if he were given an alternate channel of upward communication around his superior. Judging from McGregor's statement, benefits from this communication program would accrue to all employees in an organization regardless of their rank. Of course, top management's formal consent is necessary for establishing these channels of communication.

Others, following McGregor's cue, have made similar observations. For instance, Keith Davis notes that two types of justice predominate in organizations. The first type called executive justice is dispensed by "fair" managers. The second type called judicial justice is available through a system of appeal, hopefully independent of the hierarchial pressures of the organization's management. Significantly Davis says, "Experience seems to indicate that the judicial type is needed to protect persons from deficiencies in the executive type."[4] The similarity between Davis' judicial type system and McGregor's appeal mechanism is obvious.

William M. Evan discusses the same issue and arrives at the same conclusion as Davis and McGregor. An outline of Evan's view is useful because it is the most refined of all the statements to date.

1. The key to understanding the behavior of "organization men" (junior executives in the middle income bracket inhabiting large organizations) is their commitment to an ideology of conformity.

2. Organization men are forced to adopt this ideology because of social-structural determinants peculiar to large organizations. These determinants are:
A. Subjective performance appraisal by superiors causing subordinates to conform to perceptions of what they think will please the boss.
B. A sponsorship system of promotion.
C. The hierarchical arrangement of organizational authority structure which allows the boss to god-play with his subordinates' careers.

3. The ensuing conformity behavior resulting from these determinants is dysfunctional for the individual, the organization, and the community.

4. This being so, it is advantageous to reduce the necessity for conformity.

5. To this end, Evan suggests two solutions—procedural due process of law and the professionalization of management. The first suggestion results in a modification of organizational structure. The second suggestion represents the introduction of a third, external force into the middle-top management relationship. These suggestions are interacting and re-enforcing.[5]

Even though Evan chooses to discuss the issue in "organization men" terms, his argument is relevant for most situations where subordination and dependency are, or could become, burdensome for the individual. Indeed, this seems to be the position of still other writers who are taking "uneasy glances at performance appraisal."[6] They are saying that:

1. organizational logic demands that the superior evaluate his subordinates, but
2. this same logic establishes a "god-man" relationship in which the superior is in an inordinately powerful position to determine the fate of his subordinates, and
3. the consequence of this relationship stifles individual freedom, initiative, and growth to psychological maturity, and finally,
4. this relationship is repugnant to a society where the tradition of government by law is unalterably opposed to government by functionary.[7]

According to this interpretation all subordinates, organization men or not, suffer to a greater or lesser degree from dependence upon superiors for the distribution favors. It follows that all in such circumstances could benefit from an appeal system. Even if the appeal system is not used extensively, the simple knowledge that it is available produces a salubrious psychological state in employees.

From this brief overview it is evident that the issue of managerial justice has not been ignored by the industrial humanists. They have, in fact, contributed most to the ideological, if not the empirical, content of the subject.

The Ideology of the Justice Issue: A Summary   Administrative theorists observe that the larger an organization becomes the more effort is expended to rigidify its functional and interpersonal relationships.[8] The result is a bureaucratic organization characterized by strong functional and superior-subordinate systems of interdependencies. These systems create organizations which are collectivistic in nature, bonded by power and formal authority.

In such a setting the freedom of subordinates is considerably reduced with respect to their superiors. Instead of freedom, a state of dependency is substituted which is crucial and often objectionable. It is crucial because the integrity and effectiveness of the organization rests upon the efficiency of coordination.* It is objectional because it is thought at times to produce dysfunctional consequences for the organization itself, for the community in which the organization functions, and especially for the people who serve in the system. In this last respect Evan says that a subordinate deprived of his right to appeal is "highly motivated to fulfill his superior's expectations even at the expense of his own ideas and wishes in order to insure positive appraisal and associated rewards."[9] Individual liberty and self-assertion are forced by organizational demands to give way to authority, discipline, and dependency.

The goal of industrial humanism is the restoration of the individual's opportunity for self-realization. This is a large order in the face of the "natural" authoritarian development of formalized organizations. Obviously much has to be modified in terms of the philosophy of the administration and the organizational structure to counteract these tendencies.

In this perspective the appeal concept is just a fragment of the industrial humanist's ideology. But the premise is clear upon which the concept is based. An avenue for individual redress of grievances is an essential adjunct to the humane atmosphere which is planned for increasing employee satisfactions at work. In the modified organization the grant of greater opportunities for satisfaction is meaningless without the added right of an employee to bypass his superior for an impartial hearing if he feels he is being treated unjustly. If appeal systems contribute to the accomplishment of this end, they advance the efficiency of coordination and reduce the objectionableness of dependency.

Systems of Appeal in Action

Operational appeal systems in private organizations are not hard to find. There are many in widely different organizational settings. Whether or not they serve the lofty purposes of industrial humanism is a consideration best postponed until

*Coordination is the classical term for the administrative acts necessary to weld diverse functions into a formal system of behavior aimed at accomplishing goals and objectives.

the later chapters. For now, to assure the reader that we are not dealing with an ephemeral subject, several programs of business firms which have been publicized are noted.

Wilfred Brown in his book *Exploration in Management* describes the appeal system at the Glacier Metal Working Plant in England.[10] Since this is a model plan it is useful to point out its general features:

1. Every member of the company (Glacier) has the right to appeal from any decision of his manager to the next level of management, and successively to higher levels of management until he reaches the Managing Director. (This constitutes three levels of appeal above the bottom rung of the hierarchy.)

2. The employee, subject to special provisions, has the final right of appeal to an Appeal Tribunal consisting of an employee representative, a management member, and a Tribunal Chairman appointed from outside the company by the Chairman of the relevant works council.

3. At each appeal hearing, the person appealing is entitled to assistance from his chosen representative, with the managers involved being present.

4. The task of the managers who hear the appeals is to come to a decision in the light of existing policy, standing orders, and precedent.

5. Either party to an appeal may refer it to a personnel officer for counselling. The personnel officer may make recommendations to both parties. But they are not binding and, if not accepted, the appeal continues to be heard in the normal way.[11]

In a company policy document[12] it is clear that every member of the company is allowed the right to appeal from any executive decision or action which affects him or which he considers unfair. In an analysis of appeals heard by the Managing Director from 1953 to 1958 not one of the 53 appeals came from members of the "Executive System" (i.e., management, in Glacierese). Forty-three appeals were from hourly rated employees; fifteen came from staff. Of course, it must be remembered that these appeals are only those which reached the "head man." There could have been executive system appeals which did not get to the top.

Another well known program is the Open Door Policy of IBM. In a recent book, Thomas J. Watson, Jr., says, "We wanted to be certain that no one got lost in the organization and, most of all, that no individual became a victim of any manager's unfairness or personal whim. In this regard, we developed what we call our 'Open Door' policy. This is a key element in our employee relations."[13]

While many open door programs are casual informal affairs, such is not the case at IBM. The method of submitting and processing complaints is clearly stated in the Employee Manual. The procedure has three steps beginning with the employee's immediate superior and ending with the Chairman of the Board.[14] A record of the type, location, and disposition of the complaints is maintained.

Western Electric runs a program exclusively for its engineering employees. Western Electric's Engineering Personnel Units occupy the key role in the administration of the appeal system. The program, they say, provides technical employees with an "alternate channel of communication" upward. EPU representatives at various plants are available to talk to engineering personnel and bring problems to the attention of local management.[15]

The Management of Conflict

Cry Haro

Adolf Berle in his book, *The 20th Century Capitalist Revolution,*[16] tells of the feudal practice allowing aggrieved people to approach the lord or king with the cry of "haro" which signified they were seeking redress of a wrong. These appeals were to the benevolence of the king's conscience because all other avenues for justice had been exhausted. Berle finds a similarity between appeals invoking the conscience of the king and appeals to the conscience of the corporation. But the problem, as he sees it, is that the rights and mechanisms necessary in calling upon the judicial conscience of the corporation are not well defined or firmly established. This does not mean that ways of resolving conflicts do not exist.

Conflicts of many descriptions, actual or potential, are present in organizations. Most of these conflicts are institutionalized to insure organizational stability. Regularized means are evolved to settle conflicts, or direct them into harmless channels, or to use them as constructive forces. Practically it makes little difference whether the means are formal or informal as long as conflicts are resolved before they erode the organization. Regularization does not imply administrative formalization. Evan has shown, for example, ". . . that a very high proportion of the respondents in the industrial laboratory—which does not have a formal appeal system—perceives a due process norm to be institutionalized and have internalized such a norm. This points to the functioning of an informal appeal system."[17]

Thus, in many organizations the cry of haro may be directed with ease and informality to key executives who act in the role of arbitrator in resolving conflicts among subordinates. But as the determinants of size and mobility are felt, informal conflict resolution is often paralleled by formalized procedures which serve similar ends. Formal systems of appeal may never fully supplant informal methods for settling complaints and ameliorating conflicts. However, the forces of bureaucratization which produce programs of procedural due process will cause administrators to reflect more carefully on their judicial function. This function has been subordinated in emphasis to the legislative (policy-making) and executive (action-evoking) in organizations, particularly business firms. The appeal systems which we have analyzed are formalized means through which the modern participant in a bureaucratic organization can "cry haro" if he feels his rights are jeopardized.

So just as the cry of haro, as an institutionalized system for the redress of grievances, was a restraint on the absolute power of the feudal ruler, so also are systems of appeal restraints on the power of administrators. However, it is indeed naive not to recognize that the amount of restraint depends entirely upon the judicial standards used by managers, where these standards come from, and the extent to which the executive and legislative functions of administration are separated from the judicial function.

While the process of bureaucratization may be the determinant of the formalization of appeal practices, it is *not* the determinant of the philosophy or spirit in which the system is administered. The goals of the system and the judicial standards which are used for appeal settlement may differ from organization to organization. The differences are attributable to the choices of the policy makers themselves. What these alternatives are is considered next.

The Judicial Goals and Standards
of Appeal Systems

Appeal systems are not inherently democratic or authoritarian. As products of an amoral process—formalization—they serve either philosophy, or some intermediate ones, equally well. The tone and spirit in which the system is administered depends on the philosophy of the executives in each organization. The philosophical alternatives upon which the administration of formal appeal systems can be based is shown in Table 1.[18]

Table 1   The Goals and Settlement Standards of Appeal Systems

Administrative Alternatives	Objectives	Judicial Settlement Standards	Source of Standards
1. Authoritarian	1. Benevolence and control	1. *Ad hoc* standards of executives hearing cases, consistent with organization's value system	1. Internally derived from organization's value system
2. Legalistic (internal)	2. Uniform and impartial application of organization law	2. Organization policy rules, regulations, and precedents	2. Internally derived from organization's value system but unbiased application assured by outside participant in appeal system
3. Legalistic (external)	3. Dilution of authoritarianism by the regulation of policy legislation and execution	3. Organization values congruent with democratic public legal statutes and precedents	3. Internally derived but with an eye to correspondence with *external* values of a democratic society the enforcement of which in the organization is assured by an outside participant in the appeal system
4. Democratic	4. Equality of satisfactions a. Release from dependence b. Self-determination	4. Liberal, democratic humanitarianism within the framework of a system of organizational due process of law	4. Externally derived from the democratic organizational milieu. Will prevail as long as organizations retain hierarchical authoritarian bias

Before we take a closer look at each alternative, the reader is reminded that most appeal programs are anticipated to contribute to the effectiveness and efficiency goals which are essential in the cooperative system. This is true even though administrators may differ on appeal philosophy.

Authoritarian   While the major character of formal organizations is hierarchy, there are many, including those in high positions of authority, who feel that leadership must be benevolent. By formalizing the appeal process, the authoritarian objective of benevolence is underscored. We might call it formalizing the access to the "conscience of the organization." Anyway, the right to formal redress is at least a modest restraint on arbitrary and unjust use of authority.

The authoritarian alternative would admit settlement of cases upon judicial standards which are derived internally from the organization's value system. That is, the "legitimate" criteria used in settling cases conform to organizational standards primarily, *although these criteria may not be uniformly applied from case to case by executives involved in the hearings.*

This situation must exist in many organizations with appeal programs. Settlement of complaints is based upon interpretations of employee "rights" which frequently either are not formally stated at all or are vaguely represented in handbooks and manuals. In any event, somewhere in the appeal network the "givers of rights" become also the "interpreters of the same rights." This arrangement prevents any serious objection from being raised against organizational values. At the same time, it gives managerial "judges" the chance to bend rules or modify precedents for the sake of benevolence in individual cases.

The authoritarian alternative has another aspect, besides benevolence, which cannot be ignored. Since the policies of an organization are executed by humans, the risk of mistakes, malpractice, injustice, and cheating is present in varying degrees. In view of this, appeal systems may also be correctly considered as control devices. This interpretation takes on added meaning when we reflect on the fact that the aggrieved party most often institutes his appeal action on technical, administrative, or personal grounds against an *agent* of the organization rather than the organization itself.

Control is certainly the point of several business policy statements I read which say that if a manager knows that his subordinates have a legitimate avenue of redress around him he will "watch his step." In other organizations, the control feature of appeal is strengthened by the institution of a control staff function like the military inspector general or the ecclesiastical visitor. It is not a coincidence that official documents in these organizations say that the soldier or the cleric has the *duty* to report administrative injustices or infractions. This statement of duty is calculated to reinforce organizational control through the appeal network.

Legalistic (Internal)   The philosophic foundation of the internal legalistic alternative is found neither in authoritarian benevolence nor in bureaucratic control. Instead this philosophy proposes the rule of law, not men, in organizations. Its goal is to insure that the law of the organization is kept through impartial hearings, objective interpretations, and equitable settlements of complaints. The aim of this philosophy is to insure administrative compliance with the policies which define the rights and govern the organization's affairs with its members.

The standards for judicial actions are derived internally from the organization's value system. In this respect, this alternative differs little from the authoritarian. *The distinction is that the internal legalistic approach seeks consistent and impartial application of organizational law to all organization members.*

The chief difficulty of this approach is implementation. In order for laws and policies to be administered impartially those who hear and decide appeal cases should not be members of the organizational hierarchy. This is probably too extreme to be realistic. So let us amend it and say that at least one decision stage, preferably the last in the appeal procedure, ought to be in the hands of responsible parties having no connection with the executive structure. They should have the power to interpret and enforce the laws and policies as these have evolved in the organization, and yet they must be detached from the hierarchy of the organization.

These provisions are necessary for the internal legalistic approach to work. First, there must be a statutory base provided by a constitution or some other kind of pact as the foundation for membership rights. In a business organization this could be as simple as a manual. Second, a file of decisions reached in all appeal cases at all steps in the procedure must be maintained as precedents for future cases. Neither of these requirements poses a problem. The third does. *It requires outside participation in conflict resolution.*

By opening the appeal procedure to an external uncommitted party in the settlement process, the crucial separation of judicial from other management activities occurs. This is an aspect of the legalistic approach which many policy makers would find hard to accept. Yet the separation of functions in the administration of an appeal network is essential if a modicum of organizational justice is sought. Just two business organizations were encountered in this study which employed this approach. The UAW's Public Review Board is a good example, structurally, of the alternative examined in this section.

Legalistic (External)   This alternative differs in two ways from the internal legalistic.

1. It adopts standards of civil law as guides for those hearing organizational appeal cases. This is where the name external legalistic comes from.
2. It implies outside participation, or veto power, in legislative as well as judicial administrative activities.

The purpose of this alternative is to mold the settlements gained through the appeal procedure into conformance with the legal criteria of the democratic society at large. The dominance of internal authoritarianism is reduced by reference to external standards of legal custom and practice. Thus an appeal may be denied on the grounds of an organization's constitution or other rules of government. But if the section of the constitution or policies upon which the case is based is not consistent with analogous civil statute or precedent, then, under this approach, the rule itself might be invalidated and the appeal sustained.[19] It is evident that the need for outside participation in the appeal process is as essential in this alternative as it is in the previous.

While this approach most certainly would dilute the authoritarianism of an organization's executive hierarchy, it would also reduce their sovereignty. If a policy is challenged in appeal and found inconsistent with or contrary to civil legal criteria, the law of organization could be overturned. It is doubtful that administrators would be willing to impose this degree of restraint upon their autonomy to legislate.

Democratic   This alternative visualizes the objective of appeal as the enhancement of the individual's satisfactions as an organizational participant. Although this goal is implied in the other alternatives, the standards of democratic judgment are the most permissive of all because they propose to reduce individual dependence and extend the opportunity for self-determination.

The judicial criteria to accomplish this do not come entirely from formal organizational values or from public law. Instead the norms are found in the *spirit* of those who are liberal and humanitarian in outlook. Of these some would be selected to participate in the appeal activity, again as members unattached and uncommitted to the organization to which the system is appended.

The democratic alternative is difficult to conceptualize. Yet its aims are not much different from the more familiar methods recommended to humanize the organization. This alternative is consistent with, and might even be considered the *judicial* extension of, McGregor's Theory Y. This means that instead of a negative atmosphere surrounding the appeal activity in its authoritarian or legalistic forms, the democratic approach would promote a positive integration of organizational and individual goals.

It would do so by operating from a framework of behavioral assumptions which differ substantially from the traditional. The attitudes guiding appeal hearings and settlements would stem more from Theory Y behavioral criteria than from standards which are implicit in the authoritarian or legalistic notions of motivation.

The reader is right if he senses that he is back on familiar ground. We have completed the circle which we began with the discussion of industrial humanism. However, there is an important difference. Industrial humanism is not offered as an explanation of why appeal systems emerge, but rather it is an administrative philosophy which could be used to govern these programs once they are evolved out of the formalization process.

The main point to be stressed in this section is when judicial criteria are internally derived and when there is no separation of the judicial from the legislative and executive functions, it is hard to foresee that the standards of conflict management would more than mildly differ, if at all, from organizational values. This situation, represented by the authoritarian alternative, imposes the minimum restraint on the hierarchy. By the same token, it may also be the least efficient in Barnard's sense.

The degree of restraint on authority increases in the other alternatives, moving from the internal legalistic, through the external legalistic, and finally to the democratic. Presumably, too, the amount of dependence is reduced progressively in each of these alternatives while, simultaneously, the chances for individual self-determination increase.

Now although I carefully noted that these alternatives represent a spirit or philosophy of administration, there are procedural prerequisites which must exist to insure that the philosophy is more than talk. The minimum procedural requirement is separation of the functions which we have mentioned several times. Somewhere in the procedure, an outsider must exercise judicial authority or the appeal system comes to little more than a form of benevolence or paternalism.

It is safe to say, with the exceptions already described, that most of the organizations comprising the targets of this analysis have not gone beyond the second alternative, the internal legalistic, in the imposition of restraint on managerial authority through the appeal device. Even here, in business organizations, redress is generally not available to a disinterested outside third party. Instead, a representative of the personnel department is often used in this role. His job is to secure a tenuous compromise between the separation of legal power on the one hand with the maintenance of vested authority and secrecy about organizational affairs on the other. His success in this capacity, by securing a modicum of detachment from organizational values and demands, is a matter requiring research.

The Challenge to Formal Authority

While formal organizations of every description in America are exerting a widening influence on the individual, the legitimacy of authority within these organizations is being questioned. It is not surprising though since part of our cultural heritage includes a suspicion of authority without counterbalancing regulation. This coupled with the desire to secure equal opportunity for self-development for all citizens would cause many to interpret bureaucratization as a threat to our democratic ideals. Thus the recommendations for authoritarian offsets multiply. So even though the process of formalization which acccounts for appeal systems and the philosophies by which they may be administered are quite different matters, the melding of the two, process and philosophy, provides a vehicle for constraint upon internal organizational authority. As such these programs are in step with the modern mood of liberalism.

Administrators themselves have not ignored the potential effects this challenge of authority may have upon the organization. The broad acceptance of such administrative devices as participation, democratic leadership, sensitivity training, and so on is evidence that policy makers believe that the unmodified structure of formal authority creates dangerous inequalities in the distribution of satisfactions to people in the organization. Dangerous to the extent that if changes in the motivational climate are not introduced, the behavior of the organization as a cooperative system will be impaired.

An appeal system as part of the modified structure and motivational climate cannot, however, be a shallow substitute for self-determination. No one is fooled when it is. An appeal system based upon Machiavellian or paternalistic premises is usually avoided as a means for resolving conflicts. Instead conflicts are settled either informally or not at all.

The difficulty with many formal programs of redress is that their values and the values of the organization in which they function are not perceived by participants as different. This is why a grin is often provoked when a person is told he can go over his superior's head if he has a problem. He is telling you that he does not believe it will do him any good or that reprisals will not be visited upon him. In summary he does not see organizational justice implemented by the formal machinery of due process.

Our skeptical friend has not, in the language of the social psychologist, internalized the values of the formal appeal system. This reaction is caused in part by structural deficiencies, mainly the failure to separate the legal functions of the organization. But the problem is deeper because rejection of a formal system of appeal adds up to a vote of "no confidence" in the management's efforts to provide objective, accessible, and systematic grounds for adjudication of disputes.

I think cynicism characterizes the attitude of many people toward formalized appeal procedures or "open-door policies." To dispel this attitude fully a democratic approach to the administration of programs may be necessary. However, this is a little rich for contemporary executives. But the demands for more restraint on arbitrary authority and greater opportunities for personal development will not go unnoticed. They will become imperative as the character of the work force continues to change. The enlarging numbers of scientific, administrative, and technical personnel will reinforce the swelling desire for freedom and satisfaction within organizations.

The first step in this direction for most organizations probably is not the democratic one. More likely, it is some form of legalism. If the organization cannot be democratized, in the literal meaning of the word, it can at least be constitutionalized. I feel this is the direction in which not a few organizations are moving. And in this transition away from unfettered authoritarianism, procedural due process is essential for the settlement of disputes which arise "under the law."

Notes and References

1. Wendell French, *The Nature and Problems of Organizational Justice,* a paper given before the Academy of Management, December, 1964. Published in the *Proceedings* of the Academy, pp. 102–109.

2. For example, see Dale S. Beach, "An Organizational Problem: Superior-Subordinate Relations," *Advanced Management,* December, 1960, pp. 12–15. At times the subject is treated under the heading of grievance procedures for non-unionized personnel: see Walter V. Ronner, "Handling Grievances in a Non-Union Plant," *Proceedings* of the Industrial Relations Research Assoc., December, 1961, pp. 306–14; and Reid L. Shaw, "A Grievance Procedure for Non-Unionized Employees," *Personnel,* July–August, 1959, pp. 66–70. Another source of information is in the office management literature: see Allen K. Trueman, "You Can Resolve Employee Grievance," *Administrative Management,* March, 1964, pp. 56–58; John B. Coyle, "Setting-up Communication and Grievance Systems," *Office Management,* two-part series, February and March, 1960, pp. 26–32 and 28–39, respectively; and Clark Nichols, "Formal Grievance Procedures: How They Operate in Non-Union Companies," *Office Executive,* October, 1958, pp. 22–26. These articles discuss either systems in operation at a company or the ways to go about designing and installing an appeal system. A union organizer would comment that these plans are proposed and used as antiunion measures. In some cases he might be right.

   Very little is available in empirical studies of appeal systems in business. The only research of this kind that I could find is an old study by the National Industrial Conference Board released through its Personnel Series as Report No. 109, *Grievance Procedures in Non-unionized Companies,* 1950.

3. Douglas McGregor, "Conditions of Effective Leadership in the Industrial Organization," *Journal of Consulting Psychology,* March–April, 1944, pp. 62–63. Copyright 1944 by the American Psychological Association, and reproduced by permission.

4. Keith Davis, *Human Relations at Work* (New York: McGraw-Hill Book Company, 1962), p. 299.

5. William M. Evan, "Organization Man and Due Process of Law," *American Sociological Review,* Vol. 26, August, 1961, pp. 540–47. Reprinted by permission.

6. For example, Thomas L. Whisler, "Performance Appraisal and the Organization Man," *Journal of Business,* January, 1958, pp. 19–27; and Douglas McGregor, "An Uneasy Look at Performance Appraisal," *Harvard Business Review,* May–June, 1957, pp. 89–94.

7. A situation where an individual simultaneously fills the roles of judge, jury, and prosecutor is opposed to the democratic notion that these roles should be performed

by different people to insure the maximum protection of a citizen's rights. It is obvious that this concept is violated in an administrative organization. In basing the authority to dispense rewards and to assign punishments upon the scalar principle, the administrative organization systematically abrogates the democratic ideal of the separation of legal powers. Therefore, it is easy to see why those who favor democracy in industry as an intrinsic part of industrial humanism seek a device to bypass the unappealable power of a superior. For an excellent historical treatment of the growth of democratic ideology in both public and private administration, see Dwight Waldo, "Development of Theory of Democratic Administration," *The American Political Science Review,* March–June, 1952, pp. 81–103.

8. See the discussion of the Merton and Gouldner models of bureaucratic behavior in James G. March and Herbert A. Simon, *Organizations* (New York: John Wiley & Sons, 1958), pp. 37–47.

   The crucial problem faced by small growing companies is establishing the jurisdictional scope of managerial positions and the delineation of the degree and type of interaction among functions. The problem may be stated in a word— formalization. Carrying this one step further, Filley points out that "after the growth rate begins to decline, the firm starts its development of the characteristic for successful maturity. This requires a rational decentralized organization structure, full functional development of institutional service objectives, written records and policies, professional management, staff functions to plan and control operations, and a fairly homogeneous employee group." Alan Filley, "A Theory of Business Growth," an unpublished paper given before the Academy of Management, Pittsburgh, December 29, 1962.

9. Evan, "Organization Man and Due Process of Law," p. 543.

10. Wilfred Brown, *Exploration in Management* (New York: John Wiley & Sons, 1960), pp. 250–73.

11. *Ibid.,* pp. 254ff.

12. *Ibid.,* p. 310.

13. Thomas J. Watson, Jr., *A Business and Its Beliefs: The Ideas that Helped Build IBM* (New York: McGraw-Hill Book Company, 1963), p. 19.

14. As stated in the IBM Manager's Manual under the heading "Employee Relations."

15. As explained in a company publication "Engineering Personnel Relations," *Notes,* November, 1962.

16. A. A. Berle, Jr., *The 20th Century Capitalist Revolution* (New York: Harcourt Brace Jovanovich, 1954), chap. 3.

17. William M. Evan, "Due Process of Law in a Government and an Industrial Research Organization," *Proceedings of the Academy of Management,* 1965, p. 115.

18. An approach suggested by Walter E. Oberer, "Union Democracy and the Rule of Law," *Democracy and Public Review* (New York: The Fund for the Republic, 1960).

19. This is a difficult proposal so let us pose a hypothetical case. Suppose an employee objects to having his psyche probed by tests and analyses to determine his promotability within his corporation. Suppose further that his objection is grounded upon his opinion that this personnel policy and practice constitutes an invasion of his privacy. So he files an appeal, saying he should be promoted on, say, the basis of demonstrated competence in prior jobs, seniority, and the additional education he has undertaken to improve his functional expertness. *He feels that the organization invades his right to be let alone* if it goes beyond the objective concrete evidence of tenure and proficiency in establishing his promotability. Assuming the appeal goes the full route through the procedure, which it probably will, then it is up to the outside party in the corporate appeal network to decide if there is any merit to the argument by reference to the external law of privacy.

The selection of this example is not an arbitrary choice since there is considerable literature building up on this issue of tests and privacy. However, to pursue it here would be an interesting but unnecessary digression. The reader might refer to an article in the *Wall Street Journal* of February 9, 1965, for a discussion of the subject. For a treatment of the legal status of the concept of privacy, see Morris L. Ernst and Alan U. Schwartz, *Privacy: The Right to be Let Alone* (New York: The Macmillan Company, 1962).

Questions for Discussion

1. How does dominance manage conflict? What are its advantages? Disadvantages?

2. How does hierarchical appeal manage conflict? What are its advantages over dominance?

3. What developments have decreased the power of the manager to resolve conflict through hierarchical/judicial decisions?

4. How does integrative bargaining differ from distributive bargaining?

5. What are the various ways in which an organization can be restructured to prevent conflict from developing?

6. How can a manager "decouple" conflicting parties?

7. What is "unifying work flow"?

8. Sit in a local restaurant. Observe and plot the flow of work and interactions, indicating the points of stress and conflict. Redesign the work flow to reduce conflict.

9. Plot the work flow in the university registration process. Where are the points of stress for students? For administrators/secretaries? For faculty? Recommend changes to reduce stress and conflict.

10. How do transcendent objectives reduce conflict? Describe a person or situation you know by whom or where this technique was used.

11. What are the essential objectives and means of the mediator? Have you ever mediated a conflict (e.g., between family members, school friends, etc.)? What did you do? Did it work? Why?

12. Why is the incidence of conflict resolution through direct bargaining increasing in U.S. society?

13. You have seen that many writers feel that there is conflict between human needs and organizational requirements. The needs of the mature individual (for autonomy, satisfying social relationships, and self-actualization) seem to conflict with organizational requirements for hierarchy, subordination, control, and predictability. Why might managers want to alleviate such conflict? How might managers do it? Do you expect managers to make more or fewer such efforts in the future?

14. One observer of modern business has written: "The so-called private business corporation owned by many individual stockholders is in effect a private government with officials who are only loosely responsible to the owners. They are even less responsible to the citizens of the government—the employees. In spite of management's appeal to rational decision making and scientific organization, its fundamental internal administration is authoritarian. The business organization implies more of Genghis Khan than Thomas Jefferson. This centralized authority is not justified and must be replaced by a more democratic system whereby employees at all levels have guarantees of due process and representation." How would you agree or disagree with this position?

Short Cases for Discussion

The Old Ivy Review of Business

It was late Friday afternoon. Tim Haley, managing editor of the Old Ivy *Review of Business,* slipped behind his desk and unlocked the drawer containing the final drafts of the articles for the winter issue of the *Review.* Tim was in his last year of the Old Ivy School's two year course leading to a Masters in Business Administration, and he was glad that this would be his last issue of the *Review.* Certainly he had enjoyed the responsibility his position had brought to him, but somehow these last few months his work had ceased to be the fun it had once been. In fact, in the wake of the *Review's* mushrooming circulation, his job had become downright drudgery.

Tim had been instrumental in revitalizing the *Review,* having been a moving force in the upgrading of its stature. Less than two years ago, the *Review* had virtually no circulation outside the school and total annual advertising revenues of less than $1500. This issue alone would carry in excess of $2500 worth of advertising, and would find its way to the campus of virtually every major business school in the country. Admittedly the $2500 was nearly $1000 more than the projected revenues for the spring issue, but then this was a particularly attractive edition for prospective employers. The *Review* had actively promoted this issue as its recruiting edition.

Among other items the winter *Review* would include (1) two articles specifically on job hunting, (2) an article on recruiting/interviewing, and (3) 25 recruiting-oriented advertisements from some of America's most progressive organizations. The advertisements were varied in their approach, but each similar in its attempt to speak directly to the graduating MBA of the career opportunities at a specific corporation. Almost without exception, each ad included an invitation to interested MBAs to respond directly to the company. Although most of these firms would subsequently spend a day or two at the placement office interviewing all interested students, this avenue for early contact was becoming popular among aggressive firms. By soliciting resumes at this early stage, they were able to accelerate the recruiting process with those MBAs whose credentials matched the company's needs.

The idea of the special recruiting edition had been conceived by the *Review* staff during a summer brainstorming session, and it had been imaginatively (and successfully) promoted during the ensuing months. Now all was in readiness, and only the printing, reading, and hope for favorable response remained.

Tim picked up the drafts hurriedly and leafed through the typed pages until he came to the article he was looking for. Tim had spent many hours with Gene Edwards, its author, editing the article. Gene was one of Old Ivy's most gifted students, a black who had been recruited by Old Ivy's energetic director of admissions. Tim had first approached Gene with the idea for the article early last spring, only to be turned down. However, as Gene and Tim became better friends, the refusal gradually became less adamant. When Gene returned to school in September, he had produced the article that Tim now held in his hands.

Some modifications (mainly to tone down the rough language) had been made along the way, but the message remained essentially the same: Blacks were tired of having "whitey" call the shots in the neighborhoods. Everywhere black men were combining their brains and backs to produce a new kind of black power, one that would ultimately bring green power to black communities. Tim read the article one last time—it was good!

Thursday of the following week, Tim was confronted just outside the *Review* office by Ben Jackson, apparently acting as a spokesman for Old Ivy's black students. Ben was flourishing a copy of the freshly printed magazine.

Jackson: I just saw the *Review,* Tim. What do you think you are trying to do to us?

Haley: What do you mean?

Jackson: You know perfectly well what I mean. Your article that purports to speak for the black entrepreneur just HASN'T got it, baby.

Haley: Really? One of your people wrote it.

Jackson: He didn't write that and you know it as well as I do.

Haley: He did write it, Ben, and quite frankly I think it's good!

Jackson: That wouldn't surprise me, seeing as how it's your article.

Haley: I told you Gene Edwards wrote that article, Ben. I think he will verify that.

Jackson: Gene says the article was his idea but you and your people turned it upside down when you got your hands on it. By the time you got finished with it it was your article, not Gene's.

Haley: That's not so; we wrote that article together—I mean Gene wrote it, I made a few suggestions, and he changed some minor things—that was it.

Jackson: Gene doesn't agree with you. He says the article has been completely changed since he gave his approval.

Haley: I don't believe that.

Jackson: Look, Tim, all this is a waste of time. We can't let that article appear in the magazine as it is. That article makes us look like Uncle Toms and you know it. Your sheet doesn't get distributed this month.

Haley: The hell you say! This is the most important issue of the year, or of the *Review's* existence for that matter. Twenty-five companies and 400 or 500 MBAs, not to mention the *Review,* have a lot riding on this issue.

Jackson: I'm sorry about that, but twelve black MBAs have a lot riding on this issue too, and we aim to protect ourselves.

Haley: And just how do you propose to do that?

Jackson: By getting you to agree that the *Review* will be destroyed.

Haley: And what if we don't agree?

Jackson: Then we'll destroy it for you.

Haley: Now wait a minute, Jackson, just hold on. Who do you think you are anyway?

Jackson: I'm a black man speaking his mind for a change, standing up to you people. For 100 years you've been telling us how to live and act; now just when we're about to get on our own feet you've taken on yourself to tell us how we should think. Well, it won't happen that way this time, man.

Haley: You're talking nonsense, Jackson. What's gotten into you?

Jackson: How much plainer do I have to make it? We don't approve of the article, and since it purports to speak for us, we have the right to stop it.

Haley: Get serious, Jackson. This article was written by one of your people and regardless of who wrote it I think it's a good piece of work. If anyone should have a gripe, it might be some of our more conservative white classmates.

Jackson: We just don't see it that way. Do I make myself clear?

Haley: I'm getting the message. Now let me explain a few things to you. We have guaranteed our advertisers circulation of this issue to MBA students all over the country before November 1. Well, it's already the 3rd, and even if we could afford to go back to the printer, the delay would push us awfully close to the time when five of our principal advertisers are going to be on campus. You probably know that Booz, Fry, Cresap, McKinsey, and A. T. Kearney are all going to be here the week of November 20. And they start at Harvard the week before, so those issues have got to go now!

Jackson: O.K., you have your problems, too. So let's make a compromise. The article only takes up two pages. We'll cut those two pages out, plus the table of contents and your issue can go.

Haley: Let me see that copy you have.

Ben Jackson handed Tim the copy of the *Review*. Tim turned quickly to the three pages in question, only to have his worst fears realized.

Haley: Ben, there are not three pages involved, but six.

Jackson: What do you mean, six?

Haley: Each one of those pages has a back and a front. And on each of those backs there's an ad. The way things are going you won't be surprised to hear that McKinsey has one of those backs and Cresap another.

Jackson: That's too bad. You people got yourself in this fix; you're going to have to find a way out. Right now we have all of your *Reviews* in safe keeping, and we're prepared to keep them.

Question

Discuss the causes of this conflict and formulate recommendations for Haley.

The Old Ivy Challenge

In March copies of the black-covered document had generated excitement in the graduate students' lounge at the Old Ivy School of Business. The appearance of the little pamphlet, entitled "The Old Ivy Challenge," had produced animated discussion and debate among an already restless student body. It had predicted things to come and suggested changes. Now it was November, and the mood was strikingly different; disappointment was pervasive. What had happened?

The project had been conceived in January, the brain child of the then MBA Association President, Sam Zimmerman. On a Sunday afternoon, he had called a meeting of some forty students, each of whom had previously expressed interest in effecting change at Old Ivy, and outlined his plans. The group responded enthusiastically. Study groups were immediately formed to audit current Old Ivy practices and policies in three major areas: management, classroom, and environment. "The Old Ivy Challenge" was born with high hopes.

Old Ivy is a venerable and prestigious institution, known nationally and world-wide for the quality of its business education and the success of its graduates. Each September a new class of 500 aggressive and highly talented individuals arrives, champing at the bit and ready to take on anything Old Ivy can throw at them academically. But for many of the new arrivals, motivation quickly peters out, to be replaced first by dismay, then disillusionment. Many question the wisdom of their decision to attend Old Ivy; perhaps a rival institution would have lived up to expectations. By their second year in the MBA program, too many Old Ivy students have turned off completely. They sit in the back of the classroom, seldom speak up in class discussion, and generally minimize their involvement with Old Ivy. Their only apparent concern: get a good job, graduate, and get the hell out of here.

As seen by the "Challenge" group, there are several basic causes of this disaffection. The first of these hits the new student hardest: the faculty is disappointing. Old Ivy has a large faculty of reputed excellence, with many outstanding articles and books to their credit. Among them are some who pride themselves on teaching, but the majority emphasize scholarly research and/or outside consulting—to the detriment of their classroom responsibilities, many students feel. As it becomes obvious that most instructors simply are not going to be very demanding of student preparation and participation (the straight, unidirectional lecture is all too common), the typical student reacts in like manner, and mentally withdraws from the course.

The second disillusioning factor is the physical environment inside and outside the school. The University is located in a run-down, crime-ridden area of a large, drab city. The classroom building is shared with undergraduate students, and since its builders had not foreseen the rapid expansion of Old Ivy, it is cramped and overcrowded. In addition, seats are attached to the floor, all facing toward the lecturer. Communication among class members is difficult, even when the professor desires it. It is much like a high-school classroom. A new building complex for Old Ivy's graduate division has been promised every year, but the University administration is hard-pressed financially, and construction has never commenced.

Finally, to many students, it just does not seem that the Old Ivy School is managed very effectively, because of the following: registration is an incomprehensible nightmare; all official forms require the signature of a faculty advisor who never seems to be available and apparently couldn't care less about advising anyway; the school seems to be run by secretaries who are either (a) sweet old ladies, (b) consider students distinctly inferior beings, or (c) both. When the

"Challenge" study groups attempted to diagram the school's administrative structure, they found lines of authority crossed everywhere. There was no long-range planning function, no working outside advisory board. The top men in the administration seem tired and more concerned with resting on the school's laurels than forging ahead. Old Ivy appeared to have ground to a halt.

During the eight weeks of their study, the "Challenge" groups dug into these issues and their ramifications. Open meetings were heavily attended by students, and the "Challenge" group felt it had strong grass-roots support. When the booklet was published in March, it contained the study groups' findings and a list of 64 recommendations for change at Old Ivy, ranging from abolishing the thesis requirement and grading system, to hiring a director of student affairs and limiting administrative tenure. Student excitement was at a fever pitch, and it was rumored that even some faculty members supported the changes.

Upon completion of the study, the forty-man "Challenge" group dissolved, but was survived by a five-member steering committee whose task it was to attempt to get the recommendations implemented. The first one was easy: Sam Zimmerman was hired by Old Ivy as director of student affairs upon graduation in May. But the second, a recommendation to allow the business school to solicit corporate funds on its own, met defeat in a meeting with University officials.

An opportunity to implement a number of the other recommendations soon occurred, however. Following a conference with the Old Ivy dean, a joint committee was formed in June to study the administrative reorganization of the Old Ivy School. The committee consisted of students, alumni, faculty, and administrative members, and was to report its findings in the fall. The decision to join this committee was a critical one for the "Challenge" group, because it represented a potential compromise of the stated views contained in the published document. Yet any reorganization of the school would have to involve all interests—faculty, administration, and alumni—and this presented a chance to work forcefully with them and perhaps to implement several of the most important "Challenge" recommendations. Thus, the "Challenge" steering committee members became the student representatives of the joint committee.

Now it was a Saturday morning in November. Mike Hood, who had chaired one of the original "Challenge" study groups, had been a founding member of the "Challenge" steering committee, and was now a member of the joint reorganization committee, sat alone with his thoughts in the school auditorium. He and several other "Challenge" students had spent innumerable hours over the summer and fall negotiating within the joint committee. Their position had been true to the "Challenge" document: decentralization of the school to give the graduate division's director power to rejuvenate the MBA program. This position had been accepted by the faculty, administration, and alumni representatives, and was contained in the joint committee proposals, which were distributed in October and had been the subject of an intensive publicity and lobbying campaign. The joint committee felt that if the faculty would vote acceptance of the proposals, the dean would then be forced to act to implement them.

A meeting of the Old Ivy faculty had been held that morning for what Mike had thought was a vote on acceptance of the joint committee's proposals, but the professors had gone now. And so, Mike thought to himself, had hopes of seeing the reorganization proposals put into effect. As the meeting had opened, a notoriously conservative professor rose to address the committee, "Gentlemen, you realize, of course, that we are not prepared to vote on these proposals this morning. To do so would be unthinkably rash." And the debate that took place over the next several hours was fragmented, inconclusive, and showed little support for the proposals. The faculty meeting ended with no action taken—not even an agreement to meet again.

A disappointed Mike now pondered what action to recommend to his fellow students on the "Challenge" steering committee. Long ago they had adopted a policy of acting "through the proper channels" in advocating the "Challenge" recommendations. But all along they had felt strong student pressure for a protest demonstration to make demands instead of recommendations. As he sat there, Mike realized that this pressure would return, strengthened by the defeat of his moderate tactics. As steering committee chairman, Mike faced a critical decision; what to do?

Question

Formulate recommendations for Mike.

Chapter 12

Organization Development

We come now to a way of managing individual and group processes in an organization which has been called variously "planned change" or "organization development." The target of OD management is to change the beliefs and attitudes of people. Most OD practitioners hold that only people who have previously learned to trust, help, and cooperate with one another can then keep their minds on technical and structural problems, and devote their full intellectual and creative abilities to running the business. As Blake and Mouton (1967) put it, "Organization Development deliberately shifts the emphasis away from the organization's structure, from technical skill, from wherewithal and results *per se*, as it diagnoses the organization's ills. Focusing on organization purpose, the human interaction process, and organization culture, it accepts these as the areas in which problems are preventing the fullest possible integration within the organization" (p. 11).

A simplified way of viewing the OD approach would be to draw an arrow from a question in the first column of the list below to the related question in the second column.

Personal and Interpersonal (Cultural) Questions

1. Does an advertising manager see salesmen as valuable people in the organization, or does he see himself as being more important? Do salesmen see the advertising manager as helpful, or as a "hard-nosed" headquarters checker? Does the advertising manager see the salesmen as helpful?

2. Does a sales manager see the controller (financial planner) as helpful? Does the controller believe the sales manager to be a valuable person?

3. How does a head nurse in a hospital see herself in relation to the nurses? How does she *think* the nurses see her? How do the nurses *really* see her (in terms of her ability to communicate, her ability to evoke trust on the part of others, etc.)?

Structural Questions

1. What is the job of the advertising manager in introducing the new product? What is the job of the salesman in selling a new product when it is introduced?

2. What is the cost of selling? How many salesmen can we afford? How much television advertising can we afford?

3. What is the authority of the head nurse? On what kinds of actions are nurses supposed to obey her? Who works out the daily shift schedule in the ward?

The arrow would be one of causation. Thus, in question 2, we would say that if the sales manager sees the controller as a useful person, if he views the controller as helpful (instead of a policeman), and if the controller believes the sales manager to be a worthy person, then they would more likely be able to view selling the company product as a joint or team goal. The probability is much greater that they can then answer questions such as those in the second column: What is the cost of selling? How many salesmen can we afford? How much television advertising can we afford?

To summarize, we might say that organization development reverses the typical sequence of "what changes who." It is the change in personal values in the system, coupled with the change in ways in which people treat one another, which comes first. Only then is a group capable of tackling the operating problems of maximizing organizational effectiveness.

Viewed in this way, the general model for most organization development efforts is as follows:

1. Plan the change processes (done primarily by trained consultants [behavioral scientists] advising the client [top management] who approves the program).
2. Change the attitudes and habits of individuals (the ways people treat one another).
3. Change group climate or culture (the collective attitudes and habits of individuals).
4. Work out new structures, such as (a) subgoals (products, types of patient care, allocation of budget money), (b) who does what (a new specialization pattern), and (c) who has final authority over whom.
5. Solve day-to-day problems, involving (a) new demands from outside the organization, and (b) new discoveries or demands from inside the organization.

For those interested in theories and models, OD not only reverses the practical steps in applying the change process to the real world, it also reverses the dependent and independent variables. Operating procedures, costs, job descriptions, production schedules—the whole rational side of the firm—become dependent on how a group of people feel about themselves as people and about others as people. One must not expect, for example, that an operations research expert can really increase organizational effectiveness by figuring out a production schedule which is then conveyed in a memo to foremen on the assembly line; nor can a market research manager at headquarters (however much he may have studied statistics and consumer psychology) really increase company sales to the maximum by determining what customers or geographic market segment the company should concentrate upon, especially if the resulting policy he arrives at is passed on in directives to district sales managers. Rather, it is the production staff man learning how to relate to the foreman (and vice versa), or the market research man learning how to relate to the district sales manager (and vice versa) which is the key causal event in maximizing organizational effectiveness.

It should be pointed out that, as the training proceeds, OD practitioners vary greatly in the relative "mix" they seek in discussing operating problems versus discussing human and interpersonal problems. In some OD efforts, the change agent begins, for example, by discussing the technical or operational reasons why the sale of a new product did not go well, and moves rather quickly into discussing the behavioral reasons why the new product did not go well (whether the people involved have been cooperative and helpful, or uncooperative and nonhelpful). Other OD consultants may devote considerably more time to discussing operational problems, assuming that the group will get the message on interpersonal problems without explicitly confronting each other in this respect. Nevertheless, all OD efforts carry out the philosophy suggested in the above model, of placing human and cultural factors first, as the most important targets of change.

The selection by Douglas McGregor following this chapter clearly sets out the philosophy of the team as a principal determinant of organizational effectiveness. It is a team of people who analyze the various role pressures on all personnel. The team perhaps discovers that the advertising manager is indeed under pressure from the field sales force, and that the field sales managers are indeed dependent on the advertising manager. It is the team who then draws implications from these pressures and dependencies—implications for what the organization expects of each person in terms of such structural matters as job duties or responsibilities.

McGregor's instrument for directing the team's attention to its attitudes and beliefs also shows what he believes a team should work on first. He wants it to "discuss in depth each variable," such as:

In our day-to-day work

- do we trust each other? or do we suspect each other?
- do we have genuine concern for each other, or is it every man for himself?
- do we communicate openly our true feelings and thoughts, or are we guarded and cautious?
- do we listen to others or do we act on our own?
- do we accept conflicts and work them through, or do we deny, avoid, or suppress conflicts?
- does the team utilize the abilities, knowledge, and experience of each member, or does the team ignore the capabilities of some?
- does everyone understand and feel committed to work objectives, or do some fail to understand them or feel negative toward them?

Need for Organization Development

Environmental Complexity and Work Specialization

Managers today are faced with a much more turbulent technical world in the external environment. The time when customers, competitive products, distributive channels, production methods, and labor costs or skills were stable and orderly has changed to a time when product life cycles are short, new products must be developed to meet changing population patterns and tastes, and a host of other adjustments must be made. The same is true of other institutions in our society. We have changed from hospitals that met one set of needs in society to those which must cope with new and different classes of patients, new methods of medical diagnosis and treatment, and a much larger number of patients. We have changed from a U.S. Office of Education that operated under one set of social conditions to a full-fledged Department of Health, Education and Welfare which must cope with new numbers and classes of students in schools, new curriculum content, and new physical facilities on a scale not before imagined.

All of this has meant an increase in the size and complexity of organizations—of the number of specialists required, and the ability of these specialists to collectively guide the operations of the organization. No longer can a single sales vice president or regional sales manager be sufficiently acquainted in a specialized way with market research, inventory control techniques, financial cost techniques, advertising methods, or scientific product research to make wise decisions. Nor can the specialist in any one of these areas *alone* make decisions that are wise. No longer can the hospital director, the chief of internal medicine, the chief of anesthesiology, the financial controller, the head nurse or the director of the emergency ward *alone* make decisions. It is a price we pay for modern large-scale organizations that everything depends on everything else—what the emergency ward does affects the finances of the hospital, the way anesthesiologists deaden pain, and the hours doctors work in internal medicine.

This complexity and interdependence has been clearly explained by Burns and Stalker (1961) in a selection following Chapter 6. They found that organizations in the Scottish electronics industry which were *organic,* in that they had more open and fluid work relationships among people holding different internal functional positions, were the ones that were most successful in changing their production and marketing to meet the rapid developments in British and world markets.

Some writers on OD focus on the *systems* concept to explain the need for this form of management (e.g., Alderfer, 1971). They are in effect saying that all of the changes taking place in a turbulent environment do (and must) reach directly the relevant specialists inside the organization (e.g., customer information to marketing specialist, new discovery in hydrocarbon chemistry to the research department, etc.). They cannot reach only the president—it would cause an overload in his decision making, nor would he be able to comprehend the detailed *meaning* as would a specialist. The only answer is *teamwork,* with the president or general manager the one who sets up the process and procedures for *group* decision making. In most of the OD literature showing how companies go about this kind of management, it is stressed that some general manager initially sees the need for this kind of approach and at some point becomes committed to it. He is the one who, with the change agent, schedules the various meetings, attends himself, and otherwise lends official authority and procedure to its being carried out.

Another development in the environment is a rapid change in *human* culture, as contrasted with rapid technological changes. The top executives, middle managers, and employees of any organization are, after all, people who hold the beliefs, values, needs, and demands of their times, culture, and society. We need look no further than the streets of Newark or the campus at Berkeley to see that there is, indeed, a change in the way people expect to be treated. Warren Bennis (1969), one of the leading developers of the OD form of management, has this to say about this kind of environmental change:

"The environment now is busy, clogged and dense with opportunities and threats; it is turbulent, uncertain, and dynamic. The people who work for organizations are more complicated than ever before. They have needs, motives, anxieties, and to make matters even more complicated, they bring higher expectations than ever before to our institutions. The institutions themselves are changing, through the press of environmental challenges and the internal demands of its people" (p. 81).

Exchanging Commitment and
Loyalty for Satisfaction of Needs

At this point we can pull together two ideas already learned from the chapter on individual motivation and the chapter on influence. In those two chapters it was pointed out that one important kind of influence exists when an organization satisfies the human needs of another person. If a doctor in a hospital finds that many of the things he wants in life are gained by working in this particular hospital, he is more likely to develop positive attitudes toward it, and to carry out the duties and responsibilities necessary for the success of the hospital as an institution. In this sense, OD teamwork provides this doctor with much more opportunity for problem solving, for determining his own destiny through having a voice in the way the hospital operates, and for greater accomplishment than he could hope for if he worked in a single office by himself. It might, by increasing his social function in society, give him more self-esteem as well as more freedom and autonomy.

Thus, if one sees the logic of a man's relationship to his employing institution as a "psychological contract," involving the exchange by the man of his work and commitment for an offer by the institution of all of these other things, he also sees that OD might well be a key to the elusive problem of commitment and loyalty. Economists, while stressing that "economic man" works for wages and money, have always recognized that people in certain jobs also work for what they called "psychic benefits." The good court judge works for less money than many private lawyers on Wall Street, the good professor of physics works for less money than he could get with IBM or General Motors.

Overcoming Maladaptive Attitudes from the Past

A second basic force recognized by many who advocate organization development is one which is brought into the organization as part of the personality of participants when they join it—whether they be top managers, middle managers, or employees. In the process of maturation and development, certain basic attitudes derived during one's growth are deep seated, quite stable, and tend to affect one's present relations with other people. Of particular importance in organizational life are attitudes toward authority and attitudes toward intimacy (Bennis and Shepard, 1965). An overly *dependent* person—who has a pronounced feeling of comfort in having others be leaders, or in having rules and procedures to guide his life—may be in for some trouble. Since the world really is not one where a benevolent leader and rule system attends to every need of an active person, the dependent person may feel underneath a strong sense of hostility and resentment toward the organization. Or he may feel a sense of personal failure. Finally, he may vacillate between submissiveness and rebelliousness.

Conversely, an overly *counterdependent* person—one with pronounced feelings of discomfort toward people in authority, or toward rules and regulations—may also be in for some trouble. As he moves through life, running upon some "good" and some "bad" organizations (both *do* exist in the real world), he does not always act realistically in the situation around him. In his attempt to get through life, he too may vacillate between wanting more direction (submissiveness) and hating all direction (rebelliousness), always trying to make sense out of the world but feeling underneath that all organization is "bad."

Another interpersonal attitude is the one toward intimacy. One person may have learned to be overly *personal*—he cannot rest until he has stabilized a relatively high degree of intimacy with others. Another has learned to be overly *counterpersonal*—he tends to avoid any intimacy or personal talk at any cost. He is only comfortable talking about the work to be done, or the costs, or the output. But the world is not really like either man's stereotypical view. If either person clings to one or the other extreme, he may find himself vacillating between both.

Although organization development practitioners may differ in their terminology, and in how strongly they aim their efforts at changing basic attitudes, all OD efforts try to get people to see the world as it is, here-and-now, and to see themselves and others as they are, not as some stereotype.

Another effort made is to get people to learn how to learn. This is an elusive objective. Those who practice OD assume that it takes skill to see one's self, other team members, and the job to be done in realistic terms. Such skill must be learned. It is as if every day, in each specific problem that arises in a company, one has a new learning experience. He learns what *is* rather than spending his life confirming previous attitudes and beliefs. Anderson (1970) shows how feedback not only can help another person to learn, but that one must *learn* how to give feedback which is constructive, rather than destructive.

John Dewey, the famous philosopher who developed important insights about how the human mind solves problems, coined the phrase "trained incapacity" to denote how specialization has tended to block a person's ability to understand another person's job and point of view. In a company, the sales force thinks only about sales, while the finance department thinks only about costs or investments. In a hospital, the surgeons spend their lives operating, while the controller spends his life dealing with patients who pay bills or vendors who sell beds and pharmaceuticals. Dewey meant that the very training of finance men, salesmen, or surgeons (including their day-to-day experiences) builds into them a predisposition to see the whole corporation or the whole hospital from their own viewpoint, and an *incapacity* to see the needs of the organization as a whole.

Sociologists who study bureaucracy have pointed out that if a person lives in the same organization for a long time, with the same policy rules and the same job descriptions, his mind is likely to play strange tricks, to "displace" the original goal of serving the customer (or another part of the organization) with a different goal: abiding by the rule book. One of us recently appeared at Kennedy airport 15 minutes before takeoff time. At the gate, both he and the passenger agent could see that the airplane had not yet left. "I'm sorry," he was told, "closing time for the aircraft was a few minutes ago; you'll have to get the next flight to Chicago." After much heated exchange, another passenger agent, overhearing the conversation, said, "Let him on. They're delayed because of food delivery to the airplane." The first agent was not problem solving or thinking about the airline's main goal of transporting passengers. He was thinking about the rule book.

Another explanation of why large organizations might become more interested in maintaining status, prestige, and office than in solving up-to-date problems is given by Thompson in a selection following Chapter 6. According to this view, general managers have the traditional *right* to decide policies and changes in the organization, yet the *ability* to decide drifts more and more into the hands of specialists. As a result, managers engage in activity designed to maintain their perquisites and prestige, rather than in solving real operating problems.

A further explanation of the need for breaking down rigid bureaucratic practices is found in the study by Burns and Stalker (following Chapter 6). In the Scottish electronic companies, the authors found that the companies most successful in changing to meet the times (bringing out new products, developing new ways of selling, resisting the decay of producing out-of-date government products) seemed to be *organic* types of organizations, characterized by:

- loose boundaries between departments—everyone seemed concerned with everyone else's business.
- flexible job assignments—a man's role might change from time to time, depending on the kind of problem the company was trying to solve.
- commitment toward company goals, not toward departments.
- a great deal of discussion, committee meetings, and task forces which cut across divisions and jobs.

On the other hand, the less successful companies in adapting to change in the British marketplace were those "mechanistic" companies which stuck to clear and precise departmental and job descriptions, and in which the managers by their own words and behavior seemed to spend more time demonstrating loyalty and commitment to their immediate superiors than they did to thinking about and solving problems.

While various OD practitioners differ somewhat on how much stress they place on this point, there is little doubt that all such efforts attempt to decrease significantly the degree to which structural rules exist, the degree to which they actually influence human behavior, and the amount of power held by the "legal" hierarchy. This move toward sharing of power, rather than concentration of status and power, takes place in a pronounced way during the actual training or "planned change" period. And it is intended to be a more or less permanent result if the OD effort is successful. With respect to the transformation period, the selection by Greiner accompanying this chapter takes perhaps the clearest position. He states that one of the central or key goals of OD is to achieve shared power.

Management of Conflict

A final reason often cited as to why organization development is needed in modern organizations is that it is an effective way to *manage* conflict, rather than let conflict become persistent and destructive. According to this view, maladaptive interpersonal attitudes from the past, or departmental conflicts of interest, or both, tend to cause conflicts between various parties in the organization—managers versus subordinates, specialists versus specialists, one department versus another. In our society, so this reasoning goes, and especially in many work organizations, there is a built-in belief that people should not bring such conflict into the open. A sales manager who shows some hostility toward the production department when orders are late, and who says in a committee meeting, "You guys always seem uncooperative to me," is not playing by the rules. It is O.K. for him to *feel* hostile, or to make jokes behind the engineers' backs: "Those slide-rule boys are really not as important to this company as the sales managers, who earn the engineers' salaries." But if he should seriously tell them he has never felt they are very important to company success, he is violating good manners and being disruptive. Someone in the meeting is very likely to change the subject by starting to talk "business," technical matters of production scheduling, or other "objective" matters.

According to this view, such minor hostilities, if constantly swept under the rug, can build up to polarized positions, wherein each side is in a "win-lose" frame of mind. Instead of searching for creative solutions to the problems of selling and producing, or working to get each of these specialities to help one another, the parties spend much time in what appears on the surface to be politely using technical reasoning, statistical facts, or business arguments. Underneath, in reality, this kind of behavior is often directed at proving that the other side is wrong (cutting them down) while "we are the real brains around here" (building us up).

Lawrence and Lorsch (1967) place the management of conflict as a key concept in their argument on how to promote *integration* among many specialized technical processes in an organization, and among the many specialists whose interests might conflict. They have in mind a set of events that look like this:

a conflict resolution process characterized by directly confronting conflicts instead of smoothing them over and achieved by organization members *learning* how to be open and frank $\longrightarrow$ greater integration of teams and among people in diverse departments $\longrightarrow$ firms successful in adapting to a changing environment

We should be careful to distinguish between the *management* of conflict and the *elimination* of feelings of conflict. While it is true that some OD consultants (and some unrealistic managers) attempt to eliminate conflict, it is also true that most OD practitioners view overt conflict in moderate amounts not only as a fact of life, but as a source of creativity and innovation.

Methods of Organization Development

There are many approaches to organization development. All of them involve (1) gathering data about the state of operations in the organization, the state of interpersonal attitudes and behavior, or both; (2) feedback of data to the various parties involved, who then analyze it to see how the human attitude and behavior system is affecting solution of the organization's operating problems; and (3) team planning of new solutions to operating problems or new structures of duties, procedures, policies, and rules for the organization's operations.

Beyond this general similarity, there are almost as many methods of organization development as there are consultants engaging in this kind of work. While some may say that this proliferation of methods is due to the newness of this kind of management development, it is probably equally due to the fact that human behavior is a very rich and variable phenomena. It is so subject to diverse viewpoints and interpretations that we shall probably always have considerable variation among OD methods.

The first two stages above can be conveniently classed as the *diagnosis* or *unfreezing* stage of planned organization change. This is the stage in which participants in the organization look deeply at the present state of affairs in the organization—its operations, its successes and failures, and particularly the way human attitudes and relationships either foster or hinder the solving of operating problems. A number of applied behavioral scientists have used the term "unfreezing" to denote the diagnosis phase of OD. This term implies what has already been said in other parts of the book: that people in organizations have a way of becoming "frozen" into out-of-date *operating* policies, customs, and job descriptions; or "frozen" into *interpersonal attitudes* of formality (rather than reality), of competition, of ritual, or of distrust. Still other practicing OD consultants have taken the term "action research" from Kurt Lewin, a founder of this type of change philosophy, implying that OD is similar to any type of applied research except that "the relationship of researcher and subject may reverse—the subjects becoming the researchers" (Bennis, 1965). Viewed in this way, the participants on OD teams within an organization literally become researchers to discover how rigid operating practices, or rigid interpersonal attitudes, or both, are hampering organizational effectiveness. The OD consultant, on the other hand, becomes an educator, training teams in how to do research on these two types of problems.

The third stage, *action planning* or *refreezing*, is the stage when the same participants, having faced up to and eliminated some of the structural and human blocks to effective problem solving, proceed to devise *new* ways of operating—they solve patient care problems or advertising problems, and they invent new organization structures such as new job descriptions, new procedures for the flow of work, or new policies for patient care or advertising.

Diagnosis of Organizational Problems

Questionnaire Feedback Methods

One of the earlier organization development efforts was that carried out by Floyd Mann (1957) and his colleagues at the University of Michigan. They were bothered by the fact that companies were trying to improve effectiveness and change by training individual managers. The "manager development" approach did not seem to be working. According to Mann, it assumes that a manager attends training sessions, that his own attitudes and beliefs change, and that when he returns to the job his behavior will change. This change will in turn be seen by his subordinates, who will then become more effective in their jobs, and begin to contribute new and effective ways for operating the company. Yet even in training programs designed and conducted by supposedly competent people, Mann found no evidence that the attitudes and beliefs of managers changed, or that they behaved any differently when they got back on the job. In fact, his assessment of these programs pointed to the fact that certain factors *other* than attending a training program were more powerful in determining how a manager acts on the job, and how his department performs.

As a result of this recognition, the Michigan group endeavored to find a way "for changing attitudes, perceptions, and relationships among individuals in complex hierarchies without changing the personnel of the units"—in other words, a way to report findings from human relations research to organizations so that they could understand what the research meant and how to use it in day-to-day operations.

A company-wide study was made by questionnaire of employee and management attitudes. Over a period of the next two years, three different sets of data were fed back to members of the company organization: (1) information on the attitudes of 8000 workers toward their work, their managers, and fellow employees; (2) information on the feelings of first and second-line managers plus their beliefs about how to manage; and (3) attitudes and beliefs of top and intermediate managers about their own philosophies of how to manage, their role in decision making, and their problems of organizational integration.

The process which seemed to maximize the usefulness of the survey findings was an interlocking chain of conferences—a report to the president and senior officers, and then reports to successively lower hierarchical levels until the foremen and their employees were discussing the data. In these meetings, the line executive met with the group of people in a particular department to discuss the data pertaining to that department, and to all subunits for which members of the department were responsible. Members of each group were asked to help interpret the data and then decide what further meaning could be derived from it in order to formulate plans for constructive future action. Behavioral researchers attended these meetings as resource people, to help interpret the data and its meaning.

Since this effort at organization development, many innovations have been made. Nevertheless, this early effort attempted to get "families" within the organizations together for team diagnosis. And the presence of outside researchers undoubtedly had some of the effects, to be discussed later, of interrupting the "old" organization.

In a more recent effort, which also involved interviews and direct feedback, as well as questionnaires, the Boise Cascade Corporation (1970) engaged in a comprehensive organization renewal project. More than 2000 managers in this billion-dollar company completed a questionnaire for later summarization and feedback. A team of outside and inside consultants on organization development assisted in the project. Following are examples of the type of information gathered:

One part of the questionnaire dealt with what the manager thinks the present aims of the company *are*. This part also sought to find out what managers thought the broad goals of the company *should be*. Specific questions covered such items as "growing as rapidly as possible," "becoming a significant multi-national company," "long-term security for employees," "gaining a reputation as a socially concerned corporation," "achieving above-average profit in this industry," and "creating an environment that employees find stimulating and challenging."

A second part of the questionnaire dealt with how managers view the organizational climate. Managers were asked whether jobs are clearly defined and logically structured for good operations, whether a friendly atmosphere prevails, whether it is unclear as to who has authority to make a decision, whether people in the organization trust each other, whether there seems to be personal loyalty to the organization, whether subordinates' ideas are sought and used, whether upward communication is accurate and whether cooperation or competitiveness more nearly describe how people act toward each other.

A third part of the questionnaire sought to find out how a manager feels or believes about himself. Each man was asked to rate himself on a seven-point scale under each of 29 characteristics—whether the particular characteristic was "very characteristic" of himself, "somewhat characteristic" or "not at all characteristic." Examples of these characteristics are:

> Enthusiastic about what I do, getting excited about my work.
> Have many strong opinions and feelings which are important to me.
> Having many friends, giving affection and receiving it from others.
> Getting and using suggestions from others.
> Being a leader; having other people look up to me for direction; taking over when things are confused.

A fourth part sought information on the way strategic decisions at Boise are made, and the way capital is allocated. Managers marked a five-point scale—from strongly agree to strongly disagree—on the following kinds of statements:

> "I think the annual strategy process is a good thing."
> "Strategies are prepared more for the benefit of top management than for my part of the organization."
> "I have been greatly involved in this kind of decision making."

Whether the results of such a questionnaire actually influence real changes depends on what is done with the information. In this and other companies, teams of people are expected to get down to diagnosing fundamental causes of what is going on. If people in one department feel that there is not much personal loyalty to the company, the reasons for this might be explored in a nonthreatening way so as to bring about a greater degree of commitment.

Some behavioral scientists (e.g., Schein, 1969) do not believe that questionnaires are as effective as face-to-face giving of information. They feel that the categories in a questionnaire are not rich enough in content, powerful enough in force, or personal enough in impact to have a real and meaningful effect on attitudes and perceptions.

T-Groups and Sensitivity Training

Perhaps no other method in organization development has received so much attention, and been the subject of so much controversy, as T-Group or sensitivity training. The method is difficult to describe to someone who has not been through it so that he can understand or have any real feeling for what goes on and what is accomplished. Furthermore, it has numerous variations, each depending on the personality and *modus operandi* of the trainer himself. Nevertheless, no book on organizational behavior today would be complete without some attempt to explain this method of training. The selection by Schein and Bennis (1967) following this chapter is such an attempt.

One characteristic of all such efforts is that the individual is placed in an *unstructured* situation with other people. In purest form (perhaps few trainers stick to the "purest"), this means that there is no agenda, no subject to be discussed, no rules or traditions for operating, and no leader or authority figure. The trainer serves principally to remind the group (when asked or when demanded), "We are here to observe our own behavior and the behavior of others, and to learn from it." Often the presence of the trainer (and therefore the hope that "something must come of this," or the belief "this can't be sheer nonsense, though it looks like it to me") serves to keep people in the room for specified periods before the group has existed long enough for the people in it to recognize the experience as useful.

A second characteristic of most T-Group efforts is that they concentrate on "here-and-now" experiences. They do not analyze the external factors in some story a member might tell about "what it's like back in my company" or "the latest Russian-American incident." Sooner or later it is the intent of the trainer that, if such talk arises to pass the time (or to evade what is going on in the room), these subjects will be converted to such questions as, "What is John Jones doing in this room when he tells us about the personnel problems back in his company?" Or "What is Jack Smith doing here in this room when he raises the subject of Russian-American relations?" Some trainers may remind the group of the "here-and-now" rule, or others may simply let the group discover it for themselves. Sooner or later, if Jack Smith keeps talking about Russian relations, the national football league, or his recent readings in Buddhism, someone will question what he is doing.

We can imagine how such a deliberately contrived "vacuum" might reveal behavioral insights never seen before. With no family, no father, no prescribed duties or agenda, no boss, no organization, no rules, no customs, no policies, people are forced to rely only on the inner attitudes and beliefs they bring to the group. There are many theories of what happens in such a group over a period of time. Some of the goals of such training most frequently mentioned by professionals in the field are increased insight into one's own interpersonal attitudes, beliefs, or habits of behavior (including how competent and successful one is), insights into those attitudes and habits on the part of other people (including how competent and successful they are), and insights about the various processes of conflict, harmony, leadership, or followership which occur in a structureless group over time.

T-Groups are used for other reasons than organization development—and some OD efforts do not use T-Groups. However, the T-Group method, or some method which has some of its characteristics, is often used as *part* of the total OD program. One way is by having a large number of individual managers from one organization attend "stranger" labs (no one from the same company or work group) offered by the National Training Laboratories. It is thought that if many people in the same organization have developed greater interpersonal awareness and competence by attending stranger group training, two results will follow: each manager is more likely to be able to solve operating problems effectively; and the work in a stranger lab will make each manager better at going through other steps in organization development, such as confrontation meetings, chains of interlocking conferences, or action planning sessions. Each participant would already have had some experience, and would be better able to "unfreeze" in his own organization. However, stranger labs are more often used by companies for *manager* development than for *organization* development.

The most direct application of T-Groups to OD, however, is what has been called by one author, cousin, brother, and family labs (Beckhard, 1965). Cousins are people taken from "a diagonal slice of the organization, cutting through two or three vertical hierarchical levels but without a boss and subordinate being in the same group." Brother labs include people who occupy similar horizontal roles in an organization (again without bosses and subordinates in the same group). For example, a group of branch managers from the same bank, a group of nurses who are heads of wards in a hospital, or a group of territory managers in the Bureau of Indian Affairs would be brothers. Finally, family labs are made up of a whole department: the line executive and the people who report to him or her. The chief nurse in a hospital meeting with the head nurses in charge of various wards, or the chief of branch bank operations meeting with the branch managers, is a family T-Group.

The advantage of such familial T-Groups is that people get to know themselves in relation to the individuals in their own organizations, and vice versa. When the time comes to go back to work, it is thought by some trainers, these people will be better able to solve operating problems together than will men who have attended stranger laboratories. The disadvantages of familial labs compared to stranger labs include the fact that it is more difficult to get people who know each other historically to concentrate on "here and now," and the danger that unstructured experiences might generate some animosities which would jeopardize, rather than help, future work relations.

Another controversy over the use of T-Group training centers on the possibility of permanently damaging an unstable personality, and on the ethics involved in subjecting or otherwise influencing a person to expose his private attitudes in a "no agenda" situation. Beckhard (1965) would avoid such criticisms by specifying that T-Groups are inappropriate "if the goal of training is primarily to deal with a 'sick' person or one who cannot be handled in the organization, to convert a person to a new way of life, to institute rapid change in personality and/or behavior, or to produce a maverick—one with 'new ideas'—in a hostile back-home culture. . . . [but] T-Group training for teams and units within an organization tends to be appropriate where the primary goals are establishment of new norms, establishment of new values, or establishment of new ways of work—such as consensual decision-making."

T-Groups have in fact been successfully used in a wide variety of organization development efforts. Anderson (1970) shows, for example, that Procter & Gamble utilized T-Groups with beneficial results; their dangers did not materialize, at least in the opinion of the company and the trainers. The drawbacks and dangers of such training will be minimized by more rigorous certification procedures for competent trainers, and more effective ways of determining admission to such programs, based on who can benefit (or who may be harmed) by such training. The most serious problem seems to be how to maintain for people in organizations a truly voluntary choice of such training.

If, as we have said, it is almost impossible for one to have a true understanding of what goes on in a T-Group unless he has been through it, how do we "educate" a person to the point where he can make the choice? Or, if the "company" or the "boss" decides on an OD effort, how does one refuse on grounds of privacy without incurring the boss' displeasure or some form of social penalty in the form of suspicion by fellow employees?

No discussion of T-Group training would be complete without reference to the study done by Dunnette and Campbell (1968). They set out to find evidence that such training actually accomplishes the goals claimed by those who advocate it. They concluded (1) that no researcher has yet demonstrated that T-Groups have any marked effect on scores on objective attitude tests, (2) that T-Groups may result in increased self-awareness and interpersonal sensitivity, (3) that the associates of most persons who have received T-Group training report observable changes in their behavior back on the job (e.g., more openness in communication, better leadership styles), but (4) that no hard evidence exists to show that organizations have increased in productivity, output, or other organizational results.

Focused Exercises and Confrontation Meetings

Focused exercises are in one sense a halfway house between unfettered behavior in a structureless group and the more circumscribed behavior we all engage in in the real world. On the one hand, these exercises are like T-Groups. They provide experiential learning (rather than reading about or hearing about someone else's experience), and they set up a situation in which people are removed from *part* of the real world of agendas, time limits, leaders, hierarchies, quality controls, competition, scarce resources, technology, and so on. But in another way they differ from T-Groups. By creating situations which include *certain* of these things but not others, the trainer is able to design an experience which allows a group of participants to "see" things they might not otherwise see: how these constraints affect human behavior, and vice versa.

Such exercises have existed for years in the military form of "war games." These have been played by officers in training who use toy soldiers and weapons on elaborate terrain boards (some boards from the eighteenth and nineteenth centuries can be bought in European antique shops). And as all infantry trainees for World War II, Korea, and Vietnam know well, they may be played on bivouacs with "enemies" firing overhead while troops crawl on the ground, send out night patrols, or evade air attack. The fire drills in buildings, the lifeboat drills on ships, and the forced landing procedures in pilot training are all forms of "experiences" or "games" designed to let people know how it "feels" to be in a given situation. Perhaps the most elaborate simulations of real experience we have today are the ground trainers which enable airline pilots to experience everything from sudden crosswinds to loss of engine power to vertigo (loss of inner ear balance) by climbing into a cockpit on the ground, "flying" the trainer, but never leaving the earth.

A wide variety of simulated experiences have been devised which generate some specific behavior, such as competition, trust and openness, conflict, shared problem solving, hierarchical problem solving, division of scarce resources, and one-way versus two-way communication. In a selection following this chapter, Schein and Bennis discuss two such exercises. The classic computer games, devised originally to demonstrate certain economic phenomena, are played at some schools with emphasis on how a team of students behave in relation to each other during the decision-making process. These and other games have also been used to show *intergroup* relations—how one group might distrust another, how the two groups compete, and how a winning group has high cohesiveness. Conversely, a losing group often experiences an *intragroup* divisiveness, and a lack of loyalty to the leader who led the group in competition.

These experiences differ from T-Groups in a second important way. Not only is there an "agenda," but the "agenda" is imposed from the outside world. Remembering that human beings are motivated partly by what they bring to an organization and partly by what is in the organization around them, it is easy to see the importance of the externally imposed agenda. A stranger T-Group would emphasize what is within the individual, while the focused experience would enable participants to analyze both. The design imposed by the trainer can be arranged to highlight the organizational environment, enabling participants to "see" how agendas affect behavior, and vice versa.

One variation of the focused experience is the confrontation meeting. In his first selection following this chapter, Beckhard describes the conditions under which he believes that such a technique is applicable and the steps involved in such a confrontation. Notice that in Beckhard's meeting, it is the *operating* problems of an organization—hotel reservation procedures, the way financial information is funneled to subunits, and the like—which occupy most of the group's time. At the beginning, however, the consultant focuses on such human processes as problems of communication in a large organization, the need for mutual understanding, and the need for shared responsibility for future successful operations.

A quite different type of confrontation meeting focuses exclusively on the difficulties among people as they work in a complex organization. One study describes a five-day confrontation meeting between the headquarters sales executives and the field sales executives—regional managers plus division managers—in a large company (Golembiewski and Blumberg, 1967).

This company had had problems because the field sales managers often complained that sales promotion display or advertising materials were not of the quality that actually "sold" the products, or were not the kind that the field salesmen could get customers actually to display, or did not appear physically, or in newspapers, at the most advantageous *time* to help salesmen sell the products. The management recognized that these "today's irritations" could well become "tomorrow's tangled problems," so they engaged consultants in OD to institute a development effort.

The consultants had already conducted cognitive training (reading, lectures, theories) about rigidity and change in large organizations, leadership styles, and the effectiveness of counseling (rather than authority and "ordering") as a managerial style. After the confrontations, the operating problems identified during confrontation were to be followed up by core-issue task forces in a full-scale OD program.

There were 29 division sales managers who met in three groups, one with each regional manager. There was one group from the headquarters promotion department, and one group of sales department staff executives—the head of hospital sales, the head of sales personnel and training, the controller of the sales division, etc. Thus, there were five learning groups.

The first exercise involved each of these groups choosing *who* outside their group was a *relevant other*. Consultants defined "relevant other" as any position or organization unit with whom effective relations are necessary if the choosing party is to do a good job. A group of division sales managers, for example, could (and did) list the headquarters promotion group as a relevant other. After choosing, all 46 men gathered while the consultants received the reports of the five groups. They drew a 5 × 5 grid and checked off for each party who the relevant others were. They left plenty of space for listing "free" relevant others—specific persons, positions, or parts of other groups. These checkmarks were entered "in an atmosphere of tense horseplay." As the choosing proceeded, the division managers erupted. "That proves it," one shouted. "All of the regional groups chose *them* [the promotion group] but promotion didn't think we were relevant for *them*. As usual, they look only upward [to the vice president and headquarters]. They chose our regional bosses and the director of sales. But *we* aren't relevant for them." At this point, the consultants suggested that while the other groups work on the intense feelings aroused, the promotion department retire separately and evaluate its position. This evaluation was done by the "3-D Image" technique.

The 3-D technique requires that a group construct a three dimensional image of its position *vis-à-vis* another group:

1. *Describe how we see ourselves in relation to some relevant other.* The promotion department saw itself "as a united group which provides sales strategy and sales promotion materials to the division managers, designed to enhance their selling abilities," "as a vital factor in success of the division managers' selling efforts," "as cooperative allies with the division managers in achieving common selling goals," and "as dependent on division managers for important field intelligence from customers."
2. *Describe how we feel the relevant other sees us.* The promotion group saw the division managers "as not fully understanding the role and responsibility of product managers at headquarters in our marketing philosophy," "as the most important factor in any promotion effort we provide," and "as feeling frustration as a result of their not having more say in developing promotion materials."
3. *Describe how we see the relevant other.* The promotion group never got around to describing this. However, Exhibit 12-1 summarizes the third dimension for a *reverse* relationship: how field sales division managers saw the three dimensions, including the promotion department.

If we study carefully both the three-dimensional pattern for one group, and the pattern of the other group, we can see the richness of data and information that might be discussed in diagnosis sessions, such as the one that occurred when consultants suggested that groups "work on the intense feelings aroused." They scheduled 12 confrontation periods of up to 90 minutes each for relevant others to confront each other in such discussions.

Later in the confrontation, an additional technique was used—the identification of "core issues." In a general meeting of all participants, the whole group of 46 men, with the help of the consultants, developed a list of important issues to be worked on in action planning sessions. These issues were listed on large newsprint sheets. Any man present could sign up to work on this or that issue.

Exhibit 12-1   A Sample 3-D Image by One Regional Aggregate with Promotion as the Relevant Other

---

A. *How Members of Regional Aggregate 1 See Themselves in Relation to Promotion Department*

1. Circumvented
2. Manipulated
3. Receiving benefits of their efforts
4. Nonparticipating (relatively)
5. Defensive
6. Used
7. Productive
8. Instrument of their success
9. Have never taken us into their confidence in admitting that a promotion "bombed"
10. The field would like to help, but must be a two-way street

B. *How Members of Regional Aggregate 1 Feel Promotion Department Sees Them*

1. Insensitive to corporate needs
2. Noncommunicative upwards, as holding back ideas and suggestions
3. Productive in field saleswork
4. Naïf about the promotion side of business
5. Unappreciative of promotion efforts
6. As lacking understanding about their sales objectives
7. Belligerent
8. Overly independent operators
9. Not qualified to evaluate the promotions sent to us
10. Honest in opinions

C. *How Members of Regional Aggregate 1 Characterize Promotion Department*

1. Autocratic
2. Productive
3. Unappreciative of field efforts
4. Competent with "things" but not "people"
5. Industrious
6. Inflexible
7. Unrealistic
8. Naïf
9. Progressive in promotion philosophy and programs
10. Overly competitive within own department
11. Plagiarists who take field ideas but do not always give credit

---

The names on these lists became "core groups." They met to decide when and where to meet again to begin work on the issue.

Interview Methods

So far, we have seen two ways in which information (research data) is made available to participants in an organization: by questionnaire and by direct feedback (T-Groups and focused exercises) from one part of the organization to another. A third method, that of interview by an outside consultant and feedback by him to the teams, is today the principal method used by most OD consultants. In this method, the consultant interviews various people in the organization and feeds back to others, and to the whole group, certain selected or summarized information on a wide range of subjects. While some of this information pertains to operating matters ("the branch managers seem to believe that the company is charging too little for the product"), consultants are especially valuable in the feeding back of information on *human* processes in the team ("they say you won't let them have a voice in decisions such as pricing, which affect them"). Presumably, the consultant has the skill to state such feedback in a nonthreatening way, and as an outsider, he can state touchy matters in a way less likely to cause the recipient immediately to blame the other party. For both reasons, OD theory suggests, the person receiving such feedback is more likely to *think*, rather than react in an aggressive way without thinking. He is more likely to concentrate on the problem, regardless of whether it is his "fault," someone else's "fault," or both.

Another reason for using the interview method is that the human problems in an organization, which cannot readily be "seen" by untrained perceivers, or by people who have lived in a particularly structured organization, can be highlighted and emphasized. This may be accomplished by directive questioning in the interviews: "When the company charges prices so low that it keeps pressure on your plant to lower costs, doesn't that make you wonder who is doing the pricing?" Or, "That must make you feel pretty bad when you get the price list each quarter." Such emphasis can also be accomplished by selecting from interview data which information is to be reported back in feedback sessions: "One of the things we found is that most plant managers resent not being consulted on company pricing decisions."

OD consultants differ in the degree to which they stress direction or selection by the outside consultant in the OD process. Some consider them very important functions. A few deny that they seek to "filter" or "highlight" information, since their function is objective research—to discover and feed back, without bias or selectivity, all information reported to them in interviews. Regardless of this disagreement, it is highly likely that all consultants, given their training and interest in human affairs, do in fact select out, filter, or otherwise reinterpret data. It is also safe to say that, if OD is a worthy effort conducted by competent practitioners, reinterpretation is a vital part of the whole process. In fact, even in questionnaire and most direct group dynamics methods, the consultant's interpretations are an integral part of diagnosis.

Sequence of Experience and Explanation

It is perhaps a central thesis of all OD logic that people *learn* by experience, rather than by listening to lectures, reading books, or otherwise listening to the results of other people's experiences summarized in the form of theories or research principles. Few full-scale OD efforts leave out these cognitive inputs altogether, but most consultants stress the fact that they should come *after* an experience-type exercise, not before. For example, a focused exercise might be devised which places members of the team in competition with one another. Only after the group has acted out the exercise does the consultant give a lecture on how men act toward one another and feel toward one another when they are in competition. As another example, Zand et al. (1971) created temporary systems or problem-solving teams of managers and foremen in a manufacturing plant. After some problem-solving sessions, and throughout the program, the consultants scheduled a lecture on styles of supervision, an interpreted exercise on giving and receiving help, a lecture on organization theory, a film on problem solving under conflict, and an interpreted exercise showing what happens when a manager's upward influence is reduced.

There are exceptions to this principle of experience first, theory later. The first session of Beckhard's confrontations (described in his first selection following this chapter) include lectures on the problem of communication, the need for understanding, or the concept of shared responsibility for the future of the organization. This reverse in procedure is apparently thought desirable when very limited time is available for the activity, top management wishes to improve the conditions quickly, and when there is a major and rapid change in the organization (merger, change in organization structure, change in leadership) which causes confusion and expenditure of dysfunctional energy that negatively affects both productivity and morale.

A Complete Organization Development Program

In theory, at least, all OD consultants intend that organization development programs will, after the diagnosis stage, evolve into an action planning stage. After all, productive organizations do not exist only to improve human understanding, sensitivity, and diagnostic skills. The goals of productive organizations are to produce goods and services for society. And this means curing patients (a hospital), offering education (a school system), producing antibiotics (a drug company), or improving a standard of living (a government poverty bureau).

The action phase of organization development involves solving operating problems. But there is actually relatively little in the literature of OD which treats action planning in any detail. Perhaps this is because many OD consultants feel that, once the group or team becomes proficient in the human skills of joint problem solving, the planning of specific operations and procedures is "their business." On the other hand, certain OD specialists have recognized the danger of spending all efforts on diagnosis and research, and giving little attention to action planning. Such a procedure may be criticized for "all talk and no action," or be compared to the well-known criticism of "all we do is appoint another committee."

We have already referred to the interlocking chain of conferences, committees, and task forces which were set up by one consultant to deal with operating problems, and to the core-issue groups set up at the end of a confrontation meeting. The second selection by Beckhard following this chapter is one of the most comprehensive descriptions of a total program available, including both diagnosis and action phases. In an effort to change the operating practices, financial operations, policies, procedures, and job duties in a chain of 26 hotels operating internationally, the consultants set up an elaborate program. They utilized top executive conferences for the hotel chain headquarters, key executive conferences of hotel managers, problem-solving conferences within each hotel, annual goal-setting processes for each hotel and between top management and the group of hotels, management schools, technical seminars, new-hotel-management team programs (one for operating teams, one for staff teams), overhead cost-reduction teams, and a variety of other action-oriented task forces. The elaborate nature of this effort shows the amount of time and planning required if the OD logic is to be applied thoroughly to an entire organization. In studying this selection, you should be cognizant of both the types of operating subjects discussed, and the kinds of behavior the consultant sought while problem solving took place.

Another point of importance in such a full-scale action program is the fact that the hierarchical management, working with the consultant, set up a strong *structural* element in organization development. The plan of organization in this phase of OD has a great deal in common with the structural approach to managing organizations discussed in Chapter 7. To the extent that the existing hierarchy of headquarters management and subsidiary management of individual hotels is partly dictated by technology and geography (every hotel must have a management team), the OD effort must utilize the structural approach, especially in the action stages. However, the consultant in the hotel project sought to build *new* connective structures, based on what it takes to get the job done, and to integrate them with the technologically determined hierarchy.

Crucial Role of the Consultant

One of the hallmarks of organization development, and a characteristic which separates it from older management methods, is the assumption of part of the management task by an outside consultant, trained in the behavioral sciences. Some studies refer to this individual as a "change agent," a "practitioner," or an "interventionist." Whatever he is called, the literature on OD strongly suggests that OD management cannot be carried out without him.

Who is the consultant or change agent, and what functions does he perform? Authorities in the field differ as to how they describe him and his function—perhaps both his characteristics and his function in management can be looked at in different ways.

He is a man with certain *knowledge.* The chief certification agency for the profession is the National Training Laboratories, though there are undoubtedly many managers and consultants doing OD-type work who are either intuitively trained or unaware that this approach now has a name. Certification procedures at this stage are not too clear, but evidence of advanced work in the behavioral sciences, plus recommendation by some existing practitioner under whom the candidate has worked, are necessary. Within NTL, the organization development network affords the opportunity for those who do this work to meet and exchange knowledge and experience, and NTL operates a training institute in Colorado offering a month of more formal training.

The consultant is also a person with certain emotional characteristics —interests, attitudes, values, beliefs, and assumptions. These assumptions, attitudes, and interests relate to human behavior in organizations, both as it *is* and as it *ought* to be. Normative values are strong enough in the makeup of a typical OD consultant that they separate him from the behavioral scientist. While the latter usually confines himself to the descriptive or analytical *study* organizations, the OD consultant wants to *act,* to make the organization operate as he thinks it ought to operate. The orientation of the consultant can be characterized as having a strong "humanistic" quality (see for example, Raia, 1970, and Davis and Tannenbaum, 1969). According to one authority, many OD strategies "are based upon the assumptions that man is rational and reasonable; that he can be influenced by logic and knowledge; that he is responsible and will respond to the truth; and that he is loving, caring, and trusting of others" (Raia, 1970). Another puts this even more strongly: "Organization Development practitioners rely exclusively on two sources of influence, truth and love" (Bennis, 1969).

A third way of describing the consultant is in terms of skill. For example, he has worked in practical affairs enough that he is able to translate practical events into terms of human interaction theory (and vice versa), to give feedback in a way that is helpful instead of destructive, and to recognize when "the truth hurts too much."

Given these characteristics of the typical OD consultant, what functions does he perform that cannot be performed by a member of the operating team itself, or by one of the hierarchical managers? First, there is his knowledge of behavioral sciences and particularly of change methods. Second, it is thought that, because he is exempt from the intellectual and emotional biases of the organization, and partially exempt from the power (punishment) biases of an operating manager, he can bring freshness of perspective and a degree of stimulation not possible were he an operating member of the organization (Alderfer, 1971). Third, with his skill in constructive feedback, he not only can protect individuals when "too much truth hurts," he can also help demonstrate openness and truth in a way that is constructive instead of destructive. Fourth, in the diagnosis stage, he can set up a system that will actually undermine certain value systems (e.g., overemphasis on formal authority) in order to build a new value system based on open and honest communication (Greiner, 1967a, p. 83). Fifth, he can meet some of the dependency needs of a team in the early stages when the usual hierarchical bosses are not "bossing," and even be a useful model with whom team members might identify and thus learn from by imitation (Zand, 1971, p. 21).

Finally, overriding many of these other functions, the consultant serves an important function of promoting *power equalization*. He often moderates or acts as discussion leader for team meetings rather than the formal managers who do have sanctions. In fact, many consultants stress that this structural approval of higher management, in the form of permission to start an OD effort and in the form of turning the meeting over to the consultant, serves both to give *structural* support to a change effort (as opposed to the unstructured aspect), and to equalize the power among team members (Greiner, 1967b). Without such power equalization, it would be difficult for team members to "open up" and engage in the kind of exchanges that otherwise might seem threatening to higher authority (and dangerous to lower participants).

Though most OD writers stress the necessity of an outside consultant (either from outside the parent organization or as a top staff member within the organization who is not part of the operations being changed), one of the most respected earlier members of the profession did not think consultants were mandatory. Douglas McGregor first made the point that *any* trial-and-error learning of complex human interactions can be dangerous without a professional—it is dangerous for a man to try to be his own doctor or lawyer. But management of any kind (OD or otherwise) is a professional action field, and McGregor (1967) thought he had evidence that managers in the real world can produce real physical and mental dangers for people working in the organization. Therefore, he thought, self development of management teams, involving a "do-it-yourself" diagnosis of interpersonal relations using a rating scale, probably involves "no greater danger than is inherent in many widely accepted managerial policies and practices such as budgeting, cost control, promotion, or performance appraisal. . . . I believe a managerial group *can* successfully undertake its own self development, with or without the help of a behavioral scientist consultant" (p. 170).

Limitations to and Conditions for Organization Development

There is no doubt that organization development is one of the most significant *practical* techniques which depart from traditional management based on division of labor and formal authority. For years, behavioral scientists have referred to participative management and structural job enlargement as the main alternatives to traditional management. But until the advent of OD nobody made them *operational.* It is as easy to *preach* participation as it is to preach motherhood and democracy, but for the same reasons that preaching has never eliminated sin, it would be difficult to bring about participation in a bureaucratic organization by advocacy alone.

But OD has its limitations. Analysis, clarity, reality, openness, and facing up to the truth may be an alternative to closed-system stereotypical thinking, but there is no guarantee that it will work in all organizations. The viewpoint which the modern manager must take, therefore, is that this method of management has both powerful benefits and powerful limitations. The key is to try to understand when and under what circumstances such a technique will succeed.

The first set of conditions to watch for in deciding when to use OD are summarized by Greiner (1967b) (treated more fully in Greiner, 1967a). The organizations where OD has been successful were under considerable external and internal pressure to change the organization radically, long before OD consultants entered the picture. This suggests that, like the drinker who chooses on his own to go to Alcoholics Anonymous rather than have someone sell him on it, the organization itself must be searching for new ways of managing, must want help, and must call on the consultant—not vice versa. Second, the hierarchical managers must be willing to experiment with OD and become deeply involved, devoting their time and energies to the change process. It is possible to share power *too much* by relying on group dynamics alone, without including structural aspects. In the organizations which did not succeed with OD, Greiner found that some made the mistake of too much unilateral "forcing" or "selling" of OD procedures, while others went overboard in the other direction—they utilized T-Groups with virtual abdication of power, with no active participation of formal authority figures, or with data discussions that did not get to an action stage based on a combination of consensus and legitimate authority.

A second set of conditions which the wise manager should attend to concern the hiring of a consultant—whether a total outsider, or an internal staff person at headquarters who is an "outsider" to operating departments. Even some OD specialists themselves (e.g., Bennis, 1969) recognize that consultants often are ignorant, unskilled, or uninterested in that part of the world which does not fit their model of open communication and trust. Power and authority, as well as technical operations and output, are not only facts of life in most organizations but very important facts at that. Unless the consultant also possesses interest in the organization's purpose, procedures, and technical operations, he is likely either to let these take distinctly second place behind its human processes, or to let them become lost in the maze of human process techniques. OD is not an end in itself, at least to a society that wants hospital care, police protection, air transportation, and pharmaceuticals, as well as trust and harmony. The very logic of OD makes it clear that solving the organization's problems is the end value desired.

A further limitation of OD has to do with *time.* It is a process which aims at long-term changes in organizational productivity and success. If events in the environment warrant a quick and coordinated response of the entire organization, the method is probably inferior to management by structure and authority. If a Nazi bombing squadron had been detected by radar headed toward Westminster Abbey during the Battle of Britain, one would not have expected a British fighter squadron commander to call a meeting and ask his pilots, "Who do you think are your relevant others?" Nor would General Motors spend two years on developing interlocking chains of committees in response to the sudden introduction of prohibitive tariffs against U.S. automobiles around the world.

A final limitation has to do with the possibility that OD consultants might themselves become susceptible to advocating stereotyped answers to problems. One authority in the field notices that some OD consultants, having discovered a method appropriate under *certain conditions,* tend to apply the same method to any and all organizations, without regard to whether the specific organization is suitable for this kind of management. Frederick Taylor had his time and motion study, his separation of planning from operations, and his industrial engineers as the ultimate planners. Today's OD specialist has his open communications, his involvement of a team in both operations and planning, and his expert behavioral scientist in charge of the change process.

There is probably value in OD. But it should not be applied in the same way to all organizations. This chapter has sought to give the practicing manager enough understanding of organization development to know that it is one alternative for managing a complex organization and that it is useful under certain conditions.

Summary

Organization development is a philosophy and method of management which focuses on the *informal culture* of the organization, rather than on the formal structure of jobs, authority, technical procedures, and financial procedures. It attacks the prevailing attitudes, mores, and beliefs of the people in the organization as a group. Particularly, it seeks to develop such attitudes and beliefs as "other people are valuable in themselves," "other people are valuable as co-workers in getting the job done," "trust and openness are productive for me and for them," and "only if we can communicate with trust and frankness can we then solve financial problems, marketing problems, or other technical, operating, and work problems." This philosophy of management also attempts to develop certain *skills* in the organization's culture, particularly skill in giving and receiving honest feedback.

According to the OD philosophy of management, such cultural attitudes, mores, and skills are necessary *before* the members of the firm can move on to solve successfully the technical side of the business: job descriptions, the structure of authority (who can or should make certain decisions), questions of technology (what is our product line and our method of selling), or economic-financial matters (what are our income statement figures and what do they mean?).

The OD philosophy of management has arisen because of several problems which develop as organizations grow and mature. The organization's goals must change to meet the changing tastes and demands of society, yet such organizations sometimes have a tendency to train participants to be more interested in maintaining their own position in the status hierarchy. People become so specialized that they cannot deal with one another with any degree of real understanding without becoming impatient. The further one goes down the line in the hierarchy, the more starvation one finds—for *involvement* in the wider world, as opposed to the smaller world of performing in a specialized corner of the organization. The ever more complex patterns of specialization seem to defeat this desire. Both the organization and the people need some way to settle the many interpersonal and interdepartmental conflicts that arise as a result of specialization.

A number of different methods have been developed to implement OD management: questionnaire feedback, T-Groups or sensitivity training, focused exercises and confrontation meetings, interviews, and cognitive "lectures" to help people logically interpret what they have learned from the more emotional experiential methods. Finally, a complete OD program, integrating a number of these methods, culminates in team management projects in which newly trained participants proceeded to plan the authority structure, economic aspects, and technical operations of a business.

There are three essential steps involved in all of these methods, regardless of which are selected for an individual OD project: gathering data, feedback of data, and planning of new solutions.

Most authorities on OD today believe that a full-time executive, of the traditional line or staff type, cannot carry out the role of the change agent or OD practitioner. Members of the organization are likely to be unwilling or unable to practice skills or examine attitudes as required, particularly if the "manager" of the process holds a position of formal power (or if he has a stake in the existing status and operating structures).

Authorities differ as to whether this "outsider" must be a total stranger, not employed in the organization (a consultant), or whether he can be a "semi-outsider," a staff specialist in OD. Even Douglas McGregor, who believed that men could engage in a kind of do-it-yourself organization development, without the active presence of a consultant, nevertheless assumed that (1) the group initiates and maintains the process, not a "boss," and (2) the consultant's expert knowledge, reflected in the instrument or questionnaire the team uses, is a necessary adjunct.

OD is not to be construed, as some advocates unfortunately seem to imply, as a long-awaited ideal management method. It has its problems. Among these is that it is one thing to preach a philosophy and yet another to act it out in practice. Not all organizations are rigid bureaucracies in dire need of change. People in the organization must feel the need for improvement *before* an outsider attempts to impose his own "ideals." Furthermore, the ad hoc and unstructured relationships required to carry out such a program exact a high price in terms of human energy, anxiety, and effort, and a high price in terms of time commitment. They also tend to go against another of man's needs: the need for structure, stability, and familiarity. Too much uncertainty over time, with little or no familiar routine, will tax the abilities of people to work effectively. Finally, the OD effort which ignores the technical side may eventually result in the method being labeled as theoretical, unreal, or even mystical by those who work in organizations and those who manage them. The economic production of goods for outsiders in society, as well as human satisfaction inside the organization, are equally important.

These are the kinds of situations which may limit the effectiveness of the method and which any manager must consider in determining when it is appropriately used.

References

Alderfer, C. P. "Change Processes in Organizations." In *Handbook of Industrial and Organization Psychology,* ed. M. D. Dunnette (in press).

Anderson, J. "Giving and Receiving Feedback." In *Organizational Change and Development,* ed. G. W. Dalton, P. R. Lawrence, and L. E. Greiner. Irwin-Dorsey, 1970.

Beckhard, R. "The Appropriate Use of T-Groups in Organizations." A.T.N. Occasional Papers, No. 2, in *T-Group Training: Group Dynamics in Management Education,* ed. B. Blackwell. Oxford, 1965.

———. "The Confrontation Meeting." *Harvard Business Review,* March–April 1967.

Bennis, W., and H. Shepard. "A Theory of Group Development." *Human Relations,* Vol. 9, No. 4, 1965.

———. "Unsolved Problems Facing Organization Development." *The Business Quarterly,* Winter 1969.

Blake, R. R., and J. S. Mouton. "Grid Organization Development." *Personnel Administration,* January–February 1967.

Boise Cascade Corporation. *Organization Renewal Questionnaire.* Human Resources Committee, Boise, Idaho, 1970.

Davis, S., and R. Tannenbaum. "Values, Man and Organizations." *Industrial Management Review,* Winter 1969.

Dunnette, M. D., and J. P. Campbell. "Laboratory Education: Impact on People and Organizations." *Industrial Relations,* October 1968.

Golembiewski, R. T., and A. Blumberg. "Confrontation as a Training Design in Complex Organizations." *Journal of Applied Behavioral Science,* Vol. 3, No. 4, 1967.

Greiner, L. E. "Antecedents of Planned Organization Change." *Journal of Applied Behavioral Science,* Vol. 3, No. 1, 1967a.

———. "Patterns of Organization Change." *Harvard Business Review,* Vol. 45, May–June 1967b.

Lawrence, P. R., and J. W. Lorsch. *Organization and Environment.* Cambridge, Harvard University, Graduate School of Business Administration, 1967.

McGregor, D. "Team Development." In *The Professional Manager.* McGraw-Hill, 1967.

Mann, F. C. "Studying and Creating Change: A Means to Understanding Social Organization." *Research in Industrial Human Relations,* ed. C. Arensberg, S. Barkin, W. E. Chalmers, H. Willensky, J. Worthy, and B. Dennis. Harper & Row, 1957.

Raia, A. P. *Organizational Development: Some Issues and Challenges.* Unpubl. ms, November 1970.

Schein, E. H., and W. G. Bennis. *Personal and Organizational Change Through Group Methods.* Wiley, 1967.

Schein, E. H. *Process Consultation, Its Role in Organization Development.* Addison-Wesley, 1969.

Zand, D. E., M. B. Miles, and W. O. Lytle. "Development of a Collateral Problem-Solving Organization Through Use of a Temporary System." In *Proceedings of the Academy of Management,* August 1971.

Readings

Team Development

DOUGLAS McGREGOR

The skills involved in social interaction are often compared to those involved in sports like golf and tennis. Since the concern here is with team skills, the analogy to baseball or football teams might appear to be appropriate. However, these analogies are too oversimplified for our purposes. The common aspect is the necessity for practice, for experience-based learning. One cannot acquire the skills of golf without playing golf, nor can one acquire the skills of team operation without being a team member.

Let us say that a manager wishes to undertake a process of team development involving himself and all his immediate subordinates, both staff and line. In my view this is perfectly appropriate and practical. He is concerned with changing certain characteristics of this sociotechnical system. He cannot impose these conditions on the group, as we have seen. Nothing can be gained by any kind of secret manipulation of the system. The process must be public and transactional. He would begin, therefore, with an open discussion in a meeting of the whole group. He would discuss his reasons for suggesting such a process. If he were tentative, perhaps even doubtful (which would be natural), he would say so. He would encourage a discussion about its feasibility. He would ask his subordinates to express their own feelings openly, because there would be little point in the process in the face of strong reservations. If negative reactions were expressed, however tentatively, he would be careful not to override them or even try to persuade. Instead he would encourage the group to understand them fully.

He would need to be prepared with some ideas (not firm convictions) to answer questions like: "How would we go about it?" One way would be to discuss the primary task of the group with the purpose of clarifying and coming to mutual agreement about it.

If this process is to be transactional, it will involve much more than a cursory examination of the organization chart and the position description of the members' jobs. It will involve a critical, deep analysis by the whole team of the role pressures to which they are subjected and of the implications of these for what the organization expects of this unit formally and informally.

From this analysis will follow an attempt to formulate the primary task that encompasses all these expectations. If, as often happens, this proves impossible, the discussion will proceed to determine what *is* possible, from the point of view of both the team and the larger organization.

The outcome may be a conception of the team's primary task that resembles neither the formal organization chart and position descriptions nor the role expectations of the organization as experienced by the team. If the analysis conducted by the group and the manager has been thorough, they will have a persuasive rationale for seeking change in one direction or the other. The manager would normally be the person to attempt this.

If the group's conception of its primary task is acceptable, there remains the organization of work within the team. Members should be given considerable freedom in working this out themselves. The ideal would be a structure of responsibilities that is flexible enough to permit adjustment to changing situational requirements whether these arise within the team or in the wider organizational system or in the external environment of society (which of course includes the market).

The overall value of a process like this is not only the classification that results, but the growth of identification with the team and its responsibilities, and the sense of a degree of control by the group over its environment. There will have been compromises and adjustments, but the active involvement of the whole team and the sense of achievement when the task is completed provide important intrinsic rewards to all the members.

A second step—or possibly an alternative first step—would be to analyze together the current state of the group, to attempt to agree on those characteristics which require improvement.

I have seen groups make effective use of a simple rating scale like the accompanying exhibit for purposes of analysis. After a little discussion of the meaning of each of the variables, each member fills out the form anonymously, rating his personal view of the current state of the group. The ratings are then pooled and a chart prepared by a couple of members showing the mean of the ratings and the high and low "score" for each variable. On the basis of these data, the group discusses what aspects of its group operation need work.

Analyze your team (the group here in this room) by rating it on a scale (Exhibit 1) from 1 to 7 (7 being what you consider to be ideal) with respect to each of these variables. Then (with the rest of the team) discuss in depth the situation with respect to each variable, paying particular attention to those for which the average rating is below 5 or for which the range of individual ratings is particularly wide. Formulate some ideas about *why* these perceptions exist. The "whys" are likely to be quite different for different variables.

In using an approach like this, it is important to agree in advance on a ground rule that there will be no attempt to ferret out the "author" of any individual rating, although any member may *volunteer* comment about his own rating. If the group leader feels comfortable about it, his ratings might also be used. However, in most circumstances it would be advisable to wait until a fairly high degree of mutual trust and open communications is revealed by the data before attempting to analyze the leader's behavior separately.

The ratings of most groups tend to be unrealistically high on the first attempt to use an instrument like this. After some initial discussion it is usually fruitful to wait a week or two and then use it again, applying it the second time to a regular group meeting concerned with normal operating problems. A few minutes before the close of the meeting can be set aside for the purpose.

The problems that provide the agenda for meetings of the team, whatever they may be, are grist for the mill with respect to group development. The way to use them for this purpose is first to provide time for looking back directly after the group has dealt with a problem in order to examine together "how we operated." The experience is fresh; the data for examination are the behavior

Exhibit 1 Analyzing Team Effectiveness

---

1. Degree of mutual trust:
   High suspicion _____ High trust
          (1)   (7)

2. Degree of mutual support:
   Every man for himself _____ Genuine concern
                                             for each other
                 (1)   (7)

3. Communications:
   Guarded, cautious _____ Open, authentic
            (1)   (7)

   We don't listen to   We listen; we understand
   each other _____ and are understood
         (1)   (7)

4. Team objectives
   not understood by team _____ Clearly understood
                                         by team
             (1)   (7)

   Team is negative   Team is committed
   toward objectives _____ to objectives
            (1)   (7)

5. Handling conflicts within team:
   We deny, avoid, or   We accept conflicts and
   suppress conflicts _____ "work them through"
           (1)   (7)

6. Utilization of member resources:
   Our abilities, knowledge,   Our abilities, knowledge,
   and experience aren't   and experience are fully
   utilized by the team _____ utilized by the team
           (1)   (7)

7. Control methods:
   Control is imposed on us _____ We control ourselves
              (1)   (7)

8. Organizational environment:
   restrictive; pressure   Free; supportive; respect
   toward conformity _____ for individual differences
           (1)   (7)

---

of the group members (including the leader) as they carried on the normal activities of the group. The process involves comments by individual members, if they feel free to express themselves, on how they felt when this or that happened and on their reaction to the whole process.

The group will gain most from such a feedback process if they give consideration to the consequences of different kinds of feedback. One of the purposes is to help each member of the group to recognize the impact of his behavior on others. Under ordinary circumstances individuals rarely acquire this information, *particularly* with respect to an immediate and specific situation when all the details are "here and now." More often than not, an individual discovers that the reactions of others to his own words or actions are not the same as he perceived them to be. Thus the feedback provides him an opportunity to test his perceptions against reality and to modify his future behavior *if he chooses to do so.*

If this is a purpose of feedback, it is quite unlikely to be helpful if it takes the form of a critical attack that simply puts the person on the defensive and makes it unlikely that he will either understand or accept the feedback. Nor is there any help in feedback that attempts to probe the motives behind his behavior. To turn feedback into a "two-bit analysis" defeats the purpose and may be highly disturbing to the recipient.

The guiding notion is that feedback tells the other individual: "This is how your behavior affected me." The information should be authentic. If his behavior made me angry or suspicious, or if it led me to become his ally or to feel especially positive about him, or if it led me to agree or disagree with him—*I should try to help him to understand my reactions, my feelings.* If others provide him with feedback on the same basis, he may discover that my reactions were like those of others in the group or that they were quite different. (In the latter case *I* may learn something, too!) The same considerations would apply to feedback by an individual member to the rest of the group.

Honest, sincere feedback between all the members of a team (including the leader) is one of the foundations on which mutual trust is built. It is in this sense that open communications and trust are reciprocal. It may seem inconsistent to think that one can be supportive and at the same time tell another person: "Your behavior angers me." However, there is a tremendous difference between responding with anger (attacking) and feeding back information about one's feelings in the hope of correcting a situation that is interfering with group accomplishment. The same is true of a reaction of mistrust or indifference or rejection. Genuine feedback of this kind (information) *identifies a problem that can be explored* and probably solved.

I argued earlier that *absolute* open communication may be dysfunctional. In the context of the immediate situation one must always make judgments about how far to go. The problem in the ordinary situation is that feedback (if it occurs at all) is so limited and cautious that it seldom provides much help. My experience with groups that are deliberately trying to create mutual trust, support, and open communications is that most people are quite skillful in sensing intuitively when they are at the limit in a given situation. Subtle cues from the other person—gestures, flushing, particular verbal responses, and the like—are noted. In a group setting particularly, it is remarkable how often some member will respond to these cues, even if the individual giving the feedback does not, and will find ways to divert the discussion. This is fortunate because there are no simple rules for setting the limits. Human beings differ widely in the amount and kind of feedback they can accept. On the other hand, the limits are not fixed. They usually become extended substantially as mutual trust and support increase.

Of course, these skills and sensitivities are not immediately present when a group begins to use this method. Discussion of the reasons for using feedback and examination of what the reactions are as the process goes along can pretty well prevent any lasting damaging consequences.

The process of using feedback to explore and examine a just-ended group session can gradually be extended so that many difficulties arising in group operation are corrected as a matter of course almost as they happen rather than being postponed to a post mortem. Part of the skill acquired is in recognizing when it is important to interrupt an ongoing activity in order to save time and trouble later and when to refrain from doing so because it is recognized that the effects on group performance are relatively unimportant. During the initial phases of acquiring skill along these lines, groups often become unduly preoccupied and overly sensitive about the needs for feedback on minor matters. This is, however, a natural and useful part of the process of acquiring skill.

Intellectual, cognitive learning is also an integral part of effective team development. This can occur in two different ways, and both are important. I have stressed continuously throughout this volume the many ways in which beliefs, assumptions, perceptions of reality, and theories about the nature of man and organized human effort affect managerial strategy.

Thus, effective use of feedback *for purposes of team development* requires another step: generalization. The value for the group in undertaking an analysis of their behavior is not in the analysis itself, but in what can be learned from it that can be used to improve the future performance of this and any other groups with which these members may be associated. For purposes of group development it is not enough that a particular problem may have been solved. The particular problem may never appear again in exactly the same form. However, it may well appear again under other circumstances and in other guises. Will the analysis of this single experience help the group to recognize the problem in other forms and deal with it? The probability is "no," unless the group has answered for itself the question: What have we learned from this experience? The learning may pertain to the meeting that was analyzed or the process that was used for analysis, or both. The generalizations may be quite tentative, subject to modification as a result of future experience. Nevertheless, the group's conscious generalizations concerning its own learning are the rungs of the ladder it is seeking to climb.

Every time the group faces a business problem that cannot be solved easily and quickly on the basis of habit, past experience, or existing policy, there is an opportunity for team development. Blake and Mouton refer to this as the "dilemma-invention-feedback-generalization" process, and it is in many ways a model for all kinds of learning.[1] A dilemma or problem confronts the group (or the individual). If it is solved by conventional, known formulas, there is no learning. If, however, it can be solved only by some form of ingenuity or inventiveness (or if that ingenuity is used to find a new and better solution to an old problem), there is an opportunity for learning by analyzing how the solution was arrived at and generalizing on the analysis.

That is why feedback, whether simple, brief, and essentially intellectual (as it will be sometimes) or complex, time-consuming, and emotion-laden, is crucial for team development. This is what is implied by "experience-based" learning.

[1] R. R. Blake, *Tenth Proceedings of the Action Research Training Laboratory,* West Point, New York, 1960.

What Is Laboratory Training?

EDGAR SCHEIN, WARREN BENNIS

Many attempts have been made to characterize the nature of laboratory training, but most of them have not been successful for several reasons: (1) laboratories *vary tremendously* in goals, training design, delegate population, length, and setting, making it difficult to describe this experience in general; (2) laboratories attempt to provide a *total* and *integrated* learning experience for the participants, making it difficult to communicate in written words the interdependence of the many separate aspects of the laboratory training design; (3) laboratories intend to provide a learning experience which is, in part, *emotional,* and to provide the opportunity for the participants to explore the interdependence of emotional and intellectual learning. It is difficult without observing the process first-hand to describe and understand the nature of this emotional learning and its meaning to the learner.

In spite of these difficulties, it is important to attempt to communicate some of the flavor of the typical laboratory training experience. By giving a bird's-eye view of laboratory training, we hope to highlight and exemplify the differences in assumptions and methods between the laboratory approach and more traditional educational activities. For our case, we will use a typical *two-week residential* laboratory for a group such as middle level managers in industry. By residential, we mean that all the participants live at the conference center and spend their entire time in training activities. There are many other types of laboratories. We have chosen the two-week residential one as our example because it represents the most typical kind of laboratory. The primary focus of the laboratory is the *personal* learning of the individual delegate.

Arrival at the "Cultural Island"

Most laboratories are held somewhere away from the pressures of day-to-day urban living, generally in an isolated comfortable hotel or conference center. The preliminary information sent to the delegate makes it clear that the atmosphere of the laboratory is informal and that the delegate will be expected to live in, in the sense of having minimal contacts with job or family during the course of the laboratory.

When he arrives at the conference center, the delegate is assigned to a room with one or more other delegates—a situation which may be of considerable emotional significance if he has been used to staying alone when traveling or attending conventions. He is given a notebook which contains general information, schedules, and group assignments. He is also given a name tag which has only his name on it, making it clear at the outset that he is at the laboratory as a *person,* not as a representative of the organization.

Initial conversations among the delegates, perhaps while unpacking, often involve attempts to discover what the laboratory is all about and how expert others are about it. The range of responses is likely to be from complete ignorance and confusion among some, to tales of "emotional bloodbaths" among others who have undergone experiences that they believe to have been similar or who have read about T-groups in popularized articles. The uncertainty about what lies ahead is preoccupying and provokes tension.

This newness, the uncertainty, and the apprehension all work toward a situation in which the delegate arrives at his first orientation session unable to comprehend what is being said. He is too busy trying to get acclimatized and to get control of his own feelings of tension and uncertainty. Some delegates have read portions of their notebook, but these are not informative either, at this stage of the game.

First Session

The orientation session for the entire group of from 50 to 75 delegates is generally held in the early afternoon of the first day. It deals with matters of housekeeping (dining room hours, recreation facilities, how to get laundry done, and so forth), provides an opportunity to introduce the staff of the laboratory, and states in brief form the goals of the laboratory and the kinds of learning activities which hopefully will enable the delegates to achieve these goals.

For example, in a typical introduction, the "dean" of the laboratory or some other staff member points out that the *goals* of the laboratory are to create opportunities for the delegates *to learn* about the following kinds of things:

1. *Self.* The delegates' own behavior in groups and the impact which their behavior has on other members.
2. *Others.* The behavior of others in a group and the impact which their behavior has on them.
3. *Groups.* How groups work; what makes them function.
4. *Larger systems.* How organizations and larger social systems work.
5. *The learning process.* How to learn from their own experience ("learning how to learn").

These are deceptively simple goals and are in general only vaguely understood when first outlined. In discussing the *method* by which we learn in a laboratory setting, the speaker indicates that the basic difference between the laboratory and the traditional learning experience is that in the former we attempt to learn *from an analysis of our own experiences in groups* rather than from what some expert tells us. Thus, the term laboratory implies that the delegate has an opportunity to become a researcher and a student of his own and others' group behavior; he becomes both the subject and the experimenter-observer. The speaker points out that it is easier to explain this method after the delegates have had some experience in the laboratory. He then turns to an explanation of the daily schedule (see Table 1), after which he sends the delegates to their groups for the first training group (T-group) session.

The schedule which is given to the delegate will indicate the major training activities of the laboratory:

1. *T-groups.* These are basic learning groups which continue to meet

Table 1 Typical Schedule for the Week

	Sun.	Mon.	Tues.	Wed.	Thurs.	Fri.
9:00–11:00		T-group	T-group	T-group	T-group	T-group
11:00–11:30		Coffee break	Coffee break	Coffee break	Coffee break	Coffee break
11:30–12:30		General session	General session	General session	General session	General session
12:30–1:30		Lunch	Lunch	Lunch	Lunch	Lunch
1:30–3:30		T-group	T-group	Exercise	Exercise	Exercise
3:30–6:00	Opening session	Free time	Free time	Free time	Free time	Free time
6:00–7:30		Dinner	Dinner	Dinner	Dinner	Dinner
7:30–9:30	T-group	T-group	Tape listening exercise	Free	Exercise or training film	Free

throughout the course of the laboratory. They usually contain 10 to 15 members with one or two staff members or "trainers." T-groups are generally "unstructured," in the sense that the staff provides a minimum of agenda and formal leadership. [The T in T-group stands for training. Such groups have also been called D-groups (development) and study groups.]

2. *Information or theory sessions.* These are general sessions during which a staff member lectures and/or gives a demonstration to impart some concepts or ideas or research findings about an area relevant to the laboratory goals.

3. *Focused exercises.* These are activities which may involve small or large groups. They are usually introduced by a staff member who describes the learning goals and the specific activities, such as role-playing or group observation, which are to be engaged in by the delegates.

4. *Other activities.* Most laboratories involve seminars, two-man interview groups (dyads), informal bull sessions, and other activities which may be introduced during its course. Some of these will be described below in our chronicle. They are usually not included on the delegate's regular schedule because of their informal or optional status.

Scheduled activities generally take place from 9 to 12 in the morning, 1 to 3 in the afternoon, and 8 to 10 in the evening. What the schedule can only half-successfully impart, but which is crucial is the degree to which the training design is an attempt to integrate the scheduled activities, and the degree to which informal unscheduled activities form an integral part of the total training. Furthermore, the schedule itself overstates the rigidity of the laboratory. Actually, the staff communicates to delegates that they, as well as the staff, have the power to change the schedule if training needs dictate such changes.

The T-Group

The T-group is, for most delegates, the major emotional focus of their laboratory experience. From their notebooks, they discover which group they are in. Also in the notebook is a roster of all delegates including their job title and organization. Finding out who the other members of their group are, including the staff member, becomes one of the first anchors around which the delegates organize their experience. This anchor takes on additional importance as the delegate discovers the unstructured nature of the T-group.

The group meets in a room around a large table. Each person is given a name card which is placed in front of him. There is usually a tape-recorder on or near the table. When the group has settled down, the staff member gives a short introduction, usually lasting less than five minutes, in which he restates some of the learning goals. He points out that the T-group's primary task is to create learning opportunities for its members, and that it has no formal leader, preset agenda, or rules by which it must operate. It is up to the whole group, including the staff member, to decide what to do and how best to learn from its experience.

Whether he emphasizes it in the introduction or later, the trainer makes it clear that it is legitimate and likely to be profitable for the group to try to learn from its *own* experienced behavior—the "here-and-now" situation—rather than to discuss problems outside the group, from the world they left, the "there-and-then" world. The tape-recorder, which will be running at all times unless the group decides to turn it off, is available as a learning aid to enable the group to recapitulate and study some of its earlier experiences. The tapes are the property of the group and are erased at the end of the laboratory. If the staff member comments on his own role at all, he is likely to state that he does not perceive himself to be the chairman or leader of the group, but rather a person who will help the learning process in whatever way he can. [We have had to qualify so often this description of what the staff member does because of the huge variation among trainers in how they open the T-group and the kind of role they make for themselves. For a more complete discussion of the role of the trainer, the reader is referred to Chapter 16 of Schein and Bennis (1965) and to the volume on training by Bradford, Gibb, and Benne (1964).]

When the trainer finishes his introduction, the group is suddenly left to its own resources. It is difficult to describe the full emotional impact of the beginning minutes of a T-group because the members are struggling with so many emotional issues at once. They are confronted with a violation of many expectations they have taken for granted in educational settings, most of all that the trainer will define an agenda, some ground rules and some goals which are meaningful for the group. Instead, each member confronts some major problems—"what do we do and what are our goals"; "who am I to be in this unstructured situation and what kind of role should I play"; "how can I keep sufficient control over the group to prevent it from doing things which will make me too uncomfortable?"

In coping with these problems, different members use different strategies. Some ask further questions of the trainer; some try to get him to be more of a leader or guide; some lapse into an anxious watchful silence; some get angry; and some attempt to organize the group with various tasks like "introducing ourselves." As the members fill the vacuum with their behavior, they begin to generate the raw data from which they will have the opportunity to learn about themselves, their impact on others, others' reactions to them, and how groups work.

How the T-group goes about its business of creating learning opportunities during the first and subsequent sessions is hard to characterize because each group has its own unique history. It has its own particular combination of people; its own particular trainer with his own theory of learning and style of intervention; its unforeseen incidents, dilemmas, and crises. It creates, for each member, a unique set of emotional and intellectual experiences.

T-groups do have in common the kinds of issues or dilemmas which have to be resolved in the process of building a group and learning from this procedure—what to do, how to spend the time, how to distribute power, control and influence, how to develop group standards and a climate which permits maximum learning, how to develop group goals and a sense of group progress, how to keep the group process within bounds. It is the particular solutions to such dilemmas which make each group unique.

A Digression: The Learning Process in the T-Group

What does the delegate begin to learn from the unstructured group experience? In what manner does he first discover for himself the meaning of the laboratory method of learning? For some delegates, learning begins immediately with the opportunity to study their own reactions to this novel experience, and to compare their reactions with those of others. For other delegates, the learning process does not begin until they become involved in some incident in the life of the T-group in which they are confronted with unexpected feelings on the part of others, either in reaction to their own behavior or to the behavior of others. Both kinds of delegates gain an *increased awareness of their own feelings and the feelings of others.* What is this increased awareness about?

For many delegates, the learning process first focuses around the problem of *communication.* While most delegates admit at the outset that they are not as good listeners as it might be hoped, rarely do they realize how little listening they or anyone else in the group does during the early sessions. The discovery that they missed many things altogether and that various group members heard the same speaker say entirely different things is shocking and thought provoking. *They become more aware of the complexity of the communication process.*

For some delegates, the problem of communication is not as salient as the problem of structure and organization in the group. Those who wish to get the group organized often find themselves confronted by others who are comfortable in an unstructured setting and vice versa. An important first learning step for this group is the *awareness and acceptance of genuine differences in member needs, goals, and ways of approaching problems.*

Another kind of learning which occurs results from a group member getting reactions from others in areas about which he is relatively blind. The person who leaps into the early power vacuum of the group with the sincere motive of getting the group moving may discover that a number of other members perceived him as attempting to dominate and control the group. The silent member may discover that he communicates more of his feelings through his silence than he realizes, and that for many members his behavior is a subtle but powerful way of controlling the group. The person who tries to help by giving reactions to others whenever the impulse moves him may discover that others do not find his "feedback" helpful, either because it is too evaluative, too ill-timed, or too hostile in undertone. The person who hides his own feelings by being constantly analytical about what the group is doing may discover that several members view his behavior as a real barrier to group progress instead of an aid. For all of these delegates, the crucial learning process is *increased awareness of their own impact on others* which enables them to check the assumptions they have made about themselves.

Some delegates focus their learning effort on the level of group processes. They discover that group decisions are tricky things to observe and to manage intelligently. Sometimes a minority pushes the group into action because each of the silent members erroneously assumes that the silence of the others means consent. Sometimes the group votes and then acts on majority rule only to discover that the minority is effectively able to block the action. The group may elect or appoint a chairman only to discover that he is unable to control the vicissitudes of the meeting because the same members who were willing to have him be chairman discover that they are unwilling to have him exercise any kind of control. Sometimes the group sets up an agenda only to discover that the agenda tyrannizes the group and prevents it from doing what it really wants to do. Yet, no one knows how to undo the group decision, particularly if it was hard won in the first place. *Increased awareness of how groups function and the consequences of certain kinds of group action* are the learning result.

Usually these discoveries result from an emotionally taxing reconstruction of some of the earlier events in the group's life. In the process of making such a reconstruction, members learn how to be better observers of group action, learn what sorts of observation other members have made, and learn what sorts of reaction have been aroused by various incidents in the group's history. Almost in spite of themselves group members become more observant, more analytical, and more cautious in making assumptions about group behavior. They are, in this sense, *learning how to learn* from their own experience.

Out of increased awareness in all these areas comes the possibility of changed attitudes. The delegate develops new attitudes toward the learning process, toward himself, toward others, and toward groups. Out of such attitude changes will come new behavior and greater competence in dealing with others. The major learning outcomes, therefore, will be *increased awareness, changed attitudes,* and *greater interpersonal competence.*

Theory Sessions

It is a basic assumption of laboratory training that experience must precede the introduction of a theoretical concept. Equally important is the assumption that raw experience without some degree of intellectual understanding is insufficient to produce learning which is useful and can be generalized. The delegate must be able to fit his experience into a framework of concepts and ideas which will allow him to relate to situations and persons other than in the laboratory.

In order to optimize learning, delegates attend daily information or theory sessions. The content of these sessions is designed to help them understand the experiences they are having in the T-group by focusing on topics such as the following: what to observe in a group, emotional problems of becoming a member of a new group, decision making and problem solving in groups, the communication process, styles of emotional expression and presentation of self to others.

For example, after the first T-group session, the entire delegate group usually goes to a general session during which the speaker discusses in greater detail the set of assumptions which underlie the laboratory method, in particular why the T-group is so unstructured. He points out that the removal of stucture, agenda, and ground rules facilitates a *maximum exposure* of the reactions of the group members to the group situation. There is no place to hide, no agenda or set of rules behind which to obscure feelings. He also points out that merely creating a situation in which members expose some of their typical reactions does not, by itself, lead to learning. In addition, there must develop a *frank sharing of reactions and feelings* and a *climate of support and encouragement* which facilitates further exposure; there must develop a *willingness to engage in genuine mutual exploration* of group phenomena and a group atmosphere in which *experimentation* and *exploration* are viewed as positive sources of learning; there must develop a set of ground rules and a climate which permits *behavior to be viewed objectively* as data for analysis, rather than as something to be evaluated, rewarded, or punished. Finally, for the learning experience to be fully useful to the person, there must develop some degree of *intellectual understanding* of what is happening at the emotional level.

The speaker generally attempts to draw his illustrations from his own T-group experience and to show that the seemingly unique events in the groups do fit some theoretical framework and can be generalized, to some extent, to other groups in other settings. When such lectures are well done, the delegates have a genuine sense of integration with the realization that *neither the T-group nor the lectures would make complete sense without the other.* Together, they can make a potent learning experience.

In designing the content of theory sessions, the staff draws on its general knowledge of what issues the T-groups are likely to be facing at any given time and how these relate to other laboratory and back-home realities. In many instances, however, they will introduce new topics on short notice if it appears that several groups are facing some new issue which was not going to be dealt with. This requires close coordination among staff members and a sharing of what they perceive to be happening in their T-groups from day to day.

During the second week, the emphasis in theory sessions usually shifts somewhat from T-group issues to issues which arise in social systems, organizations, and communities. More attention is given to the occupational role which the delegate plays, to problems of authority and delegation, theories of management and organization, the consequences of collaboration or competition, and the like. As we will see below, an attempt is made to integrate this material with experiences generated in focused exercises.

Focused Exercises

The purpose of focused exercises is to generate some specific behavior so that a particular area can be studied (e.g., the communication process), or to practice some skill which is important for further learning (e.g., how to observe group action). An example of the former is an experiment highlighting the differences between one- and two-way communication. A delegate is asked to give some complex instructions to a group under two kinds of conditions: *one-way communi-cation*, defined by the ground rule that the group is not allowed to ask any questions during the instructions, and *two-way communication*, defined by the ground rule that the group may say anything during the instructions. The one-way and two-way conditions can then be compared in terms of accuracy of communication, length of time taken, feelings of the sender and the receivers, and so forth.

An example of the latter, practicing a skill, is an exercise on skills of observation. One half of the T-group is asked to engage in a short role-playing sequence while the other half of the group observes the interaction in terms of categories decided on prior to the exercise. If observation is the sole focus, the different observers then take time to compare their observation and discuss the possible sources of difference in them. If, in addition, the exercise is designed to practice the skill of giving feedback to make the participant group more effective, a period is set aside for the observers to report on their findings to the participants. The participants are then interviewed to obtain their reactions to the feedback, or are allowed to engage in further interaction to determine what difference, if any, the feedback has made. A final portion of the exercise is a joint discussion or a reversal of roles among the groups between that of actor and that of observer.

An exercise such as any of these involves practice in several kinds of activities: actually observing others while remaining silent, analyzing observations and reconciling differences between observers, deciding what observations to report back to the group in order to be helpful, and the actual process of giving the feedback in such a way as to maximize learning opportunities. The behavior to be watched may be left entirely to the observers or may be structured into the exercise through instructions and observational forms. Such forms deal with communication patterns, the kinds of membership roles which different people play, patterns of influence and leadership, methods of group decision, style of expressing emotions, and so forth.

Toward the end of the first week or beginning of the second week, a more complicated and extensive exercise may be introduced. One frequently used exercise is on intergroup competition. Two or three T-groups are each given instructions to produce some product—a one or two page paper on some relevant topic—which is evaluated by a panel of judges consisting of members drawn from the competing groups. For example, the instructions may be to produce a 200-word statement outlining a plan for the conversion of a highly autocratic organization into one which practices participative management techniques, or a plan for the movement of a plant from one city to another with minimum negative consequences. One product is judged the winner. The purpose of the exercise is to give the groups a chance to work on some concrete task and to explore the dynamics of inter-group competition. By the time this exercise is introduced, the groups are usually more ready to begin a concrete task and to test themselves against other groups, a situation which produces high levels of motivation for the exercise.

The group first selects one or two of its members to join the judging panel, after which it works on its product for two hours or so. In the meantime, the judges meet to develop criteria by which the product will be judged. When each group has finished, the paper is turned over to the laboratory secretary for duplication and distribution to the competing groups. In the free time after the work period, one typically sees the groups clustered in separate parts of the conference center reviewing how they worked, expressing confidence in their own product, and generally derogating (though in a joking manner) the other groups. Questionnaire data on how the groups perceive their own effectiveness and that of the other groups are gathered by the staff before the groups begin working on the product and again after they have finished.

The following morning, the groups meet to look at their own product and that of the other groups. They are told that a general session is scheduled at which time they will have a chance to argue for their product through a spokesman who will engage in a debate with spokesmen from the other competing groups. The groups spend some time electing this spokesman and developing a strategy for him to follow in the debate. During the general session, each group sits behind its spokesman and is allowed to pass notes to him but not to communicate with him in any other way. At various points during the morning, data are gathered on each group's opinion of which is the best product, and whether it feels the judges will be influenced primarily by the merit of the product or by loyalty to their group.

After the debate, the judges deliberate in front of all the groups and reach a decision. At this point, feelings run very high, particularly in the losing group or groups. Each group is sent back to its own room for 30 minutes or so to consider how it feels about the decision. In the meantime, the data gathered at various points are being tabulated in preparation for a total feedback and analysis session. After the half hour of separate group meetings, the groups are brought back into general session to be interviewed by a staff member—do they feel the decision was fair, do they feel the judges were swayed by loyalty, and so forth?

In line with the general assumption that for maximum learning the experiences which the groups have had must be analyzed and put into a framework, the final portion of the exercise is devoted to an hour or more of systematic recapitulation supported by the results of the questionnaires which had been administered at various points during the total exercise.[1] One effective way to conduct the general session is to have a staff member make some predictions about group reactions to (1) having a concrete task to perform under time pressure, (2) being in a competitive situation, and (3) actually winning or losing. He may also point out some of the strains of being a judge or being a group spokesman. The delegates are then invited to comment on the predictions—did they observe the phenomenon predicted or not, and if not, why do they feel it did not occur in their group. Finally, the questionnaire data, which also bear on the predictions, are presented. These usually support the predictions in a clear fashion and create a dramatic finale to the exercise.

In this type of exercise, an attempt is made to simulate the realities of organizations and social systems. The exercise highlights for delegates the positive and negative consequences of intergroup competition, what it feels like to be a winner or a loser, a judge or a group representative. The exercise also

---

[1]This particular intergroup competition exercise was adapted from a previously employed and systematically conducted experiment, thus permitting some predictions to be made about the outcome. The exercise was developed by Blake and Shepard and is based on experiments conducted by Muzafer Sherif.

begins to refocus the delegate on his back-home situation. Where the T-group is oriented to the here-and-now, the intergroup exercise begins to bridge the gap to the job situation with all of its intergroup conflict problems. Delegates usually have little difficulty generalizing some of their observations to labor-management negotiations, staff-line conflicts, interdepartmental rivalries, and majority-minority conflicts in committee meetings and other instances of inter-group discord.

One important learning outcome of the exercise is the discovery by most delegates that the losing group rarely changes its mind about which product was the best; rather, it rationalizes in a variety of ways reasons for its loss. Once a group becomes committed to its product, it has difficulty seeing the merit in another group's product. Even if the delegate already knows that this phe-nomenon tends to occur, his knowledge takes on a new and more significant meaning when he relates it to his own intense and often irrational feelings of loyalty to his T-group, and when he studies the nature of his own feelings and shares them with other members who have similar feelings.

The Second Week

The main task of the first week is entry into the laboratory culture. Re-entry into the back-home world is the primary task of the second week. During this week, the increasing attention on back-home problems is manifested in a variety of ways. Sometimes groups are brought together with the task of discussing how they might apply some of their new knowledge to the back-home situation. Or, meetings of groups are held at which members take turns discussing some particular back-home problem they have, while the other members attempt, through interviewing and careful diagnosis, to give help to each other on the problem. The real benefit of this kind of activity is to give the helpers practice in the art of giving help. If the problem presenter gains new insight into his back-home situation, this is a secondary gain. In some laboratory designs, a new set of groups is started with the purpose of giving every member the experience of making a transition from one group to another. The problems of re-entry into the back-home groups can then be assessed in the light of the transitional experience within the laboratory.

To support the theoretical material on problems of organizations and change, additional exercises are sometimes used. For example, to deepen under-standing of the forces which make for or restrain change, the T-groups may be asked to diagnose the forces which have led to greater openness of communi-cation in the group and those forces which have tended to prevent it. To obtain increased insight into organizational phenomena, groups may be given the task of simulating a company to market an actual product, while observers study the procedures used by the groups to establish their organization and to handle the kinds of problems that develop.

Informal Contacts

One other type of activity which takes on increasing importance as the labora-tory proceeds is the informal contact made with the staff in individual or seminar sessions. Sometimes seminars are scheduled around topics which are of particular interest to staff members. In some laboratories, the delegates survey their own needs and ask that certain seminar topics be covered by any staff member (or other delegate) who is willing to act as seminar leader. Topics, such as the role of values in business, reconciliation of problems of family and career, the place of religion in modern life, the possibility of a similarity between laboratory training and brainwashing, may be proposed. Even if no one is found to be an expert resource person in the area, the group is encouraged to meet and discuss the issue.

In addition to seminars, a variety of informal contacts with staff develop in which either small groups or individuals get together with a staff member, often the trainer of their own T-group, to discuss anything ranging from the possible applications of the laboratory method to back-home problems to more general issues like the nature of organization theory. The staff member may be asked to elaborate on a lecture he gave or discuss what is new in a given area of research. Or, he may be sought out for guidance relating to a delegate's personal problem. If the staff member feels that the pursuit of such an area would create a problem (because of the special relationship which this would imply between himself and a single member of the T-group or because he might not feel qualified to enter such a counseling relationship), he can suggest that the delegate take the problem to a particular staff member, usually a psychiatrist hired for this purpose, who holds himself more available for individual help.

Informal contacts among *delegates* are also of great importance in furthering the learning process. To facilitate such contacts, meal times, coffee breaks, cocktail hours, and periods of recreation are kept as informal as possible and are scheduled to be as long as possible. Delegates are encouraged to review and work through what is going on in their groups and what they have heard in lectures; to work out in subgroups those problems which the total T-group could not solve; to explore in greater depth issues which have arisen in the group; to get other members to elaborate on feedback which was given initially in the group; to explore with others, who have similar jobs or come from similar organizations, the relevance of things learned to the job situation.

The focus during T-group meetings is on here-and-now group events; informal times provide an opportunity to talk about there-and-then back-home problems or more general issues. Informal contacts also provide important supports. The skeptic can seek out other skeptics and share his doubts about the value of the laboratory method; the enthusiast can seek out other enthusiasts; the person who is troubled by something said to him in the group can talk it over with someone whom he perceives as being supportive. Incidentally, in those laboratories where the physical facilities require delegates to share rooms, it is found that the late evening bull sessions among roommates are one of the most meaningful of these informal contacts.

Outcomes of the Laboratory

As the laboratory draws to a close, a variety of reactions among the delegates is noticed. There are those for whom the opportunity to concentrate on themselves and their own problems has been so meaningful and so releasing that they are genuinely reluctant to see the experience end. They feel they have become better acquainted with themselves. They may not be sure how this will affect them on the job or at home, but they are sure that the experience has been very worth while.

There are others who feel they have had a revelation as to what makes other people and groups work. They have had the opportunity, for the first time perhaps, to study the reactions of others and to observe how a group must struggle with the diversity of its human resources. Sometimes such insights lead to sharply changed attitudes toward groups and group action. Outright hostility toward any form of committee often changes into a more sensitive understanding of groups, and into recognition that groups can only be effective if allowed to mature and work through their initial problems.

There are some delegates for whom the most meaningful experience has been that they have been accepted and liked by the other group members. They go back home with a renewed sense of confidence in themselves. There are others for whom the experience has been primarily disturbing because they may have discovered that they were not as persuasive, clever, or powerful as they had assumed. They will go home with more questions about themselves than they had brought, and many of these questions will remain unanswered for some time after the laboratory.

Still others will see in the laboratory some gimmicks and devices for use in back-home groups, and will attempt to utilize these in spite of entreaties from staff not to take the laboratory method as a model of how to run a work group or a business. For some of these "alumni," the gimmicks will fail; they may then turn against the laboratory method feeling it to be a fraud, without recognizing their own misuse of the method.

Some delegates will cherish the fact that the laboratory provided a two-week period during which they could leave behind their work and family and ruminate about basic issues of life. For them, it offered a retreat and an opportunity to revitalize themselves. Some delegates will find that among their fellow T-group members, roommates, or other contacts, they can now count several close friends with whom they will maintain a relationship in the future. Some of these friendships may be more intimate than any they have in their back-home situation.

Some delegates will suffer intensely during the entire laboratory period because, from their point of view, very little was actually accomplished; they will go home puzzled, confused, and still skeptical.

All delegates, whether they are aware of it or not, go home with greater skills as group observers and diagnosticians, and with greater sensitivity to the complexity of interpersonal relationships. Whether they *utilize* this increased sensitivity constructively or not depends upon them, but there is little doubt that they have acquired it. All delegates become familiar with a new approach to learning—utilizing their own experience and learning from it. All delegates finally understand why it was so difficult for others to tell them what the laboratory would be about. As they think back over their own experiences, they realize how personal and unique these have been and how difficult it will be to tell others what has transpired.

References

Bradford, L. P., J. R. Gibb, and K. D. Benne. *T-Group Theory and Laboratory Method.* Wiley, 1964.

Schein, E. H., and W. G. Bennis. *Personal and Organization Change Through Group Methods.* Wiley, 1965.

The Confrontation Meeting

RICHARD BECKHARD

One of the continuing problems facing the top management team of any organization in times of stress or major change is how to assess accurately the state of the organization's health. How are people reacting to the change? How committed are subordinate managers to the new conditions? Where are the most pressing organization problems?

In the period following a major change—such as that brought about by a change in leadership or organization structure, a merger, or the introduction of a new technology—there tends to be much confusion and an expenditure of dysfunctional energy that negatively affects both productivity and morale.

At such times, the top management group usually spends many hours together working on the business problems and finding ways of coping with the new conditions. Frequently, the process of working together under this pressure also has the effect of making the top team more cohesive.

Concurrently, these same managers tend to spend less and less time with their subordinates and with the rest of the organization. Communications decrease between the top and middle levels of management. People at the lower levels often complain that they are less in touch with what is going on than they were before the change. They feel left out. They report having less influence than before, being more unsure of their own decision-making authority, and feeling less sense of ownership in the organization. As a result of this, they tend to make fewer decisions, take fewer risks, and wait until the "smoke clears."

Recently I have experimented with an activity that allows a total management group, drawn from all levels of the organization, to take a quick reading on its own health, and—*within a matter of hours*—to set action plans for improving it. I call this a "confrontation meeting."

The activity is based on my previous experience with an action-oriented method of planned change in which information on problems and attitudes is collected and fed back to those who produced it, and steps are taken to start action plans for improvement of the condition.

Sometimes, following situations of organizational stress, the elapsed time in moving from identification of the problem to collaborative action planning must be extremely brief. The confrontation meeting can be carried out in $4\frac{1}{2}$ to 5 hours' working time, and it is designed to include the entire management of a large system in a joint action-planning program.

I have found this approach to be particularly practical in organization situations where there are large numbers in the management group and/or where it is difficult to take the entire group off the job for any length of time. The activity has been conducted several times with a one evening and one morning session—taking only $2\frac{1}{2}$ hours out of a regular working day.

"The Confrontation Meeting" by Richard Beckhard from *Harvard Business Review* (March–April 1967). © 1967 by the President and Fellows of Harvard College; all rights reserved. Reprinted by permission of *Harvard Business Review*.

The confrontation meeting discussed in this article has been used in a number of different organization situations. Experience shows that it is appropriate where:

- There is a need for the total management group to examine its own workings.
- Very limited time is available for the activity.
- Top management wishes to improve the conditions quickly.
- There is enough cohesion in the top team to ensure follow-up.
- There is real commitment to resolving the issues on the part of top management.
- The organization is experiencing, or has recently experienced, some major change.

Case Example A

The initial application of the confrontation meeting technique occurred in 1965 in a large food products company. Into this long-time family-owned and closely controlled company, there was introduced for the first time a nonfamily professional general manager. He had been promoted from the ranks of the group that had previously reported to the family-member general manager.

This change in the "management culture," which had been carefully and thoroughly prepared by the family executives, was carried out with a minimum number of problems. The new general manager and his operating heads spent many hours together and developed a quite open problem-solving climate and an effective, cohesive team. Day-to-day operations were left pretty much in the hands of their immediate subordinates, while the top group focused on planning.

A few months after the change, however, the general manager began getting some information that indicated all was not well further down in the organization. On investigation, he discovered that many middle-level managers were feeling isolated from what was going on. Many were unclear about the authority and functions of the "management committee" (his top team); some were finding it very difficult to see and consult with their bosses (his operating heads); others were not being informed of decisions made at his management committee meetings; still others were apprehensive that a new power elite was developing which in many ways was much worse than the former family managers.

In discussing this feedback information with his operating heads, the general manager found one or two who felt these issues required immediate management committee attention. But most of the members of the top team tended to minimize the information as "the usual griping," or "people needing too many decisions made for them," or "everybody always wanting to be in on everything."

The general manager then began searching for some way to—

. . . bring the whole matter into the open;

. . . determine the magnitude and potency of the total problem;

. . . give his management committee and himself a true picture of the state of the organization's attitudes and concerns;

. . . collect information on employee needs, problems, and frustrations in some organized way so that corrective actions could be taken in priority order;

. . . get his management committee members in better tune with their subordinates' feelings and attitudes, and put some pressure on the team members for continued two-way communication within their own special areas;

. . . make clear to the total organization that he—the top manager—was personally concerned;

. . . set up mechanisms by which all members of the total management group could feel that their individual needs were noticed;

. . . provide additional mechanisms for supervisors to influence the whole organization.

The confrontation meeting was created to satisfy these objectives and to minimize the time in which a large number of people would have to be away from the job.

Some 70 managers, representing the total management group, were brought together for a confrontation meeting starting at 9:00 in the morning and ending at 4:30 in the afternoon. The specific "design" for the day, which is broken down into a more detailed description in Appendix A, had the following components:

1. Climate setting—establishing willingness to participate.
2. Information collecting—getting the attitudes and feelings out in the open.
3. Information sharing—making total information available to all.
4. Priority setting and group action planning—holding work-unit sessions to set priority actions and to make timetable commitments.
5. Organization action planning—getting commitment by top management to the working of these priorities.
6. Immediate follow-up by the top management committee—planning first actions and commitments.

During the day-long affair, the group identified some 80 problems that were of concern to people throughout the organization; they selected priorities from among them; they began working on these priority issues in functional work units, and each unit produced action recommendations with timetables and targets; and they got a commitment from top management of actions on priorities that would be attended to. The top management team met immediately after the confrontation meeting to pin down the action steps and commitments.

(In subsequent applications of this confrontation meeting approach, a seventh component—a progress review—has been added, since experience has shown that it is important to reconvene the total group four to six weeks later for a progress review both from the functional units and from the top management team.)

Positive Results

The experience of the foregoing case examples, as well as that of other organizations in which the confrontation meeting technique has been applied,

demonstrates that positive results—particularly, improved operational procedures and improved organization health—frequently occur.

Operational Advantages

One of the outstanding plus factors is that procedures which have been confused
are clarified. In addition, practices which have been nonexistent are initiated.
Typical of these kinds of operational improvement, for example, are the reporting of financial information to operating units, the handling of the reservation
system at a hotel, and the inspection procedures and responsibilities in a changing manufacturing process.

Another advantage is that task forces, and/or temporary systems, are set
up as needed. These may be in the form of special teams to study the overlap
in responsibilities between two departments and to write new statements and
descriptions, or to work out a new system for handling order processing from
sales to production planning, or to examine the kinds of information that should
flow regularly from the management committee to middle management.

Still another improvement is in providing guidance to top management
as to specific areas needing priority attention. For example, "the overtime policy
set under other conditions is really impeding the achievement of organization
requirements," or "the food in the employee's cafeteria is really creating morale
problems," or "the lack of understanding of where the organization is going
and what top management's goals are is producing apathy," or "what goes on
in top management meetings does not get communicated to the middle managers."

Organization Health

In reviewing the experiences of companies where the confrontation meeting
approach has been instituted, I have perceived a number of positive results in
the area of organization health:

A high degree of open communication between various departments and
organization levels is achieved very quickly. Because people are assigned to
functional units and produce data together, it is possible to express the real
feeling of one level or group toward another, particularly if the middle echelon
believes the top wants to hear it.

The information collected is current, correct, and "checkable."

A real dialogue can exist between the top management team and the rest
of the management organization, which personalizes the top manager to the
total group.

Larger numbers of people get "ownership" of the problem, since everyone
has some influence through his unit's guidance to the top management team;
thus people feel they have made a real contribution. Even more, the requirement
that each functional unit take personal responsibility for resolving some of the
issues broadens the base of ownership.

Collaborative goal setting at several levels is demonstrated and practiced.
The mechanism provides requirements for joint goal setting within each functional unit and between top and middle managers. People report that this helps
them to understand "management by objectives" more clearly than before.

The top team can take corrective actions based on valid information. By
making real commitments and establishing check or review points, there is a

quick building of trust in management's intentions on the part of lower level managers.

There tends to be an increase in trust and confidence both toward the top management team and toward colleagues. A frequently appearing agenda item is the "need for better understanding of the job problems of other departments," and the output of these meetings is often the commitment to some "mechanism for systematic interdepartmental communication." People also report a change in their stereotypes of people in other areas.

This activity tends to be a "success experience" and thus increases total morale. The process itself, which requires interaction, contribution, and joint work on the problems and which rewards constructive criticism, tends to produce a high degree of enthusiasm and commitment. Because of this, the follow-up activities are crucial in ensuring continuation of this enthusiasm.

Potential Problems

The confrontation meeting technique produces, in a very short time, a great deal of commitment and desire for results on the part of a lot of people. Feelings tend to be more intense than in some other settings because of the concentration of time and manpower. As a result, problems can develop through misuse of the techniques.

If the top management team does not really use the information from its subordinates, or if there are great promises and little follow-up action, more harm can be caused to the organization's health than if the event were never held.

If the confrontation meeting is used as a manipulative device to give people the "feeling of participation," the act can boomerang. They will soon figure out management's intentions, and the reaction can be severe.

Another possible difficulty is that the functional units, full of enthusiasm at the meeting, set unrealistic or impractical goals and commitments. The behavior of the key man in each unit—usually a department manager or division head—is crucial in keeping suggestions in balance.

One more possible problem may appear when the functional units select a few priority issues to report out. While these issues may be the most *urgent*, they are not necessarily the most *important*. Mechanisms for working *all* of the information need to be developed within each functional unit.

Appendix A. Confrontation Meeting

Here is a detailed description of the seven components which make up the specific "design" for the day-long confrontation meeting.

Phase 1. Climate Setting

(Forty-five minutes to one hour.) At the outset, the top manager needs to communicate to the total management group his goals for the meeting, and his concern for and interest in free discussion and issue facing. He also has to assure his people that there is no punishment for open confrontation.

It is also helpful to have some form of information session or lecture by the top manager or a consultant. Appropriate subjects might deal with the problems of communication, the need for understanding, the assumptions and the goals of the total organization, the concept of shared responsibility for the future of the organization, and the opportunity for and responsibility of influencing the organization.

Phase 2. Information Collecting

(One hour.) The total group is divided into small heterogeneous units of seven or eight people. If there is a top management team that has been holding sessions regularly, it meets as a separate unit. The rest of the participants are assigned to units with a "diagonal slice" of the organization used as a basis for composition—that is, no boss and subordinate are together, and each unit contains members from every functional area.

The assignment given to each of these units is along these lines:

"Think of yourself as an individual with needs and goals. Also think as a person concerned about the total organization. What are the obstacles, 'demotivators,' poor procedures or policies, unclear goals, or poor attitudes that exist today? What different conditions, if any, would make the organization more effective and make life in the organization better?"

Each unit is instructed to select a reporter to present its results at a general information-collecting session to be held one hour later.

Phase 3. Information Sharing

(One hour.) Each reporter writes his unit's complete findings on newsprint, which is tacked up around the room.

The meeting leader suggests some categories under which all the data from all the sheets can be located. In other words, if there are 75 items, the likelihood is that these can be grouped into 6 or 7 major categories—say, by type of problem, such as "communications difficulties"; or by type of relationship, such as "problems with top management"; or by type of area involved, such as "problems in the mechanical department."

Then the meeting breaks, either for lunch or, if it happens to be an evening session, until the next morning.

During the break all the data sheets are duplicated for general distribution.

Phase 4. Priority Setting and Group Action Planning

(One hour and fifteen minutes.) The total group reconvenes for a 15-minute general session. With the meeting leader, they go through the raw data on the duplicated sheets and put category numbers by each piece of data.

People are now assigned to their functional, natural work units for a one-hour session. Manufacturing people at all levels go to one unit, everybody in sales to another, and so forth. These units are headed by a department manager or division head of that function. This means that some units may have as few as 3 people and some as many as 25. Each unit is charged to perform three specific tasks:

1. Discuss the problems and issues which affect its area. Decide on the priorities and early actions to which the group is prepared to commit itself. (They should be prepared to share this commitment with their colleagues at the general session.)

2. Identify the issues and/or problems to which the top management team should give its priority attention.
3. Decide how to communicate the results of the session to their subordinates.

Phase 5. Organization Action Planning

(One to two hours.) The total management group reconvenes in a general session, where:

1. Each functional unit reports its commitment and plans to the total group.
2. Each unit reports and lists the items that its members believe the management team should deal with first.
3. The top manager reacts to this list and makes commitments (through setting targets or assigning task forces or timetables, and so on) for action where required.
4. Each unit shares briefly its plans for communicating the results of the confrontation meeting to all subordinates.

Phase 6. Immediate Follow-up by Top Team

(One to three hours.) The top management team meets immediately after the confrontation meeting ends to plan first follow-up actions, which should then be reported back to the total management group within a few days.

Phase 7. Progress Review

(Two hours.) Follow-up with total management group four to six weeks later.

Appendix B. Sample Schedule

9:00 a.m.	Opening Remarks, by general manager Background, goals, outcomes Norms of openness and "leveling" Personal commitment to follow-up
9:10	General Session *Communications Problems in Organizations,* by general manager (or consultant) The communications process Communications breakdowns in organizations and individuals Dilemmas to be resolved Conditions for more openness
10:00	Coffee
10:15	Data Production Unit Session Sharing feelings and attitudes Identifying problems and concerns Collecting data
11:15	General Session Sharing findings from each unit (on newsprint) Developing categories on problem issues

12:15 p.m.   Lunch

2:00   General Session
                   Reviewing list of items in categories
                   Instructing functional units

2:15   Functional Unit Session
                   Listing priority actions to be taken
                   Preparing recommendations for top team
                   Planning for presentation of results at general meeting

3:15   General Session
                   Sharing recommendations of functional units
                   Listing priorities for top team action
                   Planning for communicating results of meeting to others

4:15   Closing Remarks, by general manager

4:30   Adjournment

Patterns of Organization Change

LARRY E. GREINER

Today many top managers are attempting to introduce sweeping and basic changes in the behavior and practices of the supervisors and the subordinates throughout their organizations. Whereas only a few years ago the target of organization change was limited to a small work group or a single department, especially at lower levels, the focus is now converging on the organization as a whole, reaching out to include many divisions and levels at once, and even the top managers themselves. There is a critical need at this time to understand better this complex process, especially in terms of which approaches lead to successful changes and which actions fail to achieve the desired results.

Revolutionary Process

The shifting emphasis from small- to large-scale organization change represents a significant departure from past managerial thinking. For many years, change was regarded more as an evolutionary than a revolutionary process. The evolutionary assumption reflected the view that change is a product of one minor adjustment after another, fueled by time and subtle environmental forces largely outside the direct control of management. This relatively passive philosophy of managing change is typically expressed in words like these:

"Our company is continuing to benefit from a dynamically expanding market. While our share of the market has remained the same, our sales have increased 15% over the past year. In order to handle this increased business, we have added a new marketing vice president and may have to double our sales force in the next two years."

Such an optimistic statement frequently belies an unbounding faith in a beneficent environment. Perhaps this philosophy was adequate in less competitive times, when small patchwork changes, such as replacing a manager here and there, were sufficient to maintain profitability. But now the environments around organizations are changing rapidly and are challenging managements to become far more alert and inventive than they ever were before.

Management Awakening

In recent years more and more top managements have begun to realize that fragmented changes are seldom effective in stemming the underlying tides of stagnation and complacency that can subtly creep into a profitable and growing organization. While rigid and uncreative attitudes are slow to develop, they are also slow to disappear, even in the face of frequent personnel changes. Most often these signs of decay can be recognized in managerial behavior that (a) is oriented more to the past than to the future, (b) recognizes the obligations of ritual more than the challenges of current problems, and (c) owes allegiance more to department goals than to overall company objectives.

Management's recent awakening to these danger signs has been stimulated largely by the rapidly changing tempo and quality of its environment. Consider:

- Computer technology has narrowed the decision time span.
- Mass communication has heightened public awareness of consumer products.
- New management knowledge and techniques have come into being.
- Technological discoveries have multiplied.
- New world markets have opened up.
- Social drives for equality have intensified.
- Governmental demands and regulations have increased.

As a result, many organizations are currently being challenged to shift, or even reverse, gears in order to survive, let alone prosper.

A number of top managements have come around to adopting a revolutionary attitude toward change, in order to bridge the gap between a dynamic environment and a stagnant organization. They feel that they can no longer sit back and condone organizational self-indulgence, waiting for time to heal all wounds. So, through a number of means, revolutionary attempts are now being made to transform their organizations rapidly by altering the behavior and attitudes of their line and staff personnel at all levels of management. While each organization obviously varies in its approach, the overarching goal seems to be the same: to get everyone psychologically redirected toward solving the problems and challenges of today's business environment. Here, for example, is how one company president describes his current goal for change:

"I've got to get this organization moving, and soon. Many of our managers act as if we were still selling the products that used to be our bread and butter. We're in a different business now, and I'm not sure that they realize it. Somehow we've got to start recognizing our problems, and then become more competent in solving them. This applies to everyone here, including me and the janitor. I'm starting with a massive reorganization which I hope will get us pulling together instead of in fifty separate directions."

Striking Similarities

Although there still are not many studies of organization change, the number is growing; and a survey of them shows that it is already possible to detect some striking similarities running throughout their findings. I shall report some of these similarities, under two headings:

1. *Common approaches* being used to initiate organization change.
2. *Reported results*—what happened in a number of cases of actual organization change.

I shall begin with the approaches, and then attempt to place them within the perspective of what has happened when these approaches were applied. As we shall see, only a few of the approaches used tend to facilitate successful change, but even here we find that each is aided by unplanned forces preceding and following its use. Finally, I shall conclude with some tentative interpretations as to what I think is actually taking place when an organization change occurs.

Common Approaches

In looking at the various major approaches being used to *introduce* organization change, one is immediately struck by their position along a "power distribution" continuum. At one extreme are those which rely on *unilateral* authority. More toward the middle of the continuum are the *shared* approaches. Finally, at the opposite extreme are the *delegated* approaches.

As we shall see later, the *shared* approaches tend to be emphasized in the more successful organization changes. Just why this is so is an important question we will consider in the concluding section. For now, though, let us gain a clearer picture of the various approaches as they appear most frequently in the literature of organization change.

Unilateral Action

At this extreme on the power distribution continuum, the organization change is implemented through an emphasis on the authority of a man's hierarchical position in the company. Here, the definition and solution to the problem at hand tend to be specified by the upper echelons and directed downward through formal and impersonal control mechanisms. The use of unilateral authority to introduce organization change appears in three forms.

By Decree This is probably the most commonly used approach, having its roots in centuries of practice within military and government bureaucracies and taking its authority from the formal position of the person introducing the change.

It is essentially a "one-way" announcement that is directed downward to the lower levels in the organization. The spirit of the communication reads something like "today we are this way—tomorrow we must be that way."

In its concrete form it may appear as a memorandum, lecture, policy statement, or verbal command. The general nature of the decree approach is impersonal, formal, and task-oriented. It assumes that people are highly rational and best motivated by authoritative directions. Its expectation is that people will comply in their outward behavior and that this compliance will lead to more effective results.

By Replacement Often resorted to when the decree approach fails, this involves the replacement of key persons. It is based on the assumption that organization problems tend to reside in a few strategically located individuals, and that replacing these people will bring about sweeping and basic changes. As in the decree form, this change is usually initiated at the top and directed downward by a high authority figure. At the same time, however, it tends to be somewhat more personal, since particular individuals are singled out for replacement. Nevertheless, it retains much of the formality and explicit concern for task accomplishment that is common to the decree approach. Similarly, it holds no false optimism about the ability of individuals to change their own behavior without clear outside direction.

By Structure This old and familiar change approach is currently receiving much reevaluation by behavioral scientists. In its earlier form, it involved a highly rational approach to the design of formal organization and to the layout of technology. The basic assumption here was that people behaved in close agreement with the structure and technology governing them. However, it tended to have serious drawbacks, since what seemed logical on paper was not necessarily logical for human goals.

Recently attempts have been made to alter the organizational structure in line with what is becoming known about both the logics and nonlogics of human behavior, such as engineering the job to fit the man, on the one hand, or adjusting formal authority to match informal authority, on the other hand. These attempts, however, still rely heavily on mechanisms for change that tend to be relatively formal, impersonal, and located outside the individual. At the same time, however, because of greater concern for the effects of structure on people, they can probably be characterized as more personal, subtle, and less directive than either the decree or replacement approaches.

Sharing of Power

More toward the middle of the power distribution continuum, as noted earlier, are the shared approaches, where authority is still present and used, yet there is also interaction and sharing of power. This approach to change is utilized in two forms.

By Group Decision Making Here the problems still tend to be defined unilaterally from above, but lower-level groups are usually left free to develop alternative solutions and to choose among them. The main assumption tends to be that individuals develop more commitment to action when they have a voice in the decisions that affect them. The net result is that power is shared between bosses and subordinates, though there is a division of labor between those who define the problems and those who develop the solutions.

By Group Problem Solving   This form emphasizes both the definition and the solution of problems within the context of group discussion. Here power is shared throughout the decision process, but, unlike group decision making, there is an added opportunity for lower-level subordinates to define the problem. The assumption underlying this approach is not only that people gain greater commitment from being exposed to a wider decision-making role, but also that they have significant knowledge to contribute to the definition of the problem.

Delegated Authority

At the other extreme from unilateral authority are found the delegated approaches, where almost complete responsibility for defining and acting on problems is turned over to the subordinates. These also appear in two forms.

By Case Discussion   This method focuses more on the acquisition of knowledge and skills than on the solution of specific problems at hand. An authority figure, usually a teacher or boss, uses his power only to guide a general discussion of information describing a problem situation, such as a case or a report of research results. The "teacher" refrains from imposing his own analysis or solutions on the group. Instead, he encourages individual members to arrive at their own insights, and they are left to use them as they see fit. The implicit assumption here is that individuals, through the medium of discussion about concrete situations, will develop general problem-solving skills to aid them in carrying out subsequent individual and organization changes.

By T-Group Sessions   These sessions, once conducted mainly in outside courses for representatives of many different organizations, are increasingly being used inside individual companies for effecting change. Usually, they are confined to top management, with the hope that beneficial "spill-over" will result for the rest of the organization. The primary emphasis of the T-group tends to be on increasing an individual's self-awareness and sensitivity to group social processes. Compared to the previously discussed approaches, the T-group places much less emphasis on the discussion and solution of task-related problems. Instead, the data for discussion are typically the interpersonal actions of individuals in the group; no specific task is assigned to the group.

The basic assumption underlying this approach is that exposure to a structureless situation will release unconscious emotional energies within individuals, which, in turn, will lead to self-analysis, insight, and behavioral change. The authority figure in the group, usually a professional trainer, avoids asserting his own authority in structuring the group. Instead, he often attempts to become an accepted and influential member of the group. Thus, in comparison to the other approaches, much more authority is turned over to the group, from which position it is expected to chart its own course of change in an atmosphere of great informality and highly personal exchanges.

Reported Results

As we have seen, each of the major approaches, as well as the various forms within them, rests on certain assumptions about what *should* happen when it is applied to initiate change. Now let us step back and consider what actually *does* happen—before, during, and after a particular approach is introduced.

To discover whether there are certain dimensions of organization change that might stand out against the background of characteristics unique to one company, we conducted a survey of 18 studies of organization change. Specifically, we were looking for the existence of dominant patterns of similarity and/or difference running across all of these studies. As we went along, relevant information was written down and compared with the other studies in regard to (a) the conditions leading up to an attempted change, (b) the manner in which the change was introduced, (c) the critical blocks and/or facilitators encountered during implementation, and (d) the more lasting results which appeared over a period of time.

The survey findings show some intriguing similarities and differences between those studies reporting "successful" change patterns and those disclosing "less successful" changes—i.e., failure to achieve the desired results. The successful changes generally appear as those which:

- Spread throughout the organization to include and affect many people.
- Produce positive changes in line and staff attitudes.
- Prompt people to behave more effectively in solving problems and in relating to others.
- Result in improved organization performance.

Significantly, the less successful changes fall short on all of these dimensions.

'Success' Patterns

Using the category breakdown just cited as the baseline for "success," the survey reveals some very distinct patterns in the evolution of change. In all, eight major patterns are identifiable in five studies reporting successful change, and six other success studies show quite similar characteristics, although the information contained in each is somewhat less complete. (See the Appendix for studies included in the survey.) Consider:

1. The organization, and especially top management, is under considerable external and internal pressure for improvement long before an explicit organization change is contemplated. Performance and/or morale are low. Top management seems to be groping for a solution to its problems.

2. A new man, known for his ability to introduce improvements, enters the organization, either as the official head of the organization, or as a consultant who deals directly with the head of the organization.

3. An initial act of the new man is to encourage a reexamination of past practices and current problems within the organization.

4. The head of the organization and his immediate subordinates assume a direct and highly involved role in conducting this reexamination.

5. The new man, with top management support, engages several levels of

the organization in collaborative, fact-finding, problem-solving discussions to identify and diagnose current organization problems.

6. The new man provides others with new ideas and methods for developing solutions to problems, again at many levels of the organization.

7. The solutions and decisions are developed, tested, and found creditable for solving problems on a small scale before an attempt is made to widen the scope of change to larger problems and the entire organization.

8. The change effort spreads with each success experience, and as management support grows, it is gradually absorbed permanently into the organization's way of life.

The likely significance of these similarities becomes more apparent when we consider the patterns found in the less successful organization changes. Let us briefly make this contrast before speculating further about why the successful changes seem to unfold as they do.

'Failure' Forms

Apart from their common "failure" to achieve the desired results, the most striking overall characteristic of seven less successful change studies is a singular lack of consistency—not just between studies, but within studies. Where each of the successful changes follows a similar and highly consistent route of one step building on another, the less successful changes are much less orderly (see Appendix for a list of these studies).

There are three interesting patterns of inconsistency:

1. The less successful changes begin from a variety of starting points. This is in contrast to the successful changes, which begin from a common point—i.e., strong pressure both externally and internally. Only one less successful change, for example, began with outside pressure on the organization; another originated with the hiring of a consultant; and a third started with the presence of internal pressure, but without outside pressure.

2. Another pattern of inconsistency is found in the sequence of change steps. In the successful change patterns, we observe some degree of logical consistency between steps, as each seems to make possible the next. But in the less successful changes, there are wide and seemingly illogical gaps in sequence. One study, for instance, described a big jump from the reaction to outside pressure to the installation of an unskilled newcomer who immediately attempted large-scale changes. In another case, the company lacked the presence of a newcomer to provide new methods and ideas to the organization. A third failed to achieve the cooperation and involvement of top management. And a fourth missed the step of obtaining early successes while experimenting with new change methods.

3. A final pattern of inconsistency is evident in the major approaches used to introduce change. In the successful cases, it seems fairly clear that *shared* approaches are used—i.e., authority figures seek the participation of subordinates in joint decision making. In the less successful attempts, however, the approaches used lie closer to the extreme ends of the power distribution continuum. Thus, in five less successful change studies, a *unilateral* approach (decree, replacement, structural) was used, while in two other studies a *delegated* approach (data discussion, T-group) was applied. None of the less successful change studies reported the use of a *shared* approach.

How can we use this lack of consistency in the sequence of change steps and this absence of shared power to explain the less successful change attempts? In the next section, I shall examine in greater depth the successful changes, which, unlike the less successful ones, are marked by a high degree of consistency and the use of shared power. My intent here will be not only to develop a tentative explanation of the more successful changes, but in so doing to explain the less successful attempts within the same framework.

Power Redistribution

Keeping in mind that the survey evidence on which both the successful and the less successful patterns are based is quite limited, I would like to propose a tentative explanatory scheme for viewing the change process as a whole, and also for considering specific managerial action steps within this overall process. The framework for this scheme hinges on two key notions:

1. Successful change depends basically on a *redistribution of power* within the structure of an organization. (By *power,* I mean the locus of formal authority and influence which typically is top management. By *redistribution,* I mean a significant alteration in the traditional practices that the power structure uses in making decisions. I propose that this redistribution move toward the greater use of *shared* power.)

2. Power redistribution occurs through a *developmental process of change.* (This implies that organization change is not a black to white affair occurring overnight through a single causal mechanism. Rather, as we shall see, it involves a number of phases, each containing specific elements and multiple causes that provoke a needed *reaction* from the power structure, which, in turn, sets the stage for the next phase in the process.)

Using the survey evidence from the successful patterns, I have divided the change process into six phases, each of them broken down into the particular stimulus and reaction which appear critical for moving the power structure from one phase to another. Exhibit 1 represents an abstract view of these two key notions in operation.

Exhibit 1   Dynamics of Successful Organization Change

	Phase 1	Phase 2	Phase 3	Phase 4	Phase 5	Phase 6
STIMULUS on the Power Structure	Pressure on Top Management	Intervention at the Top	Diagnosis of Problem Areas	Invention of New Solutions	Experimentation with New Solutions	Reinforcement from Positive Results
REACTION of the Power Structure	Arousal to Take Action	Reorientation to Internal Problems	Recognition of Specific Problems	Commitment to New Courses of Action	Search for Results	Acceptance of New Practices

Let us now consider how each of these phases and their specific elements make themselves evident in the patterns of successful change, as well as how their absence contributes to the less successful changes.

I. Pressure and Arousal

This initial stage indicates a need to shake the power structure at its very foundation. Until the ground under the top managers begins to shift, it seems unlikely that they will be sufficiently aroused to see the need for change, both in themselves and in the rest of the organization.

The success patterns suggest that strong pressures in areas of top management responsibility are likely to provoke the greatest concern for organization change. These pressures seem to come from two broad sources: (1) serious environmental factors, such as lower sales, stockholder discontent, or competitor breakthroughs; and (2) internal events, such as a union strike, low productivity, high costs, or interdepartmental conflict. These pressures fall into responsibility areas that top managers can readily see as reflecting on their own capability. An excerpt from one successful change study shows how this pressure and arousal process began:

"'Pressure' was the common expression used at all levels. Urgent telephone calls, telegrams, letters and memoranda were being received by the plant from central headquarters. . . . Faced with an increase in directives from above and cognizant of Plant Y's low performance position, the manager knew that he was, as he put it, 'on the spot.'"[1]

As this example points out, it is probably significant when both environmental and internal pressures exist simultaneously. When only one is present, or when the two are offsetting (e.g., high profits despite low morale), it is easier for top management to excuse the pressure as only temporary or inconsequential. However, when both are present at once, it is easier to see that the organization is not performing effectively.

The presence of severe pressure is not so clearly evident in the less successful changes. In one case, there was internal pressure for more effective working relations between top management and lower levels; yet the company was doing reasonably well from a profit standpoint. In another case, there was environmental pressure for a centralized purchasing system, but little pressure from within for such a change.

II. Intervention and Reorientation

While strong pressure may arouse the power structure, this does not provide automatic assurance that top management will see its problems or take the correct action to solve them. Quite likely, top management, when under severe pressure, may be inclined to rationalize its problems by blaming them on a group other than itself, such as "that lousy union" or "that meddling government."

As a result, we find a second stage in the successful change patterns— namely, intervention by an outsider. Important here seems to be the combination of the fact that the newcomer enters at the top of the organization and the fact that he is respected for his skills at improving organization practices. Being a newcomer probably allows him to make a relatively objective appraisal of the organization; entering at the top gives him ready access to those people who make decisions affecting the entire organization; and his being respected is likely to give added weight to his initial comments about the organization.

Thus we find the newcomer in an ideal position to reorient the power structure to its own internal problems. This occurs in the successful changes as the newcomer encourages the top managers to reexamine their past practices and current problems. The effect appears to be one of causing the power structure to suspend, at least temporarily, its traditional habit of presuming beforehand where the "real" problems reside. Otherwise, we would not find top management undertaking the third stage—identifying and diagnosing organization problems. We can see how an outsider was accomplishing this reorientation in the following comment by the plant manager in one successful change study:

"I didn't like what the consultant told me about our problems being inside the organization instead of outside. But he was an outsider, supposedly an expert at this sort of thing. So maybe he could see our problems better than we could. I asked him what we ought to do, and he said that we should begin to identify our specific problems."[2]

Three of the less successful changes missed this step. Two of the three attempted large-scale changes without the assistance of an outsider, while the third relied on an outsider who lacked the necessary expertise for reorienting top management.

III. Diagnosis and Recognition

Here, we find the power structure, from top to bottom, as well as the newcomer, joining in to assemble information and collaborate in seeking the location and causes of problems. This process begins at the top, then moves gradually down through the organizational hierarchy. Most often, this occurs in meetings attended by people from various organization levels.

A *shared* approach to power and change makes itself evident during this stage. Through consulting with subordinates on the nature of problems, the top managers are seen as indicating a willingness to involve others in the decision-making process. Discussion topics, which formerly may have been regarded as taboo, are now treated as legitimate areas for further inquiry. We see the diagnosis and recognition process taking place in this example from one successful change study:

"The manager's role in the first few months, as he saw it, was to ask questions and to find out what ideas for improvement would emerge from the group as a whole. The process of information gathering took several forms, the principal one being face-to-face conversations between the manager and his subordinates, supervisors on the lower levels, hourly workers, and union representatives. Ideas were then listed for the agenda of weekly planning sessions."[3]

The significance of this step seems to go beyond the possible intellectual benefits derived from a thorough diagnosis of organization problems. This is due to the fact that in front of every subordinate there is evidence that (a) top management is willing to change, (b) important problems are being acknowledged and faced up to, and (c) ideas from lower levels are being valued by upper levels.

The less successful changes all seem to avoid this step. For example, on the one hand, those top managements that took a *unilateral* approach seemed to presume ahead of time that they knew what the real problems were and how to fix them. On the other hand, those that took a *delegated* approach tended to abdicate responsibility by turning over authority to lower levels in such a nondirective way that subordinates seemed to question the sincerity and real interest of top management.

IV. Invention and Commitment

Once problems are recognized, it is another matter to develop effective solutions and to obtain full commitment for implementing them. Traditional practices and solutions within an organization often maintain a hold that is difficult to shed. The temptation is always there, especially for the power structure, to apply old solutions to new problems. Thus, a fourth phase—the invention of new and unique solutions which have high commitment from the power structure—seems to be necessary.

The successful changes disclose widespread and intensive searches for creative solutions, with the newcomer again playing an active role. In each instance the newcomer involves the entire management in learning and practicing new forms of behavior which seek to tap and release the creative resources of many people. Again, as in the previous phase, the method for obtaining solutions is based on a *shared* power concept. Here the emphasis is placed on the use of collaboration and participation in developing group solutions to the problems identified in Phase III.

The potency of this model for obtaining both quality decisions and high commitment to action has been demonstrated repeatedly in research. In three successful changes, the model was introduced as a part of the Phase III diagnosis sessions, with the newcomer either presenting it through his informal comments or subtly conveying it through his own guiding actions as the attention of the group turned to the search for a solution. In two other studies, formal training programs were used to introduce and to help implement the model. For all successful changes, the outcome is essentially the same—a large number of people collaborate to invent solutions that are of their own making and which have their own endorsement.

It is significant that none of the less successful changes reach this fourth stage. Instead, the seeds of failure, sown in the previous phases, grow into instances of serious resistance to change. As a result, top management in such cases falls back, gives up, or regroups for another effort. Because these studies conclude their reports at this stage, we are not able to determine the final outcome of the less successful change attempts.

V. Experimentation and Search

Each of the successful change studies reports a fifth stage—that of "reality testing" before large-scale changes are introduced. In this phase not only the validity of specific decisions made in Phase IV, but also the underlying model for making these decisions (*shared* power), falls under careful organization scrutiny. Instead of making only big decisions at the top, a number of small decisions are implemented at *all* levels of the organization. Further, these decisions tend to be regarded more as experiments than as final, irreversible decisions. People at all organization levels seem to be searching for supporting evidence in their environment—e.g., dollar savings or higher motivation—before judging the relative merits of their actions. This concern is reflected in the comment of a consultant involved in one successful change:

"As might be expected, there was something less than a smooth, unresisted, uncomplicated transition to a new pattern of leadership and organizational activity. Events as they unfolded presented a mixture of successes and failures, frustrations and satisfactions. . . . With considerable apprehension, the supervisors agreed to go along with any feasible solution the employees might propose."[4]

This atmosphere of tentativeness is understandable when we think of a power structure undergoing change. On the one hand, lower-level managers are undoubtedly concerned with whether top management will support their decisions. If lower-level managers make decisions that fail, or are subsequently reversed by top levels, then their own future careers may be in jeopardy. Or, on the other hand, if higher-level managers, who are held responsible for the survival of the firm, do not see tangible improvements, then they may revert to the status quo or seek other approaches to change.

Thus, with these experimental attempts at change and the accompanying search for signs of payoff, there begins a final stage where people receive the results and react to them.

VI. Reinforcement and Acceptance

Each of the studies of successful change reports improvements in organization performance. Furthermore, there are relatively clear indications of strong support for change from all organization levels. Obviously, positive results have a strong reinforcing effect—that is, people are rewarded and encouraged to continue and even to expand the changes they are making. We see this expansion effect occurring as more and more problems are identified and a greater number of people participate in the solution of them. Consider this comment by a foreman in one study:

"I've noticed a real difference in the hourly workers. They seem a lot more willing to work, and I can't explain just why it is, but something has happened all right. I suppose it's being treated better. My boss treats me better because he gets treated better. People above me listen to me, and I hope, at least, that I listen to my people below me."[5]

The most significant effect of this phase is probably a greater and more permanent acceptance at all levels of the underlying methods used to bring about the change. In each of the successful changes, the use of *shared* power is more of an institutionalized and continuing practice than just a "one shot" method used to introduce change. With such a reorientation in the decision-making practices of the power structure, it hardly appears likely that these organizations will "slip back" to their previous behavior.

Looking Ahead

What is needed in future changes in organization is less intuition and more consideration of the evidence that is now emerging from studies in this area. While it would be unwise to take too literally each of the major patterns identified in this article (future research will undoubtedly dispel, modify, or elaborate on them), their overall import suggests that it is time to put to bed some of the common myths about organization change. As I see it, there are four positive actions called for.

1. *We must revise our egocentric notions that organization change is heavily dependent*

on a master blueprint designed and executed in one fell swoop by an omniscient consultant or top manager.

The patterns identified here clearly indicate that change is the outgrowth of several actions, some planned and some unplanned, each related to the other and occurring over time. The successful changes begin with pressure, which is unplanned from the organization's point of view. Then the more planned stages come into focus as top management initiates a series of events designed to involve lower-level people in the problem-solving process. But, even here, there are usually unplanned events as subordinates begin to "talk back" and raise issues that top management probably does not anticipate. Moreover, there are the concluding stages of experiencing success, partly affected by conscious design but just as often due to forces outside the control of the planners.

2. *We too often assume that organization change is for "those people downstairs," who are somehow perceived as less intelligent and less productive than "those upstairs."*

Contrary to this assumption, the success patterns point to the importance of top management seeing itself as part of the organization's problems and becoming actively involved in finding solutions to them. Without the involvement and commitment of top management, it is doubtful that lower levels can see the need for change or, if they do, be willing to take the risks that such change entails.

3. *We need to reduce our fond attachment for both unilateral and delegated approaches to change.*

The *unilateral* approach, although tempting because its procedures are readily accessible to top management, generally serves only to perpetuate the myths and disadvantages of omniscience and downward thinking. On the other hand, the *delegated* approach, while appealing because of its "democratic" connotations, may remove the power structure from direct involvement in a process that calls for its strong guidance and active support.

The findings discussed in this article highlight the use of the more difficult, but perhaps more fruitful, *shared* power approach. As top managers join in to open up their power structures and their organizations to an exchange of influence between upper and lower levels, they may be unleashing new surges of energy and creativity not previously imagined.

4. *There is a need for managers, consultants, skeptics, and researchers to become less parochial in their viewpoints.*

For too long, each of us has acted as if cross-fertilization is unproductive. Much more constructive dialogue and joint effort are needed if we are to understand better and act wisely in terms of the complexities and stakes inherent in the difficult problems of introducing organization change.

Appendix: Survey of Studies

Those reporting "successful" organization changes include:

Robert R. Blake, Jane S. Mouton, Louis B. Barnes, and Larry E. Greiner, "Breakthrough in Organization Development," HBR November–December 1964, p. 133.
Robert H. Guest, *Organization Change: The Effect of Successful Leadership* (Homewood, Illinois, The Dorsey Press, Inc., 1962).

Elliott Jaques, *The Changing Culture of a Factory* (New York, The Dryden Press, Inc., 1952).

A. K. Rice, *Productivity and Social Organization: The Ahmedabad Experiment* (London, Tavistock Publications, Ltd., 1958).

S. E. Seashore and D. G. Bowers, *Changing the Structure and Functioning of an Organization* (Ann Arbor, Survey Research Center, The University of Michigan, Monograph No. 33, 1963).

Those showing similar "success" patterns, but containing somewhat less complete information:

Gene W. Dalton, Louis B. Barnes, and Abraham Zaleznik, *The Authority Structure as a Change Variable* (Paper presented at the 57th meeting of the American Sociological Association, August 1962, Washington, D.C.).

Paul R. Lawrence, *The Changing of Organization Behavior Patterns: A Case Study of Decentralization* (Boston, Division of Research, Harvard Business School, 1958).

Paul R. Lawrence et al, "Battleship Y," *Organizational Behavior and Administration* (Homewood, Illinois, The Dorsey Press, Inc.), p. 328 (1965 edition).

Floyd C. Mann, "Studying and Creating Change: A Means to Understanding Social Organization," *Research in Industrial Human Relations,* edited by C. M. Arensberg et al (New York, Harper and Brothers, 1957).

C. Sofer, *The Organization from Within* (London, Tavistock Publications, Ltd., 1961).

William F. Whyte, *Pattern for Industrial Peace* (New York, Harper and Brothers, 1951).

Included here are studies which reveal "less successful" change patterns:

Chris Argyris, *Interpersonal Competence and Organizational Effectiveness* (Homewood, Illinois, The Dorsey Press, Inc., 1962), especially pp. 254–257.

A. Gouldner, *Patterns of Industrial Bureaucracy* (Glencoe, Illinois, The Free Press, 1964).

Paul R. Lawrence et al, "The Dashman Company" and "Flint Electric," *Organizational Behavior and Administration* (Homewood, Illinois, The Dorsey Press, Inc.), p. 16 (1965 edition) and p. 600 (1961 edition).

George Strauss, "The Set-Up Man: A Case Study of Organizational Change," *Human Organization,* Vol. 13, 1954, p. 17.

A. J. M. Sykes, "The Effects of a Supervisory Training Course in Changing Supervisors' Perceptions and Expectations of the Role of Management," *Human Relations,* Vol. 15, 1962, p. 227.

William F. Whyte, *Money and Motivation* (New York, Harper and Brothers, 1955).

References

1. Robert H. Guest, *Organization Change: The Effect of Successful Leadership* (Homewood, Illinois, The Dorsey Press, Inc., 1962), p. 18.

2. From my unpublished doctoral dissertation, *Organization and Development* (Harvard Business School, June 1965).

3. Robert H. Guest, op. cit., p. 50.

4. S. E. Seashore and D. G. Bowers, *Changing the Structure and Functioning of an Organization* (Ann Arbor, Survey Research Center, The University of Michigan, Monograph No. 33, 1963), p. 29.

5. Robert H. Guest, op. cit., p. 64.

Improvement in a Decentralized Organization
RICHARD BECKHARD

In the past few years, some "giant steps" have been taken in the application of behavioral science knowledge to the problems of organization improvement and growth. It is becoming increasingly possible for organization managers to scientifically diagnose the conditions in their organization both in terms of practices, procedures, and ways of producing integrated effort and in terms of motivation, attitudes, and values of the people who make up the organization. It is also possible, from such diagnosis, to make a realistic assessment of the state of an organization's health and from this assessment to plan systematic steps for improving its health and effectiveness.

Some Assumptions About Organization Change

Organization Diagnosis
In introducing change into a system, it is assumed that the following phases of initial diagnosis would apply:

Defining the change problem;
Determining the appropriate client systems within the total organization system;
Determining each system's readiness and capacity to change;
Determining appropriate change objectives;
Assessing the change agent's own resources.

It is also assumed that for change to take place, the current status or set of conditions must be unfrozen, new inputs made available, and the system refrozen in a new set of conditions. For this to occur effectively in an organization, the education or change program needs to be organic; that is, it should grow out of itself and out of the needs identified as relevant to the organization's purposes. Specifically:

The program must be *goal-related*, that is, clearly related to organization purposes;
The program must be seen as *relevant* to *individual purposes* as well as to organization purposes by the people participating in it;
The program should have maximum *spread potential* throughout the organization.

Induction of Change
The change strategy should ensure that the organization can continue to learn from its own experience. This implies activities and tactics that provide for operating units to look at their own operations, test them against alternatives, and plan future improvement. It also implies a process of systematic information

collecting, feedback, and action planning based on the information. For such purposes the organization should be divided into learning groups such as work families, peer groups, or project groups.

Change goals need to be clearly defined in terms of the *types* of changes desired. One type is change in *organizational climate* (as evidenced in the organization's practices, its communications, its ways of handling conflict). A second type is change in *attitudes* and *values* of the people in the organization (for example, treating conflict as an appropriate and necessary condition of organization life or recognizing that frank and open communication is a desirable value). A third type is a change in *skills* (e.g., in problem solving or interpersonal relationships).

Although all of these types of change goals are existent in any organization change effort, it is important that relatively explicit priorities be established.

In the management of change it is necessary to find appropriate educational methods to achieve any of these change goals. The function of the educational consultant is to help the organization provide conditions in which it can introduce appropriate educational methods, collect more systematic data on its own organizational functioning, increase its ability to use such data in improvement planning, and build a training and educational orientation into its line management so that organization improvement becomes a way of life.

The Organization

Let us look at this particular organization, its purposes, and general structure.

The company is a medium-sized concern which operates 26 hotel properties in the United States, Canada, the Caribbean, and Great Britain. At the time the improvement program started, the company managed five hotels with about 2,000 employees. Today, its activities include hotels, motor hotels, and motor lodges, with about 7,000 employees. The period covered by this report, 1958 to 1963, was one of rapid growth resulting from the building and establishment of new hotels. The requirements for staffing, financing, and operating each new property made extreme demands on management personnel as well as on the finances of the company. Also, during this period conditions in the hotel industry changed. A rapid increase in the number of hotel and motor hotel units led to increased competition in rates and special services. These outside influences, plus rapid expansion and major investment in new properties, made the company's profit position precarious. At the time of this writing, however, a major upturn is being reported.

The organization improvement program with which we are concerned begins in the spring of 1958 and deals with the hotel division of the company. The president of the hotel division had reporting to him at central headquarters a staff consisting of the directors of five departments: operations, sales and advertising, purchasing and food, personnel employment, and controller. The general managers of each of the hotels also reported directly to the president. (See Figure 1.) The company had moved to an administratively decentralized operating policy. Each general manager was quite autonomous in terms of decision making, with the exception of a central accounting and control system and certain corporate policies relative to centralized purchasing. Large capital expenditures were approved centrally. General managers did not have actual

Figure 1   1958 Organization Chart

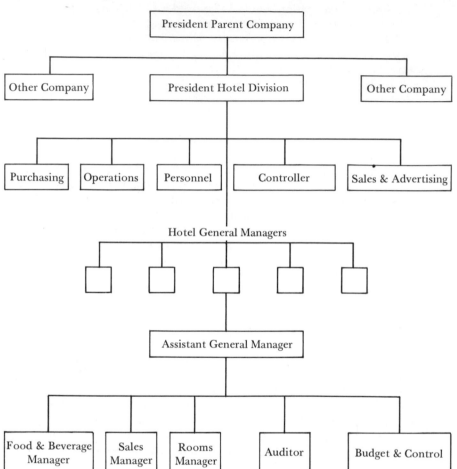

profit targets, but profit estimates were a standard procedure. Each of the hotel properties was a unique unit with very few of the characteristics of a "chain" operation.

During the period of the change effort with which this paper is concerned, the company moved into the motor hotel field, developed a motor hotel division, and later, a motor lodge division.

Identification of the Need for Improvement

The president initiated the change program. In the spring of 1958 he attended a workshop at which the consultant was a trainer. In discussing his organization, the president identified as a serious managerial problem the communication difficulties between corporate or central staff and line top managers. He felt that, although he had brought these two elements of the organization together regularly at quarterly management meetings, there still existed a lack of trust, openness, and clarity in terms of decision-making authority. The causes for these difficulties were perceived to be both organizational and interpersonal. The president also felt that the communication from the top group to second-level line managers in the hotels was not so effective as it should be. He was looking for help.

In describing his concern, the president pointed to various evidences of the problem:

"Central staff reported considerable difficulty in trying to initiate new ideas or improvement efforts into the hotels. They felt there were too many debates with general managers as to what could or could not be done in an improvement effort. In some cases staff were required to communicate *only* through general managers rather than through counterpart department heads.

"On the other hand, general managers complained to the president about the confusion caused by the central staff's coming into hotels and making recommendations and suggestions. Some general managers saw this as an intrusion by people who lacked the experience and know-how of the hotel business. In a few cases general managers had barred central staff from their hotels, unless specifically requested by the general manager.

"Although attempts had been made during the quarterly meetings to work through these problems, there seemed to be a lack of willingness to deal openly with them."

Because of the background of the hotel industry, essentially entrepreneurial, and because of the managerial styles of the general managers, relatively little direct communication existed between several of the general managers and their operating subordinates except on necessary operational matters. Furthermore, social distance was reinforced by the economics of the situation, as illustrated by the fact that the general manager's compensation is approximately 100 percent more than that of the next nearest subordinate staff member.

First Phases of the Program

Proceeding on the assumption that information collecting, feedback, and action planning are three essential steps in initiating change, the consultants suggested that a program be developed with the top group with the purposes of further defining the problem, broadening its base of information, and setting some conditions for joint planning to deal with it.

Information Collection Through Interviews

As a first step, an interview was held with each of the general managers, each of the central staff department heads, with a sample of the subordinates of the general managers, and a sample of the subordinates of the central staff heads. In each of these interviews, the respondents were told why the interview was being held, what use would be made of the data, that there would be a meeting of the general managers and central staff heads to work on improving communications and operations, and that they as individual respondents could contribute to the effectiveness of this meeting by sharing their information about the causes of difficulties and by giving their suggestions as to ways for improving communications.

In each case these interviews lasted from one to two hours, were nondirected, and ranged over a wide variety of topics. The interviewer recorded information, and at the close of the interview reported back to the respondent what he had heard. He also cleared with the respondent the information to be reported out, with the assurance that the identity of the respondent would be held confidential.

The material from all these interviews was organized into a series of management process headings such as—

1. Communications between president and line (or staff)
2. Line-staff communications
3. Location of decision making
4. Role clarification or confusion
5. Communications procedures.

The interview results were then listed under these categories and color-coded to identify the category of respondent (i.e., general manager, staff head, staff assistant, and so on).

Feedback of Information from Interviews and Initiation of Planning

A three-day meeting was convened at an off-site area. This meeting was attended by the president, the general managers, the central staff heads, and two consultants. On the first half-day of the meeting the findings from the interviews were presented. During this presentation, the members of the group could check for clarification, but no discussion of the information was allowed.

In the second phase of the meeting the group as a whole went through the list and determined the priority items. As the group analyzed the findings and the sources of information, it became clear that solutions to most of the problems listed could be achieved only through the joint efforts of those present. The type of information could not be dealt with by legislation from the top but required problem solving by all those affected. Sample items were—

From staff heads: The president expects us to introduce changes and maintain and upgrade quality but the general managers won't let us into the hotels to do it.

From general managers: The advertising policy of the corporation is ridiculous. We talk decentralization and yet we have no voice in setting our own advertising policy.

From subordinates of general managers: Where are we going in this organization? We have no feeling of belonging to a corporation but only to a hotel.

There were over 90 individual items representing issues on which the group would need to work. The process of selecting priority issues for discussion took the better part of the first day. On reconvening the first night, as a change of pace, and with the purpose of giving a framework for looking at the difficulties the group would be facing as it worked on the issues in subsequent days, the consultants introduced some theory about communications in organizations.

The second and third days were spent in digging into some of the central issues, bringing up the conflicts that existed among the various groups, and looking for areas of agreement and ways of working through the problems. This process involved identification of the causes of an issue in terms of past back-grounds of the staff and the managers, the behavior of the president, the problems of structure, and the nature of the business. The group explored possible changes in practices, procedures, and attitudes that would be required for correcting some of the problems that had been identified.

During the discussions, the consultants' contributions pinpointed how the group was functioning, guidelines for working on a problem, bringing conflict to the surface where it could be worked on, and systematic diagnosis of the causes of some of the problems that were identified.

The three days were active, volatile, and tiring. But by the end of this period, the group felt that it had made only a start and that it needed to continue. A meeting was therefore scheduled for one month later.

The second meeting was held in a hotel and was less exciting than the first. The members of the group came with the expectation of picking up where they had been, that is, with the climate of openness and problem solving that had existed at the end of the first session. They were surprised to discover that in the intervening time there had been considerable regression. In order for discussions to continue profitably, it was necessary to spend a few hours in re-establishing the earlier climate of trust.

A significant outcome of this second meeting was the top management's recognition of, and attention to, concerns of subordinates about the state of affairs. Some of the concerns that had been reported were that subordinate managers did not feel they could influence the corporate management in any significant way; that they considered their primary rewards and punishments as coming from the general manager of their hotel, that therefore their primary and almost exclusive loyalty lay there; and that they thought no one at corporate headquarters was much concerned with their needs, career plans, or current performance. Related to this, they felt little identification with the corporation's future objectives and plans, but saw their career planning in terms either of their own unit or of the total industry.

Most felt a lack of communication with counterparts in other of the organization's hotels. For example, sales managers had never had a meeting together, nor had other functional counterparts. In a number of cases, due to the entrepreneurial management style, subordinates did not see themselves as part of a management team but rather as individuals reporting to "the boss."

The management group decided that it would be desirable to set up a series of meetings, modeled after the ones they themselves were having, for the subor-dinate manager group. They set up two sets of meetings: one with sales, food, and rooms managers (customer-contact departments) and another with assistant general managers, auditors, and budget and control directors (administrative departments). Second-level central staff counterparts were assigned to meet with the relevant groups.

It was agreed that for these meetings there would again be a need for collecting information from those attending and for providing a method to feed this information back and make it available for group work. In creating these sets of conferences, the management group recognized that it would be necessary to ensure some follow-up from the output of the conferences if any real orga-nization improvement were to occur. During discussion on this point, the consultants suggested that, to deal with the feelings of lack of connection with the corporation that were repeatedly expressed by their subordinates, it might be desirable to include some face-to-face contact with the president of the division during these meetings. This was programmed into the meetings. It was also suggested that the meetings should try to deal simultaneously with a variety of stated needs, including: need for communication between counterparts, need for improved problem solving between staff and line at the same level, need for strengthening of hotel teams, and need for establishing communication between the hotel teams and the system.

The hotel managers agreed that they would report and present the plan to their teams and that they would build in follow-up meetings in the hotels so that the outputs of the conferences could be built back into the hotel organizations. To establish some identifying label, the series of meetings were called "Key Executive Conferences."

Key Executive Conferences

The methodology of these conferences was similar to that of the top management conference. Consultants interviewed the participants, organized the material by categories, and scheduled problem-solving meetings.

The first phase of each of these meetings was concerned with the feedback of information. The second phase differed slightly from the top management meetings in that the groups were asked by the consultant to go through the agenda and rate each item as—

1. An item we want to recommend to top management
2. An item we want to discuss and work through
3. An item that no longer seems relevant.

The items that were seen as ready for immediate recommendation were accumulated throughout the conference on a separate list. The items identified as needing discussion by the group became the group's major agenda during the three-day period. As each of these items was discussed, it was either attached to the list of recommendations or identified as completed and therefore eliminated from the agenda.

The cumulative list of recommendations to the corporation was presented to the president in a confrontation meeting held on the last half-day of the conference. He discussed each item and noted some action. That is, he made a decision, yes or no, or referred a question to a task force or to some other part of the organization. A specific issue will serve to illustrate this process.

One question of central concern to a number of people was: "How can we reorganize advertising policy to allow hotels to have more voice in planning their own advertising programs?"

After discussion of this issue, the group sent a delegation to the president to discuss it with him in detail. At this confrontation he announced that with the information he now had from the field (previously screened from him) he was hereby appointing a field-oriented man (a member of the group attending) as sales and advertising director to provide the needed liaison between the field and central office. This was a major policy change from highly centralized advertising direction by a corporate vice-president with little or no field consultation. It also demonstrated dramatically a successful and useful influence effort on the part of second-level management on top management.

These key executive conferences were scheduled twice a year. On the third round the groups reviewed the status of the conferences, their original purposes, and their current relevance. It was felt that the need for across-the-board problem-solving meetings had diminished as intrahotel communications improved and channels to the top were clearly opened. However, the need for technical counterpart meetings was stronger than ever.

It was decided, and agreed to by top management, that the key executive conferences would be terminated and that technical meetings on a periodically scheduled basis would be instituted.

Problem-Solving Conferences in Hotels

Emerging from these conferences was a general improvement in the communications and working effectiveness of the top team in each hotel. Some of the managers suggested that similar conferences within hotels would be profitable, and such programs were set up.

The format of these hotel "self-survey, action-planning meetings" was essentially similar to that of the meetings already described. After interviews with all middle- and first-line supervision, the information was categorized and fed back to the respondents who met in working groups composed of representatives of all departments. These groups worked through the agenda and made recommendations to top (hotel) management. The recommendations were then fed back to the top team and a confrontation meeting similar to those described above was held, but with the general manager conducting the meeting and setting the action plans.

These meetings have proved to be continuously effective and are held today on a semiannual or annual basis in all of the hotels. They have become a "way of life" for identifying current concerns, organizing work to deal with them, and planning action. The consultants' role has become that of "sponge" (collecting their data), "water faucet" (giving the information back to them), and "catalyst" (bringing all elements of management together).

A Redefinition of the Change Goals

This initial improvement effort was designed to deal with the effects of decentralization, the needs for improvement of interunit and interpersonal communications skills, and with techniques for better problem solving. The same set of goals guided the activities with the key executives and the initial efforts within the hotels.

Concurrently with the development of this program, the nature of the mission of the organization changed as the corporation went into the motor hotel business. This expansion necessitated a structural reorganization. From it emerged an organization in which two group vice-presidents reported to the president, one for motor hotels and one for hotels. (Later a motor lodge group was added.) Reporting to the group vice-president for hotels were the general managers of all the hotels and a small staff of specialists. Reporting to the group vice-president for motor hotels were the general managers of the motor hotels. Reporting to the president at a staff level were directors of corporate service: planning (for new hotels), purchasing, personnel, and sales and advertising.

During the period previously described, the president had attended a National Training Laboratories human relations laboratory and had subsequently encouraged his key executives to attend. The two group vice-presidents, several of the hotel general managers, and two or three of the staff directors had done so. As a result of these and other activities, the president became quite explicit in his desire to move the entire organization toward a management-by-objectives or Theory-Y orientation.

The president convened a two-day planning conference with the central staff directors and group vice-presidents to explore how far the organization had progressed in this direction and what would be needed to move the total culture toward a Theory-Y or management-by-objectives orientation. (See Figure 2.) At this conference the group reviewed the relationships between the president and staff and line management. These were seen to be quite improved although there were still difficulties between line management and some central office departments, and between the president and his staff. It was agreed that a periodic series of organization improvement meetings should be held with this group, with the minimum of one annual off-site conference and a series of on-site, shorter meetings.

The group recognized that a systematic target-setting[1] or goal-setting program was a necessary tool of any management-by-objectives operation. It was agreed that a unit-by-unit goal-setting process would be instituted during the coming year and that an individual performance-improvement target-setting process would be developed within the top management and corporate staff group.

A need was also felt for a program with the motor hotel management group working toward the development of a concept of team management. Another area identified was building a team for a new hotel; another was building intergroup relationships between the planning division (the corporate representatives in building and preparing a new hotel) and the general manager and his team (who take over its operation when it opens).

In looking ahead, it was obvious to all that a speed-up in the development of potential general management talent was a major organization requirement. The rapid expansion of the industry, the policy of rotation within the organization, and the proposed additional expansion for the late sixties, all combined to require acceleration in the preparation of management talent.

Management Development Training
Several factors combined to influence the next major effort:

1. The expansion program and organization policy discussed above

[1]Target setting, a management practice, reverses the traditional method of performance appraisal in which the supervisor writes the job description and evaluates the subordinate's performance against his, or the organization's, criteria for effective performance. In target setting, the subordinate develops his own position description and discusses this with his supervisor, with joint agreement on the position description. The incumbent then sets performance-improvement targets for a short period, such as six months. These improvement targets are discussed with the supervisor and become the joint goals of the supervisor and subordinate for the subordinate's performance improvement. At the end of the period, the incumbent analyzes his results in terms of goals achieved or not achieved, and this analysis provides a basis for joint discussion with the supervisor and for the joint replanning and setting of new goals for the next period. The process requires that the supervisor function as a consultant and at the same time represent organization requirements. It may produce some strain on the subordinate who must now commit himself to improvement targets rather than work toward targets set for him by either the supervisor or the organization.

Figure 2 1964 Organization Chart

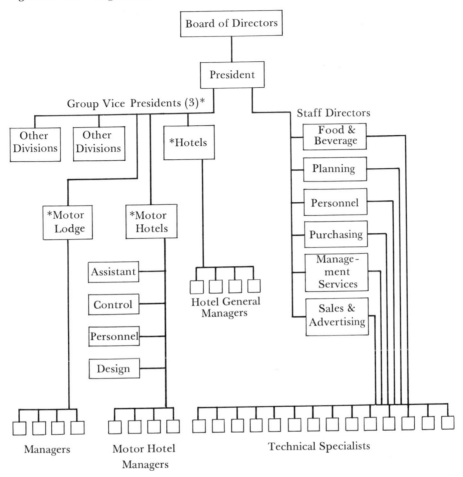

2. The experience of the president and most of the corporate staff heads with laboratory training
3. The need for additional technical development and training for new management trainees
4. The needs of existing middle managers who had come up through one phase of the business but had little training in either management or other technical phases of the business.

Organization Improvement Activities

It was therefore proposed that there should be three types of educational efforts.

Management School A one-week management workshop using laboratory training methods was scheduled. The purposes were to increase the insights of participants into the effectiveness of their own managerial behavior; to help them understand the different types of managerial styles and their effects on productivity; to help them develop some concepts of organizational effectiveness; to help make them aware of the corporate philosophy of *management by objectives* and its application to the units in which they performed; to broaden their concept of team effectiveness and team development.

These workshops were staffed by a faculty of behavioral scientists. They were scheduled for a group of 24 middle management executives selected by a task force composed of the president, the two group vice-presidents, and the personnel department head.

The first of these workshops was held in 1962 and additional workshops have since been held twice a year. The entire middle management group from the hotel and motor hotel operations and from the central staff have participated.

Technical Seminars   To deal with the broadening of technical skills, a series of technical meetings on food and beverage, budget and control, and auditing have been established. Participants from a variety of settings within the organization have attended these sessions.

Counterpart Meetings   The regularly scheduled technical counterpart meetings mentioned earlier have broadened their agenda to include some training and development work on problem solving, communications, and management. A series of special workshops on interviewing and consulting have been given to large numbers of managers.

In addition to the above specific educational efforts, the personnel office provides a central clearing house for offsite educational activities both in hotel operations and management.

Target and Goal Setting

As reported earlier, one of the major areas identified at the planning conference as needing attention was the process of goal setting in hotel units, in the field, and in individual performance improvement.

A program was established by which, on a semiannual basis, the top management of each hotel meet with the group vice-president of their division, the president of the corporation, and the key central staff, to review unit goals and jointly determine what is necessary to implement the goals for the coming year or months. This process requires the active participation of the management team within the unit. This has had the effect of building in much more involvement throughout the organization and a feeling of "ownership" in the unit and organization goals.

Personal performance improvement via systematic goal setting was established initially by the president and the group vice-presidents. This included the preparation of position descriptions by subordinates; the setting of improvement targets; the sharing of perceptions between the president and his subordinates about the reality and achievability of these various targets; their priority; and the periodic, joint review of progress toward targets. By constant evaluation of the process as well as by the refinement of the techniques employed, this has become a useful method of continuous information collecting and planning for the top group. Several of the general managers felt the method would be a helpful management tool in their hotels, and two of them introduced it within their organizations. In one case, the program included a series of training meetings for the entire management group in which they were given lectures on the process, opportunities to develop position descriptions, practice in interviews, and so forth. The process received substantial favorable lip service. However, because of pressure from the general manager to "do" the program, it met with considerable resistance in practice. As soon as the pressure abated, the program fell apart. This was one of the more dramatic failure incidents in this total effort and serves to reinforce the fact that an externally imposed program, without real involvement and participation on the part of those responsible for its implementation, is probably doomed from the start.

On the other hand, the unit goal setting which is organic to the corporate requirements has been seen as relevant by all concerned and has become an increasingly effective instrument for planning and communication among the several field units and the central office.

Team Training—Intergroup Staff and Line in New Hotels

One of the innovations in the organization improvement program has been the training of new management teams. The hotel industry is constantly developing new management teams as new properties open. It also sets up temporary systems which are established for a limited time only, such as the team that comes into existence to design and supervise the building and furnishing of a new hotel. This team goes out of existence when the hotel opens.

There were two specific sets of groups that were identified by the staff and the group vice-presidents as needing help in improving their communications and teamwork. One was the technical team responsible for the planning and construction supervision of a new hotel. The other was the general manager and his top team who would operate the hotel. A specific area of concern was the interface between these two groups (the planning team and the operating team) during the period of the final phases of construction and the preopening activities.

A series of conferences was held with the technical staff to analyze the problems of multiple authority, change-over from staff to line operation, problems of the preopening period, selection of personnel for the new hotel (previously handled by central staff), and training of staff (by central specialists or line heads). A result of these joint meetings was a series of revised procedures whereby the general manager was brought into the picture at a much earlier date, had a more active role in the selection of his own staff, and had more influence on the final design of the facility.

Training Operating Teams

The training of new hotel management operating teams was established as a high priority need. In order to understand the significance of this training, one needs a picture of previous practice.

The selection of people to serve as department heads in new hotels had been based on their proved technical competence in their own fields, such as housekeeping, engineering, food preparation, and so on. Each of the members making up a new management team came from a background of experience in which he had learned to operate *with* a particular managerial style and *under* a particular managerial style. The general manager, in each case an experienced man, had his own managerial style and ways of work which he intended to employ in his future operations. When the team came together on the job, the demands of the work required their fullest effort in the technical area. No time was spent on discussion of ways of work, relationships, communications procedures. For the first few months after the hotel opened, all the problems of a new property created similar demands and pressures. Matters of relationship, communication, and so forth usually did not get much attention by the team until well along in the first year. Consequently, considerable inefficiency might well have been avoided had better communication been established earlier among the several key members of the management team.

It was hypothesized that the effective building of a new team could be accomplished more efficiently if, as a part of their earliest experiences as a team, they could spend some time concentrating on the building of a culture. This would include explicit discussion of norms and procedures to be followed in terms of communication, decision making, and job responsibilities.

Experiments were set up with three hotels which were due to open within a year or two. In each case, the first activity of the top management team (general manager and key department heads) was to attend a two- or three-day off-site conference with the purpose clearly to begin building the management team.

The format of these conferences was as follows: After an opening statement by the head of the team (general manager), the group built an agenda of relevant concerns and problems to be tackled in the area of team effectiveness, work relationships, communications, training, and the like. Explicit attention was paid to the establishment of an open communications climate through such devices as asking each member to share with the group his reasons for taking the job, what his career aspirations were, and so on. Another mechanism was for each member to describe for the group how he saw his responsibilities and authority in the new unit. The general manager then reacted to this statement, as did the colleagues, and a consensus was arrived at relative to each job.

Other agenda items included plans for communication (staff meetings, among others); training programs for staff coordination and use of resources; clarification of practices—for example, what things needed approval; relationships to the technical planning staff; and special problems of the "opening week."

In each of these three experiments, follow-up meetings were held approximately six to eight months after the opening to check on results and to review the various commitments made at the earlier meeting. Respondents reported considerable progress toward more openness and improved communication; but, in each case, there were some regressions which were reviewed and worked through again.

As reported by the president, the corporate staff, the board of directors, the general managers involved, and the teams themselves, the openings of these three hotels were the smoothest in the corporation's history. Teams were able to deal with a much larger number of complex problems; turnover was reduced dramatically as compared with experience at previous openings in similar hotels; and, contrary to the trend for new hotels, there was virtually no turnover in the middle management groups within the first year. These activities were seen by the participants and the corporate leadership as highly useful in terms of developing the health of the organization.

Operations Improvement Committees

With the continually increased need to improve its competitive position, an operations improvement program was introduced into the organization. Profit improvement or operations improvement committees were developed in most units with rank-and-file and management participation. The mission of these committees was to develop innovations, service improvements, and more efficiency in the quality and handling of food, lodging, and service.

These activities have produced a high degree of involvement on a fairly broad base and have resulted in a considerable number of improvements in performance, in increased service and reduced costs. Management reports much more concern for profit and costs on the part of rank-and-file employees. This shows up in such ways as reduced breakage in the kitchens, less waste in handling laundry, and so on.

Overhead Cost Reduction Program

With the tightening economic conditions, due to overexpansion in the industry, there was the need for an appreciable cut in overhead costs at the central staff level.

The president brought together the heads of staff departments and told them of the amounts of cuts that would probably be required, using two figures: a minimum and a maximum. He asked each staff head, in consultation with two or three of his colleagues from other departments, to form task forces to think through what he and his department would do if the minimum cut or the maximum cut were required and also to think through what the consequences would be to the corporation this year, and for several years ahead. Staff heads were asked to include some colleagues with points of view different from their own.

A historian for this project was selected early in the program to keep a record of the processes operating throughout the program. Some bases for selection of task forces were recorded as follows:

Knowledge of the activity of the other department
Use of the services of the other department
Involvement in effects of reduction
Range of ideas and viewpoints
Challenge to certain items
Individual bias in favor of the particular department's services
Need to be involved in the decision making
Special skills
Decision-making power and importance of approval.

Following the series of task force meetings, a general meeting was held during which each staff head explained his present budget, his recommendations for reducing his budget, and the consequences on both a long- and short-term basis of these reductions.

The final results as indicated in the report were as follows: Individual department reductions range from zero to $50,000. The total effect of this program, provided all recommendations are put into effect, results in reducing the central office budget by approximately $225,000 and in reducing the number of persons employed in central office by 12.

Significant aspects of this effect, in addition to the obvious savings in dollars, are the high degree of shared commitment to the solution of the problem and the ability to cope with layoffs and belt-tightening without any loss to the viability of the organization.

Program Effects

Dramatic profit improvement was recorded in 1964, with highest earnings in the company's ten-year history. This profit was against an industry trend of stabilized profits. It is impossible to correlate this profit improvement fully with the educational effort; but it is clear that the program has made a significant contribution through developing attitudes of commitment to company objectives, a shared value of concern for costs, and a measurable increase in operating efficiency of almost all units.

Specific evidence of changes in organization climate include very low turnover in a highly mobile industry, an increase in rotation of management personnel, the promotion into higher positions of more than a hundred management people, an increase of performance effectiveness in most units in terms of costs as related to sales, more efficient staffing, and reduction of costs with no appreciable decrease of service.

There are clear indications that the organization is able to handle crises in much more effective ways. The organization has recently withstood a reorganization at the corporate level, major modifications in proposed expansion plans, major relocations of numbers of management personnel into new assignments, yet has shown an increase in performance return.

Increasingly, the units of the organization are learning from their own experience, are able to function more effectively with less dependence on outside help, and, at the same time, are making more creative use of a variety of resources within the organization.

Summary

The change effort started with the president's recognition of the need for improving problem-solving skills, interpersonal communication skills, and intergroup communication as a function of the decentralization policy. The key line management and the corporate staff management, together with the president, were seen as an initial learning group; first efforts were with them, to help identify and work through the problems of the organization as they perceived them.

The next major effort was with the subordinates of the above-mentioned key line and staff executives. Here the primary concerns (in addition to improving skills and individual effectiveness) were to change the influence pattern between middle management and the top management of the organization, to build the effectiveness of the team within each operating unit, and to establish communication links between counterparts in various segments of the system.

Building team effectiveness, improving communications, and problem solving in the several individual units made up the next major phase, with emphasis on improved linkage between the corporate headquarters and the middle line management through top management of each unit, intergroup and interpersonal communication within a unit, and vertical communication between the general manager and the rest of his team. Increased operating effectiveness in terms of better procedures and more generally shared concern for costs, controls, and efficiency were the organization goals of this phase.

The major goal shifted to moving the entire organization toward a management-by-objectives or "Theory-Y" orientation. Changing external conditions and increasing requirements for management talent also meant speeding up the preparation of existing management personnel to enable them to handle greater responsibilities.

To meet these goals, new learning groups were created. Groups of peers from across the system were brought together in one-week management laboratories for intensive exploration of their own managerial styles and of organization behavior. Technical sessions dealing with food and beverage preparation, budget and controls, auditing procedures, and so on, were held for specialists in these fields and for others in management who wished to broaden their repertoire of skills.

Goal-setting programs were introduced for all operating units on a systematic basis; and performance-improvement, target-setting sessions were instituted at the central staff level and in some of the operating units. The training of new hotel teams received major emphasis.

When economic conditions required tightening of the belt, improved efficiency throughout the organization, and reduction in overhead costs, the *total resources* of the organization were mobilized. Operations improvement committees consisting of rank-and-file management personnel in all units were set up in each hotel, and a series of task forces was developed to achieve a rather drastic cut in central staff overhead costs.

Questions for Discussion

1. What are the advantages and disadvantages of "in-house" laboratory training as compared to "stranger" laboratories?

2. What are the principal functions performed by an organization development consultant? Why is it unlikely that a line manager employed in the company could perform the same functions?

3. In deciding whether to use OD as a method of managing, the line management in a company must consider its limitations, and the conditions under which it may be applicable. What are these limitations and conditions?

4. Recalling from Chapter 7 the conditions under which "organic" or "participative" organization systems are appropriate, and the conditions under which "formal" or "directive" systems are appropriate, when would one *not* use organization development? Illustrate with a real-world example.

5. Some writers on management believe that in spite of the limitations of OD (questions 3 and 4), this technique of management is becoming *in general* more applicable in *all* organizations. What is their reasoning?

6. Organization development philosophy differs in a very important way from *structural* philosophy—OD has to do with a vision of how the organization should function, how people should behave and act, and what *causes* organizations (and people) to change. Explain this difference, and give the OD argument for why structuralist philosophy "puts the cart before the horse."

7. In what way is a nondirective T-Group a scientifically designed, closed-system experiment? In order for a feather and a lead ball to obey the laws of physics (gravity) and fall at the same speed through space, the scientist must close the system and exclude the friction of air, wind, or other forces. He does this by enclosing the falling objects in a vacuum chamber. The T-Group excludes all but certain things. What is excluded and what is included?

8. T-Groups are often criticized because a person returning to work finds his real working environment not like the atmosphere created in the laboratory "vacuum." Is this a valid criticism? Is it an invalid criticism? Is it both? Use the example from question 7: everyone knows that a feather and a lead ball do not fall at exactly the same rate—except in a vacuum.

9. Study Greiner's emphasis on *power redistribution* as part of the OD process. In what sense would this aspect of OD overcome some of Thompson's (Chapter 6) concept of conflict between line officers ("with the right to decide but not the ability") and staff officers ("with the ability to decide but not the right")?

Short Cases for Discussion

University Student Union

The snack bar in the university student union employs three students on the day shift: Jim, Jack, and Bill. Jack has concluded that Jim is hard to get along with. Jim is very intelligent, almost brilliant. Every time a problem comes up, such as rearranging the shelves or scheduling holiday shifts, he has a quick answer, and usually the best one. But he does not seem to care at all about the feelings and views of Jack and Bill. He comes out with a quick answer, tells them what it is, and then goes on to other things. Jack thinks Jim expects the other two to admire his intelligence.

Finally, Jack decided he was going to "stop playing Jim's game." Jim figured out a different way to stack the post cards sold at the snack bar counter. Jack ignored the idea, and so did Bill. In fact, they deliberately continued to put the post cards up in the same way they always had. Jack could tell by Jim's manner that he was angry, but Jim did not say anything.

Later, Jim suggested a way they might improve the candy display. Candy was stored in shelves behind the cash register. According to Jim, there were problems because the three workers bumped into each other frequently in getting at the candy, and people bunched up around the cash register, not knowing what kind of candy they wanted, "shopping" the display, and then pointing at their choice. In making his suggestion, Jim said, "You guys just don't know how to operate efficiently. Put the damn candy in two identical bunches, one at each end of the counter in front of the cash register." To Jack, he seemed deliberately sarcastic.

Jack and Bill felt that it was more important to put post cards, cigarettes, and notions such as shaving cream and chapsticks on the counter. They argued that cigarettes would cause even more of a jam-up at the cash register if put behind it on shelves, because they were higher volume sellers. So they ignored Jim's second suggestion.

Questions

1. If you were Jack, what rating would you give Jim on item 2 in Douglas McGregor's team rating scale (in the article, "Team Development")?

2. McGregor stresses a certain kind of feedback as a means of building a team. If you were Jack, and attempting to give such feedback, what would you say to Jim in the above episode?

3. If you were Bill, what rating would you give Jack on item 2 in McGregor's rating scale at the time of the episode?

Note: The above answers may be written. If they are, try to capture in your writing style the real way you would talk.

4. For additional insight into the answers to questions 1–3, the instructor may ask for volunteers to play the roles of Jim, Jack, and Bill. The remainder of the class will have responsibility for listening to *specific* things that are said during the role play. One third of the class can rate Jack on McGregor's point 2 on the rating scale, and one third can rate each of the other two characters. After the role play, each class group will report their ratings (and reasons for them) to the rest of the class.

5. In the role play in question 4, the characters undoubtedly mentioned the rearranging of shelves behind the counter, the way post cards are stored, and the way candy is displayed. These are *technological* aspects, as opposed to *human* aspects. The *organization* of the snack bar, if it is to be *developed*, must include both. Did you see any progress in the development of candy-display technology which would help the snack bar in its goal of supplying students with candy? That is, how did the characters perform in (a) the initial phase of diagnosing and solving *human* problems, and (b) in the second phase of working as a team to operate the technical aspects of the snack bar?

6. As a test of the second phase of question 5, the same three students who role played will be asked to continue. This time, see if the three make progress on settling the best arrangements to accomplish the team goal (optimizing the service of the concession to the student public).

Century National Bank

Four months ago, the president of Century National Bank decided that the bank had grown large enough that people in various departments were losing touch with each other. This resulted in bureaucratic red tape, some mixups where a customer was told one thing by one department of the bank and a contradictory thing by another department, and a feeling among employees that "everything has to be done by the book."

In dealing with this problem, the president, aided by the vice president for personnel, sent a questionnaire to 48 key managers in the bank. One section of this questionnaire was for the purpose of finding out how managers viewed themselves and their own jobs. They were asked to check, for each of the two following characteristics, whether it was "very characteristic" of himself, "somewhat characteristic," or "not at all characteristic."

	Very	Somewhat	Not at all
a) Enthusiastic about what I do; get excited about my work.	33	10	5
b) Being a leader; having other people look up to me for direction; taking over when things are confused.	19	20	9

Question

The tabulation above was made after the 48 managers returned their questionnaires. What would you, as president, conclude from this tabulation about whether you should proceed with an organization development program? Why?

Index